World Politics

Trend and Transformation

EIGHTH EDITION

WORLD POLITICS

Trend and Transformation

CHARLES W. KEGLEY, JR.
University of South Carolina

EUGENE R. WITTKOPF
Louisiana State University

BEDFORD / ST. MARTIN'S
Boston • New York

For Debbie—CWK

For Debra and Jonathan—ERW

For Bedford/St. Martin's

Executive Editor for History and Political Science: Katherine E. Kurzman
Developmental Editor: Gretchen Boger
Senior Editor, Publishing Services: Douglas Bell
Production Supervisor: Dennis Conroy
Project Management: Publisher's Studio
Cover and Text Design: Wanda Kossak
Maps: Mapping Specialists Limited
Graphics: Stratford Publishing Services, Inc.
Photo Research: Publisher's Studio
Cover Photos: (Top left) Copyright © Christopher Morris/Black Star/Time, Inc. (Top center) Copyright © Maxim Marmur/Stringer/Associated Press, AP. (Top right) Copyright © Pavel Rahman/Stringer/Associated Press, AP. (Botom) Copyright © Wally McNamee/CORBIS
Composition: Stratford Publishing Services, Inc.
Printing and Binding: R.R. Donnelley & Sons Company

President: Charles H. Christensen
Editorial Director: Joan E. Feinberg
Director of Marketing: Karen R. Melton
Director of Editing, Design, and Production: Marcia Cohen
Manager, Publishing Services: Emily Berleth

Library of Congress Control Number: 00-104286

Manufactured in the United States of America.

6 5 4 3 2 1
f e d c b a

For information, write: Bedford/St. Martin's, 75 Arlington Street,
Boston, MA 02116 (617-399-4000)

ISBN: 0-312-24735-4

Published and distributed outside North America by
MACMILLAN PRESS LTD
Houndmills, Basingstoke, Hampshire RG21 2XS and London
Companies and representatives throughout the world

ISBN: 0-333-94578-6

A catalogue record for this book is available from the British Library.

Acknowledgments

Acknowledgments and copyrights appear at the back of the book on pages A-1 and A-2, which constitute an extension of the copyright page.

PREFACE

New, new, new: "new century," "new millennium," "new world order." At the turn of the year 2000, talk about possible global transformations reached frenzied proportions. Many people stopped to contemplate the promise and peril of the global future. Yet it was unclear whether a new date on the calendar would actually signal a new epoch in world history.

Our age does not have, as yet, a name. True, we are in a "post–Cold War," "post–twentieth century" phase. But those phrases don't completely describe this period of transition. We have left something behind but do not yet possess sufficient confidence about the future to predict where global affairs are headed. Rapid changes sweeping world politics pose an enormous challenge to policymakers, scholars, and especially students. Without a single, overriding issue like the Cold War to structure thinking about global affairs, there exists little agreement about which dimensions of world politics will come to the fore in the new century.

It is the purpose of the eighth edition of *World Politics: Trend and Transformation* to establish the framework students need to put changes and continuities into perspective. The book combines the latest available data with contemporary debates in international relations to prepare students to assess the possibilities for the global future and its impact on their lives. *World Politics* aims to help them with such critical thinking by presenting the evolving relations among global actors, the historical developments that have affected those actors' relationships, and today's trends in global interactions. The major theories political scientists use to discuss international relations—realism and liberalism and their variants—frame our study. At the same time, this book incorporates the reconstructed theories newly advanced to interpret contemporary events, and resists the temptation to overly simplify world politics with a treatment that masks complexities and distorts realities.

OVERVIEW OF THE BOOK

To help students make sense of those complexities, *World Politics* is organized into five parts. Part I introduces them to the field and to the major theories of international relations. Part II presents the major actors in the global arena and discusses the processes by which those actors make decisions. Part III looks at issues of global welfare, including trade and monetary relations, the forces of globalization, human demographics, and the interplay between humans and the natural environment. Global conflict is the subject of Part IV, including national security, arms, warfare, and different theoretical approaches to peace. The text concludes with Part V, in which ten questions provoked by unfolding trends in world politics are posed to stimulate thinking about the global future.

CHANGES IN THE EIGHTH EDITION

Content and Organization

Many global changes have taken place in the twenty-four months since the publication of the seventh edition. They required us to revisit every passage and integrate the latest developments with the most current information available as the book went to press. This edition includes the most recent indices on issues ranging from human development and the empowerment of women, to the number of wars and military interventions in progress, and the rise of foreign direct investments and the economic clout of multinational corporations.

In addition, we have expanded coverage to take account of new departures in theory that attempt to interpret recent developments. Without identifying every modification in the new edition, we draw attention to the most important changes in each chapter. Those familiar with previous editions will note the following:

- Chapter 1, "Exploring Twenty-First-Century World Politics," has been rewritten to even more sharply define the multilevel, multi-issue approach of the book. The concluding five questions, which anticipate future trends in global politics, have been updated to account for recent changes in a global system rife with controversy. Some of these questions are revisited at length in the final chapter.
- Chapter 2, "Theories of World Politics," highlights the two major theoretical interpretations of world politics—the realist and liberal traditions. At the same time, we have expanded and revised coverage of alternative theories, relating them more explicitly to concrete global issues to allow students to understand the contribution of political theory to understanding international relations.
- Chapter 3, "Foreign Policy Decision Making," more instructively uses the "levels-of-analysis" framework to explain the major influences on how both states and nonstate actors, such as international organizations and multinational corporations, make policy choices to cope with changing international circumstances.
- Chapter 4, "Great-Power Rivalries and Relations," has been updated to cover recent trends in the relationships of the great powers, as the ratio of power and resources among them continues to undergo destabilizing transitions. Long-term projections summarize contending forecasts about the potential for friction as a new balance of power emerges.
- Chapter 5, "The Plight and Policy Posture of the Global South," takes a fresh, critical look at the widening gap between an impoverished and youthful southern hemisphere and a wealthy and aging northern hemisphere. We have expanded coverage of both the impact of globalization on the Global South and of the Global South countries' foreign policy responses to globalization. The chapter pays increased attention to issues of human security and human rights, such as gender equality, as these issues assume increasing significance in comparison to national security.
- Chapter 6, "Intergovernmental Organizations (IGOs)," monitors the profound changes that have accompanied the recent growth of the globe's major intergovernmental organizations. New coverage focuses on the reorganized

United Nations, the expanding European Union with its common currency and a new "Eurocorps" military force independent of NATO, and the enlarged World Trade Organization, which finds itself under increasing attack as a symbol of the problems associated with globalization and free trade.

- Chapter 7, "The Promise and Peril of Nongovernmental Organizations (NGOs)," more explicitly examines the role that ethnopolitical groups, indigenous peoples, religious groups, terrorists, and multinational corporations pose to the dominant sovereign state, as globalization elevates the importance of nonstate actors. We evaluate the potential decline in states' sovereign power as a global trend, not only in the liberal democracies of the Global North but also in the "failed states" of the Global South.
- Chapter 8, "Trade and Monetary Issues in a Globalized Political Economy," discusses how the liberalization of the marketplace has fostered extreme currency volatility, and assesses whether sustained prosperity, free trade, and the management of currency and banking crises will continue, taking into account newly evolving perspectives in commercial liberalism, mercantilism, and hegemonic stability theory. For students new to economic policy, we have added a basic explanation of monetary terms and concepts to give them a solid grounding.
- Chapter 9, "Globalization and the Disappearance of National Borders," has been revised to highlight the growing controversies between winners and losers in the process of globalization. The chapter also addresses the intensifying popular backlash against globalization and reviews divided opinions about whether it is a process that states have the power to control.
- Chapter 10, retitled "Population Politics and the Demographic Dimensions of Globalization," and Chapter 11, "Ecopolitics and the Preservation of the Global Commons," have both been revised to more closely link the discussion of changes in the rate of population growth to the question of sustaining the global ecology. We explore the opportunities and problems associated with the "birth dearth" in the aging Global North, and the continuing population explosion in many Global South countries, as they relate to new legal regimes being negotiated to control such common environmental problems as global warming, biotechnology, and genetic engineering.
- We have revised both Chapter 12, "Armed Conflict between and within States," and Chapter 13, "Military Power and National Security in the Age of Globalization," to cover recent changes in the incidence of different types of warfare, specifically expanding discussion of the wave of internal rebellions in failing states. We also discuss new military technologies that many believe have reduced international security by making new methods of warfare available, and introduce the latest available information on arms sales. Finally, the new edition features a revised comparison of the great powers' national security strategies, including the United States' refusal to sign the Comprehensive Test Ban Treaty in 1999, to take account of their new doctrines and policies at the beginning of the twenty-first century.
- Chapter 14, retitled "Coercive Diplomacy and Intervention in a World of Vanishing Borders," brings up to date the discussion of how states exercise military influence by methods short of war. The use of military intervention for humanitarian and peace-keeping purposes and the controversies sur-

rounding such interventionism are given the prominence they deserve at the start of the twenty-first century.

- Chapter 15, "The Realist Road to Security through Alliances, the Balance of Power, and Arms Control," and Chapter 16, "The Liberal Institutional Paths to Peace," have been refocused to sharpen awareness of the similarities and differences in the realist and liberal approaches to world order. We have incorporated discussions of new developments and issues, such as START III, the changing laws regarding humanitarian military intervention, and the controversies surrounding the possibility of preserving peace by promoting the enlargement of the community of liberal democratic states, which have seldom if ever waged war against one another.
- Chapter 17, retitled "Ten Questions about Twenty-First-Century Global Prospects," presents by way of conclusion a series of questions designed to generate students' critical thoughts about the trends and issues identified in the preceding chapters and the dilemmas they pose for the global future. We have thoroughly revised these ten questions and our discussion of them to present the most recent assessments of the global prospect, while relating them to enduring issues in international relations.

Design and Pedagogy

The eighth edition of *World Politics* features an attractive new interior design and a variety of pedagogic improvements to make the intellectual journey through world politics easier than ever for students.

- **Part openers provide a road map to each section's content.** The five parts in *World Politics* now each begin with a pedagogically useful, visually attractive, two-page part opener, in which we overview the topics to be covered in the chapters that follow, to give students a better understanding of the connections between the many different aspects of global politics.
- **Chapter *Topics and Themes* revised to match chapter headings.** Each chapter now begins with an outline of major topics that corresponds to the chapter headings and the titles of the featured essays, for students' ease in navigating the chapter.
- ***Controversy* boxes present essential debates.** Each chapter features one or two essays on major controversies in international relations. As a sense of change grips much of the world, discourse about international relations gives rise to questions that inspire intense debate. Each Controversy identifies a major issue on which there are opposing positions. The essay encourages students to consider rival viewpoints and develop their own opinions. Addressing both classic dilemmas in international affairs and the most heated current debates, Controversy boxes offer excellent starting points for class debates or research papers.
- **Comprehensive marginal glosses for all key terms.** Responding to the popularity of the marginal glosses introduced in the seventh edition, we now provide marginal glosses for *all* key terms in the text. For complex terms with multiple meanings, the marginal glosses provide the explanation that is most relevant in each place and cross-reference a key definition,

enabling students to compare different uses of the term to broaden their understanding of its meaning.

- **Expanded map and illustration program brings the book up to date.** Over a hundred new maps, tables, photographs, and figures and twenty-eight specially-updated maps and figures from previous editions broaden the book's coverage, provoke interest, and enable students to visualize the ideas that command attention. We have selected photographs and illustrations with an eye toward introducing the most timely topics, including a detailed caption that identifies the image and explains its relevance to the larger issues discussed in the text.
- **Updated "Where on the World Wide Web?" listings.** Responding to the new and rapidly changing information available on the Internet, the "Where on the World Wide Web?" section at the end of each chapter has been updated and expanded to list major Web sites that students can explore for further information on the topics discussed in the chapter. Researched thoroughly by Lynn Kuzma of the University of Southern Maine, each Web listing is accompanied by a lively annotation describing the site's contents and suggesting activities and research that students can pursue on the site.
- **Revised list of suggested reading.** To bring the most recent scholarship and commentary to the attention of students for further study, we provide a thoroughly revised list of authoritative books and articles, incorporating the groundbreaking research of the past two years into a list of key publications.
- **Full-color re-design.** A bright, new interior design retains the vivid look of previous editions while making greater use of photographic images in part and chapter openers, reformatting running heads for greater ease in navigating the text, and enhancing maps and figures for easier comparison and readability.

SUPPLEMENTS

Instructor's Resource Manual with Test Bank

An extensive *Instructor's Resource Manual with Test Bank* supports the eighth edition of *World Politics*. The manual includes chapter outlines to guide lectures; thematic guides suggesting a variety of approaches to covering each chapter's material; learning objectives; suggested readings for instructors; creative teaching aids for each chapter, including simulations, teaching cases, and multimedia offerings; and a test bank containing over five hundred new or revised essay and multiple-choice questions. A computerized version of the test bank portion of the manual is available on CD-ROM.

Multimedia Companion

World Politics: Trend and Transformation is accompanied by an interactive Web site that can be found at <www.bedfordstmartins.com/polisci>. This on-line ancillary for instructors and students includes chapter quizzes, flashcards for vocabulary testing, and interactive student activities for further practice with the concepts presented in the text.

ACKNOWLEDGMENTS

Many people have contributed to making the eighth edition the most timely and useful version of *World Politics* since the book was first published in 1981. In addition to those whose assistance helped establish *World Politics* as the field's leading text in its previous editions, we wish to acknowledge the special assistance and advice of those who have contributed specifically to the eighth edition.

We greatly appreciate the constructive comments and suggestions offered by reviewers. In particular, we express our gratitude to professional scholars who provided blind reviews of the revised manuscript, including Kevin Archer, David Dickson, Matthias Kaelberer, and Thomas Oatley. We also wish to thank Roger Coate and Donald Puchala at the University of South Carolina, Richard Grimmett at the Congressional Research Office, Ted Robert Gurr at the University of Maryland, Margaret G. Hermann at Syracuse University, Bjørn Møller at the Copenhagen Peace Research Institute, Jeffrey Pickering at Kansas State University, Gregory A. Raymond at Boise State University, Joseph Reap at the U.S. Department of State, Daniel Rotfield at the International Peace Research Institute, and Rodney Tomlinson at the U.S. Naval Academy, for providing and sharing data which made the update of statistical information possible. Lynn Kuzma at the University of Southern Maine diligently collected sites for the "Where on the World Wide Web?" boxes and developed the revised *Instructor's Resource Manual with Testbank* and *World Politics* Web site to accompany the text.

At Bedford/St. Martin's, Executive Editor for History and Political Science Katherine E. Kurzman, President Charles H. Christensen, and Editorial Director Joan E. Feinberg are to be thanked for applying their talents and staff to professionally producing a redesigned publication with many new stylistic features. Deserving of special gratitude are our highly skilled, dedicated, and helpful editors, Developmental Editor Gretchen Boger and Senior Editor Doug Bell, who exercised extraordinary professionalism in guiding the process that brought this edition into print. In addition, Linda DeMasi and the staff at Publisher's Studio, as well as Leslie Connor, our copyeditor, contributed immeasurably to the preparation, polish, and production of the book.

Beyond the Bedford/St. Martin's staff and their associates, we are pleased to acknowledge the enormous contribution of Ruth Cooper to the preparation of a complete manuscript, and to the research and proofreading assistance provided by Edward Ballanco, Julie Hysong, Se-Woo Pyo, Tahir Sevik, Fahrettin Súmer, Zhenghuan Zhou, and Zhiqun Zhu.

Charles W. Kegley, Jr.
Eugene R. Wittkopf

Brief Table of Contents

CONTENTS

WTO

ماكدونالدز

Controversy Boxes and Maps

CONTROVERSY BOXES

MAPS

About the Authors

CHARLES W. KEGLEY, JR. received his doctorate from Syracuse University. Currently, he is Pearce Professor of International Relations at the University of South Carolina. A past president of the International Studies Association (1993–1994), Kegley has held appointments at Georgetown University, the University of Texas, Rutgers University, and the People's University of China. He is the editor of *Controversies in International Relations Theory: Realism and the Neoliberal Challenge* (St. Martin's Press, 1995) and *The Long Postwar Peace* (1991), and has published extensively in scholarly journals. With Gregory A. Raymond, Kegley is the coauthor of *How Nations Make Peace* (St. Martin's/Worth, 1999), *A Multipolar Peace? Great-Power Politics in the Twenty-First Century* (St. Martin's Press, 1994), and *When Trust Breaks Down: Alliance Norms and World Politics* (1990).

EUGENE R. WITTKOPF received his doctorate from Syracuse University. He is currently R. Downs Poindexter Distinguished Professor of Political Science at Louisiana State University. He has also held appointments at the University of Florida and the University of North Carolina at Chapel Hill. Wittkopf is author of *Faces of Internationalism: Public Opinion and American Foreign Policy* (1990), coeditor of the third edition of *The Future of American Foreign Policy* (St. Martin's/Worth, 1999) and *The Domestic Sources of American Foreign Policy: Insights and Evidence* (1999). He has also published extensively in professional journal literature. In 1997 he received the highest award given by Louisiana State University in recognition of faculty contributions to research and scholarship when he was named the LSU Distinguished Research Master of Arts, Humanities, and Social Sciences.

Together, Kegley and Wittkopf have coauthored and edited several texts and readers for St. Martin's Press, including *American Foreign Policy: Pattern and Process,* Fifth Edition (1996); *The Future of American Foreign Policy* (1992); *The Nuclear Reader: Strategy, Weapons, War,* Second Edition (1989); and *The Domestic Sources of American Foreign Policy* (1988). They are also the coeditors of *The Global Agenda,* Sixth Edition (2001).

PART I

TREND AND TRANSFORMATION IN WORLD POLITICS

The world has moved into a new century and new millennium. How are we to think about the global future? Part I introduces you to the study of world politics in a period of rapid change. It opens a window on the many trends that are unfolding, some of them in contrary directions, whose combined force is transforming the pattern of international relations.

There are obstacles to understanding world politics accurately. Chapter 1 explains how our perceptions of global realities can lead to distortions and provides a framework for getting beyond these barriers. Within this framework, the major influences on changing international conditions are divided into three categories—the individual, the state, and the global "levels of analysis." Chapter 2 introduces the major theories that political scientists have developed over the years to help policymakers and citizens better describe, explain, and predict the evolving nature of international relations. Such theories are important, because they are the tools that can help us make sense of the complexity of world politics and interpret emerging trends and transformations.

CHAPTER 1

EXPLORING TWENTY-FIRST-CENTURY WORLD POLITICS

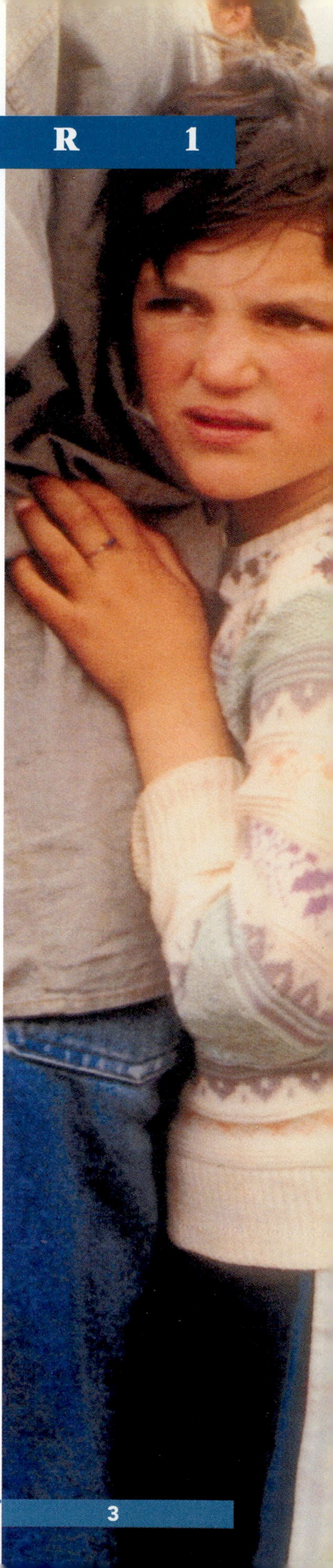

TOPICS AND THEMES

- The challenge of investigating international affairs
- How perceptions influence images of reality
- Different levels of analysis: Individuals, states, and the global system
- The book's approach: Actors, issues, and their interactions
- Facing the future: Key questions to confront

- **CONTROVERSY** WHAT IS THE "RIGHT" WAY TO MAP THE GLOBE? ALTERNATIVE PROJECTIONS OF REALITY
- **CONTROVERSY** CAN YOU MAKE A DIFFERENCE IN THE WORLD'S FUTURE?

Kosovar refugees wait for food rations.

Great things are achieved by guessing the direction of one's century.

—Giuseppe Mazzini, Italian political leader, 1848

Now the world faces new circumstances whose implications it is just beginning to discover, and the problem of order has become even more complex than before.

—Stanley Hoffmann, political scientist, 1998

Picture yourself returning home from a week's vacation on an island where you had no access to the news. You enjoyed the peace and quiet, but now you are curious about what happened while you were away. As you pick up the newspapers piled outside your door, headlines catch your eye. They tell you that in the short time you were gone, leaders of the Group of Eight (G-8) major industrial democracies concluded a historic summit, at which they argued about the proliferation of weapons, military interventionism, and the enlargement of NATO. They also squabbled over the new rules of the World Trade Organization, whose 135 members planned a new "Millennium Round" of multilateral free trade negotiations. The following day's headlines report that greenhouse gasses and global warming are producing another record heat wave and that widespread droughts are likely. The next day's headlines inform you that during its upcoming session the United Nations (UN) General Assembly plans to discuss the lack of progress on environmental issues in the seven years since the Earth Summit in Rio de Janeiro.

Turning to CNN, you hear that the United States and Russia agreed to begin a new round of negotiations for a START III treaty to reduce their long-range nuclear weapons. Surfing to another channel, you view Chinese leaders warning that if Taiwan (which China regards as a renegade province temporarily separated from the mainland) moves toward independence by departing from the "one China" policy and dealing with China on a "state-to-state" basis, China will use military force. Perplexed, you turn off the television and connect to the Internet where you learn that the peace process in Northern Ireland was interrupted by another failure to accept a negotiated agreement, that at its Singapore Summit the Sixth Asian Forum condemned North Korea when it conducted successful launches of its new Taepo Dong 2 long-range missiles, and that India and Pakistan threaten to use their nuclear weapons in war over Kashmir. Next you learn that since NATO's intervention in Kosovo, civil wars and ethnic cleansing continued in East Timor, Congo, and Iran, as a new rebellion swept Colombia. You also read that the international community's response to the suffering of the starving victims of these genocidal internal wars was once again limited and feeble. Despairing, you greet with skepticism the announcement that the United States and more than forty other countries signed an ambitious and costly plan to rebuild the Balkans after NATO's seventy-eight-day war over Kosovo. The Internet next reports that human rights organizations had succeeded in their quest to create a permanent war crimes court at the Hague to prosecute crimes against humanity, and that that court took the precedent-setting step to prevent dictators from butchering people within their territorial borders by indicting a sitting head of state—Yugoslavia's Slobodan Milosevic.

This news is not "new." It tells an old story about a sea of turmoil swept by global forces. Nevertheless, the temptation to wish that this depressing kind of chaotic world would just "go away" is overwhelming. If only the unstable world would stand still long enough for a sense of predictability and order to prevail. Alas, that does not appear likely. You cannot escape the world or control its turbulence, and you cannot single-handedly alter its character.

The scenario just described is not hypothetical. The events recorded actually occurred during the month of July 1999. Undoubtedly, many individuals experienced dismay, fear, and confusion. We are all a part of the world, and the world is an integral part of each of us. Hence, if we are to live adaptively amidst the fierce winds of global change, we must face the challenge of discovering the dynamic properties of world politics. Because every person is influenced increasingly by world events, all must confront the challenge of investigating how the global system works and how the process of globalization is remaking our political and economic world. Only through learning how our own decisions and behavior, as well as those of powerful governments and transnational actors, contribute to the global condition, and how all people and groups in turn are heavily conditioned by changes in world politics, can we address what U.S. President Bill Clinton in 1993 defined as "the question of our time—whether we can make change our friend and not our enemy."

THE INVESTIGATIVE CHALLENGE

How can we best understand the political convulsions that confront the globe's more than 6 billion people almost daily? How can we anticipate their future significance? And how can we understand which factors and forces most influence the world's future? At the beginning of the twenty-first century, we have been engulfed in futurist talk. We have been forced to use unfamiliar language—"new century," "new millennium," "new world"—and to speculate, What will the new world be like? Will it be different? As global conditions change, will the human victims and beneficiaries change in the process? Or will the patterns of the past endure?

How can we visualize our probable human destiny and see beyond the confines of our immediate time? To start, it is important to appreciate the interaction of previous ideas and events with current realities. As philosopher George Santayana cautioned, "Those who cannot remember the past are condemned to repeat it." Similarly, British Prime Minister Winston Churchill advised, "The farther backward you look, the farther forward you are likely to see." Thus, to understand the dramatic changes in world politics today and to predict how they will shape the future, we will view them in the context of a long-term perspective that examines how the **international political system**—the patterns of interaction among world political actors—has changed and how some of its fundamental characteristics have resisted change. What do evolving diplomatic practices suggest about the current state of world politics? Are the episodic shock waves throughout the world clearing the way for a truly new twenty-first-century world order? Or will many of today's dramatic disruptions ultimately prove temporary, mere spikes on the seismograph of history?

■ **international political system**
the patterns of political interaction among actors in the global arena.

We invite you to explore these questions with us. To begin our search, let us explore how the differences between continuities, changes, and cycles in world history can help us orient our effort.

Every historical period is marked to some extent by change. Now, however, the pace of change seems more rapid and its consequences more profound than ever. To many observers, the cascade of events at the start of the twenty-first century implies a revolutionary restructuring of world politics. Numerous integrative trends point to that possibility. The countries of the world are drawing closer together in communications, ideas, and trade, as the integration of national economies has produced a globalized market, forming interdependent bonds between countries and cultures. Globalization is changing the way the world works. Likewise, disintegrative trends are shaking the globe and restructuring the way it operates. The proliferation of conventional and unconventional weapons, global environmental deterioration, and the resurgence of nationalism and ethnic conflict all portend a restructuring marked by disorder. The opposing forces of integration and disintegration point toward a **transformation** in world politics as extensive and important as the system-disrupting convulsions following World Wars I and II and the **Cold War** between the United States and the former Soviet Union and their allies.

■ **transformation**
a change in the characteristic pattern of interaction among the most active participants in world politics of such magnitude that it appears that one "global system" has replaced another.

■ **Cold War**
the forty-two-year rivalry between the United States and the Soviet Union, as well as their competing coalitions, between 1949 and 1991, which sought to contain each other's expansion through an arms race, and win worldwide predominance for capitalism (U.S.) or communism (USSR).

Distinguishing meaningful transformations (true historical watersheds) from temporary changes (sudden changes that at first shock and scare everyone but then, with the passage of time, fade in importance) is difficult. The moment of transformation from one system to another is not immediately obvious. Still, certain times are especially likely candidates. Major turning points in world politics usually have occurred at the ends of major wars, which typically disrupt or destroy preexisting international arrangements. In the twentieth century, World Wars I and II and the end of the Cold War stimulated fundamental breaks with the past and set in motion major transformations providing countries with incentives to rethink seriously the premises underlying their interests, purposes, and priorities.

Despite all that is radically different at the start of the twenty-first century, much remains the same in world politics. Indeed, we often expect the future to bring about changes, only to discover certain subjects or patterns reappearing. Because "history usually makes a mockery of our hopes and expectations,"

Breaking Down Cold War Barriers New global systems sometimes emerge quickly, when a single, global-shattering development alters prevailing conditions. That happened overnight when the nuclear age began on August 6, 1945, with the U.S. atomic bombing of Hiroshima. More recently, the dismantling of the Berlin Wall in November 1989 signaled the end of the Cold War system. As exuberant citizens chipped away at the last vestiges of a divided nation, Germany moved toward reunification for the first time in over forty years, and the post–Cold War era began.

leaders must "question . . . the ways and areas in which the future is likely to resemble the past" (Jervis 1991–92).

How can we determine when an existing pattern of relationships gives way to a new international system? Following Stanley Hoffmann (1961), we will proceed by assuming that we have a new international system when we have a new answer to one of three questions: (1) *What are the system's basic units?* (e.g., states or supranational institutions for global governance); (2) *What are the predominant foreign policy goals that these units seek with respect to one another?* (e.g., territorial conquest or material gain through trade); and (3) *What can these units do to one another with their military and economic capabilities?*

These criteria might lead us to conclude that a new system has now emerged. First, new trade partnerships have been forged in Europe, the cone of South America, North America, and the Pacific Rim, and these trading blocs may behave as unitary, or independent, actors as they compete with one another. Moreover, international organizations, such as the World Trade Organization and the European Union, now sometimes flex their political muscles in contests with individual states; and transnational religious movements, such as Islamic fundamentalism, challenge the **global system** itself—a system that international law still defines as composed primarily of **states** consisting of nationality groups who perceive themselves as unified by a common language, culture, or ethnic identity. At the same time, some states have disintegrated into smaller units. In 1991, the former Soviet Union fragmented into fractious political entities searching for national identity and autonomy. Other national units could disintegrate as well—peacefully, like the former Czechoslovakia, or violently, like the former Yugoslavia.

Second, territorial conquest is no longer the predominant goal of many states' foreign policies. Instead, their emphasis has shifted from traditional military

■ global system
a worldwide system primarily of states comprising nationality groups who perceive themselves as unified by language, culture, or ethnic identity.

■ state
an independent, territorially defined community in the global system administered by a sovereign government (see p. 55).

methods of exercising influence to economic means. Meanwhile, the ideological contest between democratic capitalism and the Marxist-Leninist communism of the Cold War era no longer comprises the primary cleavage in international politics, and a major new axis has yet to become clear.

Third, the proliferation of weapons technology has profoundly altered the damage that states can inflict on one another. Great powers alone no longer control the world's most lethal weapons. Increasingly, however, the great powers' prosperity depends on economic circumstances throughout the globe, reducing their ability to control their growth rates at precisely the time when their capabilities to militarily dominate others have eroded.

The profound changes in units, goals, and capabilities of recent years have dramatically altered the ranking of states in the pecking orders that define the structure of international politics. Still, the hierarchies themselves endure. The *economic hierarchy* that divides the rich from the poor, the *political hierarchy* that separates the rulers from the ruled, the *resource hierarchy* that makes some suppliers and others dependents, and the *military asymmetries* that pit the strong against the weak all still shape the relations among states, as they have in the past. Similarly, the perpetuation of international **anarchy** in the absence of institutions to govern the globe and chronic national insecurity continue to encourage preparations for war and the use of force without international mandate. Thus change and continuity coexist, with both forces simultaneously shaping contemporary world politics.

■ **anarchy**
a condition in which the units in the global system are subjected to few if any overarching institutions to regulate their conduct (see p. 428).

The interaction of constancy and change makes it difficult to predict whether the twenty-first century will bring a wholly new and different international system. What is clear is that this interaction will determine future relations among global actors. This, perhaps, explains why **cycles** so often appear to characterize world politics: Periodic sequences of events occur that resemble patterns in earlier periods. Because the emergent international system shares many characteristics with earlier periods, historically minded observers may experience déjà vu—the illusion of having already experienced something actually being experienced for the first time.

■ **cycles**
the periodic reemergence of conditions similar to those that existed previously.

The challenge, then, is to observe unfolding global realities objectively in order to describe and explain them accurately, and hence to understand their future impact. This requires that we understand how our images of reality shape our expectations. It also requires a set of tools for analyzing the forces of constancy and change that affect our world. Thus, the remainder of this chapter will briefly examine the role that images of reality play in our understanding of world politics, and then will describe the theoretical orientation of the book. Chapter 2 will examine the theoretical perspectives we will use in this book to interpret trends and transformations in world politics.

HOW PERCEPTIONS INFLUENCE IMAGES OF REALITY

We all carry mental images of world politics—explicit or implicit, conscious or subconscious. But whatever our level of awareness, our images simplify "reality" by exaggerating some features of the real world while ignoring others. Thus we live in a world defined by our expectations and images.

These mental pictures, or perceptions, are inevitably distortions, as they cannot fully capture the complexity and configurations of even physical objects, such as the globe itself (see Controversy: What Is the "Right" Way to Map the Globe?). Thus many of our images of the world's political realities may be built on illusions and misconceptions. Even images that are now accurate can easily become outdated if we fail to recognize changes in the world. Indeed, the world's future will be determined not only by changes in the "objective" facts of world politics but also by the meaning that people ascribe to those facts, the assumptions on which they base their interpretations, and the actions that flow from these assumptions and interpretations—however accurate or inaccurate they might be.

The Nature and Sources of Images

The effort to simplify one's view of the world is inevitable and even necessary. Just as cartographers' projections simplify complex geophysical space so we can better understand the world, each of us inevitably creates a "mental map"—a habitual way of organizing information—to make sense of a confusing abundance of information. Although mental maps are neither inherently right nor wrong, they are important because we tend to react according to the way the world appears to us rather than the way it is. How we *view* the world (not what it is really like) determines our attitudes, our beliefs, and our behavior. Political leaders, too, are captives of this tendency. As Richard Ned Lebow (1981) warns, "Policymakers are prone to distort reality in accord with their needs even in situations that appear . . . relatively unambiguous."

Most of us—policymakers included—look for information that reinforces our preexisting beliefs about the world, assimilate new data into familiar images, mistakenly equate what we believe with what we know, and deny information that contradicts our expectations. We process information using **schematic reasoning;** that is, we rely on learned ways of psychologically perceiving new information and we interpret it in light of our memories (Rosenberg 1988). We use information shortcuts both to make political judgments and to help orient our attitudes and beliefs toward specific events and policy issues. A schema thus aids in the organization of information and shapes our perceptions of the world.

■ **schematic reasoning** the process of reasoning by which new information is interpreted according to a memory structure that contains a network of genetic scripts, metaphors, and stereotypical characters.

We assemble and organize information about the world to help us simplify it. This is necessary "to cope with an extraordinarily confusing world by structuring views about specific foreign policies according to [our] more general and abstract beliefs" (Hurwitz and Peffley 1987). Our preexisting values and beliefs encourage us to accept some images as accurate while rejecting from consciousness others that are incongruent with our prior beliefs, a psychological conflict known as **cognitive dissonance** (see Festinger 1957). The mind selects, screens, and filters what it perceives. Thus our view of world politics depends not only on what happens in the world but also on how we interpret and internalize those events; our mental maps inevitably help to shape our dispositions toward global issues. Several factors influence our perceptions of international relations:

■ **cognitive dissonance** the general psychological tendency to deny discrepancies between one's preexisting beliefs (cognitions) and new information.

- Our psychological needs, drives, and dispositions (e.g., trust or mistrust), which are ingrained in our personalities as a result of early childhood experiences.
- Our views of international affairs (e.g., tolerance or fear of cultural diversity) as filtered through the socialization or learning we receive as children.

CONTROVERSY

WHAT IS THE "RIGHT" WAY TO MAP THE GLOBE?

Alternative Projections of Reality

To understand the kind of controversies that can arise from the fact that different people can see different realities when they look at an issue from different perspectives, consider the continuing controversy among cartographers about how to make an accurate projection of the world. All maps of the globe are distorted, because it is impossible to perfectly represent the three-dimensional globe on a two-dimensional piece of paper. The difficulty cartographers face can be appreciated by trying to flatten an orange peel. You can only flatten it by separating pieces of the peel that were joined when it was spherical. Cartographers who try to flatten the globe on paper, without "ripping it" into separate pieces, face the same problem. Although there are a variety of ways to represent the three-dimensional object on paper, all of them involve some kind of distortion. Thus cartographers must choose among the imperfect ways of representing the globe by selecting those aspects of the world's geography

MAP 1.1
Orthographic Projection

The orthographic projection, centering on the mid-Atlantic, conveys some sense of the curvature of the earth by using rounded edges. The sizes and shapes of continents toward the outer edges of the circle are distorted to give a sense of spherical perspective.

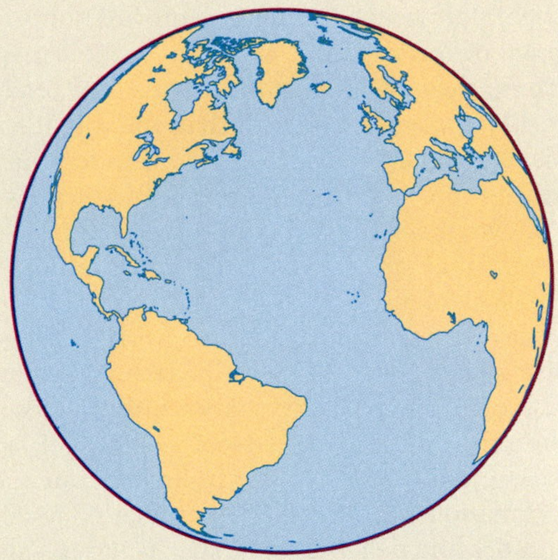

MAP 1.2
Mercator Projection

This Mercator projection, popular in sixteenth-century Europe, is a classic Eurocentric view of the world. It retained direction accurately, making it useful for navigators, but placed Europe at the center of the world and exaggerated the continent's importance relative to other land masses. Europe appears larger than South America, which is twice Europe's size, and two-thirds of the map is used to represent the northern half of the world and only one-third the southern half. Because lines of longitude were represented as parallel rather than convergent, it also greatly exaggerates the size of Greenland and Antarctica.

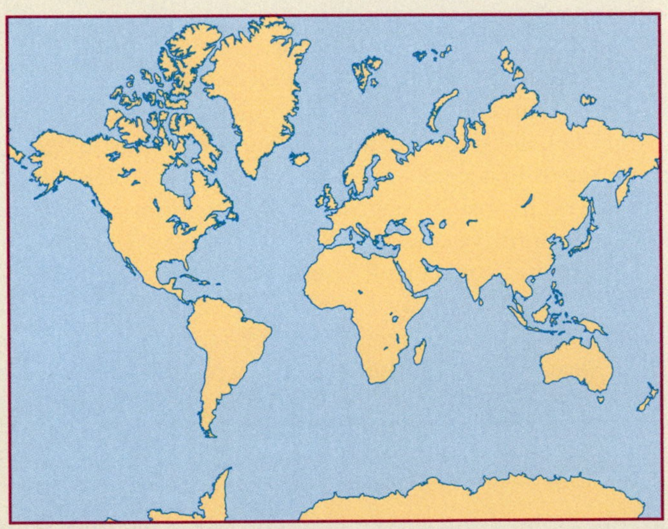

they consider most important to describe them accurately, while making adjustments to other parts.

Cartographers' ideas of what is most important in world geography have varied according to their own global perspectives. These four maps depict the distribution of the earth's land surfaces and territory, but each portrays a different image. Each is a model of reality, an abstraction that highlights some features of the globe while ignoring others. Of course, all of us confront similar types of perceptual biases as we organize our perceptions to view and interpret world politics. In examining these four ways of viewing and interpreting the globe, consider which projection you think is best. Which elements do you think are most important to preserve accurately? What does your answer indicate about your view of the world?

MAP 1.3
Peter's Projection

In the Peter's projection, each land mass appears in correct proportion in relation to all others, but it distorts the shape and position of land masses. In contrast with most geographic representations, it draws attention to the less-developed countries of the Global South where more than three-quarters of the world's population lives today.

MAP 1.4
World Time View

This map is a modified south pole projection portraying the world's twenty-four standard time zones. Note that these zones often follow state borders rather than straight latitude lines. Knowledge of time-zone differences is critical in today's age of globalization and interdependence.
SOURCE: IVN Communications, Inc.

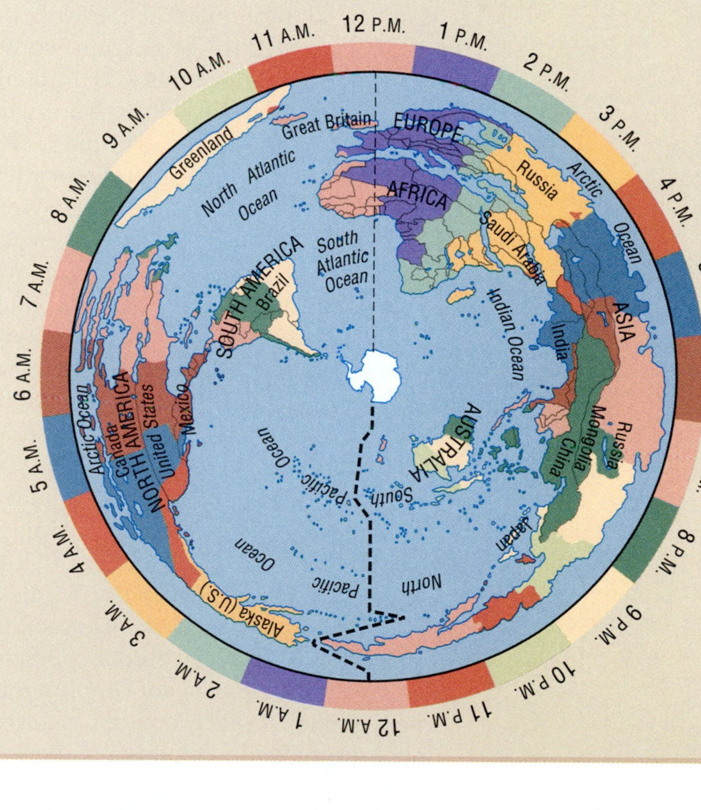

- Our images of world history as shaped by the teachers and books to which we are exposed.
- Opinions about world affairs articulated by our frequent associates, such as close friends.
- Attitudes expressed by policymakers, political pundits, and others whose expertise we respect.
- Positions we occupy and roles we perform (student, parent, bureaucrat, policymaker, diplomat, etc.).

Tolerance of ambiguity and receptivity to new ways of organizing thinking vary among individuals and personality types. Some people are receptive to diversity and therefore better able than others to revise perceptual habits to accommodate new realities. Nevertheless, to some extent, we are all prisoners of the perceptual predispositions that have shaped us and that in turn shape our attitudes, beliefs, and images of world politics. This is why political **ideologies** tend to develop and to attract adherents who join groups to express their common beliefs.

ideology
a set of core philosophical principles that a group of leaders and citizens collectively holds about politics, the interests of political actors, and the ways people ought to ethically behave.

The Role of Images in World Politics

We must be careful not to assume automatically that what applies to individuals applies to entire countries. Still, leaders' images of historical circumstances often predispose them to behave in particular ways toward others, regardless of "objective" facts. For instance, the loss of 26 million Soviet lives in the "Great Patriotic War" (as the Russians refer to World War II) created an exaggerated fear of foreign invasion, which caused a generation of Soviet policymakers to perceive U.S. defensive moves with considerable suspicion and often alarm. Similarly, the founders of the United States viewed eighteenth-century European power politics as corrupt, contributing to two seemingly contradictory tendencies later evident in U.S. foreign policy: (1) America's isolationist impulse (its disposition to withdraw from world affairs), and (2) its determination to reform the world in its own image. The former led the country to reject membership in the League of Nations after World War I; the latter gave rise to the U.S. globalist foreign policy after World War II, which committed the country to active involvement nearly everywhere on nearly every issue. Most Americans failed to recognize that others might regard such a far-reaching international policy position as arrogant or threatening; they saw only good intentions. As President Jimmy Carter once lamented, "The hardest thing for Americans to understand is that they are not better than other people."

Because leaders and citizens are prone to ignore or reinterpret information that runs counter to their beliefs and values, mutual misperceptions often fuel discord in world politics, especially when relations between countries are hostile. Distrust and suspicion arise as conflicting parties view each other in the same negative light—that is, as **mirror images** develop. This occurred in Moscow and Washington during the Cold War. Self-righteousness often leads one party to view its own actions as constructive but its adversary's responses as negative and hostile. When this occurs, conflict resolution is extraordinarily difficult, as the Cold War and the recurrent ethnic conflicts in the Balkans and elsewhere illustrate. Thus fostering peace is not simply a matter of expanding trade and other forms of transnational contact, or even of bringing political leaders together in international summits. Rather, it is a matter of changing deeply entrenched beliefs.

mirror images
the tendency of states and people in competitive interaction to perceive each other similarly—to see others the same way others see them.

Although our mental maps of world politics are resistant to change, change is possible. Overcoming old thinking habits sometimes occurs when we experience punishment or discomfort as a result of clinging to false assumptions. As Benjamin Franklin once observed, "The things that hurt, instruct." Dramatic events in particular can alter international images, sometimes drastically. The Vietnam War caused many Americans to adjust their previous images about the use of force in contemporary world politics. The defeat of the Third Reich and revelations of atrocities committed before and during World War II caused the German people to confront their past as they prepared for a democratic future imposed by the victorious allies. The use of atomic bombs against Japan in the waning days of World War II caused many to confront the horrors of modern warfare and the immorality of weapons of mass destruction. More recently, the unexpected collapse of communist rule in the Soviet Union and Eastern Europe prompted policymakers and political commentators alike to reexamine their assumptions about foreign policy priorities in a new, post–Cold War system. Often such jolting experiences encourage us to create new mental maps, perceptual filters, and criteria through which we may interpret later events and define situations.

As we shape and reshape our images of world politics and its future, we need to think critically about the foundations on which our perceptions rest. Are they accurate? Are they informed? Might they be adjusted to gain greater understanding and empathy? This rethinking is one of the challenges we face in confronting the world politics of the twenty-first century.

DIFFERENT LEVELS OF ANALYSIS

To predict which forces will dominate the future, we must recognize that many forces are operating at the same time. No trend or trouble stands alone; all interact simultaneously. The future is influenced by many determinants, each connected to the rest in a complex web of linkages. Collectively, these may produce stability by limiting the impact of any single disruptive force. If interacting forces converge, however, their combined effects can accelerate the pace of change in world politics, moving it in directions not possible otherwise.

Many international relations scholars agree that world politics can best be understood by focusing on one (or more) of three levels. Known as **levels of analysis,** this classification distinguishes: (1) individuals, (2) states or other world political actors, and (3) the entire global system.

The **individual level of analysis** refers to the personal characteristics of humans, including those responsible for making important decisions on behalf of state and nonstate actors, as well as ordinary citizens whose behavior has important political consequences. Here, for example, we may properly locate the impact of individuals' perceptions on their political attitudes, beliefs, and behavior, and explore the question of why each human being is a crucial part of the global drama, and why the study of world politics is relevant to our lives and future (see Controversy: Can You Make a Difference in the World's Future?).

The **state level of analysis** consists of the authoritative decision-making units that govern states' foreign policy processes and the internal attributes of those states (e.g., their type of government, level of economic and military

■ **levels of analysis**
the different aspects of and agents in international affairs that may be stressed in interpreting world politics and explaining global phenomena, depending on whether the analyst chooses to focus on "wholes" (the complete global system and large collectivities) or on "parts" (individual states or people) (see p. 56).

■ **individual level of analysis**
an analytical approach that emphasizes the psychological and perceptual variables motivating people such as those who make foreign policy decisions on behalf of states and other global actors.

■ **state level of analysis**
an analytical approach that emphasizes how the internal attributes of states influence their foreign policy behaviors (see p. 417).

Ethnic Warfare The twentieth century came to an end with the collapse of many "failed states" that resulted from wars between ethnic groups and state-sponsored terrorism against particular minority groups within the state's own borders. The tragic human cost of such ethnic warfare is vividly depicted in this photo of a Kosovar burying the remains of twenty-two relatives murdered by troops under Serbian dictator Slobodan Milosevic at the family's compound near Pristina, Kosovo, in June 1999. This kind of barbarism is a telling reminder that many threats to world order confront humanity throughout a globalized international community where danger abroad spells danger at home.

power, and number of nationality groups), which both shape and constrain leaders' foreign policy choices. The processes by which states make decisions regarding war and peace and their capabilities for carrying out those decisions, for instance, fall within the state level of analysis.

■ **global level of analysis**
an analytical approach that emphasizes the impact of worldwide conditions on foreign policy behavior.

The **global level of analysis** refers to the interactions of states and nonstate global actors whose behaviors ultimately shape the international political system and the levels of conflict and cooperation that characterize world politics. The capacity of rich states to dictate the choices of poor states properly falls within the global level of analysis. So does the capacity (or incapacity) of the UN to maintain peace.

Examples abound of the diverse ways in which global trends and issues are the product of influences at each level of analysis. Protectionist trade policies by an importing country increase the costs to consumers of clothing and cars and reduce the standard of living of citizens in the manufacturing states. Such policies are initiated by a *state* government (national level), but diminish the quality of life of *people* living both within the protectionist country and those living

CONTROVERSY

Can You Make a Difference in the World's Future?

Many people feel powerless, and question whether they can influence the way events and developments in world politics affect their lives. Some see themselves as victims of vast, invisible global forces beyond their control. In fact, many people think individuals are unimportant in the overall scheme of world politics, because it is difficult to imagine that one person can have an impact on global issues in the face of powerful states, organizations, and businesses. Individuals without significant money and power seem especially at a disadvantage against well-financed and widely known operations.

However, it is worth considering the rival view that we are all global citizens—that because the world depends on how we act, our actions can contribute positively to global welfare. Many philosophers have argued that everyone matters, and that each decision and action matters in influencing in a small way the overall evolution of history. Part of the reason is because the whole world is composed of each of its parts, and each individual contributes to the global consensus about basic human values in a worldwide community. Alexander Pope expressed how we learn to see beyond our immediate selfish needs, to accept our moral obligations not only to ourselves and those closest to us but also to conceptions of justice that apply to everyone, when he wrote in *An Essay on Man:*

> God loves from Whole to Parts: but human soul
> Must rise from Individual to the Whole.
> Self-love but serves the virtuous mind to wake,
> As the small pebble stirs the peaceful lake;
> The center mov'd, a circle strait succeeds,
> Another still, and still another spreads,
> Friend, parent, neighbour, first it will embrace,
> His country next, and next all human race. . . .

"If you're not part of the solution, you're part of the problem" is an adage that speaks to our involvement in the making of a more just or unjust world. How, then, should we proceed? Passivity is not an alternative because, as the British author Edmund Burke reminds us, "The only thing necessary for the triumph of evil is that good men do nothing." To make a positive contribution, and set standards for a better world, everyone must take a stand. Dr. Tony Evans, an African-American theologian, explains wisely why and how we should accept moral responsibilities to one another as global citizens if we want the benefits of living in a more just world order.

> The fact is that if you're a messed-up person and you have a family, you are going to contribute to a messed-up family. And if you're a messed-up person contributing to a messed-up family, and your family goes to church, then your messed-up family will contribute to a messed-up church.
>
> And if you're a messed-up person contributing to a messed-up family contributing to a messed-up church, and your church is in a neighborhood, then your messed-up church will lead to a messed-up neighborhood.
>
> And if you're a messed-up person contributing to a messed-up family contributing to a messed-up church leading to a messed-up neighborhood, and your neighborhood resides in a city, then your messed-up neighborhood will result in a messed-up city.
>
> Now if you're a messed-up person contributing to a messed-up family contributing to a messed-up church leading to a messed-up neighborhood resulting in a messed-up city, and your city resides in a county, then your messed-up city will cause a messed-up county.
>
> And if you're a messed-up person contributing to a messed-up family, contributing to a messed-up church leading to a messed-up neighborhood resulting in a messed-up city residing in a messed-up county, and your county is part of a state, then your county will help create a messed-up state.
>
> But that's not all. . . . If you're a messed-up person contributing to a messed-up family contributing to a messed-up church leading to a messed-up neighborhood resulting in a messed-up city residing in a messed-up county helping to create a messed-up state . . . and your nation is part of the world, your messed-up country will leave us with a messed-up world!
>
> So, if you want a better world composed of better countries, inhabited by better states, made up of better counties, composed of better cities inhabited by better neighborhoods, illuminated by better churches made up of better families, then we need to become better people. It all starts with personal responsibility! (Evans 1997, 2–3)

abroad (individual level), and reduce the level of *global* trade while threatening to precipitate retaliatory trade wars. Of course, for some developments and issues, factors and forces emanating primarily from one or two particular levels provide more analytical leverage than do those at the other(s). Accordingly, as we confront specific global issues in subsequent chapters, we will emphasize those levels of analysis that provide the most informative lens for viewing them. In the next section, we outline the path to discovery that *World Politics* will pursue.

THE BOOK'S APPROACH: ACTORS, ISSUES, AND THEIR INTERACTIONS

Because world politics is complex and our images of it are often discordant, scholars differ in their approaches to understanding the contemporary world. In this book, we adopt a multilevel, multi-issue perspective that frames the investigation by looking at: (1) the characteristics, capabilities, and interests of the principal "actors" in world politics (states and various nonstate participants in international affairs); (2) the principal welfare and security issues that populate the **global agenda;** and (3) the patterns of cooperation and contention that influence the interactions between and among actors and issues. As we probe these interactions, we will discover why **politics**—the exercise of influence to affect the distribution of particular values, such as power, prestige, or wealth—is the most pervasive and controversial aspect of international affairs.

■ **global agenda**
the primary issues, problems, and controversies on which states and humanity concentrate their attention and to which they allocate resources.

■ **politics**
to Harold Lasswell, the study of "who gets what, when, how and why?" (see p. 457).

A multilevel, multi-issue perspective is useful, not only because it takes into account the interaction of constancy and change in the new millennium, but also because it avoids dwelling on any particular events, countries, individuals, or transitory phenomena whose long-term significance is likely to diminish. Instead, the perspective seeks to identify behaviors that cohere into general global patterns—trends and transformations that measurably affect global living conditions. Thus we explore the nature of world politics from a perspective that places general patterns into a larger, lasting theoretical context, providing the conceptual tools and theories that will enable us to interpret subsequent developments.

Our journey into the dynamics of world politics begins in Chapter 2 with an overview of the major realist and liberal theoretical traditions that scholars and leaders use most to interpret world politics. This provides the intellectual background for the description, explanation, and prediction of the issues and developments that are treated in the remaining chapters.

Chapter 3 begins the analysis of actors, issues, and their interactions with a close examination of foreign policy decision-making processes *within* states, which remain the principal actors in world politics. Chapter 3 also covers the individual level of analysis, as we consider the role of leaders in making foreign policy, but the bulk of the chapter addresses how other forces at the state or domestic levels can constrain the impact of individuals.

■ **great powers**
the most powerful countries, militarily and economically, in the global system.

■ **nonstate actors**
all transnationally active groups other than states, such as organizations whose members are states and nongovernmental organizations whose members are individuals and private groups from more than one state.

We will then turn our attention to each of the types of actors in world politics and examine how their characteristics and capabilities affect their interests and influence in the world. **Great powers** (those wealthy countries with the biggest militaries) are the focus of attention in Chapter 4, "lesser powers" in Chapter 5; these chapters cover two groups of countries at the state level of analysis. In Chapters 6 and 7 we will extend this level to include **nonstate actors**—international organizations, multinational corporations, religious and enthnopolitical movements, and terrorist groups—that challenge the supremacy of states by either transcending or subverting states' sovereign control over their destinies.

The next group of chapters properly falls within the global level of analysis. Here we shift attention to global issues and inquire into how the characteristics, capabilities, and interests of the principal actors in world politics affect interactions and outcomes of the principal welfare and security issues on the global agenda. Welfare issues—the so-called **low politics** of problems relating to economics, population, and the environment—are the subjects of Chapters 8 through 11; Chapters 12 through 16 examine the so-called **high politics** of security issues—war and peace—that traditionally command attention on the global agenda.

■ **low politics**
the category of global issues related to the economic, social, demographic, and environmental aspects of relations between governments and people (see p. 247).

■ **high politics**
those issues related to the military, security, and political relations of states (see p. 247).

FACING THE FUTURE: KEY QUESTIONS TO CONFRONT AT THE DAWN OF THE NEW MILLENNIUM

Chapter 17 concludes our inquiry into the trends and transformations comprising contemporary world politics. It draws on the ideas and information presented in earlier chapters in order to address ten questions regarding the global issues that will dominate political discourse during the next decade. We anticipate those questions here by posing several that will also inform our inquiry in the chapters that follow.

Are States Obsolete?

The territorial state has been the primary actor in world politics for more than four centuries. Resurgent nationalism and civil warfare throughout the world attests to the continuing quest by national independence movements for self-governance and statehood, as the principal motive of each nationalistic separatist movement is to become a sovereign independent state. The disintegration of failed states and the creation of new members of the international community in recent years accounts for the expansion of the number of UN member states from 166 in 1991 to 189 in the year 2000. If today's fragile failed states break into even smaller separate states, the UN could have 400 to 500 members in the twenty-first century. Some estimate that the number of independent states in the global system could grow from 207 in 2000 to more than 800 by the year 2025. Others wonder if nation-states will fade in the twenty-first century, with globally engaged "citistates" assuming their place by the year 2100 as the organizing principle for world affairs (Peirce 2000).

In some respects, the territorial state is flourishing because it is still needed to give people identity, raise taxes, provide safety nets for the needy, protect the environment, and provide military security. At the same time some states are failing to adequately meet such traditional goals as providing for the poor, generating economic growth, preventing pollution, maintaining domestic stability, or countering terrorism. In fact, many have proclaimed "the end" of **state sovereignty** (Opello and Rosow 1999) and its supreme authority in the face of growing challenges from home and abroad. To them, "The one trend that is sure to dominate the coming . . . quarter-century is the decline of the power of the state" (Zakaria 1999) because "a wide variety of forces has made it increasingly difficult for any

■ **state sovereignty**
under international law, the status of states as equals in that within their territory, a state's government is subject to no higher external authority.

state to wield power over its people and address issues it once considered its sole prerogative" (Stanley Foundation 1993).

"While states may not be about to exit from the political stage, and while they may even continue to occupy center stage, they do seem likely to become vulnerable and impotent" (Rosenau 1995). The question to be confronted is if

> . . . even where sovereignty still appears intact, states [can any] longer . . . retain sole command of what transpires within their own territorial boundaries . . . The notion of the nation-state as a self-governing, autonomous unit appears to be more a normative claim than a descriptive statement. (Held et al. 1999, 8–9)

As global trends transform twenty-first-century world politics, the question is whether the state can cope with the challenges it now faces. Auguste Comte, a nineteenth-century French political philosopher, argued that societies create institutions to address problems and meet human needs. When institutions are no longer able to perform these functions, they disappear. Today, as the managerial capabilities of states fail to inspire confidence, we must ask if states have a future.

Is Globalization a Cure or a Curse?

globalization the integration of states through increasing contact, communication, and trade to create a holistic, single global system in which the process of change increasingly binds people together in a common fate (see p. 41).

interdependence a situation arising when the behavior of international actors greatly affects others with whom they have contact, so that the parties to the exchange become mutually sensitive and vulnerable to the others' actions (see p. 249).

Globalization has become a popular shorthand term to describe a number of basic dimensions of world politics; it is used as an adjective, a noun, and a verb to refer alternatively to a process, a product, a policy, or a predicament. Globalization in general describes the internationalization and integration of the global community into a single society without barriers and national boundaries. Most observers would agree with one among many possible definitions of globalization—as "the increasing scale and importance of exchanges of people, products, services, capital, and ideas across international borders" (Auguste 1999). However, globalization is perhaps also interpreted not only as a condition but in addition is best seen as the culmination of what a quarter of a century ago was commonly called **interdependence**—the increasing degree since the mid-1970s to which the quality of life within states was rapidly and visibly becoming dependent on conditions in other states.

Interdependent globalization lies at the heart of the external challenges states now face. As the range of global issues has expanded and the integration of national economies has created a worldwide market and global culture, globalization in a borderless world has reduced states' ability to govern their affairs. Mutual vulnerabilities have reduced states' autonomy by curtailing their control of their own national fates, and globalization has erased the traditional distinctions between what is national and what is international, what is private and what is public, and what is domestic and what is foreign.

From one perspective, an awareness of the common destiny of all, alongside the declining ability of many sovereign states to cope with global problems through national means, will energize efforts to put aside interstate competition. According to this reasoning, conflict will recede as humanity begins to better recognize how little protection national borders and oceans provides it against the multiple challenges arising from the global revolution in travel, communications, and trade—shared problems that can only be managed through collective, multilateral cooperation. As Thomas Friedman (1999b) argues, globalization, "with its economic integration, digital integration, its ever-widening connectivity of individuals and nations, its spreading of capitalist values and networks to the remotest corners of the world [is creating] a much stronger web of constraints on the foreign policy behavior of those nations which are plugged into the system." Consequently, because globalization makes it imperative that states cooperate, we should welcome the continued tightening of interstate linkages.

From another, more pessimistic perspective, the irreversible process of globalization will not lead to transnational collaboration. Regardless of how compelling the need or how rewarding the benefits, increased contact and the trend toward an integrated single society of states will breed enmity, not amity. According to this view, globalization empowers advantaged states but constrains the prospects of weak states, producing new inequalities in a highly stratified global hierarchy in which the gap between the wealthy and the poor continues to widen. Because its benefits will not be distributed equally, globalization will likely generate conflict between winners and losers. Intertwined economies will sour relations more often than sweeten them. Under conditions of fierce competition, scarcity, and resurgent nationalism, the temptation may be irresistible to seek isolation from the assault of globalization on national identity and autonomy by creating barriers to trade and other transactions. The temptation to achieve political benefits by military force will also continue. Thus the tightening web of globalization foretells danger as well as opportunity.

Is Technological Innovation a Blessing or a Burden?

"The dynamics of globalization unleashed by technology," James N. Rosenau (1995) concludes, "are the dominant catalyst in world affairs." The consequences, however, are not certain. Like globalization, which technology engenders, technological innovation solves some problems but causes others. Not only can technological innovations create new ways of preventing or treating disease, but they can also enhance the sophistication and destructiveness of weapons of war. As Meg Greenfield (1997) correctly reminds us, "Illness, ignorance, and want have obviously not been eliminated. But millions upon millions of people living today, who not all that long ago would have been direly afflicted by all three, will never know them in anything like their once common form if they know them at all." Nevertheless, no generation but ours has faced the kind of random violence made possible and accessible by modern weapons technology.

Discoveries in microelectronics, information processing, transportation, energy, agriculture, communications, medicine, and biotechnology profoundly affect our lives and shape our future (Dyson 1997). They have united the globe into a single international market and common culture, while paradoxically breaking down people's sense of citizenship and community (Barber 1995). "There appears to be a fundamental lag between the current rate of technological change and the rate of adjustment to these changes among decision makers" (Blumenthal 1988). Technological change requires proper and constructive management, but is this possible in a greedy, disintegrative world in which science and technology are often selfishly exploited without serious consideration of their impact on and ethical consequences for humanity at large?

Will Geo-Economics Supersede Geopolitics?

Throughout modern history, states have competed with one another militarily for position and prominence in the hierarchy of international power. For more than three centuries, world politics has been largely a record of preparing for, waging, and recovering from interstate war. Military might was equated with prestige and influence, and military conquest became the means to economic as well as political preeminence.

In the view of some, the battlefield in world politics has shifted to economic issues. National destinies will be determined by commercial competition, not military conquest. If issues of **geo-economics** (the distribution of wealth) become more important than conventional issues of **geopolitics** (the distribution of political and military power), will states' foreign policies also change? If wealth is converted into political muscle, nationalistic pride can give rise to competition and self-assertiveness. But economic interdependence and tight commercial relationships can also collapse into trade disputes and political rivalry. Nevertheless, the apparent shift of priorities to the economic dimensions of world politics is certain to alter the distribution of twenty-first-century global power. This shift is also likely to increase the porousness of national borders.

■ **geo-economics**
the relationship between geography and the economic conditions and behavior of states that define their levels of production, trade, and consumption of goods and services.

■ **geopolitics**
the relationship between geography and politics and their consequences for states' national interests and relative power.

What Constitutes Human Well-Being on an Ecologically Fragile Planet?

The worldwide quest for **human rights** requires people and governments to define and distinguish the fundamental values to which they are entitled. Throughout history, many have placed money and prosperity as their first priority. However, that value preference has been challenged, and the once popular **limits-to-growth proposition**—the belief that the world cannot forever increase its productive capacity—has been replaced by the maxim of sustainability. Sustainability emphasizes "the growth of limits" in the global ecology (the total pattern of relations between organisms and their environment on earth). Thus **sustainable development** means learning to live off the earth's interest without encroaching on its capital, in order that the planet can continue to provide the means to life that makes the pursuit of other values such as political freedom and religious principles possible.

Gross national product (GNP)—the total monetary value of goods and services produced in a state during a specified period, usually a year—is the common measure of national economic well-being. It is an index of relative standards of living "closely bound up with human welfare. . . . Human welfare has dimensions other than the economic one. But it is widely held that the economic element is *very* important, and that the stronger the economy the greater the contribution to human welfare" (Daly and Cobb 1989). Indeed, many states' values are highly materialistic; money is perceived as a means to a secure and happy national existence—almost a human rights entitlement. To the inhabitants of most Global South less-developed countries, growth in GNP may mean more food, better housing, improved education, and an increased standard of living. However, affluent people in the Global North already enjoy these basic amenities; therefore, additional income usually allows them to satisfy comparatively trivial needs. When basic needs are fulfilled, conspicuous consumption and greed pose a danger to other values.

■ **human rights**
political rights and civil liberties recognized internationally as inalienable for individuals in all countries (see p. 526).

■ **limits-to-growth proposition**
the theory that the earth's capacity to support life has natural limits and that if important resources such as fresh water are depleted, many will perish.

■ **sustainable development**
economic growth that does not deplete the resources needed to maintain growth (see p. 368).

■ **gross national product (GNP)**
the total monetary value of goods and services produced in a state during a specified period (see p. 137).

Looking beyond Earth's Problems As we consider the future, we must ask ourselves whether technological innovation is inevitably the answer to our concerns. Although we are now able to send satellites into space and receive photos from planets we will never visit, we remain unable to eliminate hatred or aggression, or to achieve peace on earth.

The global impact of population growth, as well as the continued quest for economic growth, are great. Whereas people in poor countries make few demands on world resources, people in rich countries contribute greatly to the depletion of the world's resources and the global pollution to maintain their high standard of living. In both cases, continued population growth is detrimental—for poor societies, because it inhibits increases in personal income and welfare; for rich societies, because it further burdens the earth's delicate ecological system. Unbridled exploitation and consumption, disregarding responsibility to others, are ultimately self-destructive. As Soviet President Mikhail Gorbachev warned in 1988, we must halt "humanity's aggression against nature."

These ideas challenge the core values of Western civilization. Although sustainable development is an attractive goal, even it will be hard to realize. Sustainable economic welfare requires economic growth managed to limit natural resource depletion and environmental damage, while protecting people's rights of leisure and liberty. But can this kind of growth in a finite world proceed infinitely? How long can finite energy sources sustain uncontrolled consumption before automobiles sputter to a stop, industries grind to a halt, and lights go out? How many pollutants can the atmosphere absorb before irreparable environmental damage results? And how many people can a delicately balanced ecosystem support?

Understanding today's world requires a willingness to confront complexity. A true but complicated idea always has less chance of success than a simple but false one, the French political sociologist Alexis de Tocqueville (1969) cautioned in 1835. The challenge is difficult but the rewards warrant the effort. Humankind's ability to chart a more rewarding future is contingent on its ability to entertain complex ideas, to free itself from the sometimes paralyzing grip of the past, and to develop a questioning attitude about rival perspectives on international realities. On that hopeful yet introspective note, we begin our exploration of world politics in a new millennium.

KEY TERMS

international political system
Cold War
transformation
global system
state
anarchy
cycles
schematic reasoning
cognitive dissonance
ideology
mirror images
levels of analysis
individual level of analysis
state level of analysis
global level of analysis
global agenda
politics
great powers
nonstate actors
low politics
high politics
state sovereignty
globalization
interdependence
geo-economics
geopolitics
human rights
limits-to-growth proposition
sustainable development
gross national product (GNP)

SUGGESTED READING

Blumenfeld, Yorick, ed. *Scanning the Future: Prospects for Tomorrow.* London: Thames & Hudson, 1999.

Cusimano, Maryann K., ed. *Beyond Sovereignty: Issues for a Global Agenda.* Boston: Bedford/St. Martin's, 2000.

Head, David, Anthony McGraw, David Goldblatt, and Jonathan Perraton. *Global Transformations.* Stanford, Calif.: Stanford University Press, 1999.

Holsti, Ole R., Randolph M. Siverson, and Alexander L. George, eds. *Change in the International System.* Boulder, Colo.: Westview Press, 1980.

Hoffmann, Stanley. *World Disorders: Troubled Peace in the Post–Cold War Era.* Lanham, Md.: Rowman & Littlefield, 1998.

Hughes, Barry B. *International Futures: Choices in the Face of Uncertainty,* 3rd ed. Boulder, Colo.: Westview Press, 1999.

Kegley, Charles W., Jr., and Eugene R. Wittkopf, eds. *The Global Agenda: Issues and Perspectives,* 6th ed. New York: McGraw-Hill, 2001.

Knutsen, Tørbjørn L. *The Rise and Fall of World Orders.* Manchester, Eng.: Manchester University Press, 1999.

National Geographic Society. *National Geographic Atlas of the World,* 7th ed. Washington, D.C.: National Geographic Society, 2000.

Opello, Walter C., Jr., and Stephen J. Rosow. *The Nation-State and Global Order.* Boulder, Colo.: Lynne Rienner, 1999.

Rosenau, James N. *Along the Domestic-Foreign Frontier: Exploring Governance in a Turbulent World.* Cambridge, Eng.: Cambridge University Press, 1997.

Worldwatch Institute. *State of the World 2000.* New York: Norton, 2000.

WHERE ON THE WORLD WIDE WEB?

The World Wide Web's (www or Web) features make it a powerful tool for providing access to global information sources. Using the Web, you have instant access to documentation of important international events and agreements. On-line information is current and often more complex than traditional sources. It quickly reflects the changing nature of international events. The Web's international reach also permits users to locate opinions and perspectives from individuals across the United States and around the world. Many from the international community post their work on the Web. Every day more sources become available online as individuals and institutions discover the wonders of the Web.

The "Where on the World Wide Web?" sections that accompany each chapter provide you with interesting Web links to explore. Through this investigation, you will become an active participant in the globalization of world information (see Chapter 9 for a discussion of the Internet's role in the globalization process). You will also gain a greater understanding of the concepts and terms discussed in *World Politics*.

As you begin to examine the trends and transformation of world politics, it is important that you understand the evolution of international events and keep abreast of the ever-changing world of international politics. The Web links listed here will help you analyze current events.

American Journalism Review News Link
http://www.newslink.org/news.html

If you are interested in "going to the source" for your news, check out the *American Journalism Review*'s Web site. This site provides links to electronic newspapers from the United States or anywhere in the world. Even campus papers are accessible through this site. You can read the news in a foreign language or try to find an English version. You may want to compare the same news story found in different newspapers around the world to see how different countries interpret the same event.

CNN Interactive World News
http://www.cnn.com/WORLD/

Surf the Web site of the news organization that changed the way world news is reported by providing constant, minute-by-minute coverage of breaking news stories from around the world. CNN's World News main page is divided according to world region and reports the top stories in each area. Over the course of a week, compare and contrast the content of the top stories from each region. Do you see a pattern concerning the type of news stories reported for each area?

Foreign Affairs Online
http://www.people.virginia.edu/~rjb3v/rjb.html

This comprehensive Web site has been specifically designed to assist students and other individuals interested in international law, international relations, and U.S. foreign policy. It has links to general references, map resources, foreign states, the United Nations system, international organizations, international legal entities, think tanks, and media resources. As a useful gateway to numerous international affairs resources on the Web, you may want to bookmark this site.

The National Geographic Society
http://www.nationalgeographic.com/maps/index.html

Publisher of the popular *National Geographic* magazine, the Society has created an impressive Web tool called the Map Machine, one of the best interactive map sets on the Web. Viewers can choose many different types of interactive maps. For instance, the Dynamic Maps, which use geographic information systems (GIS), display population densities, ecoregions, weather patterns, earthquake fault lines, mineral deposits, and other features anywhere in the world. The Atlas Maps identify 191 independent states and provide a brief overview of each state. A quick click anywhere on the map gives key geographic, demographic, and economic data. As Chapter 1 explains, all maps focus on specific features while ignoring others, which leads to distortions. Compare the Map Machine maps with those found in the Controversy: What Is the "Right" Way to Map the Globe? on pp. 10–11. Are the "dynamic" maps more accurate representations of reality? What distortions do they depict?

National Public Radio Online
http://www.npr.org/

As an alternative to reading the news, access National Public Radio Online. This site lets you listen to the top news stories and is updated every hour. You may also want to take a minute to cruise the discussion area and give your thoughts on the headline stories. You will need to download the RealAudio player to listen to the news stories at this site.

New York Times on the Web
http://www.nytimes.com

"All the news that's fit to print" is available on-line following a free registration. International news stories are easily accessed by clicking on the "International" news category. Keep in mind that the *Times* is a news source produced in the United States and may have American biases. While you read the news stories, think of ways in which they may have an "American slant."

University of Texas Library On-line Map Collection
http://www.lib.utexas.edu/Libs/PCL/Map_collection/Map_collection.html

If you've ever wondered exactly where Rwanda, Kosovo, Taiwan, or Pakistan was, this site can help. The Perry-Castaneda Library Map Collection of the University of Texas at Austin is an extensive collection of electronic maps. It features regional as well as state maps according to political and shaded relief criteria. When reading about a specific country in *World Politics*, make sure you can locate the country and identify its neighbors. This will give you a better understanding of international events.

CHAPTER 2

THEORIES OF WORLD POLITICS

TOPICS AND THEMES

- Thinking theoretically to interpret global issues
- The liberal orientation
- The realist orientation
- The neorealist extension of realism
- The neoclassical extension of realism
- The neoliberal revision of liberalism
- Alternative theories
- International politics in a world of change

- **CONTROVERSY** CAN BEHAVIORAL SCIENCE ADVANCE THE STUDY OF INTERNATIONAL RELATIONS?
- **CONTROVERSY** NEOLIBERALISM VERSUS NEOREALISM: WHICH THEORY MAKES THE MOST REASONABLE ASSUMPTIONS?
- **CONTROVERSY** WHAT'S MISSING IN REALIST THEORIES OF INTERSTATE RELATIONS? THE FEMINIST CRITIQUE

The State of the Union address

It's important that we take a hard, clear look . . . not at some simple world, either of universal goodwill or of universal hostility, but the complex, changing, and sometimes dangerous world that really exists.

—JIMMY CARTER, U.S. president, 1980

The present generation, and even more its successors, encounter a special challenge. For we are living through not only an exceptional period of fluidity in international relations but through an even more profound upheaval in how publics and leaders view the world around them.

—HENRY A. KISSINGER, former U.S. secretary of state, 1999

Imagine yourself the newly elected president of the United States. You are scheduled to deliver the State of the Union address on your views of the current world situation and your foreign policy to deal with it. You face the task of both defining those aspects of international affairs most worthy of attention and explaining the reasons for their priority. To convince citizens these issues are important, you must present them as part of a larger picture of the world. Therefore, based on your perceptions of world politics, you must identify a general framework from which to consider global issues. You must, in short, think *theoretically.* At the same time, you must be careful, because your interpretations will necessarily depend on assumptions about international realities that your citizens might find questionable. The effort to explain the world, predict new global problems, and sell others on a policy to deal with them is bound to result in controversy because even reasonable people often see realities differently.

When leaders face these kinds of intellectual challenges, they fortunately benefit from the existence of a body of theoretically informed ideas from which they can draw guidance. In this chapter we distinguish among the major theoretical perspectives policymakers and scholars use to interpret international relations. Since the perceived "realities" of international affairs that these theories seek to explain influence their content, we will examine how perceived changes in underlying international conditions have shaped various theories. In addition, our review of contending political theories will identify the intellectual heritage that informs this book.

UNDERSTANDING WORLD POLITICS

Social scientists construct different theories to make international events understandable. Over time, a **paradigm,** or dominant way of looking at a particular subject, such as international relations, arises to influence judgments regarding which characteristics of the subject are most important, what puzzles need to be solved, and what criteria should govern social scientists' investigations. These paradigms or "fundamental assumptions scholars make about the world they are studying" (Vasquez, 1997) tend eventually to be revised in order to explain new developments in world affairs. Thus, the theories that guide the thinking of policymakers and scholars in different historical circumstances tell us much about world politics itself.

■ **paradigm**
derived from the Greek *paradeigma* meaning an example, a model, or an essential pattern, a paradigm structures thoughts about an area of inquiry (see p. 368).

The Elusive Quest for Theory

Throughout history, paradigms have been revised or abandoned when their assertions have failed to mirror the prevailing patterns of international behavior. Major wars have been especially potent in bringing about significant changes in the theoretical interpretation of world affairs. "Every war . . . has been followed in due course by skeptical reassessments of supposedly sacred assumptions" (Schlesinger 1986) and has influenced "what ideas and values will predominate, thereby determining the ethos of succeeding ages" (Gilpin 1981). Three such system-transforming wars dominated the twentieth century: World War I, World War II, and the Cold War. Each has shaped policymakers' perceptions of world politics and each has provided lessons critical to developing policy programs that can best preserve world order in the twenty-first century.

This chapter will concentrate on the two core perspectives that throughout history have most influenced thinking about international affairs and that continue to guide theorizing: liberalism and realism and their neoliberal and neorealist variants that have commanded a large following in the last two decades.

The Evolution of Theoretical Inquiry

When the formal study of international relations began at the dawn of the twentieth century, the world abounded with optimism. Many people believed that peace and prosperity had taken root and would persist. The Hague peace conferences in 1899 and 1907 had inspired hope of controlling arms and sparing Europe another series of wars like those between 1848 and 1870. Moreover, numerous individuals—including the Scottish-American industrialist Andrew Carnegie, who gave much of his fortune to the cause of world peace—assumed that as industrialization progressed and the costs and risks of war increased, the chance of protracted war among the great powers would decline dramatically (see also Angell 1910).

In those tranquil times, students of international relations studied history to glean insight on the events of the day. The study of international relations consisted mainly of commentary about personalities and events, past and present. Rarely did scholars seek to generalize theoretically about the "lessons" of history or about the principles or "laws" that might account for states' characteristic responses to similar stimuli or influences. Sir Halford Mackinder (1919) and Alfred Thayer Mahan (1890) were exceptions. Both sought to generate theoretical propositions pertaining to the influence of geographic factors on national power and international politics—efforts that laid the foundations for the study of political geography, which survives today as an important approach to world politics (see Demko and Wood 1994).

■ **current history approach**
a focus on the description of contemporary and particular historical events rather than theoretical explanations to explain international relations.

■ **theory**
a set of hypotheses postulating the relationship between variables or conditions, advanced to describe, explain, or predict phenomena and make prescriptions about how positive changes ought to be engineered to realize particular ethical principles (see p. 250).

The large-scale death and destruction that World War I exacted from 1914 to 1918 destroyed the sense of security that had made the **current history approach** popular. This catastrophic war was a painful lesson that stimulated the search for knowledge to address contemporary policy problems in a theoretical context. However interesting descriptions of recent or past wars might be, they were of doubtful use to a world in search of ways to prevent wars of mass destruction. For those purposes, policymakers and scholars needed a **theory**—a statement attempting to account for general phenomena or patterns rather than explaining unique or individual circumstances—that could reliably predict war and instruct leaders on the best policies to prevent it.

LIBERALISM

World War I initiated a paradigmatic revolution in the study of international relations, in which several perspectives competed for attention. While the current history approach continued to claim some disciples in the waning days of World War I, after Russia's Bolshevik Revolution Marxist-Leninist thought became increasingly influential, with its critique of capitalism's creation of inequality, class conflict, and imperialistic war. In the 1930s, with the rise of Adolf Hitler in Germany, national socialism (or fascism) also challenged conventional European thinking about world politics. Nazism, the German variant of national socialism, was particularly provocative. Not only did Nazism glorify the role of the state (as opposed to that of the individual) in political life, it also championed war as an instrument of national policy.

■ **liberalism**
a paradigm predicated on the hope that the application of reason and universal ethics to international relations can lead to a more orderly, just, and cooperative world, and that international anarchy and war can be policed by institutional reforms that empower international organizations and laws.

■ **politics**
to liberal idealists, the search for agreement about shared values to foster cooperation within a global community (see p. 457).

The Liberal Worldview

Emerging as dominant, however, was a perspective known as **liberalism.** At the core of liberalism is an emphasis on the impact of ideas on behavior, the equality and liberty of the individual, and the need to protect people from excessive state regulation. Liberalism views the individual as the seat of moral value and virtue and asserts that human beings should be treated as ends rather than means. It emphasizes ethical principle over the pursuit of power and institutions over capabilities as forces shaping interstate relations, and defines **politics** at the

Pioneers in the Liberal Quest for World Order Influenced by David Hume and Jean-Jacques Rousseau, Immanuel Kant (left) in *Perpetual Peace* (1795) helped to redefine modern liberal theory by advocating global (not state) citizenship, free trade, and a federation of democracies as a means to peace. Richard Cobden (right) primarily foresaw the possibility of peace across borders; in his view, if contact and communication among people could expand through free trade, so too would international friendship and peace, secured by prosperity that would create interdependence and eliminate the need for military forces to pursue rivalries.

international level more as a struggle for consensus than a struggle for power and prestige.

Because advocates of liberalism were inspired by their interest in ideals, after World War I they are sometimes referred to as **idealists,** even if they were a diverse group within the larger liberal tradition. Post–World War I idealism, as advocated by such scholars and policymakers as Alfred Zimmerman, Norman Angell, James T. Shotwell, and Woodrow Wilson, derived from ancient liberal philosophy and has been interpreted variously in different periods. These idealists drew their philosophy from such liberal thinkers as Immanuel Kant, Thomas Jefferson, James Madison, John Stuart Mill, John Locke, David Hume, Jean-Jacques Rousseau, and Adam Smith (see Doyle 1995, Howard 1978, and Zacher and Matthew 1995).

■ **idealists**
people inspired by the liberal theoretical tradition who believe that the pursuit of ideals like world peace can change the world by reducing the disorder often exhibited in world politics.

Collectively, the post–World War I liberal idealists embraced a worldview that emphasized the power of ideas in controlling global destiny, based on the following beliefs:

1. Human nature is essentially "good" or altruistic, and people are therefore capable of mutual aid and collaboration through reason and ethically inspired education.

2. The fundamental human concern for others' welfare makes progress possible.
3. Sinful or wicked human behavior, such as violence, is the product not of flawed people but of evil institutions that encourage people to act selfishly and to harm others.
4. War and international anarchy are not inevitable and war's frequency can be reduced by strengthening the institutional arrangements that encourage its disappearance.
5. War is a global problem requiring collective or multilateral, rather than national, efforts to control it.
6. Reforms must be inspired by a compassionate ethical concern for the welfare and security of all people, and this humanitarian motive requires the inclusion of morality in statecraft.
7. International society must reorganize itself in order to eliminate the institutions that make war likely, and states must reform their political systems so that democratic governance and civil liberties within states can protect human rights and help pacify relations among states.

While not all liberal idealists subscribed to each of these tenets with equal conviction, they shared a moralistic, optimistic, and universalistic image of international affairs as taking place within a global community.

The Liberal Reform Program

Although liberal idealists after World War I differed significantly in their prescriptions for reforming the international political system (see Herz 1951), they generally fell into one of three groups. The first group advocated creating international institutions to replace the anarchical and war-prone balance-of-power system, characterized by coalitions of independent states formed to wage war or to defend a weaker coalition partner from attack. In place of this unregulated competitive system, idealists sought to create a new one based on **collective security.** This approach dealt with the problem of war by declaring any state's aggression an aggression against all, who would act in concert to thwart the aggressor. The League of Nations was the institutional embodiment of collective security through international organization, reflecting simultaneously the liberal idealists' emphasis on international institutions and the possibility of international cooperation for global problem solving.

■ **collective security** a security regime agreed to by the great powers that sets rules for keeping peace, guided by the principle that an act of aggression by any state will be met by a collective response from the rest (see p. 559).

A second group emphasized the use of legal processes such as mediation and arbitration to settle disputes and avoid armed conflict. This facet of the idealists' policy prescriptions was illustrated by the creation in 1921 of the Permanent Court of International Justice to litigate interstate conflicts and by the ratification of the **Kellogg-Briand Pact** of 1928, which "outlawed" war as an instrument of national policy.

■ **Kellogg-Briand Pact** a multilateral treaty negotiated in 1928 that outlawed war as a method for settling interstate conflicts.

A third group followed the biblical injunction that states should beat their swords into plowshares and sought disarmament as a means to ending war. This orientation was exemplified by efforts during the 1920s, such as those negotiated at the Washington and London naval conferences, to secure arms control and disarmament agreements.

Several corollary ideas gave definition to the liberals' emphasis on encouraging global cooperation through international institutions, law, and disarmament. These included:

- The need to substitute attitudes that stressed the unity of humankind for those that stressed parochial national loyalties to independent sovereign states.
- The use of the power of ideas through education to arouse world public opinion against warfare.
- The promotion of free international trade in place of economic nationalism.
- The replacement of secret diplomacy by a system of "open covenants, openly arrived at."
- The termination of interlocking bilateral alliances and the power balances they sought to achieve.

In seeking a more peaceful world, some liberal reformers promoted the ideal of **self-determination**—giving nationalities the right through voting to become independent **states**—as a means to redraw the globe's political geography to make **nations'** borders conform to ethnic groupings. Related to this was U.S. president Woodrow Wilson's call for democratic domestic institutions. "Making the world safe for democracy," liberals believed, would also make it secure and free from war, because democracies do not fight one another. Wilson's celebrated Fourteen Points speech to Congress in 1918 proposed the creation of the League of Nations and, with it, the pursuit of other liberal idealists' aims such as free trade to create wealth and a global harmony of states' interests. This speech, perhaps better than any other statement, expressed the idealistic sentiments of the liberal worldview and program.

Although a tone of idealism dominated policy rhetoric and academic discussions during the interwar period, with the exception of the League of Nations and the precedent-setting Washington Naval Disarmament Treaties, little of the liberal reform program was ever seriously attempted, and even less of it was achieved. When the winds of international change again shifted and the Axis Powers pursued world conquest, enthusiasm for liberal idealism as a worldview receded.

self-determination
the principle that the global community is obligated to give nationalities their own governments (see p. 639).

state
a legal entity with a permanent population, a well-defined territory, and a government capable of managing sovereign authority over the nations or nationality groups living within its legal borders (see p. 55).

nation
a collection of people who, on the basis of ethnic, linguistic, or cultural affinity, perceive themselves to be members of the same group (see p. 55).

REALISM

The drive for global conquest that led to World War II provoked strong criticism of the liberal idealist paradigm. Critics blamed the outbreak of war on what they believed to be the so-called idealists' naive legalistic and moralistic assumptions about the possibility of peace and progress through human aspiration, and alleged that idealists were utopians who neglected the harsh realities of power politics (see Carr 1939). The lessons the critics drew from the interwar period shaped a new set of perceptions and beliefs.

Advocates of the new, ascendant paradigm known as **realism,** or **realpolitik** as a specific philosophy, emerged to frame an intellectual movement whose message reads like the antithesis of idealism. Among the principal prophets of this new worldview were E. H. Carr (1939), George F. Kennan (1951, 1954), Hans J. Morgenthau (1948), Reinhold Niebuhr (1947), and Kenneth W. Thompson (1960). Realism deserves careful scrutiny because it continues to guide much thought about world politics.

realism
a paradigm based on the premise that world politics is essentially and unchangeably a struggle among self-interested states for power and position under anarchy, with each competing state pursuing its own national interests (see p. 457).

realpolitik
the theoretical outlook prescribing that countries should prepare for war in order to preserve peace.

The Realist Worldview

As a political theory, realism can trace its intellectual roots to the ancient Greek historian Thucydides and his account of the Peloponnesian Wars between Athens and Sparta (431–404 B.C.E.), the writings of Kautilya (minister to the Maurya emperor of India more than two thousand years ago), and especially the sixteenth-century political thought of the Italian theorist Niccoló Machiavelli and the English philosopher Thomas Hobbes.

Realism, as applied to contemporary world politics, views the state as the most important actor on the world stage since it answers to no higher political authority. Moreover, conflicts of interests among states are assumed to be inevitable. Realism also emphasizes the ways in which the anarchical nature of international politics dictates the choices that foreign policymakers, as rational problem solvers who must calculate their interest in terms of power, must make. (See Chapter 3 for discussion of the "rational" actor.)

Within the realist paradigm, the purpose of statecraft is national survival in a hostile environment. To this end, no means is more important than the acquisition of **power,** and no principle is more important than **self-help.** In this conception, **state sovereignty,** a cornerstone of international law, gives heads of state the freedom—and responsibility—to do whatever is necessary to advance the state's interests and survival.

■ **power**
the factors that enable one actor to manipulate another actor's behavior against its preferences.

■ **self-help**
the principle that in anarchy actors must rely on themselves (see p. 661).

■ **state sovereignty**
under international law, the principle that the governments of states are subject to no higher external authority (see p. 17).

To the hard-core realist, respect for moral principles is a wasteful and dangerous interference in the rational pursuit of national self-advantage. To these proponents of power politics, questions about the relative virtues of the values within this or that ideological system cannot be allowed to interfere with sound policy making. A state's philosophical or ethical preferences are neither good nor bad—what matters is whether they serve its self-interest. Thus, the game of international politics revolves around the pursuit of power: acquiring it, increasing it, projecting it, and using it to bend others to one's will. At the extreme, realism appears to accept war as normal and rejects morality as it pertains to relations between individuals.

At the risk of oversimplification, realism's message can be summarized in the form of ten assumptions and related propositions:

1. People are by nature narrowly selfish and ethically flawed, and cannot free themselves from the sinful fact that they are driven to watch out for themselves and compete with others for self-advantage.
2. Of all people's evil ways, none are more prevalent, inexorable, or dangerous than their instinctive lust for power and their desire to dominate others.
3. The possibility of eradicating the instinct for power is a utopian aspiration.
4. International politics is—as Thomas Hobbes put it—a struggle for power, "a war of all against all."
5. The primary obligation of every state—the goal to which all other national objectives should be subordinated—is to promote its **national interest,** and to acquire power for this purpose.
6. The anarchical nature of the international system dictates that states acquire sufficient military capabilities to deter attack by potential enemies and to exercise influence over others.

■ **national interest**
the goals that states pursue to maximize what is selfishly best for their country.

Realist Pioneers of Power Politics In *The Prince* (1532) and *The Leviathan* (1651) Niccoló Machiavelli and Thomas Hobbes, respectively, emphasized a political calculus based on interest, prudence, power, and expediency above all other considerations. This formed the foundation of what became a growing body of modern realist thinking that accepts the drive for power over others as necessary and wise statecraft.

7. Economics is less relevant to national security than is military might; economic growth is important primarily as a means of acquiring national power and prestige.
8. Allies might increase a state's ability to defend itself, but their loyalty and reliability should not be assumed.
9. States should never entrust the task of self-protection to international security organizations or international law and should resist efforts to regulate international behavior through global governance.
10. If all states seek to maximize power, stability will result by maintaining a balance of power, lubricated by shifts in the formation and decay of opposing alliances.

Realism in the Nuclear Age

The dour and pessimistic realist thinking that dominated policy making and academic discourse in the 1940s and 1950s fit the needs of a pessimistic age. World War II, the onset of rivalry between the United States and the Soviet Union, the expansion of the Cold War into a global struggle between East and West, the stockpiling of nuclear weapons, and the periodic crises that threatened to erupt into global violence all confirmed the realists' emphasis on the inevitability of conflict, the poor prospects for cooperation, and the divergence of national interests among incorrigibly selfish, power-seeking states.

The realists' interpretations appeared particularly persuasive after World War II, given the prevailing patterns of conflictual interstate relations. States and their incessant competition were accordingly seen as the defining elements of global reality; all other aspects of world politics became secondary. At the same time, the view that a threatening international environment demanded that foreign policy take precedence over domestic problems also appeared cogent. As the historical imperatives of "power politics" required unceasing attention to the threat of war, the logic of realpolitik asserted that military security was the essence of world politics.

The Limitations of Realism

However persuasive the realists' arguments about the essential properties of international politics, their contentions and conclusions were frequently at odds and even contradictory.

> Critics . . . noted a lack of precision and even contradictions in the way classical realists use such concepts as "power," "national interest," and "balance of power." They also see possible contradictions between the central descriptive and prescriptive elements of classical realism. On the one hand, as Hans Morgenthau put it, nations and their leaders "think and act in terms of interests defined as power," but on the other, diplomats are urged to exercise prudence and self-restraint, as well as to recognize the legitimate national interests of other nations. Obviously, then, power plays a central role in classical realism. But the correlation between the relative power balance and political outcomes is often less than compelling, suggesting the need to enrich analyses with other variables. (O. Holsti 2001, 125)

Thus, once analysis moved beyond the belief that people are wicked and the rhetoric requiring that foreign policy serve the national interest, important questions remained: What policies best serve the national interest? Do alliances encourage peace or instability? Do arms promote national security or provoke costly arms races and war? Are states more prone to act aggressively when they are strong or weak? Are the interests of states better served through competition or through cooperation? If humankind is unchanging, then how do we explain the observable evolution and transformation of the international system? Indeed, how do we explain the growth of collaborative multilateral institutions, economic expansion, and states' observable willingness to abide by ethical principles and agreements rather than to exploit others ruthlessly when the opportunity arises?

Because many of the assumptions of the realist paradigm were not testable, realism began to be questioned (Brooks 1997; Vasquez 1997). Realism offered no criteria for determining what data were significant and what epistemological rules to follow to interpret relevant information. Even the policy recommendations that purportedly flowed from its logic were often divergent. Realists themselves, for example, were sharply divided as to whether U.S. intervention in Vietnam served American national interests and whether nuclear weapons contributed to international security.

A growing number of critics also pointed out that realism did not account for significant new developments in world politics. For instance, it could not explain the construction of new liberal trade and political institutions in Western Europe in the 1950s and 1960s, where the cooperative pursuit of mutual advantage rather than narrow self-interest appeared to dominate (at least in economic, if not always in military, affairs). Other critics began to worry about realism's tendency to disregard ethical principles and about the material and social costs that some of its policy prescriptions seemed to impose, such as retarded economic growth resulting from unrestrained military expenditures. Consequently, by the end of the 1960s, realism found itself bombarded by criticism, especially by **behavioral scientists** who sought to replace realist thought and polemics with theories tested against evidence (see Controversy: Can Behavioral Science Advance the Study of International Relations?).

■ **behavioral scientists** scholars who apply scientific methods to the study of world politics.

Despite realism's shortcomings, much of the world continues to think about world politics in realist terms, especially in times of global tension. This happened, for example, in the early 1980s when the Cold War competition between the United States and the Soviet Union entered an embittered new phase and their arms race accelerated. Because realism provides great insight into the drive for national security through military means, it tends to be used to explain such phenomena as the outbreak of bloody wars in the former Yugoslavia in the 1990s.

■ **neorealism** a theoretical account of states' behavior that explains it as determined by differences in their relative power instead of by other factors, such as their values, types of government, or domestic circumstances (see p. 500).

Two schools of thought within the realist theoretical tradition have recently arisen to overcome realism's recognized limitations and to reconstruct it as a general theory: "neorealism" and "neoclassical realism." **Neorealism** emphasizes the anarchic nature of global society without governance rather than the traditional realist emphasis on the unceasing lust for power inherent in human nature in its explanation for why interstate conflict persists. For this reason, neorealism is sometimes referred to as **structural realism** because it emphasizes the influence of the global power structure on the behavior of states within it. The second reformulated version of realism, known as **neotraditional realism,** reacted against the limitations of structural realism by returning to the original roots of realism, which placed considerable emphasis on the ways leaders of states made foreign policy decisions.

■ **structural realism** a theory that emphasizes the influence of the world power structure on the behavior of the states within the global hierarchy, defined primarily by the distribution of power (see p. 431).

■ **neotraditional realism** a body of recent realist theorizing that departs from neorealism by emphasizing the motives behind states' foreign policies more than global structure and that focuses on the internal influences on states' external behavior instead of the global determinants of states' foreign behavior.

THE NEOREALIST OR "STRUCTURAL" EXTENSION OF REALISM

In his influential book *Theory of International Politics* (1979), the pioneer of neorealism, Kenneth N. Waltz, set out to convert the loose and disjointed body of realist "thought" into a formal "theory" (Waltz 1995). "To systematize political realism into a rigorous, deductive systemic theory of international politics" (Keohane 1986b), neorealism dismisses explanations developed at the individual and state levels of analysis and argues that explanations at the global system level are sufficient to account for the main trends in world politics. As Waltz (1995) expressed his neorealist conceptualization of the determinants of international behavior, "international structure emerges from the interaction of states and then constrains them from taking certain actions while propelling them toward others."

CONTROVERSY

CAN BEHAVIORAL SCIENCE ADVANCE THE STUDY OF INTERNATIONAL RELATIONS?

How should scholars build theories to interpret international behavior? The answer to that question has never been satisfactorily resolved, and the long-standing debate about how best to construct theories of international relations continues today. Some scholars, known as "postmodern deconstructionists," challenge the ability of intellectuals to provide a satisfactory theoretical account of why states and people act as they do in international relations. These scholars devote their efforts to criticizing and "deconstructing" the theories of world politics to expose their inherent limitations. Most scholars remain motivated by the theoretical quest to interpret and comprehend the complexities of international relations, and challenge the pessimistic view that world politics defies meaningful understanding, despite the obstacles and limits to knowledge. What do you think? Is the scientific analysis of patterns of international relations a realistic undertaking? Or are explanations of international relations impossible, as deconstructionists argue? In determining your opinion, take into consideration the progression of this intellectual debate over the past four decades.

This evolving epistemological controversy took an important step in the 1960s and early 1970s when dissatisfaction with realism's shortcomings intensified and a movement known as **behavioralism** arose to challenge realism, which the behavioralists called "traditionalism," and other modes of studying international relations. Behavioralism was not a new theory of international relations so much as a new method of studying them, based largely on the application of scientific methods to the study of global affairs (see Knorr and Rosenau 1969; Knorr and Verba 1961).

Behavioralism advances principles and procedures for investigating international phenomena to reach generalizations or statements about international regularities that hold across time and place. Science, the behavioralists claim, is primarily a generalizing activity. From this perspective—a view consistent with that of many "traditional" realists and liberals—a theory of international relations should state the relationship between two or more variables that specifies the conditions under which the relationship(s) hold and explain why the relationship(s) should hold. To uncover such theories, behavioralists lean toward using comparative cross-national analyses rather than case studies of particular countries at particular times. Behavioralists also stress the need for data about the characteristics of countries and how they behave toward one another. Hence, the behavioral movement encourages the comparative and quantitative study of international relations (see, for example, Rosenau 1980; Singer 1968).

What makes behavioralism innovative is its attitude toward the purposes of inquiry: replacing subjective beliefs with verifiable knowledge, supplanting impressions and intuition with testable evidence, and substituting data and reproducible information for mere opinion. In this sense, behavioralists embrace liberalism's "high regard for modern science" and its "attacks against superstition and authority" (Hall 1993). In place of appeals to the "expert" opinion of authorities, behavioral scientists seek to acquire knowledge cumulatively by suspending judgments about truths or values until they have sufficient evidence to support them. They attempt to overcome the tendency of traditional inquiry to select facts and cases to fit preexisting hunches. Instead, all available data, those which contradict as well as those which support existing theoretical hypotheses, are to be examined. Knowledge, they argue, would advance best by theorists assuming a cautious, skeptical attitude toward any empirical statement. The slogans "Let the data, not the armchair theorist, speak," and "Seek evidence, but distrust it" represent the behavioral posture toward the acquisition of knowledge.

Although some behavioral research speaks directly to the moral issues that differentiate realism and liberalism, it is sometimes criticized for neglecting the ethical aspects of poverty, hunger, violence, and other global problems. This accusation led to a **postbehavioral movement** which called for a new research agenda that would focus on new issues (see Easton 1969). Nonetheless, postbehavioralists rarely have recommended discarding scientific methods, despite the harsh criticism of behavioral science by "postmodern deconstructionists."

In neorealism, as in realism, anarchy or the absence of central institutions above states is the most important and enduring property of the structure of the system. States remain the primary actors, acting according to the principle of self-help and seeking to ensure their own survival. Thus, it is the neorealists' view that states do not differ in the tasks they face, only in their capabilities. Capabilities define the position of states in the system, and the distribution of capabilities defines the structure of the system and shapes the ways the units interact with one another.

Power also remains a central concept in neorealism. However, the quest for power is not considered an end in itself, as in realism; nor does it derive from human nature. Instead, states always pursue power as a means of survival. As Waltz (1979) explains, the "means fall into two categories: internal efforts (moves to increase economic capability, to increase military strength, to develop clever strategies) and external efforts (moves to strengthen and enlarge one's own alliance or to weaken and shrink an opposing one)." Furthermore, because the instinct for survival drives states, neorealism asserts that balances of power form automatically, regardless of whether "some or all states consciously aim to establish and maintain a balance, or whether some or all states aim for universal domination" (Waltz 1979). Once the global system is formed, its structure "becomes a force that the units may not be able to control; it constrains their behavior and interposes itself between their intentions and the outcomes of their actions" (Ruggie 1983).

Although neorealists recognize that states' goals sometimes "fluctuate with the changing currents of domestic politics, are prey to the vagaries of a shifting cast of political leaders, and are influenced by the outcomes of bureaucratic struggles," they contend that such factors as whether governments are democracies or dictatorships tell little about the process whereby states come to pursue the goal of balancing power with power. Instead, "structural constraints explain why the [same] methods are repeatedly used despite differences in the persons and states who use them" (Waltz 1979).

> In its stress on the structure of the international system, that is, the state of anarchy among sovereign states, [neo]realism attaches little or no importance to what is going on inside states—what kind of regimes are in power, what kind of ideologies prevail, what kind of leadership is provided. According to [neo]realists, the foreign policies of all states are basically driven by the same systemic factors—they are like so many billiard balls, obeying the same laws of political geometry and physics. (Harries 1995, 13)

Neorealist theory also helps to explain why the prospects for international cooperation and change often appear so dim and why states are naturally wary of others and strive to compete. The anarchical structure of the system compels states to be sensitive to their *relative position* in the distribution of power.

> When faced with the possibility of cooperating for mutual gain, states that feel insecure must ask how the gain will be divided. They are compelled to ask not "Will both of us gain?" but "Who will gain more?" If an expected gain is to be divided, say, in the ratio of two to one, one state may use its disproportionate gain to implement a policy intended to damage or destroy

behavioralism
an approach to the study of international relations that emphasizes the application of scientific methods (see p. 410).

postbehavioral movement
an approach to the study of international relations that calls for increased attention to the policy relevance of scientific research.

> the other. Even the prospect of large absolute gains for both parties does not elicit their cooperation so long as each fears how the other will use its increased capabilities. (Waltz 1979, 105; see also Snidal 1993)

Impediments to global cooperation thus result not from the parties' attitudes toward potential collaborative efforts, but rather from the insecurity that the anarchical system breeds. "The condition of insecurity—at the least, the uncertainty of each about the other's future intentions and actions—works against their cooperation" (Waltz 1979), as does states' fear of dependence on others.

THE NEOCLASSICAL EXTENSION OF REALISM

Alongside neorealism, another group of realists who share a dim view of cooperation in world politics has arisen, advocating what is called neotraditional realism. This theoretical movement seeks to transcend Waltzian neorealism's exclusive focus on the global level of analysis, which they argue incorrectly neglects classical realism's attention to the determinants of foreign policy at the individual and state levels of analysis (see Vasquez 1998). To neoclassical theorists the sources of states' foreign policy choices are best explained not by changes in the global structure, but by leaders' perception of national interests and capabilities: "Statesmen, not states, are the primary actors in international affairs, and their perceptions of shifts in power, rather than objective measures, are critical" (Zakaria 1998). Hence, "a new breed of realist scholars have embraced the richer formulation of traditional, pre-Waltzian realists, who focus more on foreign policy than systemic phenomena. While not abandoning Waltz's insights about international structure and its consequences, neoclassical realists have added [factors at the state and individual levels of analysis] such as domestic politics . . . , state power and intentions, and statesmen's perceptions of the relative distribution of capabilities . . . to better explain historical puzzles and foreign policy decision making" (Schweller 1999).

Many scholars and policymakers disagree with the view of the neorealists and the neoclassical realists about the prospects for international cooperation. They point out that the record suggests that patterns can change and that increased interdependence can lead to even higher levels of cooperation. This expectation lies behind the so-called neoliberal challenge to realism and neorealism (Doyle and Ikenberry 1997; Kegley 1995).

NEOLIBERALISM

In the last decade of the twentieth century, dissatisfaction with realism and neorealism began to rise. Arguing that it was time for a new, more rigorous liberal alternative to realism, critics pointed to several shortcomings: (1) power-politics perspectives failed to predict the peaceful end of the Cold War and international social change in general; (2) research suggested that the "underlying theory of war and peace [of realism and neorealism was] flawed" (Vasquez

1993) because realists "oversimplified the concept of power and misunderstood the lessons of history" (Kober 1990); and (3) it appeared that realism's approach would "not be an adequate guide for the future of international politics" (Jervis 1992), because the broadened global agenda included many questions and problems that realist theory could not cover. The problems of AIDS, ecological deterioration, global warming, economic underdevelopment, and the globalization of trade and markets were among those for which the realistic approach was seen as deficient.

Asking "Is realism finished?" (Zakaria 1992–93), these critics also saw neorealism as "a research enterprise in crisis" (James 1993; Legro and Moravscik 1999). But they went beyond the call to rethink and revise these theories by advocating that "the recovery of liberalism" (Little 1993) be treated as a theoretical goal in international relations. This view gained a following among policymakers. For example, in accord with Francis Fukuyama's conclusion (1992b) that there were "good reasons for examining aspects of the liberal international legacy once again," U.S. President Bill Clinton in 1995 maintained that "In a world where freedom, not tyranny, is on the march, the cynical calculus of pure power politics simply does not compute. It is ill-suited to the new era."

In light of this growing sentiment, in the early 1990s **neoliberalism,** a new approach to world politics that concentrates on the ways international organizations and other nonstate actors promote international cooperation, emerged. This analytic departure goes by several labels including "neoliberal institutionalism" (Grieco 1995), "neoidealism" (Kegley 1993), and "neo-Wilsonian idealism" (Fukuyama 1992a).

neoliberalism
a perspective that accounts for the way international institutions promote global change, cooperation, peace, and prosperity through collective programs for reforms (see p. 366).

Neoliberalism seeks to build theories of international relations by giving the basic tenets of classical liberalism and post–World War I liberal idealism a fresh examination. Taking heart in the international prohibition, through community consensus, of such previously entrenched practices as slavery, piracy, dueling, colonialism, the slaughter of certain animals, and unrestrained exploitation of the planet's ecology, neoliberalism emphasizes the prospects for progress, peace, and prosperity. Studies of regional integration—processes whereby sovereign states might be politically unified—began to flourish in the 1950s and 1960s, paving the way for the new liberal theories that emerged in the 1990s. The expansion of trade, communication, information, technology, and immigrant labor propelled Europeans to sacrifice portions of their sovereign independence to create a new political community out of previously separate units. These developments were outside of realism's worldview, creating conditions that made the call for a theory grounded in the liberal tradition convincing to many who had previously been skeptical of realism.

Neoliberalism departs from neorealism on many assumptions (see Controversy: Neoliberalism versus Neorealism). In particular, neoliberalism focuses on the ways in which influences such as democratic governance, public opinion, mass education, free trade, liberal commercial enterprise, international law and organization, arms control and disarmament, collective security and multilateral diplomacy, and ethically inspired statecraft can improve life on our planet. Because they perceive change in global conditions as progressing through cooperative efforts, neoliberal theorists maintain that the ideas and ideals of the liberal legacy today can describe, explain, predict, and prescribe international conduct in ways that they could not during the conflict-ridden Cold War (see Moravcsik 1997).

CONTROVERSY

Neoliberalism versus Neorealism

Which Theory Makes the Most Reasonable Assumptions?

The issues dividing neoliberal and neorealist theorizing center, according to David Baldwin (1993, 4–8) on the different assumptions they make about the following six topics. Looking at the world, which set of assumptions do you think is the most accurate for interpreting twenty-first century world politics?

- *The Nature and Consequences of Anarchy.* Whereas everyone recognizes that the global system is anarchical because effective institutions for global governance are lacking, neorealists argue that anarchy does not matter much and in fact may be preferable to the restraints of world government. Neoliberals see anarchy as a big problem that can be reformed through creation of strong global institutions.
- *International Cooperation.* Although neorealists and neoliberals agree that international cooperation is possible, neorealists think cooperation is difficult to sustain whereas neoliberals believe cooperation can be expected because collaboration produces rewards that reduce the temptation to selfishly compete.
- *Relative versus Absolute Gains.* Both neorealists and neoliberals are concerned with relative gain as well as absolute gain. Neorealists believe that the desire to get ahead of their competitor by obtaining relative gains is the primary motive, while neoliberals believe that states are motivated by the search for opportunities to cooperate that will produce absolute gain for all parties to the cooperative exchange.
- *Priority of State Goals.* Both national security and national economic prosperity are seen as important state goals by neorealists and neoliberals, but neorealists stress security as the most important, while neoliberals believe states place a greater priority on economic welfare.
- *Intentions versus Capabilities.* Contemporary neorealists maintain that the distribution of states' capabilities is the primary determinant of their behavior and international outcomes. Neoliberals maintain that states' intentions, interests, information, and ideals are more influential than is the distribution of capabilities.
- *Institutions and Regimes.* Both neorealists and neoliberals recognize that states have created a variety of new international regimes and institutions to regulate their relations since World War II. Neoliberals believe that institutions such as the World Trade Organization create norms that are binding on their members and that change patterns of international politics. On the other hand, neorealists emphasize that organizations like the UN are arenas where states carry out their traditional competition and political rivalry for influence.

Like realism and neorealism, neoliberalism does not represent a cohesive intellectual movement or school of thought. Neoliberals operate from different assumptions, examining different aspects of the processes through which international change and cooperation might be promoted. Some, like neorealists, embrace a structural theory that examines the characteristics of the global system. Others concentrate on the characteristics of the units and subunits that comprise it, such as the types of governments (democracies or dictatorships) and the leaders who govern states. Still other neoliberals give primary attention to the influence of international institutions such as the UN and nonstate actors such as multinational corporations. All neoliberals, however, share an interest in probing the conditions under which the convergent and overlapping interests among otherwise sovereign political actors may result in cooperation.

To illuminate these similarities and differences among neoliberals, we will examine two theoretical perspectives that paved the way for neoliberalism's acceptance and are a part of its orientation: "transnational interdependence" and "international regimes." For the sake of brevity, we have selected only these two examples from among the many other divergent stands within neoliberal theorizing (see Zacher and Matthew 1995), such as the feminist critique of conventional theories in general and of realism in particular (see Controversy: What's Missing in Realist Theories of Interstate Relations?).

Transnational Interdependence as a Liberal Worldview

In the 1970s, a new analytical perspective known as "transnational relations" arose to question realism's key assumption that states are the only important actors on the global stage. With **complex interdependence** as its central concept, this liberal theory argued that nonstate actors, such as multinational corporations and transnational banks, are "important not only because of their activities in pursuit of their own interests, but also because they act as transmission belts, making government policies in various countries more sensitive to one another" (Keohane and Nye 1988, 2001). The proliferation of ties among states that became increasingly dependent on one another, in the process that is now called **globalization,** encouraged acceptance of transnational interdependence as an alternative to realism because it was becoming clear that as the sovereign control of states was eroding, a theory of international relations needed to account for much more than state-to-state relations. In this sense, transnational interdependence represented a holistic conception of world politics as the sum of its many interacting parts in a global society (see O. Holsti 2001).

■ **complex interdependence** a theory stressing the complex ways in which the growing ties among transnational actors makes them vulnerable to each other's actions and sensitive to each other's needs.

■ **globalization** the integration and growing interdependence of states through their increasing contact and trade that is creating a single united global society within a single culture so as to tie people together in a common fate and to reduce through this process the capacity of states to control their national destinies.

The transnational interdependence school also questioned whether national security issues were truly dominant in states' decision-making agendas. Under conditions of mutual vulnerability, it seemed that states' foreign policy agendas had become "larger and more diverse." Alongside the threat of war, trade, monetary, and environmental issues began to crowd the global agenda to such an extent that they were beginning to make a broader range of "governments' policies, even those previously considered merely domestic, impinge on one another" (Keohane and Nye 1988). In addition, this neoliberal perspective disputed the popular notion that military force was the only means of exercising influence in international politics, particularly among the industrialized democracies. It was argued that "Intense relationships of mutual influence exist between these countries, but in most of them force is irrelevant or unimportant as an instrument of policy" (Keohane and Nye 1988, 2001).

Advocates of the transnational interdependence perspective extended many of these insights in order to account for the growing role of transnational institutions in global affairs, such as multinational corporations and human rights organizations. Thus, international institutions commanded a central place in many new liberal analyses such as Robert O. Keohane and Joseph S. Nye's (1977, 1989, 2001) *Power and Interdependence,* the definitive treatise on this new extension of liberalism. A careful reading of this pioneering theoretical book reveals that the transnational interdependence perspective does not altogether reject realism. Rather, the initial concern of its adherents is "the conditions under which the assumptions of realism were sufficient or needed to be supplemented by a more complex model of change" (Nye 1987; see also Keohane 1983). Keohane and Nye drew on realism, in part, to account for the willingness of states to see their interests served by the creation of international regimes, or the norms for behavior that are created when cooperation becomes institutionalized and actors expect them to be followed, even though this necessitates a sacrifice of sovereignty.

CONTROVERSY

What's Missing in Realist Theories of Interstate Relations?

The Feminist Critique

Many scholars are dissatisfied with existing theories of world politics because nearly all fail, in their opinion, to give sufficient attention to certain important factors and forces. No theory can possibly cover everything comprehensively; however, if a theory ignores a key variable or issue in the effort to simplify the essential features of world politics, that theory will fail to capture the true complexity of international relations. Yet people disagree about what is essential. Determining which features should be emphasized is controversial, because certain questions are more interesting to some students than others (as the debate between realists and liberals illustrates).

Do you think mainstream realism and liberalism ignore any crucial factors in world politics? To stimulate your thinking about what is essential and what has potentially been ignored, consider the issue of gender. Until recently, most theories paid little attention to this variable, and thus failed to account for such crucial trends as the chronic and widening inequalities in income and freedom between men and women.

Feminist theory, a body of scholarship that emphasizes the importance of gender as a factor in world politics, arose in the 1960s in response to the pronounced realist depersonalization of state-centered accounts of foreign policy. In particular, feminist theory attacked the exclusion of women in discussions about public and international affairs as well as the injustice and unequal treatment of women this prejudice caused. The mainstream realist literature on world politics underestimated or ignored the plight and contributions of women, treating differences in men's and women's status, beliefs, and behaviors as unimportant. Gender roles were also ignored, along with the evidence that sexism is a pillar of the war system (Reardon 1985). In the realists' masculine image of sovereign rulers, "Fame, wealth, and women were prizes to be won in battle. For the typical prince, war was a means to reputation and glory" (Tickner 1999). In the feminist critique, a remedy for this problem might be to give women the prominence and power in policy making that traditional practices denied them (see Beckman and D'Amico 1994; Peterson and Runyan 1993).

As feminist theory crystallized, it moved away from focusing on a history of discrimination against women and began to direct much of its criticism at realism. In particular, many gender studies alleged that realism, formulated and dominated by males, ignored the human roots of global conditions and promoted an essentially masculine interpretation of international relations that was inattentive to human rights and rife with rationales for aggression.

Derived in part from liberal principles supportive of fair play, justice, and the philosophical acceptance of love over power, feminist theory moved beyond this initial critique of realism's bias to chart an independent theoretical course (Keohane 1989). This perspective has focused on the performance of women as leaders of government and as members of infantry combat units (Grant and Newland 1991), as well as on theoretical explorations of the plight of women in business and in the less developed countries of the Global South.

Perhaps of greatest influence in the field of international relations, however, has been feminist theory's rejection of the realist preoccupation with states' military strategies in favor of developing strategies for world security (see Tickner 1992). In this sense, feminist theory, like neoliberalism generally, is motivated by the quest for discovering paths to greater international cooperation. In liberating conventional theory from its narrow focus, can feminist theory open a window on the full range of international activity and point the way toward a fuller appreciation of the ways in which human beings influence the global condition?

■ **feminist theory**
a body of scholarship that emphasizes gender in the study of world politics (see p. 418).

Transnational interdependence has become a central component of the neoliberal perspective and continues to be widely used to interpret cooperative agreements between states under the continuing twenty-first-century conditions of anarchy and fears of dependence and exploitation.

A Need for International Regimes? This is the way an artist imagines the city of Cologne, Germany, will look in the year 2050, after global warming due to the greenhouse effect has melted polar ice caps, raised ocean levels, and altered Western Europe's climate. Global warming is a transnational problem that cannot be controlled without multilateral, interstate cooperation. The rules of international regimes are designed to enforce such cooperation, and the liberal institutionalism of regime theory investigates how such regimes are created and sustained.

International Regimes

Although the international system is still characterized by anarchy, its nature is more properly conceptualized as an ordered anarchy, and the world as a whole as an "anarchical society" (Bull 1977), because cooperation, not conflict, is often the observable outcome of relations among states.

Given this reality, the question arises: How can **international regimes** based on coordinated cooperation be established and preserved? Interest in this question derives from two goals: first, "a desire to understand the extent to which mutually accepted constraints affect states' behaviors" (Zacher 1987), and second, a desire to devise strategies for creating a less disorderly "world order."

■ **international regimes** a perspective that explains the benefits of actors supporting particular rules to regulate a specific international activity, such as disposal of toxic wastes.

Regimes are institutionalized or regularized patterns of cooperation in a given issue area, as reflected by established rules. Because the international regime perspective necessarily looks primarily at global institutions and the ways in which norms influence states to behave according to more global than national interests, it is perhaps best viewed as an attempt to reconcile the liberal and realist perspectives on world politics (Haggard and Simmons 1987).

The global trade and monetary rules created during and after World War II are vivid examples of international regulatory regimes. These rules, as well as particular sectors within the trade system, have been the focus of considerable inquiry from the regime perspective. Together, the trade and monetary regimes comprised a Liberal International Economic Order (LIEO) that limited government intervention in the world political economy and otherwise facilitated the free flow of goods and capital across national boundaries. The General Agreement on Tariffs and Trade (GATT) that preceded the World Trade Organization (WTO) and the International Monetary Fund (IMF) played important institutional roles in the LIEO and reconfirmed the importance of international institutions in fostering transnational cooperation (see Chapter 8 for elaboration).

Most illustrations of the regime perspective appear in the low politics arena of economic and humanitarian relationships; until recently, relatively few "security regimes" (Jervis 1982) had emerged in the high politics defense issue area. Early exceptions were the nuclear nonproliferation regime and the regime that the United States and the Soviet Union used to manage their crises (see George 1986). But after the Cold War, the pressures of globalization can be expected to foster creation of regimes in widening areas of international conduct. This is likely to accelerate efforts to grapple theoretically with the causes and consequences of multilateral approaches to collective problem solving.

ALTERNATIVE THEORIES

Having studied the liberal and realist traditions, keep in mind that this coverage is very selective. At least seven additional major schools of thought regarding particular aspects of world politics also deserve attention, and each will be introduced—along with still other theoretical subspecialties linked to them—in later chapters where they best help to interpret the topic covered. First, as explained in Chapter 3, decision-making theory accounts for the ways leaders and other actors seek to make policy choices rationally, and the limits to this aspiration. Second, as introduced in Chapter 4, long-cycle theory seeks to explain the historical ebb and flow of world politics, global leadership, and systemwide war (Goldstein 1988; Modelski and Thompson 1996). The rise and fall of the great powers and empires is its central concern. Third, dependency theory, first treated in Chapter 5, examines the pattern of dominance and dependence that characterizes the unequal relationship between the world's rich and poor states (Packenham 1992). Fourth, to understand how cooperation among states is encouraged to deal with problems primarily in the realm of low politics (Chapters 8–11), hegemonic stability theory, a hybrid of liberal/neorealist theory (Gill 1993b), examines what happens when a clearly predominant state, a "hegemon," exercises leadership and control of the international system by setting and enforcing the rules governing international trade, finance, investment, and other issues, such as environmental regulation (see Gilpin 1981; Levy 2001). Fifth, to expand this coverage and move to other topics dealing with global security, world-system theory looks at system dynamics from a long-term, structural perspective, emphasizing its economic underpinnings, to explain the Western capitalist societies' rise to dominance and the lack of economic development in many other geographic areas (Chapters 5–11) and their military repercussions (Chapter 12) (see Wallerstein 1980). Sixth, to systematically organize inquiry about how states fit into international phenomena from

■ **epistemology** the philosophical examination of how knowledge is acquired and the analytic principles governing the study of phenomena.

diverse levels of analysis, advocates of the comparative study of foreign policy seek to probe the similarities and differences in states' international circumstances, national attributes and capabilities, foreign policy decision-making processes, and individual policymakers (see Hermann, Kegley, and Rosenau 1987). Finally, a variety of theoretical approaches to methodological issues in **epistemology,** such as behavioralism and **constructivism,** seek to identify a better intellectual framework for comprehending the nature of world politics.

■ **constructivism**
an approach emphasizing the importance of agents (people and groups) and the shared meanings they construct to define their identities, interests, and institutions—understandings that influence their international behavior.

INTERNATIONAL POLITICS IN A WORLD OF CHANGE

To understand our changing world and to make reasonable prognoses about the future, we must begin by arming ourselves with an array of information and conceptual tools, entertaining rival interpretations of world politics, and questioning the assumptions on which these contending worldviews rest. Because there are a large (and growing) number of alternative, and sometimes incompatible, ways of organizing theoretical inquiry about world politics, the challenge of capturing the world's political problems cannot be reduced to any one simple yet compelling account, such as the four major theoretical traditions stressed here (see Table 2.1). Each paradigmatic effort to do so in the past, whether derived from liberalism or from realism, has ultimately been abandoned as developments in world affairs eroded its continuing relevance. Although grand theories fade with the passage of time, they often regain their attractiveness when global transformations make them useful once again. In fact, world politics is so resistant to clear, comprehensive, and convincing analysis that some so-called **deconstructionists** contend that international complexity defies description, explanation, and prediction (see Controversy: Can Behavioral Science Advance the Study of International Relations?, p. 36). Deconstructionists share the philosophical view that all peoples' conceptions of global realities are relative to their understandings and that, because there is no objective principle the validity of which is independent of one's own personal point of view, any interpretation is as valid as any other and there is no point in attempting to develop a shared conception of the world.

Most other scholars continue to struggle in the pursuit of theory and knowledge about international affairs. For example, scholars adhering to **chaos theory** attempt to find new methods for modeling the kind of turbulent global change that is occurring in the world. In addition, an increasing number of theorists have concluded that international relations can best be interpreted through **social constructivism**—an emerging paradigm that attempts to bridge the gap between neoliberal and neorealist theories by accepting many key assumptions shared by both approaches while critically rejecting realism's failure to pay attention to the powerful role of ideas and norms in world politics. Constructivists emphasize the importance of shared ideas and understandings that are developed between actors on the world stage through their interactions. These shared experiences define their interests, identities, and images of the world in which they interact (Wendt 1992; see also Hopf 1998, Onuf 1989 and 2001, and S. Smith 1997). Constructivism is helpful because it reminds us that how we

■ **deconstruction**
postmodern theory that the complexity of the world system renders precise description impossible, and that the purpose of scholarship is to understand actors' motives by deconstructing their textual statements.

■ **chaos theory**
the application of mathematical methods to identify underlying, episodically recurring patterns in rapidly changing and seemingly unconnected relationships (as many global phenomena appear) in order to better interpret complex reality.

■ **social constructivism**
a liberal-realist theoretical approach advocated by Alexander Wendt that sees self-interested states as the key actors in world politics; their actions are determined not by anarchy but by the ways states socially "construct" and then respond to the meanings they give to power politics, so that as their definitions change, cooperative practices can evolve.

TABLE 2.1

The Quest for Theory: Four Major Perspectives

Feature	*Realism*	*Neorealism*	*Liberalism*	*Neoliberalism*
Key Units	Independent states	The international system's structure	Institutions transcending states	Individuals; "penetrated" states and nonstate transnational actors
Core Concern	War and security	Struggle for position and power under anarchy	Institutionalizing peace	Fostering interstate cooperation on the globe's shared economic, social, and ecological problems
Major Approach	Balance of power	Balance of terror; military preparedness, and deterrence	International law; international organization; democratization	Complex interdependence and regimes
Outlook on Global Prospects	Pessimistic/ stability	Pessimistic	Optimistic/progress	Expectation of cooperation and creation of a global community
Motives of Actors	National interests; zero-sum competition; security; power	Power, prestige, and advantage (relative gains) over other states	Collaboration; mutual aid; meeting human needs	Global interests (absolute gains); justice; peace and prosperity; liberty; morality
Central Concepts	Structural anarchy; power; national interests; balance of power; polarity	Structural anarchy; rational choice; arms races	Collective security world order, law; integration; international organization	Transnational relations; law; free markets; interdependence; integration; liberal republican rule; human rights; gender
Prescriptions	Increase national power; resist reduction of national autonomy	Preserve nuclear deterrence; avoid disarmament and supernational organizations	Institutional reform	Develop regimes and promote democracy and international institutions to coordinate collective responses to global problems

think about the world matters. All theories are necessarily socially constructed based on communication among the agents in international relations, and these constructions of shared meanings through social learning provide states and other actors with the mental models of international politics on which they act. This method of viewing international politics represents a welcome theoretical departure, because it reminds us that shared images influence the ways actors in the global arena see themselves and behave (Checkel 1998). Further, this emphasis on subjective beliefs helps us appreciate that the practices in statecraft and the identities of global actors or agents are products of shared ideas rather than,

Defending Reason against Deconstructionist Criticism Pope John Paul II is shown here signing the "Fides et Ratio" encyclical in October 1998 that defends using reason to discover bedrock truths. Arguing that faith and reason are not incompatible, the statement describes deconstructionism as a nihilistic philosophy that breeds skepticism because it questions our ability to know anything for certain and rejects "the pursuit of truth through reason." Yet in a bewildering, complex world, it is easy to appreciate why some theoreticians give up the effort to discover the underlying principles of world politics, claiming that the challenge is hopeless.

as the realists would have it, simply products of the objective or material structure of the international system. As we move into the twenty-first century, it is likely to become increasingly popular to interpret world politics from a constructivist theory that focuses on the collective norms and culture of people and state actors. Those shared norms will define their reality and influence their relations within that constructed vision (see Desch 1998).

As we seek to understand the changing global conditions, we must be humble in recognizing the limitations of our understandings of world politics and at the same time inquisitive about its character. The task of interpretation is complicated because the world is itself complex. As one scholar frames the challenge:

> Conceptually speaking, world affairs today can be likened to a disassembled jigsaw puzzle scattered on a table before us. Each piece shows a fragment of a broad picture that as yet remains indiscernible. Some pieces depict resurgent nationalism; others show spreading democracy; some picture genocide; others portray prosperity through trade and investment; some picture nuclear disarmament; others picture nuclear proliferation; some indicate a reinvigorated United Nations; others show the UN still enfeebled and ineffective; some describe cultural globalization; others predict clashing civilizations.
>
> How do these pieces fit together, and what picture do they exhibit when they are appropriately fitted? (Puchala 1994, 17)

All theories are maps of possible futures. Theories can guide us in fitting the pieces together to form an accurate picture. However, in evaluating the usefulness of any theory to interpret global conditions, the historical overview in this chapter suggests that it would be wrong to oversimplify or to assume that a particular theory will remain useful in the future. Nonetheless, as the American poet Robert Frost observed in 1911, any belief we cling to long enough is likely to be true again someday, because "most of the change we think we see in life is due to truths being in and out of favor." So in our theoretical exploration of world politics, we must critically assess the accuracy of our impressions, avoiding the temptation to embrace one worldview and abandon another without any assurance that their relative worth is permanently fixed.

KEY TERMS

paradigm
current history approach
theory
liberalism
politics
idealists
collective security
Kellogg-Briand Pact
self-determination
state
nation
realism
realpolitik
power
self-help
state sovereignty
national interest
behavioral scientists
neorealism
structural realism
neotraditional realism
behavioralism
postbehavioral movement
neoliberalism
complex interdependence
globalization
feminist theory
international regimes
epistomology
constructivism
deconstruction
chaos theory
social constructivism

SUGGESTED READING

Beitz, Charles R. *Political Theory and International Relations,* rev. ed. Princeton, N.J.: Princeton University Press, 1999.

Dougherty, James E., and Robert L. Pfaltzgraff, Jr. *Contending Theories of International Relations,* 5th ed. New York: Addison-Wesley-Longman, 2001.

Doyle, Michael W. *Ways of War and Peace.* New York: Norton, 1997.

Ferguson, Yale H., and Richard W. Mansbach. *The Elusive Quest: Theory and International Politics.* Columbia: University of South Carolina Press, 1988.

Ion, Judith, ed. *International Feminist Journal of Politics,* published quarterly.

Jackson, Robert, and Georg Sørensen. *Introduction to International Relations.* Oxford, Eng.: Oxford University Press, 1999.

Jarvis, D. S. L. *International Relations and the Challenge of Postmodernism: Defending the Discipline.* Columbia: University of South Carolina Press, 2000.

Jervis, Robert. "Realism, Neoliberalism, and Cooperation: Understanding the Debate," *International Security* 24 (Summer 1999): 42–63.

Kegley, Charles W., Jr., ed. *Controversies in International Relations Theory: Realism and the Neoliberal Challenge.* New York: St. Martin's Press, 1995.

Keohane, Robert O., and Joseph S. Nye, Jr. *Power and Interdependence: World Politics in Transition,* 2nd ed. Glenview, Ill.: Scott, Foresman/Little, Brown, 1989.

Neumann, Iver B., and Ole Weaver, eds. *The Future of International Relations: Masters in the Making?* London: Routledge, 1997.

Peterson, V. Spike, and Anne Sisson Runyan. *Global Gender Issues,* 2nd ed. Boulder, Colo.: Perseus Books, 1999.

Puchala, Donald J., ed. *Visions of International Relations: Assessing an Academic Field.* Columbia: University of South Carolina Press, 2001.

Tickner, J. Ann. "Searching for the Princess: Feminist Perspectives in International Relations," *Harvard International Review* 21 (Fall 1999): 44–48.

Vasquez, John A. *The Power of Power Politics: From Classical Realism to Neotraditionalism.* Cambridge, Eng.: Cambridge University Press, 1998.

Viotti, Paul R., and Mark V. Kauppi. *International Relations Theory,* 3rd ed. Boston: Allyn & Bacon, 1999.

WHERE ON THE WORLD WIDE WEB?

Contemporary Philosophy, Critical Theory, and Postmodern Thought
http://www.cudenver.edu/~mryder/itc_data/postmodern.html

The University of Colorado at Denver's School of Education has created a Web site that helps students understand the ideas behind critical theory and postmodern thought. Read about the main authors of postmodern thought and then access their works.

Data on the Net
http://odwin.ucsd.edu/idata/

Try your hand at being a behavioral social scientist. The University of California at San Diego has created a gateway Web site from which you can browse the collection of 813 Internet sites of numerous social science statistical data. On the homepage, type in a topic area that interests you and receive data that is relevant to your topic area.

Feminist Theory and International Studies
http://csf.colorado.edu/isa/ftgs/

This is the homepage of the Feminist Theory and Gender Studies Section (FTGSS) of the International Studies Association. Through this site you can access the archives of FEMISA, a moderated discussion list where individuals discuss issues related to gender and international studies. You can also subscribe to the FEMISA list and join the lively debate.

Feminist Theory Web Site
http://www.cddc.vt.edu/feminism/

The Center for Digital Discourse and Culture at Virginia Tech University hosts the award-winning Feminist Theory Web Site. This site provides one of the most extensive lists of research materials and information for students, activists, and scholars interested in women's conditions and struggles around the world, with a staggering 5,425 bibliographical entries and 593 links to other Internet sites. Its stated goals are to encourage research and dialogue between individuals in different countries around the world. True to its international focus, the site can be accessed in English, Spanish, or French. Those interested can read complete bibliographies from various fields as well as obtain information on women's movements and activities anywhere in the world. As noted on page 42, much literature on world politics has ignored the plight and contributions of women. This Web site will undoubtedly contribute to remedying this situation.

Machiavelli On-line
http://www.sas.upenn.edu/~pgrose/mach/

The writings of Nicolo Machiavelli (1469–1527) are often cited as the base of realist thinking in international relations. As this chapter explains, the realist worldview is often primarily concerned with a state's drive for power. Visit Machiavelli On-line for a complete informational resource on Machiavelli's life and times. There is also a link to his famous book on how to rule, *The Prince,* which you can read on-line.

President Woodrow Wilson
http://gi.grolier.com/presidents/aae/bios/28pwils.html

As Chapter 2 notes, Woodrow Wilson's celebrated Fourteen Points speech before a joint session of Congress on January 8, 1918 "expressed the sentiments of the liberal world view and program." The *Academic American Encyclopedia,* produced by Grolier Online, features this speech along with information on Wilson's life and times. Take a moment to read the Fourteen Points. In retrospect, did Wilson's speech aim to prevent another war or establish American international dominance in a new world order? Which philosophy do you think underlies current U.S. foreign policy, liberalism or realism?

PART II

The Actors and Their Relations

Shakespeare said that "all the world's a stage and all the men and women merely players." When it comes to international politics, not just people, but also organizations, groups, and countries have a variety of roles to play on the global stage. Part II identifies the major actors in world politics today and describes the roles they perform and the policies they are pursuing.

Each chapter in Part II focuses on a prominent type of global actor. We begin with states (Chapter 3), using them as an example to show the processes all transnational actors use to make foreign policy decisions. We also identify the factors that sometimes interfere with the actors' ability to make rational choices about their interests and policies. In Chapter 4 special attention is given to the actors with the greatest military and economic capabilities, the great powers. In comparison, Chapter 5 deals with the weaker, economically less-developed countries known collectively as the Global South, because the majority of them are located in the earth's southern hemisphere. Next we examine the growing role of nonstate actors—intergovernmental organizations such as the United Nations and European Union (Chapter 6)—and nongovernmental organizations (Chapter 7) of private actors such as Greenpeace and Amnesty International, whose members actively work for global changes. This broad category also includes multinational corporations, ethnopolitical groups, religious movements, and international terrorist groups.

CHAPTER 3

FOREIGN POLICY DECISION MAKING

TOPICS AND THEMES

- The emergence of the modern state system
- The global and domestic determinants of states' foreign policy behavior
- The unitary actor and rational decision making
- The bureaucratic politics of foreign policy decision making
- The role of leaders in foreign policy decision making
- Constraints on foreign policy making: Problems and prospects

- **CONTROVERSY** ARE DEMOCRACIES DEFICIENT IN FOREIGN AFFAIRS?
- **CONTROVERSY** DO LEADERS MAKE A DIFFERENCE?

British Parliament opens with a more democratic House of Lords, November 1999.

Foreign policy is the system of activities evolved by communities for changing the behavior of other states and for adjusting their own activities to the international environment.

—George Modelski, political scientist, 1962

Much of the anguish of foreign policy results from the need to establish priorities among competing, sometimes conflicting, necessities.

—Henry A. Kissinger, former U.S. secretary of state, 1999

■ **actor**
a group, unit, or organization that plays a major role in world politics.

In studying world politics we typically use the term **actor** to refer to the agents who are the globe's primary performers. These transnational players include countries (for example, the United States and Japan), international organizations (the United Nations, or UN, and the Nordic Council), multinational corporations (General Motors and Sony), as well as nongovernmental international organizations (the World Wildlife Federation), indigenous nonstate nationalities (the Kurds in Iran, Iraq, and Turkey), and terrorist groups (the Abu Nidal Organization, or ANO). The conventional image is that of a stage on which players in the global drama act out their assigned roles. The leading actors dominate center stage, and the supporting players move along the periphery.

We will discuss each type of actor in later chapters, but here we will focus on countries, usually called "states." We particularly emphasize the ways states make foreign policy decisions designed to cope with challenges from abroad. The processes by which states decide on foreign policy will illuminate the factors that influence how other types of transnational actors make foreign policy choices as well. States demand primary attention, however, because international law gives them special status as the principal holders of economic and military capabilities in world affairs, and assigns to states alone the legal right to use armed force.

THE EMERGENCE OF THE MODERN STATE SYSTEM

As a network of relationships among independent territorial units, the modern state system was born with the Peace of Westphalia in 1648, which ended the Thirty Years' War in Europe. Thereafter, European rulers refused to recognize the secular authority of the Roman Catholic Church, replacing the system of papal governance in the Middle Ages with geographically and politically separate states that recognized no superior authority. The newly independent states were all given the same legal rights: territory under their sole control, unrestricted control of their domestic affairs, and the freedom to conduct foreign relations and negotiate treaties with other states. The concept of **state sovereignty**—that no one is above the state—captures these legal rights.

The Westphalian system still colors every dimension of world politics, and provides the terminology used to describe the primary units in international affairs. Although the term "nation-state" is often used interchangeably with "state" and "nation," technically the three are different. A **state** is a legal entity that enjoys a permanent population, a well-defined territory, and a government capable of exercising sovereignty. A **nation** is a collection of people who, on the basis of ethnic, linguistic, or cultural affinity, perceive themselves to be members of the same group. Thus the term nation-state implies a convergence between territorial states and the psychological identification of people within them. However, in employing this familiar terminology, we should exercise caution because this condition is relatively rare; there are few independent states comprising a single nationality. As we shall explain in Chapter 7, most states are populated by many nations, and some nations are not states. These "nonstate nations" are ethnic groups, such as Native American tribes in the United States, Sikhs in India, or Basques in Spain, composed of people without sovereign power over the territory in which they live.

When we speak generically about **foreign policy** and the decision-making processes that produce it, we mean the goals that officials heading states (and other transnational actors) seek abroad, the values that underlie those goals, and the means or instruments used to pursue them. To begin our inquiry into how foreign policy choices are made, we first consider the setting for states' choices and the circumstances outside national borders that make such choices necessary. Next we look at decision making as a rational process before considering two ways of viewing national decision making: the bureaucratic politics and the history-making individual models. We conclude by examining how states' national attributes influence their foreign policy behavior.

■ **state sovereignty**
a state's supreme authority to manage internal affairs and foreign relations (see p. 17).

■ **state**
a legal entity with a permanent population, a well-defined territory, and a government capable of exercising sovereignty.

■ **nation**
a collection of people who, on the basis of ethnic, linguistic, or cultural affinity, perceive themselves to be members of the same group.

■ **foreign policy**
the decisions governing authorities make to realize international goals.

THE GLOBAL AND DOMESTIC DETERMINANTS OF STATES' FOREIGN POLICY BEHAVIOR

Geostrategic location, military might, economic prowess, and system of government are all variables that affect foreign policy choices. Still, due to the diversity of states, as well as their different locations and positions within the contemporary state system, it is difficult to generalize about the influence of any one factor or combination of factors.

levels of analysis
the different aspects of and agents in international affairs that may be stressed in interpreting world politics and explaining global phenomena, depending on whether the analyst chooses to focus on "wholes" (the complete global system and large collectivities) or on "parts" (individual states or people).

intermestic
those issues confronting a state that are simultaneously international and domestic.

To determine the relative impact of specific factors under different circumstances, we must first distinguish between the international and internal influences on policy choices. Note the **levels of analysis** pictured in Figure 3.1. In classifying the determinants not only of states' foreign policies but also of trends in world politics generally, the levels-of-analysis concept introduced in Chapter 1 helps to describe the multiple influences on states' decision-making processes. Recall that states and the global system make up two distinct levels: the state level encompasses domestic characteristics, and the global or international system level encompasses interstate relations and changes in these relations over time. Although these two traditionally discrete realms have become increasingly fused in what is called **intermestic** politics, as the need for leaders to coordinate their domestic and foreign policies has increased with the **globalization** of twenty-first-century international relations, this categorical distinction is still useful for purposes of analysis.

Global or "external" influences on foreign policy include all activities occurring beyond a state's borders that structure the choices its officials make. Such factors as the content of international law, the number of military alliances, destruction of the forests and animal species, and the changing levels of international trade sometimes profoundly affect the choices of decisionmakers.

FIGURE 3.1
The Major Sources of States' Foreign Policy Decisions: Influences at Three Levels

The factors that shape states' foreign policies can be categorized at three basic levels. At the global level are those structural features of the international system such as the prevalence of civil wars and the extent of trade interdependence. At the state level are internal or domestic influences such as the state's type of government or the opinions of its citizens. At the individual level are the characteristics of the leader—his or her personal beliefs, values, and personality. All three levels of influence simultaneously affect decisions, but their relative weight usually depends on the issues and circumstances at the time of decision.

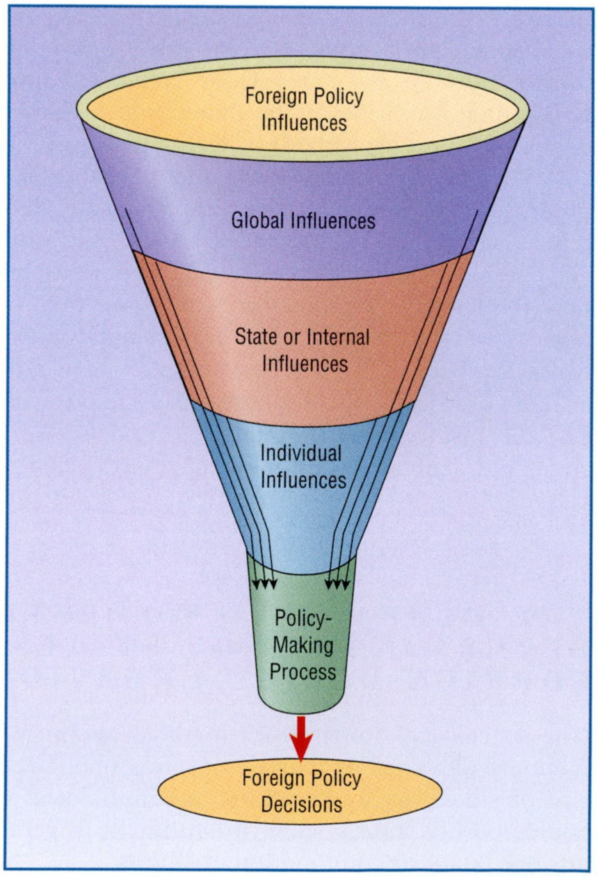

Internal or "domestic" influences, on the other hand, are those that exist at the level of the state, not the system. Here attention focuses on variations in **states' attributes,** such as military capabilities, level of economic development, and types of government, that may influence different states' foreign policy behavior. Examples of both types of influences follow.

globalization
the accelerating process by which increasing interstate interconnectedness has eroded the traditional distinction between states' domestic and international affairs (see p. 41).

states' attributes
state characteristics that shape foreign policy behavior, such as their size, wealth, and the extent to which their leaders are accountable to their citizens in comparison with other states.

Geopolitics

One of the most important influences on a state's foreign policy behavior is its location and physical terrain. The presence of natural frontiers, for example, may profoundly guide policymakers' choices (see Map 3.1). Consider the United States, which has prospered because vast oceans separate it from Europe and Asia. The advantage of having oceans as barriers to foreign intervention, combined with the absence of militarily powerful neighbors, permitted the United States to develop into an industrial giant and to practice safely an isolationist foreign policy for over 150 years. Consider also mountainous Switzerland, whose topography has made neutrality a compelling foreign policy posture.

Similarly, maintaining autonomy from continental politics has been an enduring theme in the foreign policy of Great Britain, an island country whose physical separation from Europe served historically as a buffer separating it from entanglement in major-power disputes on the Continent. Preserving this protective shield has been a priority for Britain and helps to explain why Great Britain has been so hesitant in the past twenty years to accepting full integration in the European Union (EU) and adopting its currency to the euro (see Chapters 6 and 16).

Most countries are not insular, however; they have many states on their borders, denying them the option of noninvolvement in world affairs. Germany, which sits in the geographic center of Europe, historically has found its domestic political system and foreign policy preferences profoundly affected by its geostrategic position. In the twentieth century alone, even before the unification of East and West, Germany had "undergone five radical changes in political personality—from Wilhelm II's empire to the Weimar Republic, from Hitler's *Reich* of a Thousand Years to its two postwar successors, the Federal Republic of Germany . . . and the German Democratic Republic" (Joffe 1985).

In much the same way, extended frontiers with the former Soviet Union shaped the foreign policies of China and Finland. Finland's neutrality in the Cold War helped ensure its survival in the face of a powerful and threatening neighbor. China, on the other hand, has long regarded its relationship with the now defunct Soviet Union as unequal, and in the late 1960s the two communist giants clashed militarily as the Chinese sought to rectify past injustices. The "unequal treaties" between China and outside powers, which encapsulate other perceived injustices, resulted in part from China's vast size and indefensible borders, which made it an easy target for the great powers that had carved it into spheres of influence in previous centuries.

Like China, the Latin American countries reside geographically near a much stronger power, the United States, whose capabilities are in part a function of geophysical resources. Latin America has long been the object of studied interest and frequent intervention by the giant to the north. The U.S. presence provoked a bitter response among Latin American countries for many decades, because they felt they could not compete on an equal footing with the U.S.

MAP 3.1
Geographic Influences on Foreign Policy

How countries act toward others is shaped by the number of neighboring states on their borders and whether they are protected from invasion by natural barriers such as mountains and oceans. This map suggests how the separation of the United States from Eurasia has encouraged an isolationist policy during many periods in U.S. history. Note also how topography, location, and other geopolitical factors may have influenced the foreign policy priorities of Great Britain, Germany, China, Finland, and states in South America—hypotheses advanced by the geopolitics approach to international politics.

economic and military powerhouse. Their foreign policy of resistance to so-called Yankee **imperialism** was driven by their vulnerable circumstances. Understandably, many other poor Global South countries without many resources also see that, given their weak geo-economic condition, their foreign policy goals should be geared to opposing imperialism—what former Egyptian President Gamal Abdel Nasser defined as "the subjugation of small nations to the interests of the big ones."

■ **imperialism**
intentional imposition of one state's power over another, traditionally through territorial conquest, but more recently through economic domination, denying the victim population freedom to have a voice in the conquering regime's decisions.

History is replete with other examples of geography's influence on states' foreign policy goals, which is why geopolitical theories are useful (see Demko and Wood 1994). The **geopolitics** school of realist thought and political geography generally stresses the influence of geographic factors on state power and international conduct. Illustrative of early geopolitical thinking is Alfred Thayer Mahan's (1890) *The Influence of Sea Power in History,* which maintained that control of the seas shaped national power. Thus states with extensive coastlines and ports enjoyed a competitive advantage. Later geopoliticians, such as Sir Halford Mackinder (1919) and Nicholas Spykman (1944), stressed that not only location but also topography, size (territory and population), climate, and distance between states are powerful determinants of the foreign policies of individual countries. The underlying principle behind the geopolitical perspective is self-evident: Leaders' perceptions of available foreign policy options are influ-

■ **geopolitics**
the theoretical postulate that states' foreign policies are determined by their location, natural resources, and physical environment.

enced by the geopolitical circumstances that define their states' place on the world stage.

Geopolitics is only one aspect of the global environment that may influence foreign policy. In other chapters we will discuss additional global factors. Here, we comment briefly on three internal attributes of states that influence their foreign policies: military capabilities, level of economic development, and type of government.

Military Capabilities

The proposition that states' internal capabilities shape their foreign policy priorities is supported by the fact that states' preparations for war strongly influence their later use of force (see Levy 2001; Vasquez 1993). Thus while all states may seek similar goals, their ability to realize them will vary according to their military capabilities.

Because military capabilities limit a state's range of prudent policy choices, they act as a mediating factor on leaders' national security decisions. For instance, in the 1980s Libyan leader Muammar Qaddafi repeatedly provoked the United States through anti-American and anti-Israeli rhetoric and by supporting various terrorist activities. Qaddafi was able to act as he did largely because neither bureaucratic organizations nor a mobilized public existed in Libya to constrain his personal whims and militaristic foreign policy preferences. However, Qaddafi was doubtlessly more highly constrained by the outside world than were the leaders in the more militarily capable countries toward whom his anger was directed. Limited military muscle compared with the United States precluded the kinds of belligerent behaviors he threatened to practice.

Conversely, Saddam Hussein, the Iraqi dictator, made strenuous efforts to build Iraq's military might (partly with the help of U.S. arms sales) and by 1990 had built the fourth-largest army in the world. Thus the invasion of Kuwait became a feasible foreign policy option. In the end, however, even Iraq's impressive military power proved ineffective against a vastly superior coalition of military forces, headed by the United States, which forced Saddam Hussein to capitulate and withdraw from the conquered territory. The conflict reignited in the late 1990s when a defiant and increasingly armed Iraq resisted UN inspection of its weapons-production facilities, and the UN relaxed its sanctions on the export of Iraqi oil in 2000.

Economic Characteristics

The level of economic and industrial development a state enjoys affects the foreign policy goals it can pursue. Generally, the more economically developed a state is, the more likely it is to play an activist role in the global political economy. Rich states have interests that extend far beyond their borders and typically possess the means to pursue and protect them. Not coincidentally, states that enjoy industrial capabilities and extensive involvement in international trade also tend to be militarily powerful—in part because military might is a function of economic capabilities. Before India and Pakistan became nuclear weapons states, only the world's most scientifically sophisticated industrial economies had produced nuclear weapons, which many regard as the ultimate expression of military prowess. In this sense nuclear weapons were the *result* of being powerful, not its cause.

Military Intervention for Both Power and Principle? In early 1999 Serbian dictator Slobodan Milosevic escalated what the nineteen NATO countries called a campaign of terror against Serbia's Albanian minority, and launched *Operation Allied Force* in response to what NATO defined on April 24 as "a fundamental challenge to the values for which NATO has stood since its inception: democracy, human rights and the rule of law." Shown here are jubilant Albanian Kosovars greeting German troops arriving in Prizen, Kosovo, on June 13, to aid in their defense. NATO's response illustrated the continuing importance of military capabilities to defend ideals as well as the principle that arsenals and armies do not necessarily give a warmonger the power to freely destroy the lives of ethnic minorities.

For four decades after World War II, the United States and the Soviet Union stood out as superpowers precisely because they benefited from a combination of vast economic and military capabilities, including extensive nuclear weapons capabilities. This enabled both states to practice unrestrained globalism; their "imperial reach" and interventionist behavior were seemingly unconstrained by limited wealth or resources. In fact, historically major powers (rich states) have been involved in foreign conflict more frequently than minor powers (poor states). For this reason, **gross national product (GNP)** is often used in combination with other factors to identify great powers, and by itself is an important element in predicting the extensiveness of states' global interests and involvements.

■ **gross national product (GNP)** measure of a state's production of goods and services within a given period of time (see p. 137).

Although economically advanced states are more active globally, this does not mean that their privileged circumstances dictate adventuresome policies. Rich states are often "satisfied" ones that have much to lose from the onset of revolutionary change or global instability and that usually perceive the status quo as best serving their interests (Wolfers 1962). As a result, they often forge international economic policies to protect and expand their envied position at the pinnacle of the global hierarchy.

Levels of productivity and prosperity also affect the foreign policies of the poor states at the bottom of the hierarchy. Some dependent states respond to their economic weakness by complying subserviently with the wishes of the rich on whom they depend. Others rebel defiantly, sometimes succeeding (despite their disadvantaged bargaining position) in resisting the efforts by great powers to control their international behavior.

Thus generalizations about the economic foundations of states' international political behavior often prove inaccurate. Although levels of economic development vary widely among states in the global system, they alone do not determine foreign policies. Instead, leaders' perceptions of the opportunities and constraints that their states' economic resources provide may more powerfully influence their foreign policy choices.

Type of Government

A third important attribute affecting states' international behavior is their political system. Although neorealism predicts that all states will act similarly to protect their interests, a state's type of government demonstrably constrains important choices, including whether the use of force is threatened and whether the threat is carried out. Here the important distinction is between **constitutional democracy** (representative government) on one end of the spectrum and **autocratic rule** (authoritarian or totalitarian) on the other.

In neither democratic (sometimes called "open") nor autocratic ("closed") political systems can political leaders survive long without the support of organized domestic political interests, and sometimes the mass citizenry. But in democratic systems those interests are likely to be politically potent, spread beyond the government itself, and active in their pressure on the government to make policy choices that benefit them. Public opinion, interest groups, and the mass media are a more visible part of the policy-making process in democratic systems. Similarly, the electoral process in democratic societies more meaningfully frames choices and produces results about who will lead than typically occurs in authoritarian regimes, where the real choices are made by a few elites behind closed doors. In short, in a democracy, public opinions and preferences may matter and, therefore, differences in who is allowed to participate and how much they exercise their right to participate are critical determinants of foreign policy choices (see Ray 1995; Russett 2001).

Compare, for example, the foreign policy of Saudi Arabia, controlled by a king and royal family, with that of Switzerland, governed by a multiparty democratic process. In the former, foreign policy decisions have sometimes been bold and unexpected, as exemplified by the Saudi royal family's revolutionary policies in summoning U.S. military forces to its territory during the 1991 Persian Gulf War, in contravention of long-standing Arab policies designed to prevent Western encroachments against Muslim lands. In Switzerland, where voting and mass political participation heavily influence decisions about Switzerland's international activities, the government has pursued the policy of neutrality without deviation since 1815.

Although public preferences help shape democratic societies' foreign policies, so too does **elitism** (Mills 1956). Often, even in democratic governments, decisions are made by a small ruling elite; this is especially true when international crises erupt. Military-industrial complexes, obtrusively evident in many countries, are examples of elite groups sometimes believed to exercise disproportionate control over defense policy making in both turbulent and calm times. Elitism's rival model, known as **pluralism,** sees policy making as an upward-flowing process in which competitive domestic groups pressure the government for policies responsive to their interests and needs. Pluralism is a widespread phenomenon in democratic societies, although its effects are sometimes difficult to pinpoint.

Foreign Policy Performance in Democracies. The proposition that domestic stimuli, and not simply international events, are a source of foreign

■ **constitutional democracy**
government processes that allow people through their elected representatives to exercise power and influence the state's policies.

■ **autocratic rule**
a system of authoritarian or totalitarian government where unlimited power is concentrated in a single person.

■ **elitism**
the argument that because a "power elite" really controls democratic governments for its own interests, ordinary citizens are given participation without power, involvement without influence.

■ **pluralism**
a model of the policy-making process that highlights the impact of competitive domestic groups in pressuring the government for policies responsive to their interests and needs.

policy is not novel. In ancient Greece, for instance, the realist historian Thucydides observed that what happened within the Greek city-states often did more to shape their external behavior than what each did to the others. He added that Greek leaders frequently concentrated their efforts on influencing the political climate within their own polities rather than on managing relations with other Greek city-states. Similarly, leaders today sometimes make foreign policy decisions for domestic political purposes—as, for example, when bold or aggressive acts abroad are intended to influence election outcomes at home or to divert public attention from economic woes. This is sometimes called the "scapegoat" phenomenon or the **diversionary theory of war** (Levy 1989b).

■ **diversionary theory of war**
the contention that leaders initiate conflict abroad as a way of increasing national cohesion at home.

Some see the intrusion of domestic politics into foreign policy making as a disadvantage of democratic political systems that undermines their ability to deal decisively with crises or to bargain effectively with less democratic adversaries and allies (see Controversy: Are Democracies Deficient in Foreign Affairs?). Democracies are subject to inertia. They move slowly on issues, because so many disparate elements are involved in decision making and officials are responsible to a variety of public opinions. A crisis sufficient enough to sway a large portion of people rapidly may need to occur in order for large changes in policy to come about. As the French political sociologist Alexis de Tocqueville argued in 1835, democracies may be inclined to "impulse rather than prudence" because they overreact to perceived external dangers once they recognize them. "There are two things that a democratic people will always find difficult," de Tocqueville mused, "to start a war and to end it." In contrast, authoritarian governments can "make decisions more rapidly, ensure domestic compliance with their decisions, and perhaps be more consistent in their foreign policy" (Jensen 1982). But there is a cost: Nondemocracies "often are less effective in developing an innovative foreign policy because of subordinates' pervasive fear of raising questions." In short, the concentration of power and the suppression of public opposition can be dangerous as well as advantageous.

The Spread of Democracy and Its Foreign Policy Consequences. The impact of government type on foreign policy choice has taken on great significance as the twenty-first century dawns, following the rapid conversion of many dictatorships to democratic rule. These liberal government conversions have occurred in three successive "waves" since the 1800s. The first wave occurred between 1878 and 1926 and the second between 1943 and 1962. "Even in the rich world, in 1900 democracy scarcely existed. Only six countries out of 43 then recognized as nation-states had something that began to deserve the name, and even there the suffrage was invariably limited, with some men and all women excluded. The rich world's democratic growth took place only after 1945, when Germany, Italy and Japan joined the fray" (*Economist,* September 11, 1999, 7). This inaugurated democratization's "third wave" of growth (Huntington 1991b; see Vanhanen 2000), during which the global spread of democratic governance really began to accelerate. In 1980, only 37 of the world's 121 countries were democratic, accounting for a mere 35 percent of the world's population. But by 2000, 144 of the 192 countries monitored by Freedom House were democratic, covering nearly 60 percent of the world's population. During that twenty-year span, more than three-fourths of the countries in the world became elective governments with more than half of the world's population able to choose their government leaders by the ballot (see Map 3.2).

CONTROVERSY

Are Democracies Deficient in Foreign Affairs?

History suggests that democracies enjoy faithful allies and lose fewer wars than do nondemocracies but, despite these achievements, democracies may make foreign policy choices in ways that are less rational and efficient than autocracies (see Siverson and Emmons 1991). For this reason, one realist thesis argues that democracies are decidedly inferior to nondemocratic regimes. Does the nature of democratic rule help or hinder those governments' capacities to realize their goals under anarchy? In evaluating this controversy, consider the views of a leading American policymaker and realist political scientist, George F. Kennan, who advanced the following thesis:

> I sometimes wonder whether a democracy is not uncomfortably similar to one of those prehistoric monsters with a body as long as this room and a brain the size of a pin. He lies there in his comfortable primeval mud and pays little attention to his environment; he is slow to wrath—in fact, you practically have to whack his tail off to make him aware that his interests are being disturbed; but, once he grasps this, he lies about him with such blind determination that he not only destroys his adversary but largely wrecks his native habitat. You wonder whether it would not have been wiser for him to have taken a little more interest in what was going on at an earlier date and to have seen whether he could not have prevented some of these situations from arising instead of proceeding from an undiscriminating indifference to a holy wrath equally undiscriminating. (Kennan 1951, 59)

Against this criticism of democratic governments' tendency to react without foresight or moderation in foreign policy, defenders of liberal democratic governance such as Immanuel Kant, Thomas Jefferson, and Woodrow Wilson have argued just the opposite: that giving people power through the ballot and a voice in the making of foreign policy decisions restrains leaders in those countries from extreme or excessive choices, such as initiating a war on a whim. Thus, to liberals, democratization makes a positive contribution, enabling the leader of a democracy to bargain successfully with nondemocracies, since other states know that democratic governments are likely to have the support of the people and to honor their agreements.

What do you think? Are democratic procedures for making foreign policy decisions an aid or a handicap? What arguments and evidence can you provide to support your general conclusion about this timeless controversy?

As the tide of democratization spread worldwide, the sea change has prompted some observers to speculate that we may be witnessing the **end of history**—meaning "the end of mankind's ideological evolution and the universalization of Western liberal democracy as the final form of government" (Fukuyama 1989). The contagious expansion of democratic states could end, of course, because many of these fledgling new democracies are fragile, and some are faltering. If they do survive, however, and if new democratic governments take root elsewhere, a transformation of the historic pattern of international relations could occur in the twenty-first century, because changes in domestic political institutions often precede changes in foreign policy behavior (see Gowa 1999). The recent growth of democracy has emboldened neoliberals to predict that a **democratic peace** will develop—that a new century increasingly dominated by "liberal democracies" will be a safer century. Their reasons for this prophecy vary. Yet most neoliberal reformers rely on the logic of Immanuel Kant outlined in his 1795 treatise *Perpetual Peace*. In this pioneering liberal theoretical statement, Kant posited that democracies would act very differently than nondemocracies in their foreign relations: they would form a separate peace with each other. The basis for this prediction rested on Kant's recognition that in democracies leaders

■ **end of history**
the thesis advanced by Francis Fukuyama that because liberal democracy and a market economy are the only workable options for modern societies, the contest with centrally planned governance has ended (see p. 110).

■ **democratic peace**
the theory that although democratic states sometimes wage wars against other states, they do not fight each other (see p. 424).

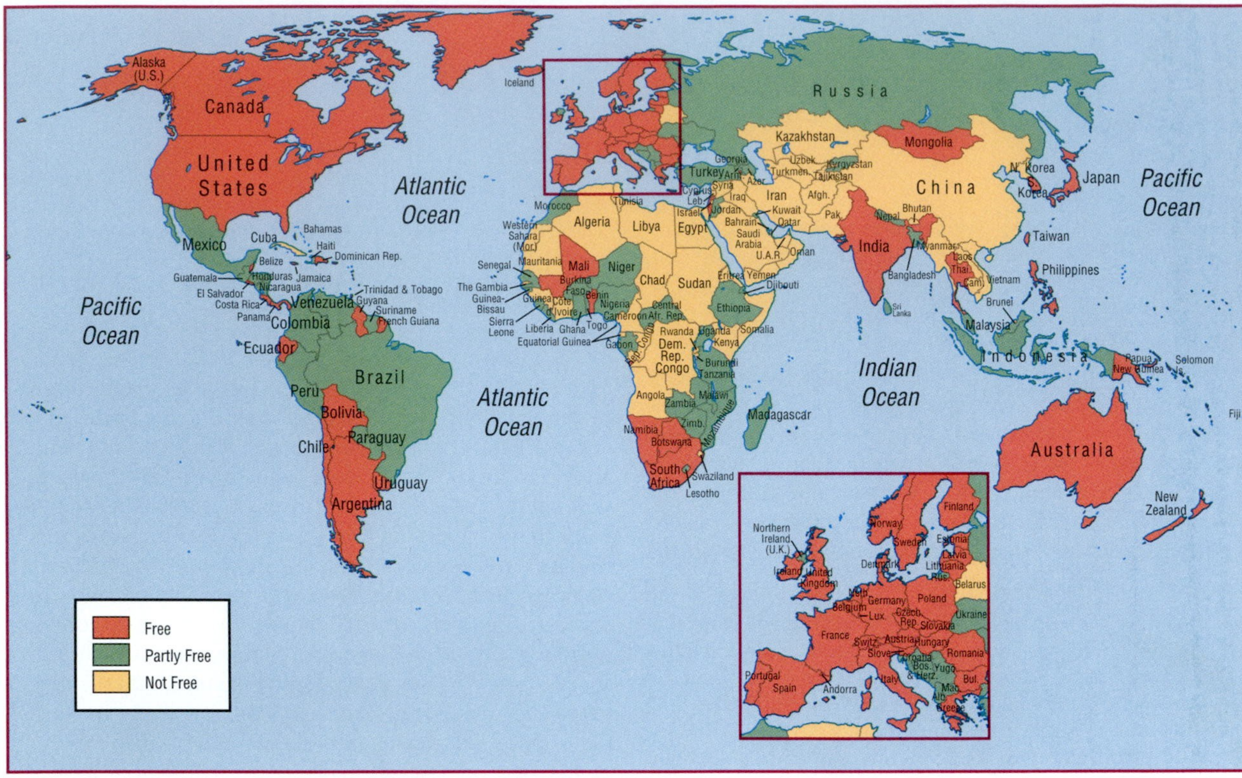

MAP 3.2

The Flow of Freedom: Democratic Liberty at the Dawn of a New Century

Throughout most of modern history the majority of states were ruled autocratically and the people living in them were not free. However, since the mid-1950s, an increasing number of states have undertaken political reforms leading to transitions toward democratic governance and civil liberties. This map shows the location in the year 2000 of eighty-five "free" countries whose governments provide their citizens with a high degree of political and economic freedom and safeguard basic civil liberties, fifty-nine "partly free" electoral democracies, and forty-eight "not free" states, where citizens' human rights and liberties are systematically abused or denied. Liberal democratic peace theory predicts that the spread of liberty, if it continues, will produce peaceful relations among the growing community of the liberal democracies whose leaders are accountable to the public for their election and for approval of their policies.

SOURCE: Adapted from index provided Freedom House, an international nongovernmental organization dedicated to strengthening democratic institutions.

are accountable to the public, and that "having two distinct domestic institutions, freedom of discussion with regular competitive elections of those empowered to make war" (Owen 1997), democracies would permit ordinary citizens to constrain leaders from initiating wars. Because citizens have to supply the soldiers and bear the human and financial cost of imperialistic policies, they would choose not to wage war, especially against other liberal democracies similarly constrained by norms and institutions that respect compromise and civil liberties. As Kant might have argued, "When those who fought and paid for war were granted the right to decide on war, the world would finally have peace" (Owen 1997). From this reasoning derived the neoliberal democratic peace argument that liberal democracies are natural forces for international peace.

Much empirical evidence supports the **neoliberal** proposition that, as stated in 1994 by President Bill Clinton, "Democracies don't attack each other." Whereas liberal democracies fight wars often with nondemocracies (Small and Singer 1976), in the last two centuries there rarely if ever has been a major war waged by one democracy against another (Gowa 1999; Ray 1995; Russett 2001), thus posing a serious challenge to realism's assumption that when it comes to war liberal democracies are no different from illiberal states. Consequently, there is reason to believe that should the growth of democratization continue throughout the world, this trend could make the twenty-first century hospitable to the preservation of international peace.

■ neoliberalism
a perspective that accounts for the way international institutions promote global change, cooperation, peace, and prosperity through collective action (see p. 366).

However, we must be careful not to assume that the historically strong linkage between democracy and peace will necessarily hold in the future. As Samuel Huntington (1989) warns, "The 'democratic zone of peace' argument is valid as far as it goes, but may not go all that far." Democracies are prone to aggression during times of economic and domestic crisis (Morgan and Campbell 1991), and there have been some important exceptions to the general rule that democratic regimes are less bellicose (Wright 1942). Hitler came to power in Germany in 1933 through the ballot and then proceeded to wage the most destructive war in history. In addition, the record of democratic states' active participation in colonial wars undermines liberalism's expectation that democratic rule is an antidote to imperialism (see Chan 1984 and 1997). So, too, does democratic states' frequent practice of military intervention short of war (Kegley and Hermann 1997). Indeed, critics note that the longest surviving democracy, the United States, initiated or supported military or paramilitary actions against elected governments in Chile, Grenada, Nicaragua, and Panama. Consequently, we must suspend judgment on the question of whether a world of democracies will necessarily be a more peaceful world.

Nevertheless, the overall record shows that, contrary to realism's premise, the type of government, and more specifically whether leaders are accountable to opposition groups through multiparty elections, strongly influences the kinds of goals these states pursue abroad (see Snyder 1991). Citizens' freedom constrains their leaders' choices and influences liberal democracies' patterns of international interactions. Many developments in world politics examined in later chapters will draw further attention to the internal roots of external behavior.

Having described the international settings to which policymakers respond and the internal factors that influence their decisions, we now turn to how foreign policy decisions are reached. We begin with the rational model of decision making.

THE UNITARY ACTOR AND RATIONAL DECISION MAKING

According to realist theorizing, the primary goal of foreign policy is to ensure state survival. From this viewpoint, strategic calculations about national security are the primary determinants of policymakers' choices. Domestic politics and the process of policy making itself are of secondary concern.

States as Unitary Actors

Realism, in both its classical and neorealist forms, emphasizes that the international environment determines state action. It assumes that foreign policy making consists primarily of adjusting the state to the pressures of an anarchical world system whose essential properties will not vary. Accordingly, it presumes that all states and the individuals responsible for their foreign policies confront the problem of national survival in similar ways. Thus all decisionmakers are essentially alike in their approach to foreign policy making:

> If they follow the [decision] rules, we need know nothing more about them. In essence, if the decision maker behaves rationally, the observer, knowing the rules of rationality, can rehearse the decisional process in his own mind, and, if he knows the decision maker's goals, can both predict the decision and understand why that particular decision was made. (Verba 1969, 225)

Because realists believe that leaders' goals and their corresponding approach to foreign policy choices are the same, the decision-making processes of each state can be studied as though it were a **unitary actor**—a homogenous or monolithic unit with few or no important internal differences that affect its choices. One way to picture this assumption is to think of states as billiard balls and the table on which they interact as the state system. The balls (states) continuously clash and collide with one another, and the actions of each are determined by its interactions with the others, not by what occurs inside it. According to this realist view, the leaders who make foreign policy, the types of governments they head, the characteristics of their societies, and the internal economic and political conditions of the states they lead are unimportant.

■ **unitary actor**
a transnational actor (usually a sovereign state) assumed to be internally united, so that changes in its internal circumstances do not influence its foreign policy as much as do the decisions that actor's leaders make to cope with changes in its global environment.

Policy Making as Rational Choice

The decision-making processes of unitary actors that determine national interests are typically described as rational. We define rationality or **rational choice** here as purposeful, goal-directed behavior exhibited when "the individual responding to an international event . . . uses the best information available and chooses from the universe of possible responses that alternative most likely to maximize his [or her] goals" (Verba 1969). Scholars describe rationality as a sequence of decision-making activities involving the following intellectual steps:

■ **rational choice**
decision-making procedures guided by careful definition of situations, weighing of goals, consideration of all alternatives, and selection of the options most likely to achieve the highest goals.

1. *Problem Recognition and Definition.* The need to decide begins when policymakers perceive an external problem and attempt to define objectively its distinguishing characteristics. Objectivity requires full information about the actions, motivations, and capabilities of other actors as well as the character of the international environment and trends within it. The search for the information must be exhaustive, and all the facts relevant to the problem must be gathered.
2. *Goal Selection.* Next, those responsible for making foreign policy choices must determine what they want to accomplish. This disarmingly simple requirement is often difficult. It requires the identification and ranking of *all* values (such as security, democracy, and economic well-being) in a hierarchy from most to least preferred.

3. *Identification of Alternatives.* Rationality also requires the compilation of an exhaustive list of *all* available policy options and an estimate of the costs associated with each alternative.
4. *Choice.* Finally, rationality requires selecting the single alternative with the best chance of achieving the desired goal(s). For this purpose, policymakers must conduct a rigorous means-ends, cost-benefit analysis guided by an accurate prediction of the probable success of each option.

Policymakers often describe their own behavior as resulting from a rational decision-making process designed to reach the "best" decision possible. Indeed, some past foreign policy decisions do reveal elements of this idealized process, described well by former U.S. Secretary of State Henry Kissinger when he observed that

> . . . an effective decision-making process must . . . reflect well-thought-out policy choices—that is, they must answer these questions: What are we trying to achieve, or what are we trying to prevent? What consequences do we expect from this decision, and what steps do we have in mind for dealing with them? What is the cost of the proposed action? Are we willing to pay that price, and for what length of time? (Kissinger 1999, 1067)

The 1962 Cuban missile crisis, for example, illustrates several ways in which the deliberations of key U.S. policymakers conformed to a rational process (Allison and Zelikow 1999). Once Washington discovered the presence of Soviet missiles in Cuba, President John F. Kennedy formed a crisis decision-making group and charged it to "set aside all other tasks to make a prompt and intensive survey of the dangers and all possible courses of action." Six options were ultimately identified: do nothing; exert diplomatic pressure; make a secret approach to the Cuban leader Fidel Castro; invade Cuba; launch a surgical air strike against the missiles; or blockade Cuba. Before the group could choose among these six, it had to prioritize goals. Was removal of the Soviet missiles, retaliation against Castro or maintaining the balance of power the objective? Or did the missiles pose little threat to vital U.S. interests? Until it was determined that the missiles posed a serious threat to national security, "do nothing" remained an option.

Once the advisers agreed that their goal was removing the missiles, their discussion turned to evaluating a surgical air strike versus a blockade. They eventually chose the latter because of its presumed advantages, including the demonstration of firmness it permitted the United States and the flexibility about further choices it allowed both parties.

President Bill Clinton's decision to commit the United States to participate in and lead NATO's military intervention in Kosovo following acts of genocide by Yugoslavia dictator Slobodan Milosevic's Serbian troops against the Albanian Kosovar minority in 1999 is another example of crisis decision making that conforms in part to the model of rational choice. As in the Cuban missile crisis, the "do nothing" option was dismissed by the president and his advisers. The Clinton administration decided that intervention was necessary if the global community was to establish the principle that a sovereign government could not legally violate the human rights of people living within its territory or, worse still, slaughter them. Instead, much of the debate among senior officials focused on diplomatic and economic retaliation against Yugoslavia and

Diplomatic Ties — Rituals in a Global Diplomatic Culture Israeli Prime Minister Yitzhak Rabin, Egyptian President Hosni Mubarak, Jordan's King Hussein, U.S. President Bill Clinton, and the Palestine Liberation Organization's Yasser Arafat made history by signing an accord in September 1995 to expand Palestinian self-rule on the West Bank. The agreement was reached through step-by-step bargaining to realize common objectives presumably carefully decided on by rational choice. Fateful diplomatic ties, like neckties, can sometimes go askew, despite the best intentions. Five months later, the celebratory mood of the moment vanished when Rabin was assassinated by a terrorist as punishment for his act of courage.

possible covert action to topple Milosevic. Clinton chose to affirm the sanctity of human rights law by militarily resisting Milosevic's genocide. He ordered the deployment of U.S. troops for three clear goals: (1) to help eighteen other NATO allies defend the Kosovars against further aggression; (2) to defend respect for international law; and (3) to establish the right of military intervention for human rights protection as a principle for global order in the twenty-first century. Eventually those decisions gave way to a single choice from among the identified alternatives: air strikes and massive bombardment to force Yugoslavia to stop the human slaughter, surrender, and accept NATO's military occupation of Kosovo. Whether the decision proved wise was highly debated, but few observers doubted that the Clinton administration had attempted to reach what they thought was the "best" decision through a rational policy-making process.

Impediments to Rational Choice

Despite the apparent application of rationality in these crises, rational choice is often more an idealized standard than an accurate description of real-world behavior. Theodore Sorenson—one of President Kennedy's closest advisers and a participant in the Cuban missile deliberations—has written not only about the steps policymakers in the Kennedy administration followed as they sought to emulate the process of rational choice but also of how actual decision making often departed from it. He described an eight-step process for policy making that is consistent with the model we have described: (1) agreeing on the facts; (2) agreeing on the overall policy objective; (3) precisely defining the problems; (4) canvassing all possible solutions; (5) listing the possible consequences that flow from each solution; (6) recommending one option; (7) communicating the option selected; and (8) providing for its execution. But he explained how difficult it is to follow these steps, because:

> [e]ach step cannot be taken in order. The facts may be in doubt or dispute. Several policies, all good, may conflict. Several means, all bad, may be all that are open. Value judgments may differ. Stated goals may be imprecise. There may be many interpretations of what is right, what is possible, and what is in the national interest. (Sorensen 1963, 19–20)

Despite the virtues rational choice promises, the impediments to its realization in foreign policy making are substantial, which is why an eminent historian concluded a "phenomenon noticeable throughout history regardless of place or period is the pursuit by governments of policies contrary to their own interests" (Tuchman 1984). In fact, **bounded rationality** is typical (Simon 1982 and 1997). Some of the barriers that make errors in foreign policy so common are human, deriving from deficiencies in the intelligence, capability, and psychological needs and aspirations of foreign policy decisionmakers. Others are organizational, since most decisions require group agreement about the national interest and the wisest course of action. Reaching agreement is not easy, however, as reasonable people with different values often disagree about goals, preferences, and the probable results of alternative options. Thus the impediments to rational policy making are not to be underestimated.

■ **bounded rationality** the concept that decisionmakers' capacity to choose the best option is often constrained by many human and organizational obstacles.

Scrutiny of the actual process of decision making reveals other hindrances. Available information is often insufficient to recognize emergent problems accurately, resulting in decisions made on the basis of incomplete information. Moreover, the available information is often inaccurate, because the bureaucratic organizations political leaders depend on for advice screen, sort, and rearrange it. Compounding the problem is decisionmakers' susceptibility to **cognitive dissonance**—they are psychologically prone to block out negative, or dissonant, information and perceptions about their preferred choice and to look instead for information that justifies that choice. This explains why policymakers sometimes pay little heed to warnings and overlook information about dangers, so that they repeat their past intellectual mistakes.

■ **cognitive dissonance** the general psychological tendency to deny discrepancies between one's preexisting beliefs (cognitions) and new information (see p. 9).

In addition, determining what goals best serve national interests is difficult: "Decision making often takes place within an atmosphere marked by value-complexity and uncertainty. The existence of competing values about a single issue forces value trade-offs; uncertainty refers to the absence of complete and well-organized information on which to base a confident policy choice" (Walker 1991).

Furthermore, decisionmakers' inability to rapidly gather and digest large quantities of information constrains their capacity to make informed choices. Because policymakers work with overloaded **policy agendas** and short deadlines, the search for policy options is seldom exhaustive. "There is little time for leaders to reflect," observes former U.S. Secretary of State Henry Kissinger (1979). "They are locked in an endless battle in which the urgent constantly gains on the important. The public life of every political figure is a continual struggle to rescue an element of choice from the pressure of circumstance." In

■ **policy agenda** the changing list of problems or issues to which governments pay special attention at any given moment.

the choice phase, then, decisionmakers rarely make value-maximizing choices. Instead of selecting the option with the best chance of success, they typically end their evaluation as soon as an alternative appears that seems superior to those already considered. Herbert Simon (1957) describes this as **satisficing** behavior. Rather than "optimizing" by seeking the best alternative, decisionmakers are routinely content to choose the first option that meets minimally acceptable standards. Because they frequently face "unresolvable" choices that preclude satisfaction across competing preferences, often only "admissible" ones appear available (see Levi 1990).

■ **satisficing** the tendency for decisionmakers to choose the first available alternative that meets minimum acceptable standards.

The ability to make decisions is hindered by individuals' difficulties in abandoning formed opinions and their tendency to overreact in crises. **Prospect theory** informs us that when making choices, decisionmakers proceed by "framing" their choices from a perceived "reference point" based on past experiences about potential gains and losses, and react differently about what they expect to gain or lose from particular choices by overvaluing losses relative to comparable gains. Because "people tend to value what they have more than comparable things they do not have, [there results an] observed tendency toward status quo choices" (Levy 1997). Prospect theory suggests that leaders do not make decisions according to the rational-choice model; they let their needs and expectations affect when they will be receptive to taking risks and when they will be psychologically reluctant to take the risk of making policy changes to achieve gains. One implication of this theory and evidence is that when leaders strike out by taking risks to initiate bold new foreign policy directions, they will have great difficulty admitting and correcting those choices if they later prove to be mistaken. Like investors who take big risks in the hope of making big profits but hold losing investments too long, policymakers view the prospects of new policies hopefully but cling to failed policies long after their deficiencies have become apparent. This—along with the "sunk-cost fallacy" that having paid for something, people are unwilling to waste it no matter what the consequences, as well as people's tendency to select the option that looks preferable judging by some past reference point rather than one with better prospects for future gains—may account for leaders' reluctance to make and implement corrective policy decisions for fear of public criticism (Bostdorff 1993; also Levy 1992; Stein and Pauly 1993).

■ **prospect theory** the social psychological theory that international decision making is constrained by formed opinions and tendencies to overreact in crises, that decisions tend to be made based on the perceived prospects of choices to fulfill objectives, and that policymakers engage in risk-averse behavior in making choices about probable gains but are risk-acceptant when making choices about anticipated losses.

The assumption that states are unitary actors partially explains the discrepancy between the theory and practice of rational decision making. Most leaders must meet the often incompatible demands of domestic politics and external diplomacy, and it is seldom possible to make policy decisions that respond rationally to both sets of goals. Domestic policy traditionally referred to governmental decisions affecting people's behavior within the state's borders, foreign policy to external relations. However, in an age of globalization and state interdependence, it is often difficult to know where domestic policy ends and foreign policy begins. Policies at home often have many consequences abroad. Similarly, foreign activities usually heavily influence a state's internal condition. This is why many leaders are likely to fuse the two sectors in contemplating policy decisions.

■ **two-level games** a concept referring to the growing need for national policymakers to make decisions that will meet both domestic and foreign goals.

To better capture the way most leaders proceed as they make policy decisions, Robert D. Putnam coined the phrase **two-level games.** Challenging the assumptions of realism, he asserted that leaders should formulate policies simultaneously in both the diplomatic and domestic arenas, and should make those choices in accordance with the rules dictated by the "game."

> At the national level, domestic groups pursue their interests by pressuring the government to adopt favorable policies, and politicians seek power by constructing coalitions among these groups. At the international level, national governments seek to maximize their own ability to satisfy domestic pressures, while minimizing the adverse consequences of foreign developments. Neither of the two games can be ignored by central decision-makers so long as their countries remain interdependent, yet sovereign. (Putnam 1988, 434)

In addition to the complications undermining the separation of foreign and domestic decision making, states are administered by individuals with varying beliefs, values, preferences, and psychological needs, and such differences generate disagreements about goals and alternatives that are seldom resolved through tidy, orderly, rational processes. These procedures may be better described as **muddling through,** or making incremental policy changes through small steps (Lindblom 1979). As one former U.S. policymaker put it, "Rather than through grand decisions or grand alternatives, policy changes seem to come through a series of slight modifications of existing policy, with new policy emerging slowly and haltingly by small and usually tentative steps, a process of trial and error in which policy zigs and zags, reverses itself, and then moves forward" (Hilsman 1967).

muddling through the tendency for leaders to make foreign policy decisions by trial-and-error adjustments in an attempt to cope with challenges.

Despite the image that policymakers seek to project, the actual practice of foreign policy decision making is an exercise that lends itself to miscalculations, errors, and fiascoes. Policymakers tend "to avoid new interpretations of the environment, to select and act upon traditional goals, to limit the search for alternatives to a small number of moderate ones, and finally to take risks which involve low costs" (Coplin 1971). Thus, although policymakers can sometimes absorb new information quickly under great pressure and take calculated risks through deliberate planning, more often the degree of rationality "bears little relationship to the world in which officials conduct their deliberations" (Rosenau 1980).

Although rational foreign policy making is more an ideal than a reality, we can still assume that policymakers aspire to rational decision-making behavior, which they may occasionally approximate. Indeed, as a working proposition, it is useful to accept rationality as a picture of how the decision process *should* work as well as a description of key elements of how it *does* work (see Table 3.1).

THE BUREAUCRATIC POLITICS OF FOREIGN POLICY DECISION MAKING

Picture yourself as a head of state charged with managing your nation's relations with the rest of the world. To make the right choices, you must seek information and advice, and you must see that the actions your decisions generate are carried out properly. Who can aid you in these tasks? Out of necessity, you must turn to those with the expertise you lack.

In today's world, states' extensive political, military, and economic relations require dependence on large-scale organizations. Leaders turn to these organizations for information and advice as they face critical foreign policy choices.

TABLE 3.1

Foreign Policy Decision Making in Theory and Practice

Ideal Rational Process	*Actual Common Practice*
Accurate, comprehensive information	Distorted, incomplete information
Clear definition of national interests and goals	Personal motivations and organizational interests bias national goals
Exhaustive analysis of all options	Limited number of options considered; none thoroughly analyzed
Selection of optimal course of action for producing desired results	Course of action selected by political bargaining and compromise
Effective statement of decision and its rationale to mobilize domestic support	Confusing and contradictory statements of decision, often framed for media consumption
Careful monitoring of the decision's implementation by foreign affairs bureaucracies	Neglect of the tedious task of managing the decision's implementation by foreign affairs bureaucracies
Instantaneous evaluation of consequences followed by correction of errors	Superficial policy evaluation, uncertain responsibility, poor follow-through, and delayed correction

Although this is more true of major powers than of small states, even those without large budgets and complex foreign policy bureaucracies seldom make decisions without the advice and assistance of many individuals and administrative agencies (Korany 1986). Organizations perform vital services, enhancing the state's capacity to cope with changing global circumstances.

In the United States, for instance, the State Department, Defense Department, and Central Intelligence Agency are all key participants in the foreign policy machinery. Other agencies also bear responsibility for specialized aspects of U.S. foreign relations, such as the Treasury, Commerce, and Agriculture departments. Similar agencies characterize the foreign affairs machinery of most other major powers, whose governments face many of the same foreign policy management challenges as the United States.

Bureaucratic Efficiency and Rationality

Bureaucratic management of foreign relations is not new. However, with the internationalization of domestic politics during the twentieth century, the growth of large-scale organizations to manage foreign relations has spread. Bureaucratic procedures based on the theoretical work of the German social scientist Max Weber are commonplace, primarily because they are perceived to enhance rational decision making and efficient administration.

■ **bureaucracies** the agencies, regulatory commissions, and departments that conduct the functions of a central government.

Bureaucracies increase efficiency and rationality by assigning responsibility for different tasks to different people. They define rules and standard operating procedures that specify how tasks are to be performed; they rely on record systems to gather and store information; they divide authority among different organizations to avoid duplication of effort; and they often lead to meritocracies by hiring and promoting the most capable individuals. Bureaucracies also permit the luxury of engaging in forward planning designed to determine long-term needs and the means to attain them. Unlike heads of state, whose roles require attention to the crisis of the moment, bureaucrats are able to consider the future as well as the present. The presence of several organizations can also result in **multiple advocacy** of rival choices (George 1972), thus improving the chance that all possible policy options will be considered.

■ **multiple advocacy** the concept that better and more rational choices are made when decisions are reached in a group context that allows advocates of differing alternatives to be heard, so that the feasibility of rival options receives critical evaluation.

The Limits of Bureaucratic Organization

What emerges from our description of bureaucracy is another idealized picture of the policy-making process. Before jumping to the conclusion that bureaucratic decision making is a modern blessing, however, we should emphasize that the foregoing propositions tell us how bureaucratic decision making should occur; they do not tell us how it does occur. The actual practice and the foreign policy choices that result reveal burdens to bureaucracy as well as benefits.

Consider again the 1962 Cuban missile crisis, probably the single most threatening crisis in the post–World War II era. The method that U.S. policymakers used in orchestrating a response is often viewed as having nearly approximated the ideal of rational choice. From another decision-making perspective, however, the missile crisis reveals how decision making by and within organizational contexts sometimes compromises rather than facilitates rational choice.

In his well-known book on the missile crisis, *Essence of Decision* (1971), Harvard political scientist Graham Allison identifies two elements in the **bureaucratic politics model** (see also Allison and Zelikow 1999; Caldwell 1977; C. Hermann 1988). One, which he calls "organizational process," reflects the constraints that organizations and coalitions of organizations in **policy networks** place on decisionmakers' choices. The other, "governmental politics," draws attention to the "pulling and hauling" that occurs among the key participants and **caucuses** of aligned bureaucracies in the decision process.

■ **bureaucratic politics model** a description of decision making that sees foreign policy choices as based on bargaining and compromises among government agencies.

One way in which large-scale bureaucratic organizations contribute to the policy-making process is by devising **standard operating procedures (SOPs)**—established methods to be followed in the performance of designated tasks. For example, once the Kennedy administration opted for a naval quarantine of Cuba, the Navy could carry out the president's decision according to previously devised procedures. These routines, however, effectively limit the range of viable policy choices. Rather than expanding the number of policy alternatives in a manner consistent with the logic of rational decision making, what organizations are prepared to do shapes what is and is not considered possible. In the Cuban crisis, a surgical air strike was seen as preferable to the blockade, but when the Air Force confessed that it could not guarantee complete success in taking out the missiles, the alternative was dropped.

■ **policy networks** leaders and organized interests (such as lobbies) that form temporary alliances to influence a particular policy decision.

■ **caucuses** informal groups that individuals in government join to promote their common interests.

Governmental politics, the second element in the bureaucratic politics model, is related to the organizational character of foreign policy making in complex societies. Not surprisingly, participants in the deliberations that lead to policy choices often define issues and favor policy alternatives that reflect their organizational affiliations. "Where you stand depends on where you sit" is a favorite aphorism reflecting these bureaucratic imperatives. Consequently, many students of governmental politics observe that professional diplomats typically favor diplomatic approaches to policy problems, while military officers routinely favor military solutions.

■ **standard operating procedures (SOPs)** rules for reaching decisions about particular types of situations.

Collective Decision Making During crises that threaten a country's national security, decisions usually are made by the head of state and a small group of advisers rather than by large-scale bureaucracies. But at times critical choices are reached by large decision-making groups, such as here at the fiftieth anniversary NATO summit on April 23, 1999, in Washington, D.C., at which allied leaders labored to make the tough decision about intervening to contain the crisis in Kosovo. A collective decision was reached through a process that displayed some of the characteristics of "groupthink" (see p. 76).

Because the players in the game of governmental politics are responsible for protecting the nation's security, they are "obliged to fight for what they are convinced is right." The consequence is that "different groups pulling in different directions produce a result, or better a resultant—a mixture of conflicting preferences and unequal power of various individuals—distinct from what any person or group intended" (Allison 1971). Rather than being a value-maximizing process, then, policy making is itself intensely political. Thus one explanation of why states make the choices they do lies not in their behavior vis-à-vis one another but within their own governments. And rather than presupposing the existence of a unitary actor, "it is necessary to identify the games and players, to display the coalitions, bargains, and compromises, and to convey some feel for the confusion" (Allison 1971). From this perspective, the decision to blockade Cuba was as much a product of who favored the choice as of any inherent logic that may have commended it. Once Robert Kennedy (the president's brother and the attorney general), Theodore Sorensen (the president's special counsel and "alter ego"), and Secretary of Defense Robert McNamara united behind the blockade, how could the president have chosen otherwise?

"Who favored what" also colored President George Bush's decision in 1991 to dispatch troops to Saudi Arabia. Although key Pentagon officials might have been expected to favor the use of force, some—specifically Dick Cheney, secretary of defense, and Colin Powell, the four-star general who was chairman of the Joint Chiefs of Staff—only reluctantly supported the military option. Instead, members of the president's White House staff, notably Brent Scowcroft (the president's national security adviser and a retired air force lieutenant general) and the president himself (a World War II navy pilot) were the principal advocates of a military response (Woodward 1991). Scowcroft continued to push a reluctant military as the crisis evolved, until in the fall, the strategic plan changed from defense to offense.

The disastrous Vietnam War, which the professional military regarded as a debacle in part because it lacked public support at home and a clear political objective abroad, helps to explain the Pentagon's nonaggressiveness on the military option. General Powell, who served President Ronald Reagan as national security adviser and believed that "there is no legitimate use of military force without a political objective," apparently gave so much political advice during the early days of the crisis over Kuwait that "Cheney firmly suggested that the president would be better served if Powell offered more military advice" (Woodward and Atkinson 1990).

In some sense, what the military could offer constrained the Bush administration in much the same way it did Kennedy. For many years the Pentagon had been preparing for "low-intensity" conflicts in jungle or forested terrain. Thus, its SOPs were ill suited to mechanized warfare in the flat, open, and featureless desert terrain of the Middle East.

Daunting logistical obstacles confronted the Pentagon as it contemplated a mission in a distant region without U.S. military bases. The gut response of Powell and others during the early hours of the crisis was despair about the absence of preparations. How, then, to proceed? As in Cuba, the choice was shaped by previous decisions. The United States relied on a plan first devised in the early 1980s. A massive air- and sealift of military personnel and equipment and ground deployment of heavy armor and antitank weapons became the basis for Operation Desert Storm (Woodward and Atkinson 1990). Once the president had ordered troops to the Persian Gulf region, a process was under way that the professional military could support and execute, and it became their standard for operations.

Attributes of Bureaucratic Behavior

In addition to their influence on the policy choices of political leaders, bureaucratic organizations possess several other characteristics that affect the decision-making environment. One view proposes that bureaucratic agencies are parochial and that every administrative unit within a state's foreign policy-making bureaucracy seeks to promote its own purposes and power. Organizational needs, such as large staffs and budgets, come before the state's needs, sometimes encouraging the sacrifice of national interests to bureaucratic interests, as bureaucrats come to see their own interests as the state's. Bureaucracies fight for survival, even when their usefulness has vanished.

> Programs that don't concoct some new argument or other for their continuing indispensability also tend to survive. This is because of [an] immutable law of government: even the most anachronistic, abysmal, extravagant and counterproductive government program will do at least one thing that is hard to assault. (Greenfield 1995)

Bureaucratic parochialism breeds competition among the agencies charged with foreign policy responsibilities. Far from being neutral or impartial managers, desiring only to carry out orders from the head of state, bureaucratic organizations frequently take policy positions designed to increase their own influence relative to that of other agencies. Characteristically, they are driven to enlarge their prerogatives and expand the conception of their mission, seeking to take on other units' responsibilities and powers.

To protect their own interests, bureaucratic organizations attempt to reduce interference from and penetration by the political leaders to whom they report as well as from other government agencies. Because knowledge is power, a common device for promoting organizational exclusivity is to hide inner workings and policy activities from others. The "invisible government" operating within the U.S. National Security Council during the Reagan administration illustrates this syndrome. Lieutenant Colonel Oliver North used his authority as a staff member of the council to orchestrate a secret arms-for-hostages deal with the Iranian government, part of what became popularly known as the Iran-contra affair.

The natural inclination of professionals who work in large organizations is to adapt their outlook and beliefs to those prevailing where they work. Every bureaucracy develops a shared "mind-set" or dominant way of looking at reality akin to the **groupthink** characteristic that small groups often develop (Janis 1982). An institutional mind-set discourages creativity, dissent, and independent thinking; it encourages reliance on standard operating procedures and deference to precedent rather than the exploration of new options to meet new challenges. This results in policy decisions that rarely deviate from conventional preferences.

■ **groupthink**
the propensity for members of a group to accept and agree with the group's prevailing attitudes, rather than speaking out for what they believe (see p. 414).

The Consequences of Bureaucratic Policy Making

A corollary of the notion that bureaucracies are often self-serving and guardians of the status quo is the idea that they defy directives by the political authorities they are supposed to serve. To thwart unpopular demands by authorities, bureaucracies often slow down and act inefficiently. At other times, bureaucratic sabotage is direct and immediate, again as vividly illustrated by the Cuban missile crisis. While President Kennedy sought to orchestrate U.S. action and bargaining, his bureaucracy in general, and the navy in particular, were in fact controlling events by doing as they wished.

> [The bureaucracy chose] to obey the orders it liked and ignore or stretch others. Thus, after a tense argument with the navy, Kennedy ordered the blockade line moved closer to Cuba so that the Russians might have more time to draw back. Having lost the argument with the president, the navy simply ignored his order. Unbeknownst to Kennedy, the navy was also at work forcing Soviet submarines to surface long before Kennedy authorized any contact with Soviet ships. And despite the president's order to halt all provocative intelligence, an American U-2 plane entered Soviet airspace at the height of the crisis. When Kennedy began to realize that he was not in full control, he asked his secretary of defense to see if he could find out just what the navy was doing. McNamara then made his first visit to the navy command post in the Pentagon. In a heated exchange, the chief of naval operations suggested that McNamara return to his office and let the navy run the blockade. (Gelb and Halperin 1973, 256)

Bureaucratic stubbornness is not unique to democracies. The resistance of bureaucracies to change is one of the major problems that reformers in the Soviet Union and the other centralized communist countries of Eastern Europe encountered, impairing their efforts to chart new policy directions and to remain in power. The foreign policy process in China, also a centralized communist government, operates similarly. It is "subject to the same vicissitudes of subjective perception, organizational conflict, bureaucratic politics, and factional infighting that bedevil other governments, perhaps more so given its size" (Whiting 1985). And in the United States nearly all chief executives have complained at some time about how the bureaucracy has undercut their policies, as Ronald Reagan did when he bemoaned that "one of the hardest things in a government this size is to know that down there, underneath, is the permanent structure that's resisting everything you're doing." The implementation of foreign policy innovations thus poses a major challenge to most leaders (see Smith and Clarke 1985).

Bureaucratic resistance is not the only inertial force promoting status quo foreign policies. The dynamics of governmental politics, which reduce policy choices to the outcome of a political tug of war, also retard the prospects for change. From the perspective of the participants, decision making is a high-stakes political game in which differences are often settled at the least common denominator instead of by rational cost-benefit calculations. As former U.S. Secretary of State Henry Kissinger described the process:

> Each of the contending factions within the bureaucracy has a maximum incentive to state its case in its most extreme form because the ultimate outcome depends, to a considerable extent, on a bargaining process. The premium placed on advocacy turns decision making into a series of adjustments among special interests—a process more suited to domestic than to foreign policy. . . . The outcome usually depends more on the pressure or the persuasiveness of the contending advocates than on a concept of overall purpose. (Kissinger 1969, 268)

Thus it is not surprising that bureaucracies throughout the world are frequently the object of criticism by both the political leaders they ostensibly serve and the citizens whose lives they so often affect.

THE ROLE OF LEADERS IN FOREIGN POLICY DECISION MAKING

The course of history is determined by the decisions of political elites. Leaders and the kind of leadership they exert shape the way in which foreign policies are made and the consequent behavior of states in world politics. "There is properly no history, only biography" is the way Ralph Waldo Emerson encapsulated the view that individual leaders move history.

history-making individuals model an interpretation of foreign policy behavior that equates states' actions with the preferences and initiatives of the highest government officials.

Leaders as Makers and Movers of World History

This **history-making individuals model** of policy decision making equates states' actions with the preferences and initiatives of the highest government officials. We expect leaders to lead, and we assume new leaders will make a

Nixon Doctrine President Richard Nixon's position that U.S. allies should bear a greater share of the burden for their defense.

Reagan Doctrine the Reagan administration's pledge of U.S. support for anticommunist insurgents who sought to overthrow Soviet-supported governments.

Clinton Doctrine the Clinton administration's policy of active engagement in world affairs to support enlargement of the peaceful liberal democratic community (see p. 509).

procedural rationality a method of decision making based on having perfect information and carefully weighing all possible courses of action.

instrumental rationality a conceptualization of rationality that emphasizes the tendency for decisionmakers to compare options with one another and select the one that has the best chance of succeeding.

difference. We reinforce this image when we routinely attach the names of leaders to policies, as though the leaders were synonymous with the state itself, as well as when we ascribe most successes and failures in foreign affairs to the leaders in charge at the time they occur. The equation of U.S. foreign policy with the **Nixon Doctrine** in the 1970s, the **Reagan Doctrine** in the 1980s, and the **Clinton Doctrine** in the 1990s are recent examples.

Citizens are not alone in thinking that leaders are the decisive determinants of states' foreign policies and, by extension, world history. Leaders themselves seek to create impressions of their own self-importance while attributing extraordinary powers to other leaders. The assumptions they make about the personalities of their counterparts, consciously or unconsciously, in turn influence their own behavior (Wendzel 1980), as political psychologists who study the impact of leaders' perceptions and personalities on their foreign policy preferences demonstrate (see Kelman 1965).

One of the dilemmas that leader-driven explanations of foreign policy behavior poses is that history's movers and shakers often pursue decidedly irrational policies. The classic example is Adolf Hitler, whose ruthless determination to seek military conquest of the entire European continent proved disastrous for Germany. How do we square this kind of behavior with the logic of realism, which says that survival is the paramount goal of all states and that all leaders engage in rational decision making? If the realists are correct, even defects in states' foreign policy processes cannot easily explain such wide divergences between the decisions leaders sometimes make and what cold cost-benefit calculations would predict.

We can explain this divergence in part by distinguishing between procedural rationality and instrumental rationality (Zagare 1990). **Procedural rationality** is the foundation of the realists' billiard-ball image of world politics. It views all states as acting similarly because all decisionmakers engage in the same "cool and clearheaded ends-means calculation" (Verba 1969) based on a careful weighing of all possible alternative courses of action. **Instrumental rationality** is a more limited view, which says simply that individuals have preferences and, when faced with two or more alternatives, they will choose the one they believe will yield the preferred outcome.

The implications of these seemingly semantic differences are important. The idea of instrumental rationality demonstrates that rationality does not "connote superhuman calculating ability, omniscience, or an Olympian view of the world," as is often assumed when the rational-actor model we have described is applied to real-world situations (Zagare 1990). They also suggest that an individual's actions may be rational even though the process of decision making and its product may appear decidedly irrational. Why did Libya's leader, the mercurial Muammar Qaddafi, repeatedly challenge the United States, almost goading President Ronald Reagan into a military strike in 1986? Because, we can postulate, Qaddafi's actions were consistent with his preferences, regardless of how "irrational" it was for a fourth-rate military power to take on the world's preeminent superpower. This and many other examples serve as a reminder of the importance of the human factor in understanding how decisions are made. Temptation, lack of self-control, anger, fear of getting hurt, religious conviction, bad habits, overconfidence—all play a part in determining why people make the kinds of decisions they do (Kegley and Raymond 1999).

Factors Affecting the Capacity to Lead

Despite the popularity of the history-making individuals model, we must be wary of ascribing too much importance to individual leaders. Their influence is likely to be subtler, a probability summarized by U.S. President Bill Clinton in 1998 when he observed, "Great presidents don't do great things. Great presidents get a lot of other people to do great things." Henry Kissinger, once described as "the most powerful individual in the world in the 1970s" (Isaak 1975), in a commencement address at the University of South Carolina in May 1985 urged against placing too much reliance on personalities:

> [There is] a profound American temptation to believe that foreign policy is a subdivision of psychiatry and that relations among nations are like relations among people. But the problem [of easing protracted conflicts between states] is not so simple. Tensions . . . must have some objective causes, and unless we can remove these causes, no personal relationship can possibly deal with them. We are [not] doing . . . ourselves a favor by reducing the issues to a contest of personalities.

Most leaders operate under a variety of political, psychological, and circumstantial constraints that limit what they can accomplish and reduce their control over events. In this context, Emmet John Hughes (1972), an adviser to President Dwight D. Eisenhower, concluded that "all of [America's past presidents] from the most venturesome to the most reticent have shared one disconcerting experience: the discovery of the limits and restraints—decreed by law, by history, and by circumstances—that sometimes can blur their clearest designs or dull their sharpest purposes." Abraham Lincoln in 1864 summarized his presidential experience with the conclusion, "I have not controlled events, events have controlled me."

The question at issue is not whether political elites lead or whether they can make a difference. They clearly do both. But leaders are not in complete control, and their influence is severely constrained. Thus personality and personal political preferences do not determine foreign policy directly. The relevant question, then, is not whether leaders' personal characteristics make a difference, but rather under what conditions their characteristics are influential. As Margaret G. Hermann has observed, the impact of leaders is modified by at least six factors:

> (1) what their world view is, (2) what their political style is like, (3) what motivates them to have the position they do, (4) whether they are interested in and have any training in foreign affairs, (5) what the foreign policy climate was like when the leader was starting out his or her political career, and (6) how the leader was socialized into his or her present position. World view, political style, and motivation tell us something about the leader's personality; the other characteristics give information about the leader's previous experiences and background. (Hermann 1988, 268)

The impact of leaders' personal characteristics on their state's foreign policy generally increases when their authority and legitimacy are widely accepted by citizens or, in authoritarian or totalitarian regimes, when leaders are protected from broad public criticism. Moreover, certain circumstances enhance individuals' potential influence. Among them are new situations that free leaders from conventional approaches to defining the situation; complex situations involving many different factors; and situations without social sanctions, which permit freedom of choice because norms defining the range of permissible options are unclear (DiRenzo 1974).

■ **political efficacy** the extent to which policymakers' self-confidence instills in them the belief that they can effectively make rational choices.

A leader's **political efficacy** or self-image—that person's belief in his or her own ability to control events politically—combined with the citizenry's relative desire for leadership, will also influence the degree to which personal values and psychological needs govern decision making (DeRivera 1968). For example, when public opinion strongly favors a powerful leader, and when the head of state has an exceptional need for admiration, foreign policy will more likely reflect that leader's inner needs. Thus Kaiser Wilhelm II's narcissistic personality allegedly met the German people's desire for a symbolically powerful leader, and German public preferences in turn influenced the foreign policy that Germany pursued during Wilhelm's reign, ending in World War I (Baron and Pletsch 1985).

Other factors undoubtedly influence how much leaders can shape their states' choices. For instance, when leaders believe that their own interests and welfare are at stake, they tend to respond in terms of their private needs and psychological drives. When circumstances are stable, however, and when leaders' egos are not entangled with policy outcomes, the influence of their personal characteristics is less apparent.

The amount of information available about a particular situation is also important. Without pertinent information, policy is likely to be based on leaders' personal likes or dislikes. Conversely, the more information leaders have about international affairs, the more likely they are to engage in rational decision making (Verba 1969).

Similarly, the timing of a leader's assumption of power is significant. When an individual first assumes a leadership position, the formal requirements of that role are least likely to restrict what he or she can do. That is especially true during the "honeymoon" period routinely given to new heads of state, during which time they are relatively free of criticism and excessive pressure. Moreover, when a leader assumes office following a dramatic event (a landslide election, for example, or the assassination of a predecessor), he or she can institute policies almost with a free hand, as "constituency criticism is held in abeyance during this time" (Hermann 1976).

A national crisis is a potent circumstance that increases a leader's control over foreign policy making. Decision making during crises is typically centralized and handled exclusively by the top leadership. Crucial information is often unavailable, and leaders see themselves as responsible for outcomes. Not surprisingly, great leaders (e.g., Napoleon Bonaparte, Winston Churchill, and Franklin D. Roosevelt) customarily emerge during periods of extreme tumult. A crisis can liberate a leader from the constraints that normally would inhibit his or her capacity to control events or engineer foreign policy change.

History abounds with examples of the seminal importance of political leaders who emerge in different times and places and under different circumstances to play critical roles in shaping world history. Mikhail Gorbachev dramatically illustrates an individual's capacity to change the course of history. Many experts

CONTROVERSY

Do Leaders Make a Difference?

Some theorists, such as **neorealists,** embrace the assumption of rationality and assume that any leader will respond to a choice in the same way: the situation structures the reaction to the existing costs and benefits of any choice. But does this assumption square with the facts? What do we know about the impact of people's perceptions and values on the way they view choices? Political psychology tells us that the same option is likely to have different value to different leaders. Does this mean that different leaders would respond differently to similar situations?

Consider the example of Richard Nixon. In 1971, Americans took to the streets outside the White House to protest the immorality of Nixon's massive bombing of Vietnam. His reaction to this perceived threat was to shield himself from the voice of the people, without success, as it happened. Nixon complained that "nobody can know what it means for a president to be sitting in that White House working late at night and to have hundreds of thousands of demonstrators charging through the streets. Not even earplugs could block the noise."

Earlier, on a rainy afternoon in 1962, John F. Kennedy faced a similar citizen protest. Americans had gathered in front of the White House for a Ban the Bomb demonstration. His response was to send out urns of coffee and doughnuts and invite the leaders of the protest to come inside to state their case, believing that a democracy should encourage dissent and debate.

Nixon saw protesters as a threat; Kennedy saw them as an opportunity. This comparison suggests that the type of leader can make a difference in determining the kinds of choices likely to be made in response to similar situations. More important than each president's treatment of the protesters, however, was whether he actually changed his policy decisions based on the protests. Although Kennedy was hospitable to protesters, he did not ban nuclear weapons; in fact, military spending under Kennedy grew to consume half of the federal budget. Many would protest that Kennedy alone could not be expected to eliminate nuclear weapons—that the zeitgeist was dominated by fear of the Soviet Union and intense concern for national security. The protesters in 1971, however, were more in keeping with the spirit of the times. Although they alone may not have persuaded Nixon to alter his policies in Vietnam, widespread protest and discontentment with the war, as well as America's inability to win, eventually prompted Nixon to order the gradual withdrawal of U.S. troops, ending American participation in the Vietnam War. These outcomes suggest that leaders are captive to zeitgeist, or larger forces that drive international relations in their times.

What do you think? Did Kennedy and Nixon choose courses of action that reflected who they were as individuals? Or would any president in their respective eras have made similar choices?

believe that the Cold War could not have been brought to an end, nor Communist Party rule in Moscow terminated and the Soviet state set on a path toward democracy and free enterprise, had it not been for Gorbachev's vision, courage, and commitment to engineering these revolutionary, system-transforming changes (Bundy 1990). Ironically, those reforms led to his loss of power when the Soviet Union imploded in 1991.

■ **neorealism**
a theoretical account of states' behavior as determined by differences in their relative power (see p. 500).

Refinements to the History-Making Individuals Model

Having said that the history-making individuals model may be compelling, we must be cautious and remember that leaders are not all-powerful determinants of states' foreign policy behavior. Rather, their personal influence varies with the context, and often the context is more influential than the leader (see Controversy: Do Leaders Make a Difference?). The "great person" versus **zeitgeist** (spirit of the times) debate is pertinent here. At the core of this enduring controversy is the question of whether certain times are conducive to the emergence of leaders or whether famous leaders would have an impact whenever and wherever they lived (see Greenstein 1987). That question may be unanswerable but it reminds us at least that multiple factors affect states' foreign policy decisions. The history-making individuals model alone appears too simple an explanation of how states react to challenges from abroad.

■ **zeitgeist**
the "spirit of the times"or the dominant cultural norms assumed to influence the behavior of people living in particular periods.

CONSTRAINTS ON FOREIGN POLICY MAKING: PROBLEMS AND PROSPECTS

Can states respond to the demands that external challenges and internal politics simultaneously place on their leaders? For many reasons, that capability is increasingly strained.

Foreign policy choice occurs in an environment of uncertainty and multiple, competing interests. On occasion, it is also made in situations when policymakers are caught by surprise and a quick decision is needed. Preoccupied with sunk costs, short-run results, and postdecisional rationalization, the stress these conditions produce impairs leaders' cognitive abilities and may cause them to react emotionally rather than analytically.

The trends and transformations currently unfolding in world politics are the products of countless decisions made daily throughout the world. Some decisions are more consequential than others, and some actors are more important than others. Throughout history, great powers such as the United States have at times stood at the center of the world political stage, possessing the combination of natural resources, military might, and the means to project power worldwide that earned them great-power status. How such major powers have responded to one another has had profound consequences for the entire drama of world politics. To better understand that, we turn our attention next to the dynamics of great-power rivalry on the world stage.

KEY TERMS

actor
state sovereignty
state
nation
foreign policy
levels of analysis
intermestic
globalization
imperialism
geopolitics
gross national product (GNP)
constitutional democracy
autocratic rule
elitism
pluralism

diversionary theory of war
end of history
democratic peace
neoliberalism
unitary actor
rational choice
bounded rationality
cognitive dissonance
policy agenda
satisficing
prospect theory
two-level games
muddling through
bureaucracies
multiple advocacy
bureaucratic politics model
policy networks
caucuses
standard operating procedures (SOPs)
groupthink
history-making individuals model
Nixon Doctrine
Reagan Doctrine
Clinton Doctrine
procedural rationality
instrumental rationality
political efficacy
neorealism
zeitgeist

SUGGESTED READING

Allison, Graham, and Philip Zelikow. *Essence of Decision: Explaining the Cuban Missile Crisis,* 2nd ed. New York: Longman, 1999.

George, Alexander L. *Bridging the Gap: Theory and Practice in Foreign Policy.* Washington, D.C.: U.S. Institute of Peace, 1993.

Gallhofer, Irmstraud N., and William E. Saris. *Foreign Policy Decision Making.* Westport, Conn.: Greenwood, 1999.

Hermann, Charles F., Charles W. Kegley, Jr., and James N. Rosenau, eds. *New Directions in the Study of Foreign Policy.* Boston: Allen & Unwin, 1987.

Hilsman, Roger. *The Politics of Policy Making in Defense and Foreign Affairs: Conceptual Models and Bureaucratic Politics,* 2nd ed. Englewood Cliffs, N.J.: Prentice Hall, 1990.

Jensen, Lloyd. *Explaining Foreign Policy.* Englewood Cliffs, N.J.: Prentice Hall, 1982.

Kegley, Charles W., Jr., and Gregory A. Raymond. *How Nations Make Peace.* Boston: Bedford/St. Martin's, 1999.

Korany, Bahgat. *How Foreign Policy Decisions Are Made in the Third World.* Boulder, Colo.: Westview Press, 1986.

Levy, Jack S. "Prospect Theory, Rational Choice, and International Relations," *International Studies Quarterly* (March 1997): 87–112.

Neack, Laura, Jeanne A. K. Hey and Patrick J. Haney, eds. *Foreign Policy Analysis: Continuity and Change in Its Second Generation.* Englewood Cliffs, N.J.: Prentice-Hall, 1995.

Ray, James Lee. *Democracies and International Conflict.* Columbia: University of South Carolina Press, 1995.

Rosati, Jerel A., Joe D. Hagan, and Martin W. Sampson III, eds. *Foreign Policy Restructuring: How Governments Respond to Global Change.* Columbia: University of South Carolina Press, 1997.

t'Hart, Paul, Eric K. Stern, and Bengt Sundelius, eds. *Beyond Groupthink: Political Group Dynamics and Foreign Policy-Making.* Ann Arbor: University of Michigan Press, 1997.

WHERE ON THE WORLD WIDE WEB?

Cuban Missile Crisis
http://hyperion.advanced.org/11046/

The Cuban Missile Crisis is often cited as an event that brought the superpowers to the brink of nuclear war. This site provides an in-depth account and analysis of the crisis and the actors and issues involved. Read dossiers of the primary players, hear segments of the ExComm meeting, and see U-2 spy plane photos. At the end, take an on-line quiz to see how well you understand the crisis.

Freedom, Democracy, Peace; Power, Democide, and War

http://www2.hawaii.edu/~rummel/

The democratic peace theory presented in Chapter 3 contends that "although democratic states sometimes wage wars against other states, they do not fight each other" (see pp. 63–65). Political scientist Rudolph J. Rummel has devoted his career to research on the causes and conditions of collective violence and war with a view toward helping bring about their resolution or elimination; he supports the democratic peace proposition. Visit his Web site to analyze his work. What evidence do you think supports the democratic peace proposition? How persuasive are his arguments? *Caution:* Some of the pictures on the site contain graphic violence.

Freedom House

http://www.freedomhouse.org/

Founded by Eleanor Roosevelt and Wendell Willkie, this nonprofit organization has been concerned with threats to peace and democracy. Each year since 1972, Freedom House has published comparative ratings for countries and territories around the world, evaluating levels of political rights and civil liberties. Map 3.2 (p. 64) in your text uses data on the spread of democratic liberty throughout the world provided by Freedom House. Examine specific countries' "freedom records." Which have radically improved? Why do you think this is so?

The Presidents: PBS's *The American Experience*

http://www.pbs.org/wgbh/amex/presidents/indexjs.html

This inclusive Web site features some of the most prominent U.S. presidents of the twentieth century, including Theodore Roosevelt, Franklin Roosevelt, Dwight Eisenhower, Harry Truman, John Kennedy, Lyndon Johnson, Richard Nixon, and Ronald Reagan. Sections focus on the U.S. foreign policy achievements of each president. Chapter 3 introduces the history-making individuals model of government that equates a state's foreign policy with the preferences and initiatives of the highest government officials. Familiarize yourself with the foreign policy achievements of some U.S. presidents. Do you believe the history-making individuals model is a legitimate explanation of foreign policy? What are the limits to the model?

C H A P T E R 4

Great-Power Rivalries and Relations

Topics and Themes

- The quest for great-power hegemony
  - Long-cycle theory
  - Hegemonic stability theory
- The causes and consequences of World War I
  - Structuralism
  - Rational choice and great-power relations
- The causes and consequences of World War II
- The causes, characteristics, and conflicts of the Cold War
- The future of great-power politics: A cold peace?

- **Controversy** Was Ideology the Primary Source of East-West Conflict?
- **Controversy** Was Military Containment Necessary?
- **Controversy** Why Did the Cold War End Peacefully?

The Big Three (Winston Churchill, Franklin Roosevelt, and Joseph Stalin) discuss peace at Yalta, 1945.

A profound disparity is already defining itself between the strategic and economic rank-orders of the major powers. . . . An emerging multipolar system characterized by strengthening rivalry will last until 2010–2020 and then be challenged by a new division of the world. . . .

—Alpo M. Rusi, foreign policy adviser to the former president of Finland, 2000

We're in the middle of a transition that will be obvious to historians one hundred years from now. . . . We are now moving into a . . . world in which power and influence [are] diffused among a multiplicity of states. . . . Unless we recognize what's taking place . . . the problems of the next twenty years will eat us alive.

—Lawrence Eagleburger, U.S. deputy secretary of state, 1989

Who's number one? Who's gaining on the leader? What does it mean for the future if the strongest is seriously challenged for predominant position?

These are the kinds of questions sports fans often ask when the rankings of the top teams are adjusted after the preceding week's competition. World leaders also adopt what former U.S. Secretary of State Dean Rusk once called a "football stadium approach to diplomacy." And many people throughout the world habitually make comparisons of countries, asking which states are the biggest, strongest, wealthiest, and most militarily powerful and evaluating which states are rising and which are falling relative to one another. When making such rankings, both groups are looking at world politics through the lens of realism. They see a globe of competitors, with winners and losers in an ancient contest for supremacy. And they look most closely at the shifting rankings at the very top of the international hierarchy of power—at the rivalry and struggle among the "great powers." Moreover, they picture this conflict as continual. As

Arnold J. Toynbee's (1954) famous cyclical theory of history explains: "The most emphatic punctuation in a uniform series of events recurring in one repetitive cycle after another is the outbreak of a great war in which one power that has forged ahead of all its rivals makes so formidable a bid for world domination that it evokes an opposing coalition of all the other powers."

Toynbee's conclusion lies at the center of realism. The starting point for understanding world politics, maintains Hans J. Morgenthau (1985), the leading post–World War II classical realist theorist, is to recognize that "all history shows that nations active in international politics are continuously preparing for, actively involved in, or recovering from organized violence in the form of war." Cycles of war and peace colored twentieth-century world politics, with three global wars breaking out. World Wars I and II were fought with fire and blood; the Cold War was fought by less destructive means but with equal intensity. U.S. Secretary of State James A. Baker noted in late 1991, "For the third time this century, we have ended a war—this time a cold one—between the great powers." Each of these three global wars set in motion major transformations in world politics. In this chapter we explore the causes and consequences of these past great-power rivalries. By examining their origins and impact, we can better anticipate whether in the twenty-first century the great powers will again fail to control their rivalries and the world will experience another global war—a dangerous but real possibility. As British Foreign Secretary Douglas Hurd warned in 1993, "The familiar threats might reoccur."

THE QUEST FOR GREAT-POWER HEGEMONY

Great-power war was not unique to the twentieth century. Changes in the balance of power over the past five hundred years have regularly preceded war's outbreak. For this reason, the relationship between the great powers' rise and fall and global instability is a core concern in theories of world politics.

One viewpoint, **long-cycle theory,** seeks to explain why over the past five centuries periods of war have been followed by periods of peace, with shifts in the cycle usually occurring in concert with changes in the major states' relative power (see Modelski and Thompson 1989, 1996, 1999). During this long cycle, each global war led to the emergence of a victorious **hegemon,** a dominant global leader capable of dictating "the rules and arrangements by which international relations, political and economic, are conducted" (Goldstein 1988; compare Nye 2001). With its acquisition of unrivaled power, the hegemon reshapes the existing system by creating and enforcing rules to preserve not only world order but also its own dominant position.

■ **long-cycle theory**
a theory that focuses on the rise and fall of the leading global power as the central political process of the modern world system (see p. 432).

■ **hegemon**
a single, overwhelmingly powerful state that exercises predominate influence over other global actors (see p. 432).

Hegemony characteristically imposes an extraordinary tax on the world leader, which must bear the costs of maintaining economic and political order while protecting its position and preserving its empire. In time, as the weight of global responsibilities takes its toll, new rivals rise to challenge the increasingly vulnerable world leader. Historically, this struggle for power has set the stage for another global war, the demise of one hegemon, and the ascent of another.

Long-cycle theory also draws attention to the fact that "world politics has rarely been reordered without a major war" (Jervis 1991–1992). "Only after such a total breakdown has the international situation been sufficiently fluid to induce leaders and supporting publics of dominant nations to join seriously in the task of reorganizing international society to avoid a repetition of the terrible events just experienced" (Falk 1970). Table 4.1 summarizes the cyclical rise and fall of great powers, their global wars, and their subsequent efforts to restore order.

The central premise of long-cycle theory is disarmingly simple, and for this reason it is not without critics. Must great powers rise and fall as if by the law of gravity—what goes up must come down? There is something disturbingly deter-

TABLE 4.1

The Evolution of Great-Power Rivalry for World Leadership, 1495–2025

Dates	*Preponderant State(s) Seeking Hegemony*	*Other Powers Resisting Domination*	*Global War*	*New Order after Global War*
1495–1540	Portugal	Spain, Valois, France, Burgundy, England, Venice	Wars of Italy and the Indian Ocean, 1494–1517	Treaty of Tordesillas, 1517
1560–1609	Spain	The Netherlands, France, England	Spanish-Dutch Wars, 1580–1608	Truce of 1609; Evangelical Union and the Catholic League formed
1610–1648	Holy Roman Empire (Hapsburg dynasty in Spain and Austria-Hungary)	Shifting ad hoc coalitions of mostly Protestant states (Sweden, Holland) and German principalities as well as Catholic France against remnants of papal rule	Thirty Years' War, 1618–1648	Peace of Westphalia, 1648
1650–1713	France (Louis XIV)	The United Provinces, England,the Hapsburg Empire, Spain, major German states, Russia	Wars of the Grand Alliance, 1688–1713	Treaty of Utrecht, 1713
1792–1815	France (Napoleon)	Great Britain, Prussia, Austria, Russia	Napoleonic Wars, 1792–1815	Congress of Vienna and Concert of Europe, 1815
1871–1914	Germany, Austria-Hungary, Turkey	Great Britain, France, Russia, United States	World War I, 1914–1918	Treaty of Versailles creating League of Nations, 1919
1933–1945	Germany, Japan, Italy	Great Britain, France, Soviet Union, United States	World War II, 1939–1945	Bretton Woods, 1944; United Nations, 1945; Potsdam, 1945
1945–2010	United States, Soviet Union	Great Britain, France, China, Japan	Cold War, 1945–1991	NATO/Partnerships for Peace, 1995; World Trade Organization, 1995
2010–2025	United States, China	European Union, Japan, Russia	A cold peace or hegemonic war, 2000–2025?	A new security regime to preserve world order?

ministic in a proposition that implies that global destiny is beyond policy-makers' control. Fundamental hypotheses drawn from long-cycle theory are difficult to confirm. Long-cycle theorists disagree on whether economic, military, or domestic factors produce these cycles, as well as about their comparative influence in different historical epochs (see Lundestad 1994). Still, long-cycle theory provides important insights into a fundamental continuity in world politics and provokes questions about whether this entrenched cycle can be broken. It also invites critical consideration of **hegemonic stability theory,** which assumes that a stable world order requires a dominant global leader to keep peace, punish aggressors who challenge the status quo, and prevent the explosive competition of **enduring rivalries** between competing great powers from escalating into a major systemwide war. Many great powers have become entangled in long-term struggles "to occupy the same territory, control the same markets, or monopolize overlapping positions of influence [and] in the process they [have] become competitors for these objectives." The persisting clashes between Britain and France (1066–1904), France and Germany (1815–1955), and the United States and Japan (1905–1945) are examples of enduring rivalries that historically have produced a significant degree of interstate conflict. Long-cycle theory and hegemonic stability theory enable us to see the dynamics of great-power rivalries "from the standpoint of the present, future, and the past . . . to better understand all the other things that happen in international relations" (Thompson 1999b). For this purpose, this chapter inspects the three great-power wars of the twentieth century and the lessons these uncontained rivalries suggest for the twenty-first century.

■ **hegemonic stability theory**
a body of theory that maintains that the establishment of hegemony for global dominance by a single great power is a necessary condition for global order in commercial transactions and international military security (see p. 557).

■ **enduring rivalries**
prolonged competition between great powers or other pairs of countries whose perpetual conflicting interests often lead to war.

THE FIRST WORLD WAR

World War I rumbled onto the global stage when a Serbian nationalist seeking to free his ethnic group from Austrian rule assassinated Archduke Ferdinand, heir to the Hapsburg throne of the Austrian-Hungarian Empire, at Sarajevo in June 1914 (the same location where NATO's 1999 intervention in Yugoslavia was centered). This assassination sparked a series of moves and countermoves by states and empires distrustful of each other's intentions in the two months that followed, which shattered world peace.

Before the assassination, two hostile alliances had already formed, pitting Germany, Austria-Hungary, and the Ottoman Empire against France, Britain, and Russia. The strategic choices of the two alliances culminated in World War I, the "origins, course, and consequences [of which] are central to an understanding of the twentieth century" (Kennedy 1999). By the time the longest European war in a century had ended, nearly 10 million people had died, three empires had crumbled, new states had been born, seven decades of Communist rule in Russia had begun, and the world geopolitical map had been redrawn in ways that paved the way for the rise of Adolf Hitler in Nazi Germany.

The Causes of World War I

How can such a catastrophic war be explained? Although the answers are numerous, many converge around structural explanations, which hold that World War I was inadvertent, not the result of anyone's master plan. It was a

War and the Collapse of Great-Power Empires Global wars topple governments. The end of the Cold War in 1991 was followed by the rejection of communist rule in Russia and the creation of a fledgling democracy. Pictured here is the statue of the founder of the USSR's intelligence agency, the KGB—a symbol of communist power—which was moved from its prominent place to the "sculpture graveyard" where the Russian government keeps retired Soviet icons.

war bred by uncertainty and circumstances beyond the control of those involved, one that people neither wanted nor expected. Some revisionist historians, using **counterfactual reasoning** (Ferguson 1999), regard World War I as far from inevitable. One called it "a tragic and unnecessary conflict . . . because the train of events that led to its outbreak might have been broken at any point during the five weeks of crisis that preceded the first clash of arms, had prudence or common goodwill found a voice" (Keegan 1999).

■ **counterfactual reasoning** speculations about historical events and developments that ask how the world might have changed had certain momentous foreign policy choices not been taken or had other conditions prevailed (see p. 521).

■ **structuralism** the proposition that states' behavior is shaped primarily by the changes in the properties of the global system, instead of by individual heads of states or by changes in states' internal characteristics.

Structuralism. **Structuralism** is a neorealist theory that sees the changing distribution of power within the global system as the primary factor determining states' behavior. The power distribution determines whether coalitions will form and peace will prevail. Many historians find a structural interpretation framed at the global level of analysis convincing because on the eve of World War I "the sort of military system that existed in Europe at the time—a system of interlocking mobilizations and of war plans that placed a great emphasis on rapid offensive action—directly led to a conflict that might otherwise have been avoided" (Trachtenberg 1990–91).

Proponents of structuralism emphasize that the great powers' prior rearmament efforts as well as their alliances and counteralliances—the Triple Alliance of Germany, Austria-Hungary, and Italy, initiated in 1882 and renewed in 1902, and the Entente Cordiale between Britain and France, forged in 1904—created a momentum that, along with the pressures created by the mobilization of armies and arms races, dragged European statesmen toward war (Tuchman 1962).

A related element in the structuralist explanation focuses on the nineteenth century, when Britain dominated world politics. An island country isolated by temperament, tradition, and geography from Continental affairs, Britain's sea power gave it command of the world's shipping lanes and control of a vast empire stretching from the Mediterranean to Southeast Asia. This dominance helped to deter aggression. However, Germany would mount a challenge to British power.

After becoming a unified country in 1871, Germany prospered and used its growing wealth to create a formidable army and navy. With strength came ambition and resentment of British preeminence. As the predominant military and industrial power on the European continent, Germany sought to compete for international position and status. As Kaiser William II proclaimed in 1898, Germany had "great tasks outside the narrow boundaries of old Europe." With Germany ascendant, the balance of power shifted as its rising power and global aspirations altered the European geopolitical landscape.

Germany was not the only newly emergent power at the turn of the century, however. Russia was also expanding and becoming a threat to Germany. The decline in power of the Austro-Hungarian Empire, Germany's only ally, heightened Germany's fear of Russia—thus its strong reaction to Archduke Ferdinand's assassination. Germany became convinced that a short, localized, and victorious war was possible, fearing an unfavorable shift in the balance of power in the event of a long war. Accordingly, while the advantages seemed clear-cut, Germany gave Austria-Hungary a "blank check" to crush Serbia, which proved to be a serious miscalculation.

To Germany's imperial rulers, the risk involved in the blank check made sense from the viewpoint of preserving the Austro-Hungarian Empire. The disintegration of the empire would have left Germany isolated, without an ally. Unfortunately for Germany, its guarantee provoked an unexpected reaction from France and Russia, as the two powers joined forces to defend the Slavs. Britain then abandoned its traditional "splendid isolation" and joined France and Russia in the Triple Entente in opposing Germany and its allied Central Powers. Although the immediate objective was to defend Belgian neutrality, the war later expanded across the ocean when in April 1917 the United States, reacting to German submarine warfare, entered the conflict. For the first time ever, war became truly global in scope.

This chain reaction and the rapidity of escalation that led to World War I fit the interpretation that it was an "inadvertent war." Simply put, European leaders were not in full control of their own fate. Still, historians ask why they miscalculated so badly. Did they simply fail to recognize their primary interest in successfully managing the crisis? If so, was this because their alliances gave them a false sense of assurance, blinding them to danger and dragging them into a conflict that was not a part of anyone's design?

Rational Choice. Rational choice theory provides an alternative interpretation of World War I. From this perspective, framed at the individual level of analysis, the war's outbreak was a result of German elites' preference for a war with France and Russia in order to consolidate Germany's position on the continent, confirm its status as a world power, and divert domestic attention from its internal troubles (Kaiser 1990). "It was the men gathered at the Imperial Palace in Berlin," Volker R. Berghahn (1995) concludes, "who pushed Europe over the brink."

If the **rational choice** model of decision making offers an accurate interpretation, then World War I is best seen as a consequence of the purposive goal of rival great powers to compete against one another for global power, a preference that realists believe is an "iron law of history." It resulted from "an attempt

■ **rational choice**
the theory that decision-makers choose on the basis of what they perceive to be the best interests for themselves and their states, based on their expectations about the relative usefulness of alternative options for realizing goals. Sometimes called "expected-utility theory," this model derives from realist theories (see p. 66).

by Germany to secure its position before an increasingly powerful Russia had achieved a position of equality with Germany (which the latter expected to happen by 1917)" (Levy 1998b).

As these alternative interpretations suggest, the causes of World War I remain in dispute. Structural explanations, which emphasize the global distribution of power, and rational choice explanations, which direct attention to the calculations and goals of particular leaders, partially help us to understand the sequences that produced the world's first truly global war. We must, however, consider additional factors that, in association with these underlying causes, led to the outbreak of war that Barbara Tuchman (1962) called "the guns of August."

nationalism
a mindset glorifying a particular state and the nationality group living in it, which sees the state's interests as a supreme value (see p. 633).

Other Explanations. At the state level of analysis, some historians argue that domestic factors within countries were influential causes. In particular, many view the growth of **nationalism,** especially in southeastern Europe, as having created a climate of opinion that made war likely. Different groups began to champion their own state above all others. As nationalistic feelings intensified, they aroused long-suppressed ethnic and national hatreds, which strained European statesmen's ability to avoid war.

Domestic unrest inflamed these nationalistic passions, as did the pressure for war applied by munitions makers who played on nationalistic sentiments (Blainey 1988). The Austro-Hungarian Empire's reaction to the assassination crisis suggests the potency of national passions, which fed Austria-Hungary's diabolic image of the enemy, its hypersensitivity about the preservation of the empire, and its overconfidence in its military capabilities.

The Germans and Russians were also driven by intense nationalism, an uncritically passionate, patriotic love of country that caused them to make serious miscalculations. In particular, Germany's lack of empathy prevented it from understanding "the strength of the Russians' pride, their fear of humiliation if they allowed the Germans and Austrians to destroy their little protégé, Serbia, and the intensity of Russian anger at the tricky, deceptive way the Germans and Austrians went about their aggression" (White 1990).

Despite these national passions, World War I would not likely have unfolded without Anglo-German commercial rivalry, the Franco-Russian alliance, Germany's blank check to Austria-Hungary, and—perhaps most important—the formation of two entangling alliances. "One cannot conceive of the onset of World War I without the presence of the Triple Entente, which existed as an alliance of ideologically dissimilar governments" uniting Britain, France, and Russia (Midlarsky 1988). Consequently, the division of the multipolar balance-of-power system that drew the growing number of great-power contenders into **bipolar** coalitions—and the absence of a hegemon to maintain order—may have made war inevitable, even though "political leaders in each of the great powers . . . preferred a peaceful settlement" of their differences (Levy 1990–91).

bipolar
an international system with two dominant power centers.

The Consequences of World War I

World War I destroyed both life and property and changed the face of Europe (see Map 4.1). In its wake, three empires—the Austro-Hungarian, Russian, and Ottoman (Turkish)—collapsed, and in their place the independent states of Poland, Czechoslovakia, and Yugoslavia emerged. In addition, the countries of

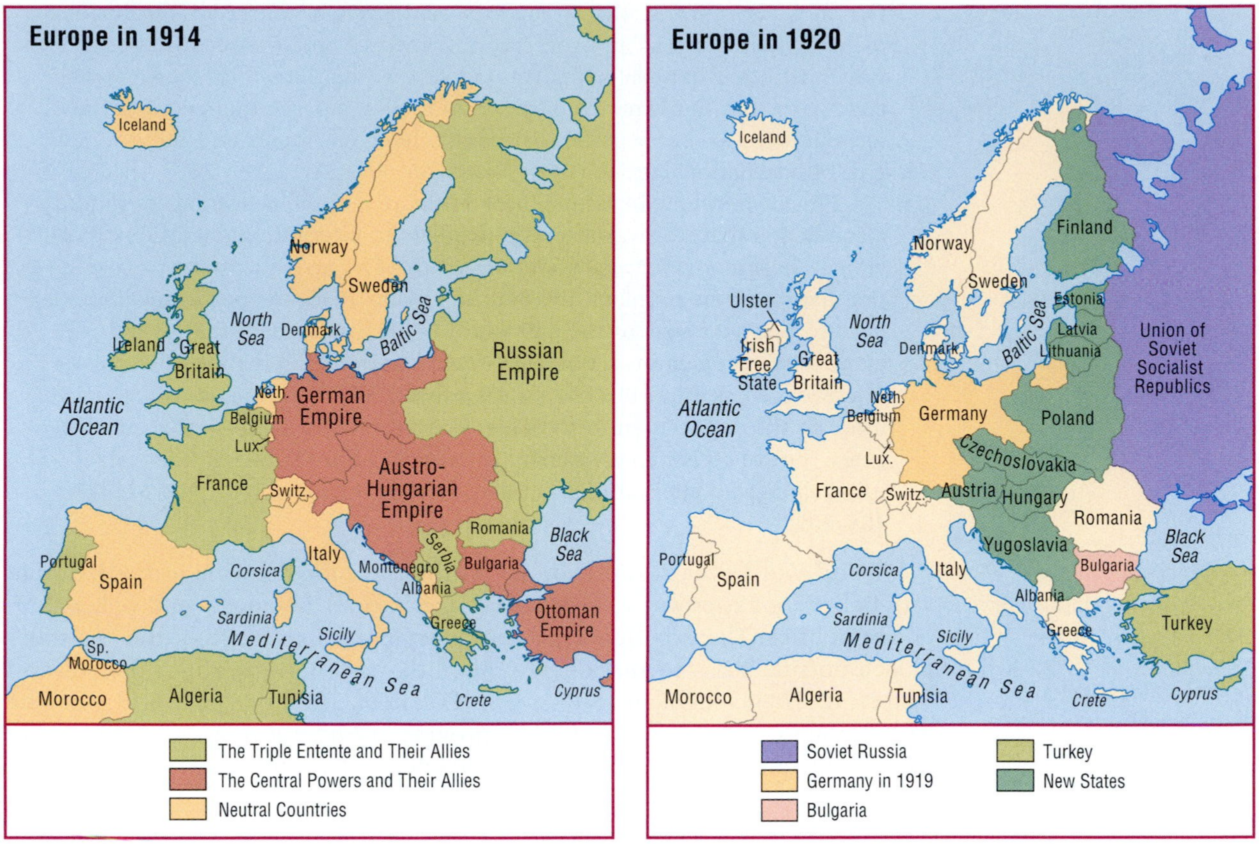

MAP 4.1
Territorial Changes in Europe following World War I

World War I redrew the boundaries of Europe. The map on the left shows state boundaries on the eve of the war in 1914, as well as the members of the two major opposing coalitions that formed. When the guns fell silent after the war, the victors met in Versailles and drafted a punitive peace settlement that stripped vast territories from the defeated German and Austro-Hungarian Empires, as well as from the western front of the Russian Empire, which disintegrated in the Bolshevik revolution that deposed the czar and brought the communists into power in the new Union of Soviet Socialist Republics (USSR). The map on the right shows the new borders in 1920, with the nine new states that emerged from the war.

Finland, Estonia, Latvia, and Lithuania were born. The war also contributed to the overthrow of the Russian czar in 1917 by the Bolsheviks. The emergence of communism under the leadership of Vladimir I. Lenin produced a change in government and ideology that would have consequences for another seventy years.

Despite its costs, the coalition consisting of Britain, France, Russia, and (later) the United States and Italy succeeded in defeating the threat of domination posed by the Central Powers (Germany, Austria-Hungary, Turkey, and their allies). Moreover, the war set the stage for a determined effort to build a new international system that could prevent another war.

> For most Europeans, the Great War had been a source of disillusionment. . . . When it was all over, few remained to be convinced that such a war must never happen again. Among vast populations there was a strong conviction that this time the parties had to plan a peace that could not just terminate a war, but a peace that could change attitudes and build a new type of international order. . . .
>
> For the first time in history, broad publics and the peacemakers shared a conviction that war was a central problem in international relations. Previously, hegemony, the aggressive activities of a particular state, or revolution had been the problem. In 1648, 1713, and 1815, the peacemakers had tried to resolve issues of the past and to construct orders that would preclude their reappearance. But in 1919 expectations ran higher. The sources of war were less important than the war itself. There was a necessity to look more to the future than to the past. The problem was not just to build a peace, but to construct a peaceful international order that would successfully manage all international conflicts of the future. (Holsti 1991, 175–176; 208–209)

■ **realism**
the school of thought which maintains that because interstate competition is natural states should prepare for war in order to avoid it (see p. 457).

World War I evoked revulsion for war and for the doctrine of **realism** that rationalized great-power rivalry, arms races, secret alliances, and balance-of-power politics. The experience led the policymakers gathered at the Versailles Palace outside Paris to reevaluate realpolitik assumptions about the rules of statecraft. They sought instead to guard against the threat of world war and global domination through a reform program of liberal internationalism that would cultivate political and commercial cooperation among the great powers (Nikovich 1999).

■ **Kellogg-Briand Pact**
a multilateral treaty negotiated in 1928 that outlawed war as a method for settling interstate conflicts (see p. 30).

The two decades following World War I were the high point of liberal idealism, as reflected in Woodrow Wilson's "Fourteen Points," creation of the League of Nations, the Washington Naval Conference, and the **Kellogg-Briand Pact** (see Chapter 2). Nevertheless, the liberal idealists' proposals failed to deter the resumption of great-power rivalry. Another system-transforming global war was on the horizon.

THE SECOND WORLD WAR

Although it lost World War I, Germany did not lose its desire for global status and influence. On the contrary, it was intensified. Thus conditions were ripe for the second great-power war of the twentieth century, as Germany again pursued an aggressive course.

Global in scope, World War II was a struggle for power cast in the image of realism. It pitted a fascist coalition striving for world supremacy—the Axis trio of Germany, Japan, and Italy—against an unlikely "grand alliance" of four great powers who united despite their incompatible ideologies—communism in the case of the Soviet Union and democratic capitalism in the case of Britain, France, and the United States.

The world's fate hinged on the outcome of this massive effort to meet the Axis threat of world conquest and restore the balance of power. The Allied powers achieved success with a six-year ordeal, but at a terrible cost: each day

23,000 lives were lost, as the war resulted in the death of 53 million people worldwide (for an account of the campaigns that finally led to victory, see Weinberg 1994).

The Causes of World War II

Several factors revived Germany's hegemonic ambitions. Domestically, German nationalism inflamed latent **irredentism** and rationalized the expansion of German borders, both to regain provinces ceded to others and to absorb Germans living in Austria, Czechoslovakia, and Poland. The rise of **fascism**—the Nazi regime's ideology championing racism, flag, fatherland, nationalism, and imperialism—animated this renewed imperialistic push. That set of beliefs glorified the "collective will" of the nation and preached the most extreme version of realism, ***machtpolitik*** (power politics), to justify the forceful expansion of the German state.

Germany also resented the punitive terms imposed by the victors of World War I (France, Great Britain, Italy, Japan, and the United States). Reflecting French demands, the Peace of Paris (the Versailles treaty) insisted on the destruction of Germany's armed forces, the loss of territory (such as Alsace-Lorraine, which Germany had absorbed following the Franco-Prussian war of 1870–1871), and the imposition of heavy reparations to compensate the Allies for the damage that German militarism had exacted. In addition, the Austro-Hungarian Empire was splintered into divided political units.

Not only was the Peace of Paris punitive, more significantly and painfully, it prevented Germany's reentry into the international system as a coequal member; Germany was denied membership in the League of Nations until 1926. As a result of its exclusion, Germany sought to recover its rightful status as a great power by force.

Proximate Causes. Why did the victorious great powers permit German rearmament? A key reason was that Britain's hope for Anglo-American collaboration to maintain world order vanished when the United States repudiated the Versailles peace treaty and retreated to a policy of **isolationism,** withdrawing from active international involements. As a result, Britain and France each fought for its own advantage in the treatment of Germany. While France wanted to deter Germany's reentry into the international system and prevent its recovery, Britain, in contrast, preferred to preserve the new balance of power by encouraging German rearmament and revival as a counterweight against the chance that France or the Soviet Union might dominate continental Europe.

Acquiescence to German rearmament and other militaristic maneuvers led to the policy of **appeasement** or pacifying potential aggressors with concessions. Adolf Hitler, the German dictator who by the mid-1930s controlled Germany's fate, pledged not to expand German territory by force. He betrayed that promise in March 1938 when he forced Austria into union with Germany (the *Anschluss*). Shortly thereafter he demanded the annexation of the German-populated area of Sudetenland in Czechoslovakia (see Map 4.2). Fear of further German expansion led to the September 1938 Munich Conference attended by Hitler, British Prime Minister Neville Chamberlain, and leaders from France and Italy (Czechoslovakia was not invited). Based on the erroneous conviction

■ irredentism
movement by an ethnonational group to regain control of territory by force so that existing state boundaries will no longer divide the group.

■ fascism
a far-right ideology that promotes extreme nationalism and the establishment of an authoritarian society built around a single party with dictatorial leadership.

■ machtpolitik
the German realist philosophy in statecraft that sees the expansion of state power and territory by use of armed force as a legitimate goal.

■ isolationism
a policy of withdrawing from active participation with other actors in world affairs and instead concentrating state efforts on managing internal affairs.

■ appeasement
a strategy of making concessions to an aggressor state without retaliation in the hope that, satisfied, it will not make additional claims on the territory of its neighbors.

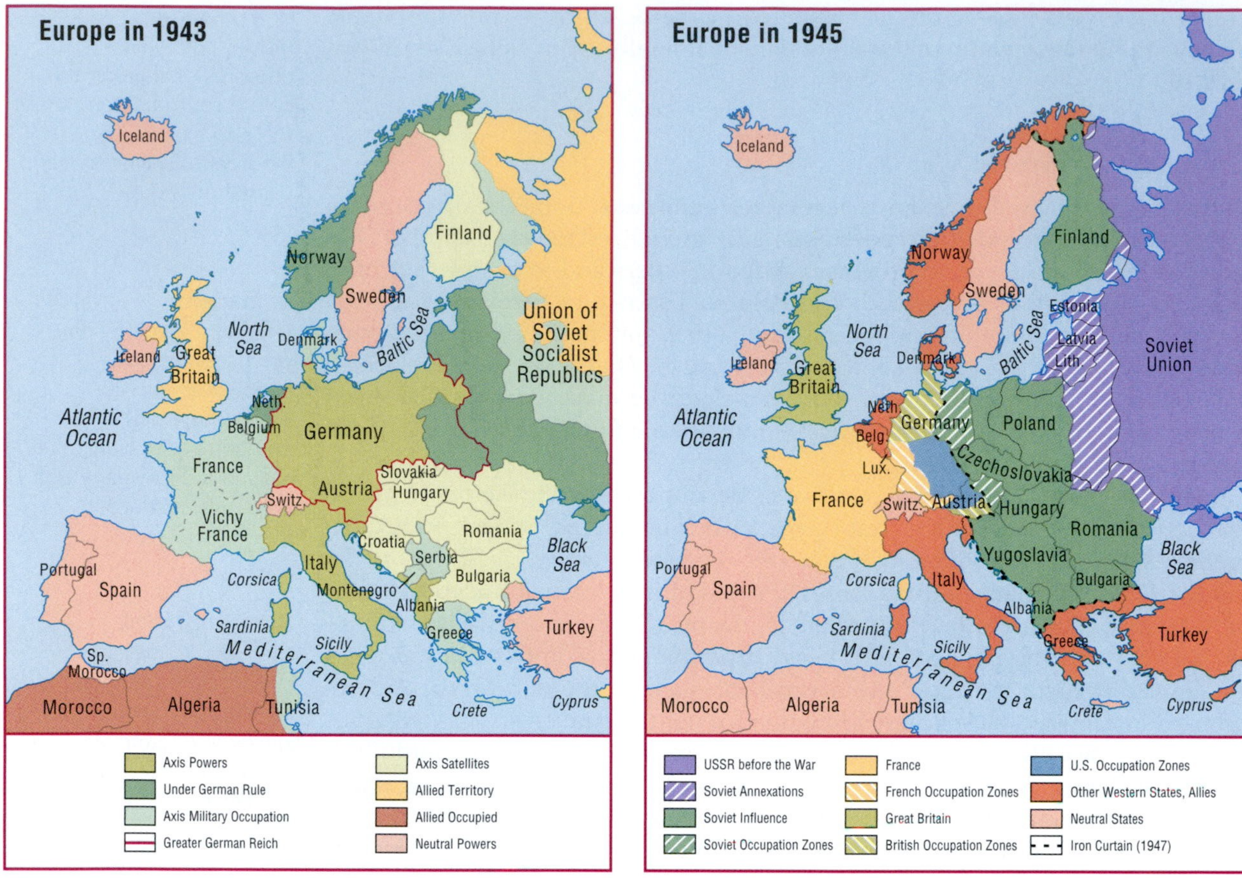

MAP 4.2
World War II Redraws the Map of Europe

The Axis coalition of great powers, composed of Germany, Italy and Japan, sought to conquer and divide the world in World War II, and almost succeeded. The map on the left shows the extent of German expansion in Europe at the height of its aggression in 1943, when Nazi Germany ruled and occupied Europe from the Atlantic Ocean and Baltic Sea to the Soviet Union's borders. The map on the right shows the new configuration of Europe after the "Grand Coalition" of Allied forces—Great Britain, the United States, and the Soviet Union—defeated the Axis's bid for supremacy. The Allies partitioned Germany into four sections occupied by British, French, Russian, and American troops and carved out other territorial changes that returned to the Soviet Union most of the land that it had lost at the end of World War I. Later, Germany was divided into two independent countries, the Federal Republic of Germany (West Germany) and the German Democratic Republic (East Germany), which were reunited in 1989 in a step that led to the Cold War's end in 1991 when the Soviet Union collapsed. Japan, having been devastated by atomic bombs and then occupied by the United States, was also then removed from the game of great-power politics.

that appeasement would halt further German expansionism and lead to "peace in our time," Chamberlain and the others agreed to Hitler's demands.

Rather than satisfying Germany, appeasement whetted its appetite and that of the newly-formed fascist coalition of Germany, Italy, and Japan, which aimed to overthrow the international status quo. Disillusioned with Western liberalism and the Paris settlements, and suffering economically from the effects of the Great Depression of the 1930s, Japan embraced militarism. In the might-makes-right climate that Germany's imperialistic quest for national aggrandizement helped to create, Japanese nationalists led their country on the path to imperialism and colonialism. Japan's invasions of Manchuria in 1931 and China proper in 1937 were followed by Italy's absorption of Abyssinia in 1935 and Albania in 1939, and both Germany and Italy intervened in the 1936–1939 Spanish civil war on the side of the fascists, headed by General Francisco Franco, while the Soviet Union supported antifascist forces.

After Germany occupied the rest of Czechoslovakia in March 1939, Britain and France belatedly reacted by forming an alliance to protect the next likely victim, Poland. They also opened negotiations with Moscow in hopes of enticing the Soviet Union to join the alliance, but failed. Then, on August 23, 1939, Hitler, a fascist, and the Soviet dictator Joseph Stalin, a communist, stunned the world with the news that they had signed a nonaggression pact. Now certain that Britain and France would not intervene, Hitler promptly invaded Poland, on September 1, 1939. Britain and France, honoring their pledge to defend the Poles, declared war on Germany two days later. World War II had begun.

The war expanded rapidly as Hitler turned his forces to the Balkans, North Africa, and westward. The powerful, mechanized German troops invaded Norway and marched through Denmark, Belgium, Luxembourg, and the Netherlands. They swept around France's defensive barrier, the Maginot line, and forced the British to evacuate a sizable expeditionary force from the French beaches at Dunkirk. Paris itself fell in June 1940, and in the months that followed, the German air force, the Luftwaffe, pounded Britain in an attempt to force it into submission as well. Instead of invading Britain, however, the Nazi troops launched a surprise attack on the Soviet Union, Hitler's former ally, in June 1941.

On December 7, 1941, Japan launched a surprise assault on the United States at Pearl Harbor. Almost immediately, Germany also declared war on the United States. The unprovoked Japanese assault and the German challenge ended U.S. aloofness and isolationism, enabling President Franklin Roosevelt to forge a coalition with Britain and the Soviet Union to oppose the fascists.

Underlying Causes. Many historians regard the reemergence of **multipolarity** in power distribution as a key factor in the onset and expansion of World War II. The post–World War I global system was placed "at risk when the sovereign states, which were its components, became too numerous and unequal in power and resources, particularly when (as happened after 1919) the great powers were reduced in number and new, lesser states proliferated" (Calvocoressi, Wint, and Pritchard 1989). In 1914, Europe had only twenty-two key states, but by 1921 the number nearly doubled. When combined with resentment over Versailles, the Russian Revolution, and the rise of fascism, the increased number of states and the resurgence of nationalistic revolts and crises made "the interwar years the most violent period in international relations since the Thirty Years' War and the wars of the French Revolution and Napoleon" (Holsti 1991).

■ **multipolarity**
the distribution of global power into three or more great-power centers, with other states allied with one of the rivals (see p. 569).

The collapse of the international economic system during the 1930s also contributed to the war. Great Britain found itself unequal to the leadership and regulatory roles it had performed in the world political economy before World

The Rise of Hitler and German Nationalism In the 1930s the nationalistic ideologies of national socialism and fascism—realist philosophies that regarded the state as supreme, accepted dictatorship, and called for expansion at the expense of neighboring countries—took root in Germany and Italy. Consistent with the realist view that states have an inherent right to expand, Adolf Hitler's propaganda experts staged dramatic political rallies to glorify the Führer (leader), persuade the German people of the need to persecute the Jews, and expand German borders by armament and aggression.

War I. Although the United States was the logical successor, its refusal to exercise leadership hastened the war. "The Depression of 1929–1931 was followed in 1933 by a world Monetary and Economic Conference whose failures—engineered by the United States—deepened the gloom, accelerated nationalist protectionism, and promoted revolution" (Calvocoressi, Wint, and Pritchard 1989). In this depressed global environment, heightened by deteriorating economic circumstances at home, Germany and Japan sought solutions through **imperialism** abroad.

■ **imperialism**
the policy of expanding state power through the conquest of foreign territory (see p. 58).

The League of Nations' failure to mount a collective response to the acts of aggression symbolized the weak institutional barriers to war. When Germany withdrew from the League of Nations in 1933, followed by Italy in 1937, war clouds gathered and the League was powerless to dispel them.

The Soviet Union's invasion of neutral Finland in 1939 provoked public indignation. In a final act of retaliation, the League of Nations expelled the Soviet Union, but the burden of defense fell on the shoulders of the victim. Ninety thousand fiercely independent Finns gave their lives in the victorious "Winter War" while the rest of the world watched in astonishment.

At the state level of analysis, psychological forces also led to World War II. These included "the domination of civilian discourse by military propaganda that primed the world for war," the "great wave of hypernationalism [that] swept over Europe [as] each state taught itself a mythical history while denigrating that of others," and the demise of democratic governance (Van Evera 1990–91).

In the final analysis, however, the importance of leaders stands out. The war would not have been possible without Adolf Hitler and his plans to conquer the world by force. Hence "German responsibility for the Second World War is in a class of its own" (Calvocoressi, Wint, and Pritchard 1989). Professing the superiority of Germans as a "master race" and virulent anti-Semitism and anticommunism, Hitler waged war to create an empire that could resolve the historic competition and precarious coexistence of the great powers in Europe by eliminating Germany's rivals.

> The broad vision of the Thousand-Year Reich was . . . of a vastly expanded—and continually expanding—German core, extending deep into Russia, with a number of vassal states and regions, including France, the Low Countries, Scandinavia, central Europe, and the Balkans, that would provide resources and labor for the core. There was to be no civilizing mission in German imperialism. On the contrary, the lesser peoples were to be taught only to do menial labor or, as Hitler once joked, educated sufficiently to read the road signs so they wouldn't get run over by German automobile traffic. The lowest of the low, the Poles and Jews, were to be exterminated. . . .
>
> To Hitler . . . the purpose of policy was to destroy the system and to reconstitute it on racial lines, with a vastly expanded Germany running a distinctly hierarchical and exploitative order. Vestiges of sovereignty might remain, but they would be fig leaves covering a monolithic order. German occupation policies during the war, whereby conquered nations were reduced to satellites, satrapies, and reservoirs of slave labor, were the practical application of Hitler's conception of the new world order. They were not improvised or planned for reasons of military necessity. (Holsti 1991, 224–225)

The Consequences of World War II

Having faced ruinous losses in Russia and a massive Allied bombing campaign at home, Germany's Thousand-Year Reich lay in ruins by May 1945. By August, the U.S. atomic bombing of Hiroshima and Nagasaki forced Japan to end its war of conquest as well.

The Allied victory over the Axis redistributed power and reordered borders, resulting in a new geopolitical terrain. The Soviet Union absorbed nearly six hundred thousand square meters of territory from the Baltic states of Estonia, Latvia, and Lithuania, and from Finland, Czechoslovakia, Poland, and Romania—recovering what Russia had lost in the 1918 Treaty of Brest-Litovsk after World War I. Poland, a victim of Soviet expansionism, was compensated with land taken from Germany. Germany itself was divided into occupation zones that eventually provided the basis for its partition into East and West Germany. Finally, pro-Soviet regimes assumed power throughout Eastern Europe (see Map 4.2, p. 96). In the Far East, the Soviet Union took the four Kurile Islands—or the "Northern Territories," as Japan calls them—from Japan, and Korea was divided into Soviet and U.S. occupation zones at the thirty-eighth parallel.

The end of World War II also generated uncertainty and mistrust. The agreements governing goals, strategy, and obligations that had guided the Allied effort began to erode even as victory neared. Victory only magnified the great powers' growing distrust of one another's intentions in an environment of ill-defined borders, altered allegiances, power vacuums, and economic ruin.

■ **Yalta Conference** the 1945 summit meeting among Franklin D. Roosevelt, Joseph Stalin, and Winston Churchill to resolve postwar territorial issues and voting procedures in the United Nations to collectively manage world order.

The "Big Three" leaders—Winston Churchill, Franklin Roosevelt, and Joseph Stalin—met at the **Yalta Conference** in February 1945 to design a new world order, but the vague compromises they reached concealed the differences percolating below the surface. Following Roosevelt's death in April and Germany's unconditional surrender in May, the Big Three (with the United States now represented by Harry Truman) met again at Potsdam in July 1945. The meeting ended without agreement, and the facade of Allied unity began to fade.

World War II, like previous great-power wars, paved the way for a new global system. The Allies' plans for a new postwar structure of peace had begun even as the war raged, and as early as 1943 the Four Power Declaration advanced principles for allied collaboration after the war. Their determination to create a new international organization to manage the postwar international order gave birth to the United Nations (UN). Consistent with the expectation that the great powers would cooperate to manage world affairs, China was promised a seat on the UN Security Council along with France and the Big Three. The purpose of the Security Council was to guarantee that all of the dominant states would share responsibility for keeping the global peace.

After the war, the United States and the Soviet Union remained the two great powers that were still strong, with the capacity to impose their will. The other major-power victors, especially Great Britain, had exhausted themselves and slid from the apex of the world-power hierarchy. The vanquished, Germany and Japan, also fell from the ranks of the great powers. Thus, as the French political sociologist Alexis de Tocqueville had foreseen in 1835, the Americans and Russians now held in their hands the destinies of half of mankind. In comparison, all other states were dwarfs. In what eventually became known as the Cold War, Washington and Moscow used the fledgling UN not to keep the peace, but to pursue their competition with each other. As the third and last great-power war of the twentieth century, the Cold War's lessons still cast shadows over the twenty-first-century geostrategic landscape.

THE COLD WAR

As World War II drew to a close in 1945, it became increasingly clear that a new era of international politics was dawning. Unparalleled in scope and unprecedented in destructiveness, the second great war of the twentieth century not only had brought about a system dominated by two superstates, the United States and the Soviet Union, it had also hastened the disintegration of the great colonial empires assembled by imperialist states in previous centuries, thereby emancipating many peoples from foreign rule. The emergent international system, unlike earlier ones, featured a bipolar distribution of power consisting of many sovereign states outside the European core area that were dominated by the two most powerful. In addition, the advent of nuclear weapons radically changed the role that threats of warfare would play in world politics. Out of these circumstances grew the competition between the United States and the Soviet Union for hegemonic leadership.

The Causes of the Cold War

Determining the origins of the twentieth century's third hegemonic battle for domination is difficult because the historical evidence lends itself to different interpretations (see Gaddis 1997; Melanson 1983). Nonetheless, an evaluation of several proposed causes can help us to understand the sources of great-power rivalries and to explain why this one, unlike other twentieth-century conflicts, ended without great-power violence.

A Conflict of Interests. Realism provides one structural explanation of the **Cold War.** The **power transition** that propelled the United States and the Soviet Union to the top of the international hierarchy made each naturally suspicious of the other, and their rivalry inescapable. Circumstances gave each superpower reasons to fear and to struggle against the other's potential global leadership.

But was the competition truly necessary and predetermined? The United States and the Soviet Union each had demonstrated an ability to subordinate ideological differences and competition for power to larger purposes during World War II (Gaddis 1997). Neither had sought unilateral advantage relentlessly, while both had expressed their hope that cooperation would continue and had reached agreements toward that purpose. President Roosevelt, for example, advocated preserving accommodation through an informal accord to let each superpower enjoy dominant influence in its own **sphere of influence,** or specified area of the globe. Rules written into the UN Charter, obligating the United States and Soviet Union to share responsibility for preserving global peace through the UN Security Council, further reflected the expectation of continued cooperation.

If cooperation was the superpowers' hope and aspiration when World War II ended, then why did they fail to achieve it? To answer that question, we must go beyond the logic of realpolitik and probe other explanations of the origins of the Cold War.

Ideological Incompatibilities. A second interpretation holds that the Cold War was simply an extension of the superpowers' mutual disdain for each other's professed beliefs about politics and economics. As U.S. Secretary of State James F. Byrnes argued at the conclusion of World War II, "there is too much difference in the ideologies of the U.S. and Russia to work out a long-term program of cooperation." To the extent that such assumptions were widely held in both Washington and Moscow, as they undoubtedly were, ideological differences made the Cold War a conflict "not only between two powerful states, but also between two different social systems" (Jervis 1991).

U.S. animosity toward the Soviet Union was stimulated by the 1917 Bolshevik revolution, which brought to power a government that embraced the Marxist critique of capitalistic imperialism. Whether real or imagined, U.S. fears of Marxism stimulated the emergence of anticommunism as an opposing ideology (Commager 1983; Morgenthau 1983). Accordingly, the United States embarked on a missionary crusade of its own, to contain and ultimately remove the atheistic communist menace from the face of the earth.

American foreign policy was fueled by the fear that communism's appeal to Europeans and the world's less fortunate countries would make its continued

■ **Cold War**
the forty-two-year (1949–1991) rivalry between the United States and the Soviet Union, as well as their competing coalitions, which sought to contain each other's expansion and win worldwide predominance (see p. 6).

■ **power transition**
a narrowing of the ratio of military capabilities between great-power rivals that is thought to increase the probability of war between them (see p. 494).

■ **sphere of influence**
a region of the globe dominated by a great power.

spread likely. This prophecy was popularized in the 1960s as the **domino theory,** the view that one country's fall to communism would cause its neighbors to fall like a row of dominoes, thus bringing the entire world under communist domination unless checked by U.S. power.

domino theory
a metaphor popular during the Cold War which predicted that if one state fell to communism, its neighbors would also fall in a chain reaction, like a row of falling dominoes.

Similarly, Soviet policy was fueled by the belief that capitalism could not coexist with communism. The purpose of Soviet policy, therefore, was to push the pace of the historical process in which communism eventually would prevail. However, Soviet planners did not believe that this historical outcome was guaranteed. They felt that the capitalist states, led by the United States, sought to encircle the Soviet Union and smother communism in its cradle, and that it was the Soviet obligation to resist. As a result, ideological incompatibility may have ruled out compromise as an option (see Controversy: Was Ideology the Primary Source of East-West Conflict?). Although the adversaries may have viewed "ideology more as a justification for action than as a guide to action," once the interests that they shared disappeared, "ideology did become the chief means which differentiated friend from foe" (Gaddis 1983).

Misperceptions. A third explanation describes the Cold War as rooted in psychological factors, particularly in the superpowers' misperceptions of each other's motives. In this view, conflicting interests and ideologies were secondary to misunderstandings in propelling the Cold War.

Mistrustful actors are prone to see only virtue in their own actions and only malice in those of their adversaries. When such **mirror images** exist, hostility is inevitable (Bronfenbrenner 1971). Moreover, when perceptions of an adversary's evil intentions become accepted as truth, **self-fulfilling prophecies** can develop. Prophecies are sometimes self-fulfilling because the future can be affected by the way it is anticipated. This tendency is illustrated by arms races: mistakenly fearing that a rival is preparing for an offensive war, a potential victim then arms in defense, thereby provoking the fearful rival to fulfill the prophecy by defensively building more weapons. The result is a classic illustration of the **security dilemma,** as each enemy's efforts to increase its own security by arming actually leads to a decline in security on both sides.

mirror images
the tendency of states and people in competitive interaction to perceive each other similarly—to see others the same way they see themselves (see p. 12).

self-fulfilling prophecy
the tendency for one's expectations to evoke behavior that helps to make the expectations become true (see p. 268).

security dilemma
the central problem faced by all sovereign states in an anarchic global system in which a state's arming for ostensibly defensive purposes provokes other states to arm in response, with the result that the national security of all declines as their armaments increase.

Both mirror images and self-fulfilling prophecies contributed heavily to the onset of the Cold War. The two countries' leaders imposed their definitions of reality on events and then became captives of those visions. As expectations shaped how leaders interpreted developments, what they saw influenced what they got. George F. Kennan, the American ambassador to the Soviet Union in 1952, noted that misread signals were common on both sides:

> The Marshall Plan, the preparations for the setting up of a West German government, and the first moves toward the establishment of NATO were taken in Moscow as the beginnings of a campaign to deprive the Soviet Union of the fruits of its victory over Germany. The Soviet crackdown on Czechoslovakia (1948) and the mounting of the Berlin blockade, both essentially defensive . . . reactions to these Western moves, were then similarly misread on the Western side. Shortly thereafter there came the crisis of the Korean War, where the Soviet attempt to employ a satellite military force in civil combat to its own advantage, by way of reaction to the American decision to establish a permanent military presence in Japan, was read in Washington as the beginning of the final Soviet push for world conquest;

CONTROVERSY

Was Ideology the Primary Source of East-West Conflict?

Cold War America was gripped by a "Great Fear" not simply of the Soviet Union but of communism. Senator Joseph McCarthy led the most infamous hunt for communist sympathizers in government, Hollywood production companies blacklisted supposed communist sympathizers, and average American citizens were often required to take loyalty oaths at their offices. Everywhere communism became synonymous with treasonous, un-American activity. As the nuclear arms race escalated and the U.S. government took military action to contain the Soviet Union, its justification was almost always expressed in terms of ideology. The threat, as the population learned to perceive it, was that of an atheistic, communistic system that challenged the fundamental American principles of democratic capitalism. The other side also couched its Cold War rhetoric in terms of ideology, objecting to the imperialistic, capitalist system that the Soviets said America planned to impose on the whole world.

Some would argue that fear of the other side's world dominance may have been more important in the Cold War than pure ideology. Both the American and the Soviet governments may have entered the Cold War to secure their relative power in the world order as much as to protect pure principles. After all, the United States and the Soviet Union had managed to transcend differing ideologies when they served as allies in World War II. After World War II, however, a power vacuum drew them into conflict with each other, and as they competed, ideological justifications surfaced.

Everyone has a psychological need to clarify their values and define them through the lens of an **ideology** or a belief system that expresses their convictions and enables them to explain what is of interest to them. Realism, liberalism, Marxism-Leninism are all examples of such ideologies of international politics. Ideologies help us to interpret life and its meaning, and are for that reason indispensable for organizing thought and values. But commitment to an ideology may at times cause hatred and hostility. Institutional proponents of particular ideologies are prone to perceive other ideologies competitively—as challenges to the truth of their own ideology's core beliefs. However, ideology can also become an excuse for less noble ambitions or for general fears. Although scholars are still debating the causes of the Cold War, we need to ask whether it was, in fact, an ideological contest over ideas or a more general contest for power—in which the two governments proselytized about communism and capitalism to win peoples' hearts and minds.

What do you think? Was the Cold War really an ideological contest between international communism and the free-market capitalism espoused by the liberal democracies or were there other, more powerful forces involved? In considering your opinion, take into account the end of the Cold War, in which the Soviet communistic system crumbled. Communist theoretician Vladimir Lenin described the predicament that he perceived to underlie the Cold War—prophetically, it turned out—when he predicted: "As long as capitalism and socialism exist, we cannot live in peace; in the end, either one or the other will triumph—a funeral dirge will be sung either over the Soviet Republic or over world capitalism."

> whereas the active American military response, provoked by this move, appeared in Moscow . . . as a threat to the Soviet position in both Manchuria and in eastern Siberia. (Kennan 1976, 683–684)

Thus, in the Cold War's formative stage, U.S. leaders and their allies in the West saw the many crises that erupted as part of a Soviet plan for world domination. The Soviets saw these same crises altogether differently—as tests of their resolve to ward off Western efforts to encircle and destroy their socialist experiment. Mistrust led to misperceptions, which in turn bred conflict. And to the extent that the Cold War originated in conflicting images and in each superpower's insensitivity to the impact of its actions on the other's fears, it is difficult

■ ideology
a set of core philosophical principles that leaders and citizens collectively hold about politics, the interests of political actors, and the ways people ought to ethically behave (see p. 12).

to assign blame for the deterioration of Soviet-American relations. Were both countries responsible because both were victims of their misperceptions? If so, then the Cold War was not simply a U.S. response to communist aggression (the orthodox American view), nor was it simply a product of postwar American assertiveness (the orthodox Soviet and revisionist historians' position; see Schlesinger 1986). Because each of the great powers felt threatened, and each had legitimate reasons to regard the other with suspicion, it is useful to view the Cold War as a conflict over reciprocal anxieties bred by the way policymakers on both sides interpreted the other's actions.

Additional factors beyond those rooted in divergent interests, ideologies, and images undoubtedly combined to produce this explosive Soviet-American hegemonic rivalry. Scholars have yet to sort out their relative causal influence. However, to grasp more completely the dynamics of this great-power rivalry in particular (and others in general), it is useful to move beyond its causes and examine its character.

The Characteristics of the Cold War

Although the character of the Cold War evolved over its duration, several conspicuous patterns persisted that illustrate the larger historical pattern of great-power rivalries (Thompson 1999b).

- Periods of intense conflict alternated with periods of relative cooperation; reciprocal, action-reaction exchanges were also evident (friendly U.S. initiatives toward the Soviet Union were reciprocated in kind).
- For reasons of expediency, both rivals were willing to disregard their respective professed ideologies whenever their perceived national interests rationalized such inconsistencies; for example, each backed allies with political systems antithetical to its own when the necessities of power politics seemed to justify doing so.
- Both rivals consistently made avoidance of all-out war their highest priority. Through a gradual learning process involving push and shove, restraint and reward, tough bargaining and calm negotiation, the superpowers created a **security regime.**

■ **security regime**
norms and rules for interaction agreed to by a set of states to increase their security (see p. 555).

These characteristics become visible when we inspect the evolution of the superpowers' relationship. For this, we divide the Cold War into three chronological phases, shown in Figure 4.1.

Confrontation, 1945–1962. A brief period of wary Soviet-American friendship soon gave way to mutual antagonism when the Cold War began. In this short period of **unipolarity**—one characterized by a single dominant power center in the international system—the United States alone possessed the capacity to devastate its adversaries with the atomic bomb.

■ **unipolarity**
a condition in which an international system has a single dominant power hegemon capable of dominating all other states (see p. 571).

Despite this restraining factor, all pretense of collaboration rapidly vanished as the superpowers' vital security interests collided in countries outside their clearly defined respective spheres of influence. At this critical juncture, George F. Kennan, then a diplomat in the American embassy in Moscow, sent to Washington his famous "long telegram" assessing the sources of Soviet conduct. Kennan's ideas were circulated widely in 1947, when the influential jour-

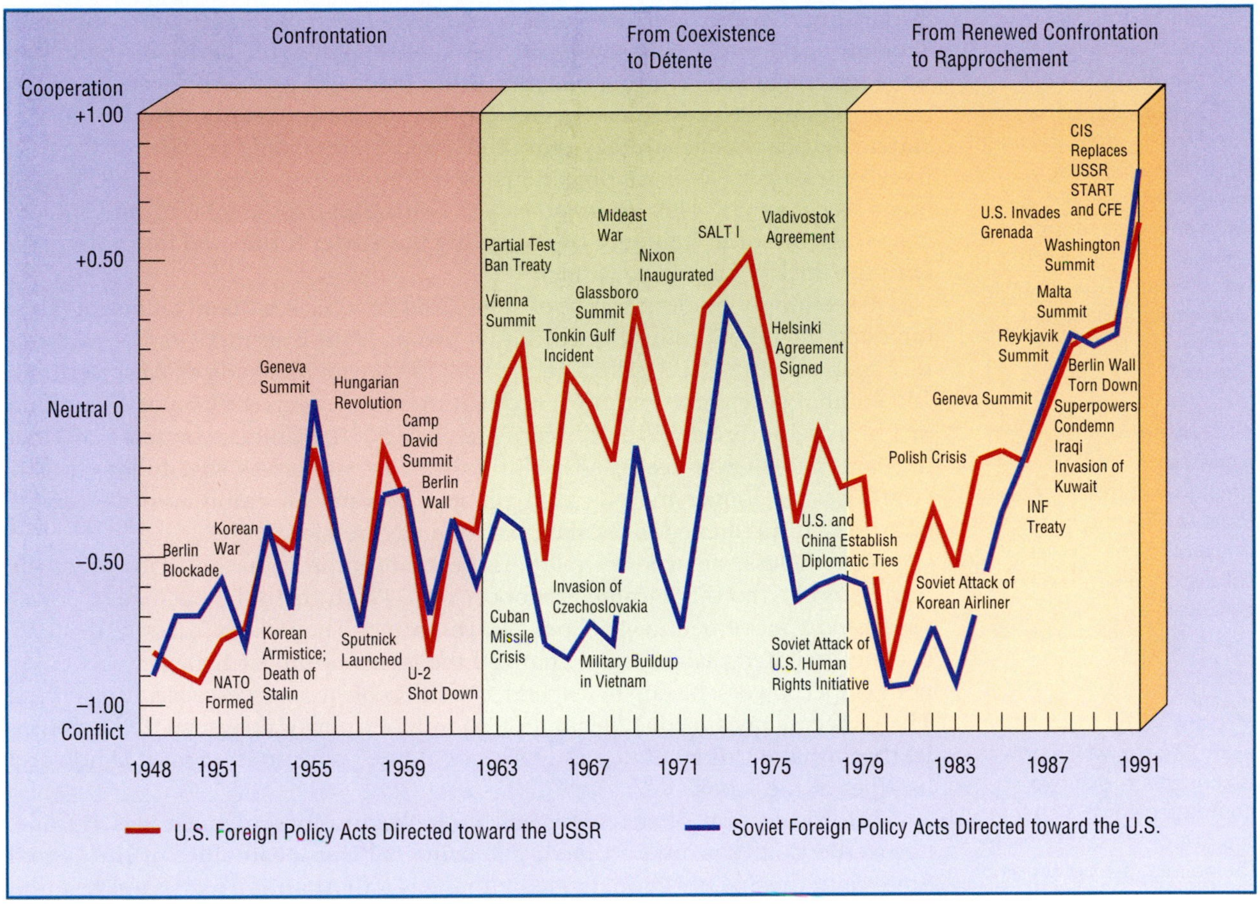

FIGURE 4.1

U.S.–Soviet Relations during the Cold War, 1948–1991

The evolution of U.S.–Soviet relations during the Cold War displays a series of shifts between periods of conflict and cooperation. As this figure shows, each superpower's behavior toward the other tended to be reciprocal, and, for most periods prior to 1983, confrontation prevailed over cooperation.

nal *Foreign Affairs* published his views in an article signed simply "X." In this article, Kennan argued that Soviet leaders forever would feel insecure about their political ability to maintain power against forces both within Soviet society and in the outside world. Their insecurity would lead to an activist—and perhaps aggressive—Soviet foreign policy. However, the United States had the power to increase the strains under which the Soviet leadership would have to operate, which could lead to a gradual mellowing or final end of Soviet power. Thus, Kennan concluded: "In these circumstances it is clear that the main element of any United States policy toward the Soviet Union must be that of a long-term, patient but firm and vigilant *containment* of Russian expansive tendencies" (Kennan 1947, emphasis added).

Soon thereafter, President Harry S Truman made Kennan's assessment the cornerstone of American postwar foreign policy. Provoked in part by violence in

Turkey and Greece, which he and others believed to be communist inspired, Truman declared, "I believe that it must be the policy of the United States to support free peoples who are resisting attempted subjugation by armed minorities or by outside pressures." Eventually known as the **Truman Doctrine,** this statement defined the strategy that the United States would pursue for the next forty years, over Kennan's objections (see Controversy: Was Military Containment Necessary?). This strategy, called **containment,** sought to prevent the expansion of Soviet influence by encircling the Soviet Union and intimidating it with the threat of a military attack.

■ **Truman Doctrine**
the declaration by President Harry S Truman that U.S. foreign policy would use intervention to support peoples who allied with the United States against external subjugation.

■ **containment**
a strategy to prevent a great power rival from using force to alter the balance of power and increase its sphere of influence (see p. 498).

A seemingly endless series of new Cold War crises soon followed. They included the Soviet refusal to withdraw troops from Iran in 1946; the communist coup d'état in Czechoslovakia in 1948; the Soviet blockade of West Berlin in June of that year; the communist acquisition of power on the Chinese mainland in 1949; the outbreak of the Korean War in 1950; the Chinese invasion of Tibet in 1950; and the on-again, off-again Taiwan Straits crises that followed. The "war" was no longer merely "cold"; it had become an embittered worldwide quarrel that threatened to escalate into open aggression.

Nonetheless, superpower relations began to improve in the 1950s. After the Soviets broke the U.S. atomic monopoly in 1949, shifts in the balance of power prompted a movement away from confrontation. The risks of massive destruction necessitated restraint and changed the terms of the struggle. In particular, both superpowers began to expend considerable resources recruiting allies. Their success produced a distribution of military power characterized by **bipolarity,** with the United States and its allies at one pole and the Soviet Union and its allies at the other.

■ **bipolarity**
a condition in which power is concentrated in two competing centers so that the rest of the states define their allegiances in terms of their relationships with both (see p. 561).

The focal point of the superpowers' jockeying for influence was Europe, where the Cold War first erupted. The principal European allies of the United States and the Soviet Union divided into the North Atlantic Treaty Organization (NATO) and the Warsaw Treaty Pact, respectively. These alliances became the cornerstones of the superpowers' external policies, as nearly all of the European members of each alliance—grateful for protection and defense—yielded to their superpower patrons.

To a lesser extent, alliance formation outside of Europe involved other states in the two titans' contest. The United States in particular sought to contain Soviet (and Chinese) influence on the Eurasian landmass by building a ring of allies, including Iran and South Korea, on the very borders of the communist world. In return, the United States promised to protect these new client states from external attack through a strategy known as **extended deterrence.** Thus the Cold War expanded across the entire globe.

■ **extended deterrence**
a great power's commitment to its allies to use its military might to prevent them from being attacked by an enemy.

In the rigid two-bloc system of the 1950s, the superpowers often talked as if war were imminent, but they both acted cautiously (especially after the Korean War). President Eisenhower and his secretary of state, John Foster Dulles, pursued a strategy termed "rollback," which promised to move what was called the "Iron Curtain" separating East and West by "liberating" the "captive nations" of Eastern Europe. They pledged to respond to communist aggression with "massive retaliation," and criticized the allegedly "soft" and "restrained" Truman Doctrine, claiming to reject containment in favor of an ambitious "winning" strategy that would finally end the confrontation with godless communism. However, containment was not replaced by a more assertive strategy. In 1956, for instance, the United States failed to respond to a call for assistance from

CONTROVERSY

Was Military Containment Necessary?

Whether a military containment strategy was appropriate remains controversial. George F. Kennan thought that U.S. leaders misinterpreted his celebrated statement. He explained:

> I . . . went to great lengths to disclaim the view, imputed to me by implication . . . that containment was a matter of stationing military forces around the Soviet borders and preventing any outbreak of Soviet military aggressiveness. I protested . . . against the implication that the Russians were aspiring to invade other areas and that the task of American policy was to prevent them from doing so. "The Russians don't want," I insisted, "to invade anyone. It is not in their tradition. They tried it once in Finland and got their fingers burned. They don't want war of any kind. Above all, they don't want the open responsibility that official invasion brings with it." (Kennan 1967, 361)

As Kennan lamented, "the image of a Stalinist Russia poised and yearning to attack the West, and deterred only by [U.S.] possession of atomic weapons, was largely a creation of the Western imagination." Cautioning against "demonizing the adversary, overestimating enemy strength and overmilitarizing the Western response" (Talbott 1990), Kennan recommended a political rather than a military containment approach.

It is worth considering whether, if Kennan's recommendations had been followed, the Cold War would have become so bitter or lasted so long.

Hungarian freedom fighters, who had revolted against Soviet control with armed resistance.

Because the Soviet Union remained strategically inferior to the United States, Nikita Khrushchev (who succeeded Stalin upon his death in 1953) pursued a policy of **peaceful coexistence** with capitalism. Nonetheless, the Soviet Union at times cautiously sought to increase its power in places where opportunities appeared to exist. As a result, the period following Stalin's death saw many Cold War confrontations, with Hungary, Cuba, Egypt, and Berlin becoming the flash points.

■ **peaceful coexistence** Soviet leader Nikita Khrushchev's 1956 doctrine that war between capitalist and communist states was not inevitable and that inter-bloc competition could be peaceful (see p. 517).

Despite the intensity and regularity of U.S.-Soviet confrontations, no threat to peace resulted in open warfare as both superpowers took accommodative steps toward improving relations. For example, the 1955 Geneva summit provided an important forum for the antagonists' meaningful dialogue about world problems, and in 1956 the Soviets dissolved the Cominform (the Communist Information Bureau, which coordinated the work of communist parties in other states).

From Coexistence to Détente, 1963–1978. Despite the Geneva conference, a dark shadow loomed over hopes for superpower peace. As the arms race accelerated, the threats to peace multiplied. In 1962, the surreptitious placement of Soviet missiles in Cuba set the stage for the greatest test of the superpowers' capacity to manage their disputes—the Cuban missile crisis. The superpowers stood eyeball to eyeball. Fortunately, one (the Soviet Union) blinked, and the crisis ended. This "catalytic" learning experience both reduced enthusiasm for waging the Cold War by military means and expanded awareness of the suicidal consequences of a nuclear war.

The growing threat of mutual destruction, in conjunction with the growing parity of American and Soviet military capabilities, made coexistence or nonexistence appear to be the only alternatives. Given this equation, finding ways to coexist became compelling. At the American University commencement exercises in 1963, U.S. President John F. Kennedy explained why tension reduction had become essential:

> Today, should total war ever break out again—no matter how—our two countries would become the primary targets. It is an ironical but accurate fact that the two strongest powers are the two in the most danger of devastation. . . . We are both caught up in a vicious and dangerous cycle in which suspicion on one side breeds suspicion on the other and new weapons beget counterweapons.
>
> In short, both the United States and its allies, and the Soviet Union and its allies, have a mutually deep interest in a just and genuine peace and in halting the arms race. . . .
>
> So let us not be blind to our differences, but let us also direct attention to our common interests and to the means by which those differences can be resolved. And if we cannot end now our differences, at least we can help make the world safe for diversity.

Kennedy signaled a shift in how the United States hoped thereafter to bargain with its adversary, and the Soviet Union reciprocally expressed its interest in more cooperative relations. Installation in 1963 of the "hot line," a direct communication system linking the White House and the Kremlin, followed. So did the 1967 Glassboro Summit and several negotiated agreements, including the 1963 Partial Test Ban Treaty, the 1967 Outer Space Treaty, and the 1968 Nuclear Nonproliferation Treaty. In addition, the superpowers agreed to accept the permanence of European borders, tacitly including those that divided Germany. Thus, in style and tone the United States and Soviet Union began to depart from past confrontational tactics, laying the foundation for détente.

■ **détente**
in general, a strategy of seeking to relax tensions between adversaries to reduce the possibility of war.

Soviet-American relations took a dramatic turn with Richard Nixon's election in 1968. Coached by his national security adviser, Henry A. Kissinger, President Nixon initiated a new approach to Soviet relations that in 1969 he officially labeled **détente.** The Soviets also adopted this term to describe their policies toward the United States.

■ **linkage strategy**
a set of assertions that claims leaders should take into account another country's overall behavior when deciding whether to reach agreement on any one specific issue.

In Kissinger's words, détente sought to create "a vested interest in cooperation and restraint," "an environment in which competitors can regulate and restrain their differences and ultimately move from competition to cooperation." To engineer the relaxation of superpower tensions, Nixon and Kissinger pursued a **linkage strategy** to bind the two rivals in a common fate by making peaceful superpower relations dependent on the continuation of mutually rewarding exchanges (such as trade concessions). Furthermore, linkage made cooperation in one policy area contingent on acceptable conduct in other areas.

The shifts in policy produced results, as relations between the Soviets and Americans "normalized." As Figure 4.1 shows, cooperative interaction became more commonplace than hostile relations. Visits, cultural exchanges, trade agreements, and joint technological ventures replaced threats, warnings, and confrontations.

■ **Strategic Arms Limitations Talks (SALT)**
two sets of agreements reached during the 1970s between the United States and the Soviet Union that established limits on strategic nuclear delivery systems.

Arms control stood at the center of the dialogue surrounding détente. The **Strategic Arms Limitation Talks (SALT),** initiated in 1969, sought to restrain the threatening, expensive, and spiraling arms race by limiting the deployment of antiballistic missiles. The talks produced two agreements, the first in 1972

Easing Tensions: U.S.-Soviet Détente As East-West tension waned, cooperation increased during the détente phase of U.S.-Soviet relations in the late 1960s. A considerable part of this departure from past confrontation was due to compromises at the bargaining table. Pictured here, President Richard Nixon, one of the architects of the U.S. "linkage" strategy along with Secretary of State Henry Kissinger, is toasting with Soviet Premier Leonid Brezhnev and fellow dignitaries at their meeting to discuss approaches to relaxing tensions between the superpowers.

(SALT I) and the second in 1979 (SALT II); however, SALT II was signed but never ratified by the United States, due to opposition in Congress. This failure underscored the substantial differences that still separated the superpowers.

From Renewed Confrontation to Rapprochement, 1979–1991. Despite the careful nurturing of détente, its spirit did not endure. In many respects, the Soviet invasion of Afghanistan in 1979 catalyzed détente's demise. As President Jimmy Carter viewed it, "Soviet aggression in Afghanistan—unless checked—confronts all the world with the most serious strategic challenge since the Cold War began." In retaliation, he advanced the **Carter Doctrine** declaring America's willingness to use military force to protect its access to oil supplies from the Persian Gulf. In addition, he attempted to organize a worldwide boycott of the 1980 Moscow Olympics and suspended U.S. grain exports to the Soviet Union.

■ **Carter Doctrine** President Jimmy Carter's declaration of U.S. willingness to use military force to protect its interests in the Persian Gulf.

Relations deteriorated dramatically thereafter. President Ronald Reagan and his Soviet counterparts (first Yuri Andropov and then Konstantin Chernenko) delivered a barrage of confrontational rhetoric. Reagan asserted that the Soviet Union "underlies all the unrest that is going on" and described the Soviet Union as "the focus of evil in the modern world." The atmosphere was punctuated by Reagan policy adviser Richard Pipes's bold challenge in 1981 that the Soviets would have to choose between "peacefully changing their communist system . . . or going to war." Soviet rhetoric was equally unrestrained and alarmist.

As talk of war increased, preparations for it escalated. The arms race resumed feverishly, at the expense of addressing domestic economic problems. The superpowers also extended the confrontation to new territory, such as

Central America, and renewed their public diplomacy (propaganda) efforts to extol the virtues of their respective systems throughout the world.

Dangerous events punctuated the renewal of conflict. The Soviets destroyed Korean Airlines flight 007 in 1983; the United States invaded Grenada soon thereafter. Arms control talks then ruptured, the Soviets boycotted the 1984 Olympic Games in Los Angeles, and the **Reagan Doctrine** pledged U.S. support for anticommunist insurgents who sought to overthrow Soviet-supported governments in Afghanistan, Angola, and Nicaragua. In addition, American leaders spoke loosely about the "winability" of a nuclear war through a "prevailing" military strategy that included the threat of a "first use" of nuclear weapons in the event of conventional war. Relations deteriorated as these moves and countermoves took their toll. The new Soviet leader, Mikhail Gorbachev, in 1985 summarized the alarming state of superpower relations by fretting that "The situation is very complex, very tense. I would even go so far as to say it is explosive."

■ Reagan Doctrine
a pledge of U.S. support for anticommunist insurgents who sought to overthrow Soviet-supported governments (see p. 78).

■ rapprochement
in diplomacy, a policy seeking to reestablish normal relations between enemies.

However, the situation did not explode. Instead, prospects for a more constructive phase improved greatly following Gorbachev's advocacy of "new thinking" in order to achieve a **rapprochement** or reconciliation of the rival states' interests. He sought to settle the Soviet Union's differences with the capitalist West in order to halt the deterioration of his country's economy and international position. Shortly thereafter, Gorbachev embarked on domestic reforms to promote democratization and the transition to a market economy, and proclaimed his desire to end the Cold War contest. "We realize that we are divided by profound historical, ideological, socioeconomic, and cultural differences," he noted in 1987 during his first visit to the United States. "But the wisdom of politics today lies in not using those differences as a pretext for confrontation, enmity, and the arms race." Soviet spokesperson Georgi Arbatov elaborated, informing the United States that "we are going to do a terrible thing to you—we are going to deprive you of an enemy."

■ Intermediate-range Nuclear Forces (INF) agreement
the 1987 disarmament agreement between the United States and the Soviet Union to remove intermediate-range nuclear forces from Europe.

Surprisingly, the Soviets did what they promised: They began to act like an ally instead of an enemy. Building on the momentum created by the **Intermediate-range Nuclear Forces (INF) agreement,** signed in 1987, the Soviet Union agreed to end its aid and support for Cuba, withdrew from Afghanistan and Eastern Europe, and announced unilateral reductions in military spending. Gorbachev also agreed to two new disarmament agreements, **START (Strategic Arms Reduction) Treaty** for deep cuts in strategic arsenals, and the **Conventional Forces in Europe (CFE) Treaty** to reduce the Soviet presence in Europe (see Chapter 15 for a description of these agreements). In addition, the Soviet Union liberalized its emigration policies and permitted greater religious freedom.

■ START (Strategic Arms Reduction) Treaty
a series of negotiations that led to a 1991 treaty, followed by ongoing negotiations and subsequent treaties, to reduce U.S. and Soviet strategic forces (see p. 582).

■ Conventional Forces in Europe (CFE) Treaty
a 1992 treaty that set ceilings on five categories of conventional arms.

The pace of steps to rapprochement then accelerated, and the "normalization" of Soviet-American relations moved rapidly. The Cold War—which began in Europe and centered on Europe for forty-five years—ended there in 1991 when the Soviet Union dissolved and all communist governments in the Soviet bloc in Eastern Europe accepted capitalist free market principles and initiated liberal democratic reforms. To nearly everyone's astonishment, the Soviet Union acquiesced in the defeat of communism and the triumph of liberalism (see Controversy: Why Did the Cold War End Peacefully?). The conclusion of the enduring rivalry between East and West, and with it the end of the seventy-year ideological dispute as well, represented such a history-transforming event that the **end of history** was proclaimed (Fukuyama 1992b).

■ end of history
the thesis that economic and political liberalism have triumphed as an accepted philosophy throughout the world, ending the contest between those who advocate market democracies and those who advocate centrally planned governance.

CONTROVERSY

Why Did the Cold War End Peacefully?

How history is remembered is important because those memories shape future decisions about the management of great-power rivalries. Why did the Cold War end without the use of armed force? That question remains a puzzle that still provokes much controversy, in part because the Cold War's abrupt end came as such a surprise to most observers and, in the unanticipated outcome, also undermined confidence in the adequacy of conventional **realist theories** that argued that no great power would ever accept without a fight the loss of position to another hegemonic rival.

What do you think? What was the cause of the Cold War's collapse? In considering your view on this issue, take into account some divergent opinions.

From one perspective, the policies George Kennan recommended in his famous "X" article now appear prophetic. In his version of nonmilitary containment, Kennan anticipated that this would "promote tendencies which must eventually find their outlet in either the breakup of or the gradual mellowing of Soviet power." Many believe that this was precisely what did happen, albeit more than forty years later!

Neorealists, in contrast, emphasize the contribution that nuclear weapons, and the West's superior military power and extended deterrence through alliances, made to forcing the Soviet Union's surrender. In 1991, for example, an adviser to U.S. President Reagan, Richard Perle, articulated the realist view in his contention that people "who argued for nuclear deterrence and serious military capabilities contributed mightily to the position of strength that eventually led the Soviet leadership to choose a less bellicose, less menacing approach to international politics."

Liberals and neoliberals voice another interpretation about causes, as Ted Galen Carpenter (1991) did when he observed that many Russian demonstrators "who sought to reject communist rule looked to the American system for inspiration. But the source of that inspiration was America's reputation as a haven for the values of limited government, not Washington's $300-billion-a-year military budget and its network of global military bases."

Although no consensus has materialized about the ways in which these factors individually or in combination put an end to the Cold War, a fundamental question resides at the center of this postmortem. Did military containment force the Soviet Union into submission? Or did Soviet leaders succumb to the inherent political weaknesses of communism, which caused an internal economic malaise that left them unable to conduct an imperial policy abroad or retain communist control at home? In other words, was the end of Communist Party rule accepted because of the intimidation of U.S. military strength? Or was the outcome produced by other political and economic influences within the Soviet Union, as suggested in 1991 by Georgi Arbatov, director of the USSR's Institute for the USA and Canada Studies, who countered from the realist perspective by arguing "that President Reagan's 'tough' policy and intensified arms race . . . persuaded communists to 'give up' is sheer nonsense. Quite to the contrary, this policy made the life for reformers, for all who yearned for democratic changes in their life, much more difficult . . . The conservatives and reactionaries were given predominant influence. . . . Reagan made it practically impossible to start reforms after Brezhnev's death (Andropov had such plans) and made things more difficult for Gorbachev to cut military expenditures."

Sorting out the contribution of different causes to ending the Cold War will doubtless intrigue historians for decades, just as determining the causes for its onset has done. The lessons drawn from this forty-five-year drama remain important because they affect how leaders are likely to manage new great-power rivalries in the twenty-first century.

realist theory the view that states are unitary global actors in relentless competition with each other for position and prosperity in the international hierarchy (see p. 306).

The failed conservative coup against Gorbachev in August 1991 put the nail in the coffin of Communist Party control in Moscow, the very heartland of the international communist movement. As communism was repudiated in the Soviet Union, a new age began. Communism was in retreat, and as a result massive changes swept world politics, producing long-term consequences. Without resistance, the Berlin Wall came down, Germany reunited, and the Warsaw Pact dissolved.

The collapse of the Cold War suggested something quite different from the lesson of the twentieth century's two world wars which had implied that great-power rivalries are doomed to end in armed conflict. The Cold War was different; it had come to an end peacefully, suggesting that it is possible for great-power rivals to reconcile their competitive differences without warfare.

The Consequences of the Cold War

The end of the Cold War liberated both the United States and the Soviet Union from a rivalry that had exacted an enormous toll and reduced their economic strength relative to other ascending great powers, such as China, the European Union, and Japan (see Map 4.3). In this sense, both Cold War superpowers "lost" (see Lebow and Stein 1994).

The collapse of the East-West contest left the world facing unfamiliar circumstances. No longer was there "a clear and present danger to delineate the purpose of power, and this basic shift invalidated the framework for much of the thought and action about international affairs in the East and West since World War II" (Oberdorfer 1991).

In accepting the devolution of its external empire, the Soviet Union has made the most dramatic peaceful retreat from power in history. The immediate consequence of the Cold War's end is a transformed global hierarchy in which the former Soviet Union is no longer a challenger to U.S. hegemonic leadership.

THE FUTURE OF GREAT-POWER POLITICS: A COLD PEACE?

The end of the Cold War thus has altered the face of world affairs in profound and diverse ways. Its disappearance into the dustbin of history inspired hope for international peace but, at the same time, raised the specter of new kinds of global instability. As then President George Bush lamented in November 1991, "The collapse of communism has thrown open a Pandora's box of ancient ethnic hatreds, resentment, even revenge."

One consequence warrants particular attention: Following Russia's decline, can we expect another fifty years of great-power peace? Or will the transformed balance of power be a prelude in the twenty-first century to new great-power rivalries and possibly war?

Scenarios for the Twenty-First Century

A peaceful future is not certain. The insights of long-cycle and realist theories predict pessimistically that prevailing trends in the diffusion of economic power will lead to renewed competition, conflict, and perhaps even warfare among the great powers, and that the range of new problems and potential threats will multiply. As political scientist Robert Jervis explains:

> Cyclical thinking suggests that, freed from the constraints of the Cold War, world politics will return to earlier patterns. Many of the basic generaliza-

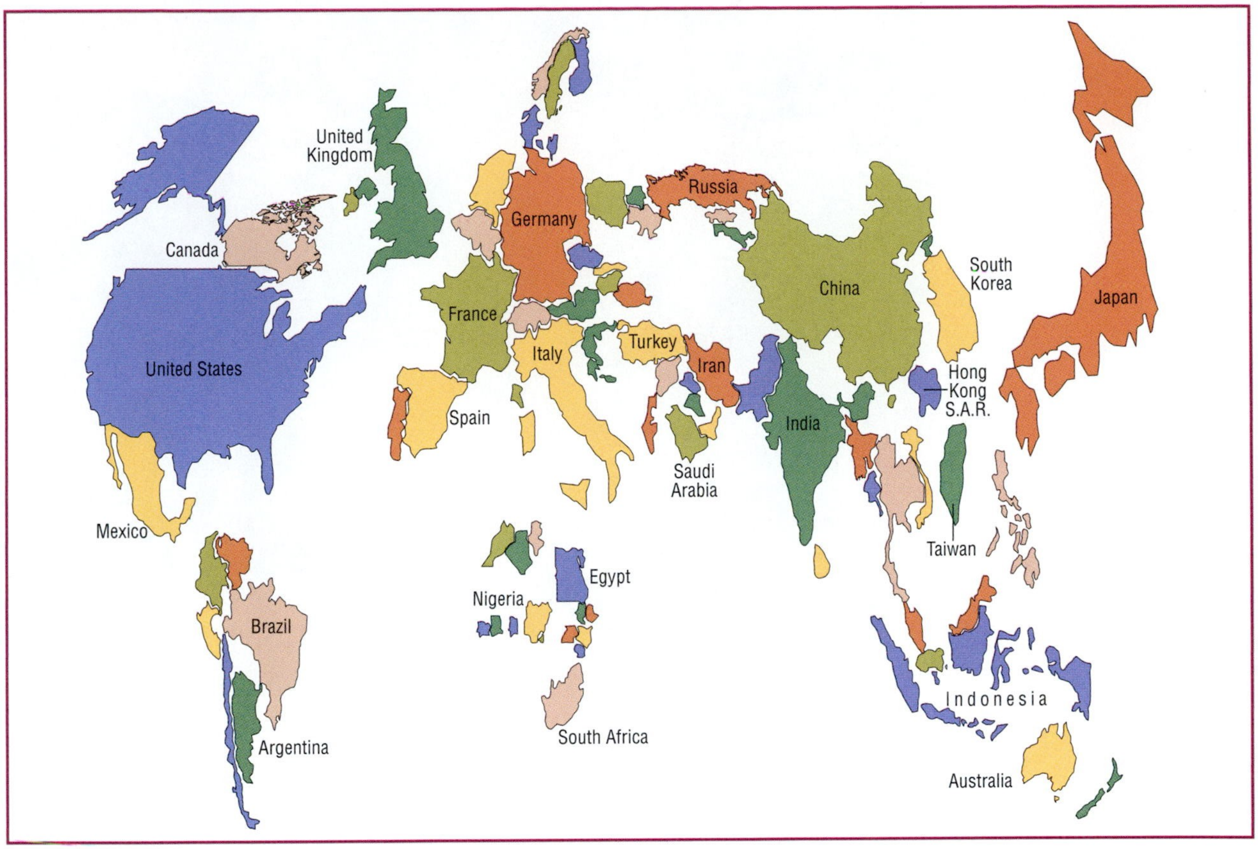

MAP 4.3

Emerging Centers of Power in a New International Hierarchy

Which countries are powerful and which are relatively weak can be estimated by different kinds of indicators. One common approach to predicting the power potential of states (i.e., their ability to project power and exercise influence in the world) is to measure and compare the size of their economies. This map depicts the distribution of power in 1997. The relative size of each country indicates proportional size of gross domestic product measured by purchasing power parities. In this estimate, the United States, Japan, China, Germany are the economic powerhouses, and Russia is a secondary power, ranking below Italy, and India, among others.

Note: Not all countries are identified, and many countries are not represented.
SOURCE: Map adapted from *Handbook of International Economic Statistics* (1999), 14.

tions of international politics remain unaltered: It is still anarchic in the sense that there is no international sovereign that can make and enforce laws and agreements. The security dilemma remains as well, with the problems it creates for states who would like to cooperate but whose security requirements do not mesh. Many specific causes of conflict also remain, including desires for greater prestige, economic rivalries, hostile nationalisms, divergent perspectives on and incompatible standards of legitimacy, religious animosities, and territorial ambitions. To put it more generally, both aggression and spirals of insecurity and tension can still disturb the peace. (Jervis 1991–92, 46)

A New Global Hegemon? China is a rising economic giant that many expect to become the globe's wealthiest country. In the West this has generated a new kind of "Red scare"—the fear that as China becomes a modern military power it will seek hegemony and use force to cause trouble abroad. Shown here at the seventy-second anniversary of the Chinese army in August 1999 is a symbol of China's potential to project power—a show of strength at Tiananmen Square.

To realists, great-power rivalry for power and position is likely to resume because the international anarchy that promotes it continues to shape the international conduct of states. Realists also foresee probable instability resulting from the changes unfolding in the international system's structure if U.S. hegemony continues to decay. As rivals rise to challenge U.S. leadership, a new structure will emerge.

A Twenty-First-Century Multipolar World

While the distribution of power in the Cold War system was bipolar, the post-Cold War world promises to be very different. Russia's demise produced a new unipolar structure, fleeting though it may be. In early 1991, when it victoriously fought the Persian Gulf War, the United States basked in a "unipolar moment." It was the "one first-rate power [with] no prospect in the immediate future of any power to rival it. . . . [It was] the only country with the military, diplomatic, political and economic assets to be a decisive player in any conflict in whatever part of the world it [chose] to involve itself" (Krauthammer 1991).

This condition is not likely to last into the next millennium, however. As Figure 4.2 shows, the long-term trajectories of history unmistakably point to

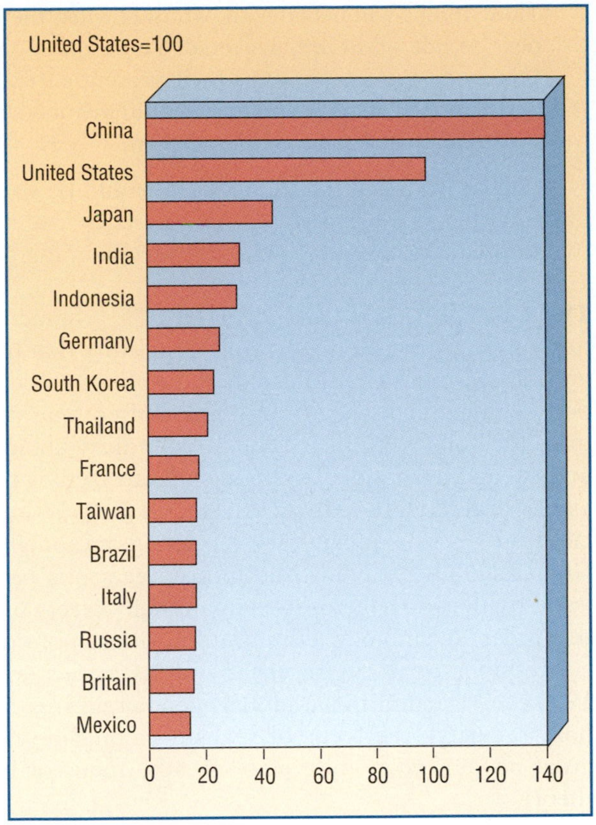

FIGURE 4.2
Projection of the Fifteen Largest Global Economies by 2020

Using purchasing power parities (PPPs) to account for differences in countries' price levels, the World Bank forecasts the probable size of the largest economies. The projections show that the rank order of the largest economic powerhouses by 2020 will be substantially different from today's. The political and military consequences are not predicted, but long-cycle theory postulates that the economic changes will breed political and even military conflict.

SOURCE: McGranahan (1995), 59; see also Buzan and Segal (1998), 176.

the coming of a world in which China, and perhaps other great powers, will rapidly rise to challenge U.S. financial prominence and political clout, even if U.S. military supremacy remains unchallenged in the short run (Kaplan 1999). China, Japan, and others are growing in economic power relative to the United States, and this suggests that the pecking order of the world's countries is likely to look very different in the twenty-first century. One projection provides clues on how to draw the probable geopolitical map of the future:

> Half a century from now, the world will not be unrecognizably different from the place it is now; it will be neither the more or less frontierless globe some optimists still hope for, nor the trampling-ground of monsters some pessimists used to fear. But nor will it be the same as the world of the 45 years of the Cold War, which was a two-sided confrontation between the communist and anti-communist alliances, or the world of the 150 years before that, which was a maneuvering for supremacy among four or five countries all of which sat in the part of the map called Europe, with America and Japan joining in only near the end.
>
> The new pattern will consist of several powers, as in pre–Cold War days, but the competing powers will be spread more evenly over the map; one of these powers will start with a large lead over the others, but it is not sure how long it will keep that lead; and neither is it clear how many of the five or six possible competitors will actually decide to join in the struggle.

> These things will become known only when the two main questions of the next decade or so are answered. Those questions are whether the United States and Europe continue their present partnership, or go their separate ways; and which of the other potential members of the coming multi-power world raises its head first. (*Economist,* July 31, 1999, 4)

■ **multipolar**
an international system with more than two dominant power centers (see p. 489).

Such a future **multipolar** world would be structured very differently from previous balance-of-power distributions in which either one (unipolarity) or two (bipolarity) countries possess overwhelming power.

The Challenge of Multipolarity. The character of a new multipolar structure may be very different from the stability that has characterized the unipolar and bipolar phases of international politics since World War II. In part this is because the emergence of a number of comparatively equal great powers will introduce more complexity and uncertainty about allegiances and alignments, and "in an international system characterized by perhaps five or six major powers . . . order will have to emerge much as it did in past centuries: from a reconciliation and balancing of competing national interests" (Kissinger 1994). Global stability may also be more precarious because "international security issues will exhibit themselves in all their variety once again—issues of markets, resources, technology, ethnic animosities, political philosophy, and different conceptions of world order, as well as armies and nuclear weapons" (Carter 1990–91). The multipolar global agenda requires continuing concern about military security—the focus of realism—alongside mounting concerns about the great powers' economic relations—the focus of liberal international relations theory.

■ **security regime**
norms and rules for interaction agreed to by a set of states to increase their security (see p. 555).

Many theorists point out the dangers inherent in multipolar distributions of power. Their warnings are inspired by the historical record, which suggests that if we look to the past to anticipate the future, we have many reasons to fear the reemergence of this kind of system. Today's hopes for great-power cooperation in the new millennium have many precedents. The end of every previous great-power war has been followed by an initial hopeful burst of collaborative institution building to forge a stable new order among the victorious powers. But each of these great-power designs for a new **security regime,** constructed at the conclusion of a multipolar period's war, ultimately proved temporary when the postwar sense of urgency faded. Precedents include the Peace of Westphalia (1648), the Treaty of Utrecht (1713), the Concert of Europe (1815), the League of Nations (1919), and the UN (1945). In each case, as the great powers' relative strength changed, collaboration gave way to competition. Sooner or later, *every* previous multipolar system collapsed, as one or more of the major powers expressed dissatisfaction with the existing hierarchy, rejected the rules by which they had agreed to manage their relations, and attempted to overturn the status quo by force. Rivalry has routinely resulted in a hegemonic struggle for supremacy ending in a new catastrophic general war, each more destructive than the last. This invites the sobering conclusion that

> in a world of sovereign states a contest among them over the distribution of power is the normal condition and . . . such contests often lead to war. . . . The reasons for seeking more power are often not merely the search for security or material advantage. Among them are demands for greater prestige, respect, deference, in short, honor. Since such demands involve judg-

> ments even more subjective than those about material advantage, they are still harder to satisfy. Other reasons emerge from fear, often unclear and intangible, not always of immediate threats but also of more distant ones, against which reassurance may not be possible. The persistence of such thinking in a wide variety of states and systems over the space of millennia suggests the unwelcome conclusion that war is probably part of the human condition and likely to be with us for some time yet. (Kagan 1995, 569)

Multipolar politics looks especially menacing when we take into account the interplay of military and economic factors in the perceived rankings of the great powers. In such a system, differentiating friend from foe will be more difficult because allies in military security are likely to be rivals in trade relationships. In Lester Thurow's (1992) apt phrase, the United States, Europe, and Japan are likely to go "head to head" on the economic battlefield. In this arena we can expect China and perhaps a reascendant Russia, India, and South Korea to join the fray. The U.S.-China and U.S.-Russia disputes in late-1999 about security issues and NATO enlargement at the very time they were also arguing about "fair trade" and the use of intervention to protect human rights within national borders illustrate the tensions that can easily escalate between powers at the pinnacle of the global hierarchy.

The diffusion of wealth predicts the likely intensification of great-power political competition. Throughout history, changes in comparative economic advantage have preceded political competition. When multipolarity has existed, economic rivals have struggled to protect their wealth and have competed politically for economic position, with military conflict usually following (Rusi 1997).

A "new cold war" could emerge between any pair of great powers, such as between the globe's two major contenders for supremacy, the United States and China, if their competition escalates and they practice containment to prevent their rival's quest for hegemony. However, this kind of armed rivalry need not develop; cooperation could increase instead. Quite different and inconsistent political types of great-power relations could emerge in the economic and military spheres. The probability of economic rivalry and conflict is generally high, whereas the likelihood of security cooperation for many of these same relationships is also high. For example, the United States, Japan, and China exhibit conflict in their commercial relations but nevertheless also display continuing efforts to manage their security relations collaboratively. Table 4.2 presents a projection of the kind of cross-cutting bilateral relationships that could develop among the great powers in the twenty-first century. It estimates the probability of military cooperation and economic conflict between any pair of the five major powers.

Awareness of these different possibilities may have been behind U.S. Secretary of State Lawrence Eagleburger's warning in 1989:

> The issue . . . is how well the United States accomplishes the transition from overwhelming predominance to a position more akin to a "first among equals" status, and how well America's partners—Japan and Western Europe—adapt to their newfound importance. The change will not be easy for any of the players, as such shifts in power relationships have never been easy.

Few observers see advantages resulting from the emerging situation. As former U.S. Secretary of State Henry A. Kissinger surmised in 1993, this poses a

TABLE 4.2

The New Great-Power Chessboard: Simultaneously Unfolding Military and Economic Rivalries

	Military Rivalry						*Economic Rivalry*				
	United States	Japan	Germany	Russia	China		United States	Japan	Germany	Russia	China
United States	—					United States	—				
Japan	L	—				Japan	H	—			
Germany	M	H	—			Germany	H	H	—		
Russia	M	H	H	—		Russia	L	M	M	—	
China	H	H	H	M	—	China	H	H	M	M	—

Note: The symbols H = high, M = medium, and L = low signify the likelihood of bilateral relationships that may develop in the twenty-first century.

How the great powers will align militarily and economically in the twenty-first century is difficult to predict. A wide variety of strategic and trade relationships are possible. To complicate the task of prediction, in the year 2000 the paradox exists that many of the pairs of great powers that are the most active trade partners are also the great military rivals. This table depicts the bilateral great-power relationships in their military and economic dimensions, and illuminates the question of whether economic cooperation will help to reduce potential military competition.

serious challenge because "the United States has very little experience with a world that consists of many powers and which it can neither dominate nor from which it can simply withdraw in isolation."

Yet, we have no way of knowing whether the future will resemble the gloomy past history of multipolar systems. Patterns and practices can change, and it is possible for policymakers to learn from previous mistakes and avoid repeating them.

Responding to Multipolarity's Challenge. What, then, can the great powers do to prevent the resumption of their rivalry? What security policies should they pursue in order to avoid the dangers of shared power and rapid transitions in their position and strength in the great-power hierarchy?

The answers are highly uncertain. As we will discuss in Chapters 13–16, debate about the methods of guaranteeing international security in Washington, Beijing, Tokyo, Berlin, and Moscow today revolves around four basic options. Each is actively under consideration, and each will become more or less practical, prudent, or problematic for each great power depending on the circumstances that materialize in tomorrow's multipolar world.

A **unilateral** conception of a great power's role represents one possible option. Acting alone is especially attractive for a self-confident great power assured of its independent strength. With sufficient power, a potential hegemon can be self-reliant. Unilateralism can involve isolationism; an attempt to exert hegemonic leadership; a strategy of **selective engagement** that concentrates external involvements on vital national interests; or an effort to play the role of a "balancer" who skillfully backs one side or another in a great-power dispute, but only when necessary to maintain a military equilibrium between the other great-power disputants. At the extreme, unilateralism can lead the global leader to play the role of international bully, seeking to run the world. More commonly, unilateralism derives from the desire for control over the flexible con-

■ **unilateral**
an approach that relies on self-help, independent strategies in foreign policy (see p. 489).

■ **selective engagement**
a great-power grand strategy using economic and military power to influence only important particular situations, countries, or global issues by striking a balance between a highly interventionist "global policeman" and an uninvolved isolationist (see p. 490).

duct of a great power's foreign relations, independent of control by or pressure from other great powers. This, clearly, was the motive behind the landmark document signed by European leaders in June 1999 at the Cologne European Union (EU) Summit, which formally committed the EU to a common policy on security and defense. The purpose is to give the EU a "capacity for autonomous action," enabling it to act independently without U.S. approval or support. To implement the goal of acting unilaterally, the EU began to build its own independent "Eurocorps" military force following the Treaty of Nice in 2000.

Cultivation of a specialized relationship with another great power, similar to that between Great Britain and the United States in the twentieth century, illustrates a second approach that some pairs of great powers might pursue. The Joint Declaration on the Multipolar World and a New World Order signed by China and Russia in April 1997 suggested the kind of strategic bilateral partnerships that are likely to develop in a climate of fear in the future, as well as the most probable reasons why such alliances may be forged between powers that have suffered from frosty relations in the recent past. Convinced that a dominant United States aimed to contain their influence, and asserting that "no country should claim hegemony for itself or pursue policy from positions of strength and monopolize international affairs," Moscow and Beijing announced their agreement to warm relations by joining together to counterbalance the United States as the world's lone superpower. That announcement led to a new agreement between the United States and Japan in July 1997 to strengthen their specialized defense relationship and to the 1999 reaffirmation of that U.S.-Japanese Mutual Security Treaty and announcement that the new defense guidelines would allow Japan to provide military support in "areas surrounding Japan" such as Taiwan. When Tokyo and Washington followed their bilateral alliance in July 1999 by agreeing to cooperate in building a joint defense against ballistic missiles, Beijing responded in accordance with the realpolitik rules of balance-of-power politics. Claiming that the United States had "only one goal, the hegemonic domination of the world" propelled by military might, the enlargement and eastward expansion of NATO and strategic partnership with Japan, China retracted the hopes it had expressed a year earlier at the October 1997 summit with President Bill Clinton in Shanghai. At that meeting, China had sought "common ground despite differences" in attempting to raise Chinese-American relations "to a new level by sharing responsibility for preserving world peace." China next strengthened its new alliance with Russia to counterbalance the perceived threat of a U.S.-EU-Japanese attempt to squeeze their countries from both east and west. Such dances among global giants, with the rapid formation and expansion of short-term specialized relationships among pairs of great powers in a climate of suspicion, is exactly the kind of national security maneuvering many expect to occur in the twenty-first century under conditions of multipolarity. Still other types of specialized relations between pairs of great powers could follow, at various levels of mutual support and commitment. There are several variants of this strategic option, including informal understandings, cooperations (sometimes termed **ententes**), and alliances formalized by treaties.

A third strategy under consideration is construction of a **concert**, or a cooperative agreement among the great powers to manage the international system jointly and to prevent international disputes from escalating to war. The Concert of Europe, at its apex between 1815 and 1822, is the epitome of previous great-power efforts to pursue this path to peace.

entente
an agreement between states to consult if one is attacked by another party.

concert
a cooperative agreement among great powers to manage jointly the international system.

■ **collective security**
a security regime agreed to by the great powers setting rules for keeping peace, guided by the principle that an act of aggression by any state will be met by a collective response from the rest (see p. 559).

Finally, some policymakers recommend that today's great powers unite with the lesser powers in constructing a true system of **collective security.** The principles rationalizing the formation of the League of Nations in 1919 exemplify this multilateral approach to peace under conditions of multipolarity, as did the 1999 pledge by Russia to cooperate with NATO following the intervention in Kosovo to build a twenty-first-century security partnership.

Whichever combination of approaches predominates in the strategies forged to prevent great-power rivalries from escalating to war in a multipolar future, the ultimate outcome will not depend on the great powers alone. The policy response of other, less powerful actors is likely to be increasingly important in shaping world politics, and their role must also be examined. We begin in Chapter 5 with a consideration of the history and characteristics of those states at the bottom of the international system's hierarchy, the Global South, and of the foreign policy interests and goals that motivate their behavior.

KEY TERMS

long-cycle theory
hegemon
hegemonic stability theory
enduring rivalries
counterfactual reasoning
structuralism
rational choice
nationalism
bipolar
realism
Kellogg-Briand Pact
irredentism
fascism
machtpolitik
isolationism
appeasement
multipolarity
imperialism
Yalta Conference
Cold War
power transition
sphere of influence
domino theory
mirror images
self-fulfilling prophecy
security dilemma
ideology
security regime
unipolarity
Truman Doctrine
containment
bipolarity
extended deterrence
peaceful coexistence
détente
linkage strategy
Strategic Arms Limitation Talks (SALT)
Carter Doctrine
Reagan Doctrine
rapprochement
Intermediate-range Nuclear Forces (INF) agreement
START (Strategic Arms Reduction) Treaty
Conventional Forces in Europe (CFE) Treaty
end of history
realist theory
multipolar
security regime
unilateral
selective engagement
entente
concert
collective security

SUGGESTED READING

Art, Robert J. "Geopolitics Updated," *International Security* 23 (Winter 1999): 79–113.

Doran, Charles F. *Systems in Crisis: New Imperatives of High Politics at Century's End.* Cambridge, Mass.: Cambridge University Press, 1992.

Gaddis, John Lewis. *We Now Know: Rethinking Cold War History.* New York: Oxford University Press, 1997.

Kegley, Charles W., Jr., and Gregory A. Raymond. *A Multipolar Peace? Great-Power Politics in the Twenty-First Century.* New York: St. Martin's Press, 1994.

Kennedy, Paul. *The Rise and Fall of the Great Powers.* New York: Random House, 1987.

Kissinger, Henry. *Diplomacy.* New York: Simon & Schuster, 1994.

Larson, Deborah Welch. *Anatomy of Mistrust: U.S.-Soviet Relations during the Cold War.* Ithaca, N.Y.: Cornell University Press, 1997.

Maynes, Charles William. "The U.S. Role in the World: What Are the Choices?" 9–17 in *Great Decisions 2000.* New York: Foreign Policy Association, 2000.

Morgan, Patrick M., and Keith L. Nelson, eds. *Re-Viewing the Cold War: Domestic Factors and Foreign Policy in the East-West Confrontation.* Westport, Conn.: Praeger, 2000.

Pastor, Robert A., ed. *A Century's Journey: How the Great Powers Shape the World.* New York: Basic Books, 1999.

Ruggie, John Gerald. *Winning the Peace.* New York: Columbia University Press, 1996.

Rusi, Alpo M. *Dangerous Peace: New Rivalry in World Politics.* Boulder, Colo.: Westview Press, 1997.

Thompson, William R., "Why Rivalries Matter and What Great Power Rivalries Can Tell Us about World Politics," 3–28 in William R. Thompson, ed., *Great Power Rivalries.* Columbia: University of South Carolina Press, 1999.

WHERE ON THE WORLD WIDE WEB?

The Avalon Project—World War II
http://www.yale.edu/lawweb/avalon/wwii/wwii.htm

Yale Law School has ambitiously undertaken to collect and house digital documents relevant to the fields of law, history, economics, politics, diplomacy, and government. This site links you to documents relating to World War II. As Chapter 4 explains, the end of World War II generated much uncertainty and mistrust. While visiting the archive, read the text of the agreements reached at the Yalta Conference at which Roosevelt, Churchill, and Stalin tried to resolve territorial issues after World War II. Did the agreements reached at Yalta make the Cold War inevitable?

Cold War
http://www.cnn.com/SPECIALS/cold.war/

Chapter 4 discusses the causes, characteristics, and the consequences of the Cold War. Learn more about the most recent great-power rivalry by exploring CNN's award-winning, comprehensive, Cold War Web Site. Navigate interactive maps of the nuclear testing sites in the American Southwest. Learn more about the key players and then play an interactive game to see which Cold War players you recognize. Hear sound bites and match them to the statesman who made them. Tour Cold War capitals through 3-D images. See espionage weapons and hear real-life spy stories.

Race for the Superbomb
http://www.pbs.org/wgbh/amex/bomb/sfeature/index.html

On this highly enlightening site, PBS re-creates the competition between the United States and the Soviet Union in their race to stockpile nuclear weapons. This Web site brings home many aspects of the Cold War rivalry discussed in Chapter 4. Have you ever wondered if you could survive a nuclear blast if a bomb exploded fifty miles away? Nuclear Blast Mapper will analyze the "zones of destruction" for any location. If you survived the blast, find out if you would survive the fallout. Then, take a virtual tour of a secret government bunker maintained as shelter for lucky congressmen in case of a nuclear attack. Not scared enough? Take a Panic Quiz to determine your panic quotient.

Senator Joe McCarthy: A Multimedia Celebration
http://webcorp.com/mccarthy/

A multimedia site where students can see and hear the most famous speeches and hearings given by Joe McCarthy. This is an important site for contemporary students who have trouble understanding "what all the fuss was about."

Soviet Exhibit
http://sunsite.unc.edu/expo/soviet.exhibit/entrance.html

This Web site is a virtual tour of the Library of Congress's Soviet Archives exhibit. Go to the first floor to see the Internal Workings of the Soviet System or proceed directly to the second floor to see the Soviet Union and the United States. Shuttle buses take you to other pavilions or let you visit the Restaurant. You can even leave messages for a current or future friend at the Post Office.

The World War I Document Archive
http://www.lib.byu.edu/~rdh/wwi/

The World War I Military History List has assembled a group of primary documents from World War I. Read the treaties, scan personal reminiscences, see photos, and access links to other resources. Chapter 4 puts forth theories concerning the cause of World War I. Some state that the switching alliances in Europe brought on the war. Others claim that the rational choices of individual German leaders who wanted to consolidate power led to a declaration of war. And finally, many assert that state factors, such as the rise of nationalism in Germany, were responsible for the war. After reading the documents in the archive, which theories do you think best explain the cause of World War I?

CHAPTER 5

THE PLIGHT AND POLICY POSTURE OF THE GLOBAL SOUTH

TOPICS AND THEMES

- The colonial history of the Global South
- Global North and Global South today: Worlds apart
- The Global South's prospects
- Theoretical explanations of underdevelopment
- Development redefined
- The Global South's foreign policy response to subordination
- The Global South in the new millennium

- **CONTROVERSY** HOW SHOULD NATIONAL AND PERSONAL WEALTH BE MEASURED? GNP PER CAPITA VERSUS "PURCHASING POWER PARITY"

Uneven development in the Global South, Panama City

The great moral problem of our time is poverty. . . . It can and must be eradicated. . . . There is no need more urgent, no cause more noble.

—EVELINE HERFKENS, HILDE F. JOHNSON, CLARE SHORT, and HEIDEMARIE WIECZOREK-ZEUL, the Dutch, Norwegian, British, and German ministers for development, 1999

The world is becoming increasingly polarized between the rich and the poor—both between and within countries . . . The costs of neglecting the rapidly growing international class divide will be immense.

—JAMES GUSTAVE SPETH, United Nations Development Program administrator, 1999

The earth is divided into two hemispheres, north and south, at the equator. Life in the north is very different, in many ways, from life in the south. One American college student painfully learned this lesson during his first visit to South America, where he found a reality far different from his own experience growing up in the United States. He was moved to write:

> I spent the first 24 years of my life in South Carolina. When I left . . . for Colombia [South America], I fully expected Bogota to be like any large U.S. city, only with citizens who spoke Spanish. When I arrived there I found my expectations were wrong. I was not in the U.S., I was on Mars! I was a victim of culture shock. As a personal experience this shock was occasionally funny and sometimes sad. But after all the laughing and the crying were over, it forced me to reevaluate both my life and the society in which I live.
>
> Colombia is a poor country by American standards. It has a per capita GNP of $550 and a very unequal distribution of income. These were the facts that I knew before I left.

> But to "know" these things intellectually is much different from experiencing first-hand how they affect people's lives. It is one thing to lecture in air conditioned classrooms about the problems of world poverty. It is quite another to see four-year-old children begging or sleeping in the streets.
>
> It tore me apart emotionally to see the reality of what I had studied for so long: "low per capita GNP and maldistribution of income." What this means in human terms is children with dirty faces who beg for bread money or turn into pickpockets because the principle of private property gets blurred by empty stomachs.
>
> It means other children whose minds and bodies will never develop fully because they were malnourished as infants. It means cripples who can't even turn to thievery and must beg to stay alive. It means street vendors who sell candy and cigarettes 14 hours a day in order to feed their families.
>
> It also means well-dressed businessmen and petty bureaucrats who indifferently pass this poverty every day as they seek asylum in their fortified houses to the north of the city.
>
> It means rich people who prefer not to see the poor, except for maids and security guards.
>
> It means foreigners like me who come to Colombia and spend more in one month than the average Colombian earns in a year.
>
> It means politicians across the ideological spectrum who are so full of abstract solutions or personal greed that they forget that it is real people they are dealing with.
>
> Somewhere within the polemics of the politicians and the "objectivity" of the social scientists, the human being has been lost. (Wallace 1978, 15–16)

What created these conditions that are characteristic of the countries south of the equator? To understand possible answers we need to begin by taking into consideration the legacy and impact of **colonialism** on the peoples who were colonized by European conquerors. The now independent sovereign states in the Southern Hemisphere are almost all former colonies.

■ **colonialism** the rule of a region by an external sovereign power.

The end of colonialism is one of the most remarkable developments in twentieth-century world politics. Since World War II, more than 120 new states have emerged, many of them former colonies. As U.S. Secretary of State George Shultz observed in 1983, "An international system that had been centered on Europe for centuries, and that regarded all non-European areas as peripheral or as objects of rivalry, has become in an amazingly short span of time a truly global arena of sovereign states."

Despite their legal status as independent entities, sovereignty could not erase the colonial heritage and vulnerabilities that the former colonies faced. Indeed, the new poor states born after World War II were thrust to the international periphery. Dominated by the rich great powers at the core of an international system they had no voice in shaping, the new states viewed the inherited rules and structures as barriers to their true independence and growth.

■ **Third World** a Cold War term to describe the developing countries of Africa, Asia, the Caribbean, and Latin America.

The term **Third World** was first used to distinguish the growing number of newly emerging, economically less developed states that tended to share a colonial heritage from those identified with either the East or West in the

■ **First World**
the relatively wealthy industrialized countries that share a commitment to varying forms of democratic political institutions and developed market economies, including the United States, Japan, Canada, Australia, and New Zealand.

■ **Second World**
during the Cold War, the group of countries, including the Soviet Union and its then–Eastern European allies, that embraced central planning to propel economic growth.

■ **Global North**
a term used to refer to the world's wealthy, industrialized countries located primarily in the Northern Hemisphere.

■ **Global South**
a term now often used instead of "Third World" to designate the less-developed countries located primarily in the Southern Hemisphere.

Cold War struggle, but it soon took on largely economic connotations. The Third World had failed to advance toward levels of economic development comparable to those of the **First World** industrialized countries, like Western Europe, North America, and Japan. The so-called **Second World** consisting of the Soviet Union and its allies in other communist countries was distinguished by a communist ideological commitment to planned economic policies rather than reliance on market forces to determine the supply and demand for goods and services. Today the states comprising the former Second World have largely vanished from the global scene, with liberalism triumphant and nearly all states committed to free-market capitalism. The Second World describes the handful of "countries in transition" that have yet to join the World Trade Organization and accept its rules of free markets and free governments.

The term *Third World* carries Cold War baggage that makes it no longer useful. Today the terms **Global North,** which refers to what was previously known as the First World, and **Global South,** which refers to the rest of the world, are popular. As always, the placement of particular states within these categories is sometimes problematic. Generally, four dimensions distinguish the North and South: politics, technology, wealth, and demography.

States comprising the Global North are democratic, technologically inventive, wealthy, and aging, as their societies tend toward zero population growth (see Map 5.1). Some states in the Global South share many of these characteristics, but none shares them all. Saudi Arabia is rich but not democratic; China is aging but only a fraction of its slow-growing population has recently become wealthy; India is democratic but burdened with an enormous and growing population; and Singapore is both wealthy and technologically innovative, with a comparatively modest population growth rate, but is not democratic. Beyond these are many states that are not democratic, technologically innovative, or wealthy, but who are experiencing rapid population growth that increasingly strains overtaxed social and ecological systems. These, the least developed of the less developed countries, are sometimes described today as the "Third World's Third World." Many, but not all, are in Africa, south of the Sahara.

The Global South is home to more than 80 percent of the world's people but commands less than 20 percent of its wealth. These disparities, illustrated in Map 5.2, underlie the long festering "North-South conflict" dispute more than do political and technological differences. The contest between the wealthy North and the poor South has historically been "a politics of mutual suspicion and struggle" (Heilbroner 1991) because of the fears and resentments that differences in status and unequal opportunities to compete economically naturally arouse. These conflicts are likely to intensify if globalization continues to widen the rich-poor gap (Miller 1999).

In this chapter we examine the roots and consequences of the often stark contrasts that set the Global South apart and the foreign policy postures that flow from them. Although considerable diversity exists within the countries of the Global South, it is common to describe them as a united group quite distinct from the similarly diverse great powers. We begin with an examination of the colonial and imperial historical experiences of most developing countries that account for their subordinate international position, and the Global South's policy reaction to that circumstance.

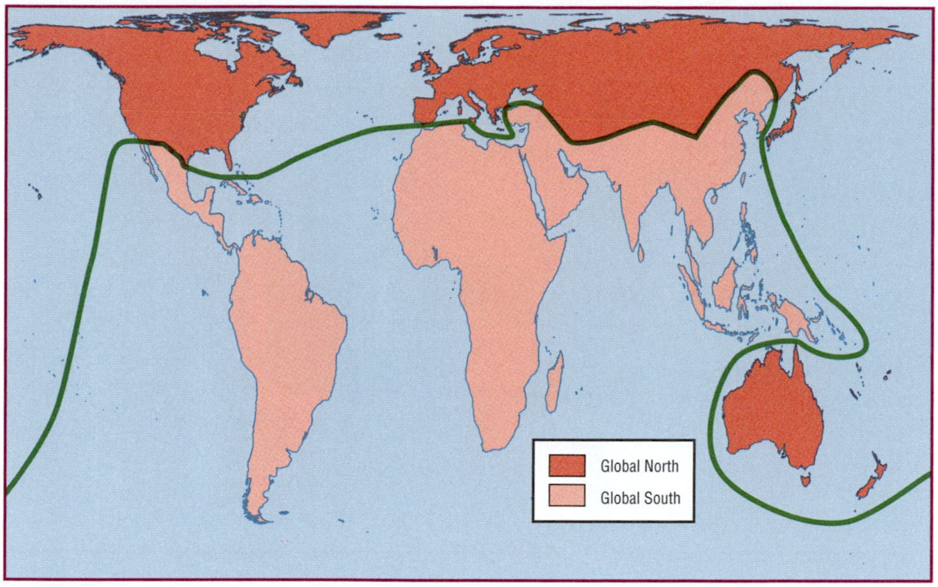

MAP 5.1
The Global North and Global South
The countries of the Global North are those that are wealthy, democratic, and technologically innovative, with declining birthrates and aging populations. In contrast, the countries in the Global South are home to 80 percent of the world's population but the impoverished people living there possess only 20 percent of the globe's wealth.

THE COLONIAL HISTORY OF THE GLOBAL SOUTH

The emergence of the Global South as an identifiable world actor is a distinctly contemporary phenomenon. Although most Latin American countries were independent before World War II, not until then did the floodgates of decolonization first open. In 1947, Great Britain granted independence to India and Pakistan, after which decolonization gathered speed. In the last half of the twentieth century a profusion of new states joined the international community as sovereign states, nearly all carved from the British, Spanish, Portuguese, Dutch, and French empires built under colonialism four hundred years ago.

Today, few colonies exist. Although the dozen or so remaining dependent territories may yet become independent members of the world community, most have populations of less than one hundred thousand and many have expressed a preference to retain their current political status. In short, the political process known as **decolonization**—the freeing of colonial peoples from their dependent status—is now complete.

■ **decolonization** the achievement of sovereign independence by countries that were once colonies of the great powers.

Most of the ethnic national conflicts now so prevalent have colonial roots, as the imperial powers drew borders within and between their domains with little regard for the national identities of the indigenous peoples. Similarly, the staggering poverty facing Global South countries may be a product of imperial pasts, when the European powers exploited their overseas territories. Although European powers have largely renounced political claims to their former colonies, many of which have become independent states, the Global North maintains an active economic presence in many countries of the Global South. Thus, as viewed through the eyes of nationalist leaders in many of the emerging states, the disparity between the rich North and the poor South is the consequence of **neocolonialism** (or **neoimperialism**)—unequal trade exchanges through which the advantaged exploit the disadvantaged by penetrating the latter's markets and by institutionalizing economic processes for this purpose.

■ **neocolonialism (neoimperialism)** the economic rather than military domination of foreign countries.

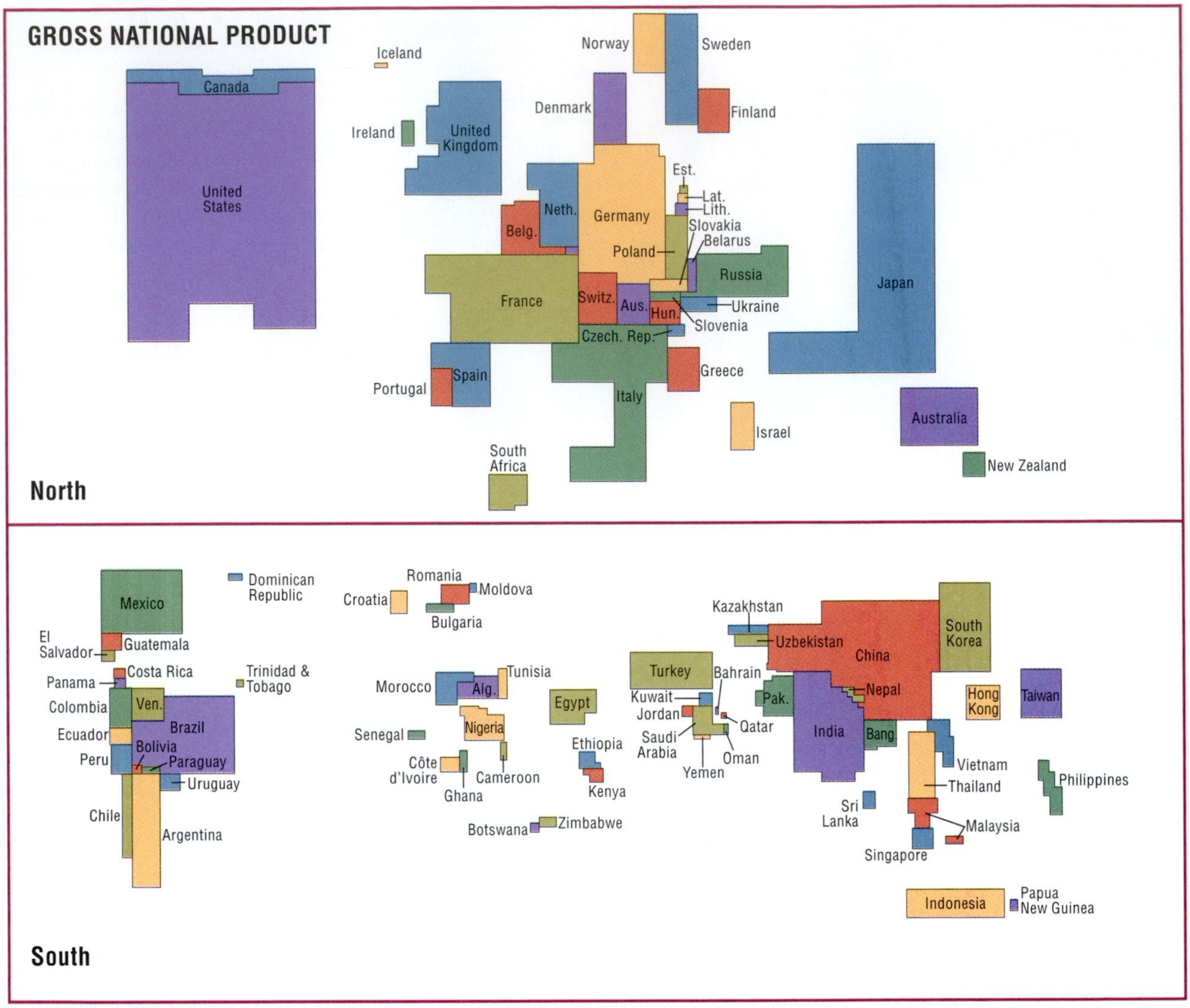

MAP 5.2
Wealth versus Population in the Global North and Global South

If the countries of the world are redrawn to reflect the size of their economies and populations, the world appears lopsided indeed: Most of the wealth is in the Global North and most of the people are in the Global South.

SOURCE: Based on data from World Bank (2000).

The First Wave of European Imperialism

The first wave of European empire building began in the late fifteenth century, as the Dutch, English, French, Portuguese, and Spanish used their military power to conquer territories for commercial gain. As scientific innovations made the European explorers' adventures possible, merchants followed in their wake, "quickly seizing upon opportunities to increase their business and profits.

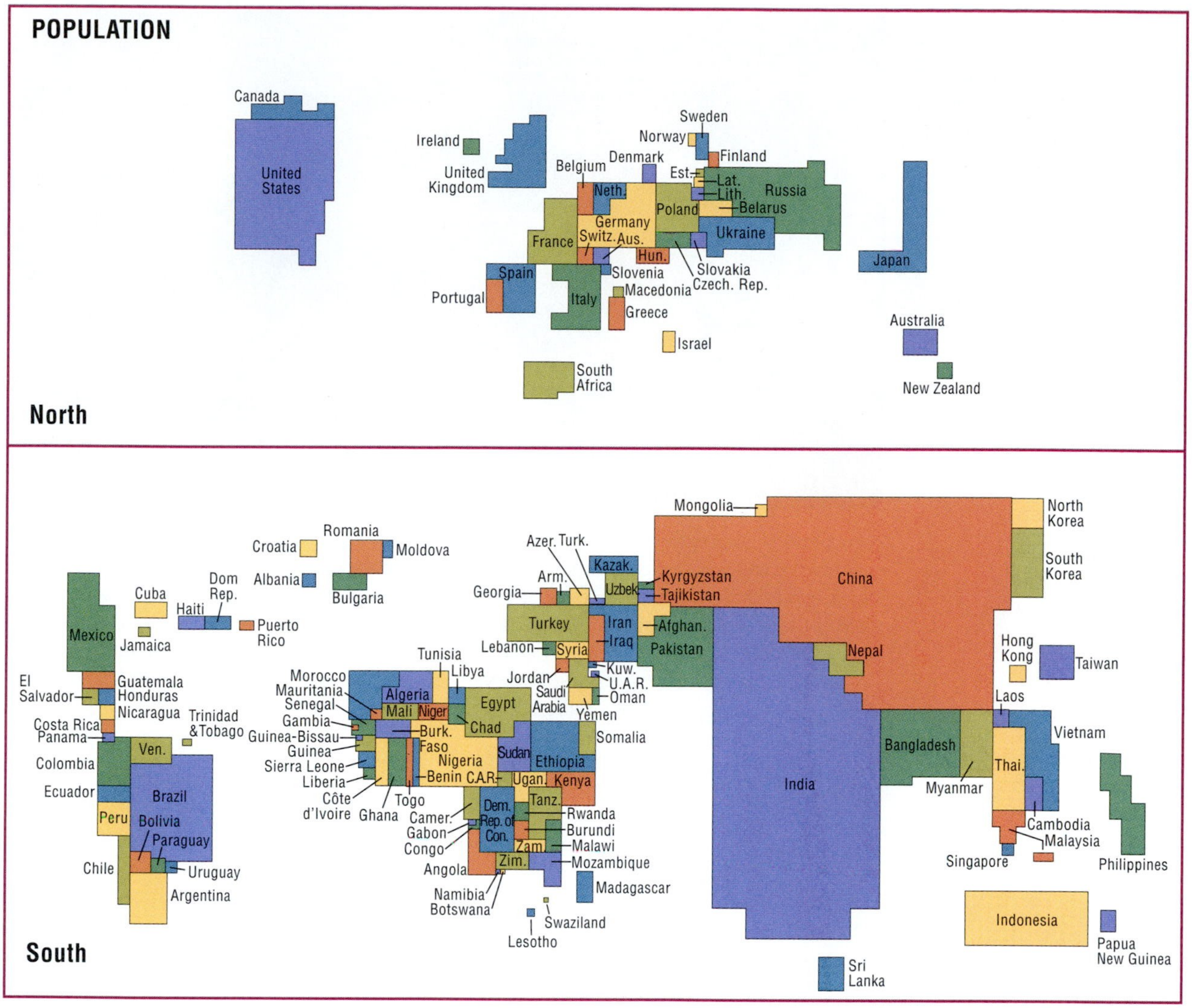

In turn, Europe's governments perceived the possibilities for increasing their own power and wealth. Commercial companies were chartered and financed, with military and naval expeditions frequently sent out after them to ensure political control of overseas territories" (Cohen 1973).

The economic strategy underlying the relationship between colonies and colonizers during this era of "classical imperialism" is known as **mercantilism:** an economic philosophy advocating government regulation of economic life to increase state power and security. European rulers believed that power flowed from the possession of national wealth measured in terms of gold and silver, and that developing mining and industry to attain a favorable balance of trade (exporting more than they imported) was the best way to accumulate the desired bullion. "Colonies were desirable in this respect because they afforded an opportunity to shut out commercial competition; they guaranteed exclusive

mercantilism
a government regulatory trade strategy for accumulating state wealth and power by encouraging exports and discouraging imports (see p. 248).

New States Even after the decolonization process runs its complete course, more new countries can be expected because many existing states are fragmenting. When World War I broke out, only sixty-two independent countries existed; at the beginning of the twenty-first century there were more than two hundred. Many new sovereign states are very small. Pictured here is the "micro" state of Nauru, which has a president, Supreme Court, and the full apparatus of government to rule its tiny population. Half the globe's countries have populations smaller than the U.S. state of Massachusetts.

access to untapped markets and sources of cheap materials (as well as, in some instances, direct sources of the precious metals themselves). Each state was determined to monopolize as many of these overseas mercantile opportunities as possible" (Cohen 1973). To maximize national power and wealth, states saw the conquest of foreign territory as a natural byproduct of active government management of the economy.

By the end of the eighteenth century the European powers had spread themselves, although thinly, throughout virtually the entire world, but the colonial empires they had built now began to crumble. Britain's thirteen North American colonies declared their independence in 1776, and most of Spain's possessions in South America won their freedom in the early nineteenth century. Nearly one hundred colonial relationships worldwide were terminated in the half-century ending in 1825 (Bergesen and Schoenberg 1980, 236).

As Europe's colonial empires dissolved, belief in the mercantilist philosophy also waned. As the Scottish political economist Adam Smith argued in his 1776 treatise, *The Wealth of Nations,* national wealth grew not through the accumulation of precious metals but rather from the capital and goods they could buy. Smith's ideas about the benefits of the "invisible hand" of the unregulated domestic and international marketplace laid much of the intellectual foundation for **classical liberal economic theory.** Following the thinking of Smith and other liberal free-trade theorists, faith in the precepts of **laissez-faire economics** (min-

■ **classical liberal economic theory**
a body of thought based on Adam Smith's ideas about the forces of supply and demand in the marketplace, emphasizing the benefits of minimal government regulation of the economy and trade.

■ **laissez-faire economics**
the philosophical principle of free markets with little governmental regulation (see p. 251).

imal government interference in the market) gained widespread acceptance (see also Chapter 8). European powers continued to hold numerous colonies, but the prevailing sentiment was now more anti- than pro-imperial.

The Second Wave of European Imperialism

Beginning in the 1870s and extending until the outbreak of World War I, a second wave of imperialism washed over the world as Europe, joined later by the United States and Japan, aggressively colonized new territories. The portion of the globe that Europeans controlled was one-third in 1800, two-thirds by 1878, and four-fifths by 1914 (Fieldhouse 1973, 3). As illustrated in Map 5.3, "in the last twenty years of the nineteenth century Europeans conquered 85 percent of Africa in a uniquely grandiose act of theft" (Goldstein 1999, 16). Africa fell under the control of seven European powers: Belgium, Britain, France, Germany, Italy, Portugal, and Spain. In all of the Far East and the Pacific, only China, Japan, and Siam (Thailand) remained outside the direct control of Europe or the United States. China, too, was divided into **spheres of influence** by the foreign great powers which carved China into separate zones of commerce they could individually control and exploit for profit, and Japan itself also imperialistically occupied Korea and Formosa (Taiwan). Elsewhere, the United States expanded across its continent, acquired Puerto Rico and the Philippines in the 1898 Spanish-American War, extended its colonial reach westward to Hawaii, leased the Panama Canal Zone "in perpetuity" from the new state of Panama (an American creation), and exercised considerable control over several Caribbean islands, notably Cuba. The preeminent imperial power, Great Britain, in a single generation expanded its empire to engulf the entire world. By 1900 the British Empire covered one-fifth of the earth's land area and comprised perhaps one-fourth of its population (Cohen 1973, 30). As British imperialists were proud to proclaim, it was an empire on which the sun never set.

■ **sphere of influence** the area dominated by a great power (see p. 101).

In contrast with classical imperialism, extraordinary competition among the imperial powers marked late-nineteenth-century "new imperialism." The European-centered industrial revolution provided the military might and economic means to subjugate foreign territories, which became important symbols of national power and prestige. In the process, the local inhabitants of the conquered lands were often ruthlessly suppressed.

> The imperial powers typically pursued their various interests overseas in a blatantly aggressive fashion. Bloody, one-sided wars with local inhabitants of contested territories were commonplace; "sporting wars," [Prussian leader Otto von] Bismarck once called them. The powers themselves rarely came into direct military conflict, but competition among them was keen, and they were perpetually involved in various diplomatic crises. In contrast to the preceding years of comparative political calm, the period after 1870 was one of unaccustomed hostility and tension. (Cohen 1973, 30)

Having abandoned their earlier acquired empires, why did most of the great powers—and those that aspired to great-power status—engage in this expensive and often vicious competition to control other peoples and territories? What explains the new imperialism? The answers are rooted in economics and politics.

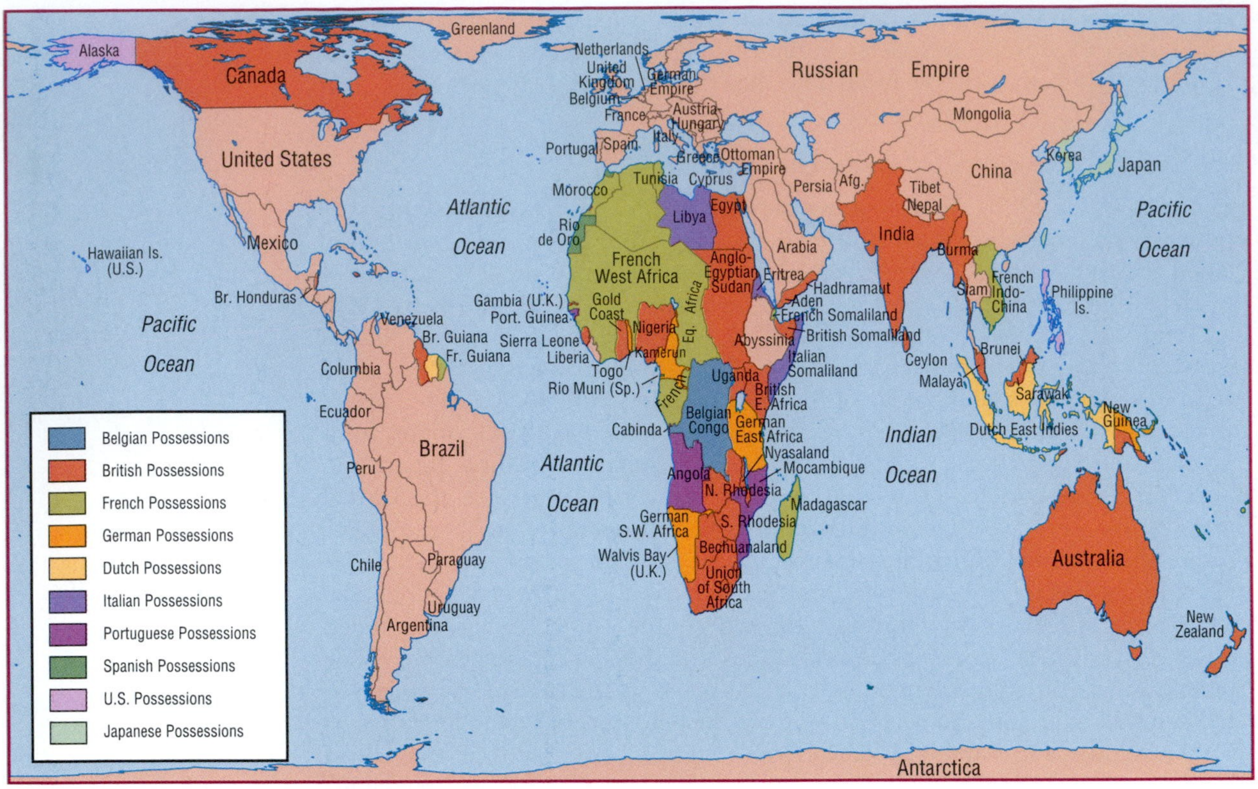

MAP 5.3
Global Imperialism, 1914
The ten major imperial powers competed for colonies throughout the globe, and on the eve of World War I their combined territories covered much of the world.

■ **communism**
an ideology maintaining that if society is organized so that every person produces according to his or her ability and consumes according to his or her needs, a community without class distinctions will emerge and sovereign states will no longer be needed.

■ **Marxism-Leninism**
communist theory as derived from the writings of Karl Marx, Vladimir I. Lenin, and their successors, which criticizes capitalism as a cause of class struggle, the exploitation of workers, colonialism, and war.

Economic Explanations for the New Imperialism. With the Industrial Revolution, capitalism grew, emphasizing the free market, private ownership of the means of production, and the accumulation of wealth. Theorists following Karl Marx, who called themselves adherents of **communism,** saw imperialism's aggressive competition as caused by capitalists' need for profitable overseas outlets for their surplus ("finance") capital. One of them was the Soviet leader Vladimir I. Lenin, who made distinctive contributions to the communist thinking later described as **Marxism-Leninism.**

In his famous 1916 monograph *Imperialism, The Highest Stage of Capitalism,* Lenin argued that military expansion abroad was produced by the "monopoly stage of capitalism." Lenin concluded that the only way to end imperialism was to abolish capitalism. Classical or liberal economists, on the other hand, regarded the new imperialism not as a product of capitalism as such but rather as "a response to certain maladjustments within the contemporary capitalist system which, given the proper will, could be corrected" (Cohen 1973). What the two perspectives shared was the belief that economics explained the new imperialism: "The fundamental problem was the presumed material needs of advanced capitalist societies—the need for cheap raw materi-

Karl Marx Challenges Imperialism Pictured on the left is the German philosopher Karl Marx (1818–1883), whose revolutionary economic theory argued that "the history of all hitherto existing society is the history of class struggle." Imperial conquest of colonial peoples could only be prevented, Marx warned, by humanity's shift from a capitalist to a socialist economy and society. Pictured on the right is the kind of imperialistic activity that provoked his wrath: ruthless, aggressive, and bent on acquiring property for profit, Britain's nineteenth-century imperial forces marched into battle to seize foreign territory.

als to feed their growing industrial complexes, for additional markets to consume their rising levels of production, and for investment outlets to absorb their rapidly accumulating capital" (Cohen 1973). Thus, from both the Marxist and classical liberal perspectives, the material needs of capitalist societies explained their imperial drive.

World-system analyses, like Marxist theories, also embrace an economic explanation. **World-system theory** postulates that a single capitalist world economy emerged during the "long 16th century" from 1450 to 1640, which created a world division of labor separating "core" (industrial) areas from those in the globe's (nonindustrial) "periphery" (Wallerstein 1974a, 1974b, 1980, 1988). Northwest Europe first emerged as the core. As the Industrial Revolution proceeded, the core states exchanged manufactured goods for raw agricultural and mineral materials secured at bargain prices by taking advantage of willing sellers and cheap labor in the colonial territories at the periphery. This perspective emphasized colonization as the principal method for imperial control over foreign lands (Boswell 1989).

■ **world-system theory** a theory that claims the perpetual and widening inequity among states is explained by capitalism's international division of labor and production, which over time allows the wealthy core countries to become richer while the peripheral states supplying raw materials and cheap labor become poorer.

World-system theory interprets the new imperialism of the late eighteenth century quite differently from the previous colonial period. "The earliest colonies were usually coastal trading posts for merchants involved in long-distance preciosity exchange with the contact periphery, such as the spice trade. Following rivers upstream, these were later superseded by settler colonies involved in the production of necessities, primarily mining and cash-crop agriculture using coerced labor." In contrast, after 1870, colonies effectively became occupation zones in which a small number of European sojourners coerced an indigenous population into production for the global economy (Boswell 1989).

Political Explanations for the New Imperialism. Political factors also explain the new imperialism. In his influential 1902 book, *Imperialism,* J. A. Hobson argued that the jockeying for power and prestige between competitive empires had always characterized the great powers' behavior in the European balance-of-power system, and that imperialism through overseas expansion was simply an extension of this inter-European competition for dominance.

By the 1800s Britain emerged from Europe's perpetual conflict as the world's leading power. It became the chief promoter of free international trade because a system with few legal barriers to exports and imports also promoted disproportionate economic growth in the core relative to the periphery (McGowan 1981). By 1870, however, Britain's superiority was on the wane. Germany emerged as a powerful industrial state, as did the United States. Understandably, Britain tried to protect its privileged position in the international division of labor in the face of growing competition from the newly emerging core states. Its efforts to maintain the status quo help to explain the second wave of imperial expansion—especially in Africa, whose partition served the imperial powers at the expense of local populations. As Africa's tragic fate illustrates, Europe's colonies were integrated into the world political economy solely for the purpose of serving the interests of the colonial powers. "The political victors controlled investment and trade, regulated currency and production, and manipulated labor, thus establishing structures of economic dependency in their colonies which would endure far longer than their actual political authority" (Spero and Hart 1997).

The British-sponsored laissez-faire system of free trade promoted rapid economic growth in a number of colonial territories, but economic development elsewhere proceeded even more rapidly. Western Europe, North America, Australia, and New Zealand were able to complete their industrial revolutions during this period and to advance as industrial societies. Thus the gap between the world's rich and poor countries began to widen.

Colonialism and Self-Determination in the Interwar Period

■ **self-determination** the doctrine that asserts nationalities have the right to determine what political authority will represent and rule them (see p. 639).

The climate of opinion turned decidedly anti-imperial when the 1917 Versailles peace settlement that ended World War I embraced the principle of national **self-determination** advocated by U.S. President Woodrow Wilson. Self-determination meant that indigenous nationalities would have the right to decide which authority would represent and rule them. Wilson and others who shared his liberal convictions believed that freedom of choice would lead to the creation of states and governments content with their territorial boundaries and therefore less inclined to make war. In practice, however, the attempt to redraw states' borders to separate nationality groups was applied almost exclusively to war-torn Europe, where six new states were created from the territory of the former Austro-Hungarian Empire (Austria, Czechoslovakia, Hungary, Poland, Romania, and the ethnically divided Yugoslavia). Other territorial adjustments were also made in Europe, but the proposition that self-determination should be extended to Europe's overseas empires did not receive serious support.

Still, the colonial territories of the powers defeated in World War I were not simply parceled out among the victorious allies, as had typically happened in the past. Instead, the territories controlled by Germany and the Ottoman Empire were transferred under League of Nations auspices to countries that would govern them as "mandates" pending their eventual self-rule. In the Middle East, France assumed the mandate for Syria, and Britain assumed it for Iraq, Transjordan, and Palestine. In Africa, most of the German colony of Tanganyika went to Britain; the West African colonies of Cameroon and Togoland were divided between Britain and France; and the Union of South Africa gained responsibility for the mandate governing German South-West Africa. In the Pacific area, Australia, New Zealand, and Japan acquired jurisdiction over the former German colonies.

Many of these territorial decisions gave rise to political conflicts during the next half-century or more. The decisions relating to the Middle East and Africa were especially crucial, as the League of Nations called for the eventual creation of a Jewish national homeland in Palestine and arranged for the transfer of control over South-West Africa (now called Namibia) to what would become the white minority regime of South Africa.

The principle implicit in the League of Nations mandate system gave birth to the idea that "colonies were a trust rather than simply a property to be exploited and treated as if its peoples had no rights of their own" (Easton 1964). This set an important precedent for the negotiations after World War II, when territories of the defeated powers placed under the United Nations (UN) trusteeship system were not absorbed by others but were promised eventual self-rule.

The End of Empire

Imperialism threatened the world again in the 1930s and early 1940s, as Germany, Japan, and Italy sought to expand their political control in Europe, Asia, and Africa. With their defeat in World War II, the threat of regional empire building receded and support for self-determination gained momentum. The decolonization process accelerated in 1947, when the British relinquished political control of the Indian subcontinent and India and Pakistan joined the international community as sovereign members. War eventually erupted between the new states as each sought to gain control over disputed territory in Kashmir. It ignited twice more, in 1965 and again in 1971, when East Pakistan broke away from West Pakistan to form the new state of Bangladesh. Violence also broke out in Indochina and Algeria in the 1950s and early 1960s as the French sought to regain control over colonial territories they had held before World War II. Similarly, bloodshed followed closely on the heels of independence in the Congo when the Belgians granted their African colony independence in 1960, and it dogged the unsuccessful efforts of Portugal to battle the winds of decolonization that swept over Africa as the 1960s wore on.

Despite these political convulsions, decolonization for the most part was not only extraordinarily rapid but also remarkably peaceful. This may be explained by World War II having sapped the economic and military vitality of many of the colonial powers. World-system analysts contend that a growing appreciation of the costs of empire also eroded support for colonial empires (Strang 1990, 1991). Regardless of the underlying cause, colonialism became less acceptable in a world increasingly dominated by rivalry between East and West. The Cold War competition for political allies and the fear of large-scale warfare gave the superpowers incentives to lobby jointly for the liberation of overseas empires. Decolonization "triumphed," as Inis Claude (1967) explains, "largely because the West [gave] priority to the containment of communism over the perpetuation of colonialism."

The UN also contributed to the "collective delegitimization" of colonialism. With colonialism already in retreat, in 1960, Global South states took advantage of their growing numbers in the UN General Assembly to secure passage of the historic Declaration on the Granting of Independence to Colonial Countries and Peoples. "The General Assembly proclaimed that the subjection of any people to alien domination was a denial of fundamental human rights, contrary to the UN Charter, and an impediment to world peace and that all subject peoples had a right to immediate and complete independence. No country cast a vote against this anticolonial manifesto. . . . It was an ideological triumph" (Riggs and Plano 1994).

As the old order crumbled—and as the leaders in the newly emancipated territories discovered that freedom did not translate automatically into autonomy, economic independence, and domestic prosperity—the conflict between the rich Global North and the emerging states of the Global South began. And it continues today. While some see future international struggle as centered on a **"clash of civilizations"** (Huntington 1996), others argue that "'civilization clash' is not so much over Jesus Christ, Confucius, or the Prophet Muhammad as it is over the unequal distribution of world power, wealth, and influence, and the perceived historical lack of respect accorded to small states and peoples by larger ones" (Fuller 1995). Whatever the major divisions in an otherwise integrating international community, one entrenched and dangerous trend will remain a cause of friction:

■ **clash of civilizations** Samuel Huntington's controversial thesis that in the twenty-first century the globe's major civilizations will conflict with one another, leading to anarchy and warfare similar to that resulting from conflicts between states over the past five hundred years.

> At the global level, it seems that the old saw is still correct: the rich get richer and the poor get children. The ratio of average income of the richest country in the world to that of the poorest has risen from about 9 to 1 at the end of the nineteenth century to at least 60 to 1 today. That is, the average family in the United States is 60 times richer than the average family in Ethiopia. Since 1950, the portion of the world's population living in poor countries grew by about 250 percent, while in rich countries the population increased by less than 50 percent. (Birdsall 2001, 19; see also Baker and Nordin 1999, 6, for another calculation that puts the rich-poor ratio at 150 to 1)

NORTH AND SOUTH TODAY: WORLDS APART

The Global South is sometimes described today as a "zone of turmoil" in large measure because, in contrast with the Global North where "peace, wealth, and democracy" prevail, most of the world's people live amidst "poverty, war, tyranny, and anarchy" (Singer and Wildavsky 1993). A particularly noteworthy difference is that the states in the Global North are democratic and rarely fight one another, whereas in the Global South, violent conflict remains rife both within and among many states.

Democracy has spread rapidly and widely since the 1980s, becoming the preferred mode of governance throughout much of the Global South. There remain many exceptions, such as China, Cuba, and Vietnam, and some of the Global South's recent additions to the liberal democratic community have governments whose commitment to regular elections and human rights are fragile. Furthermore, many Global South countries lack well-developed domestic market economies based on entrepreneurship and private enterprise. Nonetheless, because the Global North's history suggests that free markets spawn the large middle class that is a precondition for free governments (Burkhart and Lewis-Beck 1994), the continuing expansion of Global South market economies under capitalism appears likely to hasten democratization, although the continued enlargement of the liberal democratic community is not guaranteed.

Differences in technological capabilities also separate North and South. Typically, Global South countries have been unable to evolve an indigenous technology appropriate to their own resources and have been dependent on powerful Global North multinational corporations (MNCs) (see Chapter 8) to transfer technical know-how. This means that research and development expenditures are directed toward solutions of the Global North's problems, with technological advances seldom meeting the needs of the Global South (Singer and Ansari 1988). And in the Information Age, the most striking developments are again taking place in the Global North. Information technology has not been distributed equally geographically: the highest density of computer connections to the Internet is in the Global North, and the lowest is in Africa south of the Sahara, among the poorest regions of the world with 9 percent of the world's population but just 0.1 percent of the world's Internet connections (Ignatius 1999, 8; see also Chapter 9).

The fact that four-fifths of the world's population is poor is both a reflection and cause of these unequally distributed resources. To measure the disparities, the World Bank differentiates the "low-income" and "middle-income" economies in **developing countries**, whose **gross national product (GNP)** in 1998 averaged less than $785 annually per person, from the "high-income" Global North **developed countries** above this level. Among the developing countries, wide variations in economic performance (growth and inflation rates, debt burdens, export prices, and the availability of oil and other fuels, for example) and internal circumstances are evident, so it is common to further divide them by income levels. Map 5.4 estimates the geographic distribution of the world's economies measured by GNP per capita. While inspecting this distribution, keep in mind that although GNP per capita is the most widely used measure of countries' economic performance, it can be misleading as a measure of individuals' economic well-being (see Controversy: How Should National and Personal Wealth Be Measured? on page 142). Still, the portrayal reflects an undeniable fact of contemporary international realities: income is distributed very unevenly.

Numbers paint pictures and tell stories, and the data on the division between Global North and Global South point to brutal disparities and inequalities. When we compare the differences on some key indicators differentiating the low- and the middle-income developing economies from the high-income countries at the peak stage of development, we discover huge gaps (see Table 5.1).

■ **developing countries** a category used by the World bank to designate those countries with a GNP per capita (in 1998) equal to or below $785 annually.

■ **gross national product (GNP)** a measure of the production of goods and services within a given time period, which is used to delimit the geographic scope of production. GNP measures production by a state's citizens or companies, regardless of where the production occurs. An alternative measure is gross domestic product (GDP), which measures production occurring within the territory of a state, regardless of the national identity of the producers.

■ **developed countries** a category used by the World Bank to designate those countries with a GNP per capita (in 1998) above $785 annually.

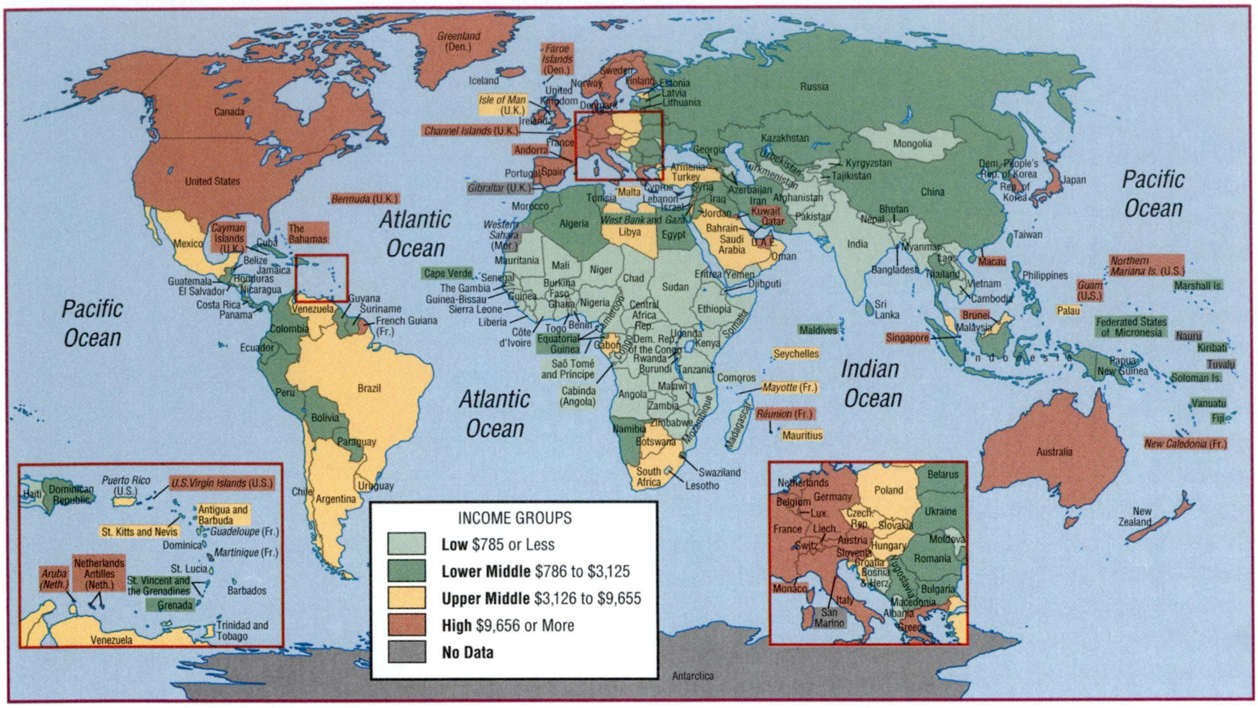

MAP 5.4
The Global Income Gap: The Geographic Distribution of Gross National Product (GNP) per Capita

The gap between wealthy and impoverished people is growing, both between and within countries, as the richest countries in the Global North have "soared to new economic heights while at least a billion people in the [Global South's] developing countries have gotten poorer" (Francis 1999), and as the difference in wealth between the top and bottom 20 percent of the world's population rose in 1998 to 74 to 1 (Baker and Nordin 1999, 6).

SOURCE: World Bank (1999b), 189.

■ **least developed of the less developed countries (LLDCs)**
the most impoverished nations in the Global South.

■ **barter**
the exchange of one good for another rather than the use of currency to buy and sell items.

This picture darkens even more when focus is shifted to the plight of the poorest in the "low-income" developing countries. More than two billion people (one-third of humanity) live in the sixty-one countries at the bottom of the global hierarchy, sometimes called by the International Monetary Fund the **least developed of the less developed countries (LLDCs),** where the average annual GNP per person is only about one U.S. dollar per day and where typically **barter** of one agricultural good for another rather than money is used for economic transactions. These countries are not "emerging" or "reemerging" to break the chains of their desperation; they are falling behind their counterparts in the developing world. The LLDCs provide an average annual income of $785 or less on which a person is expected to survive, but income inequalities within these countries are so severe that many have almost no real income (see Map 5.5).

The low-income LLDCs are not participants in the global market: they account for only 0.2 percent of world trade, and their exports are largely confined to inexpensive (nonfuel) primary products, including foodstuffs (e.g.,

TABLE 5.1

Two Worlds of Development

Characteristic	*Developing Global South*	*Developed Global North*
Number of Countries	157	50
Population (millions)	5,003	925
Land area (thousands of sq. km)	99,158	30,971
GNP ($ billions)	$6,123	$23,802
GNP per capita	$1,250	$25,700
GNP @ Purchasing Power Parity (PPP)	$15,860	$21,010
Life Expectancy at Birth (females)	67	81
Foreign Direct Investment ($ millions)	$118,774	$195,922
Exports	$1,597,906	$5,091,734
Percent of Roads Paved	24%	92%
Television Sets per 1,000 People	117	611

Where people live in the world influences how they live. As this information shows, life for people living in the developed countries of the Global North is generally much more comfortable than it is for people living in the Global South, and the future is brighter for the wealthy than for the poor.

SOURCE: World Bank (1999b), 190–231.

cocoa, coffee, and tea), minerals (e.g., copper), hides, and timber. Because these low-income countries consume most of what they produce, theirs is typically a "subsistence economy," and the prospects for change are dim because most developing countries have been bypassed by direct foreign investment and ignored by foreign aid donors (World Bank 1999).

High rates of population growth between 1990 and 1997 (2.1 percent, exceeding the average worldwide rate of 1.7 percent) contribute to the widespread poverty, because it will take only twenty-five years for the LLDCs' population to double, compared with two and a half centuries for the Global North. LLDCs' economic growth rates in the recent past have averaged less than 0.1 percent per year. Growth rates elsewhere have almost uniformly been higher. Thus the rich minority gets richer while the poorest of the poor have remained stagnant.

Life for people in the low-income LLDCs has changed little from that of their ancestors. Life expectancy at birth averages only fifty-eight years, compared with eighty-one years in the Global North. Infant mortality rates are among the highest in the world. Less than half of the adult population is literate, a proportion even lower among women. And although industrialization has recently increased, agriculture remains the dominant form of productive activity. Similarly, four out of every five people live in rural areas even as the world is undergoing rapid urbanization (World Bank 1999).

By contemporary standards, then, poverty and despair are everyday experiences for those on the bottom tier of the Global South. The facts speak for themselves: "Among the 4.4 billion people in developing countries around the world, three-fifths live in communities lacking basic sanitation; one-third go without safe drinking water; one-quarter lack adequate housing; one-fifth are undernourished; and 1.3 billion live on less than $1 a day. Nearly one-third of the people in the poorest countries, mostly in Sub-Saharan Africa, can expect to die by age 40" (Speth 1999a, 6).

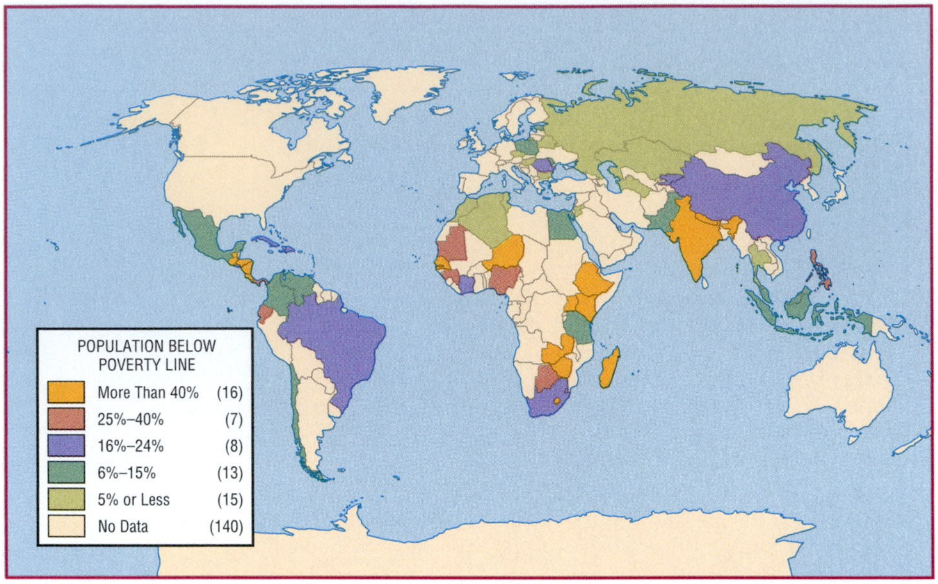

MAP 5.5
A Sea of Despair: The Location of Extreme Poverty in the World

Extreme poverty does know boundaries: The least fortunate and most impoverished people in the world, earning less than $1 per day, live primarily in the least developed countries of the Global South, although income inequality varies enormously among developing countries. For example, "In Eastern Europe and the former Soviet Union, incomes have become sharply less equal in recent years, [and] countries as diverse as Brazil, Bangladesh, China and Malaysia have seen inequality increase over the past decade" (*Economist,* June 12, 1999, 98).

SOURCE: *Development Indicators,* May 5, 1998; <http://www.oecd.org/dac/Indicators/htm/map1.htr>.

THE GLOBAL SOUTH'S PROSPECTS

Despite wide differences, a daunting scale of poverty, misery, and marginalization is evident across the Global South, from which only a fraction of its countries have begun to escape. For many people living there, the future is bleak, and the opportunities and choices most basic to freedom from fear and poverty are unavailable. As a group the Global South developing countries are thus experiencing quite different rates of development than the Global North; the fortunes of some are plummeting while others pursuing different paths and strategies are emerging and are poised to enter the ranks of the Global North developed countries. Nonetheless, global trends reveal clearly that in the last twenty years more than sixty countries are worse off than they were and are falling even further behind the levels achieved by the countries in the Global North (Miller 1999). What are we to expect about prospects from a situation in which, in 1995, 161 countries had GNPs less than the amount spent worldwide at Wal-Mart (UNDP 1997, 3; *Harper's,* October 1996, 13)? Simply put, the gap between rich and poor is increasing:

> In the past 15 years, per capita income has declined in more than 100 countries and individual consumption has dropped by about one percent annually in more than 60. The number of poor people will increase sharply . . . to more than 100 million from 40 million, if current trends continue, according to World Bank estimates. The number of Indonesians living on less than $1 a day will jump to 34 million in 1999 from 13 million in 1997. . . . Africa's growth for 1998, once expected to exceed 4 percent, has in fact been closer to 2.2 percent. In Latin America, growth forecasts have been scaled down from 5.3 percent before the global financial crisis to 2.6 percent for 1999. (Speth 1999a, 6)

For a substantial portion of humanity, suffering is an everyday experience, without sufficient food, shelter, sanitation, safe water, or health care. Severely malnourished and often illiterate, many live in ecologically poisoned areas in which they will die at an early age unless they manage to join the millions of refugees who escape their impoverished homelands each year.

However, this situation is not inevitable. Global trends do point to the potential for some developing countries to escape such miserable conditions. The poverty of the LLDCs contrasts starkly with the comparative wealth of the Global South states that have fossil fuels to consume and export. The sixteen developing-country exporters of oil and other fuels, and especially the twelve members of the Organization of Petroleum Exporting Countries (OPEC), have escaped the LLDCs' grim fate. Although many fall into the lower-middle or upper-middle income groups, some—notably OPEC members Kuwait, Qatar, and the United Arab Emirates—have risen to the high-income group, with standards of living rivaling those of Global North countries. Another category of Global South countries that inspires hope are the emerging or "middle-income" economies, or the so-called **newly industrialized economies (NIEs)** particularly in Asia, that have experienced even greater success than the oil-exporting countries. Their achievement lies in moving beyond the export of primary products—characteristic of both the LLDCs and the oil exporters—to the export of manufactured goods. Today the NIEs are among the largest exporters of manufactured goods and the most prosperous members of the Global South, and have climbed from the periphery into the **semiperiphery.** The so-called **Asian Tigers**—South Korea, Singapore, Taiwan, and Hong Kong prior to its 1997 reunification with China—have taken extraordinary advantage of comparatively low wage rates to aggressively promote export-led economic growth. Pursuing strategies similar to the imperial powers of the past, the governments' neomercantilist practices include protecting infant industries from foreign competition and providing financial incentives for manufacturing industries. Spectacular economic growth virtually unparalleled elsewhere has followed, and by 1996 the NIEs commanded over 10 percent of world trade and 3.4 percent of world output (IMF 1997, 120). With their population growth generally in check, the Asian Tigers have joined the ranks of the world's wealthiest states, and still other "new tigers" such as India are emerging, as exports and foreign investment have stimulated a booming economy (see Strasser and Mazumdar 1999). Likewise, some of the **countries in transition,** the twenty-eight remnants of the former Second World in Central and Eastern Europe, are successfully engineering economic reforms and are harnessing their citizens' skills to chart a promising future.

■ **newly industrialized economies (NIEs)**
the most prosperous members of the Global South, which have become important exporters of manufactured goods as well as important markets for the major industrialized countries that export capital goods (see p. 311).

■ **semiperiphery**
to world-system theorists, countries midway between the rich "core" or center and the poor "periphery" in the global hierarchy, at which foreign investments are targeted when labor wages and production costs become too high in the prosperous core regions.

■ **Asian Tigers**
the four Asian NIEs that experienced far greater rates of economic growth during the 1980s than the more advanced industrial societies of the Global North.

■ **countries in transition**
the remnant states of the former communist countries (Second World) in Central and Eastern Europe that are undertaking economic reforms to introduce capitalism.

CONTROVERSY

How Should National and Personal Wealth Be Measured?

GNP per Capita versus "Purchasing Power Parity"

It is difficult to estimate whether you are better or worse off than people living in other countries. A continuing issue is how to reach conclusions about your income and what it means in other countries, as well as how your country as a whole compares with other states.

The most widely used international yardstick of national wealth is gross national product (GNP) per capita. Much of this measure's popularity stems from its availability. GNP is the total of all goods and services produced by a country's economy in a given year—but that's all it is. The measure does not directly address how the average consumer in a country is faring. GNP per capita is a good indicator for comparing large gaps in national wealth among countries. An African country with only $300 GNP per capita, for example, is obviously worse off than an industrialized country with a far higher value. But the measure's usefulness ends there.

GNP per capita is often mislabeled as "per capita income," suggesting that it is the average money income for a person in a country. This mislabeling implies that GNP per capita can be used as a type of standard-of-living measure, but it does not measure living standards in a meaningful way. For example, 1997 GNP per capita in Switzerland was $44,320 and in Canada only $19,280—quite a difference. Comparing the value of money in Switzerland with its worth in Canada suggests that the average person in Switzerland was more than twice as well off as the average Canadian. But can the average Swiss citizen actually buy two times more goods and services of the same quantity and quality than the average Canadian? Not necessarily. It depends on how much goods cost in Canada versus Switzerland. If a pair of shoes costs $50 in Canada, but the same pair of shoes costs $100 in Switzerland, then Canadians can enjoy the same product even though they make less money per capita.

Economists have worked for years to develop another internationally comparable measure of living standards that will account for the different costs of living in different countries. The model they developed is called **purchasing power parity (PPP).** Although based on complex econometric calculations, simply put, PPP compares the cost of goods given the purchasing power of each country's currency to what the same things might cost in the United States. It attempts to determine what level of goods and services people living in different regions can enjoy, regardless of the absolute value of their per capita GNP.

One major caveat is that PPP does not take into account the quality of such goods. The quality of a Russian Lada automobile compared with a Nissan Sentra or Ford Taurus is an obvious example. The comparative size of apartments in Europe with those in the United States is another. Likewise, the size of each country's economy in comparison with the others can look very different if PPP is used instead of GNP. "Once differences in the local purchasing power of currencies are taken into account, China's economy looks much bigger. In 1997 China's GNP, measured at purchasing power parity (PPP) was $3.8 trillion. . . . This makes it the second-biggest economy in the world, ahead of Japan's $3.1 trillion, but roughly half America's GNP of $7.8 trillion. Most emerging market economies look relatively larger when measured on a PPP basis, because their exchange rates tend to be undervalued relative to the dollar. Indeed, seven of the world's 15 biggest economies are in the emerging world" (*Economist,* May 8, 1999, 110, citing data from the World Bank).

emerging markets the Global South states whose domestic political economies have grown rapidly as a result of liberal economic reforms and foreign investment.

Thus, remarkable accomplishments have been made within some of the Global South's regions and countries, reducing the disparity between poor and rich, women and men, rural and urban. Coexisting with continuing poverty are pockets of impressive growth. Indeed, the term **emerging markets** has arisen to identify this growing subset of countries that have started to shed the remnants of perpetual despair because their domestic political economies are particularly ripe for development.

While neither GNP nor PPP provides a perfect picture of a country's standard of living, these measures give an interesting snapshot of economic well-being across countries. GNP and PPP provide some surprisingly different conclusions, as the figures comparing some selected Global North and Global South countries below illustrates. Which do you think is the better measure?

Comparison of GNP per Capita and Purchasing Power Parity, Selected Countries

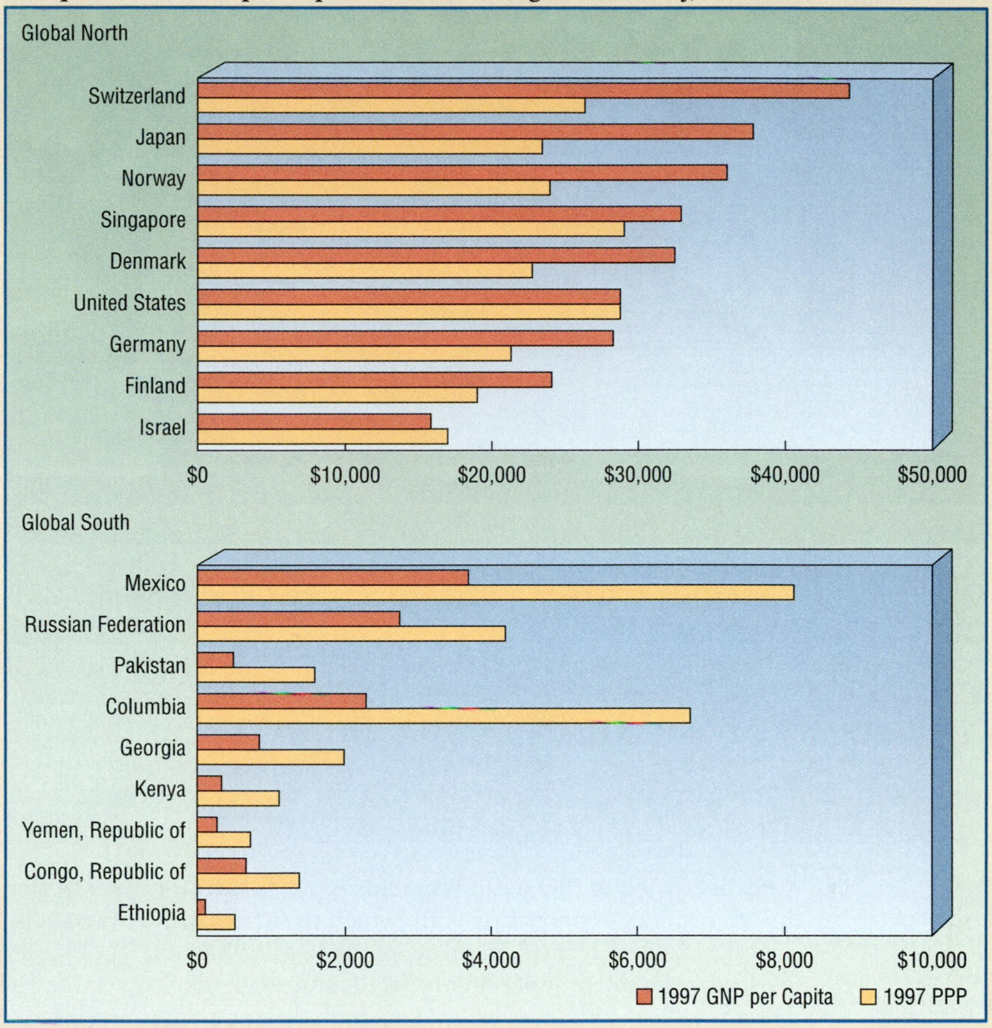

Note: The U.S. dollar is used as the standard.
SOURCE: World Bank (1999b), 190–191.

Neither geography nor current levels of economic performance define the emerging markets with great potential. What distinguishes these countries on the verge of economic revolution is that their governments and local elites have stabilized the value of their currencies, brought inflation under control, and privatized the businesses once owned by the government. In addition, they have become receptive to foreign investment, an attitude that represents a fundamental shift in thinking about the causes of and cures for underdevelopment once prevalent throughout the Global South, and

purchasing power parity (PPP) an index that calculates the true rate of exchange among currencies when parity (when what can be purchased is the same) is achieved; the index determines what can be bought with a unit of each currency.

Low Wages and Higher Trade Given a competitive advantage by the availability of a large and compliant workforce used to long hours, tedious work, and low pay, newly industrialized economies in Asia have been able to promote aggressive export marketing strategies that capitalize on low manufacturing costs.

inspires hope that advances can be engineered to erase the conditions of underdevelopment.

The possibilities for progress suggested by this mixed record of hope and unspeakable despair beg the question of why development has been so rare and recent.

THEORETICAL EXPLANATIONS OF UNDERDEVELOPMENT

■ **development**
the processes through which a country increases its capacity to meet its citizens' basic human needs and raise their standard of living.

Our discussion to this point implicitly equates **development** with a state's ability "to produce economic wealth, which in turn transforms society from a subsistence- or agricultural-based economy to one where most of society's wealth is derived from the production of manufactured goods and services" (Balaam and Veseth 1996). Urban populations, high literacy rates, well-fed people, and economies driven increasingly by the service sector mark today's developed economies. Why has the Global South lagged so far behind the Global North in its comparative level of well-being and development? And why have the development experiences even within the Global South differed so widely?

The diversity evident in the Global South invites the conclusion that underdevelopment is explained by a combination of factors within developing countries and in their relationships with the Global North. Some theorists explain the underdevelopment of most developing economies alongside the escape of others by looking primarily at differences between Global South states. Other theorists focus on the position of developing countries in the global political economy. We shall briefly discuss three variants on these interpretations, each of which has influenced policy thinking during the past half-century: classical economic development theory, structuralist theories of dominance and dependence, and neoclassical theory.

Classical Economic Development Theory

Based on the classical Western definition of development as increasing increments of per capita GNP, liberal economic development theories of **modernization** first emerged in the early post–World War II era. They argued that the major barriers to development were posed by the Global South countries' own internal characteristics. To overcome these barriers, most classical theorists recommended that the wealthy countries supply various "missing components" of development, such as investment capital through foreign aid or private foreign direct investment (Todaro 2000).

■ **modernization** a view of development popular in the Global North's liberal democracies that argues that wealth is created through efficient production, free enterprise, and free trade, and that countries' relative ability to create wealth depends on technological innovation and education more than on natural endowments such as climate and resources.

Once sufficient capital was accumulated to promote economic growth, these liberal theorists predicted that its benefits would eventually "trickle down" to broad segments of society. In this way, everyone, not just a privileged few, would enjoy the benefits of rising affluence. Walt W. Rostow, an economic historian and U.S. policymaker, formalized this theory in his influential book *The Stages of Economic Growth* (1960). He predicted that traditional societies beginning the path to development would inevitably pass through various stages by means of the free market and would eventually "take off" to become similar to the mass-consumption societies of the capitalist Global North. Even though the rich are likely to get richer, it was argued, as incomes in the world as a whole grow, the odds increase that a preindustrialized economy will grow faster and eventually reduce the gap between it and richer countries. That prognosis and the policies on which it was based were ultimately rejected by the impoverished Global South, which did not accept the classical liberal argument that the Global North became prosperous and assumed control of global economic power because their open societies concentrated on work, invention, skill, and investment in schools and tools to make them winners in the global marketplace (see Landes 1998; Thurow 1999). Economists in the Global South were persuaded by a rival interpretation of why some countries are so rich and the rest are so poor—the structural theories that attribute the Global South's plight to the links between developing countries and the global political economy.

Structural Theories

Two prongs of structuralism merit attention, as both locate the causes and potential cures of most developing countries' persistent underdevelopment in their positions of relative dominance and dependence in the global hierarchy. The first is dependency theory and its liberal variant, called "dualism." The second, which we have already introduced, is world-system theory.

■ **dependency theory** a theory that less developed countries are exploited because global capitalism makes them dependent on the rich countries, which create exploitative rules for trade and production.

Dependency Theory and Dualism. **Dependency theory** builds on Lenin's theory of imperialism, but goes beyond it to account for changes that have occurred since Lenin first wrote his Marxist interpretation of capitalism as a cause of inequality and domination. Its central proposition is that the relationship between the advanced capitalist societies at the core of the world political economy and the developing countries at the periphery is exploitative, and that the underdevelopment of the Global South has been caused by world capitalism's impact: the division of the globe into two halves, one modern and the other backward.

Although the dependency theory literature is vast and arouses many controversies (see Caporaso and Levine 1992; Packenham 1992), dependency theorists all reject Rostow's stages-of-growth thesis, arguing that underdevelopment "is not a stalled stage of linear development, a question of precapitalism, retarded or backward development, but rather a [product of the less developed countries'] structural position in a hierarchical world division of labor" (Shannon 1989). In short, the Global South's underdevelopment results from its subordinate position in a world political economy dominated by capitalistic industrialized countries.

Andre Gunder Frank (1969) wrote a definitive interpretation of chronic underdevelopment in Latin America; he argued that "the now-developed countries were never underdeveloped, though they may have been undeveloped." The reason, he asserted, was colonialism—the historical expansion of the capitalist system that "effectively and entirely penetrated even the apparently most isolated sectors of the underdeveloped world."

Other theorists—frequently called *dependentistas*—shared Frank's concern about the "enslavement" of the Global South by the capitalist Global North. "The relation of interdependence between two or more economies, and between these and world trade," Theotonio Dos Santos (1970) argued, "assumes the form of dependence when some countries (the dominant ones) can expand and can be self-sustaining, while others (the dependent ones) can do this only as a reflection of that expansion, which can have either a positive or a negative effect on their immediate development." Hence, **dependency** is seen as resulting from a situation "in which the economy of certain countries is conditioned by the development and expansion of another economy to which the former is subjected."

■ **dependency**
a condition of retarded economic growth believed to result from the Global South's subordination and structural exploitation by the Global North's advanced capitalistic market economies, making the Global South especially vulnerable to cycles of expansion and contraction.

Dependent countries are vulnerable to penetration by outside forces. Dependency theorists argue that the overseas branches of giant MNCs headquartered in the Global North are the primary agents of neocolonial penetration because they transfer profits from the penetrated societies to the penetrators. Foreign investment—whether private or in the form of aid from other governments—is also an instrument of penetration. Technological dependence and "cultural imperialism," through which Global South societies become saturated with ideas and values alien to their indigenous cultures, are among the consequences. Once penetration by advanced capitalist states has occurred, continues the dependency theory argument, the inherently unequal exchanges that bind the exploiters and the exploited are sustained by elites within the penetrated societies, who sacrifice their country's welfare for personal gain.

The argument that a privileged few benefit from dependency at the expense of their societies is logically similar to **dualism,** which even liberal theorists find persuasive. Dualism refers to the existence of two separate economic and social sectors operating side by side. Dual societies typically have a rural, impoverished, and neglected sector operating alongside an urban, developing, or advanced sector—but with little interaction between the two. Thus whatever growth occurs in the industrial sector in dual societies "neither initiates a corresponding growth process in the rural sector nor generates sufficient employment to prevent a growing population in the stagnant sectors" (Singer and Ansari 1988). MNCs contribute to dualism by promoting "the interests of the small number of well-paid modern-sector workers against the interests of the rest by widening wage differentials . . . and to worsen the imbalance between

■ **dualism**
the existence of a rural, impoverished, and neglected sector of society alongside an urban, developing, or modernizing sector, with little interaction between the two.

A Dual Society In the 1990s Brazil, South America's largest country, has moved beyond its days of dictators and hyperdebt, and has become an emerging market seeking through its size, resources, and foreign investment in its privatized market to develop into an economic giant in the global economy. But like many developing countries, Brazil remains a dual economy, with a small advanced sector coexisting alongside an impoverished one, such as the Favela Rochina slum in Rio de Janeiro pictured here—in 1997 the largest continuous slum in South America. The World Bank cites Brazil as having the world's largest gap between rich and poor.

rural and urban economic opportunities by locating primarily in urban areas and contributing to the flow of rural-urban migration" (Todaro 1994).

Like dependency theorists, those who emphasize Global South dualism reason that this economic condition stems from the colonial past, when the imperial powers regarded themselves as the best producers of manufactured goods and their colonies as the best suppliers of basic foodstuffs and raw materials. This relationship produced few "spread effects" in the colonial economies' secondary and tertiary sectors. Eventually, rapid population growth overwhelmed the ability of the colonies' rising incomes to generate continued economic growth (Higgins and Higgins 1979). Dependency theorists nonetheless reject the dualist argument as the most convincing explanation of the Global South countries' subordinate international position. Instead, they see the division into dual "modern" and "traditional" sectors as a consequence of a larger causal force—the impact of a "single international capitalist economy" that determines the destinies of states.

World-System Theory. World-system theorists, who also emphasize the structural level of analysis of the Global South's development difficulties, share dependency theorists' view that the world is divided into a core (the advanced capitalist states), a periphery (the developing states), and a semiperiphery composed of ascending countries climbing from the periphery and declining countries falling from the ranks of the wealthy core. However, they take a longer-term perspective on the emergence of disparities between the two and the forces that determine where states are positioned in the global division of labor, treating the actors in world politics in terms of classes much as Karl Marx did.

For world-system theory a critical issue is how states fit into the international division of labor. "Economic activities in each part of a true world-economy depend on and make possible the activities of the other parts. Each part or area has acquired a specialized role producing goods that it trades to others to obtain what it needs. Thus, the world-economy is tied together by a complex network of global economic exchanges" (Shannon 1989).

The core-periphery distinction is particularly important. "Within the world division of labor, core states specialize in the production of the most 'advanced' goods, which involves the use of the most sophisticated technologies and highly mechanized methods of production ('capital-intensive' production). At least until recently, this meant that core states specialized in the production of sophisticated manufactured goods." Within the periphery, on the other hand, economic activities "are relatively less technologically sophisticated and more 'labor intensive' . . . For most of the modern era, production for export was concentrated on raw materials and agricultural commodities" (Shannon 1989). Historically, states on the periphery have also been militarily inferior to core states and less well-organized administratively, which limited their ability to compete with the capitalist states.

World-system theorists cannot easily explain the industrialization now taking place in the periphery's emerging markets. To account for this, they have coined the term semiperiphery to accommodate geographic areas or countries (such as the NIEs) that are moving in an intermediate position between the core and the periphery. Dependency theorists also have difficulty explaining these countries' growth. To interpret this anomaly, they sometimes use the term **dependent development** to describe the industrial development of peripheral areas in a system otherwise dominated by the Global North. The term suggests the possibility of either growing or declining prosperity, but not outside the confines of a continuing dominance-dependence relationship between North and South.

■ **dependent development**
the industrialization of peripheral areas within the confines of the dominance-dependence relationship between North and South, which enables the poor to become wealthier without ever catching up to the core Global North countries.

Neoclassical Development Theory

Structural theories, particularly popular during the 1970s, helped to galvanize leaders throughout the Global South to lobby for reforms of the global political economy and the multilateral institutions that help to run it, such as the World Bank and the International Monetary Fund. By the 1980s, however, these same institutions increasingly embraced neoclassical theorists who advocated reducing government interference in the economic life of the Global South.

> The [neoclassical theorists] argue that by permitting competitive free markets to flourish, privatizing state-owned enterprises, promoting free trade and export expansion, welcoming investors from developed countries, and eliminating the plethora of government regulations and price distortions in . . . product and financial markets, both economic efficiency and economic growth will be stimulated. . . . What is needed, therefore, is not a

> reform of the international economic system or a restructuring of dualistic developing economies or an increase in foreign aid or attempts to control population growth or a more effective central planning system. Rather, it is simply a matter of promoting free markets and laissez-faire economics within the context of permissive governments that allow the "magic of the marketplace" and the "invisible hand" of market prices to guide resource allocation and stimulate economic development. (Todaro 1994, 85–86)

Neoclassical theorists could point to the success of the free-market practices Asian NIEs used to free themselves from the chains of poverty. Although the Asian Tiger governments routinely intervene in the marketplace, their export-led path to remarkable economic growth has encouraged others to emulate their strategies. In addition, the emerging markets have in some ways fulfilled the neoclassical predictions that market economies will thrive where government management of the market is minimal, and that entrepreneurial successes are more likely to occur where there is political freedom. Studies of the relationship between development and democracy tend to confirm the liberal argument (see, e.g., UNDP 1991; Moon and Dixon 1985).

The achievements of the NIEs and the emerging markets suggest that economic progress is within the grasp of Global South countries (see Chapter 8). Still, neoclassical theory cannot explain one of the international economic system's most striking features: as noted, at the start of the twenty-first century, "growth, unprecedented in its scale and diversity, has been badly distributed, leaving . . . gaping inequalities" (UNDP 1998). "By the late-1990s the fifth of the world's people living in the highest-income countries had 86 percent of world's GDP, the bottom fifth just 1 percent" (UNDP 1999, 3). Add to this the knowledge that nearly all of the world's population growth in the next century will occur in the Global South, and it is hard to imagine how the gap could close. Given the grim future of much of the Global South, "the greatest challenge global society faces today is preventing this fault line [separating the Global North and Global South] from erupting into a world-shaking crisis" (Kennedy 1994).

DEVELOPMENT REDEFINED

If the economic chasm separating rich and poor states cannot be bridged, does this mean that development is an impossible dream for 80 percent of humanity? Or do we need to broaden our understanding of development to move beyond its classic materialistic definition as accumulation of wealth? What ultimately provides for material and spiritual satisfaction? These are questions about which there are many philosophical controversies, and they lie at the heart of debates about how states compare in providing for their citizens' human rights to "life, liberty, and the pursuit of happiness."

In looking at how these cherished values are distributed by states to people throughout the world, the UN Development Program (UNDP) maintains that human development occurs when people's choices are expanded. At all levels of development, this occurs when people can live long in good health, acquire knowledge, and have access to the resources needed for a decent lifestyle. When people are denied these choices, no matter what their incomes are, many other opportunities vanish.

Unless one takes this approach to development into account, it is easy to overlook a remarkable accomplishment: global consumption doubled in the twentieth-century's last twenty-five years, making for enormous progress for opportunities and welfare. This achievement has led to some corresponding improvements in the way people now live in the Global South:

> A child born today in a developing country can expect to live 16 years longer than a child born 35 years ago. Developing countries have covered as much distance in human development during the past 30 years as the industrial world managed over than a century. Their infant mortality rate has been more than halved since 1960. The lives of more than 3 million children are being saved each year thanks to the extension of basic immunization over the past two decades. Child malnutrition rates have declined by a quarter. Combined primary and secondary school enrollment has more than doubled. And the share of rural families with access to safe water has risen from 10 percent to about 60 percent. Every region has made progress. (World Bank 1999b, 19)

Such evidence forces consideration of the thesis that the human dimension of development is as important as is the economic dimension of national development. It argues that people and their needs should not be valued in the same way as states value how their national incomes compare with other states.

Assessing Human Development

The human dimension of development first gained attention in the 1970s, partly in response to the growing popularity of dependency theory, and partly in reaction to the realization that "more is not better" (UNDP 1995). Advocates of a **basic human needs** perspective required new ways to measure development beyond those focusing exclusively on economic indicators. In 1990, Mahbud ul Haq at the UNDP constructed a **human development index (HDI)** to measure states' comparative ability to provide for citizens' well-being. Successive *Human Development Reports* have provoked fresh debate about the meaning of human development in national and international forums, including, for example, the 1992 UN Conference on Environment and Development, the 1994 UN Conference on Population and Development, and the 1995 World Summit for Social Development.

■ **basic human needs** adequate food intake (in terms of calories, proteins, and vitamins), safe drinking water, sufficient clothing and shelter, literacy, sanitation, health care, employment, and dignity.

■ **human development index (HDI)** an index that uses life expectancy, literacy, average number of years of schooling, and income to assess a country's performance in providing for people's welfare and security.

The HDI, as the UNDP defines it in its latest (1999) version with "better data," continues to seek to capture as many aspects of human development as possible in one simple, composite index and to rank human development achievements. The concept of human development is much deeper and richer than what can be captured in any composite index or even by a detailed set of statistical indicators. Yet to monitor progress in human development, a simple tool is needed. Thus, the HDI reflects achievements in the most basic human capabilities—leading a long life, being knowledgeable, and enjoying a decent standard of living. Three variables have been chosen to represent those dimensions—life expectancy, educational attainment, and income.

The HDI is a more comprehensive measure than per capita income. Income is only a means to human development, not an end. Nor is it the sum total of human lives. Thus by focusing on areas beyond income and treating income as a proxy for a decent standard of living, the HDI provides a more comprehensive picture of human life than income does.

With normalization of the values of the variables that make up the HDI, its value ranges from 0 to 1. The HDI value for a country shows the distance that it has already traveled towards the maximum possible value of 1 and allows for comparison with other countries. The difference between the value achieved by a country and the maximum possible value shows how far it has to go; the challenge for every country is to find ways to reduce that discrepancy (UNDP 1999).

If we look at the position of countries in terms of their ability to contribute to the human development of the people living within their borders, as measured by the HDI, we derive quite a different picture of the way personal welfare is provided for in different countries (see Table 5.2 and Figure 5.1). These indicators raise important questions about the relationship of national economic growth to human development. The index assumes that "the need is not so much for more consumption or for less, but for a different pattern of consumption—consumption for human development . . . Poor people and poor countries need to accelerate the growth of their consumption, but they need not follow the path trodden by the rich and high-growth economies . . . And patterns of consumption that harm society and reinforce inequalities and poverty can be changed" (UNDP 1998, iii).

Human Development and Economic Growth

When countries are grouped and ranked according to their human development performance, their ranking corresponds to their per capita GDP levels, but not perfectly. Clearly, the level of human development is highest in the Global North, where economic prosperity is also highest on average; conversely, the quality of life is generally lower in the Global South where per capita economic output is substantially lower. However, "the link between economic prosperity and human development is neither automatic nor obvious. Two countries with similar income per capita can have very different HDI values; countries with similar HDI values can have very different income levels. . . . Of the 174 countries, 92 rank higher on the HDI than on GDP per capita (PPP $), suggesting that these countries have been effective in converting income into human development. But for 77 countries the HDI rank is lower than the GDP per capita (PPP $) rank. These countries have been less successful in translating economic prosperity into better lives for people" (UNDP 1999, 129). In short, income alone is not a good indicator of human development. Some maintain that "redistributive" policies to meet basic human needs or otherwise enhance human welfare and growth-oriented policies through trickle-down effects work at cross purposes—the latter can only be attained at the expense of the former. Others question the trickle-down hypothesis while accepting the view that meeting basic human needs promotes long-term economic growth (see Moon and Dixon 1992).

Human Development in the Age of Globalization

Neoclassical development theory notwithstanding, the advent of global capital and the **globalization** process that is integrating the world's economies has led to widespread speculation that globalization will provide a cure for the chronic poverty of the low-income Global South. There exists "a widely shared image of globalization—a worldwide process of converging incomes and lifestyles driven

■ **globalization**
the integration of states through increasing contact, communication, and trade to create a holistic, single global system in which the process of change increasingly binds people together in a common fate (see p. 41).

TABLE 5.2

Three Levels of Human Development: The 1999 Report on the Fastest and Slowest Progress in Selected Countries

County		*1975 HDI*	*1997 HDI*	*Rate of Change 1975–1997*	*Overall 1997 HDI Rank*
Starting from High Human Development (0.800–1.000)					
Fastest Progress	Australia	0.84	0.92	52.0	7
	Norway	0.85	0.93	51.5	2
	Canada	0.86	0.93	50.5	1
Slowest Progress	Austria	0.84	0.90	42.0	16
	New Zealand	0.84	0.90	37.0	18
	Denmark	0.86	0.91	31.5	15
Starting from Medium Human Development (0.500–0.799)					
Fastest Progress	Singapore	0.74	0.89	57.5	22
	Korea, Rep. of	0.68	0.85	54.0	30
	Hong Kong, China (SAR)	0.76	0.88	51.0	24
Slowest Progress	South Africa	0.64	0.70	16.0	101
	Romania	0.72	0.75	11.0	68
	Zimbabwe	0.54	0.56	4.5	130
Starting from Low Human Development (0–0.499)					
Fastest Progress	Indonesia	0.47	0.68	40.0	105
	Egypt	0.43	0.62	32.5	120
	Swaziland	0.50	0.64	29.0	113
Slowest Progress	Burundi	0.28	0.32	6.0	170
	Central African Republic	0.34	0.38	5.5	165
	Zambia	0.45	0.43	–4.9	151

by even larger international flows of goods, images, capital, and people—as formidable equalizer [because] greater economic openness has made small parts of the changing world full-fledged members of the global village . . . so that globalized islands of prosperity are thriving in many developing nations" (Heredia 1999). However, globalization may not be benefitting the countries that most need help. Capital may flow more freely around the world, but some argue that it does not flow to the places where it has been scarce. A skeptical political economist from Mexico cautions: "Developing countries today are a much more heterogeneous group than at the beginning of the postwar period, [but] globalization is not helping them become more equal. The poorest are not catching up the fastest. . . . More and more people across the planet have become increasingly exposed to the amenities of the global marketplace, although mostly as permanent window-shoppers and silent spectators. The large majority of humankind, however, is rapidly being left outside and far behind" (Heredia 1999).

Like the controversy about whether globalization is bringing benefits or misery (see Chapter 9), how to define development is an ideological and policy issue that colors much of the debate about the roots of global inequality and rival approaches for its alleviation.

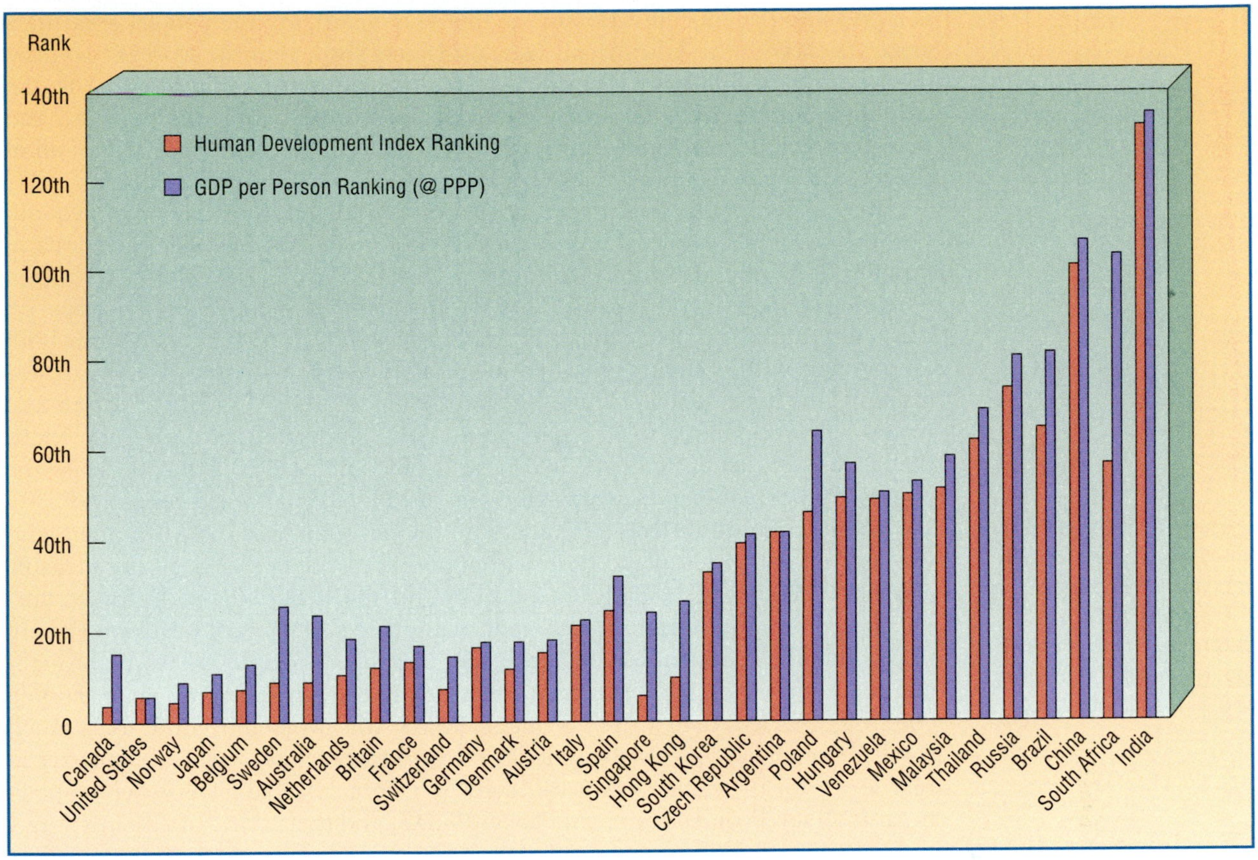

FIGURE 5.1
The Human Development Index

When one takes into account the human welfare of populations, as indicated by the Human Development Index, countries stack up somewhat differently in the calculation of development than when one uses GDP. Although there is generally a correlation between national wealth and human welfare, as indicated by the bar graph, it is not exact: Canada has the highest standard of living as measured by HDI but ranks only thirteenth in GDP. Singapore, on the other hand, ranks fourth in GDP but only twenty-second in HDI. As the table shows, countries' levels of human development are changing at different rates. Note, for example, that Singapore's standards of living are improving rapidly, however, showing that countries at all levels of current development have the potential to improve rapidly, to remain stagnant, or—as in the case of Zambia—to decline.

SOURCE: UNDP (1999), 130, 136–137; World Bank (1999b), 191–251; *Economist* (July 17, 1999), 96.

Inequalities. Neither GNP per capita nor HDI are able to measure inequalities within societies. Just as wealth is distributed unevenly at the international level, it is often concentrated in the hands of a few elites in the Global South. Although income inequalities are difficult to measure precisely, the existing evidence suggests that the degree of income inequality is at least twice as great in the Global South as in the Global North, and the disparity is increasing. Contrary to some predictions, globalization is not leading to income convergence; it is increasing the concentration of income and wealth among people, creating a separate class of the "ultra-rich." New estimates show that the world's two hundred richest people have a combined wealth of over $1 trillion, equal to the combined annual income of 41 percent of the world's people (2.5 billion), and that the three richest people have assets that exceed the combined GNP of all of the least developed countries (UNDP 1999, 38).

Just as per capita measures of economic production mask income inequalities, the HDI fails to reveal important regional, racial, and gender variations in human development within countries. The figures on income distribution nonetheless describe the same kind of inequalities. Again, the evidence on inequality mirrors the unequal and uneven levels of human development both among and within countries, where disparities are just as stark. In Brazil, for example, the poorest 50 percent of the population received 18 percent of national income in 1960, falling to 11.6 percent in 1995. In Costa Rica during the 1980s the richest 20 percent enjoyed a per capita income of PPP $14,400, while the poorest 20 percent had an average income of PPP $1,340 (World Bank 1999, 29).

■ **gender inequalities** differences between men and women in opportunity and reward that are determined by the values that guide states' foreign and domestic policies.

Gender inequalities—differences in living standards between men and women—remain widespread both within and across states, despite the measurable improvement in the daily lot and future prospects of millions of women during the past several decades. Although many facets of human development are improving, the prevalent worldwide gender gap remains especially wide throughout and within the Global South. Women's share of earned income in developing countries was less than a third of men's. Worse still, women account for a much smaller proportion of the nonagricultural workforce than men, and their pay in that sector for the same work is routinely less. Females hold fewer teaching positions at all levels of education and fewer Ph.D.s, and their share of administrative and managerial jobs is minuscule. Much the same holds true in politics, where women hold 10 percent of the seats in parliaments worldwide and only 5 percent of national government posts (UNDP 1999, 145–146; World Bank 1999b, 113, 155). The reason: "the current institutional, legal, and socioeconomic constraints to [women's] access to opportunities" (UNDP 1995). Furthermore, gender differences continue at the most basic levels of human development: more girls than boys die at a young age, females' access to adequate health care is more restricted, and women face more barriers to education at all levels. Thus it is easy to conclude that women remain victims of abuse and discrimination nearly everywhere.

Human Development or Human Despair? The general record of HDI changes presents an arresting picture of unprecedented human progress and unspeakable human misery, of humanity's advance on several fronts juxtaposed with its retreat on others, of a breathtaking globalization of prosperity side by side with a depressing globalization of poverty and deprivation. Most glaring are the stark inequalities in income and wealth as the gaps between the rich and poor countries and between rich and poor people continue to widen. But that provides only a crude reflection of the simultaneously unfolding trends toward both progress and decline. Consider, and balance, the checkered record from 1990 to 1997. On the positive side, the number of developing countries with a life expectancy of more than seventy years more than doubled, from twenty-two to forty-nine, and the proportion of people in developing countries living under democratic governance rose from two-thirds to three-fourths. On the negative side of this account, more than 80 million people lacked access to health ser-

The Gender Gap in Human Development Women throughout the world have every reason to protest the unequal treatment and opportunities they receive in nearly all countries, and have mobilized to lobby for human rights and changes in policy to close the serious "gender gap in employment." Here, in 1997, women demonstrators in Seoul, South Korea, give voice to their unfair treatment.

vices, 2.6 billion access to basic sanitation, more than 850 million adults were illiterate and about 840 million were malnourished (UNDP 1999, 22). Although progress in human development has occurred and will likely persist, so will trends toward declining human welfare, making the start of the twenty-first century appear to be both "the best of times and the worst of times." Thus, the future of world politics will not only be a struggle between the Global North and Global South but also a contest between those who see global regress as inevitable and those who see global progress as possible.

THE GLOBAL SOUTH'S FOREIGN POLICY RESPONSE

The vast political, economic, and social differences separating North and South indicate that the Global South is "weak, vulnerable, and insecure—with these traits being the function of both domestic and external factors" (Ayoob 1995). Coping with this insecurity has long been a primary foreign policy goal of Global South states, and efforts to overcome these insecurities have often brought the Global South into contention with the Global North. Ironically, the end of the Cold War magnified the challenge developing countries face, because the end of Soviet-American rivalry reduced the great powers' security interest in providing economic aid to Southern countries. Without foreign assitance, the Global South has experienced a burst of new armed conflicts in the last decade. The globalization of finance and trade threatens to further expand the economic vulnerabilities of poor Global South states in the new millennium.

As realists insist, power and wealth are states' core motives and are realized through military and economic prowess. Strategies designed to maximize power and prosperity continue to preoccupy foreign policy thinking in the Global South, where a variety of open and closed economies and democracies and dictatorships coexist, and different states take different approaches to increasing prosperity within a globalized marketplace. Let us examine how the Global South countries are pursuing their objectives, particularly in their relationships with the Global North.

In Search of Power

The states emerging after World War II struggled on separate tracks to find a foreign policy approach that could provide them with the power and prosperity they lacked. The **nonaligned states** were determined to strike a neutral course in the Cold War contest, while a broader group (including, for example, many Latin American states allied with the United States that had secured independence in the nineteenth century) concentrated their efforts more directly on severing their economic dominance by and dependence on the Global North.

■ **nonaligned states** countries that do not participate in military alliances with rival blocs for fear that formal alliance will lead them to unnecessary involvement in war.

Nonalignment. The nonalignment movement began in 1955, when twenty-nine Asian and African countries met in Bandung, Indonesia, to devise a strategy to combat colonialism. In 1961 leaders from twenty-five countries, mostly former colonies, met in Belgrade, Yugoslavia, where they created a lasting political coalition, the **Nonaligned Movement (NAM),** whose membership would later grow to more than one hundred countries.

■ **Nonaligned Movement (NAM)** a group of more than one hundred newly independent, mostly less developed states that joined together as a group of neutrals to avoid entanglement with the superpowers' competing alliances in the Cold War and to advance the Global South's common interests in economic cooperation and growth.

Because the new states sought to avoid entrapment in the Cold War, they tried through nonalignment to maximize their own gains while minimizing their costs. The strategy energized both the United States and the Soviet Union to renew their efforts to woo the uncommitted "neutrals" to their own network of allies. Nonalignment in effect enabled developing states to play one superpower off the other in order to gain advantage for themselves. The Cold War competitors became willing players in a bipolar **zero-sum** contest where one side's gains were the other's loss, often offering economic and military aid to win friends and influence allies.

■ **zero-sum** the perception in a rivalry that if one side gains, the other side loses (see p. 490).

The Cold War's end ended much of the competitive rationale for providing foreign aid and eroded the bargaining leverage nonalignment had provided the Global South. As a strategy, nonalignment "died" with the Cold War. "More than that, the way the East-West rivalry ended, with the values and systems of the West vindicated and triumphant, undermined the very basis of the nonaligned movement, which had adopted as its foundation a moral neutrality between the two blocs" (Chubin 1998).

Although the original justification for nonalignment no longer exists, the passions for the improvement of the Global South behind it live on. As the NAM prepared in late 1995 for its eleventh conference, at Cartagena, Colombia, its leaders claimed that the ideals envisaged by its founders remained unchanged. "When the Nonaligned Movement began, it was inspired by one motive—that developing countries could take decisions and positions in international politics depending on their own interests and not according to one or the other of the superpowers," the hosts announced at the opening ceremonies, "This continues to be valid."

The challenge facing the nonaligned states today is how to promote their interests in a world where few listen to their voices. The nonaligned Global South can complain, but its bargaining power to engineer institutional reforms is limited. This weakness is displayed in the UN, where the most influence the

Global South has mustered has symbolically been to delay serious proposals to make Germany and Japan permanent members of the Security Council by insisting that a nonaligned state or one of the larger developing countries (such as Brazil, Indonesia, Mexico, or South Africa) also be given a seat among the mighty. Weak states have some vocal power in numbers, but no clout or control.

This weakness represents a shift from the past, when the numerical majority of the Global South enabled it to exercise greater power within the UN than any of its members could have wielded individually. Nonalignment further enhanced that influence because the Soviet Union had often sided with the developing states in the General Assembly, particularly on decolonization issues. Now, however, the locus of power is firmly lodged in the U.S.-dominated Security Council, and the United States can veto most important resolutions originating in the General Assembly, where the Global South commands an overwhelming majority. This has intensified the developing countries' fears about many of the great powers' current activities within their territorial borders, such as "humanitarian" military intervention to cope with human suffering or to punish Global South governments that violate the human rights of their own people. That the great powers are developing a new generation of weapons of mass destruction while insisting that the Global South not participate in this arms race has also bred resentment. Thus, the Global South worries that the twenty-first century will witness "the reemergence of a more open and explicit form of imperialism, in which national sovereignty is more readily overridden by a hegemonic power pursuing its own self-defined national interest" (Bienefeld 1994).

Zones of Turmoil. These concerns are rooted in past experience: many developing countries felt betrayed and invaded when they became the battleground on which the superpowers conducted covert activities, paramilitary operations, and proxy wars. The Global South became the world's killing fields; more than 90 percent of the inter- and intrastate conflicts and 90 percent of the casualties in the past half-century occurred within it (see also Chapter 12). More than one hundred violent conflicts of various magnitude, claiming millions of victims, have been recorded in the Global South during the twentieth century's last decade (Wallensteen and Sollenberg 1999, 593–595). Although virtually every region of the world has experienced the horrors of these wars, since 1989 they have been concentrated almost exclusively within and between the fragile states—and would-be states—of the Global South.

Following the ethnonational genocidal war in Bosnia-Herzegovina, the United States, its NATO allies, and the other great powers have struggled to develop a **doctrine** to guide decisions about when, where, why, and how they should become militarily involved within the borders of sovereign Global South states where this kind of destruction is occurring. Now the great powers must determine if they should intervene in the Global South's **failed states** that are experiencing civil wars and ethnic cleansings, especially when their vital interests, such as access to oil, demand their attention. Indifference would leave the Global South highly vulnerable to violence, because since 1940 "enemies in civil wars have almost always failed to reach successful negotiated solutions to their conflicts unless an outside power guaranteed their safety during the ensuing transition period" (Walter 1997).

Arms Acquisitions. Faced with seemingly endless conflict at home or abroad, it is not surprising that the Global South has joined the rest of the

■ **doctrine**
a set of principles identifying the purposes to which a country will put its military power in the world, including identification of the conditions under which that country is prepared to use military force to achieve its foreign policy objectives (see p. 522).

■ **failed states**
countries whose governments have so mismanaged policy that their citizens, in rebellion, threaten to disintegrate the state (see p.632).

world's quest to acquire modern weapons of war—including in some cases (China, India, Iraq, North Korea, Pakistan) nuclear weapons. As a result, the burden of military spending (measured by the ratio of military expenditures to GNP) is highest among those least able to bear it. In the Global South military spending typically exceeds expenditures on health and education; impoverished states facing ethnic, religious, or tribal strife at home are quite prepared to sacrifice expenditures for economic development in order to acquire weapons.

Until recently, few Global South states produced their own modern weapons of war; instead, they imported them. The United States and the Soviet Union were the principal weapons suppliers during the Cold War, often providing arms to would-be friends and allies as outright grants. Beginning in the 1970s, in the aftermath of the Vietnam War, the United States began to sell arms to others, particularly Middle Eastern oil-exporting countries such as Iran and Saudi Arabia whose newfound wealth enabled them to buy huge quantities of the most sophisticated conventional weapons. In addition, the United States targeted its sale of weapons at the volatile Middle East region to make it a bulwark against communist expansionism, and supplied Israel with sophisticated weapons to protect it from a possible attack by newly armed Arab states. Elsewhere, the United States sold weapons as part of a program designed to shore up states facing communist threats (sometimes actual, sometimes imagined) without also having to supply American troops (as in Vietnam). Predictably, the Soviets often responded by supplying weapons to the neighbors of the U.S. arms recipients. In the Middle East, the Soviet Union became the chief weapons provider to the Arab states committed to the destruction of Israel, notably Syria and Iraq.

Expenditures on the weapons of war dropped markedly in most Global North countries when the Cold War ended. Major reductions in the relative burden of military spending were particularly pronounced for most states. But not in the Global South, where the percent of government revenue allocated to defense spending actually rose. As worldwide spending declined, so did arms purchases from foreign suppliers. Here again, the Global South was in a category by itself, with the recent trend toward expansion of military budgets and arms purchases throughout the Global South, alongside reductions in the more stable regions of the Global North:

> Relationships between arms suppliers and recipients continue to evolve in reaction to changing political, military, and economic circumstances. Despite global changes since the Cold War's end, the developing world continues to be the primary focus of foreign arms sales activity by conventional weapons suppliers. During the [1991–1998] period, conventional arms transfers to developing nations have comprised 69.4 percent of the value of all international arms transfers [and] in the period from 1995–1998, *deliveries* of conventional arms to developing nations represented 76.7 percent of the value of all international arms deliveries. In 1998, arms deliveries to developing nations constituted over 77.8 percent of the value of all such arms deliveries worldwide. (Grimmett 1999, 1; emphasis added)

peace dividend the global savings from arms expenditure reductions made possible by the decline of the threat of probable war.

As before, insecurity fed by internal wars fought by separatist minority groups seeking independence remains the primary reason for weapons acquisition in many Global South states, and, particularly in these states, the human costs of preparing for war are exceptionally high. The Global South countries had hoped to reap the benefits of the **peace dividend** at the end of the Cold

War's Human Impact
Innocent noncombatants, especially women and children, are most often the primary victims of violent conflict in the Global South. Their protection has usually required humanitarian military intervention by an outside power. Here a starving Somalian mother and child in 1997 wait for relief supplies delivered by U.S. military aircraft to a refugee camp in Wafir, Kenya.

War, anticipating that the savings the great powers realized as they cut their military expenditures would release large sums for use in bettering the economic and human condition of the world's less fortunate. But their hopes were quickly dashed. Although expenditures on the weapons of war were cut, the "dividends" were not "reinvested" in the Global South's economic development.

The Search for Wealth in a Globalized World

The persistent underdevelopment of most developing states underlies their drive for greater wealth, a better life for their people, and a higher position in the hierarchy of global power. Breaking out of their dependent status and pursuing their own industrial development remains a foreign policy priority of most Global South developing countries.

To this end, some states (particularly those in Latin America) pursued development through an **import-substitution industrialization** strategy designed to encourage domestic entrepreneurs to manufacture products traditionally imported from abroad. Governments (often dictatorships) became heavily involved in managing their economies and in some cases became the owners and operators of industry. Import-substitution industrialization eventually fell from favor, in part because manufacturers often found that they still had to rely on Global North technology and even component parts to produce goods for their domestic markets. The recent preference is for **export-led industrialization,** based on the realization that "what had enriched the rich was not their insulation from imports (rich countries do, in fact, import massively all sorts of goods) but their success in manufactured exports, where higher prices could be commanded than for [Global South] raw materials" (Sklair 1991).

■ **import-substitution industrialization**
a strategy for economic development that involves encouraging domestic entrepreneurs to manufacture products traditionally imported from abroad.

■ **export-led industrialization**
a growth strategy that concentrates on developing domestic export industries capable of competing in overseas markets.

As exemplified by the NIEs, the shift toward export-led growth strategies has transformed many Global South countries from being suppliers of raw materials into manufacturers of products already available in the Global North. Thus a new international division of labor is emerging as production, capital, labor, and technology are increasingly integrated worldwide and decision making has become transnational. "The old ideas of national autonomy, economic independence, self-reliance, and self-sufficiency have become obsolete as the national economies [have] become increasingly integrated" (Dorraj 1995).

Not all Global South economies are positioned to survive in this highly competitive globalized market. Many of the least developed countries remain heavily dependent on raw materials and other primary products for their export earnings, and even some of the NIEs have not moved beyond the dependent development stage, as their export goods are in the old, declining industries of the Global North whose technology is easily transferred to the semiperiphery. "While some may benefit from such integration and prosper, others may become more vulnerable to crises and fluctuations prevalent in capitalist economic cycles. Impoverished and dependent, . . . much of the [Global South] is ill-equipped to reap the benefits of global interdependence" (Dorraj 1995).

How to cope with dominance and dependence thus remains a key concern for many developing Global South countries. As they search for status and economic security, the Global South's key strategies in their relations with the Global North warrant attention.

■ **Group of 77 (G-77)** the coalition of Third World countries that sponsored the 1963 Joint Declaration of Developing Countries calling for reforms to allow greater equity in North-South trade.

■ **New International Economic Order (NIEO)** the 1974 policy resolution in the UN that called for a North-South dialogue to open the way for the less developed countries of the Global South to participate more fully in the making of international economic policy.

■ **Liberal International Economic Order (LIEO)** the set of regimes created after World War II, designed to promote monetary stability and reduce barriers to the free flow of trade and capital.

A New International Economic Order. The emerging nations of the Global South were born into a political-economic order with rules they had no voice in creating. Beginning in the 1950s they began to seek the means to control their own economic futures, centering their efforts on the UN where their growing numbers gave them greater influence than they could otherwise command. In the 1960s they formed a coalition of the world's poor, the **Group of 77** (known in diplomatic circles simply as the G-77) and used their voting power to convene a UN Conference on Trade and Development (UNCTAD), which later became a permanent UN organization through which the Global South could express its interests concerning development issues.

A decade later the G-77 (now numbering more than 120 countries) again used its UN numerical majority to push for a **New International Economic Order (NIEO)** to counter the **Liberal International Economic Order (LIEO)** championed by the United States and the other capitalist powers since World War II. Motivated by the oil-exporting countries' rising bargaining "commodity power," the Global South sought to compel the Global North to abandon practices that it perceived as perpetuating dominance and dependence. Later, the heated debate shifted as the Global South began to question who would govern the distribution of world wealth and how they would make their choices. Not surprisingly, the Global North rebuffed the South's reform efforts, and the North-South exchange gradually degenerated into a dialogue of the deaf.

The Global South's determination to revise the existing rules is now little more than a footnote to the history of a struggle between rich and poor states. Many of the NIEO issues remain on the global agenda, as do key philosophical controversies about the extent to which states should manage international economic transactions. Whereas the liberal philosophy underlying the LIEO recommends limited government intervention, "economic nationalists" advocate that their states act aggressively to promote national prosperity. "The nationalist considers relative gain to be more important than mutual gain [and seeks] to change the rules or regimes governing international economic relations in order to benefit themselves disproportionately with respect to other economic powers" (Gilpin 2001). Clearly that competitive viewpoint remains popular in many Global South countries (as well as some in the North), even as privatization and a return to market mechanisms rather than state-run enterprises have become widely accepted as the most effective method for generating growth. As we will discover in Chapter 8, the tension between liberalism and mercantilism applies broadly to core contemporary issues in the world political economy.

Regional Trade Regimes. With the failure of reform envisioned by the NIEO, the integration of Global South countries into the globalization process will occur according to the rules dictated by the Global North. Are there alternatives? Can regional arrangements enable Global South states to take advantage of growing economic interdependence to achieve their development goals?

To promote growth through regional economic agreements, the global economy began in the 1990s to subdivide into three "trade blocs"—one in Europe, with the European Union (EU) as its hub; a second in the Americas, with the United States at the center; and a third in East Asia, with Japan and China dominant. Consider some recent developments:

- *In the Americas:* The North American Free Trade Agreement (NAFTA), formalized in 1993, brought Canada, Mexico, and the United States into a single free-trade area whose market size rivals that of the EU (see Chapter 6). Plans envision early twenty-first-century regime expansion to create a hemisphere-wide free-trade area, in which tariffs among member countries are eliminated.
- *Also in the Americas:* The Mercosur agreement, which links Argentina, Brazil, Paraguay, and Uruguay (Latin America's largest trade bloc), and which hopes to incorporate the Andean Group (Bolivia, Colombia, Ecuador, Peru, and Venezuela) in its free-trade union.
- *In Asia:* The association of Asia-Pacific Economic Cooperation (APEC), an informal forum created in 1989 that now encompasses eighteen states (including the United States), has committed itself to creating a free-trade zone during the next twenty-five years.
- *Also in Asia:* The seven members of the Association of Southeast Asian Nations (ASEAN), first established in 1967 by Brunei, Indonesia, Malaysia, the Philippines, Singapore, and Thailand and now including Vietnam, have agreed to set up a free-trade area by 2003.
- *In Africa:* The Southern African Development Community (SADC), formed in 1980 and now encompassing more than twelve countries, has pledged to develop a free-trade area and common currency by the end of the century.

Will the lofty expectations of these regional politico-economic groups be realized? Political will and shared visions have proven in the past to be indispensable elements in successful regional trade regimes. Economic complementarity is another essential component, as the goal is to stimulate greater trade among the members of the free-trade area, not simply between it and others. If one or more members export products that each of the others wants, the chances of the regime's success are greater; if, on the other hand, they all tend to export the same products or to have virtually no trade with one another (typically the case in Africa), failure is more likely.

Prospects for the success of regional trade regimes seem greatest when Global South countries cobble their futures to Northern states—but, complain Global South leaders, on terms that the North dictates. That conclusion hardly bodes well for regional economic agreements as an effective method for balancing the North-South relationship.

Trade, Aid, Investment—or Nothing?

The developing countries have long pleaded for "trade, not aid" to improve their international position, turning to the NIEs' experience to support the view that access to the Global North's markets is critical to economic growth in the Global South. But many Global South countries have not improved their lot, often for two major reasons. First, market access has become increasingly difficult because domestic pressure groups in Global South countries have lobbied their governments to reduce imports of developing countries' products that compete with their own industries. Trade may be preferred to aid, but political barriers often interfere with free trade.

Second, the character and distribution of foreign aid have changed in the twentieth century's final decade. Nevertheless, criticism of its effectiveness and effects has risen, and consequently levels of foreign aid have stagnated. **Foreign aid** comes in a variety of forms and is used for a variety of purposes. Some aid consists of outright grants of money, some of loans at concessional rates, and some of shared technical expertise. Although most foreign aid is bilateral and is termed **official development assistance (ODA)**—meaning the money flows directly from one country to another—an increasing portion is now channeled through international institutions such as the World Bank, and hence is known as "multilateral aid." Moreover, the purposes of aid are as varied as its forms. Commonly stated foreign aid goals include not only the reduction of poverty through economic development, but also human development, environmental protection, reduced military spending, enhanced economic management, the development of private enterprise, increased power for women, the promotion of democratic governance and human rights, and humanitarian disaster relief and assistance to refugees. However, security objectives traditionally have figured prominently as motives of donors in the allocation of both economic aid and military assistance, and still do. For example, the United States continues to target Israel and Egypt as major recipients to symbolize friendship, maintain a balance of power, and influence the Middle East peace process.

■ **foreign aid**
economic assistance in the form of loans and grants provided by a donor country to a recipient country for a variety of purposes.

■ **official development assistance (ODA)**
grants or loans to countries from other countries, usually channeled through multilateral aid organizations, for the primary purpose of promoting economic development and welfare.

The assumption that development will support other goals, such as fostering solidarity among allies and promoting commercial advantage, free markets, or democratization, still underpins most donors' assistance programs. Today, however, many of these traditional justifications are under widespread attack in numerous donor countries, particularly in the United States, which has now been overtaken by Japan as the world's most generous donor country of bilateral aid through multilateral institutions, and where overall global official development assistance has in fact declined since peaking in 1991 (see Figure 5.2). "The poor economic performance of many traditional aid recipients (and some aid agencies) has tried the patience of supporters of aid programs and

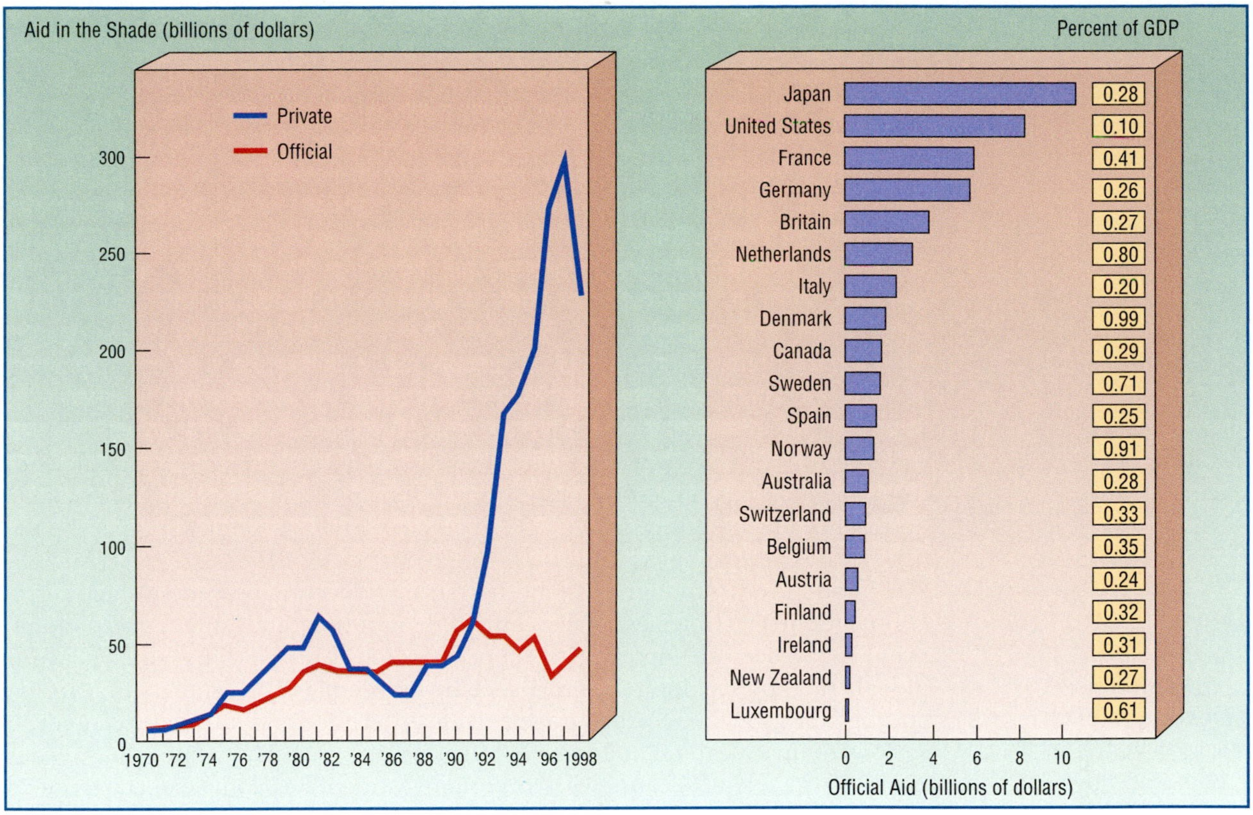

FIGURE 5.2
The Fluctuating Level of Bilateral and Multilateral Aid to Developing Countries since 1970

As the trend line on the left shows, official aid from Global North donors to the Global South increased only moderately from 1970 until 1998, when it grew to $51.5 billion. In contrast, private financial flows of resources into the developing countries soared from 1990 to 1996 and in 1998 were over four times the amount of official aid. The bar graph on the right shows the major donors' contributions to Global South foreign aid in 1998, which amounted to 0.23 percent of their combined GDPs in comparison with 0.33 percent given in 1992. "Measured relative to national income, Denmark dug deepest, dispensing 0.99 percent of its GDP in official aid. America was the stingiest: it gave a measly 0.1 percent" (*Economist*, July 26, 1999, 24; see also *Economist*, February 26, 2000, 123).
SOURCES: World Bank and OECD as reported in the *Economist* (July 3, 1999; 93; and July 26, 1999, 24).

increased skepticism about the effectiveness of aid" (World Bank 1996). Donors expect to see positive results, yet

> [o]ver the past 50 years rich nations have given $1 trillion in aid to poor ones. This stupendous sum has failed spectacularly to improve the lot of its intended beneficiaries. Aid should have boosted recipient countries' growth rates and thereby helped millions to escape from poverty. Yet countless studies have failed to find a link between aid and faster economic growth. Poor countries that receive lots of aid do no better, on average, than those that receive very little. (*Economist,* June 26, 1999, 24)

In all, the shift to market-oriented models has led many donors to conclude that foreign aid is no longer as needed, and may even be detrimental. The emergent climate of opinion, moreover, has spawned more "conditionality," or demands that recipient countries must meet to receive aid. The result is that with the erosion of assistance from donor countries, the poorest countries are not being protected from these declines and the prospects for increased aid flows appear dim. Adding to the probable demise of foreign aid is changing attitudes within many Global South countries. Developing countries chafe under the conditions or "strings" attached to donors' aid, believing that aid from rich countries was their right in repayment for years of unequal exchange perpetrated through colonialism and imperial rule. Recently, however, many Global South leaders have joined Global North critics of foreign aid, interpreting it as an instrument of neocolonialism and neoimperialism, resenting the conditionality criteria for receiving aid imposed by the International Monetary Fund and other multilateral institutions, and they have joined the chorus of experts advocating trade and investment as substitutes for aid. Without lobbying, the expansion of assistance above the current low level of only 0.9 percent of all developing countries' GNPs (UNDP 1999, 196) appears unlikely.

In addition to foreign aid, another strategy occupying center stage in the Global South's strategies for escaping deprivation and stagnant economic growth has been to increase its export earnings and gain a greater share of global trade by seeking **foreign direct investment (FDI).** The goal of an FDI strategy for growth is to encourage private enterprise and multinational corporations to invest capital in domestic business ventures. The strategy has always been controversial, because with foreign investment has come external control, the erosion of governments' sovereignty, and potentially, the exports of profits abroad (see Chapters 8 and 9). However, despite the risks, many developing countries have relaxed restrictions in order to attract foreign investors, with emphasis placed less on liberalizing investment restrictions and encouraging open domestic economic competition than on offering tax and cash enticements and opportunities for joint ventures (see Moran 1999). This has stimulated a surge in the flow of private capital to the Global South, rising severalfold in the 1990s (see Figure 5.3), although the richest 20 percent of the globe receives 68 percent of FDI and the poorest only 1 percent (UNDP 1999, 2).

■ **foreign direct investment (FDI)**
an investment in a country involving a long-term relationship and control of an enterprise by nonresidents and including equity capital, reinvestment of earnings, other long-term capital, and short-term capital as shown in the balance of payments.

The impact of this new infusion of foreign investments in the developing countries has been substantial, given the relatively small economies of the Global South. It has paved the way for emerging markets in the Global South to expand their rates of economic development despite the resistance of local industries in the Global South threatened by the competition and critics who have complained about the income inequalities that the investments are causing. Such fears and consequences notwithstanding, an intensified push among the Global South developing countries to compete for foreign investment capital in order to liberate themselves from dependence and destitution seems likely.

The prospects for either foreign aid or for foreign direct investments to contribute to the future development of, and relief of poverty in, the Global South will depend on a number of other factors. Foremost is the extent to which the staggering level of debt facing many Global South countries can be managed. The World Bank classifies more than forty countries, 80 percent of them in Africa, as burdened by "unsustainable debt." These countries are in dire need of relief, paying an average of 40 percent of their annual government budgets for

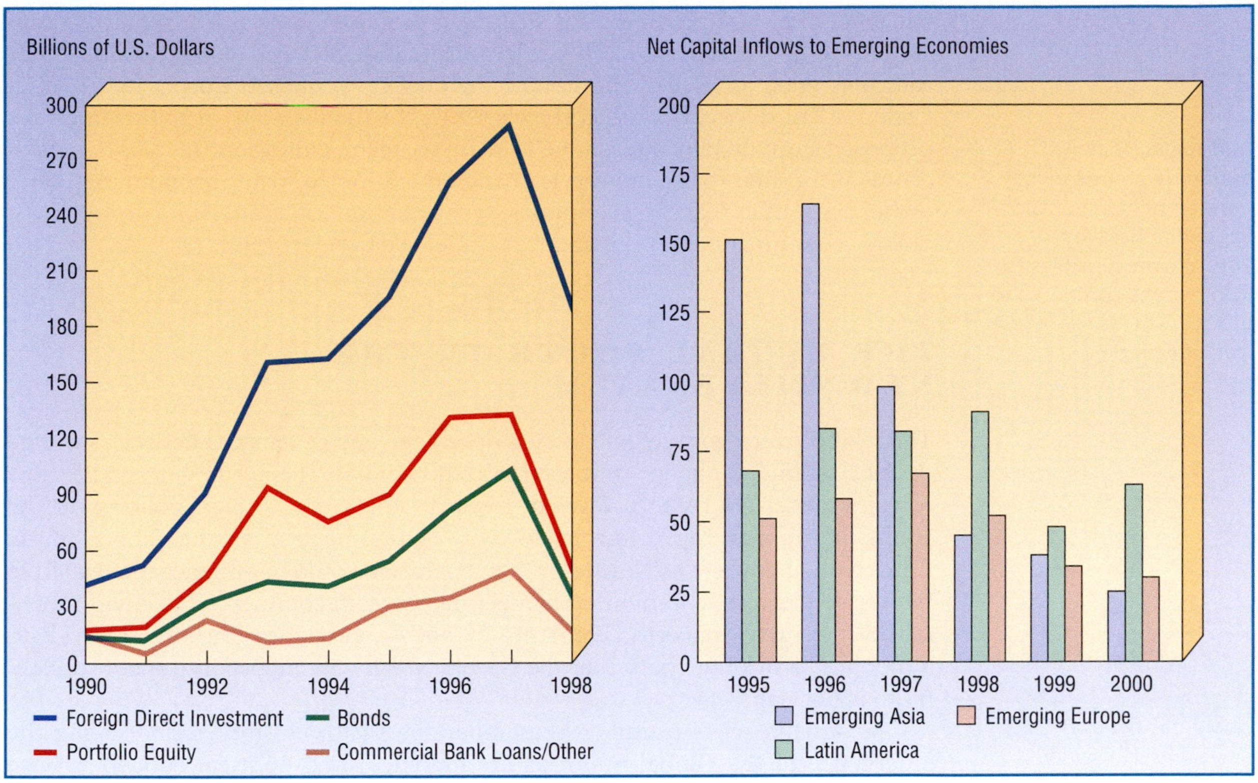

FIGURE 5.3
The Rise and Fall of Foreign Capital Investments in the Global South since 1990
Many Global South countries have sought to attract private investment capital from abroad to stimulate economic growth. Net long-term flows of capital into the developing countries dropped precipitously near the end of the twentieth century, after rising steadily since 1990, but FDI has remained at historically high levels. The chart on the right displays changes in the distribution of investments crossing borders to three regions of the developing Global South through 2000, and shows that capital inflows were expected to climb 75 percent to around $120 billion from 1999, their lowest level in the 1990s.
SOURCES: World Bank; Smithers (1999), 105; Economist (1999b), 101.

debt service (*New York Times*, April 30, 1999, A30). The external debt burden for all developing countries exceeds $2.2 trillion, or 46 percent of their total GNP (Speth 1999b, 6), and poses a threat to sustained growth in the globalized economy. It was the magnitude of this threat which prompted the Group of Eight (G-8) wealthy industrialized democracies to launch at their June 1999 summit the so-called Cologne Initiative to assist the **Heavily Indebted Poor Countries (HIPCs).** British Prime Minister Tony Blair labeled this initiative "the biggest step forward in debt relief and help to the poorest countries that we have seen in many years." Whether this initiative and others (e.g., the World Bank's 1996 program for the same purpose and the International Monetary Fund's Enhanced Structural Adjustment Facility), will succeed will also depend on the degree to which the Global South countries can undertake, with minimal corruption, the often painful liberalizing political reforms for democratic governance that are

Heavily Indebted Poor Countries (HIPCs) the subset of countries identified by the World Bank's Debtor Reporting System whose ratios of government debt to gross national product are so substantial that they cannot meet their payment obligations without experiencing political instability and economic collapse.

widely seen as a requirement for sustained economic growth (Kim and Wolfensohn 1999). Other parts of the equation include the prospects for still other reforms—such as implementation of the OECD's proposed Corporate Conduct Code for Third World Nations (Lewis 1999), or the capacity of Latin America's proposed **Fourth Way** alternative to neoliberalism, calling for increases in government funding for social services and education to foster economic growth, while accepting market economies, privatization of state-run corporations, global economic integration, and free trade (see Conger 1999).

■ **Fourth Way**
a strategy proposed for development in the Global South emphasizing government subsidies to help citizens contribute to growth within a free-trade market economy.

THE GLOBAL SOUTH IN THE NEW MILLENNIUM

The relationships between the world's developed and developing countries will no doubt continue to change in the globalized twenty-first century, but exactly how remains uncertain. A turn inward, toward isolationist foreign policies, in the Global North could lead to a posture of "benign neglect" of the Global South. Conversely, a new era of North-South cooperation could commence, dedicated to finding solutions to common problems ranging from commercial to environmental and security concerns. Elements of both approaches are already evident, although the ultimate path that the Global North will choose in the new millennium is unclear.

Meanwhile, it is useful to remember the historical forces underlying the emergence of the Global South as an analytical and political concept. Those who care to regard themselves as its members share important characteristics and experiences. Most were colonized by people of another race, experienced varying degrees of poverty and hunger, and felt powerless in a world system dominated by the affluent countries that once controlled them, and perhaps still do. Considerable change occurred among the newly emergent states as the post–World War II decolonization proceeded, but much also remains the same. Thus, the concept "Third World" continues to describe a state of mind that will galvanize the Global South in the twenty-first century as it seeks to overcome the disorder and destitution that affect so many of its members.

KEY TERMS

colonialism
Third World
First World
Second World
Global North
Global South
decolonization
neocolonialism (neoimperialism)
mercantilism
classical liberal economic theory
laissez-faire economics
sphere of influence
communism
Marxism-Leninism
world-system theory
self-determination
clash of civilizations
developing countries
gross national product (GNP)
developed countries
least developed of the less developed countries (LLDCs)
barter
newly industrialized economies (NIEs)
semiperiphery
Asian Tigers
countries in transition
purchasing power parity (PPP)
emerging markets
development
modernization

dependency theory
dependency
dualism
dependent development
basic human needs
human development index (HDI)
globalization
gender inequalities
nonaligned states
Nonaligned Movement (NAM)
zero-sum
doctrine
failed states
peace dividend
import-substitution industrialization
export-led industrialization
Group of 77
New International Economic Order (NIEO)
Liberal International Economic Order (LIEO)
foreign aid
official development assistance (ODA)
foreign direct investment (FDI)
Heavily Indebted Poor Countries (HIPCs)
Fourth Way

SUGGESTED READING

Chicote, Ronald H. *Comparative Inquiry to Politics and Political Economy.* Boulder, Colo.: Westview Press, 1999.

Crump, Andy. *The A–Z of World Development.* London: New Internationalist Publications, 1998.

Enloe, Cynthia. *Maneuvers: The International Politics of Militarizing Women's Lives.* Berkeley: University of California Press, 2000.

Journal of Third World Studies: A Biannual Periodical on Development in the Third World. Americus, Ga.: Association of Third World Studies.

Landes, David S. *The Wealth and Poverty of Nations: Why Some Are So Rich and Some So Poor.* New York: Norton, 1998.

Moran, Theodore H. *Foreign Direct Investment and Development: The New Policy Agenda for Developing Countries.* Washington, D.C.: Institute for International Economics, 1998.

Packenham, Robert A. *The Dependency Movement: Scholarship and Politics in Dependency Studies.* Cambridge, Mass.: Harvard University Press, 1992.

Qadir, Shahid, ed. *Third World Quarterly: Journal of Emerging Areas,* five issues published annually. Oxford, Eng.: Carfax Publishing.

Rodrik, Dani. *The New Global Economy and Developing Countries.* Washington, D.C.: Overseas Council, 1999.

Ryrie, William. *First World, Third World.* 2nd ed. London: Macmillan, 1999.

Schraeder, Peter J., Steven W. Hook, and Bruce Taylor. "Clarifying the Foreign Aid Puzzle," *World Politics* 50 (January 1998): 294–323.

Sen, Amartya. *Development as Freedom.* New York: Knopf, 1999.

Thurow, Lester C. *Building Wealth: The New Rules for Individuals, Companies, and Nations in a Knowledge-Based Economy.* New York: HarperCollins, 1999.

Todaro, Michael P. *Economic Development,* 7th ed. New York: Addison Wesley, 2000.

Weatherby, Joseph N., et. al. *The Other World: Issues and Politics of the Developing World,* 4th ed. New York: Longman, 2000.

World Bank, *Assessing Aid: What Works, What Doesn't, and Why.* New York: Oxford University Press, 1999.

WHERE ON THE WORLD WIDE WEB?

The Age of Imperialism

http://www.smplanet.com/imperialism/toc.html

Chapter 5 begins with a discussion of European imperialism and its effects on the Global South. To extend your analysis of imperialism, review a Small Planet's Web site. Recommended by the History Channel, this site chronicles American expansion in the Pacific, the Spanish-American War, the Boxer Rebellion, and U.S. intervention in Latin America. See historic photos of the battleship *Maine,* maps of the regions, and portraits of the participants. Read letters, anti-imperialist essays from the past, and cartoons. You can even download movie clips.

Many U.S. citizens have trouble understanding the plight of the Global South. Use the following Web sites to familiarize yourself with these countries and the problems they face. Your might choose a country from each of the following regions: Latin America, Asia, Africa, and the Middle East. Using the Web sites listed here, compare and contrast each of the countries in terms of political and economic structures. Keep the following questions in mind: What type of government does each country have? Which industrial revolution has it experienced? What primary goods does each country import and export? Based on your findings, can you identify the biggest obstacles for each country in the development process?

African Studies WWW
http://www.sas.upenn.edu/African_Studies/AS.html

The University of Pennsylvania's African Studies Center has created a Web site that provides extensive links to country-specific information as well as a bulletin board that lists current events and important documents. A multimedia archive allows you to view African sculptures. Check out the Alligator Head from Nigeria. Why is the Standing Male Figure from Zaire impaled on so many blades?

Asian Studies WWW Virtual Library
http://coombs.anu.edu.au/WWWVL-AsianStudies.html

This global collaborative project provides bibliographic and hypertext access to scholarly documents, resources, and information systems concerned with or relevant to Asian Studies. The Asian Studies WWW Virtual Library Web site is divided according to global, regional, and country-specific areas. It provides a wealth of information on the region as well as specific countries. This site is well monitored, and each link is checked for its accuracy and content.

The Center for Middle Eastern Studies
http://menic.utexas.edu/mes.html

The Middle East Network Information Center at the University of Texas at Austin is an inclusive source for general as well as country-specific information. Read about various countries' history, culture, business, energy resources, and government. View maps and scan the newspapers of the region. Learn more about Islam, Judaism, and Christianity and how these religions interact in the region. Click on the Arts and Culture link and hear Arabic spoken on numerous radio stations. Or try your hand at Interactive Arabic Texts by accessing the Modern Standard Arabic Page.

Political Database of the Americas
http://www.georgetown.edu/pdba/

A joint project of Georgetown University, the Organization of American States, and the Canadian Foundation for the Americas, this database provides documentary and statistical political information on Latin America, including constitutions, electoral laws, political parties, legislative and executive branch information, and election data. There is also a section on international affairs where you can contact embassies and consulates.

NetAid
http://www.netaid.org/index.htm

NetAid is a new, long-term effort to use the unique networking capabilities of the Internet to promote development and alleviate extreme poverty across the world. NetAid issues periodic calls to action on items of urgency and focuses attention on what works. On October 9, 1999, the NetAid concert featured more than two dozen of the world's leading musical artists performing simultaneously in London, Geneva, and New York to draw attention to world poverty and a new tool to fight it—the Internet. Their mission was to educate the global public on the problems faced by poor communities in the Global South and the means by which organizations and individuals can bring about dramatic reductions in world poverty in our lifetime. Visit this Web site to see Bono, the Crows (Black Crowes, Sheryl Crow, the Counting Crows), Jewel, David Bowie, Puff Daddy, Bush, and others in concert. Watch and listen to backstage interviews. After the entertainment, read about efforts aimed at ending hunger, helping refugees, saving the environment, security human rights, and relieving debt. This site also suggests actions you can take to address some of these issues.

The following Web sites provide general information on international development.

United Nations Conference on Trade and Development (UNCTAD)
http://www.unctad.org/en/enhome.htm

From the UNCTAD homepage, go to the Least Developed Countries link and examine the backgrounds of the countries that the United Nations has deemed the poorest countries in the world. Then, view the Activities that UNCTAD has planned in order to help these countries. Based on your study of international relations, do you think the Trust Fund will work?

United Nations Development Program (UNDP)

http://www.undp.org/

This United Nations branch helps countries in their efforts to achieve sustainable human development. As discussed in Chapter 5, the fulfillment of basic human needs (food, water, clothing, shelter, sanitation, health care, employment, and dignity) are important measures of a country's development level. The UNDP focuses its efforts on assisting countries in the Global South to design and carry out national development programs. Choose a Focus Area to explore: poverty eradication in China, empowerment of women in Cambodia, environmental protection in Africa, or enhanced governance in many Global South countries. Which projects do you think have had the greatest impact on development?

U.S. Agency for International Development (USAID)

http://www.info.usaid.gov/

USAID is the federal government agency that implements foreign economic and humanitarian assistance programs to advance the political and economic interests of the United States. It assists countries recovering from disaster, trying to escape poverty, and engaging in democratic reforms. From the homepage, click on Regions and Countries, then choose the interactive map. Now you are able to explore U.S. aid efforts in each country of the world. What are the U.S. aid priorities in each region? Do you think aid should be tied to advancing U.S. interests or given to the needy without strings attached?

Virtual Library on International Development

http://w3.acdi-cida.gc.ca/Virtual.nsf/

This Canadian site outlines international development issues by region, organization, or topic. You can click on the outlines to discover links to organizations, news, and resources. The reference desk advises you of upcoming conferences and events related to international development and links you to libraries, periodicals, and reports of value in the study of international development.

CHAPTER 6

INTERGOVERNMENTAL ORGANIZATIONS (IGOs)

TOPICS AND THEMES

- What are IGOs?
- The United Nations
- The European Union
- Other regional organizations

- **CONTROVERSY** WHO SHOULD BE ALLOWED TO JOIN THE UN? THE CASE OF TAIWAN

UN meeting on the NATO bombing of Kosovo, March 1999

One thing is sure. . . . Global complexity [is creating a] global governance crisis [that] will have to be solved through new ways of working together globally, and bold departures from old, trusted concepts.

—Jean-Francois Rischard, World Bank vice president for Europe, 1999

Globalization is a source of new challenges for humanity. . . . Only a global organization is capable of meeting global challenges. . . . When we act together, we are stronger and less vulnerable to individual calamity.

—Kofi Annan, United Nations secretary-general, 1997

The 1648 Peace of Westphalia, which ended the Thirty Years' War, also ended the secular authority of the Pope by creating sovereign and independent territorial states. The history of world politics for the past 350 years has largely been a chronicle of interactions among states, which remain the dominant political organizations in the world. States' interests, capabilities, and goals significantly shape world politics. However, the supremacy of the state has been severely challenged in recent years. When European states started to integrate in the 1950s and later in February 1992 when the Maastricht treaty on European Union (EU) was signed, they moved a step away from the absolute sovereign control of states over their territory, and toward the reassertion of authority by supranational institutions. Increasingly, world affairs are being influenced by organizations that transcend national boundaries—universal international organizations such as the United Nations (UN) and regional organizations such as the EU. Diverse in scope and purpose, these actors perform independent roles and increasingly exert global influence.

INTERNATIONAL ORGANIZATIONS: AN INTRODUCTION

There are two principal types of international organizations: **intergovernmental organizations (IGOs),** whose members are states, and **nongovernmental organizations (NGOs),** whose members are private individuals and groups. Neither type is unique to the twentieth century, although both are now more pervasive. The Union of International Organizations, which maintains comprehensive, up-to-date information on both types, records that their numbers increased sharply during the nineteenth century, as international commerce and communications grew alongside industrialization. In 1909, there were 37 IGOs and 176 NGOs. By 1960 there were 154 IGOs and 1,255 NGOs, and at the start of 2000 these numbers had risen to 251 and 27,077, respectively (see Figure 6.1).

intergovernment organizations (IGOs) institutions created and joined by governments, which give them authority to make collective decisions to manage particular problem(s) on the global agenda.

nongovernmental organizations (NGOs) transnational organizations of private citizens maintaining consultative status with the United Nations that work toward common interests (see p. 202).

In interpreting these trends, keep in mind that it is not easy to identify international organizations. In principle, IGOs are defined not only by the fact that their members are states, but also by their permanence and institutional procedures; IGOs meet at relatively regular intervals, and have specified procedures for making decisions and a permanent secretariat or headquarters staff (Jacobson 1984), although they "do not have direct access to many of the material resources normally available to states" (Young 1995). If these criteria were relaxed, the number of IGOs would far surpass the number of organizations just cited, as would the number of NGOs. An additional 6,164 international bodies ("special type") would qualify for inclusion as IGOs, as would more than 38,133 other nongovernmental associations that share characteristics with NGOs (*Yearbook of International Organizations 1999/2000,* Vol. 3, 1636–1637.)

This growth in transnational organizations has created a complex network of overlapping memberships. The cooperative activities of these "networks of interdependence" (Jacobson 1984) span the entire range of global issues: trade, defense, disarmament, economic development, agriculture, health, culture, human rights, the arts, illegal drugs, tourism, labor, women's plight, education, debt, the environment, crime, humanitarian aid, civilian crisis relief, telecommunications, science, globalization, immigration, and refugees, to name just a few.

While more than 87 percent of all the transnational organizations now in operation are nongovernmental, the remaining 13 percent are more important because their members are states. The smaller subset of IGOs that governments create will remain preeminent as long as the preeminence of states themselves persists, because IGOs "derive their importance from their character as associations of states" (Jacobson 1984), which gives them whatever authority IGOs exercise.

IGOs vary widely in size and purpose. Only thirty-five qualify as "intercontinental organizations" and only thirty-six are, like the UN, "universal membership" IGOs. The rest, accounting for more than 72 percent of the total, are limited in their scope and confined to particular regions. Table 6.1 illustrates these differences. The variation among the organizations in each subcategory is great, particularly with single-purpose, limited-membership IGOs. The North Atlantic Treaty Organization (NATO), for example, is primarily a military alliance, while others, such as the Organization of American States (OAS), promote both economic development and political reforms. Still, most IGOs

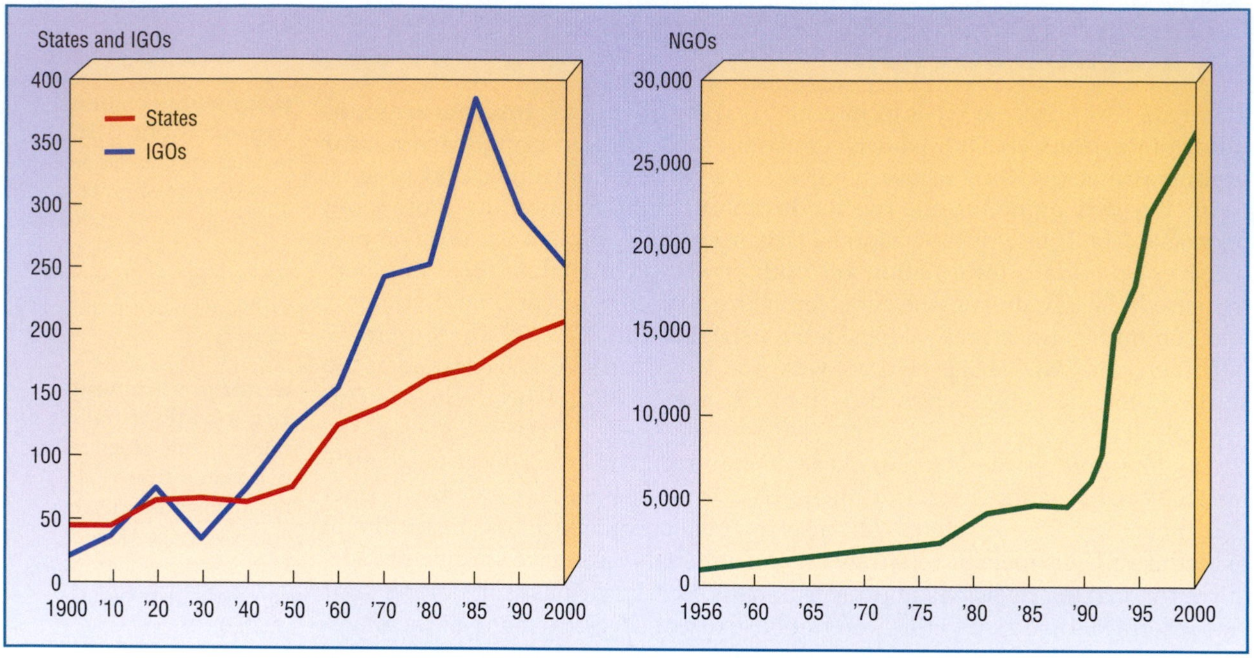

FIGURE 6.1
The Number of States, IGOs, and NGOs since 1900

The number of independent states increased greatly in the twentieth century—especially since the decolonization movement began after World War II—but the number of intergovernmental organizations (IGOs) and especially nongovernmental organizations (NGOs) has grown even more rapidly.

SOURCES: States, extrapolated from Enriquez (1999), Vanhanen (2000), and Gleditsch and Ward (1999); IGOs, *Yearbook of International Organizations, 1999/2000,* and moving averages from selected prior volumes; NGOs, *Economist* (December 11, 1999), 20.

engage in a comparatively narrow range of activities defined primarily as economic and social goals, such as the management of trade, transportation, and other types of functional cooperation. In this sense IGOs are agents, as well as reflections, of the global social and economic interdependence produced by the expansion of activities that transcend state borders.

NGOs also differ widely. Due to their number and diversity, they are even more difficult than IGOs to classify. In 1999, the Union of International Associations categorized 8.4 percent of 5,766 "conventional" NGOs as universal membership organizations, with most of the remaining NGOs classified as intracontinental or regionally oriented membership organizations. Functionally, NGOs span virtually every facet of modern political, social, and economic activity in an increasingly borderless globalized world, ranging from earth sciences to health care, language, history, culture, theology, law, ethics, security, and defense.

It is useful to think of NGOs as intersocietal organizations that help promote agreements among states on issues of international public policy. Many NGOs interact formally with IGOs. For instance, more than one thousand NGOs actively consult with various agencies of the extensive United Nations system and maintain offices in hundreds of cities. The partnership between

TABLE 6.1

A Simple Classification of Intergovernmental Organizations (IGOs)

Geographic Scope of Membership	*Range of Stated Purpose* Multiple Purposes	Single Purpose
Global	United Nations World Trade Organization UNESCO Organization of the Islamic Conference	World Health Organization International Labor Organization International Monetary Fund Universal Postal Union
Interregional, regional, subregional	European Union Organization for Security and Cooperation in Europe Organization of American States Organization of African Unity League of Arab States Association of Southeast Asian Nations	European Space Agency Nordic Council North Atlantic Treaty Organization International Olive Oil Council International North Pacific Coffee Organization African Groundnut Council

NGOs and IGOs enables both types to work (and lobby) together in pursuit of common policies and programs.

Although widespread geographically, NGOs are most active in the advanced Global North industrial democracies. "This is so because open political systems, ones in which there is societal pluralism, are more likely to allow their citizens to participate in non-governmental organizations, and such [democratic governments] are highly correlated with relatively high levels of economic development" (Jacobson 1984).

In this chapter, we will discuss some prominent and representative IGOs, including the UN, the EU, and various other regional organizations. In Chapter 7 we shall investigate in greater depth the impact of NGOs. The purpose of these chapters is not simply to describe these actors, but to question the extent to which their activities undermine states' continuing autonomy. Thus, the focus throughout will be on governments' capacity to manage global change and the role of international organizations in that process.

THE UNITED NATIONS

United Nations (UN) the preeminent global, multipurpose IGO, established in 1945, consisting of six major organs and numerous specialized agencies, conferences, and commissions.

The **United Nations (UN)** is the best-known international organization. Special characteristics distinguish it from most others, beginning with the fact that its membership includes almost all independent states. The end of the Cold War helped the cause of universality, when in 1991 Latvia, Lithuania, Estonia, North Korea, and South Korea—long denied a place in the UN—finally gained admission, and the next year the breakup of the Soviet Union enabled the fourteen newly independent non-Russian republics of the former Soviet Union to join also. In the year 2000, the organization reached 189, and will probably grow further when and if long-standing controversies about the status of potential new members are settled (see Controversy: Who Should Be Allowed to Join the UN?).

In addition to its nearly universal membership, the UN is also a multipurpose organization. As Article 1 of the UN Charter states, its objectives are to:

- Maintain international peace and security.
- Develop friendly relations among nations based on respect for the principle of equal rights and self-determination of peoples.
- Achieve international cooperation in solving international problems of an economic, social, cultural, or humanitarian character, and in promoting and encouraging respect for human rights and for fundamental freedoms for all.
- Function as a center for harmonizing the actions of nations in the attainment of these common ends.

These ideals have carried the UN into nearly every corner of the complex network of interstate relations. Its conference machinery has become permanent; it has provided a mechanism for the management of international conflict; and it has become involved in a broad range of global welfare issues.

Peace and security figured prominently in the thinking of those responsible for creating the UN and its predecessor, the League of Nations. Following each twentieth-century global war, world leaders have created new institutions to keep peace. The liberal conviction that war is not inevitable but can be eliminated by reforming the anarchical structures that encourage it inspired both efforts. The first, the League of Nations, sought to prevent a recurrence of the catastrophic First World War by replacing the balance-of-power system with one based on **collective security.** When it failed to restrain Germany, Japan, and Italy during the 1930s, the League collapsed.

■ **collective security** a principle endorsed by a group of states who agree that they will jointly punish states that breach international peace (see p. 559).

At the start of World War II the U.S., British, and Russian allies began planning for a new international organization—the UN—to maintain the postwar peace after victory. However, faith in the UN's ability to maintain international peace and security quickly eroded. The world organization soon became paralyzed by the unforeseen Cold War conflict between the United States and the Soviet Union.

The five major powers allied against Germany and Japan during World War II (the United States, the Soviet Union, Britain, France, and China) became permanent members of the Security Council and reserved the right to veto the UN General Assembly's recommendations. This formula reflected the assumption that the major powers would act together to provide collective global security. Consequently, unanimous agreement among the five permanent members was essential, for without it the council would be deadlocked and no action could occur. As it turned out, such agreement was seldom reached.

False Start: The United Nations during the Cold War

The Security Council rapidly fell victim to the Cold War. Between 1945 and 1955, the Soviet Union exercised its veto power seventy-seven times to prevent action on matters with which it disagreed. In all, it accounted for three-fourths

CONTROVERSY

Who Should Be Allowed to Join the UN?

The Case of Taiwan

Almost every country, it seems, wants to be a member of the United Nations (Switzerland being the major exception). However, membership requires support from the powerful existing members of the organization, and the politics governing this admission process can be highly conflictual.

The leaders who first drafted the UN Charter after World War II envisioned a universal organization open for membership to all countries willing to respect the charter's principles. Under such a design, politics and alliances with great powers were not to be a factor in determining eligibility. From the beginning of the Cold War, however, the great powers on the Security Council began to challenge that view of inclusion, acting in terms of their national interests in deciding who should be allowed to join the UN. Such realpolitik political considerations continue to influence decisions about new members today, as in the troublesome case of Taiwan, which seeks UN membership and recognition but is unlikely to gain it because of opposition by China.

When Chiang Kai-shek and his Nationalist troops fled mainland China in the wake of the Communist revolution in 1949, he established an alternative government on the island of Formosa (renamed Taiwan). Chiang declared it to be the true Chinese government, thus perpetuating the fiction of two Chinas. Fearing the spread of communism, the United States refused to recognize the government of Mao Tse-Tung on mainland China and supported Taiwan. Mainland China declared Taiwan a Chinese province in rebellion. Only in the 1970s did President Richard Nixon, on the advice of Secretary of State Henry Kissinger, recognize the legitimacy of the Chinese government, easing tensions between the two great powers. The status of Taiwan, however, has remained ambiguous and continues to be a source of tension. The problem reached new heights in late 1999 when Taiwan declared itself a separate state—a position that China found unacceptable.

If Taiwan is a separate state, as it insists, presumably it should be allowed membership into the UN. But because China, as a powerful nation represented on the Security Council, insists it is not an independent state, Taiwan is unlikely to receive a seat. As more states splinter into smaller, breakaway republics, questions of statehood and membership in the UN will continue. The great powers will likely continue to exert significant influence in the decisions. Should they? Whose definition of statehood should be recognized? What rules do you think should govern UN admission decisions? In considering your answer, reflect upon the following commentary on UN membership regarding Taiwan.

> It may be a mystery why any country should want to join the United Nations. Paying dues and being shot at in the name of peace would seem to have limited appeal. But joining the club has become part of growing up. Palau became independent [in 1994] and was immediately welcomed into the UN, once officials discovered where it was. All the more reason to consider the strange case of Taiwan, a poor little rich country eternally condemned to wait in the cold; an outsider wistfully looking in at the club's [189] members busily making important speeches to each other.
>
> Most of these countries would probably be happy enough to allow Taiwan in were it not for opposition by China, which says that Taiwan is not a proper country at all, but a rebel province pretending to be a country. It is an odd notion. Taiwan is clearly a country, and rather a successful one: the world's ninth-largest provider of overseas investment, much of it in China itself, and with foreign reserves about equal to Japan's. It [has shaken] off its old authoritarianism and [has turned] into a robust democracy.
>
> There's the rub. Taiwan's new freedoms, with the emergence of politicians unafraid to speak their minds, have alarmed China. The Beijing government's long-held vision of a "greater China" incorporating Taiwan, along with Hong Kong and Macau, has become blurred. Back in 1987 China and Taiwan had seemed to be reaching an accommodation, through unofficial talks in third countries. But as democracy [grew] in Taiwan, China's attitude has become chillier. Threats to invade the island made [were in 2000] for the first time since the 1970s.
>
> Taiwan must take some of the blame for its confusing status. Officially, it still calls itself the Republic of China and its rulers claim to be China's only legitimate government. Not surprisingly, this irritates the authorities in Beijing, always sensitive to challenges to their own legitimacy. But Taiwan accepts that it is being academic. It no longer parades the fiction that it rules all China. (*Economist*, December 10, 1994, 16)

Meeting Place for the World The United Nations headquarters in New York is home to the Security Council, the General Assembly, the Secretariat, and a variety of departments and other agencies. Created by liberals and realists who sought to direct global change through a universal international organization, the UN has evolved over its fifty-plus-year life span into a huge bureaucracy with a global agenda now so large that the architects who drafted the UN Charter at the 1946 San Francisco Conference would hardly recognize their creation. In the twenty-first century, as in 1946, the question persists as to whether the UN is adequately prepared and empowered to lead in global governance.

of the 149 vetoes cast in the first three decades of the UN's existence. But obstruction did not come from the Soviet Union alone. During the UN's formative period, the United States did not have to veto Security Council actions it opposed because it could count on its "hidden veto" by easily persuading a sufficient majority of other allied council members to vote negatively. In doing so it avoided the stigma of casting a single blocking vote. This ability derived from the composition of the Security Council, on whose nine (later fifteen) members the United States could easily depend to provide a pro-Western majority. When the UN's membership grew and that support was no longer ensured, the United States itself became obstructionist, and after 1970 began to veto resolutions with which it disagreed. By the time the Cold War ended in 1991, the United States had exercised its veto power seventy-two times, twice as often since 1966 as all other permanent council members combined. As a result, the Security Council was often paralyzed, as vetoes severely restricted the UN's ability to undertake collective action. This impotence was aggravated by repeated financial crises caused by both superpowers' refusal to pay their mandated fees. Together, the East-West conflict and chronic financial problems during the Cold War destroyed the UN's capacity to operate as its creators had hoped.

The growing membership of the UN also reduced its capacity for concerted action. As its size increased, the organization's membership became less homogeneous. This process increased sharply with the Fifteenth General Assembly in 1960, when seventeen new states joined the UN, nearly all of them African. By 1985 well over half of the organization's members came from Africa and Asia; in 1945, less than one-fourth came from these two regions, and their domination has increased since (see Figure 6.2). Thereafter, the Global South increasingly dominated the UN, giving rise to the North-South dispute. Between 1960 and 1990, the UN experienced considerable disunity, which proved to be a great obstacle to collective action.

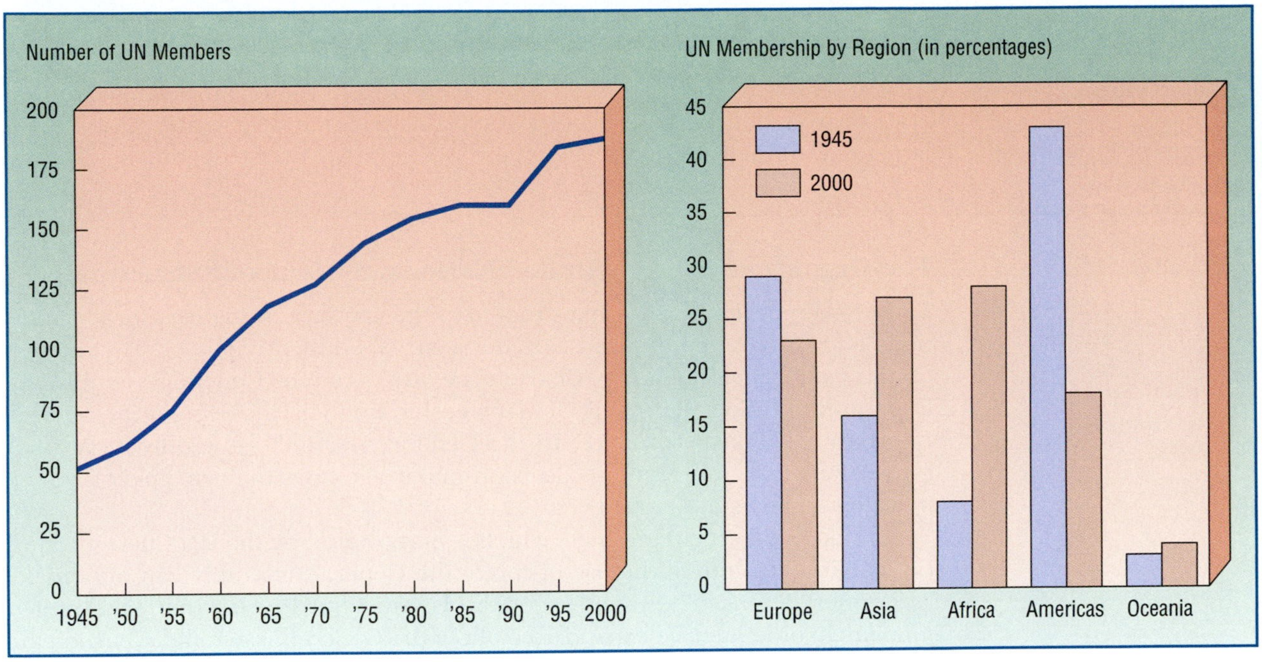

FIGURE 6.2
The Changing Membership of the United Nations, 1945–2000
Since the UN was created in 1945, its membership has grown from 51 to 189 states (see figure on left), a figure that has increasingly included countries from the Global South (see figure on right). This shift has influenced the kinds of interests and issues the UN has confronted, expanding the global agenda from the priorities of the great powers in the Global North to include those important to the developing states in the Global South.
SOURCE: United Nations.

Fresh Start? The United Nations after the Cold War

The three barriers to the UN's performance—great-power rivalry, insufficient funds, and disunity—were somewhat reduced when the Cold War ended. The great powers on the Security Council at last began to set aside their differences in order to maintain international peace. How far the United States and the Soviet Union had progressed became strikingly clear in 1990 when they joined forces to organize a collective UN effort to turn back Iraq's aggression in Kuwait. With Russia's repudiation of communism, collaborative crisis-management activities increased exponentially. The former antagonists' new cooperative attitude and renewed efforts to empower the UN to preserve world order and promote global prosperity were reflected in their mutual advocacy of **consensus decision making** in the Security Council.

■ **consensus decision making**
voting by voice without a record of individual members' formal positions, in order to reach agreement without generating criticism from opponents within the members' domestic systems.

Bolstered by the Security Council's demonstration of "the capacity to initiate collective measures essential for the maintenance of peace in a new world order" (Russett and Sutterlin 1991), as well as the Clinton administration's endorsement of what former UN Ambassador Madeleine Albright termed "assertive multilateralism," the prospects for an enhanced UN role appeared promising. However, as the UN's delayed and weak peacekeeping operations in the Balkans and elsewhere illustrated, huge obstacles remained to orchestrating a response to the awesome challenges facing the global community, especially the rampant ethnic warfare and genocide breaking out within many **failed states** throughout the world in the 1990s. As Secretary-General Boutros-Ghali lamented in August 1995, "Everywhere we work, we are struggling against the culture of death."

failed states countries with ineffective governments that have collapsed in the face of internal rebellion and anarchy (see p. 632).

The Organization of the United Nations: System and Structure

The UN's limitations are perhaps rooted in the ways it is organized for its ambitious and wide-ranging purposes. The Security Council is one of six principal organs established by the UN Charter; the others are the General Assembly, the Economic and Social Council, the Trusteeship Council, the Secretariat, and the International Court of Justice. In the General Assembly—the only organ that represents all member states—decision making follows the principle of majority rule, with no state given a veto.

Unlike the Security Council, which is empowered by the UN Charter to initiate actions including the use of force, the General Assembly can only make recommendations. The founders of the UN did not foresee that this limited mandate would later be expanded to allow the General Assembly to participate with the Security Council in managing security. The General Assembly, which has grown in numbers and importance, has assumed wider responsibilities and is now the primary body for addressing security as well as social and economic problems. The growth of the General Assembly's power may not be sufficient, however. As Secretary-General Kofi Annan noted in Tokyo in May 1997, the original UN design is outdated: it "reflects the world of 1945 and not the economic and political realities of today," and this failure to adapt to changing times lies at the core of complaints that the UN is unprepared to control the threats facing humanity in the twenty-first century.

That inadequacy is not necessarily permanent, however. Look at the UN's history. In response to the challenge of managing the world's many problems, the UN has already demonstrated its capacity to adapt by evolving into an extraordinarily complex network of overlapping institutions, some of which (the UN Children's Fund or UNICEF or the United Nations University, for example) fulfill their mission in part through NGOs. The UN has also increasingly come to rely on the many NGOs that are not under its formal authority. NGOs are now competing for dollars "that might otherwise go to UN bodies, but often assuming its role," as they did when "they pushed for the recent treaty to ban anti-personnel land mines and for the new world criminal court" (*Economist*, August 8, 1999, 20). This involvement and collaboration with NGOs blurs the line between governmental and nongovernmental functions, but UN-NGO cooperation helps the UN's mission. In the process, the UN has become not one organization but a decentralized conglomerate of countless committees, bureaus, boards, commissions, centers, institutes, offices, and agencies scattered around the globe, with each of its many specialized activities managed from offices in various cities (see Map 6.1). If any of these various units in the UN's widespread family occupies a central role in the UN's overall structure, it is the General Assembly.

The increase in UN bodies and activities paralleled the growth of international interdependence and cross-cutting linkages since World War II, and the

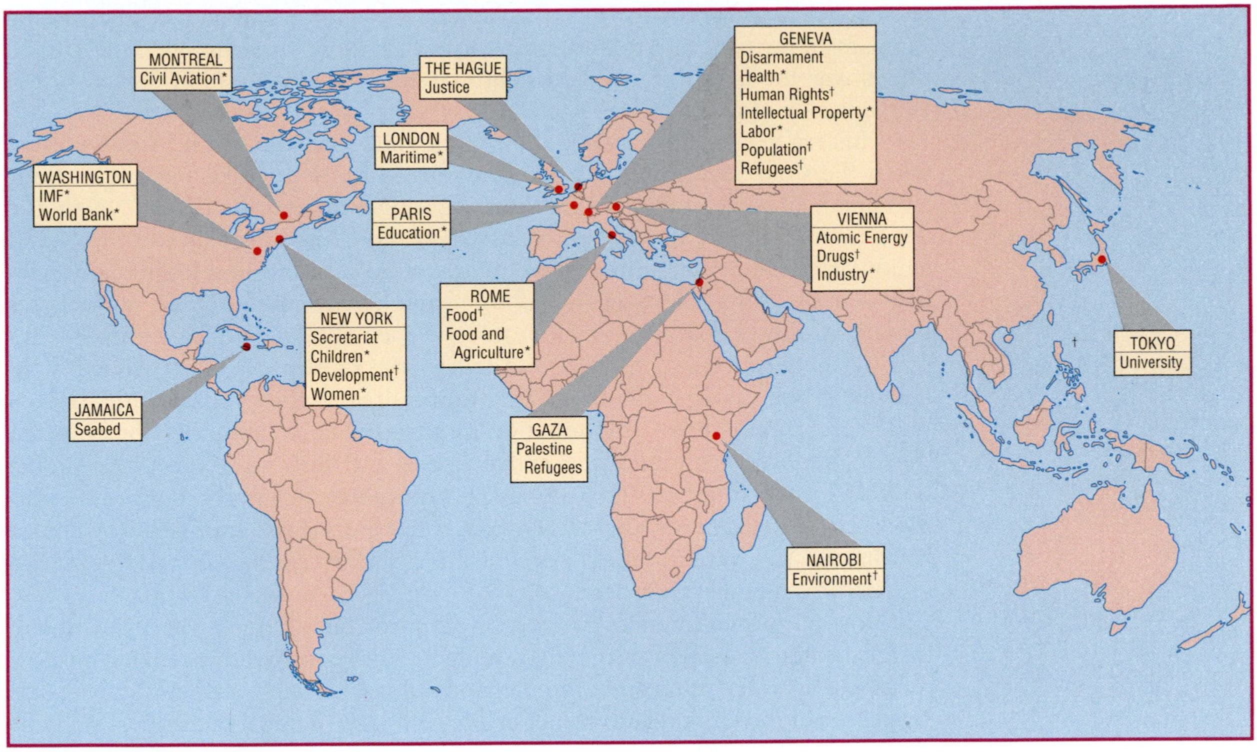

MAP 6.1
The UN's Global Network

In the words of Secretary-General Kofi Annan, "The global agenda has never been so varied, so pressing or so complex. It demands of the international community new approaches, new resources and new commitments of political will." Given this twenty-first-century reality, the United Nations has spread its administrative arm to every corner of the globe in order to fulfill its expanded mission of serving what Annan has called "a noble experiment in human cooperation."

*Specialized agencies.
†Funds and programs.
SOURCE: *The UN Handbook.*

ways in which the UN's growing membership used it to accomplish their own aims. Countries in the Global South, for instance—seizing advantage of their growing numbers under the one-state, one-vote rules of the General Assembly—began to guide UN involvement in directions of particular concern to them. This was reflected in the enormous growth of diverse affiliated agencies created to address the full array of the world's problems and needs.

The Global South countries' use of the UN forum to further their aims and interests regarding decolonization and economic development contrasted with the U.S. view of the UN as a platform for pursuing its own Cold War strategies. During the 1970s the United States suffered a series of defeats. In 1971, the General Assembly voted to seat Communist China. In 1974, the General Assembly extended permanent observer status to the Palestine Liberation Organization against U.S. opposition. In 1975, the General Assembly went on record branding Zionism "a form of racism and racial discrimination." And in 1983, the United States was the target of an overwhelmingly approved resolution deploring the U.S. invasion of Grenada.

This era of struggle between the Global South and the United States shifted when the Cold War ended. Although control of UN peacekeeping operations and financial support of UN operations no longer divides the Global North and the Global South in the same way as when the United States (and the Soviet Union) had a singular military agenda in mind and the developing countries had a quite different social, economic, and environmental one, differences remain. Today, a coalition of the less developed Global South countries comprising three-fourths of the UN and led by the **Group of 77** previously nonaligned states, along with the "Fifth Committee," which deals with the UN budget, continue to resist domination by the Global North and to protest that the UN ignores economic and social needs and fails to respect the Global South's special interests. The Global South's power in numbers gives it enormous clout because, in the 1999 words of Deputy Secretary-General Louise Fréchette, "You have to remember that this is a universal organization that has to reflect its members' wishes."

Group of 77 (G-77) a coalition of the world's poor countries formed in 1964 to press for concessions from wealthy nations (see p. 160).

North-South differences over perceived priorities are most clearly exhibited in the heated debate over the UN's budget. This controversy centers on how members should interpret the organization's charter, which states that "expenses of the Organization shall be borne by the members as apportioned by the General Assembly."

The UN budget consists of three distinct elements: the regular budget, the peacekeeping budget, and the budget for voluntary programs. States contribute to the voluntary programs and some of the peacekeeping activities as they see fit. The regular budget and other peacekeeping activities are subject to assessments.

The precise mechanism by which assessments have been determined is complicated, but historically assessments were generally allocated according to states' capacity to pay. Although this formula is under attack in many wealthy states, it still governs. Thus the United States, which has the greatest resources, contributes 25 percent of the regular UN budget (and is also the primary contributor to UN peacekeeping and voluntary programs), whereas the poorest members pay the minimum (0.01 percent) and contribute only $13,000 annually. By this agreement, the richest states pay more than three-fourths of the UN's current $1.3 billion regular budget, "although many fairly prosperous countries escape lightly. China pays just 0.9 percent of the total (less than Belgium)" (*Economist*, August 8, 1999, 22).

Resistance to this budgetary formula for funding UN activities has always existed. It has grown progressively worse, in large part because when the General Assembly apportions expenses, it does so according to majority rule. The problem is that those with the most votes (the less developed countries) do not have the money, and the most prosperous countries do not have the votes. Consider how wide these disparities had grown by July 2000. For the years from 1998 to 2000, the ten largest contributors to the UN commanded only ten votes, but were expected to pay 75 percent of its cost. At the other end of the spectrum, the poorest members paid only 25 percent of the cost but commanded 175 votes. This long-standing imbalance has led to many fierce financial disputes in the past between the more numerous Global South developing countries that wielded considerable influence over the kinds of issues on which the UN's attention and resources were focused, and the great powers' growing concern about the UN's priorities, administrative efficiency, and expenses. The wealthy members charged that the existing budget procedures institutionalize a system of taxation without fair representation. The critics countered with the argument that the great-power members should bear financial responsibilities commensurate with their wealth and influence.

At issue, of course, is not simply money, which is paltry (averaging less than twenty cents for each person in the world each year). Differences in images of what is important and which states should have political influence is the real issue. Poor states argue that needs should determine expenditure levels rather than the other way around. Major contributors, sensitive to the amounts asked of them and the purposes to which the funds are put, do not want to pay for programs they oppose. The United States in particular is the most vocal about its dissatisfaction, and in 2000 was still in arrears more than $1.2 billion—a debt that had averaged nearly $2 billion each year since 1993 when the United States first refused to pay its financial obligations. U.S. hostility toward the UN and its management and agenda was not inconsistent with previous U.S. retribution. Earlier, the Untied States had gone even further to register its disapproval with what it saw as the anti-Western drift of many UN bodies by withdrawing its membership in them. In the 1970s, for example, the Carter administration left the International Labor Organization in an attempt to influence the direction of its policies, and during the Reagan administration the United States also withdrew from the 159-member UN Educational, Scientific and Cultural Organization (UNESCO) in response to what it regarded as the politicization of the body and its hostility toward Western values (including, in particular, freedom of communication), thereby depriving UNESCO of one-fourth of its budget.

Even though the Global South countries usually managed to set the agenda in the General Assembly, like the United States they also regularly failed to pay for it or to spend time lobbying for political support from other important UN groups. In fact, in the 1990s about 90 percent of the Global South members were also in arrears.

In response to persisting cash-flow problems and rising complaints about the UN's "bloated bureaucracy" and inefficient administration, Secretary-General Kofi Annan announced "bold reforms—the most extensive and far-reaching reforms in the history of the Organization." His initiative sought to consolidate the programs under his control, reduce costs, correct corruption and waste, and reassign administrative responsibilities to different units in order to make the UN more efficient. This reform included a $123 million reduction in the 1998–1999 biennium budget on the heels of a four-year freeze and the elimination of one thousand posts above the nearly two thousand positions previously cut to reduce the staff an additional 25 percent, from ten thousand in 1996 to eight thousand. In addition, as a component of the highly detailed document entitled *Renewing the United Nations: A Programme for Reform,* Annan also begged the General Assembly to establish a commission to revise the mandates of the specialized agencies that are beyond the secretary-general's authority to reform (these kinds of changes require decisions by member states), and convened a Millennium Assembly in 2000, along with a companion People's

Assembly to define the twenty-first-century policy agenda and procedures for the UN. These massive reforms also cut the Secretariat's administrative costs by one-third, from 38 percent of the regular budget to 25 percent by 2000–2001, putting the savings into a development fund for poor countries, and adjusted the assessments of some Global North members: the United States still pays 25 percent of the regular budget, but Japan now pays 18 percent, Germany 9.6 percent, France 6.5 percent, Russia only 2.9 percent, and China only 0.9 percent. As Figure 6.3 shows, the reorganization plan merged the score of disparate programs into five categories and created the UN's first deputy secretary-general position. The new budget for the 189 members puts the UN financial house on a firmer if leaner foundation.

The future of the UN nonetheless remains uncertain. The U.S. Congress continues to resist paying America's arrears, and to make matters worse wide divergences among the General Assembly members continue to pose a well-entrenched obstacle to major changes in the way the UN works. However, given the promise of Kofi Annan's reform package and budget cutbacks, many supporters feel optimistic about the organization's long-term prospects, because past crises have been overcome and the UN's many important previous contributions to world peace and development have given most countries a large stake in its survival. The great gap between the mandates that the UN's members ordered, and the means they allowed for fulfilling them, may yet be closed. Failure would spell disaster.

The United Nations' Shifting Purposes and Priorities

The history of the UN reflects the fact that both rich countries and developing countries have successfully used the organization to promote their own foreign policy goals, and this proud record has bred considerable confidence throughout the world in the UN's future capacity to manage an ever-changing and growing agenda. However, the UN's ambitions may exceed its meager resources. The UN has been asked to address an expanding set of pressing military and nonmilitary problems, and its plate is full. Consider the wide array of world conferences that the organization has been asked to sponsor during the past three decades, keeping in mind that the issues can be expected to grow even larger in the twenty-first century: human environment (1972), law of the sea (1973), population (1974, 1984, 1994, 1999), food (1974, 1976), women (1975, 1980, 1985, 1995), human settlements (1976), basic human needs (1976), water (1977), desertification (1977), disarmament (1978, 1982, 1988), racism and racial discrimination (1978), technical cooperation among developing countries (1978), agrarian reform and rural development (1974, 1979), science and technology for development (1979), new and renewable sources of energy (1981), least developed countries (1981), aging (1982), the peaceful uses of outer space (1982), Palestine (1947, 1982), the peaceful uses of nuclear energy (1983), the prevention of crime and the treatment of offenders (1985), drug abuse and illicit trafficking in drugs (1987, 1990, 1998), the protection of children (1990), the environment and economic development (1992), transnational corporations (1992), indigenous peoples (1992, 1994), internationally organized crime (1994), social development (1995), housing (1996), human rights (1993, 1997), global warming (1992, 1997), and international trafficking of children for prostitution (2000).

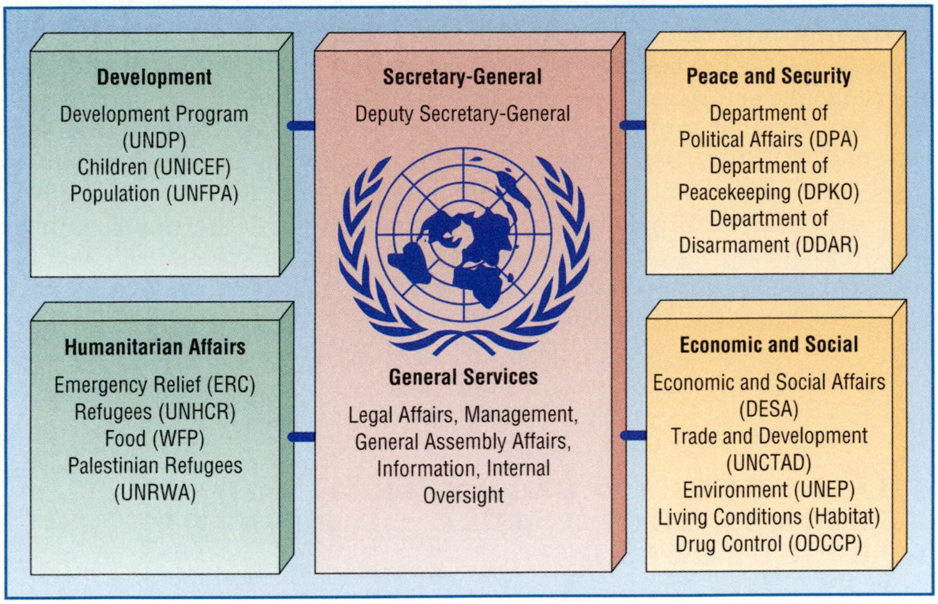

FIGURE 6.3
Secretary-General Kofi Annan's Reform for UN Administration

To offset criticism, "narrow the gap between aspiration and accomplishment," and restore the UN to a sound financial footing, Secretary-General Kofi Annan proposed and won acceptance for the reorganization and streamlining of the many UN agencies under his authority. Arguing that "to succeed in the new century, . . . the United Nations must undergo fundamental, not piecemeal, reform," Annan introduced massive cost-saving reforms that "downsized" the UN's organization by establishing five "executive groups" to make most of the important decisions. The reforms created a cabinet-style managerial chain of command, and also enabled a French Canadian, Louise Fréchette, to be appointed the first deputy secretary-general in the UN's history in 1998.

These conferences, in effect, comprise a list of "the most vital issues of present world conditions," and "represent a beginning in a long and evolving process of keeping within manageable proportions the major problems of humanity" (Bennett 1988).

In contemplating the UN's future agenda, it is sobering to reflect on Kofi Annan's warning that "The global agenda has never been so varied, so pressing or so complex. It demands of the international community new approaches, new resources and new commitments of political will." It is also sobering, given the UN's history, to recall that the agenda of issues that the UN is asked to address is likely to continue to be controversial and divisive. The UN is likely to remain an arena for heated exchanges between the Global North and the Global South, and the lack of consensus is likely to compromise the organization's capacity to forge new approaches and generate new resources to solve new global problems.

In the twenty-first century, the UN is likely to continue to play an active role both in the areas of social and economic enhancement and of peace and security. As we will examine in Chapter 16, however, the prospects for future UN peacekeeping are uncertain, and the capacity for the globe's most powerful IGO to engineer progress in the social and economic realm is also likely to be severely tested. The challenge will be great, because the UN is expected to serve the economic and social development needs of 189 states and 6 billion people with less money than the annual budget for the State University of New York system (UNDP 1997, 93). In the final analysis, the UN can be no more than the mandates and power that the member states give to it. As one high-level UN civil servant, Brian Urquhart, described the world's political dilemma, "Either the UN is vital to a more stable and equitable world and should be given the means to do the job, or peoples and governments should be encouraged to look elsewhere. But is there really an alternative?"

■ **European Union (EU)** the major regional IGO in Europe whose state members have granted it wide authority to make economic and political policy.

THE EUROPEAN UNION AS A MODEL REGIONAL IGO: A RITE OF PASSAGE FOR "EUROLAND"?

■ **security community** a group of states sharing similar values built through habits of collaboration that have become institutionalized to such an extent that all states in the community expect any disputes between its members to be settled peacefully at the bargaining table rather than on the battlefield.

■ **Third Way** an approach to governance advocated primarily by European leaders such as British Prime Minister Tony Blair and France's Socialist Prime Minister Lionel Jostin who, while recognizing few alternatives to liberal capitalism, seek to soften the cruel social impact of free-market individualism by progressively allowing government intervention to preserve social justice and the rights of individuals to freedom from fear of the deprivations caused by disruptions in the global economy.

The tug-of-war between individual states and groups of states within the UN is a reminder of an underlying principle—IGOs are run by the states that join them. This severely inhibits the IGOs' ability to rise above interstate competition and independently pursue their own purposes. In the words of Inis Claude (1967), "The United Nations has no purposes—and can have none—of its own." This is even truer of other IGOs. Because they cannot act autonomously and lack the legitimacy and capability for independent global governance, IGOs are often viewed more as instruments of states' foreign policies and arenas for debate than as independent actors.

When states dominate international organizations, as in the UN, the prospects for international cooperation decline because, as realist theorists emphasize, states typically resist any organizational actions that compromise their vital interests. This limits IGOs' capabilities for multilateral decision making to engineer global change.

A rival hypothesis—that cooperation among powerful states is possible and that international organizations help produce it—emerges from neoliberal theory. This viewpoint is especially pertinent to the **European Union (EU),** known before 1994 as the European Community (EC). The EU is a good example of the powerful role regional IGOs can sometimes play in international relations. In many respects the EU is unique, if for no other reason than that it stands as the globe's greatest example of peaceful international cooperation producing an integrated **security community** with a single economy and a common currency, one that is dedicated to liberal democratic governance and shares a preference for free-market capitalism tempered in Europe's search for a **Third Way** philosophical commitment to other values such as national equity, community, and compassion for human suffering. Moreover, the EU, or what has become known as "Euroland," is not strictly speaking a free-standing supranational organization for the collective management of European domestic and foreign affairs. The EU coexists with a large number of other European IGOs, in which it is nested and with which it jointly makes decisions. Of these, the fifty-five-member **Organization for Security and Cooperation in Europe (OSCE),** the nineteen-member NATO, and the forty-one-member Council of Europe stand as regional institutions of equal European partners, free of dividing lines, designed to manage regional security and promote the human rights of minorities through democratization. In this overlapping network of European IGOs, the EU nonetheless is prominent as the primary example of a powerful regional institution.

The process of European integration began with the creation of the European Coal and Steel Community (ECSC) in 1951, the European Atomic Energy Community (Euratom) in 1957, and the European Economic Community (EEC) in 1957. Since the late 1960s, the three have shared common organizational structures, and, in successive steps, came to be called "the European Community." Its membership has grown and its geographical scope has broadened as the EU has expanded in a series of waves to encompass fifteen countries as of 1997: Belgium, France, Germany, Italy, Luxembourg, and the Netherlands (the original "six"); Denmark, Ireland, and the United Kingdom (which joined in 1973); Greece (1981); Portugal and Spain (1986); and Austria, Finland, and Sweden (1995). At its April 1998 summit in Brussels, the EU reached a new milestone in its path toward enlargement when it formally opened negotiations aimed at bringing up to ten countries from Eastern and Central Europe plus Cyprus into its membership, pending the applicants' ability to meet the EU's economic conditions for entry and provide satisfactory indication of commitment to democracy. This move will change the face of Europe, ending the continent's postwar division and increasing the EU's population by 50 percent. The EU also then agreed to a two-tier approach to expansion, with "slow-track" applicants engaged in "preparatory talks" to join the front rank if they quickly make the required reforms, and other countries such as Turkey, which had been seeking membership since 1964, encouraged to continue negotiations.

Organization for Security and Cooperation in Europe (OSCE)
a multilateral institution that led in the transformation of Europe from a system of counterpoised military alliances to one based on common principles for maintaining security and promoting human rights and democracy.

Organizational Components and Decision-Making Procedures

The EU's institutional structure has changed over time as the organization has grown and expanded its authority over its members, to transform the EU toward governance beyond the nation-state. The principal institutions for governance, as shown in Figure 6.4, include a Council of Ministers, the European Commission, a European Parliament, and a Court of Justice. The EU's central administrative unit, the Council of Ministers, consists of cabinet ministers drawn from the EU's member states, who participate when the most important decisions are made. In this respect, the EU is an association of states similar to the UN. But the EU is more than this, as evidenced by its other elements and decision-making procedures. In the process of "enlargement," the EU's authority over its members has grown so that the EU is truly much more than the sum of its parts.

Because the Council of Ministers represents the governments of the EU's member states, it retains final authority over the policy-making decisions. The Council sets general policy guidelines for the **European Commission,** which consists of twenty commissioners (two each from Britain, France, Germany, Italy, and Spain, and one each from the remaining member states). Commissioners are nominated by EU member governments and must be approved by the European Parliament. Headquartered in Brussels, the European Commission was created to construct common economic policies for the original six member states and to oversee their administration. Today the primary functions of the

European Commission
the executive organ administratively responsible for the European Union.

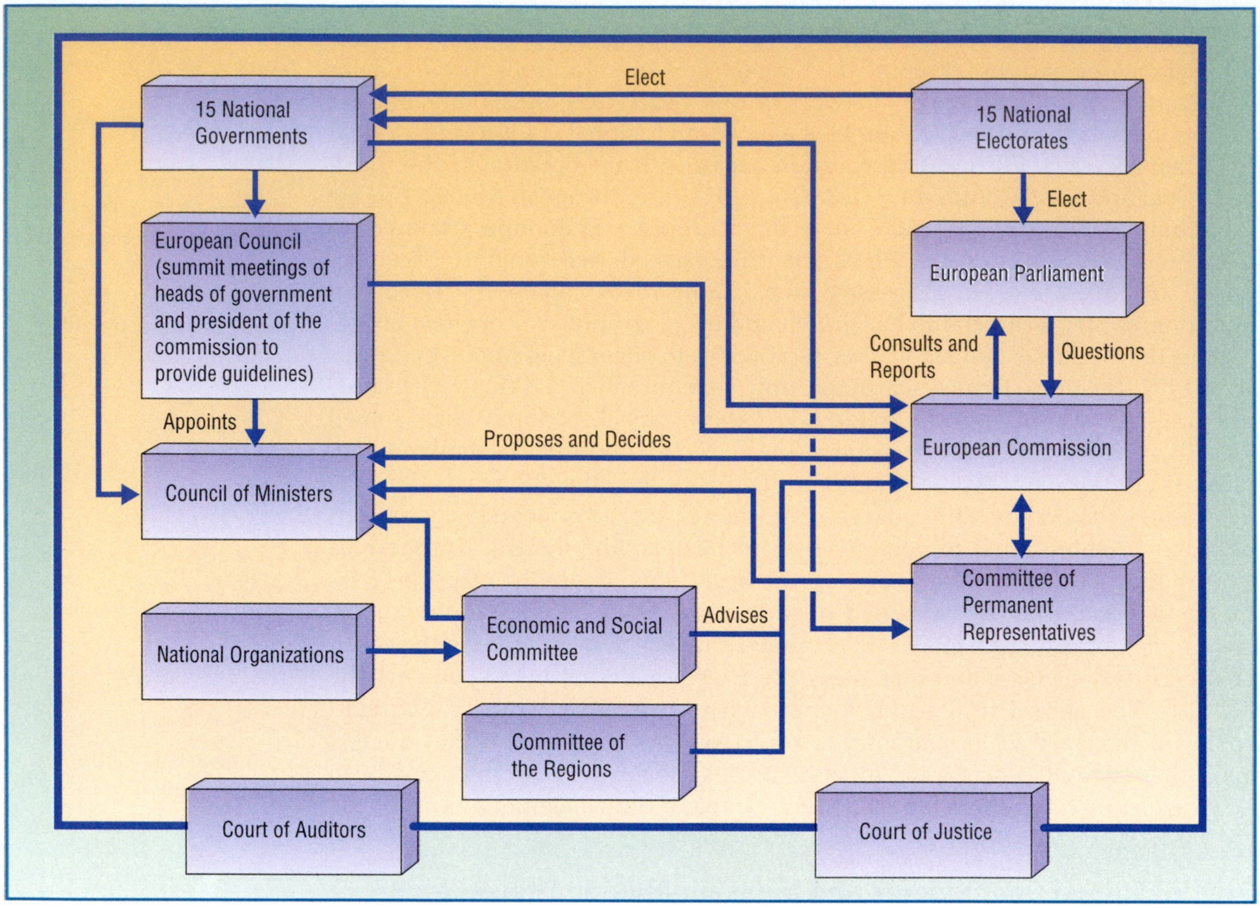

FIGURE 6.4
The European Union's Governmental Structure
The EU is a complex organization, with different responsibilities performed by various units. This figure charts the principal institutions and the relationships among them that collectively lead to EU decisions and policies.
SOURCE: *Economist* (October 23, 1999), 16.

European Commission are to propose new laws for the EU, oversee EU treaties, and execute the decrees of the European Council. A professional staff of seventeen thousand civil-service "Eurocrats," who in principle owe loyalty to the EU rather than to its national constituents, assists the Commission's administrative bureaucracy in proposing and directing decision making (by majority vote) for the EU and the Council of Ministers. The Commission proposes legislation, implements EU policies, and represents the European Union in international trade negotiations. It also manages the EU's budget, which, in contrast with most international organizations, derives part of its revenues from sources not under the control of member states.

The European Parliament represents the political parties and public opinion within Europe. It has existed from the beginning of Europe's journey toward political unification, although at its creation this legislative body was

No State Is (Really) an Island Small island states such as Thuru Island in the Maldives may appear to be tiny paradises. However, they are exceptionally vulnerable to both natural catastrophes and human threats. If international organizations such as the UN will not help to protect them, who will?

appointed rather than elected and had very little power. That is no longer the case. The European Parliament is now chosen in a direct election by the nearly 300 million citizens of the EU's member states. Its 626 deputies debate issues at the monumental $1.2 billion glass headquarters in Brussels and at a lavish Strasbourg palace in the same way that national legislative bodies do under liberal democratic governments. Although the European Parliament has grown in prominence and power as European integration has progressed, it shares authority with the Council of Ministers representing member governments. Still, the Parliament's influence has increased over time. The deputies elected through universal suffrage pass laws with the Council, approve the EU's budget (monitored by the Court of Auditors in Luxembourg), oversee the European Commission, and can overturn its acts. This last element in the Parliament's authority gives it substantial clout, which it has not been hesitant to exercise. The European Parliament sometimes denounces European Commission activities, as it did in July 1999 when the Parliament accused the previous group of commissioners of cronyism and corruption, forced their resignation, and appointed a new Commission to create a "new era."

The European Court of Justice in Luxembourg has also grown in prominence and power as European integration has gathered depth and breadth. From the start, the court was given responsibility for adjudicating claims and conflicts among EU governments as well as between those governments and the new institutions the EU created. Comprising fifteen judges, the court interprets EU law for national courts and rules on legal questions that arise within the EU's institutions and, in an important departure from past traditions, hears and rules on cases concerning individual citizens. The fact that its decisions are binding distinguishes the European Court of Justice from most other international tribunals.

In practice, two decision-making procedures have been followed for the adoption of EU directives and regulations: consultation and cooperation. Which of the two procedures is followed to adopt regulations depends on the nature of the proposal under consideration, with the principal difference being that the European Parliament plays a greater role in the cooperative than in the consultive process. Under both procedures, however, the twenty commissioners of the European Commission in Brussels have been the driving force in European integration.

The political unification of Europe has been built step-by-step as the EU has marched toward ever greater unity. Moving beyond the nation-state toward a single integrated European federation has not been smooth, and "tensions persisted, and still do, over how far and how fast Europe ought to move toward government beyond the nation-states, over how large the European Union ought to be, over the balance of initiative and authority among the central institutions (and the balance of responsibility between the central institutions and national authorities) and about how the benefits and burdens of forging greater unity ought to be distributed" (Puchala 2001). These obstacles not withstanding, the progress has been remarkable. It is noteworthy that although "the various continental structures—the EU and Parliament, and so on—are still a few posts short of constituting a true government, Europe has come far from its start as a congeries of independent states with clashing territorial and ideological ambitions. 'European-ness' is an increasingly viable identity, and Europe is an increasingly solid confederation, reminiscent in some ways of the early United States" (*New Yorker,* July 12, 1999, 22). To grasp the magnitude of this change and its character, we need to look more closely at the nature of governance within the EU.

Supranationalism or Pooled Sovereignty?

How, then, are the EU's structures and decision-making procedures best described, as compared to the UN and other international organizations? The EU has the power to make some decisions binding on its members without being subject to their individual approval. In this sense it is a "supranational organization." That is, it is not an organization of or among states, but one that goes beyond them to supersede the individual countries that comprise it.

Although the EU incorporates some supranational elements, the term **pooled sovereignty** (Keohane and Hoffmann 1991) better captures its essence, as states remain paramount in its institutional structures and decision-making procedures. The transfers of full authority to a central body were until recently rather modest, and critical decisions are still made in the Council of Ministers where states dominate. Most EU decisions continue to depend on national governments for implementation. Sovereignty is nonetheless shared in the sense that decision-making responsibility is now spread among governments and between them and the EU's institutions.

■ **pooled sovereignty** legal authority granted to an IGO by its members to make collective decisions regarding specified aspects of public policy heretofore made exclusively by each sovereign government.

Awareness that EU members decide by majority rule on some issues is critical to an understanding of pooled sovereignty. A major obstacle to effective decision making in the past was that most substantive proposals required unanimous approval. That rule enabled member states to protect their national interests as they alone defined them. For instance, France took advantage of this provision to thwart EC action in the late 1960s by simply refusing to send a minister to its meetings. The resulting impasse, called the "empty chair" crisis, spurred the development of new decision-making procedures.

Today, in a radical departure from past practices, and despite recurrent fears that a minority will block the will of the majority, reaching a consensus is easier because the EU requires only a qualified voting majority on most internal market decisions (with votes weighted according to country size):

> Unlike [typical] international organizations, the European [Union] as a whole has gained some share of states' sovereignty: The member states no longer have supremacy over all other authorities within their traditional territory, nor are they independent of outside authorities. Its institutions have some of the authority normally associated with institutions of sovereign governments: On certain issues individual states can no longer veto proposals before the Council [of Ministers]; members of the Commission are independent figures rather than instructed agents. (Keohane and Hoffmann 1991, 13)

The EU's nature is also described by its functions. On the one hand, it is so distinctly different from traditional international organizations that it is virtually in a class by itself. On the other, it has self-evidently not yet crystallized into a single "United States of Europe," with a single federal government. The legal meaning of sovereignty holds that the state alone has dominion over its internal affairs and control over the policies for its foreign relations. That level of sovereignty remains more an ambition rather than an achievement. Although "much of European political rhetoric these days builds on the illusion of unity from Lisbon to Vladivostok—a Europe with no walls—in reality . . . the integration of Europe needs a renewed vision of its future, a 'new frontier' that could attract the energies and ambitions of the Continent's leaders and a 'new deal' to reaffirm solidarity among its nations and a sense of belonging among its people" (Janning 1999).

Europe: An Economic Giant

Military security was uppermost in the minds of those who sought to forge a new Europe out of the ashes of World War II. Still, the EU has scored its most dramatic successes on the economic front. In 1999, the European Union's (EU) fifteen members represented a combined gross national product (GNP) of $7 trillion; with 6.4 percent (combined) of the world's total population, the EU accounted for 40 percent of total international trade (Economist 1999b, 39). The EU is the largest and richest single consumer market in the world. The EU's total gross domestic product and its population then exceeded those of the North American Free Trade Agreement, its closest economic rival, and the gap will widen if and when enlargement to an EU of twenty-six or more states is concluded.

As previously noted, the expanded EU builds on previous precedents. In 1991, the seven members of the **European Free Trade Association (EFTA),** created in 1960 as a counterpoint to the EEC, concluded a treaty with the EU to create the world's largest trading area. The agreement anticipated a single European "common market" that would have eliminated trade barriers among nineteen countries and nearly 400 million people. Although the treaty did not allow the EFTA countries (then Austria, Finland, Iceland, Liechtenstein, Norway, Sweden, and Switzerland) power in setting EU trade policies, it set the stage for their participation in the benefits of the single market, eliminating barriers to

■ **European Free Trade Association (EFTA)**
an organization created by seven Western European states in 1960 to counter the European Economic Community by eliminating trade restrictions among them over time; united with the EU in 1994.

the movement of money, products, and workers within the EU. In addition, the treaty eased the way for former EFTA members to join the EU as full partners, which Austria, Sweden, and Finland did in January 1995.

The EU's membership and geographical boundaries will expand further after the six new states accepted for fast-track membership at the December 1997 Luxembourg Summit (the Czech Republic, Cyprus, Estonia, Hungary, Poland, and Slovenia) are joined later by the five other states invited on a slower track schedule (Bulgaria, Latvia, Lithuania, Romania, and Slovakia). In addition, the EU continues negotiations with Norway, Switzerland, Turkey, and Malta, and sitting on the sidelines potentially seeking membership are Russia and the fourteen other former Soviet republics, providing they can meet the democratic and economic requirements for inclusion. As Map 6.2 suggests, the probable expansion of the European Union would mend many of the geopolitical divisions of this once war-torn continent.

Beyond continuing discussions regarding formal enlargement, other countries have signed treaties that provide them with direct ties to the EU. The EU is also linked to a large number of developing countries in Africa, the Caribbean, and the Pacific (ACP) through the 1975 **Lomé Convention.** The Lomé IV Convention provides the ACP countries tariff-free access to the EU single market without the necessity of reciprocal concessions for EU exports to their economies. The EU's Center for Industrial Development also provides a commodity price stabilization scheme and foreign aid. In addition to the ACP countries, the EU has agreements with several other countries throughout the Global South and has signed a cooperative agreement with seven members of the Association of Southeast Asian Nations covering trade, economic, and development issues.

■ **Lomé Convention** the series of agreements inspired by the NIEO movement that links forty-six developing countries to Europe to help the African, Caribbean, and Pacific (ACP) countries stabilize their export earnings and to provide them with financial and technical assistance.

Despite this legacy of successful integration and enlargement, the disintegrative forces of nationalism have constantly retarded progress. Resistance to the spirit and timetable of recent treaties continues to undermine supporters' optimism about establishing a truly borderless European common market, with a single currency and monetary system governed by a central political institution. The rewards of integration and enlargement are huge because, in the words of German Foreign Minister Klaus Kinkel, they would create the opportunity to extend "peace, democratic stability, and prosperity across all Europe." However, those benefits could impose equally huge potential costs and risks, especially to those EU members in southern and eastern Europe which do not presently share the same level of prosperity as the more industrialized EU members in the north. This disparity and division became apparent in December 1997 when the EU members narrowly avoided a divisive split over how they would coordinate their economic policies after they switched to the new common currency, the euro, in 1999. They avoided a rupture when in the first round of the Economic and Monetary Union (EMU) negotiations, the eleven members that officially adopted the euro formed a special euro council and agreed to continue negotiations with the four members expected to keep their national currencies until at least the July 1, 2002, deadline for all EU national currencies to be abolished.

Despite these persisting problems, the creation of the euro signals a huge step forward in "Euroland's" economic integration. The advent of a single European currency stands as a symbol of unity, and, by removing exchange-rate uncertainty from the European market, the euro creates predictability that gives the European currency the same status that the American dollar has

MAP 6.2

The Enlarged European Union and Its Links to Europe's Economic Associations

After growing to fifteen members, its "Agenda 2000" prepares the EU for enlargement eastward to include as many as twenty-six members in the twenty-first century. Indeed, in 2000 Poland, Hungary, the Czech Republic, Slovenia, Estonia, and Cyprus were negotiating the final terms for their inclusion, and if the other applicants succeed in undertaking the significant economic and political reforms required for EU membership, the "common European home" could stretch across the entire continent and include all the former communist countries in central Europe. Note that many of the states likely to join the EU have association agreements with it already and that others are members of the European Free Trade Association (EFTA).

[1] Serbia and Montenegro have asserted the formation of a joint independent state, but this entity hs not been formally recognized as a state by the United States.

[2] Estonia, Poland, Czech Republic, Hungary, Slovenia, and Cyprus have begun formal negotiations for EU membership.

[3] Includes Iceland (not shown).

[4] Includes Cyprus (not shown).

enjoyed in the twentieth century. Likewise, the euro takes another step toward the pooling of sovereignty because it reduces prospects "for different European economies to grow at different rates at different times in different ways.

Depressed countries will not be able to borrow enough or devalue their way out of recession; overheated economics may see their interest rates cut. Countries with high unemployment may see their interest rates hiked for reasons that have nothing to do with their economic needs" (*New Republic,* January 25, 1999, 7). The new single currency for eleven EU members is "genuinely historic, an epic moment [because] it is the first time that countries of anything like this number, size or global economic weight have gathered together to share a currency, and thus to pool their monetary sovereignty. It is arguably the most momentous currency innovation since the establishment of the United States dollar in 1792" (*Economist,* January 2, 1999, 16).

The reforms initiated with the slogan "Europe 1992" started the EU's movement from a **customs union** permitting the free movement of workers toward a genuine **common market** in which financial frontiers are completely abolished. Such a genuine common market requires the removal of countless regulations interfering with transborder exchanges long apparent in Europe, including restraints on the free movement of purchased goods. It also requires the harmonization of product standards (e.g., uniform socket sizes for electrical appliances), variations in rules governing taxation and capital movements, regulations on transport standards (e.g., rules governing truckers' driving hours, rest periods, and driving teams), and the like. Such inhibitions historically safeguarded national autonomy and perpetuated nationalistic rivalries; their elimination would further pool sovereignty within the EU. In this context, the substitution of majority rule in the Council of Ministers for the previous practice of consensus decision making takes on added meaning. Majority rule, reaffirmed in the Single European Act, prevents individual states from vetoing key decisions.

■ **customs union**
a market in which sovereign states agree to remove taxes on goods exported across the borders of the union's members.

■ **common market**
a form of economic integration in which restrictions on the free movement of commodities, capital, and labor among member states are completely abolished.

Yet, as noted, nationalistic resistance continues. More than a few skeptics predict that the EU's ambitious plans will ultimately fail or fall short of the goal of unity. These skeptics point to the possibility that the eleven-country caucus of single-currency countries will open a new division between them and the EU's four other members, and that enlargement eastward will create an EU too big and diverse to effectively govern its members. Although historical forces are driving the integration process forward, many obstacles to the full union of a greater Europe remain.

Europe: Military Midget or Superpower?

Since 1970 the EU's members have sought to construct a coordinated and common position on foreign policy issues. This collective spirit, known as **European Political Cooperation (EPC),** emerged at the Paris Summits of 1972 and 1974 to establish regular meetings between EU foreign ministers. Nonetheless, states often went their own way, and members failed to speak with a single voice on foreign policy issues.

■ **European Political Cooperation (EPC)**
the ongoing effort of European Union members to devise a common position on foreign policy issues through regular meetings among EU foreign ministers.

To overcome this failure, the EU agreed to what became known as its **Common Foreign and Security Policy (CFSP),** which defines as the EU's objectives safeguarding "the common values, fundamental interests, and independence of the Union," strengthening the EU's security, preserving "world peace and international security [and promoting] international cooperation to develop and consolidate democracy and the rule of law, and respect for human rights and fundamental freedoms." To fulfill these goals, the EU must further

■ **Common Foreign and Security Policy (CFSP)**
the agreement reached by the European Union that defines the goals in foreign and defense policy the EU pledges jointly to pursue.

redefine its foreign policy mission and the extents to which it will use its political and military power, which means reaching a consensus about its military **doctrine** and about the EU's relationship with the numerous other European security IGOs that presently coexist (see Figure 6.5). Of these European defense organizations, NATO is the most important.

When the Soviet security threat and the Cold War ended, the EU's diverse members no longer had a common external challenge to unite them, and NATO's very survival became a subject of debate. Since then, however, the NATO allies have reaffirmed their commitment to a broadened agenda for the defense organization. At the October 1993 summit in Travemuende, Germany, the NATO defense ministers endorsed a U.S. plan known as the **Partnership for Peace (PfP),** which offered limited military NATO "partnerships" to virtually any interested European country, including Russia and the former Warsaw Pact states. The eager new partners began participating in NATO peacekeeping missions and crisis-management operations, even though they were not given the same commitment to defend their borders guaranteed to NATO's full members. The new plan helped to alleviate fears that the alliance would disintegrate, given the hapless way in which the whole EU and NATO had slept when the former Yugoslavia was splintering prior to U.S. intervention. The PfP also prepared the way for the 1999 admission of Poland, Hungary, and the Czech Republic to full membership (an enlargement that heightened Russia's fears of exclusion and encirclement, and after the Kosovo intervention, alarmed China, as explained in Chapter 15). The PfP laid the groundwork for creation of the **Euro-Atlantic Partnership Council (EAPC),** replacing the PfP with "stronger, more cooperative partnerships . . . in decision making" among its forty-four partners which are allied with NATO's nineteen core members. The level of cooperation to which the EU, NATO, and EAPC member countries aspired was partially fulfilled in 1999 when, after much difficulty, the coalition reached the necessary degree of agreement for the allies to work together militarily to intervene in the Kosovo crisis. However, that experience bred renewed intercoalition discord and revealed the problems Europe still faces in forging a joint defense policy for common purposes. Even though the EU and NATO declared victory, they were humiliated by Europe's dependence on American military power. For this reason, there was "no wonder that right after NATO's Kosovo victory the European Union declared its intention to form its own military force capable of acting independently of the United States" (Friedman 1999a; see also Medley 1999). In reaction, the EU vowed at its Cologne Summit in June 1999 to become a military power and to move toward a truly unified common policy on security and defense that would give it the "capacity for autonomous action, backed up by credible military forces." "This is a big step in the history of the European Union," claimed German Deputy Foreign Minister Guenther Verhegen. What remains to be tested is whether in the twenty-first century the EU will indeed take this bold step toward superpower status.

The ten-country European military pact known as the **Western European Union (WEU)** is another symbol of the EU's proclaimed resolve to act in unity on defense problems. The WEU, which in 1994 made nine former Warsaw Pact countries associate partners, is scheduled to merge with the EU in 2001, bolstering Europe's ability to provide a common defense and reduce European military dependence on the United States. The forty-one member **Council of Europe,** founded in 1949 to promote greater unity and to safeguard Europe's cultural

■ **doctrine**
a set of principles identifyng the purposes to which a country or an IGO will put its military power in the world, including identification of the conditions under which that actor is prepared to use military force to achieve its foreign policy objectives (see p. 522).

■ **Partnership for Peace (PfP)**
a plan proposed in 1993 by the United States that established limited military partnerships between NATO and the former communist countries that had been allies in the Warsaw Pact.

■ **Euro-Atlantic Partnership Council (EAPC)**
a coordinating institution within NATO created in 1998 to manage the common political, military, financial, and security issues confronting Europe.

■ **Western European Union (WEU)**
a European military pact composed of ten member and eighteen associate member countries.

■ **Council of Europe**
an organization founded in 1949, whose members now include forty states, for the purpose of promoting unity and preserving Europe's cultural heritage.

heritage, also plays an advisory role in European decision making. Thus the countries of Europe find themselves involved in a variety of overlapping security organizations, and critics point out that this very complexity interferes with the creation and coordination of a common European security policy (see Figure 6.5). Although NATO seeks to continue to lead in defense policy making, the members of the EU have pledged to develop a capacity to act independently, without the United States, in military matters and to do so from a common EU defense policy.

Closer cooperation on foreign and national security policy is a prerequisite to achieving the dream of a "United States of Europe." Differences continue to make a unified EU foreign and defense policy elusive, and even the form of a potential European government for a common European citizenship remains a divisive, unresolved issue. Still, the idea of a single Europe remains compelling for many Europeans who are haunted by the specter of European nationalities and states that have been fighting each other ever since the Pax Romana collapsed eighteen hundred years ago. Consolidation could be in Europe's future. But so could disintegration and the resurrection of intra-European discord and perhaps even a surge of civil wars.

OTHER REGIONAL ORGANIZATIONS

Since Europe's 1950s initiatives toward economic and political integration, a dozen or so regional economic schemes have been created in various other parts of the world, notably among states in the Global South. Most seek to stimulate regional economic growth. The major regional organizations in the Global South include:

- The Asia-Pacific Economic Cooperation (APEC) forum, created in 1989 as a gathering of twelve states without a defined goal. APEC's membership has grown to eighteen countries (including the United States) that collectively account for 40 percent of the globe's population and more than half of global GDP. At its November 1994 meeting in Jakarta, APEC set for itself the explicit goal of free trade.
- The Association of Southeast Asian Nations (ASEAN), established in 1967 by five founding members to promote regional economic, social, and cultural cooperation, and later, in 1999, to create a free-trade zone among its ten Southeast Asian members as a counterweight outside the orbit of Japan, China, the United States and other great powers, so ASEAN could compete as a bloc in international trade. ASEAN's expansion has created an identity crisis, with fears of new divisions between the older "haves" and the newer "have-not" members, which include not only communist Vietnam, Laos, and Cambodia but also the impoverished dictatorship of Myanmar (formerly Burma). ASEAN today struggles with political, economic, and environmental problems that beset the region and that cannot be managed without the combined efforts of this regional IGO.
- The Caribbean Community and Common Market (CARICOM), established in 1973 to promote economic development and integration among its fourteen members.
- The Council of Arab Economic Unity (CAEU), established in 1964 from a 1957 accord to promote economic integration among its twelve Arab members.

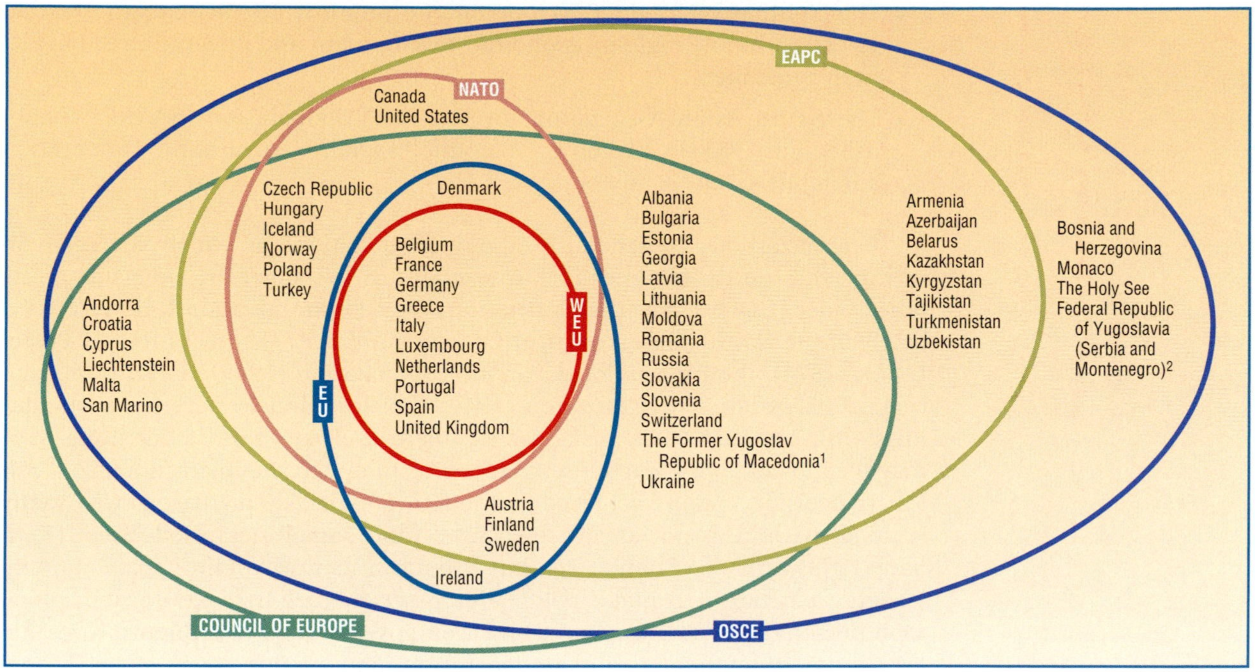

FIGURE 6.5

Overlapping Memberships in Europe's Major International Organizations

Since World War II, Europe has built, in a series of steps, an increasing number of political, military, and economic organizations, encompassing more and more countries throughout an enlarged geographic network of institutions. The overlapping architecture includes OSCE, NATO, EAPC, the Council of Europe, the EU, and the Western European Union defense organizations. As Anne-Else Holjberg in NATO's Political Affairs Division complained in 1997, "there is still a certain degree of rivalry between [these] different organizations," and the multilayered structure has made collective decision making difficult.

[1]Turkey recognizes the Republic of Macedonia by its constitutional name.
[2]Suspended.

- The Economic Community of West African States (ECOWAS), established in 1975 to promote regional economic cooperation among its seventeen members.
- The Organization of the Islamic Conference (OIC) coordinates a large number of activities among fifty Islamic states (plus the Palestine Liberation Organization) for the purpose of promoting Islamic solidarity in economic, social, cultural, and political affairs. While not technically a regional IGO, the OIC orchestrates preventive diplomacy, but does not condone the use of terrorism, and is not concerned with promoting fundamentalist Islamic religious principles.
- The Latin American Integration Association (LAIA), also known as *Asociación Latinoamericana de Integración* (ALADI), established in 1981 to promote freer regional trade among its eleven members.

- The Southern African Development Community (SADC), established in 1992 to promote regional economic development and integration among its twelve members.
- The South Asian Association for Regional Cooperation (SAARC), established in 1985 to promote economic, social, and cultural cooperation among its seven members.

It is hazardous to generalize about organizations as widely divergent in membership and sometimes in purpose as this list suggests, alongside many other, older IGOs such as the International Telecommunication Union founded in 1865, the World Meteorological Organization (1873), the Universal Postal Union (1874), the International Labour Organization (1919), and the International Civil Aviation Organization (1944) that function to perform particular missions. Regional IGOs seek to coordinate their programs, but none have managed to collaborate at a level that begins to match the institutionalized collective decision making achieved by the EU. The particular reasons why many regional IGOs are "not always successful [and sometimes] ineffective" (Keohane 1998) vary (see Chapter 16), but at bottom they are all limited by national leaders' reluctance to make politically costly choices that would undermine their personal popularity at home and their governments' sovereignty. Nonetheless, these attempts at regional cooperation demonstrate many states' acceptance of the fact that they cannot individually resolve many of the problems that confront them collectively.

Because the state is clearly failing to manage many transnational policy problems, it finds itself ironically acting as the primary agent of the same cooperative management efforts that are eroding the state's power. Collective problem solving through the growth and expanding power of IGOs is likely to continue. Globalization and the force of a shrinking, borderless world are increasing the influence of international institutions; in turn, IGOs' expanding webs of interdependence are infringing on the power of states and changing the ways in which they network on the global stage. These IGOs and processes promise to transform world politics, which is why "almost any discussion of public policy nowadays seems to begin and end with the same idea: The state is in retreat [and] its power to rule is fading" (Crook 1997). Another set of agents in the transnational transformation and globalization of world politics—nonstate actors such as NGOs, ethnonational movements, and multinational corporations—are also highly active and increasingly influential. In Chapter 7 we turn our attention to their behavior and impact.

KEY TERMS

intergovernmental organizations (IGOs)
nongovernmental organizations (NGOs)
United Nations (UN)
collective security
consensus decision making
failed states
Group of 77 (G-77)
European Union (EU)
security community
Third Way
Organization for Security and Cooperation in Europe (OSCE)
European Commission
pooled sovereignty
European Free Trade Association (EFTA)

Lomé Convention
customs union
common market
European Political Cooperation (EPC)
Common Foreign and Security Policy (CFSP)
doctrine
Partnership for Peace (PfP)
Euro-Atlantic Partnership Council (EAPC)
Western European Union (WEU)
Council of Europe

SUGGESTED READING

Caporaso, James A. *Challenges and Dilemmas of European Union.* Boulder, Colo.: Westview Press, 2000.

Claude, Inis L., Jr., *Swords into Plowshares: The Problems and Progress of International Organizations.* New York: Random House, 1984.

Diehl, Paul F., ed. *The Politics of Global Governance: International Organization in an Interdependent World.* Boulder, Colo.: Lynne Rienner, 1997.

Keohane, Robert O. "International Institutions: Can Interdependence Work?," *Foreign Policy* 110 (Spring 1998): 82–96.

Krasner, Stephen D. *Sovereignty: Organized Hypocrisy.* Princeton, N.J.: Princeton University Press, 1999.

Medley, Richard. "Europe's Next Big Idea: Strategy and Economics Point to a European Military," *Foreign Affairs* 78 (September/October 1999): 18–22.

Mingst, Karen A., and Margaret P. Karns. *The United Nations in the Post–Cold War Era.* Boulder, Colo.: Westview Press, 1995.

Pease, Kelly-Kate S. *International Organizations: Perspectives on Governance in the Twenty-First Century.* Upper Saddle River, N.J.: Prentice-Hall, 2000.

Piening, Christopher. *Global Europe: The European Union in World Affairs.* Boulder, Colo.: Lynne Rienner, 1998.

Pond, Elizabeth. *The Rebirth of Europe.* Washington, D.C.: Brookings, 1999.

Ruggle, John Gerald. *Constructing the World Polity: Essays on International Institutionalization.* London: Routledge, 1998.

Weiss, Thomas G., David P. Forsythe, and Roger A. Coate. *The United Nations and Changing World Politics,* 3rd ed. Boulder, Colo.: Westview Press, 2000.

Weiss, Tom, Neil McFarlane, and W. Andy Knight, eds. *Global Governance,* journal published quarterly. Boulder, Colo.: Lynne Rienner.

Ziring, Lawrence, Robert E. Riggs, and Jack C. Plano. *The United Nations: International Organization and World Politics,* 3rd ed. New York: Harcourt, 2000.

WHERE ON THE WORLD WIDE WEB?

The following is a small sample of Web sites for intergovernmental organizations (IGOs) like those described in Table 6.1 (see p. 175).

European Union

http://europa.eu.int/index.htm

The EU is an IGO with regional membership and multiple purposes. Chapter 6 characterizes the authority structure of the EU as one of pooled sovereignty, under which the member states grant the EU legal authority to make some collective decisions for them. After entering the Europa Web site, explore the main institutions of the EU. How does the Court of Justice differ from the UN's International Court of Justice?

International Monetary Fund

http://www.imf.org/exteranl/about.htm

The International Monetary Fund (IMF) is an IGO with global membership that was created to promote international monetary cooperation and facilitate the expansion and balanced growth of international trade by promoting exchange stability. It does this by making monetary resources temporarily available to its members. Click on the Lending link on the IMF's homepage. Which countries have received the most IMF support? Why do you think this is so?

North Atlantic Treaty Organization
http://www.nato.int

The North Atlantic Treaty Organization (NATO) is a military alliance that includes the European states, the United States, and Canada. It was originally formed to protect Europe from the Soviet threat after World War II. Since the end of the Cold War, it has been restructured and now has an auxiliary membership with the establishment of the Partnership for Peace (PfP). To see PfP's membership, click on Welcome to NATO link from the NATO homepage and then click on the Partnership for Peace area in the image map. What characteristics do the 41 PfP member countries share? Although once a regional collective defense organization, NATO has had to redefine its mission since the end of the Cold War. NATO's involvement in Bosnia was the first venture into new terrain. Many question whether it is appropriate for an organization designed for mutual self-protection from external attack to be involved in policing civil wars in Europe. What do you think?

Organization of American States
http://www.oas.org/

The Organization of American States (OAS) is a multipurpose IGO with regional members from North and South America. It is the "principal forum in the hemisphere for political, economic, and social dialogue." As you can see from the homepage, the OAS is concerned with issues such as democracy, human rights, trade, environment, and education. It sees its major challenges as drugs, corruption, poverty, and landmines. Explore one of these challenges. How might the United States and other hemispheric countries differ in their views of the challenge and the best way to solve it?

United Nations
http://www.un.org/

The United Nations (UN) is an IGO with global membership that performs multiple purposes. The UN Web site is organized according to the organization's primary concerns: peace and security, international law, humanitarian affairs, economic and social development, and human rights. Chapter 6 has introduced you to the major UN organs—the General Assembly, the Security Council, Economic and Social Council, and Secretariat. Which organ focuses on which areas of concern?

World Health Organization
http://www.who.int/

The main goal of the World Health Organization (WHO) is the attainment by all peoples of the highest possible level of health. It defines health as the "state of complete physical, mental, and social well-being and not merely the absence of disease or infirmity." The WHO has been hailed as one of the best examples of how an international organization can benefit the world community. Review the WHO's major achievements and the challenges it faces. Do you think it is possible for the WHO to achieve its goals? Do you agree with its expanded definition of health that includes social well-being?

The World Trade Organization
http://www.wto.org/

The World Trade Organization (WTO) is an IGO with a global membership and multiple purposes. Its mission is to ensure that trade flows between states as smoothly, predictably, and freely as possible. Decision making within the WTO is by consensus among all 135 member countries. Trade agreements are then ratified by members' parliaments. The WTO also uses a dispute settlement process that focuses on interpreting agreements and ensuring that member countries' trade policies follow them. The third WTO conference was held in Seattle in 1999. Click on the Webcast to see and hear the proceedings. What are the main points of contention between the Global North and the Global South?

CHAPTER 7

The Promise and Peril of Nongovernmental Organizations (NGOs)

TOPICS AND THEMES

- Nationalism, nationality, and ethnicity
- Religious movements
- International terrorists
- Multinational corporations (MNCs)
- NGOs: Saviors of stranglers of the state?

- **CONTROVERSY** ARE RELIGIOUS MOVEMENTS CAUSES OF WAR OR SOURCES OF TRANSNATIONAL HARMONY?
- **CONTROVERSY** ARE MULTINATIONAL CORPORATIONS A POSITIVE FORCE FOR THE WORLD? BALANCING CLAIMS AND CRITICISMS

Pakistani religious leader Sami-ul-Haq and followers

The protection of the nation against destruction from without and disruption from within is the overriding concern. . . . Nothing can be tolerated that might threaten the coherence of the nation.

—HANS J. MORGENTHAU, realist scholar, 1967

[Nonstate actors] are gaining economic and political power to decide their own futures. Faced with popular demand for greater self-determination, national governments around the world are under pressure to devolve power. . . . In this context, globalization is like a giant wave that can either capsize nations or carry them forward on its crest.

—SHAHID YUSUF, World Bank senior economic adviser, 1999

If you are like many other people in the world, there is at least one and possibly more world problems that are of great concern to you. You would like to see the world change. How can you help make the world a better place? You are likely to realize that you cannot engineer global changes all by yourself. However, you probably recognize that other people share your concerns and that by joining together with them you can exercise power; you can join with other, like-minded people in the world and raise your collective voices.

nongovernmental organizations (NGOs) transnational organizations of private citizens joined together to work toward common goals; they include professional associations, foundations, multinational corporations, or internationally active groups in different states.

In today's world, increasing numbers of people have found that through joining private interest groups they can participate in the global system and lobby to influence international decision making. They have joined as members of one or more **nongovernmental organizations (NGOs),** of which there are over 27,000 now in existence worldwide. NGOs are private international actors whose members are not states, but are instead volunteers drawn from the populations of two or more states who have formed organizations to promote their shared interests and ideals in order to influence the policies of state governments and intergovernmental organizations (IGOs).

These NGOs tackle many global problems, seeking changes in the world for causes such as disarmament, women's rights, environmental protection, and human development and human rights. Most of them pursue objectives that are highly respected and constructive, and therefore do not provoke controversy or arouse much opposition. For example, NGOs such as Amnesty International, the International Chamber of Commerce, Greenpeace, the Red Cross, Save the Children, the World Wildlife Federation, and Global YouthConnect (to support young people who are victims of human rights abuses) enjoy widespread popular support. Others, however, are more controversial because they push for changes which, were they to succeed, would threaten the interests of other groups who have a stake in preserving the status quo. For example, NGOs such as the Union of Concerned Scientists and Doctors Without Borders are interested in reducing military spending, and this threatens the budgets of members of the "military-industrial complex" whose jobs and income depend on continued high government spending on defense. Hence, many NGOs work at cross-purposes in a competitive struggle to redefine the global agenda.

What makes NGOs increasingly prominent on the world stage is that through their bargaining activities they have managed to successfully produce a number of substantial changes in international relations. Their efforts have at times led to the successful creation of **regimes** or new sets of rules that help to regulate many transnational problems. At the same time, the demands of NGOs have shaken the sovereign control of state governments and reduced states' authority over their foreign policies. This challenge to states by minority racial or religious NGOs has been especially severe in fragile or failing states where revolt by NGOs has led to the collapse of the state, and even in some strong states NGO pressure has led to the **devolution** of the central government's power.

regimes norms and rules for interaction agreed to by a set of states.

devolution deliberate transfer of powers held by a central government to regional or nonstate bodies (see p. 639).

This chapter explores the issues and controversies surrounding NGOs as nonstate actors in world affairs, a category that includes many different types of players in the game of world politics:

> On the most basic level, nonstate [actors] are associations of individuals and/or groups that are not established by agreements among states. This broad definition includes such disparate entities as transnational corporations and the business associations they establish to promote their interests, professional associations, ethnic groups, major religious organizations, terrorist groups, and social movements. (Riddell-Dixon 1995, 289)

Because NGOs are diverse does not mean that they defy analysis. True, "NGOs espouse an incongruous set of ideologies, agendas, and causes [and] as such creating a broad definition for this 'wild assortment' of organizations—in different contexts referred to as private voluntary organizations, civil society, and the nonprofit sector—is no simple task" (Runyan 1999). Nonetheless, despite NGOs' varying roles and identity, the story of such organizations in general can and must be told because they are growing in numbers and activities and having an increasing impact on world politics. Nonprofit NGOs "are now influencing decisions and helping to set agendas that were once determined solely by governments and corporations—from policies on international trade and investment to initiatives on literacy, international aid, and human rights. . . . NGOs have used their flexibility, small scale, technical expertise, and connections to the grass roots to spark something of an 'organization revolution'—forging an effective middle ground between the state and the free market" (Runyan 1999).

This chapter will concentrate only on the major NGOs whose political pressure on states to accept their claims arouses the most debate worldwide. Today a small subset of increasingly active and self-assertive major **nonstate actors** provokes the most controversy. To simplify our task, we will thus examine four of the most visible politically active nonstate actors: ethnopolitical groups, religious movements, terrorists, and multinational corporations.

■ **nonstate actors** all transnationally active groups other than states, including both IGOs and NGOs (see p. 16).

In examining these four major categories of NGO actors, consider whether world politics is undergoing a transformation as these political units compete for influence with the territorial state, which has been dominant for the past 350 years. The question is critically important because if, in the future, nonstate actors gain greater autonomy and power over states' resources and policy making, the state-centric structure of the international system will corrode, and the consequences of eroding state sovereignty are difficult to predict. The activities of these four NGO categories have been responsible in many ways for increasingly calling into question the idea that the state has full and exclusive control over its destiny. NGOs are making borders porous and states vulnerable both to external pressures and to challenges from within their boundaries. As NGOs rise in numbers and influence, a key question is whether what may be termed a "nongovernmental global society" will democratize, or disrupt, global governance.

> Today the state-centric world no longer predominates. The skill revolution, the worldwide authority crises, and other sources of turbulence have led to a bifurcation of the international system into two global structures, one the long-standing state-centric world of sovereign states and the other a complex multicentric world of diverse, relatively autonomous actors replete with structures, processes, and rules of their own in "globalized space." The actors of the multicentric world consist of NGOs, multinational corporations, ethnic minorities, subnational governments and bureaucracies, professional societies, incipient communities, and the like. Individually, and sometimes jointly, they compete, conflict, cooperate, or otherwise interact with the sovereignty-bound actors of the state-centric world. (Rosenau 1998, 159)

Let us look at the major NGOs to better evaluate if they are contributing to the erosion of state sovereignty and whether their impact spells promise, or peril, for twenty-first-century world politics.

NATIONALISM, NATIONALITY, AND ETHNICITY

The images of the all-powerful state and of governments as sovereign and autonomous rulers of unified nations are not very satisfactory. These images exaggerate the extent to which the state resembles a **unitary actor,** as realists often ask us to picture it. In truth, the unitary actor conception is misleading, because many states are divided internally and highly penetrated from abroad,

■ **unitary actor** the perception of states as culturally and racially homogeneous, solidified in their joint pursuit of common internal and foreign policy objectives (see p. 66).

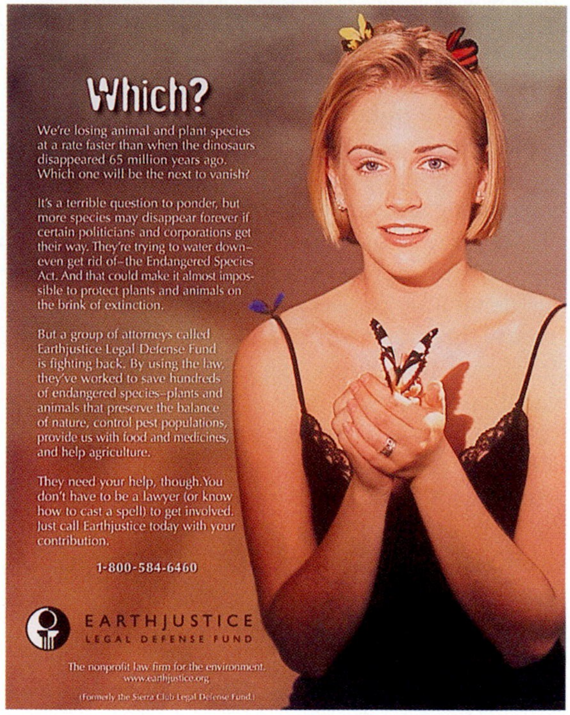

Grassroots Recruitment for Global Change NGOs are nonprofit, grassroots groups that advocate a wide variety of causes in order to set the global agenda in ways consistent with their ideology. In this advertisement, the Earthjustice Legal Defense Fund seeks to protect endangered species of plants and animals. Over 27,000 NGOs are active throughout the globe.

and few are tightly unified and capable of acting as a single body with a common purpose.

Many political scientists see a pressing "need to deal with the consequences of the declining ability of various governments to govern," and to confront the fact that one of the main forces contributing to "the erosion of effective government and of public confidence in government is the seeming insolvable nature of ethnic and religious differences that make political and social peace in more and more states a problematic exercise" (Shultz and Olson 1994). It has also been suggested that we must face the possibility that the all-powerful state of this century is a "historical anomaly [that] may be sickly and pale" as nationalistic sentiments strengthen and spread (Mead 1995).

Although the state unquestionably remains the most visible actor in world affairs, **nationalism** and nationality are potent cultural factors defining the core loyalties and identities of many people that influence how states act. Many people pledge their primary allegiance not to the state and government that rules them, but rather to a politically active minority group with which they most associate themselves. One broad category of such national groups is **ethnopolitical groups** whose members share a common nationality, language, cultural tradition, and kinship ties. They view themselves as members of their nationality first and of their state only secondarily—a definition that follows the interpretation of E. K. Francis (1976), who maintains that "cultural affinities, [which] manifest in shared linguistic, religious, racial, or other markers . . . enable one community to distinguish itself from others." As Okwudiba Nnoli (1993) elaborates on the meaning of ethnonationalism, **ethnicity** is "a phenomenon associated with contact between cultural-linguistic communal groups . . . characterized

■ **nationalism**
sentimental devotion to the welfare of one's own nation, without concern for the common interest of all nations and states in the global community (see p. 633).

■ **ethnopolitical groups**
people whose identity is primarily defined by their sense of sharing a common nationality, language, cultural heritage, and kinship ties.

■ **ethnicity**
perceptions of likeness among members of a particular racial or linguistic group, leading them to distinguish themselves from those in other kinship or cultural groups.

by cultural prejudice and social discrimination. Underlying these characteristics are the feelings of pride in the in-group, and the exclusiveness of its members. It is a phenomenon linked . . . to forms of affiliation and identification built around ties of real or putative kinship."

■ **ethnic nationalism** devotion to a cultural, ethnic, or linguistic community within an existing state.

Acknowledgment of the importance of **ethnic nationalism** (people's loyalty to and identification with a particular ethnic nationality group) in world affairs reduces the relevance of the unitary state. Many states are divided, multiethnic societies made up of a variety of politically active groups that seek, if not outright independence, a greater level of regional autonomy and a greater voice in the social and foreign policies of the state. At the end of the twentieth century, "nearly three-quarters of the world's larger countries (116 of 161) had politically significant minorities," and 275 minority groups—comprising one-sixth of the world's population—were at risk from persecution worldwide (Gurr 2001, 177). Relations between **ethnic groups** are a key element in the equation of relations between NGOs and the state, as contact is customarily widespread between groups who define their identity by their common ancestry. These divisions and the lack of unity within states make thinking of international relations as exclusively interactions between unified states dubious.

■ **ethnic group** a group of people of the same nationality who share a common culture, set of ancestors, or language.

The Fourth World

■ **indigenous peoples** the native ethnic and cultural populations living within countries controlled by others; referred to as the Fourth World (see p. 639).

Indigenous peoples are the ethnic and cultural groups that were native to a geographic location now controlled by another state or political group. The globe is populated by an estimated six thousand separate indigenous nations, each of which has "a unique language and culture and strong, often spiritual, ties to an ancestral homeland. In most cases indigenous people were at one time politically sovereign and economically self-sufficient." Today there are an estimated 300 million indigenous people, more than 5 percent of the world's population, scattered in more than seventy countries; some have placed the number as high as 600 million (Watson 1997, 389; *The State of Indigenous People* 2000). This segment of global society is conventionally referred to as the **Fourth World** to heighten awareness of the poverty and deprivation that confront many native or tribal indigenous peoples (Wilmer 1993).

■ **Fourth World** a term used to recognize the native national groups residing in many so-called united states who, although often minorities, occupied the state's territory first and refuse to accept domination, seeking instead to create a new state for themselves by splitting existing states or to gain greater political freedom to govern themselves.

Indigenous peoples often feel persecuted because they are not permitted full political participation and representation in the states where they reside, and in some cases they feel that their livelihoods, lands, cultures, and lives are threatened. Aroused nationalists are now fighting back across the globe in rebellion against the injustice, misery, and prejudice they perceive the state to have perpetrated against them. The pervasiveness of ethnic nations alongside states is so commonplace that many feel the voice of the people behind the indigenous national movements they lead must be given its due. Fourth World liberation movements are active in many countries throughout the globe (see Table 7.1). "For most indigenous peoples, the central issue in this clash of civilizations is land" (Watson 1997). Most seek a state or, more often, a regional government, of their own. In part, this quest is inspired by the evidence that between 1900 and 1987 about 130 million indigenous people were slaughtered by state-sponsored **genocide** in their own countries (Rummel 1994).

■ **genocide** the deliberate extermination of an ethnic or minority group.

This is not to suggest that all indigenous groups are bent on tearing existing states apart, or on using violence to attain power. The members of many such movements are divided about objectives, and militants who are prepared to

TABLE 7.1

The Risks of New or Escalating Wars between Indigenous Ethnic Groups and States

Region and Groups	*Groups in Ethnic Wars in 1998 and at Future Risk*	*Highest-Risk Groups in 1998*
Western Democracies: thirty-one ethno-political groups	No groups in ethnic wars; five groups at medium risk	Basques in France Basques in Spain
Eastern Europe and Former USSR: fifty-nine ethnopolitical groups	Two groups in ethnic wars; eight groups at high risk; seven groups at medium risk	Armenians in Nagorno–Karabakh Kosovars in Yugoslavia Russians in Estonia Crimean Tatars Crimean Russians Bosnian Serbs
Southeast and Pacific Asia: thirty-four ethno-political groups	Five groups in ethnic wars; three groups at high risk; twelve groups at medium risk	Uighers in China Timorese in Indonesia Aboriginal Taiwanese
West and South Asia: twenty-five ethno-political groups	Eleven groups in ethnic wars; six groups at high risk; thirteen groups at medium risk	Hazaras, Tajiks, and Uzbeks in Afghanistan Kashmiris in India Tripuras and Scheduled tribes in India
North Africa and Middle East: twenty-eight ethnopolitical groups	Three groups in ethnic wars; six groups at high risk; two groups at medium risk	Kurds in Turkey Shi'a in Iraq Shi'a in Lebanon Palestinians in Gaza and the West Bank Kurds in Iraq Arabs in Israel
Africa South of the Sahara: sixty-seven ethnopolitical groups	Eleven groups in ethnic wars; twelve groups at high risk; eight groups at medium risk	Ogani in Nigeria Tutsi in Congo-Kinshasa Ovimbundu in Angola Yoruba in Nigeria Hutu in Burundi Afar in Ethiopia
Latin America and Caribbean: thirty-two ethnopolitical groups	No groups in ethnic wars; one group at high risk; eleven groups at medium risk	Miskitos in Nicaragua Maya in Mexico Indigenous highlanders in Ecuador

This inventory of conflicts between rebels and states at the start of 1999 warns that since 1991, although internal wars fought by indigenous minorities are increasingly being resolved through third-party mediation or internal negotiations, the risks for new and/or escalating ethnic wars persist. No more than six of the highest-risk groups in each region are listed here.

SOURCE: *Peoples versus States* and "Managing Conflict in Ethnically Divided Societies," courtesy of Ted Robert Gurr (2000 and 2001).

fight for greater autonomy are usually in a minority within these groups. In fact, most Fourth World indigenous movements are committed to gaining sub-state autonomy, not sovereignty, and seek only more representative clout in

Indigenous Peoples Organize Many subnational groups of nations and indigenous peoples reside on the territory of existing states which govern them. To protect their human rights and national identity, Fourth World groups have organized meetings such as the World Conference of Indigenous Peoples in Rio de Janeiro, Brazil, in May 1992. As a result of their lobbying, the UN named 1993 the International Year of the World's Indigenous Peoples.

redirecting the policies and allocation of resources within existing states. Increasingly, these repressed Fourth World minorities are using the conventional tactics of social movements (such as mass mobilization and protest), and are eliciting the support of NGOs and IGOs to pressure states to recognize their claims and protect their civil liberties and human rights. Moreover, a substantial number of indigenous movements in the last decade have negotiated settlements resulting in devolution by the state, in which the protagonists gained concessions for greater local political power in exchange for accepting the sovereignty of the state. Examples include the Miskitos in Nicaragua, the Gagauz in Moldova, most regional separatists in Ethiopia, and others in India's Assam region.

It is difficult to foresee what the wave of internal discontent and rise of politically active minority protests will ultimately bring. Many have spawned governmental decentralization, weakened the sovereign authority of states, and compounded leaders' difficulties in constructing a coherent foreign policy that adequately represents diverse ethnic and minority interests. But on the whole, devolution—the granting of political power to increase local self-governance to ethnopolitical national groups and indigenous peoples—has served more often to keep countries together rather than break them up. The devolution and decentralization of state control in response to minority discontent has strengthened the state in the European region where separatist movements have been especially rampant in the 1990s since the Cold War glue of state loyalties dissolved. For instance, the separatist Northern League has made electoral inroads, but devolution from Rome has solidified the national unity of Italy; similarly, devolution has enabled the powerful region of Catalonia within Spain to muscle its way onto the European stage as an independent actor, and likewise Scotland's 1997 establishment of its own Parliament (with the power to make laws regarding internal affairs) was heralded by Scottish nationalists as a bold step in the rebirth of the nation through the weakening of its union with the United Kingdom. However, here and elsewhere in Europe (as in France, where the state government in Paris has loosened its grip through devolution to pacify nationalist separatist movements by creating twenty-two new mainland regions with their own budgets), experience

> suggests that devolution has proved widely popular without generally leading to secession; indeed, it can help to hold a country together. When strong regional or national identities, silent or suppressed for many years, are suddenly given a voice, the paradoxical result has often been greater harmony and a greater desire to stick together rather than anguish, chaos and disintegration. The end of the Cold War and the inexorable rise of the European Union have both weakened the grip of Europe's main states but without threatening to break them up, except when involuntary unions fragmented after communists lost control. (*Economist,* September 20, 1997, 53)

Europe—one of the world's most stable but ethnopolitcally divided regions—could well signal the path other regions could travel in the twenty-first century. But from Kosovo to Kurdistan, where rebels vie for independence we observe what may be the wave of the future: freedom fighters impatient with the map they have inherited, struggling to become a state—ironically at precisely the time when a globalized economy and culture are transforming the traditional idea and ideal of statehood, nationhood, and ethnic identity. As U.S. President Bill Clinton put it in 1993, "Economic and technological forces all over the globe are compelling the world toward integration while ethnic and religious tensions tear nations apart." The question facing humanity is the ethical issue of who should be sovereign, the rulers or the ruled. The problem is of crisis proportions. Finnish President Martii Ahtisaari in 1999 described the contemporary circumstances well when he observed, "In recent years, sadly, we have increasingly often faced the problem of failed state situations where a state with all its institutions has imploded or broken down. Instead of authority and order, chaos, fighting between political cliques and ethnic groups, even outright war, has prevailed."

Ethnopolitical Challengers to the State

It is extremely difficult to classify and count the abundant variety of politically active movements by **nonstate nations** (Bertelsen 1977) struggling for power and/or statehood. Perhaps the best way of making a rough estimate is by observing linguistic similarity. A huge number of ethnolinguistic divisions separate cultures. "Measured by spoken languages, the single best indicator of a distinct culture, all the world's people belong to 6,000 cultures; 4,000 to 5,000 of these are indigenous ones. Of the [more than 6] billion humans on the planet, some 190 to 625 million are indigenous people" (Durning 1993, 81).

■ **nonstate nations** national or ethnic groups struggling to obtain power and/or statehood.

Still, this indicator may be somewhat misleading, since the belief systems and backgrounds that incite ethnopolitical movements by indigenous peoples are varied and often overlapping. Beyond language, these movements are based on numerous combinations of cultural, racial, and religious orientations. This is why indigenous ethnopolitical movements pursue many different goals.

One characteristic of ethnopolitical movements stands out as a defining attribute amidst these differences: most transcend the existing borders that separate the more than two hundred sovereign states currently recognized as independent under international law. Indigenous peoples, as measured by the proportion of a country's total population in which minority ethnic, national, or racial groups comprise a significant percentage of the majority of the population, are scattered widely within many of the globe's pluralistic states (see Map 7.1 on p. 212). Indigenous peoples such as the sizable Kurdish minorities of Turkey, Iraq, and Syria have members living in more than one of the globe's existing independent states. Linked together by common ancestry across national borders, these peoples form transnational **cultural domains** that share a common heritage and place higher value on ideals other than patriotic loyalty to particular states. Our world is composed of at least eight distinct transnational cultural communities including European, Chinese, Russian, Hispanic, Islamic, Hindu, and both Black African and South African identities (Chaliand and Rageau 1993, 37).

■ **cultural domains** ancestral groups that share a common heritage and values and recognize no national borders.

Given the reality of cultural and ethnic diversity within the world, some observers have sketched a pessimistic scenario for the world's future, in which an epidemic wave of violent clashes will errupt between ethnic groups within states (Kaplan 1994). In another, even more gloomy, scenario, dramatically popularized by Samuel P. Huntington (1996), we will witness a **clash of civilizations** (Huntington 1999b). According to Huntington, in the twenty-first century the main fault line dividing the globe and the chief source of international conflict "will not be primarily ideological or economic" but rather cultural, between "nations and groups of different civilizations." In his view, because "people identify with cultural groups: tribes, ethnic groups, religious communities, nations, and civilizations . . . we'll never have a universal civilization." Huntington argues that globalization is not leading to what "V. S. Naipaul called a 'universal civilization,' the cultural coming together of humanity and the increasing acceptance of common values, beliefs, and institutions by people throughout the world." Instead, as peoples panic in reaction to globalization, Huntington foresees combat between and among seven or eight major civilizations that are becoming the principal actors in world affairs (see Map 7.2 on p. 214). The clash will be far removed from the Cold War's ideological confrontation between the East and West. Rather, "the single most dangerous source of instability in the world" will be between states which are members of these separate civilizations (Huntington 1999b), and it is more likely that the next world war will "be between China and the West or the West and Islam, or as Huntington fears, between the West and most of the Rest" (Felipe Fernandez-Armesto, as cited in Barber 1998, who provides a trenchant critique of Huntington's argument). Whereas many agree with Huntington (1999a) when he argues that "almost everywhere in the contemporary world people are espousing cultural and civilizational identities [that are increasingly challenging] multicivilizational states," other students of world politics question the clash of civilizations thesis, citing contrary evidence that states belonging to similar civilizations are actually more likely to fight each other than those of different civilizations (Henderson and Tucker 1999).

■ **clash of civilizations** political scientist Samuel Huntington's controversial thesis that in the twenty-first century the globe's major civilizations will conflict with one another, leading to anarchy and warfare similar to that resulting from conflicts between states over the past five centuries (see p. 136).

National Disintegration and Global Instability

In many cases, Fourth World political activism has resulted in the devolution of state sovereignty and fragmentation of the territorial integrity of existing states. In those countries where indigenous minority groups have gained a grant of internal self-government, the achievement of a measure of quasi-autonomy and a homeland relatively secure from persecution has fostered the protection of human rights and, ironically, has strengthened the state because formerly separatist peoples have been provided joint institutions of governance. However, in less stable countries balkanization, disunion, and even anarchy have resulted.

When people identify with the culture of their nationality more intensely than they do with their country, separatist revolts by peoples struggling for **self-determination** can be expected. Keep in mind that indigenous peoples are highly mobilized because "they were largely pushed to inaccessible and unproductive lands by earlier waves of colonization [and] now find that even these lands are coveted by outsiders" (Watson 1997). In response, they have pursued self-determination to protect themselves and control the resources of their territories. This quest for greater self-governance can sometimes be achieved through the peaceful separation of formerly unified states, as almost happened in November 1995 when a slim majority of Quebec's voters upheld Canadian unity, and did occur in Czechoslovakia on December 31, 1992, when that country split peacefully, through the so-called velvet divorce, into the independent Czech Republic and Slovakia. However, aroused nationalist passions can also escalate to violence. An example is the bloody warfare that has racked the former Yugoslavia since 1991, with the Bosnian Serbs and Croats both committing atrocities in the name of **ethnic cleansing**—a program of genocide to murder the rival nationality. The tribal warfare in Kosovo, Burundi, Somalia, and Rwanda also epitomizes the recent wave of human destruction that results when ancient hatreds erupt into warfare. What Italian President Oscar Luigi Scalfaro described in 1997 as a new "danger of racial, religious, and tribal hatred" follows the tragic pattern of genocides since World War II. Genocide caused the death of 500,000 to 1,100,000 ethnic minorities in the Soviet Union between 1943 and 1947, 80,000 to 1,000,000 ethnic Chinese and communists in Indonesia between 1965 and 1966, and 100,000 to 282,000 Kurds in Iraq between 1984 and 1991 (Barbara Harff, as cited in Sadowaski 1998, 18).

These divisions of states into segregated fragments along ethnic and cultural lines are different from the political partitions that resulted in the division of Korea, Vietnam, Germany, and China into separate states. Many states, in short, are inherently fragile, because they are weak coalitions of multiple nationalities that can splinter (Chatterjee 1993). Consider the degree to which minority groups compose many states; for example, the share of indigenous populations in Bolivia is 70 percent; Peru, 40 percent; Mexico, 12 percent; the Philippines, 9 percent; Canada, 4 percent. Cultural diversity is also captured by the number of distinct languages spoken in "megadiversity" countries, of which Indonesia's 670, Nigeria's 410, India's 380, Australia's 250, and Brazil's 210 are exceptional examples (Durning 1993, 83, 86). To speak of these states as culturally, linguistically, or politically "united" would be an exaggeration. Forging a consensus behind a consistent foreign policy is a challenge for many nationally diverse countries, because a definition of state interests that represents the divergent needs of minority populations is inherently difficult.

self-determination the doctrine that asserts that nationalities have the right to determine what political authority will represent and rule them (see p. 639).

ethnic cleansing the extermination of an ethnic minority group by the state, in violation of international law since the mid-1990s, before which governments could treat the people within their territory as they wished.

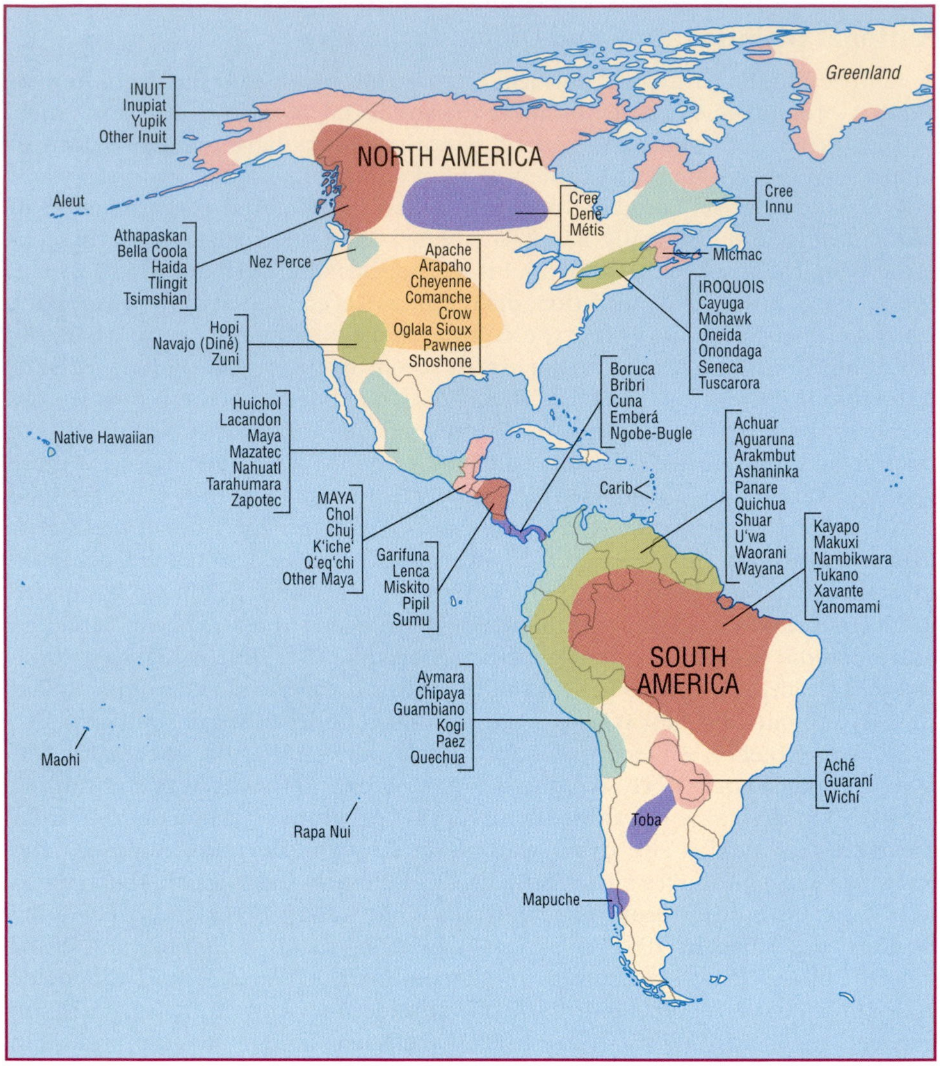

MAP 7.1

The Indigenous Cultures of the Fourth World

More than five thousand indigenous peoples are living in many countries throughout the globe and are concentrated regionally. This map only hints at their diversity. Though marginalized in most societies, these people have survived. Says Julian Burger of the UN's Office of the High Commissioner for Human Rights, "All over the world indigenous peoples are asserting their cultural identity, claiming their right to control their futures, and struggling to regain their ancestral lands" (Davis 1999, 66). The magnitude of the challenge that racial and national pluralism poses to the survival of existing state borders is hard to estimate, but because many states are culturally and ethnically diverse, it could be explosive. Many minority groups and indigenous peoples long denied self-determination are seeking to govern themselves by pursuing independence through separatist movements. If every major "racial or ethnic group won independence," U.S. President Bill Clinton observed in October 1999, "we might have 800 countries in the world and have a very difficult time having a functioning economy."

Note: Colors indicate regional concentrations of indigenous peoples.

SOURCE: Julian Burger, United Nations (in Davis 1999, 66–67).

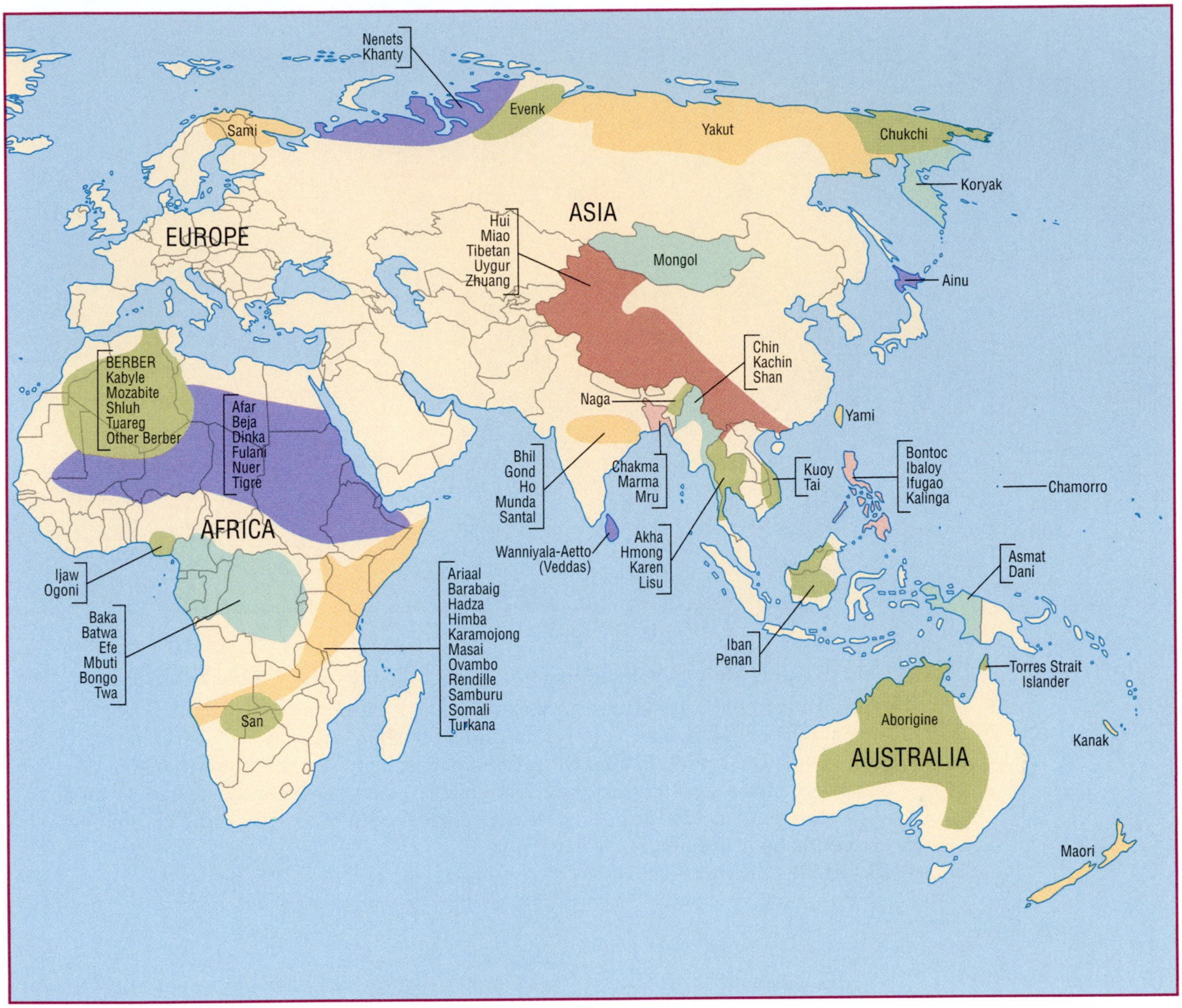

The long-term conflict between the Palestine Liberation Organization (PLO) and the state of Israel illustrates the potential for very different kinds of consequences to result from the existence of Fourth World ethnic pluralism. For four decades the Palestinian nation sought by every means available, including terrorism and war, to create a state from the territories that Israel claimed and controlled. That search cost many lives but failed to create independence. Eventually, through dialogue and negotiation, a proposed comprehensive peace accord was brokered in September 1993. Israel and Jordan then agreed to permit the Palestinians to form a government and create a new state in the West Bank territory. The accord symbolized the possibility for nationalities to become independent states through discussion and compromise rather than force and provides a potential model for other independence movements. But the peace process fell apart in the wake of the assassination of Israeli Prime Minister Yitzhak Rabin by a Jewish extremist in November 1995.

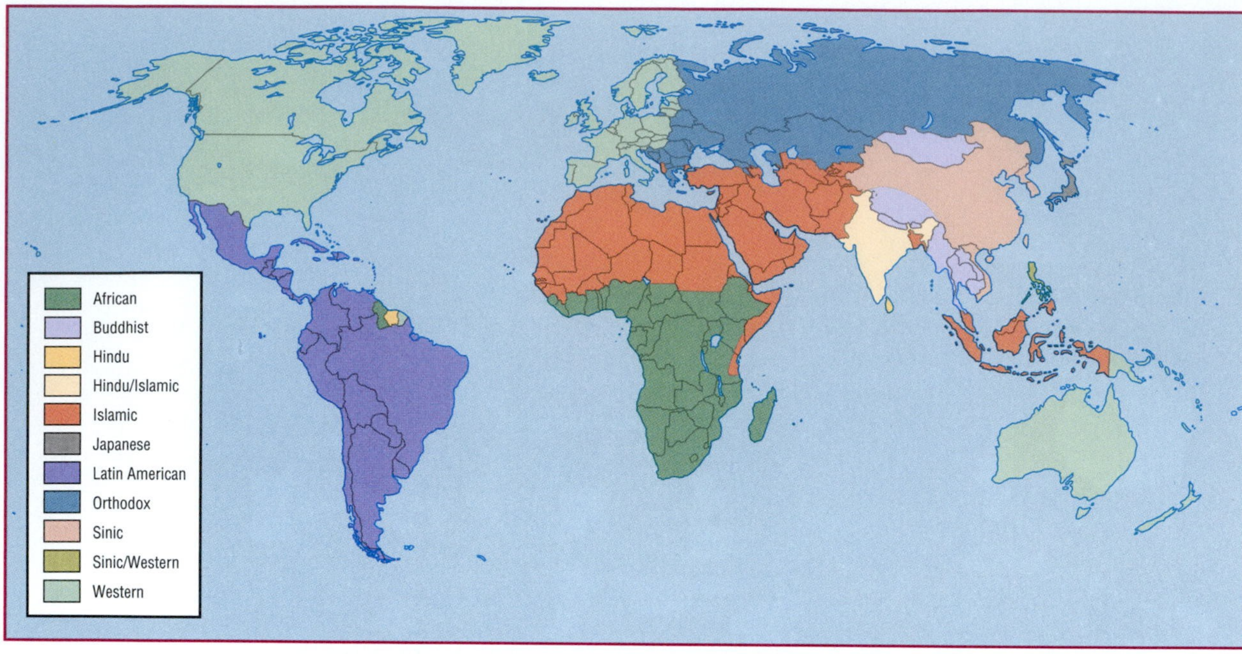

MAP 7.2
The World's Major Civilizations: Will Their Clash Create Global Disorder?
According to the controversial thesis of Samuel P. Huntington, a global war in the twenty-first century is likely to result from a "clash of civilizations." This map shows the location of the world's major civilizations, according to Huntington—the Sinic or Chinese, Japanese, Hindu, Islamic, Buddhist, Western, Latin American, the Orthodox Christians in Eastern Europe and Russia, African, Sinic/Western in the Phillippines, and Hindu/Islamic in India.
SOURCE: Huntington (1999b), 17.

Racism and intolerance could spawn a new era of tribal terrorism and warfare. In this grim scenario, the lack of the Cold War stalemate to hold such ethnic conflicts in check will render states powerless to suppress ancient rivalries and animosities. The ethnic wars between Armenians and Azerbaijanis in 1993, which brought Russia, Turkey, and Iran perilously close to combat, and the separatist revolt in Georgia to create an independent state of Abkazia, foreshadow future transpolitical ethnic turmoil in many other places. Russia appears particularly vulnerable to ethnopolitical revolts in the nine republics where Russians make up less than 50 percent of the population, such as Chechnya—a Muslim republic that has been in conflict with Moscow for over two hundred years. If and when disintegration results in the future, the earth's geopolitical boundaries will have to be redrawn by cartographers.

■ interethnic competition
a struggle for supremacy within a geographic area between two or more ethnic groups.

Although **interethnic competition** is a phenomenon that dates back to biblical times, it is a plague of the post–World War II era. Some of the world's most explosive flashpoints are the products of disputes between groups in multiethnic and culturally heterogenous countries, such as Afghanistan, Belgium, Canada, Nigeria, Russia, Somalia, Spain, Sri Lanka, and the United Kingdom, to name a few. Ethnopolitical cleavages have produced a surge of serious con-

Ethnic Cleansing Hate and hostility have traditionally led to terrorism and genocide. Racial and ethnic prejudice have commonly resulted in intercommunal warfare, such as the U.S. government's policy of expulsion and extermination of Native Americans, Nazi Germany's annihilation of 6 million Jews, and Japan's death marches and enslavement of those it conquered in the early victories of World War II. More recently, in 1994 ethnic conflict escalated to genocide in Rwanda as the Hutu militia attacked the Tutsi, and later as the Tutsi-dominated Rwandan Patriotic Front retaliated against the Hutus. This photo depicts the results of one such bloodbath, where as many as 1 million Tutsis died.

flicts since 1945. According to *The Minorities at Risk Project* (see Gurr 1993, 2000), over 450 ethnopolitical minority groups have been involved in serious, often violent, struggles since 1945. Ethnopolitical struggles that turn to violent rebellion had been a growing problem since the mid-1950s (see Figure 7.1). Two-thirds of the ethnopolitical armed conflicts erupted between 1989 and 1993 (peaking immediately after the Cold War ended in 1991), but, encouragingly, the frequency of new ethnonational wars has been declining from an average of ten each year in the late 1980s to only an average of four each year since 1995. Even more promisingly, between 1991 and 1998 eighteen of the most deadly and protracted of all ethnopolitical wars—secessionist revolts—were settled through negotiations and another ten were held in check through cease-fire agreements (Gurr 2001). In early 1999 only fourteen such wars for independence were being fought although there remain many risks of new and escalating ethnic wars at century's end (see Table 7.1 on page 207).

The inherent **ethnocentrism** underlying ethnonationalism—the belief that one's nationality is special and superior and that others are secondary and inferior—breeds ethnic conflict. Nationalists find it easy to condone marginalizing and oppressing "outside" nationalities, and ethnocentric peoples are prone to reject conciliation and compromise with other nationalities. This barrier to

ethnocentricism a parochial outlook that neatively evaluates foreign cultures and ethnic groups according to one's own cultural values, which are assumed to be superior (see p. 656).

FIGURE 7.1
Trends in the Outbreak, Continuation, and Settlement of Ethnopolitical Wars, 1956–1998

In the second half of the twentieth century, ethnopolitical wars became a prominent feature of the international landscape, with an episodic wave occurring primarily in the Global South and, since 1991, in the failed state of the former Yugoslavia and the disintegrated former Soviet Union.

SOURCE: "Managing Conflict in Ethnically Divided Societies," courtesy of Ted Robert Gurr (2001).

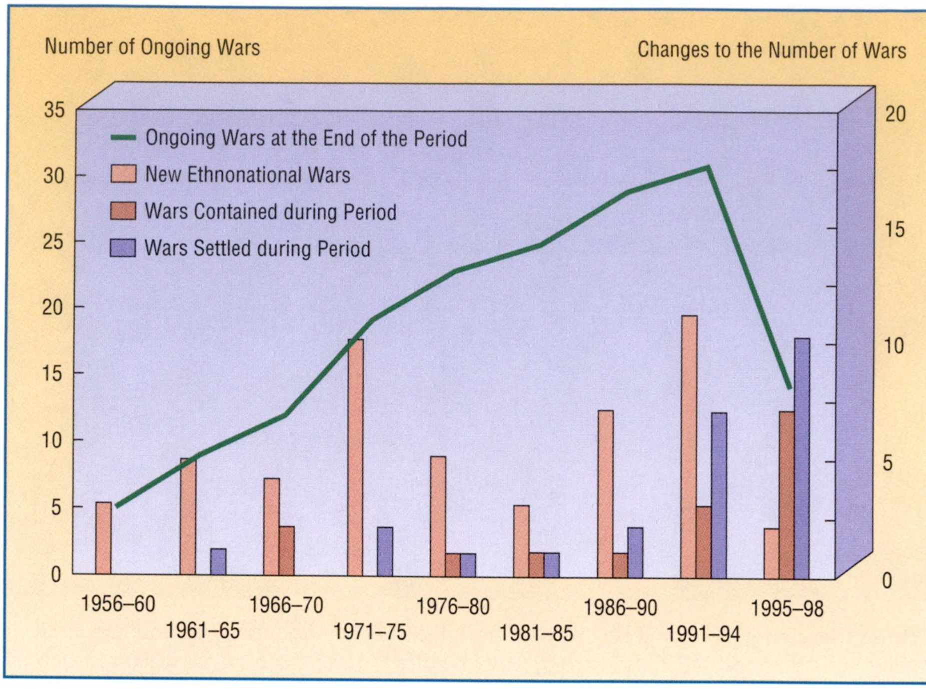

cooperation and its conflict-generating consequences was highly evident between 1993 and 1995 in the crumbling peace talks and escalating warfare in the Balkans, as negotiations among the Serbs, Croats, and Bosnians produced no concessions until NATO used force to propel the combatants to the bargaining table. Efforts at negotiation collapsed after NATO's peacekeeping forces withdrew, and to stop the bloodbath the United States and its NATO allies sent interventionary forces to end the atrocities. In Kosovo as well as in many other explosive situations where ethnic conflicts threaten to break states apart (for example, Indonesia and Montenegro), NATO and the world face difficult choices about when and where to intervene to stop civil wars that descend into the slaughter of helpless civilians, but those choices must be made. As British Prime Minister Tony Blair explained in April 1999: "We either allow ethnic cleansing to succeed, or we say that the world community has an obligation to stop this violent nationalism."

■ **displaced people** those who have been forced to flee their homes because their lives and/or liberty were at risk but, unlike refugees, they remain within their own countries because they cannot or do not wish to cross an international border; legally, displaced people fall under the sovereignty of their own government, even though that government may persecute them due to race, nationality, religion, or political beliefs.

If clashes between ethnic groups spread and intensify, it is likely that violence also will spread, and the number of internally **displaced people** (estimated by the UN High Commissioner on Refugees at over 21 million in 2000) will grow. If so, the forces of disunion and disintegration could overwhelm the power of the state, which has previously bound diverse nationalities into a common purpose. To the extent that conflict within and between ethnically disunited and divided states becomes a major axis on which twenty-first-century world politics revolves, the power and independence of the state can be expected to decline exponentially in a new era of global anarchy or lawlessness (Barber 1995). The perils should not be underestimated. As Russian Foreign Minister Andrei V. Kozyrev warned the United Nations (UN) in September 1993, the threat of ethnic violence today is "no less serious than the threat of nuclear war was yesterday." The existence of over 450 ethnopolitical minority movements in two-thirds of the globe's states (Gurr 2000) alongside the spoken use by diverse ethnonational and indigenous peoples of at least five thousand distinct languages (Supplement to *National Geographic,* August 1999) punctuates the potential peril of separatist rebellion, as does the evidence that since 1945 about one-third of all armed conflicts were internal or succession revolts (see Chapter 12).

RELIGIOUS MOVEMENTS

In theory, religion would seem a natural worldwide force for global unity and harmony. Yet millions have died in the name of religion. The Crusades between the eleventh and fourteenth centuries were originally justified by Pope Urban II in 1095 to combat Muslim aggression, but the fighting left millions of Christians and Muslims dead and, "in terms of atrocities, the two sides were about even [as both religions embraced] an ideology in which fighting was an act of self-sanctification" (*Economist,* January 5, 1996). Similarly, the "not-so-holy wars" in the religious conflicts during the Thirty Years' War (1618–1648) between Catholics and Protestants killed nearly one-fourth of all Europeans.

Many of the world's nearly 6 billion people are affiliated in some form with a **religious movement**—a politically active organization based on strong religious convictions. At the most abstract level, a religion is a system of thought shared by a group that provides its members an object of devotion and a code of behavior by which they can ethically judge their actions. This definition points to commonalities across the great diversity of organized religions in the world, but it fails to capture that diversity. The world's principal religions vary greatly in the theological doctrines or beliefs they embrace. They also differ widely in the size of their followings, in the geographical locations where they are most prevalent (see Map 7.3), and in the extent to which they engage in political efforts to direct international affairs.

■ **religious movement** a set of beliefs, practices, and ideas administered politically by a religious group to promote the worship of its conception of a transcendent diety or principles of conduct.

These differences make it risky to generalize about the impact of religious movements on world affairs. Those who study religious movements comparatively note that a system of belief provides religious followers with their main source of identity, and that this identification with and devotion to their religion springs from the natural human need to find a set of values with which to evaluate the meaning of life and the consequences of choices. Unfortunately this need sometimes leads believers of a religious creed to perceive the values of their own religion as superior to those of others, which often leads to intolerance. The proponents of most religious movements believe that their religion should be universal—that is, accepted by everyone throughout the world. To confirm their faith in their religious movement's natural superiority, many organized religions actively proselytize to convert nonbelievers to their faith, engaging in evangelical crusades to win followers of other religions over to their beliefs. Conversion is usually achieved by persuasion, through missionary activities. But at times conversion has been achieved by the sword, tarnishing the reputations of some international religious movements (see Controversy: Are Religious Movements Causes of War or Sources of Transnational Harmony? on p. 219).

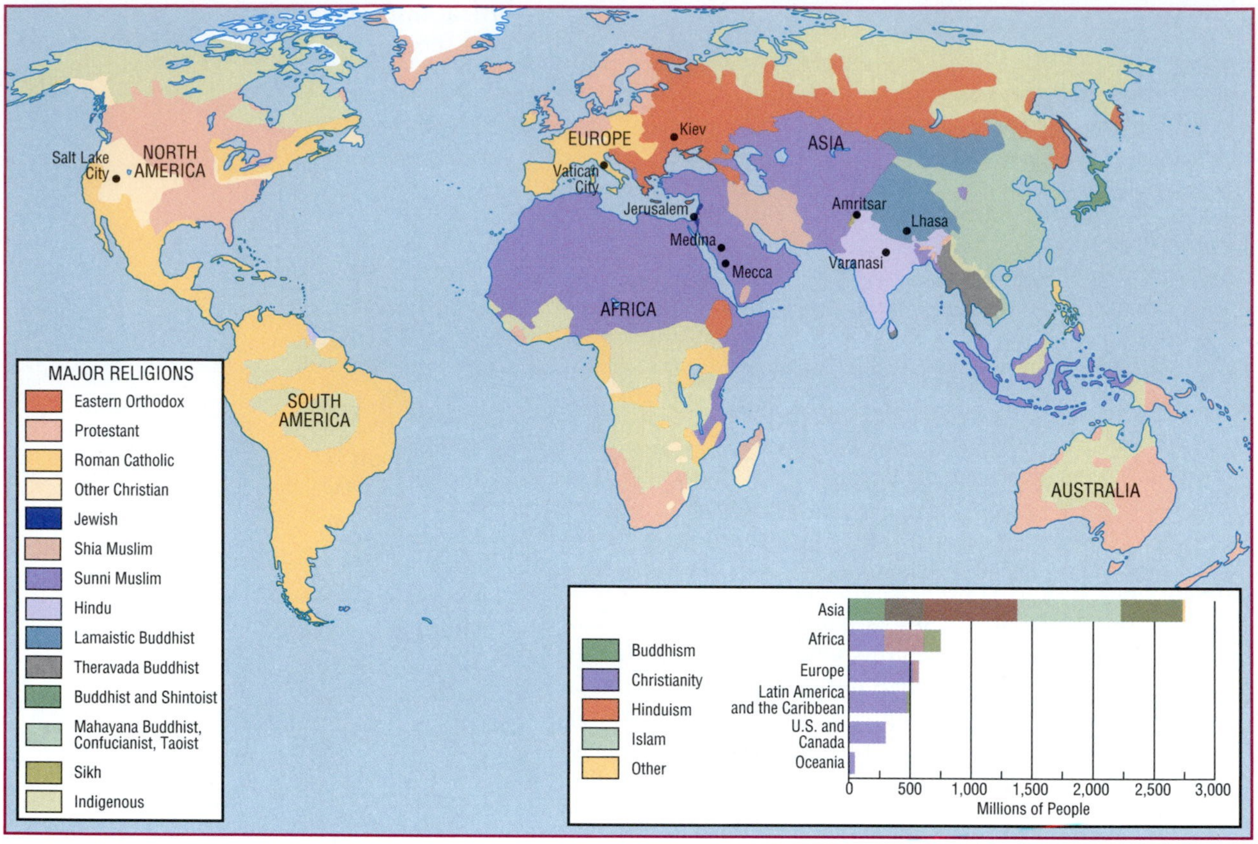

MAP 7.3
Major Religions of the World

People everywhere seek a power higher than themselves to give meaning and purpose to their lives, and many accept one or another of the world's major religions for this purpose. There are compelling reasons for the quest in an otherwise rootless and chaotic world, because life for many people is shallow without a deity to respect and a religious code of conduct to follow. This map shows where the world's major religious affiliations have attracted a dominant following. The chart on the bottom right provides an estimate of the number of people who adhere to the four largest religions in the world today—Buddhism, Christianity, Hinduism, and Islam. Christianity spread from Europe to all continents of the world over the course of five hundred years of conquest and missionary efforts. Meanwhile, high birthrates in Asia and Africa make Islam the world's fastest growing major religion. Losing out to Christianity and Islam have been a variety of indigenous religions.

SOURCE: Supplement to *National Geographic*, August 1999.

In evaluating the impact of religious movements on international affairs, it is important to distinguish carefully the high ideals of their doctrines from the activities of the people who head these religious bodies. The two realms are not the same, and each can be judged fairly only against the standards they set for themselves. To condemn what large-scale religious movements sometimes do administratively when they abuse the principles of the religions they manage does not mean that the principles themselves deserve condemnation. Moreover,

CONTROVERSY

Are Religious Movements Causes of War or Sources of Transnational Harmony?

Recently, debate over the relationship of religion to international politics has increased, partly because some of the most explosive flash points on the globe are in the countries and regions where long-standing and seemingly uncontrollable violent conflicts between religious groups prevail. Religions, and religious bodies as NGO global actors, have become a topic of much discussion. Consider Northern Ireland, where violence continues at the same time that Catholics and Protestants bargain for a peaceful solution to a very old conflict; the Balkans, where Croatian Catholics, Serb Orthodox Christians, and Bosnian and Albanian Muslims carry out blood feuds; Pakistan and India, where the Muslim destruction of Christian churches has provoked acts of revenge; and India, where Hindu extremists have attacked churches and Muslim mosques. "To do harm, to promote violence and conflict in the name of religion," said Pope John Paul II in Egypt after fighting between Christians and Muslims left twenty-three people dead in February 2000, "is a terrible contradiction and a great offense against God. But past and present history give us many examples of such misuse of religion."

It is difficult to understand the religious origins of violence because most people equate religion with peace, compassion, and forgiveness, not hatred or intolerance. Indeed, because high ideals inspire the believers of nearly all the world's major religious movements, many of the principles religions espouse are very similar and conducive to peaceful relations between people. They all voice respect and reverence for the sanctity of life and acceptance of all people as creations of a deity as equals, regardless of race or color. These are noble ideals. Religions speak to universal principles, across time and place—to enduring values in changing times. Moreover, they recognize no boundaries for their eternal validity—no north, south, east, or west—but only true virtue wherever found, and the relevance of moral precepts (e.g., the prohibition of killing and the value of working for the betterment of humankind) throughout the world.

If all the world's great religious movements espouse universalistic ideals, why are those same religions increasingly criticized as sources of international conflict—of exclusivism, hatred, terror, and war? This, in the age of religious conflict and political violence, is a percolating controversy. What do you think?

In evaluating the role of religious NGOs in international affairs, consider first the view of sociologists of religion who contend that religious hostility results from the fact that universalistic religions are managed by organizations that often adopt a particularistic and dogmatic outlook (see Juergensmeyer 1993; also Schwartz 1997). The virtues that religions uphold ironically can become weapons against those who do not hold such views. Followers of a religion may conceive the world and history through an ideological lens that views one deity protecting a single people against inferior others and, in an effort to believe in unshakable doctrines, reject the attempt to separate what they wish to be true from what they or other religions think to be true. This mentality inspires an ethic that justifies violence, plunder, and conquest, in part because outsiders tend to be seen as threatening rivals, whose loyalty and allegiance to other deities represents a challenge to their own religion's claim of universality. In a word, religious movements often practice intolerance—disrespect for diversity and the right of people to freely embrace another religion's beliefs. The next logical step is for fanatics to paint these imagined enemies as evil, unworthy of mercy, and to justify brutal violence against them.

However, using this violence as an argument against religion is controversial. It is dangerous to accept stereotypes of religious groups as responsible for relentless barrages of terrorism. Paganistic and atheistic societies recognizing no higher deity have equally long histories of waging violent wars against external enemies and their own people. Meanwhile, many religions perform ably the mission of peace making, and in fact most religious bodies have historically coexisted peacefully for centuries.

It is important for you to weigh objectively the evidence about the impact of religious NGOs on world affairs. In so doing, take into account the impact of this controversy on theories of world politics and world order. The inclination of extremist religious movements to evoke prejudice and aggression has led some realist theorists of international politics to conclude that such movements are more a menace than a pacific influence. Observing that most wars have been fought in the name of religion, these realist critics ask the world to acknowledge the viciousness and mean-spiritedness of followers who betray their religion's humanistic and global values by championing a style of religious thought which denies that morality is about nourishing life, not destroying it. What do you think?

although many students of international relations draw a causal linkage between the activities of religious movements and the outbreak of political conflict and violence (Juergensmeyer 1993; Schwartz 1997), this does not apply to all religions. Consider the Hindu ideology of tolerance of different religions, which teaches that there are many paths to truth and accepts pluralism among diverse populations. Similarly, Buddhism preaches pacifism, as did early Christianity, which prohibited Christians from serving in the armies of the Roman Empire (later, by the fourth century, only Christians were permitted to serve, as church and state became allies). But, the propensity for religious institutions to subordinate their beliefs to the state in order to survive and increase public popularity notwithstanding, many observers maintain that otherwise pacificist and humanitarian religions at times are inclined to oppose each other violently, despite their professed doctrines of tolerance. When they do, religious movements become sources of international tension, especially when they become radical—heavily involved in political action on a global scale and fanatically dedicated to the promotion of their cause. The leaders of **extreme militant religious movements** are convinced that those who do not share their convictions must be punished and that compromise is unacceptable. Richard Shultz and William Olson explain:

extreme militant religious movements politically active organizations based on strong religious convictions whose members are fanatically devoted to the global promotion of their religious beliefs.

> While not all radical religious movements involved in politics are alike, they share certain similar characteristics:
>
> 1. Militant religious political movements tend to view existing government authority as corrupt and illegitimate because it is secular and not sufficiently rigorous in upholding religious authority or religiously sanctioned social and moral values.
> 2. They attack the inability of government to address the domestic ills of the society in which the movement exists. In many cases the religious movement substitutes itself for the government at the local level and is involved in education, health, and other social welfare programs. . . .
> 3. They subscribe to a particular set of behavior and opinions that they believe political authority must reflect, promote, and protect in all governmental and social activities. This generally means that government and all of its domestic and foreign activities must be in the hands of believers or subject to their close oversight.
> 4. They are universalists; unlike ethnic movements, they tend to see their views as part of the inheritance of everyone who is a believer. This tends to give them a transstate motivation, a factor that then translates their views on legitimacy of political authority into a larger context for action. In some cases, this means that international boundaries are not recognized as barriers to the propagation of the faith, even if this means they resort to violence.
> 5. They are exclusionists; they relegate all conflicting opinions on appropriate political and social order to the margins, if they do not exclude them altogether. This means second-class citizenship for any nonbeliever in any society where such a view predominates.
> 6. Finally, they are militant, willing to use coercion to achieve the only true end. (Shultz and Olson 1994, 9–10)

Although militant religious movements are not the only nonstate actors whose ideologies and activities may contribute to violence, many experts

The Fusion of Church and State Religion, politics, and violence are seldom seen as contributing to one another. But in many countries, religious bodies are supported by the armies of the state and the state supports the transnational activities of religious movements. Consider South America, for instance, where the powerful Roman Catholic Church has often worked hand in hand with the governments the church supports. At the same time, proponents of "liberation theology" have joined forces with revolutionary groups in the so-called Marxist-Catholic alliance to bring about reforms in the repressive governments they oppose.

believe that they tend to stimulate five specific types of international activities. The first is **irredentism**—the attempt by a dominant religion or ethnic group to reclaim territory in an adjacent region once possessed but later lost from a foreign state that now controls it. The group often rationalizes the use of force for this purpose. The second is **secession** or **separative revolts**—the attempt by a religious (or ethnic) minority to break away from an internationally recognized state. Here, again, force is sometimes used, often with arms and aid supplied by third parties that support the secessionist goals. When these separative revolts succeed, states disintegrate into two or more new political units. The third type of international activity that militant religions tend to incite is **migration**—the departure of religious minorities from their countries of origin to escape persecution. Whether they move by force or by choice, the result—a fourth consequence of militant religion—is the same: The emigrants create **diasporas** or communities that live abroad in host countries but maintain economic, political, and emotional ties with their homelands. Finally, a fifth effect of militant religions is **international terrorism** in the form of support for radical coreligionists abroad.

If we critically inspect the compound consequences of the activities of militant religious movements, we come away with the impression that religious

■ **irredentism**
the efforts by an ethnonational or religious group to regain control of territory by force so that existing state boundaries will no longer separate the group.

■ **secession/separative revolts**
the attempt by a religious or ethnic minority to seek independence from an existing state.

■ **migration**
movement from one place of abode to another, sometimes by religious minorities to escape persecution.

■ **diaspora**
a dispersed immigrant community residing outside its homeland while continuing to identify with its country of origin.

■ **international terrorism**
the use of terrorism against targets in other countries.

movements not only bring people together but also divide them. Religious movements often challenge state authority, and religious-driven separatism can tear countries apart. The possible result, some predict, is that over time "the world may fracture into 500 states from the current 200" (UNDP 1994). Others put the ultimate number lower but talk of a new kind of state—something akin to "a corporate holding company—with the central government little more than a shell and power residing in the regions" (Davis 1994).

Against this prophecy, we must contemplate another dimension of the sometimes close connection between religions and states: Many states actively support particular religions while repressing minority religions. It is important to recognize just how closely states and religions are allied in many countries, with each reinforcing the other's power. And this observation, in turn, leads us to consider how terrorist groups sometimes influence the relationships between states and militant religions.

INTERNATIONAL TERRORISTS

Terrorist groups are another kind of nonstate actor on the global stage, whose activities exacerbate international tensions and undermine the state's authority and power. Terrorist groups are difficult to identify because they operate covertly and because, like ethnopolitical national movements and religious groups, their motives, tactics, and membership differ widely. However, **terrorism** is commonly defined as seeking to further political objectives through the threat or use of violence, usually in opposition to state governments.

■ **terrorism**
criminal acts and threats against a targeted actor for the purpose of arousing fear in order to get the target to accept the terrorists' demands.

Terrorism was known in ancient times, as evident in the assassination of tyrants in ancient Greece and Rome, and by the Zealots of Palestine and the Hashashin of medieval Islam. In the nineteenth century, terrorism became associated with anarchist bombings and with murders and destruction of property by nationalist groups such as the Armenians and Turks. Today terrorism is a strategy practiced by a diverse group of movements (see Table 7.2). The religious, ethnic, or political movements and minorities now practicing terrorism seek to obtain the advantages of the majority, and to extract revenge against those states and majority populations that the terrorist groups perceive as oppressors. Terrorist groups seek the political freedom, privilege, and property they think persecution has denied them.

Whereas religious fanaticism is responsible for approximately 20 percent of international terrorist incidents (James 1995, 6), the primary goals of most terrorist groups are independence and statehood. Terrorists are often the "international homeless," whose main objective is to obtain for themselves a territory and state they can control. But it would be a mistake to lump all terrorist movements together; although they share violent tactics, often crossing national borders, terrorist movements are more diverse than they are similar.

■ **international organized crime (IOC)**
organized crime syndicates that use technology to cooperatively network with each other throughout the world.

One increasingly active category of terrorist group is **international organized crime (IOC).** In the "borderless" globalized world, organized crime syndicates can easily use sophisticated computer and telecommunications technology to network with one another to expand their operations and profits. "Globalization creates new and exciting opportunities, and among the most enterprising and imaginative opportunists are the world's criminals. . . . Lowering

TABLE 7.2

Tribal Terrorists and Unholy Warriors: Some Active Terrorist Groups

Group	*Description*
Abu Nidal Organization (ANO)	Led by Sabri al-Banna, the ANO was headquartered in Iraq (1974–1983), Syria (1983–1987), and now Libya, and operates internationally to coordinate the activities of various other Muslim terrorist groups.
Armed Islamic Group	An extremist group that seeks to overthrow the secular Algerian government and replace it with an Islamic state.
Basque Fatherland and Liberty (ETA)	Founded in 1959, and once committed to Marxism, the group seeks to create an independent homeland in Spain's Basque region.
HAMAS (Islamic Resistance Movement)	Emerging in 1987 from the Palestinian branch of the Muslim Brotherhood, HAMAS pursues—often by violent means—the goal of an Islamic Palestinian state in place of Israel.
Hizballah (Party of God)	Radical Shia religious group seeking to establish an Iranian-style Islamic Republic in Lebanon.
Kach and Kahane Chai	A right-wing Jewish extremist movement seeking to restore the biblical state of Israel and to halt the peace process in Palestine. A member of Eyal (an offshoot of the radical Kach movement) assassinated Israeli Prime Minister Yitzhak Rabin in November 1995.
Party of Democratic Kampuchea (Khmer Rouge)	Communist insurgents hoping to destabilize the Cambodian government. Under Pol Pot's leadership, a campaign of genocide killed more than 1 million people in the late 1970s.
Provisional Irish Republican Army (PIRA)	Radical group formed in 1969 as the secret armed wing of Sinn Féin, the legal political movement seeking to remove British forces from Northern Ireland and unify Ireland.
Sendero Luminoso (Shining Path)	Guerrilla insurgency formed in the late 1960s by a former university professor whose stated goals are ridding Peru of foreign influences, destroying existing Peruvian institutions, and replacing them with a peasant revolutionary regime.
Al Qaeda	A global terrorist organization funded by Saudi millionaire Osama bin Laden, Al Qaeda (meaning in Arabic "the base") works on its own and with the Egyptian Islamic Jihad and other alleged terrorist organizations in at least twenty-four countries, including the United States, to promote its extremist religious cause; the terrorist group has been accused of truck bombings that shattered two U.S. embassies in East Africa in August 1998.

These descriptions of some terrorist movements active in the 1990s are provided by the U.S. Department of State's counterterrorism office. Although not exhaustive, they convey the degree to which terrorist groups seek a combination of religious, ethnic, and political goals that generally aim to challenge the authority of existing states.

the barriers to international trade and the transit of goods across borders is generally seen as a good thing. But it also helps the luxury car highjacked on a Johannesburg street to reappear for sale in Moscow" (UNDP 1999).

The ability of global gangsters to succeed in pursuit of wealth through the use of terror and death has become a serious global problem, even though in 1999 the UN International Drug Control Program reported that its campaign against crops used for illegal cocaine and heroin had begun to cut into the profits of illegal drug cartels (Wren 1999). In November 1994, the UN sponsored a conference in Naples, Italy, to confront the growing menace of international organized crime. Attended by more than eight hundred delegates from 136 countries and thirty international organizations, the conference alerted the international community to the growth of what then UN Secretary-General Boutros Boutros-Ghali termed an "empire of criminals," whose criminal activities ranged from slavery to trafficking in weapons, human organs, toxic waste, illegal drugs, and nuclear materials. The profits from international crime are staggering: "Dirty money makes the criminal underworld go around. Between $500 billion and $1.5 trillion (or 5 percent of gross world product) may be laundered every year" (*Economist,* August 28, 1999, 17). Perhaps this is why international organized crime, once in retreat, is now "reorganized," poised with new vast multinational networks "with departments of foreign relations" to create a new underworld; "organized crime," observes expert Phil Williams, today "is the HIV of the modern state" (Johnson 1999).

International organized crime represents a new kind of NGO—new, according to Claire Sterling in *Thieves' World* (1994), in the sense that criminal organizations that were once local (such as the Italian-Sicilian Mafias, the Japanese Yakuza, the Chinese Triads, and the Colombian cocaine cartels) are now internationally linked in a global network that cooperates to exploit the institutional weaknesses of a decentralized state system. According to Sterling's evidence, there is a "planetwide criminal consortium" that is without precedent, running by its own rules, outside the law, to victimize the international community. Its motive is pure profit, the search for easy money by any means necessary, which breeds a code of conduct that accepts violence as an honorable necessity.

The absence of an animating ideology beyond wealth does not mean that IOC groups and ethnic and terrorist groups are disconnected, however. In quest of ideals rather than money, ethnopolitical groups may take advantage of the networks of organized crime for their own ends:

> Ethnonational minority groups pursuing either separation from or political realignment within an existing state require resources. Through arrangements with organized crime, these movements can gain access to arms, information, and the means to help finance their operations. There is ample evidence that this is happening in Peru, Turkey, Lebanon, the Balkans, and elsewhere. An illustrative example of these types of interconnections is found in the links in heroin trafficking from Southwest Asia. Here Afghan groups, usually Pathans, have links to Pakistani, Iranian, or Indian groups who help in production and transiting. These groups, in turn, have links to Kurdish or Palestinian groups that help move heroin through Iran, Lebanon, or Turkey to Europe. In return, the various resistance movements in Turkey, Iran, and Afghanistan receive capital with which to fund their operations. They are convenient relationships.

> Criminal organizations likewise find advantages in these ties. The presence of violent ethnic conflict and government turmoil provides opportunities and incentives for criminal activities. In situations where government and law enforcement [are] ineffective, criminal organizations thrive. In Pakistan, for example, government authority is excluded from tribal areas, and it is precisely in these areas where organized drug production and smuggling are most evident. Burma shows a similar pattern. In Peru, Colombian drug traffickers work with the Sendero Luminoso [terrorists] to impair government enforcement efforts, not only against drug smuggling, but also against the very presence of government itself.
>
> IOCs benefit from other by-products of ethnic conflict, state dissolution, and borderless globalization. One such by-product is the population migration these conflicts generate. European countries harboring large refugee populations have identified a spectrum of organized criminal activities taking place within these communities, and the immigrant groups themselves are frequently the victims of these criminal ventures. Ethnic diaspora communities abroad serve as operational bases and safe havens for criminal organizations. (Shultz and Olson 1994, 28–29)

Another attribute of modern or **postmodern terrorism** (Laqueur 1998) and its relationship to existing states is the ability of many terrorist organizations and international crime syndicates to take advantage of corrupt officials in state governments and work with them to their mutual advantage. Many states suffer from official corruption at the highest level of government; Russia after the Soviet Union collapsed and Indonesia in 1999 under the Suharto regime are conspicuous examples. In what has become a wave of crime known in Russia as *koruptsiya,* "today's new Russians" have amassed billions through plunder and crony capitalism (Schmemann 1999) and organized crime has become so woven into Russian life that the presence of a Russian "state-criminal complex" has emerged and threatens to infect the rest of the world (*Economist,* August 28, 1999). International organized crime and terrorism could not survive were it not for the assistance they receive from corrupt state leaders; in fact, the alliances that have been built between the two have made many reformers worry that payoff and theft have become accepted as normal in many countries.

postmodern terrorism
the prediction that in the twenty-first century technology has improved the prospects for terrorists to use new weapons to threaten their adversaries for political purposes (see p. 450).

Viewing contemporary IOCs and terrorist NGOs in this light, it is safe to conclude that the activities of most of these nonstate actors are undermining the authority and sovereignty of legitimate existing states. However, **state terrorism** must also be included in any objective assessment, for some of the most ruthless acts of violent terrorism have been practiced by states' governments against people within their own borders. Historical examples of state terrorism include the "reign of terror" by the French revolutionary government in 1793 against the counterrevolutionary opposition, the violence practiced by Russian Bolsheviks after 1917 against their opponents (especially by the repressive regime of Joseph Stalin), and the actions of the genocidal Nazi regime of Adolf Hitler in Germany, which killed millions in the 1930s and 1940s. States, in short, can and have fought back against opposition to their sovereign authority with terrorist tactics sometimes more militant and destructive than those used by insurgents and revolutionaries, and have used **state-sponsored terrorism** to support their governments' foreign policy goals against foreign adversaries.

state terrorism
sovereign states' use of their armed forces and police to rule through fear and terror over targeted population groups within their borders.

state-sponsored terrorism
formal assistance, training, and arming of foreign terrorists by a state to achieve foreign policy goals (see p. 613).

Palestine — A Hot Spot for Terrorist Activity Terrorists are active NGOs, most of whom are dedicated to the creation of a homeland for a particular ethnic group or religious movement. On the left, a HAMAS activist works for an Islamic state in place of Israel; at center a member of the *intifadeh,* the Islamic movement that put Palestinians on the path to seeing that their nationalist dream is fulfilled; on the right is Menara Circle in the center of Ramallah, the unofficial capital of the West Bank, where the Palestinians hope their sacrifices for statehood will consummate in a new state capital.

We should therefore not underestimate states' capacity and willingness to combat by force challengers to their sovereignty and perceived national interests.

MULTINATIONAL CORPORATIONS

■ **multinational corporations (MNCs)** private businesses headquartered in one state that invest and operate extensively in other states.

Multinational corporations (MNCs)—business enterprises organized in one society with activities in another growing out of direct investment abroad—are a fourth type of nonstate actor. MNCs have grown dramatically in scope and potential influence with the expansion of the world political economy since World War II. As a result, they have provoked considerable discussion, at times animosity, and at other times enthusiastic acceptance. As advocates of liberal free trade and as active contributors to the globalization of world politics, MNCs generate both credit for the positive aspects of free trade and globalization and blame for their costs.

The Size and Scope of MNCs

■ **foreign direct investment (FDI)** the sum of capital investments by nonresidents into a country through such transactions as the purchase of factories that entail long-term commitments (see p. 164).

The numbers and immense size of MNCs add to the controversy surrounding their role and impact. At the close of the twentieth century the UN estimated that more than 53,000 MNCs and their 450,000 foreign affiliates had global assets in excess of $13 trillion and global sales of more than $9.5 trillion. This volume of foreign investments and sales accounted for more than one-fifth of the globe's economy and one-third of the world's exports (United Nations 1998, 2–3; Francis 1997, 8). The top one hundred multinationals own nearly $2 trillion of assets outside their home countries and a quarter of the world's stock of all **foreign direct investment (FDI).** MNCs also employed more than 73 million people, although most of the existing firms that operate internationally employ fewer than 250 people (Stopford 2000, 13–14). It has been estimated that 20 percent of all MNC employees work in the Global North, and this is a telling characteristic of the interests and priorities of MNCs. There exists a "clear geographic pattern: eight of the ten most global corporations are European, and among the ten largest global corporations [as indexed by the percent of sales outside the parent country,] five are American and four are Japanese. . . . With all the talk about globalization, today most multinational corporations are 'flag planters,' colonial outposts of basically domestic companies with some plant, or mines, or sales organizations in a few foreign lands" (Jain and Chelminski 1999, 9). However, MNCs are very important NGOs in today's globalized world because each MNC job typically generates additional jobs. The Nike footwear company, for example, employs about 9,000 people on its core staff but another 75,000 through subcontracting. Conservatively, then, MNCs can be expected to generate one additional job for each job in the corporation, bringing the number of jobs associated with MNCs to at least 150 million.

MNC expansion has been facilitated by **transnational banks (TNBs)** whose revenues and assets are primarily generated by financial transactions in the international economy. TNBs have become major forces in the world political economy and have contributed to the globalization process that has led to financial integration worldwide at the same time that it has made international banks critical to global economic stability (as the collapse of lending following occasional banking crises and the costs of recapitalizing, reorganizing, or liquidating insolvent banks by foreign countries illustrates). At the start of 1999, the combined assets of the world's twenty largest banks exceeded $425 trillion, a staggering figure attesting to the consolidation of the control of financial resources in a highly globalized economy. International banking is highly profitable, and the major banks in the world have formed strategic alliances and begun to merge in order to maximize their already-huge revenues. In 1998 the mergers among TNBs in the United States, the euro-currency area, Japan, and Britain exceeded $250 billion, and the consolidation of global banking is proceeding through slow but steady consolidations (*Economist,* August 28, 1999, 55–56; see also Figure 7.2). The TNBs funnel trade and help to reduce the meaning of states' borders in making each state's economy dependent on other states' economies by transferring capital through international loans and investments. Their activity helps to redistribute wealth and income in the world economy, contributing to the economic development of some states and the stagnation of others. One feared consequence in the Global South is that the TNBs advance the rich Global North at the South's expense; in 1999, the richest 20 percent of countries received 68 percent of foreign direct investment, and the poorest 20 percent of countries received only 1 percent (UNDP 1999, 2). Like MNCs, therefore, TNBs spread the rewards of globalization unequally and inequitably, increasing wealth for a select group of countries and marginalizing the others.

■ **transnational banks (TNBs)**
the globe's top banking firms, whose financial activities are concentrated in transactions that cross state borders.

Through their loans to the private sector, TNBs have made capital highly mobile and expanded the capacity of MNCs to lead the way in converging the incomes, tastes, lifestyles, and consumer products in the global marketplace. As MNCs have grown in scope and power, concern has understandably been raised about whether their efforts to remove national barriers to foreign investments and trade is undermining the ability of seemingly sovereign states to control their own economies and therefore their own fates and cultures. Is it possible that MNCs are shaking the very foundations of the present international

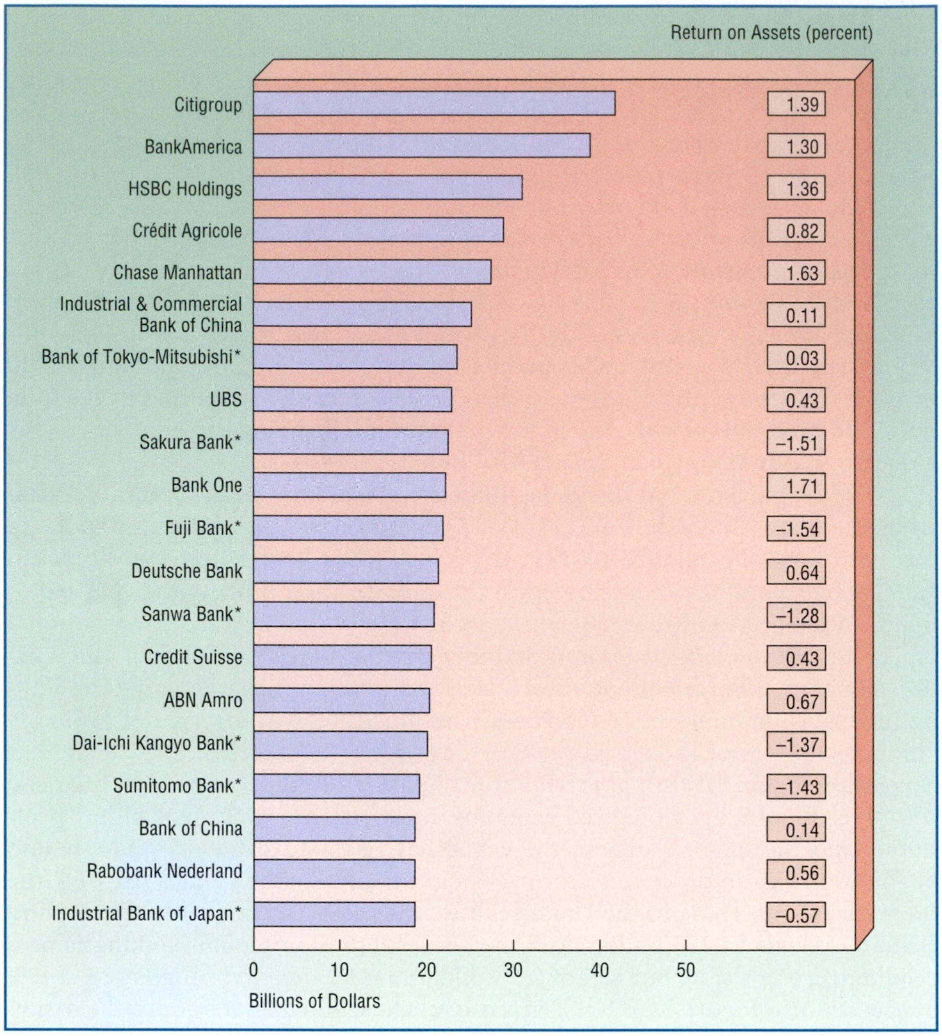

FIGURE 7.2
The World's Top Twenty Banks, 1999

Commercial banks are a part of the process of globalization, and their locations mirror the centers of financial clout in the global economy. The current trend is for the world's biggest banks to merge in order to increase their market share and influence. In 1999, Citigroup became the globe's largest commercial bank as a result of the Citigroup/Travelers merger; by late 1999, however, three Japanese banks which had already formed an alliance were conducting negotiations to create the world's biggest bank, which would have total assets of $1.3 trillion. BankAmerica rose from seventh to second after it merged. Note that of the top twenty banks, seven are Japanese, four American; Switzerland, the Netherlands and China have two each, and Britain, Germany, and France each have one.

Note: Banks are ranked according to their core capital holdings in billions of dollars at the end of 1998. Banks with an asterisk show data for end of March, 1999.
SOURCE: *Economist* (July 10, 1999), 99.

system? Or is this question perhaps based on exaggerated estimates of the MNCs' influence and therefore unwarranted?

The benefits and costs attributed to MNCs as they have risen to a position of prominence since World War II have been many and complex, and this has made them highly controversial nonstate actors (see Controversy: Are Multinational Corporations a Positive Force for the World?). Here we examine four major issues: MNCs' global reach and economic power, their effects on host and home countries, their involvement in politics, and their long-run influence on world politics.

MNCs' Global Reach and Economic Power

The modern MNC characteristically maintains an elaborate overseas network of affiliates to coordinate manufacturing and marketing globally. The creation of the European Economic Community (EEC) in 1957 stimulated this form of business organization and the internationalization of production that it fostered. Because the original six EEC members hoped to create a common external tariff wall around their common market, it made economic sense for U.S. firms to build production facilities in Europe. In this way they could remain competitive by selling their wares as domestic rather than foreign products, with their additional tariff costs. Ultimately, "the primary drive behind the overseas expansion of today's giant corporations is maximization of corporate growth and the suppression of foreign as well as domestic competition" (Gilpin 1975).

The reasons for direct investments overseas are more complex than this explanation suggests. According to **product-cycle theory,** overseas expansion is essentially a defensive maneuver designed to forestall foreign competitors and thus maintain the global competitiveness of domestically produced products. This theory views MNCs as having an edge in the initial stages of developing and producing a new product but then having to relocate production abroad to protect export markets from the foreign competitors that naturally arise as the relevant technology becomes more widespread or imitated. In the final phase of the product cycle, "production has become sufficiently routinized so that the comparative advantage shifts to relatively low-skilled, low-wage, and labor-intensive economies. This is now the case, for example, in textiles, electronic components, and footwear" (Gilpin 1975; see also Vernon 1971).

■ **product-cycle theory** the proposition that manufacturers export production overseas in order to compete with foreign producers of the same product and, at the same time, maintain their share of the goods their industries produce.

The world's giant producing, trading, and servicing corporations have become the agents of the globalization of production. Table 7.3 illustrates their economic and perhaps political importance in world politics, ranking firms by annual sales and states by GNP. The profile shows that 50 percent of the world's top one hundred economic entities are MNCs. Among the top fifty entries, multinationals account for only fourteen, but in the next fifty, they account for thirty-six. Their financial clout thus rivals or exceeds that of many countries; indeed, "sales of the ten largest corporations exceed the combined GNP of the 100 smallest countries" (*World Watch,* January/ February 1996, 37).

Although the growth of multinational firms is a global phenomenon, the Global North is home to about 90 percent of MNC parent corporations. Historically, the United States has been the home country for most of the largest multinationals, and in 1996 was the headquarters for 162 of the globe's 500 largest MNCs, followed by Japan (126), France (42), Germany (41), and Britain (34) (*Fortune,* August 4, 1997, F1). Together these five liberal democracies account for 80 percent of all parent corporations, and also account for a similar share of both the stock and flow of foreign direct investment.

Foreign direct investment (FDI)—formally defined as "ownership of assets in one country by residents of another for purposes of controlling the use of

CONTROVERSY

Are Multinational Corporations a Positive Force for the World?

Balancing Claims and Criticisms

MNCs have been alternately praised and condemned, depending on how their performance is viewed. The record is mixed and can be evaluated on different criteria. Following is a "balance sheet" summarizing the major arguments, for and against MNCs. Using this summary of contending interpretations, you can easily see why the role and impact of MNCs as important NGOs is so controversial. What do you think? Do MNCs help or harm the international community's welfare?

Positive

- Increase the volume of world trade.
- Assist the aggregation of investment capital that can fund development.
- Finance loans and service international debt.
- Lobby for free trade and the removal of barriers to trade, such as tariffs.
- Underwrite research and development that allows technological innovation.
- Introduce and dispense advanced technology to less developed countries.
- Reduce the costs of goods by encouraging their production according to the principle of comparative advantage.
- Generate employment.
- Encourage the training of workers.
- Produce new goods and expand opportunities for their purchase through the internationalization of production.
- Disseminate marketing expertise and mass advertising methods worldwide.
- Promote national revenue and economic growth; facilitate the modernization of less developed countries.
- Generate income and wealth.
- Advocate peaceful relations between and among states in order to preserve an orderly environment conducive to trade and profits.
- Break down national barriers and accelerate the globalization of the international economy and culture and the rules that govern international commerce.

Negative

- Give rise to oligopolistic conglomerations that reduce competition and free enterprise.
- Raise capital in host countries (thereby depriving local industries of investment capital) but export profits to home countries.
- Breed debtors and make the poor dependent on those providing loans.
- Limit the availability of commodities by monopolizing their production and controlling their distribution in the world marketplace.
- Create "sanctuary markets" that restrict and channel other investments to give MNCs an unfair advantage.
- Export technology ill suited to underdeveloped economies.
- Inhibit the growth of infant industries and local technological expertise in less developed countries while making Global South countries dependent on Global North technology.
- Conspire to create cartels that contribute to inflation.
- Curtail employment by driving labor competition from the market.
- Limit workers' wages.
- Limit the supply of raw materials available in international markets.
- Erode traditional cultures and national differences, leaving in their place a homogenized world culture dominated by consumer-oriented values.
- Widen the gap between rich and poor countries.
- Increase the wealth of local elites at the expense of the poor.
- Support and rationalize repressive regimes in the name of stability and order.
- Challenge national sovereignty and jeopardize the autonomy of the states.
- Create cartels with other MNCs that share markets in order to cut competition.

those assets" (Graham and Krugman 1995)—measures the investment activities of MNCs. The "stock" of FDI reflects the accumulation of past patterns of MNC investments, as revealed, for example, in the value of factories and equipment built up over a period of time. The "flow" of FDI reveals MNCs' current

TABLE 7.3

Countries and Corporations: A Ranking by Size of Economy and Revenues

Rank	*County/Corporation*	*GNP/Sales (billions of dollars)*	*Rank*	*County/Corporation*	*GNP/Sales (billions of dollars)*
1	United States	7,921.3	51	Venezuela	81.3
2	Japan	4,089.9	52	Malaysia	79.8
3	Germany	2,122.7	53	Eygpt	79.2
4	France	1,466.2	54	Philippines	78.9
5	United Kingdom	1,263.8	55	AXA	78.7
6	Italy	1,166.2	56	CITIGROUP	76.4
7	China	928.9	57	VOLKSWAGEN	76.3
8	Brazil	758.0	58	NIPPON TELEGRAPH & TELEGRAM	76.1
9	Canada	612.2	59	Chile	71.3
10	Spain	553.7	60	BP AMOCO	68.3
11	India	421.3	61	NISSHO IWAI	67.7
12	Netherlands	388.7	62	Ireland	67.5
13	Mexico	380.9	63	NIPPON LIFE INSURANCE	66.3
14	Australia	380.6	64	SIEMENS	66.0
15	Korea, Rep.	369.9	65	ALLIANZ	64.9
16	Russian Federation	337.9	66	Pakistan	63.2
17	Argentina	324.1	67	HITACHI	62.4
18	Switzerland	284.8	68	Peru	61.1
19	Belgium	259.0	69	U.S. POSTAL SERVICE	60.1
20	Sweden	226.9	70	MATSUSHITA ELECTRIC IND.	59.8
21	Austria	217.2	71	PHILIP MORRIS	57.8
22	Turkey	200.5	72	ING GROUP	56.5
23	Denmark	176.4	73	BOEING	56.2
24	GENERAL MOTORS	161.3	74	New Zealand	55.8
25	Hong Kong, China	158.3	75	AT&T	53.6
26	DAIMLER CHRYSLER	154.6	76	SONY	53.2
27	Norway	152.1	77	METRO	52.1
28	Poland	150.8	78	Czech Republic	51.8
29	FORD MOTOR	144.4	79	NISSAN MOTOR	51.5
30	WAL-MART STORES	139.2	80	FIAT	51.0
31	Indonesia	138.5	81	BANK OF AMERICA	50.8
32	Thailand	134.4	82	NESTLE	49.6
33	Finland	124.3	83	CREDIT SUISSE	49.1
34	Greece	122.9	84	HONDA MOTOR	48.7
35	South Africa	119.0	85	ASSICURAZIONI GENERALI	48.5
36	Iran	109.6	86	MOBIL	47.7
37	MISTUI	109.4	87	HEWLETT-PACKARD	47.1
38	ITOCHU	108.8	88	Algeria	46.5
39	MITSUBISHI	107.2	89	Hungary	45.6
40	Portugal	106.4	90	DEUTSCHE BANK	45.2
41	Colombia	106.1	91	UNILEVER	44.9
42	EXXON	100.7	92	STATE FARM INSURANCE	44.6
43	GENERAL ELECTRIC	100.5	93	DAI-ICHI MUTUAL LIFE INSURANCE	44.5
44	TOYOTA MOTOR	99.7	94	Bangladesh	44.0
45	Israel	95.2	95	VEBA GROUP	43.4
46	Singapore	95.1	96	HSBC HOLDINGS	43.3
47	ROYAL DUTCH/SHELL GROUP	93.7	97	FORTIS	43.2
48	ARUBENI	93.6	98	Ukraine	42.7
49	SUMITOMO	89.0	99	TOSHIBA	41.5
50	IBM	81.7	100	RENAULT	41.4

By integrating production and marketing their products worldwide, MNCs are dominating the global economy. As a result, MNCs rival many countries in wealth and are translating that income into influence as NGO actors. Note that in the recent frenzied wave of MNC mergers and acquisitions, half the top corporations (shown in capial letters) had sales as large as the GNP of the fifty most wealthy countries by 1998; just two years earlier, only 37 percent of the globe's largest one hundred economic entities were MNCs. This trend suggests that "every day the line between companies and countries blurs a bit more . . . as the walls around the world disappear. . . . The sheer size and power that some of these companies are amassing," observes Thomas L. Friedman (2000), leaves few ways to prevent "big monopolies from overwhelming consumers and preventing big business from overwhelming democratic government."

SOURCE: MNC sales, *Fortune* (June 1999; <www.pathfinder.com/fortune/fortune 500/>); countries GDP, World Bank (2000).

investment transactions. The FDI stocks thus reveal the current structure of global production and the primary locus of economic activity, while FDI flows provide insight into their changing patterns.

In the late 1990s, the MNCs' new FDI increased by about $400 billion each year, climbing by 25 percent in 1999 from $660 billion in 1998 to reach $827 billion worldwide (*Economist,* February 12, 2000, 105). Building on their past accumulation, most foreign investment stock today is heavily concentrated in the Global North, which is the source of most investment capital (outflows) and its favored target (inflows). In particular, the Japan-European Union-North America triad dominates global investments, as it does the interregional flow of global trade (see Chapter 8). This pattern replaces an earlier "bipolar" investment configuration, in which the United States and a handful of European countries (acting independently of one another) dominated the investment world. By the end of the 1980s, however, Europe began increasingly to act as a unified entity, and Japan actually surpassed the United States, with much of its investment directed at the United States itself.

The current tripolar investment pattern emerged from the corporate preferences of each partner to consolidate its own market hold and to gain a foothold in the other two regions. The United States and the European Union (EU) have shown a preference for investing in each other rather than Japan, and Japan has preferred the United States to Europe. The result is a serious imbalance between Japan and the other two partners, with the outward flow of stocks from Japan much greater than the inward flow. Because of these imbalances, competition among the three economic blocs, as well as political struggle, is likely to become increasingly fierce (Thurow 1992).

As major corporations in the United States, Europe, and Japan pursued market strategies to control their existing markets and expansion in new regional markets, they also adopted strategies that sought to construct regionally integrated core networks of affiliates clustered around their home countries. This has led to the creation of regionalized networks for production and marketing across many industries as the cartellike market-sharing arrangements of globe-spanning MNC networks converged practices but hindered openly competitive markets.

As a result of this clustering strategy and the growth of cross-border MNC mergers and acquisitions, the globe's consolidated MNCs are the major force behind FDI. In 1997, fifty-eight mergers between MNCs occurred in excess of $1 billion each, with most of the enlarged MNCs resulting from these mergers totaling $236 billion concentrated in the financial services, insurance, the life sciences, and the telecommunications industries (UNDP 1999, 26). FDI propelled by the MNCs has gone largely to regions in the wealthy Global North rather than to the poorer regions in the Global South, the most impoverished of which, with only 20 percent of world income, received less than 1 percent of all foreign direct investments (UNDP 1999, 2). A major consequence is that FDI is now increasingly regional, and local markets are protected in opaque ways. Each of the principal host countries in eastern Europe and the Global South receives the bulk of its funds from a single member of the investment triad, typically the one geographically closest to it. The effect is to reinforce—perhaps to cause—the growing regionalization of the world political economy across a range of dimensions, not only in investment but also in finance, labor, and trade (Doremus et al. 1998; see also Chapter 8).

The Effects of MNCs on Home and Host Nations

In addition to their global reach and economic power, MNCs' domestic impact on both home and host countries is a matter of widespread concern. MNCs allegedly exercise their power at great cost to their home or parent countries. Charges against them include shifting productive facilities abroad to avoid labor unions' demands for higher wages. According to this view, because capital is more mobile than labor, the practice of exporting production from industrially advanced countries to industrially backward countries—where labor is cheap and unions weak or nonexistent—causes structural unemployment in the advanced countries. Others contend, however, that MNCs help reduce balance-of-payments deficits, create new employment opportunities, promote competition in both domestic and foreign markets, and reduce rather than widen income inequalities between rich and poor states and within both.

If home countries have incurred both costs and benefits, have host countries shared similar experiences? "As privileged organizations," David E. Apter and Louis W. Goodman (1976) note, MNCs "hold a unique position among growth-inducing institutions able to affect the direction of development." This implies that MNCs may promote development as much as they impede it. It is nonetheless true that countries in the Global South historically viewed MNCs with suspicion. This attitude has changed noticeably in recent years. MNCs are more important to the developing countries' overall GNP and to their most advanced economic sectors than they are to the developed states' economies, and realization of the opportunities their investments can create has altered the traditional fear in the Global South of MNCs as neocolonial agents that endanger national sovereignty and undermine local prosperity. Global South countries from Mexico to Malaysia are "rolling out the welcome mat for global companies in the quest for rapid growth" (Francis 1997), despite the many risks and costs that MNCs' penetrations incur (Heredia 1997).

Politics and Multinational Corporations

A lingering concern regarding MNCs' role is their involvement in the domestic political affairs of local or host countries. In some instances this concern has extended to MNCs' involvement in the domestic politics of their home countries, where they actively lobby their governments for more liberal trade and investment policies that will enhance the profitability of their business activities abroad. In turn, both host and home governments have sometimes used MNCs as instruments in their foreign policy strategies.

Perhaps the most notorious instance of an MNC's intervention in the politics of a host state occurred in Chile in the early 1970s. There, International Telephone and Telegraph (ITT) tried to protect its interests in the profitable Chiltelco telephone company by seeking to prevent the election of Marxist-oriented Salvador Allende as president and later by seeking his overthrow. ITT's efforts to undermine Allende included giving monetary support to his political opponents and, once Allende was elected, pressuring the U.S. government to disrupt the Chilean economy. Eventually Allende was overthrown by a military dictatorship.

At times MNCs' practices have been embarrassing to home countries—as when the West German government found that a German firm had sold mustard gas–manufacturing equipment to Libya. On other occasions they seemed to defy the home country—as when the French subsidiary of Dresser Industries of

Dallas, Texas, exported energy technology to the Soviet Union in defiance of a U.S. government effort to thwart the sale.

In addition, MNCs often lobby their home governments for policies that back their disputes with host governments, although they are not always successful in these endeavors. The U.S. stipulation, made in the early 1970s, that foreign aid would be cut to any country that nationalized U.S. overseas investments without just compensation is representative of the tendency for home-state governments to support their own MNCs' overseas activities.

More broadly, MNCs have assisted in promoting free trade. In this sense, they have been active participants in the process by which governments have reached agreements on rules liberalizing economic transactions in the global marketplace, and active participants in the globalization process.

However, at another level, MNCs headquartered in one country have sometimes worked at cross-purposes with their parent governments by serving the wishes of the host government. During the 1973–1974 oil crisis, for example, the governments of the Organization of Petroleum Exporting Countries (OPEC) received assistance from the multinational oil companies to achieve OPEC's goal of using oil as a political weapon against the West. As the corporations reaped huge profits, their home countries suffered greatly.

The political role of the MNC in home and host countries is difficult to characterize, and varies around the globe. Perhaps the conclusion that best describes its impact is one that pictures the MNC not only as a threat to state power, but also as "a stimulant to the further extension of state power in the economic realm" (Gilpin 1985).

> Only the state can defend corporate interests in international negotiations over trade, investment, and market access. Agreements over such things as airline routes, the opening of banking establishments, and the right to sell insurance are not decided by corporate actors who gather around a table; they are determined by diplomats and bureaucrats. Corporations must turn to governments when they have interests to protect or advance. (Kapstein 1991–1992, 56)

Still, the blurring of the boundaries between internal and external affairs adds potency to the political role that MNCs unavoidably play as actors at the intersection of foreign and domestic policy, and the symbolic invasion of national borders by MNCs can be expected to arouse the anger of many local nationalists who fear the loss of income, jobs, and control to foreign corporate interests.

MNCs' Influence

Because multinationals often make decisions over which national political leaders have little control, a fourth significant issue regarding MNCs is whether their influence will lead to the erosion of the international system's major structural foundation—the principle that the state alone should be sovereign. Because "the reach and influence of multinationals, large and small, is far greater than the official statistics suggest [and] the relationship between governments and multinationals is characterized by a complex distribution of benefits," states have every reason to feel that MNCs are stripping away their sovereign control inasmuch as "multinational corporations increasingly demand the 'freedom' they need to optimize their operations across borders" (Stopford 2000).

The question of control is especially pertinent to countries in the Global South, although it is not limited to them. As one senior U.S. foreign policy official declared at the time of the Dresser Industries controversy, "Basically we're in an impossible situation. You don't want to get rid of the advantages of this international economic system, but if you try to exercise control for foreign policy reasons, you cut across sovereign frontiers."

Addressing the suspicion that multinationals "steal" U.S. technology and fail to "generate or retain wealth and quality jobs within [U.S.] borders," the U.S. Office of Technology Assessment in 1993 called for new rules to "balance interests . . . between nations and firms" (Dentzer 1993). However, the MNCs' complex patterns of ownership and licensing arrangements make the problem unmanageable, because it is often difficult to equate the MNCs' interests with particular national jurisdictions (Reich 1990). General Electric, for example, one of the most "American" of all U.S. MNCs, has coproduction agreements with Nuovo Pignone of Italy, Mitsubishi and Hitachi of Japan, and Mannessmann and AEG Telefunken of Germany, and in 1998 Daimler-Benz of Germany and the Chrysler Corporation in the United States agreed to a merger that stimulated a wave of new international merger negotiations among other automobile manufacturers. Controlling such a complex pattern of interrelationships, joint ventures, and shared ownership for any particular national purpose is nearly impossible. Part of the reason is that "about one-third of the 1996 world $6 trillion trade in goods and services occurs within multinationals—from one branch to another, [and] trade between different multinationals accounts for another third of world trade" (Francis 1997, 8). Joint production and **strategic corporate alliances** to create temporary phantom "virtual corporations" complicates the problem of identity. "The internationalization of the economy—which the U.S. spearheaded—has rendered obsolete old ideas of economic warfare," Richard J. Barnet, coauthor of *Global Reach* (Barnet and Müller 1974), observed in 1982. "You can't find targets any more, and if you aim at a target you often find it's yourself."

■ **strategic corporate alliances**
cooperation between MNCs and foreign companies in the same industry driven by the quest by MNCs to compete for production and sales overseas.

The multinationals' potential long-run influence is depicted in *Global Dreams: Imperial Corporations and the New World Order:*

> By acquiring earth-spanning technologies, by developing products that can be produced anywhere and sold everywhere, by spreading credit around the world, and by connecting global channels of communication that can penetrate any village or neighborhood, these institutions we normally think of as economic rather than political, private rather than public, are becoming the world empires of the twenty-first century. The architects and managers of these space-age business enterprises understand that the balance of power in world politics has shifted in recent years from territorially bound governments to companies that can roam the world. As the hopes and pretensions of government shrink almost everywhere, these imperial corporations are occupying public space and exerting a more profound influence over the lives of ever larger numbers of people. (Barnet and Cavanagh 1994, 14)

Whether the corporate visionaries who manage the MNCs will help to create a more prosperous, peaceful, and just world—as free-trade liberal theorists hope and others, whose interests are threatened by a new, globalized political

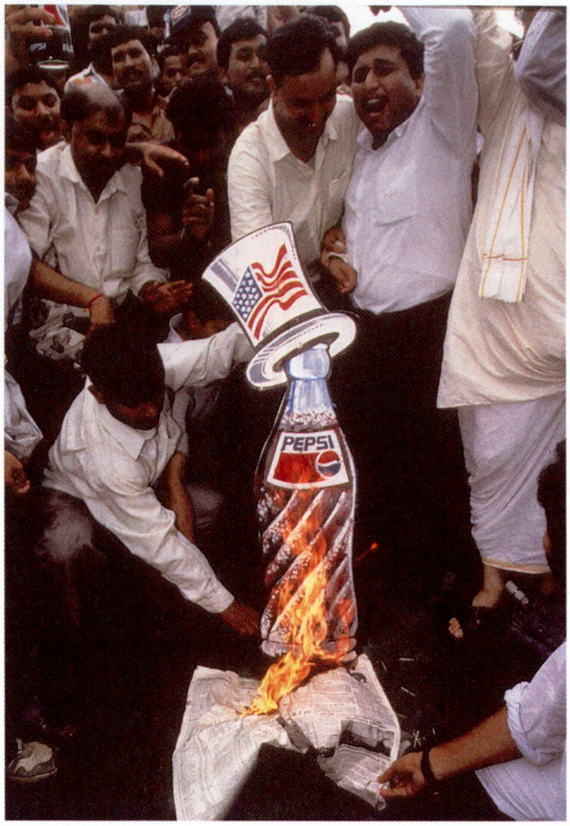

Not the Choice of a New Generation Many nationalists blame multinational corporations for the problems of their countries' economies and social conditions. Foreign firms often face a backlash. In 1995, Hindu nationalists in India—the world's largest democracy—protested economic reforms that would open the country's borders to liberal trade and investment. These and other opponents pledged to drive some of the world's best-known brands out of the Indian market.

economy, fear—is debatable. "For some, the global corporation holds the promise of lifting [humankind] out of poverty and bringing the good life to everyone. For others, these corporations have become a law unto themselves; they are miniempires which exploit all for the benefit of a few" (Gilpin 1975).

The existence of multinational corporations "has become a fact of life. They are now permanent—and influential—players in the international arena" (Spero and Hart 1997). Because MNC's "globalized financial markets have greatly heightened the structural power of capital holders and reduced the policy options open to governments" (Heredia 1997), their challenge to the existing international system of states should not be taken lightly. The UN Commission on Transnational Corporations forcefully poses the issue:

> A growing number of international norms has produced a body of international soft law on transnational corporations; it is, however, limited in scope and does not adequately match the globalization of business activity. In an era of globalization, it is increasingly difficult to distinguish between national and international issues of governance. The capacity of governments to manage their economies and achieve national objectives in areas ranging from fiscal policy to environmental control is being strained by the growing importance of transnational corporations in the international economy. Many issues related to corporate responsibility cannot be resolved satisfactorily in the context of a single national legal regime. (Commission on Transnational Corporations 1991, 33)

As multinational corporations continue to be significant players in world politics, international structures will be needed to deal with the issues raised by an economic and business sector that has turned global.

NGOS: SAVIORS OR STRANGLERS OF THE STATE?

Because ethnopolitical movements, religious groups, international terrorists, and multinational corporations are sapping the state's authority, NGOs are undermining the very institutional pillars on which the state system has rested for the previous 350 years. An accurate conceptualization of contemporary world politics must acknowledge the growing influence of NGOs and IGOs as partners and independent actors, as it becomes increasingly misleading "to view the world as consisting of territorial units each exerting supreme authority within its borders" (Falk 1993).

Like IGOs, NGOs are helping to transform traditional patterns of international relations. Exactly how their growing numbers and activity under conditions of accelerating globalization are creating changes in world politics remains undetermined, however. Indeed, as NGOs have succeeded in pushing for a greater voice in international decision making and global governance, assessments about the benefits and costs of their rising power and participation have provoked considerable controversy. Some see NGOs' contribution as beneficial to humanity when they serve humanitarian causes; this is the positive image that UN Secretary-General Kofi Annan expressed when he argued that the "partnership between the UN and the NGOs is vital because we face new enemies—the forces of what I call 'uncivil' society." Critics complain that many NGOs, some of them powerful and wealthy, cause harm because they promote their own interests at the expense of humanity's collective interests. This image is expressed by those who typically portray MNCs as "inherently exploitative . . . globetrotting sweatshop operators, indifferent polluters, and systematic tax evaders" (Stopford 2000). "A growing number of non-profit [NGOs] are funded and controlled by corporate interests [and these] trade groups employ four times as many people as environmental groups do. . . . Many NGOs now operate as little more than industry front groups, such as the Global Climate Coalition (which was set up by the fossil-fuel industry to stifle climate change-negotiations)" (Runyan 1999).

Controversies about the potential promise and/or peril of the rising influences of NGOs are likely to mount because, although NGOs are all international organizations whose members are not states, their differences outweigh their similarities and this means that some NGOs create solutions for global problems and others create problems. In thinking about and evaluating NGOs' future role, it is useful to keep in mind that

> NGOs are diverse, heterogeneous, and independent. They tend to focus around particular issues or causes. They vary widely in organizational structure, size, and membership. They are diverse in mission, level of resources, methods of operating, governance, constituencies, effectiveness, and credibility. Some NGOs develop ongoing partnerships with governments and

> receive large amounts of government funding, raising questions of their independence. Others have rather adversarial relationships with governments, perhaps affecting their ability to influence government policy. Some are transnational, and others are national or local. Most transnational NGOs are supportive of the United Nations, but some U.S. national ones seek to undermine UN credibility and activities. (Stanley Foundation 1999, 8)

Having observed their diversity and wide-ranging impact, one generalization certainly is apt: NGOs pose a threat to the overriding prominence of states in the management of world affairs. "There is every indication," Czech President Václav Havel forcefully argued in July 1999, "that the glory of the nation-state as the culmination of every national community's history . . . has already passed its peak [and] that human beings are more important than the state. In this new world, people—regardless of borders—are connected in millions of different ways: through trade, finance, property, and information."

IGOs and NGOs are together changing the face of international affairs and reshaping the global agenda, as a coalition of 160 NGOs from all regions did in October 1998 when they met in Toronto to organize to control the shipment of small arms that they believed "are causing misery and destruction all over the world." These global actors are collectively interested in turning the world of states upside down (Clegg 1999). The question for the twenty-first century is whether the nation-state system will survive, given the challenges from IGOs, NGOs, and the gales of globalization to their continuing domination. Consider one among many assessments:

> Even if a few states can still defend their territory against an invading army, not even the most powerful can protect its people and cities against a devastating surprise attack by guided missiles, and none can control the flow of images and ideas that shape human tastes and values. The globalized "presence" of Madonna, McDonald's, and Mickey Mouse make a mockery of sovereignty as exclusive territorial control. A few governments do their best to insulate their populations from such influences, but their efforts are growing less effective and run counter to democratizing demands that are growing more difficult to resist. . . . Interdependence and the interpenetration of domestic and international politics, the mobility and globalization of capital and information, and the rising influence of transnational social movements and organizations are among the factors that make it anachronistic to analyze politics as if territorial supremacy continues to be a generalized condition or a useful fiction. In particular, sovereignty, with its stress on the inside/outside distinction as between domestic and international society, seems more misleading than illuminating under current conditions. (Falk 1993, 853)

This by no means indicates that the era of state dominance is over, however. States retain a (near) monopoly on the use of coercive force in the international system, and they continue to shape the transnational interactions of nonstate actors. The state still molds the activities of nonstate actors more than its behavior is molded by them. It "may be anachronistic, but we have yet to develop an alternative form of societal organization that is able to provide its members with both wealth and power" (Kapstein 1991–1992). It is also true that "a gain in power by nonstate actors does not necessarily translate into a loss of power for the state" (Slaughter 1997). We must conclude that whereas it would be premature to abandon the focus on the state in international politics, it would be equally mistaken to exaggerate the state's power as a determinant of the globe's fate and dismiss the expanding role that nonstate actors are playing within the tightening web of interdependent globalization that is eroding the power of states. We cannot ignore the shifts occurring "away from the state—up, down, and sideways—to supra-state, sub-state, and, above all non-state actors—new players that have multiple allegiances and global reach" (Slaughter 1997; also Mathews 1997). The next chapter examines how trade and currency issues are changing in the new globalized market, making it difficult to distinguish corporations, countries, and other actors in an era of collapsing states and reemergent nations.

KEY TERMS

nongovernmental organizations (NGOs)
regimes
devolution
nonstate actors
unitary actor
nationalism
ethnopolitical groups
ethnicity
ethnic nationalism
ethnic group
indigenous peoples
Fourth World
genocide
nonstate nations
cultural domains
clash of civilizations
self-determination
ethnic cleansing
interethnic competition
ethnocentrism
displaced people
religious movement
extreme militant religious movements
irredentism
secession/separative revolts
migration
diaspora
international terrorism
terrorism
international organized crime (IOC)
postmodern terrorism
state terrorism
state-sponsored terrorism
multinational corporations (MNCs)
foreign direct investment (FDI)
transnational banks (TNBs)
product-cycle theory
strategic corporate alliances

SUGGESTED READING

Appleby, R. Scott. *The Ambivalence of the Sacred: Religion, Violence, and Reconciliation*. Boulder, Colo.: Rowman & Littlefield, 2000.

Barnet, Richard J., and John Cavanagh. *Global Dreams: Imperial Corporations and the New World Order.* New York: Simon & Schuster, 1994.

Boli, John, and George M. Thomas, eds. *Constructing World Culture: International Nongovernmental Organizations since 1875*. Stanford, Calif.: Stanford University Press, 1999.

Doremus, Paul N., William W. Keller, Louis W. Pauly, and Simon Reich. *The Myth of the Global Corporation*. Princeton, N.J.: Princeton University Press, 1998.

Eller, David. *From Culture to Ethnicity to Conflict: An Anthropological Perspective on International Ethnic Conflict*. Ann Arbor: University of Michigan Press, 1999.

Gurr, Ted Robert. *Peoples versus States: Minorities at Risk in the New Century.* Washington, D.C.: United States Institute of Press, 2000.

Huntington, Samuel P. *The Clash of Civilizations and the Remaking of World Order.* New York: Simon & Schuster, 1996.

Keohane, Robert O. "International Institutions: Can Interdependence Work?" *Foreign Policy* 110 (Spring 1998): 82–96.

Rudolph, Susanne Hoeber, and James Piscatori, eds. *Transnational Religion and Fading States.* Boulder, Colo.: Westview Press, 1997.

Smith, Anthony D., ed. *Nations and Nationalism: Journal of the Association for the Study of Ethnicity and Nationalism,* published three times annually. New York: Cambridge University Press.

The State of Indigenous People. Olympia, Wash.: Center for World Indigenous Studies, a nonprofit organization which issues bimonthly reports that can be accessed at <www.soroptimist.org>.

Teske, Robin L., and Mary Ann Tétreault, eds. *Feminist Approaches to Social Movements, Community and Power: Vol. 1, Conscious Acts and the Politics of Social Change.* Columbia: University of South Carolina Press, 2000.

Williams, Phil, ed. *Transnational Organized Crime,* quarterly journal. London: Frank Cass.

Wilmer, Franke. *The Indigenous Voice in World Politics.* Newbury Park, Calif.: Sage, 1993.

WHERE ON THE WORLD WIDE WEB?

Academic Info Religion
http://www.academicinfo.net/religindex.html

Many American students are unfamiliar with the belief systems of non-Western religions. As you look at Map 7.3 of the world's principal religions, do you wonder what the difference is between Lamaistic and Theravada Buddhists? Find out by visiting the Academic Info Religion Web site. This site links you with Internet resources for the study of the world's religions. Click on the World Scriptures and then Religious Texts to read passages from the Koran and the Old and New Testaments. Compare and contrast Taoist, Zen, Mormon, Hindu, Gnostic, and Nag Hammadi texts. If your tastes lean more toward mythology and alchemy, you will find them here, too.

Amnesty International
http://www.organic.com/Non.profits/Amnesty/index.html

Amnesty International (AI) is an international nongovernmental organization (NGO) with a global reach and a specific purpose. Its activities are concentrated on prisoners around the world who are detained solely for their beliefs, color, sex, ethnic origin, language, or religion. Amnesty International advocates the release of all prisoners of conscience, the availability of a fair and prompt trial for political prisoners, and the abolishment of the death penalty, torture, and other cruel and inhuman treatment of prisoners. Go to The Amnesty Gallery and click on photos to read and hear real-life stories of individuals who were unjustly detained.

Ethnic World Survey
http://www.partal.com/ciemen/ethnic.html

Organized by continent, this site links to information on all ethnic groups, including sites about ethnic conflicts. In Asia, read about the conflict between Tibet and China and Kashmir and India. In Europe, review the conflicts that the Basques have with the Spanish government, and that the Corsicans have with the Italian authorities. In the Americas, examine the combative Pipil in El Salvador and the Mayans in Mexico. In exploring this Web site, you will be amazed at the extent and number of ethnic groups. Why do you think that some ethnic groups turn to violence and others do not?

Fourth World Documentation Project
http://www.cwis.org/fwdp.html

The Center for World Indigenous Studies created this Web site to document and make available important materials relating to the social, political, strategic, economic, and human rights problems that indigenous peoples face. The site is organized according to region and has links to international agreements and resolutions.

Nathanson Center for the Study of Organized Crime and Corruption
http://www.yorku.ca/nathanson/

International organized crime is an increasingly influential nonstate actor for which the "creed is greed." The Nathanson Center at York University in Canada analyzes organized crime and corruption as part of its commitment to educate the public. Focusing primarily on North American organized crime, this site has an extensive bibliography of articles, books, and reports that is a good start for anyone researching this topic. It also offers links to Web sites on different international criminal organizations, including the Italian-Sicilian Mafia, the Japanese Yakuza, the Chinese Triads, and outlaw motorcycle gangs. Alternatively, it lists links by specific type of crime.

NativeWeb

http://www.nativeweb.org

The NativeWeb has both a resource center and a community center. Research the native peoples of the world by clicking on the Nations/Peoples link in the resource center, or visit the community center to discuss current issues on the message board. You can also participate in an on-line chat.

Patterns of Global Terrorism

http://www.usis.usemb.se/terror/

The U.S. Department of State has compiled a Web site that reviews region-specific information on terrorism from 1995 through 1999. Choose a year, then view appendices for a chronology of terrorist attacks, background information on specific terrorist groups, and attack and casualty statistics. Choose a terrorist group. What are its demands? Should the United States ever negotiate with terrorists? Why or why not?

Terrorism Research Center

http://www.terrorism.com/terrorism/research.html

This site is a good source for research on terrorism and links to other Web sources on terrorism. Look at the Terrorist Profiles for profiles of groups and the Definition of Terrorism controversy. Keep in mind that one group's "freedom fighters" may be another group's "terrorists."

WTO

PART III

THE POLITICS OF GLOBAL WELFARE

What factors most affect the welfare of the world's people? World politics may be played out on a large stage, but with the expansion of international commerce and communication, a new era of globalization has arisen, knitting the world into a tight web of interdependence. Money, goods, and people travel across national borders at an accelerating pace. The effects of globalization are felt locally because to an increasing extent what happens in one place influences what happens every place, and how people live in one place affects how people live everywhere else. The chapters in Part III draw attention to "human security"—the welfare of the peoples of the world—and the ways that state-to-state relations and global institutions are transforming humanity's living standards and future prospects. This section explores how changes in international trade and monetary affairs (Chapter 8), population demographics (Chapter 10), and the earth's ecological system (Chapter 11) interact to improve for some but decrease for others the quality of life, the degree of liberty, and the expectation of personal security. In looking at each of these elements of global welfare, we give special consideration to the impact of globalization (Chapter 9) and evaluate its benefits, costs, and probable effect on human prosperity.

CHAPTER 8

Trade and Monetary Issues in a Globalized Political Economy

TOPICS AND THEMES

- **The global context for interpreting contemporary world economic change**
  Past commercial philosophy
  Liberal versus mercantile values
  Hegemony: A precondition for economic order and free trade?
- **The changing free-trade regime**
- **Monetary matters: Can regimes promote trade and growth?**
- **The fate of free trade: Triumph or trouble?**

- **Controversy** Globalization's Growing Pains: Is the World Trade Organization a Friend or Foe?

Protest at the World Trade Organization conference, Seattle, November 1999

The architecture of the international finance system must be reformed to reduce its susceptibility to crises. . . . The ultimate key is not economics or finance, but politics—the art of developing support for strong policy.

—Robert Rubin, U.S. treasury secretary, 1999

The idea of economic competition among nations is flawed. Companies compete. But economically, countries depend on each other.

—Robert J. Samuelson, political economist, 1998

As leaders throughout the world planned for the twenty-first century, they faced an unfamiliar opportunity. Much of the world expected economic growth. Expanding international trade in the 1990s had transformed the ways people were living and interacting. Newly affluent people and emerging middle classes were basking in the freedom of a promising future. Much of the world set its sights on generating even more prosperity, while confronting the awesome task of reducing the huge gap between the rich and poor and of preserving the peace that allowed such vigorous economic growth. The world concentrated on finding new ways of making money, not war.

The quest for wealth is an ageless pursuit. Because it provides the means by which many other prized values can be realized, the successful management of economics lies at the center of how governments define their national interests. What practices (and underlying philosophies justifying them) should they embrace to regulate commercial and monetary activities within their borders? And what policies should each state adopt to influence trading and financial exchanges with other states?

■ **political economy** the study of the relationship between politics and economics.

These are the principal concerns of **political economy.** To introduce this topic, this chapter will first look at the ways in which the global economic system has evolved. This will allow us to then investigate how trade and monetary activities in today's growing globalized marketplace are creating new issues, and the promise and peril inherent in how these issues will be addressed in the twenty-first century.

THE GLOBAL CONTEXT FOR INTERPRETING CONTEMPORARY WORLD ECONOMIC CHANGE

Rapid changes in the world force people to think about and interpret world politics in fresh ways. Of all the many recent changes, perhaps none has been more profound and far-reaching than the post–World War II phenomenon known as **globalization**—"the increasingly close international integration of markets both for goods and services, and for capital" (IMF 1997). The growth of the interdependence of states' economies can be viewed as the recent culmination of a trend that began more than a century ago, but its current level is unprecedented. As states' economies have become more closely linked, basic ideas about states, markets, trade, and currency exchange mechanisms are being reexamined. **International political economy**—"the study of the inequality in power and wealth between peoples and nations and the patterns of collective power and learning that change this inequality" (Isaak 1995) is increasingly important because it is at this vortex of politics and economics that controversies in world politics often find their most heated expression. The contests between rich and poor, Global North and Global South, and supplier and producer have risen to prominence. While some might say that the **high politics** governing military confrontation, superpower struggle, and the quest for national security in an insecure strategic environment remain a necessary preoccupation, most would also agree that the turbulent world of **low politics,** where the economic game of world politics is played out, has assumed new relevance. The strong undercurrents in the latter are reshaping the former. The dramatic growth of international trade and the increasingly interlocked nature of the world's economy compel attention to economic transactions. Today, high interest rates in one country lead to high interest rates in others, and a stock market free fall starting in Asia will spread to New York and London. Depression abroad means recession at home. Inflation is shared everywhere, and it seems to be beyond the control of any single actor. The balance of fiscal power is now as pertinent to national security and the quality of life as the global balance of military power. These are some of the consequences of the growing international interdependence known as "globalization."

■ globalization
the integration of national markets into an interdependent global market without borders (see p. 41).

■ international political economy
the study of the intersection of politics and economics that illuminates the reasons why changes occur in the distribution of states' wealth and power.

■ high politics
geostrategic issues of national and international security as related to war and peace.

■ low politics
the category of global issues related to the economic, social, demographic, and environmental aspects of relations between governments and people.

Globalization has led to rediscovery of theories of political economy as an approach to understanding contemporary world affairs, and to the reexamination of such classic mid-nineteenth-century studies as John Stuart Mill's *Principles of Political Economy* and Karl Marx's *A Contribution to the Critique of Political Economy.* This reconsideration stems from the growing awareness that the conventional categories of politics and economics can no longer be separated. They do not form a meaningful dichotomy. The two realms are insuperably joined in an era of globalization that challenges states, because now "much of politics is economics, and most of economics is politics" (Lindblom 1979).

In this transformed context politics (states) and economics (markets) are merging. Global commerce has grown by an average of nearly 7 percent each year in the 1990s to over $8 trillion annually, and is projected to grow by 6.3 percent in 2002 (IMF 1999, 243). The relentless march in the volume of international commerce has made trade increasingly important to countries' economies. Trade comprises a growing share of the global economy, now accounting for 37 percent of global gross domestic product, up from 27 percent in 1980 (Stokes 2000, 90, 93). States in markets have become fused in an integrated international political economy. Expanding at a rate that far exceeds that of world output, trade is the most visible symbol and cause of globalization and interdependence. World trade properly deserves our primary attention, as do the dynamics of the floating **international monetary system** through which foreign currencies and credits are calculated when capital moves across borders through trade, investments, and loans. For inquiry, we need to first step backward and understand how globalization is influencing ideas about states' trade and monetary policies, which are rooted in past thinking. As the World Bank (1997) observes, "Around the globe, the state is in the spotlight. Far-reaching developments in the global economy have us revisiting basic questions about government: what its role should be, what it can and cannot do, and how best to do it." In this chapter we will focus on the critical role of the United States in shaping the contest between liberalism and mercantilism as alternative political economy philosophies underlying the different trade and monetary strategies that states pursue in their quest for power and wealth.

■ **international monetary system** the financial procedures governing the exchange and conversion of national currencies so that they can be bought and sold for one another to calculate the value of currencies and credits when capital is transferred across borders through trade, investment, and loans.

The Shadow of Past Commercial Policy Philosophy

In July 1944, forty-four states allied in war against the Axis powers met in the New Hampshire resort community of Bretton Woods. Their purpose was to devise new rules and institutions to govern international trade and monetary relations after World War II. As the world's preeminent economic and military power, the United States played the leading role. Its proposals were shaped by its perception of the causes of the 1930s' economic catastrophe and its beliefs about the role the U.S. dollar and economy should play in the postwar world. The United States sought free trade, open markets, and monetary stability—all central tenets of what would become the "Bretton Woods system"—based on the theoretical premises of **commercial liberalism,** which advocates free markets with few barriers to private trade and capital flows.

■ **commercial liberalism** an economic theory advocating free markets and the removal of barriers to the flow of trade and capital as a locomotive for prosperity.

Britain also played an important role at the conference. Led by John Maynard Keynes—whose theories about the state's role in managing inflation, unemployment, and growth influenced a generation of economic thinking throughout the capitalist world—the British delegation won support for the principle of strong government action by states facing economic problems. That ideology conforms less closely with liberalism than with the principles of **mercantilism,** which assign states a greater role than markets in managing economic interactions and accepts protectionist trade policies to expand exports and limit imports as a strategy for acquiring national wealth.

■ **mercantilism** a popular theory in the seventeenth century preaching that trading states should increase their wealth and power by expanding exports and protecting their domestic economy from imports.

Despite these differences, the rules established at Bretton Woods reflected a remarkable level of agreement and governed international economic relations for the next twenty-five years because they rested on three political bases (Spero and Hart 1997). First, power was concentrated in the rich Western European and North American countries, which reduced the number of states whose agreement was necessary for effective management by restricting the potential challenges by Japan, the Global South, and the then-communist states of Eastern Europe and the Soviet Union. Second, the system's operation was facilitated by the dominant states' shared preference for an open international economy with limited government intervention. The onset of the Cold War helped cement Western unity, because a common external enemy led the Western industrial countries to perceive economic cooperation as necessary for both prosperity and military security. That perception promoted a willingness to share economic burdens. Third, Bretton Woods worked because the United States assumed the burdens of leadership and others willingly accepted that leadership to ensure American military support.

The political bases of the Bretton Woods system crumbled in 1972 when the United States suspended the convertibility of the dollar into gold and abandoned the system of fixed currency exchange rates at its core. Since then, as floating exchange rates and growing capital mobility have made monetary mechanisms unstable, more chaotic processes of international economic relations have materialized. Still, commercial liberalism's preference for market mechanisms over government intervention remains widely accepted today. Democracy and the urge to privatize and otherwise reduce government regulation of markets has spread worldwide since the Cold War collapsed, and multinational corporations (MNCs) are serving as a powerful pillar in support of continuing strength of the liberal rules of the global trade regime. Thus it is still useful to characterize the contemporary international economic system as a **Liberal International Economic Order (LIEO)**—one based on such free market principles as openness and nondiscriminatory trade.

Liberal International Economic Order (LIEO) the set of regimes created after World War II, designed to promote monetary stability and reduce barriers to the free flow of trade and capital.

Not all states consistently support the liberal tenet that governments should not interfere by managing trade flows because they fear the potential costs of free trade. Commercial liberalism is under attack in many states, including some of liberalism's unenthusiastic proponents, which are pressured domestically to protect industries and employment at home. When the president of the United States calls the king of Saudi Arabia to secure a multibillion-dollar sale of U.S.-built passenger jets—as Bill Clinton did—free trade is victimized. When the World Trade Organization fails to agree on a new round of trade liberalization negotiations, as occurred in December 1999 at its Seattle conference, mercantilism holds sway. States and markets continue to coexist in tension with one another, as they always have in a world of competitive sovereign states. Globalization has not eliminated the urge to compete, because states fear that **interdependence**—a condition of mutual sensitivity and vulnerability (Keohane and Nye 1989)—will compromise their sovereignty and security. "Sensitivity" means that economic phenomena that occur in one society are readily transmitted to another through their mutual interactions (e.g., inflation), and governments cannot control their transnational reverberations. "Vulnerability" results when deliberate changes in the policies (e.g., trade embargoes) of one state politically affect another. Interdependence thus encourages states to maximize their gains through international exchanges while minimizing their sensitivity and vulnerability. States' trade policies are naturally influenced by the selfish desire to increase the domestic benefits of international economic transactions and to lessen their adverse consequences, even if this will undermine the expansion of a global capitalist economy propelled by free trade.

interdependence a situation in which the behavior of international actors greatly affects others with whom they have contact, making all parties mutually sensitive and vulnerable to the others' actions.

The Clash between Liberal and Mercantile Values

How should states rationally cope in the globalized political economy to best manage economic change? The choices inspire different philosophies and policies. They force governments to attempt to reconcile the overriding need for states to cooperate with others in trade liberalization if they are to maximize their wealth with each state's natural competitive desire to put its own welfare first.

Most controversies in international political economy are ultimately reducible to the competing ideologies of liberalism and mercantilism, which represent "fundamentally different . . . conceptions of the relationships among society, state, and market" (Gilpin 2001). A comparison of the logic behind the two theoretical traditions can help us to appreciate why a reconciliation or balance is so hard to achieve, why particular protectionist domestic interests sacrifice collective prosperity in order to maximize their own parochial gains, and why others criticize mercantilism as self-defeating.

■ theory
a set of conclusions derived from assumptions (axioms) and/or evidence about some phenomenon, including its character, causes, and probable consequences and their ethical implications.

Commercial Liberalism. Commercial liberalism as a political **theory** explains economics by building on the presumption that humankind's natural inclination is to cooperate in order to increase prosperity and enlarge individual liberty under law. Consequently, it is closely related to liberal theory (described in Chapter 2), which is based on the assumption that individuals and groups usually make decisions on the basis of rational calculations through the application of intellect to analysis of available facts. Commercial liberalism asserts that through mutually beneficial exchanges people can benefit and the problems of capitalism—boom-and-bust cycles, trade wars, and poverty—can be solved. Commercial liberal theory has many roots and variations, but all liberal thinkers agree that the promotion of free international trade to lift the poor from poverty and to expand political liberties is one of the globe's "great causes" (see Bhagwati 1999).

Adam Smith, the eighteenth-century political economist who helped define the precepts of classical liberalism as well as modern-day economics, used the metaphor of the unregulated market's "invisible hand" to show how the collective or public interest can be served by humans' natural tendency to "truck, barter, and exchange" in pursuit of private gain. Hence the importance of "free" markets, which produce collective as well as private gain. David Ricardo, a nineteenth-century British political economist, added an important corollary to liberal thought as applied to the international economy. Ricardo demonstrated conclusively that when all states specialize in the production of those goods in which they enjoy a **comparative advantage** and trade them for goods in which others enjoy an advantage, a net gain in welfare for both states, in the form of higher living standards, will result. The principle of comparative advantage underpins commercial liberalism's advocacy of free trade as a method for capital accumulation. Material progress is realized and mutual gains are achieved, according to this principle, providing countries specialize in the production of what they can produce least expensively and are willing to purchase goods that are costly for them to produce from other countries, and, in addition, do not restrict the flow of trade across borders.

■ comparative advantage
the concept in liberal economics that a state will benefit if it specializes in those goods it can produce comparatively cheaply and acquires through trade goods that it can only produce at a higher cost.

Liberalism maintains that open markets and free trade are both advantageous and the engines of economic progress. As Benjamin Franklin summarized commercial liberal theory more than two centuries ago, "No nation was ever ruined by trade." Another way of expressing this idea is to say that each country should specialize in producing those goods in which it has the greatest comparative cost advantage or least comparative cost disadvantage, and trade with others. The assumption is that trade competition is good for all. Competition stimulates technological innovation to improve production efficiency in order to meet the competition for trade of other producers, and in the long run the world's output and income will increase and everyone's standard of living will rise providing all abide by the rules of free trade and open markets. Commercial liberalism recognizes that in the short run free trade will result in unequal rewards for some and produce inequalities in countries' rate of growth, but argues that the long-term gains for all in a **laissez-faire economic** system of free markets are most important.

■ **laissez-faire economics** from a French phrase (meaning literally "let do") that Adam Smith and other commercial liberals in the eighteenth century used to describe the advantages of free-wheeling capitalism without government interference in economic affairs.

Why does free trade produce benefits for trade partners who specialize in the production of goods for which they each have comparative advantage? Consider a hypothetical illustration of Japan and the United States, each of which produces cameras and computers but with different worker productivity (output per hour) for each country, as shown in the first column of Table 8.1.

Clearly Japan has an absolute advantage in both products, as Japanese workers are more productive in turning out cameras and computers than the American workers are. Does this mean the two countries cannot benefit by trading with one another? If trade does occur, should each country continue to allocate its resources as in the past? The answer to both questions is no.

Each country should specialize in producing that item in which it has the greatest comparative cost advantage or least comparative cost disadvantage, and trade for others. Because Japan is three times more productive in cameras than computers, it should direct more of its resources into manufacturing that industry. One cost of doing so is lost computer output, but Japan can turn out three additional cameras for every computer given up. The United States, on the other hand, can obtain only two computers. Like their Japanese counterparts, American workers are also more productive in making cameras than computers. Still, U.S. resources should be directed to computers because the United States is at a smaller disadvantage compared with Japan in this area. If the United States specializes in computers and Japan in cameras and they trade with one another, each will benefit. The following scenario shows why.

Begin with one hundred workers in each industry without specialization or trade (second column). Next specialize production by shifting ten Japanese

TABLE 8.1

Comparative Advantage and the Gains from Free Trade

	Worker Productivity per Hour		*Before Specialization*		*Specialization, No Trade*		*Specialization with Trade*	
Country	Camera	Computer	Camera	Computer	Camera	Computer	Camera	Computer
Japan	9	3	900	300	990	270	910	300
United States	4	2	400	200	320	240	400	210

workers from computer to camera production and shifting twenty American workers from camera production to computers (third column). Then permit free trade so that eighty Japanese-manufactured cameras are exported to the United States and thirty U.S. computers are exported to Japan. With specialization *and* free trade the benefits to both countries improve.

By shifting Japanese resources into the production of cameras and U.S. resources into computers and allowing trade, the same total allocations will cause camera and computer output to rise ten units each (fourth column). The reason is because resources are now being used more efficiently. Benefits to both countries can be realized when each trades some of its additional output for the other's. Japan ends up with more cameras than before specialization and trade and the same number of computers, while the United States finds itself with more computers and the same number of cameras. More output in both countries means higher living standards.

Liberals such as Smith, Ricardo, and Franklin believed that markets work best when free of government interference. They reasoned that economic processes governing the production, distribution, and consumption of goods and services operate according to certain natural laws. They saw **politics** as necessary if crass, and argued that while governments often performed their key tasks poorly, they had the capacity to overcome their historic proclivity to abuse power and could instead become engines for prosperity—providing they would not exercise a heavy hand in regulating the marketplace. Today people subscribing to these views are described as conservatives, not liberals. The tenets described here are those of "classical" liberalism. The hallmark of commercial liberal theory, then, is its commitment "to free markets and minimal state intervention. . . . Liberals believe economics is progressive and politics is regressive. Thus they conceive of progress as divorced from politics and based on the evolution of the market" (Gilpin 2001).

■ **politics**
the exercise of power (see p. 457).

Transferred to the international level, these principles suggest that trade and other forms of economic relations "are a source of peaceful relations among nations because the mutual benefits of trade and expanding interdependence among national economies will tend to foster cooperative relations. . . . A liberal international economy will have a moderating influence on international politics as it creates bonds of mutual interests and a commitment to the status quo" (Gilpin 2001). Thus, trade liberalization is believed to produce many economic and political benefits: the removal of trade restrictions, currency devaluations, and other reforms generate rapid export and economic growth because they promote competition, improve resource allocations, reduce production costs, generate pressures for increased production efficiencies, attract foreign capital and expertise, provide foreign exchange needed for imports, and promote more equal access to scarce resources. These economic benefits are believed to have positive political consequences, leading to the growth of civil liberties and democratic governance (Todaro 2000).

There is a fly in this liberal ointment, however. Although commercial liberal theory promises that the "invisible hand" will maximize efficiency so that everyone will gain, it does not promise that everyone will gain equally. Instead, "everyone will gain in accordance with his or her contribution to the whole, but . . . not everyone will gain equally because individual productivities differ. Under free exchange, society as a whole will be more wealthy, but individuals will be rewarded in terms of their marginal productivity and relative contribution to the overall social product" (Gilpin 2001). This applies at the international level as well: The gains from international trade may be distributed quite unequally, even if the principle of comparative advantage governs. Commercial liberal theory ignores these differences, as it is concerned with **absolute gains** rather than **relative gains.** Other theorists, however, are more concerned with the distribution of economic rewards.

■ **absolute gains** a measure of the degree to which all participants in an exchange become better off.

■ **relative gains** a measure of how much some participants in an exchange benefit in comparison to others.

Mercantilism. Mercantilism is an economic philosophy deeply entrenched in the long story of states' quest for power and wealth. Its theoretical underpinnings prompted Adam Smith to write his famous critique in *The Wealth of Nations,* and its practice prompted rebellious American colonists to dump British tea into the Boston harbor in 1773.

Mercantilism advocates government regulation of economic life to increase state power and security. It emerged in Europe as the leading political economy philosophy after the decline of feudalism and helped to stimulate the first wave of Europe's imperialist expansion, which began in the fifteenth century. Accumulating gold and silver was seen as the route to state power and wealth, and imperialistically acquiring overseas colonies was seen as a means to that end.

While states no longer try to stockpile precious metals, many continue to intervene in the marketplace. In the contemporary context, then, **neomercantilism** refers to "a trade policy whereby a state seeks to maintain a balance-of-trade surplus and to promote domestic production and employment by reducing imports, stimulating home production, and promoting exports" (Walters and Blake 1992). Its advocates are sometimes called "economic nationalists." In their view, states must compete for position and power, and economic resources are the source of state power. From this it follows that "economic activities are and should be subordinate to the goal of state building and the interests of the state. All nationalists ascribe to the primacy of the state, of national security, and of military power in the functioning of the international system" (Gilpin 2001).

■ **neomercantilism** a contemporary version of classical mercantilism which advocates promoting domestic production and a balance-of-payment surplus by subsidizing exports and using tariffs and nontarriff barriers to reduce imports.

As an ideology of political economy, mercantilism shares much in common with political realism: Realists and mercantilists both see the state as the principal world actor; both view the international system as anarchical; and both dwell on the aggressively competitive drive of people and states for advantage. "Economic nationalists . . . stress the role of power in the rise of a market and the conflictual nature of international economic relations; they argue that economic interdependence must have a political foundation and that it creates yet another arena of interstate conflict, increases national vulnerability, and constitutes a mechanism that one society can employ to dominate another" (Gilpin 2001).

While commercial liberals emphasize the mutual benefits of cooperative trade agreements, mercantilists are more concerned that the gains realized by one side of the bargain will come at the expense of the other. For them, relative gains are more important than both parties' absolute gains. An American economic nationalist, for instance, would complain about a trade agreement that promised the United States a 5 percent growth in income and the Chinese 6 percent. Although the bargain would ensure an eventual increase in U.S. living standards, its position compared with China's would erode. Indeed, projected over the long run, such seemingly small differences would eventually lead to

China's replacement of the United States as the world's largest economy—an outcome highly unacceptable to American economic nationalists. Calculations such as these explain why achieving mutual gains through international cooperation often encounters stiff resistance from domestic groups seeking to protect their profits from foreign competition. It also explains why specific, negatively affected domestic producers lobby for mercantilist measures, and why they sometimes succeed against the unorganized interests of consumers who benefit from free trade.

Protectionism is the generic term used to describe a number of mercantilist policies designed to protect domestic producers from the influx of foreign goods. The following are some common protectionist strategies:

- **Beggar-thy-neighbor policies** seek to enhance domestic welfare by promoting trade surpluses that can be realized only at other countries' expense. They reflect a government's efforts to reduce unemployment through currency devaluations, tariffs, quotas, export subsidies, and other strategies that adversely affect its trade partners. These protective strategies encourage unequal exchanges between exporters and importers (see Chapter 5).
- **Import quotas** unilaterally specify the quantity of a particular product that can be imported from abroad. In the late 1950s, for example, the United States established import quotas on oil, arguing that they were necessary to protect U.S. national security. Hence the government, rather than the marketplace, determined the amount and source of imports.
- **Export quotas** result from negotiated agreements between producers and consumers and restrict the flow of products (e.g., shoes or sugar) from the former to the latter. An **orderly market arrangement (OMA)** is a formal agreement in which a country agrees to limit the export of products that might impair workers in the importing country, often under specific rules designed to monitor and manage trade flows. Exporting countries are willing to accept such restrictions in exchange for concessions on other fronts from the importing countries. The Multi-Fiber Arrangement (MFA) is an example of an elaborate OMA that restricts exports of textiles and apparel. It originated in the early 1960s, when the United States formalized earlier, informal **voluntary export restrictions (VERs)** negotiated with Japan and Hong Kong to protect domestic producers from cheap cotton imports. The quota system was later extended to other importing and exporting countries and then, in the 1970s, to other fibers, when it became the MFA.
- Import and export quotas are representative of a broader category of trade restrictions known as **nontariff barriers (NTBs)** that discriminate against imports without direct tax levies. As complex societies strive to protect the welfare of their citizens through numerous and often complex government regulations regarding health and safety, foreign-produced goods frequently cannot compete. NTBs are now a more important form of general trade protectionism than tariffs that impose taxes on commodity imports to shelter particular domestic industries from foreign competition.
- Among developing countries, whose domestic industrialization goals may be hindered by the absence of protection from the Global North's more efficient

protectionism a policy of creating barriers to foreign trade, such as tariffs and quotas, that protect local industries from competition.

beggar-thy-neighbor policies the attempt to promote trade surpluses by trade policies that cause trade partners to suffer trade deficits.

import quotas nontariff barriers to free trade that involve limits on the quantity of particular products that can be imported.

export quotas barriers to free trade agreed to by two trading states to protect their domestic producers.

orderly market arrangements (OMAs) voluntary export restrictions that involve a government-to-government agreement and often specific rules of management.

voluntary export restrictions (VERs) a protectionist measure popular in the 1980s and early 1990s, in which exporting countries agree to restrict shipments of a particular product to a country to deter it from imposing an even more onerous import quota.

nontariff barriers (NTBs) measures that discriminate against imports without direct tax levies and are beyond the scope of international regulation.

firms, the **infant industry** argument is often used to justify mercantilist trade policies. According to this argument, tariffs or other forms of protection are necessary to nurture young industries until they eventually mature and lower production costs to compete effectively in the global marketplace. Import-substitution industrialization policies, once popular in Latin America and elsewhere, often depended on protection of infant industries (see Chapter 5).

- In the Global North, creating comparative advantages now motivates the use of what is known as **strategic trade policy** as a neomercantilist means of ensuring that a country's industries will remain competitive. Strategic trade is a form of government industrial policy that targets subsidies toward particular industries so they gain a competitive edge over foreign producers. Two protectionist strategies that are increasingly used are **countervailing duties,** the imposition of tariffs to offset alleged subsidies by foreign producers, and **antidumping duties** imposed to counter the alleged sale of products at below the cost of production.

infant industry a newly established industry that is not yet strong enough to compete effectively in the global marketplace.

strategic trade policy an industrial policy that targets government subsidies toward particular industries so as to gain competitive advantage over foreign producers.

countervailing duties tariffs imposed by a government to offset suspected subsidies provided by foreign governments to their producers.

antidumping duties duties imposed to offset another state's alleged selling of a product at below the cost to produce it.

Realist theory helps to account for states' impulse to practice mercantilist and neomercantilist protectionism. Recall that **realism** argues that states often shun cooperation because international anarchy without global governance creates fear: Threatened states mistrust one another's motives. Moreover, in the self-help international system, states alone are responsible for their survival and well-being. As a result, uncertainty about others' expansionist aims encourages each state to spend "a portion of its effort, not forwarding its own good, but in providing the means of protecting itself against others" (Waltz 1979).

The insecurity that breeds competition rather than cooperation is often exhibited in international economic relations. Those who see states' power and wealth as inextricably linked conclude that "even if nation-states do not fear for their physical survival, they worry that a decrease in their power capabilities relative to those of other states will compromise their political autonomy, expose them to the influence attempts of others, or lessen their ability to prevail in political disputes with allies and adversaries" (Mastanduno 1991). Thus many states are "defensively positional actors" that seek not only to promote their domestic well-being but also to defend their rank (position) in comparison with others (see Grieco 1995).

realism the theoretical tradition that operates from the assumption that competitive states seek self-advantage and are unlikely to cooperate (see p. 457).

The relative gains issue speaks to the difficulties of achieving international cooperation under anarchical conditions, and explains why some domestic producers vigorously oppose liberal (open) international economies despite the evidence that free trade promotes economic growth (Quinn 1997). Different countries therefore practice dissimilar economic policies. Some endorse free trade, and others impose protectionist barriers; some see an unregulated market as the best method for protecting the greatest good for the greatest number; others seek to tilt the playing field to their own advantage.

hegemonic stability theory the proposition that free trade and interstate peace depend on the existence of a predominant great power willing and able to use economic and military strength to promote global stability (see p. 557).

Hegemony: A Precondition for Economic Order and Free Trade?

Hegemonic stability theory, a blend of liberalism and mercantilism, holds that when a single state ascends to hold a preponderance of military and economic power such that a **hegemon** emerges, international economic stability based on liberal principles can materialize to alleviate the fears of nationalistic mercantilists. Unlike mercantilism, this realist worldview follows the logic of

hegemon a single, overwhelmingly powerful state that exercises predominant influence over other global actors (see p. 432).

Freak Food or Unfair Foreign Trade? A Greenpeace activist in France protests the import of genetically modified corn, which the United States produces for export around the globe. Although most economists today believe the more trade the better, in many countries the public thinks simply that exports are good and imports, which they see as threatening jobs and environmental standards, are bad. Foreign trade clearly helps countries grow more wealthy, but trade causes harm to some domestic groups and NGOs, which react by lobbying against it.

long-cycle theory the proposition based on the evidence that great powers rise to positions of hegemonic global leadership, but eventually decline when their leadership is challenged by ascendant rivals (see p. 432).

hegemony the ability of one state to dominate rules and arrangements governing international economics and politics.

long-cycle theory (see Chapter 4) in viewing the balancing of power among competing actors in anarchy as the key to global economic order, but accepts the likelihood that order can best emerge at those phases in the long-term redistribution of global power when an all-powerful single hegemon uses its position to enforce free-trade rules. Hegemonic stability theory thus "assumes that a liberal economic system cannot be self-sustaining but must be maintained over the long term through the actions of the dominant economy" (Gilpin 2001).

Hegemony is the ability to "dictate, or at least dominate, the rules and arrangements by which international relations, political and economic, are conducted" (Goldstein 1988). In the world economy it occurs when a single great power garners a sufficient preponderance of material resources so that it can dominate the international flow of raw materials, capital, and trade.

From its preponderant position, a hegemon is able to promote rules for the whole global system that protect the hegemon's own interests. Hegemons such as the United States (and Britain before it), whose domestic economies are based on capitalist principles, have championed liberal international economic systems, because their comparatively greater control of technology, capital, and raw materials has given them more opportunities to profit from a system free of mercantilist restraints. When they have enforced such free-trade rules, the hegemon's economies typically have served as "engines of growth" for others in the "liberal train."

However, historically hegemons have also had special responsibilities. They have had to coordinate states' **macroeconomic** policies, manage the international monetary system to enable one state's money to be exchanged for others', make sure that countries facing balance-of-payments deficits (imbalances in their financial inflows and outflows) could find the credits necessary to finance their deficits, and serve as lenders of last resort during financial crises. When the most powerful liberal states could not perform these tasks, they have often backtracked toward more closed (protected or regulated) domestic economies, and in doing so have undermined the open international system that was previously advantageous to them (Block 1977). This kind of departure historically has made tariffs, monetary regulations, and other mercantilist policies more widespread, and thereby undermined the LIEO regime. In short, hegemonic states have not only had the greatest capacity to make a free-trade regime succeed but in the past they have also had the greatest responsibility for its effective operation and preservation. To interpret whether hegemonic stability theory is likely to hold in the future, a closer look at the theory's logic is useful.

■ **macroeconomics** the study of aggregate economic indicators such as GDP, the money supply, and the balance of trade that governments monitor to measure changes in the national economy.

The Hegemonic Pillars of Free Markets and Free Trade. Nearly all economic theories accept particular principles about the preconditions for fostering the free movement of goods across national borders. A core concept that informs discussion is that of public or **collective goods**—benefits that everyone shares and from which no one can be excluded selectively. National security is one such collective good that governments try to provide for all of their citizens, regardless of the resources that individuals contribute through taxation. In the realm of economic analysis, an open international economy permitting the relatively free movement of goods, services, and capital is similarly seen as a desirable collective good, inasmuch as it permits economic benefits for all states that would not be available if the global economy were closed to the trade.

■ **collective goods** goods such as safe drinking water from which everyone benefits (see p. 395).

According to hegemonic stability theory, the collective good of an open global economy needs a single, dominant power—a hegemon—to remain open and liberal. If a hegemon does not exist or is unwilling to use its power to provide this collective good, states will be tempted to "free ride" rather than contribute to maintaining the liberal international economy. A major way in which the hegemon pays may be to open its own market to less expensive imported goods even if other countries free ride by not opening their own markets. And if enough states take this easy route, the entire structure may collapse.

The analogy of a public park helps us to clarify this principle. If there were no central government to provide for the maintenance of the park, individuals themselves would have to cooperate to keep the park in order (the trees trimmed, the lawn mowed, and so on). But some may try to come and enjoy the benefits of the park without pitching in. If enough people realize that they can get away with this—that they can enjoy a beautiful park without helping with its upkeep—it will not be long before the once beautiful park looks shabby. Cooperation to provide a public good is thus difficult. This is also the case with the collective good of a liberal international economy, because many states that enjoy the collective good of an orderly, open, free market economy pay little or

■ **free riders**
those who enjoy the benefits of collective goods but pay little or nothing for them.

■ **zero-sum**
an exchange in which what one competitor gains is lost by the other party to the exchange (see p. 490).

nothing for it. These are known as **free riders.** A hegemon typically tolerates free riders, partly because the benefits that the hegemon provides, such as a stable global currency, encourage other states to accept the leader's dictates. Thus both gain, much as liberalism sees the benefits of cooperation as a "positive-sum" outcome because both sides to a bargain stand to gain from their exchanges. If the costs of leadership begin to multiply, however, a hegemon will tend to become less tolerant of others' free riding. In such a situation cooperation will increasingly be seen as one-sided or **zero-sum** because most of the benefits come at the expense of the hegemon. Then the open global economy will crumble amidst a competitive race for individual gain at others' expense.

Charles Kindleberger (1973), an international economist, first theorized about the need for a preponderant liberal hegemon to maintain order and stability. In his explanation of the 1930s Great Depression, Kindleberger concluded that "the international economic and monetary system needs leadership, a country which is prepared, consciously or unconsciously, . . . to set standards of conduct for other countries; and to seek to get others to follow them, to take on an undue share of the burdens of the system, and in particular to take on its support in adversity." Britain played this role from 1815 until the outbreak of World War I in 1914, and the United States assumed the British mantle in the decades immediately following World War II. In the interwar years, however, Britain was unable to play its previous leadership role, and the United States, although capable of leadership, was unwilling to exercise it. The void, Kindleberger concluded, was a principal cause of the "width and depth" of the Great Depression throughout the world in the 1930s.

The Causes of Hegemonic Decline. Although hegemonic powers benefit from the liberal economic systems that their power promotes, the very success of liberalism eventually erodes the pillars that support it.

> Economic competition and the price mechanism drive the market economy toward ever higher levels of productive efficiency, economic growth, and the integration of national markets. In time, the market produces profound shifts in the location of economic activities and affects the international redistribution of economic and industrial power. The unleashing of market forces transforms the political framework itself, undermines the hegemonic power, and creates a new political environment to which the world must eventually adjust. With the inevitable shift in the international distribution of economic and military power from the core to rising nations in the periphery and elsewhere, the capacity of the hegemon to maintain the system decreases. Capitalism and the market system thus tend to destroy the political foundations on which they must ultimately rest. (Gilpin 1987, 77–78)

The leading economic power's ability to adapt is critical to maintaining its dominant position. Britain was unable to adapt, and fell from its top-ranked position. Is the United States destined to suffer the same fate? Many contend that the signs of potential U.S. hegemonic decline should not be ignored, even though at the twenty-first century's dawn the United States still stood as an economic superpower, with no apparent end in sight to the longest-running economic expansion in U.S. history, which saw America's GNP increase by 33 percent between 1991 and 2000. One indicator of decline, however, is the U.S.

share of world output, which has fallen steadily since World War II ended. In 1947, the United States accounted for nearly 50 percent of the combined gross world product. By 1960, its share had slipped to 28 percent, by 1970 to 25 percent, and "by the 1990s to 20 percent or less—less than of what it had been at its peak and less than it was at the time of the Spanish-American War, when the United States first emerged as a world power" (D. White 1998, 42). Another symptom of the U.S. erosion in the international pecking order is that the U.S. share of world financial reserves has declined. The United States went from being the globe's greatest creditor country in 1980 to the world's largest debtor by 1990, and remains "the biggest debtor nation in history" (D. White 1998). A third symptom of U.S. decline is the fact that its external indebtedness (a measure in the difference in value between U.S. investments abroad and foreign investments in the United States) has also steadily risen during the 1990s to record levels; at the start of 1999 foreign indebtedness reached $1.24 trillion (*Economist,* July 3, 1999, 5). Fourth, at $271.3 billion, the U.S. trade deficit at the start of 2000 reached the highest level ever, increasing by 65 percent in 1999 to widen the surging gap by more than $100 billion from 1998 as the booming U.S. economy pushed up consumer demand for foreign goods. Finally, alongside these debt burdens and trade imbalances, U.S. investment in public infrastructure to stimulate future growth is lower than that of all the other G-7 industrialized powerhouses, a problem that is causing the United States to lose "its ability to compete with other economies because of its low savings rate and insufficient investment in education" (Thurow 1998). These trends suggest that U.S. advantages in the global marketplace will not continue: "The U.S. clearly is the world's strongest economy, but weak spots are visible as we look to the decades ahead" (Weidenbaum 1999).

Because in many areas essential to the preservation of hegemony—control over capital, markets and competitive production—U.S. preponderance may be waning, a number of "declinist" analysts remain convinced of Paul Kennedy's popular argument that **imperial overstretch** is likely to cause America's fall from its preeminent position at the pinnacle of global economic power (1987). As Kennedy argued, "The United States now runs the risk that the sum total of [its] global interests and obligations is nowadays far larger than the country's power to defend them all simultaneously." This prediction derives from a principle suggested by past hegemonic experiences, namely "that a power that wants to remain number one for generation after generation requires not just military capability, not just national will, but also a flourishing and efficient economic base, strong finances and a healthy social fabric, for it is upon such foundations that the country's military strength rests in the long term" (Kennedy 1992).

■ **imperial overstretch** Paul Kennedy's thesis that hegemons decline because they make costly global commitments in excess of their ability to fulfill them.

Kennedy's popular declinist thesis was attacked by critics who saw the parallels between the American and earlier British experiences as unfair and as undervaluing continued U.S. dynamism (see Nye 2001). Still, the rise of economic rivals to U.S. hegemonic leadership, partly as a result of America's declining share of world wealth, low domestic savings rate, and poor educational performance, does not bode well for continuing U.S. economic dominance. Most projections of the coming rise and fall of states' future global position agree with the view that "Russia has fallen, American power and wealth are in slow relative decline, but China and the European Union are rising" (Hughes 2000).

An undisputed hegemonic power typically can afford to be less concerned about its relative power position than others. It is therefore less likely to attempt to maximize its share of the global market than are aspiring hegemons or other economic powers threatened by an erosion in their relative power. As a hegemon's dominance erodes, however, its trade and other economic policies can be expected to change. The United States once tolerated—indeed, encouraged—other states to practice mercantile policies as it sought to cement Western solidarity during the Cold War. Today it is less willing to assume the burdens of maintaining the liberal international economic order it once championed, emphasizing competitiveness more than support for political allies.

The Uncertain Consequences of Hegemonic Decline. What happens when a hegemon's preponderant power declines? Domestically we would expect it to abandon the torch of commercial liberalism as the forces of economic nationalism gain politically. Internationally, hegemonic stability theory predicts that disorder will result, because hegemonic leadership is "the cement that holds the system together" (Gilpin 1987). In extreme instances, armed conflict may follow; for example, the hegemonic decline of Britain and the absence of U.S. leadership may have precipitated the two world wars of the twentieth century.

An orderly and stable world political economy existed from the end of World War II until the early 1970s, when U.S. hegemony was unchallenged. Since then, however, American dominance has waned, and international economic relations have been wracked by periodic crises and instability. Still, the system has not collapsed, as it did in the years between World Wars I and II. Is this because the processes of hegemonic decline have yet to play themselves out? Or, as some would argue, is the decline of American power a myth? Or is it because the institutions and rules put into place to govern the liberal order during the period of American hegemony have now taken on a life of their own? The last view is the most convincing one to commercial liberals, who believe that the rise of a liberal international regime and embedded network of complementary institutions to support its open rules explains the persistence of economic order and growth, even though American hegemony may be fading (Strange 1996).

The power of that conviction resides in the fact that the commercial liberalism institutionalized in the original Bretton Woods system is continuing to gain strength, despite the relative decline of U.S. hegemony. True, "America's defection could throw the process into reverse" (Bergsten 1997). However, even in the absence of a U.S. hegemon pushing for trade liberalization, and even in the possible face of the declining U.S. hegemon succumbing to the temptations of (free-riding) mercantilism, trade liberalization is now too deeply entrenched for it to collapse easily. The free-trade regime has too many supporters, including powerful MNCs, for that regime to need a single hegemonic protector to preserve free trade as it did in the past two hundred years. Institutionalized globalization has progressed to a level that makes the continuation of a liberal trading system likely, because too many states and multilateral institutions have an enormous stake in its preservation. "Built-in restraints on imposing new trade barriers have never been greater" (Stokes 2000).

■ **international regime** the set of rules, norms, and decision-making procedures that coordinates state behavior in such issue areas as international trade.

International regimes are created when states devise rules for cooperation even under international anarchy. Although most of the liberal international regimes (rules and institutions) that govern international trade today first developed during the era of U.S. dominance, they have continued to flourish. "By providing more information, establishing mechanisms for monitoring and generating shared expectations, institutions can create an environment in which interstate cooperation is possible even without a single dominant leader" (Krasner 1993). The free-trade regime may no longer depend on the existence of an all-powerful hegemon.

To better probe that hypothesis and understand the likely future of global economics, let us now inspect how those international trade and monetary rules have evolved from mere pledges to reduce trade barriers to become entrenched customary policy practices.

THE CHANGING FREE-TRADE REGIME

In the period immediately following World War II, when the United States became the world's new political hegemon, it simultaneously became the preeminent voice in international trade affairs. The liberal trading system the United States chose to promote rejected the zero-sum, beggar-thy-neighbor competitive economic nationalism widely seen as the major factor in deepening and perpetuating the economic depression of the 1930s. Removing barriers to trade became a priority and led to the recurrent rounds of trade negotiations that cumulatively produced remarkable reductions in tariff rates. As the large U.S. market was opened to foreign producers, other countries' economies grew, and rising trade contributed to a climate that encouraged others to open their markets also.

That movement toward free trade progressed in a series of steps. At the time of the Bretton Woods negotiations, the United States envisioned a new International Trade Organization (ITO) that would seek lower restrictions on trade and set rules of commerce. The organization was stillborn, however. The proposed trading scheme, popularly known as the Havana Charter, failed to win the approval of the U.S. Congress: "Protectionists opposed the arrangement for being too liberal, and liberals were against it for being too protectionist. . . . Without U.S. support the ITO was dead" (Isaak 1995).

Without the ITO, the United States needed to find another institutional base from which to create and enhance a liberalized trade regime. It turned to the **General Agreement on Tariffs and Trade (GATT)** that, after its birth in the late 1940s, became the principal international organization designed to promote and protect free trade in the postwar LIEO.

■ **General Agreement on Tariffs and Trade (GATT)** an international organization affiliated with the United Nations that promotes international trade and tariff reductions.

GATT was never intended to be a formal institution with enforcement powers. Instead, a premium was placed on negotiations and reaching consensus to settle disputes among parties to the agreement, which was first and foremost a commercial treaty. As the trading system changed and disputes multiplied, though, GATT—under pressure from the United States—increasingly became involved in dispute settlement following increasingly legalistic procedures. Those rules put into law an evolving regime whose primary mission has been increasing free trade.

The United States, the principal catalyst to the GATT negotiating rounds, opened its own market to others and tolerated their free riding. For example, the United States knowingly acquiesced in Japan's protectionist trade practices and Europe's discrimination against many U.S. exports, because restoring European and Japanese economic vitality was the first U.S. foreign policy goal.

In the poisoned Cold War atmosphere, the superpowers were primarily concerned with securing the loyalty of allies, even when that meant subsidizing their growth, and thus the long-term economic benefits of their revitalization outweighed the short-term costs. Thus the United States not only permitted but actually encouraged others' relative gains.

The history of the emergence of a global free trade regime in the second half of the twentieth century is a history of starts and stops along the progressive path toward creating a truly open trade system through the reduction of barriers to the free flow of goods across national borders. The progress toward the negotiation of increasingly lower tariffs has encountered resistance along the way, but in 1994 the GATT sessions in the **Uruguay Round** of negotiations that had begun in 1986 culminated in the 1995 creation of the **World Trade Organization (WTO).** A new free-trade organization with "teeth," the WTO has made a huge difference in the way the world conducts its business (see Table 8.2), and that agreement was the most comprehensive trade deal in history, covering everything from paper clips to jet aircraft. The very bulk of the document symbolized its breadth: "The Final Act signed in Marrakesh, Morocco, on 15 April, 1994, weighed 385 pounds and included over 22,000 pages" (Jackson 1994, 131).

■ **Uruguay Round**
the multilateral trade negotiations of GATT that began in 1986 and concluded in 1994 with the creation of the WTO.

■ **World Trade Organization (WTO)**
a multilateral agency that monitors the implementation of trade agreements and settles disputes among trade partners.

The new WTO represents a breathtaking step in free-trade management, although it has also provoked much controversy (see Controversy: Globalization's Growing Pains). The WTO extended GATT's coverage to products, sectors, and conditions of trade not previously covered adequately. The WTO also enhanced previous dispute-settlement procedures by making the findings of its arbitration panels binding on the domestic laws of participating states (GATT's findings were not binding). And the WTO deals with the problem of free riding by being available only to states that belong to GATT, subscribe to all of the Uruguay Round agreements, and make market access commitments (under the old GATT system, free riding was possible when some small states were permitted to benefit from trade liberalization without having to make contributions of their own). Finally, the WTO embodied certain "legislative powers" that removed the need for prolonged negotiations that result in large "packages" embracing multiple concessions, as in previous multilateral negotiating sessions. Now it is possible simply to amend existing rules one at a time. Thus the WTO extended the GATT structure in a manner consistent with what was once envisioned for the failed ITO, as there is now "an explicit treaty-charter agreement establishing an international organization for trade, which can take its place beside the other Bretton Woods organizations" (Jackson 1994).

Fear of failure and its consequence for the trade regime and individual countries' economic and political stability provided important incentives for the accord's acceptance, which proponents hailed as a big step toward keeping the liberal trade regime afloat in an increasingly competitive and globalized world economy. The anticipated advantages of lower free-trade barriers figured prominently, since the evidence speaks loudly to the proposition that both exports and imports contribute to higher standards of living. Hopes that the Uruguay Round would stimulate the expansion of global output by billions of dollars were fulfilled sooner than predicted—even as the negotiations continued.

In the end, then, the Uruguay Round that created the World Trade Organization struck a blow for liberalism. It may also have struck a blow for hegemony because the agreement that outlawed a great deal of free riding (neomercantilism) was to the U.S. hegemon's advantage, as the United States derived greater

TABLE 8.2 AND FIGURE 8.1

Round and Round: A GATT-WTO Chronology

Date	*Summary*
1947	Birth of the GATT, signed by twenty-three couuntries on October 30th at the Palais des Nations in Geneva.
1948	The GATT comes into force. First meeting of its members in Havana, Cuba.
1949	Second round of talks at Annecy, France. Some five thousand tariff cuts agreed to; ten new countries admitted.
1950–51	Third round at Torquay, England. Members exchange 8,700 trade concessions and welcome four new countries.
1956	Fourth round at Geneva. Tariff cuts worth $1.3 trillion at today's prices.
1960–62	The Dillon Round, named after U.S. Undersecretary of State Douglas Dillon, who proposed the talks. A further 4,400 tariff cuts.
1964–67	The Kennedy Round. Many industrial tariffs halved. Signed by fifty countries. Code on dumping agreed to separately.
1973–79	The Tokyo Round, involving ninety-nine countries. First serious discussion of nontariff trade barriers, such as subsidies and licensing requirements. Average tariff on manufactured goods in the nine biggest markets cut from 7 percent to 4.7 percent.
1986–93	The Uruguay Round. Further cuts in industrial tariffs, export subsidies, licensing, and customs valuation. First agreements on trade in services and intellectual property.
1995	Formation of WTO with power to settle disputes between members.
1997	Agreements concluded on telecommunications services, information technology, and financial services.
1999	The "Millennium Round" convenes at Seattle in November to organize for a new round of multilateral trade negotiations. Thousands demonstrate against globalization and trade liberalization, including numerous NGOs pressuring the WTO to advance their agendas.
2000	The WTO has 135 members, and more than 30 other states including China are seeking to join, as the WTO sought to put aside the acrimony that erupted in Seattle and begin a series of negotiations, expected to last three to four years, on revamping trade rules on agricultural goods and services.

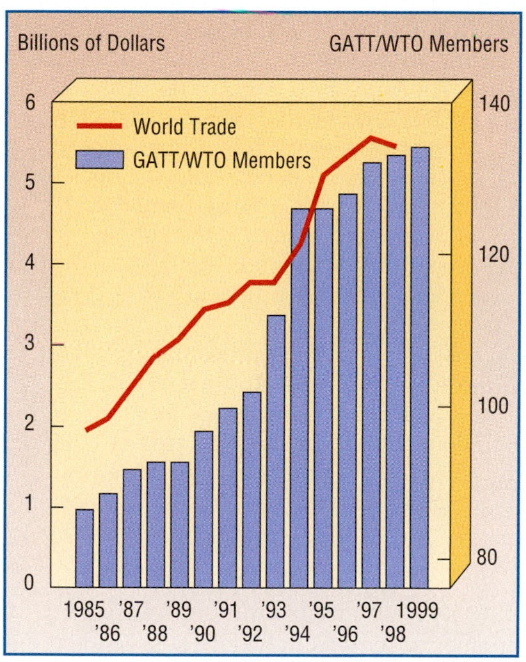

The liberalization of the international trading system is the product of cooperative efforts within the framework of the General Agreement on Tariffs and Trade, as shown in this summary of the major GATT multilateral negotiating rounds since its creation in 1947 (top) and the growth of trade among the WTO's members since 1985 (left). The free-trade regime has greatly aided the expansion of global trade, which more than doubled in the last fifteen years of the twentieth century. One indicator of the growing magnitude of trade interdependence is the fact that in 1950 exports accounted for 8 percent of all countries' GDP and in 1999 they accounted for 26.4 percent of countries' GDPs (WTO, *Economist*, November 27, 1999, 21).

SOURCE: Adapted from *The Economist* (May 16, 1998), 22 (top insert); (August 28, 1998), 52 (left insert).

relative gains from the successful conclusion of the pathbreaking multilateral negotiations. The irony of this step toward trade liberalization was that the new rules and institutions incorporated in the WTO made it increasingly difficult and

CONTROVERSY

Globalization's Growing Pains

Is the World Trade Organization a Friend or Foe?

In late November 1999, the 135 member countries of the World Trade Organization (WTO) and 30 additional observer states made final preparations to stage in Seattle what was billed as the Millennium Round on trade negotiations—the follow-up to the Uruguay Round of trade talks completed in 1993. At the time the mood was optimistic. The meeting promised to celebrate the free-trade regime for the global marketplace and the contributions that lower trade barriers arguably had made to the growth of international exports and, for many members (particularly the United States), their longest and largest peacetime economic expansion in the twentieth century. In fact, consensus had grown around the globe prior to the WTO conference, it seemed, that free trade produced economic growth, even if growth rates were destined to be uneven. There appeared to be widespread recognition that

> Every country in history that has raised its living standards—including the United States—has done so by hitching its wagon to the world economy. . . . During the past 40 years, the world has seen a massive reduction in trade barriers—and consequently the biggest and longest economic boon in history. Between 1950 and 1998, world exports of manufactured goods multiplied 34-fold and world economic output increased eighteenfold. All this has meant rising standards of living for people around the world, but most especially those in the West and the United States. (Zakaria 1998a, 40)

A half-century of generally rising prosperity had generated a climate of enthusiasm for the power of free trade. Fears of imports tend to recede in good economic times, and, with the best decade ever, most leaders in the twilight of the twentieth century emphasized the sunnier side of free trade. Advocates share the conviction that free trade is the magical key to curing the world's economical and social ills. According to the prevailing consensus, countries, companies, and consumers have much to gain by a globalized economy freed from restraints on the exchange of goods across borders. A world without walls promotes prosperity and welfare. Negotiators expected added benefits from a new trade round that could slash tariffs and other trade barriers in agriculture, manufactured goods, and services. Hence, hopes were riding high in 1999 that the WTO's members would be able to agree on new ways to further liberalized trade.

That mood and the seeming consensus on which it based was shattered when the Seattle trade talks opened. An estimated fifty thousand to one hundred thousand protesters and grassroots anti-WTO activists, who differed widely in their special interests (the poor, environment, labor, women, indigenous people), joined hands to shout their common opposition to the general idea of globalization and free trade. A plane trailed a banner proclaiming "People Over Profits: Stop WTO" as part of what became known as "The Battle in Seattle" or, alternatively, the "Carnival against Capitalism." A tirade against open trade ensued.

The Seattle conference will be remembered as the moment when the debate over the benefits and costs of the globalized economy rose to the pinnacle of the global agenda. The immediate target of the demonstrations was the WTO; however, the organization itself was simply a convenient symbol of a much larger sea of discontent. The WTO protests—and the failure of the WTO conference attendees to compromise on tightly held positions and agree on even a minimal accord—exposed the deep divisions about the best ways to open global commerce and adopt new rules at a time of rapid change.

Controversies about globalization, free trade, and global governance are multiple. At the core is the question of whether a globalized economy is inevitable and, if so, an antidote to suffering or an enemy of human welfare. The debates are explosive, because everyone is affected, but in quite different ways. Many are enjoying

costly for the United States to extricate its economy from the growing force of the global economy on which U.S. prosperity increasingly depends. Trade liberalization is thus likely to continue, with or without U.S. support, because "globalization and multinationalization have reduced the powers of all governments to regulate behavior and set independent economic policies. Companies are no longer wedded to any one economy" (Thurow 1998). As former U.S. Trade Rep-

the boom years under liberalized trade engineered by the WTO's sweeping power to enforce international trade agreements, but the celebration is confined largely to the top—the privileged, powerful, and prosperous. Many others see themselves as clear victims of an open global economy, as when a factory closes and workers lose their jobs. Those discontented with globalized free trade include a diverse coalition of protestors, many of whom harbor very specific concerns about wages, the environment, and human rights issues. Labor leaders contend that the WTO is sacrificing worker rights; environmental groups complain that when green values collide with world commerce, environmental standards are left out of trade negotiations; and human rights activists accuse the WTO of serving the preferences of MNCs for erasing trade barriers in ways that fail to protect human rights. In addition, enraged trade ministers from the Global South's developing countries see a Global North conspiracy in the WTO's efforts to adopt core labor standards, because the less developed Global South views such high-sounding rules as a method to impose high tariffs on their products and take away the comparative advantage Global South developing nations enjoy with lower wage scales.

These, and other issues, are certain to continue as major controversies. What do you think? Is the WTO a valuable tool for improving global governance and human welfare or a threat? Is the WTO and the free trade practices it promotes too strong or too weak? Does the WTO put corporate greed and profits above human rights and environmental protection, as critics charge? Or do you agree with WTO Director General Mike Moore's defense of free trade, and his warning against what he called a "false debate" between working people and the WTO, when he maintained "Trade is the ally of working people, not their enemy. As living standards improve, so does education, health, the environment and labor standards." What direction should global trade take?

resentative Mickey Kantor predicted in November 1997, "There will still be progress, because there are companies around the world that share an interest in getting rid of the political obstacles to doing business. The only question is whether those deals will be struck with us, or around us."

Trade squabbles will nonetheless continue despite overwhelming profits from trade liberalization. There are many tricks to free trade, and contentious issues will inevitably cast the spotlight on the continuing frictions caused by a shrinking globe of competitive states. Free trade generates new jobs and wealth, but laissez-faire international capitalism also brings unprecedented risks.

MONETARY MATTERS: CAN REGIMES PROMOTE TRADE AND GROWTH?

States cannot always trade as they wish. The flow of exports (and imports) depends on many factors, such as the level of tariffs, quotas, and duties of others that restrict sales abroad and, of course, on changes in global demand and prices for the goods and services that countries' producers sell in the global marketplace. The mechanisms for setting the currency exchange rates by which the value of traded goods are priced comprise another key structural factor that heavily influences international trade. Indeed, the **monetary system** is crucial for international trade, for without a stable and predictable method of calculating the value of sales and foreign investments, those transactions become too risky, causing trade and investment activities to fall. As the World Bank notes, the success of international trade and "market reforms depends on the health of the financial system" (1996).

■ **monetary system**
a stable and predictable method for calculating the value of sales and foreign investments across national currencies.

The Nuts and Bolts of Monetary Policy

Monetary and financial policies are woven into a complex set of relationships between states and the international system, and, because monetary and currency issues have their own specialized technical terminology, they are difficult to understand. However, the essentials are rather basic:

> **Monetary policy** works on two principal economic variables: the aggregate supply of money in circulation and the level of interest rates. The **money supply** (currency plus commercial bank demand deposits) is thought to be directly related to the level of economic activity in the sense that a greater money supply induces expanded economic activity by enabling people to purchase more goods and services. This in essence is the *monetarist theory* of economic activity. Its advocates argue that by controlling the growth of the money supply, governments can regulate their nations' economic activity and control inflation. (Todaro 2000, 657)

■ **monetary policy**
the decisions made by states' central banks to regulate the national economy and control inflation using policies such as changing the money supply and interest rates.

■ **money supply**
the total amount of currency in circulation in a state, calculated to include demand deposits, such as checking accounts, in commercial banks and time deposits, such as savings accounts and bonds, in savings banks.

■ **exchange rate**
the rate at which one state's currency is exchanged for another state's currency in the global marketplace.

To understand the importance of monetary policies as a determinant of states' trade, growth rates, and wealth consider why **exchange rates** (see Table 8.3) fluctuate and the impact of these currency fluctuations. Money works in several ways and serves different purposes. First, money must be widely accepted, so that people earning it can use it to buy goods and services from others. Second, money must serve to store value, so that people will be willing to keep some of their wealth in the form of money. Third, money must act as a standard of deferred payment, so that people will be willing to lend money knowing that when the money is repaid in the future, it will still have purchasing power.

Inflation occurs when the government creates too much money in relation to the goods and services produced in the economy. As money becomes more

TABLE 8.3

Currency Concerns: Concepts for Conversing about International Exchange Rates and Balance-of-Payments Issues

Term	*Concept*
Balance of Payments	A calculation summarizing a country's financial transactions with the external world, determined by the level of credits (export earnings, profits from foreign investment, receipts of foreign aid) minus the country's total international debts (imports, interest payments on international debts, foreign direct investments, and the like). A favorable balance of payments is achieved when a country's international credits exceed its national debits, as recorded in its current account (the market value of exports and imports with the rest of the world) and its capital account (the ratio of a country's private and foreign investments flowing into and outside the country).
Balance-of-Trade Deficit	A situation that results from the emergence of an imbalance between a country's imports and exports when a state buys more from abroad than it sells. The merchandise balance measures only the value of goods and services bought and sold abroad, but because trade in services has grown rapidly in recent years an accurate calculation of balance-of-trade deficits or surpluses now requires that the difference between the value of services imported and exported also be calculated. To correct a payments deficit, a country has available three basic but painful options: (1) its government can initiate deflationary policies at home by raising interest rates to tighten budgets; (2) it can restrict the outflow of money by imposing higher tariffs, import quotas, or other restrictions; or (3) it can borrow in capital markets or liquidate its foreign exchange reserves.
Central Bank	The major "financial institution [in a state] responsible for issuing currency, managing foreign reserves, implementing monetary policy, and providing banking services to the government and commercial banks" (Todaro 2000).
Devaluation	The lowering of the official exchange rate of one country's currency relative to the value of all other states' currencies, usually in the hope that the devaluation will encourage foreigners to purchase products through trade at the artificially reduced price.
Exchange Rate	The rate at which one state's currency is exchanged for another state's currency in the global marketplace. For 1 U.S. dollar, you might receive 1.5 Swiss francs or 9 Mexican pesos. Exchange rates are subject to rapid fluctuations, usually changing daily, though to small degrees. One day your 1 U.S. dollar might buy 1.51 Swiss francs and the next day 1.54 Swiss francs.
External Debt	"Debt owed by a country to non-residents repayable in foreign currency, goods and services" (UNDP 1999).
Fixed Exchange Rate	A system in which a government sets the value of its currency at a fixed rate for exchange in relation to another country's currency (usually the U.S. dollar, but in the late-nineteenth century against the gold standard when national currency values were defined in terms of the gold coinage that was used as money), so that the exchange value is not free to fluctuate in the global money market.
Floating Exchange Rate	The system that replaced the Bretton Woods system of fixed exchange rates in the early 1970s, when the link between the dollar and gold was severed. Market forces, rather than government actions, are expected to adjust the relative value of states' currencies to reflect the underlying strengths and weaknesses of their economies. In principle, a floating exchange rate is based on the expectation that imbalances in states' payments to one another will more or less automatically adjust themselves, but in practice states have intervened frequently to ensure monetary stability and flexibility.
Managed Exchange Rate System	The kind of system constructed by the European Union (EU) when it created the single European currency, the euro. The European Monetary System (EMS) links the currencies of EU members whose governments pledge to stabilize currency values through government intervention if necessary. In practice, the system has proven stable when EU governments have exercised the necessary will to operate it effectively.
Official Exchange Rate	The rate at which a state's central bank agrees to buy and sell its currency in exchange for a unit of another country's currency such as the U.S. dollar.

plentiful and thus less acceptable, it cannot serve effectively to store value or to satisfy debts or as a medium of exchange. Governments work to ensure that their currencies do the jobs they are intended to do. This means, among other things, that they try to maintain an inflation-free environment.

In the international monetary system, movements in a state's exchange rate occur in part when changes develop in peoples' assessment of the national currency's underlying economic strength or the ability of its government to maintain the value of its money. A deficit in a country's balance of payments, for example, would likely cause a decline in the value of its currency relative to that of others. This happens when the supply of the currency is greater than the demand for it. Similarly, when those engaged in international economic transactions change their expectations about a currency's future value, they might reschedule their lending and borrowing. Fluctuations in the exchange rate could follow.

Speculators—those who buy and sell money in an effort to make it—may also affect the international stability of a country's currency. Speculators make money by guessing the future. If, for instance, they believe that the Japanese yen will be worth more in three months than it is now, they can buy yen today and sell them for a profit three months later. Conversely, if they believe that the yen will be worth less in three months, they can sell yen today for a certain number of dollars and then buy back the same yen in three months for fewer dollars, making a profit.

Speculators base their decisions on a number of factors. One is their reading of the health of the currency in which they are speculating. If they believe the U.S. dollar is weak because the U.S. economy itself is weak, they may conclude that policymakers will permit the dollar to depreciate. A closely related consideration is whether a government is perceived as having the political will to carry out monetary policies that will ensure the value of its money, particularly against inflationary pressures or interest-group opposition. If speculators think a government will not exercise prudent leadership, they will be inclined to sell dollars now and buy them back later at the (anticipated) lower price. In the process, speculators may create **self-fulfilling prophecies:** They may "prove" that the dollar needs to depreciate in value simply because of the volume of seemingly unwanted dollars offered for sale. The globalization of finance now also encourages managers of investment portfolios to move funds from one currency to another in order to realize gains from differences in states' interest rates—including their anticipation of how interest rates might change.

■ **self-fulfilling prophecy**
the tendency for one's expectations to evoke behavior that helps to make the prediction come true.

In the same way that governments try to protect the value of their currencies at home, they try to protect them internationally by intervening in currency markets. Their willingness to do so is important to importers and exporters, who depend on orderliness and predictability in the value of the currencies they deal in to carry out transnational exchanges. Governments intervene when countries' central banks buy or sell currencies to change the value of their own currencies in relation to those of others. Unlike speculators, however, governments are pledged not to manipulate exchange rates so as to gain unfair advantages, for states' reputations as custodians of monetary stability are valuable. Whether governments can affect their currencies' values in the face of large transnational movements of capital is, however, increasingly questionable.

The Bretton Woods Monetary System

When the leaders of the capitalist West met at Bretton Woods, they were acutely aware of the need to create a reliable mechanism for determining the value of countries' currencies in relation to one another, and agreed to a set of concepts to define monetary and currency policy for conducting international trade and finance. Recognizing that a shared system and vocabulary was a necessary precondition for trade, and from it post–World War II economic recovery and prosperity, the negotiating parties agreed that the postwar monetary system should be based on **fixed exchange rates,** and assigned governments primary responsibility for enforcing its rules. In addition, they foresaw the need to create what later became the **International Monetary Fund (IMF),** to help states maintain equilibrium in their balance of payments and stability in their exchange rates with one another. The International Bank for Reconstruction and Development, known as the **World Bank,** was also created to aid recovery from the war.

fixed exchange rates a system under which states establish the parity of their currencies and commit to keeping fluctuations in their exchange rates within narrow limits.

Today the IMF and World Bank are important, if controversial, players in the global monetary and financial systems. Their primary missions are to promote Global South development and serve as "lenders of last resort" when its member states face financial crises, providing those seeking assistance meet the often painful conditions requiring domestic adjustments to strengthen their liberal economies' export markets. In the period immediately after World War II, these institutions commanded too little authority and too few resources to cope with the enormous devastation of the war. The United States stepped into the breach.

International Monetary Fund (IMF) a financial agency with 182 members affiliated with the United Nations, formed in 1945, to promote international monetary cooperation, free trade, exchange rate stability, and democratic rule by providing financial assistance and loans to countries facing financial crises.

The U.S. dollar became the key to the hegemonic role that the United States eagerly assumed as manager of the international monetary system. Backed by a vigorous and healthy economy, a fixed relationship between gold and the dollar (pegged at $35 per ounce of gold), and the U.S. commitment to exchange gold for dollars at any time (known as "dollar convertibility"), the dollar became "as good as gold." In fact, others preferred dollars to gold for use in managing their balance-of-payments and savings accounts. Dollars earned interest, which gold did not; they did not incur storage and insurance costs; and they were needed to buy imports necessary for survival and postwar reconstruction. Thus the postwar economic system was a dollar-based system with the dollar a "parallel currency" universally accepted as the "currency against which every other country sold or redeemed its own national currency in the exchange markets" (Triffin 1978–1979). Dollars became the international reserve used by monetary authorities in most countries, as well as the primary "working balances" used by private banks, corporations, and individuals for international trade and capital transactions.

World Bank also known as the International Bank of Reconstruction and Development (IBRD), the World Bank is the globe's major IGO for financing economic growth in the Global South.

To maintain the value of their currencies, central banks in other countries either bought or sold their own currencies, using the dollar to raise or depress their value. Thus the Bretton Woods monetary regime was based on fixed exchange rates, and ultimately required a measure of government intervention for its preservation.

To get U.S. dollars into the hands of those who needed them most, the Marshall Plan provided Western European states billions of dollars in aid to buy the U.S. goods necessary for rebuilding their war-torn economies. The United States also encouraged deficits in its own balance of payments as a way of providing **international liquidity** in the form of dollars.

international liquidity reserve assets used to settle international accounts.

In addition to providing liquidity, the United States assumed a disproportionate share of the burden of rejuvenating Western Europe and Japan. It supported European and Japanese trade competitiveness, permitted certain forms of protectionism (such as Japanese restrictions on importing U.S. products), and condoned discrimination against the dollar (as in the European Payments Union, which promoted trade within Europe at the expense of trade with the United States). The United States willingly incurred these leadership costs and others' free riding because subsidizing economic growth in Europe and Japan would widen the U.S. export markets and strengthen the West against communism's possible popular appeal.

Although this system worked well, with the United States operating as the world's banker, the costs grew as the enormous number of dollars held by others made the U.S. economy increasingly vulnerable to financial shocks from abroad. As the British had discovered before, U.S. leadership made devaluing the dollar without hurting U.S. allies difficult; nor could inflationary or deflationary pressures at home be managed without impairing allies abroad. This reduced the United States' ability to use the normal methods available to other states for dealing with the disruption caused by deficits in a country's balance of trade, such as adjusting interest and currency exchange rates.

The Decline of U.S. Financial Hegemony and the End of Bretton Woods

As early as 1960 it was clear that the dollar's top currency status could not be sustained by U.S. hegemony. A number of developments combined to destroy the monetary system, leading to a crisis in which the collapse of one country's economy and currency leads—in a modern version of the **commercial domino theory**—to "fiscal contagion" that spreads uncontrollably around the world, wreaking havoc on global capitalism. The fall of fiscal dominos rippling through the world economy has become a common experience in a tightly interconnected international monetary system, in which capital and currency move instantaneously outside borders at the slightest sign of fiscal troubles. In any imploding national market, when one country's currency reserves are depleted, it sets in motion panic abroad as investors reduce their holdings and the flight of capital brings down other countries in a chain reaction (Sanger 1998). Because for the first time in history a single, integrated global economic system is emerging, the deficiencies of global financial institutions with unstable fixed and floating currencies have become apparent, and not much is being done to revise and reform the shaky existing global financial architecture. In a world of increasingly mobile capital, volatility in capital flows lies at the heart of the prevailing international financial crisis and threatens, in the absence of international financial regulation, the continuation of world economic growth.

■ **commercial domino theory**
the notion that under conditions of globalization the depletion of one country's currency reserves panics investors worldwide and spreads like a contagious disease to other countries, which, in a chain reaction, witness the decline of their own currency reserves as the flight of capital also reduces the value of their currency.

To understand the perils of today's global financial crisis, it is instructive to briefly look backward at its origins and the pivotal role that U.S. monetary policy as the globe's financial hegemon played in the evolution of the international monetary system. "Much of the international relations literature concerned with prospects for international monetary reform can be read as a search for an alternative to hegemony as a basis for international monetary stability" (Eichengreen 2000), and the need for a reformed system stems in large part from the failure of the United States to adjust its policies so it could continue to serve as a hegemonic stabilizing force in international finance.

What led to this failure? First, the cost of extensive U.S. military intervention, foreign economic and military aid, and massive private investments produced increasing balance-of-payments deficits. Second, the possibility of a U.S. devaluation of the dollar made others less confident in its currency and less willing to hold dollars as a reserve currency. The Global North's increasing monetary and financial interdependence permitted the central bankers and finance ministers from the leading economic powers to devise various ad hoc solutions (such as currency swaps) to deal with their common problems and to create Special Drawing Rights (SDRs) in the IMF (reserve assets popularly known as "paper gold") to grow international liquidity by means other than increasing the outflow of dollars from the United States. Third, Europe and Japan had completely recovered, and because recovery made their currencies convertible again, U.S. monetary dominance and the dollar's privileged position were increasingly unacceptable politically; the return to convertibility meant that alternatives to the dollar (such as the German mark and Japanese yen) for savings and exchange were now available.

Although the United States sought to stave off challenges to its leadership role, its own deteriorating economic situation as a consequence of the costs of its global military involvements made it increasingly difficult. Mounting inflation—caused in part by the unwillingness of the Johnson administration to raise taxes to pay for either the Vietnam War or the Great Society domestic engineering initiative—drove up the price of U.S.-produced goods and reduced their relative competitiveness overseas. In 1971, for the first time in the twentieth century, the United States suffered a trade deficit of $2 billion, which worsened the next year. Predictably, demands by industrial, labor, and agricultural interests for protectionist trade measures grew. Simultaneously, the U.S. position in the global marketplace was deteriorating, as its share of international trade declined and Europe's and Japan's increased. America could no longer unilaterally regulate international monetary affairs.

The United States aggressively sought to shore up its sagging position. In August 1971, President Richard M. Nixon abruptly announced that the United States would no longer exchange dollars for gold. He also imposed a surcharge on imports into the United States as part of a strategy designed to force a realignment of others' currency exchange rates. These startling and unexpected decisions shocked the other Western industrial countries, which had not been consulted, and promptly ended the Bretton Woods system.

The Impact of Floating Exchange Rates

With the price of gold no longer fixed and dollar convertibility no longer guaranteed, the Bretton Woods system gave way to a much larger set of liberal rules and oversight institutions based on **floating exchange rates.** Market forces, rather than government intervention, were now expected to determine currency values. The theory underlying this sea change was that a country experiencing adverse economic conditions will see the value of its currency decline in the marketplace in response to the choices of traders, bankers, and businesspeople. This will make its exports cheaper and its imports more expensive, which in turn will pull its currency's value back toward equilibrium—all without the

■ floating exchange rates
an unmanaged process where market forces rather than governments influence the relative rate of exchange for currencies between countries.

need for central bankers to support their currencies. In this way it was hoped that the politically humiliating devaluations of the past could be avoided.

Policymakers did not foresee that the new rules would introduce an unparalleled degree of uncertainty and unpredictability into international monetary affairs. Two "oil shocks" induced by the Organization of Petroleum Exporting Nations (OPEC) and the subsequent debt crisis that many Global South countries and others faced raised apprehension about the viability of an international economy clumsily managed by various groups of industrial states and quasi-official negotiating forums. These fears were compounded by the absence of hegemonic U.S. leadership and the beginning of the erratic and nerve-wracking fluctuation of the dollar's value.

■ **stagflation**
a situtation in which economic stagnation and high inflation occur at the same time and the usual tendency for an economic downturn to drive down prices does not occur.

These fears proved to be well-founded. Global economic recession followed each oil shock. Ironically, however, inflation persisted. **Stagflation** was coined as a term to describe the strange and strangled situation. In response, the leading industrial powers relied on fiscal and monetary adjustments to stimulate economic recovery and to avoid politically unacceptable unemployment levels. But after the second oil shock triggered unprecedented inflation and the longest and most severe economic downturn since the 1930s Great Depression, efforts shifted to controlling inflation through strict monetarist policies (i.e., policies designed to limit the money supply in the economy). Large fiscal deficits, sharply higher interest rates, and higher unemployment rates followed.

All the Global North countries suffered these problems, which also spread to the Global South developing countries that borrowed extensively from abroad to pay for the increased cost of energy. Borrowing was possible because the billions of "petrodollars" flowed to the oil-producing states, and private banks and various multilateral institutions "recycled" them. In the process, however, many states assumed ominous debt burdens just when interest rates on loans climbed. Beginning in the 1970s, escalating in the 1980s, and persisting through the 1990s have been a rising wave of financial crises, both in currency and banking (see Figure 8.2). These have been compounded by massive defaults by countries unable to service their debts—a chronic problem that has pushed the international monetary regime to the brink of destruction.

High U.S. interest rates compared with other countries contributed not only to the Global South's debt burden but also to the rising demand for the U.S. dollar. Renewed U.S. economic growth, a sharp reduction in inflation, and the perception of the United States as a comparatively safe haven for financial investments also helped to restore faith in the dollar. Foreign investors therefore rushed to acquire the dollars necessary to take advantage of profitable investment opportunities in the United States, driving the mid-1980s value of the dollar to new heights. This situation contrasted sharply with the 1970s when fears of the huge U.S. foreign indebtedness drove down the exchange rate.

For the United States, the dollar's appreciation was a mixed blessing because it increased the cost of U.S. exports to foreign buyers, reducing the competitiveness of American products in overseas markets. Tens of thousands of jobs were lost, and record trade deficits ($122 billion in 1985, $145 billion in 1986, and exceeding $340 billion in 2000) occurred as imports from abroad became relatively cheaper and hence more attractive to American consumers. The budget deficit of the U.S. government also climbed to record levels at this time, topping $200 billion each year in the 1980s and mid-1990s until a budget

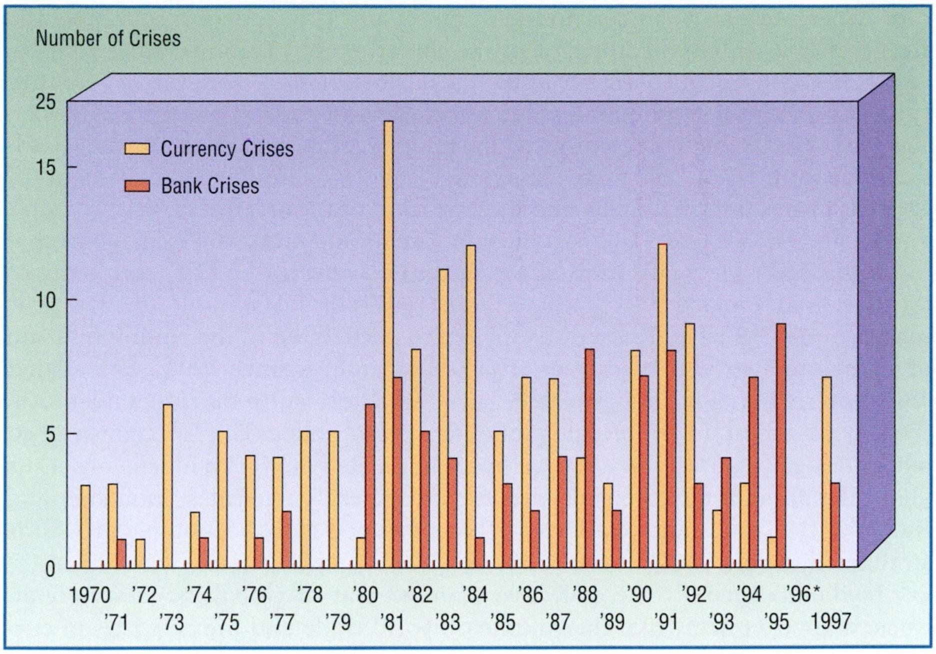

FIGURE 8.2

The Spread of Banking and Currency Crises since 1970

Financial crises have become increasingly frequent around the world as a result of the inability of states to manage debt, inflation, interest, and income in a volatile international monetary environment of mobile capital and wild currency exchange rate gyrations. In the past thirty years, more than one hundred major episodes of banking insolvency occurred in ninety developing and emerging countries, partly as a consequence of their increasing exposure to external financial pressures. The financial cost of these crises in terms of the percentage of GDP loss has been huge, with the toll in Argentina (1980–1982), Chile (1981–1983), Uruguay (1981–1984), Israel (1977–1983), and Côte d'lvoire (1988–1991) exceeding 30 percent. The disastrous debts generated by banking and currency disruptions forced governments to suffer, on average, direct losses of 14.6 percent of their GDP for each crisis and more than a 5 percent decline in output growth after each crisis (World Bank 1999, 126).

*Data not availabale for 1996.

SOURCE: World Bank (1999), 125.

surplus was realized in 1999 during a booming economy that enabled the United States to begin to retire some of its nearly $6 trillion accumulated debt.

In a normally functioning market, the combination of a strong dollar and severe trade imbalance would set in motion self-corrective processes that would return the dollar to its equilibrium value. Growing U.S. imports, for example—although beneficial to America's trade partners in generating jobs and thus stimulating their return to economic growth—should create upward pressure on the value of others' currencies. Conversely, a drop in U.S. exports should ease the demand for dollars, thereby reducing the dollar's value in exchange markets. These mechanisms did not work as they should have because high U.S. interest rates persisted as a result of continuing high military spending.

In response to the growing awareness of the extent to which the health of others' economies depended on the value of the dollar internationally (which in turn depended on the underlying strength of the U.S. economy), in 1985 the Group of Five (or G-5—composed of the United States, Britain, France, Japan, and West Germany) met secretly at the Plaza Hotel in New York City. There they agreed to mount a coordinated effort to bring down the overvalued U.S. dollar. The landmark agreement committed the major economic powers to greater collective coordination of their economic policies through management of exchange rates internationally and interest rates domestically.

Japan also became a full partner in international monetary management, a move that led to formalization of the **Group of Seven** (the **G-7,** consisting of the G-5 plus Canada and Italy). At the 1997 annual summit the G-7 was renamed the **G-8** when Russia was invited to participate in the common forum of leading industrial democracies. The G-8's meetings since 1999, such as that convened in Tokyo in January 2000, have failed to inspire much confidence in the group's ability to coordinate global monetary policy. The G-8, constrained by domestic pressures, has not developed the capacity to reach much consensus about the difficult next steps needed to manage exchange rates, monetary and fiscal policies, and trade relations so that sustained global economic growth is stimulated (Strom 2000).

■ **Group of Seven (G-7)/ Group of Eight (G-8)** a group of advance industrialized democracies composed of the United States, Britain, France, Japan, Germany, Canada, and Italy that meets in regular economic summit conferences; since 1997, known as the G-8 with the addition of Russia.

In the absence of true collective management of global monetary conditions, it appears likely that the volume of world trade and the activities of currency speculators (who use sophisticated global electronic technologies and rely on about two thousand "hedge funds" to make profits in currency trading) will increasingly determine national currency values. An average of over $1.5 trillion in currency trading occurs each day—a transfer of capital greater than one-fourth of the world's average *weekly* level of international trade. International sales of stocks and bonds have mushroomed as well, and promise to rise through increased investor trading on the Internet. In the volatile world of increasingly mobile capital, wide fluctuations in national currencies' exchange rates have become common. The globalization of finance and the removal of barriers to capital flows across borders expose national economies to shocks, with little hope that such volatility will vanish.

Current Efforts at Monetary Reform

Many proposals have been advanced for reforming the international monetary system. Reforms are needed to help cushion the aftershocks of the rapid movement of investment funds among countries that creates booms and busts, such as the 1980s Latin American debt crisis and the global crisis that followed on the heels of the 1997–1998 flight of capital from Asia. Some see reversion to the pre–World War I gold standard as preferable to the current system of floating exchange rates with highly fluctuating currencies. Others recommend something like the Bretton Woods system of fixed but adjustable rates. What these and other proposals seek is a mechanism for creating the currency stability and flexibility on which prosperity through trade depends, and which the current system has failed to achieve. "There is little agreement on what to do about the exchange rate system. All appraisals conclude that the performance of the world economy could be improved if policy discipline were strengthened and if the frequency and size of exchange rate misalignments could be reduced. But there is little consensus on how to bring that about" (Goldstein 1995). With

The Domino Effect in Global Finance When a country's banks go bankrupt and its economy collapses, foreign capital flees in panic. No worldwide central bank exists to cushion such crashes. Money problems in one country lead to money problems in others, provoking currency depreciations and plunges in stock prices at home and abroad. Here stunned brokers react to the January 1998 plummet of Hong Kong stocks that caused the key indexes elsewhere in Asia, London, Frankfort, New York, and Paris to fall. Described as "the worst international financial crisis in fifty years [which] took global finance to the edge of collapse," it is worrisome that "since then, reforms of the financial system have been few and far between" (Altman and Cutter 1999).

global democratization, most governments face domestic pressures to sacrifice such goals as unemployment reduction for exchange rate stability, so it seems likely that floating exchange rates, with all their costs and uncertainties, are here to stay. As one observer notes,

> The world is a far different place than it was when currency rates were fixed during the first quarter century after World War II. At that time, governments maintained strict controls over the flow of capital across their borders. Today, money sloshes around the world . . . because of the widely accepted view that growth will be maximized if capital is free to seek the highest returns. And whatever action is taken to limit "hot" money flows, few if any experts believe the broad trend can or should be reversed. (Blustein 1999a, 6)

FROM CURRENCY CONCERNS TO TRADE TROUBLES IN THE TWENTY-FIRST CENTURY

Emerging Unilateral Trade Policies

To anticipate the future, we can look at the **unilateral** strategies of individual countries and at the regional strategies of groups of countries or blocs.

■ **unilateral**
a state's policies to manage foreign policy problems independently through self-help measures (see p. 489).

In the past, the United States led the way to the decline of protectionist tariffs in the industrialized world (see Figure 8.3). However, the United States has not consistently advocated free trade; in reaction to its increasingly shaky global position in the 1980s, it began to practice "aggressive unilateralism" by retaliating against states perceived to be engaging in unfair trade practices. The Omnibus Trade Act incorporated a bellicose "Super 301" provision that required the president to identify countries believed to be engaging in unfair trade practices and to force them to either negotiate remedies or face U.S. retaliation. This is symptomatic of the fragility of commitments to free trade, because the Super 301 provision was "almost unanimously viewed abroad as a clear violation of the GATT" (Walters and Blake 1992). Since then, however, the United States has begun to act under the milder, less accusatory "ordinary" 301 legislation (which does not carry automatic retaliatory penalties), but has still initiated hundreds of complaints, and in 1998 and the first seven months of 1999 initiated seventy-seven antidumping investigations while the U.S. Congress passed restrictive steel quota legislation and Washington battled the EU over trade in bananas, hormone-treated beef, and genetically modified crops. Hence, free trade remains under challenge.

The continuing trade imbalance between Japan (long viewed as the preeminent neomercantilist power) and the United States—which runs into the tens of billions of dollars each year—reinforced the U.S. assertion that Japan's protectionist trade policies closed the Japanese market to U.S. exports. American firms particularly resent Japan's intimate government-business alliance and its cross-share holding practice known as *keiretsu,* which results in informal corporate bargains that make foreign penetration difficult. Nonetheless, nearly thirty new trade agreements were subsequently reached under a mix of 301 and Super 301 retaliatory threats that have permitted American exports to Japan to increase considerably in recent years. These bilateral sectional agreements

FIGURE 8.3
The Decline of Tariffs in the Industrialized Countries, 1940 Projected to 2000

Tariffs have declined dramatically since the peak period of economic nationalism in the 1930s. With average tariff levels among industrialized countries declining to less than 5 percent by 2000 (compared with 40 percent in 1940), tariffs have become a comparatively unimportant restraint on international trade.

SOURCE: Office of the U.S. Trade Representative, citing estimates by the Center for International Economics.

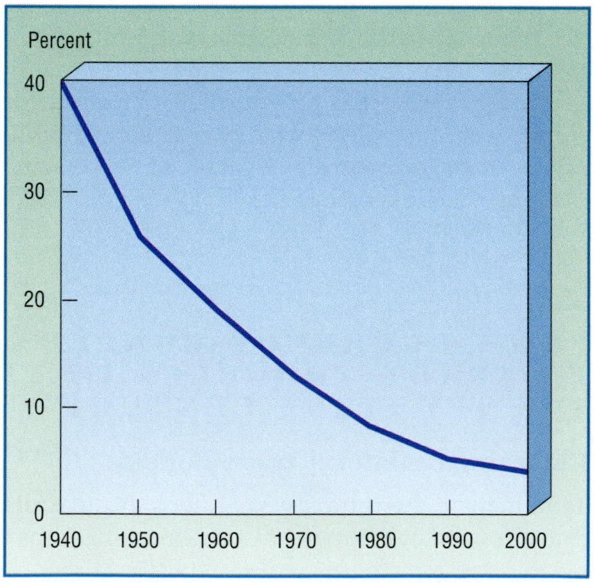

included the Structural Impediments Initiative (SII), launched in 1989 shortly after Japan was named as one of three countries engaging in unfair trade practices under Super 301 (Brazil and India were the others). Hence, U.S. trade policy reflects twin instincts: to push for trade liberalization in foreign markets, and to cushion the impact of imports on the U.S. economy and employment rate. The stakes are high; in 1997, the Commerce Department estimated that one in five U.S. jobs was supported by trade. Awareness of this dependence was behind the Clinton administration's elusive 1997 search for **fast-track negotiating authority** from Congress. "At issue," Clinton argued, "is America's leadership and credibility in the eyes of our competitors." Clinton's failure to obtain from Congress greater power to negotiate trade agreements illustrated the power of domestic trade protectionists and the fragility of free-trade agreements, despite the strongly pro-free-trade support of U.S. corporations which complained that without fast-track authority, huge opportunities for new trade deals would be lost and the U.S. economy would be hurt. "I'm concerned," reported one U.S. manufacturer, "that we'll end up exporting jobs rather than products" (Stevenson 1997). In 1999, Alan Greenspan, chair of the U.S. Federal Reserve Board, echoed the sentiment; warning, "I am concerned about the recent evident weakening of support for free trade in this country," he argued that it sometimes may be necessary for pockets of workers to suffer in order for the nation to prosper. How U.S. trade partners and rivals view the American commitment to free trade will shape their own trade policies, and whether they will choose free trade over protectionism. Tough negotiations and counter-

fast-track negotiating authority
a concession by the U.S. Congress permitting the president to negotiate reciprocal tariff-reduction agreements with other countries which, when granted, enables the United States to reach bilateral trade treaties more easily.

Warning: Made in the U.S.A. The Japanese regard foreign products as inferior to those produced domestically. This makes it difficult for those who export to Japan to compete with local firms, even if their products are of equal or superior quality. The Japanese perpetuate this restraint on trade by labeling retail goods with little flags that show the country of origin and by placing imported goods in separate sections of stores.

charges plague U.S.-China exports, as well as the relationships between many other active international trade partners.

Domestic economic policies tend to shape many countries' foreign trade policies. Observe in this context how much countries differ in the extent to which they regulate their national economies within their borders and the degree to which the level of economic freedom within states predicts the level of growth they experience as well as their willingness to open their domestic markets to foreign imports to elevate their citizens' standard of living. Overwhelming evidence shows that economic freedom makes for prosperity; those countries which do not interfere with trade at home tend to have the highest average economic growth rates (see Map 8.1). Not only does liberalism in economic policy pay financial dividends, but it also has the side benefit of fostering political freedom. Ranking 161 countries according to their economic freedom shows that "those countries that are most economically free generally are also the most politically free. Similarly, those countries that are most economically repressed also tend to be the most politically repressed." Alternatively stated, "political reform precedes economic reform and makes it more lasting [and] economic reform, with its higher income levels, leads to a demand for political reform" (Bryan Johnson and James Gwartney, respectively, as cited in Francis 1999).

Given these seemingly clear-cut economic advantages to free markets and free trade, it is difficult to understand why many governments protectively resist open markets. The answer lies in the fact that trade is profoundly treacherous, and appears in the eye of the beholder to be inherently unfair. Trade unions in wealthy Global North states complain that the lower wages of the Global South countries give them "unfair" advantages and, for their part, the less developed Global South states complain that they cannot "fairly" compete against their more productive, technologically advanced Global North counterparts. Hence, the age-old debate between free traders and mercantilists is likely to persist as a global issue in the brutally competitive globalized world economy.

Emerging Regional Trade Policies. One possibility for partial reform is the formation of **regional currency unions** to try to stabilize today's extraordinarily erratic exchange rate fluctuations. These would avoid the pitfalls of the tactic many emerging economies have tried—a hybrid experiment to loosely tie their exchange rate either to a single foreign currency such as the U.S. dollar or to a basket of currencies. This so-called limited flexibility compromised approach did not meet with success, and the chaos of floating-rate volatility has renewed interest in the idea that regional financial supervision and regulation within a currency bloc or union offers a better solution in the absence of a global exchange rate regime. Much of that confidence is based on the experience of the European Union (EU), which has gone the farthest in the creation of a regional currency union.

■ **regional currency union**
the pooling of sovereignty to create a common currency (such as the EU's euro) and single monetary system for members in a region, regulated by a regional central bank within the currency bloc to reduce the likelihood of large-scale liquidity crises.

The European Monetary System (EMS), launched in 1979 by the European Community, blends elements of the Bretton Woods system of fixed exchange rates and the post–Bretton Woods system of floating rates. Short-term fluctuations are guided by the marketplace, but the EMS requires that political consultations precede realignments of European currencies. Hence it is a "managed" system aimed at eliminating all fifteen EU national currencies by 2002, replac-

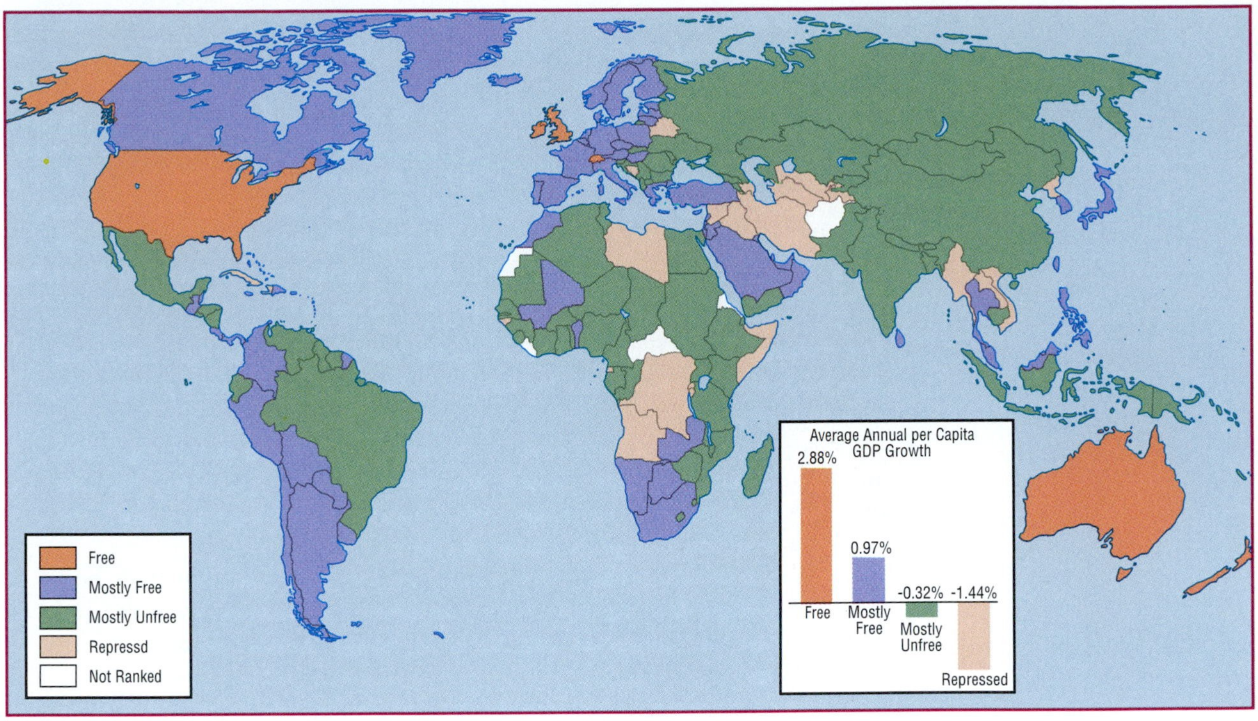

MAP 8.1
Countries Ranked by Their Economic Freedom

The Heritage Foundation and the *Wall Street Journal* produce an annual "Index of Economic Freedom" that classifies countries according to their levels of government control over economic activity on ten indicators of government restrictions, including trade policy, taxation, foreign investment rules, and wage and price controls. A country can score between 1 (most free) and 5 (least free) in each category. This map shows the distribution of countries on this scale at the start of 2000. The chart on the bottom right provides convincing evidence from 1980 through 1993 that economic freedom generates economic prosperity, reaffirming the conclusion that "countries that open their economies have enjoyed annual growth of several percentage points more than those that remained closed. This is true both across the entire developing world and within its regional components" (Bergsten 2000).

SOURCE: Dillin (2000), 13, citing the Heritage Foundation and the *Wall Street Journal*; Francis (1999).

ing them with the single "euro" currency, which would reduce Europeans' need for foreign exchange reserves and raise the value of the euro against the U.S. dollar. This currency integration could serve as a model for *global* monetary management, provided that the many disappointments the EU experienced until recently in its journey to a single currency can be avoided and the EU's creation of a Europe-wide central bank and currency based on a system of managed exchange rates begins to bear fruit and become a precursor of a new global monetary regime.

In December 1997, the WTO, mobilized into action by the spread of the Asian fiscal crisis that threatened to destroy the entire global economy, hammered out a last-minute pact to open the members' banking, insurance, and securities markets to more foreign competition and to introduce more responsibility over the management of international monetary affairs. That kind of agreement could represent the future, but the transition from architecture to action has yet to be made. Japanese Deputy Minister of Finance Eisuke Sakakibara warned at the 1999 summit of high-powered political and business leaders in Davos, Switzerland, it is "important to proceed speedily on the issue of a new international financial architecture," but it is doubtful that his recommendation will be followed. As U.S. Treasury Secretary Robert Rubin complained in 1999, there are "no easy answers and no magic wands for overhauling financial institutions to make the world safe for global capitalism."

> The message from the economics mainstream about floating currencies thus boils down to this: Make the best of it, because the system's going to be around a long time.
>
> Yes, the number of currencies in the world may shrink in coming years, and the number of currency boards may grow, as some countries conclude that they are willing to surrender their monetary sovereignty to quell the tempests besetting foreign exchange markets.
>
> But economists predict most countries will conclude that their best course is to make floating rates more tolerable—for example, by increasing opportunities for companies and banks to hedge themselves against currency swings.
>
> "There's no perfect arrangement, but the way in which the tide is moving is clear," says Barry Eichengreen, a professor at the University of California at Berkeley. "The task is for countries to build institutions and markets so they can live with greater exchange rate variability, rather than to deny that variable exchange rates are the wave of the future." (Blustein 1999a, 7)

North American Free Trade Agreement (NAFTA)
an agreement that brings Mexico into the free-trade zone linking Canada and the United States.

The United States has also led the way toward building regional arrangements in response to its changing position in the global political economy. These include the 1984 Caribbean Basin Initiative to reduce tariffs and provide tax incentives to promote industry and trade; free-trade agreements with Israel and Canada concluded in 1987 and 1989, respectively; and the **North American Free Trade Agreement (NAFTA),** signed by Canada, Mexico, and the United States in 1993.

NAFTA's purpose was to intertwine Mexico and Canada with the United States as a prelude to a wider Western Hemispheric economic partnership, in part to balance the challenge of the emerging European-wide common market. This challenge began to grow in the mid-1980s when European leaders committed to creating a single market and followed this with the Maastricht agreement to develop a single European currency. With enlargement of its membership eastward accepted in 1998, the EU escalated its push toward the creation of a continent-wide economic union.

In the Pacific Rim, the Asia-Pacific Economic Cooperation (APEC) forum, whose eighteen members make up half the world economy, has agreed to achieve "free and open trade and investment" by the year 2020. Already the growing antagonism between the United States and China on military as well as economic issues stands as an obstacle to the goals of making APEC the world's largest free-trade area. Meanwhile, the United States and the thirty-three Western Hemispheric democracies agreed at the 1994 Miami Summit of the Americas to build a **Free Trade Area of the Americas (FTAA)** in that region by 2005. The highly successful Mercosur free-trade zone in the cone of South America (whose four member countries—Argentina, Brazil, Paraguay, and Uruguay and two associate members, Chile and Bolivia—expanded trade in 1998 to $18.2 billion from only $3.6 billion in 1991) and the enlarged ten-member Association of Southeast Asian Nations (ASEAN) free-trade region are the other major multilateral regional trading blocs (see Map 8.2).

■ **Free Trade Area of the Americas (FTAA)** a set of rules to promote free trade among thirty-four democracies in North and South America.

Many feel that NAFTA and other regional free-trade zones are consistent with GATT's rules, and see regional regimes as vital pieces in the step toward a free-trade agreement for the entire global economy—as suggested by the 1999 trade talks that began at the Rio de Janeiro summit of forty-eight European and Latin American countries to create a free-trade zone between the two regions through "bilateral, gradual, and reciprocal trade liberalism." Others see the division of the globe into competing trade blocs as an obstacle to the integration of trade zones, fretting that the EU-South American negotiations will not succeed and that existing regional free-trade zones actually violate the WTO's nondiscrimination principle by moving away from free trade toward closure and inter-bloc competition. In particular, the critics fear that further development of regionalized markets centered on Asia, Europe, and North America could split globalized trade into exclusionary competitive trade blocs. Already more than one-third of world trade takes place within four major regions (see Figure 8.4), with more than half of all imports in East Asia going to other East Asian countries, imports within Western Europe accounting for almost 70 percent of the EU's trade, and two-fifths of all imports in North America originating within the region (*Handbook of International Economic Statistics* 1999, 71). The United Nations vocalized this fear in its world economic survey, observing in 1991 that "Today the question is not whether these blocs will be formed, but rather how encompassing they will be and how to ensure that they will not harm the [global] trading system."

The ultimate impact of the trend toward regionalization of the world political economy, both nationally and globally, remains uncertain. Some analysts, pointing to the dispute-settlement provisions of NAFTA and its side agreements on the environment and other matters, see that agreement as the precursor of future efforts to negotiate settlements on issues that will likely undermine the free-trade regime and thereby plague world growth in the years ahead. Others are concerned with the possible impact of the economic regional centers on security relationships. One line of reasoning—which builds on the logic of strategic trade theory—suggests that "bitter economic rivalry" is a likely outcome of a triangular world political economy because of fear that "there can be *enduring* national winners and losers from trade competition" (Borrus et al. 1992). The result would be mercantile rivalry among the world's principal trading blocs, in which "fear of one another" may be the only force binding them together.

Those outside the globe's three major regional trading blocs have ample reason to be concerned about this regionalization. "For the developing countries, the prospect of a world divided into separate regional centers is disconcerting. It leaves too many countries out of the system altogether, and even those it encompasses are left relatively weaker as their bargaining power is divided. So, even though developing countries in the past have regarded the GATT as a 'rich man's club,' today they see it as a guardian for the clear and fair

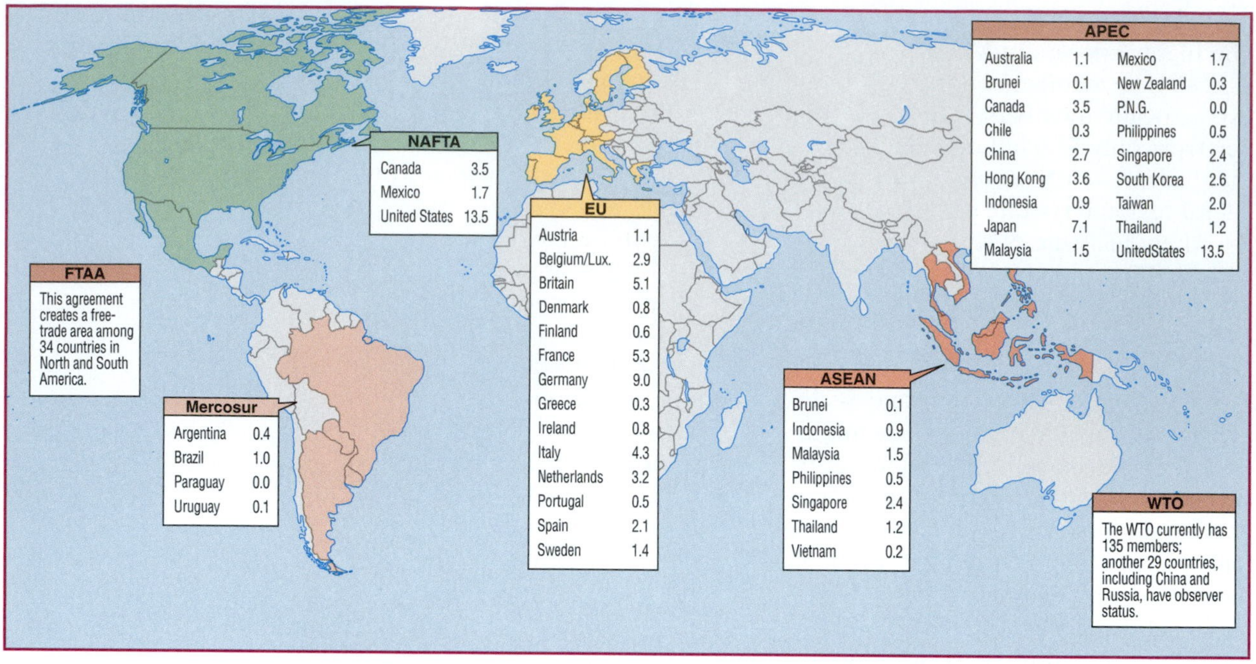

MAP 8.2

Regional Free-Trade Blocs: Building Blocks or Road Blocks for Economic Growth?

Dynamic rates of economic growth have recently occurred in a number of regions where agreements have been reached to reduce tariff barriers. Regional trade agreements represent a major trend: "In the past fifty years, 153 regional trade agreements have been notified to the GATT or the WTO of which most are still in force. Almost half of these . . . have been set up since 1990" (*Economist,* October 3, 1998, 19). This map identifies the six largest regional free-trade blocs that have instituted trade liberalization, as promoted by the 135-members in the World Trade Organization, and records the percentage of total world trade of the trading bloc's member countries in 1996. Numbers represent percentage of world trade.

Note: FTAA = Free Trade Area of the Americas; NAFTA = North American Free Trade Agreement; EU = European Union; ASEAN = Association of Southeast Asian Nations; APEC = Asia-Pacific Economic Cooperation; WTO = World Trade Organization.

SOURCE: *Economist* (September 27, 1997), 23.

rules they need if they are to enter the international arena successfully" (Philips and Tucker 1991). Beyond GATT, and now the 135-member WTO, however, developing countries have also spawned a growing number of regional economic cooperation schemes of their own, as discussed in Chapter 5. But their chances of superseding existing bilateral and multilateral agreements are poor.

THE FATE OF FREE TRADE: TRIUMPH OR TROUBLE?

The exponential growth of world trade in the second half of the twentieth century has contributed measurably to an unprecedented rise in global economic prosperity. Between 1970 and 1998 the value of world trade has grown at an

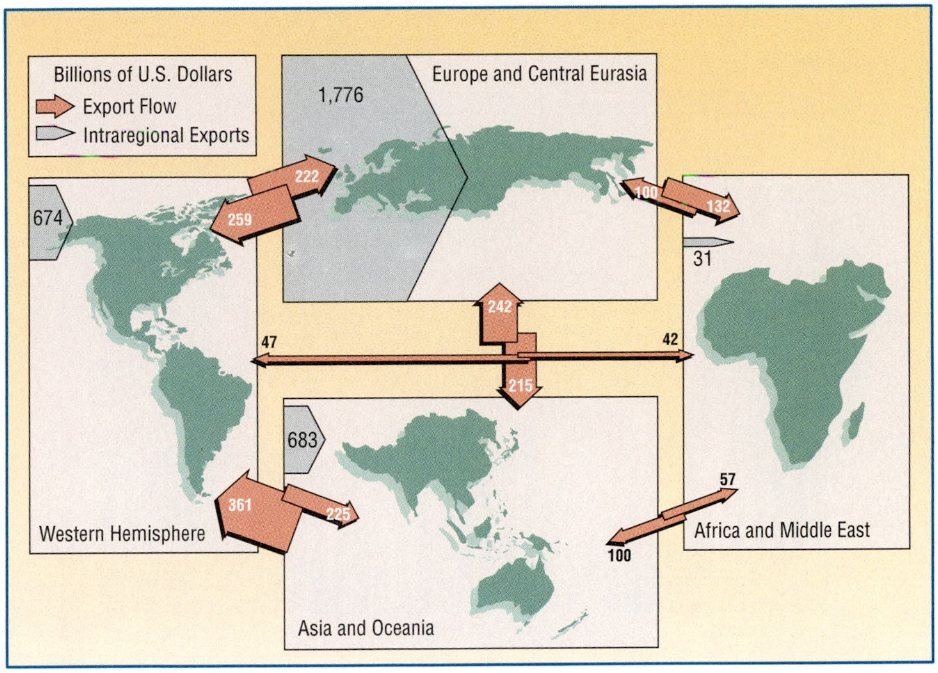

FIGURE 8.4
The Regionalization of International Trade: Share of Exports within and between Major Areas
Increasingly, trade is concentrated within particular regions more than between them. The flows are not even, as in 1999 the dollar value of exports varied in direction and balance across the major trade regions.
Note: Width of arrows scaled to dollar value of exports.
SOURCE: *Handbook of International Economic Statistics (1998)*, 74.

average rate of 4.8 percent annually, and is expected to grow between 1999 and 2004 by another 5.9 percent each year. In the same period, world real GNP has increased each year an average 3.7 percent, and is projected to grow an average of 4.4 percent each year between 1999 and 2004 (IMF 1997, 205; 1999, 243). Reductions in barriers to free trade are expected to accelerate these trends, specifically if world trade continues to expand three times faster than real world output, as it did in 1997 (*Economist*, March 28, 1998) (see Figure 8.5). The World Bank (1995a) predicts "trade integration"—the difference between growth rates in trade and gross national (or gross world) product—will bind national economies ever more tightly in interdependent economic relationships.

These projections assume that the process of liberalizing the global political economy will continue. Progress, however, remains problematic if the forces of neomercantilism also remain vibrant. Although hegemonic stability theory would predict that a U.S. leadership decline will inevitably be followed by the liberal trade regime's closure, a collapse of free trade is unlikely. The liberal trade regime endures with the support of global institutions such as the WTO and liberal regional regimes such as FTAA.

Many states see advantages in rejecting mercantilism and accepting instead the **most-favored-nation (MFN) principle** (which holds that the tariff preferences granted to one state must be granted to all others exporting the same product) as well as the **reciprocity** norm (countries will reduce their own tariffs in return for another's reductions) and **nondiscrimination** rule (goods produced at home and abroad are to be treated the same).

"Free trade is about raising living standards; it is about looking after people better," Mike Moore, the WTO director argued in July 1999 in an attempt to better defend the benefits of free trade. However, free trade is attractive only if everyone, developed Global North and developing Global South countries alike,

■ **most-favored-nation (MFN) principle**
unconditional nondiscriminatory treatment in trade between contracting parties guaranteed by GATT; in 1997, U.S. Sen. Daniel Patrick Moynihan introduced legislation to replace the term with "normal trade relations" to better reflect its true meaning.

■ **reciprocity**
a principle that requires countries to reduce their own tariffs in return for another's reductions.

■ **nondiscrimination**
a principle for trade that proclaims that goods produced at home and abroad are to be treated the same for import and export agreements.

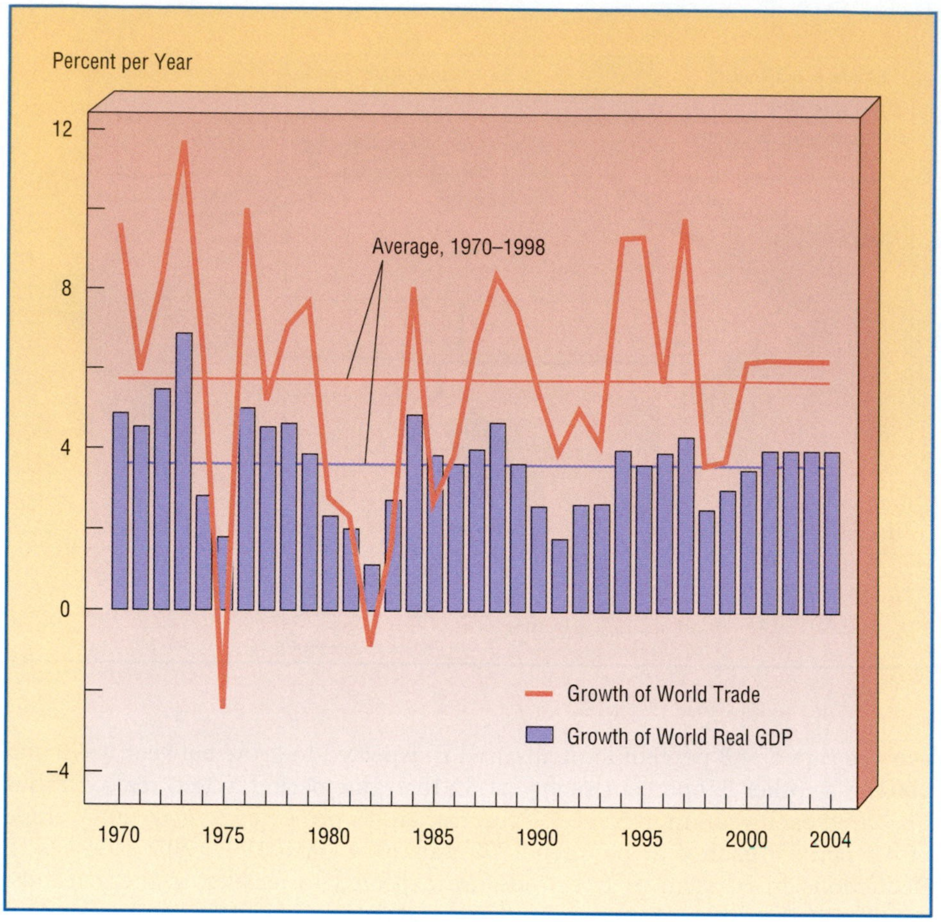

FIGURE 8.5
Global Economic Prospects: The Growth of Trade and Wealth

In almost all years since 1970, the volume of world trade has grown; in fact, between 1970 and 1998 it expanded nearly 4 percent on average each year. The expansion of global trade has contributed to the growth of the world economy as measured here in terms of world real GDP. Although the global economy experienced a recent slowdown, that slump between 1996 and 1997 was the mildest of the four that had occurred in the past three decades, and projections between 2001 through 2004 are optimistic about another period of sustained expansion at 4 percent each year. World trade is expected to grow even faster between 2001 and 2004, at 6.3 percent each year (IMF 1999, 243). However, although trade integration is deepening, the benefits of a booming global economy are unevenly distributed, as some countries are not participating in the expansion at the same level as the global trend in the growth of world trade.

Note: Growth rates beyond 1998 are projections.
SOURCE: International Monetary Fund (1999), 3, 243.

can benefit. Recall the principle of comparative advantage is a central tenet of free trade, because specialization and trade are viewed as permitting trading states to enjoy a higher standard of living than they would otherwise (see Table 8.1, p. 251). Still, as we have seen, many states remain tempted to enhance their domestic well-being by protectionist means even though, according to commercial liberalism, their relations with their trade partners will be undermined, reducing the benefits free trade would otherwise provide to both. "Trade may be global," warn Ramesh Thakur and Steve Lee (2000), but "politics is still local." If neomercantilism spreads, the preservation of the free-trade regime is unlikely throughout the twenty-first century.

The simultaneous pursuit of liberalism and mercantilism today shows states' determination to reap the benefits of interdependence while minimizing its costs. It also reveals the tension between states and markets, between the promise that everyone will benefit and the fear that the benefits will not be equally distributed. As noted earlier, the absence of world government encourages each state to be more concerned with how it fares competitively in relation to other states—its relative gains—than collectively with its absolute gains. These simple yet powerful ideas shed light on the reasons why the United States, the principal advocate of free trade in the post–World War II era, has increasingly engaged in neomercantilism and protectionism, and in 1999 seemed bent on waging a trade war with Europe (over the issue of banana imports!). Fearful of others' free riding, the United States looks more like an "ordinary country" than a hegemonic power, despite the fact that it remains the largest economic market and one of the world's leading exporting countries.

Premises for a Future Global Economy

Six premises dictate the boundaries within which the global economy is likely to vary in the future. First, free trade contributes to economic growth, and trade protection reduces prosperity in the long run. Second, the future will depend heavily on the rules the leading economic powers choose to support to govern trade and monetary policy. The choices are between the contrasting philosophies of commercial liberalism without burdensome regulation, and mercantilist and neomercantilist approaches that seek protectionism. Third, the position of the globe's largest economy, the United States, will likely remain pivotal in the equation, for how this (rising or declining?) hegemon makes economic policy will influence the direction in which others' trade and monetary policies are likely to move. Fourth, the activities of powerful and wealthy mobile MNCs in foreign investment and trade will increasingly determine economic flows; these activities and pressure for continuing trade liberalization are increasingly beyond the control of state governments, whose sovereign power is eroding. Fifth, nonstate commercial and monetary actors (for example, transnational banks, many of which are negotiating mergers to consolidate their power), will provide much of the lubrication that can keep the global trade engine humming. Finally, globalization is likely to accelerate, and as competition expands wealth and reduces the costs of both products and labor, the economic fate of the globe's 6 billion people will be tied together in increasingly interdependent ties, making the welfare of any one important to the welfare of all.

Global Economic Destiny?

The United States, Europe, and Japan have advocated quite different philosophies toward states and markets over the years, and their policies have evolved as their circumstances in the global economy have changed over time. At times, Japan has embraced mercantilism (even as it talked of liberalization), the United States has touted liberalism (even as it practiced mercantilism), and Europe historically has stood midway between the two (but looked more inward than outward). Increasingly, economic nationalism "could propel the preeminent economic powers—and the rest of the world with them—into an era of 'real-economik,' in which parochial economic interests drive governments to pursue marginal advantage in an international system marked by growing interdependencies" (Peterson 1998). Whether a collision of these competing capitalisms can be averted is questionable, especially if the relative position of American economic power declines in a country where a clear majority of Americans (56 percent) are protectionists and only 37 percent are free-trade supporters. Protectionist pressure is rising in the United States and elsewhere—public opinion shows 48 percent worldwide now favor protectionism (*Economist,* January 25, 1999, 36). The erosion of U.S. hegemonical management, the rise of protectionist pressure, and other instabilities in the international political economy "do not augur well for the level of cooperation necessary to avoid the neomercantilist confrontation that could flow from competing national policies" (Peterson 1998). "Historically, recession is the midwife of protectionism. In good times, peoples and nations are happy to enjoy the benefits of open trade. Come bad times, they are tempted to minimize short-run pain through protection" (*Economist,* January 2, 1999). Unfortunately for the fate of the liberal international regime, the threats to global prosperity are multiplying at the same time that the dependency of countries on volatile foreign capital is creating an inherently unstable situation and the volume of world trade is fluctuating in periodic swings between expansion and contraction. If global trade experiences anemic growth or, worse, declines, this slump will cause the demand for exports to drop, and the world's consumers are likely to seek to cushion the impact of the slowdown by turning away from the free-trade regime that engineered their previous period of unprecedented growth.

The architecture of the LIEO constructed at Bretton Woods a half-century ago appeared to depend not only on a consensus about the appropriate shape of the world political economy but also on U.S. leadership. The United States is still the dominant state in the world political economy and continues to perform many hegemonic functions: It tries to maintain a comparatively open market for others' goods, manage the international monetary system, provide capital to would-be borrowers facing financial stress, and coordinate economic policies among the world's leading economies. Today, however, U.S. willingness to absorb the costs of leadership has waned, and its ability to affect global economic outcomes in preferred directions is simply not what it once was. Both the United States and the world must adjust to the decline of American hegemony, and must resist the temptation to return to mercantilist free riding and protectionist trade policies.

> For the world at large, the drift of American trade policy is worrying. Rising protectionism invites retaliation. A deadlock on further liberalization encourages backsliding. Emerging economies, . . . Brazil, China and Russia have all recently tightened import controls. The protectionist instincts of the EU and Japan are undimmed. Over the past fifty years, America has led successive efforts to free world trade. Unless it reclaims that mantle, the prospects for keeping trade as free as it is, let alone for freeing it further, will remain grim. (*Economist,* January 30, 1999, 65)

China in a Capitalist Global Market China has a booming free-market economy under communist political control, and its vast market is now closely tied to the global economy. It is seeking membership in the 135-member WTO, at the same time the WTO is insisting, as a price for membership, that China make large-scale concessions that would allow foreign companies to sell stock, deliver packages commercially, and sell telecommunications across the breadth of China. Much of the future may hinge on whether negotiations can integrate China into the free-trade regime.

However, a new wave of mercantilism and trade wars is not preordained. A number of other important developments are also likely to influence the future direction of the world political economy, and these, in combination, are likely to sustain and strengthen the liberal free-trade regime that has contributed to global economic growth. World commerce has become globalized; global financial flows outstrip trade transactions within countries; and market forces almost everywhere are now being given a freer reign to determine economic outcomes. With trade growing rapidly in the absence of barriers, and with the expansion of free-trade areas, pressure to preserve the liberal trade regime has increased. Multinational corporations are playing a larger role in the continuing growth of commercial liberalism worldwide, and they are supported in this aspiration by the powerful WTO, the conversion of eastern Europe and China to acceptance of freer trade, and the opening up of restrictive markets to exports. All these developments suggest that the prospects for the momentum of commercial liberalism to gain strength are promising.

Some theorists believe that the spread of liberal market philosophies will eliminate the need for new institutions to cope with the changed and changing world political economy. Others caution that the unregulated market should not be considered the ideal and universal arrangement for economic activity, because coordinating institutions are needed to manage sustained growth (Hollingsworth and Boyer 1997). The task of reaching agreement about economic principles is made more daunting by the absence of a true consensus about what the world political economy should look like, as the continuing contest between liberalism and mercantilism (as well as the conflict between rich and poor countries) illustrates. Furthermore, the globalization of commerce and finance increasingly seems to shape, rather than be shaped by, states' policies—thus challenging the sovereign prerogatives of states themselves.

The face of the future thus remains uncertain. If liberals are correct, the process of rapid globalization already on the horizon will hasten the trend toward about interdependence and integration and, with that, the prospects for economic prosperity and political harmony. If mercantilists are right, however, an emerging era of geo-economics will increase states' vulnerability, and thus the likelihood of political conflict and states' efforts to dominate others. What the future holds is hard to foresee, because the various rules for trade and currency are likely to change in the twenty-first century, and these changes will undercut the usefulness of past economic philosophies. The world seems to be spinning out of control in a sea change of rapid globalization that hides the decisions that affect our daily lives. In the next chapter we will examine further how globalization is entangling the functions of governments and markets and making it difficult to tell the difference between countries and corporations.

KEY TERMS

political economy
globalization
international political economy
high politics
low politics
international monetary system
commercial liberalism
mercantilism
Liberal International Economic Order (LIEO)
interdependence
theory
comparative advantage
laissez-faire economics
politics
absolute gains/relative gains
neomercantilism
protectionism
- beggar-thy-neighbor policies
- import quotas
- export quotas
- orderly market arrangements (OMAs)
- voluntary export restrictions (VERs)
- nontariff barriers (NTBs)
- infant industry
- strategic trade policy
- countervailing duties
- antidumping duties

realism
hegemonic stability theory
hegemon
long-cycle theory
hegemony
macroeconomics
collective goods
free riders
zero-sum
imperial overstretch
international regime
General Agreement on Tariffs and Trade (GATT)
Uruguay Round
World Trade Organization (WTO)
monetary system
monetary policy
money supply
exchange rate
self-fulfilling prophecy
fixed exchange rates
International Monetary Fund (IMF)
World Bank
international liquidity
commercial domino theory
floating exchange rates
stagflation
Group of Seven (G-7)/Group of Eight (G-8)
unilateral
fast-track negotiating authority
regional currency union
North American Free Trade Agreement (NAFTA)
Free Trade Area of the Americas (FTAA)
most-favored-nation (MFN) principle
reciprocity
nondiscrimination

SUGGESTED READING

Bhagwati, Jagdish, Krishna Provin, and Arviad Paragariya, eds. *Trading Blocs.* Cambridge, Mass.: MIT Press, 1999.

Caporaso, James A., and David P. Levine. *Theories of Political Economy.* New York: Cambridge University Press, 1992.

Cohen, Benjamin J. *The Geography of Money.* Ithaca, N.Y.: Cornell University Press, 2000.

Eichengreen, Barry. *Globalizing Capital: A History of the International Monetary System.* Princeton, N.J.: Princeton University Press, 1996.

Gilpin, Robert. "Three Ideologies of Political Economy," pp. 269–286 in Charles W. Kegley, Jr. and Eugene A. Wittkopf (eds.), *The Global Agenda,* 5th ed. Boston: McGraw-Hill, 2001.

Hodges, Michael R., John H. Kirton, and Joseph P. Daniels. *The G8's Role in the New Millenium.* Brookfield, Vt.: Ashgate, 2000.

Irwin, Douglas A. *Against the Tide: An Intellectual History of Free Trade.* Princeton, N.J.: Princeton University Press, 1996.

Isaak, Robert A. *Managing World Economic Change: International Political Economy,* 3rd ed. Upper Saddle River, N.J.: Prentice Hall, 2000.

Lipson, Charles, and Benjamin J. Cohen, eds. *Theory and Structure in International Political Economy.* Cambridge, Mass.: MIT Press, 1999.

Milner, Helen. "International Political Economy: Beyond Hegemonic Stability," *Foreign Policy* 110 (Spring 1998): 112–124.

Solomon, Robert. *The Transformation of the World Economy,* 2nd ed. New York: St. Martin's Press, 1999.

Spero, Joan Edelman, and Jeffrey Hart. *The Politics of International Economic Relations,* 5th ed. New York: St. Martin's Press, 1997.

Thurow, Lester C. *The Future of Capitalism: How Today's Economic Forces Shape Tomorrow's World.* New York: Penguin Books, 1996.

WHERE ON THE WORLD WIDE WEB?

Exchange Rates
http://www.x-rates.com

There is no common international currency for carrying on financial transactions. Currency rates of exchange show the value of one country's currency in relation to another's. The Exchange Rates site allows you to compare currencies for thirty-five different countries. Using this site, see how the euro, the currency of the European Union, is doing in relation to the U.S. dollar, or use the Customs Table to compare the U.S. dollar with all other currencies. For fun, you can click on Photos to see what a Belgian franc looks like, or can even order foreign currencies before your trip abroad.

Mercosur
http://www.americasnet.com/mauritz/mercosur

Mercosur is one of the regional free-trade blocs described in the chapter. Operating in South America, its core members are Argentina, Paraguay, Uruguay and Brazil. Its objectives are the free transit of production goods, services and factors between the member states, lifting of non-tariff barriers, adopting a common trade policy with regard to nonmember states or groups of states, and the coordination of positions in regional and international commercial and economic meetings. Visit Mercosur's Web site to get an idea of the role and functions of a trading bloc. Read about the history of Mercosur and some of the problems this trading bloc faces. Look at Map 8.2. What are the other major trading blocs? Do you think free-trade blocs promote economic growth?

Organization for Economic Cooperation and Development
http://www.oecd.org/

The Organization for Economic Cooperation and Development (OECD) began with the purpose of rebuilding war-ravaged economies after World War II and administering the distribution of the Marshall

Plan's aid to Europe. Today, the OECD promotes policies that contribute to the expansion of world trade on a nondiscriminatory basis. It provides a forum in which the governments of the twenty-nine member states can compare their experiences and further the principles of a market economy. From the OECD's homepage, you can access the largest source of comparative statistical data on the industrialized countries. Look at the Frequently Requested Statistics to compare economies.

Trade Resources

http://www.usitc.gov/tr/tr.htm

The United States International Trade Commission (USITC) has created an information referral service for those seeking information related to international trade and investment. Interested in investing in a chemical company in Canada? Want to export tractors to Russia? This Web site provides Internet resources to help those interested in international trade and investment to obtain information on their client country, research various products, access trade assistance, understand patent law, or view international law.

U.S. Trade Representative

http://www.ustr.gov/

The Office of the U.S. Trade Representative (USTR) is responsible for "developing and coordinating U.S. international trade, commodity, and direct investment policy, and leading or directing negotiations with other countries on such matters." Learn about the history of the U.S. Trade Representative, read speeches by the current representative and by Charlene Barshefsky and other past trade representatives, and scan the trade agreements the United States has with many other countries of the world.

World Bank

http://www.worldbank.org/

The World Bank is the world's largest source of development assistance, providing nearly $30 billion in loans annually. The Bank was first created to aid European countries in their recovery from World War II. Today the Bank's mission is to help developing countries achieve stable, sustainable, and equitable growth. Its main focus is to help the poorest people and the poorest countries to grow economically. Explore this Web site to find out the eligibility requirements for borrowing money. What are some of the criteria?

World Trade Organization

http://www.wto.org/

The World Trade Organization (WTO) is a multilateral, global intergovernmental organization (IGO). The WTO's main purpose is to administer trade agreements between countries, monitor trade policies, and provide technical assistance and training for developing countries. Unlike many international organizations, the WTO has a mechanism for settling international disputes with limited enforcement abilities. Click on the Dispute Settlement link on the homepage to review Overview of the State-of-Play of WTO Disputes. In how many disputes is the United States the defendant? In how many is the United States the complainant?

CHAPTER 9

Globalization and the Disappearance of National Borders

TOPICS AND THEMES

- What is globalization?
- The globalization of finance
- The globalization of trade
- The globalization of production
- The globalization of labor
- Globalization and the state: What future?

- **Controversy** Does Globalization Mean the End of the Age of States?
- **Controversy** Is Globalization Producing Prosperity or Poverty?

The first McDonald's franchise opens in Lebanon.

Globalization is a double-edged sword: a powerful vehicle that raises economic growth, spreads new technology, and increases living standards in rich and poor countries alike, but also an immensely controversial process that assaults national sovereignty, erodes local culture and tradition, and threatens economic and social stability.

—Robert J. Samuelson, political economist, 2000

There is a saying that all politics is local. But increasingly, all local politics has global consequences. And those global consequences, in turn, affect the quality of local life everywhere.

—Kofi Annan, secretary-general of the United Nations, 1998

Stock prices tumble as foreign investors sell investments across borders with lightning speed, while your parents fret about their ability to meet their bills. Industrial and financial tycoons merge their multinational companies to form a global business colossus, and you discover that your local bank is now controlled overseas and your new employer is headquartered abroad and plans to restructure by cutting the workforce. As the Federal Reserve System lowers U.S. interest rates, skittish currency traders sell billions of dollars and buy euros. Another U.S. manufacturer shifts production overseas, substituting foreign workers without trade unions for local union workers. A bomb explodes in your hometown, and a friend's family member dies from the violence believed caused by foreign terrorists. Meanwhile, clad in Levi jeans and Calvin Klein shirts, university students in Istanbul chat with friends in America on cellular phones as they sip raki in a local bar, while the music of Hootie and the Blowfish plays in the background.

What in the world is going on? The answer: globalization. Capital, commerce, advanced technology, and information are spreading worldwide at record speeds, producing the complexity and chaos associated with what is today widely known as **globalization.** "Globalization" is shorthand for a cluster of interconnected phenomena that together are transforming twenty-first-century world politics. It is used to describe, alternatively, a process, a policy, a predicament, and the product of vast, invisible forces at work in international affairs. Most would probably agree that globalization is a permanent trend leading to a global phenomenon—"the overarching international system shaping the domestic politics and foreign relations of virtually every country [that involves] the inexorable integration of markets, nation-states and technologies to a degree never witnessed before, in a way that is enabling individuals, corporations and nation-states to reach around the world farther, faster, deeper and cheaper than ever before" (Friedman 1999b).

■ **globalization** according to the International Monetary Fund, "the increasingly close international integration of markets both for goods and services and for capital" (see p. 41).

Globalization is a hot topic because money, goods, people, technology, and ideas are moving across national borders at an accelerating pace. As the world is rapidly becoming interconnected, linked tighter and tighter into a single, integrated global community and market, globalization is transforming world affairs in profound ways. This interdependence creates both possibilities and problems. On the one hand, globalization is uniting the world and generating unprecedented new levels of wealth. On the other hand, globalization is making national boundaries and state governments less important and, by creating some winners and many losers, it is also producing greater inequalities. Globalization is leading to the simultaneous integration and disintegration of states, to the growth of some states' power and the erosion of many other states' authority, and few global actors know how to adaptively respond to the force of globalization's changes.

It is understandable, therefore, that globalization is so controversial. It portends two very different possible futures. In one optimistic scenario, **neoliberal theory** sees sovereignty at bay as the globalization of markets and cultures transcends contemporary geopolitical boundaries and erodes the meaning of national identity, creating "global citizens" who assign loyalty to the common interests of all peoples. In the other, more pessimistic forecast, states will compete with one another to attain or retain the trappings of independence from and control over the homogenizing forces now sweeping the world. This competition will divide the world even as countries become more alike, making some wealthy and stable but others poorer and fragile. The cascading cross-border activities that make for global interdependence will be considered disruptive and will represent "a fundamental qualitative change in the international system, predicting perhaps the end of the nation-state" (Reinicke 1997).

■ **neoliberal theory** a philosophy that maintains that peaceful change with prosperity can be encouraged through cooperation in institutions that knit the states and peoples of the world together into a true global community (see p. 423).

The economic side of globalization dominates the headlines of financial pages and computer trade journals. It is found in "that loose combination of free-trade agreements, the Internet, and the integration of financial markets that is erasing borders and uniting the world into a single, lucrative, but brutally competitive, marketplace" (Friedman 1996). The causes and consequences of globalization extend beyond economics, though. Globalization stems from "the onrush of economic and ecological forces that demand integration and uniformity and that mesmerize the world with fast music, fast computers, and fast food—with MTV, Macintosh, and McDonald's, pressing nations into one commercially homogenous global network: one McWorld tied together by technology, ecology, communications, and commerce" (Barber 1995). Such forces imply nothing less than a redistribution of global economic power "which will increasingly translate into a redistribution of political power" (Schwab and Smadja 1996).

In this and the next two chapters we will examine the diverse forces propelling the rapid globalization now sweeping the world, and explore whether a globalized "new economy" will sweep away the old order based on sovereign states. In considering whether the state will have a future (see Controversy: Does Globalization Mean the End of the Age of States?), this chapter will look primarily at the economic influence of international trade, investment, finance, production, and labor and their impact on markets, growth, and global governance. Chapters 10 and 11 broaden the coverage to encompass the demographic (population) and ecopolitical (environmental) dimensions of a globalizing world. All three chapters repeatedly ask how globalization is likely to affect the well-being of the states and people of the Global North and Global South, as well as the prospects for cooperation and conflict. Before looking at globalization's consequences, however, we must first inspect its causes.

WHAT IS GLOBALIZATION?

■ **global village** a popular image used to describe the growth of awareness that all people share a common fate, stemming from a holistic perspective that the world is an integrated and interdependent whole.

Rapid and unrestrained communication is a hallmark of the **global village**—a metaphor used by many futurologists to portray a world in which borders will vanish and the world will become a single community. The major source of this global transformation is the growing speed and flow of communications, because "by drastically reducing the importance of proximity, the new technologies change people's perceptions of community" (Mathews 1997). Do cellular phones and other means of transnational communication portend consensus, and, perhaps, an integrated global village? Will life in the emergent wired global village be an improvement over what we now know? Or is the vision of such a global village, in which shared information breeds understanding and peace, pure mythology? Worse, will the virus of interconnectiveness within globalization do away with private life, erasing what remains of identity, individualism, and independence?

The Global Information Age

Cellular phones are becoming available worldwide, enabling many in the world who have never before made a phone call to communicate instantly with others. The "wireless world" of cellular phones which use radio waves rather than installed lines is growing almost 50 percent yearly, allowing communication between rural areas in developing Global South countries and "wired" Global North countries where connected telephone lines are already abundant. The direct linkage of nearly 800 million telephones to the global phone network, which has expanded 4–7 percent a year for the past four decades (*Vital Signs 1999*, 92), with more than 100 million new mobile telephone connections added each year worldwide (*Economist*, October 9, 1999, 6), comprises still another element in the larger revolution in telecommunications that is shrinking our world. "The death of distance as a determinant of the cost of communications will probably be the single most important economic force shaping society in the first half of the [twenty-first] century," according to the *Economist* (September 30, 1995). "It will alter, in ways that are only dimly imaginable, decisions about where people live and work; concepts of national borders; patterns of

The World at One's Fingertips The revolution in telecommunications has contributed to "the death of distance," as virtually instantaneous communications are possible nearly everywhere. Here, in a remote and desolate region of northern Kenya, a Samburu warrior makes a call on his cellular telephone.

international trade. Its effects will be as pervasive as those of the discovery of electricity."

Computers are another significant symbol of globalization. They are also its most potent agents. No area of the world and no arena of politics, economics, society, or culture is immune from the pervasive influence of computer technology. Even victims of ethnopolitical conflict and natural disasters in the most remote corners of the world are connected to others by the laptop computers that relief workers from the International Federation of Red Cross and Red Crescent Societies bring with them.

More than 200 million computers are in use today; more than 95 percent are personal computers (PCs), which have replaced the mainframes of yesteryear. Their number is growing by the millions annually, propelled in no small measure by miniaturization. Microprocessors in today's PCs are incredibly small and growing more powerful at a phenomenal rate. "Computers owe their growth and impact to a phenomenon dubbed Moore's Law (after Gordon Moore, the founder of Intel), which says that computing power and capacity double every eighteen months. This exponential growth has led to the digital revolution, and it has only just begun" (*Economist,* July 1, 1995, 4).

The freedom people enjoy with personal computers and their ability to tap into emerging technologies without government intervention is most apparent on the Internet. Individuals routinely "surf the Net" without constraints, creating a global, electronic web of people, ideas, and interactions—a **cyberspace**—unencumbered by state borders. The Internet was developed in the late 1960s at the initiative of the U.S. Department of Defense. Its intent was to enable scientists and engineers working on military contracts to share computers, resources, and

■ **cyberspace**
the metaphorical term used to describe the global electronic web of people, ideas, and interactions on the Internet, which is unencumbered by the borders of the geopolitical world.

CONTROVERSY

Does Globalization Mean the End of the Age of States?

What does globalization today mean for the survival of the state? To some thinkers "it's the end of sovereignty [which] has seen the rise of the European state as the epitome of political organization. The twenty-first century will see the end of state sovereignty as we have known it" (Howell 1998). Still others believe that globalization is simply a new manifestation of old patterns, one that "in many ways can be viewed as a resumption of a trend observed in the world economy a century ago . . . The trends we have been observing in recent decades are in a sense taking us back to the future" (IMF 1997).

Consider this question as informed by the observations of journalist Neal R. Peirce, who attended the fiftieth Salzburg Seminar of global leaders in 1997 to contemplate the state's future in the face of transformative globalization. Peirce issued this provocative summary of the debate, which provides a good framework to consider rival ideas about globalization's causes, likely consequences, and probable impact on the survival of the nation-state.

> Is the nation-state at the end of its 500-year run? Is it about to succumb to rapid-fire economic globalization, resurgent regions or to ethnic and tribal rivalries?
>
> Not entirely, say midcareer professionals from some thirty-two nations who came here in March [1997] to debate the nation-state's furture at the elegant eighteenth-century palace that has been the site of the Salzburg Seminar for fifty years.
>
> Whether from advanced or undeveloped, Western or Eastern nations, most participants agreed we'll still need nation-states to give people identity, raise taxes, provide social safety nets, protect the environment and guarantee internal security.
>
> But for a peek into the deep uncertainties of the twenty-first century and the astounding array of forces now undermining the nation-states, this conference was a remarkable tour de force.
>
> Leading the parade of transformative change are globalization and its accomplices. The computer and telecommunications revolutions enable instant worldwide communications to create new relationships, new economics, whether central governments like them or not.
>
> Multinational corporations now assemble goods from plants across the globe and have moved heavily into services, too—law, accounting, advertising, computer consultation—as if the world were borderless.
>
> Financial markets are also globalized. Where nation-states once sought to set exchange rates, private traders

ideas—the latter through e-mail, a way of sending messages electronically. Designed to survive a nuclear war, information was transmitted in small "packages" through different routes, making it difficult to eavesdrop on the data and messages sent.

The popularity of the Internet spread slowly through the academic world, which by the mid-1980s was its principal user. Two innovations then revolutionized the ease with which the Internet could be used, propelling its popularity beyond universities. One was Swiss software engineer Tim Berners-Lee's invention of the World Wide Web and "hypertext" to link documents with one another. The other was a software program known as Mosaic (written primarily by Marc Andreesen, an undergraduate student at the University of Illinois), which provides user-friendly access to the Web and the Net. In 1994, commercial companies surpassed universities as the leading users of the Internet. Today it is the functional equivalent of the "information superhighway" telecommunications specialists have long anticipated and promised.

Use of the Internet has grown—fueled by the growth of personal computers in homes and businesses—from less than 100,000 Internet hosts in 1988 to some 43 million at the start of 1999, wiring together an estimated 147 million people.

now control currency flows—at a scarcely believable level of $1.3 trillion a day.

The nation-states fatefully shrank their own power by creating supernational institutions such as the United Nations, World Trade Organization and World Bank. Each creates its own cadres of civil servants unaccountable to any single state.

Now comes a rise of influential, globally active non-governmental organizations—the NGOs—ranging from Greenpeace to Amnesty International to animal rights groups. They got official UNrecognition at the Rio Earth Summit in 1992; now they're negotiating to get a voice in official UNdeliberations. Yet the NGOs, like multinationals, are mostly based in Europe and North America, feeding off cutting-edge technology, setting new global standards without much accountability to anyone.

Globalization is creating immense wealth. Yet countries unwilling or unequipped to become technologically connected—many in Africa today, for example—face "marginalization," another word for isolation and poverty.

At the Salzburg sessions there was real unease about globalization—a fear that the world order now emerging would be too cruel, too amoral, too exclusive in its power-wielding.

Anil Saldanha, a corporate executive from India, gave voice to these concerns.

"Man is not well," Mr. Saldanha said. "He is going through a process of insularity—insecurity, fright, fear. He doesn't know what's thrust on him, he must cope. So we need to look inward, to express our individuality, spirituality. If we do not put a human face on globalization, bring humanity to the forefront, we may not have far to go."

A global market does not create a global community, another speaker commented.

Yet the conference made it clear that the erosion of the nation-state is not only coming from above, it's creeping up from below.

One force is the rise of subnational regions impatient with the bureaucracy and unresponsiveness of large national governments. Nimble city-states—the "Asian tigers" of Hong Kong, Taiwan and Singapore, for example—have been recent models of success. In 1970, four U.S. states had trade offices abroad. Now virtually all do and all have official standing in the World Trade Organization.

Ethnic, racial and religious groups grasping for power are perhaps an even greater pressure from below. The end of the Cold War untapped myriad ethnic nationalistic tensions.

Indeed, we may end up with more nation-states. The United Nations had 166 member "states" in 1991. It . . . has 185 [now 187], and it could one day end up with 400 or more, just because of ethnic divisions. But how many will be viable nations? And what does the developed world do about the collapse of countries [that are] worlds removed from its sleek globalization?

New hybrid structures—African, Asian or Latin American emulations of the European Union, for example—may be needed.

Perhaps we'll see forms of community as unknown now as the nation-state was when it burst on the scene in the sixteenth century.

SOURCE: Peirce (1997), 189.

"Since 1995, the Internet has grown roughly 50 percent each year, after fifteen years of more than doubling in size annually. Today one in every forty people on the planet has access to this global electronic network [and] analysts predict Internet usage will expand another 13-fold by 2002" (*Vital Signs 1999*, 94). Because "the Internet is the fastest-growing tool of communication ever," by 2001 the number of users is certain to reach more than 700 million (UNDP 1999, 58).

Communication technologies are driving much of the globalization process and are the underlying force in the global race for knowledge in the twenty-first century's Information Age:

> Communications technology set this era of globalization apart form any other. The Internet, mobile phones, and satellite networks have shrunk space and time. Bringing together computers and communications unleashed an unprecedented explosion of ways to communicate at the start of the 1990s. Since then tremendous productivity gains, ever-falling costs and rapidly growing networks of computers have transformed the computing and communications sector. If the automobile industry had the same productivity growth, a car today would cost $3. (UNDP 1999, 57–58)

To some enthusiasts, the advantages of the communications revolution are, through globalization, a blessing for humanity. Far-reaching changes are in store "as the communications revolution turns digital promises . . . to connect everything to everything else, creating . . . a tremendous force for human development for all those connected—by providing information, enabling empowerment, and raising productivity" (UNDP 1999). "Enthusiasts see a sort of digital Utopia, not because everything is admirable, but because [the communications revolution] defies centralized authority" (*Economist,* July 1, 1995). Envisioning the Information Age and globalization as liberating, advocates for the promotion of globalization as a policy regard it as a leveling factor that allows small businesses to successfully compete in the global marketplace, empowering the globe's 27,000 nongovernmental organizations (NGOs) "using the network to fire up debates and rally instant responses, bringing a new lobbying power to previously silent voices on the global stage, [and] at the same time [fostering] closer community formation [by allowing] a diversity of voices and cultures to be aired" (UNDP 1999). The Internet expands information and communication in ways that threaten dictatorial governments' rule, as China discovered when it sought to muzzle Web networking by the Falun Gong religious movement in late 1999 (Crossette 1999).

Critics, on the other hand, warn that even as Internet commerce grows toward $3 trillion by 2003 (*Economist,* June 26, 1999, 33), the communications revolution is widening the gap between the rich and the poor, leading to the "globalization of poverty" (Chossudovsky 1997) and the destruction of local culture. They point to the probability that although computer technology and communication are agents of rapid globalization, these forces accentuate the already wide differences in countries' abilities to shape (and be shaped by) a computer-driven world. As shown in Figure 9.1 for example, the spread of the Internet is heavily concentrated in the Global North and a handful of newly industrialized economies, primarily in Asia. Thus the communication revolution through computer technology suggests the peril that globalization will be increasingly uneven, benefiting a few privileged countries while putting the rest at a great disadvantage. For example, the doors to the communication revolution for small entrepreneurs in developing countries remain closed, creating a "digital divide" where one-third of the world's 6 billion people are denied access (Brown 2000, 10). The Global North is the primary beneficiary. In particular, because it spawned the Internet, the United States is home to over half of all Internet users (*Vital Signs 1999,* 94), and remains in the vanguard of the telecommunications revolution. Consequently, many other countries fear that America's technological and information edge provide it with the means to continue to dominate global culture, politics, and military affairs in the twenty-first century to the great disadvantage of its rivals. Other critics complain that the growing electronic network has created a new global condition known as **virtuality,** defined by Claude Moisey as "the ability to create a fictitious world using one's computers." In such a world one can conceal one's true identity, which threatens to make the activities of international organized crime and terrorist groups easier (see Moisy 1997).

■ **virtuality**
imagery created by computer technology of objects and phenomena that produces a fictitious picture of actual things, people, and experiences.

The Media: Markets or Monopoly?

Ours is often described as the Information Age, but a remarkably large portion of the information we receive is controlled by a remarkably small number of media sources. In the United States, despite more than 25,000 media outlets,

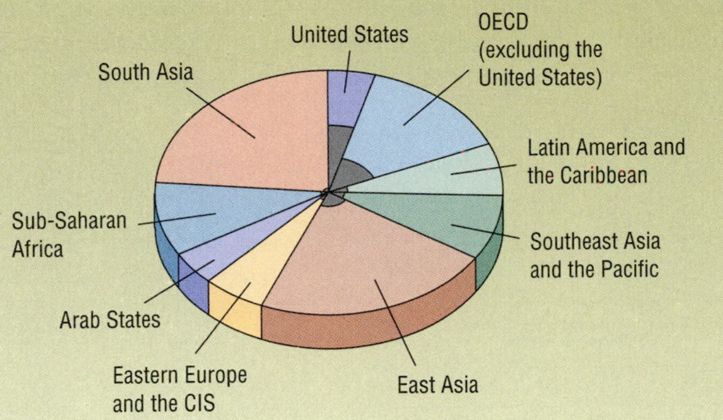

	Regional Population (as a percentage of world population)	Internet Users (as a percentage of regional population)
United States	4.7	26.3
OECD (excluding United States)	14.1	6.9
Latin America and the Caribbean	6.8	0.8
Southeast Asia and the Pacific	8.6	0.5
East Asia	22.2	0.4
Eastern Europe and the CIS	5.8	0.4
Arab States	4.5	0.2
Sub-Saharan Africa	9.7	0.1
South Asia	23.5	0.04

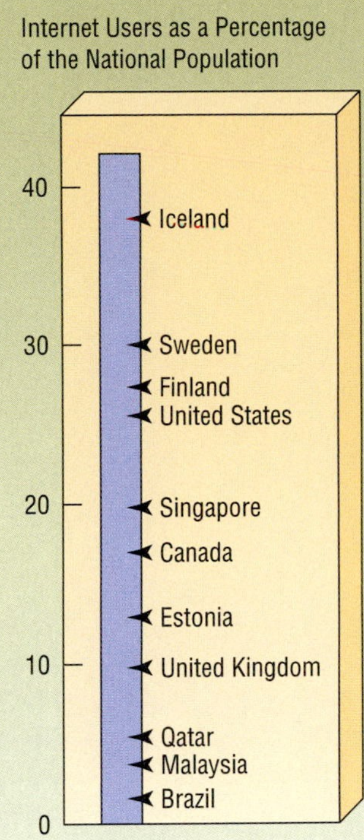

FIGURE 9.1

Does the Concentration of Internet Connections Produce an Elite Enclave?

The Information Age has made it possible for people, corporations, and institutions to communicate with one another and transact business through the Internet almost instantaneously nearly everywhere in the world, but access to this technology is very unevenly distributed. The slices in this pie graph indicate the percentage of the population living in each region, while the dark inner wedges show the percentage of Internet users worldwide living in each region. Note that the United States and the OECD countries comprise 19 percent of the world's population but include 91 percent of its Internet users. In fact, only 2.4 percent of people worldwide use the Internet at all. As the United Nations notes, "Geographic barriers may have fallen for communications, but a new barrier has emerged, an invisible barrier that is like a world wide web, embracing the connected and silently—almost imperceptibly—excluding the rest."

The pie chart represents world population.
Pie slices show regional shares of world population.
Dark wedges show Internet users.

Note: The Czech Republic, Hungary, Mexico, Poland, the Republic of Korea, and Turkey are included in the OECD and not in the regional aggregates.

SOURCE: UNDP (1999), 63; based on data supplied by NUA 1999, Network Wizards 1998, and IDC 1999.

only "twenty-three corporations control most of the business in daily newspapers, magazines, television, books, and motion pictures" (Bagdikian 1992, 4), and as corporate America merges its media sources into ever larger and fewer units—as witnessed in Disney Corporation's buyout of the ABC broadcasting network, as well as Vicacom's acquisition of the CBS broadcasting network and the Time Warner–America Online merger—fewer and fewer corporate executives will control what Americans hear and see about the world around them. The world's population may become a captive audience to what a few telecommunication corporate giants choose to present as information. Already the Information Age's landscape is heavily colored by the fact that ownership of media sources worldwide is increasingly concentrated in a smaller number of huge national and multinational corporations. In the early 1980s, they numbered about fifty, and by the mid-1990s had shrunk to only twenty. In some media services ownership is even more monopolized; for example, there are only thirteen "root name servers" (computers holding the routing information for the entire Internet that allows each computer to connect to every other computer) in the entire world (Shannon 1999). Although thousands of potential sources of information about politics, society, and culture are available, the influence of such media midgets is negligible compared to that of the giants. This, it would appear, gives the rich Global North and, in particular the United States, extraordinary power over the way people throughout the world think, structuring what they believe and how they view the world.

The media's impact on the global diffusion of Western culture is widely seen as influential, as the handful of news and information agencies operate like a giant circulatory system, pumping ideas, information, and ideals from the wealthy center to the remote periphery in the Global South. This global reach is nowhere more striking than in the fact that although the Internet reaches all over the world, only 6 percent of the most visited Web sites in 1999 were physically outside the United States (Shannon 1999, 6). The media's power is also attributed to CNN (Cable News Network), the twenty-four-hour news channel beamed around the world, and MTV which has been called "one of the first global television channels [to give] rise to a global teenage culture linked through music" (Etheredge 1999). Indeed, the recent merger of giant telecommunications companies concentrates further the control of information in the hands of conglomerates. The January 2000 merger of America Online and Time Warner, for example, gives it enormous clout with financial resources one-fourth larger than the annual budget of France (*Harper's,* March 2000, 19). What Global South opponents of globalization complain about is not so much modernization and trade; rather, they oppose "corporate globalization" dictated by MNCs which, they contend, ignores the values and needs of the vast majority in the developing world.

The type of power the media wields over international affairs is, in fact, a specific and limited type of power. Scholarship shows that the media influence what people *think about* more than what they *think*. In this way, the media primarily functions to *set the agenda* of public discussion about public affairs instead of determining public opinion. In the process of **agenda setting** the media demonstrably shape international public policy. For example, global broadcasts of violence and repression in Kosovo were often viewed as a cause of NATO's military intervention in 1999, and for the mobilization of foreign opposition in September 1999 to the reign of terror in East Timor following that island's vote for independence. These examples of the positive contribution of information technology to international peacekeeping aside, some people caution that this kind of "virtual diplomacy," possible because of the development of a "global brain" circulating common information through 1,700 communica-

■ **agenda setting**
the thesis that by their ability to identify and publicize issues, the communications media determine the problems that receive attention by governments and international organizations.

tion satellites weaving an information web around the globe (J. Peterson 1999), has real limitations. One critic has described the impact of CNN and the media this way:

> In foreign policy circles these days one often hears that the advent of instantaneous and global technology has given the news media far greater influence in international relations than ever before, robbing diplomacy of its rightful place at the helm in the process. Observers of international affairs call it the CNN curve. . . . It suggests that when CNN floods the airwaves with news of a foreign crisis, it evokes an emotional outcry from the public to "do something." Under the spell of the CNN curve, goes this refrain, policymakers have no choice but to redirect their attention to the crisis at hand or risk unpopularity, whether or not such revision is merited by policy considerations. (Neuman 1995–1996, 109)

Control of television and other media sources by the United States and a small number of European countries became the focus of hot dispute with the Global South during the 1980s. Dissatisfied with the media coverage it received from Global North news agencies and resentful of Northern domination of other forms of communication, Global South leaders demanded a **New World Information and Communication Order (NWICO)** to create a new regime with fair rules to right the imbalance of the information flows from North to South. The image of the South painted by such sources, they believed, fostered Northern values, such as consumerism and conspicuous consumption, that perpetuated the South's dependence on the North. As the North-South conflict brewed, the United States angrily withdrew from the United Nations Educational, Scientific, and Cultural Organization (UNESCO), in part as a rejection of its role in promoting the new communications order.

New World Information and Communication Order (NWICO) the controversial 1980 call by the less developed Global South to combat what was termed "cultural imperialism" by circumscribing the news and information disseminated by the Western transnational news agencies.

The NWICO has since receded on the global agenda, but the issues remain very much alive in NGOs concerned about the concentration of so much media power in so few hands. In 1995, Hollywood was able to beam the Academy Awards around the world to over a billion people, and American evangelist Billy Graham preached via electronic links to a similar number in over 185 countries. The new global information infrastructure is "especially disturbing because dominance in 'global' products implies not just the ability to ship products around the world, but dominance in cultural exports. This dominance provides the potential to displace indigenous culture with a tide of largely Western, largely consumerist, global conformity. Perhaps globalization is just a nice word that multinational corporations use to hide their efforts to infect the entire world with the cultural virus of commercialism" (Mowlana 1995).

Whatever its true character, the nearly $800 billion global telecommunications industry is without question the major vehicle for the rapid spread of ideas, information, and images worldwide. It also plays a role in the transfer of institutions and generation of income, as exhibited by the World Trade Organization's (WTO) World Telecom Pact. Issued by nearly seventy countries, the accord to open the industry to the free market creates a new regime that ends government and private telecommunication monopolies in many states and has pumped new funds into the global economy by slashing phone costs to consumers and creating countless jobs. Estimating that liberalization could add $1 trillion, or 4 percent, to the value of world economic output over the next decade, WTO Director-General Renato Ruggiero in 1997 proclaimed that the accord "is good news for the international economy, it is good news for businesses and it is good news for the ordinary people around the world." Many, of course, agree with this assessment, and see global telecommunications liberating minds, expanding choices, penetrating societies closed to diplomatic communication, and creating a single, more united, homogenized global culture. Others disagree, however. They note that the airwaves can broadcast divisive messages as well as unifying ones, and that what is said is more important than how much is said.

One counterpoint to the "McWorld" of transnational media consumerism is "Jihad"—a world driven by "parochial hatreds," not "universalizing markets" (Barber 1995). In this context, it is sobering to note that the Ayatollah Khomeini, author of the revival of Islamic fundamentalism that swept the shah of Iran from power in 1979, "combined his access to networks of mosques and bazaars with that of electronic communication and cassette tapes" to carry on a successful long-distance bid to create an Iranian theocracy (Mowlana 1995).

Hence, because globalized communications and information may be used as tools for conflict and revolution as well as for community and peace, the creation of "a world without boundaries where everybody will know everything about everybody else" may not necessarily be a better world (Moisy 1997). We must ask, would the world be better or worse if it were to become an increasingly impersonal place, with "rootless, atomistic individuals floating free of any ties to society, . . . a world without ties of history, language, culture and kinship, in which it is costless for people and objects to move around?" (*Economist*, September 20, 1997, 29).

Global Health or Global Infection?

Humankind and the threat of disease have always coexisted uneasily. In the early 1990s, for example, in Kikwit, Zaire, the deadly Ebola virus—after lying dormant for twenty years—broke out and ravaged its victims with massive hemorrhaging and certain death. Globalization not only heightens awareness of health risks, but actually multiplies them. Truck drivers in India are primary agents for the AIDS (acquired immune deficiency syndrome) epidemic in that country and elsewhere in Asia. Rapid urbanization in much of the world also contributes to the rapid spread of diseases. Growing numbers of refugees forced into unsanitary camps are ravaged by cholera and other diseases that can prove as deadly as the violent ethnic conflicts they flee. Excessive population growth forces people to move into habitats where unknown microorganisms and killer viruses await them. Millions of airline travelers share cabin-sealed environments filled with the carriers of potentially fatal diseases. A shrinking globe, in short, has made the spread of disease across borders rapid, frequent, and difficult to control:

> It is somewhat ironic that, in the face of an ongoing biomedical revolution, traditional diseases are making a comeback and new microbes are evolving to challenge human immune systems. The World Health Organization estimates that one-quarter of the world's population is subject to chronic intestinal parasitic infections. Of the nearly twenty million annual deaths due to communicable diseases, resurgent tuberculosis kills three million people annually, malaria two million, and hepatitis one million. (Pirages 1998, 393)

Meanwhile, the AIDS virus has become global in scope. "The number of people infected with HIV—the virus that causes AIDS—has climbed to nearly 50 million; cumulative AIDS deaths stand at over 14 million and, given that 34 million people currently have HIV, the number is expected to keep climbing" (*Vital Signs 1999*, 102). AIDS strikes most virulently in the impoverished Global South among youthful wage earners who are the foundation of the labor force for development, but it undermines economic growth everywhere on the planet. The human toll from AIDS-related diseases, according to the United Nations (UN), has been most severe in Sub-Saharan Africa, where "the devastation wrought by the disease has translated into a stunning drop of 25 years in life expectancy, from 65 years before the epidemic started in the mid-1980s to an estimated 39 years today" (Tucker 1999, A11).

Many also view narcotic use as a disease. The illicit use of drugs is widespread, hugely profitable, and difficult to control in a borderless world. Fueled by major production and distribution complexes in the Andes and southwest and southeast Asia, the narcotics industry generates profits estimated at $400 billion annually (Mathews 1997, 57). As profits have grown, traffickers' power has expanded, leading to other worrisome developments. Among them are "the [widening] impact of the illicit drug trade on illegal economic structures and processes in major producing or transit countries; the increasing political corruption in such countries; the growing intrusion of narcocriminal enterprises into the realm of the state and the law . . . ; the successes of narcotics businesses in innovation, avoiding detection, and increasing operating efficiency; and . . . the growing transnational cooperation among criminal empires that deal in drugs and other black-market items" (Lee 1995). **International organized crime (IOC)** syndicates have profited enormously by the opportunities created by globalization.

■ **international organized crime (IOC)**
crime syndicates specializing in the use of technology to cooperatively network with each other throughout the world (see p. 222).

Global Migration

The movement of populations across frontiers has reached unprecedented proportions, producing a **global migration crisis** as more than 22 million people qualified for and received refugee assistance in 1998 (*Vital Signs 1999*, 106). The flood of people leaving their homeland for another country raises a host of moral issues, such as the ethnic balance inside host countries, the meaning of citizenship and sovereignty, the distribution of income, labor supply, xenophobia, the impact of multiculturalism, protection of basic human rights and prevention of exploitation, and the potential for large flows of migrants and refugees from **failed states** to undermine democratic governance and state stability. Particularly troubling is the moral inconsistency between liberal democracies that simultaneously defend the fundamental right of refugees to emigrate and the absolute right of sovereign states to control their borders (see Weiner 1995).

■ **global migration crisis**
a crisis stemming from the growing number of people moving from their home country to another country straining the ability of the host countries to absorb the foreign migrants.

■ **failed states**
countries whose governments no longer enjoy support from their rebelling citizens and from displaced peoples who either flee the country or organize revolts to disintegrate the state into smaller independent units (see p. 632).

As "national sovereignty is eroded from above by the mobility of capital, goods, and information across national boundaries" (Sandel 1996), whether existing institutions of global governance are able to cope with globalization's multiple challenges is a hotly contested issue. Meanwhile, the capacity of the state to cope with the forces of rapid change is also being tested. As we turn our attention to the globalization of finance, trade, production, and labor, we will find further evidence that "globalization is uneven. It unites but it also divides, creating winners here and losers there." And in an anarchical international political system, "there is no global civil society that can be called on to support global governance" (Sørensen 1995). Like politics and markets, then, politics and the process of globalization are intimately intertwined, as "even the most powerful states cannot escape the imperatives of the global economy" (Sandel 1996). Meanwhile, realization of truly civic-spirited community in the global village remains elusive.

THE GLOBALIZATION OF FINANCE

Global finance encompasses "all types of cross-border portfolio-type transactions—borrowing and lending, trading of currencies or other monetary claims, and the provision of commercial banking or other financial services. It also includes capital flows associated with foreign direct investment—transactions involving significant control of producing enterprises" (Cohen 1996). The **globalization of finance** refers to the increasing transnationalization or centralization of financial markets through the worldwide integration of capital flows. The central characteristic of the emerging consolidated system of financial arrangements is that it is not centered on a single state. Thus globalization implies the growth of a single, unified world market. While telecommunications specialists talk about the "death of distance," financial specialists talk about the "end of geography," which "refers to a state of economic development where geographic location no longer matters in finance" (O'Brien 1992).

■ **globalization of finance**
the increasing transnationalization of financial markets.

Evidence of financial globalization abounds. Although trade has grown dramatically since World War II, the volume of cross-border capital flows has increased even more. Financial flows now greatly exceed the volume of trade by sixty times and the gap continues to widen. Similarly, cross-border transactions in bonds and equities have increased at an astonishing rate over the past twenty years. In the mid-1990s, "$1,300 billion (roughly the equivalent of the French annual GNP) were being exchanged daily, compared to $18 billion at the beginning of the 1970s" (Pfetsch 1999, 3). "Each day well over a trillion dollars flows around the world, exceeding the volume of trade by 60 times" (Eizenstat 1999, 6).

Further evidence of financial globalization is the astonishing recent increases in the daily turnover on the foreign exchange market. On many days, private currency traders may exchange as much as $2 trillion to make profits through **arbitrage** on the basis of minute shifts in the value of states' currencies, and their activity continues to climb steadily. Consequently, interconnected markets require more than ever a reliable system of money to conduct business across borders while coping with an array of fluctuating national currencies. "It has become a well-known fact that the daily turnover on the currency markets now often exceeds the global stock of official foreign exchange reserves—so what chance have central banks in influencing exchange rates by buying and selling currency in the markets?" (*Economist*, September 10, 1997).

■ **arbitrage**
the selling of one currency (or product) and purchase of another to make a profit on the changing exchange rates; traders ("arbitrageurs") help to keep states' currencies in balance through their speculative efforts to buy large quantities of devalued currencies and sell them in countries where they are valued more highly.

As the transnational economy becomes integrated, "most national central banks are now irrelevant [because] the world's money is essentially controlled by three key institutions: the U.S. Federal Reserve Board, the Bank of Japan, and the German Bundesbank, and global capital markets centered in London, Tokyo, and New York are facilitating increased internationalization in every area of finance" (Thurow 1998). "National" securities markets have also been integrated and have lost their meaning as a consequence of the globalization of finance. Foreign investors' activities in U.S. stock markets during the 1980s increased by more than $300 billion. They also set new records in Japan, growing from 4.6 billion yen in 1980 to more than 54 billion in 1987. Between 1980 and 1990 the market value of shares (known as "capitalization") on world stock markets increased from $2.5 to $8.2 trillion. "New York's capitalization doubled, London's more than tripled, and Tokyo's increased tenfold" (Sobel 1994, 50–51). Amidst this growth in transactions, a rise or fall in any national security market now routinely causes a similar change in the others' indexes. In addition, new financial instruments have emerged, leading to new markets in which they are bought and sold. "Derivatives" are one example. These are complex financial instruments that combine speculation in "options" and "futures" designed to hedge against volatility in financial markets, but they require no actual purchase of the underlying securities (stocks and bonds). Derivatives now account for trillions of dollars in cross-border transactions and "are rapidly becoming one of the most globalized financial markets" (Cerny 1994). The buzz of money in motion is certain to rise as the cost of international transactions plummets with automated online trading and competition intensifies for making equity purchases; transactions that presently cost about $2 are projected to drop to only a 30 cent commission on the Internet (Sivy 1999, 71).

As these illustrations suggest, markets are being profoundly transformed by the rapid acceleration of financial globalization, and markets are becoming "increasingly volatile and subject to reversals" (World Bank 1999b). We may not yet have experienced the end of geography, but clearly financial globalization "has put governments distinctly on the defensive, eroding much of the authority of the contemporary sovereign state" (Cohen 1996). What explains these changes? Analysts generally agree that three critical developments account for the globalization of finance. First, the oil crisis of 1973–1974 and the OPEC decade that followed unleashed a rapid increase in global financial flows and stimulated new patterns of global investments and new financial management procedures. Second, beginning in the 1970s and accelerating in the 1980s, the basic philosophy governing financial and capital movements began to include the value of "deregulating" markets in adherence with commercial liberalism's tenet that markets operate best when free of government interference. Third, "the computerization of finance" (O'Brien 1992) became "the electronic equivalent of nuts and bolts that [altered] the culture of production, competition, and innovation . . . in all of the other sectors of economy and society" (Cerny 1994) because financial transactions and contracts across borders could be processed instantly on a computer screen.

Many economists see the increased mobility of capital as proof that markets become more efficient as they widen. From their perspective, the exploding volume of international financial transactions encourages deregulation and liberalization of global markets and the convergence of monetary and fiscal policies, particularly in the Global North. This is known as the **capital mobility hypothesis**—that the free or unregulated flow of money across borders is influential in the globalization of finance. A corollary hypothesis is that the technological revolution has created **electronic cash** in the form of global electronic debit and credit systems, "smart" credit cards, and true digital money, and that

capital mobility hypothesis the proposition that MNCs' movement of investment capital has led to the globalization of finance.

electronic cash the instantaneous transfer of money for transnational purchases by computers and electronic telecommunications that, unregulated, leads to global financial crises, corruption, and crime because these exchanges cannot be easily detected by traditional accounting methods.

digital world economy a system based largely on globalized electronic debt and credit systems.

in the new **digital world economy** "the risks of fraud, money-laundering, and other financial crises are markedly increased" (Kobrin 1997).

A contributing factor to the transnational movement of capital has been the growing preference of states to relax legal constraints on international capital. The rules governing foreign capital transactions have been progressively liberalized, as many countries have loosened restraints on international capital, speeding the pace at which finance has been globalized. An increasing percentage of the world's governments have deregulated their control over their domestic economies and opened their markets to foreign capital. "The number of countries with liberal or mostly liberal capital regimes [few government restrictions on the size and timing of transactions] has grown from nine to thirty in the past two decades, while the number of countries with relatively restrictive rules [meaning that investments by foreigners or foreign investments by domestic residents require official approval] has dropped sharply, from seventy-three to fifty-three" (World Bank 1997, 134; see also Chapter 8 for data on the national distribution of economic freedom and privatization).

Despite the general liberalization of rules governing foreign capital transactions, the impact of those rules has applied differently in the volume of international capital received by different states and regions, with capital flowing rapidly to perceived targets of opportunity as they materialize in various pockets of the Global North and the Global South (see Map 9.1).

> Just as countries differ markedly with respect to growth in trade, so there is considerable disparity in countries' ability to attract foreign capital. Although worldwide private and official capital flows have expanded by about a factor of ten in the past two decades, developing regions have fared unequally in attracting these flows. Much of the expansion has been in private flows, and among developing regions most of these go to East Asia and Latin America. One estimate suggests that more than half the population of the developing world has been little touched by this aspect of globalization. (World Bank 1997, 134)

Because the accelerating mobility of capital means that financial markets are no longer centered within states, the globalized financial system is not subject to regulation by any one state in particular. Most states are losing their grip on their capacity to control the flow and level of finance in their national economies. The globalization of finance has expanded the power of private markets and corporations no longer tied to any one country, "thereby increasingly undermining state power itself and institutionalizing that of the global marketplace. . . . Having set up the conditions in which more open international financial markets were established in the 1970s and 1980s, [states] are now having difficulty controlling their own creations" (Cerny 1994).

realist theory the view that states are sovereign, unitary global actors in relentless competition with each other for position and prosperity in the international hierarchy, able to engineer policies to promote their own interests at the expense of other states.

Thus as financial globalization has taken on a life of its own, states' economic policy choices are constrained—much as **realist theory** argues that the distribution of military power constrains their choices in the quest for self-preservation against competitors' weapons. In other words, the international mobility of capital has modified states' circumstances by rewarding some actors and punishing others much as military power once did; it also undermines the assumption of classical realist theory that states are autonomous, unitary actors free to regulate their internal economic affairs: Globalization limits "the ability of governments to restrict—or even control—economic activity" (Thurow 1998).

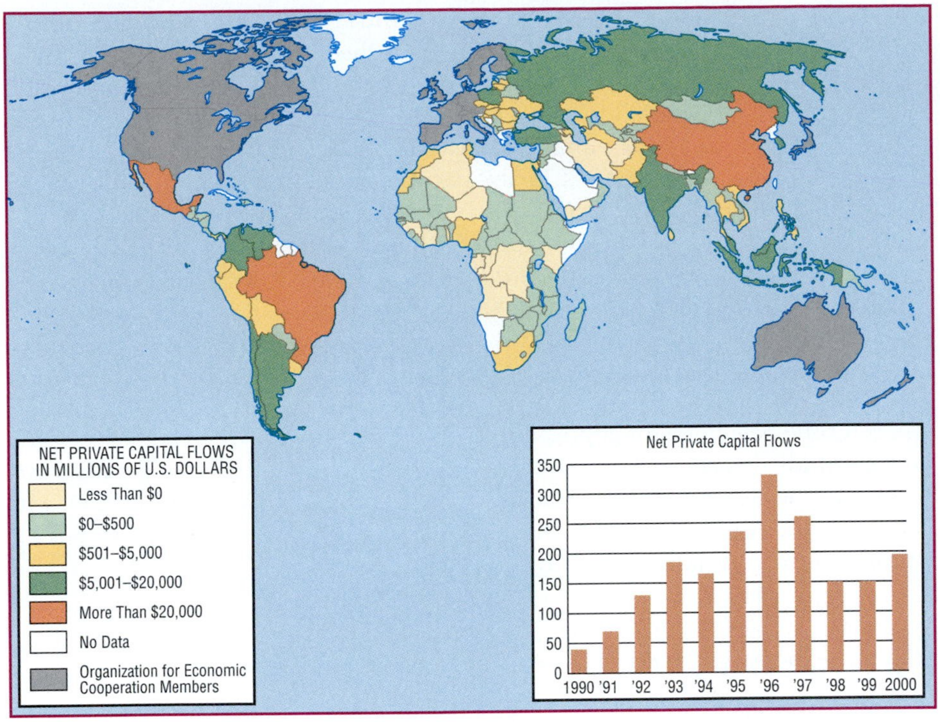

MAP 9.1
The Flow of Finance to Developing Countries

The movement of capital across borders has expanded to target investment opportunities in the globalized political economy, with the bulk of the money landing in the rich Global North. However, a select number of Global South developing countries are now favored recipients. This map shows the total volume of capital flows in millions of dollars for each developing country, a reminder that this portion of the volume of capital flows "must be assessed by its effect on people's lives [and] although an integrated global economy may be more efficient, . . . it also may be less comfortable for many people" (World Bank 1998). Capital flows internationally through loans by commercial banks and private creditors, and through foreign direct investments (FDI) in businesses located in countries different from the investors. The graph to the bottom right reports the volume of private capital that has been funneled into the emerging market economies between 1990 and 2000. Note that net private capital rose to an estimated $193 billion in 2000, with Latin America the expected recipient of 46 percent and the Asia/Pacific the projected recipient of just over 30 percent (*Economist*, February 5, 2000, 102). In contrast, cross-border investments in the form of FDI is much larger, and serves as a telling symbol of the globalization of finance. In 1999, total world FDI surged to $827 billion from $660 billion in 1998 (*Economist*, February 12, 200, 105). The expansion in the levels of private capital flow and FDI attest to the extent to which, increasingly, finance recognizes few borders.

SOURCE: Allen (2000), 52; *Economist* (February 5, 2000), 102.

States' diminishing ability to regulate financial markets, control the international conduct of national business enterprises, and manage the global character of their national economies was vividly illustrated by the Global South's debt crisis in the 1980s. In the wake of excessive borrowing to repay their loans from foreign sources, many Global South countries discovered how much they could be victimized by "capital flight" during the worldwide 1980s recession, when the money they needed to service the interest payments owed on their growing debt simply failed to materialize. Their sovereignty was put at risk by their dependence on foreign finance. The crisis—as well as the plunging currencies and stock markets that put East Asian tiger economies in a deep freeze in 1998—call into question the soundness of the international financial and banking system and dramatically underscored the extent to which all countries had become *mutually sensitive* and *mutually vulnerable* in a globalized, interdependent financial world. This example suggests the growing need for more routinized multilateral mechanisms for policy coordination and cooperation. As global finance becomes increasingly interlocked through massive cross-border transactions beyond the immediate reach of state regulation, such mechanisms will offer the best hope for coping with potential future crises. "The near-instant flow of funds determines who, if anyone, will prosper and who will suffer, and this power holds poor nations at its mercy," warns Robert A. Levine (1999), who predicts that "the interaction between disintegrative economies and starving people and the self-interested rich states will be explosive."

THE GLOBALIZATION OF TRADE

Technological changes have led to the integration of states' economic markets. However, the extraordinary pace at which the countries of the world have linked their markets can be attributed to more than the increased speed of transport and communication. The expansion of markets at a global level, and the convergence of commodity prices across countries, has been driven by the worldwide reduction of tariff rates that has made the expansion of international trade possible. Recall that:

> After World War II, the General Agreement on Tariffs and Trade (GATT) was created by the international community, along with the IMF, the World Bank, and other international organizations. Based on the principles of multilateral cooperation, the GATT had a mandate to roll back tariffs from their prewar peaks and to continue reducing them in the future. The GATT was extremely successful in 1947 in the first Geneva Round in reducing tariffs by 35 percent. Successive rounds in the 1950s, 1960s (the Kennedy Round), and the 1970s (Tokyo Round) and the recent Uruguay Round have virtually eliminated tariffs on manufactured goods. The World Trade Organization (WTO), which succeeded GATT in 1994, is currently engaged in reducing nontariff barriers and protection, including in areas not covered by the GATT. (IMF 1997, 113)

■ **commercial liberalism** an economic theory advocating free markets and the removal of barriers to the flow of trade and capital as a locomotive for prosperity.

The WTO has enlarged its membership, and the 135 countries that have agreed to adhere to its free-trade rules are spread across the globe, with important applicants such as China eagerly seeking entry (see Map 9.2). If and when this expansion process is complete, the globalization of trade will escalate even further and faster.

In historical perspective, the globalization of trade serves as testimony to the wisdom of **commercial liberalism,** which held that trade liberalization to

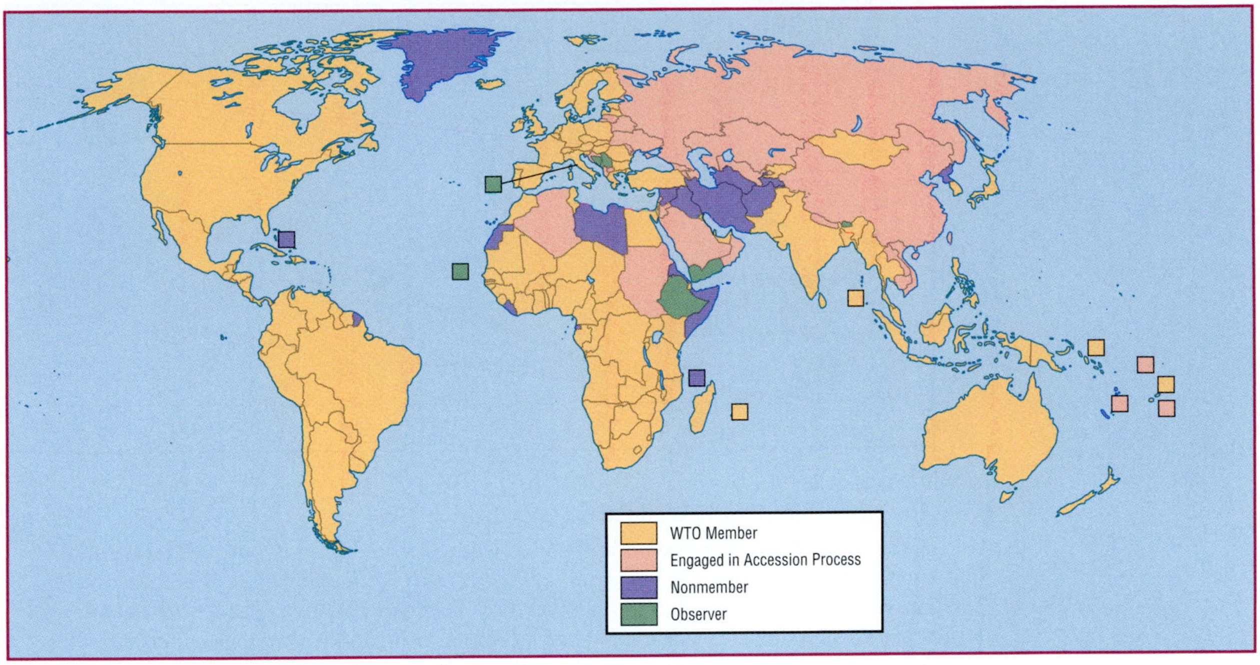

MAP 9.2
Countries Affiliated with the World Trade Organization

Most states are already members of the World Trade Organization, whose purpose is to promote free trade throughout the world. Most of the remaining states are applicants, and when (and if) they join, the volume of trade will climb, contributing further to the integration of the world market.

SOURCE: World Trade Organization, <www.wto.org/wto/about/organsn6.htm> (February 20, 2000).

remove barriers to exports would permit the free trade crucial to growing prosperity. The reduction of tariff rates since World War II (see Chapter 8) permitted international trade and world output to grow hand in hand. Growing international trade has propelled widespread advances in global welfare during the past half-century, and its expansion has been particularly rapid recently. Even during the early 1990s, when the world experienced a recession in economic growth, world trade growth barely slowed (see Figure 9.2). Despite the 1997 Asian financial crisis, world trade volume grew by 7 percent in real terms in 1998, above the 5.5 percent increase in 1996 and the second highest rate in more than twenty years (World Bank 1999, 2). World trade climbed another 3.7 percent in 1999, and was projected to increase an average of 6.3 percent each year between 2001 and 2004 (IMF 1999, 243). The growth and globalization of trade has pushed economic growth to new highs, which many experts believe will continue into the next century (see also Figure 8.5, p. 284).

Trade globalization through the liberalization of trade rules has truly transformed the way the world works, thinks, and consumes. It has altered peoples' standards of living, as the volume of goods and services crossing borders

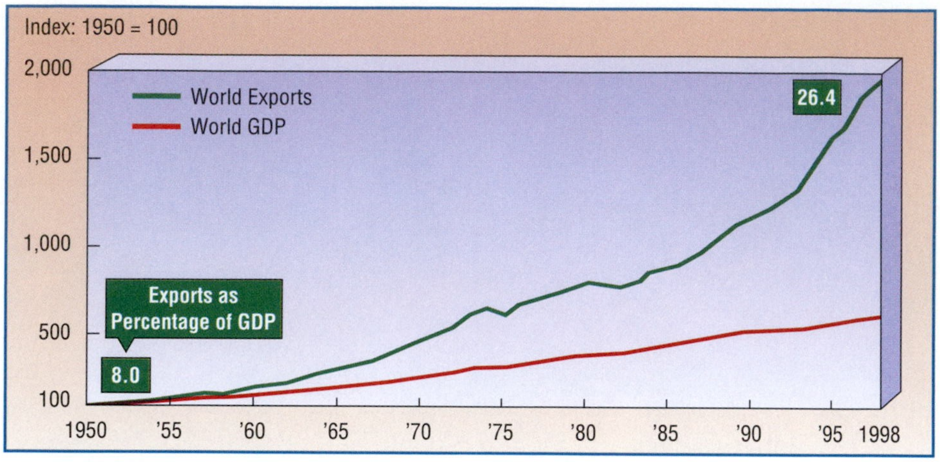

FIGURE 9.2

The Growth of World Trade and Output since 1950

Since 1950, the annual increase in global trade has consistently outpaced the annual increase in global economic output; at century's close, as indexed in this measure between 1950 and 1998 based on WTO data. Over the past five decades "the share of trade flows relative to world GNP has increased continuously and especially rapidly during economic upswings" (Petit and Soete 1999), and the ratio of global trade to total world GDP (imports and exports) is now estimated at as high as 40 percent (Stokes 2000, 93). That ratio is expected to widen, according to the International Monetary Fund, which predicts that between 2001 and 2004 world trade will grow 6.3 percent each year and world GDP will grow 4 percent each year (IMF 1999, 243). As a result of these trends in trade integration, states' domestic welfare has become more tighlty interdependent as nearly all states have increasingly become more involved in foreign trade and more closely integrated into the global political economy. Note, as an indicator of the rising level of trade interdependence alongside the globalization of trade, that in 1950 exports comprised 8 percent of worldwide GDP; by 1998 exports accounted for 26.4 percent of world GDP.

SOURCE: United Nations (1995a), 35; and (1999), 2.

has climbed with reductions in the obstacles to free trade. As two reports summarize,

> if shop windows everywhere seem to be filled with imports, there is a reason. International trade has been growing at a startling pace. While the global economy has been expanding at a bit over 3 percent a year, the volume of trade has been rising at a compound annual rate of about twice that. In 1996 some $5.2 trillion of goods was sent from one country to another, up from $2 trillion a decade earlier. Foreign products, from meat to machinery, play a more important role in almost every economy in the world, and foreign markets now tempt businesses that never much worried about sales beyond their nation's borders. . . .
>
> Time was when trade flows were of interest mainly to economic experts and executives of big corporations. But over the past few years, the movement of goods and services across national boundaries has become the subject of intense public attention all over the world. To the public at large,

trade is the most obvious manifestation of a globalizing world economy. (*Economist,* November 8 and 15, 1997, 85)

There is a serious downside to the globalization of trade and the economic growth it has stimulated, however. As shown in Chapter 8, the gains from trade are uneven because "capitalism is motivated by inequality: the economically fit are expected to drive the economically unfit out of existence" (Thurow 1998). As a result, domestic protectionist measures designed to cushion or curtail the unfavorable effects of the rapid globalization of trade abound in the most victimized countries and regions. Although the primary winner, the Global North has often taken the lead in these neomercantilist measures, usually targeting the rapidly growing economies in the Global South—particularly in Asia. For the **newly industrialized economies (NIEs)** in Asia and other emerging markets, however, the globalization of trade has become the preferred route to economic advancement, and they have energetically sought to attract multinational corporations' foreign direct investment to help them better compete for exports in the global market, despite the costly consequences for the poor (see also Chapter 5).

Trade integration is a measure of the extent to which growth rate in world trade expands faster than does the growth rate of world gross domestic product. As trade integration grows, so does interdependence as states' exports account for an increasing proportion of their gross domestic product. As the index in Figure 9.2 shows, in the last half of the twentieth century trade integration has risen dramatically; in fact, the speed of integration has accelerated, because the growth of world trade has far outpaced the growth in world population. The increasing dependence of states' economies on exports is a reflection of the globalization of international trade, which knits the world together in a tight web of international interdependence. The globalization of trade means that states' prosperity depends increasingly on the demand of other states to import the goods manufactured locally.

Countries differ in the degree to which their economies become integrated through trade in the global political economy. It is important to note that the pace of trade integration has been sharply higher in the Global South than in the Global North, reflecting the less developed Global South's increasing contribution to world trade—a trend expected to continue (see Figure 9.3). This also means that the Global South is becoming increasingly important to growing economic prosperity in the Global North. Some Global South countries' imports matter more than others, inasmuch as differences exist in the extent to which Global South countries are participants in the global marketplace. Eastern Europe, Central Asia, and East Asia have integrated into the global political economy most rapidly; North Africa, Sub-Saharan Africa, and the Middle East lag far behind. "The global economy created in the 1990s by the spread of markets . . . and more open trade have yet to prove that it distributes its fruits more evenly: the rich still get richer and the poor get poorer—only faster" (Hoagland 1999b).

The differences among these groups reflect their historical experiences and the different strategies of development each has chosen (see Chapter 5). They also reflect changes in technology and consumer demands in a global economy. High-technology electronic goods (i.e., data-processing equipment, telecommunications equipment, and semiconductors and microprocessors) make up an increasing proportion of trade in manufactured goods. Here, the twenty-eight

■ **newly industrialized economies (NIEs)** states such as Singapore and South Korea that have successfully grown into advanced industrialized societies, and as wealthy countries are now members of the Global North and competitive players in global trade and investments, no longer in need of development assistance.

■ **trade integration** the higher rate of growth in trade than in gross domestic product that makes trade increasingly important to prosperity throughout the world.

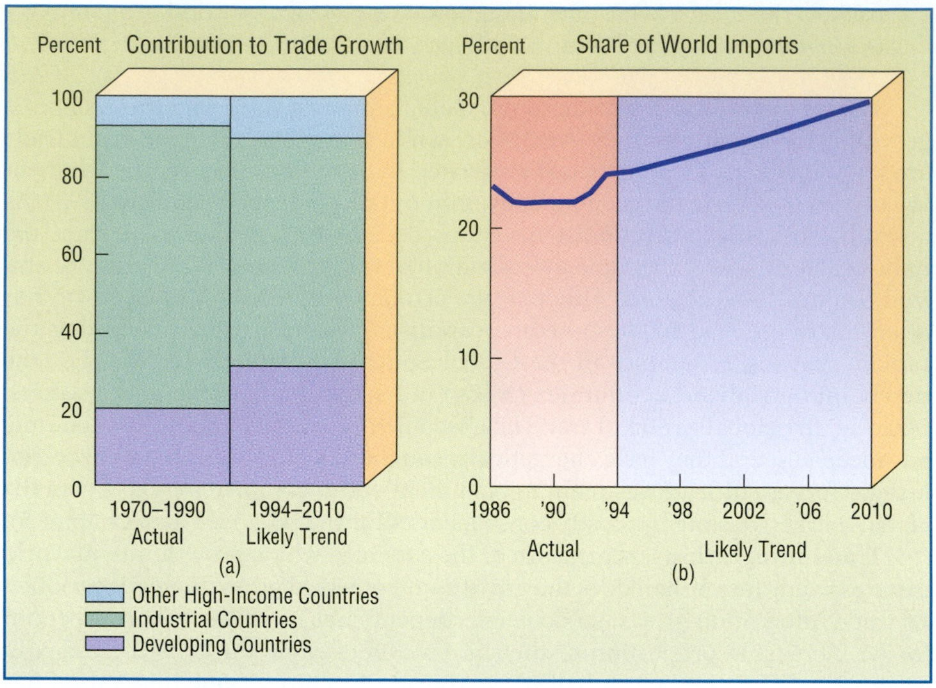

FIGURE 9.3
The Global South in World Trade

In recent years, international trade has grown more rapidly than the production of goods and services. The Global South's contribution to world trade growth and its rising share of world imports reveal its growing importance to the world political economy.

SOURCE: World Bank (1995a), 58; UNDP (1999), 26.

advanced Global North economies have cornered the market as the major suppliers, accounting for nearly 80 percent of world exports in goods and services in 1996 (IMF 1997, 120). The United States and Japan lead the pack, followed by the European Union (EU) countries. However, globalization has altered these patterns, creating new winners in the creation of new products and in their command of the market.

As noted, the Global South's share of global trade has grown (from 23 percent in 1985 to 28 percent in 1998), and is projected to expand in the future. The developing countries share of global exports in manufactured products has also grown (increasing from 10 percent in 1980 to 25 percent in 1997). In this context the Global South's growth in the share of *new* products for exports is especially impressive; as a result of recent industrialization, that share has expanded from less than 12 percent in 1980 to more than 21 percent according to the latest estimates in 1999 (World Bank 1999, 198). In the development and export of new products Asia has taken the lead; the three Asian tigers and the new "cubs"—Malaysia, Thailand, and India—account for nearly two-thirds of all developing countries' exports. In short, Asian NIEs and emerging markets, now well integrated with rapid technological upgrading of exports into the globalization of trade, have been winners.

Trade in services also promises to make new winners. Because the United States enjoys comparative advantages in this area, it has been a strong advocate of bringing services under the liberalizing rules of the WTO. Trade in services has already expanded more than threefold since 1980, with the Global North reaping most of the benefits, even though the Global South has increased its share of this growing trade even more rapidly. The spread of information technology and the comparatively lower wage costs in developing economies are among the reasons

Opportunity Lost? Globalization has transformed world production and employment patterns, moving both manufacturing and jobs across borders in response to MNCs' perceptions of changing investment opportunities. These changes have provoked various responses, many negative, because change frightens people and threatens established interests. One example appears in the photo on the left where Fiat automobiles manufactured by the Italian-based carmaker in Rio de Janeiro await export to Europe. Fiat is one of many European companies that have moved production to Brazil, whose economy leads the Mercosur free-trade bloc. The rich countries in the Global North fear that manufacturing is passing into the hands of the poor Global South countries where production is inexpensive, and are lobbying against globalization that makes production seemingly come from everywhere and go everywhere. Globalization often wreaks havoc on local economies and leads to protests against the economic volatility it engenders, as shown at right in Brazil.

why the World Bank predicts that developing countries will capture an increasing share of world trade in the first two decades of the twenty-first century. In the case of services, then, it appears that—at least for the time being—Global North and Global South will both reap the growing profits from the globalization of trade.

It would be terribly inaccurate to picture trade globalization as a panacea for poverty, however. It is not proving to be a path to wealth for many developing countries, and wide disparities exist among them in their trade linkages to the world. Globalization "has changed the distribution of these gains from trade. There are clear winners and losers, both between and within countries. More trade with developing countries hurts low-skilled workers while simultaneously increasing the incomes of more highly skilled workers" (Held et al., 1999). A backlash to these growing inequalities is to be expected, and many groups in most Global South countries see themselves as victims of an integrated trade world. "Globalization is proceeding largely for the benefit of the dynamic and powerful countries" (UNDP 1997), and the Global South's poorer countries are not participating in the advantages that globalization is providing the winners. The losers, "poor countries and poor people," often find their interests neglected. The Controversy Box: Is Globalization Producing Prosperity or Poverty? frames the issues surrounding the painful costs of trade globalization for the Global South's poor countries. While the shares of global exports of the Asian NIEs and the rapidly industrialized economies have increased between 1968 and 1996, the

CONTROVERSY

Is Globalization Producing Prosperity or Poverty?

Many people recommend globalization as a form of international public policy because they believe that its consequences are basically good for humankind. However, critics argue that globalization's costs far outweigh its benefits. In particular, a major controversy revolves around the question of whether globalization punishes countries and people who are already poor by actually increasing their poverty. Despite the evidence that half a century of increasing globalization has been associated with unprecedented growth and general prosperity, others argue that this property has come at the great expense of some people and regions. According to "anti-globalists," writes Paul Krugman (2000), "again and again you see the less attractive features of the modern world contrasted with an imagined pre-globalization Arcadia of happy villagers living in harmony with nature."

Examine the evidence presented in Chapter 5 on the Global South, Chapter 8 on income inequality, and in this chapter. What do you think? Has globalization led to the "stark disparities between rich and poor, . . . with the fifth of the world's people living in the highest income countries [getting] 8.6 percent of world GDP [and] the bottom fifth just 1 percent?" (UNDP 1999, 2). Or, is poverty in the world due to other causes besides globalization? In evaluating your assessment, consider how the UN Development Program describes the characteristics of contemporary globalization and the issues it creates:

> A dominant economic theme of the 1990s, globalization encapsulates both a description and a prescription. The description is the widening and deepening of international flows of trade, finance and information in a single, integrated global market. The prescription is to liberalize national and global markets in the belief that free flows of trade, finance and information will produce the best outcome for growth and human welfare. All is presented with an air of inevitability and overwhelming conviction. Not since the heyday of free trade in the nineteenth century has economic theory elicited such widespread certainty.
>
> The principles of free global markets are nevertheless applied selectively. If this were not so, the global market for unskilled labor would be as free as the market for industrial country exports or capital. Global negotiations are moving rapidly toward a free world market in foreign investments and services. But intervention in agriculture and textiles, an obstacle to developing countries, remains high. Lacking power, poor countries and poor people too often find their interests neglected and undermined.
>
> Globalization has its winners and its losers. With the expansion of trade and foreign investment, developing countries have seen the gaps among themselves widen. Meanwhile, in many industrial countries unemployment has soared to levels not seen since the 1930s, and income inequality to levels not recorded since the last century.
>
> A rising tide of wealth is supposed to lift all boats. But some are more seaworthy than others. The yachts and ocean liners are indeed rising in response to new opportunities, but the rafts and rowboats are taking on water—and some are sinking fast.
>
> Inequality is not inherent in globalization. Because liberalization exposes domestic producers to volatile global markets and to capital flows that are large relative to the economy, it increases risks—but it also increases potential rewards. For poverty eradication the challenge is to identify policies that enable poor people to participate in markets on more equitable terms, nationally and globally.
>
> Globalization has many aspects. . . . Its economic impact on poor nations and poor people is staggering.
>
> For the world the benefits of liberalization should exceed the costs. During 1995–2001 the results of the Uruguay Round of the GATT (General Agreement on Tariffs and Trade) are expected to increase global income by an estimated $212–$510 billion—gains from greater efficiency and higher rates of return on capital, as well as from the expansion of trade.
>
> The overall gains obscure a more complex balance sheet of winners and losers. Projected losses are heavily outweighed by the gains, but those losses will be concentrated in a group of countries that can least afford them—and for some the costs will be significant. The least developed countries stand to lose up to $600 million a year, and Sub-Saharan Africa $1.2 billion.
>
> This scenario has disturbing implications for poverty and human welfare. Foreign exchange losses will translate into pressure on incomes, a diminishing ability to sustain imports and increased dependence on aid at a time when aid itself is under severe pressure. Revenue from trade will be lost, undermining the capacity of governments to develop the economic and social infrastructure on which sustained reduction in human poverty depends.

SOURCE: UNDP (1997), 82–83.

shares of most of the other 127 developing countries have been "roughly flat or have declined," and their "integration with the world economy has been rather slow" (IMF 1997, 73–74). If globalization is to continue, and it appears highly likely, then perhaps in the long run globalization's success will depend on large "transfers of capital, tangible and intangible alike," from the Global North to the Global South (Reinicke 1997).

THE GLOBALIZATION OF PRODUCTION

In the early 1990s, Ford Motor Company launched a program called Ford 2000. Its proclaimed purpose was to transform the world's second-largest industrial firm into its first truly international corporation. Management control would no longer be centered in Dearborn, Michigan, but rather dispersed throughout the world. Ford's chairman Alex Trotman—himself from Scotland—proudly proclaimed that "there's not an American in charge of any of our national companies in Europe." Ford engineered changes in its product line as well. Unlike most multinational corporations (MNCs) today, which manufacture and sell products tailored for particular regional markets (as does the Toyota corporation), Ford developed manufacturing capabilities that reduced duplication in different national settings. This permitted greater standardization and moved the new automobile along the path toward a "world car." Reduced costs and greater efficiency were the goals, setting a model for production and sales for other MNCs to emulate.

Ford's push to become a truly international corporation arguably represents the "highest stage" of corporate development in the globalized economy of the twenty-first century. According to Harvard University's Christopher Bartlett, MNCs evolved through four stages. The initial period was one of corporate colonialism, when European MNCs directed their investments toward colonies. This was followed, after World War II, by the nationalistic period, in which U.S. companies dominated the manufacture of goods and sold them in foreign markets. Today, as noted, most multinationals are stressing manufacturing and selling products tailored for particular regional markets. From a management point of view, MNCs' overseas operations are "appendages" of a centralized hub. Ford's movement into the fourth stage of MNC development is designed to disperse the hub, much as production facilities themselves are now dispersed worldwide. MNCs are replacing national corporations, because the sales of large corporations are geared to the global market, a large proportion of their revenues are generated from sales outside the countries where they are headquartered, and the growing globalization of production is transforming the international political economy:

> Global exports may be more important than ever, but transnational production is now worth even more. To sell to another country, increasingly you have to move there; this is the main way to sell goods and services abroad. The multinational corporation has taken economic interdependence to new levels. Today, 53,000 multinational corporations and 450,000 foreign subsidiaries sell $9.5 trillion of goods and services across the globe every year. Multinational corporations account for at least 20 percent of world production and 70 percent of world trade. A quarter to a third of world trade is intrafirm trade between branches of multinationals. (Held et al., 1999, 135)

What needs to be added to this picture is the modern mobility of the MNCs' mode of production. Beginning in the 1980s, the MNCs began to move their manufacturing plants overseas to meet the cost of competition in foreign markets. This led to a trend toward **strategic corporate alliances** with foreign companies in the same industry. As political economist Neil Richardson observed in the mid-1990s,

■ **strategic corporate alliances** cooperation between MNCs and foreign companies in the same industry, driven by the movement of MNC manufacturing overseas (see p. 235).

> Some of these are long-term partnerships, anchored in equity ownership—thus, Ford now owns 25 percent of rival Mazda while Honda owns 20 percent of rival Rover. Other alliances are more transient and project-specific, giving rise to the term "virtual corporations." Generally speaking, there are two purposes these various alliances can serve. First, an alliance with a rival may serve to achieve economies of scale. The Chrysler-Mitsubishi assembly plant in Illinois produces virtually identical cars under different nameplates for the two companies. (Originally the Diamond-Star assembly plant in Normal, Illinois, was equally owned by each firm. In 1991, Chrysler sold its half of the plant to Mitsubishi on the condition that certain Chrysler components continue to be used there and that Chrysler-badged vehicles continue to be produced there.) Second, an alliance can allow each firm to complement the other's most distinctive talents and simultaneously learn from its partner's expertise. In addition, these alliances are often complex: Mitsubishi works with Chrysler in North America and meanwhile cooperates in far-flung electronic and automotive ventures with Germany's Daimler-Benz [with which it later merged] and in automobile coproduction with the Volvo-Renault alliance in the Netherlands.
>
> These cases show that states are being drawn into disputes that are given new form by the growth of those global alliances. Policymakers can easily misunderstand the consequences of their [efforts to arrest foreign imports when] they are seemingly oblivious to the mobility of relevant firms even as they futilely expend diplomatic good will in sometimes rancorous negotiations with other governments. . . .
>
> What is a member of the U.S. Congress to think when lobbied by the "Big Three" U.S. automakers for much higher tariff protection against Japanese minivans? Would the official know that Ford and Nissan jointly produce a minivan in the United States already? That the Dodge Colt minivan is imported from Japan? Would she or he appreciate that, because Japanese minivans have only a very small market share in the United States, Detroit would gain little from such a diplomatically costly decision? Few government leaders in the major trading states are likely to have such trade expertise. (N. Richardson 1995, 286–287, 289)

As the multinational corporation has evolved, it has been the primary agent of the globalization of production, propelling as well the extraordinary growth in trade and capital mobility witnessed during the past half-century. "While in the 1960s and 1970s foreign direct investment closely correlated with world output and trade, it expanded at an average of 16 percent annually between 1985 and 1995, compared with 2 percent and 7 percent, respectively, for output and trade" (Reinicke 1997, 128). Today more than fifty thousand MNC parent companies are now linked with each other in **virtual corporations** and alliances of co-ownership and coproduction. These corporate networks of MNCs pursue truly global strategies for financial gain, often through long-term

■ **virtual corporations** agreements between otherwise competitive MNCs, often temporary, to join forces and skills to coproduce and export particular products in the borderless global marketplace.

supplier agreements and licensing and franchising contracts through the MNCs' international alliances and joint foreign direct investment strategies; today "about 70 percent of world trade is intra-industry or inter-firm" (Reinicke 1997, 128). As they funnel large financial flows across national borders, these global corporate conglomerates are integrating national economies into a single global market. The outward flow of **foreign direct investment (FDI)** stock attributable to their more than 450,000 foreign affiliates has increased rapidly. "Foreign direct investment topped $400 billion in 1997, seven times the level in real terms in the 1970s. Portfolio and other short-term capital flows [have grown] substantially, and now total more than $2 trillion in gross terms, almost three times those in the 1980s" (UNDP 1999, 25). Most of this MNC investment in search of profit continues to flow into the Global North, and the MNCs headquarted there provide the primary source for the outward flow of FDI (see Figure 9.4).

■ **foreign direct investment (FDI)** purchase of stock, property, or assets in another country, with a goal of long-term involvement in the economy of that country (see p. 164).

The reason for the concentration of FDI in the Global North is self-interest: Profits are MNCs' primary motivation, and their investment returns are likely to be greatest in the Global North, where a combination of affluence and political stability reduces investment risks. Still, the Global South is the recipient of considerable, and rapidly growing, FDI. Although the amounts fluctuate on a yearly basis, the 1990s have generally seen a return to the expansive pattern of 1971 to 1981, when a growing number of developing countries came to be viewed as targets of investment opportunity, and inflows between 1990 and 1997 totaled $938 billion (*Newsweek*, November 10, 1997, 35).

> Net private capital flows to developing countries (excluding the Asian NIEs) averaged about $150 billion a year over 1993–1996 and almost hit $200 billion in 1996—nearly a sixfold increase from the average annual inflow over 1983–1989. In fact, capital flows to one country, China, were larger in 1996 than they were to all developing countries as recently as 1989. These capital inflows roughly doubled in relation to developing country GDP between 1985 and 1996. Unlike in the 1970s and early 1980s when most capital flows represented bank lending, the largest flows in recent years have been in equity and portfolio investments. Such private capital flows rose from a low of ½ of 1 percent of developing country GDP in 1983–1989 to 2–4 percent of GDP in each of the years 1994–1996. Foreign direct investment has posted the largest rise. This has flowed overwhelmingly toward the emerging market countries that have been experiencing relatively fast economic growth. Asian developing countries received almost twice the net private capital inflows as a percentage of their GDP that African countries received over 1990–1996. Liberalization of financial markets in both recipient and source countries has helped to spur this growing capital market integration. Successful developing countries increasingly have lifted controls on cross-border flows, especially on capital inflows, and removed restrictions on payments for current account transactions. (IMF 1997, 73)

The impact of FDI on creating an interconnected global capital market extends beyond money. With it comes technology, managerial expertise, and employment opportunities. Champions of MNCs view these as contributions to the development of less developed economies. Not surprisingly, many Global South countries often actively seek MNC investment capital and the other perquisites that flow from it. MNCs are especially important to those who seek

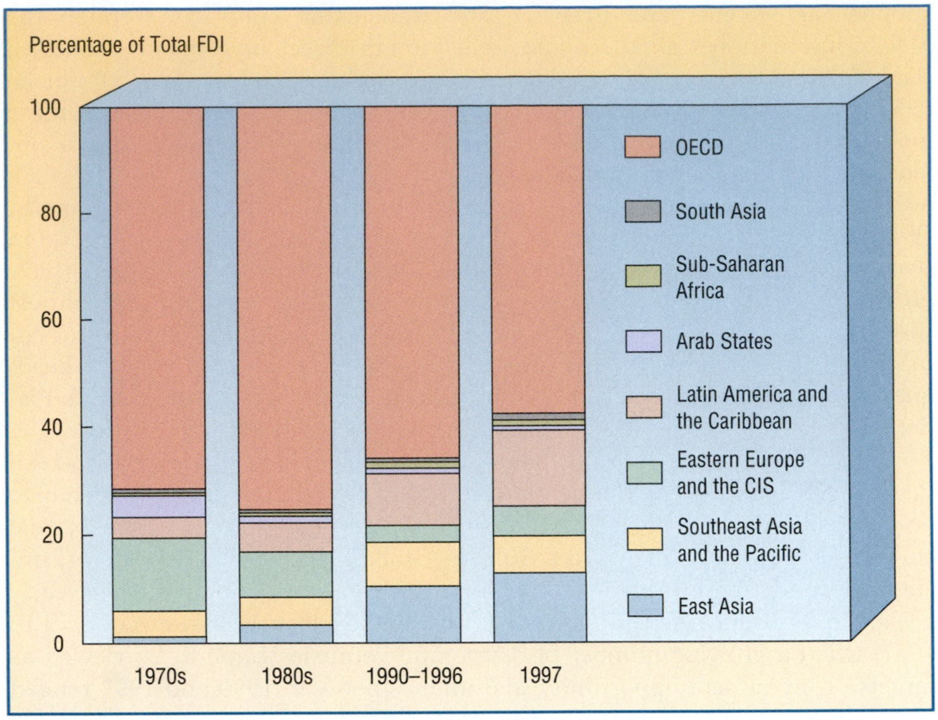

FIGURE 9.4

The Changing Distribution of Foreign Direct Investment since 1970

FDI is primarily directed toward countries in the rich Global North, from which almost all the flows originate, although the level to developing countries has risen several-fold in the twentieth century's last decade (World Bank 1999b). The flows of investment from MNCs into and out of the twenty-nine wealthy OECD industrialized, market-economy countries in the Global North reached a new record level in 1998; investments into the OECD countries rose 7.1 percent to $465 billion and outflow increased 4.2 percent to $566 billion (*Economist,* August 7, 1999, 89). That situation persisted in 1999, when FDI worldwide rose to $827 billion with the largest investments again concentrated in the Global North (*Economist,* February 12, 2000, 105). The people living in the top 20 percent high-income countries benefited from 6.8 percent of foreign investment; in contrast, the bottom 20 percent of the poorest sixty-five countries' share of total global FDI was only 1 percent (UNDP 1999, 2, 3).

SOURCE: UNDP (1999), 26.

to emulate the economic success of the NIEs, which depend on an ability to sustain growth in exports. Foreign capital is critical to this goal.

Although many countries aggressively compete for foreign investments by MNCs, they also recognize that FDI can come with costs and that MNCs might take advantage of the states where they elect to conduct overseas business. "Enormous size confers great economic and sometimes political power on MNCs vis-à-vis the countries in which they operate" (Todaro 2000), which can skew outcomes in unfavorable directions (see Korten 1995). Critics of MNCs also worry that the presumed economic benefits from FDI often mask adverse social and economic consequences. For example, the charge was made in the 1970s that the Swiss-based Nestle corporation (with factories in more than

Trade Links Former Enemies The developing countries once shunned foreign investments, fearing their adverse economic and political consequences, but no longer. Even Vietnam, once a bitter communist enemy of the capitalistic United States, now welcomes American investment dollars.

eighty countries) targeted Global South mothers as a high-growth marketing opportunity and aggressively promoted its powdered baby formula, even when that formula proved harmful. A transnational boycott of Nestle products was organized by the Infant Formula Action Committee (INFACT) NGO based in the United States (see Lopez, Smith, and Pagnucco 1995). These and other MNC investment and business practices lie behind the fear of MNCs' activities. Critics "see these giant corporations not as needed agents of economic change but more as vehicles of antidevelopment. Multinationals, they argue, reinforce dualistic economic structures and exacerbate domestic inequalities with wrong products and inappropriate technology" (Todaro 2000).

These critics contend that MNCs exact a cost not only on the Global South but also on the Global North (recall Controversy: Are Multinational Corporations a Positive Force for the World?, p. 230). They note that while corporate executives often have a "broad vision and understanding of global issues," they have little appreciation of, or concern for, "the long-term social or political consequences of what their companies make or what they do" (Barnet and Cavanagh 1994; see also Barnet and Müller 1974). These allegedly include a host of maladies, including environmental degradation, a maldistribution of global resources, and social disintegration. Further, critics complain that MNCs are beyond the control of national political leaders.

> The formidable power and mobility of global corporations are undermining the effectiveness of national governments to carry out essential policies on behalf of their people. Leaders of nation-states are losing much of the control over their own territory they once had. More and more, they must conform to the demands of the outside world because the outsiders are

> already inside the gates. Business enterprises that routinely operate across borders are linking far-flung pieces of territory into a new world economy that bypasses all sorts of established political arrangements and conventions. (Barnet and Cavanagh 1994, 19)

Nonetheless, some corporate visionaries extol the transnational virtues and the positive contribution they claim MNCs make by encouraging replacement of narrow nationalistic values with those of a truly global culture. To the extent that this influence is operative, MNCs' globalization of production and investment will lead to the transfer of people's loyalties from individual countries to the world as a whole. By challenging "the operational sovereignty of a government, that is, its ability to exercise sovereignty in the daily affairs of politics" (Reinicke 1997), the globalization of production builds bridges across the politics that divide states—providing a common ground for people to cooperate. This would fulfill the humanist vision of international harmony resulting from acceptance of everyone's shared humanity and destiny. "There are no longer any national flag carriers," in the words of Kenichi Ohmae, a Japanese management consultant. "Corporations must serve their customers, not governments."

THE GLOBALIZATION OF LABOR

In his manifesto on the evils of capitalism, Karl Marx urged the workers of the world to unite, throwing off the chains imposed by the oppressive owners of capital. The assumption was that workers everywhere were members of the same disadvantaged class who shared a common purpose and vision. But that assumption is not as accurate today. As the liberalization and rapid integration of markets throughout the world proceed, labor markets will be profoundly affected. Competition—not solidarity—has intensified. Because the spread of globalization is uneven, some employees will be winners, many others losers.

As recently as the 1970s one-third of the world's workers were insulated from the rest of the world through centralized economic planning, as in the former Eastern bloc, and through restrictive trade barriers and the regulation of capital markets elsewhere. "Today, three giant population blocs—China, the republics of the former Soviet Union, and India—with nearly half the world's labor force among them, are entering the global market, and many other countries from Mexico to Indonesia have already established deep linkages." The World Bank (1995, 50) estimated that at the start of the twenty-first century, more than 90 percent of the world's workers would be part of the global economic mainstream.

Accommodating the influx of new workers will be difficult, because the growth of trade does not automatically create more employment and better wages (UNDP 1999). Already "the world is experiencing the worst employment crisis since the 1930s," according to a former U.S. secretary of labor. "Almost one-third of the Earth's 2.8 billion workers are either jobless or underemployed, and many of those who are employed work for very low wages with little prospect for advancement" (Marshall 1995). The prospects for rising wages remain especially grim for women (UNDP 1999). The lack of jobs is a worldwide problem, even in the Global North. For example, sustained economic

Child Labor in a Global System Globalization is sped not only by the rapid expansion of technology but by the availability of cheap labor in some countries, which take advantage of their peoples' low wages to make products highly competitive in the globalized marketplace. Here a child labors at near slave wages in Bangladesh, producing goods that cost less than those made where labor unions protect workers. Such practices have mercantilist nationalists and free-trade critics up in arms, even though open global markets encourage them.

growth has not reduced Europe's chronic unemployment, which for the last decade has left about 12 percent of the labor force idle. Unemployment and **underemployment** rates are lower in the United States, but the real wages of most U.S. workers have fallen over the past two decades. Mass unemployment characterizes conditions in many other countries, and throughout much of the the Global South employment growth has slowed and wage rates have fallen. With a world population of 6 billion, "national governments face the daunting task of creating nearly 30 million additional jobs each year for the next 50 years. . . . In a situation of labor surplus, the quality of jobs may suffer. Workers will settle for lower wages, longer hours, fewer benefits and less control over work activities. As global economic integration proceeds, surplus labor anywhere can weaken labor's bargaining power everywhere. Rapid technological developments and globalization have also decreased demand for some kinds of labor" (Brown and Halweil 1999, 9).

■ **underemployment** a condition critics trace to trade globalization in which a large portion of the labor force only works part time at low pay in occupations below their skill level.

The costs of deteriorating employment rates are high. "In both poor and rich countries dislocations from economic and corporate restructuring, and from dismantling the institutions of social protection, have meant greater insecurity in jobs and incomes" (UNDP 1999). "Globalization has exposed a deep fault line between groups who have the skills and mobility to flourish in global markets and those who either do not have these advantages or perceive the expansion of unregulated markets as inimical to social stability" (Rodrik 1997b). For the skilled, "salaries and work styles will converge among people high up in the demographic pyramid" (Sivy 1999); for the unskilled at the bottom, low wages and unemployment are likely a shared experience. High levels of joblessness produced by global economic integration result in human suffering and hopelessness, rising inequality within and between countries, and deteriorating social cohesion, domestic disintegration, and corroding democratic institutions. Growing global interdependence in one country affects the economic circumstances of workers in others as well:

> During that first era of openness, labor was far more mobile than today (it was a time of mass migration). Now highly skilled and professional workers are mobile, either physically or via computer, but most countries no longer welcome unskilled immigrants.

> Meanwhile, companies that once were anchored in their communities can easily pick up and relocate. In fact companies which do not go where they can manufacture and operate most efficiently will soon be overtaken by those which do.
>
> So capital can move, but labor can't; business executives are in a strong bargaining position, but workers aren't; and the result is pretty much what you would expect. (Hiatt 1997, 8)

Multinational corporations have been a primary vehicle of growing global interdependence that benefits some workers at the relative expense of others' wages. This forecast about the success of the rich and powerful that makes workers the losers, and that makes "the hollowing of the middle class a feature of income distribution in many countries" (Rodrik 1997b), has been fulfilled in the global economy; "wage inequality between skilled and unskilled labor is a global trend." Part of the reason is because MNCs easily move manufacturing sites and technical know-how to developing countries, where labor is cheap and their ability to control wages and move production has been facilitated by cross-border mergers and acquisitions. Consolidation has become "a striking trend and a major driver of FDI," and in 1997 there were fifty-eight major corporate mergers that each exceeded $1 billion (UNDP 1999, 26). Inasmuch as MNC mergers exceeded $26 trillion in 1998 (*Economist*, January 9, 1999, 22), enormous opportunities have been created for the new, larger transnational conglomerates to cut jobs and engage in monopolistic policies, despite antitrust regulation laws and increasing cross-border cooperation by trade unions to oppose these practices (see Carr 1999). Powerful interest groups have at times succeeded in curtailing these kinds of opportunistic MNC mergers. For example, the Pentagon's 1999 opposition to the merger of Lockheed Martin and Northrup Gruman, the two leading arms manufacturers in the world, blocked their plans to merge.

Of the 8 million jobs created by MNCs between 1985 and 1992, 5 million were in the Global South. In countries as diverse as Argentina, Barbados, Botswana, Indonesia, Malaysia, Mauritius, Mexico, the Philippines, Singapore, and Sri Lanka, multinationals account for one-fifth of the manufacturing sector employment (World Bank 1995, 62). These workers have benefited from the new job opportunities created. In a world of highly mobile capital, however, this also makes unskilled laborers with low wages, and the countries where they are employed, vulnerable. "Many developing countries fear that increased competition for funds by other developing countries will lead to a rise in footloose investments, prone to leave at the slightest shock. . . . This problem is especially acute in low-skill industries such as garments and footwear, where firm-specific knowledge is slight and exit costs are low."

Such fears, born of experience, are all too real in the Global North. Workers there also fear losing their jobs due to cheap imports made possible by lower-cost production in the Global South or because the companies they work for will relocate abroad. The irony is that economic growth has been rekindled since the recession of the early 1990s. For many, however, this has been a time of "jobless growth." And even if they keep their jobs, employees often blame cheap foreign labor for their own lack of pay hikes and resultant stagnating living standards.

Wage rates differ widely throughout the world, and "gaps in income between the poorest and richest people and countries have continued to widen.

In 1960 the world's people within the richest countries had 30 times the income of the poorest 20 percent—in 1997, 74 times as much" (UNDP 1999, 36). It is difficult to assess the impact of wage rates in different countries on one another, because labor trends are affected not only by trade but also by technological developments, trends in labor productivity, and migration. However, economic theory does predict that, as a result of international trade, the wage rates in poor countries will eventually be pulled up somewhat. Meanwhile, wage rates for unskilled workers in rich countries will come down. "The logic behind this is that trade affects the relative rewards of factors of production by changing the relative price of goods. Opening up to trade increases the price of labor-intensive goods in poor, labor-rich countries, which, as a consequence, shift their resources to the production of labor-intensive goods. This, in turn, raises demand for labor in poor countries, and hence raises relative wages. As relative prices of goods converge in rich and poor countries, so do wages" (Diwan and Revenga 1995). In short, as a consequence of trade, wage rates should tend toward convergence. For some, this means a gain in welfare; for others, it means lost income.

Empirical studies of wage rates in different countries support these expectations (for a summary, see Diwan and Revenga 1995). They also show that increased competition from producers in developing countries is responsible in part for declining wages for labor and growing income inequality in Australia, Canada, and the United States, as well as for the persistence of high levels of unemployment in Europe. Where analysts disagree is in their determination of what part trade competition plays in these problems. "Most analyses conclude that trade with developing countries can explain only 10 to 30 percent of the industrial countries' labor market difficulties, but some studies come up with more extreme results—on both sides of the argument" (Diwan and Revenga 1995).

With protectionist sentiments widespread in the Global North, countries in the Global South worry that their own hopes for economic advancement cannot be realized unless and until the Global North relaxes its multitude of restrictive trade barriers. Interestingly, however, concern for the impact of low wage rates is no longer confined to the Global North. Faced with the prospect of huge numbers of low-wage Chinese workers entering the workforce, some Global South countries have also embraced protectionist trade practices. Thus the challenge of globalization promises to shape the global political agenda in the twenty-first century.

GLOBALIZATION AND THE STATE: WHAT FUTURE?

Rapid globalization, fueled in large measure by technological revolutions, is likely to continue. Analysts differ on whether globalization is desirable or despicable, depending in part on the scenarios about the future world order that globalization will help create and the political perspectives that inform their worldviews. Some analysts focus on the benefits of globalization for economic well-being; others focus on its unevenness and the prospects for marginalizing large numbers of peoples and states. Some focus on the challenge globalization

In Defense of Jobs at Home Free trade and globalization are seen as threats to the job security of some workers, who seek protection to preserve their employment in vulnerable, relatively uncompetitive sectors of the global market. In 1993, American workers demonstrated against the North American Free Trade Agreement (NAFTA). If such protests succeed around the globe, free-trade agreements are likely to unravel.

poses to an international system founded on the sovereign territorial state; others are more hopeful about the state's resilience and the prospects for global governance to cope with the challenge of steering globalization in rewarding directions. We can expect the controversies about globalization's alleged virtues and vices, benefits and costs, to heighten as finance, population, trade, labor, and culture continue to converge globally. While globalization has narrowed distance between the world's people, some have gained and others have lost ground. The global village is not proving to be an equally hospitable home for everyone. The losers resisting "corporate citizenship" or "stakeholder capitalism" are mounting a backlash, even though "no one can predict globalization's outcome" (Pfaff 1996). "Globalization rides mankind, but drives people to take refuge from its powerful forces" (Schlesinger 1997). Winners in the game of trade and investment play down the costs of global integration, while protectionist critics of free trade and open capitalist markets deny its benefits, and the debate about globalization's problematic impact has intensified without resolution as the debaters have hardened their positions without listening to the counterarguments.

The key question is really about fairness, ethics, and justice, not about the benefits of free trade, which both rich and poor countries recognize as they competitively seek to gain a larger share of the global export market. The evidence about the costs and payoffs is mixed because globalization refers to different phenomena, the outcomes of which are open to interpretation. While many issues remain uncertain, it *is* clear that globalization is not altogether a "win-win" situation. Therefore, the debate will continue.

Is globalization eroding the ability of even the rich states to control their economic and political fortunes? To be sure, a world of vanishing borders challenges all territorial states, rich and poor alike. However, states still rule and govern the institutions and laws that shape changes in the world economy. States remain the globe's major political unit, and some observers see the power of the state as being as strong as ever, even in the era of global interdependency that has forced states to reorganize themselves to more effectively manage international transactions (see Gelber 1998). Globalization may even strengthen the size and economic power of states. The age of big government is not dead.

> At the beginning of [the twentieth] century government spending in today's industrial countries accounted for less than one-tenth of national income. [In 1997] in the same countries, the government's share of output was roughly half. Decade by decade, the change in the government's share of the economy moved in one direction only: up. During war it went up; during peace it went up. Between 1920 and the mid-1930s, years of greatly diminished trade and international economic contact, it went up. Between 1960 and 1980, as global trade and finance expanded, it went up. Between 1980 and 1990, as this breeze of globalization became a strong wind, it went up again. Between 1990 and 1996, as the wind became a gale, it went up some more. (*Economist,* September 20, 1997, 7)

The expansion of governmental control over states' spending notwithstanding, globalization has arguably reduced the sovereign control of states over activities within their borders and their relations with other states and nonstate actors.

Globalization reduces the capacity of states to exercise political power over the territory in which private-sector actors operate. This loss of control probably means that, "Probing further into the future, including the future of the nation-state itself, one must recognize that globalization has ended the nation-state's monopoly over internal sovereignty, which was formerly guaranteed by territory. This change deprives external sovereignty of its functional value. The nation-state as an externally sovereign actor in the international system will become a thing of the past" (Reinicke 1997).

International regimes such as those that evolved after World War II to promote global governance in monetary and trade affairs may also prove effective management strategies for coping with the challenge of globalization. Because "globalization implies that everyone and everything is more closely connected than ever before but on a foundation that is still shaky," a more effective architecture for global governance needs to be created (Garten 1999). A key issue is whether states can find a focal point, a norm, around which cooperation could coalesce. Liberal theorists, who focus on the mutual gains stemming from international cooperation, are optimistic about the possibilities. Realists and neomercantilists, who are concerned more with relative gains than absolute gains, are more pessimistic. But all accounts agree on one proposition: "that the communications and technology revolution that facilitates the flow of capital, information, and jobs across old national boundaries will force a redefinition of the role of states [because] the process of globalization is remaking the economic world and inevitably will reshape the political world as well" (Broder 1999).

There is another troublesome side to globalization: its impact on the global environment. This chapter began by asking whether globalization is the route to a global village—one free of conflict and intent only on improving villagers' welfare—or whether this is mere mythology. *Global pillage* is an alternative description of the probable consequences that will flow from cascading globalization. The costs of rapidly accelerating consumption promoted by free trade and the ethos of consumerism are not sustainable. Will that force—the possibility of destroying the planet's very life-support systems—ultimately doom humanity's future? The next two chapters investigate possible answers to this question.

KEY TERMS

globalization
neoliberal theory
global village
cyberspace
virtuality
agenda setting
New World Information and Communication Order (NWICO)
international organized crime (IOC)
global migration crisis
failed states
globalization of finance
arbitrage
capital mobility hypothesis
electronic cash
digital world economy
realist theory
commercial liberalism
newly industrialized economies (NIEs)
trade integration
strategic corporate alliances
virtual corporations
foreign direct investment (FDI)
underemployment

SUGGESTED READING

Chossudovsky, Michel. *The Globalisation of Poverty.* London: Zed Books, 1997.

Etheredge, Lloyd S., ed. *Politics in Wired Nations.* New Brunswick, N.J.: Transaction Books, 1998.

Friedman, Thomas L. *The Lexus and the Olive Tree: Understanding Globalization.* New York: Farrar, Straus, Giroux, 1999.

Held, David, Anthony McGrew, David Goldblatt, and Jonathan Perraton. *Global Transformations: Politics, Economics and Culture.* Stanford, Calif.: Stanford University Press, 1999.

Keohane, Robert O., and Joseph S. Nye, Jr. "Globalization: What's New? What's Hot? (And so What)," *Foreign Policy* 118 (Spring 2000): 104–109.

Mittelman, James H., ed. *The Globalization Syndrome: Transformation and Resistance.* Princeton, N.J.: Princeton University Press, 2000.

Odell, John. *Negotiating the World Economy.* Ithaca, N.Y.: Cornell University Press, 2000.

Rosenau, James N. *Along the Domestic-Foreign Frontier: Exploring Governance in a Turbulent World.* Cambridge, Eng.: Cambridge University Press, 1997.

Sachs, Jeffrey. "International Economics: Unlocking the Mysteries of Globalization" *Foreign Policy* 110 (Spring 1998): 97–111.

Sassen, Saskia. *Globalization and Its Discontents.* New York: New Press, 1998.

Schaeffer, Robert K. *Understanding Globalization.* Oxford, Eng.: Rowman & Littlefield, 1997.

Waltz, Kenneth N. "Globalization and Governance," *PS: Political Science and Politics* 32 (December 1999): 693–700.

Wienner, Jarrod, ed. *Global Society: Journal of Interdisciplinary International Relations,* published three times a year. Oxfordshire, Eng.: Carfax Publishing.

Young, Patrick with Thomas Theys. *Capital Market Revolution.* Upper Saddle River, N.J.: Prentice-Hall, 1999.

WHERE ON THE WORLD WIDE WEB?

LaborNet

http://www.labornet.apc.org/

LaborNet provides labor news from around the world, Internet services, and Internet training to those interested in workers' causes. Want to be a sympathetic striker? Click on the Strike Page and find out the who, what, where, and why of current strikes anywhere in the world. This Web site also has extensive links to international labor unions. Want to form a student union organization? This is the place to look for support and more information. It also gives the reader a sense of how the Internet has contributed to the globalization of labor.

Migration Dialogue

http://migration.ucdavis.edu/

The University of California at Davis has created a Web site that "promotes an informed discussion of the issues associated with international migration by providing unbiased and timely information on immigration and integration issues." Most useful to you at this site is Migration News, which has up-to-date reports on migration issues in various states and regions of the world. Its archive allows you to search news by year and month, so you can track migration issues over time. Based on your exploration of the site's offerings, do you think there is a "global migration crisis"?

The Progress of Nations

http://www.unicef.org/pon99/

As described in the chapter, AIDS is a disease that has spread around the world through the process of globalization. The United Nations Children's Fund (UNICEF) has created a Web site that details the devastating impact of HIV/AIDS on children. Use this site to analyze the effects of AIDS on children in a variety of countries. Charts present a cross-country comparison of the number of children orphaned by AIDS and the impact it has had on their lives. What country's children are most affected by the AIDS epidemic?

Telecom Information Resources on the Internet

http://china.si.umich.edu/telecom/telecom-info.html

The University of Michigan has produced a Web site that references information sources related to technical, economic, public policy, and social aspects of telecommunications (voice, data, video, wired, wireless, cable television, and satellite). Map 9.1 displays the uneven distribution of Internet connections around the world, offering evidence to support the concern that the globalization of telecommunications will be concentrated in the Global North. As you visit the Telecom site, see if you can find additional evidence that substantiates this concern. Click on Broadcasters to link to every television and radio broadcaster in the world. Count how many broadcasters are in each country; you will be amazed at the number in the United States.

CHAPTER 10

POPULATION POLITICS AND THE DEMOGRAPHIC DIMENSIONS OF GLOBALIZATION

TOPICS AND THEMES

- The tragedy of the global commons
- Global demographic trends
- Further factors affecting population
  HIV/AIDS
  Migration
- How population policy colors world politics
- The international response to population issues
  The subordinate status of women and its consequences
  The ICPD program of action

- **CONTROVERSY** HOW MANY PEOPLE CAN THE EARTH SUPPORT?

A railway station in Bombay, India, on the day world population reached 6 billion, October 12, 1999.

If fertility remained at current levels, [world] population would reach the absurd figure of 296 billion in just 150 years. . . . There are six billion of us already, a number the world strains to support.

—Bill McKibben, futurist, 1998

Reducing population growth [helps] both to stimulate economic growth and to reduce levels of poverty and income inequality.

—Steven W. Sinding, Rockefeller Foundation director of population sciences, 1999

Increasing numbers of people are populating the planet, and globalization is bringing them closer together in an interconnected, interdependent, and crowded global village. Population growth is transforming how people interact. At the same time, the planet's **carrying capacity**—its ability to support human and other life forms—is not unlimited, so the population explosion threatens to undermine humanity's long-term prospects for survival. The bulk of **demographic** evidence points to the possibility that unrestrained population growth will result in lost economic opportunities, environmental degradation, domestic strife, and incentives—perhaps imperatives—for governmental restraints on individuals' freedom to make choices about having children. A world interdependent economically as well as ecopolitically is certain to share the costs of unrestrained population growth, and this problem has made population policy a key political issue on the global agenda of the twenty-first century.

■ **carrying capacity** the maximum biomass that can be supported by a given territory.

■ **demography** the study of population changes, their sources, and their impact.

This chapter and the next explore how changes in demography, the environment, and resources influence world politics. Here we focus on demographic variables—how global trends in births, deaths, migration, and their correlates are likely to shape the world's future. This sets the stage for Chapter 11, in which we examine the relationship between environmental and resource trends and the widely shared goals of security and development.

POPULATION GROWTH AS A GLOBAL POLITICAL PROBLEM: THE TRAGEDY OF THE COMMONS

The **tragedy of the commons** is a metaphor that highlights the potential impact of human behavior on the planet's resources and its delicately balanced ecological systems. It is a kind of shorthand for situations in which "people so impinge on each other in pursuing their own interests that collectively they might be better off if they could be restrained, but no one gains individually by self-restraint." The commons metaphor is a part of a broad set of situations "in which some of the costs or damages of what people do occur beyond their purview, and they either don't know or don't care about them" (Schelling 1978).

■ **tragedy of the commons** a metaphor, widely used to explain the impact of human behavior on ecological systems, that says that rational self-interested behavior by individuals may have a destructive collective impact.

First articulated in 1833 by English political economist William Foster Lloyd and later extended to contemporary problems by human ecologist Garrett Hardin, the *common* dates back to medieval English villages, where the "green" was common property on which all villagers could graze their cattle. Freedom of access to the commons was a cherished village value, and sharing the common grazing area worked well as long as the number of cattle did not exceed the land's carrying capacity. Should that happen, the pasture would be ruined and the number of cattle the common property could sustain would be drastically reduced. Which path would the village herders take—preserving the village green or ruining it? In the absence of restraints on human freedom—and assuming the villagers were driven by the profit motive—herders had a maximum incentive to increase their stock as much as possible. Although the village green eventually would be destroyed if they all behaved this way, in the short run the addition of one more animal would produce a personal gain whose costs would be borne by everyone. Self-interest thus encouraged all herders to increase their stock indiscriminately and discouraged self-sacrifice for the general welfare. In the end, however, the collective impact of their individual efforts to maximize private gain led to more cattle on the village green than it could sustain, with the inevitable result: destruction of the common property. "Ruin is the destination toward which all men rush," Hardin (1968) concluded, "each pursuing his own best interest in a society that believes in the freedom of the commons."

The tragedy of the commons provides insight into numerous global issues created by population pressure. How many people can the earth support? What are the costs of population growth to human freedom, human welfare, and many environmental issues (see Soroos 2001), ranging from excessive fishing of the oceans to transboundary pollution caused when industries spew toxic wastes into the atmosphere? Procreation is a major "unregulated" freedom. "The most important aspect of necessity that we must now recognize," Hardin (1968) wrote, "is the necessity of abandoning the commons in breeding. Freedom to breed will bring ruin to all. . . . The only way we can preserve and nurture other and more precious freedoms is by relinquishing the freedom to breed, and that very soon. . . . Only so, can we put an end to this aspect of the tragedy of the commons."

■ **ethics**
the criteria by which right and wrong behavior and motives are distinguished (see p. 606).

Not everyone will agree with the **ethics** of Hardin's arguments (see also Hardin 1993). Indeed, the freedom to procreate is a major unregulated *decision,* and few choices are more intensely personal, valued, or intimately tied to the social and cultural fabric of a society than those that free people make about marriage and family. Some regard the freedom to parent as a human right. Others claim that controls on family size are unnecessary because the ultimate carrying capacity of the global ecosystem is unknown and the impact of unregulated population growth on social well-being and environmental quality remains unclear. For this reason, **politics** governs debates about population policies. To understand why this issue has become so controversial, it is helpful to trace the global trends in population growth that have made the topic so problematic.

■ **politics**
the type of situation or issue that arises when people have opposing views about a problem and each conflicting party seeks to resolve the dispute to its own satisfaction at the other party's expense (see p. 457).

ASSESSING GLOBAL DEMOGRAPHIC TRENDS

The dramatic growth in world population in the twentieth century was historically unprecedented. It took 2 million years for the world population to reach 1 billion in 1804, but only until 1927 to reach 2 billion. Since then, additional billions have been added even more rapidly: 3 billion was reached by 1960, 4 billion in 1974, and 5 billion in 1987 (see Figure 10.1). The sixth billionth human arrived on the eve of the twenty-first century. How is this series of ever larger, increases possible? Because world population grows by nearly ten thousand *each hour of every day* and is increasing at a record pace; "we add a New York city every month, almost a Mexico every year, almost an India every decade" (McKibben 1998, 56). If present trends continue uninterrupted, world population will grow to 7.5 billion in 2015, hit 9.8 billion in 2050, and reach 10 billion only a few years later—about the time most of today's college students will be drawing retirement benefits. Indeed, most students reading this book will have witnessed the largest population surge ever to have occurred in a single generation—theirs.

As difficult as it may be to imagine a world with half again as many people as today, 10 billion is less than what was once projected for the middle of the twenty-first century. The latest projection—what the United Nations (UN) calls its "medium variant" (the middle line among the three population projections in Figure 10.1)—depends on the assumption that the world fertility rate will continue to decline, as it has for more than a decade, and will eventually settle at a point where couples only replace themselves. Without that, population growth could be much more rapid in the first half of the twenty-first century, reaching 11.9 billion in the year 2050 (the top line in Figure 10.1), nearly five times the 1950 population. In either case, world population will continue to grow throughout the twenty-first century and into the twenty-second. On the other hand, should birthrates slow more rapidly, world population would also grow more slowly and eventually settle at a level much lower than now seems most likely (the bottom line in Figure 10.1).

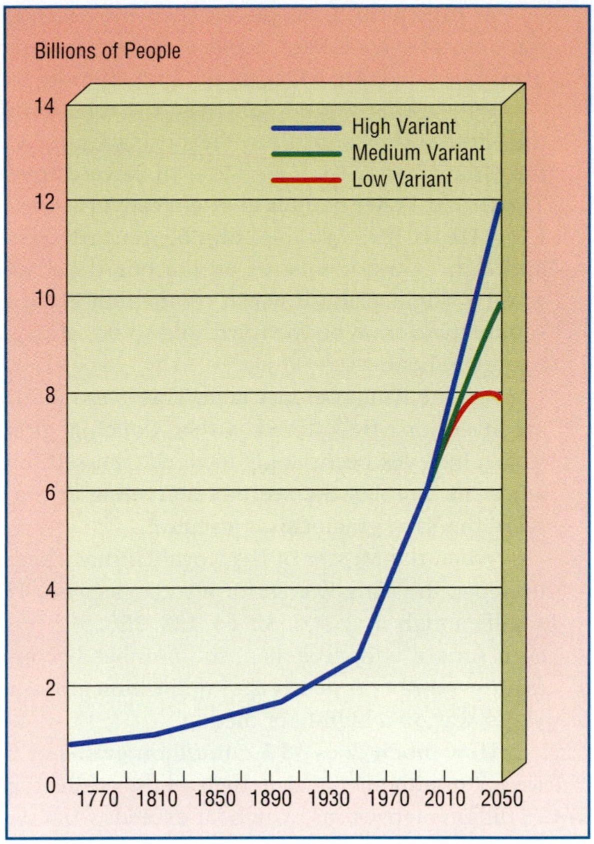

FIGURE 10.1 World Population Growth, 1750 to 1999 and Projected to 2050

World population in the twentieth century has grown from fewer than 2 billion people to 6 billion, with each billion added in less time than the previous billion. Between 2 and 4 billion more will be added between now and the fifth decade of the twenty-first century. Changes in world fertility rates and life spans will determine the exact number.

SOURCE: Adapted from United Nations (1995), 101, 226–227, 234–235, 242–243.

Understanding Growth Rates: The Persian Chessboard

The rapid growth of world population since 1927 is described by a simple mathematical principle articulated in 1798 by the Reverend Thomas Malthus: unchecked, population increases in a geometric or exponential ratio (e.g., 1 to 2, 2 to 4, 4 to 8, etc.), whereas subsistence increases in only an arithmetic ratio (1 to 2, 2 to 3, 3 to 4). When population increases at such a geometric rate, the acceleration can be staggering. Carl Sagan provides a telling illustration of this principle governing growth rates with a parable he termed "The Secret of the Persian Chessboard":

> The way I first heard the story, it happened in ancient Persia. But it may have been India, or even China. Anyway, it happened a long time ago. The Grand Vizier, the principal adviser to the King, had invented a new game. It was played with moving pieces on a board of 64 squares. The most important piece was the King. The next most important piece was the Grand Vizier—just what we might expect of a game invented by a Grand Vizier. The object of the game was to capture the enemy King, and so the game was called, in Persian, shahmat—shah for king, mat for dead. Death to the King. In Russia it is still called shakhmaty, which perhaps conveys a lingering revolutionary ardor. Even in English there is an echo of the name—the final move is called "checkmate." The game, of course, is chess.

> As time passed, the pieces, their moves and the rules evolved. There is, for example, no longer a piece called the Grand Vizier—it has become transmogrified into a Queen, with much more formidable powers.
>
> Why a king should delight in the creation of a game called "Death to the King" is a mystery. But, the story goes, he was so pleased that he asked the Grand Vizier to name his own reward for such a splendid invention. The Grand Vizier had his answer ready: He was a humble man, he told the King. He wished only for a humble reward. Gesturing to the eight columns and eight rows of squares on the board he devised, he asked that he be given a single grain of wheat on the first square, twice that on the second square, twice that on the third, and so on, until each square had its complement of wheat.
>
> No, the King remonstrated. This is too modest a prize for so important an invention. He offered jewels, dancing girls, palaces. But the Grand Vizier, his eyes becomingly lowered, refused them all. It was little piles of wheat he wanted. So, secretly marveling at the unselfishness of his counselor, the King graciously consented.
>
> When the Master of the Royal Granary began to count out the grains, however, the King was in for a rude surprise. The number of grains starts small enough: 1, 2, 4, 8, 32, 64, 128, 256, 512, 1,024. . . . But by the time the 64th square is approached, the number becomes colossal, staggering. In fact the number is nearly 18.5 quintillion grains of wheat. Maybe the Grand Vizier was on a high-fiber diet.
>
> How much does 18.5 quintillion grains of wheat weigh? If each grain were 2 millimeters in size, then all the grains together would weigh around 75 billion metric tons, which far exceeds what could have been stored in the King's granaries. In fact, this is the equivalent of about 150 years of the world's present wheat production. (Sagan 1989, 14)

To picture in another way how growth rates unfold, consider how money deposited in a savings account grows as it earns interest not only on the original investment but also on the interest payments. If each of our ancestors had put a mere 10 dollars in the bank for us two hundred years ago, and it accrued a steady 6 percent annual interest, today we would all be millionaires! Population grows in the same way: It is a function of increases in the original number of people plus those accruing from past population growth. Thus a population growing at a 1 percent rate will double in sixty-nine years, while a population growing at a 2 percent rate will double in only thirty-five years. (The impact of different growth rates on doubling times can be calculated by dividing 69 by the percentage of growth.)

The principles that define growth rates explain why "growth is the defining feature of the twentieth century, and has become the *de facto* organizing principle for societies around the world. Although growth rates have risen and fallen, the total scale of human activity has expanded continually, reaching levels that would have been unimaginable in earlier centuries" (Brown et al. 1999). The story of population growth is told in its statistics: The annual rate of population growth in the twentieth century increased from less than 1 percent in 1900 to a peak of 2.2 percent in 1964. It has since dropped to 1.4 percent since then. Despite the change in rate, however, the absolute number of people added continued to grow, from 16 million in 1900 to a peak of 87 million in 1990. It has fallen to 80 million new people per year and is expected to remain at that level for another two decades (Brown et al. 1999, 8). These figures tell us that the planet in the twenty-first century will have more people, well beyond the 6 billion already roaming the planet. Yet the feared "population explosion" once believed certain to overwhelm the earth's resources is now expected to be far less dramatic than once thought by the year 2050.

If a catastrophic population explosion is not necessarily assured and the probability of continuing population growth to overwhelm a crowded planet is receding, why then does population remain such a political powder keg in world politics? The answers are numerous, but several salient features about population dynamics make demographic change the source of new global issues and problems.

The Demographic Divide between Global North and Global South

One key problem has to do with the fact that population growth rates are not the same throughout the world. Population is growing much more rapidly in the developing Global South countries than in the wealthy countries in the Global North, and the differentials are widening because in the next century nearly all the increase will take place in the Global South (mainly in its burgeoning cities) while the population of the industrialized world is actually expected to decline. In fact, population growth figures

> . . . for individual countries vary more than at any time in history. In some thirty-two countries, human numbers have stabilized, while in others they are projected to double or triple. With the exception of Japan, all the countries in the stable group are in Europe. The number of people in a dozen or so countries, including Russia, Japan, and Germany, is actually projected to decline somewhat over the next half-century. In another forty countries, which account for nearly 40 percent of the global total, fertility has dropped to at least replacement level—roughly two children per couple. Among the countries in this category are China and the United States, the world's first and third most populous nations. In contrast to this group, some developing countries are projected to triple their populations over the next half-century. For example, Ethiopia's current population of 59 million is due to reach 213 million in 2050, while Pakistan's 147 million are likely to become 357 million, surpassing the projected population of the United States before 2050. Nigeria, meanwhile, is projected to go from 122 million today to 339 million—more people than in all of Africa in 1950. The largest absolute increase is anticipated for India, which is likely to add nearly 600 million by 2050, eclipsing China as the most populous country. Scores of smaller countries also face potentially overwhelming population growth. (Brown et al. 1999, 8–9)

The globe has become, and will remain, demographically divided as the incremental contributions of the Global South to the globe's population is responsible for almost all of that increase. "Whereas 79 percent of the annual increase in world population between 1950 and 1955 originated in the less developed regions, 95 percent of the increment between 1990 and 1995 originated in those regions. It is expected that by 2045–2050 *all* the net population growth in the world will arise in the less developed regions, as the population of the more developed regions is expected to be declining in absolute numbers" (United Nations 1995a, 147). This "demographic divide," as projected in Figure 10.2, explains a large part of the problem making population such a hot political issue.

Because population growth is occurring in precisely those countries least able to support a growing number of people, the high fertility rate in the developing world means that global population cannot be expected to stabilize until it falls below replacement-level fertility. In 1999, the worldwide average number of children born to a woman during her lifetime—the total **fertility rate**—was around 3.0, at which rate the world population would double in forty-seven years. However, "these global summaries disguise two different worlds: the rich and the poor" (Cohen 1998). Although the world's population added 78 million people in 1998 (equal to another Germany), "nearly all of these people were added in the developing countries, already home to 4.85 billion people—more than 80 percent of the world" (*Vital Signs 1999,* 98). Hence, global population growth is the result of new births in the developing Global South, where the average fertility rate was on average 3.4 children for each mother, in contrast to the wealthy developed Global North where the fertility rate has actually declined to 1.6 children for each woman, which is below **replacement-level fertility** (each couple replacing itself with two children).

■ **fertility rate** the average number of children born to a given group of women in a lifetime.

■ **replacement-level fertility** one couple replacing itself with two children.

These numbers are sharply lower than in the 1960s and 1970s, thus helping to slow the rate of global population growth to its present level. Still, "world population can be stable only if fertility rates around the world average out to 2.1 children per woman" to fall to replacement level (Singer 1999). Yet throughout much of the Global South, the preferred family size remains far in excess not only of the replacement level but also of the present world fertility rate of about 3 percent. Among the world's largest states, for example, China is the only Global South country that has achieved the replacement plateau. The numbers are especially startling in sub-Saharan African states such as Nigeria, where the region's fertility rate stood at 6.2 in 1995.

The developing countries' high fertility rates have important economic consequences. Those higher rates in the Global South combined with the sheer number of children already born are largely responsible for the fact that fractious differences in wealth between the Global South and the Global North are likely to widen. Almost all the problems in the North-South dispute can be traced to these stark differences in wealth, and the disparities in income and economic growth are directly linked to the differentials in population growth rate. A brief look at these dynamics completes the picture underlying the global problem of ongoing political conflict between the haves and the have-nots.

Population Momentum

The surge in the Global South's population in the twentieth century is easily explained as a combination of high birthrates and rapidly falling death rates. But to understand the population surge projected throughout the twenty-first century—when birth rates throughout the world will decline—we have to understand the force of **population momentum,** the continued growth of population for decades into the future because of the large numbers of women now entering their childbearing years. Like the inertia of a descending airliner when it first touches down on the runway, population growth simply cannot be halted

■ **population momentum** the concept that population growth will continue for several decades after replacement-level fertility is achieved.

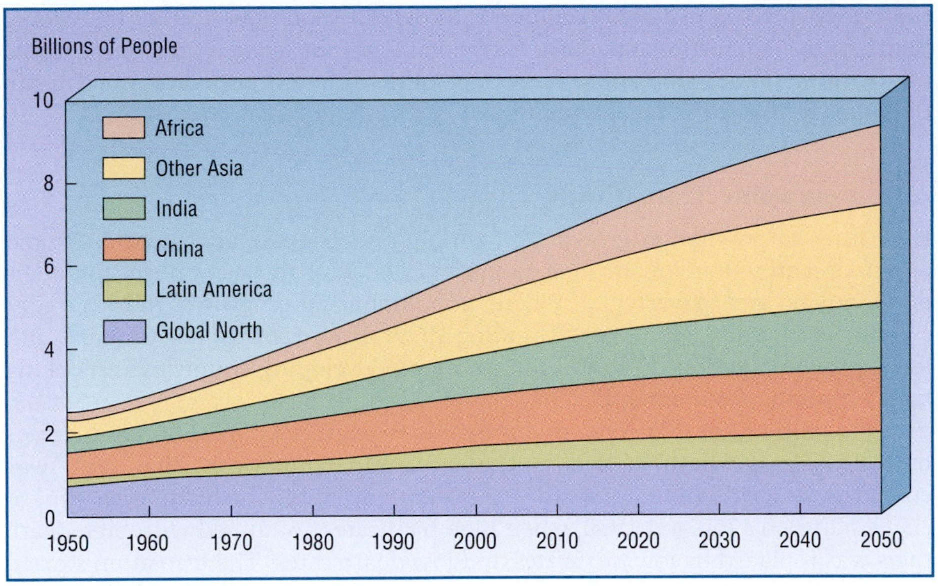

FIGURE 10.2
The Demographic Divide, 1950–2050

Nearly all of the world's population growth in the next half-century will occur in the Global South, with Africa growing most rapidly. By the middle of the twenty-first century, the absolute number of people in the Global North is expected to be declining.

Note: Projections are based on United Nations medium variant estimates shown in Figure 10.1.

SOURCE: Adapted from United Nations (1995b), 213–214, 588, 674.

even with an immediate, full application of the brakes. Instead, many years of high fertility mean that more women will be entering their reproductive years than in the past. Not until the size of the generation giving birth to children is no larger than the generation among which deaths are occurring will the population "airplane" come to a halt.

The impact of the existing base population on future growth was made evident in 1998. That year, world population increased even though the rate of growth had fallen to 1.4 percent from the record high of 2.2 percent in 1964: the 2.2 percent growth rate in 1964 added 69 million more people, but the 1.4 percent growth rate in 1998 added 78 million people, swelling the global total to 5.92 billion (*Vital Signs 1999*, 98). Hence, the momentum created by the past population base limits the significance of a declining growth rate.

Western Europe and Sub-Saharan Africa also illustrate the force of population momentum. Africa's demographic profile is one of rapid population growth, as each new age group (cohort) contains more people than the one before it. Thus, even if individual African couples choose to have fewer children than their parents, Africa's population will continue to grow because there are now more men and women of childbearing age than ever before. In contrast, Europe's population profile is one of slow growth, as recent cohorts have been smaller than preceding ones. In fact, Europe has moved beyond replacement-level fertility to become a "declining" population, described by low birthrates and a growing number of people who survive middle age. A product of an extended period of low birthrates, low death rates, and increased longevity, Europe's age structure is best described as that of a "mature" or "old" society, where the low birthrates and aging populations have caused alarms that "there are too few newborns in Europe to renew populations" (Specter 1998).

As the Global North generally ages, much of the Global South continues to mirror the Sub-Saharan African profile. Because each cohort is typically larger than the one before it, the number of young men and women entering their reproductive years will also continue to grow. The consequences of the Global South's now proportionately larger fertile age groups is why the demographic momentum already in place will produce quite different population profiles in the developed and the developing worlds.

A Demographic Transition?

High rates of population growth are, simply put, punitive and painful. "Rapid population growth in low-income countries condemns those countries to underdevelopment and poverty. . . . Where populations have grown most rapidly, economies have done the worst" (Sinding 1999). How can the poor Global South escape the population explosion that in many developing countries is blocking their economic development?

■ **demographic transition**
the low or stable population levels that tend to be achieved when the ratio of birthrates to death rates undergoes significant change.

One path out of this economic prison is to engineer population reductions by following the path known as **demographic transition.** That term was coined to describe the change that Europe and, later, North America experienced between 1750 and 1930, when high birthrates combined with high death rates was replaced by low birthrates and low death rates. The transition started when death rates began to fall—presumably due to economic growth, rising living standards, and improved disease control. Although the potential for substantial population growth was high, birthrates soon began to decline as well. During this phase of the demographic transition, the rate of population growth slowed. In fact, growth rates rarely exceeded 1.5 percent per year.

Demographic transition is now under way virtually everywhere in the world (Lutz 1994), but at much different rates in different countries and regions. With the exception of about twenty-five states now at near-replacement levels, the experience of the Global South differs greatly from that of Europe and North America, where death rates declined slowly. In most of the Global South, death rates have declined rapidly, largely as a result of more effective "death-control" measures introduced by the outside world. A population explosion inevitably followed.

The experience of the Indian Ocean island of Mauritius illustrates the interplay of changing birth and death rates as underlying long-term factors in demographic transitions. Following the eradication of malaria and the introduction of modern medical technology after World War II, the death rate dropped abruptly; however, birthrates remained high, and the population of Mauritius grew rapidly. It was not until much later when the fertility rate fell that the average number of children born to each woman declined from six to less than three, slowing the growth rate of Mauritius's population. India provides another example of the barriers to slowing the rate at which population increases until the full effects of a demographic transition occur. India's total fertility rate dropped from 4.3 in 1985 to 3.2 in 1996 but because of India's already massive population size, nearly 25 million children were born that year. Despite the drop in fertility, India's population is expected to reach 1.5 billion by 2050 (*Vital Signs 1997*, 80).

There are two ways that changes in birth and death rates enable demographic transitions to develop. First, a decline in death rates can itself stimulate a decline in birthrates. When people begin to expect to live longer lives, couples begin "to realize that more of their children will live to adulthood, and therefore, to feel secure that they can have fewer births and still achieve their desired number of surviving children" (Lutz 1994). Second, demographic transitions are a by-product of **modernization,** which produces value changes about the preferred size of family. In traditional low-income societies children are economic bonuses because they contribute to the family income; as modernization proceeds, they can become economic burdens, inhibiting social mobility and capital accumulation. "In most every country where people have moved from traditional ways of life to modern ones, they are choosing to have too few children to replace themselves." Modernization changes family values and drives fertility rates toward the replacement level; a demographic transition then commences followed by low or no population growth. "As long as people prefer saving effort and money by having fewer children, population will continue to decline" (Singer 1999).

■ **modernization** a view of development popular in the Global North's liberal democracies that argues that wealth is created through efficient production, free enterprise, and free trade, and that countries' relative ability to create wealth depends on technological innovation and education.

These two paths to demographic transitions are not mutually exclusive. They may in fact be at work simultaneously in much of the Global South, where declines in birth and death rates have often occurred in tandem. Mauritius is again instructive: Its fertility rate fell by half in a single decade "on a strictly voluntary basis—the result of high levels of literacy and education for women—together with successful family-planning programs" (Lutz 1994). Demographic transitions typically involve four phases: (1) high birthrate, high death rate; (2) high birthrate, falling death rate; (3) declining birthrate, relatively low death rate; (4) low birthrate, low death rate. Yet in such different places as Costa Rica in Central America, Tunisia in North Africa, and Sri Lanka in South Asia, some Global South countries are seemingly stuck between the second and third stages of the transition: Death rates have fallen to very low levels, but fertility rates seem to have stabilized well above replacement level. Does the reason lie in social attitudes toward family size that remain unchanged by modernization—unlike in Europe, North America, or some newly emerging economies (NIEs) in the Global South? Or is it caused by inadequate education and family-planning programs?

In both cases, women's role in society is critical, as are changes that occur in the values that national cultures embrace. Affecting both of these determinants is the political economy of family practice. Economics is probably the most important factor influencing which additional Global South countries will undergo demographic transitions. The level of poverty is a barrier to population control, because in the most impoverished countries children add to a family's labor force and provide future security for parents, especially for those who live in societies that have no public programs for the elderly. When the infant mortality rate is high, the incentives to have many offspring are even greater: The larger the number of children born, the greater the chance that some will survive. Infant and child (under-five) mortality rates have declined dramatically in the past three decades (UNDP 1999), but improvements have been slowest where poverty and population growth are most pervasive. Continuing population growth plagues vast numbers of people who remain extremely vulnerable to crushing poverty. "Measured by the common standard of $1 a day, 1.3 billion people in the developing world live in extreme poverty. Most of these people are in Asia. Eighty percent of the world's poor live in twelve countries—and 62 percent live in China and India. Many countries will be able to reduce poverty if they can sustain recent [economic] growth rates and avoid worsening income distribution, but others [the poorest of the poor in high-population growth countries] will need to grow much faster" (World Bank 1998, 14–15). The demographic divide between Global North and Global South is entrenched, and until the disparity is closed world population is likely to remain a global problem that breeds new disputes and difficulties.

An island of economic abundance surrounded by a sea of misery is bound to be precarious. But there are other trends underway that could make this forecast of an increasingly crowded planet, with poor countries growing in population and poverty while rich countries grow their wealth and reduce their population, less accurate. Many of the contemporary statistics and projections pointing to future population problems are purely demographic, and they can change in unpredictable ways. Furthermore, world population growth can and will change when human values change and policies are enacted that promote such value changes. For example, "the empowerment and education of women has now been accepted as a key contribution to reducing population growth [and many now see the value of] dividing the wealth and resources of the world more fairly" (Crump 1998).

In addition, the future of world politics may hinge on natural forces that have little to do with human values and choices but which nonetheless can transform the ways population growth and decline influence global decisions. Everything we now believe about the population problem could become obsolete if other demographic changes occur. "The old assumptions about world population trends need to be resolved. One thing is clear: the world is in for some rapid downsizing" and population redistributions (Singer 1999). We next identify some other global developments that could alter the debate over whether population really is a problem.

THE CHANGING POPULATION PYRAMID: FURTHER TRENDS AFFECTING POPULATION

Demographers emphasize fertility rates (births), mortality rates (deaths), and migration as the three basic factors that determine all population changes. Having already outlined some of the consequences of human choices about fertility, we need to look at the impact of mortality and migration more closely.

The Global Spread of HIV/AIDS

■ human immunodeficiency virus (HIV) a virus that can progress to acquired immune deficiency syndrome (AIDS).

■ acquired immune deficiency syndrome (AIDS) an often fatal condition that can result from infection with the human immunodeficiency virus (HIV).

Although infant and child mortality rates remain discouragingly high in much of the developing world, at least they are decreasing. Life expectancy at birth each year since 1950 has increased on a global average, climbing to a record peak at the start of 1999 to sixty-six years (*Vital Signs 1999*, 100); on the other side of the ledger, world population has swelled as a consequence. However, this trend in rising longevity could reverse if globally transmittable diseases cut into the extension of life spans made possible by improvements in health care, nutrition, water quality, and public sanitation. Throughout history the spread of bacteria, parasites, viruses, plagues, and diseases to various ecospheres, regardless of state borders, have suspended development or brought down once-mighty states and empires (see Watts 1998; Oldstone 1998). This possibility is made no more evident than in the spread of the **human immunodeficiency virus (HIV),** the virus that causes **AIDS (acquired immune deficiency syndrome).**

Since the onset of the AIDS pandemic in the late 1970s, the UN estimates the occurrence of new infections to be 18,000 each day and more than 5.8 million each year. The number of those already HIV-infected is believed to have climbed to 50 million. Because 34 million of those infected are alive today, a record number of new HIV infections and AIDS deaths have been recorded each year since 1980 and "is expected to keep climbing" (*Vital Signs 1999,* 102). As many as 150 million globally could be infected with the often fatal virus in the year 2000 (Pear 1997, 1). Two-thirds of those infected live in Africa, and, "barring a medical miracle, future AIDS deaths . . . will bring population growth to a halt. In Asia, the number of infected people expands rapidly [where] thriving commercial sex industries and growing drug use fuel the epidemics. . . . In India and China, the virus continues to spread beyond high-risk urban populations, such as prostitutes and intravenous drug users, to the general population where it is more difficult and costlier to contain" (*Vital Signs 1999,* 102).

More than 90 percent of new infections occur in the developing countries of the Global South, but the contagion respects no borders and is a truly global epidemic, killing throughout the world (see Map 10.1). Are world death rates thus destined to rise in the future, reversing the upward trend in world population? "Bacteria, parasites, and viruses exploit appropriate ecospheres wherever they find them, regardless of national boundaries" (Garrett 1988). The "age of AIDS" is a sobering reminder that population and power are heavily determined by natural phenomena in an era where what occurs anywhere often has consequences everywhere. The spread and control of infectious diseases—AIDS, Lassa fever, Ebola, mad cow disease, and so on—must be viewed as a global issue.

The spread of AIDS is difficult to predict because many cases go undiagnosed or unreported, particularly in the Global South. Furthermore, the virus that causes AIDS is hard to detect because of its long incubation period. The length of time between HIV infection and the possible progression to AIDS averages about ten years. Consequently, even if HIV infections could be immediately halted, the AIDS pandemic would continue. Three-quarters of new infections are the result of heterosexual contact, with approximately 3,500 women becoming infected each day. Of infants born to women with HIV/AIDS, 25 to 35 percent become infected in utero, during birth, or through breastfeeding (*Vital Signs 1997,* 84). HIV/AIDS has a certain, dark future, because "about 10 percent of all new infections are in children under 15, and more than half, the remainder, are in people 15 to 24" (Pear 1997, 6).

As the cumulative impact of HIV infections grows, the societal costs of AIDS climb. The ruinous economic effects in particular regions pose a threat to the entire global market economy because large portions of populations are unable to work and die young. In some African countries such as Kenya, Zimbabwe, and Botswana, one in four adults is infected and life expectancy has declined by one-third or more (Brown et al. 2000, 5–16). In addition, AIDS's impact on social structures and economic performance is even more devastating than its victims' numbers suggests; its spread mostly affects young and middle-aged people, thus heavily reducing income generation, family caregiving, and food production in countries where agriculture remains labor intensive.

HIV populations are likely to grow and AIDS will take a heavy toll, but it will not stop the world's relentless march toward an ever-larger total population in the mid-twenty-first century. Even in most countries where HIV infections

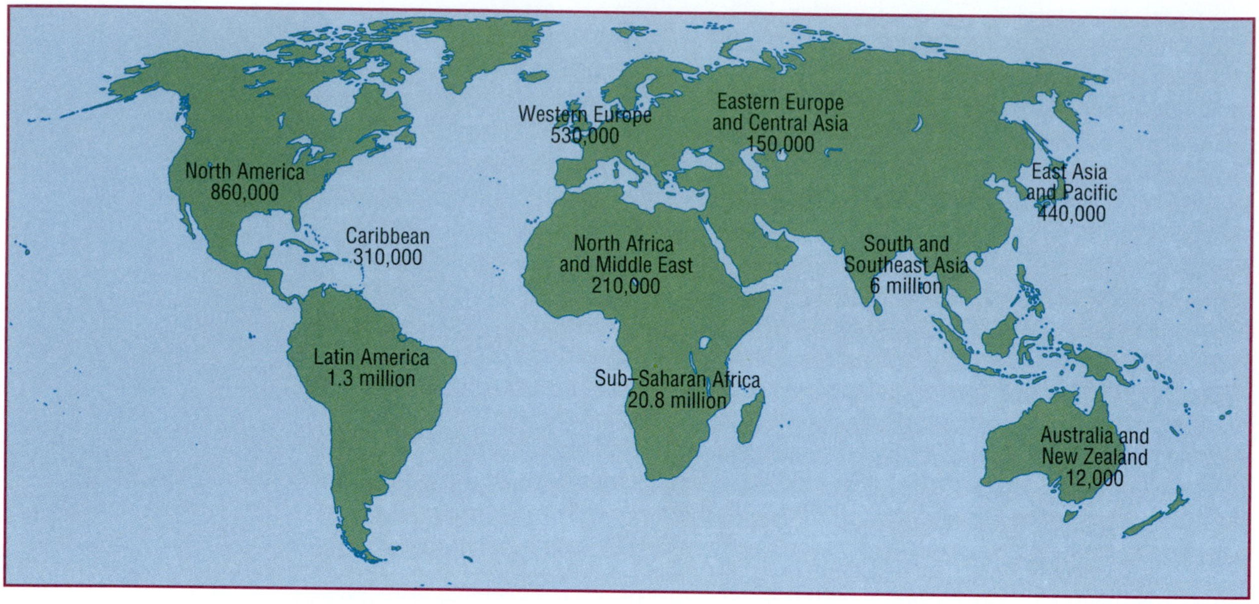

MAP 10.1
Global Levels of HIV

In 1997, the United Nations doubled its previous estimates of new cases of HIV infection. The estimated number of people who will die from AIDS worldwide was put at 2.3 million in 1997—up more than 50 percent from the 1.5 million who died from the disease in 1996. Africa is at the epicenter of the pandemic, where, "barring a medical miracle, these countries will lose one-fifth or more of their adult population" in the first decade of the twenty-first century (Brown et al. 2000, 4). However, as shown, no region of the world is unaffected by the rapid spread of this often fatal disease.

SOURCE: *International Herald Tribune* (November 27, 1997), 1.

are highest, national populations are likely to grow, because these countries also have the highest growth rates and population momentum.

Migration

Migration figures less prominently in long-range population projections, but is nonetheless relevant, as it becomes pervasive and politically controversial in many countries. Britain and France, for example, continue to receive large numbers of immigrants from their former colonies, while Israel has absorbed a flood of immigrants, particularly from Russia. The Middle Eastern oil producers also have received large numbers of migrants in recent years. And the United States, historically a refuge from religious and political persecution and a mecca of economic opportunity, continues to provide a home for millions from throughout the world. The 1980s witnessed the largest immigration into the United States since early in the twentieth century, but with an important difference: In the early part of the century nearly all of the immigrants came from Europe; since the 1980s, 80 percent came from Asia and Latin America, stimulated in part by the end of the Vietnam War and by political turmoil and civil strife in Cuba, El Salvador, Guatemala, Haiti, and Nicaragua.

The number of legal immigrants is difficult to determine but is believed to be in excess of 100 million, while the number of illegal immigrants is probably around 10 million. Thus "about 125 million people live outside the countries where they were born—it is as if the entire population of Japan had packed up and left" (Kane, 1995).

Migrants are of two types: refugees and those in search of economic opportunity. **Refugees** are individuals whose race, religion, nationality, membership in a particular social group, or political opinions makes them targets of persecution, and who escape by living outside the country of their origin or nationality and are unable to return to it. According to the UN High Commissioner for Refugees, the world's refugee population has grown since 1960, swelling rapidly since 1992 to an all-time peak of 27.4 million in 1995, after which it declined in 1999 to the still-staggering number of 21.5 million (see Figure 10.3). Combined, the totals between 1960 and 1999 exceed 360 million refugees, not counting another 56 million returnees (former refugees who have returned home) or 20 to 30 million internally **displaced people** living in situations similar to those of refugees but held hostage in their own countries and prevented from crossing their national border to freedom (*Vital Signs 1999,* 106).

■ **refugees**
people who flee for safety to another country because of a well-founded fear of persecution.

■ **displaced people**
people involuntarily uprooted from their homes but still living in their own countries (see p. 216).

Refugees and displaced persons alike are often the victims of war. The Persian Gulf War, for example, created a refugee population of 5 million. The war in Afghanistan caused a peak flight of 6.3 million people, and civil conflict and genocide in Rwanda in 1994 left more than 1.7 million still classified as refugees in 1997 (*Vital Signs 1997,* 82). The persecution, ethnic cleansing, and armed conflict that accompanied the breakup of the former Yugoslavia uprooted nearly 3 million victims, moving Europe to the list of continents with large numbers of refugees (6.1 million in 1998) for the first time since World War II (*Vital Signs 1999,* 106).

War—particularly ethnopolitical conflicts, which account for a large proportion of the world's refugees and displaced people—are one of the primary forces that propel many to make the difficult decision to flee their own homelands, especially where ethnic and religious conflicts erupt in failed states. If we understood the causes of internal and interstate war (a topic explored in Chapters 7 and 12), we could better understand the underlying roots of what many now see as a "global migration crisis" (Weiner 1995).

Human rights abuses must figure prominently in any assessment of why millions of people make the difficult decision to leave their homelands. "Refugees know that they cannot expect, at home, the protection of the police, access to a fair trial, redress of grievances through the courts, prosecution of those who violate their rights, or public assistance in the face of disaster. . . . Forcing people to flee is a violation of the human right to remain peacefully in one's home. The direct denial of other basic rights, including the rights of civilians not to be targeted in military actions, often provides the immediate impetus for flight" (Newland 1994).

■ **human rights**
the political rights and civil liberties recognized by the international community as inalienable and valid for individuals in all countries by virtue of their humanness (see p. 526).

People also leave home in search of opportunity. Legal migrants—particularly young people in the Global South without productive employment—are among those leaving at record rates. Germany and the United States are favored host (receiving) states, but nearly all of the states in western Europe and Japan have experienced a rising tide of migrants in recent years. Migration is occurring increasingly within the Global South. In fact, the bulk of today's migrants move from one developing country to another in search of opportunity (Weiner

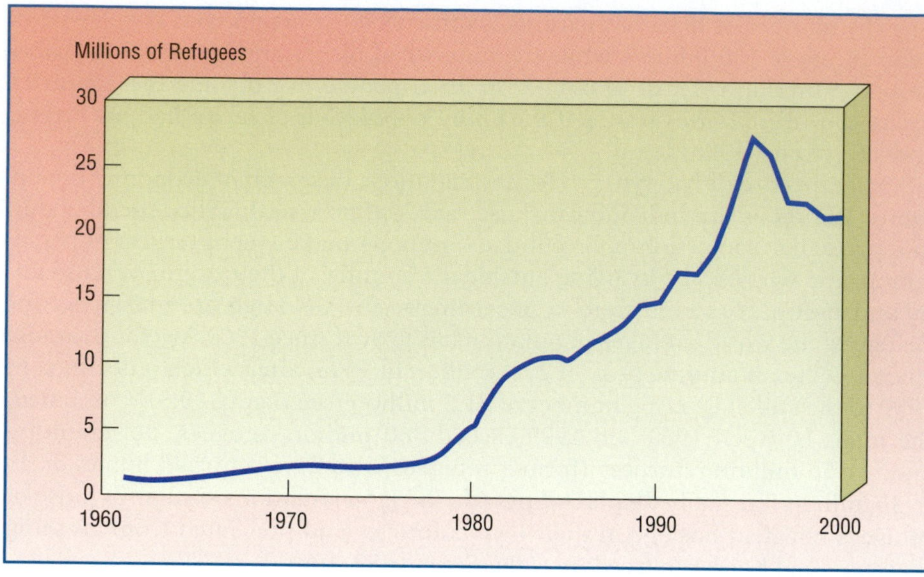

FIGURE 10.3
The Globe's Refugee Population, 1960–2000

The number of refugees receiving assistance from the United Nations has risen exponentially in the last four decades of the twentieth century. More than 350 million people have fled their home countries to avoid persecution. This mass exodus is a symptom of human rights abuses worldwide and a symbol of the globalization process that is creating a borderless world. Meanwhile, one estimate suggests that another 47 million people have been internally displaced, living like refugees in their own countries (Kidron and Segal 1995, 103).

SOURCE: UN High Commissioner for Refugees.

1995). But everywhere the pattern is the same: People leave poorer states in search of higher-paying jobs in richer states.

Migrants traveling to faraway lands often take jobs shunned by local inhabitants. Typically this means migrants earn less than the native people but more than they would earn in their homelands, even when performing the same tasks. Host countries sometimes welcome migrants (as Europe did during the 1970s' "guest worker" era) not only because they accept low wages for undesirable jobs, but also because in many places the host pays little if anything for migrants' health, education, and welfare needs. On the other hand, the home (sending) countries sometimes encourage people to emigrate as a way of reducing unemployment or exporting unwanted elements of the population, such as criminals. Often, however, many of those who leave their home states are the best educated and most talented, causing a serious "brain drain" that is rarely, if ever, reversed.

Migrants typically send considerable portions of their income to their families at home. "By the end of the [1980s], remittances [money sent home] amounted to more than $65 billion a year according to a World Bank study, second only to crude oil in their value to the world's economy, and larger than all official development assistance. Almost half of this money went to developing countries" (Kane 1995, 34).

Refugees of War In search of safety and freedom, more than two hundred thousand refugees flooded into Tanzania after civil war erupted in Rwanda in April 1994. Sparked by the death of the country's president in a suspicious plane crash, ethnic conflicts between the Hutu majority and Tutsi minority led to genocide as well as mass migration before the year was out.

Although receiving countries can benefit economically from migration (see Passel and Fix 1994), the influx of foreigners has become a matter of growing controversy everywhere.

> In many countries, citizens have become fearful that they are now being invaded not by armies and tanks but by migrants who speak other languages, worship other gods, belong to other cultures, and, they fear, will take their jobs, occupy their land, live off the welfare system, and threaten their way of life, their environment, and even their polity. . . . Virtually every country in western Europe now has a right-wing antiforeign political party or movement. . . .
>
> The sense of crisis is not confined to advanced industrial societies. . . . In portions of Pakistan, India, Bangladesh, Thailand, Mauritania, Senegal, Congo, Nigeria, and Libya, local citizens or their governments have turned against foreigners. (Weiner 1995, 2–3)

With **xenophobia** (fear of foreigners) on the rise, as illustrated by the Freedom Party under Jörg Haider in Austria whose racial rhetoric provoked condemnation by the EU in 2000, many among the growing number of refugees seeking asylum are finding the doors to safe havens closing. Security concerns stimulated by terrorist fears are sometimes at work—as in the United States, where many believe the New York World Trade Center bombing would not have occurred had immigration controls been tighter. More often, asylum seekers "are seen as migrants looking for better economic conditions rather than as

■ **xenophobia** the fearful dislike, disrespect, and disregard for members of a foreign nationality, ethnic, or linguistic group.

refugees with a well-founded fear of being persecuted" (UNDP 1994b). Those seeking political refuge in the United States also have suffered "guilt by association," as a wave of illegal immigrants has contributed to the rising tide of anti-immigrant sentiments in a country born of immigrants (see Clad 1994). Thus thousands of refugees from Haiti and Cuba, who earlier would have found safe haven in the United States, have been repatriated to their homelands or otherwise denied a chance to apply for political **asylum** in the United States.

■ **asylum**
protection given to refugees escaping the threat of persecution in their own country.

A combination of push and pull factors has propelled migration to the forefront of the globalization of population dynamics. Human rights violations, environmental degradation, international war, and ethnonational clashes and **atrocities** within states—all in some sense related to the Global South's rapidly expanding population—*push* millions beyond their homelands. They also are *pulled* abroad by the promise of political freedom and economic opportunity elsewhere, particularly in the Global North. Indeed, the recent growth of immigration "to the North from the South is related to the 'shrinking' of the world (through revolutions in communication and transport), reduction in economic obstacles to labor movements (despite the increase in political barriers), and the growing reach and absorptive power of international capitalism (even as economic politics in the North has turned more inward-looking and nationalistic)" (Sen 1994). Population growth may encourage outward migration, but "to try to explain the increase in immigration pressure by the growth rate of total population in the [Global South] is to close one's eyes to the deep changes that have occurred—and are occurring—in the world in which we live, and the rapid internationalization of its cultures and economies that accompanies those changes." Nonetheless, to many countries in the Global North, immigration has become the population "problem," and shutting the door is increasingly viewed as a solution.

■ **atrocities**
brutal and savage acts against targeted citizen groups or prisoners of war, defined as illegal under interanational law.

HOW POPULATION POLICY COLORS WORLD POLITICS

Migration is the primary way in which the globalization of population dynamics occurs, but population politics affect the globalized world in many other ways. Population is an issue area high on the global agenda. The importance and impact of population policy as a political problem is illustrated across many dimensions of world politics. Two, which cross the divide between the so-called **high politics** of international security and the **low politics** of the political economy of global food security, provide examples of the controversies caused by population changes in international affairs.

■ **high politics**
geostrategic issues of national and international security related to war and peace (see p. 247).

■ **low politics**
the category of global issues related to the economic, social, demographic, and environmental aspects of relations between governments and people (see p. 247).

The Demography of National Security Issues

Almost 98 percent of the growth in world population is now occurring in the Global South's developing countries, and this disproportionate rate of increase is projected to continue. As rapid population growth in the Global South makes the countries of the developed Global North a declining fraction of world population, concerns about the consequences for national security have risen. Realists argue that a country's population size is an important source of political power. The shrinking of the world's more economically prosperous states, as low fertility rates and aging populations in the Global North make it difficult to maintain large armies, may reduce their military power relative to the Global South, whose abundant youth can provide ample supplies of soldiers to fight the wars of the twenty-first century (see Table 10.1 and Figure 10.4).

Ironically, Global South economic progress over the next several decades may also accelerate a shift of the **balance of power** toward those experiencing rapid population growth. Some, in fact, already perceive power to have shifted toward those most prone to reject the Global North's values and to engage the West in a **clash of civilizations** (Huntington 1999). Most likely to convert population power into military power are those NIEs in the Global South where population increases coupled with rapid economic growth will give them advantages and global political clout in bargaining with the Global North. "Simple arithmetic demonstrates Western folly," a deputy secretary in Singapore's Foreign Ministry has written. "The West has 800 million people; the rest make up almost 4.7 billion. . . . No Western society would accept a situation where 15 percent of its population legislated for the remaining 85 percent" (cited in Connelly and Kennedy 1994).

■ **balance of power**
a measure of the amount of military power states or blocs hold in relation to each other (see p. 619).

■ **clash of civilizations**
political scientist Samuel Huntington's controversial thesis that in the twenty-first century the globe's major civilizations will conflict with one another, leading to anarchy and warfare similar to that resulting from conflicts between states over the past five hundred years (see p. 136).

The Demography of Global Food Security: The Clash of Optimists and Pessimists

The impact of population growth on national security and environmental quality has long been in dispute in international politics, and remains so. Particularly hot in recent years has been a new set of unconventional questions: Is the planet running out of food? If world population grows to 9 billion and food supplies are depleted, will too many people mean that many will be underfed and undernourished? Who will eat and who will starve? These kinds of questions make for a continuing controversy in international politics, with **neo-Malthusians** alarmed about future shortages of sufficient food debating **cornucopians** who claim these pessimists' concerns are unwarranted (see Controversy: How Many People Can the Earth Support?).

■ **neo-Malthusians**
pessimists who warn of the global ecopolitical implications of uncontrolled growth (see p. 368).

■ **cornucopians**
optimists who question limits-to-growth analyses and contend that markets effectively maintain a balance between population, resources, and the environment (see p. 368).

Determining which perspective is "right" is difficult, as history does not provide a clear answer. Furthermore, the range of opinion and conviction separating them is less clear than the labels suggest. As noted in Chapter 5, for example, the absolute gap in income between Global North and Global South continues, but the gap in human development between rich and poor countries has narrowed. Moreover, the relative economic position of many heavily populated countries within the Global South has improved with time, as their economies have grown more rapidly than their populations, but the total number of people living in absolute poverty continues to grow.

To make matters more complicated, consider whether overpopulation alone is really a cause of most current problems, or if instead it is just one factor that aggravates other problems, including unsustainable resource consumption, impractical government policies, political instability, and inadequate technology. The second viewpoint is suggested by the fact that the gloomiest of Thomas Malthus's predictions, made two centuries ago—that the world's population would eventually outstrip its capacity to produce enough food to sustain its growing numbers—has not come true. Malthus based his prognosis on what he regarded as the simple mathematical fact that population grows exponentially while agricultural output grows only arithmetically. He did not foresee that agricultural output would also grow at an increasing rate due to technological innovations.

TABLE 10.1 AND FIGURE 10.4
Rank by Size of the Twenty Largest Countries and Their Projected Population in 2050

	1998		*2050*	
Rank	Country	Population (million)	Country	Population (million)
1	China	1,255	India	1,533
2	India	976	China	1,517
3	United States	274	Pakistan	357
4	Indonesia	207	United States	348
5	Brazil	165	Nigeria	339
6	Russia	148	Indonesia	318
7	Pakistan	147	Brazil	243
8	Japan	126	Bangladesh	218
9	Bangladesh	124	Ethiopia	213
10	Nigeria	122	Iran	170
11	Mexico	96	The Congo	165
12	Germany	82	Mexico	154
13	Vietnam	78	Philippines	131
14	Iran	73	Vietnam	130
15	Philippines	72	Egypt	115
16	Egypt	66	Russia	114
17	Turkey	64	Japan	110
18	Thailand	62	Turkey	98
19	France	60	South Africa	91
20	Ethiopia	59	Tanzania	89

SOURCE: United Nations, as presented in Brown et al. (1999), 9; and Constable (1999), 16.

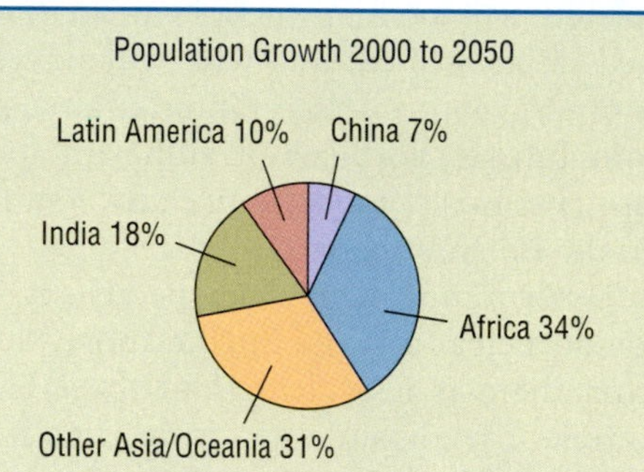

This forecast by the United Nations projects a new global hierarchy of population by state in the year 2050. Note that India is expected to surpass China's population about the year 2035, making the globe's so-called largest democracy the largest country in the world. According to realists, the power of states measured in their ability to compete militarily depends in part on the size of each state's relative population, from which governments recruit soldiers and sailors to wage wars. If this realist assumption is correct and if present population-growth trends continue in some Global South countries while other countries experience reductions in their population, someday the weak will be strong and the strong will be weak.

SOURCE: United Nations, as presented in Brown et al. (1999), 9; and Constable (1999), 16.

■ **green revolution** the introduction of new, high-yield grains to Global South developing countries.

Increases in the world's food output have been especially remarkable since World War II, far outstripping the largest-ever expansion of world population. The greatest gains occurred as a result of the increased productivity of farmers in the Global North. However, the Global South also obtained impressive results by expanding the acreage devoted to agriculture and, later, by introducing new high-yield strains of wheat and rice—what we now call the **"green revolution."** By the 1980s Indonesia, once a massive importer of food, had largely left the import market, and India, once regarded as a permanent

CONTROVERSY

How Many People Can the Earth Support?

Are there limits to the size of world population beyond which humanity will perish? Two thousand years ago, when the earth had about the same number of people as the United States does today, few would have pondered that question. They do now, however, because with 8 to 10 billion people expected to live on the Earth and consume what can be grown on it in the twenty-first century, the possibility has arisen that there will not be enough food to feed the world. If so, food scarcities will lead to famine and mass starvation, and countries will engage in "food fights" over agriculture products.

It is unclear whether this grim outcome will materialize, however. Demographic and environmental scientists are divided in their evaluations about the planet's future carrying capacity—the limits on its ability to supply the resources to sustain life on a planet teeming with a growing human population. The two major broadly defined groups of analysts approach these issues quite differently. Taking their name and orientation from Thomas Malthus and his classic 1798 *Essay on the Principle of Population,* the first group, neo-Malthusians, believe that world population is pushing against the earth's resources, straining its ability to meet the needs of this generation and the next. Sometimes called "growth pessimists," many neo-Malthusian ecologists point to a host of disconcerting facts about the present global condition: "Since Malthus wrote, the human population has grown by a factor of six, and total human energy use by a factor of one hundred or so. . . . The forest cover of the earth has been cut by a third and the area of undisturbed wetlands by half. The composition of the atmosphere has been altered by human-generated pollution. Hundreds of millions of people have starved to death; thousands of species have gone extinct" (Meadows 1993).

In contrast with the pessimism of neo-Malthusians, the second group, the cornucopians (many of whom are economists and otherwise known as "growth optimists") emphasize quite different global trends. Observing that global life expectancy has more than doubled since 1950 to sixty-six years and "a person born today will live twenty years—43 percent—longer than a person born in 1950" (*Vital Signs 1999,* 100), they conclude that rapid population growth has occurred not because human beings suddenly started breeding like rabbits but because they finally stopped dropping like flies. Despite the growth of global population from 1.6 billion in 1900 to more than 6 billion in 2000, cornucopians argue that "global health and productivity have exploded. Today human beings eat better, produce more, and consume more than ever. . . . 'Overpopulation' is a problem that has been misidentified and misdefined. The term has no scientific definition or clear meaning. The problems typically associated with overpopulation (hungry families, squalid and overcrowded living conditions) are more properly understood as issues of poverty." Although some blame dwindling natural resources for the reversals and catastrophes that have recently befallen heavily populated low-income countries, such episodes are directly traceable to the policies or practices of presiding governments (Eberstadt 1995).

States' policies and practices surrounding population will have an impact. Some governments understandably view too many people as a problem and will seek to control population growth. Other countries are facing the threat of shrinking populations and see additional people as critical to their future. These differences in national needs make population policies highly contentious, especially because divergent population policies affect everyone and will determine whether technological advances will be sufficient for the earth to provide enough resources for its people.

candidate for the international dole, had actually become a modest grain exporter.

Continued growth in world food production is uncertain, yet it is necessary if output is to keep pace with an expanding world population and improved living standards. Huge quantities of food will be necessary for a world that with today's population already finds 790 million people enduring hunger (Diouf 2000, 8).

Genetic Engineering in Agriculture A farmer in Tienman, China, cultivates a field using a new breed of cow, developed by researchers in Africa, that is strong enough to work in the field without reducing its capacity to produce milk or to breed. Many enthusiasts of genetically modified or transgenetic livestock and crops believe such new products will feed a growing world population. Critics, on the other hand, complain that genetic engineering through biotechnology is dangerous because it is harmful to public health and actually endangers the environment. "Far from being a solution to the world's hunger problem," complain some experts (Rosset 1999; see also Chapter 11), "the rapid introduction of genetically engineered crops may actually threaten agriculture and food security."

Cornucopians argue that continued advances can be expected as current resources are used more efficiently and high-yield farming practices continue to spread. They cite as evidence the green revolution resulting from scientific advances since the 1950s, such as pest-resistant hybrids that have raised crop yields per acre substantially for key grains such as rice, maize, wheat and rye. And they foresee few reasons why cross-breeding, biotechnology, and genetic engineering should fail to boost yields considerably in the future, while at the same time introducing new, efficient methods for protecting the environment from destruction. Among the impressive record of past accomplishments, particularly impressive is the degree to which world food production has grown. Shortages notwithstanding, "the half-century since 1945 has been a golden era of technological and economic wonders. For example, in constant prices, with the price in 1990 set equal to 100, total food commodity prices fell from 196 in 1975 to 76 in 1992. . . . For many economists, the decline proves that human welfare is improving" (Cohen 1998, 29). This achievement is well summarized, paradoxically, by the world's leading neo-Malthusian, Lester Brown:

> When [the twentieth] century began, each American farmer produced enough food to feed seven other people in the United States and abroad. Today, a U.S. farmer feeds 96 people. Staggering gains in agricultural productivity in the United States and elsewhere have underpinned the emergence of the modern world as we known it. Just as the discovery of agriculture itself set the stage for the emergence of early civilization, these gains in agricultural productivity have facilitated the emergence of our modern global civilization.
>
> This [was] a revolutionary century for world agriculture. Draft animals have largely been replaced by tractors; traditional varieties of corn, wheat, and rice have given way to high-yielding varieties; and world irrigated area has multiplied sixfold since 1900. The use of chemical fertilizers—virtually unheard of in 1900—now accounts for an estimated 40 percent of world grain production.

> Technological advances have tripled the productivity of world cropland during this century. They have helped expand the world grain harvest from less than 400 million tons in 1900 to nearly 1.9 billion tons in 1998. Indeed, farmers have expanded grain production five times as much since 1900 as during the preceding 10,000 years since agriculture began. (Brown et al. 1999, 115)

Neo-Maulthusians such as Lester Brown are quick to balance this optimistic picture with counterclaims, arguing that agricultural and other biological systems such as ocean fisheries will be unable to meet rising demand. Realizing the goal of global **food security** is in jeopardy, they point to the major disturbing trend that underlies their concern: Although food production has increased steadily, production per person has dropped significantly and is expected to decline precipitously by 2050 (see Figure 10.5). World food production may have grown by nearly 30 percent since the 1980s, but per capita production has remained stagnant and this means that because of continuing population growth food supplies will be inadequate to feed the world.

■ **food security**
access by all people at all times to enough food for an active, healthy life.

Neo-Malthusians point to other developments that suggest a less-than-rosy future, including the impact of rising affluence on global food supplies and the resources required to provide them. As wealth increases, people move up the **food ladder,** shifting their preferences from beans and rice to steak and chicken, asparagus and apricots. The culinary preferences of more affluent people also translate into proportionately higher demands on agricultural lands and water resources. Still, ascending the food ladder is the shape of things to come.

■ **food ladder**
the idea that as personal income increases, people change their diet to consume grains indirectly through meat rather than directly.

> China's meat consumption is currently rising by 3 million tons (and 10 percent) per year. Chinese meat consumption has traditionally been very low, but rising per-capita incomes are putting more meat within the reach of many more consumers. Indians do not eat much meat because of their predominant Hindu religion, but the demand for dairy products is rising by 2 million tons per year. Indonesia is Islamic, so its residents do not eat pork, and it has no extensive grazing lands for beef, but poultry consumption is rising at double-digit rates. All told, Asia's diet upgrading is the biggest surge in farm resource demand the world has ever seen. . . . And each ton of added protein demand will require three to five added tons of grain and oilseed production to provide feed to produce the additional animal protein. (Avery 1995, 51–52)

Thus, even as world population growth begins to level off, pressures on world food systems will continue their forward momentum.

Can the world's food-producing systems sustain the growing demand stimulated by population growth and rising affluence? The Worldwatch Institute warns that the earth's carrying capacity is limited and that its limits are rapidly approaching (see Brown et al. 1999). It argues that diminishing returns from fertilizer applications combined with soil erosion, growing water scarcity, and other environmental stresses already undermine the ability of national agricultural systems to provide for a growing world population.

China—which accounts for more than one-fifth of humanity—is especially worrisome. Drawing on the experience of Japan, South Korea, and Taiwan, Brown (1995) argues that the transformation of China from an agricultural to

FIGURE 10.5
Total Grain per Person since 1950, with Projections to 2050

Many human ecologists are concerned that there will not be sufficient food to feed the world in the twenty-first century. "Between 1950 and 1998, the grain harvested area per person worldwide shrank from 0.23 hectares to 0.12 hectares. For most countries this was not a problem because unprecedented rises in land productivity more than offset the shrinkage. Given the marked loss of momentum in raising land productivity since 1990, however, there is reason to doubt whether future increases can offset the projected shrinkage in cropland per person to 0.07 hectares by 2050" (L. Brown 1999, 121).

SOURCE: L. Brown (1999), 121.

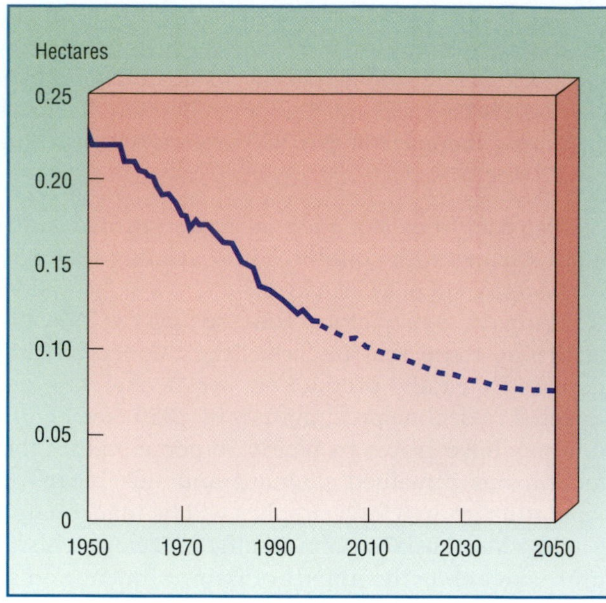

an industrial society has caused its food consumption to quickly outstrip production. Increasingly, then, China has had to turn to the world marketplace to feed its billion-plus residents. Evidence is seen in China's exponentially growing food imports from the United States, contributing to record U.S. agricultural exports. American farmers doubtless profited, but in a tightly integrated world market based on free-trade logic, prices everywhere can be expected to rise sharply as demand exceeds supply. Who feeds China may thus determine who goes hungry.

Africa's experience already seems to vindicate neo-Malthusians' pessimism. The continent's food production increased by less than 2 percent annually during the 1970s, but its population grew by nearly 3 percent. Starvation and death became daily occurrences in broad stretches of the Sahel, ranging from Ethiopia in the east to Mauritania in the west. The situation was repeated a decade later when, in Ethiopia in particular, the world witnessed the tragic specter of tens of thousands suffering and dying from malnutrition and famine at a time of unprecedented food surpluses worldwide.

As population growth has moved in concert with environmental degradation, Sub-Saharan Africa has experienced the tragedy of the commons in all of its most remorseless manifestations. Civil strife, ethnic bloodletting, and war have characterized postcolonial Africa, as conflicts affecting tens of millions of people have ravaged one-third or more of the countries in the region since the 1970s. In some cases, as in Ethiopia, Somalia, and the Sudan, food was actively used as a political weapon. The UN-U.S. humanitarian intervention in Somalia in 1992–1994 sought to curb these practices, but with limited success. Thus the words of Shun Chetty of the UN High Commissioner for Refugees retain their tragic pertinence: "He who controls roads controls food. He who controls food controls the people."

Growth optimists reject the Malthusian analogy as applied to Africa, particularly the prophecy that excessive population growth causes food deficits. War is not the *consequence* but the *cause* of famine, malnutrition, and starvation, cornucopians argue. "Famines come about when political systems fail to encourage agriculture and distribution successfully. And those political failures have a pattern: They occur in centralized, authoritarian systems. Free-market economics do not produce famines" (Avery 1995). Asia's recent experience also seems to vindicate cornucopian logic. The continent's per capita food production has outstripped that of all other world regions since the early 1980s, with China and Vietnam leading the pack as each moved toward market-based agricultural systems—and this despite large population increases.

Still, millions go hungry each day. Nearly 800 million people in Africa, Asia, Latin America, and the Middle East—representing 20 percent of humanity—suffer chronic undernutrition (UNDP 2000). Neo-Malthusians urge that, on moral grounds alone, population growth must be stemmed so that those who now suffer most can be relieved. In practice, however, the issue is not a lack of food but its maldistribution. According to the microeconomic principle known as **Engels's law,** poorer families typically spend a much higher percentage of their budget on food than do higher income groups. Yet the ability to acquire more food depends on having the income necessary to buy it. "Most people who stop eating do so not because there is insufficient food grown in the world but because they no longer grow it themselves and do not have the money to buy it" (Barnet 1980). From this perspective, poverty—not overpopulation—is the cause of the food deficits so many countries and people experience. But what causes poverty? And what are its cures? Neo-Malthusians and cornucopians both speak to this issue, and each offers a rival interpretation about if and how **sustainable development**—meeting the present generation's need without compromising the ability of future generations to meet their needs—can best be achieved. Both perspectives recognize the danger of **ecological overshoot** if the earth's carrying capacity is destroyed by excessive consumption and overpopulation, and both acknowledge the threat presented worldwide by continuing soil erosion, **desertification,** and **deforestation** if ecological degradation is not arrested (see Chapter 11). However, neo-Malthusians and cornucopians disagree about the magnitude of the potential population-environmental problem and how best to cope with it. But who is right?

THE INTERNATIONAL RESPONSE TO POPULATION ISSUES

A quarter-century has passed since the world community convened its first World Population Conference to address the world's growing population, then already concentrated in the Global South. Meeting in Bucharest in 1974, many delegates from the Global South concluded from Europe's and North America's demographic transitions that declining fertility rates flowed more or less automatically from economic growth. Thus they understandably prescribed policies that focused on economic development rather than population control. They called on the Global North for assistance in their economic development, reasoning that the population problem would then take care of itself. The slogan "development is the best contraceptive" reflected the prevailing view. Many in the Global North, on the other hand, advocated a more direct attack on what

■ Engels's law
the Marxist economist Friedrich Engels's principle of consumption, which predicts that poor people spend their limited income on necessary goods, whereas the rich spend wealth on unnecessary luxuries.

■ sustainable development
economic growth engineered by policies and practices that do not destroy the environment in order to subsidize quick development and short-term profits for producers (see p. 368).

■ ecological overshoot
exploitation of natural resources to a point that exceeds the earth's carrying capacity.

■ desertification
the creation of deserts due to soil erosion, overfarming, and deforestation, which convert cropland to nonproductive, arid sand (see p. 389).

■ deforestation
the destruction of forests (see p. 388).

they saw as "the population problem"—namely, excessive population growth that erodes economic opportunities and imperils other values.

A decade later, a second World Population Conference was held in Mexico City. By then a new consensus had converged around the critical importance of family planning. Curiously, the United States, previously a major advocate of this viewpoint, departed from this emerging global consensus. Reflecting the conservative political sentiments prevalent in Washington at the time, the U.S. delegation asserted that free-market principles should take precedence over government intervention in economic and population matters. The Reagan adminstration also vigorously opposed abortion as an approach to family planning. China became the object of special ire, prompted by a television exposé of its family-planning practices, which included "human rights abuses . . . [ranging] from mandatory sterilization and abortion to forced insertions of IUDs, all committed in the name of slowing the country's runaway population growth" (Moffett 1994). The United States began to withhold support for multilateral as well as bilateral efforts to assist family-planning programs in developing countries, slowing their spread throughout the Global South.

Although the views of the United States in 1984 clearly represented a minority perspective, they reflected growing dissatisfaction with earlier neo-Malthusian analyses of the global ecopolitical implications of population growth. Instead, the U.S. position in Mexico City reflected that of cornucopians, who argue that human ingenuity has developed resource-saving (or -substituting) innovations in response to shortages created by population growth, so that population growth is a stimulus, not a deterrent, to economic advancement.

The United States reversed its course following Bill Clinton's election in 1992. Restrictions that denied U.S. funds to some family-planning organizations because of abortion-related activities were lifted almost immediately. Bilateral and **multilateral** aid designed to support population activities soon began to flow more liberally. The Clinton administration also embraced the premise—effectively denied during the 1980s—that population pressures aggravate social, economic, and environmental problems and may cause political instability. Robert D. Kaplan's (1994) shockingly pessimistic account of "the coming anarchy" in West Africa, stimulated by overpopulation and environmental degradation, not only captured the attention of Washington policymakers but also encapsulated their convictions.

■ **multilateral** actions and activities pursued by three or more states to cooperatively manage common problems.

The debate between optimists and pessimists continues. By 1994, however, when the UN convened its third decennial World Population Conference in Cairo, it had moved in new directions. As suggested by the conference title, "International Conference on Population and Development (ICPD)," population and development were now to be considered together. Thus the ICPD moved beyond population numbers and demographic targets, embracing instead the view that population stabilization can be achieved only in the larger context of human development and sustainable economic growth. In 1999, the UN General Assembly resumed its debate about its previous plans to limit world population growth, with developing Global South countries remaining deeply divided over proposed population-control programs. Some Global North developed countries also took issue with Secretary-General Kofi Annan's position in the opening session that "We have to stabilize the population of this planet." That same year, more than one hundred countries gathered at the Hague to review problems in carrying out the consensus commitment that emerged at the 1994 Cairo conference, which emphasized the need to take a humane, non-coercive approach to population stabilization.

The Subordinate Status of Women and Its Consequences

In all population conferences in the twentieth century's final decade, the critical role of women was recognized and a global consensus emerged about the need to improve the status of women if population control and human development were to progress. The road to the Hague was marked by signposts that increasingly depicted the right of women to control their own bodies and reproductive fate as a basic human right, recognizable under international law (see Table 10.2). It was also marked by incontrovertible evidence that women's status in society, and especially their education, have an important influence on preferences toward family size.

> Having an education usually means that women delay marriage, seek wage-paying jobs, learn about and have more favorable attitudes toward family planning, and have better communication with their husbands when they marry. Educated women have fewer infant deaths; high infant mortality is associated with high fertility. Similarly, when women have wage-paying jobs, they tend to have fewer children (and conversely, women with fewer children find it easier to work). (Population Reference Bureau 1981, 5)

Nevertheless, as measured by the UN's **gender empowerment index,** women throughout the world continue to be disadvantaged relative to men across a broad spectrum of educational statistics, such as literacy rates, school and college enrollments, and targeted educational resources. Women also enjoy less access to advanced study and training in professional fields, such as science, engineering, law, and business. In addition, within occupational groups, they are almost always in less prestigious jobs, they face formidable barriers to political involvement, and everywhere they receive less pay than men. Although these and other gender differences have narrowed in recent years, in most countries **gender inequalities** remain firmly rooted.

▪ gender empowerment index the UN Development Program's attempt to measure the extent of gender equality across the globe's countries, based on estimates of women's relative economic status, high-paying employment, and access to professional and parliamentary positions.

▪ gender inequalities differences of opportunity and reward for men and women that are determined by the values that guide states' foreign and domestic policies (see p. 154).

Addressing women's rights is difficult because the issues touch deeply entrenched as well as widely divergent religious and cultural beliefs. In many Islamic countries, for example, women must hide their faces with veils in public, and women and men are often completely separated in social and religious activities. For many in Western countries, these traditions are difficult to understand. On the other hand, Western conceptions of feminism and women's rights, typically focused on social, political, and economic equality of the sexes, are foreign to women elsewhere, where the issues are personal and the goals pragmatic: "access to capital, the right of inheritance, basic education for girls, a voice in the political establishment and medical systems that let them make choices, especially in reproductive health" (Crossette 1995).

Despite the pitfalls and minefields, the ICPD Program of Action—endorsed by 180 countries—addressed issues of gender equality and "empowerment" as well as women's reproductive rights. This was a historic step toward global recognition of the critical role that women play in both development and population stabilization. Noting that "in all parts of the world, women are facing threats to their lives, health, and well-being as a result of being overburdened

TABLE 10.2

Human Rights and Women's Rights: A Quarter-Century of Progress

Year	*Conference*	*Outcome*
1968	United Nations International Conference on Human Rights (Teheran)	The UN explicitly addresses the issue of "human reproduction." The Teheran Declaration states: "Parents have a basic human right to decide freely and responsibly on the number and spacing of their children and a right to adequate education and information in this respect."
1974	World Population Conference (Bucharest)	From "parents," the focus shifts to "couples and individuals," who have a right to the "means" as well as the information and education needed to decide on the number and spacing of their children. The notion of responsibility is also introduced: "The responsibility of couples and individuals in the exercise of this right takes into account the needs of their living and future children, and their responsibilities towards the community."
1975	International Women's Year Conference (Mexico City)	Launching the UN Decade for Women, the conference emphasizes reproductive choice, bodily integrity, and reproductive autonomy: "The human body, whether that of woman or man, is inviolable, and respect for it is a fundamental element of human dignity and freedom."
1979	Convention on the Elimination of All Forms of Discrimination against Women (Women's Convention)	An unambiguous goal of the convention is equality between women and men in their right and ability to control reproduction. The convention's thirty articles address educational, economic, social, cultural, civic, and political discrimination. Article 12 refers to women's reproductive rights and calls on countries that have ratified the convention to "take all appropriate measures to eliminate discrimination against women in the field of health care in order to ensure, on a basis of equality of men and women, access to health care services, including those related to family planning." Article 16 urges the elimination of "discrimination against women in all matters relating to marriage and family relations."
1984	World Population Conference (Mexico City)	Conference recommendations emphasize the responsibilities of governments and individuals alike: "The experience of the past ten years suggests that governments can do more to assist people in making their reproductive decisions in a responsible way." Making family planning more available is viewed "as a matter of urgency."
1992	United Nations Conference on Environment and Development (Rio)	Agenda 21, the draft of the meeting's official document, includes discussion of family planning and highlights quality, calling for "women-centered, women-managed, safe and accessible, responsible planning of family size and services."
1993	United Nations World Conference on Human Rights (Vienna)	The Vienna Declaration includes nine paragraphs on "The Equal Status and Human Rights of Women," and, for the first time, violence against women is recognized as a human-rights abuse.
1994	International Conference on Population and Development (Cairo)	ICPD Program of Action "reaffirms the basic human right of all couples and individuals to decide freely and responsibly the number and spacing of their children and to have the information, education, and means to do so."
1995	United Nations Fourth World Conference on Women (Beijing)	Sets a wide-ranging, ambitious agenda for promoting human development by addressing gender inequality and women's rights.
1999	United Nations Conference on World Population (The Hague)	Drafts recommendations on humane assistance for international family planning programs in light of trend toward the slowing of world population growth and the possibility that global population could start to decline late in the twenty-first century.

SOURCES: UN Population Fund (1994), 19; (1995), 2; updated to 2000.

Women March for Suffrage . . . in 1998 Although recently, substantial progress toward resolving issues regarding gender inequalities and injustices has been made, the global community still has a long way to go. New Zealand was the first country to give women the right to vote, in 1893. In 1998, women in Kuwait still sought to secure the same civil liberty.

with work and of their lack of power and influence," the conference also called for "the elimination of all kinds of violence against women."

In 1995, in Beijing, the UN convened its fourth World Conference on Women, the largest-ever gathering of women. Many of the issues regarding women's rights, along with the arguments provoked by differing religious and cultural traditions (including some thought to have been resolved in Cairo), resurfaced during the conference. Nonetheless, its very occurrence continued to focus attention on gender issues and the concept of **gender empowerment**—the conviction that "only when the potential of all human beings is fully realized can we talk of true human development" (UNDP 1995).

■ **gender empowerment** the attempt to give women the same political power as men in the societies in which they live.

The ICPD Program of Action

Surprisingly, the precedent-setting 1994 Cairo debates paid little attention to many issues which by then had become common fare in global population forums—perhaps because the contentious issue of abortion rights commanded center stage during the conference. Among the standards were issues of environmental quality, resource conservation, demographic sources of political instability and ethnic conflict, urbanization, and structural inequalities between the Global North and Global South. Many did figure into the goals articulated in the ICPD Program of Action. Nonetheless, others now also emerged prominently among the key objectives around which a global consensus was achieved:

- Establishing a long-term goal of stabilizing population growth levels consistent with sustainable development;
- Establishing an international partnership for sustainable development that recognizes the responsibility of the North to address wasteful resource use in conjunction with the South's addressing high rates of population growth;
- Developing a comprehensive approach for national efforts and international assistance programs that includes:

  —addressing the unmet need and demand for family planning and reproductive health services;

  —strategies for preventing HIV/AIDS infection;

  —child survival and women's health needs;

  —the need to advance the rights and economic, political, and social roles of women;

  —improving the education of girls and women; and

  —increasing male responsibility in family planning and childrearing.
- Mobilizing institutional capability and financial resources necessary to implement the above goals. (U.S. Department of State 1994, 9)

The Program of Action also set out specific goals to be achieved by 2015 that deal with access to primary school education, family-planning services, reproductive health, infant and child mortality, maternal mortality, and life expectancy.

The proposals contained in the Program of Action were only recommendations and thus not binding on governments. Indeed, few could be expected to act on all of them, particularly given the enormous resources their realization demands. By 2000, the expenditures on family planning alone were expected to balloon to $10 billion, nearly double the amount spent in the early 1990s. Even greater sums will be required to meet the goals of increased access to primary education and to health care (including that required by the growing number of HIV/AIDS patients). Global South countries cannot be expected to meet these demands by themselves, and others—meaning governments in the Global North—will be asked to supplement their resources. However, domestic political support for foreign aid among donor countries has virtually disappeared.

Mounting a sustained effort to stem the growth of world population thus remains a formidable challenge. But the goal itself is no longer in serious dispute, as the global community has now agreed that the concurrent growth of human population and demands on the planet threatens to exceed some of the natural limits on the earth's carrying capacity. The world community has also now, in the age of globalization, begun to accept the once controversial view that "the real problems are poverty and inequality. Too many people are too poor to buy the food that is available or lack [environmentally safe and productive] land on which to grow it themselves" (Rosset 1999). Reaffirmed at the 1999 Hague conference, this level of consensus about population politics and policies is a rather remarkable achievement given the comparatively short time in which the "population problem" has been on the global agenda, as well as the disparate interests and values that motivate states' behavior on the issues it encompasses.

A Prescription for Optimism or Pessimism?

Neo-Malthusians and cornucopians paint quite different visions of our future. Might both be right? Rapidly expanding populations stress environmental systems, exacerbate poverty, and encourage reproduction to hedge against the future. Economic development, on the other hand, discourages large families, stimulating reduced birthrates and hence declining population growth rates. So, too, do government family-planning policies. Where each of us chooses to focus attention—dictated by our perceptual lens—will in turn frame our policy prescriptions.

The world community has made great strides in recent decades in recognizing the complex causes and consequences of rapid population growth. Whether it has the will and shared vision to cope with the problems and expand the possibilities remains to be seen. Meanwhile, an interdependent and rapidly globalizing world promises that none will be immune to world population trends and dynamics, even as the effects of population growth play out on the natural environment on which we depend. Population politics are linked directly to the issue of protecting the planet's ecology, which we examine in the next chapter.

KEY TERMS

carrying capacity
demography
tragedy of the commons
ethics
politics
fertility rate
replacement-level fertility
population momentum
demographic transition
modernization
human immunodeficiency virus (HIV)
acquired immune deficiency syndrome (AIDS)
refugees
displaced people
human rights
xenophobia
asylum
atrocities
high politics
low politics
balance of power
clash of civilizations
neo-Malthusians
cornucopians
green revolution
food security
food ladder
Engels's law
sustainable development
ecological overshoot
desertification
deforestation
multilateral
gender empowerment index
gender inequalities
gender empowerment

SUGGESTED READING

Brown, Lester R., Gary Gardner, and Brian Halweil. *Beyond Malthus: Nineteen Dimensions of the Population Challenge.* New York: Norton, 1999.

Buvinić, Mayra. "Women in Poverty: A New Global Underclass," *Foreign Policy* 108 (Fall 1997): 38–52.

Carrying Capacity Network. *The Carrying Capacity Briefing Book.* Washington, D.C.: Carrying Capacity Network, 1997.

Cohen, Joel E. *How Many People Can the Earth Support?* New York: Norton, 1997.

Demeny, Paul, ed. *Population and Development Review,* a quarterly journal examining population dynamics and socioeconomic change. New York: Population Council.

Diamond, Jared. *Guns, Germs, and Steel: The Fates of Human Societies.* New York: Norton, 1997.

Easterbrook, Gregg. "Overpopulation Is No Problem—In the Long Run," *New Republic,* October 11, 1999, 22–28.

Ehrlich, Paul, Anne H. Ehrlich, and Gretchen C. Daily. *The Stork and the Plow.* New York: Putnam, 1995.

Garrett, Laurie. *The Coming Plague: Newly Emerging Diseases in a World Out of Balance,* rev. ed. London: Virago, 2000.

Hyndman, Jennifer. *Managing Displacement: Refugees and the Politics of Humanitarianism.* Minneapolis: Univesity of Minnesota Press, 2000.

McKibben, Bill. "The Future of Population: A Special Moment in History," *Atlantic Monthly* May 1998, 55–78.

Oldstone, Michael B. A. *Viruses, Plagues, and History.* New York: Oxford University Press, 1998.

Switzer, Jacqueline Vaughn. *Environmental Politics: Domestic and Global Dimensions,* 3rd ed. New York: Bedford/St. Martin's, 2001.

World Bank. *Confronting AIDS: Public Priorities in a Global Epidemic.* New York: Oxford University Press, 1997.

WHERE ON THE WORLD WIDE WEB?

Beijing '95: Women, Power, and Change
http://www.womensnet.org/beijing/

WomensNet brings you a Web site devoted to the implementation and follow-up of the 1995 UN Fourth World Conference on Women. Through this site, interested individuals can read the Final Report on the Fourth World Conference on Women or examine the influence that nongovernmental organizations had on the issues presented at the conference and some of the problems they experienced. Click on Implementing the Platform for Action and read the Summary. Then, examine one of the following issues at length: poverty, education, health, violence, economy, power, armed conflict, human rights, media, environment, or The Girl-Child. Explore the Web links provided to gather more information.

International Data Base
http://www.census.gov/ipc/www/idbnew.html

The U.S. Census Bureau offers you the chance to use their computerized bank of demographic data for all countries of the world. From their homepage you can look at the Summary Demographic Data to see totals in population and rates of growth for each country. Click on "Population Pyramids" to compare countries according to their population pyramids. First, choose the United States. What age groups had the largest concentration of people in 1997? Does this change in the year 2025? What about in the year 2050 (when you will probably be retired)? Is there a big difference between male and female populations? Now, choose a country in Africa. How is the pyramid for this country different from the one for the United States? How does it change across time? What conclusions can you draw about the problems each of the countries may face given the number of citizens in different age categories in different time periods?

UNAIDS
http://www.unaids.org/

UNAIDS is a joint program of the UN and a leading advocate for worldwide action against HIV/AIDS. Its mission is to support and strengthen an exapnded response to the global AIDS epidemic. UNAIDS devises programs that will prevent the spread of HIV, provide care and support for those affected by the disease, and alleviate the socioeconomic and human impact of the epidemic. Explore this Web site to read the global HIV/AIDS surveillance by country and find out about the World AIDS Campaign. What effect do you think AIDS will have on population growth rates?

The United Nations and the Status of Women: Setting the Global Gender Agenda
http://www.un.org/Conferences/Women/PubInfo/Status/Home.htm

Table 10.2 chronicles a quarter-century of progress on women's rights. As you can see, the UN and its programs have provided the most important international forums on women's rights. This Web site explains the major UN programs that advance women's rights, including the Committee on the Elimination of Discrimination against Women, UN

Actions for Women, Commission on the Status of Women, Women in Development, and the Convention on the Elimination of All Forms of Discrimination against Women.

United Nations High Commissioner for Refugees
http://www.unhcr.ch/

Any study of population dynamics requires that one consider migration. The UN High Commissioner for Refugees leads and coordinates international action for the worldwide protection of refugees and the resolution of refugee problems. This Web site offers a wealth of information on refugees and is a good place to start examining the issues involved. From the homepage you can explore The World by clicking a region on the map to reach country-specific information about refugees. The Statistics link gives you current numbers on refugees worldwide as well as by country. Explore the Witness link to see an award winning multimedia series of documentaries entitled Roads to Refuge. Finally, click on Images to see what it is like to be a refugee.

World POPClock Projection
http://www.census.gov/cgi-bin/ipc/popclockw

The U.S. Census Bureau's World Population Clock projects the world population every second of every day. Look at the number of people in the world. Then, hit the Reload button on the top of your Web browser. How many more people were born in the time that it took you to *read* the number of people in the world? Click Reload again. How many more people were born?

CHAPTER 11

ECOPOLITICS AND THE PRESERVATION OF THE GLOBAL COMMONS

TOPICS AND THEMES

- Environmental security and sustainable development
- The ecopolitics of energy
- The ecopolitics of the atmosphere
- The ecopolitics of forests and biodiversity
- Trade, the environment, and sustainable development
- Toward sustainability

- **CONTROVERSY** ARE NATIONAL SECURITY, ENVIRONMENTAL SECURITY, AND HUMAN SECURITY COMPETING GOALS?
- **CONTROVERSY** CAN GLOBALIZATION BE GREEN? FREE TRADE AND SUSTAINABLE DEVELOPMENT

An oil platform is towed to an offshore oil field in Niteroi, Brazil.

The bright promise of a new century is clouded by unprecedented threats to the stability of the natural world. Rapid deforestation, falling water tables, and accelerating climate change could undermine economies around the world in the decades ahead.

—LESTER BROWN and CHRISTOPHER FLAVIN, Worldwatch Institute, senior researchers, 1999

Environmental change has always been with us. What is new today is that some of the greatest threats are global—and any effective response will have to be global too. . . . Most forms of environmental degradation were largely local until the middle of [the twentieth] century. Since then, the globalization of environmental degradation has accelerated.

—DAVID HELD, ANTHONY MCGREW, DAVID GOLDBLATT, and JONATHON PERRATON, British social scientists, 2000

When American astronauts first viewed the Earth from the Apollo spacecraft, they remarked to millions of listeners about the "blue planet" they saw through their small windows and how the clouds and continents flowed into one another without regard to the political boundaries humans had imposed on a pristine planet. Those images are often replayed. However, the improvement in space technology has also enabled us to see uncomfortable images—of atmospheric poisons that encircle the globe; of violent winter and summer storms pounding islands and continents with relentless fury; of massive holes in the ozone shield that protects humans from dangerous ultraviolet rays; of vanishing forests and widening deserts. The same satellite technology enables military commanders to target their opponents in warfare, in order to defend state borders.

Responsibility for warfare clearly lies at the doorstep of humankind. Are environmental problems also our doing? Will the expanding world popula-

The View from Afar People on the planet collectively face many threats to survival, one of which is the threat posed by heat-trapping greenhouse gases that contribute to climate change and destructive global warming. Taken from a NASA global satellite surveillance system, this photo shows how integrated the globalized, borderless planet appears from outer space. NASA monitors the geophysical and biological conditions that will affect the Earth's climate and the prospects for sustaining human life.

tion—which "has grown more since 1950 than it did in the previous four million years" (McKibben 1998)—be responsible for the destruction of the global environment in the twenty-first century? Or will the consumption habits and the high-pollution industrialization of the Global North producing excessive toxic waste be the primary causes of environmental damage? There is no consensus on these issues. Not surprisingly, then, there is no more consensus on how states ought to cope with ecological degradation than on how they should deal with the globalization of demographic, economic, and political transformations.

This chapter explores global environmental challenges and responses to them, broadly described by the concept of **ecopolitics**—the intersection of ecology and politics. Ecology deals with the impact of human activity on the environment. Politics, as we have seen, is concerned with the exercise of power. Ecopolitics, then, centers on how political actors influence perceptions of, and policy responses to, their environments.

■ **ecopolitics**
the political issues surrounding how the global environment should be managed.

Peoples and states today face a broad range of environmental and resource challenges. This discussion will cover a limited yet representative sample including issues related to nonrenewable resources, common properties, and renewable resources—in seeking to understand how ecology and politics interact to shape our future. Not surprisingly, politics emerges as a powerful force that permeates all dimensions of environmental and resource issues, ranging from the evaluation of scientific evidence to prescriptions for dealing with that evidence. The text goes on to examine the alternative strategies states have adopted for coping with environmental stress in an anarchical international system and how environmental issues are linked to other values that states prize, notably security and economic and social well-being.

ENVIRONMENTAL SECURITY AND SUSTAINABLE DEVELOPMENT: AN OVERVIEW

"Security" means freedom from fear. It also means freedom from risk and danger. Since the mid-1900s, because fear of a nuclear holocaust has haunted much of the world, security has been conventionally equated with "national security." The danger posed by the threat of war requires national strategies to cope with the struggle for state power central to **realism.** Today many analysts urge people to adopt a broader conception of what constitutes security at both the state and global levels.

One view suggests that threats to national security should encompass actions or events that "degrade the quality of life for the inhabitants of a state . . . or narrow the range of policy choices available to the government of a state or . . . private, nongovernmental entities (persons, groups, corporations) within the state" (Ullman 1983). This is the politics of scarcity, which predicts that future international conflict will likely be caused by resource scarcities—restricted access to food, oil, and water, for example—rather than by overt military challenges.

Compelling as this unconventional viewpoint may be, scarcity continues to be studied primarily from a state-centric ecopolitical perspective. **Environmental security** is a useful concept to broaden the definition of national security, pushing our vision beyond borders and their protection. Focusing on the transboundary character of challenges to preserving the global environment, it recognizes that "threats to global life systems such as global warming, ozone depletion, and the loss of tropical forests and marine habitats are just as important to the future of humankind as the threat of nuclear catastrophe" (Porter and Brown 1996) (see Controversy: Are National Security, Environmental Security, and Human Security Competing Goals?). Because environmental degradation undercuts states' economic well-being and the quality of life all governments seek for their citizens, it invites a **neoliberal** interpretation of how states can cooperate with intergovernmental organizations (IGOs) and nongovernmental organizations (NGOs) to preserve the global environment (Zacher and Matthew 1995). Because the effort by the neoliberal **epistemic community** to redefine "security" moves beyond realism's popular state-centric conception of international politics, the enterprise is understandably controversial.

■ **realism**
a school of theoretical thought emphasizing the supreme importance of states as unitary, sovereign actors and militarily competitive states' division by solid borders (see p. 457).

■ **environmental security**
a concept recognizing that environmental threats to global life systems are as important as the threat of armed conflicts.

■ **neoliberalism**
seeing the globe as an integrated whole, without meaningful national boundaries; this viewpoint attempts to explain international cooperation and change through the mutual activities of states, IGOs, and NGOs.

■ **epistemic community**
a group of experts from around the world who, based on their knowledge, develop a shared understanding of a problem on the global agenda and a set of preferences for responding to it.

CONTROVERSY

Are National Security, Environmental Security, and Human Security Competing Goals?

How should "security" be defined? Policymakers disagree. Some see security primarily in terms of "national security"; others in terms of "environmental security" or "human security." The basis for the disagreement is competing conceptions of who and what is most important on the global agenda. One tradition gives states first priority and assumes that protecting national security must be put ahead of cooperation with others to manage shared problems such as environmental issues. Other groups challenge this conception and give primacy to the security of individual people, arguing that environmental protectionism must therefore be seen as a global priority, because all people depend on a clean, healthy environment for survival.

What do you think? In considering the issue, take into consideration the following interpretation, which frames the issue in the contemporary policy debate within national capitals and international organizations (IGOs and NGOs).

> The traditional concept of national security that evolved during the Cold War viewed security as a function of the successful pursuit of interstate power competition.... Environmental security represents a significant departure from this approach to national security. It addresses two distinct issues: the environmental factors behind potentially violent conflicts, and the impact of global environmental degradation on the well-being of societies and economies. The idea that environmental degradation is a security issue when it is a cause of violent conflict appears to be consistent with the traditional definition of national security. However, ... [the] focus on threats that do not involve an enemy state or political entity disturbs many theorists and practitioners of national security, for whom the only issues that should be viewed as "security" issues are those that revolve around conflict itself....
>
> The case for environmental security rests primarily on evidence that there has been serious degradation of natural resources (fresh water, soils, forests, fishery resources, and biological diversity) and vital life-support systems (the ozone layer, climate system, oceans, and atmosphere) as a result of the recent acceleration of global economic activities. These global physical changes could have far-reaching effects in the long run.
>
> Each of these environmental threats to global well-being is subject to significant empirical and scientific uncertainty.... The uncertainties ... are comparable, however, to those associated with most military threats that national security establishments prepare for. Military planning is based on "worst-case" contingencies that are considered relatively unlikely to occur, yet military preparations for such contingencies are justified as a necessary insurance policy or "hedge" against uncertainty....
>
> The relationship between scarce natural resources and international conflict is not a new issue. But unlike traditional national security thinking about such conflict, which focuses on nonrenewable resources like minerals and petroleum, the environmental security approach addresses renewable resources—those that need not be depleted if managed sustainably.

SOURCE: Porter (1995), 218–220.

Human Courage in the Face of Urbanization

Global environmental issues pose another controversy, one that engages the competing perspectives of optimistic **cornucopians** and pessimistic **neo-Malthusians.** Cornucopians believe that if free markets and free trade are practiced, ecological imbalances that threaten humankind will be corrected. For them, prices are the key adjustment mechanism that in time produces the greatest good for the greatest number of people. Neo-Malthusians, on the other hand, share more in common with liberal internationalists and mercantilists. For them, markets' failure to account for the cost of excessive exploitation of both renewable and nonrenewable resources requires intervention by nonmarket agents. More fundamentally, it requires revision of the "dominant social paradigm," which says "first, that the free market will always maximize social welfare, and second, that there is not only an infinite supply of natural resources but also of 'sinks' for disposing the wastes from exploiting those resources" (Porter and Brown 1996).

■ **cornucopians** economists who question limits-to-growth analyses and who argue that markets effectively maintain a balance between population pressures and preservation of the global environment.

■ **neo-Malthusians** ecological pessimists who warn of the ecopolitical dangers of uncontrolled growth in population, consumption, and pollution.

The dominant social **paradigm** is under serious attack by environmental activists. It is also under attack internationally. **Sustainable development** is now popularly perceived as an alternative to unlimited growth, a concept that enjoys widespread support among governments and a broad range of NGOs that are particularly active in shaping the global environmental agenda. Its heritage is traceable to *Our Common Future,* the 1987 report of the World Commission on Environment and Development, popularly known as the Brundtland Commission after the Norwegian prime minister who chaired it. The commission concluded that the world cannot sustain the growth required to meet the needs and aspirations of the world's growing population unless it adopts radically different approaches to basic issues of economic expansion, equity, resource management, energy efficiency, and the like. Rejecting the "limits of growth" maxim popular among neo-Malthusians during the 1970s, it emphasized instead "the growth of limits." The commission defined a "sustainable society" as one that "meets the needs of the present without compromising the ability of future generations to meet their own needs."

■ **paradigm** a common scholarly way of organizing perceptions about the characteristics and causes of a particular phenomenon for the purpose of studying it and managing its effects.

■ **sustainable development** the expansion of income and wealth in ways that do not destroy the resources provided by the environment.

The Brundtland Commission report is an important landmark in the rapid emergence of environmental issues as global concerns. The process began in earnest in 1972, when the United Nations (UN) General Assembly convened the first UN Conference on the Human Environment in Stockholm. Conferences have since been held on a wide range of environmental topics, with scores of treaties negotiated and new international agencies put into place to promote cooperation and monitor environmental developments.

A second milestone in the challenge to the dominant social paradigm was the **Earth Summit,** which took place in Rio de Janeiro, Brazil, in 1992—the twentieth anniversary of the Stockholm conference on the environment. Formally known as the UN Conference on Environment and Development (UNCED), the meeting brought together more than 150 states, fourteen hundred nongovernmental organizations, and some eight thousand journalists. A program of action agreed on at Rio, *Agenda 21,* embodies a political commitment to a broad range of environmental and development goals. Prior to the Earth Summit, the environment and development had been treated separately—and often regarded as being in conflict with each other, as development frequently imperils and degrades the environment. Now the concept of *sustainability* galvanized a simultaneous treatment of environmental and development issues. Recognition of the interrelatedness of global welfare issues continued at

■ **Earth Summit** an international meeting held in 1992 in Rio de Janeiro, Brazil, aimed at creating a program of action to address a broad range of environmental and developmental issues.

Dos and Don'ts of Sustainable Farming Deforestation and inappropriate farming techniques often lead to degradation of soils, causing excessive erosion and desertification, as shown in the picture on the left. Appropriate farming techniques, such as Indonesia's traditional methods of terracing farmlands, illustrated on the right, can limit the damage, even in a densely populated and growing society.

the 1994 Cairo International Conference on Population and Development (ICPD). The proposition that all politics—even global politics—are local, and that protection of the earth's environment is a primary international security issue, was reiterated at the 1997 "Rio Plus Five" UN Earth Summit and the follow-up 1999 UN population conference at the Hague, when the commitment was reaffirmed to treat population, economic development, and environmental preservation as policies that needed to be coordinated at the global level, as well as to build on environmental preservation by adding new safeguards beyond the 240 international treaties already in place (Brown et al. 2000, 201).

Because sustainability means living off the earth's interest without encroaching on its capital, it draws attention to meeting current needs without depriving future generations of the resources necessary for their survival. Literally hundreds of books and articles have asked how this ambitious goal can be achieved. A common thread throughout this literature is that sustainability cannot be realized without dramatic changes in the social, economic, and political practices throughout an increasingly interconnected world. Is that possible? Are individuals willing to sacrifice personal welfare for the common good? Will they sacrifice now to enrich their heirs? The **tragedy of the commons** described in Chapter 10 provides little basis for optimism, whether applied to individuals or states, suggesting that greed and the striving for **relative gains** by some in the absence of regulation leads to reductions in everyone's **absolute gains** and possibly their destruction. Add to this the fact that the anarchy of international politics without global governance discourages states from cooperating with one another out of fear that some will gain more than others, and it becomes clear that while environmental problems often cross national boundaries they remain hostage to institutions too weak to effectively manage the shared threats.

To better understand the multiple tensions that global environmental problems pose in an anarchical world and how competing perceptions of security

■ **tragedy of the commons**
the ruin that results when people are free to overexploit shared (common) resources, without regulation of their equal access to them (see p. 331).

■ **relative gains**
a measure of how much some participants in an exchange benefit in comparison to others (see p. 253).

■ **absolute gains**
a measure of the degree to which all participants in an exchange become better off (see p. 253).

and markets shape responses to them, we turn our attention to three interrelated clusters of problems on the global ecopolitical agenda: oil and energy, climate change and ozone depletion, and biodiversity and deforestation. The first involves conflict over a scarce, nonrenewable resource in the tradition of commonplace definitions of national security. The other two broaden the net to encompass what many analysts regard as threats to environmental security within the **global commons.** The latter two clusters illustrate the problems and pitfalls that states and nonstate actors (IGOs and NGOs) face as they seek sustainable development of common properties and renewable resources. Following this we will examine the controversy surrounding the impact of international trade on sustainable development.

■ **global commons** the entire environment considered to be the common heritage and property of the human race on the planet Earth, including the ocean floor under international waters, the Antarctic, and the celestial bodies in outer space.

THE ECOPOLITICS OF ENERGY

In April 1990, the average price for a barrel of internationally traded crude oil was less than fifteen dollars. Five months later—stimulated by Iraq's invasion of the tiny oil sheikdom of Kuwait—it rose to more than forty dollars. For the third time in less than two decades, the world suffered an "oil shock" when the price paid for the most widely used commercial energy source skyrocketed.

The Persian Gulf War underscored the importance of oil to the economic security of states dependent on foreign energy supplies and hence to their national security. For example, U.S. President George Bush—under whose multilateral leadership Iraq's aggression was foiled—never openly admitted that oil was the main reason for his decision to oppose Iraq's Saddam Hussein, but he did acknowledge that short-sighted energy policies had made the United States unduly dependent on Middle Eastern oil to fuel its industrial economy.

Oil also figured prominently in Iraq's own security calculations and hence in Saddam Hussein's decision to invade Kuwait. Iraq's eight-year war with Iran, which ended in 1988, had caused severe domestic economic dislocations and a mounting foreign debt burden. Lower oil prices, caused in part by increased production by other OPEC members, made it more difficult for Iraq to meet its obligations. The Iraqi dictator turned to aggression as a quick fix for his country's economic ills by attempting to seize the vast wealth of Kuwait, including its $100 billion in foreign assets. Political goals also motivated Saddam Hussein, including his aspiration to dominate the Arab world. Thus, control over Kuwaiti oil was a means to an end as well as an end in itself. The effort once more plunged the Middle East into open warfare, causing worldwide alarm that mobilized nearly forty countries to support the UN-authorized military response to Iraq's aggression.

The Persian Gulf War culminated two decades of Middle Eastern turmoil in which access to its prized energy resources often figured prominently. That concern remains. Indeed, it is not an exaggeration to suggest that prospects for global prosperity and peace depend on the preservation of order in the volatile Middle East, whose oil is especially critical to the economic fortunes of the Global North. Ensuring access to the region's oil is thus a national security priority for the developed countries. At issue is the ability to protect the region's vast oil fields from terrorist or other attacks, to avert a repetition of the internal political disruptions that have often plagued the region, and to secure the sea lanes along which oil is shipped.

Kuwait's Oily Aftermath Kuwait, one of the twelve oil-exporting members of OPEC, experienced widespread pollution when some of its oil wells were destroyed in the 1991 Persian Gulf War. Wars destroy not only people and property, but also the environment.

Global Patterns of Oil Consumption

The criticality of oil to the Global North generally and the United States in particular is evident from the disproportionate share of world energy resources they consume. Europe uses more than twice as much energy per capita as the Global South, while Canada and the United States use more than six times as much. The differences parallel the gap between the globe's rich and poor countries, apparent in so many other dimensions of a globalized world (BP Amoco, <bpamoco.com>, August 24, 1999).

Throughout the twentieth century, demand for and consumption of oil spiraled upward. It hit an all-time high of 3.3 billion tons (64 million barrels per day) in 1996, when oil supplied about 85 percent of the world's commercial energy and the industrialization of many emerging Global South economies contributed to the increase. Throughout that century, the global shift to oil was propelled by the aggressive production and promotion of a small group of multinational corporations (MNCs), known as the "majors," whose number shrunk even in the merger frenzy that resulted in the corporate marriages of Exxon with Mobile, BP with Amoco and ARCO, and Total Fina with Elf. Their operations encompassed every aspect of the business, from exploration to the retail sales of products at their gas stations. Their search for, production of, and marketing of low-cost oil was for decades largely unhindered. Concessions from countries in the oil-rich Middle East and elsewhere were easy to get. The communist states were virtually the only oil-producing countries that barred them. The oil companies were thus able to maintain the price of oil at a level profitable for themselves, even though it declined relative to other commodities. An abundant supply of oil at low prices facilitated the recovery of western Europe and Japan from World War II and encouraged consumers to use energy-intensive technologies, such as the private automobile. An enormous growth in the worldwide demand for and consumption of energy followed.

The continuing search for and exploitation of new oil deposits were necessary to meet the high growth in demand. The incentives for developing petroleum reserves outside the Middle East waned, however, as the real cost of oil failed to keep pace with increases in the cost of other commodities, goods, and services. And incentives for developing technologies for alternative energy sources, such as coal, were virtually nonexistent. Eventually this contributed to the rise of the Organization of Petroleum Exporting Countries (OPEC) as an important actor in the energy market, as alternatives to the resources it controlled could not easily be replaced. For nearly a decade—until the global price of oil plunged sharply in the mid-1980s—the oil cartel was a pivotal actor not only in energy markets but also in the world political economy generally. Then in March 1999, OPEC cut production to limit supplies and oil prices tripled within a year, showing that OPEC could once again make oil a critical political issue.

Running on Empty: Is Energy Security an Elusive Goal?

Oil will likely play an important role in the global energy picture well into the twenty-first century. This raises questions about OPEC's potential future role as a price setter and production leader. The historical record leads us to be cautious in predicting the cartel's future role, but signs point toward its continuing importance. The threat is not that another oil crisis is inevitable soon, because although oil is an exhaustible energy resource, it is unlikely that OPEC will keep prices rising by creating severe shortages over the long term. In the past, additions to oil reserves have increased faster than oil has been used.

> The problem is not that we are about to "run out" of oil. The problem is that the world's conventional oil resources are concentrated in relatively few countries who are able to manipulate the economic scarcity of oil to their advantage and to the disadvantage of other countries and who have done so in the past. Our best estimates of the totality of the world's conventional oil resources indicate that OPEC countries own more than half of them. Published, credible estimates of OPEC's share range from a low of 55 percent to a high of 64 percent. The difference is due to greater optimism on the part of analysts at the US Geological Survey about the extent of petroleum resources in the former Soviet Union and, to a lesser extent, in the United States, Canada, Mexico, and China.
>
> Because OPEC members are drawing down their reserves at half the rate of the rest of the world's oil producers, it seems almost inevitable that OPEC's share of the world oil market will grow. For example, the US Energy Information Administration predicts that OPEC's share of the world oil market will rise from its current level of 42 percent to reach 48 percent by 2005, and will climb to 52 percent by 2010. (Greene 1997, 18)

These trends mean that OPEC is critical to global oil supply, the Middle East is critical to OPEC, and countries such as the United States (whose oil inventories hit a twenty-three-year low in 2000) that depend on oil imports from this volatile, unstable source are highly vulnerable to disruptions.

OPEC's future role could change significantly, however, as its political and economic clout and finances depend heavily on factors largely outside its control: changes in global demand (consumption) and supply. And we may now be witnessing the advent of a potentially historic juncture that could overturn the place of oil in the twenty-first century's global political economy.

Global demand for the world's proven reserves of oil has weakened at a time when explorations have uncovered new supplies of oil and the cost of oil has fallen nearly in half since 1981, when oil costs comprised about 8 percent of global economic output. The world's declining dependence on oil comes as a great relief to all countries dependent on imported oil to fuel their future economic growth, who vividly recall the pain caused by the "shocks" of 1973 and 1979–1980 when OPEC quadrupled the price of oil and brought much of the industrialized Global North and many Global South importers to their knees as available supplies grew scarce. Times have changed in the twenty-first century, even though between 1999 and 2000 OPEC closed ranks and took about 6.5 percent of world oil production off the market. "World energy needs are projected to double in the next several decades, but no credible geologist foresees a doubling of world oil production, which is expected to peak within the next few decades" (Brown and Flavin 1999, 6). The petroleum picture on the planet is undergoing a massive transformation (see Figure 11.1), and this presages enormous future transformations in the ways the global community will meet its growth energy needs throughout the twenty-first century.

The transforming global energy system, indeed, may be in the process of reinvention. Consider the magnitude of the transition:

> Fossil fuels—coal, oil, and natural gas—that are dug or pumped from the ground, then burned in engines or furnaces, provide 90 percent or more of the energy in most industrial countries and 75 percent of energy worldwide. They are led by petroleum, the most convenient and ubiquitous among them—an energy source that has shaped the twentieth century, and that now seems irreplaceable. But . . . energy forecasts can overlook what later seems obvious. A close examination of technological, economic, social, and environmental trends suggests that we may already be in the early stages of a major global energy transition—one that is likely to accelerate early in the next century.
>
> To understand energy in world history is to expect the unexpected. And as we live in a particularly dynamic period, the least likely scenario may be that the energy picture 100 years from now will closely resemble that of today. Although the future remains, as always, far from crystal clear, the broad outlines of a new energy system may now be emerging, thanks in part to a series of revolutionary new technologies and approaches. These developments suggest that our future energy economy may be highly efficient and decentralized, using a range of sophisticated electronics. The primary energy resources for this system may be the most abundant ones on Earth: the sun, the wind, and other "renewable" sources of energy. And the main fuel for this twenty-first century economy could be hydrogen, the lightest and most abundant element in the universe.
>
> This transition would in some sense be a return to our roots. *Homo sapiens* has relied for most of its existence on a virtually limitless flow of renewable energy resource—muscles, plants, sun, wind, and water—to

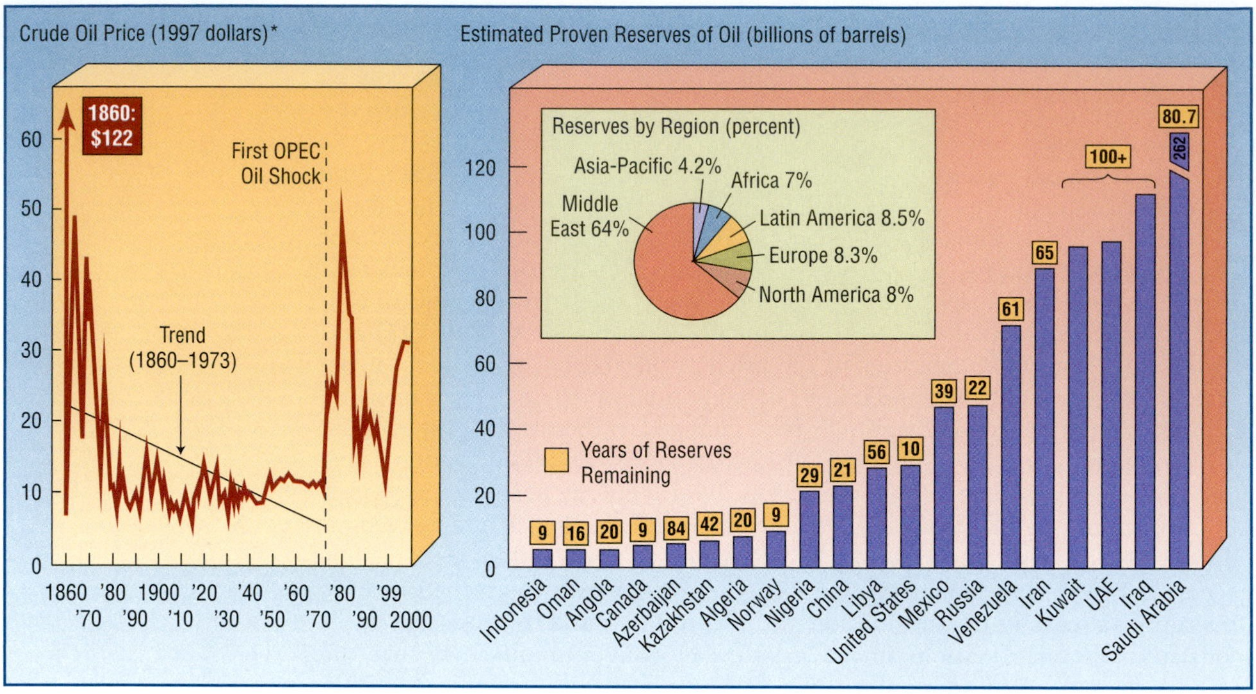

FIGURE 11.1
Crude Oil Prices since 1861 and the Growth of Proven Oil Reserves
In the 110-year period between 1860 and 1970, the availability of cheap oil relative to other sources of energy made oil the primary engine for industrialization (left). The two oil shocks in the 1970-1980 period skyrocketed the price of oil. In the 1980s, crude oil prices returned to their relatively low historic levels, until they tripled between 1999 and early 2000 to over thirty dollars a barrel. Demand rose in 1999 by "only 0.1 percent globally, the lowest in five years" (*Economist*, July 3, 1999, 92). Meanwhile, estimated proven reserves of oil worldwide (right) are abundant because exploration has discovered new supplies of the finite energy source available for extraction.
*Per barrel price 1860–1973 equals average U.S. wellhead price; 1974–1998 is Arab Light on a freight on board (fob) basis.
SOURCES: Adapted from the *Economist* (March 6, 1999), 23, and (July 3, 1999), 92, with crude oil prices since July 1999 based on Primark Datastream.

> meet its basic needs for shelter, heat, cooking, lighting, and movement. The relatively recent transition to coal that began in Europe in the seventeenth century marked a major shift to dependence on a finite stock of fossilized fuels whose remaining energy is now equivalent to less than 11 days of sunshine. From a millennial perspective, today's hydrocarbon-based civilization is but a brief interlude in human history. (Flavin and Dunn 1999, 23)

The impact of such a global transformation would be huge, overturning the past 125-year pattern in world energy development and consumption. Could the era of "big oil" really be ending? That could well be the case:

> A growing number of energy analysts and industry officials now argue that energy markets are beginning the inevitable long-run shift away from fossil

> fuels. In a remarkable speech in Houston in early 1999, Mike Bowlin, Chairman and CEO of the ARCO oil company, said, "We've embarked on the beginning of the Last Days of the Age of Oil." Bowlin went on to say that the world is moving "along the spectrum away from carbon, and headed toward hydrogen and other forms of energy." (*Vital Signs 1999,* 48).

At the start of the twenty-first century, just seven years after the Rio Earth Summit, awareness has expanded about the overwhelming environmental problems the world faces. With this recognition has come acceptance by many companies and countries that proactive environmental protection through the sustainable use of resources makes environmental sense. Growing public alarm about the true cost of fossil fuels in light of the danger of global warming has created greater acceptance of measures which protect the earth's biosphere as the best chance for sustained human progress. Physical restraints appear to make a conversion away from dependence on fossil fuels, especially oil, necessary:

> A peak in world oil production early in the new century would reverberate through the energy system. The problem is not just the large amount of oil currently used—67 million barrels daily—but the intent of many developing countries, most lacking much oil of their own, to increase their use of automobiles and trucks. Meeting the growing needs of China, India, and the rest of the developing world in the way industrial countries' demands are met today would require a tripling of world oil production, even assuming no increases in industrial-country use. Yet capacity in 2020 is unlikely to be much above current levels—and may well be declining.
>
> Long before we completely run out of fossil fuels, however, the environmental and health burdens of using them may force us toward a cleaner energy system. Fossil fuel burning is the main source of air pollution and a leading cause of water and land degradation. Combustion of coal and oil produces carbon monoxide and tiny particles that have been implicated in lung cancer and other respiratory problems; nitrogen and sulfur oxides create urban smog, and bring acid rain that has damaged forests extensively. Oil spills, refinery operations, and coal mining release toxic materials that impair water quality. Increasingly, oil exploration disrupts fragile ecosystems and coal mining removes entire mountains. Although modern pollution controls have improved air quality in most industrial countries in recent decades, the deadly experiences of London and Pittsburgh are now being repeated in Mexico City, São Paulo, New Delhi, Bangkok, and many other cities in the developing world. Each year, coal burning is estimated to kill 178,000 people prematurely in China alone. (Flavin and Dunn 1999, 25)

What this transformation thus portends is a global shift from oil to unconventional sources (such as tar sands and shale) and renewable forms of energy. In the latter category solar, tidal, and wind power, as well as geothermal energy and bioconversion, are among the alternatives to oil most likely someday to become technologically and economically viable. Their development would reduce dependence on oil from the volatile Middle East and reduce anxieties over possible scarcity. However, the comparatively low price of oil—and its projected stability in the wake of OPEC's March 2000 decision to incrase oil output by 6.5 percent—discourages their development. Meanwhile, coal, natural gas, hydropower and nuclear power are the principal alternatives to oil; although, as

Figure 11.2 shows, advocates of reliance on environmentally friendly, renewable energy supplies picture a radically different pattern in the twenty-first century than that which prevailed in the twentieth century.

Coal. Coal is the chief fossil fuel alternative to oil. Based on the current ratio of reserves to production, sufficient oil to provide the world's needs will only last until about 2040, but coal will last for more than two centuries. "Coal's share of world energy, which peaked at 62 percent in 1910, is down to 23 percent, roughly where it was in 1860" (Dunn 1999, 8). Oil's current share is 30 percent and natural gas, 22 percent.

Although trade in coal increased sharply during the 1980s, most is consumed where it is produced, making coal less susceptible to supply disruptions than oil. China, the United States, and Russia account for almost 60 percent of coal reserves, which, as noted, are so abundant that some experts expect supplies to last at least one thousand years.

Although the use of coal increased sharply in the aftermath of the first oil shock, the social costs—known as **externalities**—associated with its widespread use are substantial. Coal is a major pollutant of the atmosphere, for example, as it contributes heavily to the acidification of precipitation and to the release of carbon that contributes to global warming. "Coal is the most carbon-intensive fossil fuel, releasing 29 percent more carbon per unit of energy than oil, and 80 percent more than natural gas. It accounts for 43 percent of annual global carbon emissions" (Dunn 1999, 10). As a result of environmental concerns and tighter regulations, coal is a poor alternative to oil worldwide. Nonetheless, some countries such as China that have large supplies of coal continue to rely on it to fuel rapid growth, despite heavy pollution that sparks the ire of the rest of the world, which must bear the environmental consequences.

■ **externalities** the side effects produced by economic activities, especially costs such as pollution.

Natural Gas. Natural gas is cleaner and more convenient to use than either coal or oil. Based on the current ratio of reserves to production, natural gas supplies are likely to last for more than sixty years, and production is expected to rise from 2 billion tons of oil equivalent in 2000 to 2.6 billion by 2010 (Economist 1999b, 89). Unlike coal, however, natural gas is concentrated in a small number of regions, and this means that its continued development as a source of energy will depend heavily on export trade.

The two largest natural gas markets are the United States and Russia. In 2000, these two countries together consumed about two-thirds of global production, and Russia, which is also the major producer, possesses the largest proven reserves of gas. In comparison, the United States has less than 4 percent of world reserves. Historically, the United States has met virtually all of its need for gas from domestic sources. It seems likely, though, that it will have to look increasingly to imports to meet its high demand. As with oil, the Middle East is a likely source, as it holds nearly one-third of the world's proven reserves but consumes only 6 percent of world production.

Getting gas from the wellhead to consumers is a primary problem. Pipelines are the preferred method of transport, but they are massive and expensive engineering projects that also pose environmental dangers and thus encounter resistance. Liquefied natural gas is an alternative—perhaps the only one for trans-

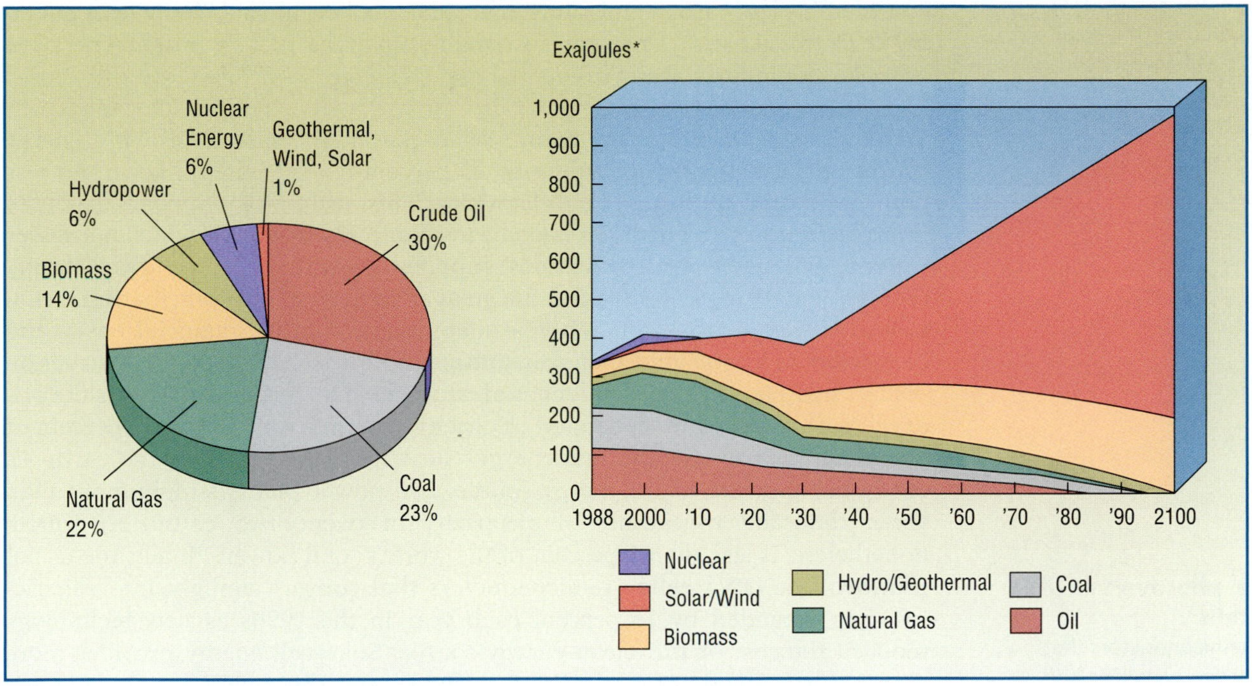

FIGURE 11.2

Phasing Out Fossil Fuels? The Potential for Renewable Energy to Supply the World's Energy Needs by the Year 2100

The global economy's need for energy continues to rise, requiring more energy than is ultimately available from nonrenewable resources. Thus rising demand is likely to change the current distribution of sources on which the world relies to meet its energy needs (left). As the Fossil Free Energy Scenario prediction (right) suggests, it would be possible to tap renewable sources to meet the world's entire energy needs by the end of the twenty-first century. For example, it is estimated that more than fifty Global South countries could produce as much energy from the biomass residues generated by sugar production as they presently obtain from oil; that less than 5 percent of the globe's small-scale hydropower has been exploited; and that land-based wind turbines could provide 20 million megawatt-hours of electricity each year—twice as much as the world consumed in 1987 (Crump 1998, 223). Renewable energy from replacable sources also has the advantage of doing relatively little damage to the environment. Whether these sources of energy will actually be harnessed remains to be seen, because the relatively low financial cost of using the planet's nonrenewable resources (like oil, which takes millions of years to form) makes them economically attractive.

*A joule is a unit of work or energy, equivalent to 0.239 calories (1 exajoule equals 10^{18} joules).
Note: Percentages do not equal 100 due to rounding errors.
SOURCE: Adapted from Crump (1998), 193 (left) and 223 (right).

shipment from the Middle East to North America or to the growing European and Japanese markets—but experts disagree about its safety. That concern, combined with cost considerations and sensitivity to dependence on OPEC sources, has limited the development of liquefied natural gas. Still, because natural gas produces considerably less carbon emissions than either coal or oil, and "is the least polluting of the fossil fuels . . . natural gas remains a popular fuel for power generation as well as for industrial and residential use" (*Vital Signs 1999,* 48).

Wind, Water, Earth, and Sun. Wind power, the fastest growing energy source in the 1990s, is expanding by 25 percent a year, but still generates less than 1 percent of the globe's electricity. This technology appears likely to improve as new wind turbines become available. Hydropower, which harnesses water to generate electricity and now supplies one-fifth of the world's electricity (Brown et al. 1998, 179–180), has the great advantage of not contributing to pollution. However, limits on water availability, prohibitive financial costs, and controversies about land management and soil loss due to dam construction restrict hydropower development as an alternative to fossil fuels. This is the primary reason that water-generated electricity accounts for less than 3 percent of global energy use. Geothermal energy—heat from the center of the earth—is costly but growing as an energy source; 250 power plants supply more than seven thousand megawatts of electricity in twenty-two countries, which, nonetheless, is less than 1 percent of the world's total power. Finally, the use of **photovoltaic (PV) cells**—semiconductors that convert sunlight into electricity—has expanded by 16 percent each year in the 1990s as new technology reduced the cost of this clean energy source. Solar-cell energy provides more than 150 megawatts of electricity worldwide, and this nonpolluting source is particularly efficient in supplying energy in developing countries where approximately 2 billion people live without access to electricity (*Vital Signs 1999,* 54).

■ **photovoltaic (PV) cells** semiconductors that convert sunlight into electricity.

Wind, water, earth, and sun thus seem destined to grow as sources for meeting the world's increasing need for energy, despite the great financial expenses for their continued development.

Nuclear Power. Between 1997 and 1998, 438 nuclear reactors throughout the world provided about 6 percent of the globe's energy; an additional 33 new reactors were under construction, while 86 were in the process of being dismantled. Those in operation combined to generate 343,000 megawatts of energy, with the highest consumption in the United States, followed by France, Japan, and Russia. If China carries out its ambitious plans to build an additional fifty nuclear reactors by 2020, the globe's most populated country will take the lead in nuclear generating capacity and consumption (*Vital Signs 1999,* 50).

Among known technologies, nuclear energy was once seen as the leading alternative to fossil fuel dependence, but that is no longer the case. Technical and financial problems have forced some countries to reduce or abandon their programs, and in others the political climate has turned markedly against nuclear power, with safety a principal point of contention. Well-publicized nuclear accidents in the United States at the Three Mile Island nuclear power plant in Pennsylvania in 1979 and at Chernobyl in Ukraine in 1986, and no less than five major accidents between 1995 and 1999 at Japan's fifty-two nuclear power plants (which supply about a third of Japan's electricity) dramatized the potential dangers of nuclear power. "A few governments still support nuclear power, but the number is dwindling, with each passing year" (*Vital Signs 1999,* 50).

Catastrophe was averted at Three Mile Island, but even without the threatened meltdown of the reactor core, the accident released the largest-ever level of radioactive contamination by the U.S. commercial nuclear industry. At Chernobyl, however, catastrophe did strike. Thousands are believed to have been killed; hundreds of thousands were forced to evacuate their homes; and the radioactive fallout—"the equivalent of ten Hiroshima bombs"—"left a swath of agricultural land the size of Holland permanently poisoned" (Dobbs 1991, 10). Radioactive fallout spread beyond the Ukraine as well, multiplying the geographical scope and number of those ravaged by the catastrophe and its long-term consequences. Nine years after the disaster, it was estimated that "Chernobyl will be the longest, most high-tech and expensive environmental cleanup the world has attempted—costing billions of dollars and taking perhaps one hundred years to complete" (Rupert 1995). And in Japan, political support for nuclear power has steadily fallen since the series of accidents between 1995 and 2000, while Green Party environmental activists have led a crusade to shut down nuclear power plants and reactors in Germany and throughout Europe. The Greens' argument: Nuclear energy produces lethal wastes that endanger future generations for centuries because there is no way to render them harmless, and the meltdown of a nuclear reactor is a catastrophic possibility.

Concerns about the risks of nuclear power extend beyond the safety of nuclear energy as a means of generating electricity. How and where to dispose of highly radioactive nuclear wastes, for example, is a contentious and unresolved issue virtually everywhere. No safe procedure for handling radioactive nuclear waste—some of which remains dangerous for hundreds of thousands of years—has yet been devised. In the meantime, large quantities have accumulated, posing a substantial threat to environmental safety. The end of the Cold War has compounded the issue, as the dismantling of both nuclear weapons and the facilities that produced them requires means of disposal. Local communities often cry "not in my back yard" (NIMBY is the popular acronym). The issue is no less contentious internationally, as disposal of nuclear and other toxic wastes figures prominently on the global ecopolitical agenda as a divisive issue between the Global North (which prefers to dump wastes outside its own territory) and the Global South (which would prefer not to be the dump—but often is).

A related fear is that countries that do not now possess nuclear know-how might acquire it, thus gaining the means to develop nuclear weapons. While nuclear weapons proliferation is essentially a national security issue, it is linked technologically to nuclear power production for peaceful purposes. Nuclear-generating facilities produce weapons-grade material, specifically highly enriched uranium and plutonium. Neither of these materials, which can be used to create a nuclear weapon, is used commercially as fuel in the current generation of nuclear power reactors. Still, the fear persists that eventually weapons-grade material will place within reach the construction of tens of thousands of nuclear bombs. It was this concern that prompted the United States (with the help of South Korea and Japan) to give North Korea—a longtime political-military adversary—nuclear reactors less susceptible to nuclear weapons production than those North Korea was developing in its indigenous nuclear program.

The brief exploration of the "energy problematique" demonstrates the centrality of the politics of scarcity in contemporary world politics. In an environmentally interdependent world without strong global governing institutions, where actions anywhere have external costs almost everywhere, the challenge of managing the global commons has reached unprecedented levels. Common property resources and their preservation will be a core concern and security issue in the twenty-first century.

THE ECOPOLITICS OF THE ATMOSPHERE

■ **global warming** the gradual rise in world temperature, a suspected consequence of greenhouse gases trapping heat emitted from Earth that would otherwise escape into outer space.

The scores of government negotiators and nongovernmental representatives who converged on Rio de Janeiro in 1992 came in the wake of the hottest decade on record. For years scientists had warned that **global warming**—the gradual rise in world temperature—would cause destructive changes in world climatological patterns and that rising sea levels, melting glaciers, and freak storms would provoke widespread changes in the globe's political and economic systems and relationships. Perhaps because they had been burned by the heat of the 1980s, negotiators agreed at Rio to a Framework Convention on Climate Change whose purpose was to address the human causes of climate change by reducing emissions of carbon dioxide and other greenhouse gases.

Three years later, new data and technology narrowed the disagreement concerning the extent of climate change, and two thousand of the world's top climate scientists concluded that the balance of evidence shows a discernible human influence. In response to many ecological alarm bells, in December 1997, representatives of 160 governments met in Kyoto, Japan, to hammer out a new agreement on curbing the pollutants blamed for global warming. That agreement had little impact, and the 1999 climate talks in Bonn did little better: they called for shifts away from fossil fuels to renewable sources of energy, but envisioned a mere 5 percent reduction in carbon emissions by the industrialized countries beginning in 2008.

Climate Change

Although major gaps in our knowledge of climate change remain, few climate scientists think the world can afford to wait for answers. The changes are substantial, and threatening. Most scientists believe that the gradual rise in the earth's temperature, especially evident since the onset of the Industrial Revolution, is caused by an increase in human-made gases released into the atmosphere, altering its insulating effects. The atmosphere permits radiation from the sun to penetrate to the earth, but gas molecules form the equivalent of a greenhouse roof by trapping heat remitted from Earth that would otherwise escape into outer space. Carbon dioxide (CO_2) accounts for the bulk of the gases that contribute to the **greenhouse effect,** with chlorofluorocarbons (CFCs) composing much of the rest. As the amount of these gases released into the atmosphere has grown, the global temperature has risen. As shown in Figure 11.3, the temperature of the atmosphere on the earth's surface has increased nearly a half degree since 1950; eleven of the hottest years since record keeping began in 1866 have occurred since 1987, with 1998 and 1999 setting new records in the 1990s—"the warmest decade in the past 600 years" (*Vital Signs 1999,* 58).

■ **greenhouse effect** the phenomenon producing planetary warming when gases released by burning fossil fuels act as a blanket in the atmosphere, thereby increasing temperature.

The globe's temperature is now between 0.3 and 0.6 degrees Celsius higher than it was in 1880, and is projected to further increase by 3.6 degrees Celsius by 2100 if preventive action is not taken (Soroos 2001). Although CO_2 is the principal greenhouse gas, concentrations of methane in the atmosphere are growing more rapidly. Methane gas emissions arise from livestock populations, rice cultivation, and the production and transportation of natural gas. Interestingly, the largest concentrations of methane are not in the atmosphere but locked in ice, permafrost, and coastal marine sediments. This raises the possibility that warming will cause more methane to be released into the atmos-

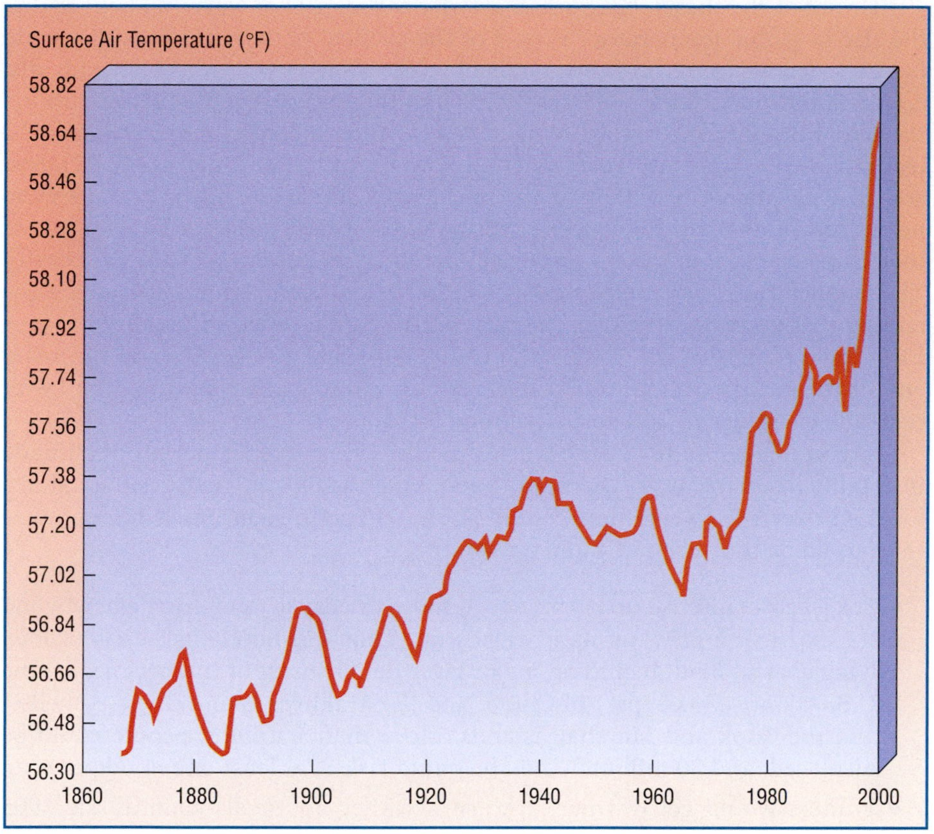

FIGURE 11.3
Rising Temperatures since 1860

The World Meteorological Organization (WMO) monitors average global surface temperatures at thousands of sites around the world, and its records strongly indicate that so-called global warming is not a myth. For nearly 150 years, the globe's temperature has seesawed up and down, usually by tiny fractions of degrees. But since the mid-1970s, the mercury has largely been on the rise, and the WMO predicts that the average global surface temperature could jump 3.6 degrees Celsius by the end of the twenty-first century—more than triple the rise of the past one hundred years.

Note: Five-year averages of global temperatures.

SOURCE: Adapted from World Resources Institute, Repetto and Lash (1997), 93; *Vital Signs 1999*, 59.

phere, which would then reinforce the process because of methane's strong warming potential.

> Since some greenhouse gases stay aloft for long periods and because the oceans store a huge amount of heat, warming will continue and persist irreversibly for centuries even after accumulation stops. Consequently, the observable change in the climate, at any time before equilibrium is restored, will be much less than what emissions up to that point have made inevitable. Put simply, the climate problem will always be worse than it appears to be. (Repetto and Lash 1997, 85)

Critics of the thesis that human activity causes global warming believe that the rise in global temperature is part of the cyclical pattern changes the world has experienced for tens of thousands of years. That view has been steadily discredited, however. Since 1988, hundreds of atmospheric scientists from around the world organized several UN agencies to study global climate change. The team, known as the Intergovernmental Panel on Climate Change (IPCC), first conclusively stated in 1995 its belief that global climate trends are "unlikely to be entirely due to natural causes," that humans are to blame for at least part of the problem, and that the consequences are likely to be very harmful and costly. The implications were self-evident: Without significant efforts to reduce the emission of greenhouse gases, the increase in global temperatures by the year 2100 could be equivalent to that which ended the last ice age. Even at the lower end of the panel's estimates (1.4 degrees Fahrenheit), the rise would be faster than any experienced in recorded human history.

According to the IPCC, the world has already entered a period of climatic instability likely to cause "widespread economic, social, and environmental dislocation over the twenty-first century." The effects of continued temperature rises could be both dramatic and devastating:

- Sea levels could rise up to three feet, mostly because of melting glaciers and the expansion of water as it warms up. That will flood vast areas of low-lying coastal land, including major river deltas; most of the beaches on the U.S. Atlantic Coast; part of China; and the Maldives island, the Seychelles, and the Cook and Marshall islands. More than 1 million people could be displaced, and 30 million would be put at risk of at least one flood per year.
- Winters would get warmer . . . warm-weather hot spells such as the 1995 summer heat wave that killed five hundred people in Chicago would become more frequent and more severe.
- Rainfall would increase globally, but only the areas already prone to flooding would flood more often and more severely, with freak storms such as the 1997 El Niño surge of storms in the Pacific and the 1997 flooding in the Dakotas becoming more common. Since water evaporates more easily in a warmer world, drought-prone regions would become even dryer. As oceans heat, hurricanes, which draw their energy from warm oceans, would become even stronger.
- Entire ecosystems would vanish from the planet, and a hotter earth would drive some plants to higher latitudes and altitudes and require farmers to irrigate and change their crops and agriculture practices.
- The combination of flooding and droughts will cause tropical diseases such as malaria and dengue fever to flourish in previously temperate regions that were formerly too cold for their insect carriers.

Climate-Change Culprits. It is clear that the politics of agreements to reduce the threat of global warming are charged because the economics and financial stakes are enormous and every proposal generates stiff opposition. However, the basic physical dynamics behind the problem are rather simple. CO_2 emissions are the principle culprits in global warming. That is, when coal, oil, and natural gas fossil fuels are burned to generate energy, carbon reacts with oxygen to form CO_2, trapping thermal radiation that would otherwise escape into outer space and causing surface temperature to rise. Other major greenhouse gases include chlorofluorocarbons (CFCs) and methane, but CO_2 is believed to contribute about half of all greenhouse concentrations that generate the rising surface temperatures which affect both weather and climate.

CO_2 emissions from the burning of fossil fuels have climbed steadily, rising fourfold since 1950. The industrial Global North states are the principal sources of global carbon emissions, accounting for 73 percent of global CO_2 emissions (*Fortune,* December 8, 1997, 113); the United States emits more CO_2 into the atmosphere than any other state. In large measure because of its big buildings, 125 million cars, and relatively inefficient industries, the U.S. CO_2 emissions per person are nearly four times those in western Europe, and five times the world average. Elsewhere, China is a major and growing source of concern because coal emits more atmospheric pollutants than other fossil fuels, and three-fourths of China's energy for its fast-growing economy comes from coal. China now accounts for about 15 percent of all greenhouse gas emissions, making it the fastest-growing major contributor to global warming, even though its emissions per person remain one-seventh of those in the United States.

To combat the danger of accelerating global warming, more than 160 states signed the 1992 UN Framework Convention on Climate Change, which seeks to contain greenhouse gases at levels that will avoid threatening climate change, and aimed to return emissions to 1990 levels. But that agreement did not go far enough and most industrial countries were expected to miss their targets for reductions; in fact, yearly CO_2 emissions were predicted to reach "9 billion tons by 2010—49 percent above 1990 levels" (*Vital Signs 1997,* 58). To strengthen the 1992 Climate Change Treaty, the 1997 Kyoto Protocol was reached, requiring twenty-eight industrial countries to reduce their greenhouse gas emissions from 1990 levels between 2008 and 2012. If adhered to, the United States would cut emissions by 7 percent, the European Union by 8 percent, and Japan by 6 percent, and the protocol asked China, India, and other developing economies to voluntarily set sizable reduction targets. The November 1998 climate talks in Buenos Aires went a step further; 160 states adopted a "plan of action" to set rules for carbon sinks, emission trading, and a "clean development mechanism" for carbon control. However, "carbon-cutting strategies have yet to address the need for major energy innovation and a plan for resources" (*Vital Signs 1999,* 60).

Coal is a major source of atmospheric sulfur and nitrogen oxides as well. These pollutants return to Earth, typically after traveling long distances, in the form of **acid rain,** which adds to the acidification of lakes, the corrosion of materials and structures, and the impairment of ecosystems. Acid rain is a serious problem in much of China. Because the oxides that cause it are also transboundary pollutants, China's domestic energy policies have become a major irritant in its relations with its neighbors, particularly South Korea and Japan. Nonetheless, China plans to increase the amount of coal it burns by nearly 900 million tons a year by 2010. Other Asian states are following in its path, including populous India which, like China, has sizable coal deposits. Already China and India account for 14 percent of global greenhouse emissions, and their combined share of CO_2 emissions is expected to grow. "Human activity has now

■ **acid rain** precipitation that has been made acidic through contact with sulfur dioxide and nitrogen oxides.

Thawing Polar Ice Caps Global emissions of carbon dioxide and other greenhouse gases are rising and contributing to global warming. The long-term consequences are grim; if the earth continues to heat, oceans will rise and land will be submerged. Pictured here is the Bering Glacier at the edge of Vitus Lake in Alaska, which according to Greenpeace has shrunk about forty feet in length during the past century due to global warming.

added more than 200 billion tons of carbon to the atmosphere since 1950. Among industrial nations, responsible for 45 percent of global carbon emissions, output increased 8.1 percent between 1990 and 1998. The United States, the world's leading emitter with 27 percent of the overall total, saw output rise 11.8 percent between 1990 and 1998. . . . Developing countries held a 41 percent share of global carbon emissions, and saw a 39.1 percent rise in output between 1990 and 1998" (*Vital Signs 1999,* 60). Hence, global warming will remain a hot topic on the global agenda.

The Science and Politics of Climate Change. Global climate change contains the elements of a classic tragedy of the commons: It was intended by none yet is seemingly beyond the control of all who must bear its costs. Four strategies are available for avoiding the ruin common properties face when excessively exploited for private gain:

1. *Voluntary restraints,* which come about "through education about the ecological consequences of irresponsible actions and by bringing social pres-

sures to bear on members of the community who have not moderated their actions" (Soroos 2001).

2. *Regulations* that restrict the use of common properties, including penalties for violators.
3. *Partitioning* responsibility for the common property so that those who most profit from its exploitation also pay the costs of its preservation.
4. *Common ownership* of the property, which limits access to those with a share in ownership and who in turn share in the profits. "Under such an arrangement, the community as a whole would not only receive all the profits but also absorb all the costs of [excessive exploitation]" (Soroos 2001).

Each of these strategies for averting a commons tragedy has played a part in states' efforts to cope with the environmental challenges they collectively face. In the case of climate change, however—arguably the most threatening commons tragedy of all—global efforts remain confined to largely voluntary restraints. Because education and social pressures are particularly important here, the role of the IPCC in determining that the world has already entered a period of climatic instability due to rising temperatures takes on added significance. As one prominent environmentalist observed, "The IPCC's influence stems from its unique design. It combines in a single institution independent scientists acting on their professional knowledge with policymakers acting on behalf of governments. Science is separated and protected from political tinkering and at the same time thrust under policymakers' noses. Without realizing what they were doing, governments created in the IPCC an institution that forces them to confront a phenomenon many—if not most—would prefer to ignore" (Mathews 1996).

The Kyoto Protocol of 1997 amending the 1992 Earth Summit set an ambitious goal: stabilizing the overall concentration of greenhouse gases in the atmosphere as well as reducing their emissions worldwide. Despite expectations, many experts criticized the treaty's modest goals, and little progress has been made in realizing the voluntary restraints agreed to after the climate-control talks in Buenos Aires in 1998 and Bonn in 1999, which failed to produce agreements with real muscle. European states, previously at the forefront of efforts to reduce carbon emissions, began to waffle and the United States interpreted the provisions of these treaties to mean that carbon emissions could actually increase if they were offset by reductions in other emissions. Thus, the subtle shift from "binding limits" to rather vague "targets" and "goals" threatens to reduce the impact of recent treaties, despite rapid increases in greenhouse gas emissions.

Strengthening the barrier to effective global action is the fact that the ecopolitical dispute between the Global North and Global South is colored by widely discrepant perceptions and political interests. The South sees the Global North—correctly—as the primary culprit in previous greenhouse emissions, while the Global North sees the Global South—also correctly—as the primary source of rising new emissions, thus negating any benefits that might be realized by altering its own behavior today. Since 1988 greenhouse emissions from the Global South have increased and, as noted, these industrializing Global

South countries' share of global energy is rising faster than those of the Global North. Increased coal burning by China and India alone could undermine any efforts to deal with long-term problems.

The developing Global South basically rejected the Kyoto Protocol outright, in large measure in reaction to the Global North's perceived unwillingness to bear the costs of reshaping their $1 trillion dollar fossil fuel economies (Warrack 1998, 31). Friction generated by the search for financial profit at the expense of environmental protection and by disagreements between North and South thus continue to undermine the prospects for the global community to set binding limits on greenhouse emissions in the future.

Ozone Protection

ozone layer
the protective layer of the upper atmosphere that shields the Earth from the sun's harmful impact on living organisms.

States' efforts to cope with depletion of the atmosphere's protective **ozone layer** share similarities with the story of climate change. In this case, however, an international regime has emerged and has been progressively strengthened as scientific evidence pointing toward the environmental damage caused by human activity continues to mount.

Ozone is a pollutant in the lower atmosphere, but in the upper atmosphere it provides the Earth with a critical layer of protection against the sun's harmful ultraviolet radiation. Scientists have discovered a marked depletion of the ozone layer—most notably an "ozone hole" over Antarctica which grows at times to be larger than the continental United States—and they have conclusively linked the thinning of the layer to CFCs, a related family of compounds known as halons, hydrochlorofluorocarbons (HCFCs), methyl bromide, and other chemicals. Depletion of the ozone layer exposes humans to increased health hazards of various sorts, particularly skin cancer, and threatens other forms of marine and terrestrial life. The release of many ozone-depleting gases also adds measurably to the accumulation of greenhouse gases that threaten dramatic climate change through global warming.

United Nations Environment Program (UNEP)
a UN agency created in 1972 to study environmental deterioration and propose regulations to protect the global environment.

Scientists began to link halons and CFCs to ozone depletion in the early 1970s. Even before their hypotheses were conclusively confirmed, the **United Nations Environment Program** (UNEP, a UN agency created in the aftermath of the 1972 Stockholm conference) sought some form of regulatory action. The scientific uncertainty surrounding the issue eased the sense of urgency some felt, and differences of policy in the United States (where bans were placed on some CFCs, such as aerosol propellants) and Europe (where they were not) slowed efforts to devise controls. Nevertheless, in 1985 the Vienna Convention on Protection of the Ozone Layer, whose purpose was to control ozone-modifying substances, was concluded. This landmark decision "represented the first international effort to deal formally with an environmental danger before it erupted" (Benedick 1991).

Two years later an even more significant agreement was reached, the Montreal Protocol on Substances That Deplete the Ozone Layer, signed by twenty-three states and the Commission of the European Community. The signatories agreed to reduce their CFC emissions to one-half of their 1986 levels by 2000. The agreement was widely heralded, as its parties accounted for more than 80 percent of global CFC emissions. Even further cuts were proposed later, with an agreement for a 1996 phaseout of CFC production in the Global North and in the Global South by around 2010. Subsequent agreements called for the phaseout of HCFCs. Originally developed because they were believed to be ozone-friendly alternatives to CFCs and a bridge to further scientific breakthroughs, HCFCs will be phased out completely by 2030 under current agreements (although many European states would prefer to speed up the timetable). Agreement was also reached in late 1995 to completely eliminate by 2010 production of methyl bromide, an ozone-depleting chemical widely used as an all-purpose pesticide.

The rapid move since 1985 to restrict the use of ozone-depleting chemicals contradicts the behavior the tragedy of the commons metaphor would lead us to expect. Rather than exploiting a common property (the atmosphere), states have successfully put their long-term collective interests in environmental protection ahead of short-term individual interests in protecting investments and jobs in the chemical industry.

As remarkable as this achievement is, implementation of the ozone regime still faces challenges. Notably, in spite of reductions in CFCs over the past decade, the ozone hole over Antarctica has continued to expand. Nature will eventually mend the atmospheric damage done by prior ozone-depleting chemical emissions, but it will take decades. Meanwhile, under the current international regime, depletion of the protective ozone shield is expected to accelerate before it begins to regenerate itself. An increase in sulfur particles due to volcanic eruptions (such as Mount Pinatubo in the Philippines in 1991 and Montserrat in 1997) and the burning of fossil fuels are contributing factors. The use of HCFCs as transition chemicals may also be debilitating. Although these compounds do not last as long as CFCs (whose ozone-depleting chemical reactions can last a century or more), they do most of their damage in ten to twenty years—precisely the time frame in which the ozone shield is already at greatest risk (Gurney 1996)—and they contribute markedly to global warming. Some states, however, notably the United States, are unwilling to shorten the time frame for elimination of HCFCs so as to permit the industries that have heavily invested in alternatives to CFCs to recover their investments (Porter and Brown 1996).

A second issue turns on the differing interests of developed and developing countries. Global production of CFCs declined sharply in the 1990s as the largest producers (and consumers) prepared for their complete phaseout. This, for the most part, has now been achieved. Production in the Global South, on the other hand, is surging. Demand is growing for refrigerators, air conditioners, and other products using CFCs. Current CFC production in the Global South is still comparatively low. However, as it increases between now and 2010, it will offset the gains realized by stopping production in the North. Developed countries agreed to provide aid to the developing countries to help them adopt CFC alternatives, but thus far they have failed to provide all of the resources promised. Without this support, many in the Global South may not be able to keep their end of the global bargain. Meanwhile, a significant illegal trade in both virgin and recycled CFCs has emerged, threatening to further undermine the positive effects of the ozone regime (Porter and Brown 1996).

Despite these challenges to the ozone regime, it stands as a significant achievement in international environmental cooperation. Can it serve as a model for breakthroughs on other issues, notably climate change? The success of the ozone initiative is widely attributed to the growing body of scientific evidence supporting the theory, combined with what some see as the absence of a significant requirement for changes in behavior or substantial costs. Containing other environmental threats meets resistance because the costs to vested interests are excessive. Again, consider the example of global warming. "There's a better scientific consensus on this than any other issue I know—except maybe Newton's second law of dynamics," observed D. James Baker of the U.S. National Oceanic Administration. "Man has reached the point where his impact on the climate can be as significant as nature's" (Warrick 1997). Yet, despite this consensus about the benefits of reducing the effects of global warming, many countries have failed to ratify the 1997 Kyoto Protocol to bolster the 1992 Convention on Climate Change or subsequent "action plans," and developing countries such as China and India are not even required to make a binding commitment to its provisions. Hence global efforts to avert the tragedy of the commons on atmospheric issues are inadequate. Continued conflicts are predicted in efforts to negotiate new treaties to protect forests and the Earth's biological heritage.

THE ECOPOLITICS OF FORESTS AND BIODIVERSITY

The world's forests play a critical role in the earth's complex ecological systems as well as in humankind's relationship with the environment and its well-being. Forests are intimately tied to preserving the earth's biodiversity and to protecting the atmosphere and land resources. For these reasons they have been an ecological issue of rising importance on the global agenda. Some rules have emerged to guide international behavior in the preservation of biodiversity, but issues concerning forests have proven much more difficult to address.

Shrinking Forests and Dust Bowls

Are the world's forests at risk of destruction, either through commercial exploitation or at the hands of local populations? Information is inconclusive, but estimates based on trends during the 1980s point toward considerable **deforestation** in the United States and throughout much of the Global South. Each minute, on average, 52 acres of the world's forests are lost (*Time,* April 13, 1998, 199). Destruction of tropical rain forests in such places as Brazil, Indonesia, and Malaysia is a matter of special concern, as much of the world's genetic heritage is found there. Ironically, commercial logging to sell lumber and other wood products in the global marketplace is a major cause of deforestation, but "why the virgin forest is being cut down is not so much the simple pursuit of profit but a set of perverse economic incentives. . . . The sort of policies that might help countries reduce their rate of deforestation are the sort of policies that are likely to promote economic growth. The desire to promote economic growth stands in the way of efforts to stop deforestation, despite the evidence that in the long run the countries that limit the rates at which they cut their forests are the one that expand their rates of economic growth the fastest" (*Economist,* March 21, 1998, 10–11).

■ **deforestation**
"the permanent depletion of the ground cover of trees to less than 10 percent" (World Resources Institute).

The representatives sent to the Earth Summit hoped to secure an easy victory on a statement of principle for global forest conservation, but opposition quickly developed to the principle that all countries were responsible for protecting national forests in the global interest. The Global South objected vigorously.

Led by Malaysia—a principal exporter of tropical wood products—the South resisted an effort to establish the legal principle that the world's forests are a common property resource, the "common heritage of mankind." Malaysia and others in the Global South feared that accepting that principle as applied to forests would give the Global North "some right to interfere in the management of the tropical forest countries' resources." In the end, the Earth Summit dropped "both the idea of international guidelines for forest management and any reference to trade in 'sustainably managed' forest products" (Porter and Brown 1996). The situation today is largely unchanged. The International Tropical Timber Organization (ITTO) remains the principal international forum for addressing transnational issues (notably trade) in timber products, but it is dominated largely by the timber interests themselves.

Meanwhile, high population growth rates, industrialization, and urbanization increase pressure to farm forests and marginal land less suited to cultivation and lead to deforestation and **desertification,** which make an increasing portion of the Earth's land mass deserts that are useless for agricultural productivity or wildlife habitats. Soil degradation has stripped more than 3 billion acres of the Earth's surface from productive farming, and "soil erosion and pollution are problems not just in developing countries with high population densities and increasing use of marginal lands but in the more highly developed regions of mechanized industrial agriculture as well" (Allen 2000). "Since 1950, 11 percent of the planet's vegetation (approximately [2.9 billion acres]) has suffered land degradation" (Crump 1998, 78). Map 11.1 shows the regions of the globe where deforestation and desertification are occuring most rapidly. Based on previous trends, it has been estimated that an area about the size of one-fourth to one-half of an American football field is deforested each time another person is added to the world population. This means that the addition of another billion people will require between 1.2 million to 2.5 million square kilometers of additional land for food production and other uses (J. Cohen 1995, 338). In the Global North, reforestation has alleviated some of the danger. This is not the case in many cash-starved Global South countries, which sell timber for income and to make room for their growing populations seemingly without concern for the long-term consequences of the destruction of their forests. The World Wide Fund for Nature (WWFN), a London-based environmental NGO, called 1997 "the year the world caught fire," complaining that more tropical forests were deliberately burned that year than in any other year in recorded history, 80 percent by multinational corporations (MNCs) clearing land for planting or development. Up to 12.4 million acres of forest were burned in Indonesia and Brazil alone in what the WWFN termed a "planetary disaster that is destroying our insurance for the future."

desertification the loss of agricultural land and forests when the cutting of timber, overcultivation and overgrazing strip the land of its soil-preserving vegative cover, so that soil erosion and degradation make once-green fields and forests into barren, unproductive dust bowls.

The clearing and burning of tropical rain forests to make room for farms and ranches is especially troublesome from the viewpoint of climate change. Green plants remove CO_2 from the atmosphere during photosynthesis. The natural processes that remove greenhouse gases are destroyed when forests

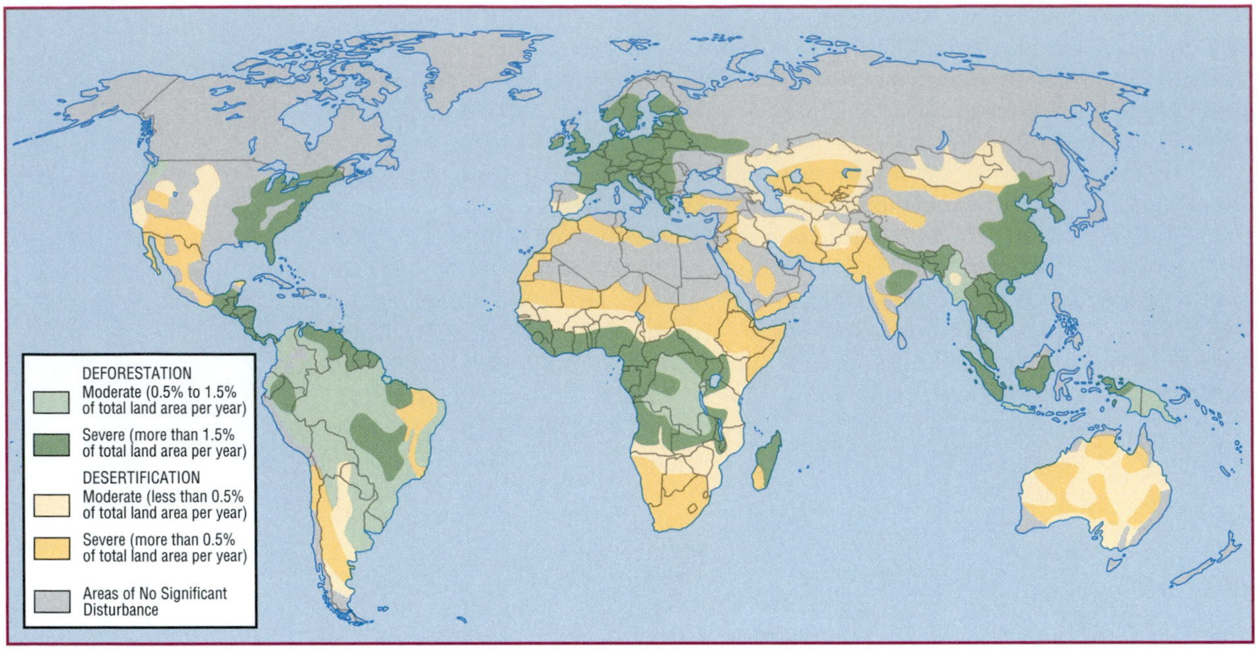

MAP 11.1
The Deforestation and Desertification of the Planet
Deforestation and desertification are global phenomena, destroying vast stretches of green forests and fields and turning them into brown deserts. "The rate of soil erosion is much higher in the Global South than the Global North. Worldwide, more than 10 million acres of farmland are becoming unproductive deserts each year" (Seck 1999, 9), and tropical forests in Central and South America, Africa, and Southeast Asia are being cleared at an alarming rate. The UN Convention to Combat Desertification (CCD), signed in November 1999 by 159 states at the treaty conference in Recife, Brazil, seeks to stop the spread of deserts, which now cover 2 million square miles inhabited by one-third of the world's population (Hottelet 1999, 8).
SOURCE: Allen (2000), 82.

are cut down, and, as the forests decay or are burned, the amount of CO_2 discharged into the atmosphere increases. This makes deforestation doubly destructive. Furthermore, the cattle raised on the newly deforested land add to the staggering volume of methane released into the atmosphere, which also contributes to global warming. Nonetheless, the World Resources Institute reports that the rate of tropical deforestation during the 1980s was so rapid that "an area three times the size of France was converted to other uses" (Knickerbocker 1994, 7).

■ **biodiversity** term used to describe the variety of species and genetic strains of the planetary ecosystem.

Biodiversity

Biodiversity, or biological diversity, is an umbrella term that refers to the earth's variety of life. Technically it encompasses three basic levels of organization in living systems: genetic diversity, species diversity, and ecosystem diver-

Deforestation Destruction of the world's forests contributes to climate change through global warming and threatens the earth's biodiversity and genetic heritage. Lumbering for commercial purposes exacts a toll on forests, but deforestation due to the expansion of agriculture to meet the needs of a growing population may be a more critical threat.

sity. Until recently public attention has been focused almost exclusively on preserving species diversity. Efforts to protect endangered species from extinction and conservation programs designed to protect old-growth forests, tallgrass prairies, wetlands, coastal habitats, coral reefs, and similar areas are illustrative.

Forests, especially tropical forests, are especially important to preserving biodiversity because they are home to countless species of animals and plants, many of them still unknown. Scientists believe that the global habitat contains between 8 and 10 million species. Of these, only about 1.5 million have been named, and most of them are in the temperate regions of North America, Europe, Russia, and Australia (Edwards 1995, 215). Destruction of tropical forests, where two-thirds to three-fourths of all species are believed to live, thus threatens the destruction of much of the world's biological diversity and genetic heritage. There exists overwhelming, alarming evidence that "environmental deterioration is taking a growing toll on a wide range of living organisms. Of the 242,000 plant species surveyed by the World Conservation Union in 1997, some 33,000, or 14 percent, are threatened with extinction, mainly as a result of clearing land for housing, roads, and industries. This mass extinction is disrupting nature's ability to provide essential ecosystem services, ranging from pollination to flood control" (Brown and Flavin 1999, 6).

Many experts worry that, due mainly to human activities, "the world is on the verge of an episode of major species extinction, rivaling five other documented periods over the past half-billion years during which a significant portion of global fauna and flora were wiped out," each time requiring "ten million years or more for the number of species to return to the level of diversity existing prior to the event." Others doubt the imminence of a massive die-out, pointing out that only a small fraction of the earth's species have actually disappeared over the past several centuries. Indeed, optimistic cornucopians argue that species extinction may not be bad news, as new species may evolve that will prove even more beneficial to humanity (McKibben 1998).

Although threats to biodiversity have implications for all species, and thus the issue resembles threats to other common property resources, biodiversity's distributional characteristics also make it different from other issues. In particular, because the Earth's biological heritage is concentrated in the tropics, the Global South has a special interest in this issue. It also has a growing concern about protecting its interest in the face of recent developments. "Traditionally, the genetic character of the many species of plants and animals have been considered a part of the common heritage of humankind, but increasingly they have become the objects of an enclosure movement that is seeking to enclose, privatize, and reduce the building blocks of life to marketable products" (Miller 1995).

■ **enclosure movement** the claiming of common properties by states or private interests.

Toward Enclosure: The Stakes. MNCs in the Global North are major players in the **enclosure movement.** In India, for example, products from the neem tree "for centuries . . . have been used locally for medicine, contraception, toiletries, timber, fuel, and insecticide. Its chemical properties have never been patented in India, but since 1985 U.S. and Japanese firms have taken out more than a dozen U.S. patents for a variety of neem compounds" (Miller 1995). Ironically, local Indian populations must now compete with MNCs for products long readily available to them, often at sharply higher prices.

Pharmaceutical companies have also laid claim to resources in the Global South. They actively explore plants, microbes, and other living organisms in tropical forests for possible use in prescription drugs. "This is a lucrative field; about 25 percent of the prescription drugs used in the United States have active ingredients extracted or derived from plants" (Miller 1995, 110). An example of a particularly successful project was Eli Lilly's development of drugs from the rosy periwinkle found in Madagascar's rain forest to treat childhood leukemia. Sales of the drugs amounted to about $100 million annually—although Madagascar received nothing for the use of its biological resource. Averting repetition of Madagascar's experience is a central concern among developing countries.

■ **genetic engineering** research geared to discover seeds for new types of plants and animals for sale and use as substitutes for naturally produced products.

■ **transgenetic crops** new crops with improved characteristics created artificially through genetic engineering, which combines genes from species that would not naturally interbreed.

The rapid growth of biotechnology has added incentives for preserving the earth's biological diversity so as to maintain a wide gene pool from which to develop new medical and agricultural products. At the same time, however, **genetic engineering** has made major strides in the race to develop hybrid seeds for new plants. Genetically modified or genetically engineered **transgenetic crops**

> have been altered by inserting genes to express a desired trait, such as herbicide tolerance or increased oil content. Unlike crop varieties developed through traditional plant breeding, transgenetics often contain genes from unrelated species—of plant, animal, bacteria, or other origin—with which the crop could not reproduce naturally. (*Vital Signs 1999,* 122)

British Protest of Transgenetic Crops In 1999 the United States and the European Union engaged in a "food fight" over the issue of hormone-treated beef and genetically altered soybeans the United States exported to Europe. The EU retaliated by banning the importation of bananas from the Americas. Activists dumped four tons of genetically altered soybeans produced in the United States outside 10 Downing Street, the home of British Prime Minister Tony Blair, to protest his assertion that bioengineered food was safe to eat.

Like the computer revolution, geneticists could revolutionize agriculture and transform the capability of the planet to feed the globe's growing population. This could increase **food security** and restore contaminated soils and polluted seas. However, two concerns about transgenetic crop engineering make the growing prevalence of commercially grown and globally marketed genetic agriculture production a rising controversy on the global agenda. The first is ethical: "How much should science manipulate nature to care for mankind" (Belsie, 1999)? Are gene-spliced plants and hormone-treated beef safe, or do they interfere with nature in ways that will prove unhealthy and ultimately harmful? "From England to India," cautions one analyst of transgenetic crops, "farmers and activists have destroyed transgenetic test plots in protest. Many governments have exercised caution over possible risks to ecological and human health" (*Vital Signs 1999*). The second issue is economic: Biogenetical engineering of harvests threatens to disrupt established trade and profits. Most transgenetically altered foods and crops (primarily soybeans, beef, corn, and cotton) produced in North America are sold abroad in other countries' grocery stores. Farmers and scientists increasingly must look to the Global South for primitive germ plasm (the genetic material containing hereditary information).

■ **food security** access by all people at all times to enough food for an active, healthy life (see p. 351).

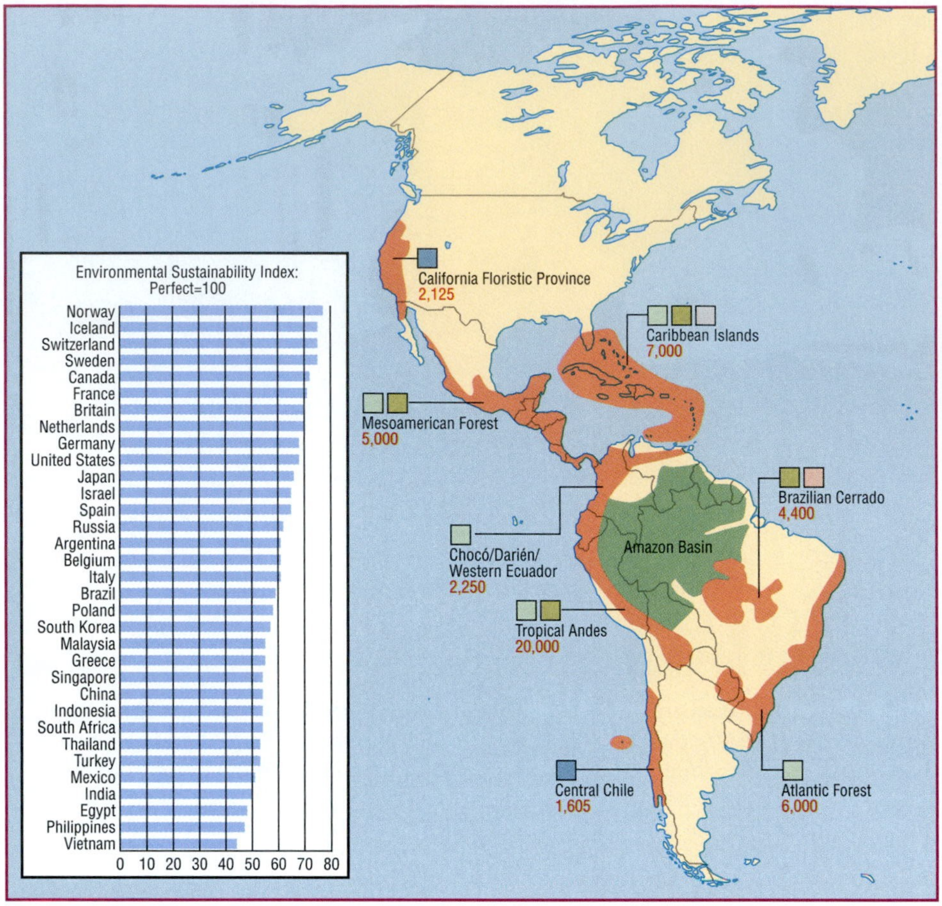

MAP 11.2
Biodiversity Bastions and Endangered Biodiversity Hot Spots

Because the survival of a large number of plant and animal species is threatened, biodiversity has become a hot global issue. The map shows the geographic spread and magnitude of the problem, with "biodiversity hot spots"—biologically rich areas that have been disturbed by human activity—identified in diverse ecosystem types. To the left is a ranking of countries based on five measures of "environmental sustainability" that estimates how well they are managing the environmental problems they face.

Note: Numbers under respective ecosysem types indicate number of plant species that are unique to each hot spot.

SOURCE: *Time* (December 14, 1998), 63–64; *Economist* (January 29, 2000), 126.

They assume that, as with the high seas, this primitive germ plasm is the common property of humankind. These genetic resources are used to produce genetically altered seeds for the international market. Since these are now patented and are private property, they can then be sold back to [Global South] consumers. The genetically altered seeds often need expensive additives such as chemical fertilizers and pesticides, which are often environmentally as well as financially costly. The picture for [Global South] agriculture deteriorates further when developing-country farmers focus on

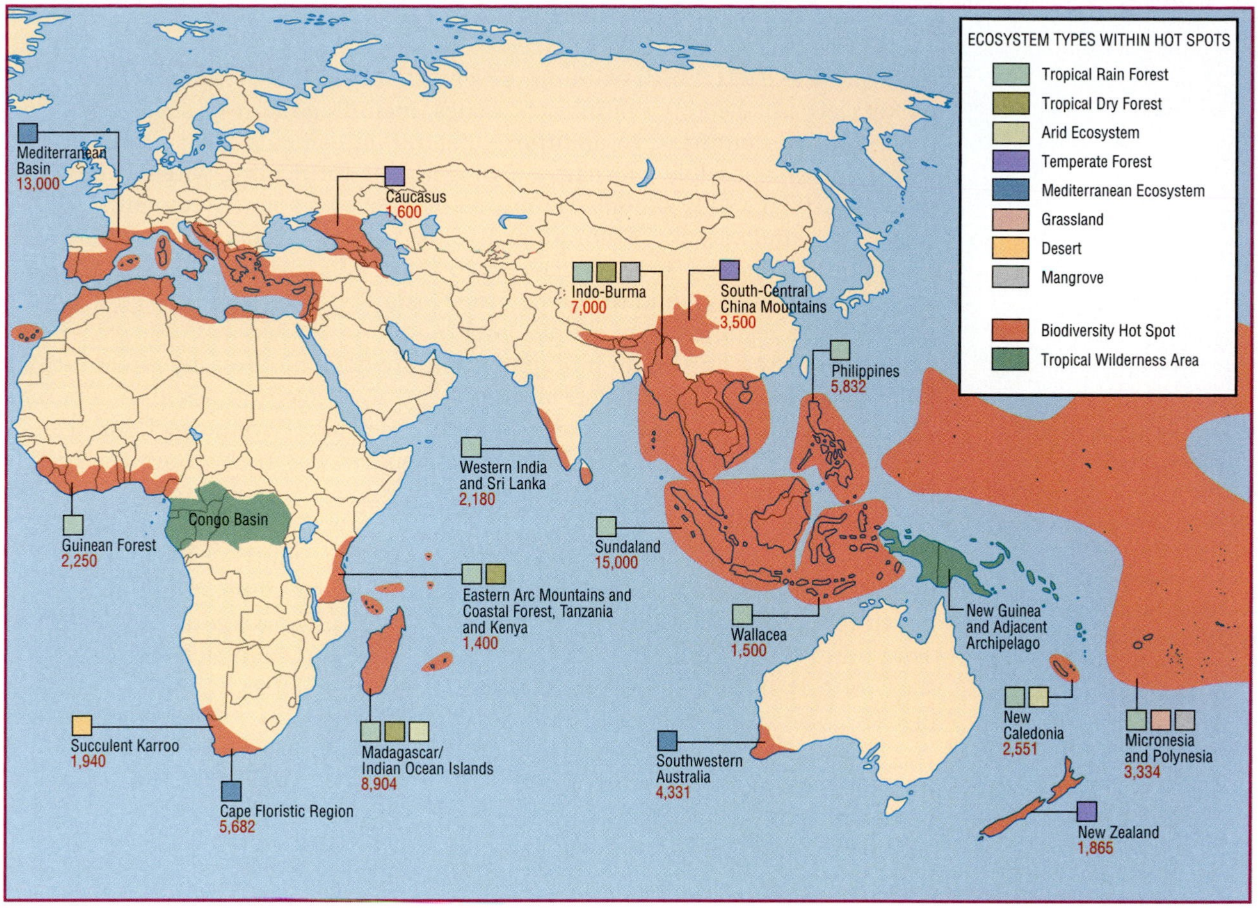

hybrid varieties to the detriment of, and at the risk of causing the disappearance of, the old varieties. (Miller 1995, 112)

Biogenetic engineering threatens to escalate the loss of global diversity. Biological resources—animal and plant species—are distributed unevenly in the world. Map 11.2 shows the location of major "biodiversity bastions," where more than half the Earth's species are found, primarily tropical wilderness territories laden with plant and animal species, covering only 2 percent of the land. It also shows the location of "biodiversity hot spots" where human activity threatens to disturb and potentially destroy many species that international law defines as a **collective good,** a resource for all humanity. According to the United Nations, about fifty thousand plant and animal species become extinct each year. This issue will intensify as the global community wrestles with the ethics of biodiversity preservation and management policies. The issue is also likely to influence and possibly poison relations between the Global North, where transgenetic crops are manufactured, and the Global South.

collective goods resources such as safe drinking water from which everyone benefits .

Toward Preservation: The International Response. Biodiversity has been a focus of global attention since the 1972 Stockholm conference. Between then and the 1992 Earth Summit, several conferences were held and agreements were reached on a number of issues, including many of special concern to developing countries. In addition, bilateral agreements have set important precedents for possible alternative arrangements for dealing with the competing interests at stake. Among the most innovative was an agreement between Costa Rica and Merck Corporation, the world's largest pharmaceutical firm. The company agreed to pay for access to Costa Rica's rich tropical forests for drug-related research and to compensate Costa Rica with royalty payments for any products resulting from this research.

What set the Earth Summit apart from previous biodiversity efforts at the international level was the special treatment now given the issue. A separate **Convention on Biodiversity** set forth a comprehensive framework for preservation of biodiversity. The road to the convention was rocky, however, as the Global North and South repeatedly clashed. Especially contentious was a proposal to use a recently created **Global Environment Facility (GEF)** within the World Bank, a joint enterprise with the UN Environment (UNEP) and Development (UNDP) Programs, as the instrument for resource transfers from North to South to meet the objectives spelled out in the biodiversity convention as well as in other Earth Summit documents. The developing countries protested that the World Bank heavily favors the interests of the Global North, which is its principal source of funds.

■ **Convention on Biodiversity**
a 1993 treaty obligating ratifying states to rules for sharing the profits of biotechnological discoveries and protecting endangered species and habitats.

■ **Global Environment Facility (GEF)**
an instrument for resource transfers from Global North to Global South, as spelled out in the Convention on Biodiversity.

Ratified by 161 countries, the Convention on Biodiversity spells out guidelines for sharing the profits of biotechnology between the Global North and South. It also commits governments to devise national strategies for conserving species and habitats, protecting endangered species, expanding protected areas and repairing damaged ones, and promoting public awareness of the need to protect the Earth's heritage.

Still, much remains to be done. Although food production is rising and most people are living longer and healthier lives,

> These gains are threatened by a growing scarcity of fresh water and a loss of topsoil and productive farmland. According to the UN, one-third of the world's population does not have an adequate supply of clean water, and two-thirds will be deprived of it by 2010 unless action is taken. Some 3.7 billion acres of farmland—nearly 30 percent of the world's vegetated surface—are now degraded to some degree.
>
> Air and water quality is generally improving in rich countries. But despite substantial reforestation in those countries and a recent slowing of deforestation globally, forest loss continues worldwide.
>
> Each year, according to the United Nations, an area the size of Nepal is cut or burned. Ocean pollution threatens the health and livelihood of the two-thirds of humanity living near coastlines, and about 60 percent of commercial fisheries are overfished or fully fished and in danger of depletion. Toxic chemicals still pose significant threats. (Stevens 1997, 4)

The obstacles to overcoming the human habits that have reduced environmental security are many. This was illustrated in 1999 in Cartagena, Colombia, when the attempt to forge a proposed Biosafety Protocol failed. The "biotech" treaty was the first to seek to regulate trade in genetically modified products, but the United States and a handful of other big agricultural-exporting countries rejected this global regime, even though it had the support of more than 130 other countries more concerned about the environment than about business profits (Pollack, 1999). Part of the problem with creating rules to protect the environment and life on the planet is due to the fact that scientific uncertainty abounds about how (or even whether) species can be saved. Balancing the interests of those who seek access to genetic materials with those who have a stake in the profits of biotechnology must still be resolved. And agreements on mechanisms to finance the obligations of biodiversity-protection regimes and creating an institutional mechanism to oversee their implementation must still be reached. As one environmental specialist astutely observes, "governments of most nations . . . recognize the need for rules to preserve those aspects of the global environment that are beyond the jurisdiction of any state." However, they "often balk at agreeing to specific regulations and complying with them" to avert environmental tragedies (Soroos 2001). At the conclusion of the 1997 Rio Plus Five Earth Summit, observers sadly noted that "with some important exceptions, environmental trends [had] changed little since the 1992 Rio gathering" (Stevens 1997), and that the magnitude of the corrections needed to preserve the global commons is huge (see Table 11.1).

TRADE, THE ENVIRONMENT, AND SUSTAINABLE DEVELOPMENT

This chapter began by posing the question of whether national security and environmental security are compatible objectives. A similar contrast may be drawn between free trade and sustainable development. Do these values complement one another, or are they in conflict? The question is especially pertinent in a rapidly globalizing world in which trade increasingly links politics, economics, societies, and cultures in complex interdependencies.

Liberal economic theory argues that free trade produces benefits. If all states specialize in the production of goods in which they enjoy comparative advantages and trade them with others who enjoy advantages in other products, all will prosper. Following this logic, commercial liberals conclude that free trade increases prosperity, and wealth contributes to the capacity to manage the environment well. "Growth enables governments to tax and to raise resources for a variety of objectives, including the abatement of pollution and the general protection of the environment. Without such revenues, little can be achieved, no matter how pure one's motives may be" (Bhagwati 1993).

Environmentalists question commercial liberal economists' logic, especially because they see economic growth and environmental protection as goals at cross-purposes. "Free traders seek to maximize profits and production without regard for considerations that represent hidden social and environmental costs [and fail to appreciate] that growth is increasing environmental costs

TABLE 11.1

A Post-Rio Report Card on a Sustainable Global Commons

Area	*Status*
Poverty	Gaps between rich and poor continue to grow. More than 1.1 billion people—20 percent of the world's population—live on the equivalent of less than $1 a day.
Consumption	Twenty percent of the world's people consume 80 percent of its resources. Some large developing countries are moving rapidly toward high-consumption lifestyles.
Population	Fertility rates are declining more rapidly than expected in most regions, but population-growth rates still strain natural resources in some countries.
Forests	Forest loss has declined, but 33.8 million acres of forest—about the size of Nepal—are cut or burned yearly.
Fresh Water	By 2025, two-thirds of the population could live in countries facing moderate or severe water stress.
Oceans	About 60 percent of fish stocks are overfished or fully fished. Marine pollution continues to pose a serious problem.
Climate	Global emissions of carbon dioxide, and other greenhouse gases, are rising.
Energy	Rapid growth in fossil fuel use in many developing countries is leading to severe pollution. Energy consumption is projected to more than double by 2050.
Land	World food production is rising, but more than 800 million people still suffer from hunger and malnutrition. Pesticides, poor farming methods, and desertification—the degradation of drylands—have taken a heavy toll.
Toxics	About 3 million tons of toxic and hazardous waste cross national borders each year.
Biodiversity	About fifty thousand plant and animal species are lost each year.

SOURCE: United Nations, as summarized in the *Christian Science Monitor* (June 24, 1997), 11.

faster than benefits from production—thereby making us poorer, not richer" (Daly 1993).

Beyond the issue of the gains from and costs of trade, environmentalists and liberal economists differ in their assessments of the wisdom of using trade to promote environmental standards (see Controversy: Can Globalization Be Green?). Liberal economists see such efforts as market distortions, while environmentalists view them as useful instruments for correcting market failures, such as markets' inability to compensate for the externalities of environmental exploitation (e.g., atmospheric pollution by chemical companies). Some countries, however, particularly in the Global South, view the use of trade mechanisms to protect the environment as yet another way in which the rich states block entry into lucrative Global North markets, thus keeping the Global South permanently disadvantaged (Durbin 1995).

Trade-offs must sometimes be made between goals that, in principle, all seem designed to increase human well-being. However, another interpretation maintains that trade encourages states to live beyond their means. It "magnifies the ecological effects of production by expanding the market for commodities beyond national boundaries. . . . It allows nations that have depleted their resource bases or passed strict laws protecting them to reach past their borders for desired products, effectively shifting the environmental impacts of consumption to someone else's backyard" (French 1994). These concerns provoked Leon Brittan, the European Union commissioner for exernal trade, in 1999 to argue that "the economic case for pursuing the process of trade liberalization is an overwhelming one. But it is impossible to ignore the fact that . . . there are widespread fears of the social and environmental consequences of the combination of liberalization and globalization."

What happens when everyone does the same thing? The tragedy of the commons metaphor suggests a bleak future. Is ruin the destination toward which humankind rushes?

TOWARD SUSTAINABILITY

Sustainable development promises a much brighter future. Although the goal remains distant and elusive, governments' and nonstate actors' acceptance of the concept throughout the world invites environmentally sensitive responses to the challenges posed. Differences between the rich countries of the Global North and the rapidly growing states in the Global South will continue to spark controversy. Contention will be especially pronounced on issues involving the transfer of resources and technology—as called for to deal with climate change, ozone depletion, biodiversity, and a host of other specific problem areas. This controversy will arise in part from differing perceptions as to who is responsible for what.

There is little doubt that the Global South, with rapidly growing populations and rising affluence, faces increasingly serious environmental challenges. Nonetheless, the trend is already "toward better environmental policies, increased investment in environmental infrastructure and technology, and the pursuit generally of economic development alternatives that minimize environmental impacts" (Helman 1995).

The Global North faces serious environmental challenges as well, as its consumption levels far exceed those of other states. Interestingly, though, as the industrialized countries move into the information age and their economies shift away from "dirty" manufacturing to much cleaner service-oriented activities, the adverse environmental consequences of their economic activities will diminish, or at least they will decline locally. Trade with other states, however, will ensure continuing pressures on global resources and the environmental burdens they pose.

CONTROVERSY

Can Globalization Be Green?

Free Trade and Sustainable Development

The links between trade and the environment raise three main questions, about which much disagreement exists, yet the global community is increasingly pressured to debate. In an age when choices often involve the lesser of two evils, assessment of trade-offs and payoffs between competing values is necessary. What do you think about the three questions posed by the World Bank that follow? How would you choose if you had to make policy choices for your country and for the global community?

1. What are the environmental effects of trade liberalization?

The fear that these effects are generally negative has led to calls for amending trade policies to take explicit account of environmental goals. Recent controversies have concerned the negative effects of the . . . North American Free Trade Agreement [NAFTA] on air and water quality in Mexico and the southwestern United States, of liberalized cassava exports to the [EU] on soil erosion in Thailand, and of exchange rate depreciation on deforestation in Ghana. But using trade restrictions to address environmental problems is inefficient and usually ineffective. Liberalized trade fosters greater efficiency and higher productivity and may actually reduce pollution by encouraging the growth of less-polluting industries and the adoption and diffusion of cleaner technologies.

In these and other examples, the primary cause of environmental problems is not liberalized trade but failure of markets to price the environment appropriately. . . . Indeed, modifying trade policies to deal with environmental problems may worsen degradation. Thus, restricting the export of logs, as in Indonesia, raises returns to the domestic wood-processing industry and may contribute to inefficient and high-cost production that could worsen deforestation. Usually, more direct instruments than trade policies are available for combating deforestation, soil erosion, or industrial pollution.

2. Should trade policies be used to influence environmental standards in other countries?

The arguments noted above apply here as well and are strengthened by another consideration: Some variation in environmental standards across regions and coun-

The key to reducing the stress that economic growth places on the environment may be replacing our current ideas about markets with the concept of a steady-state economy. "A steady-state economy is one whose throughput [the speed at which resources are consumed] remains constant at a level that neither depletes the environment beyond its regenerative capacity nor pollutes it beyond its absorptive capacity" (Daly 1993). This is sustainable development (qualitative improvements) without growth (quantitative increases in the use or consumption of materials), in its essence. "An economy that is steady in scale may still continue to develop a greater capacity to satisfy human wants by increasing the efficiency of its resource use, by improving social institutions, and by clarifying its ethical priorities—but not by increasing resource throughput." Is the world ready for such a revolution in thinking? Even if it is, can the revolution be achieved? As one futurist put the question,

> The bottom-line argument goes like this: the next fifty years are a special time. They will decide how strong and healthy the planet will be for centuries to come. . . . so it's the task of those of us alive right now to deal with this spe-

tries is justified by differences in priorities and in capacities to assimilate pollutants or cope with resource degradation. When countries (typically, the bigger and richer ones) use trade policy to impose their environmental standards, the effect is to protect domestic producers from foreign competition. Applying the same standards to domestic production and imports may be justified when, as with cars or pesticides, consumption leads to environmental damage. But even there, environmental concerns do not warrant uniformity across countries.

Evidence shows that developing countries do not compete for foreign investment in "dirty" industries by lowering their environmental standards. . . . Rather, anecdotal data . . . suggest the opposite: Because it is cheaper for multinational corporations to use the same technologies as they do in industrial countries, these firms can be potent sources of environmental improvement.

3. Should trade policies be used to enforce or implement international environmental agreements?

Trade measures to implement environmental agreements include the Montreal Protocol, which phases out ozone-depleting chemicals; the Basel Convention for controlling the transboundary movement and the disposal of hazardous wastes; and the Convention on International Trade in Endangered Species (CITES), which supports the embargo on ivory trade. The use of trade instruments could be justified in some of these cases. For instance, restricting trade in hazardous and toxic wastes . . . is appropriate if the capacities of many countries to monitor and dispose of these wastes are in doubt. But in most countries, the scale of such trade is small in comparison with the volume of hazardous wastes being generated domestically. Therefore, the concern should be to minimize the production of these wastes and to devise ways of ensuring their safe disposal. A total ban on all trade in hazardous and toxic wastes would be counterproductive because it would prevent the development of collective arrangements for treatment and disposal, even where individual countries, as in western Europe, can specialize in safe and low-cost disposal.

The ban on trade in ivory to protect the African elephant also involves difficult tradeoffs. Available evidence shows that ivory prices have fallen and poaching has declined since the ban became effective. But countries such as Botswana, South Africa, and Zimbabwe have argued that the ivory ban, by raising prices in the long run, will simply make poaching more lucrative. . . . These countries also claim that the ban discriminates against their efforts to manage their elephant herds sustainably by using revenue from hunting and tourism to enrich local people and finance law enforcement.

SOURCE: World Bank (1992), 67.

cial phase, to squeeze us through the next fifty years. . . . We need in these fifty years to be working simultaneously on all parts of the equation—our ways of life, on our technologies and on our population. (McKibben 1998, 78)

KEY TERMS

ecopolitics
realism
environmental security
neoliberalism
epistemic community
cornucopians
neo-Malthusians
paradigm
sustainable development
Earth Summit
tragedy of the commons
relative gains
absolute gains
global commons
externalities
photovoltaic (PV) cells
global warming
greenhouse effect
acid rain
ozone layer

United Nations Environment Program
deforestation
desertification
biodiversity
enclosure movement
genetic engineering
transgenetic crops
food security
collective goods
Convention on Biodiversity
Global Environment Facility (GEF)

SUGGESTED READING

Bright, Chris. *Life Out of Bounds: Bioinvasion in a Borderless World.* Washington, D.C.: Worldwatch, 1999.

Brown, Lester R., Michael Renner, and Brian Halweil. *Vital Signs 1999: The Environmental Trends That Are Shaping Our Future.* New York: Norton, 1999.

Foster, Gregory D., and Louise B. Wise. "Sustainable Security: Transnational Environmental Threats and Foreign Policy," *Harvard International Review* 21 (Fall 1999): 20–23.

French, Hilary. *Vanishing Borders: Protecting the Planet in the Age of Globalization.* Washington, D.C.: Worldwatch Institute, 2000.

Goldsmith, Edward, and Peter Bunyard, eds. *The Ecologist,* bimonthly journal. Cambridge, Mass.: MIT Press.

Gore, Al. *Earth in the Balance: Ecology and the Human Spirit.* Boston: Houghton Mifflin, 1992.

Journal of International Affairs, Fueling the 21st Century: The New Political Economy of Energy. New York: Columbia University School of Public and International Affairs, Fall 1999.

Litfin, Karen T., ed. *The Greening of Sovereignty in World Politics.* Cambridge, Mass.: MIT Press, 1998.

Renner, Michael. *Fighting for Survival: Environmental Decline, Social Conflict, and the New Age of Insecurity.* Washington, D.C.: Worldwatch, 1999.

Roodman, David Malin. *The Natural Wealth of Nations: Harnessing the Market for the Environment.* Washington, D.C.: Worldwatch, 1999.

United Nations Environment Program. *Global Environment Outlook.* New York: Oxford University Press, 2000.

Young, Oran R., ed. *The Effectiveness of International Environmental Regimes.* Cambridge, Mass.: MIT Press, 1999.

WHERE ON THE WORLD WIDE WEB?

Earth Times
http://www.earthtimes.org/

Earth Times is an independent international electronic newspaper devoted to reporting global and national issues relating to the environment, sustainable development, population, human rights, and current affairs. This award-winning site will give you up-to-date reports on and analyses of ecological issues. It is a very good resource on current events.

Greenpeace
http://www.greenpeace.org/

Greenpeace is an international nongovernmental organization (NGO) committed to global environmental advocacy. Its operation focuses on protecting the oceans and forests, phasing out use of fossil fuels, and promoting renewable energies in order to stop climate change. Visit this site to see how a nongovernmental actor affects global environmental issues. Find out how you can become a cyber-activist!

IISDnet
http://iisd1.iisd.ca/

The International Institute for Sustainable Development (IISD) has produced a Web site to help users learn about sustainable development, provide information on controversial topics, explore issues in environmental management, and show how businesses can turn sustainability into a competitive advantage. The site also includes a link to multimedia resources. To get to this module, click on SD Overview on the homepage, then History and Institutions. On this page you will find a link to the Sustainable Development Timeline, an especially interesting section. Here you can follow how our society has tried to integrate protection of the environment with the establishment of healthy societies and economies. Is there a specific event that you believe has crystallized global thinking on sustainable development? Which decade do you believe has seen the greatest advances? Follow some of the timeline links and read about the organizations that have been at the forefront of environmental protection.

Millennium
http://tectonic.nationalgeographic.com/2000/index.cfm

At the dawn of the new millennium, the National Geographic Society has produced a Web site that focuses on the important issues that confront humankind. Among these is climate change. Debates rage over whether changes in the atmosphere are a threat to ecological security. Form your own opinion as you explore the Society's on-line Laboratory. A quick study of the carbon cycle can help you understand how humans have affected the functioning of the atmosphere. Read about the analysis of ice cores from Antarctica showing that temperatures and carbon dioxide levels have risen and fallen together over the centuries. View a computer model that depicts how conditions on Earth could change with a rise in carbon dioxide levels. Compare the atmospheres of Earth and Venus. What is the major difference between the two sister planets?

Rainforest Action Network
http://www.ran.org/ran

The mission of the Rainforest Action Network is to protect the Earth's rain forests and support the rights of rain forest inhabitants through education, grassroots organizing, and nonviolent direct action. Visit the network's Web site and learn about the threats to rain forests and read about the campaigns that this group is waging. Take a quiz to see how proficient you are on rain forest issues. Learn what you can do to help protect the world's rain forests.

The Worldwatch Institute
http://www.worldwatch.org/

One of the leading publications on the environment is now on-line. The Worldwatch Institute is dedicated to fostering the evolution of an environmentally sustainable society. Scan the most recent articles from the *World Watch* magazine or access alerts and press briefings.

GLOBAL CONFLICT AND ITS MANAGEMENT

The threat of violence and warfare casts a dark cloud over many people throughout the world, who live in fear of aggression from terrorists, a neighboring state, or even from their own government, bent on persecuting its citizens because of their nationality or religion. National and international security—freedom from fear of a military attack—remains precarious in the twenty-first century. Millions of people are the victims of aggression, and millions more have had to flee as refugees to seek sanctuary from the ravages of war.

Part IV explores the changing character of armed conflict and war (Chapter 12), looking closely at the growing number of prolonged civil wars in failing states that undermine national security and threaten human security. Chapter 13 addresses the strategies of states to provide for defense through military expenditures and to produce and import armaments. It discusses the changing national security strategies of the great powers in light of anxieties about a new age of nuclear proliferation and the rising danger posed by weapons of mass destruction, such as biological and chemical weapons. Chapter 14 examines how states seek to coerce other states to agree to their demands or to refrain from behaving in an undesired way by such means as economic sanctions or military interventions. Finally, we consider the alternative paths to peace prescribed by the realist (Chapter 15) and liberal (Chapter 16) theoretical traditions.

CHAPTER 12

Armed Conflict between and within States

Topics and Themes

- Armed conflict: Continuities and change
- The causes of armed conflict: Rival theories
- Armed conflict within states: Civil wars, uncivil methods
- Terrorism
- The human tragedy of violent conflict

- **Controversy** Does Nationalistic Love of Country Cause War with Foreign Nations?
- **Controversy** Does Civil Strife Breed External Aggression? The Diversionary Theory of War Debated

Australian peacemaker and East Timorese refugees

Mankind must put an end to war or war will put an end to mankind.

—John F. Kennedy, U.S. president, 1961

Sovereignty carries with it many rights, but killing and torturing innocent people are not among them. Serious and repeated abuses of human rights are everybody's business.

—Madeleine Albright, U.S. secretary of state, 2000

It is a rare day when a daily newspaper does not report another horrifying story of the use of armed force somewhere in the world. Since 1945 not a single day has gone by without war—a continuous saga of violent conflicts that in 1992 led U.S. President George Bush to lament that "only the dead have seen the end of conflict." And the frequency of mass slaughter in war had not declined as the twentieth century drew to a close. At the start of 1999, thirty-six major armed conflicts were active in thirty-one locations throughout the world, including Afghanistan, Iraq, and East Timor (Wallensteen and Sollenberg 1999, 593), and twenty-eight other areas of high tension were also raging with armed violence (*Christian Science Monitor,* February 12, 1999, 12–13). The bloodletting persisted in March 2000, when six states sent armies to fight in the oil- and diamond-rich Congo, whose autocratic regime was undergoing a civil war at the same time nine Congo rebel groups were fighting to overthrow governments in neighboring countries and UN peacekeepers were preparing to contain what was widely called "Africa's First World War." Given war's widespread occurrence, it is little wonder that so many people think of international politics as armed aggression.

In *On War,* Prussian strategist Karl von Clausewitz advanced his famous dictum that war is merely an extension of diplomacy by other means—"a form of communication between countries," albeit an extreme form. This insight underscores the realist belief that **war** is an instrument for states to use to resolve their conflicts. War, however, is the deadliest instrument of conflict resolution, and its onset usually means that persuasion and negotiations have failed.

■ **war**
a condition arising within states (civil war) or between states (interstate war) when actors use violent means to destroy their opponents or coerce them into submission.

In international relations, **conflict** regularly occurs when actors interact and disputes over incompatible interests arise. In and of itself, conflict (like **politics**—the exercise of influence) is not necessarily threatening, because war and conflict are different. Conflict may be seen as inevitable and occurs when two parties perceive differences between themselves and seek to resolve those differences to their own satisfaction. Some conflict results whenever people interact and may be generated by religious, ideological, ethnic, economic, political, or territorial issues; therefore we should not regard it as abnormal. Nor should we regard conflict as necessarily destructive, since it can promote social solidarity, creative thinking, learning, and communication—all factors critical to the resolution of disputes and the cultivation of cooperation (Coser 1956). However, the costs of conflict do become threatening when the partners turn to arms to settle their perceived irreconcilable differences. When that happens, violence occurs, and we enter the separate sphere of warfare.

■ **conflict**
discord, often arising in international relations over perceived incompatibilities of interest.

■ **politics**
activities aimed at getting another actor to do something it would not otherwise do (see p. 457).

This chapter explores the challenge that armed conflicts pose in world affairs, examining the character, causes, and magnitude of international violence, as well as changes in it over time. It investigates three primary ways that **armed conflict** is most often used: *wars* between states, *civil wars* within states, and *terrorism.* The next chapters consider the ways in which states and other global actors respond to this challenge and the major approaches they have taken for preventing violent conflicts and for containing and terminating those that erupt.

■ **armed conflict**
combat between the military forces of two or more states or groups.

ARMED CONFLICT IN THE WORLD: CONTINUITIES AND CHANGE

Our understanding of the amount of armed conflict occurring globally depends in part on the definitions scholars use to establish types and thresholds. One broad measure of war provides a disturbing estimate that includes domestic and foreign incidents of armed conflict resulting in death to both soldiers and civilians. It shows that

> As the twentieth century [raced] to a close, it already [stood] out as the most productive *and* destructive century on record. No other comes close to it in terms of social progress—in the education, health, and wealth it has provided for the population. Yet it is also evident that no other century on record equals the twentieth in uncivilized civil violence, in the number of conflicts waged, the hordes of refugees created, the millions of people killed in wars, and the vast expenditures for "defense." (Sivard 1996, 7)

■ **behavioralism**
the methodological research movement to incorporate rigorous scientific analysis into the study of world politics in order to base conclusions about patterns on measurement, data, and evidence rather than on speculation and subjective belief.

These grim statistics can be put into perspective by observing trends in the number of wars breaking out each year, based on quantitative inventories from **behavioralism.** Different definitions and indicators produce slightly different estimates of frequencies, but agree that many new wars have broken out each year since World War II. In general, the incidence of war has risen in the second half of the twentieth century (*Vital Signs 1999,* 113). From 1950 through 1998, by one calculation conducted at the University of Hamburg, no less than four hundred separate wars occurred in the second half of the twentieth century. The number of armed conflicts throughout the globe peaked in 1992 at fifty-two—a level almost five times that of the 1950s (when they averaged eleven each year) and more than three times the average number of fifteen each year during the 1960s. More than thirty-one conflicts occurred each year in the 1970s, more than forty in the 1980s, and more than forty-four each year in the 1990s.

A good measure of the globalization of international violence is obtained by considering the number of wars underway each year. This index paints an especially depressing portrait, because many active wars that started much earlier have persisted for years. Take into account the fact that of the nearly 50 wars and armed conflicts active in 1998, "26 had their origin during the 1990s, and another 8 during the 1980s. But some conflicts are far more protracted: 8 started in the 1970s, 5 during the 1960s, and 1 goes back to the 1950s" (*Vital Signs 1999,* 112). Hence, the number of armed conflicts throughout the globe involving the military of a state government appears much more widespread and frequent when the total number still raging—those underway, many across several years and even decades—are compared with the smaller number of new wars that are initiated.

The frequency of the outbreak of wars and their continuation since World War II suggests why United Nations (UN) Secretary-General Boutros Boutros-Ghali described the contemporary global system as a "culture of death." Although the location, duration, size, and frequency has changed over time in the past fifty years, wars have been recurrent as well as constantly destructive. Consider the most deadly armed conflicts—those claiming more than one hundred thousand lives. From 1945 to 1998, nine such large-scale wars were underway each year on average, a frequency that has remained relatively constant, averaging 8.5 each year in the 1960s, 7.3 in the 1970s, and 10.1 in the 1980s; in the 1990s, the number has declined from 11 in 1991 to 7 in 1994 (Kane 1995) and 1 at the start of 1998 (*Defense Monitor* 27 [1998], 3).

In the short span of only a single century, death and destruction have been the twentieth century's most cruel characteristic. Estimates of the deaths from as many as 650 total armed conflicts between 1900 and today are difficult to make, but most historians believe these wars combined to take the lives of at least 125 million people, with a rising proportion of the victims of warfare being civilian noncombatants instead of armed forces (Sivard 1996; *Vital Signs 1999*). "The twentieth century has been history's most violent: "By one analysis, the number of war deaths during the post-1945 period has been more than twice that in the nineteenth century and seven times that in the eighteenth century" (Kane 1995, 19).

Figure 12.1 charts the number of armed conflicts globally from three perspectives. The first takes a long-term perspective, looking at the changes over the six hundred years from 1400 to 2000. It identifies, by decade, the outbreak of 2,566

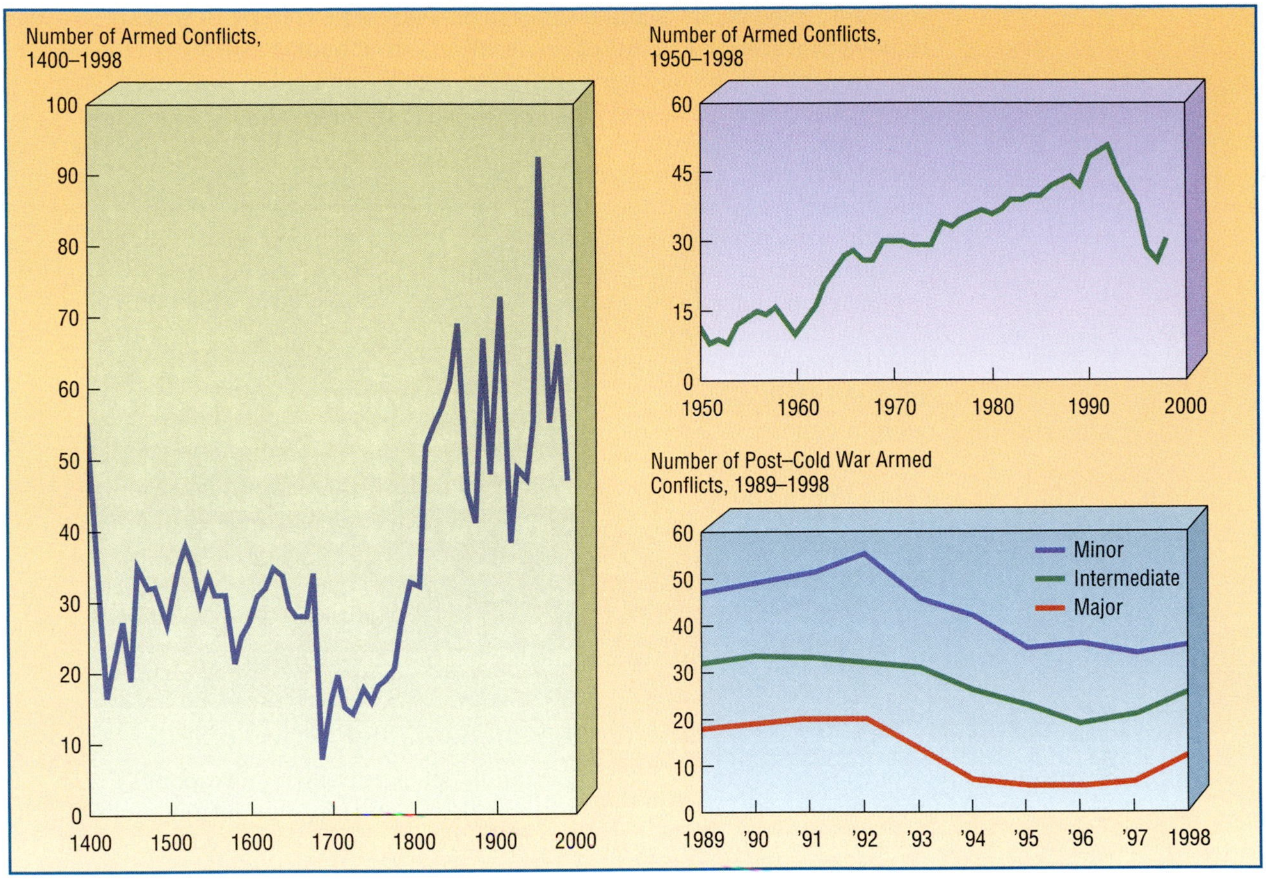

FIGURE 12.1

The Changing Frequency of Armed Conflicts on Three Scales

Armed conflict between states has been around for as long as sovereign states have existed, as the trends in the figure at left of armed conflicts between 1400 and 2000 demonstrate. That six-century profile breaks down 2,566 individual wars by the decade in which they began, and shows that the number dropped considerably in the late 1600s in the aftermath of the Thirty Years' War, but has risen sharply in the three centuries since, peaking in the 1960s. The top right figure reports contemporary changes in the number of wars each year between 1950 and 1998, revealing that the last half of the twentieth century was anything but peaceful. The frequency of wars has risen steadily since 1950 for a total of 400, and hit an all-time high of 52 in 1992, after which total armed conflicts worldwide have declined slightly; at the beginning of 1999, 31 wars were underway. The post–Cold War period, beginning in 1989 after the Berlin Wall was torn down, is of special interest because past patterns of armed conflict fueled by superpower ideological rivalry have begun to change as conflict has begun to erupt from other causes. The figure at bottom right records a total of 108 armed conflicts worldwide, arranged in three categories: major wars with more than one thousand battle-related deaths in a given year; intermediate armed conflicts with more than one thousand battle deaths but fewer than that level in any single year, and minor armed conflicts with battle-related deaths below one thousand during each war's entire history. It is important to note that nearly all of the total 108 armed conflicts, 92 (85 percent), were internal armed conflicts that took place within a single state's borders; the remaining 7 interstate wars were between opposing countries such as India and Pakistan in 1997 (Wallensteen and Sollenberg 1999, 597, 594).

SOURCE: Left, Brecke (1999), 8; top right, University of Hamburg, presented in *Vital Signs 1999* (1999), 112; bottom right, Conflict Data Project at the Uppsala University, Sweden, Wallensteen and Sollenberg (1999), 594.

separate armed conflicts and testifies to the entrenched nature of warfare as a continuous characteristic of human civilization throughout the history of the modern state-system. The second figure inventories the rising number of armed conflicts each year between 1950 and 1998. The third figure pinpoints the frequency of 108 total armed conflicts worldwide in the decade of special interest since the Cold War ended with the collapse of the Soviet Union in 1991. These inventories report, in different ways, what the mass media tell us; that violence and international insecurity are likely to remain core concerns in the twenty-first century.

Of particular concern to international security are global trends in wars between established states (such as Iraq's 1990 attack on Kuwait and the Gulf War that followed). Armed interstate conflicts that cross borders and result in one thousand or more battle fatalities have been far less frequent between 1945 and 1998 than all types of armed conflicts in general. Since World War II, 104 such interstate wars were under way annually during this period, with, on average, 2.5 occurring each year in the 1950s, 2.6 in the 1960s, 2.9 in the 1970s, 3.1 in the 1980s, and 1.2 in the 1990s (Worldwatch database diskette 1999; Wallensteen and Sollenberg 1999, 594). This tells us that although the post–World War II period has not been peaceful, most armed conflicts have been civil wars *within* states instead of wars *between* two recognized countries. While we will look separately at internal wars, let us first look more closely at the characteristics and causes of armed conflicts between states.

The Changing Character of Armed Conflict between States

Over the course of history, armed conflicts have changed in response to innovations in military technology and their dispersion throughout the globe. In the twentieth century, increasingly destructive modern weaponry has transformed contemporary warfare in major ways:

- First, although the average duration of interstate wars remained "remarkably steady" from 1500 (Brecke 1999), after World War II the length of major armed conflicts between states shortened. Presumably, the increasing technological capacity of militarily powerful countries to inflict massive destruction has forced many armed conflicts to end sooner, even though recently many lower-scale wars between weaker Global South countries have lasted for lengthy periods.
- Second, the average number of countries involved in major wars has fallen sharply since World War II. This is observable both in the types of and number of countries that now participate in armed conflicts.
- Third, armed conflicts have become increasingly concentrated geographically and now almost exclusively involve the Global South's less developed countries. Since 1945, nine out of ten wars have been in the weak or failed states of the Global South (Worldwatch 1999 database diskette). Since 1990, most armed conflicts have occurred in Asia and Africa, the region with the globe's highest number of states, largest populations, and lowest levels of income; thirteen wars were underway in Africa in 1999 (*Harper's*, July 1999, 17).
- Fourth, *large-scale* armed conflicts inflicting widespread destruction have become less frequent, reversing the historic pattern that characterized the nineteenth century (when war between the great powers was more common, included more participants, and often took a large toll in human lives).

Saddam Hussein Addresses Iraqi Soldiers Iraqi dictator Saddam Hussein in 1991 financed a plan to rapidly develop a nuclear weapons arsenal for use against the United States and its allies. Nuclear proliferation appeared to be an omen for the future when in 1998 India and Pakistan became nuclear powers. This prompted fears that other countries would follow and that the so-called nuclear peace that has prevailed for nearly six decades might end.

- Fifth, the goals of many states in waging war have changed since previous centuries, perhaps as a consequence of war's rising destructiveness and financial costs, as well as the danger that aggression will provoke external intervention and undermine the warring state's international reputation. "A large number of the most powerful states," writes British diplomat Robert Cooper (*International Herald Tribune,* September 18, 1997, 8), "no longer want to fight or conquer. Acquiring territory is no longer of interest. Acquiring subject populations would be for most states a nightmare."

This last change raises questions as to why wars between the great powers have ceased.

Nuclear Weapons and the Obsolescence of Great-Power War?

Paradoxically, since 1945 the world's most powerful countries have been the most constrained in their use of military strength against one another. Some people believe that the creation of nuclear weapons has produced this outcome. For example, British Prime Minister Winston Churchill articulated this thesis in 1953 when he confessed that on occasion he had "the odd thought that the annihilating character of [nuclear weapons] may bring an utterly unforeseeable security to mankind. . . . It may be that when the advance of destructive weapons enables everyone to kill anybody else no one will want to kill anyone at all." Whatever its causes, peace among the great powers has prevailed since 1945, with a "zone of peace" emerging among them alongside a "zone of turmoil" in the rest of the world.

In early 1992, U.S. President George Bush observed at the UN that "today the threat of global nuclear war is more distant than ever before." As Melvin Laird, U.S. Secretary of Defense in the Nixon administration, observed, "Nuclear weapons . . . are useless for military purposes." This does not assure us, however, that the threat of wars of mass destruction has disappeared. Increasing numbers of countries in the Global South's large zone of turmoil are now stockpiling weapons of mass destruction, overtly or covertly, for defense and, possibly, aggression (see Chapter 13). Admittedly, many countries are very risk averse when it comes to actually using these lethal weapons, because doing so could easily result in their own destruction. However, even though most nuclear states seek not to win but rather to avoid loss, there is no guarantee that **deterrence** (dissuasion by means of military threat) will succeed forever, or that a radical government that acquires nuclear weapons will not use them. By the laws of probability, moreover, the longer nuclear arsenals exist, the more probable it is that a nuclear exchange will occur: the question is not *if*, but *when*. The odds of a nuclear holocaust occurring through a fatal error (whether of judgment, miscalculation, or accident) are high. The limits to **rational choice** under conditions of crisis heighten the potential dangers, as does the tendency for large-scale organizations and military bureaucracies to make high-risk decisions about war through **groupthink** collective choices. If these pessimistic considerations are included in assessments of the future, then we must question if the world has escaped nuclear devastation largely by sheer luck—"less a consequence of intelligent policy than a fortunate concatenation of conditions" (Singer 1991).

These apocalyptic thoughts suggest that the widespread belief that nuclear weapons have preserved peace—a **pax atomica**—may be a fanciful myth (see Vasquez 1991). Also questionable is the corollary proposition that as "the fear of escalating nuclear power reaches further down, [it will inhibit] also the use of lesser force for lesser ends and goals" (Majeed 1991). If the trends in armed conflicts since 1945 tell us anything, it is that recourse to force and scenes of human carnage beamed to TV screens are likely to continue, even if the proportion of armed conflicts between states declines relative to internal armed conflicts within states. Destruction and death remain rampant. People, it seems, remain willing to kill through organized violence, especially today in the Global South, where poverty and less stable governments prevail.

What ends motivate human beings to continue to resort to force, given the unspeakable casualties? The question provokes a more fundamental set of related questions about the causes of aggression generally. Accordingly, it is useful to review contending theories about the sources from which armed conflicts arise.

■ deterrence
a military strategy in which the primary purpose is to prevent a foreign adversary's attack.

■ rational choice
the assumption that decisionmakers make choices through cool-headed calculations of costs and benefits and pick the options that have the best chance of realizing preferred goals (see p. 66).

■ groupthink
the propensity for members of a decision-making group to accept and agree with the group's prevailing attitudes, rather than speaking out for what they believe would be the most rational choice.

■ pax atomica
the notion that nuclear weapons have preserved peace.

THE CAUSES OF ARMED CONFLICT: RIVAL THEORIES

Throughout history efforts have been made to explain why states resort to force. Inventories of war's origins invariably conclude that they are incomplete (see Blainey 1988; Howard 1983; Van Evera 1999 Vasquez 1993; Waltz 1954), in part because most agree that war is rooted in multiple sources at various **levels of analysis.** For our purposes, the most plausible causes are divided here into three major levels or categories: individuals, states, and the global system.

The First Level of Analysis: Individuals' Human Nature

In a sense, all wars between states originate from the decisions of national leaders, whose choices ultimately determine whether armed conflict will occur. We must therefore consider the relationship of war to individuals and their choices, and for this, questions about human nature are central.

The repeated outbreak of war has led some, such as psychologist Sigmund Freud (1968), to conclude that aggression is an instinctive part of human nature that stems from humans' genetic programming and psychological makeup. Identifying Homo sapiens as the deadliest species, ethologists (those who study animal behavior in order to understand human behavior) such as Konrad Lorenz (1963) similarly argue that humankind is one of the few species practicing **intraspecific aggression** (routine killing of its own kind), in comparison with most other species, which practice **interspecific aggression** (killing only other species, except in the most unusual circumstances—cannibalism in certain tropical fishes being one exception). Ethologists are joined in their interpretation by those **realists** who assume that the drive for power is innate and cannot be eliminated. They therefore accept the conclusion suggested by Charles Darwin's theories of evolution and natural selection: Life entails a struggle for survival of the fittest, and natural selection eliminates the traits that interfere with successful competition, such as **pacifism,** which rejects the right of people to kill in order to obtain power.

Many question these theories on both empirical and logical grounds. If aggression is an inevitable impulse deriving from human nature, then should not all humans exhibit this genetically determined behavior? This, of course, is rarely the case; many individuals are consistently nonaggressive, and most, adhering to the ethical position that killing is evil, neither murder nor accept others' killing on behalf of the state. In fact, at some fundamental, genetic level, argues Francis Fukuyama (1999a), human beings are built for consensus, not for conflict: "People feel intensely uncomfortable if they live in a society that doesn't have moral rules." In addition, liberal theory and social science research suggest that genetics fails to explain why individuals may be belligerent only at certain times. Social Darwinism's interpretation of the biological influences on human behavior can be countered by examining why people cooperate and act morally. As James Q. Wilson (1993) argues, Darwinian **survival of the fittest** realist theory overlooks the fact that "the moral sense must have adaptive value; if it did not, natural selection would have worked against people who had such useless traits as sympathy, self-control, or a desire for fairness in favor of those with the opposite tendencies."

Although the **nature versus nurture** controversy regarding the biological bases of aggression has not been resolved (see Caspary 1993; Nelson 1974; Ridley 1998; and Somit 1990), most social scientists now strongly disagree with this realist premise that humans are essentially selfish and aggressive and that people murder and kill because of their innate genetic drives to act out aggressively. Instead, the majority of social scientists conclude that war occurs only where it is a learned habit; violence is a possible part of humankind's cultural

■ **levels of analysis**
the interpretation of the sources of international phenomena that looks separately at the influences of individuals, the characteristics of states, or the global system (see p. 56).

■ **intraspecific aggression**
killing members of one's own species.

■ **interspecific aggression**
killing members of species other than one's own.

■ **realism**
the theory that states are driven to compete for power through war and imperialism because of human nature, which is flawed by the urge to engage in aggression (see p. 457).

■ **pacifism**
the liberal idealist school of ethical thought that recognizes no conditions that justify the taking of another human's life, even when authorized by a head of state.

■ **survival of the fittest**
a realist concept derived from Charles Darwin's theory of evolution that advises that ruthless competition is ethically acceptable to survive, even if the actions violate moral commands not to kill.

■ **nature versus nurture**
the controversy over whether human behavior is determined more by the biological basis of "human nature" than it is nurtured by the environmental conditions that humans experience.

heritage rather than a product of biological nature. The 1986 *Seville Statement*, endorsed by more than a dozen professional scholarly associations, maintains that "it is scientifically incorrect" to say that "we have inherited a tendency to make war from our animal ancestors," "that war or any other violent behavior is genetically programmed into our human nature," "that humans have a 'violent brain,' " or "that war is caused by 'instinct' or any single motivation" (see Somit 1990). Ted Robert Gurr (1970) expresses the thesis, supported by behavioral research, that the "capacity, but not the need, for violence appears to be biologically entrenched in humans." Aggression is a propensity acquired early in life as a result of **socialization** and, therefore, is a learned rather than biologically determined behavior.

socialization the processes by which people learn the beliefs, values, and behaviors that are acceptable in a given society.

Individuals' willingness to sacrifice their lives in war out of a sense of duty to their leaders and country is one of history's puzzles. "The fog of war" is what the Russian author Leo Tolstoy and others have called the fact that people will give their lives in struggles, large and small, whose importance and purpose are sometimes not understood. Clearly, this self-sacrifice stems from learned beliefs that some convictions—such as loyalty to the state—are worth dying for. "It has been widely observed that soldiers fight—and noncombatants assent to war—not out of aggressiveness but obedience" (Caspary 1993). This, however, does not make human nature a cause of war, even if such learned habits of obedience are grounds for participation in the aggression authorized by others, and even if at times the mass public's jingoistic enthusiasm for aggression against foreign adversaries encourages leaders to start wars.

If human nature is not a direct cause of interstate conflict, how then do we explain the enduring rivalries and the repetitive recourse to genocide in some areas? For example, what accounts for the heritage of hatred in the Balkans where obsessive and indignant murder appears to have been a way of life for centuries? The Balkans suffer from a reputation for blood feuds that has been passed down from generation to generation, punctuated by repeated acts of atrocity, that arguably began in the Battle of Kosovo when the Turks advanced west toward Vienna in 1389, vanquished the Serbs, and left their bodies to the crows. Since then, this territory has lived by a code of revenge: an eye for an eye. The ethnic cleansing and brutal destruction forms a cult of violence that links the past to the present.

It is the bloody history of territories such as the Balkans that inspires anthropologists to inquire if territoriality drives human aggression. Could it be that the genocide in Kosovo in 1999 stemmed from "an innate human aggression, inherited from our animal ancestors, to possess territory believed to be one's own"? Robert Ardrey (1966), the playwright turned anthropologist, proposed the notion of human territorial aggression in *The Territorial Imperative*, published in the 1960s. The controversial best-seller argued that "the territorial instincts of animals apply equally to man. . . . Simply put, Mr. Ardrey's theory proposes that humans, like animals, are compelled by instinct to possess and defend territory they believe belongs exclusively to them" (Levingston 1999). The **territorial imperative** has been resurrected as a theory to account for the kinds of ethnic wars that rage across the globe in so many regions today, even though some scientists are critical of the methods by which these conclusions have been reached. Whether the territorial instincts to think geopolitically by declaring "this place is mine" and to act aggressively to defend a territory is truly an inherited "territorial imperative" (Ardrey 1966) is likely to be debated

territorial imperative the term coined by anthropologist Robert Ardrey to popularize the proposition that people and nations will defend to the death their territory for the same reasons animals do.

as philosophers and policymakers attempt to control today's tribal warriors who are willing to kill to defend territory.

Many scholars using behavioral methods to study international relations question the belief that entire nationalities are predisposed to war—that **national character** predetermines national aggression. National character—the shared attributes and values of members of a nationality—can express itself in different ways and can also change. Sweden and Switzerland have managed conflict without recourse to war since 1809 and 1815, respectively, whereas formerly they were aggressive. And until its invasion by China in 1949, Tibet had negotiated its foreign disputes peacefully for eight hundred consecutive years. This suggests that violence is not an inborn characteristic of particular peoples that predestines periodic outbreaks of aggression. Many states have escaped the tragedy of war; in fact, since 1500 more than one in five have never experienced war (Sivard 1991, 20). This variation across states over five centuries suggests that war is not endemic and unavoidable: "A vision of a ubiquitous struggle for power or of a determining systemic structure explains recurrence without accounting for non-recurrence or the great deviations from an average pattern of recurrence" (Holsti 1991).

national character the collective characteristics ascribed to the people within a state.

Nobel Prize winner Ralph Bunche, a U.S. policymaker, argued before the UN that "there are no warlike people—just warlike leaders." Similarly, St. Thomas More declared in the sixteenth century that "the common folk do not go to war of their own accord, but are driven to it by the madness of kings." But explaining the role of leaders in making war is not quite that simple, as leaders usually make foreign policies within groups. The social-psychological and bureaucratic setting for decision making and the global environment may exert "an influence independent of the actions and beliefs of individual policymakers. . . . War seems less like something decisionmakers choose than something that somehow happens to them," even as it happens "through them," through the choices they make (Beer 1981).

The decision for war is better explained, then, not by individual leaders' aggressiveness or by aggressive national character, but by the many political pressures that influence the government leaders who "ultimately decide the great questions of war and peace" (Holsti 1991). Therefore, it is relevant to ask, what domestic factors encourage policymakers to "choose war"—to see foreign aggression as the most rational choice for realizing foreign policy goals.

The Second Level of Analysis: States' Internal Characteristics

Conventional wisdom holds that variations in states' governments, sizes, ideologies, geographical locations, population dynamics, ethnic homogeneity, wealth, economic performance, military capabilities, and level of educational attainment influence whether they will engage in war. Drawing on the possibility suggested by Russian political theorist Peter Kropotkin in 1884 that "the word *state* is identical with the word *war*" and the evidence that war has contributed to the rise of the state (Porter 1994), we need to examine some theories addressing the internal characteristics of states that influence leaders' choices regarding the use of force. Implicit in this approach to explaining armed conflict at the **state level of analysis** is the assumption (embraced by "the comparative study of foreign policy" perspective relied on to discuss foreign policy decision making in Chapter 3) that differences in the types or classes of states will determine

state level of analysis an analytical approach to the study of world politics that emphasizes how the internal attributes of states explain their foreign policy behaviors.

neorealism
the so-called structural version of realism that explains state conduct as a function of changes in the global system's structure, such as shifts in the distribution of states' miliary capabilities (see p. 500).

whether they will engage in war. To argue that the prospects for war are influenced most heavily by national attributes and the types of leaders making decisions for states is to challenge the **neorealist** premise that international circumstances are the most powerful determinants of warfare, and that domestic factors have no influence.

Duration of Independence. New states are more likely to initiate wars than are mature states (Wright 1942), and the birth of new and smaller states has been a trend in the last half of the twentieth century from which many, if not most, of today's armed conflicts have arisen. "Three-quarters of the flags woven into military uniforms, painted on planes and saluted in classrooms throughout the world today did not exist 50 years ago" (Enriquez 1999, 12). Drives to settle long-standing internal grievances and territorial disputes by force often follow the acquisition of independence: Between 1945 and 1992, all but one of sixty civil wars were fought in emergent states, and nearly one-fourth of them became internationalized as the bloodletting expanded across borders (Singer 1991, 59, 79). Because the national upheavals and revolutions that produce new states are most common in the newly independent countries of the Global South, it is not surprising that these states "are much more likely to be involved in international conflict" (Gurr 1994). The wave of armed conflicts occurring today is explained by the tendency for civil strife within new states to conform to the past historical pattern of generating foreign wars. In the past two centuries, newly independent countries have typically gone through a period of internal political upheaval following their acquisition of sovereign independence, and this has often served as a catalyst to subsequent foreign aggression as leaders try to divert public attention to fears of neighboring enemies.

Cultural Determinants, Feminist Theory, and the Decay of Moral Constraints. The cultural and ethical traditions of their peoples strongly influence the international behavior of modern countries. In the state system governed by the rules championed by realism, moral constraints on the use of force do not command wide acceptance. Instead, most governments have encouraged their populations to accept whatever decisions their leaders deem necessary for national security, including warfare against adversaries. We need to take seriously the potentially powerful cultural origins of armed conflict. Does history support the theory that the prevailing dominant cultural systems in the world, rooted in realism, glorify the state and aggression and, as a consequence, make violence more probable?

feminist theory
a body of scholarship emerging from the social feminist movement to promote the political equality of women with men, critiquing sexual biases and challenging gender roles that encourage female subordination and warfare.

Advocates of the cultural origins of war argue that most people in most societies live an everday experience of disengagement, or "numbness," which disinclines them to oppose their leaders' decisions to wage war. The modern state thus organizes its society to accept war and "builds a culture that affirms death" and accepts senseless carnage (Caspary 1993). In contrast, critics operating from the perspective of **feminist theories** of international relations argue that the foundation of war worldwide, alongside cultural numbing, is rooted in the masculine ethos of realism, which prepares people to accept war and to respect the warrior as a hero (see especially Enloe 2000 and Tickner 1997). Gender roles, they assert, supported by realist values contribute to the prevalence of militarism and warfare:

> According to feminist critics, international relations theory as it has evolved incorporates "masculinist" prejudices at each of its three levels of analysis: man, the state, and war. Realists are "androcentric" in arguing that the propensity for conflict is universal in human nature ("man"); that the logic and the morality of sovereign states are not identical to those of individuals ("the state"); and that the world is an anarchy in which sovereign states must be prepared to rely on self-help, including organized violence ("war"). Feminist theorists would stress the nurturing and cooperative aspects—the conventionally feminine aspects—of human nature; they would expose the artificiality of notions of sovereignty, and their connection with patriarchy and militarism; and they would replace the narrow realist emphasis on security, especially military security, with a redefinition of security as universal social justice. (Lind 1993, 37)

To feminists and other theorists about the causes of war who embrace a cultural interpretation, the penchant for warfare does not evolve in a vacuum but is produced by the ways in which societies shape their populations' beliefs and norms. Many governments, through the educational programs they fund in schools and other institutions, indoctrinate values in their political culture that condone the practice of war. Ironically, in a world of diverse national cultures, the messages of obedience and of duty to make sacrifices to the state through such **cultural conditioning** are common. States disseminate the belief that their right to make war should not be questioned and that the ethical principles of religious and secular philosophies prohibiting violence should be disregarded. Consequently, critics stress the existence of powerful institutions that prepare individuals to subconsciously accept warfare as necessary and legitimate.

■ **cultural conditioning** the impact of national traditions and moral principles on the behavior of states, under the assumption that culture affects national decision making about issues such as the acceptability of aggression.

Poverty. A country's level of economic development also affects the probability of its involvement in war. Historically, the most warlike states have been poor, and this pattern persists, as the locale of warfare has shifted since 1945 to the developing countries at the Global South's periphery. As U.S. Secretary of Defense Robert S. McNamara explained in 1966, "there is no question but that there is evidence of a relationship between violence and economic backwardness."

Before we conclude that poverty always breeds war, however, we must note that the *most* impoverished countries have been the least prone to start wars with their neighbors. The poorest countries cannot vent their frustrations aggressively because they lack the military or economic resources to do so. Thus the poorest states, like the wealthiest, cannot afford to wage war, though for quite different reasons. The former lack the means; the latter hold weapons too destructive to use.

This pattern does not mean that the poorest countries will always remain peaceful. If the past is a guide to the future, then the impoverished countries that develop economically will be those most likely to acquire arms and engage in future external wars. In particular, many studies suggest that states are likely to initiate foreign wars *after* sustained periods of economic growth—that is, during periods of rising prosperity, when they can most afford them (Cashman 1993). This signals danger if countries in the Global South develop rapidly and direct the new resources toward armament, as India and Pakistan chose to do in 1998, rather than investments in sustained development.

Afghan Guerrilla Fighters Many people believe that "violence begets violence"—that once aggression is accepted, fighters are prone to practice armed conflict in the future against foreign or domestic enemies. Here guerrilla units in Afghanistan prepare for a military attack against the ruling Afghan government. Funding for the fighters who ousted Soviet troops from Afghanistan provided a springboard for today's eager terrorists, who are conditioned by past experience and training to use force to achieve their objectives against foes, unconcerned that their aggression might be immoral.

Militarization. The age-old question of whether the acquisition of military power leads to war or peace is as timely as ever at the start of the twenty-first century. As Chapter 13 explains, the race for the most advanced military technology in the highly industrialized countries is no longer confined there. It is now highly active in the Global South where the developing countries are racing to acquire weapons. In the 1990s, the poor states in the Global South have been by far the biggest customers in the global trade in arms. During the period from 1995 through 1998, the developing Global South countries accounted for 77 percent of all arms deliveries worldwide, which in 1998 alone were valued at $23.2 billion (Grimmett 1999, 76, 1). Corrupt Global South dictatorships have exploited natural resources to "buy, largely from abroad, military power with which to keep their people in order, challenge neighbors and, all too often, keep themselves in power" (Neild 2000). The impact of arms transfers and military expansion on their human development and their national security has been devastating (Blanton 1999), as the acquisition of arms has been followed by the outbreak of many civil and interstate wars in those same countries which have followed the realist's dictum that to obtain peace it is necessary to prepare for war. This has renewed concerns about whether the continued dispersion of weapons will increase the probability of new wars.

As developing countries in the Global South accumulate the economic resources to equip their military establishments, many experts believe that war will become more frequent before it becomes less so. This prediction stems from the evidence that fundamental changes in military capability are an important determinant of the onset of war (Vasquez 1993), especially as reflected in the historical pattern in Europe.

During its transition to the peak of development, Europe was the location of the world's most frequent and deadly wars. The major European states armed themselves heavily and were engaged in warfare about 65 percent of the time in the sixteenth and seventeenth centuries (Wright 1942). Between 1816 and 1945, three-fifths of all interstate wars took place in Europe, with one erupting on average every other year (Singer 1991, 58). Not coincidentally, this happened when the developing states of Europe were most energetically arming in competition with one another. Perhaps as a consequence, the great powers—those with the largest armed forces—were the most involved in, and most often initiated, war (Cashman 1993). Since 1945, however, with the exception of war among the now-independent units of the former Yugoslavia, interstate war has not occurred in Europe. As the European countries moved up the ladder of development, they moved away from war with one another (internal conflict is another matter).

In contrast, the developing countries now resemble Europe prior to 1945. If the Global South follows the European pattern, the immediate future may well witness a peaceful, developed world surrounded by a violent, less developed world.

Economic System. Does the character of states' economic systems influence the frequency of warfare? The question has provoked controversy for centuries. Particularly since Marxism took root in Russia following the Bolshevik revolution in 1917, communist theoreticians claimed that capitalism was the primary cause of war—that capitalists practice imperialism and colonialism and, as they were fond of quoting Vladimir Lenin's 1916 explanation of World War I, war is caused by imperialistic capitalists' effort "to divert the attention of the laboring masses from the domestic political crisis" of collapsing incomes under capitalism. According to the **communist theory of imperialism,** capitalism produces surplus capital. The need to export it stimulates wars to capture and protect foreign markets. Thus **laissez-faire economics**—based on the philosophical principle of free markets with little governmental regulation of the marketplace—rationalized militarism and imperialism for economic gain. Citing the demonstrable frequency with which wealthy capitalist societies engaged in aggression, Marxists believed that the only way to end international war was to end capitalism.

communist theory of imperialism
the Marxist-Leninist economic interpretation of imperialist wars of conquest as driven by capitalism's need for foreign markets to generate capital.

Contrary to Marxist theory is commercial liberalism's conviction that free market systems promote peace, not war. Defenders of capitalism have long believed that free market countries that practice free trade abroad are more pacific. The reasons are multiple, but they center on the premise that commercial enterprises are natural lobbyists for world peace because their profits depend on it. War interferes with trade, blocks profit, destroys property, causes inflation, consumes scarce resources, and encourages big government and counterproductive regulation of business activity. By extension, this reasoning continues, as government regulation of internal markets declines, prosperity will increase and fewer wars will occur (see Chapter 8).

laissez-faire economics
the philosophical principle of free markets with little governmental regulation of the marketplace (see p. 251).

The evidence for these rival theories is, not surprisingly, mixed. Conclusions depend in part on perceptions regarding economic influences on international behavior, in part because alternative perspectives focus on different dimensions of the linkage. This controversy was at the heart of the ideological debate between East and West during the Cold War, when the relative virtues and vices of two radically different economic systems—socialism and capitalism—were uppermost in people's minds. At the time, communists cited the previous record of wars initiated by capitalistic countries (e.g., Germany, Japan, and the United States in Vietnam) to lend credence to the Marxist interpretation, while ignoring the pacificity of other capitalist states such as Switzerland.

Marxist theory also did not explain communist states' embarrassingly frequent use of force. The Soviet Union invaded Finland in 1939 and Afghanistan in 1979; North Korea attacked South Korea in 1950; Communist China attacked Tibet in 1959; Vietnam invaded Cambodia in 1975; and Cuba intervened militarily in Africa in the 1980s. Moreover, communist states repeatedly clashed with one another during the Cold War, for example, China and the Soviet Union in 1969, China and Vietnam in 1979 and 1987, the Soviet Union and Hungary in 1956, and the Soviet Union and Czechoslovakia in 1968. Communist or socialist systems participated in roughly 25 percent of all interstate wars between 1945 and 1967, even though only about 15 percent of all countries had socialist economies (Cashman 1993, 133). Thus the thesis that socialist or communist states are inherently nonaggressive failed empirically.

Communism's failure to produce economic prosperity also hastened its rejection in Eastern Europe and in the very heartland of the communist experiment, the Soviet Union. With capitalism's triumph over communism, a phase of history appeared to have ended (Fukuyama 1992b). By 1998, only Cuba and North Korea still fully endorsed communist economic principles; although communism could yet prove resurgent, all other former advocates appear committed to free market economies.

The end of the Cold War did not end the historic debate about the link between economics and war. The issue of economic influences on international behavior remains, and this basic theoretical question is likely to command increasing interest, especially given the "shift in the relevance and usefulness of different power resources, with military power declining and economic power increasing in importance" (Huntington 1991a).

Globalization, through which the growing economic interdependence of countries has tightly linked states' growth rates, has intensified the debate about the relationship between trade and international armed conflict. Although "most leaders still cling to the long-standing belief that expanding economic ties will cement the bonds of friendship between and within nations that make resort to arms unfathomable," observe Katherine Barbieri and Gerald Schneider (1999), "in contrast, realist and Marxist critics reject the liberal view" that the opening of free market economies within states and increased levels of trade between them will produce peace (see Chapters 8 and 9). Even though substantial evidence exists to support "the liberals' belief that economic interdependence [and economic and political freedom] have important pacific benefits" (Oneal and Russett 1999), that conclusion is unlikely to be widely accepted by the many poor Global South countries who maintain that under interdependent globalization the wealthy will profit disproportionally from trade, at their expense. This **relative gains** argument insists conflict is produced because the benefits of economic exchanges are distributed unequally (the rich get richer and the poor get poorer), and trade-war disputes and even

■ **relative gains**
a situation in which some participants benefit more than others (see p. 253).

wars are likely to undermine world peace. The future will tell if free markets and free trade will generate international conflict or cooperation in the globalized twenty-first century.

Type of Government. Realist and especially neorealist theories discount the importance of government type as an influence on war and peace. Not so with liberalism, especially **neoliberal theories,** which disagree stridently. Indeed, the liberal tradition assigns great weight to the kind of political institutions that govern states as a factor that powerfully shapes the kinds of foreign policies states formulate. Recall that neoliberalism predicts that "free" democratically ruled governments (and free trade) will promote peaceful interstate relations. This perspective prescribes that states *should* reform their governments and economies by liberalizing them (giving citizens power through the ballot to choose their leaders and commercial enterprises freedom to conduct business with minimal government interference in the marketplace). Liberty in governance and the economy is seen as beneficial—not only because human dignity and civil liberties are virtues in their own right, but because when embraced in policy choices, these values produce consequences that make for a better life. According to liberal theorists, liberal political and economic institutions promote cooperation, peace, and prosperity.

■ **neoliberal theories** the "new" liberal theories stressing the critical impact of free governments and free trade in promoting peace and prosperity through democratically managed institutions, following the liberal world politics philosophies of Immanuel Kant, Thomas Jefferson, James Madison, and Woodrow Wilson.

This belief and policy recommendation is rooted deeply in liberal intellectual history. It follows the argument carefully advanced by the eighteenth-century German philosopher Immanuel Kant, whose influential essay, *Perpetual Peace,* published in 1795, summarized the basis for liberal theory's view of how lasting peace between sovereign, competitive states could be created, even under conditions of global anarchy that would otherwise encourage conflict and war. Kant reasoned that a government with a "republican constitution," or what we today call a democracy, which permits all people to vote in freely contested elections so that leaders are chosen by popular vote among a citizenship enjoying civil rights and civil liberties, produces foreign policy decisions that are far less inclined to initiate wars than do centrally ruled dictatorships and monarchies. Indeed, when a government is accountable to the people, Kant predicted, heads of state will be reluctant to wage war because public opinion will restrain rulers. Why? Wars are fought by common people, who as soldiers are asked to die for their country, and the mass public bearing the human and financial costs of wars made by leaders crave peace and prosperity more than death and poverty. In democracies, where the voice of the people is heard, opposition to unnecessary warfare abroad deters an adventuresome ruler from choosing to use armed force. Hence, Kant's solution to the problem of war was to recommend that states give power to the people to democratically control their fates and fortunes. If liberal democracy (and free trade) spread worldwide, world politics would become peaceful, and a truly new world order would emerge.

Kant was joined by other liberal reformers, such as Thomas Jefferson, James Madison, and Woodrow Wilson in the United States—all of whom believed that an "empire of liberty" (as Madison pictured a growing community of liberal democracies) would be one freed of the curse of war, and that if democratic institutions spread throughout the world, the entire past pattern of belligerent international relations would be replaced by a new pacific pattern.

These liberal and neoliberal predictions have been fulfilled by the passage of time since they were first advanced. "We now have solid evidence that democracies do not make war on each other" (Russett 2001). Much research has been conducted that convincingly shows that "although preventive war has been the preferred response of declining authoritarian leaders, no democracy has ever initiated such a war" against another democratic state (Schweller 1992). True, democracies experience disagreements with each other often, and one or more of the disputing parties have become boiling mad over the issue; but they have always resolved their differences at the bargaining table rather than on the battlefield (Dixon 1994; Doyle 1997; Weart 1998). The demonstrated capacity of democracies to settle their disputes peacefully provides the cornerstone for what is known as the **democratic peace** proposition (Ray 1995). This proposition holds that democratic governance *is* a strong pillar of global peace, and that if and when the globe is ruled by a larger and larger proportion of democratic governments, lasting peace within this enlarged liberal community will result. As Bruce Russett summarizes,

■ **democratic peace** the liberal theory that lasting peace depends on the deepening of liberal democratic institutions within states and their diffusion throughout the globe, given the "iron law" that democracies do not wage wars against each other.

> Democracies are unlikely to engage in any kind of militarized disputes *with each other* or to let any such disputes escalate into war. They rarely even skirmish. Pairs of democratic states have been only one-eighth as likely as other kinds of states to threaten to use force against each other, and only one-tenth as likely actually to do so. Established democracies fought *no wars* against one another during the entire twentieth century.
>
> The more democratic each state is, the more peaceful their relations are likely to be. Democracies are more likely to employ "democratic" means of peaceful conflict resolution. They are readier to reciprocate each other's behavior, to accept third-party mediation or good offices in settling disputes, and to accept binding third-party arbitration and adjudication. Careful statistical analyses of countries' behavior have shown that democracies' relatively peaceful relations toward each other are not spuriously caused by some other influence such as sharing high levels of wealth, or rapid growth, or ties of alliance. The phenomenon of peace between democracies is not limited just to the rich industrialized states of the Global North. It was not maintained simply by pressure from a common adversary in the Cold War, and it has outlasted that threat. (Russett 2001, 235)

The "democratic peace" proposition is based on a theoretical explanation of the influence of democracy in foreign policy making, as well as a prediction about democratization's potential impact on world politics in the future. Again, Russett summarizes the thinking behind this neoliberal argument.

> The phenomenon of democratic peace can be explained by the pervasiveness of normative restraints on conflict between democracies. That explanation extends to the international arena the cultural norms of live-and-let-live and peaceful conflict resolution that operate within democracies. The phenomenon of democratic peace can also be explained by the role of institutional restraints on democracies' decisions to go to war. Those restraints insure that any state in a conflict of interest with another democracy can expect ample time for conflict-resolution processes to be effective, and [democracies' political decision-making processes are relatively transparent]. These two influences reinforce each other. The spread of democratic norms and practices in the world, if consolidated, should reduce the frequency of violent conflict and war. Where normative restraints are weak,

> democratic institutions may provide the necessary additional restraints on the use of violence against other democratic states.
>
> To the degree that countries once ruled by autocratic systems become democratic, the absence of war among democracies comes to bear on any discussion of the future of international relations. The statement that in the modern international system democracies have almost never fought each other represents a complex phenomenon: (1) Democracies rarely fight each other (an empirical statement) because (2) they have other means of resolving conflicts between them and therefore don't need to fight each other (a prudential cost-benefit statement), and (3) they perceive that democracies should not fight each other (a normative statement about principles of right behavior), which reinforces the empirical statement. By this reasoning, the more democracies there are in the world, the fewer potential adversaries democracies will have and the wider the zone of peace will be. (Russett 2001, 235–236)

In viewing the promising prospects for a democratic peace, it is important to note that its proponents do not see democratization as a panacea. Neoliberals qualify the assessment. They acknowledge that democracies do sometimes start wars and are not always pacific in dealing with other states—"It appears that democracies fight as often as do other types of states" (Morgan and Schwebach 1992; Small and Singer 1976; Wright 1942), because they have often been engaged in "defensive" or preventive wars against aggressive dictatorships. Moreover, democracies have actively practiced imperialism by taking colonies by force and have frequently used covert and overt military intervention in the internal affairs of other states—both democratic and nondemocratic (Kegley and Hermann 1997). "Democracies frequently resort to violence in their relations with authoritarian states. But the relations between stable democracies are qualitatively different" (Russett 2001). The democratic peace specifies only that democracies seldom, if ever, fight *each other.* Ballots serve as a barrier against the use of bullets and bombs by one democracy against another.

Faith in democratization as an antidote to armed conflict has grown in the past several decades, not only as a result of growing recognition of research findings, but also in association with the global diffusion of democratic governance over the past two centuries (see Figure 12.2). A third wave of democratic reforms began to sweep the globe in the 1970s. Whereas by 1980 only 37 of the world's 121 countries, accounting for 35 percent of the world's population, were democracies, that picture had changed considerably at the end of the twentieth century as nearly one-third of the previously nondemocratic countries on the planet converted their political systems to democratic rule. According to annual measures of each state's degree of freedom provided by the influential research organization Freedom House, at the start of 2000, no less than 144 "free" and "partly free" governments among 192 states were ruled democratically; this tells us that three-fourths of the globe's governments, in whose territory 60 percent of the world's population resided, determined their leaders by free elections and provided their citizens with basic political rights and civil liberties.

This wave of democratization since the 1970s has provoked speculation that Western liberal democracy eventually will become universal, "the final form of government" (Fukuyama 1992b). As the growth of democracy spreads

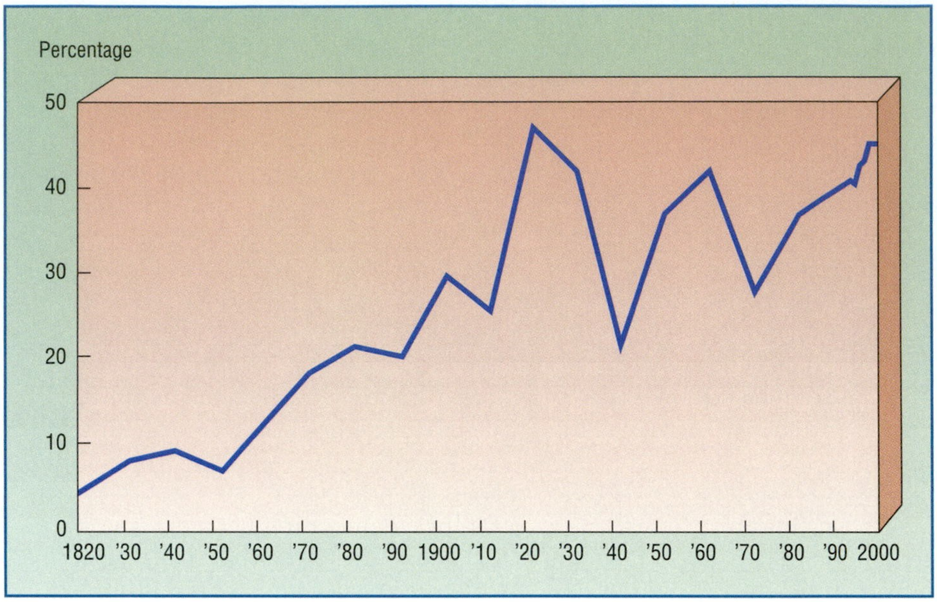

FIGURE 12.2
Fully "Free" Democracies as a Percentage of the World's Governments
Throughout most of modern history, states have been ruled by monarchies, despots, dictators, and autocrats. But beginning in the twentieth century, democratization has spread sporadically in a series of three waves—with an increasing percentage of the world now "freely" ruled by democratic institutions that support civil liberties and empower voters to restrict leaders' freedom to initiate wars (Vanhanen 2000). If democratic countries were defined by less stringent criteria to include "partly free" or less-than-full democratic practices, then 75 percent of states would be classified as democratic in 2000.
SOURCE: Polity III data (Jaggers and Gurr 1995), extended by Freedom House since 1993 as calculated by Harvey Starr.

to the Global South, hope has risen that the transition to democratic rule will usher in a new era of truly peaceful world politics. Indeed, this liberal doctrine has been embedded in the foreign policy of the United States and the other liberal democracies in the Group of Seven (G-7) (i.e., Britain, Canada, France, Germany, Italy, and Japan, alongside the "eighth" member, the fledgling Russian democracy), which have defined the promotion of democracy elsewhere as one of their central purposes and strategies for preventing future wars. In President Bill Clinton's 1994 State of the Union address, for example, he cited the absence of war between democracies as a justification for promoting democratization around the globe, and this neoliberal principle has been endorsed by the World Bank, the International Monetary Fund, North Atlantic Treaty Organization (NATO), the European Union (EU), and now the UN, all of which advocate defining democracy as a "human right" or entitlement that all states are obligated to protect (see Chapter 16).

Although the experience of Western Europe since World War II has helped make "the enlargement" of the liberal democratic community a policy goal, predicated on the discovery that democratic states will not engage in war with one another, we must still be cautious of quick assumptions that democracy will necessarily serve as an altogether reliable barrier to war in the twenty-first century. Fragile new democracies sometimes fall prey to internal instability, as ethnic and national passions spill over into turmoil, and at times have put into office leaders who stepped on the human rights of the people who elected them. And the fact that leaders in elective democracies are accountable to public approval and electoral rejection does not guarantee that they will not use force to settle disputes with other democracies:

> It was, after all, the democratization of conflict in the nineteenth century that restored a ferocity to warfare unknown since the seventeenth century; the bloodiest war in American history remains the one fought between two (by today's standards flawed) democracies—the Civil War. Concentration camps appeared during another conflict between two limited democracies, the Boer War. World War I was launched by two regimes—Wilhelmine Germany and Austria-Hungary—that had greater representation and more equitable legal systems than those of many important states today. And even when modern liberal democracies go to war they do not necessarily moderate the scope of the violence they apply; indeed, sensitivity to their own casualties sometimes leads to profligate uses of firepower or violent efforts to end wars quickly. Shaky democracies fight each other all the time. . . . We must remind ourselves just how peculiar the wealthy and secure democracies of the West are, how painful their evolution to stability and the horror of war with each other has been. Perhaps other countries will find short-cuts to those conditions, but it would be foolish to assume they will. (E. Cohen 1998, 39)

Thus it would be premature and overly optimistic to assume that the growth of democracy will automatically produce a more peaceful world.

Yet another concern is the frequency with which democratic states have intervened militarily, not only in authoritarian states but in other democratic states as well, in order to force democratic reform. Waging wars to spread democracy, as Woodrow Wilson did when he sent U.S. Marines into Mexico "to teach them to elect good governments," will not make for a more peaceful world. And the democratic peace could collapse because "countries do not become mature democracies overnight. More typically, they go through a rocky transitional period, where democratic control over foreign policy is partial, where mass politics mixes in a volatile way with authoritarian elite politics, and where democratization suffers reversals. In this transitional phase of democratization, countries become more aggressive and war-prone, not less, and they do fight wars with democratic states" (Mansfield and Snyder 1995).

Nationalism. **Nationalism**—love of and loyalty to a nation—is widely believed to be the cauldron from which wars often spring (Van Evera 1994; see also Chapters 4 and 7). "The tendency of the vast majority of people to center their supreme loyalties on the nation-state," Jack S. Levy explains, is a powerful catalyst to war. When people "acquire an intense commitment to the power and prosperity of the state [and] this commitment is strengthened by national myths emphasizing the moral, physical, and political strength of the state and by individuals' feelings of powerlessness and their consequent tendency to seek their identity and fulfillment through the state, . . . nationalism contributes to war" (Levy 1989a).

■ **nationalism**
sentimental devotion to the welfare of one's own nation, without concern for the common interest of all nations and states in the global community (see p. 633).

The connection between nationalism and war has a long history and provokes much debate (see Controversy: Does Nationalistic Love of Country Cause War with Foreign Nations?), but it has been especially pronounced in the twentieth century. The English essayist Aldous Huxley once termed nationalism "the religion of the twentieth century." Today, nationalism is particularly virulent and intense, and arguably, it and racism are "the most powerful movements in our world today, cutting across many social systems" (Gardels 1991).

Most armed conflicts today are fed by nationalist sentiments that promote "war fever . . . accompanied by overt hostility and contempt toward a caricatured image of the enemy," out of which sadistic violence and genocide have historically emanated (Caspary 1993). This entrenched linkage leads some to argue that "nationalism has often generated aggression abroad [and] has given us some three dozen costly wars in the Middle East since 1945" (Yoder 1991). And the danger could escalate. Nationalism's threat to world order led former Soviet President Mikhail Gorbachev to warn in May 1992 that "the demons of nationalism are coming alive again, and they are putting the stability of the international system to the test. Even the United States itself is not immune from the dangerous nationalism."

This discussion of the characteristics of states that influence their proclivity for war does not exhaust the subject. Many other potential causes internal to the state exist. But however important domestic influences might be as a source of war, many believe that the nature of the international system is even more critical.

■ **global level of analysis**
an analytical approach to world politics that emphasizes the impact of global conditions on foreign policy behavior (see p. 14).

■ **self-help**
the principle that in anarchy states in the global system must rely on themselves (see p. 661).

■ **security dilemma**
the tendency of states to view the defensive arming of adversaries as threatening, and when they arm in response, everyone's security declines (see p. 102).

■ **anarchy**
at the global level, the absence of institutions for global governance with the power to enforce rules and regulate disputes between states to insure that international relations are peaceful.

The Third Level of Analysis: Cycles of War and Peace in the Global System

Classical realism and neotraditional realism emphasize that the roots of armed conflict rest in human nature. In contrast, neorealism sees war springing from changes at the **global level of analysis,** that is, as a product of the decentralized character of the international system that requires sovereign states to rely on **self-help** for their security.

> Although different realist theories often generate conflicting predictions, they share a core of common assumptions: The key actors in world politics are sovereign states that act rationally to advance their security, power, and wealth in a conflictual international system that lacks a legitimate governmental authority to regulate conflicts or enforce agreements.
>
> For realists, wars can occur not only because some states prefer war to peace, but also because of unintended consequences of actions by those who prefer peace to war and are more interested in preserving their position than in enhancing it. Even defensively motivated efforts by states to provide for their own security through armaments, alliances, and deterrent threats are often perceived as threatening and lead to counteractions and conflict spirals that are difficult to reverse. This is the **"security dilemma"**—the possibility that a state's actions to provide for its security may result in a decrease in the security of all states, including itself. (Levy 1998b, 145)

International **anarchy** may promote war's outbreak, but it fails to provide a complete explanation of changes in the levels of war and peace over time or

CONTROVERSY

DOES NATIONALISTIC LOVE OF COUNTRY CAUSE WAR WITH FOREIGN NATIONS?

What does patriotism mean? The most familiar definition is popularly expressed as "love for one's country." Often, it involves "love for the nation or nationality of the people living in a particular state," especially when the population of that state primarily comprises a single ethnonational racial or linguistic group. Because "love" for valued objects of affection, such as a person's homeland, is widely seen as a virtue, it is understandable why governments everywhere teach young citizens that love for country is a moral duty—it fosters a sense of political community. Nationalism encourages internal harmony and political stability, and thereby makes a positive contribution to civic solidarity and domestic peace. On these grounds, nationalism is not controversial. However, critics of nationalism find patriotism to be potentially dangerous in its extreme form. Superpatriots, these critics warn, are hyper-nationalists who measure their patriotism by the degree of hatred and opposition exhibited toward foreign nations and by the blind approval of every policy and practice of the "patriot's" own nation. In this sense, nationalistic patriotism can ignore transcendent moral principles such as the love for all humanity, even toward one's enemies, as preached by Jesus Christ in the Sermon on the Mount and other religious leaders such as Muhammad, the founder of Islam, and the legendary King Solomon in Judaism. If so, then is nationalistic superpatriotism sometimes a cause of war between nations? What do you think? In contemplating your opinion about this controversial issue over values—about whether nationalism and internationalism are mutually exclusive, and whether nationalism makes for war by undermining justice under law for the world of nations—take into consideration the view of Karl Deutsch, a German-born immigrant and famous scholar who taught for many years at Harvard University. Deutsch, an authority on nationalism, described nationalism's linkage to armed conflict in these moving words:

> *Nationalism* is an attitude of mind, a pattern of attention and desires. It arises in response to a condition of society and to a particular stage in its development. It is a predisposition to pay far more attention to messages about one's own people, or to messages from its members, than to messages from or about any other people. At the same time, it is a desire to have one's own people get any and all values that are available. The extreme nationalist wants his people to have all the power, all the wealth, and all the well-being for which there is any competition. He wants his people to command all the respect and deference from others; he tends to claim all rectitude and virtue for it, as well as all enlightenment and skill; and he gives it a monopoly of his affection. In short, he totally identifies himself with his nation. Though he may be willing to sacrifice himself for it, his nationalism is a form of egotism written large. . . .
>
> Even if most people are not extreme nationalists, nationalism has altered the world in many ways. Nationalism has not only increased the number of countries on the face of the earth, it has helped to diminish the number of its inhabitants. All major wars in the twentieth century have been fought in its name. . . .
>
> Nationalism is in potential conflict with all philosophies or religions—such as Christianity—which teach universal standards of truth and of right and wrong, regardless of nation, race, or tribe. Early in the nineteenth century a gallant American naval officer, Stephen Decatur, proposed the toast, "Our country! In her intercourse with foreign nations, may she be always in the right, but our country, right or wrong." Nearly 150 years later the United States Third Army, marching into Germany following the collapse of the Nazi regime, liberated the huge concentration camp at Buchenwald. Over the main entrance to that place of torture and death, the Nazi elite guard had thoughtfully written, "My Country, Right or Wrong." (Deutsch 1974, 124–125)

In confronting the impact of nationalism on armed conflict, we need to recognize its dual character: It is a force that (1) binds nations and nationalities together in common bonds, and (2) divides nation against nation, nationality against nationality, and is used to justify armed conflicts against other nations.

why particular wars are fought. To capture war's many structural determinants, we must consider how and why systems change. This requires us to explore the impact of the distribution of military capabilities, balances (and imbalances) of power, the number of alliances and international organizations, and the rules of

Nationalism's Dark Side Under the Fascist dictatorship of Adolf Hitler, the Nazi government glorified the state and claimed that the German people were a superior race. What followed from this extreme form of nationalism was war against Germany's neighbors and the campaign of genocide against the Jews and other ethnic minorities. Here, U.S. troops under the command of General George Patton arrive to liberate the concentration camp at Buchenwald in May 1945, but not in time to save the lives of the prisoners the Nazi elite guard had put to death in the gas chambers.

international law. At issue is how these factors—the system's characteristics and institutions—combine to influence changes in war's frequency. We will examine many of these factors in Chapters 15 and 16. Here we focus on cycles of war and peace at the international level and the structural determinants of armed conflict.

Does Violence Breed Violence? The adage "violence breeds violence" reflects the notion that the seeds of future wars are found in past wars. From this perspective World War II was an outgrowth of World War I, and the successive wars in the Middle East were seemingly little more than one war, with each battle stimulated by its predecessor. Because the frequency of past wars is correlated with the incidence of wars in later periods, war appears to be contagious and its future outbreak inevitable. If so, then something within the dynamics of world politics—its anarchical nature, its weak legal system, its uneven distribution of power, inevitable destabilizing changes in the principal actors' relative power, or some combination of structural attributes—makes the state system a war system.

Those believing in war's inevitability often cite the historical fact that war has been so repetitive. We cannot, however, safely infer that past wars have *caused* later wars. The fact that a war precedes a later one does not mean that it caused the one that followed.

Nor does war's recurrence throughout history necessarily mean we will always have it. War is not a universal institution (see Etzioni 1968; Kluckhohn 1944; Mead 1968; Sumner 1968); as we have seen, some societies have never known war, and others have been immune to it for prolonged periods. Moreover, since 1945 the outbreak of armed conflicts between states has greatly declined, despite the large increase in the number of independent countries. This indicates that armed conflict is not necessarily inevitable and that historical forces do not control people's freedom of choice or experiences.

Power Transitions. These trends notwithstanding, when changes have occurred in the major states' military capabilities, war has often resulted. Although not inevitable, war has been likely whenever competitive states' power ratios (the differentials between their capabilities) have narrowed. Dubbed the **power transition theory,** this explanation rooted in **structural realism** holds that

> an even distribution of political, economic, and military capabilities between contending groups of states is likely to increase the probability of war; peace is preserved best when there is an imbalance of national capabilities between disadvantaged and advantaged nations; the aggressor will come from a small group of dissatisfied strong countries; and it is the weaker, rather than the stronger, power that is most likely to be the aggressor. (Organski and Kugler 1980, 19)

■ power transition theory
the theory that war is likely when a dominant great power is threatened by the rapid growth of a rival's capabilities, which reduces the difference in their relative power (see p. 494).

■ structural realism
a neorealist theory that emphasizes the influence of the structure of world power on the behavior of the states within it.

During the transition from developing to developed status, emergent challengers can achieve through force the recognition that their newly formed muscles allow them. Conversely, established powers ruled by risk-acceptant leaders are often willing to employ force to put the brakes on their relative decline. Thus when advancing and retreating states seek to cope with the changes in their relative power, war between the rising challenger(s) and the declining power(s) has become especially likely. For example, the rapid changes in the power and status that produced the division of Europe among seven great powers nearly equal in military strength are often (along with the alliances they nurtured) interpreted as the tinderbox from which World War I ignited.

As explained in Chapter 15, rapid shifts in the global distribution of military power have often preceded outbursts of aggression, especially when the new distribution nears approximate parity (equality) and thereby tempts the rivals to wage war against their hegemonic challengers. According to the power transition theory, periods in which rivals' military capabilities are nearly balanced create "the necessary conditions for global war, while gross inequality assures peace or, in the worst case, an asymmetric, limited war" (Kugler 1993). Moreover, transitions in states' relative capabilities can potentially lead the weaker party to start a war in order either to overtake its rival or to protect itself from domination. Presumably, the uncertainty created by a rough equilibrium prompts the challenger's (usually unsuccessful) effort to wage war against a stronger opponent. Equally persistent is the power transition theory's observation that advantages have shifted from the attacker to the defender: "In earlier centuries the aggressor seemed to have a 50-50 chance of winning the war, but this no longer holds. The chances of the starter being victorious are shrinking. In the 1980s only 18 percent of the starters were winners" (Sivard 1991, 20). As in the past (e.g., Japan's attack and subjugation of China in 1931 and 1937), there are notable exceptions: "Since 1945, six out of twenty wars have secured decisive advantage for the initiator (the Vietnam, Six Day, Bangladesh, Yom Kippur/Ramadan, Falklands, and Persian Gulf wars)" (Ziegler 1995).

Cyclical Theories. If war is recurrent but not necessarily inevitable, are there other international factors besides power transitions that might also explain changes over time in its outbreak? The absence of a clear trend in its frequency since the late fifteenth century, and its periodic outbreak after intermittent stretches of peace, suggest that world history seesaws between long cycles of war and peace. This provides a third structural explanation of war's onset.

The more recent formal analysis of such cycles is known as **long-cycle theory.** As noted in Chapter 4, its advocates argue that cycles of world leadership and global war have existed over the past five centuries, with a "general war" erupting approximately once every century, although at irregular intervals (Hopkins and Wallerstein 1996; Modelski 1987b; Modelski and Thompson 1996). Long-cycle theory seeks to explain how an all-powerful invisible hand built into the system's dynamics causes such peaks and valleys. Although this theory embraces many contending explanations (see Goldstein 1988), they converge on the proposition that some combination of systemic properties (economic, military, and political) produce the frequency with which major wars have erupted periodically throughout modern history.

■ **long-cycle theory**
an interpretation of world history that focuses on repeating patterns of interstate behavior, such as the outbreak of systemwide general wars at regular intervals, after long periods during which other patterns (global peace) were dominant.

The long-cycle perspective is based on the fact that a great power has risen to a hegemonic position about every one hundred years. Using as a measure of dominance the possession of disproportionate sea power, we observe the rise of a single **hegemon** regularly appearing after particular hegemonic periods (see Figure 12.3). Portugal and the Netherlands rose at the beginning of the sixteenth and seventeenth centuries, respectively; Britain climbed to dominance at the beginning of both the eighteenth and nineteenth centuries; and the United States became a world leader at the end of World War II. During their reigns, these hegemonic powers monopolized military power and trade and determined the system's rules. Yet no hegemonic power has retained its top-dog position for more than three or four decades. In each cycle, overcommitments, the costs of empire, and ultimately the appearance of rivals led to the delegitimation of the hegemon's authority and to the deconcentration of power globally. As challengers to the hegemon's rule grew in strength, a "global war" has erupted after a long period of peace in each century since 1400. At the conclusion of each previous general war, a new world leader emerged dominant (Modelski 1978, 1987b), and the cyclical process began anew.

■ **hegemon**
a single dominant military and economic state that uses its unrivaled power to create and enforce rules aimed at preserving the existing world order and its own position in that order.

Such deterministic theories have intuitive appeal. It seems plausible, for instance, that just as long-term downswings and recoveries in business cycles profoundly affect subsequent behaviors and conditions, wars will produce aftereffects that may last for generations. The idea that a country at war will become exhausted and lose its enthusiasm for another war, but only for a time, is known as the **war weariness hypothesis** (Blainey 1988). Italian historian Luigi da Porto expresses one version: "Peace brings riches; riches bring pride; pride brings anger; anger brings war; war brings poverty; poverty brings humanity; humanity brings peace; peace, as I have said, brings riches, and so the world's affairs go round." Because it takes time to move through these stages, alternating periods of enthusiasm for war and weariness of war appear to be influenced by learning, forgetting, and aging.

■ **war weariness hypothesis**
the contention that a state at war will become exhausted and lose its enthusiasm for another war, but only for a time.

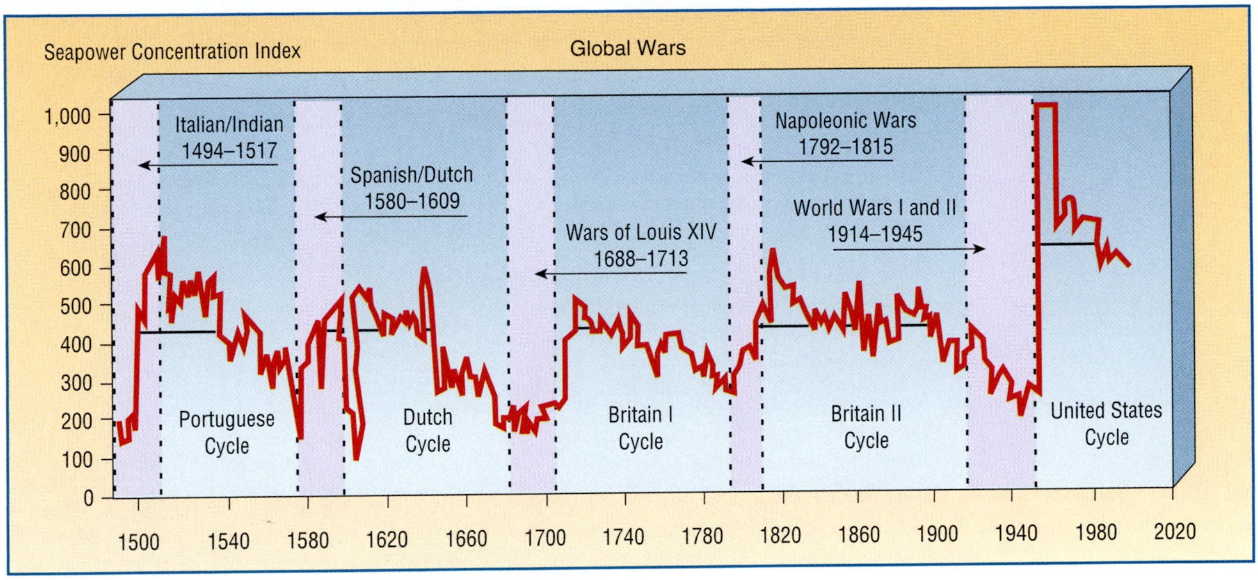

FIGURE 12.3
The Long Cycle of Global Leadership and Global War, 1494–2000
Over the past five hundred years, five great powers have risen to control the international system by dominating it. However, none of these powerful states (except Britain) has managed to reign for long. The past pattern shows that within a generation, the leader's grip on top-dog status has slipped, and in time new rivals have risen to challenge that leadership. About every one hundred years, a global war has erupted to settle the contest. The troubling question is whether this long cycle of war can be broken in the future or whether humankind will again experience a global war to determine which great power will lead.
SOURCE: Adapted from Modelski (1987a), 6.

Empirical tests of cyclical theories produce conflicting results. Quincy Wright (1942) suggested that if cycles exist, intervals between major outbreaks of war last about fifty years. In contrast, Lewis F. Richardson (1960a) and Pitirim Sorokin (1937) estimated that cycles extend over two hundred years from peak to peak (although both were somewhat skeptical and cautioned against attaching too much causal importance to their time estimates).

The validity of cyclical interpretations depends in part on the methods used to measure war's frequency and magnitude. For example, the Correlates of War research project traced cycles in the frequency and character of war between states, breaking the state system since 1815 into six historical periods, with 1848, 1881, 1914, 1945, and 1989 marking the significant turning points scholars conventionally identify in contemporary history. Table 12.1 summarizes the data for the outbreak of interstate wars exceeding one thousand battle deaths, facilitating comparisons across these six successive periods. Measured in this restricted way, the data show that 188 interstate wars erupted between 1816 and 1998, but that the frequency was fairly stable over time until the last period (1989–1998), when these kinds of wars between states greatly declined. Furthermore, if we take the expanding number of countries in the system into account, the frequency of the

TABLE 12.1

Frequency with Which 188 Wars between States Have Begun over Six Historical Periods, 1816–1998

Period	*Key System Characteristic*	*Number of Wars Initiated*	*System Size (average number of states)*
1816–1848	Concert of Europe	33	28
1849–1881	Wars of European unification	43	39
1882–1914	Resurgent imperialism	38	40
1915–1944	The Great Depression	24	59
1945–1988	The Cold War	43	117
1989–1998	Post–Cold War multipolarity	7	192

SOURCES: Data for 1816–1988 provided courtesy of the Correlates of War project under the direction of J. David Singer and Melvin Small. Data for 1989–1998 are for wars that "concerned 'classical' interstate conflict, where two internationally recognized countries were waging an armed battle," based on Wallensteen and Sollenberg (1999), and Freedom House and Vanhanen (2000) for the number of independent states.

outbreak of wars since 1816 "actually declines from four per state per decade prior to World War II to two per state per decade since [and even less since the Berlin Wall was dismantled in 1989]. And if we control not for the number of states but the number of *pairs,* the decline appears even more dramatic" (Singer 1991, 57).

This evidence fails to establish the existence of a cycle in war's onset since 1815 (Singer 1981). Moreover, because "no cyclical patterns are apparent when we examine the military experiences of the individual nations which participated in several wars" (Small and Singer 1972), it is doubtful that the international system automatically produces recurrent cycles in wars between sovereign states.

Thus, when we adjust for the increasing number of independent states, the post–World War II and post–Cold War eras appear comparatively more peaceful than do the periods that preceded them. Or do they? A somewhat different picture emerges when attention focuses on the number of wars under way, rather than on the number of wars that start. (This measure takes into account the fact that many wars continue, or last, over two or more years.) Interstate war has been in progress almost continuously since the Congress of Vienna in 1815. Although there were eighty-four years between 1816 and 1998 in which no interstate wars began, there were only twenty in which none was in progress (Small and Singer 1982, 149; Singer 1991, 60–75; Wallensteen and Sollenberg 1999, 594). The so-called outbreak of peace in the post–Cold War era is not mythical, however, as only seven large-scale wars were under way between states in the 1989–1998 period. Thus, the available evidence "suggests not so much that discrete wars come and go with some regularity, but that, with some level of such violence almost always present, there may be certain periodic fluctuations in the amount of that violence" (Small and Singer 1982).

From several theoretical standpoints, therefore, we must question claims that warfare in the twenty-first century—whether long and destructive or short and less costly—is structurally predetermined. The historical record provides a basis for assuming that the war system may be disappearing, and that peace between countries is possible (see Modelski and Thompson 1999 for projections through the twenty-first century). Both long periods of peace and long periods of warfare have existed in the past, and either could follow in the approaching new millennium. But the most recent trends show promise that classical war between states is ceasing to dominate world affairs.

Although the disappearance of war between states is possible over the long run, armed conflict and violence may persist *inside* established states. We now turn from our exploration of the multiple causes of armed conflicts between states to examine armed conflicts within states.

ARMED CONFLICT WITHIN STATES

Civil wars—wars within states—have erupted far more frequently than have wars between states. It is these armed struggles that most often capture news headlines worldwide. The *New York Times* on May 7, 1995, for example, featured a story concluding that "for just about the first time since 1815, no great powers are at one another's throats [but] civil wars and snarling savageries continue on both sides of the Equator."

■ **civil war**
war between factions within the same country.

The Characteristics of Civil War

There is a basis in fact for this assertion. Between 1989 and 1998, internal armed conflicts over government (civil wars) or over territory (state formation conflicts) have been the most common, by far. In this period, 107 civil wars erupted, in comparison with only 7 between states. At the start of 1998, 32 civil wars were raging, and only 1 cross-border armed conflict was under way (Wallensteen and Sollenberg 1999, 594).

Civil wars resulting in at least one thousand civilian and military deaths per year occurred 231 times between 1816 and 1998 (Small and Singer 1982; Singer 1991, 66–75; Wallensteen and Sollenberg 1999). Their outbreak has been somewhat irregular. Although at least one civil war was begun in eighty-four of these years, over time civil war has become increasingly frequent (see Table 12.2). Of the civil wars since 1816, 72 percent began after 1945, with the frequency steadily climbing each decade. The estimate that "more than two-thirds of all armed conflict in the world since 1945 has taken the form of civil wars" (K. Holsti 1995, 320–321) remains close to the mark but is probably low today. However, this trend is, in part, a product of the increase in the number of independent states in the international system, which makes the incidence of civil war statistically more probable. Nonetheless, civil wars stem from similar emerging conditions, and are "generally waged around three issues":

- First, many minority ethnic groups are seeking greater autonomy or the creation of an independent state (for example, the Kurds in Turkey and Chechens in Russia).
- Second, wars are fought over control of the state. During the Cold War, the East and West fueled many such conflicts. Although superpower sponsorship has ended, active fighting in sixty-one civil wars continued without interruption from 1989 into 1999 in Afghanistan, Colombia, Peru, Sri Lanka, Sudan, and Yugoslavia (Kosovo). Wars over state control are also driven by ethnic, clan, or religious differences, as in Rwanda and Algeria.

TABLE 12.2

The Frequency and Severity of 231 Civil Wars, 1816–1998

Period	*Key System Characteristics*	*System Size (average number of states)*	*Number of Civil Wars Begun*	*System Size Battle Deaths*	*Number (percent) of Civil Wars Internationalized through Large-Scale Military Intervention*
1816–1848	Monarchies in Concert of Europe suppress democratic revolutions.	28	12	93,200	3 (25%)
1849–1881	Rising nationalism and civil wars.	39	20	2,891,600	1 (5%)
1882–1914	Imperialism and colonization.	40	18	388,000	3 (17%)
1915–1945	World wars and economic collapse.	59	14	1,631,460	4 (29%)
1946–1988	Decolonization and independence for emerging Global South countries during Cold War.	117	60	6,222,020	14 (23%)
1989–1998	Age of failed states and civil wars.	192	107	1,950,000	10 (9%)
Totals			231	13,216,000	33 (14%)

SOURCE: Data for 1816–1988 provided courtesy of the Correlates of War project under the direction of J. David Singer and Melvin Small; 1989–1998 frequencies are based on Wallenstein and Sollenberg (1998) and battle-death projections are extrapolated from Sivard (1996).

- Finally, several armed conflicts are occurring where national government has either badly eroded or completely broken down. In these "failed states" (such as Liberia and Somalia) the line between political struggle and economic banditry is blurred. Almost all quantitative inventories "include in their tallies only conflicts that involve government forces among the protagonists, at least on one side. Increasingly, however, fighting involves opposing warlords, ethnic militias, criminal organizations, and others that do not have the trappings of sovereignty and whose fighters do not wear a state's uniforms and badges" (*Vital Signs 1999*).

The number of civil wars underway provides a different picture. Referring to the same inventories cited in Table 12.2, we see that between 1816 and 1998 civil wars were in progress somewhere in the world about 90 percent of the time. During the five-year period from 1989 to 1993, a total of ninety conflicts were active in at least one year in sixty-one locations around the world, and none of these were "truly international" (Gleditsch 1995, 586). In June 1998, the ratio remained about the same: thirty-two of the thirty-six wars then being fought were civil wars without the involvement of foreign intervention, many of which had begun more than a decade earlier (Wallensteen and Sollenberg 1999). Africa's so-called First World War in 2000 involving outside intervention by six states in the Congo where a dictatorship was waging a civil war against the separate rebel groups—and the UN was assigned the impossible task of peacekeeping—may be a symbol of the internal wars of the future.

A notable characteristic of civil wars is their severity. The number of lives lost in civil violence has remained high since the Napoleonic Wars ended in 1815, and casualty rates show an alarming growth, especially since World War II. One symptom of the climbing lethality of civil rebellions is that ten of the fifteen most destructive civil wars between 1816 and 1980 occurred in the twentieth century; of those ten, seven have occurred since World War II (Small and Singer 1982, 241). The cliché that "the most savage conflicts occur in the home" captures the ugly reality, as genocide and mass slaughter aimed at depopulating entire regions have become commonplace in recent civil wars. That grim reality was illustrated in Rwanda, where "the Hutu government incited citizens to a genocidal slaughter, resulting in the murder of an estimated 500,000 people in a month's time" (Sivard 1996). Sudan provides another horrifying example of the mass slaughter of civilians that often occurs when governments seek to keep power by destroying minority opposition groups.

> A quick glimpse within Sudan's borders reveals a world of famine, slavery, torture, religious persecution, rape, massacres, pillaging and looting. . . . Sudan has been engulfed by a brutal civil war since 1983. For years, southern rebels have fought for a democratic, secular Sudan that would guarantee equal rights for those southern Sudanese who have been treated as second-class citizens for far too long.
>
> The Sudanese government, which displaced a democratically elected government in 1989, has engaged in a policy to divide and destroy the people of the predominately Christian and animist south. It uses terror against civilians as a weapon of choice and pits different ethnic groups against each other, resulting in southern factional fighting that has complicated the overall situation. The scale of death and destruction has reached staggering proportions.
>
> Credible estimates from human rights organizations suggest that 2 million people have perished, 4 million have been internally displaced, and nearly 400,000 have been forced to live in neighboring countries as refugees. Many of the displaced live without adequate food and shelter and in constant fear of government assaults. (Rice and Scheffer 1999, 6)

A second core characteristic of civil wars suggested by the case of the Sudanese civil war is their typically long duration.

> The dominant pattern is of rumbling conflicts that, from time to time across a decade, erupt viciously into action. . . . For the most part, modern [internal] war resembles a slow torture, [offering] few triumphs. . . . They simply continue. More than half the wars of the 1990s lasted more than five years, two-fifths lasted more than ten years and a quarter for more than twenty. The action is often fitful. (D. Smith 1997, 14).

A third characteristic of civil wars is their resistance to negotiated settlement. Making peace among rival factions that are struggling for power, driven by hatred, and poisoned by the inertia of prolonged killing that has become a way of life is very difficult. Civil wars rarely result in the decisive victory of one faction over another. The pattern of civil wars is that domestic enemies are rarely able to end the fighting through negotiated compromise at the bargaining table; most end on the battlefield:

> Between 1940 and 1990 55 percent of interstate wars were resolved at the bargaining table, whereas only 20 percent of civil wars reached similar solutions. Instead, most internal wars ended with the extermination, expulsion, or capitulation of the losing side. In fact, groups fighting civil wars almost always chose to fight to the finish unless an outside power stepped in to guarantee a peace agreement. If a third party agreed to enforce the terms of a peace treaty, negotiations always succeeded regardless of the initial goals, ideology, or ethnicity of the participants. If a third party did not intervene, these talks usually failed. (Walter 1997, 335)

The growing frequency, severity, length, and indeterminate conclusion of the civil wars in the last decade of the twentieth century are accounted for by the multiple causes of these prolonged domestic disputes raging across the globe.

The Causes of Civil War

Civil wars stem from a wide range of ideological, demographic, religious, ethnic, economic, social-structural, and political conditions. Civil war and revolution have simultaneously been defended as instruments of justice and condemned as the immoral acceptance of violent change. They contain ingredients of both. Those who engineered the American, Russian, and Chinese revolutions claimed that violence was necessary to realize social change, political freedom, and independence; the powers from whom they sought liberation berated the immorality of their methods.

■ **relative deprivation** inequality between the wealth and status of individuals and groups, and the outrage of those at the bottom about their perceived exploitation by those at the top.

Internal Rebellion. Among the sources of civil war, internal violence is a reaction to frustration and **relative deprivation**—people's perception that they are unfairly deprived of the wealth and status that they deserve in comparison with advantaged others (Gurr 1970). When people's expectations of what they deserve rise more rapidly than their material rewards, the probability of conflict grows. That, of course, applies to most of the countries in the Global South today, where the distribution of wealth and opportunities is highly unequal (see Chapter 5).

Secessionist Revolts. Civil wars break up existing states and the parts divide into new states, a pattern of fragmentation has been going on for the past half-century. The first wave was primarily revolutions that succeeded in breaking colonies away from foreign control and occupation; the second wave has been primarily a splintering of either older or the recently emerged new states from within. Altogether, "from 1950 to 1990, 2.2 new states were created per year, up from an average of 1.2 per year from 1900 to 1950. The 1990s have seen extreme instability: From 1990 to 1998, the rate was 3.1 new countries per year. Throughout history, the dissolution of countries has been primarily a consequence of wars between states. Today, governments have more to fear from within than without. . . . Internal turmoil increasingly leads to abrupt border changes. . . . Globalization is breaking the world down into its component parts, even as it is drawing these parts closer together" (Enriquez 1999, 32, 34). The seeds of civil strife are often sown by national independence movements. "More than two

The Painful Birth of Democracy In mid-1999 East Timor voted to secede from Indonesia. The Indonesian authorities sought to prevent by violence and repression the East Timorese bid for independence, prior to intervention by UN peacekeeping forces to halt the assault on human rights of hundreds of thousands of innocent East Timorese civilians. Here a rock-wielding protester is hunted down and killed by Jakarta-backed militia.

thirds of all the armed combat in the world between 1945 and 1995 were manifestations of the state-creation enterprise" (K. Holsti 1995, 22). In the aftermath of the Cold War, unrest and discontent—long held in check at the point of a bayonet—have been released, and succession revolts have multiplied as a result. Some of these independence movements have started at the ballot box, but spilled over to violence when the presiding government used armed force to prevent separation. This happened in East Timor following the tumultuous vote in August 1999 for nationhood; 99 percent of those eligible to vote turned out in that election, and 80 percent of the fearful voters cast ballots for independence. The Javanese politicians and military generals brutally fought to crush the Timorese independence movement, ordering their militia to suppress the Timorese nationalities, attempting to escape their oppression. Violence often has been the means through which nations have been given—or denied—birth.

Nationalism and Neonationalism. Nationalism today is widely regarded as an especially potent cause of war within states as noted earlier (see also Chapter 7). However, the conditions prevailing today lead many to believe that nationalism will incite "wars of states against nations, wars of succession, and major armed uprisings to oust governments" (K. Holsti 1995) at unprecedented levels. The potential magnitude of nationalism-inspired revolutionary war is great:

> More than 95 percent of the world's . . . states are multinational, that is, composed of many nations, some unconsenting. These . . . states assert

> sovereignty over the world's three thousand to five thousand nations and peoples. . . . State governments [are pitted] against guerrilla insurgencies and indigenous nations. Most of these wars are over territory, resources, and identity, not ideology. They are hidden from most people's views because the fighting is against peoples and countries that are not even on the map. (Nietschmann 1991, 172–173)

■ **neonationalism** the expression of communal or ethnic aspirations by a dissatisfied nationality group within a given state.

If nationalism is a powerful influence on internal wars, what is termed **neonationalism** adds a new element to this traditional cause. Neonationalism and the localized conflicts it spawns differ from the nationalism previously seen in the Global South.

> Earlier stages of Third World nationalism tended to revolve around the national liberation experience, the zeal engendered by the throwing off of colonial ties. . . . Neonationalism is the product of more recent decades, going beyond classical nationalism and [including] separatist subnationalism; that is, the expression of communal/ethnic aspirations of groups within the nation-state that are unhappy with their lot: Shiites in Iraq, Sikhs in India, Unighur Turks in Chinese Turkestan. It involves strong new drives toward separatism: the Moros in the Philippines, Georgians in the [former] Soviet Union, Catholics in Northern Ireland, Hungarians in Romania, Biafra in Nigeria, even Quebec in Canada. (Fuller 1991–1992, 14–15)

This kind of destabilizing "hypernationalism" is malign because the neonationalist doctrines are used "to justify or motivate large-scale violence [or] the conquest or subjugation of other nationalities" (Snyder 1993). The civil strife that erupted in Albania, Liberia, Serbia, Sudan, and Rwanda in the mid-1990s is symptomatic of the new wave of fractional conflicts that neonationalism has ignited. The future is foretold by the recent (1990–1995) past, during which half the countries that experienced a civil war were those in which ethnic minorities comprised 10 to 50 percent of the population (D. Smith 1997, 30).

■ **ethnic warfare** violence resulting from wars between two or more ethnic groups or from state-sponsored violence to terrorize or destroy an ethnic minority.

■ **displaced people** people involuntarily uprooted from their homes but still living in their own countries (see p. 216).

Ethnonational Conflict. Since World War II, civil wars provoked by ancient ethnic and racial hatreds have been commonplace in multiethnic states. Between 1945 and 1981, 258 cases of **ethnic warfare** were observed, 40 percent of which involved high levels of violence (Carment 1993, 141). More recently, this armed conflict has reached epidemic proportions. Ted Robert Gurr (1994, 351–352) estimated that 26,759,000 refugees fled the fifty major ethnonational conflicts that were occurring in 1993–1994, each of which was responsible for an average of eighty thousand deaths. Most of the victims were innocent children. Between 1983 and 1993, some 10 million children died in civil strife (Kane 1995, 20), and the rate of killing of innocent civilian noncombatants continues to climb. Brutal assaults on civilians, including children, are escalating, and it is estimated that "today more than 90 percent of all casualties are non-combatants" (Sivard 1996, 17). Of the 40 million refugees worldwide, just over half are **displaced people**—refugees within their own countries—and "women and children are more likely to be made refugees than men" (D. Smith 1997, 26).

As U.S. President Bill Clinton observed in his June 7, 1994, speech before the French National Assembly, militant ethnic nationalism was "on the rise, transforming the healthy pride of nations, tribes, religious and ethnic groups into

Ethnic Warfare and Children Children have often been the major victims of civil strife. This photo, which received the World Press Award in 1985, depicts children caught in the ethnonational and religious civil war in Beirut, the capital of Lebanon—a country whose population is about two-thirds Muslim and one-fourth Christian, with each faction divided into further sects.

cancerous prejudice, eating away at states and leaving their people addicted to the political painkillers of violence and demagoguery." Chan Heng Chee, Singapore's former ambassador to the UN, in 1993 described the opinion shared by most experts when she observed that "with the end of the Cold War . . . the new problems haunting us will be instability arising from ethnic and religious turmoil. . . . The fault line will . . . to a large extent coincide with racial and ethnic divisions." The danger, warns Irish author Conor Cruise O'Brien (1993), resides in the fact that ethnonationalism "is something for which people are prepared to kill and die in large numbers, as Serbs, Croats, and Bosnian Muslims [did in the former Yugoslavia], and as, at an even more primordial level, warlike Somalian clansmen are doing." Thus, much of the internal revolt and ethnic warfare currently sweeping the world is less inspired by political motives and economic aims than it is by deeply rooted ethnic animosities. Ethnopolitical clashes differ greatly from the anticolonial secessionist and separatist movements of the past, and instead are often waged by irregular and private gangs committing atrocities against their neighbors. With "some 5,000 ethnic groups in the world . . . if all these groups went the way of the Kosovo Liberation Army the wars would never stop," warns Michael Hirsh (1999).

Failed States. Many fledgling governments are fragile and fall apart as they fail to effectively manage the regulatory power sovereignty under international law gives them to govern affairs within their territorial borders. Mismanagement by government administration is causing an epidemic of **failing states** throughout the globe, as disarray, discontent, and disorder have mobilized desperate populations living in conditions of anarchy to rebel. The civil wars percolated by state failure have caused as many as 113 states to dissolve or fragment into separate units between 1955 and 1994 according to the U.S. Central Intelligence Agency's "State Failure Task Force" report. In 1996 no less than another sixteen states were "high-risk" countries vulnerable to destruction through civil rebellion against a feeble government.

failing states those governments that are in danger of losing the loyalty of their citizens, who are rebelling against corruption and administrative failure, and in the process tearing the country into separate political parts.

The causes of state failure and civil disintegration are multiple, but failed states share some key characteristics. Among them, the CIA "State Failure Task Force" report finds that

- Democracy generally lowers the risk of state failure; autocracy increases it.
- Poor democracies, however, are more unstable than either rich democracies or poor nondemocracies, and poor democracies that do not improve living standards are exceptionally vulnerable.
- The best predictor of failure is high infant mortality.
- High levels of trade openness seem to inoculate any kind of regime against failure. States that have fair rules allowing a high degree of international trade gain stability.
- The existence of a "youth bulge"—a large proportion of young adults in the population—increases the risk of ethnic war because large pools of underemployed youth are easily mobilized into action.
- Mass killings are often associated with low levels of trade openness, in part, because countries with little foreign trade are usually of little concern to the international community. (Zimmerman 1996, 46)

Inasmuch as many of the 207 sovereign states in the world have one or more of these attributes, it is likely that failing states will grow as a problem in the globalized twenty-first century, as the pressures of globalization (see Chapter 9) contribute to the conditions that are causing civil wars, state failure, and the disintegration of the global community's state members into ever smaller and more numerous units. As Map 12.1 shows, the globe is speckled with many dangerous ethnic conflicts and civil war flashpoints where countries are highly vulnerable to dissolution as a result of state failure, mismanagement, and civil revolt.

The Economic Sources of Internal Rebellions. The destabilization caused by rapid growth also helps to account for the ubiquity of internal war (see Olson 1971). In contrast with what intuition might suggest, civil violence often erupts in countries in which conditions are improving, not deteriorating. "Economic modernization," former U.S. Secretary of State Henry Kissinger stated, "leads to political instability rather than political stability." When modernization generates rising expectations that governments are unable to satisfy, civil war often follows. This is the essence of relative deprivation as a cause of internal violence, as people who feel themselves to have been denied the resources they deserve are often inclined to use force in acts of rebellion (Gurr 1970).

Having observed rapid growth as a source of civil war, we must not ignore the persistence of poverty as an ancient and continuing cause. Desperation has fomented domestic insurrection throughout all periods of history, and today, even in the period of democratization and economic growth through free trade and free markets, misery among those not sharing in the benefits is breeding revolt. "The chief causes of conflict remain—overwhelming poverty in cities and the dominance of a narrow elite in rural areas." This is made evident by the fact that 57 percent of the armed conflicts between 1990 and 1995 erupted in the poor countries ranking "low" on the UN **human development index** (HDI; see Chapter 5), and another 34 percent in the "medium-human-development" countries, in contrast to only 14 percent in the "high" countries providing relative

human development index (HDI)
an index that uses life expectancy, literacy, average number of years of schooling, and income to assess a country's performance in providing for its citizens' welfare and security.

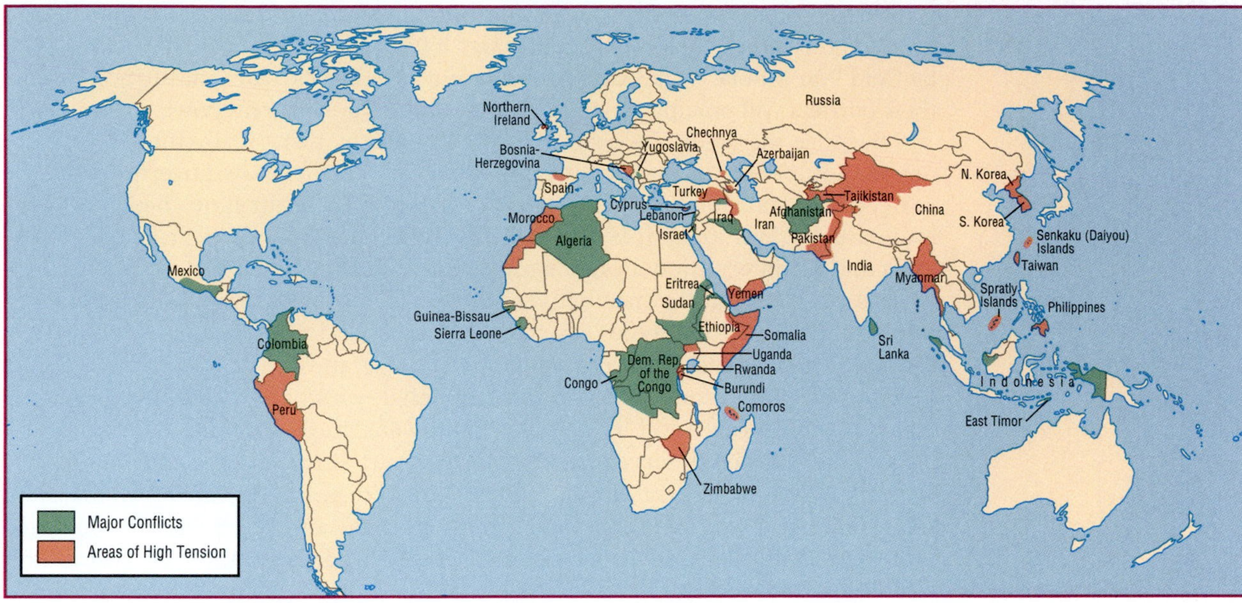

MAP 12.1
States Threatening to Collapse in Civil Wars, 1999

An increasing number of countries could break apart. State failure, defined as revolutionary or ethnic wars, mass killings, and disruptive regime changes, threatens to increase the number of countries in the twenty-first century, as failing states splinter into newly emergent states. The UN (UNDP 1994) estimates that by 2025 there may be as many as 500 sovereign states in the world. This map highlights countries where armed conflicts, mostly civil wars, threatened to explode and to implode existing states in 1999, with eighteen "major" conflicts and twenty-eight "areas of high tension" pinpointing the widespread forty-six flashpoints where existing state governments are in danger of collapsing.

SOURCE: *Christian Science Monitor* (February 12, 1999), 12–13.

prosperity, health and education for their citizens" (D. Smith 1997, 48, 50). As UN High Commissioner for Refugees Sadaka Ogata concluded in December 1997, "to establish a more peaceful, prosperous and secure world, poverty must be eliminated and income differentials reduced."

The International Dimensions of Civil War

It is tempting to think of civil war as stemming exclusively from conditions within countries. However, external factors often influence internal rebellions. "Every war has two faces. It is a conflict both between and within political systems; a conflict that is both external and internal. [It is undeniable that] internal wars affect the international system [and that] the international system affects internal wars" (Modelski 1964).

We can distinguish several phases that have influenced the linkage between changes in the global system and the incidence of civil war. First, the effects of imperialism, industrialization, nationalism, and ideology provoked the comparatively high levels of civil war between 1848 and 1870. Second, the breakup of the

European colonial empires contributed to the frequent incidence of civil war between the end of World War II and the 1960s. And today, the discipline imposed by Cold War bipolarity has disappeared, removing states' fear that turmoil within their borders will precipitate military intervention by the great powers.

Because the great powers have global interests, historically they have been prone to intervene militarily in civil wars to support friendly governments and to overthrow unfriendly ones. When they did, wars within states became internationalized. But today it is often difficult to determine where an internal war ends and an international one begins. In an interdependent, increasingly borderless world, the difference between involvement and intervention is difficult to distinguish. The two types of armed conflict are closely linked. As Table 12.2 reveals, between the Congress of Vienna (1816) and the tearing down of the Berlin Wall (1989), one out of every three civil wars has become an interstate war through intervention by an external power. More than two-thirds of these large-scale military interventions have occurred since 1945. During the Cold War, many entanglements of the United States (e.g., Lebanon, the Dominican Republic, Korea, Vietnam, Grenada, and Panama) and the Soviet Union (e.g., Hungary, Ethiopia, and Afghanistan) were responses to internal instability. Even today, the Global South remains the site of most violent conflicts and military and humanitarian interventions in the world. In response to the tragic fate of the innocent victims, the UN and NATO have intervened in multilateral operations to stop the carnage (see Chapter 16).

Many analysts believe that domestic conflicts become internationalized because leaders who experience internal opposition are inclined to provoke an international crisis in the hope that their citizens will become less rebellious if their attention is diverted to the threat of external aggression. This proposition has become known as the **diversionary theory of war** (see Controversy: Does Civil Strife Breed External Aggression? on pages 446–447).

diversionary theory of war
the contention that leaders initiate conflict abroad as a way of increasing national cohesion at home (see p. 62).

The diversionary theory of war is based on the expectation that external war will result in increased domestic support for political leaders. "To put it cynically, one could say that nothing helps a leader like a good war. It gives him his only chance of being a tyrant and being loved for it at the same time. He can introduce the most ruthless forms of control and send thousands of his followers to their deaths and still be hailed as a great protector. Nothing ties tighter the in-group bonds than an out-group threat" (Morris 1969).

The argument is logical. However, the relationship between civil and international conflict is, in practice, more complex. In general, the available evidence urges that we question the diversionary theory of war. Perhaps the most compelling reason for some doubt is that "when domestic conflict becomes extremely intense it would seem more reasonable to argue that there is a greater likelihood that a state will retreat from its foreign engagements in order to handle the situation at home" (Zinnes and Wilkenfeld 1971).

TERRORISM

terrorism
premeditated, politically motivated violence perpetrated against noncombatant targets by subnational groups or clandestine agents, usually intended to influence an audience (see p. 222).

Terrorism poses another alarming kind of violence in the contemporary world. The instruments of terror are varied and the motivations of terrorists diverse, but "experts agree that terrorism is the use or threat of violence, a method of combat or a strategy to achieve certain goals, that its aim is to induce a state of fear in the victim, that it is ruthless and does not conform to humanitarian norms, and that publicity is an essential factor in terrorist strategy" (Laqueur 1986).

Some terrorist activities, such as the 1995 bombing of the U.S. federal government building in Oklahoma City and the rampant terrorist bombings that inflicted Russia's desperate frontline fighters against random terror in 1999 and 2000, begin and end in a single country. Many, however, cross national borders. At the end of the twentieth century, terrorists targeted citizens and property in many countries, and because terrorist acts are spread throughout the globe, the risks are widespread (see Map 12.2 on p. 448).

Although terrorism has always been practiced, it emerged as a significant international problem in the 1960s (Kidder 1990) and grew to epidemic proportions in the 1970s and 1980s. Figure 12.4 (see p. 449) shows the changing frequency of terrorism in today's world, the general trend suggesting an increasing level of transnational terrorist activity from 1968, followed by a decline since 1987. International terrorist attacks during 1999 climbed 43 percent from the prior year to 392 separate terrorist acts. In 1999, 939 people were killed—one of the lowest casualty levels in recent years, the U.S. Department of State reported.

Terrorism is a tactic of the powerless against the powerful. Thus it is not surprising that political or social minorities and ethnic movements sometimes turn to acts of terrorism on behalf of their political causes (see Chapter 7). Those seeking independence and sovereign statehood, such as the Basques in Spain, typify the aspirations that animate terrorist activity. Religion also sometimes rationalizes the terrorist activities of extremist movements, such as the efforts of the Sikh groups who wish to carve out an independent state called Khalistan ("Land of the Pure") from Indian territory, and of the Islamic extremist group HAMAS to destabilize Israel and sabotage a negotiated peace between Israel and its Arab neighbors. In November 1995, right-wing Jewish fanatics in the Kach religious terrorist group assassinated Israeli Prime Minister Yitzhak Rabin to derail the peace process in Palestine.

In the industrialized world, terrorism often occurs where discrepancies in income are severe and where minority groups feel deprived of the political freedoms and privileges enjoyed by the majority. In the urbanized areas of the industrialized world, guerrilla warfare—normally associated with rural uprisings—is not a viable route to self-assertion, but terrorist tactics are.

Consideration of terrorists' motives as a disease often obscures the perception of terrorism: One person's terrorist may be another person's liberator. Ironically, both governments and countergovernment movements claim to seek liberty, and both are labeled terrorists by their opponents.

> Those who are described as terrorists, and who reject that title for themselves, make the uncomfortable point that national armed forces, fully supported by democratic opinion, have in fact employed violence and terror on a far vaster scale than what liberation movements have as yet been able to attain. The "freedom fighters" see themselves as fighting a just war. Why should they not be entitled to kill, burn, and destroy as national armies, navies, and air forces do; and why should the label "terrorist" be applied to them and not to the national militaries? (O'Brien 1977, 56–57)

CONTROVERSY

Does Civil Strife Breed External Aggression?

The Diversionary Theory of War Debated

Is there a connection between civil strife and foreign aggression? When leaders suffer conflict at home, do they attempt to contain that domestic strife by waging a war against foreigners in the hope that the international danger will take citizens' attention away from their dissatisfaction with their home government? Throughout history, many leaders have thought that there might be a causal link—that endangered dictators would be inclined to foment aggression abroad in order to retain control internally. British Prime Minister Winston Churchill thought so when he wrote "Corruption at home, aggression abroad to cover it up. . . . Sentiment by the bucketful, patriotism by the imperial pint."

There are powerful reasons for leaders to assume that national unity will rise when an external threat exists, and there are equally strong temptations for them to seek to manage domestic unrest by initiating foreign adventures. Indeed, many political advisers counsel this as a solution. For instance, the realist theorist Niccolò Machiavelli in 1513 advised leaders to undertake foreign wars whenever turmoil within their state became too great. He was echoed by the legal theorist Jean Bodin in 1593, who argued that "the best way of preserving a state, and guaranteeing it against sedition, rebellion and civil war is . . . to find an enemy against whom they can make common cause." Hermann Goering, Adolf Hitler's adviser, advocated the same idea in Nazi Germany, contending: "Voice or no voice, the people can always be brought to do the bidding of the leaders. That is easy. All you have to do is tell them they are being attacked and denounce the pacifists for lack of patriotism." Similarly, John Foster Dulles (1939), who later became U.S secretary of state, recommended "The easiest and quickest cure of internal dissension is to portray danger from abroad."

This strategy for quieting domestic unrest is controversial. Provoking a foreign war can easily backfire for a leader, mobilizing public opinion against a bellicose policy abroad and leading to protest and demonstrations. Critics warn that a manufactured war is likely to erode public confidence in the government, particularly when leaders do not enjoy a high approval rate from their constituents. And, a powerful argument can be made for an unpopular leader to exercise caution in

The difference between nationalistic "freedom fighters," whose major complaint is that they lack a country, and governments claiming to protect freedom, often lies in the eye of the beholder. This problem makes the definition of a terrorist group less obvious and more controversial, as what most distinguishes terrorist groups from liberation movements is the outcome—which faction succeeds or fails in a political struggle for power. We must keep in mind that those who are willing to use violence and terror outside the rules of warfare that have evolved over time tend to be condemned or praised, depending on whether those who condemn or praise accept or reject their cause.

The popularity of the slogan that "one person's terrorist is another's freedom fighter" notwithstanding, there is a difference. Terrorists are defined by the *means* (terror) they use, and freedom fighters by the *end* (civil liberty) they pursue. Because freedom can be fought for by moral and legal methods that respect the immunity of noncombatant targets, freedom fighters can operate differently from terrorists, who are prepared to use violence against unarmed civilians and to promote good causes by evil methods.

Although many terrorist groups today are undeniably seeking sovereignty, a broader definition of terrorism would acknowledge that many governments undertake terrorist acts, sometimes against their own people and sometimes by foreign policy, avoid the use of force overseas, and to instead cultivate a reputation for peace and cooperation in the country's relations with foreign countries. Both liberalism and realism counsel prudence in managing international conflict, and recommend, diplomacy, not war, as a means to settle international disputes as well as domestic disturbances. This position underscores the reason why many leaders are hesitant to initiate conflict abroad, fearing that a foreign war will lead to further criticism that they are intentionally undertaking military action against foreign enemies for the manipulative purpose of deflecting attention away from problems at home. In addition, the theory that leaders use foreign aggression to dampen the flame of civil unrest is also questioned by the equally compelling argument that, contrary to this theory, when leaders experience domestic strife in their country they are more prone to isolationistically withdraw from foreign military adventures than they are to initiate them, so that they can concentrate their attention on preserving internal stability.

Whether leaders actually start wars to offset domestic conflict remains a subject of debate, crucial to future policy making. At heart, these rival ideas are empirical questions. The answers are unclear. Many studies have examined the proposition that civil wars and foreign wars are linked, but few studies confirm this hypothesis (see Morgan and Bickers 1992), and for this reason the topic is controversial. What do you think? In contemplating your answer, consider that it may seem reasonable to assume "war with the outside is sometimes the last chance for a state ridden with inner antagonisms to overcome these antagonisms" (Simmel 1956), and that "statesmen may be driven to a policy of foreign conflict—if not open war—in order to defend themselves against the onslaught of domestic enemies" (Haas and Whiting 1956). Yet we cannot demonstrate that leaders undertake these diversionary actions for this purpose. "The linkage depends," Jack Levy (1989b) observes, "on the kinds of internal conditions that commonly lead to hostile external actions for diversionary purposes." For example, "democratic states are particularly likely to use force externally during an election year, especially when the election occurs at a time of economic stagnation" (Ostrom and Job 1986). To complicate this longstanding controversy even further, research shows that even this linkage holds only under particular types of circumstances.

So ask yourself in what circumstances will leaders cynically choose foreign war to preserve their personal power? Finally, take into account in evaluating the validity of the diversionary theory of war the view of one analyst, who argues that in most cases "where civil unrest preceded external conflict, war was not usually initiated by the strife-torn state. Instead, most wars were initiated by outside powers, with the internally troubled state in the role of the victim" (Cashman 1993).

supporting terrorism against other established sovereign states (see Crenshaw 1990). In fact, some states underwrite the activities of terrorist movements that advocate philosophies they embrace (or challenge the security of rival states). States have often financed, trained, equipped, and provided sanctuary for terrorists whose activities serve their foreign policy goals (see Chapter 7). The practice of such **state-sponsored terrorism** is among the charges that the United States leveled in May 2000 against Cuba, Iran, Iraq, Libya, North Korea, Syria, and Sudan. Similarly, others have accused the United States of sponsoring terrorist activities in Vietnam, Chile, El Salvador, Nicaragua, and elsewhere (Schlagheck 1990).

state-sponsored terrorism formal assistance, training, and arming of foreign terrorists by a state in order to achieve foreign policy goals (see p. 613).

Although many terrorist sanctuaries have disappeared with the end of the Cold War,

> it is unlikely that international terrorism is a passing and transitory phenomenon. The trend toward the weakening of central authority in governments, the rise in ethnic and subnational sentiments, and the increasing fractionalization of the global political process point toward its growth as a form of political protest and persuasion. Classic balance-of-power diplomacy is of little utility in dealing with it, for violent acts of small groups of people, or individuals, are difficult for governments to

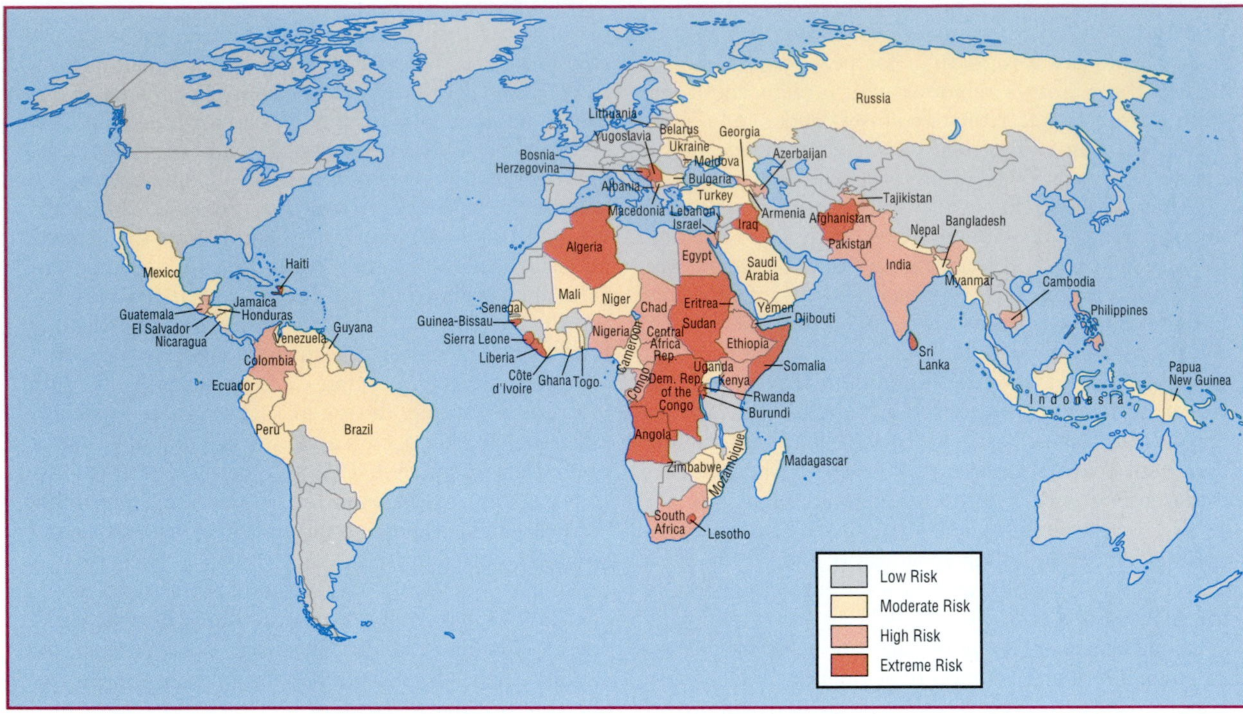

MAP 12.2
The Globalization of International Terrorism

"Terrorism is warfare by another name—the low level, low intensity use of violence for political ends," argues Dan Smith (1997) of the Oslo International Peace Research Institute. Unfortunately, this type of armed conflict is a global problem. As this map shows, security professionals rate the risk levels of terrorist violence as "high" or "extreme" in many countries, and because of this growing threat the U.S. State Department has found it necessary to issue current "travel warnings" (<http://travel.state.gov>) to advise people to avoid those countries where the risks of bombings and kidnappings are high. In 1999, about thirty countries were listed as places where the risk of a terrorist attack was high.
SOURCE: *Newsweek* (February 22, 1999), 64.

> control. International terrorism is likely to continue and to expand because in the minds of many of its perpetrators it has proven to be "successful." (Pierre 1984, 85)

Indeed, the dangers of terrorism have not waned. Libyan leader Colonel Muammar Qaddafi warned in July 1993, "Whatever takes place in America—and you will see a lot more terrorism there—is a function of perceived injustices in other parts of the world. . . . Acts of terrorism in America will be the answer, and they will be more and more violent and spectacular for television purposes around the world."

It is unlikely that the danger of terrorism will decline in the twenty-first century, and, indeed, it could easily become more deadly and harder to curb in the

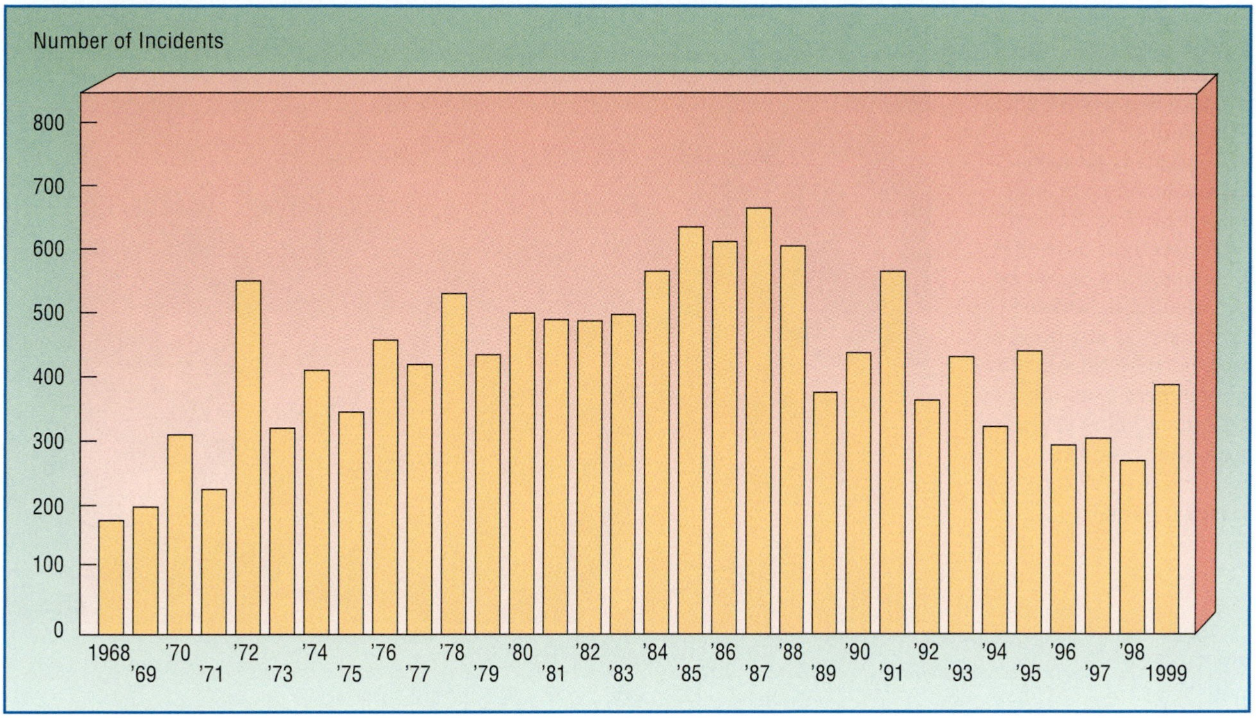

FIGURE 12.4
International Terrorist Incidents, 1968–1999

The frequency of international terrorist activity has changed over time since 1968, and the number of incidents each year has ranged between 174 (in 1968) and 665 (in 1987). These activities appear entrenched, but vary over time.

SOURCE: Office of the Coordinator for Counterterrorism, U.S. Department of State.

borderless globalized system that makes the practice of terrorism so effortless. The previous reasons for terrorist activity remain as strong as ever, and the Information Age environment makes transnational networking among terrorist groups convenient. It is also unlikely that the new International Convention for the Suppression of the Financing of Terrorism adopted by the UN in 2000 will curb terrorist activity, despite the best of intentions, in an increasingly interdependent world which facilitates the free movement of people and goods across national borders. Adding to the persistent threat is the likelihood that contemporary terrorism is also becoming more radicalized and more violent. "Any survey of the world map of terrorism—the part of the world where the most casualties occur—reveals not only growing fanaticism but also the growth of indiscriminate murder, the desire to exercise power, and sheer bloodlust. In recent years, terrorists have become less hesitant to inflict heavy casualties and cause physical destruction" (Laqueur 2001). In 1999 terror's new face was termed "catastrophic terrorism" by U.S. Secretary of Defense William Cohen to distinguish it from "the conventional type of terrorism." What makes the new game so frightening is that terrorism today is now the work of "cowards who rejoice in the agony of their victims" and are willing to use weapons of mass

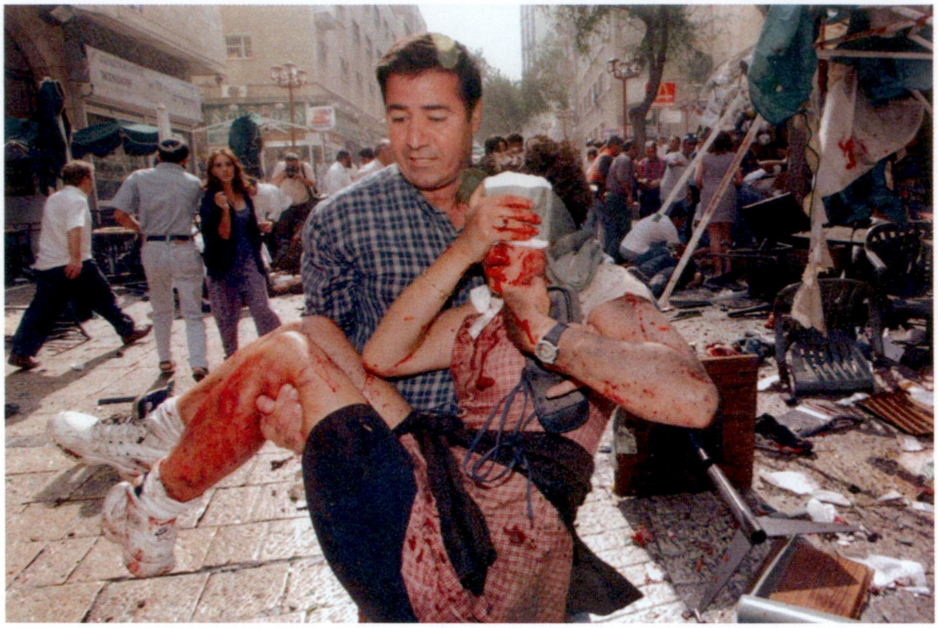

Terrorism The world has paid a fearful price for the random violence that modern terrorism inflicts. The point of terrorist campaigns is to make people feel unsafe and unsure, and to succeed, terrorists fight outside the accepted rules of war by threatening to strike anywhere, at any time, at anyone, without warning. Shown here is an innocent bystander being evacuated from the scene of a September 1997 terrorist attack in Israel.

destruction (WMD, the initials preferred to ABC for atomic, biological, chemical weapons). Hence, because terrorists now have available a variety of new tactics, such as the use of electronic threats so they can practice "cyber-terrorism" and engage in "Netwar" strategies, the dangers are climbing.

■ **postmodern terrorism**
to Walter Laqueur, the terrorism practiced by an expanding set of diverse actors with new weapons "to sow panic in a society, to weaken or even overthrow the incumbents, and to bring about political change."

International terrorism is certain to persist for still other reasons. One of the most important and potent is the condition that Walter Laqueur terms **postmodern terrorism.** This phrase describes the globalized environment which today makes terrorism easy to practice. So-called postmodern terrorism is likely to expand because the globalized international environment without meaningful barriers allows terrorists to practice their ancient trade by new rules and methods, while at the same time encouraging state-sponsored terrorism as a substitute for warfare and making the most advanced countries the most vulnerable (Laqueur 1998). Another is the rapid spread of new weapons and technology, and their easy transport across borders, which provide unprecedented opportunities for terrorists to commit atrocities and to change their tactics in response to successes in countering them. A third is the growing difficulty in a globalized system of detecting and deterring the attacks of disciplined globalized terrorist networks that are generously funded by international organized crime (IOC) syndicates to facilitate their profit in the narcotics trade (see Chapter 7). And still another is the moral ambiguity that surrounds the activities of extremist militia groups, who are glorified by some in the media for their independence and defiance of governing authority, especially in democracies protecting the rights of citizens to carry arms and express their grievances. Governments often seem reluctant to exercise the political will necessary to destroy terrorism:

> Terrorism continues, and will continue, because terrorists and their supporters make distinctions of class and race and other divisions of mankind,

> subordinating the humanity of their victims to the purposes of their cause, giving credit to the political smoke that thinly masks acts of pure bloodlust. And it continues because those who should know better refuse to recognize the distinction between aggression and rightful defense, forswearing power as if it itself were evil, when clearly it is neither good nor evil but falls easily into the service of either.
>
> Refusal to make such distinctions and to hold to them is why . . . terrorists are given the Nobel Peace Prize, and why the press refers to their retainers who attack kindergartens as "freedom fighters." . . . It is why terrorists know that the world is safe for them, that they have a good chance of success and even honor. (Helprin 1995, A14)

Terrorists appear destined to be regarded as either hated villains or as honored heroes, depending on the view of the observer. This ensures that terrorism is likely to remain a fixture of twenty-first-century international politics, and that violence will continue to cast its shadow over international relations.

THE HUMAN TRAGEDY OF VIOLENT CONFLICT

War exacts a terrible toll on human life. At the beginning of this century approximately 90 percent of war casualties were military; according to the UN, today about 90 percent of the world's war victims are innocent civilians. UNICEF reported, in *The State of the World's Children 1992,* that more than 1.5 million children were killed in wars during the 1980s, and more than 4 million were "physically disabled—limbs amputated, brains damaged, eyesight and hearing lost—through bombing, land-mines, firearms, and torture. Five million children are in refugee camps because of war: A further 12 million have lost their homes."

The tragic human consequences of violence are also revealed daily by the efforts of individuals and families seeking to escape its scourge. These are the victims of armed conflict who can be observed fleeing from one country in hopes of finding refuge, and perhaps a better life, in another country. The refugee asylum problem has now assumed global dimensions, as noted in Chapter 10. Of the twenty largest source countries of refugees in 1999, nineteen were embroiled in internal armed conflict. Religious preference, ethnic origin, and the expression of political dissent are some of the factors that motivate refugees, but armed conflict—along with poverty, persecution, and the pain of hunger and starvation—remains a paramount cause.

The ravages of war are not confined to its human victims, however. Some of its costs are economic, leaving the survivors to pay for the debts and damages. Other costs are ecological, as illustrated by the 1991 Persian Gulf War; although blackened skies have now cleared, the environmental damage may take decades to undo.

Could it be that a world so ingenious in perpetrating violence also will learn that war and violence are too costly, too destructive to continue? If so, can it discover viable paths to peace? The chapters that follow examine some of the solutions that policymakers and concerned citizens have proposed.

KEY TERMS

war
conflict
politics
armed conflict
behavioralism
deterrence
rational choice
groupthink
pax atomica
levels of analysis
intraspecific aggression
interspecific aggression
realism
pacifism
survival of the fittest
nature versus nurture
socialization
territorial imperative
national character
state level of analysis
neorealism
feminist theory
cultural conditioning
communist theory of imperialism
laissez-faire economics
relative gains
neoliberal theories
democratic peace
nationalism
global level of analysis
self-help
security dilemma
anarchy
power transition theory
structural realism
long-cycle theory
hegemon
war weariness hypothesis
civil war
relative deprivation
neonationalism
ethnic warfare
displaced people
failing states
human development index (HDI)
diversionary theory of war
terrorism
state-sponsored terrorism
postmodern terrorism

SUGGESTED READING

Art, Robert J., and Kenneth N. Waltz, eds. *The Use of Force: Military Power and International Politics*, 5th ed. Lanham, Md.: Rowman & Littlefield, 1999.

Bibble, Stephen. "The Past as Prologue: Assessing Theories of Future Warfare," *Security Studies* 8 (Autumn 1998): 1–74.

Enloe, Cynthia. *Maneuvers: The International Politics of Militarizing Women's Lives*. Berkeley: University of California Press, 2000.

Eller, Jack David. *From Culture to Ethnicity to Conflict: An Anthropological Perspective on International Ethnic Conflict*. Ann Arbor: University of Michigan Press, 1999.

Diehl, Paul F., and George Goertz. *War and Peace in International Rivalry*. Ann Arbor: University of Michigan Press, 2000.

Gilpin, Robert. *War and Change in World Politics*. Cambridge, Eng.: Cambridge University Press, 1981.

Gray, Chris Hables. *The Postmodern War: The New Politics of Conflict*. New York: Guilford, 1999.

Holsti, Kalevi J. *War, the State, and the State of War*. New York: Cambridge University Press, 1996.

Kaldor, Mary. *New and Old Wars: Organized Violence in a Global Era*. Stanford, Calif.: Stanford University Press, 1999.

Kurtz, Lester R., ed. *Encyclopedia of Violence, Peace & Conflict*. San Diego, Calif.: Academic Press, 1999.

Melko, Matthew. "Cycles of General War in World History," *International Interactions* 25 (No. 3, 1999): 287–299.

Regan, Patrick M. *Civil Wars and Foreign Powers: Outside Internvention and Interstate Conflict*. Ann Arbor: University of Michigan Press, 2000.

Van Evera, Stephen. *Causes of War: Power and the Roots of Conflict*. Ithaca, N.Y.: Cornell University Press, 1999.

Vasquez, John A. *The War Puzzle*. Cambridge, England: Cambridge University Press, 1993.

Walter, Barbara, and Jack L. Snyder, eds. *Civil War, Insecurity, and Intervention*. New York: Columbia University Press, 1999.

WHERE ON THE WORLD WIDE WEB?

CAIN Web Service
http://cain.ulst.ac.uk/index.html

The Conflict Archive on the Internet (CAIN) is a joint project of three educational institutions in the United Kingdom (the University of Ulster, the Queen's University of Belfast, and the Linen Hall Library) that seeks to provide information on the ongoing conflict in Northern Ireland, historically known as "the Troubles." There are links to descriptions of the key events and issues of this long-term conflict and background on society in Northern Ireland. The site also includes full-length articles and lectures on the conflict that would be good sources for a research paper.

Dreams of Tibet
http://www.pbs.org/wgbh/pages/frontline/shows/tibet/

PBS Online offers this very educational Web site devoted to issues surrounding Tibet and its quest for independence. View the chronology of Tibet's history starting in the year 600. Then read background about Tibetan Buddhism and find out who the Dalai Lama is. Review over ten interviews, including those with Jamyang Norbu, a Tibetan author in exile; actor Richard Gere, who is a "free Tibet" activist; and Martin Scorsese, who directed the movie *Kundun,* based on the biography of the Dalai Lama. The site includes excerpts from media articles and reports on the tenuous relationship between Tibet and the Chinese government. You can share your own thoughts in a discussion forum.

INCORE
http://www.incore.ulst.ac.uk/cds/countries/index.html

The University of Ulster has developed an Internet Guide for the Initiative on Conflict Resolution and Ethnicity that allows you to examine the most recent international conflicts and nationalist movements in detail. Clearly arranged by geographic location, this site offers information about conflict from Kosovo to Ethiopia and Eritrea. Read about the Kurds' quest for their own state. There are links to research sources, news sources, maps, nongovernmental organizations, and e-mail lists and newsgroups. You can also gather information according to theme. Want to know how war affects children? Visit the Children and Conflict link.

Institute for War and Peace Reporting
http://www.ipr.net/

Students of international relations often have a hard time getting up-to-date information from conflict areas that is not heavily censored by government agencies. The main goal of the Institute for War and Peace Reporting (IWPR) is to bring unbiased information on international conflicts to Internet users. An independent media resource, IWPR informs readers on international conflicts and supports media development in war-torn areas. Special reports provide in-depth analysis of conflict, media, and human rights issues in regions across the globe. Read reports from Central Asia, the Balkans, and the Caucasus as events unfold. There is also an extensive list of Internet links for those who want more information on the conflicts.

International Crisis Group
http://www.intl-crisis-group.org/

The International Crisis Group (ICG) is a private, multinational organization dedicated to understanding and responding to international crises. The organization's analysts conduct field research and prepare reports about ongoing conflicts that are used to make recommendations to states' decisionmakers. Currently, ICG has projects in northern and central Africa, the Balkans, and Southeast Asia. Students who are interested in these regional conflicts will find useful overviews of specific countries, reports on developments, and maps.

War, Peace, Security Guide.
http://www.cfcsc.dnd.ca/links/wars/index.html

The Canadian Forces College has created an information resource center on war and peace at this Web site. Graphical links to armed forces, peace and disarmament sites, and military information are available. Visit the clickable map of world conflicts. Choose two contemporary conflicts to explore. Who are the main combatants? What are the main issues? Can you identify any similarities between the two conflicts? Do you have any suggestions for resolution to the conflict? Are other international actors a help or a hindrance to the conflict?

CHAPTER 13

MILITARY POWER AND NATIONAL SECURITY IN THE AGE OF GLOBALIZATION

TOPICS AND THEMES

- **Power in international politics**
  What is "national security"?
  How states' military capabilities compare
  The changing nature of world power
- **The quest for military capabilities**
  Trends in military spending
  Changes in military capabilities
  Trends in weapons technology
  The proliferation problem
- **The social and economic consequences of military preparations for war**
- **The great powers' national security strategies**
  The United States' new security policies
  Russia's new strategy for a new century
  China's global clout and security posture
  Japan's search for a strategy
  Germany and the European Union search for a strategic vision
- **Can an insecure world escape the security dilemma?**

- **CONTROVERSY** A REVOLUTION IN WARFARE? THE NEXT GENERATION OF LETHAL AND NONLETHAL WEAPONS
- **CONTROVERSY** DOES MILITARY SPENDING REDUCE CITIZENS' LIVING STANDARDS?

Chinese missiles on display in Beijing

It is an unfortunate fact that we can only secure peace by preparing for war.

—John F. Kennedy, U.S. presidential candidate, 1960

I went into the British Army believing that if you want peace you must prepare for war. I now believe that if you prepare thoroughly for war you will get it.

—Sir John Frederick Maurice, British military officer, 1883

Armed conflicts are frequent and destructive. Whenever and wherever they break out, they incite tension and fear. These features explain why states are preoccupied with threats to their security and why preparing for defense is a nearly universal preoccupation. Because the anarchical international system requires that states rely on themselves for protection, **national security**—a country's psychological freedom from fear of foreign aggression—is of paramount priority. As a result, policymakers typically assign national security the most prominent place on their foreign policy agendas.

■ **national security**
a country's capacity to resist external or internal threats to its physical survival or core values.

This chapter examines why states often respond to perceived threats by arming. We begin by considering the place of power in the interdependent age of globalized world politics. We then evaluate states' efforts to reduce threats to their security, exploring in particular the great powers' security strategies in the context of general trends in military spending (and their domestic socioeconomic consequences), the arms trade, and weapons technology. Later chapters will use this discussion as a basis for exploring the dilemmas that armament acquisitions create, how states use weapons for coercive diplomacy, and which paths to peace realists and liberals advocate for escaping the danger of war.

POWER IN INTERNATIONAL POLITICS

What is this abstraction called **power,** the quest for which realists depict as states' primary motivator? Although definitions abound, power remains an ambiguous concept (see Baldwin 1989; Claude 1962; Rothgeb 1993). Nonetheless, because most leaders are schooled in realpolitik, they conventionally operate from the traditional assumption that power gives states the ability to promote and protect national interests, to win in bargaining situations, and to shape the rules governing the global system. Leaders are inclined to view power as a political phenomenon revolving around the capacity of one actor to persuade another to do what it otherwise would not. Thus, we will first evaluate this definition, which sees power as **politics**—the exercise of influence to control and dominate others.

When we view power as the means to control, it is reasonable to ask who is stronger and who is weaker, as well as which party will get its way and who will be forced to make concessions. These considerations invite the more fundamental question: What enables states to achieve their goals?

The Elements of State Power

To determine the comparative power of states, analysts usually rank them according to the capabilities or resources presumed necessary to achieve influence over others. For such purposes, multiple factors (most significantly, military and economic capability) measure countries' relative **power potential.** If we could compare each state's total capabilities, according to this logic, we could then rank them by their ability to draw on these resources to exercise influence. Such a ranking would reveal the global system's hierarchy of power, differentiating the strong from the weak, the great from the marginal.

Of all the components of state power, military capability is usually thought to be the most important. Realists regard it as the central element in states' power potential. "Throughout history, the decisive factor in the fates of nations has usually been the number, efficiency, and dispositions of fighting forces," they argue. "National influence bears a direct relationship to gross national strength; without that, the most exquisite statesmanship is likely to be of limited use" (German 1960). Because **realism** assumes that the ability to coerce is more important than the ability to reward or to purchase, realists believe that military capability is a more important source of power than economic capability. By contrast, other strategic thinkers argue that in the twenty-first century, economic competition will be increasingly more critical to national strength and human security than military competition. Accordingly, they insist the economic foundations of national security should receive primary emphasis under conditions of **globalization.**

Figure 13.1 presents two parallel rankings of the world's twenty most powerful states measured by their military spending and the size of their armed forces. Both rankings indicate what most people would likely regard as the world's most "powerful" states.

Power potential also derives from factors other than military expenditures and the number of soldiers, especially to those who argue that "advances in technology and increases in social and economic transactions will lead to a new world in which states, and their control of force, will no longer be important" (Keohane and Nye 2001). These include the size of a state's economy, its population and territorial size, geographic position, raw materials, degree of dependence on foreign

■ power
the factors that enable one state to coerce another; to realists, arms and military capabilities are the most important factor in determining which state will win a dispute (see p. 32).

■ politics
the process by which important values are upheld or compromised when two or more actors become involved in a conflict in which a gain for one party will create a partial or total loss for the other party.

■ power potential
the relative capabilities or resources held by a state that are considered necessary to its asserting influence over others.

■ realism
a paradigm based on the premise that world politics is essentially and unchangeably a struggle among self-interested states for power and position under anarchy, with each competing state single-mindedly pursuing its own national self-advantage without altruistic concern for others or sentimental attachment to moral values.

■ globalization
the processes by which the countries of the world are becoming linked to one another economically, politically, and militarily in interdependent bonds (see p. 41).

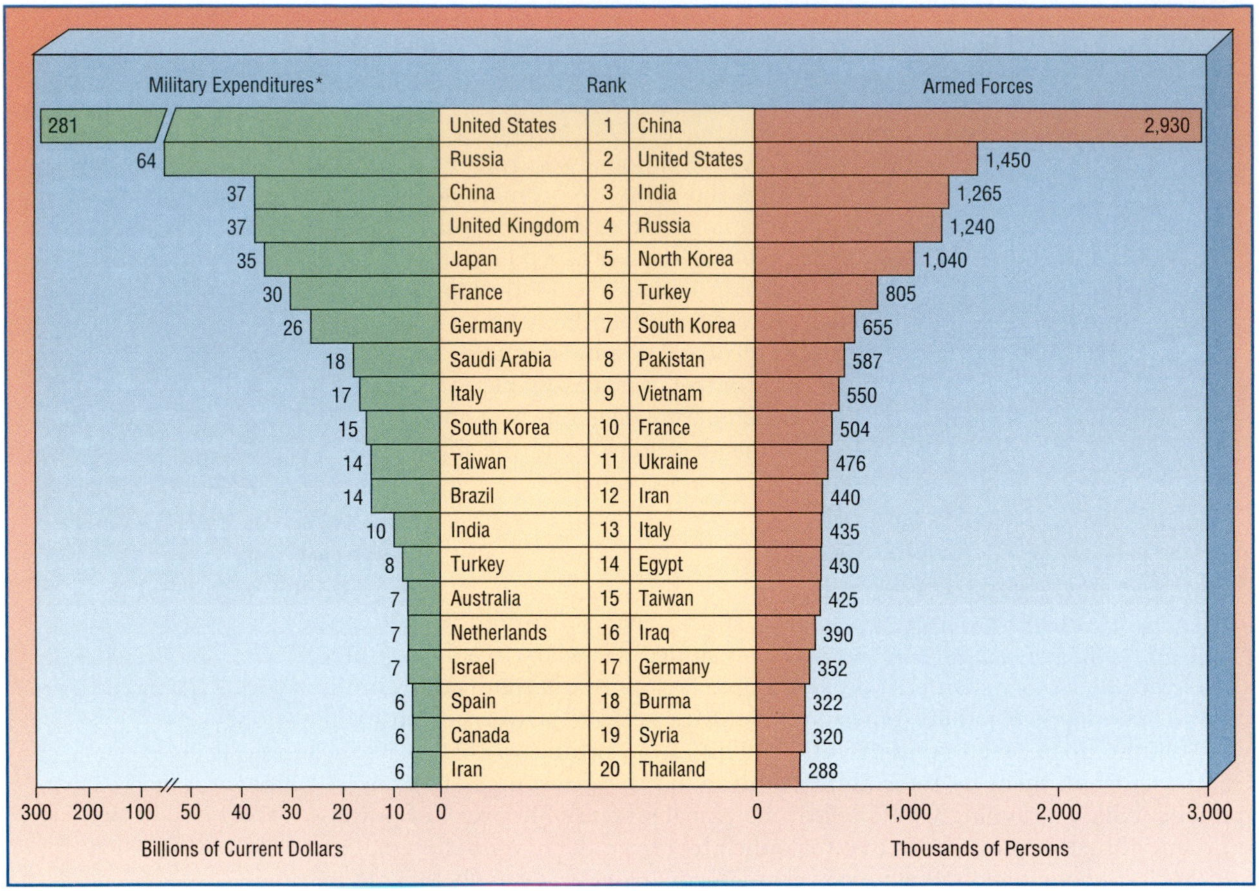

FIGURE 13.1
Arms and Armies: The Twenty States with the Largest Military Budgets and Armed Forces

All states seek a measure of safety from war, and many "purchase" large armament arsenals and armies for this purpose. States vary widely in their ability and desire to build up arms and armies, however, and on the eve of the twenty-first century many countries, fearing excessive costs, cut their military expenditures and the size of their armed forces. In 1998, the United States was the globe's biggest spender, accounting for over one-third of the world's total military expenditures of $745 billion in 1998 (SIPRI 1999, 300–315). At the same time, five countries (China, the United States, Russia, India, and North Korea) were the only states with armies of more than 1 million soldiers; these five together accounted for nearly 30 percent of the world's total of 22.8 million soldiers.

*Note change and break in scale.

SOURCE: Military spending, *Defense Monitor* (No. 1, 1999), 5; armed forces, U.S. ACDA (1997), 5.

sources of materials, technological capacity, national character, ideology, efficiency of governmental decision making, industrial productivity, volume of trade, savings and investment, educational level, and national morale and internal solidarity.

There is, however, no consensus on how best to weigh these factors. There is also no consensus as to what their relative importance should be in making com-

has directed increasing attention to the nonmilitary dimensions of national security.

If we compare military-political and trade strategies as alternative methods for realizing national security in the era of globalization, the latter begins to appear more effective as a strategy for acquiring political power and material advancement. Since 1945 only a handful of states have borne crushing military costs, while the others have gained a relative competitive edge by investing in research on the development of goods to export abroad and conserving resources by relying on allies and global institutions to provide defense against potential threats. While the United States (which in 2000 accounted for one-third of world military expenditures) has spent two-thirds of its research and development budget on military programs since the mid-1980s, European countries spent two-thirds on development of new technologies for consumers and civilians at home and abroad, and Japan's civilian product research exceeded 99 percent of all its research (SIPRI 2000; Sivard 1996, 40–41).

Military expenditures extract other **opportunity costs** as well that retard economic growth and create fiscal deficits. According to the International Monetary Fund (IMF), "military spending crowds out both private and public investment." Had U.S. military outlays remained at the 1990 levels established at the end of the Cold War, the **peace dividend** would have exceeded $400 billion in the next decade and potentially could have been made available for other purposes. The United States failed to do this, however, unlike many other countries. "Countries that made sharp cuts in military spending have also tended to reduce nonmilitary spending and their overall fiscal deficits while boosting social spending," the IMF reports (Koretz 1996). In addition to sacrificing other economic opportunities, this argument continues, military spending has direct costs, because expensive equipment quickly becomes outdated in the face of rapid technological innovations. This creates the need for even more sophisticated new weapons, the costs of which are staggering. The controversial U.S. F–22 Raptor jet, the most expensive plane in history with its $20 billion in research planning costs since 1981 (Brown 1999, 3), can be used only for large conventional battles and costs 1,500 times more to build than would upgrading an F-15 jet to twice the F-22's effectiveness (*Harper's*, October 1999, 13). Yet development of expensive new weapons such as improved stealth aircraft and many others geared to fight the last century's threats continue apace, at the expense of lost revenue for other investments and at a time of uncontested U.S. military superiority. Because "states can afford more 'butter' if they need fewer 'guns,'" Richard Rosecrance (1997) notes, "the two objectives sometimes represent trade-offs: The achievement of one may diminish the realization of the other," and the substantial costs of defense can erode national welfare—what policymakers hope to defend with military might. Conversely, commercial clout and trade competitiveness for national exports may contribute more than military might to national power in a globalized marketplace without barriers to trade; in that setting, trade bloc competition replaces the military and diplomatic struggles of the past. This is a troublesome idea, to which we will return.

In addition to economic capability, other less tangible sources of national power now figure more prominently in calculations regarding national defense, including the media empires' "power over opinion" and control of global communications and information (Bell 1995). "Political leaders and philosophers have long understood that power comes from setting the agenda and determining the

■ **opportunity costs**
the concept in decision-making theories that when the opportunity arises to use resources, what is gained for one purpose is lost for other purposes, so that every choice entails the "cost" of some lost opportunity.

■ **peace dividend**
the global savings from arms expenditures reductions made possible by the end of the Cold War (see p. 158).

■ **soft power**
the capacity for a country to get what it wants through the attraction of its ideals and ideas rather than through the exercise of coercion by means of military force or economic sanctions.

■ **hard power**
the ability to exercise influence in world politics through a state's possession of tangible resources such as military capabilities.

framework of a debate [see Chapter 9]. The ability to establish preferences tends to be associated with intangible power resources such as culture, ideology, and institutions." These intangible resources constitute **soft power,** in contrast with the **hard power** "usually associated with tangible resources like military and economic strength" (Nye 1990). Soft power is "the ability to achieve goals through attraction rather than coercion . . . by convincing others to follow or getting them to agree to norms and institutions that produce the desired behavior" (Keohane and Nye 2001). If soft power grows in relative importance in today's so-called Information Age, military force ratios will no longer translate into power potential in the way they once did.

THE QUEST FOR MILITARY CAPABILITIES

How people spend their money reveals their values. Similarly, how governments allocate their revenues reveals their priorities. Examination of national budgets discloses an unmistakable pattern: Although the sources of world political power may be changing, most states seek security by spending substantial portions of their national treasures on arms.

Trends in Military Spending

The weapons governments believe they require for national security are costly. Their willingness to purchase military protection has kept world military spending high. In 1999, the total stood at $745 billion, an amount exceeding more than $1.2 million each minute. However, world military spending could have been even higher had past levels continued. In fact, it has declined by about a third since the peak-year high of $1.36 trillion in 1987.

Another impression results if the global outlay is measured in constant dollars adjusted for inflation. The 1999 level actually shows an increase over past levels, 2.6 times that spent in 1960, 1.8 times that of the 1970 total, and 1.2 times the 1980 level. These increases appear especially noticeable in the 1980s, but on closer inspection they extend the growth rates of world military expenditures exhibited throughout the entire twentieth century. Military spending has increased fifteenfold since the mid-1930s. The growth rate exceeds that of world population, the rate of expansion of global economic output, expenditures for public health to protect people from disease, and prices (U.S. ACDA 1997; Sivard 1991, 1993, 1996).

These aggregate figures require interpretation, because the global total spent for arms and armies conceals widely varying trends for particular groups of countries. Historically, the rich countries have spent the most money on arms acquisitions, a pattern that has continued. In 1999 the Global North spent $558 billion for defense, in contrast with the developing Global South's $186 billion. Thus the developed countries' share of the world total is 75 percent. However, when measured against other factors, the differences are not so great. Both groups spent exactly 2.6 percent of their GNPs, on average, on weapons, but the Global North's military spending as a portion of government revenues stood at 9 percent and the Global South's at 13 percent. While these two groups' military spending levels are quite different, over time they are converging. The developed countries' expenditures declined 5.6 percent between 1985 and 1995, and the reduction of the developing countries fell only 1.7 percent. As Figure 13.2 reveals, the Global South's military expenditure in 1961 was about 7 percent of the world total, but by 1995 it had climbed threefold to almost 25 percent. This trend indicates that poor states are copying the

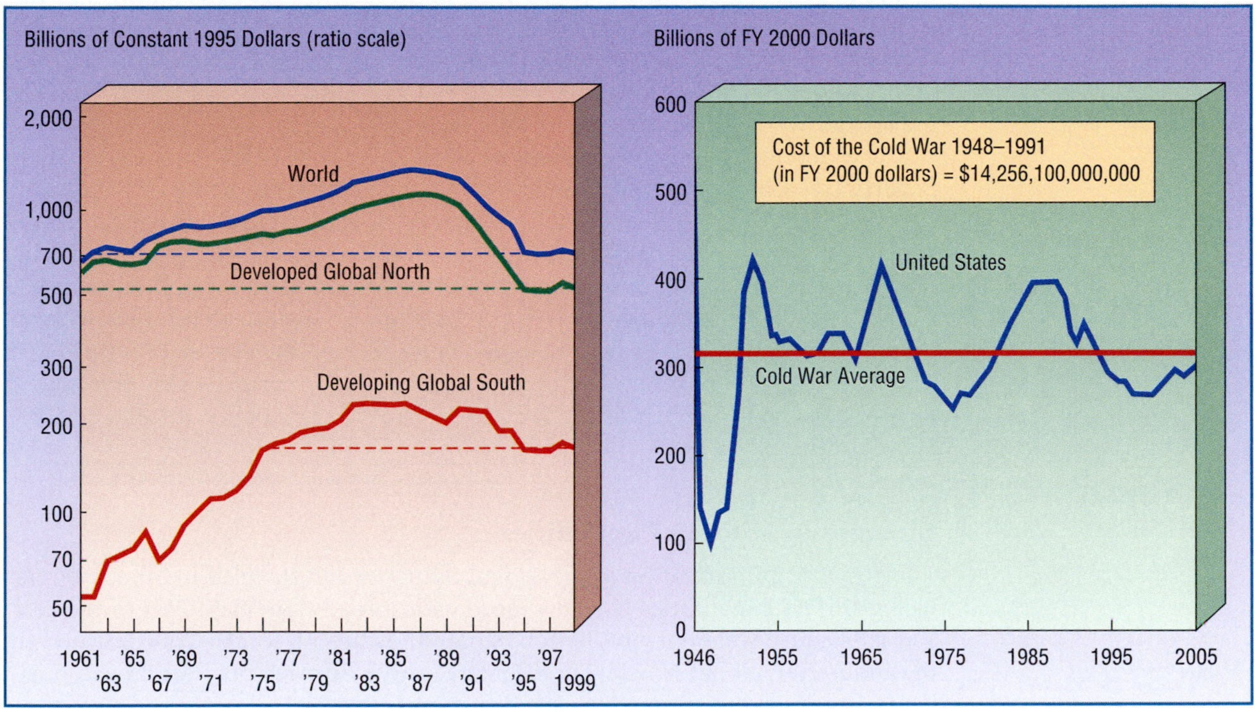

FIGURE 13.2
World and U.S. Military Expenditures

Global military budgets have fluctuated since 1960, with total expenditures worldwide peaking in 1987, after which they have fallen by about a third. Most of the recent reduction has been due to cuts in the Global North's developed economies, where, as the threat of interstate war has receded, states have allocated tax revenues toward nonmilitary threats to human security. As the trend lines on the left show, the military budgets of developing countries of the Global South have also fluctuated over time; they peaked in a 1982–1986 plateau, then declined moderately before rising since 1993 to more than $185 billion by 1999—about one-fourth of the world's total (U.S. ACDA 1997, 1–3; SIPRI 1999, 300–315). The U.S. military budget has also fluctuated as the graph on the right shows, declining rapidly after World War II only to rise again with the start of the Cold War and decline at its end. Based on current projected increases, U.S. military spending will average $300 billion each year between 1946 and 2005. U.S. military expenditures in 1999 were more than the next fifteen biggest spenders combined; Russia and China, second behind the United States in defense spending, together in 1998 allocated $180 billion less than the United States annually for their militaries.

SOURCES: 1961–1995, U.S. ACDA (1997), 1; 1996–1999 SIPRI (1999), 301, and <www.SIPRI.SC> (February 22, 2000); 2000–2005, World Bank (2000), 230–231, 252–253, 262–263; *Defense Monitor* 28 (No. 1, 1999), 4–5.

past costly military budgetary habits of the wealthiest states (U.S. ACDA 1997, 2, 49).

There are equally mixed regional and national variations in these levels and growth rates. The level of perceived threats in each region from potential or actual wars within (and, less frequently, between) states, and the spread of conventional and advanced weapons of mass destruction, exert a great impact on the rise or fall of states' levels of military spending. Similar variations are also exhibited in the rates of military expenditures across different regional organizations and military alliances. For instance, between 1985 and 1995 military expenditures for the Organization for Economic Cooperation and Development (OECD) countries fell 1.7 percent, for the Organization of Petroleum Exporting Countries (OPEC) 6.1 percent, for the North Atlantic Treaty Organization (NATO) 2.2 percent, and for the former Warsaw Pact countries 15.6 percent (U.S. ACDA 1997, 3).

The developing countries' military spending is extremely high given their poverty (see Chapter 5), resulting in large armies in the countries of the Global South that reflect their disproportionately large populations. Between 1960 and 1993, the armed forces of the developed Global North countries remained relatively constant at a little more than 10 million, and fell to 7.7 million in 1995. However, the total number of soldiers in uniform in the developing Global South nearly doubled, growing from 8.4 to 15 million—or to two-thirds of the total 22.8 million people in the armed forces in the entire world. Thirteen of the globe's twenty largest armies were in Global South countries (U.S. ACDA 1997, 7, 49).

Changes in Military Capabilities

The growing militarization of the Global South manifests itself in other ways as well. Military capabilities are now more widespread than ever. Part of the reason is because weapons-production capabilities are no longer concentrated in the industrial Global North. The Global South countries now are in the business of manufacturing modern aircraft, tanks, and missiles. A parallel change in the international arms trade and in the destructiveness of modern weapons has accelerated the spread of military capabilities around the world.

The New Arms Bazaar: The Weapons Trade at the Start of the Twenty-First Century. During the Cold War's forty-two-year period of tension, many states sought to increase their security through the purchase of arms produced by suppliers eagerly seeking allies and profits. In 1961, world arms trade was valued at $4 billion. The traffic in arms imports thereafter climbed rapidly, and peaked in 1987 at $82.4 billion (U.S. ACDA 1997, 10, 100). The end of the Cold War did not end the arms trade, however. Since 1991 the Global South developing countries have been the leading market for the traffic in arms (see Figure 13.3). Erratic jumps exist in yearly distribution over the post–Cold War period, and recent trends have followed this somewhat irregular cyclical pattern, but one pattern is striking: Today, in the face of fierce competition among an expanding number of suppliers, the world's most advanced weapons are being transferred to the Global South. The total value of all international arms deliveries between 1991 and 1998 exceeded $250 billion, of which three-quarters were exported to the developing countries (Grimmett 1999, 3).

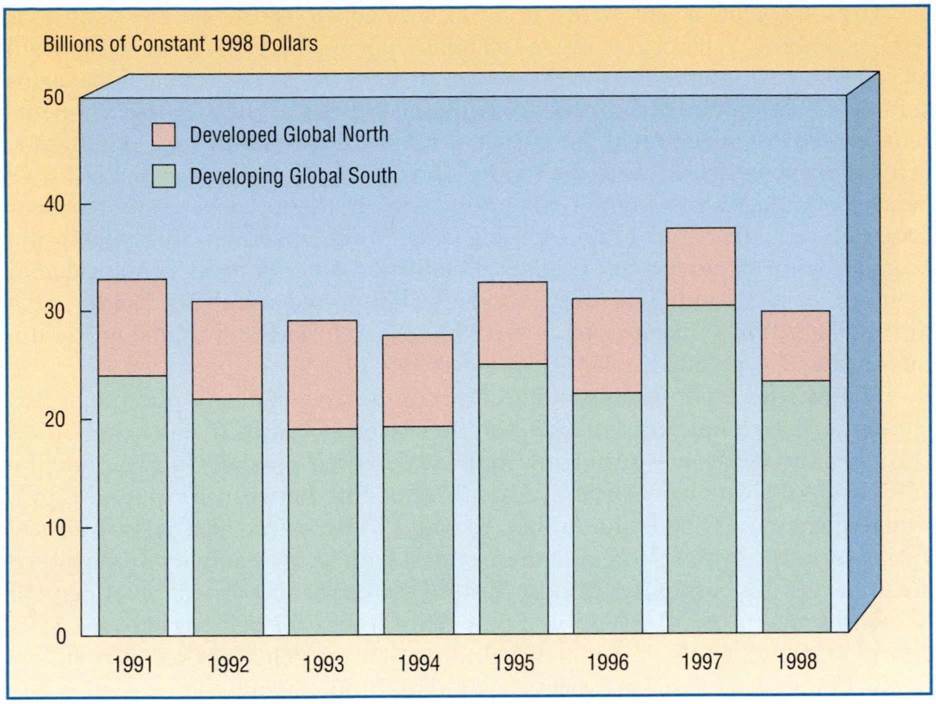

FIGURE 13.3
Arms Sales to the Global North and Global South, 1991–1998

The continuing global arms trade has led to the globalization of military capabilities throughout the Global North and Global South. "Developing world nations from 1995–1998 accounted for 76.7 percent of the value of all international arms deliveries," and in those four years exported arms totaled worldwide $131.2 billion (Grimmett 1999, 3). Many Global South countries face the fear of collapsing in a civil war or from an attack by a neighbor; in 1999, thirty-seven major armed conflicts in which at least one thousand deaths were recorded were underway, and nearly all occurred within the poorer Global South developing countries; only those between Pakistan and India and between Eritrea and Ethiopia were interstate rather than internal wars (SIPRI 1999). The least-stable states in recent years have spent a large percentage of their relatively small economies for the purchase of some of the most technologically and varied weapons of war available in the globalized arms market.

SOURCE: Grimmett (1999), 34.

Spurred by the Global South's developing countries' energetic search for armaments commensurate with those of the industrial countries, and their production of them for use at home and export abroad, the international trade in arms has fueled the dispersion of military capability throughout the globe. Weapons delivered by major suppliers to developing countries between 1991 and 1998 included 6,971 tanks and self-propelled cannon, 11,995 artillery pieces, 1,379 supersonic combat aircraft, 13,352 surface-to-air missiles, and a large number of warships, submarines, antishipping missiles, and other technologically advanced weapons systems (Grimmett 1999, 69).

The total value of arms deliveries by all suppliers to Global South countries is rising, climbing 20 percent to over $100 billion during the 1995–1998 period from $83.6 billion during the 1991–1994 period. In 1998, 78 percent of all global arms shipments were delivered to the developing countries. However, the recipients remain heavily concentrated in a subset of major Global South arms purchasers: in 1998, weapon deliveries to the top ten recipients as a group accounted for 99 percent of all deliveries in the Global South. Six of the top ten were in the Near East region, with Saudi Arabia leading that group, spending $8.7 billion and accounting for 37.5 percent of the total deliveries. In rank order of the value of their purchases, the other leading recipients of imported arms after Saudi Arabia in 1998 were Taiwan, Singapore, South Korea, Israel, Pakistan, United Arab Emirates, Qatar, Egypt, and Kuwait (Grimmett 1999, 11, 65).

The Middle East, with its numerous competitive states, is the main purchaser in the global arms market for an obvious reason: it has experienced chronic national security problems. In the wake of the Persian Gulf War and the 1993 Israeli-Palestine peace accord, rivalries endure between Egypt and Libya, Iran and Iraq, Iran and Saudi Arabia, Iraq and Kuwait, Iraq and Syria, Iraq and Turkey, and Israel and Syria, and these states' high level of activity in the global arms market has continued. Middle Eastern countries accounted for 11 percent of world arms imports in 1967, and that share rose to 77 percent between 1991 and 1994. However, the regional distribution of arms deliveries seems to follow trends in the location of the world's flashpoints, and recently the weapons trade has gravitated toward the turbulent Asian region, which now has joined the feverish rush to purchase arms, spending $33 billion (52 percent) of the global total of imports between 1995 and 1998. In fact, this rise has escalated fears that an **arms race** similar to that of the Middle East will unfold in Asia (Grimmett 1999, 58, 59). Without "clearly defined boundaries between taking prudent defensive steps to prepare for future challengers, and taking action that could be seen as threatening to other countries," the Pacific Rim could explode in a regionwide conflagration (M. Richardson 1995).

■ **arms race**
the buildup of weapons and armed forces by two or more states that threaten each other, with the competition driven by the conviction that gaining a lead is necessary for security.

It is difficult to predict future trends in arms purchases. Regular shifts in procurement have occurred rapidly in response to war and perceived threats. States' proportionate share of total weapons purchases is likely to change, depending on the location in the twenty-first century of the globe's hot spots and each state's involvement in them. Aggregate levels of world arms imports are similarly likely to be influenced by the climate of political tension and the performance of the global economy, with activity fluctuating sharply from year to year, and with weapons imported at high levels in instable regions, in countries where the risk of civil war is high, and in situations where pairs of enemy states are engaged in arms races.

Alongside changing demands of arms importers, it is also important to observe changes in the activities of arms suppliers. During the Cold War the superpowers dominated the arms export market. Between 1975 and 1989 the U.S.-Soviet share of global arms exports varied between one-half and three-fourths, and the United States alone had cornered 40 percent of the world arms export market when the Cold War ended (U.S. ACDA 1997, 19). In that period the two superpowers together "supplied an estimated $325 billion worth of arms and ammunition to the Third World" (Klare 1994, 139). But with the demise of the Soviet Union, the United States reemerged as the unrivaled "arms merchant of the world" (a phrase used by U.S. President Jimmy Carter to deplore what he

Weapons for Sale The global arms trade is big business, and it remains brisk in many regions where perceptions of threats are intense. The Middle East, which accounts for more than two-thirds of global arms sales, is a prime example. Shown here are buyers examining a model of a warship at a defense exposition in Saudi Arabia in 1997. These "arms bazaars" are a regular feature of the global weapons market.

sometimes regarded as an unsavory business). Between 1991 and 1994 the United States accounted for a higher proportion of worldwide contracts to sell arms than any other supplier, agreeing to weapons-export contracts exceeding $55 billion, or 56 percent, of the $130 billion total worldwide. However, in the twilight of the twentieth century, competition for arms sales intensified among the major weapons producers, and other major exporters began to narrow the gap with the United States. Figure 13.4 shows the magnitude of the changes in the major suppliers' share of the arms transfer agreements between the 1991–1994 and the 1995–1998 periods, in which the U.S. monopoly on agreements has apparently declined. Still, the United States continues to lead:

> In 1998, the United States led in arms transfer *agreements worldwide*, making agreements valued at $7.1 billion (30.8 percent of all such agreements), up from $5.7 billion in 1997. Germany ranked second with $5.5 billion in agreements (23.9 percent of these agreements globally), up significantly from about $600 million in 1997. France ranked third, as its arms transfer agreements worldwide dropped notably from $5 billion in 1997 to $3 billion in 1998. The United States, Germany, and France, collectively, made agreements in 1998 valued at $15.6 billion, 67.8 percent of all international arms transfer agreements made by all suppliers. (Grimmett 1999, 3)

The arms sale agreements already under contract assure that the arms trade will remain vigorous in the future, and that the United States will

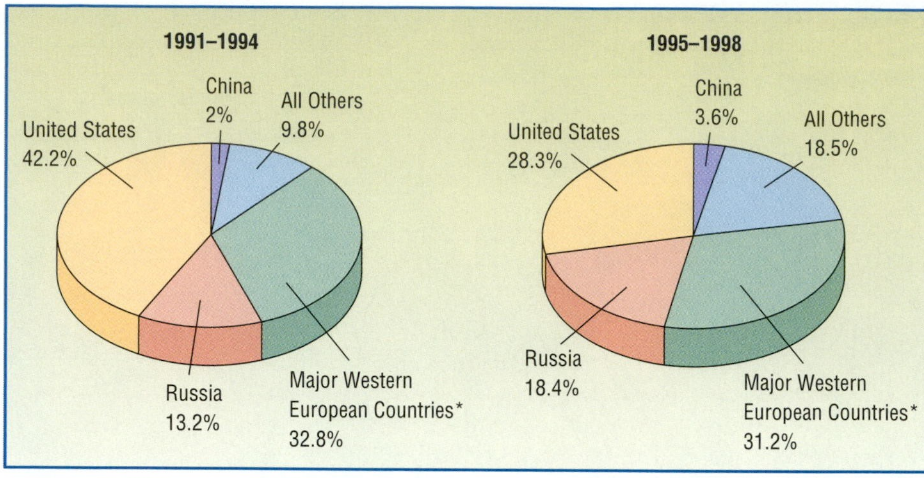

FIGURE 13.4
The Shifting Competition among Arms Suppliers: The Exporters' Percentage of Arms Transfer Agreements, 1991–1994 and 1995–1998

Weapons are moved across borders when exporters sign agreements to sell them to other countries. In the period between 1995 and 1998, the total value of all such arms transfer agreements ($100.3 billion) declined 23 percent from the preceding 1991–1994 period, when they had reached $130.6 billion. In both periods, the United States dominated the international arms trade, ranking first as the globe's leading exporter in the deliveries of weapons for the eighth year in a row.

*France, United Kingdom, Germany, and Italy.

SOURCE: Grimmett (1999), 17.

continue to be the largest exporter, followed by the other great powers. In 1998, 84 percent of the globe's annual weapons exports were sold by the big five permanent members of the United Nations (UN) Security Council.

Although the top ten major suppliers dominate the global arms market, the number of new suppliers has grown steadily, as many developing countries also now produce arms for export. By 1990 more than sixty states had entered the business of "peddling arms" (Sivard 1991, 11). Still, most of these were small producers struggling for a share of the lucrative conventional armaments trade. In fact, for the countries in the Global South, the struggle has not been very successful, considering their huge populations and combined economic clout, as in 1995 they accounted for less than 7 percent of world arms exports (Grimmett 1999, 3).

A consequence of the increased competition for arms markets is the relaxation of export controls. The UN Register of Conventional Arms, begun in 1991 to monitor the weapons exports and imports of countries, has not curbed their sale. Moreover, the illegal export of nuclear, ballistic missile, and chemical weapons technology has not abated. Diversification of suppliers, as well as the coproduction and codevelopment of weaponry through joint ventures among arms manufacturers in different countries, has ended many supplier-consumer ties that earlier had cemented patron-client diplomatic relationships. Suppliers, it seems, are now eager to sell to any purchaser.

Motives for the Arms Trade. Economic gain is an important rationale for foreign military sales, because producers sell arms abroad to subsidize their arms production at home. For example, the United States uses arms exports to offset its chronic balance-of-trade deficits, and to ensure its lead in the lucrative arms business. In 1998, it assigned 6,493 full-time federal employees to handle U.S. arms deals and spent $477,300,000 on promotional activities for U.S. arms dealers (*Harper's*, February 1998, 13). Following the disintegration of the Soviet Union, Russia sought to raise desperately needed hard currency by selling at bargain-basement prices its one product mix still in demand—weapons, weapons technology, and weapons expertise. And this aggressive sales campaign continues as "a cash-starved defense industry is selling Russian weapons to the world—latest models included" (Khripunov 1997). In February 2000, for example, Russia sold its most advanced destroyer armed with nuclear-capable missiles to China. Cash is also the primary motive among other arms suppliers, for whom ideological considerations are virtually nonexistent.

Because the sale of weapons is big business, arms manufacturers constitute a powerful domestic lobby for the continuation of arms sales. In the United States a "gunbelt" **military-industrial complex** profits at home and abroad from continued arms sales (Markusen, Hall, Campbell, and Deitrick 1991). At the same time, efforts to dismantle "the Cold War military economy" by ending "welfare" for the defense industry have encountered broad-based, coordinated resistance (Cahn 1995). As Lawrence J. Korb (1995a), who served as U.S. assistant secretary of defense for five years in the Reagan administration, explained, "The military has succeeded in inflating the threat of our foes and downplaying the contribution of our allies." Andrew Cockburn (1995) described what he saw as the unjustifiably high U.S. military budget by noting, "The problem is that the apparent goal of military spending is to direct as much money as possible into corporate coffers." In fact, many countries' civilian sectors are organized around preparations for militarization and arms manufacture and sales for the same reasons (Regan 1994).

■ **military-industrial complex**
the term coined by U.S. President Eisenhower to describe the coalition among arms manufacturers, military bureaucracies, and top government officials that promotes unnecessary defense expenditures for their own profit and power.

The end of the Cold War ironically increased states' incentives to sell arms merely for profit. Nonetheless, many states continue to sell arms (or make outright grants) for time-honored purposes: to support friendly governments, to honor allies' requests, and to cultivate cooperation. This was illustrated by U.S. arms-export policy prior to and in the aftermath of the 1990 Persian Gulf War. The United States delivered 76 percent of the $43 billion in arms sold to the Middle East between 1991 and 1994 and 62 percent of the $39 billion between 1995–1998, allegedly for the purpose of anchoring allies and preserving the military balance of power in the explosive region (Grimmett 1999, 37). However, the profit motive, fueled in part by the desire of defense contractors to maintain income in an era in which many states are reducing their defense budgets, also continues to drive the for-profit sale of weapons across borders. An underground "black market" in weapons is flourishing, and suggests the greed for money behind many defense contractors' illegal participation in the global arms trade.

The Strategic Consequences of Arms Sales. Whether the arming of other countries has accomplished all of its intended goals is open to dispute. During the Cold War, for example, the United States and the Soviet Union thought they

Runaway Costs Out of Step with Today's Military Threats? Development and deployment of many modern weapons are extremely expensive—and the profits for defense contractors can be huge. Shown here is one example: the F-22 Raptor jet fighter designed by Lockheed Martin Corporation. Critics in the U.S. Congress complain that building and buying the plane, at $85 million a copy, not counting development costs, is a waste because it is no longer needed to deal with the real threats facing the United States, such as biological terrorism. Other defense experts questioning the military-industrial complex argue that the Raptor—like the two other "gold plate" planes to be constructed during the next two decades at a cost of $340 billion (J. Brown 1999b)—are unnecessary and reckless, because rogue states can easily destroy their own "soft target" air bases, leaving no enemy targets for such jets to attack. Other skeptics about the defense industry's motives point out that to push Congress to approve sales, the Raptor's manufacturer published a flashy brochure identifying on a map all the "potential threat" states that possess the most advanced attack aircraft, but failed to acknowledge that these so-called dangerous enemies were a threat because their air forces had available U.S. fighter jets such as the F-15 and F-16, produced by the same defense contractor. For example, in December 1999 the United Arab Emirates spent $8 billion to purchase eighty F-16 fighter jets with more advanced technology than those flown by American pilots (J. Brown 1999b). The United States either sold or gave away these planes, thereby generating an arms trade boomerang that reduced U.S. security. In 1997, Lockheed Martin requested Congress to approve a license to export the F-22 Raptor stealth jet overseas; in July 1999, the House Defense Subcommittee surprised nearly everyone by voting to eliminate the $1.8 billion to build the first six of the F-22 Raptors, and the House of Representatives endorsed the decision by a vote of 379 to 45. In reaction, alarmed critics argued that U.S. military superiority remains vulnerable, and as evidence pointed to Russia's new SU-27 Flanker fighter jet—a state-of-the-art plane armed with infrared-guided missiles.

could maintain peace by spreading arms to politically pivotal recipients. Between 1983 and 1987 the United States provided arms to fifty-nine less developed countries while the Soviet Union supplied forty-two (Klare 1990, 12). Yet many of the recipients engaged in war with their neighbors or experienced internal rebellion. Of the top twenty arms importers in 1988, more than half "had governments noted for the frequent use of violence" (Sivard 1991, 17). The toll in lives from the wars in the Global South since 1945 exceeds tens of millions of people. Undoubtedly, the import of such huge arsenals of weapons from abroad aided this level of destruction. As the arms exporters "peddle death to the poor," they seldom acknowledge how this scouting for customers contradicts other proclaimed foreign policy goals. The U.S. arms export program, for example, undermines the current U.S. policy priority of promoting democracy because no less than one-third (eighteen) of the recipients of U.S. arms exports were nondemocratic governments, which purchased $13.25 billion (41 percent) of the total U.S. arms sold ($32.43 billion) in 1993 (Blanton and Kegley 1997, 94–95). Another report illustrates the contradiction between principles in the arms trade by observing that

> No sooner had the United Nations lifted its arms embargo against South Africa than Armscor, South Africa's state arms manufacturer, boasted that its weapons exports could double in a year. There was "nothing wrong," explained President Nelson Mandela, in selling arms abroad so that countries could "defend their sovereignty." And South Africa would make sure they did not get into the "wrong hands." Yet Mr. Mandela also wants to promote peace on a continent that his predecessors did so much to tear apart. As [the 1994] *Human Development Report* . . . points out, the two aims seldom make comfortable bed-mates.
>
> Too often, says the UNDP [UN Development Program] report, the rich countries—and, by African standards, South Africa is one—offer aid and promote peace in poor countries with one hand while shoveling in death with the other. The United States, France, and Britain between them sent $22 billion of aid to the poor world in 1992. The same three, plus China and Russia, the two other permanent members of the UN Security Council, also supplied 86 percent of all weaponry sold to poor countries in 1988–92. Rich-country governments often subsidize the exports of private arms makers; Mahbub ul Haq, the principal author of the report and a former finance minister of Pakistan, says the rich countries bluntly refused to tell him by how much. And many count the official "military assistance" they do admit to—meaning things like the sale of second-hand equipment or military training—as part of their "aid" for development.
>
> Nor—however scrupulous arms salesmen may be, and that is not their most famous quality—is it easy to tell who "the wrong hands" are. America spent the 1980s pouring guns into Somalia; it was by far the biggest supplier, followed by Italy. It then spent the 1990s trying to clear them out. In contravention of the UN arms embargo against it, South Africa happily sold guns, mortars and hand grenades to Rwanda for five years; France too sold the Rwandan government—whose militiamen have carried out the worst killings—mortars and light artillery, and gave technical help and French soldiers. (*Economist*, June 4, 1994, 43)

The inability of arms suppliers to control the uses to which their military hardware will be put is thus troubling. "The concern is that friends can become foes, and secrets can be stolen" (J. Brown 1999a). The United States armed both sides in several conflicts in the Global South since World War II, as did the Soviets. Moreover, loyalty is often a fragile commodity, and supplying weapons can

Deadly Conventional Arms Sales The exact extent of global trade in so-called light conventional weapons is unknown, but growing. Of the armed conflicts fought worldwide since 1990, 90 percent were fought exclusively with small arms (*Harper's*, January 2000, 11). In reaction, the UN Register of Conventional Arms in 1998 required for the first time that states' inventories and procurement of such weapons be reported. "Millions of the rifles now in the hands of the world's killers started out as legal weapons," Michael Renner (1999a) of the Worldwatch Institute warns. Shown here are M-16s from the El Salvadoran Atlacati Battalion. This U.S.-trained unit massacred eight hundred civilians at El Mozote and murdered six Jesuit priests in San Salvador in 1989. During the Reagan-Bush years, the United States supplied El Salvador with 33,000 M-16s (Lumpe 1999).

backfire, as the United States discovered when the weapons it sold to Iraq were used against U.S. forces by Saddam Hussein in the Persian Gulf War (Timmerman 1991). Likewise, in 1982 Great Britain found itself shipping military equipment to Argentina just eight days before Argentina's attack on the British-controlled Falkland Islands (Sivard 1982), and in 1998 U.S. military technology sold to China was exported to Pakistan, making possible its nuclear weapons test.

Trends in Weapons Technology

The widespread quest for armaments has created a potentially explosive global environment. The description is especially apt when we consider not only trends in defense expenditures and the arms trade but also in the destructiveness of modern weapons.

Nuclear Weapons. Technological research and development has radically expanded the destructiveness of national arsenals. The largest "blockbuster" bombs of World War II delivered a power of ten tons of TNT. The atomic bomb that leveled Hiroshima had the power of over fifteen thousand tons of TNT. Less than twenty years later, the former Soviet Union built a nuclear bomb with the explosive force of fifty-seven megatons (million tons) of TNT. As the twentieth century ended, the number of nuclear warheads worldwide had decreased to 31,535. Of these, about 14,000 were actively deployed, another 14,000 awaited eventual dismantlement, and the remainder were held in reserve. Since its 1986 peak, the size of the global nuclear arsenal (strategic and tactical warheads) has declined by 45 percent (*Bulletin of the Atomic Scientists,* March/April 2000, 79). Together, even after these cuts, those nuclear warheads available for a strike still collectively had the extraordinary explosive force of over 1.3 million Hiroshima bombs.

The use of such weapons could destroy not only entire cities and countries but, conceivably, the world's entire population. Albert Einstein, the Nobel Prize–winning physicist whose ideas were the basis for the development of nuclear weapons, was well aware of the threat they posed. He professed uncertainty about the weapons that would be used in a third world war, but was confident that in a fourth they would be "sticks and stones." He warned that inasmuch as "the unleashed power of the atom has changed everything save our modes of thinking . . . we thus drift toward unparalleled catastrophe."

The nuclear arsenals of the United States and the former Soviet Union are particularly extensive and sophisticated. When World War II ended, the United States possessed the one atomic bomb still in existence. In 1967, at the height of the U.S. **strategic stockpile,** the United States had 32,500 warheads in its arsenal. In 1986, when the Soviet Union was at its peak, it had 45,000. In addition, during the Cold War the United States and the Soviet Union each deployed thousands of tactical nuclear weapons designed for the direct support of combat operations. Their combined arsenals ranged from 25,000 in 1961 to 68,000 in 1986 (*Bulletin of the Atomic Scientists,* March/April 2000, 79).

■ **strategic stockpile** the inventory of nuclear warheads deployed for waging wars of mass destruction.

The 1987 Intermediate-range Nuclear Forces (INF) treaty began the elimination of short- and medium-range delivery vehicles from Europe. At the start of 2000, the number of operational nuclear stockpiles of the five major powers were estimated to total 31,535 strategic warheads. The U.S. arsenal had 10,500 nuclear warheads, and Russia had 20,000. In addition, France stockpiled an estimated 450 warheads; China had 400; and Britain retained 185. To this should be added the low number of nuclear warheads held by India and Pakistan as well as Israel, an "undeclared" nuclear weapons country.

The seven principal declared nuclear weapons states (the United States, the Soviet Union/Russia, Britain, France, China, India, and Pakistan) have continuously refined the deadliness of their weapons through testing. Between 1945 and 1999 they detonated a combined total of more than 2,055 nuclear explosions around the world, poisoning the planet with high levels of deadly radiation that will shorten the life spans of billions of people. The United States, which alone had conducted 1,032 nuclear tests (50 percent) in that period, suspended its testing program in August 1995, and France announced an end of its nuclear tests in January 1996. However, after the UN approved the Comprehensive Test Ban Treaty in September 1996, the United States began a round of controversial underground tests in July 1997. In October 1999, it rejected signing that nuclear arms control convention and in so doing ignited widespread fears that if the globe's previously uncontested leading nuclear superpower was preparing to resume nuclear testing, a new era of nuclear proliferation would begin, as many of the forty-three other nuclear-capable states followed the U.S. lead and resumed their suspended plans to test and build nuclear weapons.

A New Round of Nuclear Proliferation? Despite a worldwide surge in disarmament proposals since the end of the Cold War, states' quests to continue to develop and refine their nuclear arsenal have continued. On January 27, 1996, France tested its nuclear weapons in the Murura atoll of its South Pacific protectorate, Tahiti (an aerial photo of the shock waves during the test is shown here). Its decision to resume testing, justified by the proclaimed right to protect itself with weapons of mass destruction, provoked protests throughout the world. On January 29, 1996, France called a halt to its nuclear testing program and in April 1998 ratified the Comprehensive Test Ban Treaty (CTBT). But India and Pakistan rejected this treaty, and in May 1998 began testing their nuclear weapons in a surprise move that threatened to encourage Israel, Iran, Iraq, and others to acquire nuclear weapons in a new chain-reaction nuclear arms race. Then, in October 1999, the United States alarmed the world when, in a startling setback to the arms control process as arguably monumental as the 1919 Congress's rejection of U.S. membership in the League of Nations, the Senate rejected the test ban treaty, thereby opening the door to the resumption of nuclear weapons testing, production, and proliferation. In February 2000, former U.S. President Jimmy Carter warned, "It is imperative that the Nuclear Nonproliferation Treaty be reconfirmed in April. . . . This [treaty's] unraveling would exert powerful pressures even on peace-loving nations to develop a nuclear capacity."

Technological Improvements and Weapons Delivery Capabilities. Advances in weapons technology have been rapid and extraordinary. Since the advent of the atomic age, with the "gravity bombs of 1945 . . . a whole warehouse of varied weapons, each with its own special purpose" has been created. These include:

> clean bombs; dirty bombs; bombs that burrowed into the earth, seeking underground command posts; bombs that went off undersea, seeking submarines; bombs that went off high over earth, to fry the brains of electrical devices with a huge shower of electromagnetic pulses; bombs that killed tank crews with radiation but didn't flatten towns or cities; bombs delivered by guidance so precise that they could destroy anything with a known location on or near the surface of the earth. . . . The results of this tireless inven-

> tion were weapons powerful enough to threaten human life on the planet. (Powers 1994, 123)

Particularly deadly have been the technological refinements that enable states to deliver weapons as far away as nine thousand miles within one hundred feet of their targets in less than thirty minutes. In 1987, seven Western countries (Britain, Canada, France, Germany, Italy, Japan, and the United States) established the Missile Technology Control Regime (MTCR) to curtail the spread of missile technologies, especially those for the delivery of weapons of mass destruction. In 1993, the MTCR expanded its coverage to delivery systems for chemical and biological weapons. By December 1999 its formal membership included thirty-two states.

However, the MTCR is not a legally binding treaty, includes only a fraction of the missile-technology suppliers, and lacks an institution to monitor and enforce compliance with the voluntary agreement. Symptomatic of its weakness was the possession in 1993 of short- or medium-range surface-to-air missiles by twenty countries in the Global South, and the fact that more than seven of them have used missiles in warfare (Zimmerman 1994). Thus the highly threatening ballistic missile continues to be used outside meaningful international restraints.

Other technological improvements have broadened the spectrum of available weapons. The United States and Russia, for example, equipped their ballistic missiles with **multiple independently targetable reentry vehicles (MIRVs),** which enable a single missile to launch multiple warheads toward different targets simultaneously and accurately. One MIRV U.S. MX (Peacekeeper) missile could carry ten nuclear warheads—enough to wipe out a city and everything else within a fifty-mile radius. The Minuteman III missile could carry three warheads with the equivalent of three hundred kilotons explosive force; the twenty-four missiles on each Trident submarine could carry eight warheads with an explosive force of one hundred kilotons. As a result of MIRVing, the number of deliverable nuclear warheads in the nuclear powers' arsenals increased far more rapidly than the number of delivery vehicles. Taking this capacity into account, before the superpowers agreed to the START II treaty to ban MIRVed intercontinental ballistic missiles, the world's combined nuclear inventory was nearly three times larger than the number of nuclear warheads in existence. At the start of 2000, thousands of nuclear warheads were still deployed for delivery at a moment's notice, with 2,380 U.S. nuclear bombs on "high alert, including up to 200 nuclear weapons in Western Europe" (*Harper's*, January 2000, 11).

■ **multiple independently targetable reentry vehicles (MIRVs)** a technological innovation permitting many weapons to be delivered from a single missile (see p. 583).

Despite this effort to control missile capabilities, other kinds of technological improvements have led to steady increases in the speed, accuracy, range, and effectiveness of weapons. As Ruth Leger Sivard predicted,

> Now, with the improved yield-to-weight ratio, nuclear warheads can be incorporated in artillery shells with a weight of 95 pounds and a range of 18 miles. These have a yield of 2,000 tons of TNT equivalent. More powerful is the nuclear-headed cruise missile which weighs 2,650 pounds. Launched from a submarine at sea, it can travel 1,500 miles under its own power, and release up to 200,000 tons of explosives on the target. (Sivard 1991, 13)

New technologies also alter the character of weapons. Laser weapons, nuclear-armed tactical air-to-surface missiles (TASMs), Stealth air-launched cruise missiles (ACMs), and antisatellite (ASAT) weapons that can project force in and wage war from outer space, have become a part of the military landscape. In addition, a large number of innovative new weapons technologies are in use and under development—"wonder weapons" such as the so-called **nonlethal weapons** made possible by the **revolution in military technology (RMT)** and so novel that they look like they belong in science fiction (see Controversy: A Revolution in Warfare?). They include an ever-expanding inventory of "new frontier" weapons designed to fight the likely wars of the twenty-first century. They include plans to develop information-warfare squadrons to protect military computer networks from electronic sneak attacks, energy pulses to knock out or take down enemies without necessarily killing them, biofeedback beamed electromagnetic and sonic wavelengths that can modify the human behavior of targets (for example, putting people to sleep through electromagnetic heat and magnetic radiation), and underground **smart bombs** that at a speed of one thousand feet per second can penetrate a buried bunker and, at the proper millisecond after calculating the levels through which it crashes like a needle through flesh, detonate five hundred pounds of explosive to destroy an adversary's inventory of buried chemical and biological weapons. Many of these advances in the technology of warfare are already highly developed.

nonlethal weapons the wide array of "soft-kill," low-intensity methods of incapacitating an enemy's people, vehicles, communications systems, or entire cities without killing either combatants or noncombatants.

revolution in military technology (RMT) the sophisticated new weapons technologies that make fighting war without mass armies possible.

smart bombs precision-guided military technology that enables a bomb to search for its target and detonate at the precise time it can do the most damage.

Technological advances are likely to make orthodox ways of classifying weapons systems as well as prior equations for measuring power ratios obsolete. As an influential U.S. strategic report correctly predicted in 1988:

> Dramatic developments in military technology appear feasible over the next twenty years. They will be driven primarily by the further exploitation of microelectronics, in particular for sensors and information processing, and the development of directed energy. The much greater precision, range, and destructiveness of weapons could extend war across a much wider geographic area, make war much more rapid and intense, and require entirely new modes of operation. Application of new technologies to both offensive and defensive systems will pose complicated problems for designing forces and assessing enemy capabilities. (U.S. Commission on Integrated Long-Term Strategy 1988, 8)

For decades, a **firebreak** has separated conventional from nuclear wars. The term comes from the barriers of cleared land with which firefighters keep forest fires from racing out of control. In the context of modern weaponry, it is a psychological barrier whose purpose is to "prevent even the most intensive forms of conventional combat from escalating into nuclear war." As both nuclear and conventional weapons technologies advance, there is danger that the firebreak is being crossed from both directions—by a new generation of "near-nuclear" conventional weapons capable of "levels of violence approximating those of a limited nuclear conflict" and by a new generation of "near-conventional" **strategic weapons** able "to inflict damage not much greater than that of the most powerful conventional weapons" (Klare 1985).

firebreak the psychological barrier between conventional and nuclear war.

strategic weapons weapons of mass destruction that are carried on intercontinental ballistic missiles (ICBMs), submarine-launched ballistic missiles (SLBM)s, or long-range bombers and are capable of annihilating an enemy state.

The precision and power of today's conventional weapons have expanded exponentially, at precisely the moment when the revolution in military technology is leading to "the end of infantry" because, in the computer age "the sky has eyes, bullets have brains, and victory will belong to the country whose military has the better data network" (Ross 1997) (see Controversy: A Revolution in Warfare?). Note also that even as the nuclear powers retain the capacity to turn cities into glass, they increasingly rely on a variety of new cyberstrategies to deter and demobilize enemies, and are turning to **virtual nuclear arsenals** for **deterrence** of an adversary's attack. Examples include such futuristic weapons as the electromagnetic-pulse (EMP) bomb, which can be hand-delivered in a suitcase and can immobilize an entire city's computer and communications systems; computer viruses of electronics-eating microbates that can eliminate a country's telephone system; and logic bombs that can confuse and redirect traffic on the target country's air and rail system. Also planned are **information warfare (IW)** or **infowar tactics** that deploy information-age techniques "to disrupt the enemy's economy and military preparedness, perhaps without firing a shot." One example of these is the U.S. Air Force's Commando Solo psychological operations plane, which can "jam signals from the government television station and insert in its place a 'morphed' TV program, in which the enemy leader appears on the screen and makes unpopular announcements, alienating him from his people" (Waller 1995). In addition, the production, trade, and use of so-called light weapons or small conventional arms is escalating. "Because of the global upsurge in ethnic and sectarian conflict, policymakers have become more attuned to the role played by [light] arms in sparking and sustaining low-level warfare and have begun to consider new constraints on trade in these munitions. . . . Although heavy weapons sometimes play a role, most of the day-to-day fighting is performed by irregular forces armed only with rifles, grenades, machine guns, light mortars, and other 'man-portable' munitions" (Klare 1999).

virtual nuclear arsenals
the next generation of "near-nuclear" military capabilities produced by the revolution in military technology that would put strategic nuclear weapons of mass destruction at the margins of national security strategies by removing dependence on them for deterrence).

deterrence
a preventive strategy designed to dissuade an adversary from doing what it would otherwise do (see p. 414).

information warfare (IW) or infowar tactics
attacks on an adversary's telecommunications and computer networks to penetrate and degrade an enemy whose defense capabilities depend heavily on these technological systems.

Unconventional Weapons: Biological and Chemical. Biological and chemical weapons pose a special and growing threat. Each is sometimes regarded as a "poor man's atomic bomb," because they can be built at comparatively small cost and cause widespread injury and death. Despite the 1972 Biological Weapons Convention prohibiting the development, production, and stockpiling of biological weapons, "the United States, the United Kingdom, and Japan are known to have developed several types of biological weapons in the past (such stocks have since been destroyed), and Iraq and Syria are strongly suspected of stockpiling such weapons" (Fetter 1991), as is North Korea (Zimmerman 1994). Similarly, chemical weapons proliferation is a worldwide concern. In addition to Iran, Iraq, Russia, and the United States (the only states confirmed to possess chemical weapons), twenty-one other countries—mostly in the Global South—are suspected to have produced chemical weapons (Stock and De Geer 1995, 340).

International law prohibits the use of chemical weapons: The 1925 Geneva Protocol banned the use of chemical weapons in warfare, and the Chemical Weapons Convention (CWC), signed by 169 countries by January 2000, required the destruction of existing stocks. Nevertheless, legal restraints do not assure that states will forgo them. Iran's and Iraq's use of gas in warfare demonstrated this, as did Egypt's use of chemical gas weapons in Yemen in the mid-1960s. Iraq even used chemical weapons in 1989 against its own Kurdish people. Thus the firebreak against chemical warfare has already been breached.

CONTROVERSY

A Revolution in Warfare?

The Next Generation of Lethal and Nonlethal Weapons

It may seem strange, but the adage that defense planners are prone to prepare to fight and win the last war holds truth. There is a natural temptation to prepare for the "worst case" scenario, defined by the most recent war experience. That vigilant preparation seems reasonable, in principle, because military commanders are assigned the task of preparing their country for any contingency, and what better way than by perfecting the capabilities and strategies that would have ensured a quick victory over the last enemy in war, preferably at minimal loss of life? This accounts for the strong tendency for the weapons on today's drawing boards to often be suitable for waging yesterday's armed conflicts.

More controversial are innovative preparations to wage the wars of the future, when they have not yet been encountered. Yet, this challenge has been taken on boldly by defense planners in the United States who are designing new kinds of weapons to fight the wars they imagine will be fought in the twenty-first century. What makes these preparations so controversial is not the prudent vigilance that justifies developing new weapons; it is that they require costly innovations in fighting technology that have very uncertain consequences for their country's national security and for global security generally. Will the new weapons work? Will they provide for better defense? Or will they backfire, taking warfare to a new level that unintentionally reduces human security? No one can know for sure; we can only ponder these questions with **counterfactual reasoning,** guessing what will happen if radically new weapons technology becomes part of many countries' arsenals. No wonder the issue is a topic for debate.

The revolution in technology may make for a new kind of warfare. Will operations on the new battlefield be more humane? Advocates believe that by reducing the exposure of pilots to enemy antiaircraft devices, precision-guided weapons can contain killing and deter adversaries while minimizing collateral casualties to civilians. To proponents, the revolutionary new weapons technology offers great promise for preventing wars and reducing the number of deaths likely to result in the next generation of warfare. If warfare can be made less destructive, they argue, war can continue to serve as a political instrument for exercising power, in ways that make the use of military force civilized. In contrast to this argument, many critics question the effectiveness and ethics of remote and robotic killing with nonlethal arsenals. To their way of reasoning, many questions remain: Are smart bombs smart enough? Are precision weapons really effective? Or, given the high probability of technological and human error—as shown in the series of misguided NATO bombs in Belgrade that killed thousands of noncombatant civilians and leveled the Chinese Embassy in 1999—is the front edge of high-tech warfare actually rather blunt? Therefore, whether the military-technical revolution is good or bad for the preservation of peace has become a highly debatable issue.

What do you think? In contemplating your position on the promise or peril of the new weapons technology now being developed, take into consideration the kind of weapons now being planned by military engineers seeking to make technological breakthroughs that will transform the character of the battlefield of the twenty-first century. Also factor into your assessment the fact that "miniaturization has made technology more accessible

■ **counterfactual reasoning**
thought experiments to consider the consequences that probably will result if something happens that has not yet occurred such as speculating, "What if the United States once again becomes isolationistic as it did prior to World War II?" (see p. 521).

A number of factors limit the use of chemical weapons, including weather conditions and the ability to defend against them. They are nonetheless capable of causing widespread death and suffering. The use of chemical weapons (gas) during World War I, for example, produced "about one hundred thousand battle fatalities and over one million total casualties" (Fetter 1991, 15). The proliferation of ballistic missiles among regional rivals in the Middle East, Asia, and elsewhere particularly raises the danger of their use because they enable chemical weapons to be readily delivered at great distances. The possibility that these weapons might be acquired and used by terrorists poses still another kind of threat.

[and] globalization has been the engine driving its diffusion. . . . Technology and globalization have changed the instruments of power. . . . Today, almost every element of power can be acquired in the global marketplace" (Libicki 2000). The stakes have been raised by the kinds of new weapons being created. U.S. military planners speak loudly and hopefully of the revolution in military affairs (RMA), the military-technical revolution (MTR), and of Information Age warfare. These concepts refer to the goal of seeking to increase military capabilities and effectiveness by seizing the opportunities created by microprocessors, instantaneous global communications, and precision-guided munitions technologies to confront and contain the armed conflicts of the future without relying on weapons of mass destruction. To advocates who seek a kinder, gentler type of warfare, the RMA promises to transform the ways wars will be fought and the way people think about them.

To alter the nature of warfare and the conduct of military operations, enthusiasts envision RMA and MTR developing in two stages:

> The first is based on stand-off platforms, stealth, precision, information dominance, improved communications, computers, global positioning systems, digitization, "smart" weapons systems, jointness, and use of ad hoc coalitions. The second may be based on robotics, nonlethality, psychotechnology, cyberdefense, nanotechnology, "brilliant" weapons systems, hyperflexible organizations, and "fire ant warfare." If this idea is correct, change that has occurred so far will soon be dwarfed by even more fundamental transformation. (Metz and Kievit 1995, vi)

Behind the technological revolution is the belief that nonlethal weapons are practical because they can obtain intelligence from computers and advanced technologies to enable precision strikes that can "blind, immobilize, and maintain the enemy at a distance while critical targets are identified, struck, and destroyed" (Tilford 1995; for an overview, see Kokoski 1994; also Schneider and Grinter 1995). The value of these weapons was illustrated dramatically during the Persian Gulf War by the United States' use of smart bombs that could drop down chimneys, stealthy aircraft that could elude radar detection, and an airborne tracking system that could scout Iraqi military installations and movements. Their advantages also were illustrated during the 1994–1995 U.S. military intervention in Haiti, where American soldiers carried miniature video cameras on their rifles, enabling them to broadcast live images back to their headquarters and—by satellite—to the Pentagon. So-called smart bombs were used with abandon during NATO's seventy-eight-day around-the-clock random bombing of Belgrade, which ended the war in Kosovo without a single U.S. soldier losing his or her life.

Talk of stealth, precision, information dominance, and missile defense anticipates a day when robots will replace soldiers in combat and unmanned aircraft will replace pilots, roaming the globe with laser weapons to destroy ground and air targets, and "cyberdefense" through the use of smart and brilliant weapons systems will be able to make sophisticated decisions about when and how to act. In this revolution, nonlethal weapons figure prominently. Among the devices already available are "guns that shoot rubber pellets, wooden batons and tiny beanbags to disperse a crowd; stinger grenades that fire rubber pellets; sticky foam that immobilizes people; and another foam system that creates a sudslike barrier 200 feet long, 20 feet wide, and four feet high, laced with tear gas" (Graham 1995). Today's arsenal includes lasers that can blind people from a distance and a variety of biological and chemical weapons. Some advocate using the latter, arguing that a day of fever, coughing, vomiting, and internal bleeding is preferable to incineration. Still in design is a next-generation missile capable of being retargeted in flight based on intelligence from the battlefield.

At issue, now and in the future, is an ageless question: Can technology make warfare safe, or will new technological innovation pave the way to humankind's destruction?

The Proliferation Problem

Do arms acquisitions promote war? "Many amply supplied armed forces may incline governments to use force rather than to negotiate to resolve conflicts." Even so, "the possession of weapons does not guarantee their use" (Ball 1991). In fact, as Chapter 14 discusses, the primary purpose of arming is to prevent the use of force (deterrence), not to encourage it. Hence, as Michael Klare (1987) reasons, "it would be foolish to argue that increased arms transfers automatically increase the risk of war—the decision to wage war is determined by numerous factors."

■ **proliferation**
the spread of weapon capabilities from a few to many states in a chain reaction, so that an increasing number of states gain the ability to launch an attack on other states with devastating (e.g., nuclear) weapons.

■ **Nth country problem**
the addition of new nuclear states.

■ **horizontal nuclear proliferation**
an increase in the number of states that possess nuclear weapons.

■ **vertical nuclear proliferation**
an increase in the capabilities of existing nuclear powers.

■ **chain reaction arms race cycle**
arms races propelled when states increase their military capabilities to offset the expected growth of their adversaries' capabilities, which prompts other states to increase their capabilities in self-defense—an interaction that produces an upward spiral in weaponry but reduces every state's security.

■ **nonproliferation**
the absence of the development of nuclear weapons or technology by countries that do not already possess them (see p. 576).

■ **Nuclear Nonproliferation Treaty (NPT)**
an international agreement that seeks to prevent horizontal proliferation by prohibiting nuclear weapons sales, acquistions, or production.

Still, Klare continues, "There is no doubt that the widespread availability of modern arms has made it easier for potential belligerents to choose the military rather than the diplomatic option when seeking to resolve local disputes." Huge arms purchases by Iraq, for example, may have set the stage for its invasion of Kuwait and the subsequent Persian Gulf War. Iraq bought $75 billion in military equipment during the 1970s and 1980s, or nearly 10 percent of all arms transfers. "The weapons . . . may have encouraged Saddam Hussein to believe that his invasion of Kuwait would not be challenged" (Ball 1991, 20). Thus even if the arms trade and arms races do not necessarily make the world more violent, they do make it less secure (Johansen 1995). Hence the **proliferation** of arms is a serious global concern.

The Proliferation of Nuclear Weapons. The addition of new nuclear states is commonly referred to as the **Nth country problem.** The increase in the number of nuclear states is called **horizontal nuclear proliferation.** Increases in the capabilities of existing nuclear powers are referred to as **vertical nuclear proliferation.**

As Map 13.1 summarizes, in 2000 there were seven "official" members of the nuclear club—the United States, Russia, Great Britain, France, China, India, and Pakistan. In addition, Israel is a de facto or undeclared nuclear weapon state. Two others (North Korea, which agreed to freeze its nuclear program in October 1994; and Iraq, which is subject to UN monitoring) are classifiable as "states of immediate concern." In addition, Iran and Libya warrant long-term concern because they are widely suspected of having secret nuclear weapons development programs in operation.

Most countries dread the **chain reaction arms race cycle** that might lead to widespread horizontal proliferation, which increases the likelihood that one or more states will choose to use nuclear weapons or that an accident or miscalculation will lead to catastrophe. Although estimates vary, experts agree that perhaps as many as thirty other states with nuclear power facilities for energy production now have the economic and technological potential to become nuclear weapon states; the number could easily grow to forty or more following the U.S. failure in October 1999 to accept the nuclear test ban treaty—a dramatic step that suspended faith in the capacity of the thirty-year-old Nonproliferation Treaty (NPT) to remain in force over the long run. In short, the **nonproliferation** regime's future remains in great doubt despite the May 2000 renewal of the NPT treaty (see Chapter 15).

On the optimistic side of the ledger, seven states (Algeria, Argentina, Belarus, Brazil, Kazakhstan, South Africa, and Ukraine) once regarded as nuclear aspirants have now reversed their former position and joined the nonproliferation regime. On the pessimistic side, "If we totally ignore the mounting threats from nongovernmental groups and focus on nation-states alone, we can conclude that approximately twenty countries are either in or are knocking at the door of the nuclear club. We may be looking at a world in which a third to a half of all countries have some hideous weapons of mass murder locked away in their arsenals" (Toffler and Toffler 1993).

The Nonproliferation Regime. The **Nuclear Nonproliferation Treaty (NPT),** first signed in 1968, seeks to prevent further proliferation. Since the nonproliferation regime went into force on March 5, 1970, 187 states have

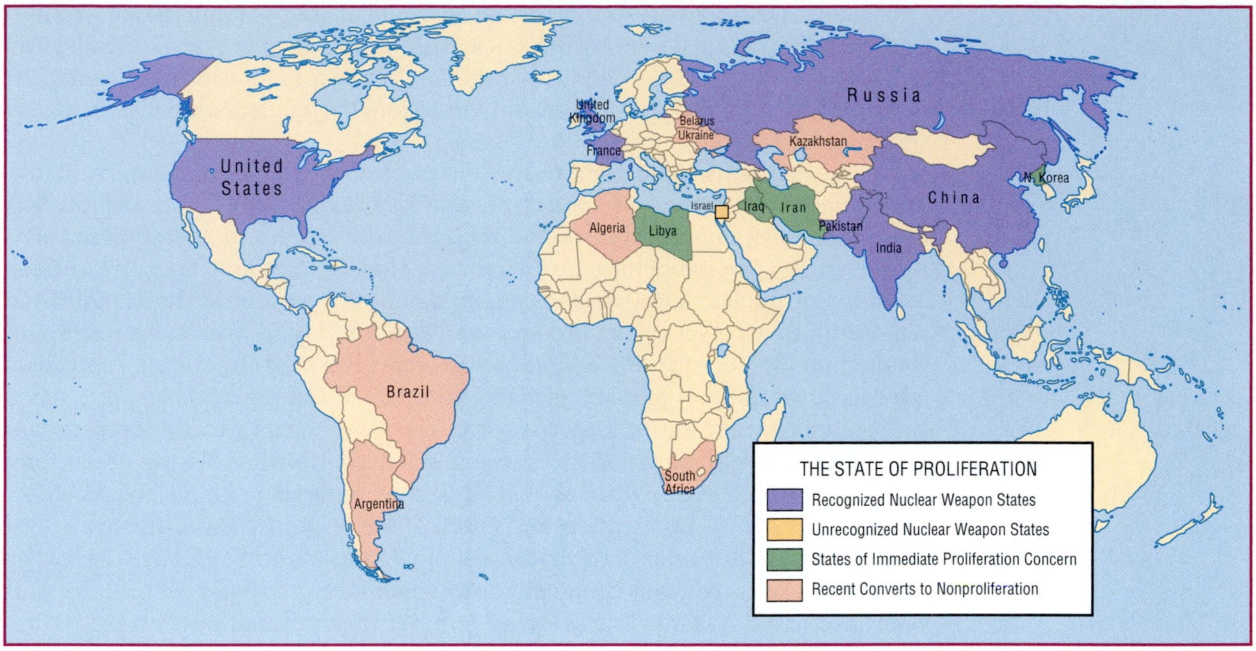

MAP 13.1
Nuclear States and the States Likely to Join the Nuclear Club

A number of countries are capable of producing nuclear weapons on short notice and are regarded as probable candidates for joining the "nuclear club" of declared nuclear weapon states. Others, such as Sweden, have long possessed the capability, but few experts consider them likely to seize the option. This map pictures the state of nuclear proliferation in the year 2000—a portrayal that may quickly become obsolete if Iran, Iraq, and other states build nuclear arsenals.

SOURCE: Projections based on predictions provided by the Arms Control Association.

become members. NPT membership is divided into two categories: nuclear weapon states and nonnuclear weapon states. Nuclear states were defined as those that manufactured and exploded a nuclear weapon prior to January 1, 1967. This definition included only China, France, Russia, the United Kingdom, and the United States—all of which are members of the NPT. All other parties to the agreement are nonnuclear weapon states.

> The NPT strikes a bargain between nuclear and non-nuclear weapon states. Under the treaty, the non-nuclear weapon states agree not to acquire nuclear weapons and to accept comprehensive International Atomic Energy Agency (IAEA) safeguards over all of their nuclear materials to ensure that they are used exclusively for peaceful purposes. In exchange, the nuclear weapon states agree to freely share the benefits of peaceful nuclear energy and technology and not to assist other states to acquire nuclear weapons. In addition, the nuclear weapon states pledged to pursue "good faith" negotiations toward an end to the arms race and toward general and complete disarmament. (Arms Control Association *Fact Sheet,* October 1, 1995, 1)

Despite the apparent success of the NPT, the obstacles to increased proliferation are fragile, as shown by the nuclear development programs of India and Pakistan in 1998, and the collapse of the nuclear test-ban's future following the U.S. rejection of the CTBT. The incentives to join the nuclear club are strong for several additional reasons.

First, the materials needed to make a nuclear weapon are widely available. This is partly due to the widespread use of nuclear technology for generating electricity. Today 428 nuclear power and research reactors are in operation in forty-four countries throughout the world (*Defense Monitor*, No. 1, 2000, 5). In addition to spreading nuclear know-how, states could choose to reprocess the uranium and plutonium that power plants produce as waste for clandestine nuclear weapons production. By the early 2000s, commercial reprocessing reactors will be producing enough plutonium to make as many as 40,000 nuclear weapons.

Second, the scientific expertise necessary for weapons development has spread with the globalization of advanced scientific training. "In the near future it will be possible to duplicate almost all past technology in all but the most forlorn of Third World backwaters, and much of the present state-of-the-art will be both intellectually and practically accessible" (Clancy and Seitz 1991–1992).

Third, export controls designed to stop technology transfer for military purposes are weak. "A large and growing number of states can now export material, equipment, technology, and services needed to develop nuclear weapons" (Potter 1992). In addition, the leaks in nuclear export controls make "a mockery of the long-revered nuclear nonproliferation regime" (Leventhal 1992). Conversion of peacetime nuclear energy programs to military purposes can occur either overtly or, as in the case of India and Pakistan, covertly. The safeguards built into the nonproliferation regime are simply inadequate to detect and prevent secret nuclear weapons development programs.

The ease with which Pakistan made a successful end run around the technology-export controls of the United States and western European governments illustrates the problem of control. In 1979, Pakistan quietly bought all the basic parts—allegedly with funds supplied by the Libyan government—necessary for a uranium-enrichment plant. Similarly, UN inspectors discovered after the Persian Gulf War that Iraq was much closer to building an atomic weapon than previously suspected, despite UN restrictions against this and Iraq's continued pledge to adhere to the rules of the nonproliferation regime. Iraq managed to resist the efforts of UN inspections, throughout 1997 and early 1998, to freely investigate possible production and storage sites for weapons of mass destruction within Iraq, as called for by the peace agreement. The Iraqi experience illustrates the obstacles to preventing the illegal proliferation of weapons, as does the record elsewhere. No less than eight countries have constructed secret nuclear production plants, underscoring the difficulties of managing effective inspections and monitoring nuclear developments (Albright 1993).

Fourth, other states have strong incentives to develop nuclear weapons similar to those once cited by the members of the nuclear club. Former French President Charles de Gaulle argued that, without an independent nuclear capability, France could not "command its own destiny." Similarly, in 1960 Britain's Labour Party leader Aneurin Bevan asserted that without the bomb Britain would go "naked into the council chambers of the world." And in 1993 North Korean President Kim Il Sung defiantly withdrew from the nonproliferation pact, refusing to allow even routine monitoring of his country's five declared nuclear sites at Yongbyon. The desire to act independently and to assert North Korea's power and independence were the primary motives. In response to President Bill Clinton's June 1994 pledge that the United States "would not allow North Korea to develop a nuclear bomb," North Korea has since dug in its heels, although for diplomatic purposes it verbally pledged to freeze its nuclear development program in October 1994.

Many nonnuclear states want the same command of their own fate and the same diplomatic influence that the nuclear powers seem to enjoy. Why, nonnuclear states ask, should they heed a nonproliferation agreement that dooms them to others' domination and security guarantees? Consider Iran's sentiments: In January 1992, its spiritual leader, the Ayatollah Ali Khamenei, declared that the United States had no business questioning the nuclear weapons program designed to make Iran the most powerful military force in the Persian Gulf. "Iran's revolutionary Muslim people recognize no false hegemony for America or any other power," he exclaimed. Similarly, in November 1993, Pakistan's Prime Minister, Benazir Bhutto, asserted that "It is degrading and humiliating to expect Pakistan to roll back its nuclear program." Pakistan developed a nuclear capability, she explained, to deter India, its archenemy. India shouldered its way into the ranks of the nuclear powers in 1998, a month after Pakistan tested the Ghaura missile, to counter the perceived threat of Pakistan and achieve the respect that India has long craved. Nuclear weapons serve as a symbol of status and power. Because of the widespread conviction rooted in realism that military might confers political stature, it is understandable why the nonnuclear powers regard the nuclear nonproliferation treaty as hypocrisy, which provides a seal of approval to the United States, Russia, China, Britain, and France for possessing nuclear weapons while denying it to all others. The underlying belief that it is acceptable to develop a nuclear capacity for deterrence, political influence and prestige was expressed in 1999 by Brajesh Mishra (national security adviser to India's Prime Minister Atal Bihari Vajpayee) when he justified India's nuclear ambitions by asserting that "In the twenty-first century a new security order is likely to arise in the Asia-Pacific region, one in which India should be granted as much respect and deference by the United States and others as is China today." It is unlikely that the nuclear threat will cease. "There's not a snowball's chance in hell we'll eliminate all nuclear weapons from the face of the earth," explains Matthew Bunn, editor of *Arms Control Today.* "That genie is long since out of the bottle and there's no chance of ever getting him back in." Moreover, a world nearing nuclear disarmament would not end the threat. "The problem is, if you eliminate them all, then any country that built just a few nuclear weapons would have enormous blackmail potential" (Davidson 1991).

THE SOCIAL AND ECONOMIC CONSEQUENCES OF MILITARY PREPARATIONS FOR WAR

Global patterns of military spending and arms acquisitions testify to the prevalence of the realist belief that power can be purchased. However, liberal and neoliberal challengers to this worldview ask: What are the effects of this belief about security on national well-being? Do military expenditures and armaments promote national prosperity and security? Or are the consequences destructive?

The Burden of Defense

relative burden of military spending a measure of the economic burden of military activities calculated by the share of each state's gross domestic product allocated to military expenditures.

The **relative burden of military spending,** the ratio of defense spending to gross domestic product (GDP), is one way to measure the sacrifices that military spending requires. As the twenty-first century commenced, the relative defense burden for the world as a whole fell to 2.6 percent, continuing a trend of consecutive reductions since 1985 (SIPRI 2000; World Bank 2000, 263). The average among developed Global North and developing Global South countries both dropped to 2.6 percent—a historic low since 1960.

It is customary to show the wide range in states' willingness to pay a heavy burden for defense by grouping them according to the share of GNP they devote to the military and then juxtaposing this relative burden with their GNP per citizen. Such studies reveal wide variations. As shown in Map 13.2, some comparatively wealthy states (e.g., Kuwait, Israel, and Brunei) bear a heavy burden. In contrast, other states that provide a high average income for their citizens (e.g., Japan, Austria, and Luxembourg) have a low defense burden. Likewise, the citizens of some very poor countries (Sierra Leone, Mozambique, and Chad) are heavily burdened, whereas those of others (Bhutan and Zaire) are not. Thus, it is difficult to generalize about the precise relationship between a country's defense burden and its citizens' standard of living, human development, or stage of development. Still, the available data do suggest two general patterns.

First, those most burdened by the costs of defense include a disproportionate share of poor countries experiencing civil or international war or security threats. Second, many of the poorest countries bear a major share of the world's military burden. Because many of those countries least able to afford weapons make the greatest sacrifices to get them, it appears that the costs of arming for national security pose "a formidable barrier" to providing for human security by alleviating the poverty and suffering. The developing countries in the late 1980s "lost to the arms race in a single year the equivalent of 187 million human-years of income" (Sivard 1991, 11). This raises questions about the social costs of expenditures to prepare for war (see Controversy: Does Military Spending Reduce Citizens' Living Standards?).

"The problem in defense spending," as President Eisenhower observed in 1956, "is to figure how far you should go without destroying from within what you are trying to defend from without." Now the concern is how downsizing military establishments geared toward Cold War competition will affect employment levels and research, development, and production opportunities in defense-related industries. The goal of **defense conversion**—redirecting budgets from armaments to internal development—is "bedeviled by two conflicting objectives: how to shift firms out of defense and into civilian pursuits, and how to preserve a mobilization base to meet conceivable future defense needs" (Adelman and Augustine 1992). The absorption of large numbers of military personnel into the domestic economy has been a matter of concern for nearly all industrialized democracies in the Global North's zone of peace.

defense conversion the process of shifting resources from the production of military goods to civilian products.

Just as excessive military spending has its costs, conversion to a much smaller, "peace-maintaining" military posture may also exact a domestic economic toll. Perhaps this explains why the Clinton administration's fiscal 2000

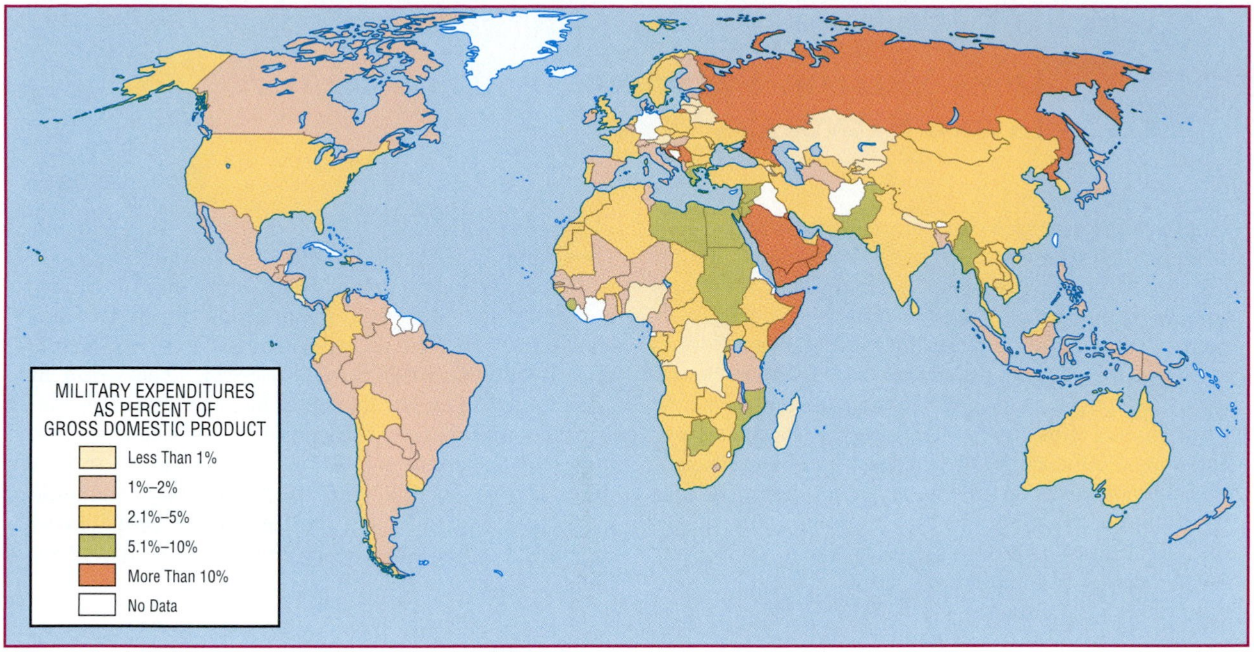

MAP 13.2

The Military Burden of Defense Expenditure on Countries around the World

States vary highly in the amount of tax revenues they extract from citizens to pay for weapons. This map shows what is known as the military burden by calculating the percentage of gross domestic product (GDP) allocated to military spending for each state. Countries where citizens are heavily burdened by taxes to pay for large armies and arsenals are those where the expectation of armed conflict *within* that country (a civilian war) or with another country (an interstate war) are high. Globally, the economic burden of defense declined in recent years to 2.6 percent on average of world GDP (<www.SIPRI.SC>, February 20, 2000). However, military spending has increased the most where people are poorest: the Global South. This preparation for war through a high military burden comes at a cost, because many economists conclude that when states spend high sums for weapons they have less money available to spend on **human security**—increasing their citizens' standards of living and life spans. "In many of the world's developing countries military expenditures have risen between 15 percent and 20 percent per year for the past few years, averaging out to 7.5 percent per year for the past quarter century. Even though many developing countries still spend less than 5 percent of their gross domestic product on defense, these funds could be put to different uses in such human development areas as housing, land reform, health care, and education" (Allen 2000, 41).

SOURCE: Allen (2000), 41; U.S. ACDA (1997), 31.

human security a concept that refers to the degrees to which the welfare of individuals is protected and advanced, in contrast to national security, which puts the interests of states first.

defense budget did not abolish a single new weapons system, and, in fact, included $112 billion in additional funding for the military through the year 2007.

Military Spending and Economic Development

How are military expenditures and economic growth linked? Many politicians and experts argue that a trade-off exists between "guns and butter"—between military spending and economic prosperity. Much evidence on the relationship

CONTROVERSY

DOES MILITARY SPENDING REDUCE CITIZENS' LIVING STANDARDS?

Many realists maintain that a strong defense makes for a strong economy and a strong and safe population. Pumping money into defense spending, they argue, is not only necessary, but constructive: it creates jobs, fuels economic growth, and increases national security. Governments are forced to set priorities when they make choices about how public funds will be spent, and it is clear from inspection of those budget decisions that a majority of the globe's countries consider it more important to spend on equipping a strong military than on investing on education and health programs that can improve the quality of their citizens' lives. Defense trumps reducing poverty, hunger, disease, and illiteracy it seems.

However, others are not convinced by this argument. They emphasize that the costs of comparatively greater resources for military preparedness cut into the ability of a state to meet the human needs of citizens and enable them to live a secure and long life. As U.S. President Dwight D. Eisenhower observed, "The world in arms is not spending money alone. It is spending the sweat of its laborers, the genius of its scientists, the hopes of its children." To assess the issues in this debate, consider the case of the global hegemonic leader, the United States, and inspect its priorities as they were defined by the proposed Fiscal Year 2000 budget (illustrated below).

President Clinton's Proposed FY 2000 Discretionary Budget

Note: Discretionary funding for Social Security and Medicare covers various administrative costs and is not related to benefits mandated by law.

SOURCE: *Defense Monitor* (No. 1, 1999), 1.

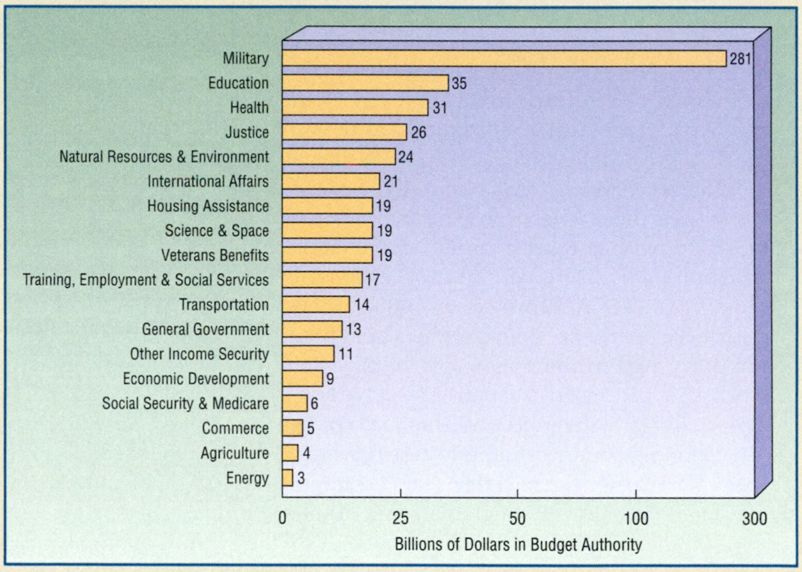

■ **guns versus growth** the trade-off between military spending and economic development, and the controversy over the extent to which spending on weapons reduces the rate of growth of a state's GNP.

points to "retarding effects through inflation, diversion of investment, use of scarce materials, and misuse of human capital" (Sivard 1979). In most developing countries, when military spending rises, the rate of economic growth declines (Deger and Smith 1983; also Payne and Sahu 1993; Väyrynen 1992) and debt increases (Snider 1991). This is due to the tendency of defense expenditures to divert resources away from growth-promoting investments and to inhibit research and development in export-generating industries.

How the leading state acts influences the choices the others will be inclined to make. It was fear of the United States' setting an example for a military buildup rather than offering the globe leadership on arms control that moved Oscar Arias, the 1987 Nobel Peace laureate and former president of Costa Rica, to write in 1999:

> World leaders must stop viewing militaristic investment as a measure of national wellbeing. And they must embrace multilateral efforts that recognize the complete and politicized nature of contemporary security questions. By maintaining a massive military-industrial complex, the United States sends the wrong signal to other countries whose national budgets desperately need to be directed toward human needs. The sad fact is that half the world's governments invest more in defense than in health programs. If we channeled just $40 billion each year away from armies and into antipoverty programs, in ten years all of the world's population would enjoy basic social services—education, health care and nutrition, potable water and sanitation. Another $40 billion each year over 10 years would provide each person on this planet with an income level above the poverty line for his or her country.

Dr. Arias's proposition that high military spending is dangerous because it reduces social welfare is amply supported by the case of the United States. Consider how the United States, the uncontested global spender on military, ranks with the rest of the globe's countries on the most-commonly used measures of **human development,** economic standing, and standard of living. Keep in mind that the United States ranks first in military spending, military technology, number of overseas military bases, training of allies' armed forces, size of naval fleet and combat aircraft, and nuclear warheads and bombs. Then inspect the U.S. rank on various nonmilitary indices, which shows that the United States is well below the achievements and position of many other countries (Sivard 1996, 40):

U.S. Rank Compared to 160 Other States

Social Development	
Percent population with safe water	1
Percent births attended by trained personnel	2
Female and male literacy rate	4
GNP per capita	5
Economic–Social Standing	
Public health expenditures per capita	8
Public education expenditures per capita	9
Public education expenditures per student	10
Maternal mortality rate	12
Infant mortality rate	13
Life expectancy	14
Percent school-age children in school	18
Under five mortality rate	18
Contraceptive prevalence	19
Percent infants with low birthweight	29
Population per physician	39
Students per teacher	39

These rankings suggest that when expenditures for arms go up, so do disease, illiteracy, and poverty (Nincic 1982; Russett 1982; UNDP 1999). Do you agree? If you were a head of state, what budget priorities would you propose for your country's national security and your citizens' human security? How would you reconcile the need for defense with the need to provide for the common welfare? The choices you would make would be difficult, because they entail a necessary tradeoff between competing values. For this reason military-spending decisions are highly controversial everywhere.

Despite this evidence, the **guns versus growth** issue remains controversial. "Previous research on the impact of military spending on the economy has produced disparate, inconsistent, and unstable results" (Chan 1987; Sandler and Hartley 1995). A strong correlation does not hold for all countries. "The effects of military expenditure on the economy," conclude Ron P. Smith and George Georgiou (1983), "depend on the nature of the expenditure, the prevailing circumstances, and the concurrent government policies." In many advanced industrial

human development the extent to which humans' ability to develop to their individual potential is protected, such that they are provided with sufficient schooling, income, and opportunity to live a full life.

Who Pays for Defense? In many countries, military spending remains exceptionally high, and maintaining a large army comes at a high cost. Poor people often lose the most. One example is the United States. In October 1999, Stansfield Turner, a former director of the Central Intelligence Agency, complained that "Since the dawn of the nuclear age, the government has spent more than $5.5 trillion on nuclear forces, more than on education, the environment and transportation combined. . . . Cutting back our current force of more than 12,000 nuclear warheads . . . could save billions for schools, health insurance for the many children who lack it, Head Start and other needed initiatives." However, that proposal's acceptance is not likely, in part because what President Dwight Eisenhower termed "the military-industrial complex" continues to shape national budgets in the United States and elsewhere. Children often suffer unmet needs or are put in harm's way. In fact, outside the United States, children are frequently required to be soldiers. "Globally, an estimated 300,000 children are involved in 36 armed conflicts from the African jungles of Angola and Sudan to the Latin American mountains of Colombia and Peru; from Afghanistan to Indonesia; the Middle East and the Balkans. Fueled by civil wars, the numbers are climbing" (Schuler 1999). Here some of the newly trained child-soldiers ride through the streets of Monrovia in Liberia in April 1996, taking up arms to wage war on behalf of their government sponsors.

economies, for instance, military spending stimulates economic growth, at least in the short run. This especially holds true during periods of unemployment, when the infusion of capital can provide jobs, training, and social infrastructure in the form of investments in highways, airports, communications, and the like.

The strain of military spending on economic growth, however, seems to be especially severe in many societies, particularly when it persists for many years (Väyrynen 1992; Ward, Davis, and Lofdahl 1995). Compare Japan with the United States and the former Soviet Union. Japan, relatively freed of the burden of funding militarization since the 1950s, expanded its economy greatly; the United States and the former Soviet Union, paying high costs for military power, fell behind economically. It appears that excessive military spending was a primary cause of the Soviet Union's demise. "No other industrialized state in the world [had] for so long spent so much of its national wealth on armaments and military forces. Soviet militarism, in harness with communism, destroyed the Soviet economy and thus hastened the self-destruction of the Soviet Empire" (Iklé 1991–1992, 28).

The end of the Cold War poses special problems for the United States, which now stands alone at the pinnacle of world power. What defense commitments and responsibilities should engage the United States now that the challenges of communist ideology and Soviet expansionism have disappeared? As noted in Chapters 4 and 8, there are no easy answers to these questions.

Maintaining a balance between military preparedness and economic revitalization presents a serious challenge not only to the United States, but also to the other major powers. A comparison of the great powers' new defense policies informs us about the ways states are thinking about national security as they prepare for the threats of the twenty-first century.

THE GREAT POWERS' NATIONAL SECURITY STRATEGIES

The threat of the Cold War turning hot has disappeared. In response, the superpowers have retired their strategic nuclear arsenals more rapidly than they have replaced them, and the size of those arsenals is scheduled to decline to their lowest levels in fifty years (see Chapter 15). As a consequence, the geostrategic landscape now bears little resemblance to the terrain of the early 1990s.

The transformed security environment has deprived the strongest states of a clear vision of how to protect their country's national interests and prosperity. In Washington, Moscow, Beijing, Tokyo, and Berlin, defense planners are struggling to construct strategies and defense doctrines.

As noted in Chapter 4, the choices range between the extremes of isolationist withdrawal from participation in world affairs to active international engagement. The options also require choices to be made between **unilateral** self-help actions on one end of the continuum, **multilateral** action with others on the other, and specialized **bilateral** alliances and ad hoc partnerships in between.

Based on the strongest powers' recent actions and statements, they appear to agree on certain fundamental priorities in the emerging twenty-first century:

- Forestalling a new major war is critical, because all other national security interests, such as prosperity, will be jeopardized if peace does not endure.
- Economic development will be of vital and growing importance to military security and to the position of each of the economic and military giants in the globe's future hierarchy of power.
- The world pyramid of power is moving toward a **multipolar** distribution, in which no hegemon will be dominant and three, four, or more great powers will share approximately equal military power.

Given the prevailing consensus about these probabilities, what sort of national security response is most likely? We will look briefly at the emerging security policies of the five major great powers.

■ **unilateral**
a go-it-alone, self-reliant strategy for dealing with threats from another actor or global problem.

■ **multilateral**
a cooperative strategy of working with allies or with collective problem-solving institutions to face threats from another actor or global problem (see p. 354).

■ **bilateral**
an intermediary strategy of working with a specific ally or in a specially created ad hoc partnership to face threats from another actor or global problem.

■ **multipolar**
an international system with distribution of power among three or more power centers.

The United States' New Security Policies

A key to understanding U.S. national security policy is America's long-term economic decline relative to an ascending China, Japan, and Germany and an integrating European Union pursuing a common security policy. To many observers, if the ten straight years of the U.S. economy's expansion in the 1990s ends, America is destined to become more imperiled than imperial. To them, "the dawn of dominance" is at hand as "the American century" ends, because the United States has seen its share of world output fall steadily "to less than it was at the time of the Spanish-American War, when the United States first emerged as a world power"; remaining "the biggest debtor nation in history," America faces stagnating living conditions and diminishing expectations (D. White 1998). Simply put, the United States must confront the reality that it faces stiff trade competition, and its rivals' economies are growing at a pace that is threatening to cut into the U.S. share of the global financial pie. In the long run, these trends could reduce U.S. influence and its ability to lead in world affairs, forcing the country to redefine its national security policy by making economic renewal at home a priority.

Yet this does not mean that military competition and threats will necessarily recede in importance, so that U.S. global strategy will shift in new directions. Former U.S. Secretary of State Lawrence Eagleburger was ahead of his time when in 1993 he predicted, "The dangers of the period into which we are going can be as unpleasant, if not as bloody, as most of the first fifty years of this century." We are returning to the raucous multipolarity more reminiscent of the nineteenth century, he warned. Given this threat, military security is likely to command as important a place in a new U.S. strategy as will trade, prosperity, and the promotion of free governments and markets throughout the world.

The trade-offs between these economic and military objectives have divided Americans about the appropriate U.S. response. Three schools of thought about America's role in global affairs continue to divide U.S. policymakers at the start of the new millennium:

> Neo-isolationists want the U.S. to deal only with threats to America's physical security, political independence, and domestic liberty. They find no such threats at present, and therefore argue that the U.S. should let other powers, and regional balances of power, take care of all the world's woes. Realists such as Henry Kissinger want the U.S. to continue to be the holder of the world balance of power, the arbiter of the main regional power groups, and the watchdog against all potential imperialistic trouble-makers. Internationalists want a greater role for multilateral institutions and more emphasis on human needs and rights, the environment and democracy. (Hoffmann 1992, 59)

Like the Clinton administration, the new presidential team of national security advisers who will take office in January 2001 will have to struggle to reconcile these divergent outlooks, and to strike a balance between the need for self-help isolationism, the impulse to flex supreme U.S. military muscle in an activist push to run the world, and the desire to promote traditional U.S. liberal ideals such as human rights, democracy and multilateral international cooperation. The quest represents a major challenge, because these goals are in many respects incompatible. They entail a **zero-sum** trade-off among choices, in which one goal can only be pursued by compromising pursuit of others. For example, the United States cannot play the role of hegemonic superpower leading the world and also isolationistically withdraw from the costs of paying for foreign aid, regional collective-security alliances, or UN peacekeeping missions; nor can the United States avoid looking hypocritical if it undertakes a massive military buildup at the same time that it preaches the ideals of arms control, disarmament, and nonproliferation for others.

■ **zero-sum**
competitive situations in which there is little room for compromise because gains for one party or one goal require a loss for another.

If the past provides a guide to the future, U.S. national security policy in the first decade of the twenty-first century is likely to continue to display a realpolitik face at the same time that it speaks in the diplomatic language of the U.S. liberal legacy. While displaying a preference for **selective engagement** on the issues and trouble spots where the United States chooses to become involved, the U.S. will isolationistically avoid intervention where the costs and risks are high (Art 1999). Power will be valued, as will principle, but action probably will be taken globally only on those international developments which the next administration defines as vital national interests. Central to U.S. national security calculations is likely to be a continuing premium placed on military preparedness; the other candidates for the presidency enthusiastically agreed with George W. Bush when, while campaigning in 1999 for the White House his

■ **selective engagement**
a national security policy that targets only special countries or situations for military action, depending on the importance of the country or problem for the intervening power.

father had previously occupied, Bush argued, "We live in a dangerous world, and the next president has to reinvigorate the military. You need a sharpened sword to deal in the dangerous world of the twenty-first century." According to this realpolitik logic, the acquisition of overwhelming military power will enable the United States to better manage the other perceived major threats to U.S. national security and realize other U.S. ideas, in order to:

- Deter the use of nuclear, biological, or chemical weapons against the United States, its forces, and its allies.
- Halt or at least slow the proliferation of such weapons.
- Pursue continuing U.S. reliance on weapons of mass destruction for deterrence and defense, as indicated by the commitment the U.S. has made to spend $4.5 billion on average *each year* through the year 2005 on nuclear arms programs (*Harper's*, September 1999, 17).
- Deter and, if necessary, defeat an aggressor state intent on conquering any country in regions important to the United States.
- Pursue the search for technological solutions to military problems through the development of smaller smart bombs, nonlethal weapons, and an improved ballistic missile defense system in outer space.
- Be capable of fighting and winning an armed conflict in at least two regions of strategic importance to the United States, in short-term military interventions that minimize American casualties.
- Prevent any other great power from challenging the hegemonic position of the United States as the leader in military power and in the globalized international political economy.
- Prepare U.S. forces to participate effectively in multilateral peace enforcement and unilateral intervention operations that could include peacekeeping, humanitarian assistance, counterdrug, and counterterrorism activities.
- Attempt to organize global intervention to stop either ethnic cleansing or genocide within other countries where corrupt governments practice state-sponsored terrorism against their own people
- Foster democratic values in other countries.
- Maintain U.S. technological superiority.

Viewed in light of this realpolitik definition of its evolving defense doctrines, the United States is committed to relying heavily on military might while attempting to build liberal ideals into the definition of its goals. This kind of "democratic realism" follows the U.S. **engagement and enlargement strategy** the Clinton Doctrine outlined to use U.S. power for humanitarian interventions throughout the world and to enlarge the community of liberal democracies. The Clinton Doctrine did not call for the United States to take on every burden throughout the world, but "to engage in some places and pass on others." U.S. national security appears destined to reaffirm the commitment to being prepared to wage two major wars simultaneously and to being able to intervene militarily around the world, while at the same time deterring an attack on the United States and selectively using U.S. troops in modest numbers to police tyranny and internal turmoil in foreign failed states where human rights abuses produce atrocities and genocidal massacres abroad.

engagement and enlargement strategy the Clinton administration's strategy that commits U.S. power to help manage conflicts throughout the world and to enlarge the community of liberal democracies.

Remote-Control Warfare? In the twenty-first century, the United States plans to preserve its commanding edge in military capabilities by building a new generation of technologically sophisticated new weapons, instead of attempting to build up an overpowering inventory of big bombs that are risky to use, in order to combat the growing threat of insurgencies within the world's failing states. A wide variety of weapons are under construction, ranging from thousand-pound bombs (the concrete, nonexplosive bombs the U.S. bombarded Iraq with in late 1999) to landmines. Some of the nonnuclear strategic weapons systems on the drawing boards "may be able to engage 1,500 targets in the first hour, if not minutes, of a conflict." Shown here is one example: "An artist's conception of an advanced unmanned aircraft system—one possibility for strategic strike with conventional explosives" (Krepinevich and Kusiak 1998).

■ **democratic peace** the theory that, because democratic states do not fight each other, the diffusion of democratic governance throughout the world will reduce the probability of war (see p. 424).

The purpose of U.S. power in the next administration will undoubtedly continue to seek to uphold universal liberal ideals by actively promoting the spread of democratic governance, based on the **democratic peace** principle. This strategy will rest also on the liberal tenet that American interests and security require liberal (free) trade in order to generate global prosperity because the prospects for peace among competitive states will improve when their continued economic growth depends heavily on an integrated and orderly global export market.

This conception of national security preserves the traditional U.S. emphasis on a strong defense and on strategic deterrence, with a rising annual defense budget, from $281 billion in 1999 to a projected military expenditure of nearly $350 billion in 2005 (*Defense Monitor*, No. 1, 1999, 5). It will aim at expanding military capabilities by developing a broad range of new conventional and nonlethal weapons made possible by the RMT to conduct precision raids on enemy targets. Moreover, it will probably continue to emphasize coercive diplomacy, alliances, and arms sales as bargaining instruments to exercise influence abroad, while striking a balance between safeguarding peace through assertive multilateralism and selective engagement. But a revised U.S. strategy is certain to place a renewed emphasis as well on containing the potential expansion of other great-power rivals and civil wars in the Global South by strengthening global institutions (NATO, the UN) and international law. The future of U.S. national security policy in the area of arms control, strategic missile defense, disarmament, and nonprolifiration is much harder to anticipate. The challenge of prediction became even more complex after the October 1999 U.S. rejection of the Comprehensive Test Ban Treaty, and the U.S. pledge to fund creation of a limited anti-ballistic missile defense to intercept and destroy from outer space missiles launched accidentally by a nuclear power or by a rogue state such as North Korea or Iraq. Critics complain that the costly missile defense system, like President Reagan's ill-fated Star Wars program to counter the Soviet nuclear threat (Fitzgerald 2000; Greenberg 2000), is misguided (see Garwin 2000).

In short, the United States will have to struggle with the dilemmas of occupying—and holding—its lonely unipolar position as the supreme superpower at the top of the global pyramid of power. It will have to avoid the extremes of isolationism and imperialism if it is to lead in the world, but resist the temptation to dominate others and thereby drive them into hostile resistance. Globalization precludes the possibility of redesigning the world to advance U.S. prominence. The U.S. standing among the community of nations remains high, and that is a source of influence; but the U.S. capacity to use military force to compel other countries to act as the United States wishes is low. The soft power that respect for U.S. ideals and ideas coupled with economic strength can provide can be the basis for the United States to fashion the globe into a prosperous and peaceful place, providing it leads by example rather than by force. Finding a global vision to chart its way in the complex twenty-first-century world that balances realist interests with liberal ideals will be America's continuing greatest challenge.

In the chaotic twenty-first century, American leaders can be expected to adapt U.S. strategy to the unknown dangers that lurk beneath the surface of turbulent global geostrategic waters. Limits on America's capacity to foresee the future—and limits on resources to take a unilateral approach to managing the new millennium's multiple security threats—suggest that a coherent strategy resting on a clear vision is likely to prove an elusive goal for the United States in the future.

Russia's New Strategy for a New Century

Russia faces a precarious geostrategic future, fraught with threats to its security on many fronts. At the start of the twenty-first century, Russia is still reeling from the revolutionary changes that occurred in the 1990s. By the end of 1991, the Union of Soviet Socialist Republics (USSR) had ceased to exist, and the Russian empire collapsed with the loss of most of its satellite allies. Overnight, Russia's superpower status vanished. Russia was no longer one of the world's foremost military powers with imperial ambitions and hopes of becoming the globe's next hegemon. The Soviet Union in 1991 had a population of 287 million people, a landmass of 8.7 million square miles, and an army of 5.5 million soldiers. Today Russia's population is about 147 million people (and declining) and it controls a landmass of 6.6 million square miles. Russia's army has lost its roar amidst a budget crisis in the new capitalistic market economy that has left Russia's 1.2 million soldiers poorly equipped and drained of morale; it is an army in "rapid decay," funded at only two-thirds what is budgeted, with the "average Russian soldier only marginally combat capable" (Pincus 1999, 18). Russia's military budget is no larger than were Kmart's U.S. sales in 1998 (*Harper's*, March 2000, 19). To add to this weakness, Russia has dismantled much of the awesome strategic nuclear stockpile that had been the backbone of its defense and deterrence strategy and the symbol of its military might. Russia also no longer benefits from the existence of reliable allies to guard its borders from external attack, facing instead an enlarged NATO alliance in its geopolitical backyard. In addition to Russia's reduced defense position, Moscow must try to rule a federation of eighty-nine regions. Consequently, there is the ever present threat of separatist independence movements led by ethnic minorities active in many of the remaining regions in Russia's shrunken empire, such as in the explosive war in the breakaway republic of Chechnya. As the danger of civil war percolates, fueled by the misery of stagnant growth rates, Kremlin leaders face a dismal strategic future.

Russian defense planners have no alternative but to make the difficult adjustment of their national security strategies to these grim realities. In the past, few great powers have experienced so painful an erosion of their power position without experiencing war. In a **power transition** of unprecedented magnitude and rapidity, Russia's sense of national security has plummeted. To manage the threats, internal strains, weaknesses, and crises, and to lessen Russia's growing fear that the United States was trying to weaken the country and to become the globe's supreme power, in January 2000 acting Russian President Vladimir Putin unveiled a new national security doctrine. Entitled *The Concept of National Security,* this document sought to make a number of accommodative revisions to the first post-Soviet security doctrine of December 1997, which attempted to construct a strategy for a humiliated Russia that had become too poor and powerless to attempt to reestablish military or economic clout beyond its borders. In the section called "Ensuring the National Security of Russia," Putin's new doctrine set the following new Russian security-policy priorities:

■ **power transition**
a situation resulting from the rapid increase or deterioration in one state's military capabilities relative to a rival's, often provoking fears that lead to warfare.

- Undertaking fundamental military reforms. Following the previous elimination of entire branches of the armed services, the meager 2000 Russian defense budget of less than $20 billion annually (about 7 percent that of the United States and less than NATO spent in 1999 for its seventy-eight-day intervention in Serbia) was cut further, with the savings put to defense conversion to stimulate domestic economic recovery and put the country back on its feet. "With luck," Mr. Putin wrote in early 2000, "Russia might hope to reach the current economic level of Portugal in fifteen years" (Lipman 2000).
- Creating smaller, more mobile, and technologically adept fighting forces to manage civil rebellions within Russia as well as along Russia's borders in what is termed the "near broad," such as war-torn Afghanistan, where potential armed conflicts threaten to undermine Russian security.
- Continuing to dismantle Russia's nuclear arsenal (with U.S. assistance) in order to alleviate other powers' fears of resurgent Russian ambitions, to repair Russia's relations with the West and seek its financial assistance, and to prevent the further proliferation of weapons of mass destruction to other countries. In April 2000, Russia ratified the START II nuclear treaty for these purposes.
- Managing a pressing new set of threats to Russia's national security, with emphasis not on international relations but on a host of domestic dangers, including economic chaos, a decay of Russian society, terrorism and crime, political polarization, and the rise of ethnic divisions.
- Lowering the nuclear threshold by modifying the language on the use of the nuclear weapons and repealing the **no first use** pledge previously made by Mikhail Gorbachev that Russia would not be the first to use nuclear

■ **no first use**
the doctrine that a nuclear state would not use its strategic weapons in the event of an attack by another state using conventional weapons.

weapons in the event of a conventional attack. Hence, for purposes of deterrence, the new doctrine allows the country's leaders to use all resisting forces "including nuclear weapons" to oppose any attack—nuclear or conventional—if other efforts fail to repel an aggressor. This strategy revises the previous doctrine, which stated that Russia would use nuclear weapons only in cases when its national sovereignty was threatened.

- Continuing its efforts to cement cooperative relationships with its European neighbors by creating institutions for democracy and a free market economy. By urging that the UN and other international institutions be strengthened, the new doctrine assumes a confrontational posture by pursuing as well the goal of working together with China, India, and France in building a counter-coalition to balance what Russia and some other great powers call the threat of U.S. hegemonial domination.

Russia's departures from its previous strategic doctrines reveal its alarm about the fact that its geostrategic position in the world has declined and its awareness of the tremendous weakness of its conventional military capabilities, which might not be able to defend the country against attack. This sense of vulnerability explains why Russia appears so defensive and defiant, as well as its new emphasis on nuclear weapons in a strategy that, security exports note, sounds very much like NATO's own security doctrines that still declare that the use of nuclear weapons remains the cornerstone of the West's security policy. At the same time, Russia's awareness of its vulnerability also explains its pronounced desire to work cooperatively with others to preserve global security.

Russia seeks to forge a multilateral approach to its many security problems. This was evidenced by its 1999 deployment abroad of ten thousand Russian soldiers in UN peacekeeping roles, while at the same time Russia seeks simultaneously to graduate from a Partner for Peace (PfP) to a full-fledged NATO member in order to prevent NATO from expanding eastward to build a new wall around an isolated Russia.

China's Global Clout and Security Posture

China figures prominently in U.S. and Russian conceptions of security.

> The rise of China, if it continues, may be the most important trend in the world for the [twenty-first] century. When historians one hundred years hence write about our time, they may well conclude that the most significant development was the emergence of a vigorous market economy—and army—in the most populous country of the world. This is particularly likely if many of the globe's leading historians and pundits a century from now do not have names like Smith but rather ones like Wu.
>
> China is the fastest growing economy in the world, with what may be the fastest growing military budget. It has nuclear weapons, border disputes with most of its neighbors, and a rapidly improving army that may—within a decade or so—be able to resolve old quarrels in its own favor. The United States has possessed the world's largest economy for more than a century, but at present trajectories China may displace it in the first half of the next century and become the number one economy in the world. (Kristof 1993, 59; see also Kaplan 1999)

China is an economic giant and potential military colossus bent on modernizing its maritime and air capabilities. China's rise and endeavors to become a global power on par with the United States has understandably heightened the concerns of the other great powers—especially Russia, which shares with China a four-thousand-mile border; Japan nearby in the China Sea; and the U.S. colossus. China seeks to reduce those states' fears about its rising capabilities as the globe's most populous and fastest growing free-market economy. China asserts that while it wants its rivals to treat the communist government with the respect due a great power, it seeks peaceful relations with all. In 1994, China signed an agreement with Russia to prevent accidental military clashes, and in 1997 it formalized the effort to ensure Russian acceptance by signing a new strategic treaty of alliance for mutual defense. Following that initiative, later in 1997 China courted a new strategic partnership with the United States; at an October Washington summit, President Jiang Zemin pledged to seek "common ground despite differences" in order to "share responsibility for preserving world peace and stability in the twenty-first century," and to underscore China's sincerity pledged to rein in nuclear and chemical exports and end the sale of cruise missiles to Iran. Underlying these Chinese efforts to prevent a new Cold War is the fear that the United States is spinning a web of security alliances around China's borders and that the United States has only one goal—"the hegemonic domination of the world" (Pomfret 1999). After the inadvertent U.S. bombing in 1999 of the Chinese Embassy in Belgrade, Chinese leaders would like U.S. leaders to listen to the advice of American scholars, who warn that "Increasingly political pressures are pushing the United States toward a self-fulfilling prophecy: Treat China as if it is inevitably hostile and dangerous, and it is more likely to become hostile and dangerous" (Seib 1999).

China has taken still other steps to alleviate the concerns of Japan, India, and the United States about how Chinese leaders might use for military purposes the resources of an economy that has doubled every eight years. In March 2000, China announced a 12.7 percent increase in military spending—the eighth straight double-digit jump—to boost the defense burden to 13 percent of the $11 billion national budget in order to modernize its army to "defend the unity of the motherland" (Hutzler 2000, A4).

Beijing's greatly expanded military spending in the 1990s has understandably heightened fears of a new "Red peril" (see Lilley and Ford 1999), especially in light of China's placement of its armed forces on "high alert" to militarily prevent Taiwan, which China regards as a renegade province, from moving away from unification toward formal independence. When in March 2000 Defense Minister Chi Haotian strengthened the Chinese People's Army's "combat readiness" and vowed to retake Taiwan by force if necessary, anxieties about Chinese militarism soared. However, many skeptics believe the danger of Chinese aggression is more of a "red herring" and these fears are overblown, because China's defense spending and military capabilities remain comparatively low. To their mind, China is more interested in economic power and diplomatic stature than territorial expansion by force.

The direction of China's policies seems geared to ensuring its rise to prominence in the Pacific Rim, as shown by its military threats in 2000 against Taiwan. To this end, China has continued to arm, preserve its nuclear weapons, and equip the globe's largest standing army (2.9 million soldiers). At the same time, China seems committed to developing the strategic and military might that the Chinese

A Hegemonic Challenger on the March? China is an ascendant superpower with the capacity to intimidate its Asian neighbors and strike fear into distant great-power rivals, who suspect that its rise to the top rankings of national economies will be followed by foreign aggressiveness. At the moment, U.S. technological advantages are so vast that China's military aspirations to equal the superpower status of the United States cannot be realized for many decades (Bracken 1999). Indeed, China is not a serious challenger to U.S. supremacy. As this photo of Chinese soldiers suggests, China's military is more stylish pomp than it is a truly modern force able to credibly project power throughout the globe. "China's military today is so outdated that much of its equipment might well have seen action in the Korean War, and many of its troops are semi-literate. The country's strategic nuclear arsenal is 300 times as small as that of the U.S. The entire arsenal packs about as much explosive power as what the U.S. stuffs into one Trident submarine. China's ballistic-missile sub (singular, not plural) hasn't been to sea for a year and would be sunk in minutes in a battle with a U.S. attack sub. The People's Republic has no aircraft carriers (the U.S. maintains 11 carrier battle groups), no long-range strategic bombers (the U.S. has 174) and funds this stumbling juggernaut with a budget of 14 cents for every dollar the U.S. spends on defense. The People's Liberation Army, says the Pentagon, is still decades away from possessing a comprehensive capability to engage and defeat a modern adversary beyond China's boundaries" (Gibney 1999, 40).

believe its status as an economic giant justifies. This attitude is evidenced by China's resistance to its Association of Southeast Asian Nations (ASEAN) neighbors' effort in 1995 to establish a nuclear-free zone in Southeast Asia.

However, despite its assertiveness and coercive diplomacy toward its neighbors China can be expected to concentrate on its internal development and trade relations, while seeking to contain domestic instability that threatens to tear apart national unity (especially if ethnic tensions and regional economic differences within China increase). Preserving domestic tranquility and growth is a priority, along with "maintaining good and friendly relations with all countries" (Grinter 1998) and avoiding becoming the next target of a U.S.-led coalition assembled to contain its rise.

As its power and wealth have grown, China has steadfastly refused to take instructions from its great-power rivals, insisting on its right to chart a foreign policy guided by its own perceptions of national interests. As yet, this does not mean that China is necessarily preparing for or planning foreign military engagement, as it argues that defense is the purpose of its military buildup and that its saber-rattling toward Taiwan is a permissible action toward a rebellious province that is part of sovereign Chinese territory. To find the safe place in the sun where it feels it belongs, China has made its priority goals for national security strategy to:

- Lobby to see that the traditional international legal rule prohibiting external interference in sovereign states' domestic affairs is respected, to safeguard against foreign intervention to punish China for disregard of its citizens' human rights and civil liberties.
- Expand China's sphere of influence in the Pacific Rim to gain the respect of its Asian neighbors, which China regards as appropriate recognition of its status as the region's preeminent power.
- Concentrate on becoming the recognized dominant country in Asia, so as to recover its lost historic **suzerainty,** or accepted deference and respect, from its neighbors. For this goal, China is energetically trying to take a giant leap forward in nuclear weapons technology, as symbolized by its August 1999 test of a missile with sufficient range to cross the Pacific Ocean, in response to the U.S. plan to place parts of Asia, including Taiwan, under an American antimissile protective shield.
- Pursue membership in the World Trade Organization (WTO) and other multilateral global institutions, in order to give China a greater voice in shaping those international organizations' future policies and decisions, and to prevent its isolation, demonization, and exclusion.
- Establish normalized diplomatic relations with the United States and deter that superpower from treating an ascendant China as an enemy to be contained in a new Cold War.

■ **suzerainty**
the claim by a powerful state to the right to exercise influence over its neighbors.

To the other great powers, these proclamations inspire divergent reactions. "Engagers" recommend efforts to further integrate China into the global economy, in the hope that this will allow China to become more prosperous and gradually become more liberal at home and reduce its hegemonial regional ambitions. "Containers" disagree, arguing that **appeasement** will encourage Chinese bellicosity, and that therefore a new **containment** policy is needed to curtail the Chinese threat before it becomes necessary to repel it by force. This reaction to China's growing clout calls, in short, for deterrence of China's potential imperial ambitions, while awaiting the day when liberal democracy comes alive within its borders to temper such pursuits.

■ **appeasement**
a strategy of deterring a potential belligerent by making concessions.

■ **containment**
a term coined by U.S. policymaker George F. Kennan for deterring Soviet Russia's expansionist aims by counterpressures, which has since become a general term used by strategists to describe the methods used to prevent an expanding great power from flexing its military muscles.

The strategic situation for China is at a crossroads. At this historical juncture, it is certain that if China's vigorous rearmament and force-modernization program, inspired by reawakened nationalist pride, continue, China's arsenal will position it to play a dominant military role in Asia and the entire world. Napoleon Bonaparte counseled in the early nineteenth century that the world should "let China sleep" because, he predicted, when China awakens, "the world will tremble." China has now awakened.

Japan's Search for a Strategy

Japan is now an economic superpower—the second richest country on earth, just behind the United States (see Table 13.1). At the start of the year 2000, its citizens enjoyed an average income far exceeding that of the average American. Yet Japan's dramatic ascent since 1950 has not been accompanied by a corresponding rise in global political and strategic weight. Since its defeat in World War II, Japan has strictly adhered to the guidelines of the **Yoshida Doctrine,** in which Prime Minister Shigeru Yoshida argued that Japanese security policy should avoid international disputes, keep a low profile on divisive global issues, and concentrate on economic pursuits.

■ **Yoshida Doctrine**
a security policy proposing that Japan should avoid international disputes, keep a low profile on divisive global issues, and concentrate on economic pursuits.

That preference continues to underlie the style behind most of Japan's strategic statements. But the new international setting has called into question the wisdom of this traditional posture—especially in light of the transformed distribution of power, with Russia's power having fallen, China's on the rise, and America's remaining predominant in the wake of the mid-1990s economic recovery. Particularly since America seems reluctant to lead in global governance, a larger Japanese role and presence are imminent, and are now being expressed.

Prime Minister Kiichi Miyazawa's policy departures in 1992 signaled a new direction for Japan's security policies. Miyazawa won passage of the Peacekeeping Operations Bill, which enabled Japan to deploy a self-defense force to participate in UN peacekeeping operations in Cambodia in 1992—the first use of Japanese armed forces abroad since World War II. Japan's acceptance of a large increase in its previous UN dues (over 20 percent in 2000), its push for inclusion as a permanent member of the UN Security Council, and its rise to the top of the world's foreign aid donors also suggest growing Japanese international activism. Such policies continued in 2000 under Prime Minister Keizo Obuchi, who set out to reverse his country's long, painful economic decline in the 1990s with bold economic reforms.

Japan seeks to discard its isolation and become an involved player in world affairs. Its rising defense expenditures and efforts to cement cordial relations with its Asian neighbors also speak to this redirection. Japan in 2000 still adhered to the policy of spending no more than 1 percent of its gross national product on defense, and remained committed to its postwar constitution, which forbids remilitarization. However, after a half-century of strict pacifism, alarmed that its neighbors' arms races are disrupting the Asian balance of power, and jittery over North Korea's launch of a three-stage long-range missile over Japan in August 1998, Japan is reconsidering how military might can contribute to national security and global standing. Japan's Self-Defense Force is impressive, with 235,000 soldiers in uniform and the Pacific's largest navy. Although it does not have advanced offensive weapons such as long-range bombers and aircraft carriers, Japan has seventeen of the most sophisticated submarines in the world. "Most analysts say that although Japan's air force and navy are numerically inferior to China's, they are more potent and will remain so for at least the next ten or twenty years" (M. Richardson 1995).

This shift in strategy worries its neighbors, who remember well Japan's history as a feared military power. Postwar Japanese pacifism could, with this military clout, give way to resurgent militarism aimed at its simmering territorial disputes with both Russia and China. Regardless of the future use of this military power, Japan faces a wide range of security concerns, which would intensify if the troubled situation in northeast Asia (especially North Korea) worsened or the United States reduced its presence in Asia. These fears are likely to prompt continuing Japanese participation in the growing Asian arms race, providing it can engineer a new era of economic expansion to regain worldwide recognition as a twenty-first-century economic powerhouse.

Predictions about Japan's emergence as a global military power with global ambitions must be offset by the reality of other restraints. The Japanese government's official projections estimate that Japan's population of 126 million in 2000 will tumble rapidly, with the "birth dearth" reducing the population to 100 million in 2050 and 67 million in 2100. Add to that the problem of Japan's continuing reliance on its fifty-three accident-prone nuclear-power processing plants for one-third of its energy, and the prospect of Japan playing a larger military role dims. Given this reality, Japanese defense planners have adapted the country's national security policies to changing global circumstances in several ways. First, Japan's security strategy seeks to further tie the country into the web of global institutions (the UN, the WTO, the G-8) on which it increasingly has depended for preservation of the global order that has made its prosperity possible. In the meantime, Japan has stepped up its efforts to lead in foreign assistance to developing Global South countries; it perceives the poor's advancement as profitable investment in its own. Japan similarly seeks to tie its security closer to America's, agreeing in 1997 to a new mutual defense treaty requiring Japanese troops to march with American troops in operations to keep the peace, and in 1999 beefing up that military alliance treaty by giving Japanese forces new authority to provide logistic support to U.S. combat forces in the vaguely defined "area around Japan." A combination of bilateralism and multilateralism have thus replaced Japan's traditional preference for unilateralism in foreign affairs.

More problematically, with its neighbors arming to the teeth, Japan has begun to have second thoughts about nuclear weapons. It balked at the Clinton administration's attempt to press for a Japanese commitment to support the indefinite and unconditional extension of the nuclear nonproliferation treaty, especially in light of the United States opening the path to nuclear weapons testing and ballistic-missile defense, which gives Japan a green light to proceed with its plans to put its own spy satellite in orbit and begin research on a planned Star Wars ballistic missile defense system. This symbolic reversal of Japanese doctrine signals the possibility of a radical departure in Japan's posture toward its future military role in the world. Indeed, as **neorealists** argue, it is extremely unlikely that Japan will refuse to develop military capabilities commensurate with its economic power and political ambitions.

neorealism the "new" version of realist theory which maintains that the distribution of military capabilities that defines the global system's structure, or its balance of power, determines the strategies of competitive states in that system.

Germany and the European Union Search for a Strategic Vision

Now united, Germany is likely to show signs of a new assertiveness once the immense costs of reunification and rebuilding the former German Democratic Republic are fully digested. Given its size, economic strength, and geographic location, the challenge for Europeans will be to find a way to absorb Germany within a broad European power-sharing arrangement. According to some analysts, however, Germany is too powerful to disappear into a wider European framework. It already accounts for almost one-half of the European Union's (EU) gross national product. In addition, its share of the EU budget is twice the amount of Great Britain and France combined. Moreover, most European states' economies are heavily linked to Germany's economy and trade, thereby giving Germany enormous leverage over the continent's economic growth. This extraordinary economic clout ensures Germany's continued dominance within any emergent amalgamated European political entity, whether it is built around the federalist idea of a supranational government or some other, more modest pan-European institutional structure. In either case, there is no set of states in the EU capable of balancing the power of a united Germany. "Too big for Europe, too small for the world" describes Germany's place in continental affairs.

If Germany's economic strength and diplomatic independence continue to grow, one consequence will be greater competition with the United States and other trade rivals. Yet this is not likely to result in a renewed push to flex German military muscle—even though Germany has one of the largest armies in Europe. Despite the parliamentary amendment to Germany's constitution, which permitted German troops to take part in international peacekeeping operations (for example, Germany's armed forces made up the second biggest contingent in NATO's 1999 peace force in Kosovo), an independent German military presence on the world stage is unlikely. Renewed militarism is even less so. Germany's armed forces are still deeply entrenched in and constrained by the joint command in NATO, the EU's joint Eurocorps armed force, and its mutual Franco-German force structure. Because Germany remains a fervent advocate of the nuclear nonproliferation regime, economic rivalry is unlikely to culminate in an arms build-up in the foreseeable future. Total European military spending is still only 60 percent of the U.S. allocation, and the billions of dollars required for the EU to catch up with U.S. military technology stand as an enormous obstacle to the ability of a European force to act unilaterally without U.S. support through NATO.

Germany likely will continue its effort to push for **collective security** with the military divisions it has created to assist multinational peacemaking units, both within Europe and globally. The drive to become a permanent member of the UN Security Council speaks to Germany's emphasis on multilateral approaches to international security; its armed force of 352,000 soldiers addresses its abiding desire to be prepared for defense. Similarly, Germany's continuing inclination to rely on the United States and NATO for a nuclear guarantee reveals a preference for cooperative partnership in international security, even as fears that the United States may not always respond has made Germany prepare to shoulder Europe's post-2000 military burden. Consciousness of its muscle and newfound status does not mean that Germany will unilaterally seek to "go it alone" in international affairs. Its heart is "Euroland," where Germany's fate and fortune most depend. German leaders "have preferred to treat the cynical pleasures of realpolitik with suspicion and to believe that foreign policy could and should be grounded in defense of virtuous principles such as democracy, self-determination, free trade, and human rights" (*Economist*, September 20, 1993). Germany's strategic approach is to reach out to Europe and to look inward to concentrate on domestic problems, consistent with the **Third Way** philosophy it shares with Great Britain and France:

> Germany is striving to project its brand of "soft power" across the continent. It has taken the lead in sponsoring early membership in the European

collective security
an agreement among states to act as allies in order to militarily prevent an aggressor from waging war (see p. 559).

Third Way
an approach to twenty-first-century governance advocated primarily by European leaders such as British Prime Minister Tony Blair and France's Socialist Prime Minister Lionel Jostin who, while recognizing few alternatives to liberal capitalism, seek to soften the cruel social impact of free-market individualism by reducing military expenditures and the deprivations caused by changes in the global economy (see p. 186).

> Union for Poland, Hungary, and the Czech Republic, a mammoth aid and a political initiative to end the long-running war between the Turkish Army and the Kurds. At the same time . . . German officials and foreign policy analysts insist [their aims] are rooted less in a grand design to stretch the clout of Berlin than in a defensive reaction to fears that turmoil among eastern neighbors will provoke a massive influx of refugees and immigrants that could ultimately threaten the future stability of Germany itself. German foreign policy these days is driven by a simple priority: to prevent poor foreigners from swamping our prosperous country," said Michael Stuermer, a former advisor to Mr. Schroeder's predecessor, Helmut Kohl. "Given the dangers of right-wing extremism, the idea is to do whatever is necessary to keep would-be immigrants from leaving their homes and heading for Germany." (Drozdiak 1999, 1)

Whatever the outcome, Europe—"a second federal, democratic superpower"—will undoubtedly be a growing force in world politics: "In the longer term, Euroland can—and probably will—look beyond its immediate borders. To be sure, it is not a military superpower like the United States, and may not be one for some time. But that reality is less significant than is often thought. The deployment of Euroland's mammoth economic resources can have a strategic impact" (Elliott 1998). Thus, a strong German aversion to militarism persists and is likely to shape Germany's security policies well into the twenty-first century. In this regard, German defense strategy differs from the posture the other great powers have assumed.

liberal institutionalism the neoliberal theory in international relations that advocates creating global institutions to promote peace and security among states.

What is more, Germany remains the most enthusiastic supporter of integration and institutional approaches to the preservation of peace. Its security strategy subscribes unflinchingly to the tenets of **liberal institutionalism:** Germany has cast its fate on the spread of international organizations, European unification, international law, disarmament, and the promotion of democracy, free markets, and free trade as the most effective strategy for assuring that a twenty-first century peace will prevail. In that sense, Germany is the leading proponent of the EU's quest to forge a common security policy. There are both dangers and opportunities embedded in that commitment, because by embracing the EU's uniform defense position Germany has cast its fate with the EU's acceptance of NATO's nuclear posture, and has aligned itself with the EU's December 1999 decision to build its own military. With Germany's support, the EU took a big step as a unitary actor by beginning plans to build a substantial military machine to secure the capacity for autonomous action in order to sever the EU's dependence on U.S. might and technology (see Medley 1999). That commitment was made concrete when the EU gave its blessing to creation of an all-European expeditionary force of 60,000 soldiers to carry out decisions made by the EU (over protest by the United States that the European Rapid Reaction Force would reduce the need for NATO and would undermine the U.S.-European alliance). Despite U.S. objections, Europe is proceeding with its strategic vision, aiming to no longer be dependent on U.S. missiles for defense.

The core group of EU, NATO, and OSCE countries see nuclear weapons as legitimate and NATO's first use of nuclear weapons doctrine to deter an attack as necessary. The wisdom or folly of Germany's strategy—and the EU's bid to become a military power—will be tested by the consequences that flow from the "nuclearization" of the EU's approach to national security.

THE SEARCH FOR SECURITY IN AN INSECURE WORLD

Preparation for war continues to command support from defense planners as an approach to peace. Rationalized by realism, the quest is understandable in a world where states alone remain responsible for their own self-defense. As President Eisenhower once noted, "until war is eliminated from international relations, unpreparedness for it is well nigh as criminal as war itself."

The fears produced by visions of national vulnerability also explain why many defense planners base their plans on worst-case analyses of others' capabilities and intentions. The urge to arm is further stimulated by defense planners' influence in the policy-making process of most countries and the tendency of political leaders to adopt the vocabulary and concepts of their military advisers. A new arms race appears to be underway at the start of the new millennium.

Asking whether military preparedness endangers, rather than ensures, national security raises an uncomfortable question that challenges the prevailing approach to national security throughout much of the world's history. Yet many experts believe such questioning is justified. To their way of thinking, now that fears of great-power war have receded, the economic and ecological dimensions of national security have assumed relatively greater prominence, and in the twenty-first century "security" should be defined more broadly so as to include both military and nonmilitary threats to human survival. Consider the argument made on behalf of a new definition of "national security":

> The concept of "security" must include protection against all major threats to human survival and well-being, not just military threats. Until now, "security"—usually addressed as "national security"—has meant the maintenance of strong military defenses against enemy invasion and attack. This approach may have served us well in the past, when such attack was seen as the only real threat to national survival; today, however, when airborne poisons released by nuclear and chemical accidents can produce widespread death and sickness (as occurred with the Bhopal and Chernobyl disasters), and when global epidemiological and environmental hazards such as AIDS and the "greenhouse effect" can jeopardize the well-being of the entire planet, this perspective appears increasingly obsolete. As individual economies become ever more enmeshed in the world economy, moreover, every society becomes more vulnerable to a global economic crisis. And, as modern telecommunications bring us all closer together, we are made acutely aware of the pain and suffering of those living under oppression, tyranny, and injustice.
>
> Given the fact that our individual security and well-being will depend to an ever-increasing extent on the world's success in mastering complex political, economic, environmental, and epidemiological problems, we must redefine "security" to embrace all of those efforts taken to enhance the long-term health and welfare of the human family. Defense against military aggression will obviously remain a vital component of security, but it must be joined by defenses against severe environmental degradation, worldwide economic crisis, and massive human suffering. Only by approaching the security dilemma from this multifaceted perspective can we develop the strategies and instruments that will be needed to promote global health and stability.

> Given the multiplicity of pressing world hazards, the concept of "national security" must be integrated with that of "world security." Until now, most people have tended to rely on the nation-state to provide protection against external threats, and have viewed their own nation's security as being adversely affected by the acquisition of power and wealth of other nations. Thus, in the interests of "national security," nation-states have often engaged in a competitive struggle to enhance their own economic and military strength at the expense of other nations' capabilities. This us-versus-them, zero-sum competition for security is naturally biased toward unilateral solutions to critical problems, frequently entailing military and/or economic coercion. In today's interdependent world, however, the quest for security is rapidly becoming a positive-sum process, whereby national well-being is achieved jointly by all countries—or not at all. (Klare and Thomas 1991, 3)

Approaches to the study of national security now frequently advocate putting these nonmilitary dimensions of the problem into the picture (for example, Shultz, Godson, and Quester 1997). At issue is whether this new way of organizing perceptions of national security is an idea whose time has come.

It is an idea certain to be given close scrutiny, because a wide spectrum of problems has risen on political agendas, and the concerns of today's foreign policymakers are arguably different and more diverse than they were just a short time ago. Former U.S. Assistant Secretary of Defense Joseph Nye (2001) argues, "Power in the twenty-first century will depend on economic growth and mastering the information revolution, not on the brute nuclear force of the twentieth century. Nuclear weapons are not a power equalizer, and they cannot be used to blast one's way into an imagined great power club." Though the danger of nuclear weapons and inter- and intrastate warfare continues, it would be foolish to neglect the dangers posed by such emergent threats as trade-bloc competition, neomercantilism, trade protectionism, the continuing impoverishment of the least developed countries, acid rain, deforestation, global warming, soaring population growth, the AIDS epidemic, international narcotic trafficking, the depletion of the earth's finite resources, and destruction of its protective ozone layer. These nonmilitary threats must command attention, as human survival may depend on addressing them.

However, the critical questions in an age of vulnerability to annihilation persist: How can states escape the prospect of destruction? How can they meet these emergent nonmilitary threats when the threat of warfare in a nationalistic age remains as pervasive as ever?

■ **common security** a concept advocating replacing the notion of states competing with one another for their own national security with collective security to promote the security of all states.

The security situation of the twenty-first century is unlikely to provide much room for maneuver. The world has yet to accept **common security** and nonoffensive defense, strategies that would eliminate offensive capabilities (Møller 1992). As demonstrated in the next chapter, many states still build weapons of attack for deterrence, even though conventional deterrence has failed frequently in the past. Moreover, contemporary deterrence theory remains based on the almost illogical premise that successful defense requires the continuing vulnerability of all states. Nonetheless, most believe that the threat system must be preserved to counter the threat, and put more faith in the realist belief that for disputes to be resolved successfully it is safer to rely on the force of arms than on the force of arguments.

Thus, security may depend as much on the control of force as on its pursuit. The next chapter examines the ways in which national leaders put armaments and arsenals to use for purposes of coercive diplomacy. It then evaluates the effectiveness of the bargaining strategies of coercive diplomacy on which states rely to defend themselves and to exercise influence over others.

KEY TERMS

national security
power
politics
power potential
realism
globalization
coercive diplomacy
opportunity costs
peace dividend
soft power
hard power
arms race
military-industrial complex
strategic stockpile
multiple independently targetable reentry vehicles (MIRVs)
nonlethal weapons
revolution in military technology (RMT)
smart bombs
firebreak
strategic weapons
virtual nuclear arsenals
deterrence
information warfare (IW) or infowar tactics
counterfactual reasoning
proliferation
Nth country problem
horizontal nuclear proliferation
vertical nuclear proliferation
chain reaction arms race cycle
nonproliferation
Nuclear Nonproliferation Treaty (NPT)
relative burden of military spending
defense conversion
human security
guns versus growth
human development
unilateral
multilateral
bilateral
multipolar
zero-sum
selective engagement
engagement and enlargement strategy
democratic peace
power transition
no first use
suzerainty
appeasement
containment
Yoshida Doctrine
neorealism
collective security
Third Way
liberal institutionalism
common security

SUGGESTED READING

Art, Robert J. "Geopolitics Updated: The Strategy of Selective Engagement," *International Security* 23 (Winter 1999): 79–113.

Beckman, Peter R., et al. *The Nuclear Predicament: Nuclear Weapons in the Twenty-First Century.* Upper Saddle River, N.J.: Prentice-Hall, 2000.

Buzan, Barry, and Eric Herring. *The Arms Dynamic in World Politics.* Boulder, Colo: Lynne Rienner, 1999.

Buzan, Barry, Ole Waever, and Jaap de Wilde. *Security: A New Framework for Analysis.* Boulder, Colo.: Lynne Rienner, 1999.

Craft, Cassady. *Weapons for Peace, Weapons for War: The Effect of Arms Transfers on War Outbreak, Involvement, and Outcomes.* New York: Routledge, 1999.

Klare, Michael T., and Yogesh Chandrani, eds. *World Security: Challenges for a New Century,* 3rd ed. New York: St. Martin's Press, 1998.

Knopf, Jeffrey W., ed. *The Nonproliferation Review,* a quarterly journal concerned with the causes, consequences, and control of the spread of weapons of mass destruction. Boulder, Colo.: Lynne Rienner.

Mutimer, David. *The Weapons State: Proliferation and the Framing of Security.* Boulder, Colo.: Lynne Rienner, 1999.

O'Hanlon, Michael. *Technological Change and the Future of Warfare.* Washington, D.C.: Brookings Institution, 1999.

Powell, Robert. *In the Shadow of Power: States and Strategies in International Politics.* Princeton, N.J.: Princeton University Press, 2000.

Ralph, Jason G. *Beyond the Security Dilemma.* Brookfield, Vt.: Ashgate, 2001.

Rosecrance, Richard. *The Rise of the Virtual State: Wealth and Power in the Coming Century.* New York: Basic Books, 1999.

Schell, Jonathan. "The Unfinished Twentieth Century: What We Have Forgotten about Nuclear Weapons," *Harper's* 300 (January 2000): 41–56.

Snyder, Craig A., ed. *Contemporary Security and Strategy.* New York: Routledge, 1999.

Weldes, Jutta, Mark Laffey, Hugh Gusterson, and Raymond Duvall, eds. *Cultures of Insecurity: States, Communities, and the Production of Danger.* Minneapolis: University of Minnesota Press, 2000.

WHERE ON THE WORLD WIDE WEB?

Arms Sales Monitoring Project
http://www.fas.org/asmp/

Concerned with the global production and trade of weapons, the Federation of American Scientists is monitoring arms transfers and making data available to the public through this Web site. Click on the U.S. Arms Sales Table. Which country is the biggest recipient of U.S. arms sales? See what was sold to whom and for how much. Why do you think that certain countries got freebies?

The Henry L. Stimson Center
http://www.stimson.org/index.html

The Henry L. Stimson Center is a nonprofit, nonpartisan research center that concentrates on the intersection of national and international security policy and technology. It provides information on chemical and biological weapons, nuclear proliferation, and missile defense systems. It houses important international agreements and searches for ways to eliminate weapons of mass destruction. An excellent site for timely information.

International Code of Conduct on Arms Transfers
http://www.basicint.org/codeindx.htm

The British American Security Information Council (BASIC) is an independent research organization that analyzes government policies and promotes public awareness of defense, disarmament, military strategy, and nuclear policies. Since the United States and the Great Britain are the suppliers of 80 percent of the world light arms trade, BASIC's main goal is to petition the United States and Great Britain to create controls for weapons transfers. Visit this Web site to explore arms transfers and learn about initiatives such as Codes of Conduct, International Action Network on Small Arms, Illicit Weapons Trafficking, and Arms Brokering.

Military Spending Clock
http://www.cdi.org/sc/javaclock.html

The Center for Defense Information, a nonprofit organization, has created a military spending clock. See what the U.S. government has spent on the military to date this year. See how much is spent every second or per day and per week.

National Commission for Economic Conversion and Disarmament
http://www.webcom.com/ncecd/

The National Commission for Economic Conversion and Disarmament is a nonprofit public organization dedicated to public education on the need to and ways to transfer military resources to civilian use. This Web site gives information on the costs associated with arms manufacturing and how monies can be better spent in other ways. Read the article comparing the exporting of arms to "green technologies" in the Fact Sheets or compare corporations and their conversion records. What is Washington's stance on this issue?

SIPRI Military Expenditure Country Graphs
http://sipri.se/projects/Milex/Introduction.html

The Stockholm International Peace Research Institute (SIPRI) monitors trends in military expenditures throughout the world. Its Web site lets you compare military expenditures and evaluate the economic burdens they pose. Choose a country from the Middle East, Far East, and Africa. How does their military spending compare to that of European countries? What conclusions can you draw?

CHAPTER 14

Coercive Diplomacy and Intervention in a World of Vanishing Borders

TOPICS AND THEMES

- Coercive diplomacy as a necessary and widespread practice
- The security dilemma
- Nuclear deterrence and defense
- Conventional armed force and the future of deterrence
- Sanctions as instruments of coercion
- Diplomatic negotiation in lieu of coercion?

- **CONTROVERSY** IS IT ETHICAL TO WAGE WAR IN ORDER TO MAKE PEACE?

Iraq under trade sanctions

All diplomacy is a continuation of war by other means.

—Chou En-Lai, premier, The People's Republic of China, 1954

[The twentieth] century has been the bloodiest in history. Over 160 million human beings have been killed in various conflicts, and that number rises each day. It is a dark history, but unless we look at it and seek to learn from it, it will only get darker.

—Robert S. McNamara, former U.S. secretary of defense, 1999

The world is a confusing place, in which states often clash over conflicting national interests. Interstate discord colors visions of contemporary international realities as countries struggle to survive and to sort out the values that should guide their policies. Unfortunately, tensions often exist between principles and power, and the chaotic globe presents many dilemmas about how to pursue ideals and protect national interests. Global politics seldom transpires according to religious creeds and high ideals. It is because the world is so confusing that so many countries, even the great powers, appear to flounder in their efforts to deal with the multiple issues on the global agenda, as they pursue not a single policy but many policies simultaneously. Those multiple policies often lack consistency and frequently appear to work at cross-purposes.

THE PLACE OF COERCIVE DIPLOMACY IN WORLD POLITICS

Picking sides in interstate competition and responding to international crises has never been easy, which is why the German philosopher Hegel once wrote that "We learn from history that men learn nothing from history." "Hegel's wisdom aside," observed journalist Carl Rowan (1999), "there are not and never have been clear and easy lessons from history on matters that involve curbing the violent and ugly side of man's nature. That is why the United States faces what [President Bill Clinton] called 'a lot of bad alternatives.' In every generation or time, leaders and peoples are required to make hard new judgments as to how much risk they will take." Making a rational choice among unsatisfactory options is never easy, but, arguably, is now more challenging in the complex age of globalization than it has been in any previous era of history.

The challenge of making rational calculations of costs and benefits of alternative policy options was vividly illustrated when the United States and Europe were put to the test of deciding what to do about Serbian dictator Slobodan Milosevic's campaign of **ethnic cleansing** against the Kosovar Albanians, over a million of whom had become refugees and **displaced people.** In Kosovo in 1999, the world community had to confront its ideals. Doing nothing was a tempting option advocated by isolationists. But that choice was rejected when the North Atlantic Treaty Organization (NATO) reached the historic decision to intervene, for the first time in its fifty-year history, by attacking a sovereign state. U.S. President Clinton outlined the **Clinton Doctrine** that rationalized this intervention, declaring, "Whether you live in Africa or Central Europe or any other place, if somebody comes after innocent civilians and tries to kill them because of their race, their ethnic background or their religion, and it's within our power to stop it, we will stop it." British Prime Minister Tony Blair echoed this approach, labeling the NATO campaign to end Milosevic's brutal mass murder of the Kosovar Albanians "a just war" and announcing that "there is no alternative to continuing until we succeed." Kosovo became the acid test for the **Third Way** approach of Western leaders (see Dahrendorf 1999) who struggled to delineate the moral principles that could guide where, how, and when strategic intervention for humanitarian purposes should be undertaken. Kosovo set a precedent because, as President Vaclav Havel of the Czech Republic noted in June 1999, "This is probably the first war that has not been waged in the name of 'national interests' but rather in the name of principles and values. . . . Kosovo has no oil fields to be coveted; no member nation in the alliance [NATO] has any territorial demands on Kosovo. . . . It is fighting out of concern for the fate of others. It is fighting because no decent person can stand by and watch the systematic state-directed murder of other people."

That said, no sooner had the seventy-eight-day, around-the-clock bombing of Yugoslavia that forced a cease-fire been concluded (and Milosevic had become the first serving head of state to be indicted for war crimes) than resistance to the future use of **coercive diplomacy** through military intervention began to mount. Critics began to voice loud opposition to United Nations (UN) Secretary-General Kofi Annan's call for "a new commitment to intervention" because "massive and systematic violation of human rights—wherever they might take place—should not be allowed to stand." Humanitarian intervention may be a moral imperative, given the kinds of horrors taking place throughout much of the world. But others—especially those schooled in realism—do not see it that way and reject moral crusades, arguing instead only for interventions that directly serve countries' vital national interests. The global community faces many hard choices in an era of humanitarian emergencies full of complexities and contradictions, which is why "there is no consensus . . . on the need to intervene in the case of gross human rights violations" (Rieff 1999).

ethnic cleansing the mass murder of an ethnic minority group by the state, in violation of international law (see p. 211).

displaced people persecuted groups who are involuntarily uprooted from their homes but still living in their own countries (see p. 216).

Clinton Doctrine a policy of active engagement in world affairs, including the use of military intervention to prevent genocide, pledging the United States to seek the enlargement of the peaceful liberal democratic community.

Third Way an approach to governance advocated primarily by European leaders such as British Prime Minister Tony Blair and France's Socialist Prime Minister Lionel Jostin who, while recognizing few alternatives to liberal capitalism, seek to soften the cruel social impact of free-market individualism and gross human rights violations such as genocide by progressively allowing government intervention to preserve social justice and the rights of individuals to freedom from fear (see p. 186).

coercive diplomacy an approach to bargaining between states engaged in a crisis in which threats or the use of limited force are made to force an adversary to reach a compromise.

Resistance to Intervention Moral imperatives may need moral pioneers, but when a great power attempts to break down the barrier of sovereign borders by intervening for humanitarian purposes it can expect to encounter great resentment and resistance. Even the threat of military intervention by a great power in the internal affairs of another state will provoke stiff opposition in the target. Here, for example, following the Indonesian militia's rampage in East Timor after that territory voted for independence in 1999, protestors fearful of a U.S. intervention burned a U.S. flag in Jakarta. Elsewhere, wherever interventionist means of coercive diplomacy are used or threatened, opposition has produced protests.

Hence, world politics in the twenty-first century remains today, as in the past, torn by conflicting values about what steps should be taken against a state that attempts to do something illegal and immoral to others in order to get its way.

This chapter inspects the ways states and other transnational actors seek to survive, to prosper, and to get their way in a ruthless world where those with whom they must interact do not always play by the rules and are not always interested in behaving ethically. Instead, their primary motive is to get what they want—seeking, often, to (1) protect themselves from attack by others; (2) to persuade others to act contrary to their self-serving interests; and (3) to convince others to agree to contracts that are not to their advantage. This domain of everyday international behavior is called coercive diplomacy. In addition to diplomatic **negotiation** designed to settle disputes at the bargaining table, it involves the most newsworthy category of activities for defense, deterrence, and bargaining—the ways most people think that **politics** unfolds globally as states make attempts to get other actors to change their behavior against their will. The occasions are unavoidably common because negotiators' efforts to peacefully resolve conflicts often fail, and the actors then turn to coercive methods to get their way. How coercive diplomacy *should* be managed, however, poses a

■ **negotiation** the process and art of discussing and debating issues when a conflict arises, in order for the disputing parties to reach a mutually satisfactory compromise agreement to resolve the issue.

■ **politics** the exercise of influence (see p. 457).

series of difficult choices, because the ethics and practical payoffs of potential decisions are unclear. This chapter will concentrate on three arenas in world politics in which coercive diplomacy is especially prominent: strategic bargaining for nuclear deterrence, the place of conventional weapons in coercion and defense, and the use of economic sanctions as a policy instrument in bargaining. The prominence of these bargaining tactics is a product of the influential impact of weapons and economic resources in the equation that separates winners and losers in interstate competition. Their mismanagement is a primary reason for the frequency of war, as argued in the concluding coverage of negotiation as a method of dispute management.

We look first at armaments and their changing role in interstate bargaining. This factor is pivotal to the survival capacity of coercively competing states, because, as documented in Chapter 12, one of the most disquieting long-term global trends is the exponential increase in the destructiveness of warfare and its human toll. Preventing such human devastation is a primary security problem for all states—powerful and weak. As noted in Chapter 13, most state defense planners rely on **realism** and respond to the danger of foreign aggression by expanding their country's military capabilities. However, in and of themselves arms will not assure peace, no matter how awesome the arsenal. To understand the predicaments that arming for war can create, the chapter first introduces the security dilemma that states face, and then examines the strategies states construct to prevent others from using arsenals against them, as well as how they use their military and economic resources in **bargaining** to exercise influence over other global actors.

■ **realism**
an approach to world politics based on the assumption that all actors are naturally eager to compete, and that they see the acquisition of weapons as a means of winning against their rivals (see p. 457).

■ **bargaining**
negotiation by states to try to settle their disputes without actually resorting to armed force.

THE SECURITY DILEMMA

What breeds the competition between states that leads to preparation for war? The eighteenth-century French political philosopher Jean-Jacques Rousseau argued that "the state . . . always feels itself weak if there is another that is stronger. Its security and preservation demand that it make itself more powerful than its neighbors. It can increase, nourish, and exercise its power only at their expense. . . . Because the grandeur of the state is purely relative, it is forced to compare itself to that of the others. . . . It becomes small or great, weak or strong, according to whether its neighbor expands or contracts, becomes stronger or declines."

Concern for relative power derives from states' desire for self-preservation, national identity, freedom from the control of others, status, and wealth. They seek these under anarchical conditions that provide little protection from the hostile designs of others. Believing that their own strength will make them secure, many states attempt to build as much military might as their resources allow, often competing with one another in military capabilities.

Although states ostensibly arm for defensive purposes, their military might is often perceived as threatening. Alarmed, their neighbors are provoked to arm in response. Thus, as Rousseau observed, security is a relative phenomenon. Such fear and its reciprocated behaviors create a predicament known as the **security dilemma** (Herz 1951), defined as the consequences that result as "each

■ **security dilemma**
the chronic distrust that actors living under anarchy feel because, without sanctions or regulatory rules, rivals will do anything, including using aggression, to get ahead, with the result that all lose their security in a climate of mistrust (see p. 102).

party's power increments are matched by the others, and all wind up with no more security than when the vicious cycle began, along with the costs incurred in having acquired and having to maintain their power" (Snyder 1984).

Some scholars also describe the dynamics of this arms competition as the **spiral model** (Jervis 1976). The imagery is apt, as it captures the tendency of defense-enhancing efforts to result in escalating arms races that diminish the security of all. Sir Edward Grey, British foreign secretary before World War I, described this process well:

■ **spiral model**
a metaphor used to describe the tendency of efforts to enhance defense to result in escalating arms races.

> The increase in armaments, that is intended in each nation to produce consciousness of strength and a sense of security, does not produce these effects. On the contrary, it produces a consciousness of the strength of other nations and a sense of fear. Fear begets suspicion and distrust and evil imaginings of all sorts, til each government feels it would be criminal and a betrayal of its own country not to take every precaution, while every government regards every precaution of every other government as evidence of hostile intent. (Grey 1925, 92)

Although the security dilemma affects all states, leaders still refuse to accept vulnerability. Searching for strength, they often proceed from the assumptions that: (1) security is a function of power; (2) power is a function of military capability; and (3) military might is a measure of national greatness. Each of these suppositions is, of course, consistent with realpolitik.

Reformers in the liberal tradition question the logic by which states engage in competitive behavior that creates and sustains the security dilemma. To them, "the central theme of international relations is not evil but tragedy. States often share a common interest, but the structure of the situation prevents them from bringing about the mutually desired situation" (Jervis 1976).

To escape this predicament, reformers adhering to **neoliberalism** call for changes in customary approaches to the problem of national security. Seeing weapons as "indefensible" (Lifton and Falk 1982), they argue that unarmed or defenseless countries enjoy a flexibility in their foreign policies that their armed neighbors do not. They are freed from the responsibilities that military power imposes and do not have to incur the costs of acquiring it. Although these countries might have to live in the constant shadow of others' missiles, they can take comfort in knowing that they are not the targets of the missiles. Appropriate in this context is President John F. Kennedy's sober warning in 1963 that, in the event of another total war, regardless of how it might begin, those most heavily armed would automatically become primary targets and victims.

■ **neoliberalism**
proponents of institutional reforms in governance, law, and economics as substitutes for warfare as an instrument of coercive diplomacy (see p. 366).

Not surprisingly, realists are less than convinced by the liberals' views. Even if leaders and defense planners recognize the threats that arming for security provokes in others, they argue that international anarchy makes these threats inevitable. Because, by definition, there is no escaping a dilemma, the security dilemma explains why states sharing a common interest in security nonetheless engage in individual actions that prevent them from realizing it.

To understand how most states confront their lack of national security, we next describe the kinds of strategies they have created. We will first examine the ways the two leading military powers, the United States and the former Soviet Union, sought during the Cold War to prevent nuclear attack through their evolving strategic doctrines regarding **nuclear deterrence.** We will then look at the strategies that other less militarily powerful states have used for purposes of

■ **nuclear deterrence**
dissuading an adversary from attacking by threatening retaliation with nuclear weapons.

conventional deterrence—prevention of an attack with conventional, nonnuclear weapons. In pursuing these topics, although nuclear and conventional deterrence are often seen as the same, most theories of the former are guided by historical investigation of cases in the latter category (Harknett 1994). It is important to keep in mind the difference

> between strategic *nuclear deterrence* (the level at which the majority of the theorizing has occurred, at which the use of intercontinental thermonuclear weapons has been threatened, and at which deterrence is usually thought to have held) and *conventional* deterrence (the level that has received considerably less attention, at which, by definition, threats to use unconventional weapons of mass destruction are excluded, and at which deterrence, arguably, has been prone to fail). . . . The range of likely cost-benefit calculations shifts dramatically when the deterrent calculus of strategic nuclear warfare is compared with regional conventional conflict. (Haffa 1992, 9)

■ **conventional deterrence** dissuading an adversary from attacking by threatening retaliation with nonnuclear weapons.

NUCLEAR DETERRENCE AND DEFENSE

The dropping of the atomic bomb on Japan on August 6, 1945, is the most important event distinguishing pre– from post–World War II international politics. In the blinding flash of a single weapon and the shadow of its mushroom cloud, the international arena was transformed from a balance-of-power to a balance-of-terror system.

In the following decades, policymakers in the nuclear states had to grapple with two central policy questions: (1) whether they should use nuclear weapons; and (2) how to prevent others from using them. The search for answers has been critical, as the failure to deter a nuclear attack would result in unimaginable destruction.

The impact of a "limited" war with today's nuclear arms would not be limited. Studies of the immediate and delayed effects of nuclear war project a post-nuclear environment too terrifying to contemplate. In the aftermath of a nuclear attack, even in a short war using a tiny fraction of any country's nuclear warheads, life as we know it would cease. The planet would be uninhabitable, because a **nuclear winter** would result, with devastating consequences:

> As bad as the prompt and local effects of nuclear war would be—the delayed and global consequences might be much worse. . . . Forest fires ignited in such a war could generate enough smoke to obscure the sun and perturb the atmosphere over large areas. . . . That smoke from the burning of modern cities would provide a still more serious threat. . . . Provided cities were targeted, even a "small" nuclear war could have disastrous climatic consequences; a global war, . . . might lower average planetary temperatures by 15° to 20°C, darken the skies sufficiently to compromise green plant photosynthesis, produce a witches' brew of chemical and radioactive poisons, and significantly deplete the protective ozone layer. These effects, which had been almost wholly overlooked by the world's military establishments, [are] described as "nuclear winter." (Sagan and Turco 1993, 369)

■ **nuclear winter** the expected freeze that would occur in the earth's climate from the fallout of smoke and dust in the event nuclear weapons were used, blocking out sunlight and destroying plant and animal life that survived the original blast.

Hiroshima In the first true test of the awful destructive capabilities of atomic weapons on cities, American forces dropped an atomic bomb on Hiroshima on August 6, 1945, in an attempt to bring World War II to a speedy close. In an instant, what later became known as "the nuclear age" was ushered in and the Japanese city lay in ruins.

It has been estimated that "the missiles on board a single [U.S.] SLBM submarine may be enough to initiate nuclear winter" (Quester 1992)—enough to end human existence. To defense planners, this prospect makes utilizing nuclear weapons for military purposes unthinkable. To the extent that nuclear states appreciate this fact, the purpose of nuclear weapons is reduced to one objective—deterring external aggression. However, many defense planners still advocate the threat of launching a nuclear strike as a declared policy option for coercive bargaining with an adversary. Today, the wisdom of a so-called first strike strategy is increasingly questionable, because military strategists recognize that if an enemy does not believe that a sane nuclear arms state would actually use its weapons in retaliation against aggression, that threat is useless as a deterrent—a bluff lacking credibility. Some experts believe that the recent voluntary reductions in the great powers' nuclear inventories have been due to the recognition that nuclear weapons are not useful as instruments in coercive bargaining. Nonetheless, those nuclear arsenals remain substantial, for whatever purpose; if all the planned cuts in nuclear weapons are implemented, the world in the first decade of the twenty-first century would still have nuclear weapons with "over 700 times the explosive power used in the twentieth century's three major wars, which killed 44 million people" (Sivard 1996, 5).

The threat of nuclear war was, and remains, particularly pertinent to the United States and Russia, today's two most heavily armed nuclear powers. Their decisions during the Cold War—the formative period that still casts its shadow on defense planning—shaped strategic thinking and doctrines both at home and elsewhere. In order to grasp the influence of past strategies on present ones, we need to first understand how the United States and the former Soviet Union used their most powerful weapons to deter each other. This will also allow us to understand the larger subject of which it is a part: how states view deterrence as a method of coercive diplomacy for **signaling**—making threats in order to intimidate a potential enemy from using its weapons aggressively.

■ **signaling**
in conflict situations, either explicit or implicit communication by states to reveal both their intentions and their capabilities.

Superpower Deterrence and Defense Policies

Although weapons of mass destruction have existed since World War II, the superpowers' postures toward them have evolved as technologies, defense needs, capabilities, and global conditions have changed. For analytical convenience, we can treat those postures in terms of three periods. The first began at the end of World War II and lasted until the **Cuban missile crisis.** U.S. nuclear superiority was the dominant characteristic of this period. The second began in 1962 and lasted until the breakup of the Soviet Union in 1991. Growing Soviet military capability was the dominant characteristic of this period (which meant that the United States no longer stood alone in its ability to annihilate another country). The third phase began in 1992, as the former Cold War antagonists and other rising great powers began to restructure their forces and revise their strategic doctrines. To better understand this new thinking, we will first examine the superpowers' strategic policies during the precedent-setting Cold War period.

■ **Cuban missile crisis**
the showdown in October 1962 between the United States and the Soviet Union over the deployment of Soviet missiles in Cuba.

Compellence, 1945–1962. Countries that enjoy military superiority often think of weapons as instruments for coercive bargaining—that is, as tools to be used for the political purpose of changing others' behavior. The United States, the world's first and, for many years, unchallenged nuclear power, was no exception. **Compellence** (Schelling 1966) described U.S. strategic doctrine when it enjoyed a clear-cut superiority in the nuclear balance of power. Compellence makes nuclear weapons instruments of political influence, used not for fighting but to get others to do what they might not otherwise do. Thus it refers to the use of nuclear weapons as instruments for "forceful persuasion" (George 1992), even if some question the ethics of a policy instrument that uses terror to pursue worthy ends such as peace (see Controversy: Is It Ethical to Wage War in Order to Make Peace?).

The United States sought to gain bargaining leverage after World War II by conveying the impression that it would actually use nuclear weapons. Its threatening posture regarding **commitments** in strategic negotiations was especially evident during the Eisenhower administration in the 1950s. To win political victories, Secretary of State John Foster Dulles practiced **brinkmanship,** deliberately threatening U.S. adversaries with nuclear destruction so that, at the brink of war, they would concede to U.S. demands.

Others went even further, seeing the new weapons of mass destruction as instruments for bargaining that could safely be used. For instance, to prevent the Soviets from also developing a hydrogen bomb, U.S. General Curtis Lemay, who would soon head the U.S. Strategic Air Command, in 1949 recommended "a nuclear Sunday punch," a preemptive strike against the Soviets. Lemay

■ **compellence**
a method of coercive diplomacy usually involving an act of war or threat to force an adversary to make concessions against its will.

■ **commitment**
a negotiator's promises during bargaining, designed to change the target's expectations about the negotiator's future behavior.

■ **brinkmanship**
the intentional, reckless taking of huge risks in bargaining with an enemy, such as threatening a nuclear attack, to compel submission.

CONTROVERSY

Is It Ethical to Wage War in Order to Make Peace?

The use of force is as old as human history. From the first recorded use of weapons by one society against another, people have debated the ethical criteria by which a **just war** can be waged without violating the principle that it is morally wrong to kill. That debate has continued in the modern state system, without a consensus emerging worldwide about the conditions under which it is morally acceptable to use armed force for political purposes. Experts in both defense and moral ethics remain divided as to the just means for containing aggression. International law, too, reflects this division of opinion (see Chapter 16).

Here we ask you to consider the controversies surrounding the ethics of peace making and peace enforcement through warfare. What do you think? Does peace sometimes require making war, or is warfare inherently evil? To frame the problem, we provide some historical examples that illustrate how policymakers have confronted these questions. Take into account first the American Civil War, in which the Union General William Tecumseh Sherman declared that "war is hell." To end the war, he sought to literally make it hell by pursuing a ruthless "march to the sea" in the American South, ravaging civilians and their communities to force surrender. To put an end to killing, Sherman believed that killing must be devastating. Only by making war terrifying, he felt, could surrender be hastened.

Many since have adopted Sherman's scorched-earth strategy to demoralize a hostile civilian population in order to subdue its army leaders. They believe that terrorism—the wanton destruction of property and people—is the most effective method of bringing an adversary to its knees.

But where does this practice to stop war end and barbarism begin? To some there are no moral limits: The ends justify the terrible means. The savagery, of course, can never be justified to its victims. Critics argue that such strategies, which overlook the traditional right of innocent noncombatants to protection from genocide, violate international law and are crimes against humanity. Classic Christian and other pacifist theologians also condemn the philosophy that condones evil methods, maintaining that a right intention does not automatically justify any means to achieve it.

The debate over the ethics of cruel destruction as a strategy arose again in the closing days of World War II. At the insistence of the head of the Allied Bomber Command, Sir Arthur "Bomber" Harris authorized the devastation of the demilitarized German city of Dresden, "roasting at least twenty-five thousand of its inhabitants in the notorious firestorm," under the conviction that "bombing German cities simply for the sake of increasing terror" and "gunning down people fleeing the burning city the morning after the British raid" would speed a German surrender. However, after the deliberate attack on "city-center churches and palaces packed with refugees," German resistance to the Allies intensified. The strategy of terrorism by flattening cities backfired: "A year of saturation bombing had not brought an uprising" against Hitler and the Nazi regime (Jenkins 1995).

Yet many defense planners feel strongly that mass destruction can produce surrender. For example, the necessity of shocking the Japanese into submission was foremost among President Harry S Truman's reasons for dropping the atomic bomb on Japan. (When informed about the plan to use the bomb to force Japan's leaders into an immediate unconditional surrender, General Dwight D. Eisenhower expressed "grave misgivings" about using this "horrible and destructive" weapon, which he saw as "completely unnecessary" [Ambrose 1995].)

---

just war
the theory originating in the Middle Ages that identifies the conditions under which it is morally permissible, or "just," for a state to go to war and the methods by which a just war might be fought.

wanted to send "an armada of planes, carrying the entire Los Alamos stockpile (numbering more than one hundred atom bombs) to destroy seventy Soviet cities" (Stengal 1995). With hydrogen weapons, the damage would have been even more devastating.

Brinkmanship was part of the overall U.S. strategic doctrine adopted by the Eisenhower administration. Known as **massive retaliation,** it advocated the use of nuclear weapons to contain communism and Soviet expansionism. Mas-

Nuclear Testing When informed of the possibility of designing a hydrogen bomb, U.S. President Truman asked, "What the hell are we waiting for?" Politicians hailed the nuclear weapon as a defensive force. However, scientists such as Robert Oppenheimer—who headed the Manhattan Project, which produced the atomic bomb—maintained that the hydrogen bomb was inherently immoral because it was a weapon of genocide that, unlike the atomic bomb, was so destructive that its use could not be restricted to military purposes. More than two thousand nuclear-weapons tests have occurred since 1945, and testing has continued. Pictured here is a 1995 French atomic test in the South Pacific of a nuclear bomb smaller than the hydrogen bomb that, in 1952, created a three-mile fireball one thousand times more powerful than the bombs used by the United States on Hiroshima and Nagasaki. In 1997, the forty-five states possessing nuclear reactors agreed to the Comprehensive Test Ban Treaty (CTBT). However, India and Pakistan conducted tests of nuclear weapons in 1998, which reduced the prospects for that treaty holding; then in October 1999, the U.S. Senate's refusal to ratify the CTBT posed a major obstacle to the treaty's entering into force.

sive retaliation was a **countervalue targeting strategy** because it aimed U.S. weapons at objects that the Soviets presumably valued most—their industrial and population centers. The alternative is a **counterforce targeting strategy,** which targets an enemy's military forces and weapons, thus sparing civilians from immediate destruction.

Massive retaliation and brinkmanship heightened Soviet fears. By 1949 the Soviet Union had broken the U.S. atomic monopoly. Thereafter, faced with U.S. belligerence, it pursued a twofold response. Following Nikita Khrushchev's rise to power in the mid-1950s, the Soviets ceased speaking of the usefulness of military power and instead pursued **peaceful coexistence** as an alternative nonmilitary strategy for continuing, by nonviolent economic and political means, the communist struggle with capitalism. Nonetheless, fearing that a nuclear exchange would destroy the Soviet Union but permit U.S. survival, Soviet leaders also expanded their nuclear arsenals. In 1957, the Soviet Union successfully

■ **massive retaliation** the Eisenhower administration's policy doctrine for containing Soviet communism by pledging to respond to any act of aggression with the most destructive capabilities available, including nuclear weapons.

■ **countervalue targeting strategy** the bargaining doctrine that declares the intention to use weapons of mass destruction against an enemy's most valued nonmilitary resources, such as the civilians and industries located in its cities.

■ **counterforce targeting strategy** targeting strategic nuclear weapons on particular military capabilities of an enemy's armed forces and arsenals.

■ **peaceful coexistence** the condition resulting from Soviet leader Nikita Khrushchev's doctrine in 1956 proclaiming that capitalist and communist states could compete economically for growth without war.

launched *Sputnik,* the world's first space satellite, demonstrating its potential ability to deliver nuclear weapons far beyond the Eurasian landmass. The superpowers' strategic competition thus took a new turn, as the United States for the first time began to face a credible military threat to its own geophysical security.

Mutual Deterrence, 1962–1983. As U.S. strategic superiority eroded, American policymakers began to question the usefulness of weapons of mass destruction for political bargaining, or for **peace enforcement** to coerce an adversary to stop fighting. They were horrified by the destruction that could result if compellence should provoke a nuclear exchange. In contrast to so-called **limited war,** waged without recourse to all weapons in a state's arsenal, the nearly suicidal Cuban missile crisis of 1962 dealt coercive diplomacy a serious blow, and undermined faith in **total war,** waged against an enemy's civilian population and economy to destroy its fighting spirit and capacity to continue. "With missiles, satellites and nuclear weapons, [it] was becoming recognized that there could be no return to the nineteenth-century belief that the military's first task is to keep war away from the country's civilians. In modern war, there are no civilians" (Drucker 1997). After the near-miss Cuban encounter, the objective of nuclear weapons shifted to preventing an attack. That is, strategic policy shifted from compellence to deterrence.

Both superpowers also pursued **extended deterrence,** protecting not only their homelands but also targets outside their adversary's defense perimeter and alliance network, to prevent an attack on their allies. Extended deterrence was especially critical to the United States, as its allies were far from its own shores and geographically close to the Soviet Union. The United States repeatedly declared that it would defend its allies. However, the credibility of its guarantee to the NATO countries in particular was often questioned. Former U.S. Secretary of State Henry Kissinger punctuated this doubt when he noted in 1979 that the U.S. promise to defend Europe with nuclear weapons involved "strategic assurances that we cannot possibly mean or if we do mean, we should not execute because if we should execute, we risk the destruction of civilization." The dubious credibility of the U.S. deterrent led some critics to advocate "decoupling" Europe from the U.S. strategic security umbrella and encouraging individual NATO countries to develop their own nuclear capabilities.

Ironically, the shift from compellence to deterrence stimulated rather than inhibited the U.S.-Soviet arms race. A deterrent strategy depends on the unquestionable ability to inflict unacceptable damage on an opponent. It requires a **second-strike capability** that enables a country to withstand an adversary's first strike and still retain the ability to retaliate with a devastating counterattack. To ensure a second-strike capability and an adversary's awareness of it, deterrence rationalized an unrestrained search for sophisticated retaliatory capabilities. Any system that could be built was built, because, as President Kennedy explained in 1961, "only when arms are sufficient beyond doubt can we be certain without doubt that they will never be employed."

To characterize the strategic balance that emerged during the 1960s and early 1970s, policymakers coined the phrase **mutual assured destruction (MAD).** It described the superpowers' essential military stalemate. Mutual deterrence, based on the principle of assured destruction, assumed the military potential for and psychological expectation of widespread death and destruc-

■ **peace enforcement**
military actions undertaken to impose a peace settlement, truce, or agreement to surrender by a warring party, or to prevent the resumption of fighting by the participants in a past war.

■ **limited war**
the restrained use of armed force, short of full-scale warfare, to obtain limited objectives.

■ **total war**
wars, such as World Wars I and II, fought with all available weapons to threaten an enemy's survival, as opposed to limited wars waged with restricted capabilities for specific objectives.

■ **extended deterrence**
strategies that seek to prevent an enemy from attacking a great power's allies, usually by pledges of retaliation (see p. 106).

■ **second-strike capability**
a state's capacity to retaliate after absorbing a first-strike attack with weapons of mass destruction.

■ **mutual assured destruction (MAD)**
a system of mutual deterrence in which both sides possess the ability to survive a first strike and launch a devastating retaliatory attack.

tion by both combatants in a nuclear exchange. Peace—or at least stability—was viewed as the product of mutual vulnerability, which was seen in turn as a precondition for successful deterrence. Each superpower sought to preserve the other's second-strike capability, trusting that neither would then dare to attack the other at the price of its own subsequent destruction.

As the United States and the Soviet Union competed with each other, the differences in their strategic capabilities narrowed. By the early 1970s a parity, or equality, developed in the two superpowers' capabilities, reinforcing the strategic assumptions of MAD. Thereafter, both armed not to gain superiority but to preserve a rough equivalence in their strategic arsenals.

The balance in the superpowers' arsenals laid the basis for negotiations on limiting strategic arms during the 1970s détente phase of the U.S.-Soviet rivalry. Two **Strategic Arms Limitation Talks (SALT)** agreements, both attempting to guarantee each superpower's second-strike capacity, were concluded during the 1970s. Although the pursuit of this shared goal posed difficulties, a precarious peace resulted. However, despite the superpowers' sometimes tacit, sometimes formal acceptance of the principles on which assured destruction rested, differences in their interpretation and practical application inevitably led to disagreements. As the strategic arms race continued into the 1980s, the concepts governing the competition began to revert from the principle of deterrence to the previous principle of compellence, which contemplated the actual use of nuclear weapons. Indeed, with superpower confrontation replacing cooperation, in the early 1980s a new debate raged regarding the role and purpose of nuclear weapons. Should nuclear weapons still be used exclusively for purposes of defense and deterrence? Or, assuming that a first-strike capability could be achieved, should they be used for offensive purposes?

■ **Strategic Arms Limitation Talks (SALT)**
the negotiations begun in 1969 between the United States and the USSR to freeze offensive weapons at existing levels and promote balanced, verifiable limits on strategic nuclear weapons (see p. 108).

Neither adversary had reason to trust the other. Each assumed that, unless deterred, its opponent would be tempted to use its arsenal for attack. As a result, bad faith and worst-case analyses governed the reformulation of strategic doctrines.

U.S. statements about the practicability of preemptive strikes and the "winnability" of a nuclear exchange alarmed the world. The atmosphere chilled as U.S. leaders spoke boldly of *damage limitation*. This concept was predicated on the belief that one way to avoid the destructive effects of nuclear weapons was to be the first to use them, destroying a portion of the adversary's weapons before they could be used in a retaliatory strike.

As U.S.-Soviet relations worsened, debate in the United States concerning the best way to protect national security with strategic weapons broke into polar positions. Although MAD continued to dominate the thinking of some, others advocated **nuclear utilization theory (NUTs),** an approach whereby nuclear weapons would not simply play a deterrent role, but could also be used in war. Such a posture was necessary, some U.S. policy advisers argued, because the Soviet Union was preparing to fight—and win—a nuclear war (Pipes 1977; c.f. Holloway 1983: Kennan 1984b). Furthermore, advocates of NUTs argued that use of nuclear weapons would not necessarily escalate to an unmanageable, all-out nuclear exchange. Instead, they reasoned that it was possible to fight a protracted "limited" nuclear war. By making nuclear weapons more usable, they argued, the United States could make nuclear threats more credible.

■ **nuclear utilization theory (NUTs)**
a body of strategic thought that claimed deterrent threats would be more credible if nuclear weapons were made more usable.

Proponents of MAD, on the other hand, held that deterrence remained the only sane purpose for nuclear weapons, and contended that any use of nuclear weapons—however limited initially—would surely escalate to an unrestrained exchange. "It is inconceivable to me," former U.S. Secretary of Defense Robert McNamara reflected, "that limited nuclear wars would remain limited—any decision to use nuclear weapons would imply a high probability of the same cataclysmic consequences as a total nuclear exchange." According to this view, the technical requirements necessary to wage a protracted limited nuclear war would surely exceed the human capacity to control it.

In addition, advocates of MAD felt that because the threatened use of even tactical nuclear weapons would lower the nuclear threshold, a nuclear strategy based on their utility in war made war more likely, thereby diminishing the weapons' deterrent capability. From this viewpoint, both superpowers were destined to live in a MAD world—even if, ironically, this meant remaining in the "mutual hostage relationship" in which their earlier weapons decisions had imprisoned them (Keeny and Panofsky 1981).

As the 1980s nuclear debate raged, U.S. and Soviet leaders both professed their commitment to avoiding nuclear war, viewing it as "unthinkable." This meant expanding the capabilities of both defensive and offensive systems. Thus each superpower continued developing and deploying the kinds of weapons that NUTs required—so-called discriminating low-yield nuclear weapons made possible by new technologies in guidance and precision. This weaponry prepared the contestants for warfare short of a massive, all-out nuclear attack and sought to provide them with effective deterrents against a conventional war.

This search for new weapons and new ideas to govern their use did little to calm fears, however. Instead, a vigorous peace movement swept Europe and North America, as mass publics on both sides of the Atlantic voiced their desire for an alternative to the threat posed by nuclear weapons. Accordingly, the purposes that NUTs strategists assigned nuclear arsenals fell into disfavor.

From Offense to Defense, 1983–1993. A new challenge to strategic thinking was launched in 1983, when U.S. President Reagan proposed building a space-based defensive shield against ballistic missiles. The **Strategic Defense Initiative (SDI),** as it was known officially, called for the development of a "Star Wars" ballistic missile defense (BMD) system using advanced space-based technologies to destroy offensive weapons launched in fear, anger, or by accident. The goal, as President Reagan defined it, was to make nuclear weapons "impotent and obsolete." Thus SDI sought to shift U.S. nuclear strategy away from reliance on offensive missiles to deterring attack—that is, away from dependence on MAD, which President Reagan deemed "morally unacceptable."

■ **Strategic Defense Initiative (SDI)**
the so-called Star Wars plan conceived by the Reagan administration to deploy an antiballistic missile system using space-based lasers that would destroy enemy nuclear missiles before they could enter the earth's atmosphere.

From the start, scientists questioned the feasibility of SDI's technological fix to the security dilemma posed by strategic weapons. There was simply no assurance that a reliable system was possible. Critics warned that the projected costs in excess of $140 billion for SDI were prohibitive and that SDI was dangerous, capable of inducing an unwarranted sense of safety, when in fact it "almost surely would not work in the event of an all-out attack." Critics also warned that SDI would stimulate development of a new generation of offensive weapons designed to overwhelm the defensive ones (Garwin 2000).

Despite this uncertainty and questionable legality, the United States continued to support SDI even after the end of the Cold War and the demise of the

Soviet Union. In the Bush administration's view, SDI still had a mission in providing "protection from limited ballistic missile assaults, whatever their source," rather than relying on "some abstract theory of deterrence." The Pentagon disagreed, pointing out the inability of a space-based system to protect against the many other ways that an enemy can deliver tactical weapons, including "short-range missiles or intermediate-range ballistic missiles that fly slightly depressed trajectories" (Fetter 1991), or even in a hand-carried suitcase.

This argument notwithstanding, the Star Wars era continued. As Lawrence J. Korb, formerly a defense secretary in the Reagan administration, complained:

> Republicans seem determined to spend additional funds [on] revival of the Strategic Defense Initiative, now known as National Missile Defense. Support for strategic defense has become a litmus test of loyalty to the Reagan legacy. . . . Thus, almost in lockstep, Republicans in Congress are voting to double the amount currently spent [on missile defense, seeking] to throw some $40 billion or $50 billion at a multisite continental defense system, although there are serious doubts about necessity and cost-effectiveness and although such a system would violate the 1972 Antiballistic Missile Treaty, negotiated by a Republican president. (Korb 1995b, 29–30)

The Shifting Strategic Situation

Thus, in some respects strategic thinking continues to rely on MAD principles, as the Clinton administration in 1998 planned to clear the way for developing advanced *high-altitude* theater missile defense (TMD) systems that would undercut the Antiballistic Missile (ABM) Treaty outlawing such strategic defenses. The Cold War, the third global conflict of the twentieth century, concluded without bloodshed. Some attributed this remarkable achievement to the effectiveness of the superpowers' deterrence strategies—the intimidating power of their weapons, which made aggression suicidal—and to the rationality of leaders, inspired by their awareness that survival was preferable to victory. Others believe that the superpowers averted apocalypse despite their awesome arsenals and deterrence doctrines rather than because of them. In fact, many of the critics of strategic nuclear deterrence (e.g., Johansen 1991; Vasquez 1991) complain that the doctrine's validity is suspect because deterrence is the nonoccurrence of an event and by definition depends on **counterfactual reasoning** that cannot be proven because they are not testable. According to this line of reasoning, "Although it can be argued that nuclear deterrence worked during the Cold War, we do not know that for sure. (The USSR may never have wished to invade Europe or to attack the United States with nuclear weapons.) It is very difficult to prove deterrent successes because that would require showing why an event did not occur" (Haffa 1992).

■ **counterfactual reasoning** thought experiments to consider the consequences that probably would have resulted had something happened that actually did not, such as speculating "What if Adolf Hitler had invaded Britain?" or "What if John F. Kennedy had not been assassinated?"

Regardless of its causes, the halt to the Cold War rivalry has ended the former adversaries' need to prepare for war against each other. In a radical change, they now perceive their interests as being served by *reducing* their armaments, not increasing them, thus signaling the start of a new age. Not long after Mikhail Gorbachev assumed power in the Soviet Union in 1985, and shortly after Reagan's Star Wars speech, the superpowers negotiated a series of dramatic new arms control agreements (see Chapter 15). Reduced fears of an attack in Europe stripped away the rationale for tactical nuclear weapons. As a result, the precedent-setting Intermediate-range Nuclear Forces (INF) Treaty, followed by the Conventional Armed Forces in Europe (CFE) agreement, and then the **START (Strategic Arms Reduction) Treaty** hastened the emergence of a strategic setting less menaced by the spectre of global warfare. In this new setting, the superpowers began to shift their strategies from nuclear deterrence to mutual safety.

■ **START (Strategic Arms Reduction) Treaty** the U.S.-Russian series of negotiations that began in 1993 and, with the 1997 START-III agreement ratified by Russia in April 2000, pledged to cut the nuclear arsenals of both sides by 80 percent of the Cold War peaks, in order to lower the risk of nuclear war by making a successful preemptive strike impossible (see p. 582).

The number of nuclear warheads worldwide has been reduced to less than 31,500 in 2000—a cut nearly in half from the peak in 1986 (see Figure 14.1). "Of these, about 20,000 are actively deployed, about 14,000 await eventual dismantlement, and the remainder are held in reserve" (*Vital Signs 1999,* 116). The United States retains 10,500 warheads, while Russia has 20,000. The other three long-standing nuclear powers—France, China and the United Kingdom, have little more than 1,000 warheads combined" (*Bulletin of the Atomic Scientists,* March/April 2000, 79). If the "deep cuts" pledged in the U.S. and Russian post-START agreements are completed in 2003 on schedule, the strategic nuclear **balance of power** in the twenty-first century would look radically different from that in the second half of the twentieth century. This will necessitate major rethinking of old assumptions underlying strategic **doctrines** defining the purposes to which weapons of mass destruction should be put.

■ **balance of power** the theory that peace and stability are most likely to be maintained when military power is distributed so that no single power or bloc can dominate the others (see p. 619).

■ **doctrine** the guidelines a great power adopts defining the conditions under which it will use military power and armed force for political purposes abroad.

Few expect a war between the great powers in the foreseeable future, although most expect wars to continue in the Global South. The great powers have sought to restructure their armed forces in order to cope with the kinds of threats and weapons with which adversaries will fight such wars. This invites additional reductions of nuclear (strategic) arsenals, U.S. help to the former Soviet republics to destroy their nuclear weapons, and collective great-power efforts to keep nuclear weapons out of the hands of aggressors. It also calls for increasing the capacity to wage conventional wars in emergent trouble spots. Military preparations have not ceased, but instead have been redirected toward short-term wars fought with increasingly sophisticated conventional weapons. The emerging strategies of the great powers now reflect their search for a new security architecture to contain regional conflicts and guard against the rising power of their rivals.

CONVENTIONAL FORCES AND THE FUTURE OF DETERRENCE

As noted in previous chapters, a number of states presently outside the circle of dominant military powers are striving to enter it, as India and Pakistan did in 1998. With ambitiously expanding armament programs, their quest for nuclear weapons and the potential collapse of the nonproliferation regime would radically transform the global security climate. Joseph Kruzel, a former U.S. defense expert who tragically lost his life in August 1995 while seeking to negotiate a peaceful solution to the warfare in the Balkans, wrote:

> Nuclear proliferation in other parts of the world must be reckoned as a high probability. The [U.S.] Central Intelligence Agency estimated that in

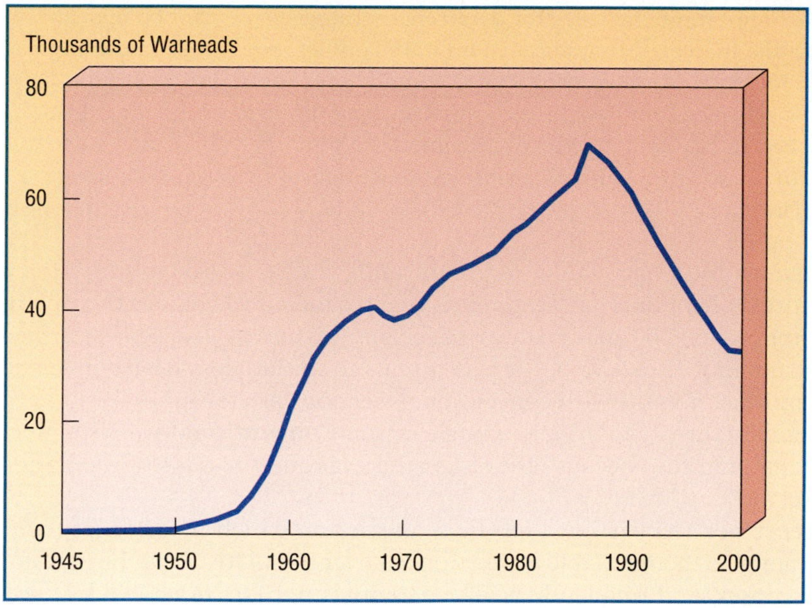

FIGURE 14.1
The Expansion and Reduction of Global Nuclear Arsenals since 1945

After addictively building inventories of nuclear weapons, the five major nuclear power states, led by the United States and Russia, have chosen to reduce the number of nuclear warheads deployed in their arsenals for strategic bargaining—to threaten, wage, or deter nuclear war. They no longer perceive huge inventories of these weapons of mass destruction as necessary for survival. It remains to be seen whether nuclear deterrence will continue, and whether technological advances will allow other kinds of weapons systems to keep the peace.

SOURCE: Robert S. Norris and William M. Arkin, adapted from their data on nuclear stockpiles as presented in the *Bulletin of the Atomic Scientists* 56 (March/April 2000), 79.

> the early 1990s over fifty countries were working on nuclear, chemical, or ballistic missile capabilities. By the end of the [twentieth] century, some number of these states will certainly develop operational weapons of mass destruction and the means to deliver them. Because nuclear forces could serve as an effective deterrent against retaliation by an outside state, more and more states may be inclined to see nuclear weapons as a serious military option. A nuclear-capable Azerbaijan, for example, could invade Armenia and present the world with a fait accompli backed by the threat of using its own nuclear weapons against any third party that would presume to meddle. (Kruzel 1993, 4)

By most assessments, controlling regional and ethnic violence is likely to provide the most compelling rationale for undertaking military action in the twenty-first century. The Global South is populated by many hypernationalist countries of growing military strength with an interest in controlling events in the areas where their primary security interests lie. This danger has increased the importance of conventional deterrence:

> The most important challenge for deterrence strategists may not be in dealing with the increased frequency of military conflict, but rather in dealing with an increased *variety* of sources of conflict. . . . Nationalist aspirations, religious cleavages, and resurgent authoritarian coups may all cut against established international political alignments. Now, and in the foreseeable future, the sources of war will have to be viewed across a variety of dimensions. (Harknett 1994, 102–103)

conventional war armed conflicts waged with nonnuclear naval, air, and ground weapons.

Many states today are failing or in turmoil, and perceive military force below the threshold of nuclear weapons as a viable means to achieve their political aims. Indeed, to the many states harboring historical grievances, armed coercion is a highly attractive option, as threats to initiate less destructive and less costly military actions with conventional weapons are far more likely to be believed than are threats to initiate a nuclear war. **Conventional war** is a more credible bargaining chip because the risks are lower and the odds of retaliation by the target also are lower.

low-intensity conflict (LIC) insurgency and counter-insurgency warfare fought with inexpensive conventional weapons that falls below the threshold of full-scale military combat between modern armies.

Deterrence is a risky game, and the strategies on which most states today depend do not give them reliable protection. Conventional force can be used for coercive purposes, and frequently is. The activity is not just practiced by weak states in the Global South; the use of conventional armed conflict short of war is a component of the great powers' bargaining strategies, as the **low-intensity conflict (LIC)** programs of the United States and others illustrate. In an interdependent world that is fraught with ethnic and religious rivalries, armed conflicts short of full-scale war are likely to erupt often, and great powers are likely to influence the outcomes of the conflicts with low-intensity bargaining tactics. Low-intensity conflict is now a symbol of warfare between the haves and have-nots, referring primarily to methods for combating terrorism, insurgency, and guerrilla activities in the Global South and failed states. Such warfare below the level of overt military operations by a state's regular army includes proxy wars, wars fought with mercenaries, psychological operations to terrorize a populace, and death squads. "What is crucial to recognize," notes Michael T. Klare (1988), "is that low-intensity conflict is a form of warfare in which your side suffers very little death or destruction, while the other side suffers as much damage as possible without producing undue hardship for your own society."

The methods through which coercive diplomacy is pursued are varied, for both deterrence and compellence. To bring about changes in other actors' behavior, states may rely on words and deeds, usually attempting to combine both. They talk tough by making threats and often act tough by using their military capabilities.

preventive diplomacy diplomatic actions taken in advance of a predictable crisis to prevent or limit violence.

It is difficult to generalize about the effectiveness of these strategies, which have worked in some situations but not others. Bargaining strategies depend on the issue, the reputation of the actor pursuing a strategy of coercive diplomacy, and the actor's commitment to its goals. The use of alternative strategies also varies with the purpose of the action. **Preventive diplomacy**—managing emergent threats by swiftly demonstrating intentions and capabilities—is one thing. The actual use of force in retaliation for acts deemed immoral, illegal, or threatening to national interests is another. Although those who initiate war often see it as a necessary instrument to pursuing national interests, it takes the game to a higher level. The escalation can either work or backfire. Consequently, the relationship between promises of rewards and military threats of destruction is complex. It works at times when the goal is war prevention as opposed to **peacekeeping** (stabilizing a threatening dispute) and peace enforcement (operations to keep terminated military hostilities from reigniting), and it fails at other times.

■ **peacekeeping** external programs by intervening forces such as UN volunteers to stabilize war-torn regions, usually with only modest resources and in ways that avoid labeling an aggressor or provoking the hostility of a great power (see p. 620).

Military Intervention

Making military threats to coerce others can be done in many forms at many levels. However, the most frequent practice is **military intervention**—sending troops onto others' territory in order to influence developments and policies there. Coercive diplomacy sometimes moves from talking to bombing, but more frequently involves sending arms, armies, and aircraft to foreign territory. Evidence suggests that this mode of coercive diplomacy has been common, if erratic, since World War II (see Figure 14.2). Altogether, nearly nine hundred individual acts of military intervention have been initiated since 1945; if the 2.4 million fatalities resulting from an average of nearly fifteen military interventions each year between 1945 and 1991 (Tillema 2001) are extrapolated, the human death-toll will exceed 3 million deaths early in the twenty-first century. Excluded from this estimate of state military interventions worldwide is an unknown number of additional **covert operations.** If these were included in the total, military interventionism would appear to be an even greater part of the way the world pictures interventionism in world affairs. That role seems destined to grow, given the rise of the use of mercenaries as "private military companies . . . working hand in glove with various governments to fight their wars in a businesslike manner" (Isenberg 2000).

■ **military intervention** overt or covert use of force by one or more countries that cross the borders of another country in order to affect the target country's government and policies.

■ **covert operations** secret activities undertaken by a state outside its borders through clandestine means to achieve specific political or military goals with respect to another.

Conceptualizing foreign overt military intervention as a form of international behavior "most closely associated with international war," Herbert Tillema (1989) includes as instances "battles involving regular foreign military forces, at least on one side" that seldom result in more than one thousand fatalities. Interventions thus include "military operations undertaken openly by a state's regular military forces within a specific foreign land in such a manner as to risk immediate combat." They exclude "less-blatant forms of international interference such as covert operations; military alerts in place; shows of force; deployments of units not immediately prepared for combat; [and] incursions across international borders that do not involve occupation of territory . . ." (Tillema 1994). Conceived in this manner, intervention is a distinct category of militarized international behavior, which: (1) involves the use of force, (2) is intrinsically hostile in motive, (3) often results in the loss of soldiers' lives, and (4) is usually described by the target as an act of war.

As a result of frequent overt and covert activity, military interventions have often heightened international tension and led to war (thirty-five cases of third-party intervention occurred between 1816 and 1988, resulting in the internationalization of twenty-five civil wars; see Small and Singer 1982; Singer 1991, 60–75). The critical question about the use of military interventions for coercive diplomacy is their probable consequences. When states intervene, does this usually help peacekeeping, peace making, and preventive diplomacy by containing serious threats from escalating to full-scale war, or providing a calming influence in a war-torn or famine-stricken failing state (as Italy's 1997 humanitarian intervention into the impoverished, insurgent neighbor across the Adriatic Sea, Albania, aimed to restore order and alleviate suffering)? Or does

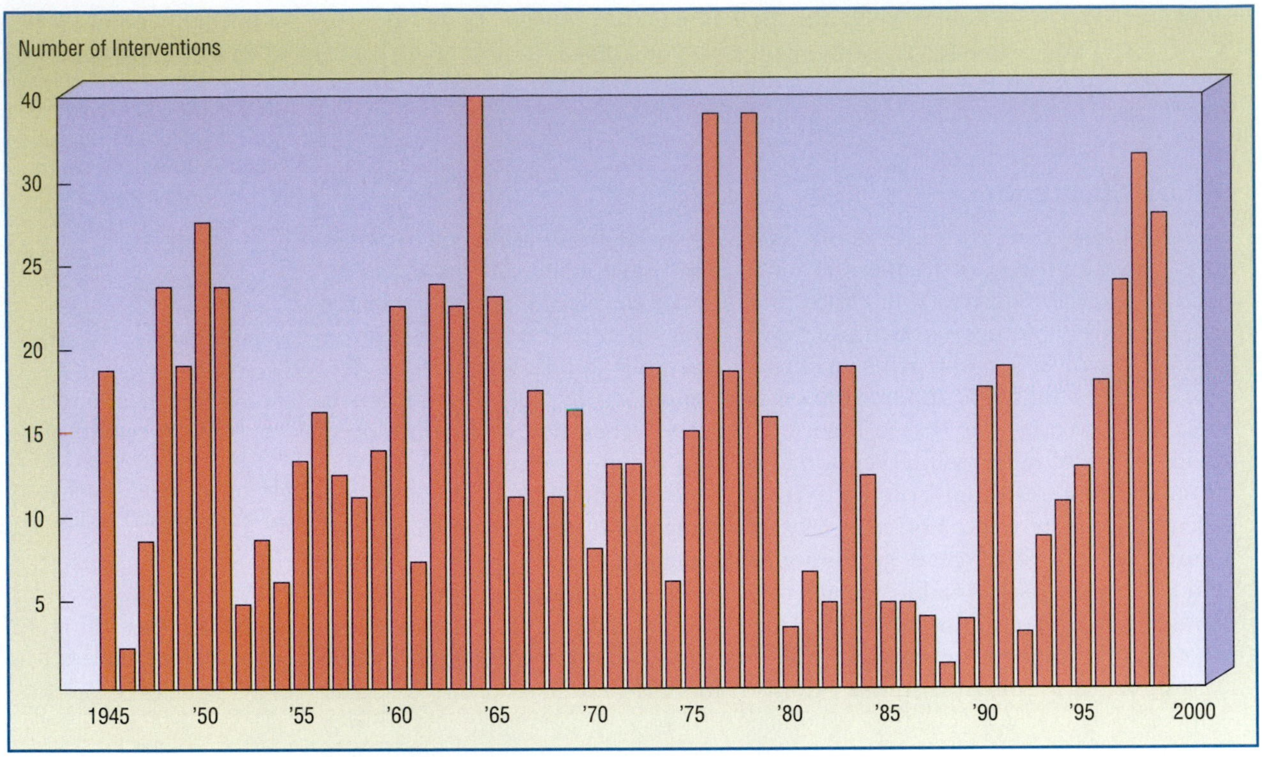

FIGURE 14.2
The Changing Incidence of Military Intervention in Coercive Diplomacy, 1945–2000

States have frequently sent their troops into the sovereign territory of other states in order to influence the target, despite the fact that military intervention has traditionally been prohibited by international law. This figure shows fluctuations in the frequency of intervention since 1946.

SOURCE: Based on Pickering (1999), with estimates for 1999 based on data from *Facts on File*.

intervention more often result not in pacification but in war? Those questions have become perhaps the most hotly debated issue in world politics at the start of the twenty-first century. In the wake of humanitarian interventions in Kosovo and East Timor in 1999, the great powers struggled unsuccessfully in an effort to reach consensus about the need to intervene in sovereign states when innocent civilians are made the victims of acts of atrocity committed by dictators and tyrants. UN Secretary-General Kofi Annan's plea in September 1999 for the permanent members of the Security Council to make "a new commitment to intervention" stirred up an already intense debate about the limits to involvement and intervention, even in the name of morality, justice, and human rights. Few question the necessity to stand up to genocide and intervene to protect the lives of persecuted peoples in theory; however, many great powers remain reluctant to pledge unconditionally to protect the **human rights** of innocent civilians. Even the United States has retreated from the blanket commitment of the Clinton Doctrine. "The real Clinton Doctrine is this: The U.S. will protect inno-

■ **human rights**
the political rights and civil liberties recognized by the international community as freedoms to which all people are entitled, even though many such inalienable privileges are not universally protected by the laws of states.

cent civilians from bullies—but only bullies that don't count geopolitically. When China oppresses Tibet, Russia ravages Chechnya or Indonesia reduces East Timor to rubble, [the United States does] not intervene" (Krauthammer 1999). In short, because the impulse to intervene for high moral and humanitarian purposes is tempting in a troubled world where evil acts and aggression are rampant, particularly in **failed states,** intervention in the name of global responsibility is likely to continue. At the same time, most great powers are likely to practice **selective engagement** by picking and choosing when and where they will be willing to militarily intervene.

In order to anticipate the extent to which interventionism will dominate international politics as a preferred method of coercive diplomacy in the future, it is helpful to examine one sure consequence that follows every act of military intervention: Each past war has begun by an act of military intervention; the by-product of every military intervention is that it produces a crisis.

International Crises

Crisis is a commonly used word that describes a situation that has reached a critical stage. More precisely, a **crisis decision** in international affairs is a decision made in a situation that (1) "threatens the high-priority goals of the decision-making unit; (2) restricts the amount of time available for response before the decision is transformed; and (3) surprises the members of the decision-making unit by its occurrence" (Hermann 1972). Most of the conspicuous military crises of our age, such as the Cuban missile crisis, the Berlin blockade, the Sino-Soviet border clash, the Formosa Straits crisis in the 1950s, and the Taiwan Straits crises in 1997 and again in 1999 exhibited these attributes. Each contained the elements of surprise, threat, and time pressure, as well as the risk of war. None of these crises crossed the line into overt large-scale military hostilities, however; all were managed successfully without escalation to war, because, arguably, the feuding parties made decisions according to **rational choice** theory. In contrast, many crises in the Global South have not been managed successfully and have escalated to war. Even with respect to crises between the great powers, the unbroken record of successful crisis management since 1945 should not necessarily instill confidence about the future. For crises to be managed successfully without escalating to war, governments, as rational actors, must be able to keep their quarrels within controllable bounds, and not let name-calling incite them to violence. There is no assurance that rationality will calm passions: "There is scant evidence that along with more lethal weapons we have evolved leaders more capable of coping with stress" (Holsti 1989). Crises can easily escalate to war because of the time pressures, inadequate information, fear and anxiety, and impulsive risk-taking that normally accompany decision-making procedures during threatening situations.

Crises result when one actor attempts to force an adversary to alter its behavior. "The strategy of coercive diplomacy . . . employs threats or limited force to persuade an opponent to call off or undo an encroachment—for example, to halt an invasion or give up territory that has been occupied" (Craig and George 1990). "Military power does not have to be used for it to be useful"; a state may succeed simply by "coercing a country by demonstrating the quantity of force and highlighting the capability of, and intention to, use force" (Majeed 1991). "Coercive diplomacy offers the possibility of achieving one's objective

failed states
countries whose governments have so mismanaged policy that they have lost the loyalty of their citizens who, in rebellion, threaten to divide the state into separate countries (see p. 632).

selective engagement
a great power grand strategy using economic and military power to influence only important particular situations, countries, or global issues, by striking a balance between a highly interventionist "global policeman" and an uninvolved isolationism when crises erupt in a great-power's sphere of influence (see p. 490).

crisis decisions
choices made in highly threatening and potentially grave situations, involving elements of surprise and restricted response time, by the highest level of authoritative decision-makers.

rational choice
the theory that decision-makers choose on the basis of what they perceive to be in the best interests of themselves and their states, and select options according to their expectations about the relative usefulness of alternative means for the realization of their preferred goals. Sometimes called "expected-utility theory," this model derives from realist theories (see p. 66).

economically, with little bloodshed, fewer political and psychological costs, and often with much less risk of escalation than does traditional military strategy" (Craig and George 1990).

The crises generated by coercive bargaining thus perform the function that war often traditionally played, namely, "to resolve without violence, or with only minimal violence, those conflicts that are too severe to be settled by ordinary diplomacy and that in earlier times would have been settled by war" (Snyder and Diesing 1977).

Figure 14.3 displays the distribution of 412 interstate crises between 1918 and 1994, revealing a continuous stream of changes "in the intensity of disruptive interactions between two or more states, with a heightened probability of military hostilities that destabilizes their relationships and challenges the structure of an international system" (Brecher 1993). Thus the frequency of international crises is sometimes measured by the incidence of **militarized disputes**—"confrontations short of war characterized by the reciprocated threat, deployment, mobilization, or use of force" (Singer 1991; also Gochman and Maoz 1984).

militarized disputes confrontations short of war characterized by the reciprocated threat, deployment, mobilization, or use of force.

gunboat diplomacy a show of military force; historically naval force.

Included in the category of militarized disputes is the practice of **gunboat diplomacy**—the high-profile sending of troops overseas to intimidate an enemy. Using the threat of force to persuade and compel is common, as many states believe that "actions speak louder than words" and that displaying one's military capabilities can convince the target to comply. The United States, for example, used shows of force 286 times between 1946 and 1984, an average of more than seven times a year (Blechman and Kaplan 1978, 547–553; Zelikow 1987, 34–36). Similarly, the former Soviet Union engaged in such behavior over 150 times between the mid-1940s and late 1970s (Kaplan 1981, 689–693). And in 1996 a bellicose China used this type of military intimidation when it conducted tests of its missiles by aiming them at a target area near a Taiwan port; in response, and to send China a warning, the United States sent two Navy aircraft carriers to the waters near the Taiwan Straits.

The evidence suggests a number of patterns. First, interstate crises were recurrent in the twentieth century, and more than four hundred such situations threatened to escalate to war across *every* region and *every* decade since World War I. Second, the incidence varied yearly, with many peaks of international tension followed by short troughs of relative calm. Third, many (in fact, most) states either provoked or experienced these threats to peace, as the 412 crises involved as initiator or target more than 850 individual states, with more than 100 states triggering at least one crisis and 125 finding themselves the principal target of the threat that provoked one or more crises. Fourth, some states (especially great powers) were the most prone to initiate crises. Finally, most crises in the twentieth century were concentrated in the Global South's developing countries; two-thirds occurred in Africa, Asia, or the Middle East, while only one-fifth occurred in Europe (Brecher and Wilkenfeld, 1997).

The use of military threat for bargaining purposes between states and the crises that result are important because crises often trigger war. Examples of violence that were preceded by a crisis include World War I (1914), Kashmir (1948), Suez (1956), Tibet (1959), the Bay of Pigs (1961), Goa (1961), Kuwait (1990), and Yugoslavia (Kosovo, 1999). More than 30 percent of all crises escalate to violence, with a large proportion (95 percent) of the most intense crises

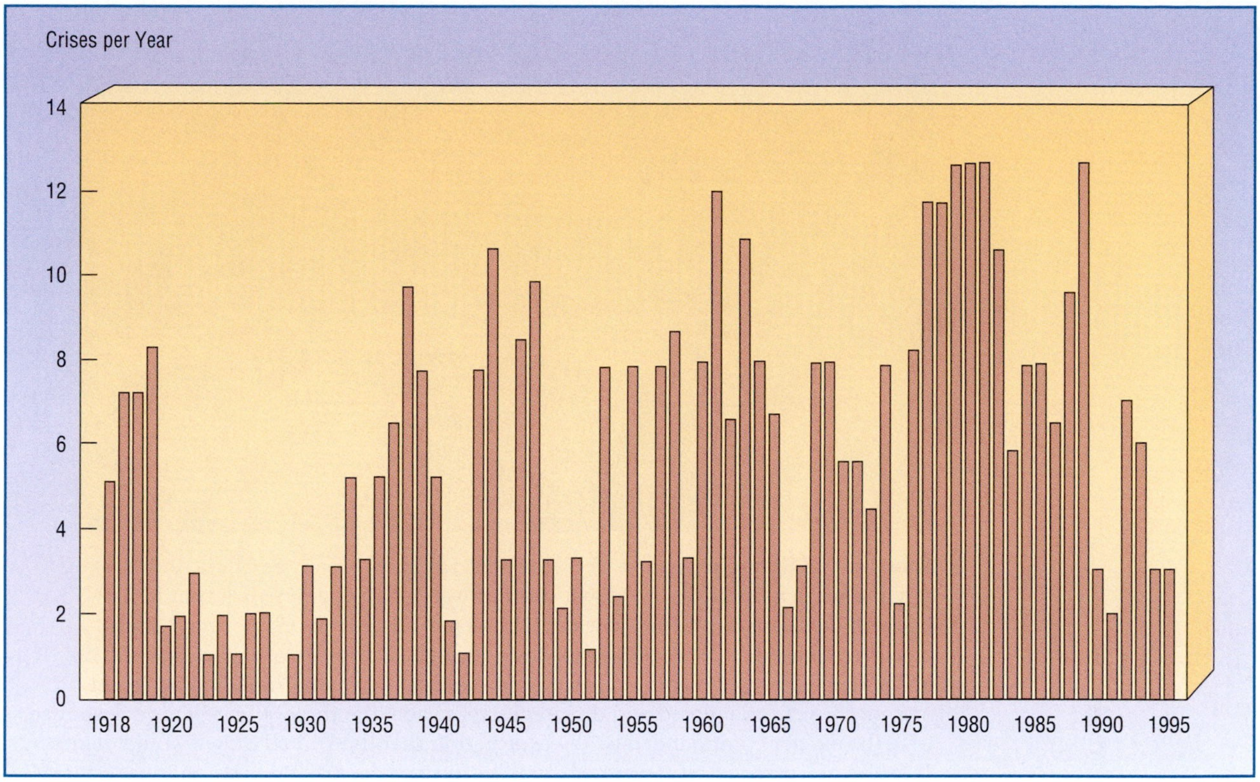

FIGURE 14.3
International Tension since World War I: The Annual Frequency of International Crises, 1918–1994

On 412 occasions, states confronted each other militarily between 1918 and 1994, in the hopes of forcing concessions. The frequency has varied over time, but its recurrence attests to states' compulsion to threaten each other with military force in the hope of getting their way. In February 2000, the world witnessed another crisis when two enemies, India and Pakistan, amassed troops on their mutual border and spoke openly of nuclear war.

SOURCE: Based on International Crisis Behavior (ICB) data, provided courtesy of Michael Brecher and Jonathan Wilkenfeld (1997).

involving the major powers (Brecher 1993, 333, 576). The lesson, in short, is that militarized disputes often lead to full-scale war rather than its deterrence, even if the latter was the threatener's original intention. Coercive diplomacy with conventional weapons is clearly a dangerous game.

If past experience is a model, then the threat of war for bargaining is likely to continue in the future, and we can predict that

> the post–Cold War subsystems will retain an abundance of conflicts within which international crises are likely to erupt. . . . The ethnic/nationalist virus has created a context for other crises in the future. . . . The conclusion is disquieting: Most anticipated international crises in the coming years are likely to erupt in violence, though its severity will vary from minor clashes to full-scale war. (Brecher 1993, 546, 548)

Tension in Taiwan In August 1997, the world held its breath as China and Taiwan squared off in a military showdown short of war. As democracy took root in Taiwan, it signaled its desire to officially declare its independence from China, and China interpreted this as a provocative act, despite nearly fifty years of separation and the uninterrupted respect for the unwritten "cease-fire" between China and its "rebel province." As China glared and threatened to invade, the threat of a military clash rose, with the danger compounded by the expectation that the United States would come to Taiwan's aid, assisted by Japanese troops because of the expanded defense pact in 1997 between Tokyo and Washington. Pictured here is an example of gunboat coercive diplomacy—new Taiwanese-made fighter jets poised for battle in August 1997 in the event of war. This crisis continued in February 2000 when China declared its intention to go to war, if necessary, to force Taiwan to proceed with unification negotiations and not seek formal independence; painting Beijing as a military menace, Taiwan in response warned that "force won't work."

The Future of Conventional Military Coercion

The sobering conclusion that international crises are likely to increase in the future raises concerns about the use of coercive bargaining by military means as a method of dispute management. Is this kind of bargaining a solution, or part of the security dilemma problem?

Policymakers today disagree about the appropriate place of coercive military bargaining in their strategic doctrines. Enthusiasts argue that the successful use of such strategies in the second half of the twentieth century argues for applying the lessons of nuclear bargaining to situations requiring deterrence in the future. Skeptics disagree, maintaining that what may have worked in the realm of strategic deterrence is unlikely to work with respect to conventional deterrence, where in all probability most of the action will center. They feel that the kinds of armed conflicts and threats most in need of deterring will be most resistant to control through the strategies that help prevent nuclear attacks. Aggressors in the future—whether they are rough, outlaw states or criminal and terrorist organizations—very likely will employ advanced telecommunication networks to operate from dispersed locations, making the threat of massive retaliatory strikes against specific geographic regions ineffective.

It will clearly be much more difficult to deter the kinds of aggression that will employ conventional weapons than to deter aggression using nuclear weapons. The key elements of deterrence require three elements: (1) *capabilities*—the possession of military resources that can make threats of military retaliation plausible; (2) *credibility*—the belief that the actor is willing to militarily defend its declared position; and (3) *communication*—the actor's ability to send a potential aggressor the clear message that it is willing to carry out its threat. In today's world, it is difficult to combine these elements to make conventional deterrence work. As Richard Harknett (1994) cautions, deterrence of conventional warfare "will succeed if threatened costs can be communicated to the challenger, assessed by the challenger, and believed by the challenger." These requirements are difficult to satisfy with the diffuse conventional warfare raging throughout the world. "Unlike during the Cold War, interests deemed vital enough to fight for will be interests that probably will lead to actual fighting."

The prolonged difficulties that the United States and its NATO allies experienced in trying to deter the Bosnian Serbs from pursuing their expansionist war in the Balkans provide a graphic example of the ineffectiveness of conventional deterrence. Talk and threats were not believed and did not work. In desperation, the frustrated NATO countries under the leadership of the Clinton administration responded to Serbian atrocities with force, initiating in September 1995 a series of air strikes, under the auspices of the United Nations and through NATO, to compel an end to Serbian defiance. Operation Joint Endeavor, the NATO assault on strategic Serb targets, applied conventional force in order to relieve the cruel siege of Sarajevo and to persuade Serbia through bombing to return to the bargaining table. As a U.S. State Department official explained, "Diplomacy was dead without force" (Fedarko 1995). But the problem was not dead. It was the defiance of Yugoslavia's Slobodan Milosevic that prompted the nineteen NATO countries in 1999 to unleash an uninterrupted series of intensive airstrikes against Yugoslavia, hoping to push the Serbian leader toward peace terms and to end the attacks by Serbian forces on ethnic Albanians in the province of Kosovo. This time, as NATO and Milosevic faced each other, it was the Yugoslavian dictator who blinked. The ability of NATO's military intervention to achieve its primary goal inspired confidence in military interventionism as a tool of diplomacy, and seemed to raise expectations that coercive bargaining using conventional military force instead of ultimatums for deterrence and compellence would be used with increasing frequency in the future. For the United States, the globe's so-called only superpower, reliance on military interventionism appeared to comprise the major military method by which it would seek to exercise influence in the international arena: since 1990 the U.S. Army has been deployed abroad three times as often as the number of "major" deployments in the entire period between 1946 and 1989 (*Harper's*, July 1999, 17).

Public opposition to and international criticism of the U.S. use of interventionary force overseas stands in the way of its practicing interventionism with abandon, however. "Intervention fatigue" and international complaints about the threat of intervention to the principle of sovereignty and the **nonintervention** norm in international law could result in the decline of this military instrument for exercising influence.

nonintervention a fundamental international legal principle, now being challenged, that traditionally has defined interference by one state in the domestic affairs of another as illegal.

Kosovar Refugees On May 4, 1999, several thousand Kosovar Albanian refugees fled their homeland to sanctuary in Albania to escape the Serbian police's attempts to exterminate them. NATO's military intervention in the Kosovo crisis to protect the ethnic minority within the territorial borders of the Federal Republic of Yugoslavia was undertaken for humanitarian goals, but provoked criticism from China, Russia, and others who complained that by violating traditional international law prohibiting external interference in the internal borders of a sovereign state, NATO was transforming international law and dismantling the meaning of borders.

Bargaining by nonmilitary methods is also likely to be tried, and perhaps will be the method of choice, given the risks of military activities and the obstacles to their effective use. Economic sanctions will figure prominently among these alternative approaches.

BOYCOTTS, NOT BULLETS, AS WEAPONS: SANCTIONS AS INSTRUMENTS OF COERCION

When the Arab members of OPEC placed an embargo on the shipment of oil to the United States and the Netherlands in 1973, their purpose was to alter these countries' policies toward the Arab-Israeli conflict. When the UN Security Council decided in August 1990 that the world organization should cease trade with Iraq, its purpose was to accomplish the immediate and unconditional withdrawal of Iraqi forces from Kuwait. Both are examples of the use of **economic sanctions**—"deliberate government actions to inflict economic deprivation on a target state or society, through the limitation or cessation of customary economic relations" (Leyton-Brown 1987).

■ **economic sanctions** the punitive use of trade or monetary measures, such as an embargo, to harm the economy of an enemy state in order to exercise influence over its policies.

We will look specifically at economic sanctions, keeping in mind that sanctions may be defined more broadly to include acts "intended to convince or compel another state to desist from engaging" in some unacceptable behavior by a wider range of methods than economic coercion. They may be military, involving the use of armed intervention; diplomatic or political (breaking formal relations); or cultural, aimed at undermining a deviant government's internal and international standing (Joyner 1995).

Economic sanctions are an increasingly popular choice from the broad array of instruments of statecraft available to governments.

> To the extent that there is a degree of optimism today about the potential effectiveness of sanctions, it is likely because of the perception shared by many that broad multilateral sanctions helped to end apartheid in South Africa, have forced Iraqi President Saddam Hussein to cooperate grudgingly (and sporadically) with the UN inspectors seeking to destroy his weapons of mass destruction, and induced Serbian leader Slobodan Milosevic to come to the negotiating table in Dayton, Ohio. Here the optimism is based on the fact that, with the end of the Cold War, it may now be possible for the United Nations to take action in defense of collective security and to protect international norms, as was originally intended. The hope is that multilateralism, combined with the relatively greater legitimacy accorded to UN enforcement actions, may restore to sanctions the leverage that they had when the United States was the dominant economic and military power in the Western world. (Elliott 1998, 50–51)

An alternative to applying military force, **sanctions** are enacted to express outrage and to change the target's behavior. Since World War I, there have been 120 observable episodes of foreign policy sanctions, 104 of which have been enacted since World War II (Hufbauer, Schott, and Elliott 1990). In the 1990s, the use of **boycotts** instead of bullets as a strategy for exercising political influence became widespread. It was illustrated by the U.S. "dual containment" policy toward Iraq and Iran (alongside the continuation of sanctions against the North African "pariah state," Libya, which was accused of sponsoring terrorism), by the 1997 U.S. effort to sever economic ties with Burma for its human rights violations, and by the April 1997 Arab foreign ministers' plan to launch a business boycott of Israel in response to its decision to move forward with a housing project in East Jerusalem.

■ **sanctions**
punitive actions by one state against another to retaliate for its previous objectionable behavior.

■ **boycotts**
concerted efforts, often organized internationally, to prevent relations such as trade with a state, to express disapproval or to coerce acceptance of certain conditions.

Despite their frequent use, most efforts to apply economic sanctions have failed. This fact has led many policy analysts to question their cost-effectiveness (Knorr 1977). Why is failure so prevalent? And why, then, have economic sanctions "become the weapon of choice in diplomatic confrontation in the wake of the Cold War" (Hoagland 1993b)? We can address these questions by looking at several prominent sanctions cases.

Superpower Sanctions: Four U.S. Failures

Between 1945 and 1990, when more than sixty cases of sanctions were undertaken, "a rate averaging better than one new action per year, more than two-thirds were initiated and maintained by the United States" (Lopez and Cortright 1995, 5). In 1998, half the world's population lived in countries that were under U.S. sanctions (*Harper's,* February 1998, 13). As Map 14.1 shows, the United States has increasingly relied on sanctions to coerce foreign countries since the 1950s, despite the frequent criticism that they often do not work and the growing awareness that "they are of limited utility in achieving foreign policy goals that depend on compelling the target country to take actions it stoutly resists [and that] the success rate importantly depends on the type of policy or government change sought" (Elliott 1998). Four conspicuous cases in which the United States applied economic sanctions illustrate their shortcomings.

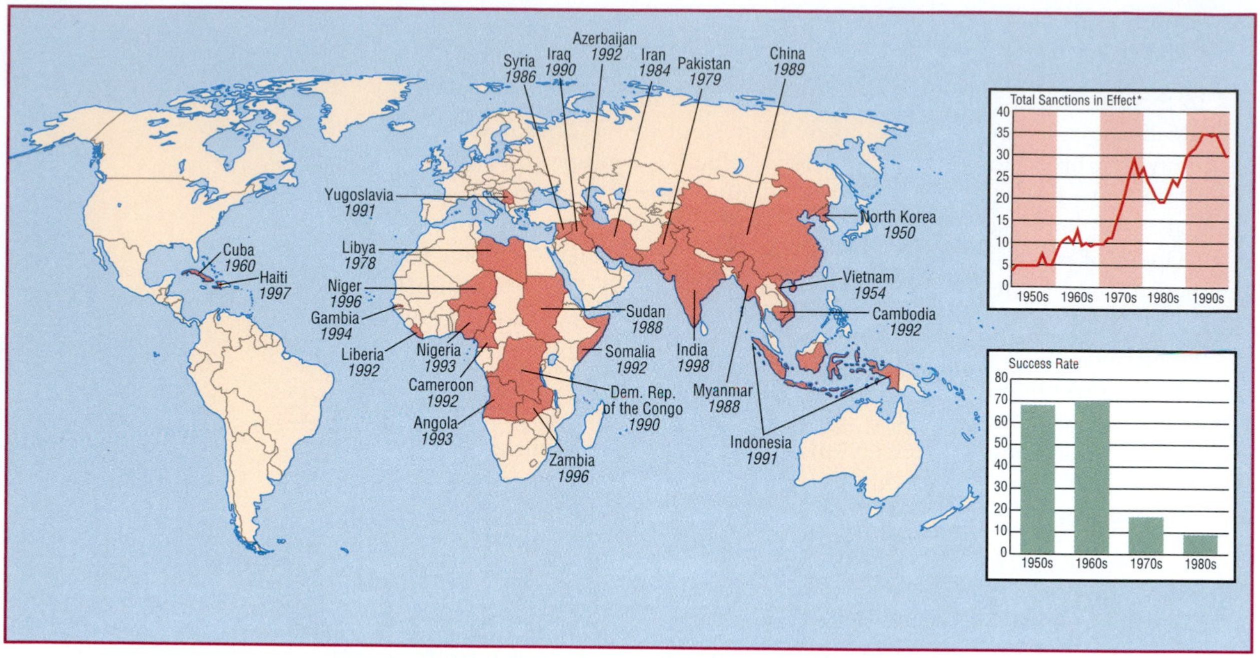

MAP 14.1

U.S. Sanctions since the 1950s and Their Rate of Success

This map shows the countries that are currently under U.S. sanctions and the year the sanctions were first imposed. Sanctions have been a major instrument of coercive diplomacy for the United States. The total number of sanctions rose until the mid-1990s, when concerns that such actions were hurting American interests and were hard to enforce led to a decline in their use. The success rate of U.S. sanctions over time has also declined sharply, as the chart at the bottom right shows. According to Kimberly Ann Elliott (1998, 50) the record is even more sobering in that "less than one in four U.S. sanctions had any success at all in the 1970s and 1980s [and] even fewer when the United States acts unilaterally . . . Although increasing international integration and declining political hegemony have eroded U.S. leverage, just over half the episodes in which the United States took a leading role from 1945 to 1970 resulted in at least partial success."

*One country may be subject to several sanctions.

SOURCE: Institute for International Economics as presented in Schmitt (1998), 1.

Cuba. The United States placed sanctions on the Castro regime shortly after it assumed power in 1960, beginning with a reduction in the amount of sugar permitted to enter the United States under its quota system. These sanctions later were extended to a full ban on all U.S. trade with Cuba, accompanied by pressure on other countries to follow suit. The U.S. goals were twofold: initially, to overthrow the Castro government; failing that, to contain the Castro revolution and Cuban interventionism in Central and South America and in Africa.

Through the late 1990s the United States remained unsuccessful in securing Castro's overthrow, and it had been only marginally successful in containing Cuba's promotion of revolution abroad. "The major accomplishment of the U.S. economic embargo . . . consisted of increasing the cost to Cuba of surviving and developing as a socialist country and of pursuing an international commitment"

(Roca 1987). Several factors helped Cuba to withstand this pressure from the globe's foremost economic and military power for over forty years. Especially potent were the Soviet Union's prolonged subsidies of "as much as $2–3 billion annually" to Cuba (Elliott 1993, 35); U.S. inability to persuade its Western allies to curtail trade with and investment in Cuba; and Castro's charismatic leadership and popular support. Although the U.S. economic sanctions extracted a heavy burden on the target, they did not accomplish their political goals.

Not only did the United States fail to get its way, but it was snubbed by its key allies. In symbolic defiance, in October 1994 they led a vote of 102 to 2 in favor of a UN resolution condemning the U.S. embargo, asserting that the embargo infringed on their sovereignty, free trade, and navigation rights; in 1995, a similar resolution passed by a vote of 117 to 3. With diminishing incentives in an era of globalization that was eroding the dividing line between domestic and international political interests, and with declining support and cooperation from others, the U.S. trade sanctions simply could not succeed. Latin America, once an obedient follower of the U.S. trade embargo against Cuba, saw that Castro was not likely to lose his grip on power in the face of outside pressure, and chose to ignore the U.S. effort to isolate Cuba and instead to develop full economic and political relations with the communist government. The United States in effect isolated itself in its bid to economically strangle the struggling Caribbean country in which "Mr. Castro himself still retains a place in the heart of most Cubans" (*Economist,* January 2, 1999). The United States is the only country in the Americas with a trade ban on Cuba, and in 1999 the sixteen-member Caribbean Community trade-bloc welcomed Cuba as a member—a move that increases the regional IGO's combined economy from $30 billion to $40 billion. At the start of the twenty-first century the verdict on the bullying by ten consecutive U.S. presidential administrations was in: the sanctions were a failure. One by one, leaders throughout the world, including Pope John Paul II in 1999, met with President Fidel Castro to negotiate economic, cultural, and tourist exchanges. "It's high time to cross the ideological divide and fully embrace Cuba as part of the hemispheric family," Jamaican Prime Minister P. J. Patterson exclaimed in July 1999. The entire global community's determined warming of relations with Cuba, rooted in economics, flies in the face of the U.S. sanctions, and illustrates the extent to which states are willing to put their financial interests ahead of their compliance with powerful allies. St. Lucia's Prime Minister Kenny Anthony described his country's thinking in 1998 by stating "the world is closing in on us. We have to look for new economic opportunities." In the case of Cuba, geoeconomics overrides geopolitics. Twenty-one states meeting at the annual Ibero-American Summit signed a 1998 joint declaration restating a "firm condemnation" of the Helms-Burton law that seeks to punish countries doing business in Cuba. Against this multilateral pressure, in 2000, the United States moved to relax rules against U.S. citizens traveling to Cuba and permitted humanitarian aid.

The Soviet Union and Afghanistan. After the Soviet Union's 1979 intervention in Afghanistan, the United States imposed a partial embargo on the sale of grain to the country and attempted to organize a boycott of the 1980 Moscow Summer Olympics. The sanctions also sought "to punish the Soviet Union while at the same time limiting the damage to the economic interests of important domestic groups" (Falkenheim 1987).

The grain embargo failed. "The Soviets did not change their policy, they simply switched suppliers and got their wheat from other countries. American farmers paid the price. Even after the embargo was lifted, American farmers never reclaimed their share of the USSR's vast market. More than 18 years later, U.S. grain exports to the former Soviet republics still have not rebounded to pre-embargo levels. Food sanctions too often miss their intended target and end up landing closer to home—among America's struggling farmers, who have seen exports drop from $59.6 billion in 1996 to a predicted $49 billion for 1999" (Weiss 1999).

The Soviet Union and Poland. Similar lessons apply to Poland. After the Polish government imposed martial law in 1981 to forestall continued labor unrest, the Reagan administration restricted U.S. government credits for Polish purchase of food and other commodities, banned high-technology exports to Poland, and suspended Poland's most-favored-nation trade status. To stiffen the sanctions' impact, the United States also targeted Poland's patron and primary trade partner, the Soviet Union. U.S. actions restricted the flow of Western goods and technology needed for the trans-Siberian gas pipeline, designed to bring Soviet energy into Western European markets, in the hope of increasing the economic strains under which both Poland and the Soviet system would have to operate.

The strategy failed to achieve these objectives, however, as the Reagan administration was forced to seek a face-saving compromise with its European allies permitting continued construction of the pipeline. The absence of consensus among the NATO allies contributed to the sanctions' failure. Other factors included the Soviet Union's ability and willingness to support its client, Poland. While the sanctions may have had some liberalizing influence on Poland, in the end the Soviet Union did not budge.

Firing Blanks: The Plot to Oust Saddam Hussein after the Kuwait Crisis. Restraints on the long-term use of economic sanctions for political purposes are illustrated by the 1990 conflict in the Middle East and its aftermath. The first response of the international community to Iraq's invasion of Kuwait was to impose sanctions, including the prohibition of all exports to and imports from Iraq except for humanitarian shipments of medicine and some food. The embargo sought to compel the Iraqi government to withdraw from Kuwait and to foment enough discontent within Iraq to cause the ouster of the Hussein regime. In the months that followed, a vigorous debate took place at the UN and in various national capitals over the utility of the sanctions. Would they force Saddam Hussein from Kuwait? How long should they be applied before resorting to military power?

Iraq was especially vulnerable to a total embargo because it imported nearly three-fourths of its food and depended almost completely on oil exports for its foreign exchange. In addition, its oil could pass through only two routes, by ship through the Persian Gulf—which was easily blockaded—or via overland pipelines to other countries. In December 1990, the director of the U.S. Central Intelligence Agency reported that "more than 90 percent of imports and 97 percent of exports have been shut off." He also reported, however, that "we see no indication that Saddam is concerned at this point that domestic discontent is growing . . . or that problems resulting from the sanctions are causing him to rethink his policy on Kuwait. . . . There is no assurance or guarantee that economic hardships will compel Saddam to change his policies or lead to internal unrest that would threaten his regime." Little more than a month later, military power took the place of economic sanctions to force Iraq from Kuwait.

During the debate over force and sanctions, two former chairmen of the U.S. Joint Chiefs of Staff urged that sanctions be given a year or more to work. "If in fact the sanctions will work in twelve to eighteen months instead of six months, the trade-off of avoiding war with its attendant sacrifices and uncertainties would, in my view, be worth it," Admiral William J. Crowe testified before the U.S. Congress. Historically, however, sanctions applied over long periods have seldom produced success. The cone of Africa, where sanctions induced South Africa to overturn its apartheid policies and external pressure led to Southern Rhodesia's transfer of power to the African majority, and the independence of Zimbabwe in 1980 are conspicuous exceptions to the historic pattern. The general conclusion is that

> Sanctions imposed slowly or incrementally may simply strengthen the target government at home as it marshals the forces of nationalism. Moreover, such measures are likely to be undercut over time either by the sender's own firms or by foreign competitors. Sanctions are generally regarded as a short-term policy, with the anticipation that normal relations will be reestablished after the resolution of the crisis. Thus, even though popular opinion in the sender country may welcome the introduction of sanctions, the longer an episode drags on, the public support for sanctions dissipates. (Hufbauer, Schott, and Elliott 1990, 100–101)

Largely for these reasons, and because of growing concern for how long the coalition against Iraq would hold together, economic sanctions were abandoned in favor of the use of overwhelming military force. Whether this was wise or foolish remains debatable. The use of military force in the Gulf War did (at an estimated cost of $57 billion) drive Iraq from Kuwait and arguably helped prevent Saddam Hussein from carrying out his crash program to build a nuclear weapon, and develop an arsenal of toxins for biological warfare, and it did contain his aggression. Nonetheless, the effort to topple the Iraqi dictator and demonize him in a **propaganda** campaign aimed at undermining his popularity failed, and his ruthless moves to retain power in Iraq succeeded. "Iraq was bombed into the Stone Age" with 89,000 tons of explosives killing more than 46,000 children (Al-Samarrai 1995), an operation "analogous to blowing up an aircraft with all passengers aboard to kill the hijacker." This case thus demonstrated the uncertain payoff of military sanctions, and it has since demonstrated the limits of economic sanctions. In 2000, Saddam Hussein was still in power, being courted by major oil companies, making huge profits buying and selling oil futures after the United Nations in the Resolution 986 "oil for food" program partially lifted its oil embargo, and exporting oil on the black market through dummy companies to needy importers in order to buy illegal arms from foreign manufacturers to protect himself and his army from his own citizens. At the same time, U.S. firms were helping to rebuild Iraq's oil industry even while air raids continued (Lynch 2000). Sanctions failed to produce compliance or submission, as the Baghdad dictator prevented UN inspectors from determining whether Iraq had complied with Security Council's demands to scrap its long-range missiles and other chemical and biological weapons of

■ **propaganda** communications used to manipulate people's thoughts, emotions, or actions.

Arming against Sanctions in Iraq In a war of words that punctuated the weakness of economic sanctions as a tool of coercive diplomacy, the Iraqi government in January 1998 called on 1 million men and women of all ages to take part in a weapons training program. Pictured here are armed Iraqi women who joined a paramilitary group in response to a call to arms by Iraqi President Saddam Hussein, who claimed his state must be ready for a U.S. attack over the issue of UN arms inspections and economic sanctions.

mass destruction under the peace settlement that ended the 1991 Gulf War. The futility of the financially crippling UN embargo to drive Saddam Hussein out of office or to open his palaces to UN inspectors, and the repeated success of Saddam's stubborn brinkmanship bargaining, highlighted the impotence of sanctions as a method of modifying unacceptable behavior against a willful foe intent on thumbing his nose at the international community. The UN sanctions did not change Iraq's policy or position, and cannot even be said to have contributed to the goals it set: Iraq's oil sales fell 22 percent short of the maximum allowed under UN sanctions, while its total oil sales since 1997 actually rose 45 percent (with the United States ranking first among countries purchasing oil from the adversary) (*Harper's,* March 1999, 17). The history of ineffectual sanctions against Iraq underscores the principles that "success importantly depends on the type of policy for government change sought [and that sanctions] are of little utility in achieving goals that depend on compelling the target country to take actions it stoutly resists" (Elliott 1998). This case explains why military force is still usually preferred as an alternative to sanctions in coercive diplomacy. It also explains why in 1999, at the same time that NATO pilots were bombing Yugoslavia, U.S. and British pilots had fired more than 1,100 missiles against 360 targets in Iraq (Myers 1999, A8). Once again, as in so many other occasions throughout history, warfare ignited from the tinderbox of failed economic diplomacy.

These four examples suggest that a superpower's successful use of economic sanctions faces substantial obstacles. The initiator often pays a high price (lost markets to exporters, increased costs to consumers) and receives a low payoff. In general, the more ambitious the goal, the less successful the efforts have been. "Sanctions are seldom effective in impairing the military potential of an important power, or in bringing about major changes in the policies of the target country" (Hufbauer, Schott, and Elliott 1990), and "have been absolutely ineffective in bringing about a change of government leadership within a target country" (Cortright and Lopez 1995).

Yet, as inventories of the use of economic sanctions indicate, states are increasingly prone to rely on them. In fact, as a high-profile, low-risk tactic of coercive diplomacy, sanctions may be the tool of choice for states seeking to make other states comply. The world may be entering "the sanctions era" (Cortright and Lopez 1995) in part because the growing volume of international commerce has made "trade-based diplomacy an increasingly prominent tool of statecraft." The advantages rationalizing the use of boycotts are suggested by cases that met with relatively greater success.

A Relatively Successful Sanction

The usefulness of economic sanctions as instruments of foreign policy has a checkered history at best. The case of South Africa illustrates the ability of sanctions at times to produce policy dividends.

South Africa and Apartheid. For many years, the white leadership in South Africa practiced a punitive policy of racial separation known as **apartheid.** To force an end to this morally unjustifiable practice, in 1963 at the behest of Third World countries, the UN imposed a voluntary arms and oil embargo against South Africa, which became mandatory in 1977.

■ **apartheid**
the former South African policy of racial separation.

Because U.S. corporations held major investments in South Africa and the United States was a primary importer of the country's rich mineral reserves, the U.S. attitude toward South Africa was of special concern to opponents of apartheid. A frequent argument in the United States concerning an appropriate response to apartheid focused on who would be the victims of internationally applied sanctions: South African blacks, already suffering under a policy of systematic racial discrimination, or the white minority regime who perpetuated apartheid. In 1981, the Reagan administration adopted a policy toward South Africa called *constructive engagement,* whose broad purpose was a soft diplomatic approach to the Pretoria regime. In 1985, however, in an unusual domestic political development, the U.S. Congress legislated, over a presidential veto, harsh mandatory sanctions against South Africa, hoping to change Reagan's policies, which Congress found objectionable.

In 1989, F. W. de Klerk, a reformer, came to power in South Africa and released Nelson Mandela, leader of the African National Congress (ANC), who had been a political prisoner for twenty-seven years. De Klerk also lifted the ban on the ANC and other anti-apartheid groups, opening the door to negotiations on political reforms between the South African government and the ANC. Thus the process of dismantling apartheid finally began and culminated in a historic agreement in 1993, which restored democracy for all South Africa's citizens and made possible black majority rule. As trade restrictions were lifted, investors rushed into the vacuum and South Africa rejoined the community of nations. It was no longer an international pariah.

Were the sanctions responsible for setting South Africa on a path toward reform and majority rule? While the sanctions were being applied, analysts' evaluations differed, but now that apartheid has been officially lifted, most believe that the sanctions eventually paid off. Apartheid ended through the concerted cooperation and economic sanctions of many states in combination with the human rights activities of international institutions and nongovernmental organizations throughout the world.

Why Sanction?

The long and generally unsuccessful history of international economic sanctions has led many critics to conclude that sanctions are a weak tool in statecraft (Elliott 1993; Førland 1993; Haass 1997). They argue that:

- A typical response to economic coercion in the sanctioned society is a heightened sense of nationalism, a *laager* mentality (circle the wagons to face oncoming enemies), which stimulates resistance in the target state.
- Sanctions sometimes hurt the disempowered people they seek to help—the country's average citizens. "Sanctions substitute for military action against rulers who have total disregard for the economic hardships faced by their subjects. The logic of the policy [unrealistically] seems to be to make unarmed citizens desperate enough to rise up and throw off brutal regimes that . . . other powers are not willing to use the world's best armies to topple" (Hoagland 1993b).
- Governments often act covertly to support the sanctioned state even as they publicly profess their support of sanctions.
- Sanctions interfere with liberal free trade and therefore profits; as barriers to globalization, sanctions are claimed by critics to reduce global prosperity and to operate as an invisible form of trade protectionism that, in the process, places an unfair burden on as many as two-thirds of the globe's population, hitting hardest the poorest most in need of the commodities at the lower prices that would result were economic sanctions not in place (see Helms 1998, 9).
- "Midsized countries can thwart sanctions, when local dictators are able to quell dissent with a powerful military and divert pain to citizens with no influence" (Hufbauer 1994).
- The credibility of the state(s) imposing sanctions is often low, given their transparent costs and the fact that "economic sanctions always involve something lost for both sides" (Howell 1995).
- Widespread and collective sustained cooperation from the international community and international organizations seldom materializes, and unilateral sanctions seldom succeed in a globalized market with many competitive suppliers of embargoed goods.

The suitability of sanctions as instruments of persuasion is therefore customarily questioned whenever they are proposed or imposed. Recent examples of their use, amidst criticism, include the OAS embargo of Haiti to force the military junta to step down (and subsequent military intervention to fulfill the objective); the embargo of North Korea to dissuade it from building a nuclear bomb; the economic sanctions against the rebel army UNITA in Angola; the use of sanctions against the Serbs that led to their acceptance of the August 1995 Dayton agreement ending the fighting in Bosnia; and U.S. threats of trade sanctions against China in 1996 in response to its shipment of cruise missiles to Iran and its missile tests near Taiwan. Despite these modest successes, critics invariably argue that "the problem with economic sanctions is that they frequently contribute little to . . . foreign policy goals while being costly and even counterproductive" (Haass 1997) Futhermore,

> . . . policymakers often have inflated expectations of what sanctions can and cannot accomplish. . . . At most there is a weak correlation between economic deprivation and political willingness to change. The *economic* impact of sanctions may be pronounced, both on the sender and the target country, but other factors in the situational context almost always overshadow the impact of sanctions in determining the *political* outcome. (Hufbauer, Schott, and Elliott 1990, 94)

If they usually spark opposition and seldom prove effective, why have "sanctions become the main tool of coercive diplomacy" (Hoagland 1996), "the most favored tool of diplomats" (Pound and El-Tahri 1994), and the "tool of choice" for the United States, which between 1993 and 1996 targeted thirty-five countries with new American sanctions (Haass 1997, 74)? One answer is that the chief alternative method of coercion, military force, is not very effective and is increasingly less popular. The threat of destruction is not very convincing because the target is unlikely to believe that it will be carried out. Moreover, if carried out, a military approach can easily backfire, taking soldiers' lives, draining government budgets, severing export earnings, and provoking public criticism at home and abroad. Simply put, military coercion to win contests with foreign foes is relatively unattractive, and the mandate for this strategy has waned except for those rare situations in which the use of force is likely to succeed in a short-term operation with few battle casualties. Hence, in comparison with military methods of coercion, economic sanctions look advantageous: "Sanctions have become a habit" because they look less costly and risky than the other options and, "once in place . . . create their own constituency" (Nathan 1997).

A second reason for the rising use of economic sanctions is a consequence of the **globalization** process that is unfolding at an accelerating rate. National economies are increasingly integrated through trade and the exchange of ideas and information (see Chapters 8 and 9). Arguably, "for the first time in history, almost all of the world's people are bound together in a global capitalist system" (Sachs 1997). This transforms the calculus of choice regarding coercion and encourages leaders to regard economic sanctions more favorably. Because globalization is making most countries dependent on trade for their own prosperity, it makes sanctions that threaten targets with the loss of an export market more effective than in the past, when countries could better withstand a foreign embargo on the purchase of their products in the global marketplace.

■ globalization
the integrative tendencies that are linking the countries of the world into increasingly tight webs of economic, political, and cultural interdependence (see p. 41).

Today, many states are highly dependent on exports for growth; they are increasingly trade dependent, and this condition makes it difficult to withstand an embargo (a government order prohibiting commerce) or a boycott that interrupts the target's export-generated income. Under these conditions, sanctions can better succeed against trade-dependent targets and countries that are highly dependent on imports of critical resources such as oil, which with rising prices in 2000 and two-thirds of known oil reserves in the Middle East made the threat of catastrophic supply disruptions a powerful tool once again. This method draws on the commercial liberal logic of James Madison and Thomas Jefferson, who advocated "peaceable coercion" against those foreign governments that would have to yield to American pressure because U.S. goods were essential to their prosperity. Economic sanctions are also gaining proponents because the number of highly vulnerable "single-commodity-dependent economies," which derive at least 40 percent of their export revenues from foreign purchase of a single product, is large (see Map 14.2).

States pursue economic sanctions in pursuit of five major policy goals:

- *Compliance* ("to force the target to alter its behavior to conform with the initiator's preferences"), as in the case of the 1982 U.S. embargo of Libya, designed to force it to end its support of terrorism.
- *Subversion* ("to remove the target's leaders . . . or overthrow the regime"), as in the case of the 1993–1994 U.S. trade embargo on Haiti.
- *Deterrence* ("to dissuade the target from repeating the disputed action in the future"), as in the case of the Soviet grain embargo by the United States.
- *International symbolism* ("to send messages to other members of the world community"), as in the case of the British sanctions against Rhodesia after its unilateral declaration of independence in 1965.
- *Domestic symbolism* ("to increase its domestic support or thwart international criticism of its foreign policies by acting decisively"), as in the case of U.S. sanctions against Iran following its seizure of U.S. diplomats in 1979 (Lindsay 1986).

Past cases of sanctions suggest that symbolism is a primary motivation behind the impulse to use this tool. Sanctions enable a leader to show leadership without bearing the costs and dangers that other policy options, particularly military force, entail. "When military options are not feasible or desirable and the initiator wants to respond forcefully to the target's behavior, sanctions provide a means of 'doing something'" (Lindsay 1986).

It is disputable whether the "symbolic utility" of economic sanctions in the face of their otherwise "apparent disutility" is a cause for applause or concern. "Critics may deride the symbolic uses of trade sanctions as empty gestures, but symbols are important in politics. This is especially so when inaction can signal weakness and silence can mark complicity" (Lindsay 1986). Thus, economic sanctions are often used even though they frequently fail to achieve the most visible aims for which they are implemented.

Nonetheless, sanctions serve important functions. They provide a policy alternative to the use of force to publicize and condemn unacceptable behavior and intolerable situations, thereby expressing outrage and making it appear that something is being done. In addition, under particular conditions such as rising globalization, "sanctions work—if imposed by a major power against a much weaker, unstable, and economically dependent foe with no friends among

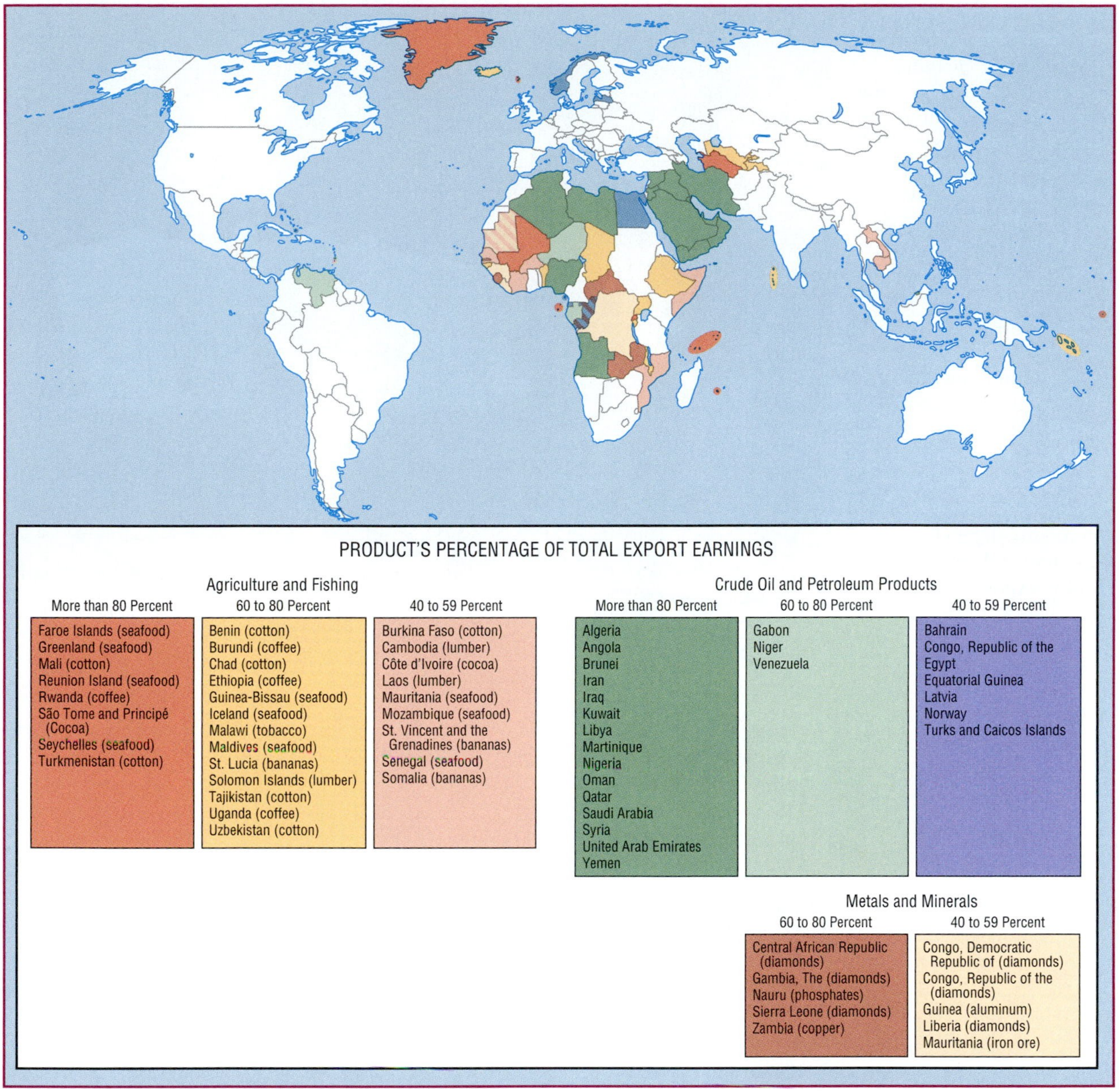

MAP 14.2

Vulnerable Single-Commodity-Dependent Economies

Many states depend on a single commodity for exports, with 40–80 percent of their trade revenue derived from the willingness of foreigners to purchase these goods. Sanctions through boycotts and embargoes, undertaken to coerce a change in the trade-dependent country's policies, can be devastating. This vulnerability has made these states especially ripe targets; because they are usually developing countries, the Global South has been the locus for many acts of economic sanctions.

Note: The countries highlighted depend on a single commodity for 40 percent or more of their export earnings.

SOURCE: *Handbook of International Economic Statistics* (1999), 72–73.

Trade Interdependence and Sanctions In this photo a tanker carrying natural gas leaves Qatar for Japan. Qatar, with huge gas reserves, hopes exports will transform its economy; Japan badly needs natural gas to propel its consumer-rich economy. Japan's dependence on foreign suppliers for desperately needed energy sources reduces its willingness to use economic sanctions to influence the policies of suppliers. The use of economic sanctions is often influenced by the relationships between commodity-dependent importers and commodity-wealthy exporters.

the rival powers" (Elliott 1993). "Sanctions can be used to deter aggression, defend human rights, and discourage nuclear proliferation" (Lopez and Cortright 1993). For these reasons we can expect sanctions to remain popular.

DIPLOMATIC NEGOTIATION IN LIEU OF COERCION?

In today's globalized economy, sanctions are popular because they offer what appears to be a proportional response to challenges in which the interests at stake are less than vital (Haass 1997). To be sure, with the danger of warfare between states receding, most of the issues that divide countries and prompt them to take action to alter the unacceptable political behavior of their targets fall into this category. The use of **soft power** or "command power" (Keohane and Nye 2001) as a means of bargaining to get other states to change their practices has gained increased recognition in international bargaining, since one country is more likely to follow another's lead because it seeks that country's markets and resources than because it fears its weapons. The National Conference of Catholic Bishops captured the growing sentiment in noting that "sanctions can offer a nonmilitary alternative to the terrible options of war or indifference when confronted with aggression or injustice."

■ **soft power**
the ability to exercise influence in world politics due to intangible resources such as culture and ideas (see p. 462).

There exists another alternative to coercive diplomacy or sanctions as methods for states to exercise influence over other countries with whom they have disputes. This is through the tried-and-true method of negotiation to resolve differences and reach a mutually satisfactory settlement. Behind the scenes, every day, members of states' foreign policy bureaucracies (ranging from heads of state meeting at summits to representatives in embassies and at international organizations) regularly convene to exchange views, consult, and communicate their positions on specific issues. These highly institutionalized channels of communication are critical to the resolution of conflicts; they rely on established procedures at the negotiating table for states to identify mutually satisfactory options and choices that can eliminate the need for the use or threatened use of punishment or even war in order for either party to a disagreement to get its way. The **diplomatic process** provides a measure through which states can bargain to find common ground. In diplomatic dialogue we thus find the most widely used instrument through which crises are managed and peace is preserved in a system that otherwise encourages states to compete, clash, and confront one another.

■ **diplomatic process** the practice of diplomacy through which states reach bargains and agreements.

Although (as with deterrence) it is difficult to identify those many cases in which diplomatic negotiation succeeds, in contemplating how states control their disagreements it is useful to remember that it may be the peacemakers convening in conferences who do the most to maintain the order we witness alongside international anarchy and ruthless violence. Diplomacy reduces international danger. Indeed, the peace-making efforts of diplomatic negotiators may result in the positive outcome of what Dr. Martin Luther King, Jr. termed the "choice between chaos and community."

This chapter reviewed four basic approaches to controlling the behavior of others, concentrating especially on the use of force. Whether for deterrence or compellence, states will continue to rely on strategic weapons to prevent their own mass destruction. They will also continue to use conventional weapons and economic sanctions to defend themselves while bargaining to protect national interests. All three of these methods of coercive diplomacy place an emphasis on capabilities—both military and economic; all three are methods for bargaining that, when used, tell us that the fourth method, diplomatic negotiation, has failed or broken down. The next chapter evaluates how these approaches to the management of armed conflict are often complemented by still other strategies advocated by realism.

KEY TERMS

ethnic cleansing
displaced people
Clinton Doctrine
Third Way
coercive diplomacy
negotiation
politics
realism
bargaining
security dilemma
spiral model
neoliberalism
nuclear deterrence
conventional deterrence
nuclear winter
signaling
Cuban missile crisis
compellence
commitment
brinkmanship
just war
massive retaliation
countervalue targeting strategy
counterforce targeting strategy
peaceful coexistence
peace enforcement
limited war
total war
extended deterrence
second-strike capability
mutual assured destruction (MAD)
Strategic Arms Limitation Talks (SALT)

nuclear utilization theory (NUTs)
Strategic Defense Initiative (SDI)
counterfactual reasoning
START (Strategic Arms Reduction) Treaty
balance of power
doctrine
conventional war
low-intensity conflict (LIC)
preventive diplomacy
peacekeeping
military intervention
covert operations
human rights
failed states
selective engagement
crisis decision
rational choice
militarized disputes
gunboat diplomacy
nonintervention
economic sanctions
sanctions
boycotts
propaganda
apartheid
globalization
soft power
diplomatic process

SUGGESTED READING

Baldwin, David A. "The Sanctions Debate and the Logic of Choice," *International Security* 24 (Winter 2000): 80–107.

Berkowitz, Bruce D., and Allan E. Goodman. "The Logic of Covert Action," *National Interest* 51 (Spring 1998): 38–46.

Brecher, Michael, and Jonathan Wilkenfeld, *A Study of Crisis*. Ann Arbor: University of Michigan Press, 1997.

Elliott, Kimberly Ann. "The Sanctions Glass: Half Full or Completely Empty?" *International Security* 23 (Summer 1998): 50–52.

Falk, Richard A. "The New Interventionism and the Third World," 189–202 in Charles W. Kegley, Jr., and Eugene R. Wittkopf, eds., *The Global Agenda*. Boston: McGraw-Hill, 2001.

Førland, Tor Egil. "The History of Economic Warfare: International Law, Effectiveness, Strategies," *Journal of Peace Research* 30 (May 1993): 151–162.

George, Alexander L. "Strategies for Preventive Diplomacy and Conflict Resolution," *PS: Political Science and Politics* 33 (March 2000): 15–19.

Harvey, Frank P., and Ben D. Mor. *Conflict in World Politics: Advances in the Study of Crisis, War, and Peace*. New York: St. Martin's Press, 1997.

Hoffmann, Stanley. *The Ethics and Politics of Humanitarian Intervention*. Chicago: University of Notre Dame Press, 1997.

Hopmann, P. Terrence. *The Negotiation Process and the Resolution of International Conflicts*. Columbia: University of South Carolina Press, 1996.

Pape, Robert A. "Why Economic Sanctions Do Not Work," *International Security* 22 (Fall 1997): 90–136.

Regan, Patrick M. *Civil Wars and Foreign Powers: Outside Intervention in Interstate Conflict*. Ann Arbor: University of Michigan Press, 2000.

Schneider, Barry R., and William L. Dowdy, eds. *Pulling Back from the Nuclear Brink: Reducing and Countering Nuclear Threats*. Portland, Oreg.: Frank Cass, 1998.

Starkey, Brigid, Mark Boyer, and Jonathan Wilkenfeld. *Negotiating a Complex World: An Introduction to International Negotiation*. Boulder, Colo.: Rowman & Littlefield, 2000.

WHERE ON THE WORLD WIDE WEB?

A-Bomb WWW Museum
http://www.csi.ad.jp/ABOMB/index.html

Visit this Japanese Web site for eyewitness accounts of the impact the first atomic bomb had on Hiroshima. The site includes pictures from the Peace Memorial Museum in Hiroshima that show the effect of the bombing and stories from survivors, many of them deeply disturbing. The A-Bomb WWW Museum was created as a perpetual reminder of the horrors of atomic bombing. It welcomes e-mail responses from all around the world.

Atomic Bomb: Decision
http://www.peak.org/~danneng/decision/decision.html

This Web site houses the available documents on the decision to use atomic bombs on the cities of Hiroshima and Nagasaki. Scan eyewitness accounts of the Trinity Test. Read what the individuals responsible for creating the bomb and for deciding to drop it had to say. See the official bombing order and hear an excerpt of President Truman's radio speech announcing the decision. Based on what you have read and heard, do you think the United States should have dropped the bomb?

Fourth Freedom Forum
http://www.fourthfreedom.org/

Are economic sanctions a useful tool in statecraft? Visit the Fourth Freedom Forum's Web site to get a pro-sanctions point of view. The Fourth Freedom Forum's works toward "a more civilized world based on the force of law rather than the law of force." It contends that the effective use of economic incentives and sanctions offers the greatest hope for creating a more secure and peaceful future. From the homepage, click on Sanctions and Incentives. Here you will find an extensive collection of articles related to international sanctions and case studies. Do you think sanctions are effective? Under what circumstances should they be used?

Missile Threats & Responses
http://www.cdiss.org/tempor1.htm

Want to know the difference between a ballistic, cruise, biological, chemical, or radiological missiles? How effective are missile defense systems? Do you want to join a forum to discuss issues relating to weapons of mass destruction (WMD)? Visit the site of the Center for Defence and International Security Studies at Cartmel College in Great Britain. It offers an overview of different WMD, raises awareness about the issues, and stimulates debate on a wide range of defence and security matters.

Remembering Nagasaki
http://www.exploratorium.edu/nagasaki/index.html

A stunning Web site, Remembering Nagasaki presents the photographs of Japanese army photographer Yosuke Yamhata, who took pictures the day after the bomb was dropped. A public forum on issues related to the atomic age includes memories from people all over the world of the moment when they heard about the explosion of the bomb and how they constructed the story in their minds, discussion of the decision to drop the bomb, the question of how to tell history, and the ethical responsibilities of scientists. This is a truly fascinating site that explores the issues from all sides.

Russian Roulette
http://www.pbs.org/wgbh/pages/frontline/shows/russia/

PBS's famous *Frontline* series is on-line with a look at the safety and security of Russia's nuclear arsenal and the potential for accidental launch or diversion of its nuclear weapons. Take a look at Russia's nuclear complex. Compare and contrast U.S. and Russian nuclear arsenals and become familiar with nuclear smuggling incidents. Read interviews with policy experts, smugglers, scientists, analysts, and law enforcement agents, and analyze Russian and U.S. articles for further perspective. On the other hand, you may not want to look at this Web site at all. As a Russian proverb states, "The less you know the better you sleep."

CHAPTER 15

THE REALIST ROAD TO SECURITY THROUGH ALLIANCES, THE BALANCE OF POWER, AND ARMS CONTROL

TOPICS AND THEMES

- Alliances and their impact on national and global security
- The balance of power
- Controlling military power through arms agreements
- Can the acquisition of allies and arms stabilize a twenty-first-century multipolar world?

- **CONTROVERSY** ARE ALLIES FRIENDS OR FOES? RECONSIDERING THE ADVANTAGES AND DISADVANTAGES OF ALLIES TO A STATE'S SECURITY
- **CONTROVERSY** IS THE BALANCE OF POWER A PRECARIOUS AND FAILED SECURITY SYSTEM?
- **CONTROVERSY** IS A UNIPOLAR, BIPOLAR, OR MULTIPOLAR SYSTEM THE MOST STABLE? THREE SCHOOLS OF THOUGHT ON THE RELATIONSHIP OF POLARITY AND INTERNATIONAL PEACE

Leonid Brezhnev and Jimmy Carter sign the SALT II Treaty, 1979.

The aim of disarmament is to increase security. All countries, regardless of their size, strength and wealth, have an equal right of security. If the great majority of developing countries cannot have security, there will never be tranquility throughout the world. Disarmament should not become a tool for stronger nations to control weaker ones. Still less should it be an instrument for a handful of countries to optimize their armaments in order to seek unilateral superiority.

—Jiang Zemin, president of China, 1999

[The quest for a preponderance of power in relation to rivals] inevitably becomes a contagious disease; for, as soon as one state increases what it calls its forces, the others immediately increase theirs, so that nothing is gained except mutual ruination.

—Charles de Montesquieu, political philosopher, 1748

■ **security dilemma** the propensity of armaments amassed by one state for ostensibly defensive purposes to be perceived by others as threatening, which drive the alarmed competitors to undertake as a countermeasure a military buildup that heightens both states' insecurities (see p. 102).

Imagine yourself as the next secretary-general of the United Nations (UN). You face responsibility for fulfilling the UN's Charter to preserve world peace. Looking at the globe, you see that many countries have the capacity to annihilate their enemies with new weapons of mass destruction whenever they wish to unleash the military power in their states' arsenal. As a consequence, you see the **security dilemma** that has been created: Due to the escalating destructive power of modern weapons, most states' sense of national security has decreased, rather than increased, and the globe's more than 6 billion people live in fear that they will not see tomorrow. What course should you counsel the UN's 189 members to pursue?

The patterns of the past five decades suggest that most states continue to reject the **liberal** and the neoliberal paths of peace, which recommend building institutions for world law, states' integration, and/or reform of governmental procedures for democratically making national security decisions (see Chapter 16). Rather, most states follow the realist road, seeing their viable choices as among three basic, time-honored options: States can (1) arm themselves; (2) form (or sever) alliances with other countries; or (3) negotiate arms control and disarmament agreements to reduce the threat of adversaries' weapons. Although most leaders usually pursue various combinations of these strategies, each nonetheless represents a distinct military approach to security.

Suspending judgment for the moment about the possible need to try other, possibly more effective nonmilitary institutional escapes from the security dilemma, how would you give advice within realism's ever popular worldview? Consider the classical and **neotraditional realist** viewpoints as the basis for your recommendations (see Chapter 2).

Up to this point, our discussion of conflict and its management has followed a logical progression. Chapter 12 began by exploring why the frequency of war makes preparations for it so necessary. Chapter 13 examined the search for national security through the acquisition of military capabilities. Chapter 14 assessed states' use of coercive diplomacy, both to realize their national goals abroad and to deter their rivals from aggression. We now concentrate on the other two military approaches to national security—the use of alliances and arms control to maintain a favorable balance of power and thereby enhance security. These approaches draw their inspiration primarily from the assumptions that realist theory makes about the most prudent paths to peace (see Table 15.1).

liberalism
a paradigm predicated on the hope that the application of reason and universal ethics to international relations can lead to a more orderly, just, and cooperative world, and that international anarchy and war can be policed by institutional reforms that empower international organizations and law (see p. 28).

neotraditional realism
the "new" version of classical realist theorizing that emphasizes leaders, their perceptions of national interests, and changes in capabilities as the primary determinants of states' foreign policies, instead of the "structural" neorealist focus on the influence of the global system (see p. 35).

TABLE 15.1

The Realist Road to Security: Assumptions and Policy Recommendations

The Realist Picture of the International Environment	
Primary global condition:	Anarchy
Probability of system change/reform:	Low
Prime actors:	States, and especially great powers
Principal actor goals:	Power over others, self-preservation, and physical security
Predominant pattern of actor interaction:	Competition and conflict
Pervasive concern:	National security
Prevalent state priorities:	Acquiring military capabilities
Popular state practice:	Use of armed force for coercive diplomacy
Realist Policy Prescription	*Premise*
Prepare for war:	If you want peace, prepare for war.
Remain vigilant:	No state is to be trusted further than its national interest.
Remain involved and actively intervene:	Isolationism is not an alternative to active global involvement.
Protect with arms:	Strive to increase military capabilities, and fight rather than submit to subordination.
Preserve the balance of power:	Do not let any state or coalition of states become predominant.
Prevent arms races from resulting in military inferiority with rivals:	Negotiate agreements with competitors to maintain a favorable military balance.

ALLIANCES AND THEIR IMPACT ON NATIONAL AND GLOBAL SECURITY

■ **alliances**
coalitions that form when two or more states combine their military capabilities and promise to coordinate their policies to increase mutual security.

Alliances are formal agreements among states to coordinate their behavior in the event of military emergencies. Alliances thus are coalitions that heed realism's first rule of statecraft: to increase military capabilities. States can do this either by acquiring arms or by acquiring allies. Although alliances are more economical because they permit the defense burden to be shared, throughout history states have vigorously pursued both methods. While alliances appear to be the preferred, least costly method for increasing military capabilities, this solution has significant disadvantages. Making alliance choices has seldom been easy, as it requires weighing the military strength, goals, and reliability of allies and adversaries alike.

Allies offer a means to counterbalance threats in an anarchical global system. Throughout history many states involved in conflicts have forged alliances with others "even in advance, against [a] probable aggressor" (Morgenthau 1959).

Alliances are "typically against, and only derivatively for, someone or something" (Liska 1962). They tend to form when two or more states face a common threat, because a mutual defense alliance can reduce the probability of being attacked (deterrence), [provide each ally] greater strength in case of attack (defense), and prevent the ally's alliance with one's adversary (preclusion)" (G. Snyder 1991).

Most alliances have not lasted long and have often dissolved when the common threat disappeared. For this reason, realists primarily see alliance formation as a strategy that includes both the recruitment and abandonment of allies. Recognizing that "alignment and dealignment are the main short-term strategies for increasing security," states have the choice of adding or expanding commitments to other states to increase their own state's security, as opposed to eliminating or reducing commitments to allies that are a drain on security (Scarborough and Bueno de Mesquita 1988). According to realpolitik logic, the best kind of alliance is one that can be dissolved easily when the threat to one's own security declines. As Britain's Lord Palmerston admonished in 1848, states "should have no eternal allies and no perpetual enemies." Their only duty, then, is to follow their interests, which may require abandoning an ally when it ceases to be useful.

The greatest risk to forming alliances is that they bind a state to a commitment that may later become disadvantageous. Throughout history, policymakers have been mindful of dangerous entanglements, because entrusting their security to the pledges of others reduces their future freedom of action. Consequently, many leaders are risk averse about making hasty commitments to a friendly government; indeed, "wise and experienced statesmen usually shy away from commitments likely to constitute limitations on a government's behavior at unknown dates in the future in the face of unpredictable situations" (Kennan 1984a). Although alliances provide some measure of protection, they also reduce a state's capacity to make accommodative realignments when conditions change. In fact, the usefulness of any alliance is destined to lessen once the common external threat that brought it together declines, as it inevitably will (Wolfers 1962). The realist tradition therefore strongly advises heads of state not to take a fixed position on temporary convergences of national interests and to forge alliances only to deal with immediate threats.

When considering whether a new alliance is a good idea—a **rational choice** in which the benefits outweigh the costs—heads of state usually recognize that such decisions are hard. The payoffs and consequences of casting their fate with another state are difficult to foresee, and in the long run, allies can easily do more harm than good (see Controversy: Are Allies Friends or Foes?).

In fact, many realists advise states to avoid alliances unless absolutely necessary for defense. They base their fears on five fundamental flaws:

rational choice a decision made by careful definition of the situation, weighing of goals, consideration of all alternatives, and selection of the options most likely to achieve the highest goals (see p. 66).

1. First, alliances enable aggressive states to combine military capabilities for aggression. This was the thinking of Adolf Hitler, who maintained that "Any alliance whose purpose is not the intention to wage war is senseless and useless." Alliances are to be feared because they allow expansionist states, counting on their allies' assistance, to act more aggressively than they otherwise would.
2. Second, alliances threaten enemies and provoke them to form counteralliances. This results in reduced security for *both* coalitions.

   > Peacetime alliances may occur in order to reduce the insecurity of anarchy or reduce armament costs. If they do, they will tend to create relations of enmity as well as alignment. Even if the initial alliance is not directed at a specific opponent, other states will perceive it as a threat and begin to behave as enemies, perhaps by forming a counteralliance. (G. Snyder 1991, 88)

3. Third, alliance formation may draw otherwise neutral parties into opposed coalitions. As a liberal theorist, U.S. President Thomas Jefferson warned, alliances can be dangerously "entangling." They require members to come to one another's aid, involving members in the wars of their partners.
4. Fourth, once states join forces, they must control the behavior of their own allies. Management of intra-alliance relations is necessary to discourage each member from reckless aggression against its enemies, threatening the security of the alliance's other members. In addition, allies must work to deter defection from the alliance and to ensure that allies' commitments to one another are faithfully honored.
5. Finally, the possibility always exists that today's ally might become tomorrow's enemy. Realists believe that all states are natural enemies, that there are no permanent friends or adversaries. The historical record is noteworthy in this respect. In the period between the Congress of Vienna in 1815 and the 1960s, wars between allies were commonplace: "More than 25 percent of coalition partners eventually [went] to war against each other" (Russett and Starr 1996, 91). Thus, when alliances form, they can increase the prospects for and the scope of war.

In a 1917 address to the U.S. Senate, President Woodrow Wilson proposed that "all nations avoid entangling alliances which would draw them into . . . a net of intrigue and selfish rivalry." In taking this position, which reflected his liberal belief that alliances and secret diplomacy transform limited conflicts into global wars with many participants, Wilson underscored the difficulties and the dangers of making alliance decisions. Despite their uncertain usefulness, many states have chosen to ally throughout history because, the risks notwithstanding, the perceived benefits to security in a time of threat justified that decision.

CONTROVERSY

ARE ALLIES FRIENDS OR FOES?

Reconsidering the Advantages and Disadvantages of Allies to a State's Security

When states make decisions about forging alliances, they must keep in mind the many risks of sharing their fate with other states. While realists generally see alliances as potentially beneficial, they caution that alliance formation is risky. A state making a defense pact with an ally, they warn, will also pay a heavy price. Creating alliances will:

- Foreclose options.
- Reduce the state's capacity to adapt to changing circumstances.
- Weaken a state's capability to influence others by decreasing the number of additional partners with which it can align.
- Eliminate the advantages in bargaining that can be derived from deliberately fostering ambiguity about one's intentions.
- Provoke the fears of adversaries.
- Entangle states in disputes with their allies' enemies.
- Interfere with the negotiation of disputes involving an ally's enemy by precluding certain issues from being placed on the agenda.
- Preserve existing rivalries.
- Stimulate envy and resentment on the part of friends who are outside the alliance and are therefore not eligible to receive its advantages.

These potential dangers explain why alliance decisions are so controversial, even when advocates enthusiastically propose that another state be sought as an ally for mutual defense. The posture of leaders about the advantage or disadvantage of alliances has depended on their personal philosophy and the country's circumstances. What do you think? What are the advantages of having alliance partners? In thinking about your options, look at the photo that follows. Pictured here, in 1796, is George Washington, the first president of the United States, advising other leaders in American government that it should be the foreign policy of the United States to "steer clear of permanent alliances." He felt that whereas a state "may safely trust to temporary alliances for extraordinary emergencies" it is an "illusion . . . to expect or calculate real favors from nation to nation." Yet, almost every state is insecure in one way or another and is tempted to recruit allies to bolster its defense capabilities and protect its power as a united friend to adversaries that threaten it.

levels of analysis variables at the global, state, and individual levels that explain why transnational actors behave as they do in international relations (see p. 56).

To best picture how alliances affect global security, it is instructive to move from the state level of analysis, which views alliance decisions from the perspective of individual state's security, to the global **level of analysis** (recall Chapters 1 and 3) by looking at the impact of alliances on the frequency of interstate war. This view focuses attention on the possible contribution of alliance formation to maintaining the balance of power.

THE BALANCE OF POWER

International anarchy makes each state responsible for its own national security. The seventeenth-century English realist philosopher Thomas Hobbes observed that this condition encourages among states a perpetual "war of all against all." Realists, neorealists, and neotraditional realists argue that reforming this system is unrealistic because international anarchy is permanent, as is the selfish drive for power over rivals. Survival and world order rest on the proper functioning of a system of shifting military alignments commonly referred to as the "balance of power."

Assumptions of Balance-of-Power Theory

Balance of power is an ambiguous concept used in a variety of ways (see Claude 1962). At its core is the idea that peace will result when military power is distributed so that no one state is strong enough to dominate the others. If one state, or a combination of states, gains enough power to threaten others, compelling incentives will exist for those threatened to disregard their superficial differences and unite in a defensive alliance. The power resulting from such collaboration would, according to this conception, deter the would-be attacker from pursuing expansionism. Thus, from the laissez-faire competition of predatory and defensive rivals would emerge a balance of contending factions, which would maintain the status quo.

■ **balance of power** the theory that peace and stability are most likely to be maintained when military power is distributed so that no single power or bloc can dominate the others (see p. 619).

Balance-of-power theory is also founded on the realist premise that weakness invites attack and that countervailing power must be used to deter potential aggressors. Because realists assume that the drive for expanded power guides every state's actions, it follows that all countries are potential adversaries, and each must strengthen its military capability to protect itself. Invariably, this reasoning rationalizes the quest for military superiority because others pursue it as well.

■ **alignments** the acceptance by a neutral state threatened by foreign enemies of a special relationship short of formal alliance with a stronger power able to protect it from attack.

On the surface, these realist assumptions appear dubious (especially to liberals). The arms races they justify can easily lead to the very outcome most feared—a destructive, global war. However, the realist policymakers in Europe who formulated classical balance-of-power theory after the Peace of Westphalia in 1648 were not irrational (Gulick 1955). They reasoned that a system founded on suspicion and competition, in which all states were independent and could make rational choices freely to advance their perceived national interests, would distribute power evenly through **alignments**—shifts by neutrals to one coalition or the other. A free-floating balance-of-power **security regime** without formal rules on how, where, and when to act for specified goals, they believed, could curtail the temptation of any actor to dominate others.

■ **security regime** norms and rules for interaction agreed to by a set of states to cooperatively increase their mutual security.

The Balance Process. In classic balance-of-power theory, fear of a third party would encourage alignments, because those threatened would need help to offset the power of the mutual adversary. An alliance would add the ally's power to the state's own and deny the addition of that power to the enemy. As alliances combine power, the offsetting coalitions would give neither a clear advantage. Therefore, aggression would appear unattractive and would be averted.

To deter an aggressor, counteralliances were expected to form easily, because states sitting on the sidelines could not risk **nonalignment.** If they

■ **nonalignment** a foreign policy posture in which states do not participate in military alliances with either of two rival blocs for fear that alliance will lead to involvement in an unnecessary war.

■ **size principle**
the propensity for competitors to form coalitions only sufficient in size to ensure victory, even if by a narrow margin, with the result that over time opposed alliances tend to remain roughly equal to one another.

■ **balancer**
under a balance-of-power system, an influential global or regional great power that throws its support in decisive fashion to a defensive coalition. This role was often played by Great Britain in the eighteenth and nineteenth centuries.

refused to ally, their own vulnerability would encourage the expansionist state to attack them at a later time. In theory, the result of these individual calculations would be the formation of coalitions approximately equal in power. This theory presumes that state actors (agents) are rational and that they elect to make policies aimed at equalizing the power of competing coalitions because of their ability to recognize states' interest in stopping aggression. The so-called **size principle** accounts for the inclination of rational actors to form coalitions only sufficient in size to ensure victory and no larger, resulting in political coalitions that are roughly equal in size (see Riker 1962).

To maintain an even distribution of power, realists recommend certain *rules* be followed to promote fluid and rapidly shifting alliances. They recognize that a balance will develop only if states practice certain behaviors. One requirement is that a great power not immediately threatened by the rise of another power or coalition perform the role of a **balancer** by offsetting the new challenger's power. Since the modern state system began in the seventeenth century, Great Britain has often played this role by consistently supporting the weaker coalition to prevent an expansionist state and its allies from achieving dominance.

In addition to needing a balancer, all states have to obey the following "essential rules": "(1) increase capabilities but negotiate rather than fight; (2) fight rather than fail to increase capabilities; (3) stop fighting rather than eliminate an essential actor; (4) oppose any coalition or single actor that tends to assume a position of predominance within the system; (5) constrain actors who subscribe to supranational organizational principles; and (6) permit defeated or constrained essential national actors to reenter the system as acceptable role partners" (Kaplan 1957).

According to these rules, competition is proper because it leads to the equalization of capabilities among the major competitors. The balance-of-power approach deals with the problem of war in a way that preserves the problem. War is a way to measure states' relative power as well as a means for changing the distribution of global power in order to preserve the essential features of the balance-of-power system itself.

The successful operation of a global balance-of-power system also presupposes some important preconditions for its successful operation. To maintain a balance, for example, Kenneth Waltz (1979) advances the neorealist thesis that "balance-of-power politics prevail whenever two, and only two, requirements are met: that the order be anarchic and that it be populated by units wishing to survive." Most other theorists hold a more complex view, and argue that the following conditions must exist:

- States must possess accurate information about others' capabilities and motives and react rationally to this information.
- There must be a sufficient number of independent states to make alliance formation and dissolution readily possible; stable balance-of-power systems usually require at least five great powers or blocs of states.
- There must be a limited geographic area.
- National leaders must have freedom of action.
- States' capabilities must be relatively equal.
- States must share a common political culture in which the rules of the security regime are recognized and respected.

- States in the system must have similar types of government and ideologies.
- States must have a weapons technology that inhibits **preemption**—quick mobilizations for war, first-strike attacks that defeat the enemy before it can organize a retaliatory response—and wars of annihilation.
- There must be no supranational institutions capable of interfering with states' alignments and realignments.

preemption a quick first-strike attack that seeks to defeat an adversary before it can organize a retaliatory response.

These preconditions characterized the environment of international politics during most periods before World War II. But do they exist today? Are the assumptions underlying classic balance-of-power theory still warranted?

The Breakdown of Power Balances. Is international order truly a product of alliance formation and power balances, as many realists (Liska 1968; Osgood 1968) believe? Or, when arms races and alliance formation combine power into contending blocs, do the aligned states find that their security actually declines and that major wars then usually erupt?

If the assumptions of the balance-of-power theory are correct, historical periods in which the basic preconditions listed above were in evidence should also have been periods in which war was less frequent. What does the historical record show?

The Eurocentric system that existed from the mid-seventeenth century until World War I is generally regarded as the "golden age" of balance-of-power politics. But even then the balance of power was always precarious at best (Dehio 1962). Indeed, the regularity of wars in Europe between the mid-1600s and the early twentieth century (the period when the necessary conditions for the "invisible hand" of the balance of power most clearly existed) reinforces the question of whether this approach brings peace or, instead, is a cause of war (see Controversy: Is the Balance of Power a Precarious and Failed Security System?). Although the classical systems may at times have prolonged the intervals of peace between conflicts and possibly limited wars' duration and damage when they occurred, a balancing of power has never kept the peace. Research shows that although during the nineteenth century alliance formation within the balance-of-power system was associated with the absence of war, throughout the first half of the twentieth century, this linkage no longer held; as many states became members of alliances, the frequency of war increased (Singer and Small 1968). However, this is not to argue that the pattern was entirely consistent in this time period. To be sure, several **long peaces**—long-lasting periods of great-power peace—occurred in Europe during the balance of power (between the Congress of Vienna in 1815 and the outbreak of war across Europe in 1848, and after the Franco-Prussian War in 1871 until 1914). An alternative explanation of the relative peace during these periods is offered by **hegemonic stability theory,** which postulates that the existence of a single, all-powerful military **hegemon** can safeguard system stability better than an equilibrium resulting from balance-of-power politics (Wohlforth 1999). At this time, it was the extraordinary dominance of power possessed and used by Great Britain, the world's hegemonic leader, that kept peace among its European rivals (Organski 1968). Whatever the causes of modern periods of peace followed by major wars, the most striking feature of the balance of power was the increasingly destructive general wars that erupted each time these balance-of-power systems collapsed.

long peaces long-lasting periods of great-power peace.

hegemonic stability theory the argument that a dominant state is necessary to enforce international cooperation, maintain international rules and regimes, and keep the peace.

hegemon a single dominant military and economic state (see p. 432).

CONTROVERSY

Is the Balance of Power a Precarious and Failed Security System?

The balance of power is an approach to preserving international peace that has been strenuously advocated by realists since the Thirty Years' War ended in 1648. The Peace of Westphalia, which ended that war, endorsed the balance of power and since then, has frequently been advocated as a strategy to prevent any one state or alliance from gaining superiority over others. Great powers often have adhered to the logic of realism—that the balance of power is the best method of perserving peace—and frequently have reaffirmed it often as the best method for reducing the frequency and duration of major wars. It would seem the balance of power must be the best solution—better than world government and other approaches recommended by liberals. However, in the course of three and a half centuries many wars broke out. The onset of these wars temporarily undermined confidence in the balance of power and aroused criticism of it as a cause of war rather than a stabilizing mechanism. Nonetheless, faith in traditional balance-of-power politics to maintain global stability has resurfaced periodically, and persists even today, despite its repeated failure to produce enduring peace. Is the balance of power a false solution?

What do you think? In evaluating your response, take into account the evaluation of perhaps the foremost expert on the balance of power, the realist political scientist Inis L. Claude, who came to this sobering conclusion:

> Balance-of-power theory is concerned mainly with the rivalries and clashes of great powers—above all—what we have come to describe as world wars, the massive military conflicts that engulf and threaten to destroy the entire multistate system. It is difficult to consider world wars as anything other than catastrophic failures, total collapses, of the balance-of-power system. They are hardly to be classed as stabilizing maneuvers or equilibrating processes, and one cannot take seriously any claim of maintaining international stability that does not entail the prevention of such disasters as the Napoleonic wars or World War I. Mention of those and similar disasters, however, frequently evokes the reminder that the would-be universal emperor—be it Louis XIV or Napoleon or Hitler—was defeated; in accordance with balance of power principles, a coalition arose to put down the challenger and maintain or restore the independence of the various states. In short, the system worked. Or did it? Is the criterion of the effectiveness of the balance of power that Germany lose its bid for conquest, or that it be deterred from precipitating World War I? It is not easy to justify the contention that a system for the management of international relations that failed to prevent the events of 1914–1918 deserves high marks as a guardian of stability or order, or peace. If the balance-of-power system does not aim at the prevention of world war, then it aims too low; if it offers no hope of maintaining the general peace, then the quest for a better system is fully warranted. (Claude 1989, 78)

The question to be asked is whether the balance of power is a reliable mechanism to prevent global war or whether there is a better approach. If so, what is it? Is it collective security, as liberal idealists such as Woodrow Wilson believed, or some other approach?

In light of the repetitious breakdown of the balance of power, it is noteworthy that the pattern of recurrent general wars ended when the nuclear era began, after World War II. Since then, war among great powers has been virtually nonexistent. Another long peace (Gaddis 1991) has taken root. Could it be that the **balance of terror** created by nuclear weapons has deterred great-power belligerence since 1945 more than the balance of power? Arguably, alliance formation and balance-of-power politics could not have caused this long peace. Rigid alliance blocs halted the rapid realignments necessary for the equilibrium that balance-of-power theory envisions. If that is so, then it seems likely that the annihilating destructiveness of nuclear weapons kept the peace since the 1950s—not the alliances and power balances that the great powers constructed.

balance of terror situations of mutual nuclear deterrence.

Equally debatable is the realist assumption underlying balance-of-power theory that countries with dominant strength will be secure. Contrary evidence suggests that rapidly arming countries may actually invite attack. In five of the nine great-power wars that occurred in the 150 years following the 1815 Congress of Vienna, the countries attacked were stronger militarily than those initiating the war (Singer and Small 1974; see also Chapter 13). This belies the premise that seeking military advantages over others deters aggression. Instead, as liberals warn, the growth of a state's military power may so terrify its adversaries that they are motivated to initiate a preemptive strike in order to prevent their defeat.

The Rise, Fall, and Revival of Collective Security as a Substitute for Power Balances

The outbreak of World War I, perhaps more than any other event, discredited balance-of-power politics and promoted the search for alternatives. The catastrophic proportions of that war led many, especially those attracted to the liberal theoretical interpretation of world politics, to view the balance-of-power mechanism as a *cause* of war instead of an instrument for its prevention. These critics cited the arms races, secret treaties, and cross-cutting alliances driving balance-of-power politics before the outbreak of the war as its immediate causes.

U.S. President Woodrow Wilson voiced the most vehement opposition to balance-of-power politics. He and other liberal reformers hoped to replace the alliances and counteralliances within the balance of power with the principle of **collective security,** a system of world order in which aggression by any state would be met by a collective response.

■ **collective security**
a global or regional security regime agreed to by the great powers setting rules for keeping peace, guided by the principle that an act of aggression by any state automatically will be met by a combined military response from the rest.

The League of Nations embodied this belief, built on the assumption that peace-loving countries could collectively deter—and, if necessary, counteract—aggression. Instead of accepting war as a legitimate instrument of national policy, collective security advocates sought to inhibit war through the threat of collective action. The theory proposed: (1) to retaliate against *any* aggression or attempt to establish hegemony—not just those acts that threatened particular countries; (2) to involve the participation of *all* member states—not just a sufficient number to stop the aggressor; and (3) to create an international organization to identify acts of aggression and to organize a military response to them—not just to let individual states decide for themselves whether to undertake self-help measures. In essence, collective security may be defined as "collective self-regulation," occurring when "a group of states attempts to reduce security threats by agreeing to collectively punish any member state that violates the system's norms" (Downs 1994). As one realist authority impartially describes the concept,

> The rock bottom principle upon which collective security is founded provides that an attack on any one state will be regarded as an attack on all states. It finds its measure in the simple doctrine of one for all and all for one. War anywhere . . . is the concern of every state.
>
> Self-help and neutrality, it should be obvious, are the exact antithesis of such a theory. States under an order of neutrality are impartial when conflict breaks out, give their blessings to combatants to fight it out, and defer judgment regarding the justice or injustice of the cause involved. Self-help in the past was often "help yourself" so far as the great powers were concerned; they enforced their own rights and more besides. In the eighteenth

> and nineteenth centuries this system was fashionable, and wars, although not eliminated, were localized whenever possible. In a more integrated world environment, a conflict anywhere has some effect on conditions of peace everywhere. A disturbance at one point upsets the equilibrium at all other points, and the adjustment of a single conflict restores the foundations of harmony at other points throughout the world. (Thompson 1953, 755)

To the disappointment of its advocates, collective security was not endorsed by the very powers that after World War I had most championed it, such as the United States. Japan's aggression against Manchuria in 1931 (and China in 1937) and Italy's invasion of Ethiopia in 1935 were widely condemned, but collective resistance was not forthcoming. Germany's invasion of Czechoslovakia and other European countries in the late 1930s elicited no collective response. When World War II broke out, collective security was discredited, and balance-of-power politics regained favor, along with realism, as the most popular approach for preserving global peace. In the wake of that deadly, global war, realists convinced many people that national self-reliance was the only trustworthy safeguard of security. They loudly preached that peace must come through states' unilateral preparations for war and use of acquired military might, to confront a potential aggressor with an abundance of power to successfully deter its aggression. U.S. President Richard Nixon was one of many leaders who reaffirmed the balance-of-power approach and rejected **multilateral** collective peacekeeping; he argued "We must remember the only time in the history of the world that we have had any extended period of peace is when there has been a balance of power. . . . It will be a safer world . . . if we have a strong, healthy United States, Europe, Soviet Union, China, and Japan, each balancing the other."

■ **multilateral** agreements among many states to cooperate for the purpose of collective action (see p. 354).

That realpolitik philosophy fell on receptive ears throughout the tense Cold War and helped to propel the worldwide arms race that characterized it. It was only after the Cold War ended in 1991 that the global community began to once again consider collective security as the preferred method for letting the UN and regional defense organizations maintain world order (see Chapter 16). Changing times in the midst of cascading **globalization** seemed to justify a return to liberal approaches. For lessons about the applicability of balance-of-power theory to today's realities, it is instructive to review the evolution of the international system's polarity structure in the post–World War II era, the world's longest period of great-power peace.

■ **globalization** the integration of states through increasing contact, communication and trade to create a holistic, single global system, which increasingly binds people together in a common fate (see p. 41).

■ **polarity** the degree to which the global system revolves around one or more extremely powerful states, or "poles," as power concentrates in a single (unipolar) center of power or is distributed between two (bipolar) main powers or among three or more (multipolar) great powers.

Models of the Balance of Power in the Second Half of the Twentieth Century

Military power can be distributed in different ways—an idea scholars call **polarity.** Historically, these have ranged from highly concentrated power on one end of the continuum to highly dispersed distributions on the other. The former have included regional empires (e.g., the Roman Empire), while an example of the latter is the approximate equality of power held by the European powers at the conclusion of the Napoleonic Wars in 1815. Following the conventional periods (e.g., Kaplan 1957; Kegley and Raymond 1994; Thompson 1988), we can identify three major distributions of international power since 1945, with a fourth probably emergent in the early twenty-first century.

Unipolarity—the United States. Most countries were devastated by World War II. The United States, however, was left in a clearly dominant position, its economy accounting for about half the world's combined gross national product (GNP). The United States was also the only country with the atomic bomb, and had demonstrated its willingness to use the new weapon. This underscored to others that it was without rival and incapable of being counterbalanced. The United States was not just stronger than *anybody*—it was stronger than *everybody*. The post–World War II power configuration was unipolar, because power was concentrated in the hands of a single hegemon. This period, however, was short-lived (although some believe that in 2000 the United States has once again regained sufficient military and economic resources to recreate a new unipolar phase, claiming to be the globe's only remaining uncontested superpower capable of preserving international peace by the application of its military might).

Bipolarity—the United States and Russia. The recovery of the Soviet economy, the growth of its military capabilities, its maintenance of a large army, and growing Soviet-U.S. rivalry soon gave rise to a new distribution of world power. The Soviets broke the U.S. monopoly on atomic weapons in 1949 and exploded a thermonuclear device in 1953, less than a year after the United States. This achievement symbolized the creation of **bipolarity** in the global system, as military capabilities were redistributed to become concentrated in the hands of two competitive "superpowers," whose capacity to massively destroy anyone made comparisons with the other great powers meaningless.

Power combined to form two opposing blocs or coalitions through **polarization** when states joined counterbalanced alliances. In interpreting these dynamics, it is important not to use the concepts of polarity and polarization interchangeably. They refer to two distinct dimensions of the primary ways in which military power is aggregated (or dispersed) at any point in time in the international system. When states independently build arms at home, their differential production rates change the system's *polarity*, or number of power centers (poles). In contrast, when states combine their arms through alliance formation, the aggregation of power through *polarization* changes the system's balance of power. A system with multiple power centers can be said to be moving toward a greater degree of polarization if its members form separate blocs whose external interactions are characterized by increasing levels of conflict while their internal interactions become more cooperative (Rapkin and Thompson with Christopherson 1989). Conversely, polarization decreases when the number of cross-cutting alignments expands. The concept of polarization is especially apt in this context because a *pole* suggests the metaphor of a magnet—it both repels and attracts.

The formation of the **North Atlantic Treaty Organization (NATO),** linking the United States to the defense of Western Europe, and the Warsaw Pact, linking the former Soviet Union in a formal alliance with its Eastern European clients, were produced by this polarization process. Through this process, states combined their military resources in two countercoalitions to reinforce a bipolar structure. The opposing blocs formed in part because the superpowers competed for allies and in part because the less powerful states looked to one superpower or the other for protection. Correspondingly, each superpower's allies gave it forward bases from which to carry on the competition. In addition,

■ **bipolarity**
the division of the balance of power into two coalitions headed by rival military powers, each seeking to contain the other's expansion.

■ **polarization**
the degree to which states cluster in alliances around the most powerful members of the state system.

■ **North Atlantic Treaty Organization (NATO)**
a military alliance created in 1949 to deter a Soviet attack on Western Europe that now seeks to maintain peace and promote democracy.

the involvement of most other states in the superpowers' struggle globalized the East-West conflict. Few states remained outside the superpowers' rival alliance networks as neutral or nonaligned countries.

By grouping the system's states into two blocs, each led by a superpower, the Cold War's bipolar structure bred insecurity among all. The balance was constantly at stake. Each bloc leader, fearing that its adversary would attain hegemony, viewed every move, however defensive, as the first step toward world conquest. **Zero-sum** conflict was endemic as both sides viewed what one side gained as a loss for the other. Both the United States and the former Soviet Union therefore attached great importance to recruiting new allies. Fear that an old ally might desert the fold was everpresent. Bipolarity left little room for compromise or maneuver and worked against the normalization of superpower relations (Waltz 1993).

■ **zero-sum**
the perception in a rivalry that if one side gains, the other side loses (see p. 490).

Bipolycentrism—Cold War Satellites. The major Cold War coalitions associated with bipolarity began to disintegrate in the 1960s and early 1970s. As their internal cohesion eroded and new centers of power emerged, a bipolycentric system came into being. **Bipolycentrism** described the continued military superiority of the two superpowers and their allies' continued reliance on their respective patrons for security. At the same time, the weaker alliance partners were afforded more room for maneuvering. Thus the term **polycentrism** was coined to describe the emergence of diverse relationships among the states subordinate to the superpowers at this second tier (e.g., the friendly relations between the United States and Romania, on the one hand, and those between France and the Soviet Union, on the other). The secondary powers also began to cultivate ties across alliance boundaries (e.g., between Poland and West Germany) to enhance their bargaining position within their own alliance. Although the superpowers remained dominant militarily, this less rigid system allowed other states to perform new foreign policy roles.

■ **bipolycentrism**
the state of military biopolarity between the United States and Soviet Union, coupled with multiple political centers of independent and non-aligned foreign policies.

■ **polycentrism**
a concept used to describe the emergence of new centers of independent power within the polarized bloc structure of the Cold War.

Rapid technological innovation in the superpowers' major weapons systems was a principal catalyst to the crumbling of the blocs. Intercontinental ballistic missiles (ICBMs), capable of delivering nuclear weapons through space from one continent to another, eroded the necessity of forward bases for striking at the heart of the adversary.

In addition, the narrowed differences in the superpowers' arsenals loosened the ties that had previously bound allies to one another. The European members of NATO in particular began to question whether the United States would, as it had pledged, protect Paris or Bonn by sacrificing New York. Under what conditions might Washington or Moscow be willing to risk a nuclear holocaust? The uncertainty became pronounced as the pledge to protect allies through **extended deterrence** seemed increasingly insincere. As former director of Central Intelligence Stansfield Turner acknowledged in 1986, "It's not conceivable that any president would risk the very existence of [the United States] in order to defend [our] European allies from a conventional assault."

■ **extended deterrence**
the protection received by a weak ally when a heavily militarized great power pledges to "extend" its capabilities to it in a defense treaty (see p. 106).

In partial response to the dilemma this posed, other states, particularly France, decided to protect themselves by developing their own nuclear capabilities. As a result, the diffusion of power already under way gathered momentum.

As these changes unfolded in the 1970s and 1980s, Cold War categories used to classify "free world" and communist countries' foreign policy alignments lost much of their relevance, as bipolycentrism implies. The acceptance of capitalism by many communist states in the late 1980s further eroded the adhesive bonds of ideology that had formerly helped these countries face their security problems from a common posture. Fissures in both blocs widened, as disputes arose in the Western alliance over strategic **doctrine,** arms control, U.S. military bases on allies' territory, and especially "out-of-area conflicts" (those beyond the traditional geographical boundaries of NATO). Not only decomposing blocs, but also declining support for the sanctity of alliance commitments in general became evident (Kegley and Raymond 1990). As fears of a new world war steadily lessened and the Cold War began to fade, leaders questioned whether defense alliances were still needed.

doctrine the guidelines a great power embraces as a strategy to specify the conditions under which it will use military power and armed force for political purposes abroad (see p. 522).

The 1989 dismantling of the Berlin Wall tore apart the post–World War II architecture of competing blocs. With the end of this division, and without a Soviet threat, the consistency of outlook and singularity of purpose that once bound NATO members together disappeared. To many critics, NATO and the Warsaw Pact had institutionalized antagonisms and perpetuated the Cold War—and were no longer needed.

Central to the unfolding debate was "the German question." According to Lord Ismay, the first secretary-general of NATO, the original purpose of the Atlantic alliance was "to keep the Russians out, the Americans in, and the Germans down." In 1990, although fearing a "Fourth Reich" (i.e., a united, powerful, and potentially expansionist German state), the Soviet Union reversed its long-standing opposition to German unification and agreed to withdraw its military forces from Europe. It did not make that dramatic concession without conditions, however. It insisted that unification be orchestrated through the active management of *all* the major World War II allies, that Germany reduce its armed forces, and that the United States keep a military presence in NATO on German soil.

Germany met all of these preconditions. In September 1990, the Four Powers (the United States, the Soviet Union, Great Britain, and France) and the two Germanys negotiated the **Two Plus Four Treaty** in Moscow, which terminated the Four Powers' rights over Germany. German leaders declared they had no territorial claims to make in Europe, including the territories in Poland that were annexed after World War II. Moreover, they pledged never to obtain nuclear weapons, and to reduce their 670,000-person armed forces to 370,000 troops (in exchange for the removal of 370,000 Soviet soldiers from Germany). Germany and the former Soviet Union also signed a bilateral treaty promising not to attack each other.

Two Plus Four Treaty the 1990 agreement between four powers (the United States, the Soviet Union, Great Britain, and France) and the two Germanys (East and West) that ended the Four Powers' rights of occupation and enabled German reunification.

The West greeted these agreements (and Soviet concessions) with enthusiasm. The agreements symbolized at once the retreat of the Soviet Union from a region (east Europe) it had long regarded as central to its security. They also symbolized the geostrategic shift of NATO influence into the heartland of the Warsaw Pact, which formally dissolved early in 1991.

In the early 1990s many perceived the need to replace NATO and the defunct Warsaw Pact with a new security arrangement. However, most leaders maintained that some configuration of a European defense architecture was still necessary to cement relationships and stabilize the rush of cascading events. Presidents George Bush and Bill Clinton, for instance, were vocal advocates of the continuing need to anchor security in alliances, pledging to keep U.S. troops in Europe and promising that the United States would remain the backbone of NATO.

Others thought a new *concert* system of conference diplomacy was needed, like the **Concert of Europe,** which the great powers created in 1815 in the wake of the Napoleonic Wars to keep the peace. Leaders in Moscow and some Western analysts recommended redefining NATO's purpose from the containment of enemies to the control of allies. For that, *all* the countries in Europe would be required to coordinate their defense policies. This would incorporate the east European and former Soviet republics pursuing democratization into a European-wide framework. It might also shift peacekeeping responsibilities from NATO to the larger Organization for Security and Cooperation in Europe (OSCE).

Concert of Europe the security system with regular conferences among Europe's great powers, formed by the great powers in Europe at the 1816 Congress of Vienna to prevent war and revolts.

An alternative scenario was the conversion of NATO from a military alliance designed for defense against a predetermined enemy to a larger collective security community. The 1991 Rome Summit moved in this direction by creating a new North Atlantic Cooperation Council (NACC) "to build genuine partnership among the North Atlantic Alliance and the countries of Central and Eastern Europe." The next meeting of defense ministers months later witnessed the members of NATO sitting at the same table with the former Warsaw Pact states and newly independent Baltic republics, facing a request from Russia to become a member.

The goal was to keep NATO alive even though the Cold War had died. The old NATO was built on the joint will to resist Soviet aggression. The new NATO sought to survive by preparing to contain ethnonational civil wars, foster disarmament, and preserve U.S. involvement in European security.

In January 1994 the historic dynamics of balance-of-power realignments again were exhibited when the four most advanced democracies in the former communist bloc (Poland, the Czech Republic, Slovakia, and Hungary) lobbied aggressively for full NATO membership. Rather than accept this effort to **bandwagon** by permitting states to abandon one alliance and join the stronger one, under U.S. advocacy NATO at that time cut a compromise deal by offering them participation and a measure of protection by becoming "peace partners" under the **Partnership for Peace (PfP)** plan. The PfP did not give the new affiliates the same guarantee of aid in the event of an attack that the sixteen existing full members enjoyed. But it became a pivotal step in the process of enlargement aimed at creating a peaceful, united, and democratic Europe. The PfP states are allowed to participate and train with NATO troops for peacekeeping and crisis-management operations (as they did in 1995 in Operation Joint Endeavor in Bosnia and Operation Allied Force in March 1999 to force Slobodan Milosevic's military machine to stop its brutal ethnic cleansing campaign in Kosovo). Seeking to avoid excluding any European states and creating another interbloc confrontation, the PfP redesigned itself for a single common defense without specifying a single common enemy.

bandwagon the tendency for weak states to seek alliance with the strongest power, irrespective of that power's ideology or form of government, in order to increase security.

Partnership for Peace (PfP) a plan proposed in 1993 by the United States that established limited military partnerships between NATO and the former Warsaw Pact countries (see p. 195).

The PfP set the stage for NATO's enlargement. The alliance's **strategic concept,** ratified at the 1999 fiftieth anniversary Washington Summit, put into words the philosophy that will guide NATO's expansion:

strategic concept NATO's 1999 set of plans identifying key strategic goals and the instruments that will be used to achieve them.

> The Alliance remains open to new members under Article 10 of the Washington Treaty. It expects to extend further invitations in coming years to nations willing and able to assume the responsibilities and obligations of membership, and as NATO determines that the inclusion of these nations would serve the overall political and strategic interests of the Alliance,

The Vestiges of Communist Power In 1998, only five countries (China, Cuba, Laos, North Korea, and Vietnam) remained members of the "communist bloc." In 1988, before the Cold War ended, that coalition consisted of fifteen countries. Pictured here is Cuba's Fidel Castro being assisted by Vietnam's General Secretary Do Muoi and a Vietnamese soldier at farewell ceremonies to a 1995 summit in Hanoi. The Cuban leader visited both China and Vietnam to observe how they had adapted Marxism to market economies. The meeting raised the question of whether communist ideology can still unify what remains of the communist bloc in a common coalition.

> strengthen its effectiveness and cohesion, and enhance overall European security and stability. To this end, NATO has established a program of activities to assist aspiring countries in their preparation for possible future membership in the context of its wider relationship with them. No European democratic country whose admission would fulfill the objectives of the Treaty will be excluded from consideration.

This commitment to enlargement put into policy a membership process that had been underway effectively since the 1997 Madrid Summit that invited the Czech Republic, Hungary, and Poland to become members and twenty-one former Warsaw Pact states, including Russia, to become Partners for Peace. As Map 15.1 shows, NATO at the start of 2001 had grown to nineteen full members. In addition, the **Euro-Atlantic Partnership Council (EAPC)** now numbers forty-four countries, and serves as the mechanism for coordinating NATO's cooperation with its partners across the full range of security problems facing twenty-first-century Europe. These include the management of crises arising from civil wars and the threats that represent "a fundamental challenge to the

Euro-Atlantic Partnership Council (EAPC)
a coordinating institution within NATO created in 1998 to manage the common political, military, financial, and security issues confronting Europe.

MAP 15.1
The Enlarged NATO and the New Geostrategic Balance of Power

The twenty-first-century geostrategic landscape has been transformed by NATO's expansion to nineteen full members and forty-four countries working as Partners for Peace. NATO now casts its security umbrella across and beyond Europe in its endeavor to create a collective security regime with states such as Russia that once were its enemies and to work with the United Nations and other IGOs for humanitarian military interventions in internal wars. Enlargement of membership and mission is reflective of NATO's resolve not to dissolve now that Cold War rivalry with the Soviet Union no longer exists. If NATO's 1999 Strategic Concept succeeds, and NATO survives by redefining itself as a coalition of liberal democracies fighting tyranny and a range of other economic, environmental, and political problems, it will defy the tendency for Europe's alliances to collapse after the defeat of a common adversary. There are challenges to this view, though. The new Russian strategic doctrine protests NATO's use of force beyond its members' borders without UN sanction.

values for which NATO has stood since its conception: democracy, human rights, and the rule of law." The new Strategic Concept summarizes NATO's approach:

> The Alliance is committed to a broad approach to security, which recognizes the importance of political, economic, social and environmental factors in addition to the indispensable defense dimension. This broad approach forms the basis for the Alliance to accomplish its fundamental security tasks effectively, and its increasing effort to develop effective cooperation with other European and Euro-Atlantic organizations as well as the United Nations. Our collective aim is to build a European security architecture in which the Alliance's contribution to the security and stability of the Euro-Atlantic area and the contribution of these other international organizations are complementary and mutually reinforcing, both in deepening relations among Euro-Atlantic countries and in managing crises.

Enlargement of both NATO's membership and its mission opens a new chapter in NATO's history. Revitalized with a larger membership and territorial reach, NATO seeks to orchestrate a cooperative approach to security among liberal democracies.

Critics of NATO's enlargement complain that NATO's expansion could backfire, undermining the security of those states it excludes. This, indeed, has been the threat perceived by Russian nationalists, who see enlargement as a new effort to contain Russia's future revival and potential military recovery of its lost Cold War empire. China, Japan, and other powers likewise have charged that the creation of a solidified military alliance in Europe without other strong military alliances to balance it poses a threat to global security. NATO asserts that these charges are unjustified because its new decision rules, giving every full member a veto over decisions regarding coercive military operations, removes the threat of a NATO preemptive strike. Other proponents of NATO and European Union enlargement claim that the maze of overlapping European security organizations (including the OSCE, the Western European Union [WEU], and the Council of Europe) are too cumbersome and slow to permit any of them to take decisive military actions outside their sphere of influence, and that these liberal democracies, moreover, are inherently pacific in values and goals. Whatever the ultimate consequences, the innovative redesign of NATO and its expansion have created a far different distribution of military power than that which existed in the bipolycentric system of the 1970s and 1980s and the bipolar system that preceded it in the 1950s and 1960s. The changes that have unfolded foretell the beginning of a new multipolar system.

Multipolarity—the Twenty-First Century? U.S. Secretary of State Lawrence Eagleburger proclaimed in 1989 that "we are now moving into . . . a world in which power and influence [are] diffused among a multiplicity of states—[a] multipolar world." A multipolar system of relatively equal powers, similar to the classical European balance-of-power system, may indeed best describe the emerging distribution of power. Such a multipolar system is likely to consist of the United States, China, Germany, Japan, and Russia (see Chapters 4 and 13), and now the European Union (EU). Following the NATO's 1999 intervention in Kosovo, many EU countries "united in spirit—against the United States . . . In Europe a quiet consensus . . . emerged that, as the German weekly *Der Spiegel* put it, 'The hegemony of the U.S. and NATO is limited as a model for the future'" (Gedman 1999; see also Medley 1999). The fifteen-country EU's plan, formulated at its 1999 Cologne Summit, to build its own Eurocorps defense arm of 60,000 soldiers to create a capacity for "autonomous action, backed by credible military force" generated a storm of protests from the United States. The United States feared that the new action plan, to be put into force in 2001 by the Treaty of Nice, which called for the EU's merger with a disbanded Western European Union (WEU), meant that the EU was likely to duplicate NATO and reduce the EU's commitment to a modernized NATO or even start the process of decoupling the EU from NATO (Gibney 1999). The EU's commissioner for external affairs, Christopher Pattern, tried to alleviate U.S. anxieties about the EU's new defense initiative when he explained that "What we're trying to do is to make sure the European voice is heard at the same strong decibel level when the European Union speaks as the world's biggest trade bloc and the biggest aid donor." The goal, and challenge, was to work out a set of rules for cooperating with, and adding to, NATO's capabilities rather than undermining or duplicating them.

The EU's assertive independence and unilateral approach, unrestrained by a very powerful ally like the United States, is precisely the kind of role usually sought by great powers in multipolar systems; the search for the capacity to compete on an equal footing with the other centers of power is characteristically strong when power is spread across three or more poles. With the effort by the EU to enter the playing field alongside the United States, China, Japan, Russia, and other regional players like Brazil and India, the game of rivalry and balancing is becoming much different from the strategies and alignments that materialize in unipolar and bipolar systems.

The relations between any pair of the great powers in a new multipolar world are difficult to predict. However, when power has been relatively evenly distributed in the past, each player has been assertive, independent, and competitive; diplomacy has displayed a nonideological, chesslike character; and conflict has been intense as each contender has feared the power of its rivals.

If a truly multipolar world develops, it is difficult to foresee how each great power's relationship with the others will evolve. Realignments—sometimes rapid—are to be expected. With the probable expansion of the number of great powers to as many as five, realist theory predicts that new cleavages will inevitably develop. It also predicts that rivalry will likely intensify as each jockeys for privilege, position, and power.

A world consisting of five or more independent and approximately equal centers of power will create an enlarged global chessboard of multiple bilateral geostrategic relationships. Such a congested landscape will be fraught with potential for conflict and confusion about the identity of friends and foes. To make the setting even more confusing, the interplay is likely to take place simultaneously on two playing fields—the first military and the second economic (recall Table 4.2 on p. 118).

In a new multipolar system, we can expect the major powers to align together against others on particular issues, as interests dictate. Behind the diplomatic smiles and handshakes, one-time friends and allies are likely to grow apart, and formally "specialized" relations are likely to dissolve. Consider the already heated U.S.-Japan-EU trade-bloc rivalry on the economic battlefield (see Chapter 8).

Multipolarity also foretells the potential alignment of former adversaries. The United States and Russia, allied victors in World War II, are now both apprehensive about the powers they defeated: Japan and Germany. Therefore, as balance-of-power theory would predict the United States and Russia have been given incentives to someday become true allies. But other realignments are also likely, as suggested by Russia's determination to restore its troubled relationship with China while at the same time seeking full NATO membership in order to deter potential Chinese expansionism. This motive was behind U.S. President Bill Clinton's May 1999 attempt to alleviate Russian fears after the bombing of Belgrade, when he wrote "The United States has a fundamental interest in a long-term positive relationship with Russia." Many other realignments are possible in a fluid, multipolar world. The range of possible alignments is suggested by the 1997 pledge by China and the United States to seek "common ground despite differences . . . by sharing responsibility for world peace"; the 1999 strengthening of the U.S.-Japanese Mutual Security Treaty; China's strengthened alliance with Russia in 1999 to move in mutual defense beyond the 1997 "Joint Declaration on the Multipolar World and the New World Order"; and the formation of a new pan-Eurasian, anti-NATO axis composed of 2.5 billion people in China and India allied with the formidable technological power of Russia, and held together by the common goal of countering the global dominance of the United States and the European allies under U.S. military protection (Marshall 1999). Many other kinds of shifting bilateral alliances and specialized relationships among pairs of great powers could emerge in the multipolar system of the twenty-first century, at various levels of commitment, that could be quite different in purpose and impact from the alternative relationships that would emerge if a great-power **concert** or a true global collective security regime were to come into being (see Chapters 4 and 16).

■ **multipolarity**
a global distribution of power in which three or more great powers or poles attain a disproportionate position of strength relative to all others, but with each power or pole approximately equal to the others.

■ **concert**
a cooperative agreement among great powers to manage jointly the international system (see p. 119).

Prospects for Peace in a Multipolar Future

As the fundamental trend toward the dispersion of global power continues, the prospects for peace will undoubtedly be affected. The emergence of a multipolar international system appears very likely, but the probable consequences are not clear, as the three different schools of thought on the relationship between polarity and global stability suggest (see Controversy: Is a Unipolar, Bipolar, or Multipolar System the Most Stable?). Because there is no real consensus on whether systems with a certain number of poles are more war-prone than others (Russett, Starr, and Kinsella 2000), it would be imprudent to conclude that a new multipolar system will necessarily produce another period of warfare or of peace.

Different types of multipolar systems can emerge, involving variant armament ratios and alliance networks. These combinations can lead to very different conditions. It is possible to imagine a wide diversity of plausible but possible geopolitical relationships in the twenty-first century (see Brzezinski 1998), and the presence or absence of a particular polarity balance by itself is unlikely to solely determine whether war clouds will gather or dissipate. For example, a new era of unipolarity could arise like that after World War II with the resurgence of the United States and its reascendence as the globe's only superpower. To hegemonic stability theorists, a unipolar concentration of power in a single hegemonic superpower would provide the global leader with

CONTROVERSY

Is a Unipolar, Bipolar, or Multipolar System the Most Stable?

Three Schools of Thought on the Relationship of Polarity and International Peace

In the early twenty-first century, a long-standing debate has intensified about which type of polarity distribution—unipolar, bipolar, or multipolar—is the most capable of preventing large-scale war. What do you think? Consider the divided opinions about this issue, as represented by the arguments in three contending schools of thought.

One interpretation holds that peace will occur when one hegemonic state acquires enough power to deter others' expansionist ambitions. This view maintains that the concentration of power reduces the chances of war because it allows a single superpower to maintain peace and manage the international system (Wohlforth 1999). The long peace under Britain's leadership in the 1800s (the Pax Britannica) and earlier, under the Roman Empire (the Pax Romana), offered support for the idea that unipolarity brings peace, and therefore inspires the hope that the twenty-first century under a Pax Americana will be stable as long as U.S. dominance prevails (Knickerbocker 1999).

In contrast, a second school of thought (e.g., Waltz 1964) maintains that bipolar systems are the most stable. According to this line of reasoning, stability, ironically, results from "the division of all nations into two camps [because it] raises the costs of war to such a high level that all but the most fundamental conflicts are resolved without resort to violence" (Bueno de Mesquita 1975). Under such stark simplicities and balanced symmetries, the two leading rivals have incentives to manage crises so that they do not escalate to war.

Those who believe that a bipolar world is inherently more stable than either its unipolar or multipolar counterparts draw support from the fact that in the bipolar environment of the 1950s, when the threat of war was endemic, major war did not occur. Extrapolating, these observers (e.g., Mearsheimer 1990) reason that because now a new multipolar distribution of global power makes it impossible to run the world from one or two centers, disorder will result:

> It is rather basic. So long as there were only two great powers, like two big battleships clumsily and cautiously circling each other, confrontations—or accidents—were easier to avoid. Now, with the global lake more crowded with ships of varying sizes, fueled by different ambitions and piloted with different degrees of navigational skill, the odds of collisions become far greater. (House 1989, A10)

A third school of thought argues that multipolar systems are the least war prone. While the reasons differ, advocates share the belief that polarized systems that either concentrate power, as in a unipolar system, or that divide the world into two antagonistic blocs, as in a bipolar system, promote struggles for dominance (see Thompson 1988; Morgenthau 1985). The peace-through-multipolarity school perceives multipolar systems as stable because they encompass a larger number of autonomous actors, giving rise to more potential alliance partners. This is seen as pacifying because it is essential to counterbalancing a would-be aggressor, as shifting alliances can occur only when there are multiple power centers (Deutsch and Singer 1964).

Abstract deductions and historical analogies can lead to contradictory conclusions, as the logic underlying these three inconsistent interpretations illustrates. The future will determine which of these rival theories is the most accurate.

the unrivaled power to police chaos and maintain international peace. Against this optimistic view currently run strong suspicions about the future stability of a unipolar world:

> Commentators were quick to recognize that a new "unipolar moment" of unprecedented U.S. power had arrived. In 1992 the Pentagon drafted a new grand strategy designed to preserve unipolarity by preventing the emergence of a global rival. But the draft plan soon ran into controversy, as com-

> mentators at home and abroad argued that any effort to preserve unipolarity was quixotic and dangerous. Officials quickly backed away from the idea and now eschew the language of primacy or predominance, speaking instead of the United States as a "leader" or the "indispensable nation."
>
> The rise and sudden demise of an official strategy for preserving primacy lends credence to the widespread belief that unipolarity is dangerous and unstable. While scholars frequently discuss unipolarity, their focus is always on its demise. For neorealists, unipolarity is the least stable of all structures because any great concentration of power threatens other states and causes them to take action to restore a balance. Other scholars grant that a large concentration of power works for peace, but they doubt that U.S. preeminence can endure. Underlying both views is the belief that U.S. preponderance is fragile and easily negated by the actions of other states. As a result, most analysts argue that unipolarity is an "illusion," a "moment" that "will not last long," or is already "giving way to multipolarity." (Wohlforth 1999, 5–6)

Whatever the duration of **unipolarity** and its consequences, it is clear that most of the globe's other powers would agree with the skeptics about the instability of world politics if the overwhelming power of the United States persists. In the view of many Chinese, Germans, and Japanese, the growing accumulation of so much political, military, economic, and cultural clout by the United States is breeding an alarming arrogance and a dangerous impulse to bully the rest of the world. Some of America's closest allies fear that U.S. dominance without interference will lead to a heavy-handed U.S. imperialism that threatens global stability.

unipolarity a condition in which an international system has a single dominant power center, or pole, able to exercise by its superior economic resources and military capability supreme authority.

Others picture the likely return of coalition politics, with a new bipolar or bipolycentric but unstable configuration emerging from the formation of a new Sino-Russian bloc, European-Russian entente, or Sino-Japanese alliance to counter an alliance spearheaded by the United States (Brzezinski 1998). Here it is possible to visualize turmoil as various states join together to restrain the American behemoth or another great-power bloc from harming others with its power. And others picture a new world order and/or disorder developing from a new multipolar division of competing systems, or, alternatively, a system breakdown because "when the Cold War ended in 1989, so did the balance of power systems . . . and the centuries-old way of looking at the world" (*Economist*, December 20, 1997, 41). It is, indeed, very difficult to predict what the twenty-first-century geostrategic chessboard will look like, and whether it will be chaotic or stable. But if the past truly is a guide to the future, the distribution of global power will exert a strong influence on the kind of global system the world will experience.

The preservation of peace by states aggregating power in order to balance power has a rather checkered history. In the long run, the resulting alliances and distributions of power have failed to avert a breakdown of world order. The great powers have persistently been drawn into wars by the collapse of the balance of power in either Europe or East Asia or both. Yet history also suggests that the prospects for peace in unipolar, bipolar, and multipolar systems depend on other factors as well. Negotiated arms agreements designed to change the existing balance of power are a critical component that could alter the tendency of multipolar systems to culminate in widespread warfare.

Russia and China Seek to Balance U.S. Power When NATO approved formal enlargement in 1997, both Russia's and China's sense of security plummeted. In reaction, the old rivals, feeling excluded, repaired their broken alliance ties by agreeing to a new "strategic partnership" aimed at rearranging the global geostrategic chessboard. Russian Premier Vickor Cheknomyrdin (right) and Chinese President Jiang Zemin met in Moscow in April 1997 to negotiate the "new world order" joint statement, which called for creation of a new "multipolar" system cemented by a new Sino-Russian axis to counter the threat of global domination by the U.S. hegemonic superpower. The logic of balance-of-power politics rationalizes the formation of these kinds of strategic unions to check the growing influence of a rising great-power rival. The same thinking inspired the 1999 common defense treaty between Japan and the United States to offset the expanding military power of China.

CONTROLLING MILITARY POWER THROUGH ARMS AGREEMENTS

Liberal reformers have often attacked the theory that power can be balanced with power to preserve world order. They have advocated instead the biblical prescription that nations should beat their swords into plowshares. The destructiveness and dispersion of today's weapons have inspired many people once again to take this tenet of liberal theory seriously. But this approach is not solely a liberal preserve. Most realists also see arms control as a way of influencing the international distribution of military power in ways that promote peace and individual states' national security. In fact, most policymakers who have negotiated arms control agreements have been realists who perceived these treaties as a prudent tool to promote their countries' security. At times, they have been the leading advocates of arms control to adjust their states' military power relative to the rivals', and to help maintain the balance of power.

Arms Control versus Disarmament

It will be useful to review the historical record of negotiators' efforts to preserve the global distribution of weapons and their uses. This will allow us to assess the implications of such negotiations for peace. However, two concepts must first be distinguished. Many people incorrectly assume that the terms "arms control" and "disarmament" are synonymous. **Arms control** refers to agreements designed to regulate arms levels either by limiting their growth or by restricting how they may be used. This is a far less ambitious endeavor than **disarmament,** which is the reduction or elimination of weapons, and **demilitarization,** which occurs when a country's war-fighting capabilities are eliminated.

> Disarmament rests on a fundamentally different philosophical premise than arms control. It envisions the drastic reduction or elimination of all weapons, looking toward the eradication of war itself. Disarmament is based on the notion that if there were no more weapons there would be no more war. This is a compelling proposition, with enough truth to give it a very long life in the history of thought about war and peace. Arms control, on the other hand, accepts the existence of weapons and the possibility of conflict. Contrary to popular impression, it is not necessarily about reducing arms levels. Arms control attempts to stabilize the status quo and to manage conflict, to encourage peaceful resolution of disputes, and limit the resort to military force. Although many visceral opponents would be shocked at the thought, arms control is fundamentally a conservative enterprise. Disarmament, by contrast, is a radical one. Disarmament seeks to overturn the status quo; arms control works to perpetuate it. (Kruzel 1991, 249)

We should also distinguish between **bilateral agreements** and **multilateral agreements.** Because the former are agreements between only two countries, they are often easier to negotiate and to enforce than are the latter, which are agreements among three or more countries. Negotiating a multilateral agreement, simultaneously binding on many states, poses many obstacles because states' security interests are very different, as are the domestic processes by which governments approve international agreements. As a result, the record of bilateral agreements is stronger than that of multilateral agreements with respect to both arms control and disarmament.

Multilateral Diplomacy: The Checkered Disarmament and Arms Control Record

It is hardly a novel idea that it is possible to control war by reducing the world's arsenals. Yet until very recently, one of the few constants in the changing international system has been the repetition with which states have advocated disarmament but failed to implement it. True, some countries in the past did reach agreements to reduce their armaments levels. For example, the Chinese states in 600 B.C.E. formed a disarmament league that produced a peaceful century for

■ **arms control**
multilateral or bilateral agreements to contain arms races by setting limits on the number and types of weapons states are permitted.

■ **disarmament**
the elimination of weapons or other means of attack.

■ **demilitarization**
the complete elimination of the military power or potential of a state.

■ **bilateral agreements**
exchanges between two states, such as arms control agreements negotiated cooperatively to set ceilings on military force levels.

■ **multilateral agreements**
cooperative compacts among many states to ensure that a concerted policy is implemented toward alleviating a common problem, such as levels of future weapons' capabilities.

the league's members, and in the Rush-Bagot Agreement of 1818 Canada and the United States disarmed the Great Lakes. Disarmament proposals also figured prominently in the League of Nations' abortive World Disarmament Conference of 1932 and rather continuously in the UN since 1946 (especially in its many "special sessions" on disarmament). Nonetheless, these kinds of achievements have been relatively rare in history. Many more countries have raced to expand their arsenals than have tried to cut them. Most disarmament is involuntary, the product of reductions imposed by the victors in the immediate aftermath of a war, as when the Allied powers attempted (unsuccessfully) to permanently disarm a defeated and demilitarized Germany after World War I.

In contrast with disarmament, there are many historical examples of arms control efforts. As early as the eleventh century, the Second Lateran Council prohibited the use of crossbows in fighting. The 1868 St. Petersburg Declaration prohibited the use of explosive bullets. In 1899 and 1907, International Peace Conferences at the Hague restricted the use of some weapons and prohibited others. The leaders of the United States, Britain, Japan, France, and Italy signed treaties at the Washington Naval Conferences (1921–1922) agreeing to adjust the relative tonnage of their fleets.

The post–World War II period saw a variety of new arms control proposals. The Baruch Plan (1946) called for the creation of a United Nations Atomic Development Authority, which would have placed atomic energy under an international authority to ensure its use for only peaceful purposes. However, the great powers never approved the proposal. The Rapacki Plan (1957) to prevent the deployment of nuclear weapons in Central Europe also failed.

Nonetheless, leaders have made recurrent efforts to resolve differences so formal arms control agreements might be realized. Prominent among them were the arms control summit meetings of the great powers, of which those between the United States and former Soviet Union—the world's nuclear superpowers—were the most frequent. Summit talks between the Cold War antagonists began in July 1955, when U.S. President Eisenhower and Soviet leader Nikita Khrushchev met in Geneva. Among other things, these summits sought and often resulted in an improved atmosphere for serious arms control negotiations. In addition, they paved the way for the ambitious agreements at the end of the Cold War to cement a new world order based on a reduced and stable military power balance.

Multilateral negotiations on particular issues have also taken on the character of institutionalized efforts to reach arms control agreements. Nine examples illustrate their range and breadth:

1. *Mutual and Balanced Force Reductions (MBFR)* The MBFR talks were conducted from 1973 to 1988 in an effort to realize force reductions between the blocs dividing Europe. Although they did not produce a treaty, during the Cold War they sustained a "consensus that arms control negotiations are a necessary component of alliance defense strategy" and "were helpful in preparing for the negotiations on Conventional Armed Forces in Europe (CFE)" (Hallenbeck and Shaver 1991).
2. *Comprehensive Test Ban Treaty (CTBT)* These negotiations have been held periodically since the late 1950s in an effort to reach agreement on a treaty banning all nuclear explosions. The Reagan administration broke off nego-

tiations in 1982, citing **verification** obstacles to public inspection of tests and the need to test nuclear weapons as long as deterrence depended on them. Nonetheless, negotiations on verification protocols resumed in November 1987, and new protocols were added to the existing Threshold Test Ban Treaty and the Peaceful Nuclear Explosions Treaty. In September 1996, the new draft Comprehensive Test Ban Treaty (CTBT) would have banned the testing of nuclear weapons, and by mid-1999 the prospects for acceptance looked favorable, with 156 countries having signed the treaty, in part because of the growing fear of nuclear proliferation. After May 1998, when India detonated three nuclear devices and Pakistan exploded two nuclear devices, it appeared likely that nuclear testing and nuclear proliferation would escalate. Fears climbed precipitously in October 1999 when the U.S. Senate voted to reject this nuclear test ban that the United States and its allies had worked side-by-side to see ratified since the days of President Eisenhower. The treaty's rejection sent shock waves through a horrified global community. Britain's government said it was "deeply disappointed" and the Japanese foreign minister said he was "extremely concerned" because the world's leading nuclear power sent a dangerous signal that was bound to encourage some of the eighteen other states with nuclear-power facilities that had not ratified the CTBT to now begin to build and test nuclear weapons. Russia, China, and even India and Pakistan had previously pledged to sign the treaty by following the U.S. leadership (Britain and France ratified the treaty in April 1998), but without a U.S. commitment, "a green light [has been given] to many countries to walk away from promises not to develop nuclear arsenals," as Peter Hain, British minister of foreign affairs, sadly concluded in 1999.

verification processes through which signatories' adherence to arms control and disarmament agreements is confirmed.

3. *Conventional Forces in Europe (CFE)* The Conventional Force Reductions in Europe negotiations, which began in 1989, produced the CFE treaty, which entered into force in late 1992. The CFE set ceilings on five categories of conventional arms (battle tanks, armored combat vehicles, artillery pieces, combat aircraft, and attack helicopters) for the thirty countries in an area stretching from the Atlantic to the Urals (the ATTU zone). The November 1999 meeting of the fifty-four members of the Organization for Security and Cooperation in Europe (OSCE) in Istanbul, Turkey, sought to replace the bloc-to-bloc CFE treaty with a system of national and territorial ceilings to prevent the potential buildup of conventional forces that could be used for offensive purposes. U.S. and Turkish officials warned, however, that adoption of the amended 1990 CFE treaty would be contingent on Russia's reduction of the weapons it had deployed along Russia's unstable southern border across the Caucasus region.

4. *Organization for Security and Cooperation in Europe (OSCE)* The OSCE emerged from the Conference on Security and Cooperation in Europe (CSCE), which began in Helsinki in 1973. Soon after, it became the leading multilateral institution for managing the transformation of Europe from a system of counterpoised alliances (NATO and the Warsaw Pact) to one based on common principles stretching across the entire continent and North America. Formalized in 1995, the fifty-four-member OSCE administers a Conflict Prevention Center and aims at a leadership role in preventive diplomacy, post-conflict rehabilitation, and regional cooperation to expand

the military, economic, democratization, and human rights provisions of the 1975 Helsinki accords. In 1999 missions were undertaken in ten countries.

5. *Nuclear Nonproliferation Treaty (NPT)* The signatories of this historic 1968 treaty have held Review Conferences every five years to discuss compliance and enforcement programs. In 1995, twenty-five years after the NPT entered into force, the review conference agreed to continue the treaty indefinitely; the 186 parties to it then identified objectives on seven issues (universality, **nonproliferation,** nuclear disarmament, nuclear-weapon-free zones, security assurances, safeguards, and peaceful uses of nuclear energy). Yet doubts remain about the NPT's ability to contain the future spread of nuclear weapons, despite the agreement in May 2000 by the five nuclear powers on the UN Security Council to eliminate their nuclear arsenals, as part of the new NPT disarmament agenda approved by 187 countries.

■ **nonproliferation** the commitment to no development of nuclear weapons or technology by countries that do not already possess them.

6. *Conference on Disarmament (CD)* The CD emerged from the bilateral U.S.–Soviet negotiations that began in 1976 to ban the production, stockpiling, and use of chemical weapons. In 1981 those closed negotiations became a part of the UN's arms control forum in Geneva. The sixty-one-member CD can be given credit for producing the 1990 U.S.-Soviet Chemical Weapons Destruction Agreement, for starting negotiations on the 1996 CTBT, and for lobbying on behalf of a comprehensive and worldwide multilateral chemical weapons disarmament convention and a worldwide ban on the production of fissile materials for use in nuclear weapons (the Fissile Material Cut-Off Treaty [FMCT]).
7. *Biological Weapons Convention (BWC)* The Review Conferences of the BWC have convened periodically since the 1972 Bacteriological (Biological) and Toxin Weapons Convention (TWC) was ratified in 1972. The TWC was the first multilateral arms control agreement aimed at prohibiting the development of an entire category of weapons of mass destruction. It banned the development, production, stockpiling, acquisition, or retention of biological and toxin weapons but did not specifically ban their use. That had already been done by the 1925 Geneva Protocol for the Prohibition of the Use in War of Asphyxiating, Poisonous, or Other Gases and of Bacteriological Methods of Warfare. The two instruments were seen as complementing each other. From these emanated the 1993 Chemical Weapons Convention (CWC). Signed by 169 countries as of January 1999, the CWC calls for the destruction of all chemical weapons by the year 2003. It is administered by the Organization for the Prevention of Chemical Weapons (OPCU) in the Hague.
8. *Missile Technology Control Regime (MTCR)* This regime is an informal arrangement among the world's most advanced suppliers of missile-related equipment to control the export of ballistic and cruise missiles and missile-related technologies. Initially designed to deter the spread of nuclear-capable missiles, the MTCR was expanded in 1993 to prevent the diffusion of missile systems for delivering chemical and biological weapons. The regime, created by seven founding countries in 1987, had since expanded to include twenty-five additional states by 1999. Following U.S. President Bill Clinton's advocacy in 1993, the 1994 Stockholm MTCR plenary meeting sought to transform the export regime into a set of rules commanding universal adherence. However, the MTCR currently relies on voluntary

Chemical Weapons Graveyard Some states see their security improved by voluntary reductions in their arsenals of weapons, as Russia and most NATO countries did in the 1990s when they chose to make deep disarmament cuts. More often, disarmament is forced and enforced by external powers' interventions and sanctions. Pictured here are the remains of some of Iraq's pre–Gulf War chemical weapons arsenal. The mustard gas bombs at Muthanna, Iraq, were uncovered and destroyed by a United Nations inspection team. The Chemical Weapons Convention (CWC), signed by 169 states in early 1999, requires existing stockpiles of these lethal weapons to be destroyed by 2003.

compliance and is neither an international treaty nor a legally binding agreement. Its weaknesses were illustrated in 1993 when the United States determined that China, which had earlier pledged to abide by the terms of the MTCR, had transferred missile components to Pakistan in violation of its provisions.

9. *United Nations Register of Conventional Arms* This registry is the first international effort to gather official information on the weapons trade since the League of Nations attempted to compile a similar list. Implemented in 1992, the register invites states to submit information voluntarily about their trade in various categories of major weapons. Each of the world's top suppliers has submitted reports. However, most of the UN's members do not regularly submit yearly reports.

Table 15.2 summarizes the major multilateral arms control agreements reached since World War II. These agreements limit the range of permissible actions and weapons systems available to states. They have also helped to slow the global arms race and paved the way for still more ambitious proposals. In addition, they contribute important confidence-building measures that reduce the political tensions underlying the urge to arm.

Bilateral Diplomacy and the Control of Nuclear Arms: Superpower Agreements

Throughout the Cold War, Soviet and U.S. arms control efforts understandably focused on ways to lessen the threat of nuclear war. These efforts intensified with the disintegration of the Soviet Union. Table 15.3 (pages 580–581) summarizes the results of these negotiations, listing the major bilateral arms control agreements between the two superpowers since 1960.

TABLE 15.2

Major Multilateral Arms Control Treaties since 1945

Date	*Agreement*	*Number of Parties (2000)*	*Principal Objectives*
1959	Antarctic Treaty	43	Prevents the military use of the Antarctic, including the testing of nuclear weapons
1963	Limited Test Ban Treaty	154	Prohibits nuclear weapons in the atmosphere, outer space, and under water
1967	Outer Space Treaty	127	Outlaws the use of outer space for testing or stationing any weapons, as well as for military maneuvers
1967	Treaty of Tlatelolco	33	Creates the Latin America Nuclear Free Zone by prohibiting the testing and possession of nuclear facilities for military purposes
1968	Nuclear Nonproliferation Treaty	187	Prevents the transfer of nuclear weapons and nuclear-weapons-production technologies to nonnuclear weapon states
1971	Seabed Treaty	117	Prohibits the deployment of weapons of mass destruction and nuclear weapons on the seabed beyond a twelve-mile coastal limit
1972	Biological Weapons Convention	169	Prohibits the production and storage of biological toxins; calls for the destruction of biological weapons stocks
1977	Environmental Modifications Convention (Enmod Convention)	85	Bans the use of technologies that could alter the earth's weather patterns, ocean currents, ozone layer, or ecology
1980	Protection of Nuclear Material Convention	53	Obligates protection of peaceful nuclear material during transport on ships or aircraft
1981	Inhumane Weapons Convention	72	Prohibits the use of such weapons as fragmentation bombs, incendiary weapons, booby traps, and mines to which civilians could be exposed
1985	South Pacific Nuclear Free Zone (Roratonga) Treaty	18	Prohibits the testing, acquisition, or deployment of nuclear weapons in the South Pacific
1986	Confidence-Building and Security-Building Measures and Disarmament in Europe (CDE) Agreement (Stockholm Accord)	54	Requires prior notification and mandatory on-site inspection of conventional military exercises in Europe

To these we might add an indeterminate number of tacit understandings about the level and use of weapons to which the two powers agreed. These understandings did not achieve the status of formal agreements but were observed by the two superpowers nonetheless. They included occasional pledges to refrain from the offensive use of nuclear arsenals, as indicated by

TABLE 15.2

(continued)

Date	*Agreement*	*Number of Parties (2000)*	*Principal Objectives*
1987	Missile Technology Control Regime (MTCR)	35	Restricts export of ballistic missiles and production facilities
1990 1992	Conventional Forces in Europe (CFE)	30	Places limits on five categories of weapons in Europe and lowers force levels
1990	Confidence- and Security-Building Measures (CSBM) Agreement	53	Improves measures for exchanging detailed informa-ition on weapons, forces, and military exercises
1991	UN Register of Conventional Arms	97	Calls on all states to submit information on seven categories of major weapons exported or imported during the previous year
1992	Open Skies Treaty	27	Permits flights by unarmed surveillance aircraft over the territory of the signatory states
1993	Chemical Weapons Convention (CWC)	169	Requires all stockpiles of chemical weapons to be destroyed within ten years
1995	Protocol to the Inhumane Weapons Convention	135	Bans some types of laser weapons that cause permanent loss of eyesight
1995	Wassenaar Export-Control Treaty	33	Regulates transfers of sensitive dual-use technologies to nonparticipating countries
1996	ASEAN Nuclear Free Zone Treaty	10	Prevents signatories in Southeast Asia from making, possessing, storing, or testing nuclear weapons
1996	Comprehensive Test Ban Treaty (CTBT)	156	Bans all testing of nuclear weapons
1996	Treaty of Pelindaba	48	Creates an African nuclear-weapon-free zone
1997	Treaty of Bangkok	10	Creates a nuclear-weapon-free zone in Southeast Asia
1998	Antipersonnel Landmines Treaty (APLT)	135	Bans the production and export of landmines and pledges plans to remove them
1999	Inter-American Convention on Transparency in Conventional Weapons Acquisitions	34	Requires all thirty-four members of the Organization of American States (OAS) to annually report all weapons acquisitions, exports, and imports

SOURCE: Stockholm International Peace Research Institute, *SIPRI Yearbooks;* Arms Control Association *Fact Files.*

President Carter's and Soviet Foreign Minister Andrei Gromyko's promises that their states would never be the first to use nuclear weapons in any conflict. Such commitments were not legally binding. Indeed, NATO based its "flexible response" strategy on the right to retaliate with nuclear weapons against an attack. More recently, in 2000, Russia's new strategic doctrine reserved the right

TABLE 15.3

Major Bilateral Arms Control Agreements between the United States and the Soviet Union/Russia

Date	*Agreement*	*Principal Objectives*
1963	Hot Line Agreement	Establishes a direct radio and telegraph communication system between the governments to be used in times of crisis
1971	Hot Line Modernization Agreement	Puts a hot line satellite communication system into operation
1971	Nuclear Accidents Agreement	Creates a process for notification of accidental or unauthorized detonation of a nuclear weapon; creates safeguards to prevent accidents
1972	Antiballistic Missile (ABM) Treaty (SALT I)	Restricts the deployment of antiballistic missile defense systems to one area and prohibits the development of a space-based ABM system
1972	SALT I Interim Agreement on Offensive Strategic Arms	Freezes the superpowers' total number of ballistic missile launchers for a five-year period
1972	Protocol to the Interim Agreement	Clarifies and strengthens prior limits on strategic arms
1972	High Seas Agreement	Creates procedures to prevent crisis-provoking incidents on the oceans
1973	Agreement on the Prevention of Nuclear War	Requires superpowers to consult if a threat of nuclear war emerges
1974	Threshold Test Ban Treaty with Protocol	Restricts the underground testing of nuclear weapons above a yield of 150 kilotons
1974	Protocol to the ABM Treaty	Reduces permitted ABMs to one site
1976	Treaty on the Limitation of Underground Explosions for Peaceful Purposes	Broadens the ban on underground nuclear testing stipulated in the 1974 Threshold Test Ban Treaty; requires on-site observers of tests with yields exceeding 150 kilotons
1977	Convention on the Prohibition of Military or Any Other Hostile Use of Environmental Modification Techniques	Bans weapons that threaten to modify the planetary ecology
1979	SALT II Treaty (never ratified)	Places ceilings on the number of strategic delivery vehicles, MIRVed missiles, long-range bombers, cruise missiles, ICBMs, and other weapons; restrains testing
1987	Nuclear Risk Reduction Centers Agreement	Creates facilities in each national capital to manage a nuclear crisis
1987	Intermediate-range Nuclear Force (INF) Treaty	Eliminates U.S. and USSR ground-level intermediate-and shorter-range nuclear weapons in Europe and permits on-site inspection to verify compliance

to use nuclear weapons in the event of an attack. Nonetheless, most understandings undeniably help enforce great-power respect for the no-first-use doctrine (as do China's vocal support for the same principle and the 1995 agreement between China and Russia to stop aiming nuclear weapons at each other). Such informal rules have paved the way to creating greater institutional controls over the use of strategic weapons.

TABLE 15.3

(continued)

Date	*Agreement*	*Principal Objectives*
1990	Chemical Weapons Destruction Agreement	Ends production of chemical weapons; commits to cutting inventories of chemical weapons in half by 2000 and to five thousand metric tons by the end of 2002
1990	Nuclear Testing Talks	New protocol improves verification procedures of prior treaties
1991	START (Strategic Arms Reduction) Treaty	Reduces arsenals of strategic nuclear weapons by about 30 percent
1992	START I Protocol	Holds Russia, Belarus, Ukraine, and Kazakhstan to strategic weapons reductions agreed to in START by the former USSR
1992	Open Skies Agreement	Permits unarmed surveillance aircraft to fly over the United States, Russia, and their allies
1992	Cooperative Threat Reduction Agreement	Provides a variety of equipment and support to assist Russia in the safe destruction of strategic delivery systems, the transportation of nuclear warheads, the physical protection of nuclear-weapon storage sites, warhead accounting, and chemical and biological weapon destruction and facility dismantlement
1993	START II	Cuts the deployed U.S. and Russian strategic nuclear warheads on each side to between 3,000 and 3,500 by the year 2003; bans multiple-warhead land-based missiles
1995	HEU Agreement	Reduces risk of diversion or theft of nuclear-weapons-grade highly enriched uranium (HEU) recovered from dismantled nuclear warheads through government purchase and use as civilian reactor fuel
1997	Fissile Material Cut-Off Treaty (FMCT)	Bans production of fissile material for nuclear weapons or other nuclear explosive devices
1997	Core Conversion Agreement	Obligates the United States to facilitate the conversion of Russia's three remaining plutonium production reactors to no longer produce weapons-grade plutonium; originally intended to be complete by the end of 2000, this project will now likely be implemented by 2002
1997	START III	Pledges the agreement that was renewed at the September 1998 Moscow Summit for the United States and Russia to deploy no more than 2,000 to 2,500 strategic nuclear warheads each on CBMs, SLBMs, and heavy bombers by December 31, 2007, pending ratification of the START II Treaty

■ **Strategic Arms Limitation Talks (SALT)** the negotiations begun in 1969 between the United States and the USSR to freeze offensive weapons at existing levels and promote balanced, verifiable limits on strategic nuclear weapons (see p. 108).

SALT. Of the superpowers' explicit, formal arms control agreements, the two so-called **Strategic Arms Limitation Talks (SALT)** agreements were precedent-setting. SALT I, signed in 1972, consisted of: (1) a treaty restricting the deployment of antiballistic missile defense systems to equal and very low levels, and (2) a five-year interim accord on strategic offensive arms that restricted intercontinental ballistic missile (ICBM) and submarine-launched ballistic missile (SLBM) launchers. The SALT I agreement was essentially a confidence-building, "stopgap" step toward a longer-term, more comprehensive treaty. The 1979 SALT II agreement, then the most extensive arms control agreement ever negotiated, sought to realize that aim. The agreement called for placing an eventual overall ceiling for each superpower of 2,250 on the number of ICBM launchers, SLBM launchers, heavy bombers, and air-to-surface ballistic missiles (ASBMs) with ranges over six hundred kilometers. These limitations reduced by as many as 8,500 the total number of strategic nuclear weapons that the United States and the Soviet Union would have possessed by 1985 without the agreement.

The obstacles to arms control were illustrated by the problems that SALT II encountered. The U.S. Senate deferred ratification of the SALT II treaty indefinitely following the 1979 Soviet invasion of Afghanistan. Although both superpowers continued to abide by the basic terms of SALT II through the early 1980s, the "final result as embodied in SALT II was a clear disappointment to the hopes generated in the early 1970s. In essence, SALT II failed to achieve actual arms reductions. Its basic fault was that it would have permitted substantial growth in the strategic forces of both sides" (U.S. Department of State 1983).

START. Against the background of what they labeled "the failed promise of SALT," U.S. leaders set the agenda for new approaches to strategic arms control. At this time, the fear inspired by the relentless arms race and frustration with the lack of progress in the arms control process increased momentum on both sides of the Atlantic for the idea of a nuclear freeze on the testing, production, and deployment of nuclear weapons. Freeze advocates were motivated by the view, expressed by one realist U.S. policymaker, that it was a "delusion" to see "nuclear weapons as just one more weapon, like any other weapon, only more destructive" (Kennan 1982). To help dispel this delusion, the American Catholic bishops composed a widely read Pastoral Letter that called for an immediate end to the arms race. It also asserted that the deliberate initiation of nuclear warfare, on however restricted a scale, could not be morally justified. As a policy proposal, a total freeze envisioned a path to disarmament that would first stop production of new weapons systems before starting to reduce the existing ones. This vision was premised on the belief that both sides' deterrent capabilities were invulnerable and that a freeze would keep them that way. Once the arms race was curtailed, it was reasoned, arms reductions could then be considered.

The **nuclear freeze movement** in the early 1980s helped set the stage for the progress that occurred in the early 1990s when the Cold War no longer constrained negotiations. In June 1982, the Reagan administration initiated a new round of arms talks aimed at significantly reducing both superpowers' strategic arsenals. Termed the **START (Strategic Arms Reduction) Treaty,** the initiative resumed the SALT process, but expanded its agenda by seeking to remove inequalities that had developed in the superpowers' weapons systems.

■ **nuclear freeze movement**
a popular revolt against the escalating strategic arms race in the 1980s that called for a suspension or freeze in building more nuclear warheads in the hopes that the threat of nuclear annihilation would be reduced.

■ **START (Strategic Arms Reduction) Treaty**
the U.S.-Russian series of negotiations that began in 1993 and, with the 1997 START-III agreement ratified by Russia in April 2000, pledged to cut the nuclear arsenals of both sides by 80 percent of the Cold War peaks, in order to lower the risk of nuclear war by making a successful preemptive strike impossible.

The Post–Cold War Disarmament Race. In September 1991, responding to widespread complaints that the START treaty barely initiated the arms reductions possible now that the threat of a Soviet attack had vanished, President Bush declared that the United States must seize "the historic opportunity now before us." Describing the Soviet Union as "no longer a realistic threat," he called long-range bombers off twenty-four-hour alert, canceled plans to deploy the long-range MX on rail cars, and offered to negotiate sharp reductions in the most dangerous kinds of globe-spanning missiles with the Soviets. Bush also proposed removing short-range nuclear weapons from U.S. bases in Europe and Asia and from U.S. Navy vessels around the world. However, Bush warned that the proposed U.S. cuts might not be made if the Soviet Union did not respond in kind. This set the stage for a showdown on a new race to disarm.

The fragmentation of the Soviet Union shortly thereafter and the improved political relationship between Russia and the United States removed the major barriers to disarmament. Instructively, the disarmament process began first through unilateral proposals and gained momentum only later through incremental accords painstakingly negotiated at the bargaining table. But when disarmament agreements finally came, they did so rapidly.

On January 25, 1992, Russian President Boris Yeltsin declared that his country "no longer considered the United States our potential adversary." He then announced the decision to stop targeting U.S. cities with nuclear missiles, clearing the way for another U.S. response. Four days later, in his State of the Union address, President Bush announced a series of unilateral arms cuts. Among them were the decision to suspend production of the B-2 bomber, halt development of the Midgetman mobile nuclear missile, and cease purchases of advanced cruise missiles. In addition, Bush canceled production of warheads used aboard Trident submarine missiles.

Yeltsin did not wait for his scheduled summit meeting with Bush at Camp David to reply to this initiative. Within hours, he recommended that the two powers reduce their nuclear arsenals to only 2,000 to 2,500 warheads each—far below the cuts called for in the START agreement and almost 50 percent greater than the reductions Bush had earlier proposed. In other statements, Yeltsin announced his intention to reduce Russian military spending to less than one-seventh of the previous year's allocation and to trim the Russian army to half its former size. To emphasize the new climate of Russian-American friendship, Yeltsin proposed creating a joint U.S.-Russian global defense system and a new international agency to oversee the orderly reduction of nuclear weapons. He also proposed eliminating strategic nuclear weapons.

Even in this hopeful climate of reciprocated reductions, obstacles remained to dismantling the weapons with which each superpower had threatened the existence of the other. The differences centered on where the cuts should be made. Bush called for the elimination of all land-based strategic missiles with **multiple independently targeted reentry vehicles (MIRVs),** the category in which Russia was strongest. But on submarine-launched missiles (SLBMs), where the United States had the advantage, Bush refused to accept reductions beyond one-third and fought the Russian quest for across-the-board cuts.

■ **multiple independently targeted reentry vehicles (MIRVs)** the technological innovation that permits many nuclear warheads to be delivered from a single ballistic missile.

The uncertain future of Russia's government further impeded progress. Even more problematic were the nuclear arsenals of other former Soviet republics. Although Ukraine, Kazakhstan, and Belarus signed the May 1992 Lisbon Protocol to the START agreement, pledging the elimination of all nuclear weapons on their territory and their willingness to join the NPT as nonnuclear states, full cooperation in complying with START was delayed and the complete dismantlement was very protracted.

Moreover, even while this progress was occurring, the superpowers continued their efforts to modernize their arsenals. The lack of realistic targets and the technological breakthrough of miniaturization made most of the discarded weapons obsolete. The former adversaries were still militarily preparing to project power in the global arena, even with the planned cuts and while the United States was assisting the Russians in destroying their strategic arsenals.

Yet, just when it appeared that the disarmament process might lose momentum, a new breakthrough was achieved. At the June 1992 Washington summit, Presidents Yeltsin and Bush made the surprise announcement that Russia and the United States would make additional deep cuts in their strategic arsenals. The formal Joint Understanding accord to the START agreement called for a 60 percent reduction of the two powers' combined total nuclear arsenals from about 15,000 to 6,500 by the year 2003 (see Figure 15.1). Even more dramatically, this so-called "Follow-on" amendment to the START agreement reshaped the strategic landscape. Signed in January 1993, START II not only cut by three-fifths the number of actual warheads in each side's strategic arsenal that had been projected under START, but it also altered drastically the kinds of weapons in each country's arsenal. Under the agreement, Russia and the United States would give up all the multiple warheads on their land-based ICBM missiles. Specifically, by banning all MIRVed ICBMs and reducing SLBM warheads to no more than 1,750, the new agreement "promised a significant enhancement of U.S.-Russian strategic stability since these missiles have long been seen as the most threatening because of their preemptive capabilities" (Keeny 1993).

If adhered to, the Follow-on START III agreement could reduce the chances of a war of annihilation by banning the nuclear weapons that both powers would be most likely to use in a preemptive strike, with the U.S. and Russian inventories each reduced by the year 2007 to 2,000–2,500 strategic warheads. The agreement would leave them with only those weapons they would be likely to use in a retaliatory strike. By reducing the probability of a nuclear war, the Start III agreement agreed to by Presidents Clinton and Yeltsin in September 1997 and ratified by Russia in April 2000, could signal the potential dawning of a new era.

The Problematic Future of Arms Control

U.S. Secretary of State Madeleine Albright warned in March 2000, "The nuclear danger clearly has not ended. We have a long way to go on the road to disarmament." As promising as some of the great powers' recent arms control agreements might appear, the history of their past negotiations testifies to the many obstacles to arms control agreements that exist. It also attests to the extent to which they are dependent on prior improvement in adversaries' political relations. That history raises questions as to whether arms control agreements can restrain the arms race in the long run. After all, these obstacles could resurface in a new multipolar system characterized by rivalry among five or more great powers and a potentially large number of new nuclear-weapon states.

Until recently, international agreements controlled only obsolete armaments or ones that the parties to the agreements had little incentive for developing in the first place. Do states purposely leave the most threatening problems outside negotiations and seek only to control the weapons they no longer deem necessary to their national security? Indeed, does the record demonstrate that

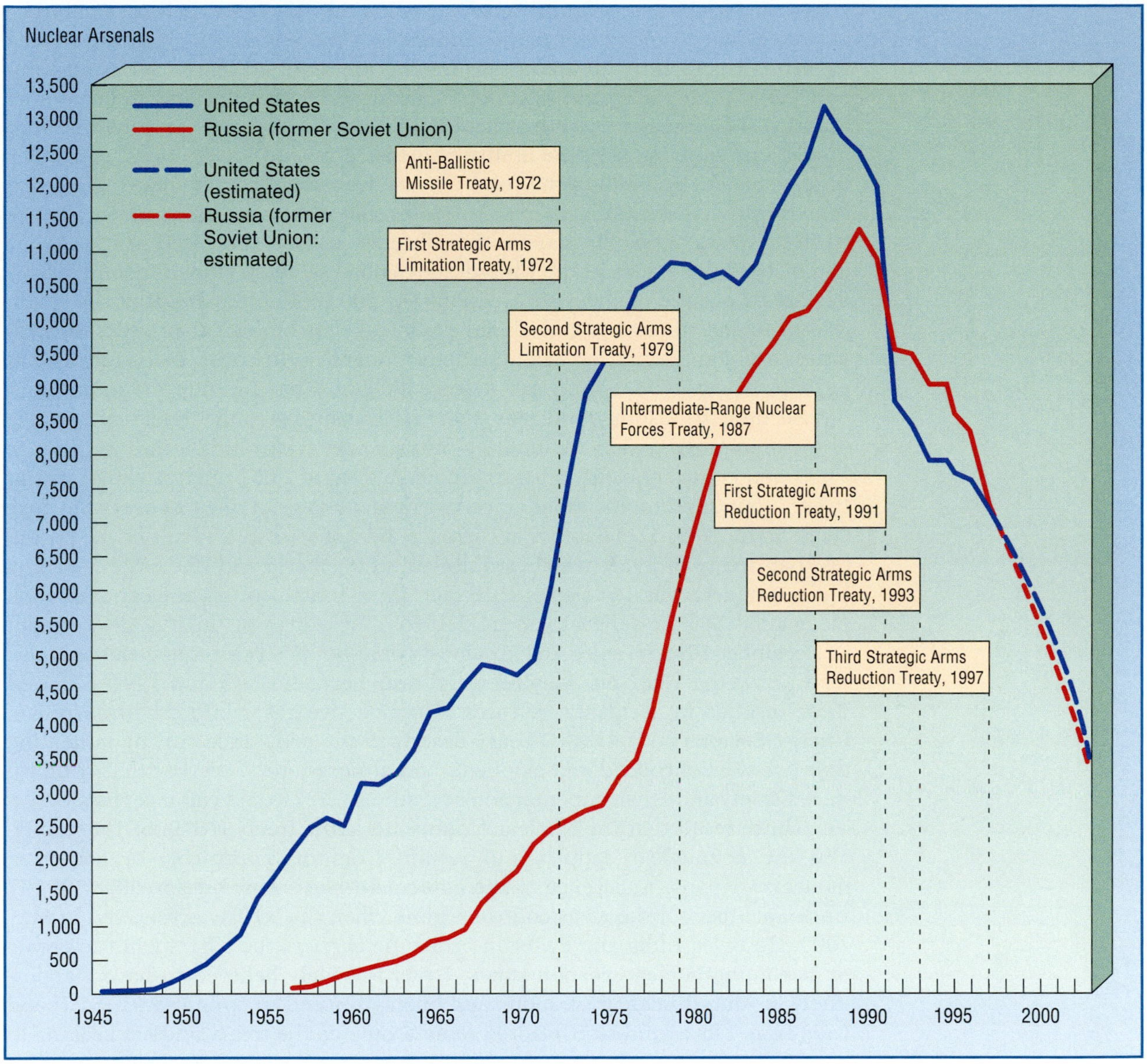

FIGURE 15.1
Countdown to Strategic Parity: The Negotiated End of the U.S.-Russian Arms Race
After decades of rapidly building the number of nuclear warheads in their arsenals, the United States and Russia have, through a series of disarmament agreements, pledged to cut dramatically the number of nuclear warheads in their stockpiles. This has inspired most of the other nuclear powers to also reduce the number of warheads they have deployed. Since its 1986 peak, the size of the global nuclear arsenal has declined by nearly 80 percent (Albright 2000, 8). However, fears that the 1990s disarmament process will be followed by a new arms race remain. As former U.S. President Jimmy Carter lamented in February 2000, "For the first time that I can remember, no series of summit meetings is underway or in preparation to seek further cuts in nuclear weapons. . . . Sad to say, the current state of affairs with regard to nuclear proliferation is not good. In fact, I think it can be said that the world is facing a nuclear crisis."
SOURCE: Based on data from Worldwatch data diskette, Arms Control Association *Fact Files,* and *SIPRI Yearbooks.*

states rarely take arms control seriously when they perceive their survival to be at stake? Many trends point to the tendency for more states to cling tenaciously to the realist belief that preparations for war are required than to accept the liberal belief that armament *reductions* can increase national and international security. The limits to arms control are illustrated by several activities that undermine confidence in the ability of arms control to lower states' capacities for causing death in the twenty-first century. Consider first that states disregard arms control conventions, even some states that were signatories to the treaties banning the weapons they later either illegally developed or used in war. At the end of 1999, for example, the United States possessed the globe's second largest declared stockpile of chemical weapons (31,500 tons) following Russia's stockpile of 40,000 tons, and additional chemical and biological production programs were suspected of being secretly under way in Iran, Iraq, Libya, and perhaps twenty other countries—despite the global ban on their manufacture.

Second, the testing of nuclear weapons also speaks to the tendency of states to make improving their weaponry a priority over controlling it (see Map 15.2). The seven known nuclear states conducted a total of 2,052 nuclear explosions in twenty-four different locations since 1945—an average of one test every ten days (*Vital Signs 1999,* 116). Note that the pace did not slow as a result of the partial test ban treaty of 1963, which prohibited atmospheric and underwater testing but not underground explosions. In fact, three-fourths of all nuclear tests took place after the ban went into effect in 1963. Disclosures by the U.S. government in December 1993 revealed 204 previously unannounced secret nuclear-weapons tests above the 1,032 officially reported tests between 1945 and 1999. Some of these resulted in accidental releases of radioactive gases into the atmosphere. Energy Secretary Hazel R. O'Leary described the arms race cult by lamenting that "we were shrouded and clouded in an atmosphere of secrecy that compromised safety and environmental considerations. . . . I would call it repression."

Third, recall that the Nuclear Nonproliferation Treaty (NPT) of 1968 obligates the nonnuclear countries to refrain from manufacturing or acquiring nuclear weapons. Adherence to the agreement had been widespread, with 187 states members of the arms control regime when the NPT was renewed in May 2000. However, India and Pakistan broke the barriers the NPT sought to create by becoming nuclear-weapon states; Israel is widely believed to have clandestinely produced nuclear weapons and openly refused to comply with NPT; and Iraq, Iran, Libya, and North Korea remain outside the treaty and are seeking to become nuclear-weapon states. In addition, even the existing nuclear states have sought to develop more imposing arsenals at the same time they were reducing the size of their arsenals. For example, in the decade since 1990, even as the United States began eliminating some of its warheads, it increased the number of Trident II warheads by 960 (*Harper's,* March 1996, 13). What is more, the superpowers have pursued invention of new technologies to create substitute deterrence forces for the previous generation of banned weapons. "The nuclear era is far from over. U.S. warhead production stopped in 1990, but new design work continues. U.S. explosive testing stopped in 1992 (and in 1990 in Russia) but new 'subcritical' tests and computer simulations may yield much of the same information. And sizeable arsenals will be retained" (*Vital Signs 1999,* 116).

If disarmament treaties are designed to eliminate the threat of mass annihilation, they have failed. For example, the START agreements would leave the United States and Russia defenseless against a handful of nuclear missiles

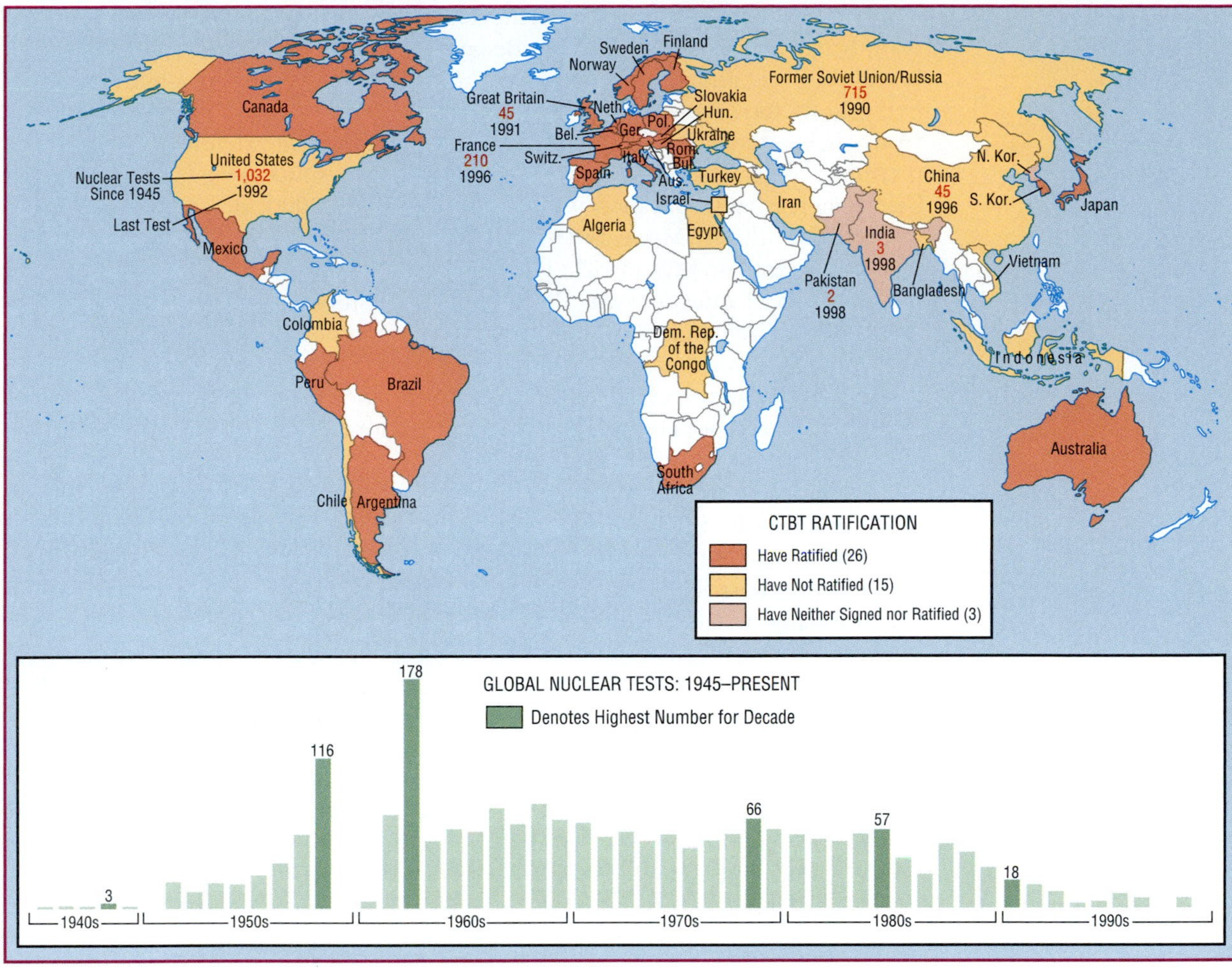

MAP 15.2

Trick or Treaty? Can Arms Control Treaties Arrest the Proliferation of Weapons?

Hope was rising in 1999 that the testing of nuclear weapons, which had been accruing since 1945 (see chart at bottom of map of the number of nuclear tests yearly), would stop if the forty-four nuclear-capable states ratified the Comprehensive Test Ban Treaty (CTBT). Those hopes dissolved that October when the U.S. Senate rejected the test ban, and in so doing opened the way for ambitious regimes like India and Pakistan to resume testing. Headlines compared the U.S. repudiation of their arms-control treaty to the same kind of partisan **intermestic** politics for domestic payoffs that prompted the U.S. rejection of the 1919 Treaty of Versailles (an isolationistic fear of multilateral treaties that arguably paved the road to World War II). The CTBT would have banned all nuclear test explosions worldwide for all time, created a multilateral global monitoring network to detect explosions and verify compliance, and allowed for on-site inspections of areas of clandestine nuclear testing. This map shows that twenty-six of the forty-four nuclear-capable states had ratified the treaty, fifteen had not ratified, and three had neither signed nor ratified, as well as the number of nuclear tests conducted by each of the seven nuclear states through 1999. With the CTBT's collapse, termed by arms-control expert Brent Scowcroft as a "pathetic blow to global arms control," the prospect of continued testing of nuclear weapons is high.

SOURCE: Arms Control Association; Stockholm International Peace Research Institute.

■ **intermestic**
those issues confronting a state that are simultaneously international and domestic, encouraging policymakers to play two-level games when making decisions (see p. 56).

launched in an accidental or unauthorized strike or by a radical regime such as Iran, Iraq, North Korea, or Libya. Because the menace of nuclear proliferation is still very real and the capacity to use these weapons could easily be acquired by ruthless terrorist groups, states' efforts to guarantee their citizens' safety from such attacks have persisted: U.S. ballistic-missile defense programs to provide a partial shield with search-and-destroy space-based lasers are still being energetically pursued with new funding in 2000, despite the fact that these violate the ABM treaty (Garwin 2000). Given their historic appetite for expanded strategic inventories, it is understandable that the nonnuclear members of the NPT question why they should remain restrained while the existing nuclear states refuse to destroy their nuclear arsenals.

Fourth, consider the sobering lessons suggested by the SALT agreements. SALT I did freeze the number of strategic launchers in operation or under construction but did not cover strategic bombers or prevent the kinds of qualitative improvements that would make quantitative thresholds meaningless. For instance, the superpowers deployed four times as many MIRVs on missiles in 1977 as when the SALT talks began, even though SALT I froze the number of delivery vehicles at the superpowers' disposal. Perhaps this troublesome outcome led Herbert Scoville, a former deputy director of the U.S. Central Intelligence Agency, to note at the time of the signing of SALT I that "arms control negotiations [were] rapidly becoming the best excuse for escalating rather than toning down the arms race." The pattern revealed in this and other developments prompted one former U.S. policymaker to conclude that "three decades of U.S.-Soviet negotiations to limit arms competition [did] little more than to codify the arms race" (Gelb 1979). This grim conclusion is validated by the existence in 2000 of seven nuclear powers whose combined strategic nuclear inventories totaled worldwide more than 14,000 warheads.

antipersonnel landmines (APLs) weapons buried below the surface of the soil that explode on contact with any person—soldier or citizen—stepping on them.

Fifth, some types of weapons have been globally recognized as counterproductive and dangerous, yet the international community has proven weak, slow, and ineffective in mobilizing sufficient clout to ban them. Consider the case of **antipersonnel landmines (APLs).** These are weapons that cannot discriminate between soldiers and civilians. Over 100 to 300 million landmines are believed to be scattered on the territory of more than seventy countries (with another 100 million in stockpiles). In the mid-1990s there was about one mine for every fifty humans on earth, and each year they killed or maimed more than 26,000 people—almost all of them civilians. In 1994, not a single state would endorse a prohibition on these deadly weapons. It took a peace activist, Jody Williams, to organize the International Campaign to Ban Landmines that produced the Convention on the Prohibition of the Use, Stockpiling, Production and Transfer of Antipersonnel Mines and Their Destruction, which was opened for signature in December 1997. For her effort to remove those landmines and ban the production of new ones, Williams was awarded the Nobel Peace Prize. But the United States, Russia, and other great powers stubbornly resisted the APL convention until a coalition of nongovernmental peace groups mounted sufficient pressure in world public opinion to coerce their consent to this epic convention. If adhered to, the challenge of enforcing the ban (signed by 135 states at the start of 2000) and the removal of APLs could prove staggering. The UN estimates they cost less than one dollar to produce but seven hundred to three thousand dollars each to remove, so the global cleanup bill could exceed $30 billion and one thousand years at the current work rates for the UN Voluntary Trust Fund to assist in mine clearance to complete its mission. Since the 1997 Antipersonnel Mine Convention entered into force in March 1999, more than 11 million landmines have been destroyed, but that is a mere dent in the huge effort still required. Hence, as with other arms control and disarmament programs, delay, disregard, and inaction seem to be part and parcel of crusades to outlaw inhumane weapons that defense planners claim are necessary for national security. And it appears that the smaller and more transportable the weapon, the tougher the task of implementing controls. The example of biological weapons illustrates the principle: the low cost and ease of secretly producing lethal bacteria, viruses, and other microbes (a kitchen lab can make enough to wipe out a city) accounts for the world's inability to stop the thirteen countries suspected of trying to develop biological arsenals (*Christian Science Monitor,* May 21, 1997, 3).

Finally, note that the various **arms control regimes** established to control the export of particular categories of weapons (such as the 1978 Nuclear Suppliers Group, the 1987 MTCR, and the 1998 European Union Dual-Use Regulation regime) are simply not very effective. The arms trade in illegal weapons is active and growing despite the barriers posed to this traffic. In 1997, for example, it was discovered that China had sold Pakistan the illegal material to build a missile plant; export controls slowed but failed to stop Iran's push for nuclear weapons capability; and Iraq's import of materials for making weapons of mass destruction showed that blocking arms trade to prevent proliferation "will be difficult if not impossible" (*Economist,* April 12, 1997, 79–82). The globalization of weapons systems, making states' capabilities increasingly sophisticated and similar, has continued apace in the so-called new arms control era, because the globalized arms trade has few barriers to dispersion (see Held et al. 2001).

■ **arms control regimes** rules accepted by the parties to treaties to prohibit the production, deployment, sale, or use of particular categories of weapons.

The experience of the past fifty years does not generate confidence in the ability of arms control agreements to reduce the number of weapons or to contain their dispersion in the next fifty years. Technology has increased the problem. Its constant movement has led to the birth of an ever-widening range of novel new weapons—increasingly smaller, deadlier, easier to conceal, and capable of destroying by means unimaginable until recently. The next generation of lethal and **nonlethal weapons** on the drawing boards will revolutionize warfare in the twenty-first century. This revolution in military technology (RMT) in the next generation of weapons was made vivid in the 1991 Persian Gulf War, which involved 600,000 troops with new high-tech weapons and ended with only 148 combat deaths. This has instilled confidence that future wars will involve "clean combat," which like a video-arcade game conveys the impression that a new generation of nonlethal weapons can make combat surgical and pristine.

■ **nonlethal weapons** the wide array of "soft-kill," low-intensity methods of incapacitating an enemy's people, vehicles, communications systems, or entire cities without killing either combatants or noncombatants (see p. 476).

War might be made to appear more acceptable to the public if stealth technology, pilotless combat airplanes, and electronic warfare keep killing from view as they did in the seventy-eight-day NATO attack on Yugoslavia in 1999 that ended with thousands of dead Serbs but not a single NATO soldier killed in combat. The new robotic and laser weapons offer little protection to innocent noncombatants who can easily become the targets. In 1995, the United States had plans to develop an antipersonnel weapon known as the Laser Countermeasure, based on a secret technology that was "cruel and inhumane even by the standards of war. It is a 40-pound portable gun that fires a beam powerful enough to burn out human retinas from up to 3,000 feet away" (Arkin 1995). By blinding people—so the rationale for the construction of this and other equally awesome new weapons goes—war could be made safe for the attacker.

Is the rationale sound? Who will protect people from ruthless aggressors using such weapons if these instruments of violence spread to ruthless terrorists and rogue governments (as they surely will on the covert arms market)? Concerns such as these reduce confidence in the ability to control the armament innovations that advanced technology makes possible, despite the 1996 agreement to ban the use (but not the production) of some types of laser weapons.

The production, stockpiling, and sale of nonlethal and revolutionary, advanced new weapons in the borderless globalized world will be ever more difficult to control. How can the international community be expected to police deadly microbes and other "poor states' nukes" such as chemical poisonous gases and contagious biological viruses that cannot be seen? Detecting an attack is the first challenge; detecting the presence of such weapons is another, much bigger problem. These will be the weapons of choice for rogue governments and terrorist groups and they are highly resistant to control. Many countries have **dual-use production technologies** such as "chemical manufacturing and processing plants and pharmaceutical laboratories which could produce deadly agents, possibly on very short notice, for use in warfare" (Sivard 1996, 27). The banning of such indiscriminate weapons of mass destruction and creation of dependable enforcement and verification procedures could pose the globe's greatest security challenge.

■ **dual-use production technologies**
technologies that have both commercial and military uses.

The primary reason for skepticism is that arms control will not be implemented without sufficient political will. And here again, the past record of low expectations and low arms control performance fails to inspire much confidence about the prospects for meaningful arms control of the twenty-first century's array of invisible, precise, and deadly killing systems. Recall the experience during the hopeful time for arms control when the superpowers' incentives for disarmament were great. Then, with "the case for cutting nuclear weapons as strong as ever," and with acceptance of the fact during the Cold War "that the nuclear balance would be firmer and cheaper to maintain with fewer weapons, not more," why is it that START II did not go further? Why couldn't the superpowers "finish what they STARTED"? (*Economist,* January 27, 1996, 17). Why do states often make decisions to arm that apparently imprison them in the grip of perpetual insecurity? On the surface, the incentives for meaningful arms control seem numerous. Significant controls would save money, reduce tension and hence the dangers of war, symbolize leaders' desire for peace, lessen health hazards, reduce the environmental hazards of nuclear waste, diminish the potential destructiveness of war, dampen the incentive for one state to seek a power advantage over others, reduce the possibility of being the target of a preemptive attack, and achieve a propaganda advantage for those advocating peace. To these we can add moral satisfaction and the opportunity to live in a less threatening global environment.

However, states did not—and perhaps still do not—significantly control the growth of arms. One indication of this is "the U.S. Arms Control and Disarmament Agency has recently been abolished, removing an often weak but at least identifiable entity to explore arms issues" (Carter 2000). There are many reasons to rely on military preparedness as a path to peace; they stem from the fear that is endemic to international anarchy. Most countries are reluctant to engage in arms limitations in a self-help system that requires each state to protect itself. Thus states find themselves caught in a vicious cycle of fear. This creates the security dilemma—a condition that is in no actor's best interest but that permits no easy escape. Its influence on behavior is potent and helps explain why military establishments often subscribe to two basic principles: "(1) 'Don't negotiate when you are behind. Why accept a permanent position of number two?' and (2) 'Don't negotiate when you are ahead. Why accept a freeze in an area of military competition when the other side has not kept up with you?'" (Barnet 1977).

Arms bargaining is a game of give-and-take, but all participants typically want to take much and give little. As a result, with the powerful restraining impact of domestic politics on the negotiation process, it is little wonder that meaningful agreements are so hard to achieve and that states develop weapons systems as bargaining chips for future negotiations. Compounding the problem is the fact that many people benefit financially from arms races and lobby against arms agreements because they could lose their jobs if military spending is cut. **Military-industrial complexes**—defense contractors, journalists, labor unions, and government employees—exist in all societies whose influence is tied to high defense spending. The resistance of military planners and defense specialists to reductions in arsenals attests to the continuing penchant of defense experts and arms manufacturers to insist that "prudence" dictates preparing for the worst contingency by retaining military preparedness at as high a level as possible. "The business of defense is defending business" is the way one analyst summarized the problem (Mulhollin 1994).

■ **military-industrial complex**
the term coined by U.S. President Eisenhower to describe the coalition among arms manufacturers, military bureaucracies, and top government officials, that promotes unnecessary defense expenditures for their own profit and power (see p. 469).

Arms control still remains a murky policy area, and the past record suggests that we should not expect too much of arms control or exaggerate its potential.

> The history of the postwar era proves that arms control, if pursued wisely and properly, can reduce the threat; it can never eliminate the risk of war altogether. Arms control is not a substitute for weapons but a complement to them. Arms and arms control, one by creating the means to inflict unacceptable damage on a potential enemy and the other by protecting that capability from enemy attack, are both necessary for national security. A defense policy that fails to pursue the two together, that emphasizes one approach to the exclusion of the other, is dangerous and incomplete. . . .
>
> True international security depends not as much on arms or arms control as on reducing as much as possible the sources of conflict in international relations and on finding effective nonviolent means of resolving the conflicts that remain. (Kruzel 1991, 268)

MILITARY POWER AND THE SEARCH FOR A TWENTY-FIRST-CENTURY PEACE

The obstacles to arms control are formidable. The idea that a disarmed world would be a more secure one does not have the force of history behind it, whereas the realist idea that military preparedness produces security does. As long as aggressive states exist, it would be imprudent to disarm. Arms control does not solve the basic problem of rivalry between states, because as long as states have and can use weapons, such agreements are little more than cooperative arrangements between adversaries. They define the competition and confine the potential destruction that war brings but do not remove the source of the conflict.

Alternatively, managing political conflicts without violence may be the key to arms control. Arms, after all, are less causes of war than symptoms of political tension: People "do not fight because they have arms. They have arms because [they are afraid and] they deem it necessary to fight" (Morgenthau 1985). From this perspective, controlling arms is contingent on removing the fears that underlie states' conflicts. The quest for national security in an anarchical world springs from states' fear of one another. Yet, because one country's security makes others insecure, nearly all states prepare for war to defend themselves. In this sense the realists' military paths to peace discussed in this chapter are intimately related to the widespread quest for armaments described in Chapter 13.

Still at issue, however, is whether world security is served by states' military search for their own national security. Perhaps the forces that propel the pursuit of peace and security through military might have sown the seeds of the world's destruction. Nothing makes the search for peace through political means more compelling. Hope may be inspired by the observations of former U.S. Secretary of Defense Robert McNamara: "We have reached the present dangerous and absurd confrontation by a long series of steps, many of which seemed rational in their time. Step by step we can undo much of the damage."

Chapter 16 examines some proposals recommended especially by liberal theorists for preventing the damage caused by arms races, power transitions, and the wars they ignite.

KEY TERMS

security dilemma
liberalism
neotraditional realism
alliances
rational choice
levels of analysis
balance of power
alignments
security regime
nonalignment
size principle
balancer
preemption
long peaces
hegemonic stability theory
hegemon
balance of terror
collective security
multilateral
globalization
polarity
bipolarity
polarization
North Atlantic Treaty Organization (NATO)
zero-sum
bipolycentrism
polycentrism
extended deterrence
doctrine
Two Plus Four Treaty
Concert of Europe
bandwagon
Partnership for Peace (PfP)
strategic concept
Euro-Atlantic Partnership Council (EAPC)
multipolarity
concert
unipolarity
arms control
disarmament
demilitarization
bilateral agreements
multilateral agreements
verification
nonproliferation
Strategic Arms Limitation Talks (SALT)
nuclear freeze movement
START (Strategic Arms Reduction) Treaty
multiple independently targeted reentry vehicles (MIRVs)
intermestic
antipersonnel landmines (APLs)
arms control regimes
nonlethal weapons
dual-use production technologies
military-industrial complex

SUGGESTED READING

Bernauer, Thomas, and Dieter Ruloff, eds. *The Politics of Positive Incentives in Arms Control.* Columbia: University of South Carolina Press, 1999.

Bracken, Paul. *Fire in the East: The Rise of Asian Military Power and the End of Western Dominance.* New York: HarperCollins, 1999.

Bueno de Mesquita, Bruce. *The War Trap.* New Haven, Conn.: Yale University Press, 1981.

Claude, Inis L., Jr. *Power and International Relations.* New York: Random House, 1962.

Diehl, Paul F., and Gary Goertz. *War and Peace in International Rivalry.* Ann Arbor: University of Michigan Press, 2000.

Haass, Richard N. "What to Do With American Primacy," 149–159 in Charles W. Kegley, Jr., and Eugene R. Wittkopf, eds., *The Global Agenda.* Boston: McGraw-Hill, 2001.

Kapstein, Ethan, and Michael Mastanduno, eds. *Unipolar Politics: Realism and State Strategies after the Cold War.* New York: Columbia University Press, 1999.

Kegley, Charles W., Jr., and Gregory A. Raymond. *A Multipolar Peace? Great-Power Politics in the Twenty-First Century.* New York: St. Martin's Press, 1994.

Pastor, Robert A., ed. *A Century's Journey: How the Great Powers Shape the World.* New York: Basic Books, 1999.

Rusi, Alpo M. *Dangerous Peace: New Rivalry in World Politics.* Boulder, Colo.: Westview Press, 1997.

Snyder, Glenn. *Alliance Politics.* Ithaca, N.Y.: Cornell University Press, 1997.

Tammen, Ronald L., et al. *Power Transitions: Strategies for the Twenty-First Century.* New York: Chatham House, 2000.

Waltz, Kenneth. N. "Globalization and American Power," *National Interest* 59 (Spring 2000): 46–56.

Wilkinson, David. "Unipolarity without Hegemony," *International Studies Review,* Special Issue, *Prospects for International Relations,* 1999, 141–172.

WHERE ON THE WORLD WIDE WEB?

Bulletin of the Atomic Scientists
http://www.bullatomsci.org/

After World War II, many of the scientists responsible for the production of the atomic bomb helped form a movement to control nuclear energy. In 1945, they founded the *Bulletin* to advocate international control of the means of nuclear production. Still published today, the *Bulletin* now appears on-line. Current and archived issues are available. While exploring this site, click on the Doomsday Clock to see how international tensions and nuclear developments have brought us alternatively closer to midnight or back from the brink. Read brief or detailed histories of technological and political developments. Scan the Nuclear Notebooks to get up-to-date facts and figures on the world's nuclear arsenals.

Center for Nonproliferation Studies (CNS)
http://cns.miis.edu/index.htm

The Center for Nonproliferation Studies (CNS) at the Monterey Institute of International Relations is the largest nongovernmental organization in the United States devoted exclusively to research and training on nonproliferation issues. At this site you will find articles on featured topics as well as summaries on CNS projects. Its extensive electronic resources are organized according to region of the world, subject (nuclear, chemical, or biological weapons), and publication type. Clicking on an image map accesses information on a specific country's nuclear, biological, and chemical weapons capabilities and its involvement in international arms control treaties. Which countries of the world are active in the production of weapons of mass destruction? Why do you think this is the case?

Federation of American Scientists
http://sun00781.dn.net/nuke/control/

Students interested in examining international arms control treaties and related issues should visit the Federation of American Scientists' (FAS) Web site to find a comprehensive archive of nuclear, chemical, and biological arms control agreements. FAS is a privately funded nonprofit policy organization engaged in analysis and advocacy on science, technology, and public policy issues that concern global security. Topics such as arms sales monitoring, chemical and biological arms, space policy, and nuclear nonproliferation and disarmament are covered extensively.

NATO
http://www.nato.int/

The North Atlantic Treaty Organization's (NATO) Web site contains information on NATO's enlargement as well as the Partnership for Peace (PfP) initiative. Click on the Partnership link to get a list of the countries participating in the PfP, read speeches from the respective countries, and get country-specific information. Also read the study on NATO enlargement. Are you convinced by the rationale for enlargement?

United Nations Conference on Disarmament
http://www.unog.ch/frames/disarm/disdoc.htm

The UN Conference on Disarmament Web page links to all the major international instruments on disarmament, from the 1949 Geneva Convention through the 1997 antipersonnel landmines convention. Read the texts of some of the most influential international agreements that seek to control or eliminate weapons of mass destruction.

United Nations Demining Database
http://www.un.org/Depts/Landmine/index.html

Antipersonnel landmines (APLs) are internationally recognized as an inhumane and counterproductive weapon. In 1997, one hundred countries signed a treaty prohibiting the production of landmines and supporting the removal of those buried in the ground, but enforcing the treaty remains a challenge. This comprehensive site explores the issues involved with demining. Click on the Country Overview to read about specific countries' problems demining their land and the origins of the mines found within their borders. See how many mines different countries have, the area contaminated, and the number of victims. Which countries have the greatest number of landmines? Why do you think this is so? Who are the biggest suppliers?

CHAPTER 16

THE LIBERAL INSTITUTIONAL PATHS TO PEACE

TOPICS AND THEMES

- International law as a means to world order
- International organizations and world order: The UN and regional organizations
- Political integration: The functional and neofunctional paths to peace
- Democracy as a means to peace
- Liberal institutions and world order

- **CONTROVERSY** LEGAL LIMITS ON SEX FOR SALE? INTERNATIONAL LAW VERSUS STATE'S RIGHTS ON PROSTITUTION

The World Court in session, 1999

My first axiom: The quest for international security involves the unconditional surrender by every nation, in a certain measure, of its liberty of action, its sovereignty that is to say, and it is clear beyond all doubt that no other road can lead to such security.

—Albert Einstein, German-born Swiss-American scientist, 1932

State sovereignty, in its most basic sense, is being redefined—not least by the forces of globalization and international cooperation. States are now widely understood to be the instruments at the service of their people, and not vice versa.

—Kofi Annan, UN secretary-general, 1999

Since antiquity, the world has pursued two primary paths to peace. The realist road emphasizes *military* solutions; the liberal road emphasizes *political* solutions. This chapter examines four principal approaches to the control of armed conflict from the liberal theoretical tradition: international law, organization, integration, and democratization (see Table 16.1). Because all four stress institutions, the new advocates of these liberal paths are sometimes referred to collectively as **neoliberal institutionalists.** While they differ in their approach to preserving twenty-first-century security, they share a fear of the historic tendency of states to make war. They are also concerned that because there is as yet "no universal international law, no global sovereign, or an effective enforcement mechanism accepted by all," war will continue to erupt (Hammond 1996).

■ **neoliberal institutionalism** the recent theoretical effort to explain how peace and prosperity instead of war might be created through law, global governance, and liberal democracies' cooperation to engineer international change.

TABLE 16.1

Liberal Paths to International Security

Prescription	*Premise*
Provide states rules of international law to regulate competition.	Interstate cooperation can be encouraged by creating rules for peaceful interaction.
Participate in the creation of international organizations.	If you want peace, prepare global institutions to keep it.
Practice collaboration to bind independent states together in integrated security communities.	Interdependence makes imperative the amalgamation of states, not their division.
Promote the spread of democratic governance.	Countries that protect their own citizens' civil liberties do not wage war against other governments that also protect their citizens' human rights.
Prepare rules to facilitate free trade.	Trade protectionism is counterproductive to prosperity and peace.
Produce agreements to reduce armaments to levels that discourage war.	States get what they plan for—beat swords into plowshares.
Provide humanitarian assistance to the impoverished.	Rich states can help themselves only by helping poor people also.
Principles are more important than power.	Principled moral behavior ultimately reap higher rewards for all because they encourage reciprocity.

INTERNATIONAL LAW AND WORLD ORDER

In 1984, the United States announced that it would unilaterally withdraw from the World Court's jurisdiction. This move followed disputes with several Central American countries after Nicaragua's accusation that the U.S. Central Intelligence Agency had illegally attempted to "overthrow and destabilize" the elected Sandinista government. Nicaragua charged in the World Court that the United States had illegally mined its ports and supplied money, military assistance, and training to the rebel *contra* forces. The United States denied the tribunal's authority. In so doing, however, it was not acting without precedent; others had done so previously. Nonetheless, by thumbing its nose at the court and the rule of law it represents, had it, as some claimed, become an "international outlaw?" Or, as others asserted, had it acted within its rights?

The World Court supported the former view. In 1984, the court ruled as follows:

> The right to sovereignty and to political independence possessed by the Republic of Nicaragua, like any other state of the region or of the world, should be fully respected and should not in any way be jeopardized by any

> military and paramilitary activities which are prohibited by the principles of international law, in particular the principle that states should refrain in their international relations from the threat or the use of force against the territorial integrity or the political independence of any state, and the principle concerning the duty not to intervene in matters within the domestic jurisdiction of a state. (*New York Times,* May 11, 1984, 8)

Yet this ruling had little effect, as neither the court nor Nicaragua had any means to enforce it. Events such as this have led many critics to conclude that international law is "weak and defenseless" (Fried 1971). Indeed, many experts—whether they are realists or liberals—skeptically ask whether international law is really law.

There are many reasons to answer this question affirmatively. Although international law is imperfect, actors regularly rely on it to redress grievances (see Joyner 2001; von Glahn 1996). Most of this activity falls within the realm of **private international law**—the regulation of routine transnational activities in such areas as commerce, communications, and travel. While largely invisible to the public, private international law is the locus for all but a small fraction of international legal activities. It is where the majority of transnational disputes are regularly settled and where the record of compliance compares favorably with that achieved in domestic legal systems.

■ **private international law**
law pertaining to routinized transnational intercourse between or among states as well as nonstate actors.

■ **public international law**
law pertaining to government-to-government relations.

In contrast, **public international law** covers issues of public order, including relations between governments and the interactions of governments with intergovernmental organizations (IGOs) and nongovernmental organizations (NGOs) such as multinational corporations. Some believe that we should use the phrase *world law* to describe the mixture of public and private, domestic and international transactions that public international law seeks to regulate in an increasingly globalized world. However, it is the regulation of government-to-government relations that dominates the headlines in discussion of public international law. This area of activity also receives most of the criticism, for here, failures—when they occur—are quite conspicuous (see Controversy: Legal Limits on Sex for Sale?). This is especially true with respect to the breakdown of peace and security. When states engage in armed conflict, criticism of its shortcomings escalates. Israeli Ambassador Abba Eban lamented that "international law is that law which the wicked do not obey and the righteous do not enforce."

Because this chapter examines the capacity of public international law to control war, our discussion will address only the laws and institutional machinery created to manage armed conflict between states. That is, it will explore that segment of public international law popularly regarded as the most deficient.

Law at the International Level: Core Principles

■ **sovereignty**
the legal doctrine that states have supreme authority to govern their internal affairs and manage their foreign relations with other states and IGOs.

Public international law is usually defined as the rules that govern the conduct of states in their relations with one another. The *corpus juris gentium* (the body of the law of nations) has grown considerably over the past four centuries, changing in response to transformations in international politics (Kaplan and Katzenbach 1961). An inventory of the basic legal principles relevant to the control of war reveals the character of the international system (for authoritative texts, see Green 1999; Higgins 1994).

CONTROVERSY

Legal Limits on Sex for Sale?

International Law versus States' Rights on Prostitution

At the edge of a new century, as an intense sense of change grips much of the world, a revolution in human affairs is occurring. The international community is attempting the awesome challenge of revising international law. Even in a world where more and more of the global population lives in good health and prosperity and is increasingly secure from territorial aggression, many others live in marked poverty and despair. The twenty-first century is home to a global dichotomy between promise and peril, achievement and affliction.

What should the global community do to address the problems that still haunt humankind? At issue is whether international law can police the many problems associated with the revolution in human affairs. Can modern perils and afflictions be brought under control by globally recognized legal doctrine? One argument holds that states should preserve their traditional sovereign right to manage human affairs within their borders as they see fit. To this way of thinking, international law should have no jurisdiction over a country's internal affairs and policies with respect to human rights. In contrast, a rival argument holds that human affairs are global affairs, and that international law should seek to protect human rights around the world, even when that regulation is resented by national governments as an unjust interference in their internal affairs.

What do you think? What are the limits of international law over the control of a state's conduct towards its citizens? What criteria should define the boundaries between global involvement and intervention that can assault national sovereignty and erode the traditions of local cultures? In contemplating your position, consider the example of the United Nations treaty being drafted at the beginning of 2000, the Convention Prohibiting the Trafficking of Women and Children for Prostitution. Sex trafficking is a serious human rights issue that has both international and national implications. Human rights groups estimate that hundreds of thousands, perhaps millions, of women and children are forced into lives of sexual exploitation. Many are transported across national borders by criminal organizations. The new treaty is designed to protect the victims of sex trafficking.

On the surface, few would question whether this treaty should be enforced, because it is designed to protect women's human rights. However, many countries have objected to the treaty because they see it as an infringement on their national sovereignty. These protestors are not alone. They are joined by a number of nongovernmental organizations (NGOs), including the National Organization for Women and the Planned Parenthood Federation of America, which complain that the wording of the treaty is too weak and in fact seeks to appease national governments. If the negotiators do not alter its wording, the treaty would make it difficult for human rights groups to prosecute prostitution rings because the terms of the treaty would deal with only a limited range of sex trafficking practices. In effect, it would legally allow states to retain primary control over issues of prostitution.

Major human issues like prostitution highlight the tension between many ethical principles and finally, between national rights versus global responsibilities to protect human rights. A daunting question of the twenty-first century is whether the states of the world will agree on rules to control shared problems through international law or whether they will continue to resist letting international law control them.

The Rules of International Law. No principle of international law is more critical than state sovereignty. **Sovereignty** means that no authority is legally above the state, except that which the state voluntarily confers on the international organizations it joins. In fact, as conceived by theoreticians schooled in the tradition of **realism** since the seventeenth century, the rules of international law were written to protect states, and permitted states "a complete freedom of action" (Parry 1968) to preserve their sovereign independence.

Nearly every legal doctrine supports and extends the cardinal principle that states are the primary subjects of international law. Although the Universal

■ **realism**
the theoretical tradition arguing that sovereign states are the most important global actors and should be unrestrained by law, principles of justice, or supranational organizations when making decisions regarding war and peace (see p. 457).

Declaration of Human Rights in 1948 expanded concern about states' treatment of individual people, states remain supreme. "Laws are made to protect the state from the individual and not the individual from the state" (Gottlieb 1982). Accordingly, the vast majority of rules address the rights and duties of states, not people. For instance, the principle of **sovereign equality** entitles each state to full respect by other states as well as equal protection by the system's legal rules. The right of independence also guarantees states' autonomy in their domestic affairs and external relations, under the logic that the independence of each presumes that of all. Similarly, the doctrine of **neutrality** permits states to avoid involvement in others' conflicts and coalitions.

Furthermore, the noninterference principle forms the basis for **nonintervention**—that is, states' duty to refrain from uninvited involvement in another's internal affairs. This sometimes abused classic rule gives governments the right to exercise jurisdiction over practically all things on, under, or above their bounded territory. (There are exceptions, however, such as **diplomatic immunity** for states' ambassadors from the domestic laws of the country where their embassies are located, and **extraterritoriality,** which allows control of embassies on other states' terrain.)

In practice, domestic jurisdiction permits a state to enact and enforce whatever laws it wishes for its own citizens. In fact, international law was so permissive toward the state's control of its domestic affairs that, prior to 1952, "there was no precedent in international law for a . . . state to assume responsibility for the crimes it committed against a minority within its jurisdiction" (Wise 1993). A citizen was not protected against the state's abuse of human rights or **crimes against humanity.** Note also that international law permits states to set their own rules for citizenship. Two basic principles govern the way nationality and citizenship are conferred: under *jus soli,* citizenship is determined by the state in whose territory the birth took place; under *jus sanguinis,* nationality is acquired by descent from a parent who is a national.

In addition, in earlier periods of modern international law, states were permitted to create whatever form of government they desired without regard to its acceptability to other states. This principle was expressed in the realpolitik language of the Treaty of Augsburg (1515) and the Westphalian Treaties (1648), which made states all-powerful by recognizing the **divine right of kings.** This doctrine was reaffirmed in the 1943 Atlantic Charter's pledge of "the right of all people to choose the form of government under which they will live." However, this rule has recently eroded, and the right of people to live under the liberties of democracy is increasingly being defined as an "entitlement" or a basic human right. At Geneva in 1999, "in a landslide victory for freedom . . . states ranging in size from Cape Verde to India came together to proclaim that all individuals have a right to democracy," thereby revising international law through a United Nations resolution and by the same vote dealing "a severe blow to those countries which continue to deny their citizens not only democracy but other fundamental human rights" (N. Rubin 1999; on the "democratic entitlement in international law," see also Sellers 1998). International law still gives states the complete freedom to regulate economic transactions within their boundaries and empowers the state to draft those living on its soil into its armed forces to fight—and die, if necessary—to defend the state.

■ **sovereign equality** the principle that states are legally entitled to equal protection under international law.

■ **neutrality** the legal doctrine that provides rights and duties for states who remain nonaligned with adversaries during wartime.

■ **nonintervention** the principle prohibiting one state from interfering in another state's internal affairs (see p. 531).

■ **diplomatic immunity** the legal doctrine that gives ambassadors immunity from the domestic laws of the countries where their embassies are located.

■ **extraterritoriality** the legal doctrine that allows states to maintain jurisdiction over their embassies in other states.

■ **crimes against humanity** a category of activities, made illegal at the Nuremberg war crime trials, condemning states that abuse the human rights of their citizens.

■ **divine right of kings** the realist doctrine that because kings are sovereign they have the right to rule their subjects authoritatively and are not accountable to the public because their rule is ordained by God.

The Montevideo Convention of 1933 on the Rights and Duties of States summarizes the major components of **statehood.** A state must possess a permanent population, a well-defined territory, and a government capable of ruling its citizens and of managing formal diplomatic relations with other states. Other rules specify how and when these conditions are satisfied. Essentially, the acquisition of statehood depends on a political entity's recognition as such by other states. Whether a state exists thus rests in the hands of other states; that is, preexisting states are entitled to extend **diplomatic recognition** to another entity. **De facto recognition** is provisional and capable of being withdrawn in the event that the recognized government is superseded by another. It does not carry with it the exchange of diplomatic representatives or other legal benefits and responsibilities. **De jure recognition,** on the other hand, extends full legal and diplomatic privileges from the granting state. This distinction emphasizes that recognition is a political tool of international law, through which approval or disapproval of a government can be expressed.

Today, with the exception of Antarctica, which is administered jointly by several states and is outside the jurisdiction of any one of them, no significant land mass remains *terra nullius* (territory belonging legally to no one). Consequently, the birth of a new state must be at the expense of an existing one. Thus, the recognition of a new state almost always means the recognition of a new government's control over a particular territory. Because recognition is a voluntary political act, **nonrecognition** is a legally institutionalized form of public insult to a government aspiring to be accepted as legitimate. It may be seen as a form of sanction against an unwanted political regime.

States are free to enter into treaty arrangements with other states. Rules specify how treaties are to be activated, interpreted, and abrogated. International law holds that treaties voluntarily entered into are binding (*pacta sunt servanda*). However, it also reserves for states the right to unilaterally terminate treaties previously agreed to, by reference to the escape clause known as *rebus sic stantibus*. This is the principle that a treaty is binding only as long as no fundamental change occurs in the circumstances that existed when it was concluded.

Procedures for Dispute Settlement. In addition to these general principles, international law provides a wide variety of legal methods for states to resolve their conflicts. The laws of negotiation do not obligate states to reach agreement or to settle their disputes peacefully. They do, however, provide rules for several conflict resolution procedures, including:

- **Mediation:** when a third party proposes a nonbinding solution to a controversy between two other states, as illustrated by U.S. President Jimmy Carter's historic mediation at the 1978 Camp David meeting between Egypt and Israel.
- **Good offices:** when a third party offers a location for discussions among disputants but does not participate in the actual negotiations, as Switzerland often does.
- **Conciliation:** when a third party assists both sides but does not offer any solution.

■ **statehood**
the legal criteria by which a country and its government become a state in the international community.

■ **diplomatic recognition**
the formal legal acceptance of a state's official status as an independent country.

■ **de facto recognition**
a government's acknowledgment of the factual existence of another state or government short of full recognition.

■ **de jure recognition**
one government's formal, legal recognition of another government or state.

■ **nonrecognition**
withholding official legal acceptance of a state as a form of sanction against that state's government.

■ **mediation**
a conflict resolution procedure in which a third party offers a nonbinding solution to the disputants.

■ **good offices**
the offering by a third party of a location for discussion among disputants.

■ **conciliation**
a conflict resolution procedure in which a third party assists both sides but proposes no solution.

■ **arbitration**
a conflict resolution procedure in which a third party makes a binding decision through an ad hoc forum.

■ **adjudication**
a conflict resolution procedure in which a third party makes a binding decision through an institutional tribunal.

- **Arbitration:** when a third party gives a binding decision through an ad hoc forum.
- **Adjudication:** when a third party offers a binding decision through an institutionalized tribunal, such as a court.

The Limitations of the International Legal System

Sovereignty and the legal principles derived from it shape and reinforce international anarchy. The nature of world politics is legally dependent on what governments choose to do with one another and the kinds of rules they voluntarily support. Throughout most of modern history, international law as constructed by realists was designed by states to protect the state, and so made sovereignty the core principle to ensure states' freedom to act in terms of their perceived national interests.

To liberal theoreticians, putting the state ahead of the global community was a serious flaw that undermined international law's potential effectiveness. Many theorists consider the international legal system institutionally defective due to its dependence on states' willingness to participate. Because formal legal institutions (like those within states) are weak at the international level, critics make the following points. First, in world politics no legislative body capable of making binding laws exists. Rules are made only when states willingly observe or embrace them in the treaties to which they voluntarily subscribe. There is no systematic method of amending or revoking treaties. Article 38 of the Statute of the International Court of Justice (or World Court) affirms this. Generally accepted as the authoritative definition of the "sources of international law," it states that international law derives from (1) custom; (2) international treaties and agreements; (3) national and international court decisions; (4) the writings of legal authorities and specialists; and (5) the "general principles" of law recognized since the Roman Empire as part of "natural law" and "right reason."

Second, in world politics no judicial body exists to authoritatively identify the rules accepted by states, record the substantive precepts reached, interpret when and how the rules apply, and identify violations. Instead, states are responsible for performing these tasks themselves. The World Court does not have the power to perform these functions without states' consent, and the UN cannot speak on judicial matters for the whole global community (even though it has recently defined a new scope for Chapter VII of the UN Charter that claims the right to make quasi-judicial authoritative interpretations of global laws).

Finally, in world politics there is no executive body capable of enforcing the rules. Rule enforcement usually occurs through the self-help actions of the victims of a transgression or with the assistance of their allies or other interested parties. No centralized enforcement procedures exist, and compliance is voluntary. The whole system rests, therefore, on states' willingness to abide by the rules to which they consent and on the ability of each to enforce through retaliatory measures the norms of behavior they value.

Consequently, states themselves—not a higher authority—determine what the rules are, when they apply, and how they should be enforced. This raises the question of greatest concern to liberal advocates of a world law: When everyone is above the law, is anyone ruled by it? It was precisely this problem that prompted UN Secretary-General Kofi Annan in his September 1999 annual address to the opening session of the General Assembly to push for abandonment of traditional "state sovereignty" and acceptance of a new conceptualization of sovereignty. He argued

> it is clear that traditional notions of sovereignty alone are not the only obstacle to effective action in humanitarian crises. No less significant are the ways in which states define their national interests. The world has changed in profound ways since the end of the Cold War, but I fear our conceptions of national interest have failed to follow suit. A new, broader definition of national interest is needed in the new century, which would induce states to find greater unity in the pursuit of common goals and values. In the context of many of the challenges facing humanity today, the collective interest is the national interest. (49–50)

Beyond the barriers to legal institutions that sovereignty poses, still other weaknesses reduce confidence in international law. Critics and reformers usually cite these additional alleged deficiencies:

- *International law lacks universality.* An effective legal system must represent the norms shared by those it governs. According to the precept of Roman law, *ubi societas, ibi jus* (where there is society, there is law), shared community values are a minimal precondition for forming a legal system. Yet the contemporary international order is culturally and ideologically pluralistic and lacks consensus on common values. Although some claim the Western-based international legal order approximates universality, state practice and the simultaneous operation of often incompatible legal traditions throughout the world contradict this claim (Bozeman 1994).
- *International law justifies the competitive pursuit of national advantage without regard to morality or justice.* As in any legal system, in international politics what is legal is not necessarily moral (see Nardin 1983). In fact, international law legitimizes the drive for hegemony and contributes to conflict (Lissitzyn 1963). The principle of **self-help** fails to check states' pursuit of power at others' expense; it is a concession to power. By accepting the view that the unbridled autonomy of sovereign independence is sacrosanct, international law follows the realists' "iron law of politics"—that legal obligations must yield to the national interest (Morgenthau 1985).

■ self-help
the principle that in anarchy actors must rely on themselves (see p. 661).

- *International law is an instrument of the powerful to oppress the weak.* In a voluntary consent system, the rules to which the powerful willingly agree are those that serve their interests. These rules therefore preserve the existing hierarchy (Friedheim 1965). For this reason, some liberal theorists claim that international law has bred the so-called **structural violence** resulting from the hierarchical organization of world politics in which the strong benefit at the expense of the weak (Galtung 1969). Enforcement is left "to the vicissitudes of the distribution of power between the violator of the law and the victim of the violation." Therefore, Hans J. Morgenthau (1985) concedes, "it makes it easy for the strong both to violate the law and to enforce it, and consequently puts the rights of the weak in jeopardy. A great power can violate the rights of a small nation without having to fear effective sanctions on the latter's part."

■ structural violence
the condition defined by Norwegian peace researcher Johan Galtung as the harm and injury caused by the global system's unregulated structure, which effectively allows strong states to victimize the weak states that cannot protect themselves.

- *International law is little more than a justification of existing practices.* When a particular behavior pattern becomes widespread, it becomes legally

positivist legal theory a theory that stresses states' customs as the most important source of law.

obligatory; rules *of* behavior become rules *for* behavior (Hoffmann 1971). Eminent legal scholar Hans Kelsen's contention that states ought to behave as they have customarily behaved (see Onuf 1982) and E. Adamson Hoebel's (1961) dictum that "what the most do, others should do" reflect the **positivist legal theory** that when a type of behavior occurs frequently, it becomes legal. In fact, the highly regarded positivist legal theorists stress states' customary practices as the most important source from which laws derive. In the absence of formal machinery for creating international rules, for evidence of what the law is, positivists observe leaders' foreign policy pronouncements, repeated usage in conventions voluntarily accepted by states, general practices (by an overwhelmingly large number of states), the judicial decisions of national and international tribunals, and legal principles stated in the resolutions of multinational assemblies such as the UN General Assembly. When the sources of international law are interpreted in this way, the actions of states shape law, not vice versa.

- *International law's ambiguity reduces law to a policy tool for propaganda purposes.* The vague, elastic wording of international law makes it easy for states to define and interpret almost any action as legitimate. "The problem here," observes Samuel S. Kim (1991), "is the lack of clarity and coherence [that enables] international law [to be] easily stretched, . . . to be a flexible fig leaf or a propaganda instrument." This ambivalence makes it possible for states to exploit international law to get what they can and to justify what they have obtained (Wright 1953).

The Relevance of International Law

International law is fraught with deficiencies. Still, we can question the proposition that it is irrelevant to contemporary international politics. States themselves do not deem public international law irrelevant. They attach considerable importance to it and expend considerable time and energy fighting over its interpretation while attempting to shape its evolution. If law were meaningless, we would not be able to point to the existence of a systematic code of rules repeatedly affirmed by states in multilateral agreements, resolutions, and declarations (see Jones 1991). These instrumentalities reflect state opinion and show that there are basic principles that states formally recognize and agree to respect.

"The reality as demonstrated through their behavior," legal scholar Christopher Joyner (2001) observes, "is that states do accept international law as law and, even more significant, in the vast majority of instances they . . . obey it." The major reason states practice self-restraint is because even the most powerful states appreciate its benefits. International reputations are important. Those who play the game of international politics by recognized rules receive rewards, whereas states that ignore international law or opportunistically break customary norms pay costs for doing as they please. Other countries will be reluctant to cooperate with them. They must also fear reprisals and retaliation by those victimized, as well as the loss of prestige. For this reason, only the most ambitious or reckless state is apt to flagrantly disregard accepted standards of conduct.

A primary reason why states value international law and affirm their commitment to it is that they need a common understanding of the "rules of the game." International law is an "institutional device for communicating to the policymakers of various states a consensus on the nature of the international system" (Coplin 1965). Law helps shape expectations, and rules reduce uncertainty and enhance predictability in international affairs. These communication functions serve every member of the international system.

While the members of the state system usually agree on certain general values, they often fail to recognize the responsibilities these values demand of them (Coplin 1966). Thus it is tempting to agree with critics who assert that the lack of supranational sanctioning powers makes international law useless for its most important function—controlling violence. However, this conclusion relies on a misleading comparison critics often draw between the international legal order's primitive institutions and states' highly centralized domestic legal systems. Comparison invites the mistaken conclusion that a formal legal structure (a centralized, "vertical system of law") is automatically superior to a decentralized, self-help, "horizontal system of law." The organizational differences between domestic (municipal) and international legal systems hide similarities and obscure the key question: Which type of legal order is more effective?

Evidence shows that unorganized or primitive legal systems succeed in containing violence and ensuring compliance with rules (see Masters 1969). Even in systems without the kinds of institutionalized procedures typically found in municipal legal systems for punishing rule violation (such as tribal societies without formal governments), sanctions often effectively regulate social relations peacefully (Barkun 1968). Thus we should not be surprised to learn that "international law is not violated more often, or to a higher degree, than the law of other systems" (Joyner 2001). The historical record demonstrates that states have regularly resolved their differences through legal procedures. In ninety-seven interstate conflicts between 1919 and 1986, 168 attempts were made by the contending parties to negotiate, mediate, adjudicate, or otherwise settle their disputes through formal procedures of conflict resolution. More impressively, sixty-eight of ninety-seven conflicts were peacefully resolved (Holsti 1988, 420). In other words, since World War I states have been able to resolve their differences 70 percent of the time by using pacific settlement procedures.

It is also clear that formal institutions for rule enforcement do not guarantee compliance. No legal system can deter all of its members from breaking existing laws. Consequently it is a mistake to expect a legal system to prevent all criminal behavior or to assert that any violation of the law proves the inadequacy of the legal structure. Law is designed to deter crime, but it is unreasonable to expect it to prevent it.

Similarly, we should not view every breakdown of international law as confirming general lawlessness. Conditions of crisis strain all legal systems, and few, when tested severely, can contain all violence. Since 1500, more people have died from civil wars than from wars between sovereign states (Sivard 1991). Today, with street crime in cities worldwide at epidemic proportions and ethnopolitical warfare within countries exacting a deadly toll against hundreds of minority groups, states' domestic legal systems are patently failing to prevent killing. Thus, the allegedly "deficient" international legal system performs its primary job—inhibiting interstate violence—more effectively than the supposedly more sophisticated domestic systems. Perhaps, then, the usual criteria by which critics assess legal systems are dubious. Should they be less concerned with structures and institutions, and more concerned with performance?

Even the most skeptical of theorists who claim that leaders act without consideration of the rules must acknowledge that legal norms help to order the process of bargaining and the formation of **security regimes**—sets of rules to contain armed conflict (see Jervis 1982; Stein 1993). At the onset of militarized disputes, law "serves as a sort of signal to tell states which of these clashes are acceptable and which are deserving of retaliation" (D'Amato 1982). Once a crisis erupts, rules eliminate the need to decide on a procedure for deciding.

security regimes the norms and rules for interaction agreed to by a set of states to increase their security (see p. 555).

At another level, public international law makes possible the routine transactions otherwise governed by private international law in such activities as international trade, foreign travel, mail flows, currency exchange, environmental protection, and debt obligations. Parties to the regimes, or rules for cooperative exchanges, in these areas regard them as binding and abide by their provisions (Kim 1991; Soroos 2001). Arguably, by restraining armed force as a possible means of resolution for a dispute, international law reduces the sources of aggression. This helps make an anarchical world more orderly.

The Legal Control of Warfare

Liberal reformers often complain that law clearly fails in the realm of behavior most resistant to legal control—conflict management. If under international law, as fashioned by realist leaders, states are "legally bound to respect each other's independence and other rights, and yet free to attack each other at will" (Brierly 1944), international law may actually encourage war. The ethical and jurisprudential **just war doctrine** from which the laws of war stem shapes discussions of contemporary public international law. Because throughout history changes in international law have followed changes in the moral consensus about the ethics of using armed force in interstate relations, it is important to understand the origins of just war theory and the way it is evolving today, before reviewing contemporary changes in the legal rules of warfare.

just war doctrine a doctrine regarding the moral conditions under which war may be undertaken and how it should be fought once it begins.

Just War Doctrine: The Changing Ethics Regarding the Use of Armed Force. Many people are confused by international law because it both prohibits and justifies the use of force. The confusion derives from the just war tradition in "Christian realism," in which the rules of war are philosophically based on **morals** (principles of behavior) and **ethics** (explanations of why these principles are proper). In the fourth century, St. Augustine questioned the strict view that those who take another's life to defend the state necessarily violate the commandment "Thou shalt not kill." He counseled that "it is the wrong-doing of the opposing party which compels the wise man to wage just wars." The Christian was obligated, he felt, to fight against evil and wickedness. To St. Augustine, the City of Man was inherently sinful, in contrast to the City of God; thus in the secular world it was sometimes permissible to kill—to punish a sin by an enemy (while still loving the sinner) to achieve a "just peace." This realist logic was extended by Pope Nicholas I, who in 866 proclaimed that any defensive war was just.

morals principles clarifying the difference between good and evil and the situations in which they are opposed.

ethics the branch of philosophy that deals with the sources, status, and justification of moral rules and how right and wrong behavior and motives may be distinguished.

From this perspective evolved the modern just war doctrine as developed by such medieval secularists as Hugo Grotius, who challenged the warring Catholic and Protestant Christian powers in the Thirty Years' War (1618–1648) to abide by humane standards of conduct, and sought to replace the two "cities," or ethical realms, of Augustine with a single global society under

War and the Birth of Modern International Law Enraged by the inhumane international conditions he witnessed during his lifetime, Dutch reformer Hugo Grotius (1583–1645) wrote *De Jure Belli et Pacis* (*On the Law of War and Peace*) in 1625 in the midst of the Thirty Years' War. His treatise called on the great powers to resolve their conflicts by judicial procedures rather than on the battlefield, and specified the legal principles he felt could encourage cooperation, peace, and more humane treatment of people. Grotius consequently became known as the "founder of international law."

national law. For Grotius, a just war was one of self-defense or punishment for inflicted damages: "No other just cause for undertaking war can there be excepting injury received." For war to be moral it must be fought by just means without harm to innocent noncombatants. From this distinction evolved the modern version of just war doctrine, consisting of two categories of argument, *jus ad bellum* (the justice of a war) and *jus in bello* (justice in a war). The former sets the criteria by which a political leader may determine whether a war should be waged. The latter specifies restraints on the range of permissible tactics to be used in fighting a just war.

These distinctions have been hotly debated since their inception. Drawing the line between murder and just war is a controversial task. Yet just war theory seeks to define these boundaries. According to this legal tradition, some circumstances in which lethal force may be justifiable are recognized under international law, which also provides guidelines for sanctioned methods.

At the core of the just war tradition is the conviction that the taking of human life may be a "lesser evil" when necessary to prevent further life-threatening aggression. St. Thomas More contended that the assassination of an evil leader responsible for starting a war was justified if it would prevent the taking of innocent lives. From this premise, a number of other principles follow. The criteria today include ten key ideas:

1. All other means to a morally just solution of conflict must be exhausted before a resort to arms can be justified.
2. War can be just only if employed to defend a stable political order or a morally preferable cause against a real threat or to restore justice after a real injury has been sustained.

3. A just war must have a reasonable chance of succeeding in these limited goals.
4. A just war must be proclaimed by a legitimate government authority.
5. War must be waged for the purpose of correcting a wrong rather than for malicious revenge.
6. Negotiations to end the war must be in continuous process as long as fighting continues.
7. Particular members of the population, especially noncombatants, must be immune from intentional attack.
8. Only legal and moral means may be employed in prosecuting the war.
9. The damage likely to be incurred from a war may not be disproportionate to the injury suffered.
10. The final goal of the war must be to reestablish peace and justice.

These ethical criteria continue to color thinking about the rules of warfare and the circumstances under which the use of armed force is legally permissible. However, the advent of nuclear and chemical or biological weapons of mass destruction that would violate many of these principles have created a crisis of relevance in just war doctrine. Fuzzy circumstances have materialized with the innovations of the **revolution in military affairs (RMA).** Because containment and prevention of violence have become the chief purpose of arms and armies today, leaders and scholars are wrestling with developing a revised just war code of conduct to deal with the new strategic realities of the twenty-first century.

revolution in military affairs (RMA)
the goal of seeking to increase military capabilities and effectiveness with new technology that does not rely on weapons of mass destruction.

Especially since World War I, the international community's tolerance of war has declined. As Figure 16.1 shows, international law has increasingly rejected the traditional legal right of states to employ force to achieve their foreign policy objectives.

This is not to suggest that the right to use force to punish wrongdoers in just war theory has been repudiated. The "neo-just war doctrine . . . no longer seriously purports to accept the view that peace is unconditionally a higher view than justice. We have returned to the medieval view that it is permissible . . . to fight to promote justice, broadly conceived. Evil ought to be overturned, and good ought to be achieved, by force if necessary" (Claude 1988). Indeed, some interpret just war theory to condone savage behavior to end a war quickly and coerce surrender. As the Prussian military theorist Karl von Clausewitz (1976) argued in his 1832 treatise, *On War,* it is necessary to use "force unsparingly, without deference against the bloodshed involved. . . . To introduce into a philosophy of war a principle of moderation would be an absurdity. War is an act of violence pushed to its utmost bounds." Yet, the modern revival of just war theory reflects the continuing quest to place legal and moral constraints on the use of armed force in order to create a moral consensus about the conditions under which ends justify means, even though "today there is a sharp difference of opinion about the criteria that should be accepted" (von Glahn 1996).

The Hague conferences of 1899 and 1907 were early developments in shaping new attitudes toward the start of armed conflict. World War I, however, revealed more than any other event the dangers inherent in the fact that "under general international law, as it stood up to 1914, any state could at any time and for any reason go to war without committing an international delinquency" (Kunz 1960).

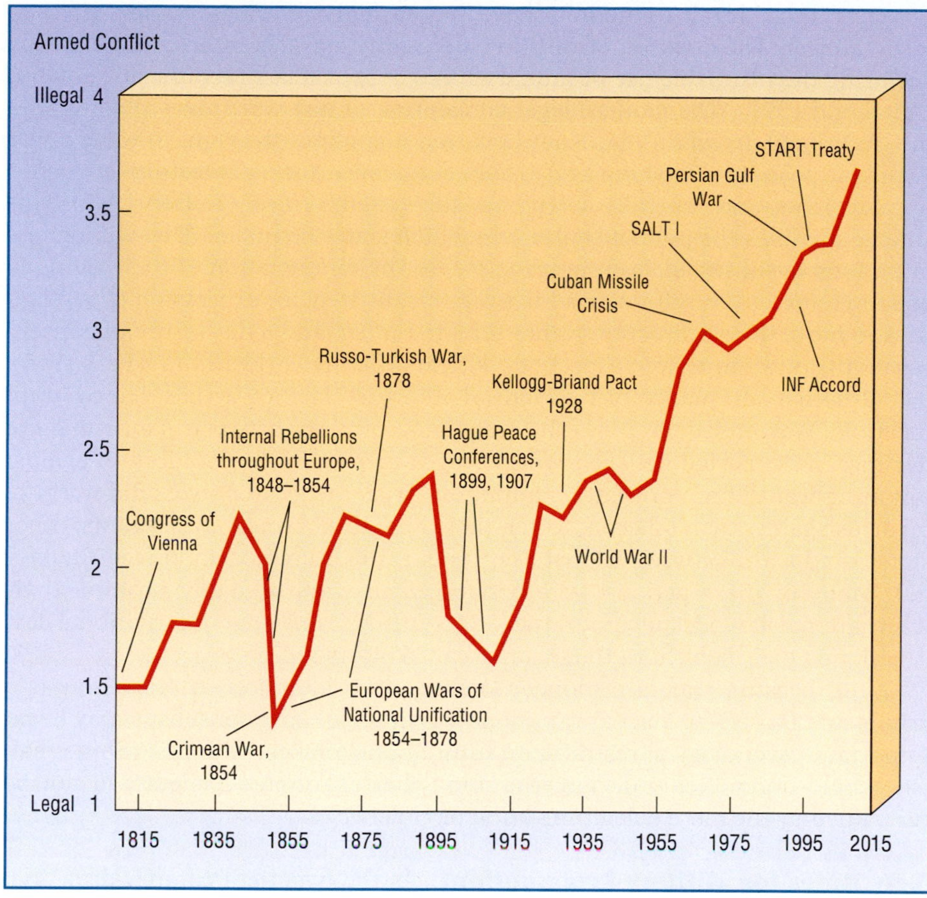

FIGURE 16.1
The Legal Prohibition of Wars of Aggression since 1815

Legal restraints on the historic right of states to start a war *(jus ad bellum)* have fluctuated over time, but only grown steadily since World War I. The experiences of the bloody twentieth century have repeatedly prompted the international community to define wars of conquest as illegal. In addition, international crises have prompted new international conventions prohibiting the traditional right of states to wage war.

SOURCE: Transnational Rules Indicators Project (TRIP), as described by Kegley and Raymond (1990, 1994).

In the aftermath of World War I, states began to reject the legal right to use force. The Covenant of the League of Nations, incorporated as Part I of the Treaty of Versailles in 1919, implemented a new regime. Articles 11 to 17 stipulated that in no case could a state resort to war until three months after a judicial determination by the League had elapsed. These articles also contained provisions subjecting any member "who committed an act of war against another member to sanctions."

Another important step was taken in 1928 in the Treaty Providing for the Renunciation of War as an Instrument of National Policy, known as the Kellogg-Briand Pact. The prohibition was reaffirmed in the 1933 Anti-War Treaty of Rio de Janeiro and in the Nuremberg war crimes trials at the end of World War II. Both spoke of war as "the supreme international crime." The UN Charter (Article 2) expanded the prohibition by unequivocally outlawing both the threat and initiation of war. At the same time, Article 39 gave the international community the right to determine "the existence of any threat to the peace, breach of the peace or act of aggression," and Article 42 authorized the Security Council "to take such action . . . as may be necessary to maintain or restore international peace and security."

military necessity the legal doctrine asserting that violation of the rules of warfare may be excused during periods of extreme emergency.

Over time, legal injunctions have increasingly restricted states' right to resort to war. The doctrine of **military necessity** clarifies international law by declaring the justifiable use of military force only as a last recourse for defense (Raymond 1999). The modern legal conception of just war thus still embraces the traditional *jus ad bellum.* Now, however, it confines the right to wage a war to the purposes of punishing aggression, deterring attack, protecting innocents' human rights, and generally defending "the system's rules" (Kelsen 1945). This change modifies the political culture in which states compete: "The willingness of nations to subscribe, even in principle, to the renunciation of their rights to use force (except in self-defense) is a significant step, an expression of willingness to move in one direction rather than the other, and a disclosure of consensus on the most important aspect of political order in world affairs" (Falk 1965).

Although acceptance of the right of states to start a war has waned, until the Cold War ended in 1989, the frequency of wars between states did not decline. In the period between World War II and 1989, the prohibition against initiating war did not prevent its initiation. True, the great powers did not take up arms against each other; however, they often used armed force against other states, and wars between Global South countries were common (see Chapter 12). Many of these actions were conducted in ways arguably prohibited by international law, despite the attacking states' claims that international law sanctioned their behavior (Tillema and Van Wingen 1982).

Still, because war is no longer licensed, the intention to make war is a crime, and those who start a war are now criminals. That consensus may be an important psychological restraint on future policymakers' choices. (Some realists would undoubtedly disagree, arguing that aggressive leaders will not be restrained by the mere delegitimization of violence.)

New Rules for Military Intervention. As the twentieth century drew to a close, the international community revised its traditional prohibition against military intervention in a fundamental way. "The belief that governments have a right, even obligation, to intervene in the affairs of other states seems to have gained great currency" (Blechman 1995). In the wake of a series of mass atrocities committed by governments against their own people, the global community asserted the right to intervene with armed force. The international community responded to the view that "the victims of armed conflicts must always remain under the protection of the principles of humanity and the dictates of public conscience." As Niels Helveg Peterson (1999), the foreign minister of Denmark, argued, the systematic violations of human rights in Iraq, Bosnia, Haiti, Kosovo, and elsewhere forced the international community into action: "Violations of human rights are a legitimate concern of the international community, and states can no longer hide behind the cozy screen of noninterference when gross systematic violations occur within their borders."

The Westphalian sanctity of state sovereignty, purporting that what a government does within its borders is its own business, has collapsed, and new rules for justified humanitarian war have been accepted, with a relaxed definition of the conditions under which a state has the right to use military intervention for moral purpose gaining acceptance in international law (see Figure 16.2). The world has made a choice on genocide, declaring organized savagery illegal: "the last fifty years have seen the rise of universally endorsed principles

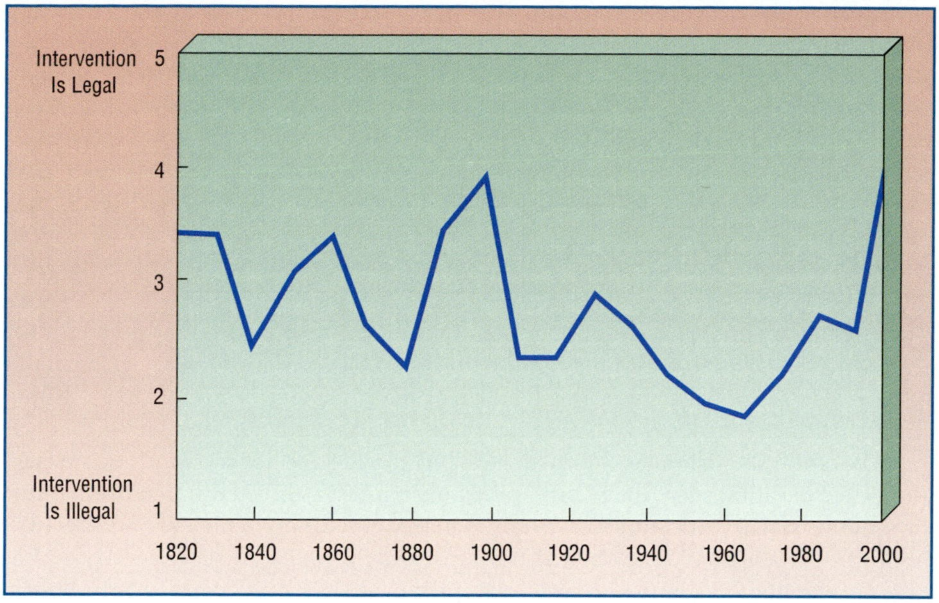

FIGURE 16.2
The Changing Status of the Nonintervention Rule in International Law since 1820
Over time, the illegality of intervening in sovereign states has changed, as determined from authoritative international law texts about the prevailing consensus regarding rules for international conduct in each period. Since 1960, international law has adopted an increasingly permissive posture toward this form of coercive diplomacy for a variety of purposes including humanitarian aid, preventing genocide, protecting civil liberties, and promoting democracy through "reform interventions."
SOURCE: Transnational Rules Indicators Project (TRIP), as measured in Kegley, Raymond, and Hermann (1998).

of conduct" defining interventionism for humanitarian wars as a legal right (Rosenberg 1999).

The Rules for War's Conduct and the Expansion of Human Rights Legislation. Laws regulating the methods that states may use in war *(jus in bello)* have also grown. These restraints include the principles of discrimination and **noncombatant immunity,** which attempt to protect innocent civilians by restricting military targets to soldiers and supplies. The laws of retaliation specify conditions under which certain practices are legitimate. One category, **reprisals** (hostile and illegal acts permitted only if made in proportionate response to a prior hostile and illegal act), stipulates procedures for military occupations, blockades, shows of force, and bombardments. Another category, **retorsion** (hostile but legal retaliatory acts made in response to similar legal acts initiated by other states), provides rules for embargoes, boycotts, import quotas, tariffs, and travel restrictions to redress grievances.

While the cynic may conclude that the laws of retaliation (particularly reprisals) are really instructions for killing, that conclusion is unwarranted.

■ **noncombatant immunity**
the legal principle that military force should not be used against innocent civilians.

■ **reprisals**
hostile and illegal retaliatory acts to punish prior illegal military actions.

■ **retorsion**
hostile but legal retaliatory acts.

Restrictions on the weapons that can be used and the permissible methods of fighting reduce killing in warfare. The message of the 1949 Geneva Convention—that even wars have limits—has been strengthened. The delegates at that historic conference to make new rules for warfare "understood that the causes of war and the problems of peace are best dealt with on their own. For war to be as merciful as possible—sparing noncombatants and, in particular, civilian populations—it is best if the law that governs the rules of war be distinct from all possible political consideration. This principle—the separation between causes of war and rules of war—became increasingly validated. . . . The world at large is so disgusted by acts of barbarity that governments and supranational bodies see it as their duty to intervene more and more to try to curb some of the more lurid atrocities that emerge here and there" (Sommaruga 1999).

The advent of a new set of legal justifications for humanitarian military intervention to protect civilians is explained by the fact that noncombatants have become the primary victims in warfare. "World War I was mass-conscription, democratic war with a vengeance, but it still was limited in its direct effect on civilians. The ratio of soldiers to civilians killed between 1914 and 1918 is about 90-to-10. In World War II, the ratio was 50-to-50. In recent years, it has been 90 civilian casualties to every 10 military losses—a reversal of the World War I ratio" (Pfaff 1999, 8). To prevent the horror of civilian casualties and contain the mass slaughter that increasingly has taken place inside national frontiers, the global community has made a radical revision in the rule of international law. For the first time international law holds leaders of countries accountable for war crimes as war criminals. Traditionally, international law prohibited leaders from allowing their militaries to undertake actions in violation of certain principles accepted by the international community, including the protection of innocent noncombatants. However, when violations occurred, there was little that could be done except to condemn such actions. Another weakness was that traditional international law did not hold government leaders to the same standards to which it held soldiers and military officers who committed atrocities against enemy civilians and captured soldiers. Although international law set standards for both individuals and states, leaders were free from jurisdiction under the doctrine of "sovereign immunity," even when their commands flouted the laws of war. Though they might behave as criminals, leaders were treated with respect because they were the people with whom the global community had to negotiate to settle conflicts.

While many people and states still commit war crimes without facing punishment, the resumption of war crime tribunals in 1993 signaled to would-be perpetrators the global community's intolerance for these atrocities. In 1999, the prosecutor's office of the UN's **International Criminal Court (ICC)** indicted seventy-seven people and arrested seven for crimes in Bosnia. Building on this step, a **permanent world criminal court** was created in the Hague to try leaders for the most terrible of mass crimes—especially acts of genocide such as those occurring in ethnopolitical conflicts. Thus a goal the UN had pursued for half a century became a reality: the world community now has an international court with teeth, through a treaty approved by more than 120 states and all major states except the United States, China, Iran, and Iraq. Moreover, heads of state are now held accountable for war crimes against humanity, removing the protection they had received under traditional international law. Ever since the Hague Tribunal's 1997 founding statute, a head of state can be

■ **International Criminal Court (ICC)**
a court established by the United Nations for indicting and administering justice to people committing war crimes in Bosnia.

■ **permanent world criminal court**
a standing international court to judge mass crimes such as genocide.

UGANDA
Idi Amin

IRAQ
Saddam Hussein

HAITI
Jean-Claude Duvallier

UNITED STATES
George Bush
(Persian Gulf War)

BRITAIN
Margaret Thatcher
(Falklands/Malvinas War)

YUGOSLAVIA
Slobodan Milosevic

Identifying War Criminals In 1994, the UN Security Council got serious about prosecuting war criminals, and created two special crimes tribunals in the Hague. Swiss criminal lawyer Carla del Ponte (left) was appointed in September 1999 as chief prosecutor for the UN's war crimes tribunals for Yugoslavia and Rwanda, where twelve cases have been judged and more than sixty other prisoners await trial. The performance of these tribunals is believed critical to the credibility of the newly created International Criminal Court. The principle that national leaders cannot get away with mass murder and torture was established after World War II at the Nuremberg and Tokyo war crimes trials, but the norm was not reinforced until the UN responded in 1999 to the genocide and state terrorism in Bosnia, Rwanda, and Tanzania by setting up special-purpose war crimes tribunals. The indictment of Chile's former president, Augusto Pinochet, in 1999 for torture and murder when a British court was offered universal jurisdiction in human rights cases was widely interpreted as a wake-up call to tyrants everywhere, despite the ailing eighty-four-year-old military dictator's release in March 2000 on humanitarian grounds. The question about precisely what behavior is proscribed for a head of state is creating a new controversy. International law still is unclear about the limits. At right are some past heads of state who potentially, according to *Time (*December 14, 1998, 42), could be called before courts to defend their use of arms, either against their own people or in wars.

charged with war crimes committed at an time the leader was in office; even a sitting head of state can now be indicted for war crimes. In fact, Slobodan Milosevic of Yugoslavia and President General Augusto Pinochet of Chile were indicted in 1999, and trials were planned in 2000 for the Khmer Rouge leaders in Cambodia, indicted for war crimes committed in the 1970s and 1980s. The criminalization of rulers' **state-sponsored terrorism** raises the legal restraints on the initiation and conduct of war to an all-time high.

The widening scope of acts now classified as **war crimes** also promises to limit the violence, savagery, and genocide that have been practiced in many recent civil wars. Consider the following examples from among more than thirty recognized rules (from von Glahn 1996), which suggest the impressive degree to which international humanitarian law has expanded for protection of and assistance to victims of armed conflicts.

■ **state-sponsored terrorism**
formal assistance, training, and arming of terrorists by a state in order to achieve foreign policy and/or domestic goals.

■ **war crimes**
acts performed during war that the international community defines as illegal crimes against humanity, including atrocities committed against an enemy's prisoners of war, civilians, or the state's own minority population.

Human Rights versus States' Rights How a state treats its own citizens was, until very recently, its own business under the nonintervention rule in international law protecting states from external interference in their domestic affairs. Now the global community has defined the humane treatment of people as a fundamental human right, and the UN Security Council has stretched the traditional definiton of threats to international peace in order to authorize various kinds of intervention to protect the universal human rights of people within states. This enlarged definition has infuriated some states who complain that their sovereign rights have been compromised. Shown here is an example of the kind of state behavior at the center of the debate: to deter crime, China's leaders have ordered the execution of hundreds of alleged criminals, and many other states have complained that this gross violation of civil liberties without fair trial warrants reprisals.

- No attacking of unarmed enemies.
- No use of forbidden arms or munitions.
- No firing on undefended localities without military significance.
- No improper use or destruction of privileged (i.e., exempt, immune) buildings for military purposes.
- No poisoning streams or wells.
- No pillaging.
- No killing or wounding military personnel who have surrendered or are disabled by wounds or sickness.
- No assassination or hiring of assassins.
- No ill-treatment of prisoners of war.
- No compelling the inhabitants of occupied enemy territory to furnish information about the armed forces of the enemy or its means of defense.

- No bombarding from the air to terrorize or attack civilian populations.
- No attacking enemy vessels that have indicated their surrender by lowering their flag.
- No destroying civilian cultural objects and places of worship.

These illustrative objections to practices once condoned move warfare away from barbarism, providing that courts and legal tribunals are willing and able to enforce humanitarian laws. The global community has impressively expanded the legal protections that have been given to people in the general area of **human rights.** As Table 16.2 shows, a large number of conventions have been enacted in the last fifty years which have steadily endowed individuals with power, rights, and respect, such that people are treated as if they are as worthy of the freedom and dignity traditionally granted by international law to states and rulers. "The old assumption that national sovereignty trumps all other principles in international relations is under attack as never before; . . . the age of human rights is upon us. In these post-communist, post-modern times, human rights seem to have become the dominant moral narrative for thinking about world affairs. No longer does national sovereignty provide blanket protection for human-rights abusers. In the eyes of many Western intellectuals, there is a New World *Moral* Order—one ruled by ideals like civil society, humanitarianism and, first and foremost, human rights" (Rieff 1999, 67).

human rights the political rights and civil liberties recognized by the international community as inalienable and valid for individuals in all countries by virtue of their humanness (see p. 526).

Law's Contribution to Peace. Cynics who contend that international law is irrelevant to the control of war overlook several dimensions of law's character. First, international law is not intended to prevent all warfare. Aggressive war is illegal, but defensive war is not. It is a mistake, therefore, to claim that international law has broken down whenever war breaks out. Second, instead of doing away with war, international law preserves it as a sanction against the breaking of rules. Thus war is a device of last resort to punish aggressors and thereby maintain the system's legal framework.

Third, international law is an institutional substitute for war. Legal procedures exist to resolve conflicts before they erupt into open hostilities. Although they cannot prevent war, they sometimes make recourse to violence unnecessary by resolving disputes that might otherwise escalate to war.

The demonstrable capacity of pacific methods to reduce the frequency of war does not mean that international adjudicative machinery is well developed or functionally effective. Nowhere is this more evident than with the International Court of Justice (ICJ), known as the World Court, which was created after World War II as the highest judicial body on earth. The World Court was an inactive judicial institution until very recently. Between 1946 and 1991 it heard only sixty-four contentious cases between states, rendered judgments on less than half of these, and handed down only nineteen advisory opinions, and over the last century has averaged only about three cases per year. Since 1991, however, the ICJ has expanded its workload, and considered cases dealing with many new issues. Even though only governments of states may apply for an appearance before the Court (and are hesitant to do so because ICJ decisions are final, without a possibility of appeal), an increasing number have done so: between 1992 and 1995, the ICJ heard twenty-four cases, and the judicial activity jumped to an average of fourteen cases each year between 1996 and 1998. The Court also became increasingly active in responding to requests for advisory

TABLE 16.2

Legal Steps in the Development of International Human Rights Protection: Some Major Conventions

Human Rights	
1948	Universal Declaration of Human Rights
1966	International Covenant on Civil and Political Rights
1966	Optional Protocol to the International Covenant on Civil and Political Rights
1969	Inter-American Convention on Human Rights
1976	International Covenant on Economic, Social, and Cultural Rights
1981	Covenant of Civil and Political Rights
1989	Second Optional Protocol to the International Covenant on Civil and Political Rights, Aiming at the Abolition of the Death Penalty
1993	Vienna Convention on Human Rights
1994	African Convention on Human and Peoples' Rights
Self-Determination	
1961	Declaration on the Granting of Independence to Colonial Countries and Peoples
Prevention of Discrimination and Protection of Minorities	
1965	International Convention on the Elimination of All Forms of Racial Discrimination
1981	Declaration on the Elimination of All Forms of Intolerance and of Discrimination Based on Religion or Belief
1993	Declaration on the Rights of Persons Belonging to National or Ethnic, Religious or Linguistic minorities
Women's Human Rights	
1953	Convention on the Political Rights of Women
1957	Convention on the Nationality of Married Women
1967	Convention on the Elimination of All Forms of Discrimination against Women
1991	Convention on the Elimination of Political, Economic, Social, Cultural, and Civil Discrimination against Women
1993	Declaration on the Elimination of Violence against Women
2000	Convention Prohibiting Trafficking of Women and Children for Prostitution
Slavery and Slavery-Like Practices	
1950	Convention for the Suppression of the Traffic of Persons and the Exploitation of the Prostitution of Others
1956	Supplementary Convention on the Abolition of Slavery, the Slave Trade, and Institutions and Practices Similar to Slavery
Rights of Prisoners and Detainees	
1977	Standard Minimum Rules for the Treatment of Prisoners

opinions; for example, in 1996 the ICJ dealt with two such issues, and rendered an advisory opinion on the highly controversial question of whether the use or threat of nuclear weapons could be declared illegal (answering that for the most part it should be). Thus, although there has been a "slight upswing in the num-

TABLE 16.2

(continued)

Protection from Torture, Ill Treatment, and Disappearance	
1975	Declaration on the Protection of All Persons from Being Subjected to Torture and Other Cruel, Inhuman, or Degrading Treatment or Punishment
1984	Convention against Torture and Other Cruel, Inhuman, or Degrading Treatment or Punishment
Rights of the Child	
1959	Declaration of the Rights of the Child
1989	Convention on the Rights of the Child
Refugees, Asylum, and Statelessness	
1951	Convention Relating to the Status of Refugees
1961	Convention on the Reduction of Statelessness
1967	Protocol Relating to the Status of Refugees
1967	Declaration of Territorial Asylum
1992	Declaration of Principles of International Law on Compensation to Refugees
War Crimes and Crimes against Humanity, Including Genocide	
1949	Convention on the Prevention and the Punishment of the Crime of Genocide
1973	Principles of International Co-Operation in the Detection, Arrest, Extradition and Punishment of Persons Guilty of War Crimes and Crimes against Humanity
1991	Convention on the Prevention and Suppression of Genocide
Law of Armed Conflict	
1950	Geneva Convention
1977	Protocols on Humanitarian Law for International Armed Conflicts and Noninternational Armed Conflicts
1983	Inhumane Weapons Convention
2000	International Convention for the Suppression of the Financing of Terrorism

The evolution of international human rights law has been rapid in the second half of the twentieth century (see Lauren 1999). This inventory of some of the major conventions since the Universal Declaration of Human Rights was proclaimed in 1948 documents this change. UN Secretary-General Kofi Annan has called the Declaration "the yardstick by which we measure human progress." Since then, progress truly has been extraordinary: according to Michael Ignatieff (1999), a "revolution in humanitarian concern" has occurred worthy of celebration because there has emerged "vast constituencies of human rights activists, development workers [and] aid experts whose moral rationale is the indivisibility of human interests and needs in an interdependent world." The growth of human rights legislation has paved the way for a new stage for human development, providing the global community can successfully transcend what Ignatieff terms human rights' "midlife crisis" by fulfilling the goals for a world order that liberal reformers have sought throughout the ages.

ber of cases on the ICJ's docket," the World Court remains underutilized, because "states do not like to litigate against other states," and "the increased number of cases per annum from two or three to something like ten only indicates a relative but minor change in the Court's utility" (Forsythe 1997).

The World Court's past impact has been marginal, partly because most judicial conflict settlements take place in the domestic courts of one of the contestants or in other international tribunals, where there is a stronger history of compliance with court decisions (Falk 1964; von Glahn 1996). Still other controversies are settled through ad hoc arbitration and mediation proceedings, and the idea of allowing international law to become less state-centric by encompassing nonstate parties has not gained sufficient support to begin to give nonstate parties (such as many displaced peoples, refugees, and other victims of war crimes) legal standing before the ICJ (Forsythe 1997). The most important reason, however, is that the World Court's jurisdiction is not compulsory. Although all UN members are members of the Court, only one-third have accepted the ICJ's compulsory jurisdiction in conflicts involving them. All but a handful of these have stipulated reservations to their acceptance, and thereby excluded the automatic jurisdiction through treaties under Article 36(1). The United States, for example, has undermined the drive to strengthen the World Court by adhering to the so-called Connally amendment, which reserves the U.S. right to determine the cases in which it will allow the court jurisdiction; the Reagan administration withdrew from a qualified grant of compulsory ICJ jurisdiction, and "neither the Bush nor Clinton administrations" since then "saw fit to return to the axiom articulated by President Eisenhower: It 'is better to lose a point now and then in an international tribunal and gain a world in which everyone lives at peace under the rule of law.' States for the most part still tend to opt for freedom over order, and to reject the notion that the most meaningful freedom is found precisely within a workable system of order" (Forsythe 1997). Exceptions occur at the regional level. For example, the European Court of Justice (ECJ) has authority over state members and acts as a legal engine for the integration of the European Union (EU), and the European Court of Human Rights, under the Council of Europe, exercises authoritative jurisdiction; in South America, the Inter-American Court on Human Rights has also considered cases.

World order in the twenty-first century will depend to a considerable extent on the uses to which states put international law. Its alleged shortcomings lie not with the laws but with their creators—states and their addiction to sovereignty as a legal right. The intentions of states acting individually or in concert, and not the slow processes by which legal development grows, will be decisive. The international community could, in principle, strengthen international law's capacity to curtail aggression. Still, many barriers remain to creating, as John F. Kennedy expressed liberal theory's hope, "a new world of law, where the strong are just and the weak secure and the peace preserved." We next consider the role of international organizations in maintaining such a world peace.

INTERNATIONAL ORGANIZATIONS AND WORLD ORDER

Liberal theorists recommend the creation of international organizations as a second political path to peace. To understand this approach, we must also understand its theoretical underpinnings. The expectations about and performance of the UN exemplify those theoretical premises.

The United Nations and the Preservation of Peace

Like its predecessor, the League of Nations, the UN's primary mission—as its charter states—is the "maintenance of international peace and security." The stipulation that membership is open to all "peace-loving" countries reaffirms this purpose, as does the charter's requirement that members "settle their international disputes by peaceful means."

Collective Security. **Collective security** is often viewed as a liberal alternative to the competitive balanced alliances that realists recommend. In a balance-of-power system, it is assumed that each state, acting in its own self-interest for its individual protection, will form coalitions offsetting others and that the resulting equilibrium will prevent war. In contrast, collective security asks each state to share responsibility for all other states' security. It "assumes that every nation perceives every challenge to the international order in the same way, and is prepared to run the same risks to preserve it" (Kissinger 1992). All states are to take joint action against any transgressor, and all are to act in concert. This presumes that the superior power of the entire community will deter those contemplating aggression or, failing this, that collective action will defeat any violator of the peace.

■ **collective security** a security regime agreed to by the great powers setting rules for keeping peace, guided by the principle that an act of aggression by any state will be met by a collective response from the rest (see p. 559).

Faced with the League's inability to put collective security into practice, realist critics attacked what they regarded as the illusory expectations on which liberal proponents had built the model. The League's failures stemmed from the U.S. refusal to join the organization; the other great powers' fear that the League's collective strength might be used against them; disagreement over objectively defining an instance of aggression in which all concurred; states' pervasive dread of inequities in sharing the risks and costs of mounting an organized response to aggression; and their tendency to voice approval of the value of general peace but to be unwilling to organize resistance except when their own security was threatened. In the final analysis, the theory's central fallacy was that it expected a state to be as anxious to see others protected as it was to protect itself. That assumption did not prove true in the period between World War I and World War II. As a result, the League of Nations never became a valid collective security system.

The architects of the UN were painfully aware of the League's disappointing experience. While they voiced support for collective security, their design restored the **balance of power** to maintain peace. The UN Charter, signed June 26, 1945, permitted any of the Security Council's five permanent members (the United States, the Soviet Union, Great Britain, France, and China) to veto and thereby block any proposed enforcement action that any of them disapproved. Because the Security Council could act in concert only when the permanent members fully agreed, the UN Charter was a concession to states' sovereign freedom:

■ **balance of power** the theory that peace and stability are most likely to be maintained when threatened states form a military coalition and thereby redistribute power to prevent any single great power hegemon or bloc from dominating the global system.

> In the final analysis, the San Francisco Conference must be described as having repudiated the doctrine of collective security as the foundation for a general, universally applicable system for the management of power in international relations. The doctrine was given ideological lip service, and a scheme was contrived for making it effective in cases of relatively minor importance. But the new organization reflected the conviction that the concept of collective security had no realistic relevance to the problems posed by conflict among the major powers. (Claude 1962, 164–165)

To further enhance the great powers' authority relative to the UN, the charter severely restricted the capacity of the General Assembly to mount collective action. The charter authorized it only to initiate studies of conflict situations, bring perceived hostilities to the attention of the Security Council, and make recommendations for initiatives to keep the peace. Moreover, it restricted the role of the secretary-general to that of chief administrative officer. Article 99 confined the secretary-general, and the working staff of the Secretariat created to aid that person, to alerting the Security Council to peace-threatening situations and to providing administrative support for the operations that the Security Council authorized.

Although the UN's structure compromises the organization's security mission, it is still much more than a mere debating society. It is also more than an arena for the conduct of power politics. During the Cold War the UN fell short of many of the ideals its more ambitious founders envisioned, principally because its two most powerful members in the Security Council, the United States and the Soviet Union, did not cooperate (see Chapter 6). Nevertheless, like any adaptive institution, it found ways to overcome the compromising legal restrictions that inhibited its capacity to preserve world order.

From Collective Security to Peacekeeping. The Korean police action in 1950 provided a glimmer of hope that the UN might overcome its institutional barriers to preserving world order. However, that episode was an intervention sponsored and fought by the United States under UN auspices and did not set a precedent for equally ambitious initiatives in later conflicts. After the disillusioning Korean experience, the UN did not undertake another "enforcement" mission to defeat an aggressor for another forty years, when it mounted a collective response to Iraq's invasion of Kuwait.

During the long period between Korea and Kuwait, the UN adaptively sought to overcome the political obstacles posed by superpower discord. Its experiments with monitoring explosive situations began during its formative period. In 1948, for example, it created the UN Truce Supervision Organization (UNTSO) to monitor the cease-fire between Israel and neighboring countries. It also created the UN Military Observer Group in India and Pakistan (UNMOGIP) to protect a cease-fire zone in Kashmir. After the Korean War, these initiatives became precedents for a new approach, called **peacekeeping.** In contrast to peace enforcement, as in Korea, peacekeeping means separating antagonists. Acting in response to the Suez crisis under the Uniting for Peace resolution, in 1956 the General Assembly created the UN Emergency Force (UNEF). It also charged the secretary-general with primary responsibility for managing this, the UN's first peacekeeping operation, to prevent the combatants from resuming fighting.

■ peacekeeping
the efforts by third parties such as the UN to intervene in civil wars and/or interstate wars or to prevent hostilities between potential belligerents from escalating, so that by acting as a buffer a negotiated settlement of the dispute can be reached.

The General Assembly designed UNEF to forestall the superpowers' competitive intrusion into a potentially explosive situation and to overcome the Security Council's inaction. This innovative approach went beyond prior UN fact-finding commissions and observer forces. It was largely improvisational, since the charter had not provided for peacekeeping activities authorized by the General Assembly and managed by the secretary-general. The principles underlying UNEF were different from collective security. The latter emphasized checking aggression through collective enforcement. UNEF, by contrast, emphasized noncoercive activities aimed at placing the UN's neutral "thin blue line" between the clashing armies to permit time for negotiations to resolve the conflict.

Success can be infectious. Following UNEF, the UN sprang into action to authorize other operations designed to prevent conflicts from reigniting. These missions have since become closely identified with the process of peacekeeping. For example, in 1958 the UN Observer Group helped to defuse the crisis in Lebanon. And in 1960 history's largest UN peacekeeping force entered the Congo to stabilize that newly independent country. In 1964, the UN sent a peacekeeping force to Cyprus. Other increasingly diverse and ambitious UN peace missions followed from these precedents (see Ratner 1997 for descriptions of these operations). Map 16.1 displays the worldwide location of more than seventy of the UN's best-known operations.

Of these operations, nearly all have successfully fulfilled their goals. UN missions have usually succeeded in creating buffers between the warring disputants, providing time for negotiating cease-fires and ensuring compliance with agreements. On many occasions they have also helped to contain conflicts that threatened to escalate to large-scale wars with additional participants. Over time, the roles associated with UN peacekeeping have evolved. Traditional or first-generation peacekeeping activities were designed to handle military matters between states; second-generation peacekeeping activities are more complex, and include a broader range of programs that have taken the UN from managing crises "during incipiency" to bolder security- and confidence-building measures, verification, legal assistance in civil wars, combating terrorism, humanitarian aid, drug interdiction, election monitoring, naval peacekeeping, and other operations beyond the activities originally envisioned.

The Changing Role of the Secretary-General. Drawing on the UN's experience with UNEF, in 1960 Secretary-General Dag Hammarskjöld of Sweden articulated his vision for a new UN role in managing peace and security, which he termed **preventive diplomacy.** Perceiving the need for the UN to take bolder conflict-avoidance measures, Hammarskjöld practiced preventive diplomacy to resolve conflicts before they reached the crisis stage (in contrast to ending wars once they erupted). His efforts were greatly inspired by his frustration with Security Council inaction.

■ **preventive diplomacy** diplomatic actions taken in advance of a predictable crisis to prevent or limit violence (see p. 524).

More than his unobtrusive predecessor, Trygve Lie of Norway (who resigned under pressure in November 1952), Hammarskjöld saw the secretary-general's role as that of an active crisis manager. He independently enlarged the defined responsibilities of the executive organ of the UN by using his "good offices" to mediate international disputes and by strengthening the UN's administrative support for peacekeeping operations.

After Hammarskjöld was killed in a tragic plane crash in September 1961, his successor, U Thant of Burma, pursued a much less activist program in his two terms of office, which ended in 1971. Constrained by increasing U.S. and Soviet pressure, U Thant concentrated on "quiet diplomacy" to manage crises that not he but the Security Council or the General Assembly identified. This approach was more akin to that which had prevailed in the early 1950s, stressing crisis response rather than crisis prevention.

The next secretary-general, Kurt Waldheim of Austria, shared U Thant's preference for avoiding offending the great powers. Waldheim did seek to resolve some interstate disputes; for example, he made efforts to obtain the

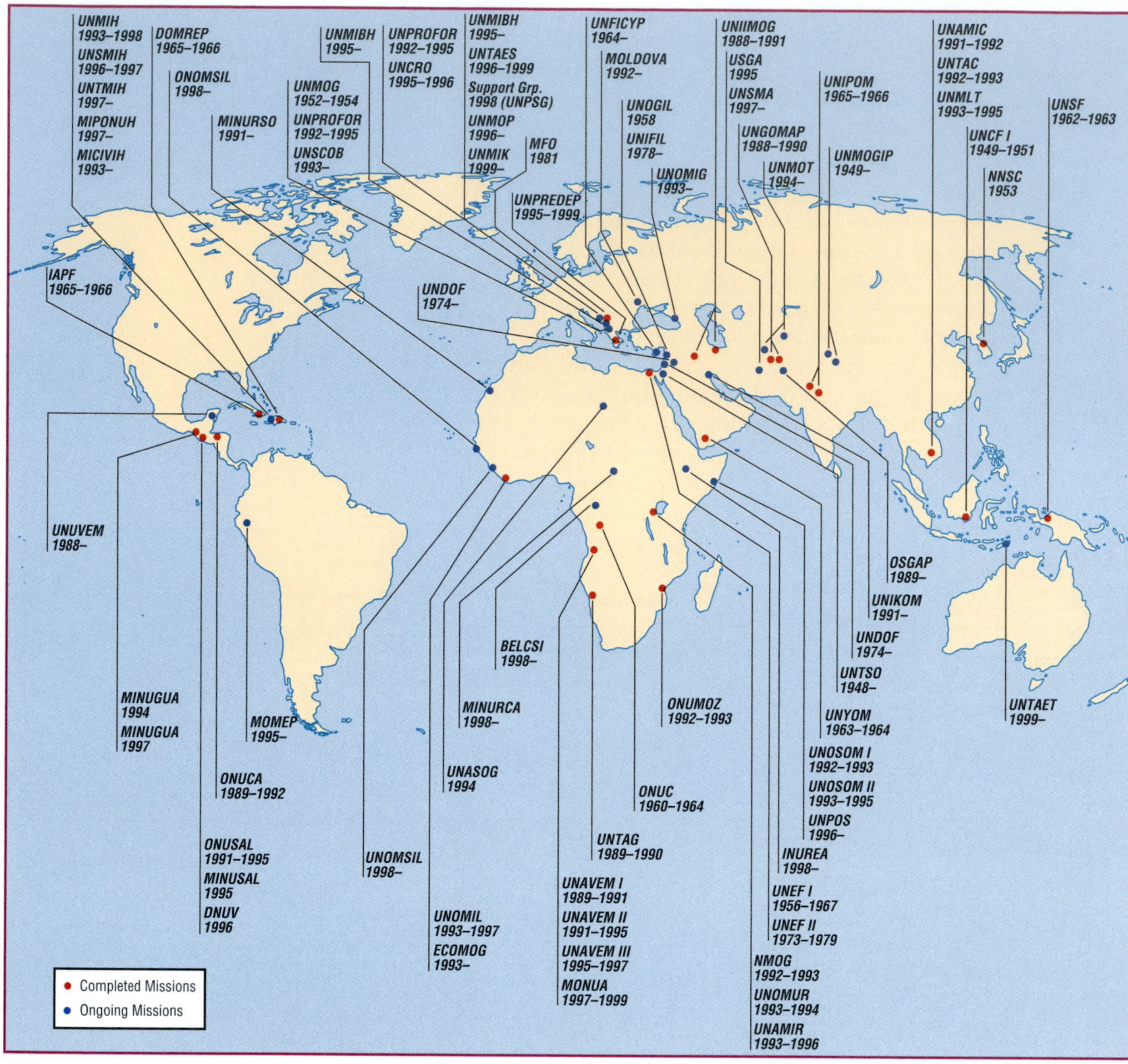

MAP 16.1
UN Peace Missions since 1948

In its first forty years, only thirteen UN peacekeeping missions were undertaken, but between 1986 and 2000 thirty-eight major new missions were launched, and as this map shows, UN peacekeepers were sent to flash points in nearly every region of the globe. Since 1989, each year, on average, more than fourteen peacekeeping operations have been active (see figure at top left). Over 750,000 persons from 110 countries have served in UN peacekeeping missions, but the cost of keeping UN Blue Helmets in the world's

release of U.S. hostages seized in Iran in 1979. His initiatives were restrained, however. In his first public statement as secretary-general, Waldheim stressed that "in this position one has to know the limits." This passivity endeared Wald-

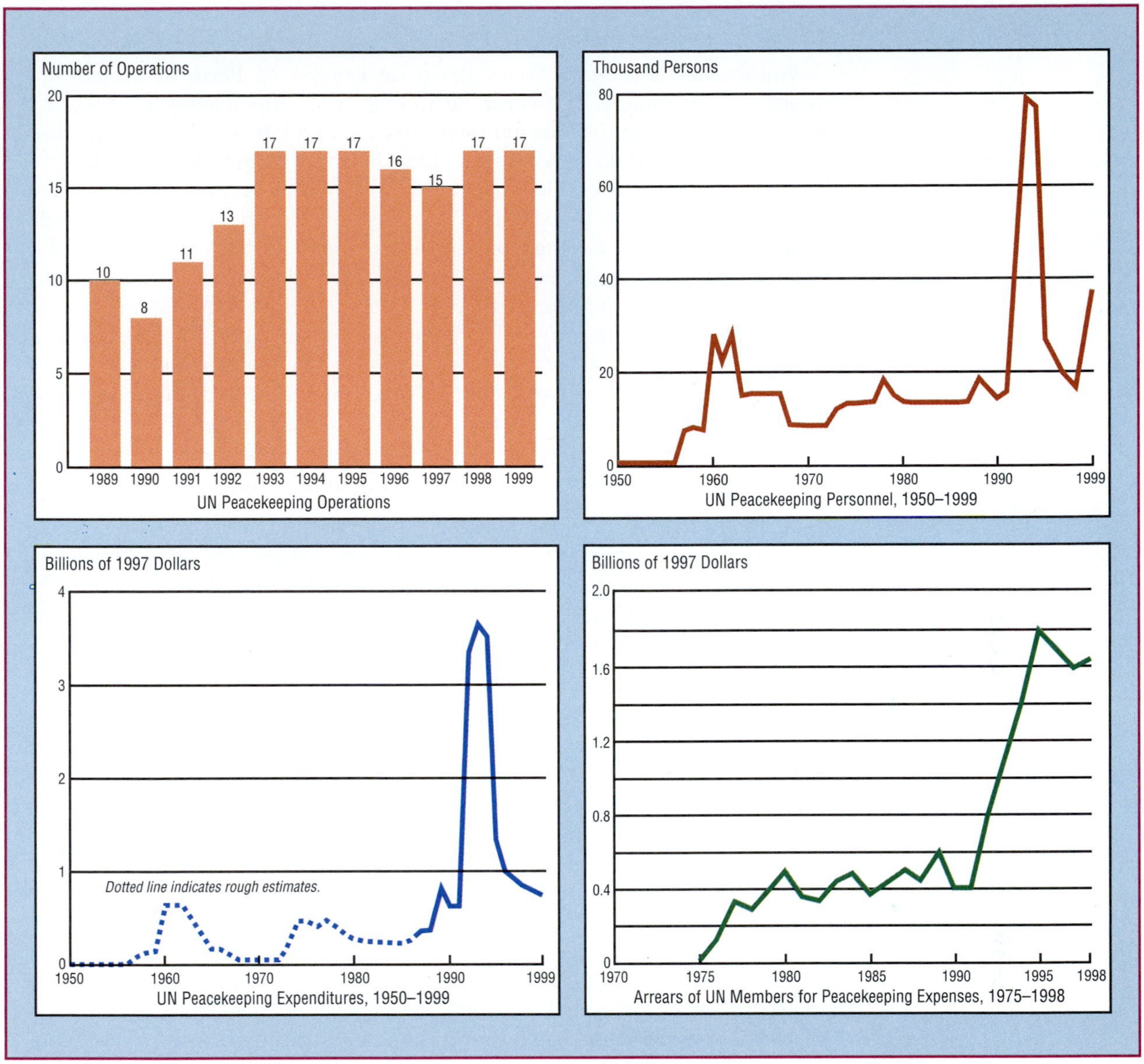

trouble spots has climbed, and so have the budget deficits of members' arrears, as the two figures at the bottom show. "In the past few years, Council members [and the United States in particular] have on the whole shown a strong aversion to getting involved in several conflicts, preferring inaction or contracting the task out to ad hoc 'coalitions of the willing'" (*Vital Signs 1999,* 114). Sadly, the need is greatest now when the resources and commitments to global peacekeeping may be declining.

SOURCE: United Nations Information Center.

---

heim to the superpowers, who rewarded his submissiveness by supporting his reappointment in 1976 and by promoting his reelection to a third term in 1981. But by this time, China—insisting on the election of a candidate from the developing countries and vowing to use its veto to prevent Waldheim's reelection—paved the way for the election of a more experienced diplomat with greater ambitions (Jakobson 1991).

Waldheim's successor, Javier Pérez de Cuéllar of Peru, also held "quiet diplomacy" in respect. Yet Pérez de Cuéllar was outspokenly critical of the "alarming succession of international crises" in which the UN was "unable to play as effective and decisive a role as the Charter certainly envisaged for it." To rectify its impotence, he called for renewed use of the Security Council that "too often [found] itself on the sidelines" because of alleged "partisanship, indecisiveness or incapacity arising from divisions among member states." He felt the Security Council should "keep an active watch on dangerous situations and, if necessary, initiate discussions with the parties" to defuse them "at an early stage before they degenerate into violence." Lamenting the fact that "the power of exposure" was the secretary-general's only authorized power under the charter, in May 1989 Pérez de Cuéllar declared, "I cannot accept that, in each and every case, we need agreement by the two great powers before we can advance." Acting on this principle, he aggressively pursued both **peace-making** and peacekeeping initiatives. He explained his approach in these terms:

■ **peace making**
the process of diplomacy, mediation, negotiation, or other forms of peaceful settlement that arranges an end to a dispute, and resolves issues that led to conflict.

> I have tried to simplify the procedures for finding peaceful solutions to international conflicts. The sequence of events is always the same. First you have to get a truce—end the hostilities. That is what we call "peace making" in diplomatic parlance. Once that is achieved and approved by the UN Security Council, we set up operations to keep the peace. That is what we call "peacekeeping."

On January 1, 1997, Kofi Annan of Ghana, formerly under-secretary for peacekeeping operations, took office as secretary-general for a five-year term. He approached the problem of managing the UN's **peace operations** enthusiastically, but he was highly aware of the administrative and budgetary constraints that limited the capacity to respond to every serious threat to peace. Using his personal humility and diplomatic charm to woo the support of the major powers, Annan concentrated his efforts on massive administrative and organizational reforms to make the UN more efficient and cost-conscious (see Chapter 6). These reforms required a more selective peacekeeping policy, and resulted in the streamlining and downsizing of existing missions and a reluctance on the part of the Security Council to launch new missions. Missions remained active in seventeen locations in 1999, but financial restraints reduced peacekeeping personnel from 78,000 at the start of 1994 to 28,000 at the start of 2000 with peacekeeping expenditures reduced from $3,547 million in 1994 to $852 million in 1998 (*Vital Signs 1999,* 115). Nonetheless, Secretary-General Annan continued to pursue plans to establish a Rapidly Deployable Mission Headquarters (RDMH) to accelerate the dispatch of UN Blue Helmets in future peace operations—a pressing need at a time (September 1999) when "35 million individuals [were] caught up in 22 humanitarian emergencies around the world" (DeVecchi and Helton 1999, 16).

■ **peace operations**
a general category encompassing both peacekeeping and peace enforcement operations undertaken to establish and maintain peace between disputants.

Cold War Obstacles to Conflict Prevention. Pérez de Cuéllar's ambitious efforts strengthened the UN's capacity to preserve world peace (Skjelsbaek 1991). Still, until the closing days of the Cold War, the UN's record of preventing and settling conflicts attested to the barriers that then existed, for "only about two out of five" of the UN's attempts to mediate conflicts succeeded (Holsti

1988, 423). Similarly, of 319 international disputes in which some fighting occurred between 1945 and 1984, only 137, or 43 percent, were referred to the UN for management. Moreover, the UN failed to control nearly half of these disputes and failed to fully settle 75 percent of them (Haas 1986, 17). Hence, the UN's peace-making achievements during the Cold War were modest at best.

Yet the achievements that were recorded demonstrate that the UN was to some extent able to transcend the substantial barriers symbolized by 246 Security Council vetoes on about one-third of its resolutions in the first fifty-one years of the UN's life. This mixed record of success and impotence showed that the UN's usefulness as an instrument of conflict management in the Cold War's inauspicious climate was greatest when a conflict:

- Did not involve the superpowers.
- Was outside the context of the East-West rivalry.
- Was important to the Security Council.
- Was intense and in danger of spreading geographically.
- Entailed fighting (albeit at a limited level).
- Centered on a decolonization dispute.
- Involved middle-sized and small states, comparatively unprepared militarily.
- Was identified as a threat to peace by the secretary-general, who led efforts to organize UN resistance to its continuation.

The record underscores the extent to which, as Trygve Lie noted in 1946, "the United Nations is no stronger than the collective will of the nations that support it. Of itself it can do nothing. It is a machinery through which nations can cooperate. It can be used and developed . . . or it can be discarded and broken."

Given this reality, it is understandable why, while the UN was a captive of Cold War competition, it directed its activities primarily toward addressing the deep-seated structural causes of war, where it could make a difference. This is seen in its "rear door" efforts to alleviate the conditions of poverty, inequality, frustration, and despair that provoke violence. The UN's greatest effort is geared toward **peace building** (creating conditions that make war unlikely) rather than peace making (ending fighting already under way). These programs are inspired by the liberal principle that improving the quality of people's lives can reduce the need for military arsenals. The conviction is expressed in the UN's work on human rights, technical assistance, refugees, decolonization, world trade, protection of children, world hunger, social discrimination, the equality of women, agricultural development, religious discrimination, disaster relief, environmental protection, and a host of other world problems that influence the quality of life and serve as potential wellsprings for aggression. "Whether or not it's equipped to shoulder the responsibility the United Nations is now in the business of nation-building [as it is asked to manage across the globe situations that] involve ethnic warring, human rights violations, forced migration, political instability, and humanitarian needs" (DeVecchi and Helton 1999).

■ **peace building** post-conflict actions, predominantly diplomatic and economic, that strengthen and rebuild governmental infrastructure and institutions in order to avoid recourse to armed conflict.

Despite its weaknesses, the UN is in many respects, as U.S. President John F. Kennedy (a realist who described himself as an "idealist without illusions") put it, "our last hope in an age where the instruments of war have far outpaced the instruments of peace." Hope for the UN gained new momentum when the end of the Cold War opened a new chapter in the quest for world order.

The UN's Blue Helmets and Multilateral Peacekeeping. The UN was a victim of superpower rivalry for more than four decades. But the end of the Cold War removed impediments to the organization's ability to fulfill its security-preserving mission. That possibility was made clear in 1990, when Iraq invaded Kuwait. The Security Council promptly passed Resolution 678, authorizing member states "to use all necessary means" to coerce Iraq's withdrawal from Kuwait. Under the authority of this resolution, on January 16, 1991, U.S. President Bush ordered an air war against Iraq's military machine, the fourth largest in the world. Forty-three days later, Iraq agreed to a cease-fire and withdrawal from Kuwait.

Bolstered by this success at collective security, optimism about the UN's capacity to take the lead in peace making started to grow. This optimism was facilitated by the shift of power from the General Assembly back to the Security Council. Acting in concert, it authorized the UN to launch nearly twice as many peacekeeping missions between 1988 and 1994 as it had in the previous forty-three years of its existence (see Table 16.3). The level of activity has remained high, with the UN managing seventeen peacekeeping operations in 1995, sixteen in 1996, fifteen in 1997, seventeen in 1998, and seventeen in 1999 (see Map 16.1 on p. 622). In 2000, the UN began preparations to augment its forces in war-torn Sierra Leone and Congo—failed states reeling from lawlessness and atrocities. The human cost for the volunteer UN peacekeepers has been high—more than 2,000 of the 750,000 peacekeeping personnel in the UN's history have sacrificed their lives while attempting to save the lives of others. One might ask how many people would have perished had these peacekeepers not been present to contain violence.

In 1992, when Boutros Boutros-Ghali became secretary-general, the UN greatly expanded its profile and agenda. Under his lobbying, the number of UN peacekeepers—its so-called Blue Helmets—increased from 14,000 to more than 75,000 by 1995. Boutros-Ghali's bold Agenda for Peace proposed creation of a standing UN "peace enforcement force" to quickly "enforce a cease-fire by taking coercive action against either party, or both, if they violate it." Under this innovation, which set the stage for **peace enforcement** operations, UN rapid deployment units would be established by the Security Council, and serve under the command of the secretary-general. Unlike traditional peacekeeping operations, however, their use could be ordered without the express consent of the disputants, and they would be trained and equipped to use force if necessary. This would enable UN forces, "by presenting a credible military threat . . . to convince all conflictual parties that violence will not succeed. . . . The military objective of the strategy, then, is to deter, dissuade, and deny (D^3)" (Ruggie 1993).

■ **peace enforcement** application of military force, or the threat of its use, normally pursuant to international authorization, to compel compliance with resolutions or sanctions designed to maintain or restore peace and order (see p. 518).

A number of barriers to these ambitious security goals exist. The first is political—the expanded size of the UN complicates decision making. Between 1992 and 2000, twenty-four countries joined the UN. This swelled the UN to 189 members, ranging in size from geographic giants such as Russia and China to microstates such as Andorra, Palau, and Eritrea. In addition, the 2000 proposals to expand the Security Council to eight or more permanent members (a move to make it more representative by bringing in Germany, Japan, and perhaps leading Global South countries) would make agreements about new peacekeeping ventures difficult, because great powers' interests are often incompatible and the prospect for reaching a consensus declines as the size of a group increases. Even if the post–Cold War environment is more hospitable to

TABLE 16.3

The Rise and Decline of the UN's Peacekeeping Role, 1988–2000

	1988	*1994*	*2000**
Security Council peacekeeping resolutions for new operations adopted	15	78	4
Disputes and conflicts in which the UN was actively involved in preventive diplomacy or peace making	11	28	54
Peacekeeping operations deployed	5	17	17
Military personnel under UN flag	9,600	73,000	28,000
Countries contributing military and police personnel	26	76	83
UN annual budget for peace-keeping operations	$230,000,000	$3,610,000,000	$1,560,000
Countries in which the UN undertook electoral activities	0	21	8
Sanctions administered by the Security Council	1	7	9

*Through June 2000.

The UN has been active as a global peacekeeper, especially since the Cold War ended. More than three out of every four major peacekeeping operations in the UN's history were launched in the 1990s. However, the number of missions decreased due to the growing reluctance of the Security Council to commit resources and personnel. In the first half of 2000, the seventeen UN operations, such as the risky Congo mission to restore order and prevent genocide in what has been called "Africa's First World War," were so underfunded and restrained that the missions were limited primarily to monitoring ceasefires and troop withdrawals and creating buffer zones. The large-scale missions of the early 1990s that ambitiously undertook the disarmament and demilitarization of combatants may be ending at the start of the twenty-first century, to the dismay of UN supporters (Shawcross 2000) and to the applause of critics (Boot 2000). Instead, the UN's unhappy lot in early 2000 was to perform perilous police duties in strife-torn failing states far from the great powers' core security concerns—in four intractable places on three continents (East Timor, Kosovo, Sierra Leone, and Congo)—where the dangers are highest and the chance of success is the lowest (Crossette 2000). Unfortunately, the hot spots where peacekeeping operations are desperately needed appear likely to multiply, and, as Secretary-General Kofi Annan bemoaned in 2000, "Only when it is too late do we value prevention."

SOURCE: UN Department of Public Information.

global security enforcement than in the past, implementing collective security through the UN will not be easy.

As in the past, there remains the temptation for members to support only those peacekeeping efforts that affect their own immediate security interests. For example, the September 1993 U.S. Presidential Decision Directive 13 prohibited contributing U.S. military units to a permanent standby force such as that authorized by Article 43 of the UN Charter. The United States issued this prohibition despite more than fifteen other UN members having earlier agreed to provide fifty-four thousand troops. The decision by the United States thus increased the gap between the UN's aspirations for maintaining peace and its capabilities, since "without U.S. leadership and power, the United Nations lacks muscle," but with it, ironically, "the United Nations loses its independent identity" (Gelb 1993).

The second constraint to realizing the UN's security goals is organizational. The UN remains poorly designed to carry out a full-fledged peace and security

Superclerk to the World Running the United Nations as secretary-general is perhaps the most challenging job in the world. In 1997, that position changed hands, as Kofi Annan of Ghana (at right) replaced Boutros Boutros-Ghali. Annan undertook massive reforms while seeking, with reduced finances, "to maintain the organization's capacity to manage existing operations and, if necessary, to launch new operations." As a key element in his organizational reform package, Annan won approval for the appointment of Louise Frechette (at left) as the UN's first deputy secretary-general.

program. Its goals have exceeded the institutional apparatus. UN troops no longer just patrol truce lines. Now they also monitor elections, promote democratic reforms, disperse information technology like the Internet, protect human rights, train local police, guard humanitarian relief deliveries, and take up arms against those who get in their way—all without sufficient technical and logistical support.

The danger of becoming overwhelmed by this ambitious agenda was illustrated in the UN mission in the former Yugoslavia (UNPROFUR). In 1992, forty thousand Blue Helmets were sent to stop the carnage threatening to kill millions. They were unprepared in training and did not have the authorization required to get the job done. It was only after NATO's September 1995 air strikes and the alliance's Operation Joint Endeavor got under way in January 1996 that the prospects for peace brightened. UNPROFUR showed that UN peace-making initiatives are destined to fail unless the great powers provide the needed resources.

The third barrier is financial. The UN's peacekeeping budget is less than the amount it takes to run the New York City police, fire department, and prisons. This lack of funds works against a managerial security role for the UN. Indeed, the UN cannot pay for its expanded list of expensive peace missions, let alone assume responsibility for new initiatives. In 1987 peacekeeping cost UN members $240 million in assessments; by 1996 the bill had risen to $3.6 billion, and at that time eighty UN members were in arrears. The United States owed 60 percent of the UN debt in January 2000. Although half the peacekeeping missions the UN had ever undertaken occurred between 1993 and 1997, the organization was financially crippled and nearing bankruptcy, and unable to find the funds to carry out the peacekeeping function the Security Council had asked of it.

In this climate, the retrenchment in peace operation activities that began in 1997 under Secretary-General Kofi Annan's reforms is likely to continue, with the prospects for the presence of the understaffed, underfunded, and overwhelmed Blue Helmets in future global hot spots becoming more remote. The trend for the future probably appears, under these restraints, in the growing

International Peacekeepers on the March In response to desperate pleas for help, the UN has selectively authorized peacekeeping forces to intervene. In September 1999, Australian soldiers marched off to lead the UN-authorized peacekeeping force in East Timor, where after voting four to one for independence from Indonesia, the people in East Timor were killed and raped in an act of state-sponsored terrorism. This mission restored order, and democracy was born.

tendency to deploy UN peacekeeping missions "alongside non-UN forces, and in others the 'coalition of the willing'—dispatched by regional organizations or composed of ad hoc coalitions of states [to] entirely replace the United Nations. This has raised questions about in whose interest these forces are acting and whether they can be held accountable. By far the largest non-UN operation remains SFOR, the NATO-led force in Bosnia. It deploys about 33,000 soldiers and cost an estimated $4 billion in 1998. Altogether, at least twenty-nine non-UN observer, peacekeeping, and peace enforcement missions were active in 1997" (*Vital Signs 1999,* 114).

The UN's problems raise concerns about its future ability to police the many ethnic conflicts and potential civil (and interstate) wars on the horizon. The UN is not yet a true collective security organization. Its blueprint for global involvement is just that—a blueprint. It is a design without a realistic structure, and the UN is not yet empowered for the high purposes it has been asked to perform. Currently, its advocates' expectations exceed its capabilities.

Impeding the UN's success are the same forces that have eroded past collective security mechanisms. In the face of aggression, many states have sought to "free ride" on the defense efforts of others, and have only supported collective efforts when their own immediate security was at stake. If countries do not act on the perception that violence and injustice anywhere are threats everywhere, the prospects for collective responses are poor. As Ramesh Thakur, vice rector of the United Nations University in Tokyo, observed, "For cynics, the United Nations exists so that nations that are unable to do anything individually can get together to decide that nothing can be done collectively. The price of inaction on a grand scale is paid by the peoples of Bosnia, Rwanda, and others. Yet its greatest strength is clear: It is the only universal forum for global cooperation and management. The global public goods of peace, prosperity, sustainable developments, and good governance cannot be achieved by any single country acting on its own. For the United Nations to succeed, the world community must match the demands made on it by the means given to it. The organization has to strike a balance between realism and idealism. It will be incapacitated if it alienates its most important members, in particular the United States. UN decisions must reflect current realities of military and economic power. But the organization also risks losing all credibility if it compromises core values." Still, it is likely that powerful members of the international community may, at times, practice **selective engagement** by responding to some of the threats and human suffering caused by interstate aggression and civil strife but not others (Art 1999). "Opponents of the United Nations, who have long argued that it should not act as a world government, will object. But, while less than perfect, the United Nations is the only global mechanism for effective collaboration in circumstances where states are reluctant or ill-placed to act alone" (DeVecchi and Helton 1999). The reasons underlying this assessment are summarized by the view that,

■ selective engagement a state's choosing to intervene militarily in some situations but declining to do so in others (see p. 490).

> In the great uncertainties and disorders that lie ahead, the United Nations, for all its shortcomings, will be called on again and again, because there is no other global institution, because there is a severe limit to what even the strongest powers wish to take on themselves. . . . Either the UN is vital to a more stable and equitable world and should be given the means to do its job, or peoples and governments should be encouraged to look elsewhere. But is there really an alternative? (Urquhart 1994, 33)

Actually, there is a conspicuous alternative. The great powers' reluctance to equip the UN to contain civil wars lends credence to the 1995 prophecy of Karel Kovanda (the Czech Republic's UN ambassador), that the "important issues are going to be taken care of by regional organizations . . . with the United Nations giving its blessings."

Regional Security Organizations and Conflict Management

If the UN reflects the lack of shared values and common purpose characteristic of a global community, perhaps regional organizations, whose members already share some interests and cultural traditions, offer better prospects. The kinds of wars raging today do not lend themselves to control by a worldwide body, because these conflicts are now almost entirely civil wars. The UN was designed to manage only interstate wars; it was not organized or legally authorized to intervene in battles within sovereign borders. This, however, is not the case for regional institutions; regional IGOs see their security interests vitally affected by armed conflicts within countries in their area or adjacent to it, and historically have shown the determination and discipline to police bitter civil conflicts "in their backyards." Hence, regional security organizations can be expected to play an increasingly larger role in the future security affairs of their regions.

During the Cold War, the North Atlantic Treaty Organization (NATO) and the Warsaw Pact were the best-known regional security organizations. Others now include the Organization for Security and Cooperation in Europe (OSCE), the ANZUS pact (Australia, New Zealand, and the United States), the Southeast Asia Treaty Organization (SEATO), and the Commonwealth of Independent States (CIS) made up of the former members of the Soviet Union. Regional organizations with somewhat broader political mandates beyond defense include the Organization of American States (OAS), the League of Arab States, the Organization of African Unity (OAU), the Nordic Council, the Association of Southeast Asian Nations (ASEAN), and the Gulf Cooperation Council.

Although Article 51 of the UN Charter encourages the creation of regional organizations for collective self-defense, it would be misleading to describe NATO and the other regional organizations as a substitute collective security instrument for the UN. They are not. More accurately, **regional collective defense** systems are designed to deter a potential common threat to the region's peace, one typically identified in advance.

regional collective defense
organizations and military alliances within a specific region created to preserve peace and security for their members collectively.

Many of today's regional security organizations are influenced by a decline in their members' perception of a clearly identifiable external enemy or common threat. A sign of the times was NATO's response to the virtual disappearance of the Soviet threat it was created to prevent, and confusion over how to deal with domestic instability within individual countries, which some see as a growing threat (Rosa 2000). NATO's enlargement through the Partnership for Peace (PfP) program (see Chapter 15) did not strengthen NATO's capacity to act as a regional alliance for collective security. The new "peace partners" were not offered the security guarantee that NATO's full members enjoy—that an attack on one would be considered an attack on all. Thus NATO's security-protecting capacity remains in doubt, and skeptics ask what the military alliance's purposes are without an agreed-upon external enemy beyond humanitarian intervention and peacekeeping within NATO's sphere of influence.

The ambiguous European security setting is marked by numerous ethnopolitical conflicts and separatist revolts, as in Bosnia and other areas of Europe. NATO was not designed to deal with this kind of vague internal threat. Its original charter envisioned only one purpose—mutual self-protection from external attack; it never defined policing civil wars as a goal. Consequently, it is not surprising that the nineteen full member states and the twenty-five associated Partners for Peace have been reluctant to call on NATO to intervene to contain ethnic warfare. However, they eventually overcame that reluctance in December 1995, when NATO took charge of all military operations in Bosnia-Herzegovina from the UN and in March 1999 when it performed the same task at Kosovo. These actions confirmed NATO's mission, adapting the alliance to an expanded purpose and giving it a new lease on life. Nonetheless, doubt remains as to whether NATO will be willing to undertake similar interventions to contain ethnic violence *within* other countries, especially if its membership grows any further (see Chapter 15). In the start of the twenty-first century, NATO is seeking to become both an alliance of security and an alliance for promoting the liberal democratic values of the region's countries. NATO's current goals are to expand its capabilities for new missions, to embrace Europe's emerging democracies as members, and to build a collaborative relationship with Russia.

Likewise, in other regional mutual security systems, controversies among the coalition partners about the identity of "the enemy" and the conditions warranting intervention raise doubts about their capacity to engineer collective defense projects. These doubts are fueled by the history of regional organizations in peacemaking efforts. Between 1945 and 1984, of 291 armed conflicts involving military units, only 68 (or 23 percent) were handled by regional organizations; regional organizations were unable to halt 77 percent of these high-intensity armed conflicts (Holsti 1992, 353). This record suggests that although

The Interventionist Road to Peace? The chaos and killing in failed states provoke widespread concern, but until recently many states and IGOs have been reluctant to intervene militarily to keep the peace in civil wars outside their spheres of influence. NATO's 1999 humanitarian intervention in Kosovo is an exception—the first time that alliance used force "out of area" to prevent a campaign of state-sponsored terror against an ethnic minority. Here a British tank heading to the Kosovo border in June 1999 is greeted by jubilant Albanian Kosovars thankful that NATO's KFOR (Kosovo Force) peacekeepers appeared on the scene to rescue them. The mission was supported by three hundred Eurocorps soldiers provided by the EU, made up largely of French and German officers, in what became the first mission of the EU's newly created Rapid Reaction Force. Humanitarian military interventions like this could become frequent now that international law has relaxed traditional prohibitions against external interference in the internal affairs of an established state.

regional collective defense institutions were, to some extent, created to overcome the deficiencies of global institutions, they may not be able to perform that task any better than global institutions.

The crisis in Kosovo again exemplifies the obstacles that regional organizations often face. This case and others suggest that regional organizations have the capacity to bring conflict under control when their members are in agreement. However, it also indicates that they often lack the consensus and political will to control controversial conflicts, and require pressure from world public opinion mobilized in global organizations such as the UN to take action. The future of peacekeeping in regional settings may best be predicted by the experience in Africa—the scene of widespread violence within **failed states** in the 1990s. Here, a combination of unilateral interventions by a single power (for example, the 1997 African Crisis Response Initiative [ACRI] by the United

■ **failed states** countries whose governments have so mismanaged policy that they have lost the loyalty of their citizens and face anarchy and revolution.

States), alongside UN and other regionally organized peacekeeping forces, smothered most of the flames of civil wars that erupted following the genocidal massacres in the 1994 Rwandan civil war.

In the twenty-first century, regional collective defense institutions, assisted by unilateral peacekeeping forces from particular interested states, and now supported by mercenaries that regional organizations and states hire or "outsource" from private multinational corporations (Isenberg 2000), may help to build a global security community in which the expectation of peace exceeds the expectation of war. The processes through which such metamorphoses might occur are addressed by the functional and neofunctional approaches to peace within the liberal paradigm.

POLITICAL INTEGRATION: THE FUNCTIONAL AND NEOFUNCTIONAL PATHS TO PEACE

Political integration refers to either the process or the product of efforts to build new political communities and supranational institutions that transcend the state. Their purposes are to remove states' incentives for war and to engineer reform programs to transform international institutions from instruments *of* states to structures *over* them.

World Federalism: A Single Global Government

Integration in its various forms does not necessarily make a frontal attack on the state by proposing to replace it with some central authority. That radical remedy is represented by **world federalism,** a school of thought advocating the merger of previously sovereign states into a single integrated federal union. Federalists follow the liberal conviction of Albert Einstein "that there is no salvation for civilization, or even the human race, other than the creation of a world government."

Federalists reason that if people value an **absolute gain** such as humanity's survival more highly than a **relative gain** such as an individual's state's national advantage over its rivals, they will willingly transfer their loyalty to a supranational authority to dismantle the anarchical system of competitive territorial states that produces war. "World government," they believe, "is not only possible, it is inevitable," because it appeals to the patriotism of people who "love their national heritages so deeply that they wish to preserve them in safety for the common good" (Ferencz and Keyes 1991).

It is not surprising that ardent adherents to **nationalism** have vehemently attacked the revolutionary federalist "top-down" peace plan. Because it seeks to subvert the system of sovereign states, the plan threatens many entrenched interests. More abstractly, other critics reject the world federalists' proposition that governments are bad but people are good, wise, and enlightened (see Claude 1971). Likewise, they question the assumption that the need for changes will automatically lead to global institutional innovation.

Many of the globe's 27,000 **nongovernmental organizations (NGOs)** are sympathetic to peace plans that seek to reduce the capability of states to make

■ **political integration** the processes and activities by which the populations of two or more states transfer their loyalties to a merged political and economic unit.

■ **world federalism** a school of thought advocating the merger of previously sovereign states into a single federal union.

■ **absolute gains** conditions in which all participants in exchanges become better off (see p. 253).

■ **relative gains** conditions in which some participants benefit more than others (see p. 253).

■ **nationalism** the feeling of loyalty to a particular state and/or nationality or ethnic group, to the exclusion of attachment to other states, universal religious values, or the collective welfare of all people.

■ **nongovernmental organizations (NGOs)** transnational organizations of private citizens maintaining consultative status with the UN; they include professional associations, foundations, multinational corporations, and internationally active groups in different states joined together to work toward common interests (see p. 202).

wars. Some accept the bold view of NGOs like United World Federalists that still actively promote creation of a world government. Nevertheless, aversion to war and raised consciousness of its dangers have not mobilized widespread grassroots enthusiasm for this radical step. Other approaches to reforming the world political system have attracted more adherents.

Functionalism

functionalism the theory advanced by David Mitrany and others explaining how people can come to value transnational institutions (IGOs, integrated or merged states) and the steps to giving those institutions authority to provide the public goods (for example, security) previously supplied by their state.

Classical functionalism is a rival but complementary reform movement associated with liberalism. In contrast to federalism, **functionalism** is not directed toward creating a world federal structure with all its constitutional paraphernalia. Rather, it seeks to build "peace by pieces" through transnational organizations that emphasize the "sharing of sovereignty" instead of its surrender. Functionalism advocates a "bottom-up," evolutionary strategy for building cooperative ties among states.

According to functionalists, technical experts, rather than professional diplomats, are the best agents for building collaborative links across national borders. They see diplomats as being overly protective of their country's national interests at the expense of collective human interests. Rather than addressing the immediate sources of national insecurity, the functionalists' peace plan calls for transnational cooperation in technical (primarily social and economic) areas as a first step. Habits of cooperation learned in one technical area (such as telecommunications or medicine), they assume, will "spill over" into others—especially if the experience is mutually beneficial and demonstrates the potential advantages of cooperation in other areas (such as transportation and communication).

To enhance the probability that cooperative endeavors will prove rewarding, the functionalist plan recommends that less difficult tasks be tackled first. It assumes that successful mastering of one problem will encourage attacking other problems collaboratively. If the process continues unabated, the bonds among countries will multiply, because no government would oppose a web of functional organizations that provide such clear-cut benefits to its citizens. Thus, "the mission of functionalism is to make peace possible by organizing particular layers of human social life in accordance with their particular requirements, breaking down the artificialities of the zoning arrangements associated with the principle of sovereignty" (Claude 1971). Its intellectual parent, David Mitrany (1966), argued in *A Working Peace System* (first published in 1943) that functionalism is based on self-interest.

> Functionalism proposes not to squelch but to utilize national selfishness; it asks governments not to give up sovereignty which belongs to their peoples but to acquire benefits for their peoples which were hitherto unavailable, not to reduce their power to defend their citizens but to expand their competence to serve them. It intimates that the basic requirement for peace is that states have the wit to cooperate in pursuit of national interests that coincide with those of other states rather than the will to compromise national interests that conflict with those of others. (Claude 1971, 386)

Persuaded by the logic of this argument, far-sighted liberals such as Jean Monnet applied functionalist theory to begin the process by which war-prone Europe began to form an integrated "security community" after World War II (Deutsch et al. 2001).

The permanent problem-solving organizations created in the 1800s, such as the Rhine River Commission (1804), the Danube River Commission (1857), the International Telegraphic Union (1865), and the Universal Post Union (1874), suggested a process by which states might cooperate to enjoy mutual benefits and hence to launch the more ambitious experiments that functionalists anticipated. Their lessons informed the early organizational ideology that also inspired the missions assigned to the UN's specialized agencies (such as the World Health Organization) and the growth of **intergovernmental organizations (IGOs)** and NGOs generally.

Functionalism, as originally formulated, did not pertain to **multinational corporations (MNCs),** the institutions some now consider the "dominant governance institutions on the planet" (Korten 1995). However, many now believe that MNCs' roles in the integration of states' economies and the globalization of world politics are consistent with functionalist logic. Individuals who manage global corporations often think and speak of themselves as a "revolutionary class," possessing a holistic, cosmopolitan, or supranational vision of the earth that challenges traditional nationalism (Barnet and Müller 1974). This **ideology** and the corresponding slogan "Down with borders" are based on the assumption that the world can be managed as a single, integrated market. From it comes a view of the world that sees global corporations as the primary catalysts to a borderless world opposed to governments that interfere unnecessarily with the free flow of capital and technology. According to this perspective, MNCs' investments and trade promote the growing level of cooperation and compromise exhibited between otherwise competitive states that is creating the emerging global culture—a culture that is eroding state sovereignty as states' economies become interdependent and states' foreign policies become increasingly **intermestic** (simultaneously international and domestic).

Critics charge that as a theory of peace and world order, functionalism does not take into account some important political realities. First, they question its assumption about the causes of war. Functionalism argues that poverty and the lack of public goods cause war. Critics question this assumption. They counter that war may instead cause poverty and the lack of public goods. Addressing issues of poverty may not alleviate war, they also argue, especially if the rapid acquisition of wealth enables dissatisified states to build armies for war.

Second, functionalism assumes that political differences among countries will be dissolved by the habits of cooperation learned by experts organized transnationally to cope with technical problems such as global warming, environmental deterioration, or contagious disease. The reality, say critics, is that technical cooperation is often more strongly influenced by politics than the other way around. The U.S. withdrawal from the International Labor Organization (ILO) and the UN Educational, Scientific, and Cultural Organization (UNESCO) because that hegemon felt that those IGOs were too politicized illustrates the entrenched primacy of political competition.

As skeptics conclude, functionalists are naive to argue that technical (functional) undertakings and political affairs can be separated. If technical cooperation becomes as important to state welfare as the functionalists argue that it will, states will assume an active role in technical developments. Welfare and power cannot be separated, because the solution of economic and social problems cannot be divorced from political considerations. The expansion of transnational institutions' authority and competency at the expense of national

■ **intergovernmental organizations (IGOs)** international organizations whose members are states, such as the World Trade Organization (see p. 173).

■ **multinational corporations (MNCs)** business enterprises headquartered in one state that invest and operate extensively in other states (see p. 226).

■ **ideology** a set of core philosophical principles collectively held about the ways people and governments ought to behave ethically and politically (see p. 12).

■ **intermestic politics** those issues confronting a state that are simultaneously international and domestic (see p. 56).

governments and state sovereignty is, therefore, unlikely. Functionalism, in short, is an idea whose time has passed.

Neofunctionalism

A new, albeit derivative, theory arose in the 1950s to question the assumption that ever-expanding functional needs for joint action to address property rights, health, technological change, and other shared problems would force the resolution of political disputes. Termed **neofunctionalism,** the reconstructed liberal theory sought to directly address the political factors that dominate the process of merging formerly independent states.

■ neofunctionalism the revised functional theory which explains that the IGOs states create to manage common problems provide benefits that exert new pressures for further political integration, the creation of additional IGOs, and the globalization of international relations in an expanding network of interdependence that reduces states' incentives to wage war.

> *Neofunctionalism* holds that political institutions and policies should be crafted so that they lead to further integration through the process of . . . "the expansive logic of sector integration." For example, [the first] president of the ECSC [European Coal and Steel Community], [Jean] Monnet, sought to use the integration of the coal and steel markets of the six member countries as a lever to promote the integration of their social security and transport policies, arguing that such action was essential to eliminate distortions in coal and steel prices. [The] neofunctionalism of Monnet and others [had] as its ultimate goal . . . the creation of a federal state. (Jacobson 1984, 66)

Neofunctionalism thus proposes to accelerate the processes leading to new supranational communities by purposely pushing for cooperation in politically controversial areas, rather than by avoiding them. It advocates bringing political pressure to bear at crucial decision points to persuade opponents of the greater benefits of forming a larger community among formerly independent national members.

The European Experience. Europe is the preeminent example of the application of neofunctionalist principles to the development of an integrated political community. Within a single generation, cooperation across European borders steadily progressed toward a single European economic market with a single currency and toward the promise of a politically integrated Europe in the formal regional institution known as the **European Union (EU)** (see Chapter 6). The 1992 Maastricht Treaty on European Union set the stage for EU "enlargement." In 1995, Austria, Finland, and Sweden joined the EU, swelling its membership to fifteen countries, and in 1998 the EU took the next step in its ambitious enlargement goals when, in a historic milestone, the EU agreed to a two-tier approach to admitting twelve new states in the next decade into the community of EU liberal democracies (providing they can meet the conditions for democratic and free-market reforms that the EU set for inclusion). Other applicants are expected to follow Turkey's continuing pursuit of membership (see Map 16.2).

■ European Union (EU) a regional organization created by the merger of the European Coal and Steel Community, the European Atomic Energy Community, and the European Economic Community, called the European Community until 1993 (see p. 186).

The Maastricht Treaty, which entered into force in November 1993, created the EU as the umbrella organization for the European Community's diverse institutions. The treaty established a timetable for completing in 1999 a single-market Economic and Monetary Union (EMU) that created the single "euro" currency, the most potent symbol of Europe's new dynamism. In the wake of the Kosovo crisis in 1999, fifteen EU countries (eleven of which were also NATO members) came to the conclusion that it was necessary to cooperate not just in

MAP 16.2
A European Union on the Verge of Enlargement

The European Union is a premier example of a supranational regional organization. It has grown from the six states that formed the European Economic Community in 1957 to twenty-two countries designated for inclusion, and in 2000, no less than six other applicants are applying for membership. The package for enlargement, known as *Agenda 2000,* sets goals for the European Union's growth well into the twenty-first century.

finance and economics but also in defense and foreign policy. Having previously endorsed the goal of creating the Common Foreign and Security Policy (CFSP), the EU took the next step toward integration and independence as a unitary actor by creating the Eurocorps expeditionary force of 60,000 soldiers to carry out EU decisions. The Treaty of Nice in 2001 established the permanent structure, modeled on NATO, to organize and train the European Rapid Reaction Force, so it can be fully operational by 2003 and prepared for deployment. The WEU is scheduled to disband and become part of the EU's new military apparatus. This new military machine is designed to allow the EU to end its dependence on U.S. might, speak with a single voice on national strategy, and serve as a symbol of Europe's capacity to act unilaterally on the world stage (Bonnart 2000).

These ambitious goals notwithstanding, progress toward full integration proved difficult. As Jacques Delors, former president of the European Commission, lamented in December 1995, "Building Europe has never been a long, calm river. There are moments of stagnation, of crises." It is unclear whether the dream of true European unity in a much wider confederation to include eastern Europe and to encompass twenty-eight states by 2010 will become a reality. Contributing to the pessimism are chronic suspicion, selfishness, and tenacious national memories of the dark side of Europe's twentieth-century history. Furthermore, EU states are aware of the potential for interdependence to provoke competition and struggles for advantage, and disagreement about the desirability of true political unification remains. For the next courageous and integrative actions to be taken, the fifteen EU legislatures will have to take aditional steps toward unity by further encroaching on members' national sovereignty.

Even if Europeans do not soon realize their aspiration to political union, Europe has already constructed a **security community** in which the expectation of war between states has vanished from one of the historically most violence-prone regions of the world (Deutsch et al. 1957, 2001). The onset of armed conflict between the EU's democracies is very unlikely. Still, how deep and geographically wide this integrative process will go is highly uncertain (see Chapter 6). In addition, the uncertain membership of this "common European home" is likely to prove consequential for European security because there is a danger that the "one Europe" proponents envisioned will in fact be two Europes, one rich and stable and the other poor and unstable. That could create future conflicts not unlike those of the past, unless the threat of failed states on the EU's periphery and, potentially, within some EU countries themselves is averted. Optimists nonetheless have many reasons to celebrate Europe's ability to leave behind the tragic cycle of rivalry and mistrust that haunted it for centuries. A European "identity" with shared beliefs has developed: the nation-state is losing ground as "a serious sense of European citizenship, along with the rights that go with it, seems to be laying the basis of a supranational identity" (Cohen 2000).

■ **security community**
a group of states whose high level of noninstitutionalized collaboration results in the settlement of disputes by compromise rather than by force (see p. 186).

The Preconditions for Regional Integration. The record of previous integrative experiments demonstrates that the factors promoting (or inhibiting) successful integration efforts are many and their mixture complex. It is not enough that two or more countries choose to interact cooperatively. Research indicates that the probability of such cooperative behavior resulting in integration is remote without geographical proximity, steady economic growth, similar political systems, supportive public opinion led by enthusiastic leaders, cultural homogeneity, internal political stability, similar experiences in historical and internal social development, compatible forms of government and economic systems, similar levels of military preparedness and economic resources, a shared perception of a common external threat, bureaucratic compatibilities, and previous collaborative efforts (Cobb and Elder 1970; Deutsch et al. 1953). While not all of these conditions must be present for integration to occur, the absence of more than a few considerably reduces the chances of success. The integration of two or more societies—let alone entire world regions—is, in short, not easily accomplished.

European institution building nonetheless has served as a model for the application of the neofunctionalist approach to integration in other regions, including Africa, Asia, the Caribbean, and South America. However, current evidence suggests that political integration may be peculiarly relevant to the Global North's advanced industrial democracies but of doubtful applicability to the developing countries of the Global South. The record, moreover, indicates that even where conditions are favorable there is no guarantee that integration will proceed automatically. As noted, even in Europe high hopes have alternated with periods of disillusionment. When momentum has occurred, **spillover**—

■ **spillover**
the propensity for successful integration across one area of cooperation between states to propel further integration in other areas.

involving either the deepening of ties in one functional area or their expansion to another to ensure the members' satisfaction with the integrative process—has led to further integration. But there is no inherent expansive momentum in integration schemes. Thus, **spillback** (when a regional integration scheme fails, as in the case of the East African Community) and **spillaround** (when a regional integration scheme stagnates or its activities in one area work against integration in another) are also possible.

■ **spillback**
the reversal of previous steps toward integration, reducing the number of sectors in which integrating states are engaged in cooperative exchanges.

■ **spillaround**
the stagnation or encapsulation of regional integration activities.

Political Disintegration

The substantial difficulty that most regions have experienced in achieving a level of institution building similar to that of the EU suggests the magnitude of existing barriers to creating new political communities out of previously divided ones. Furthermore, the paradox that the planet is dividing precipitately and coming together reluctantly at the very same moment confounds predictions. We are witnessing a convulsive splintering of states, as hundreds of ethnic nationalities are currently seeking autonomy. Consider Europe, where in 1991 hypernationalism led to the creation of fifteen newly independent countries. Since then five additional European states have been created from the former Yugoslavia. Between 1990 and 1998, the rate of new-country creation as a consequence of civil wars within states was 3.1 new countries each year (Enriquez 1999, 30). Ironically, this fragmentation occurred in precisely the same period when elsewhere political units were reintegrating, as Hong Kong in 1997 and Macao in 2000 did when, after centuries of colonialism, they once again became a part of China.

■ **indigenous peoples**
the native ethnic and cultural inhabitant populations within countries ruled by a government controlled by others, known as the "Fourth World."

The surge of ethnic and religious secessionist movements tearing countries apart is not confined to eastern and southern Europe. Disintegration of many of the globe's 207 currently separate states could multiply the number of independent countries to as many as 500 by the year 2025, according to UN estimates. With fewer than twenty-five countries ethnically homogeneous and with three thousand to five thousand **indigenous peoples** interested in securing a sovereign homeland, the prospects are high that **political disintegration** will continue, especially if the number of failed states where central governing institutions have imploded in a sea of chaos continues to rise (see Chapters 7 and 12). This division of the globe into more and more smaller states could be slowed if existing states accepted **devolution** (the granting of greater political power to quasi-autonomous regions), as many central governments have done for the purpose of containing separatist revolts. However, in many countries where governmental institutions are fragile, the leadership has refused to accept devolution and repressed by force the minority peoples seeking to share power. In these the hypernationalist quest for independence under the banner of the **self-determination** principle threatens to dismember some formerly integrated sovereign states, including such widely dissimilar states as Canada, Russia, Spain, South Africa, and the United Kingdom, where minorities (the proportion of a state's population made up by different ethnic, nationality, or racial groups) are often a repressed subclass ripe for revolution. About a third of the globe's countries contain restless, politically repressed minorities struggling at various levels for human rights and independence (see Allen 1998; Gurr 2000, 2001). Such struggles and revolutions are not new, of course. The U.S. Civil War between 1861 and 1865 and the thirty-year civil war in Ethiopia that

■ **political disintegration**
the separation of a failed state into fragments to create two or more newly independent countries.

■ **devolution**
states' granting of political power to ethnopolitical national groups and indigenous people under the expectation that greater autonomy for them in particular regions will curtail their quest for independence as a new state.

■ **self-determination**
the standard advocated strenuously in U.S. President Woodrow Wilson's "14 Points" address that national and ethnic groups have a right to statehood so they can govern themselves as independent countries.

enabled Eritrea to gain independence in 1991 remind us that states may either integrate into larger unions or disintegrate into smaller states. Hence, there is little reason to expect integrative processes, once underway, to automatically continue by the force of their own momentum. Globalization, uneven growth rates, and income inequalities could easily pull history in the opposite direction, toward the disintegration of states to create many new national flags.

A DEMOCRATIC PEACE

The liberal path to peace historically has focused on the global or structural characteristics of international society, such as anarchy, as most in need of institutional reform. For this reason liberalism is closely associated with international law, organization, and integration. But a fourth institutional approach is also central to the liberal tradition: that the types of governments in the world predict the probability of armed conflict. It matters—and matters greatly—whether states are ruled democratically, because if so, the world will become peaceful. (This liberal thesis, of course, runs directly counter to the assumptions of realism and especially neorealism that states' forms of government do not have much influence on their foreign relations (see Chapter 2). They believe that governments—whether democratic or autocratic—respond similarly to similar security threats.)

democratic peace the theory that, because democratic states do not fight each other, the diffusion of democratic governance throughout the world will reduce the probability of war (see p. 424).

The liberal ideas underlying expectations about a **democratic peace** spring from convictions that first were popularized in the late eighteenth century, the age of democratic revolution against absolute monarchy. Then—when only the fledgling United States, Switzerland, and Republican France could reasonably be counted as democratic—liberal enthusiasts voiced their belief that the spread through the world of democratically governed states would reduce the frequency of war. This was the prediction German philosopher Immanuel Kant made in 1795 in *Perpetual Peace,* arguing that democratic governments with "republican" constitutions ruled through elections by the consent of the governed would form a league to keep peace—building alliances with one another and resolving any serious conflicts at the bargaining table instead of the battlefield. Similarly, a future U.S. president, James Madison, in 1792 advocated free governments to cooperatively change world politics when he argued that "in the advent of republican governments [would be found] not only the prospect of a radical decline in the role played by war but the prospect as well of a virtual revolution in the conduct of diplomacy" (Tucker and Hendrickson 1990).

Liberal and now neoliberal policymakers have taken heart in the spread of democracy as the preferred and now most popular kind of institution for governing states throughout the world. Since the mid-1970s freedom and civil liberties have grown, in a series of transitions, and today the enlarged community of liberal democracies makes up a healthy majority with nearly three-quarters of the globe's governments ruled by free or partially free institutions (see Figure 16.3).

behavioralism an approach to the study of international relations that emphasizes the application of scientific methods (see p. 410).

This enlargement of the percentage of free and partially free countries has made liberal institutionalists especially hopeful that a democratic peace can be a reliable anchor for twenty-first-century international security. The basis for their hope springs from the evidence generated by quantitative **behavioral** research that demonstrates convincingly that "well-established democracies

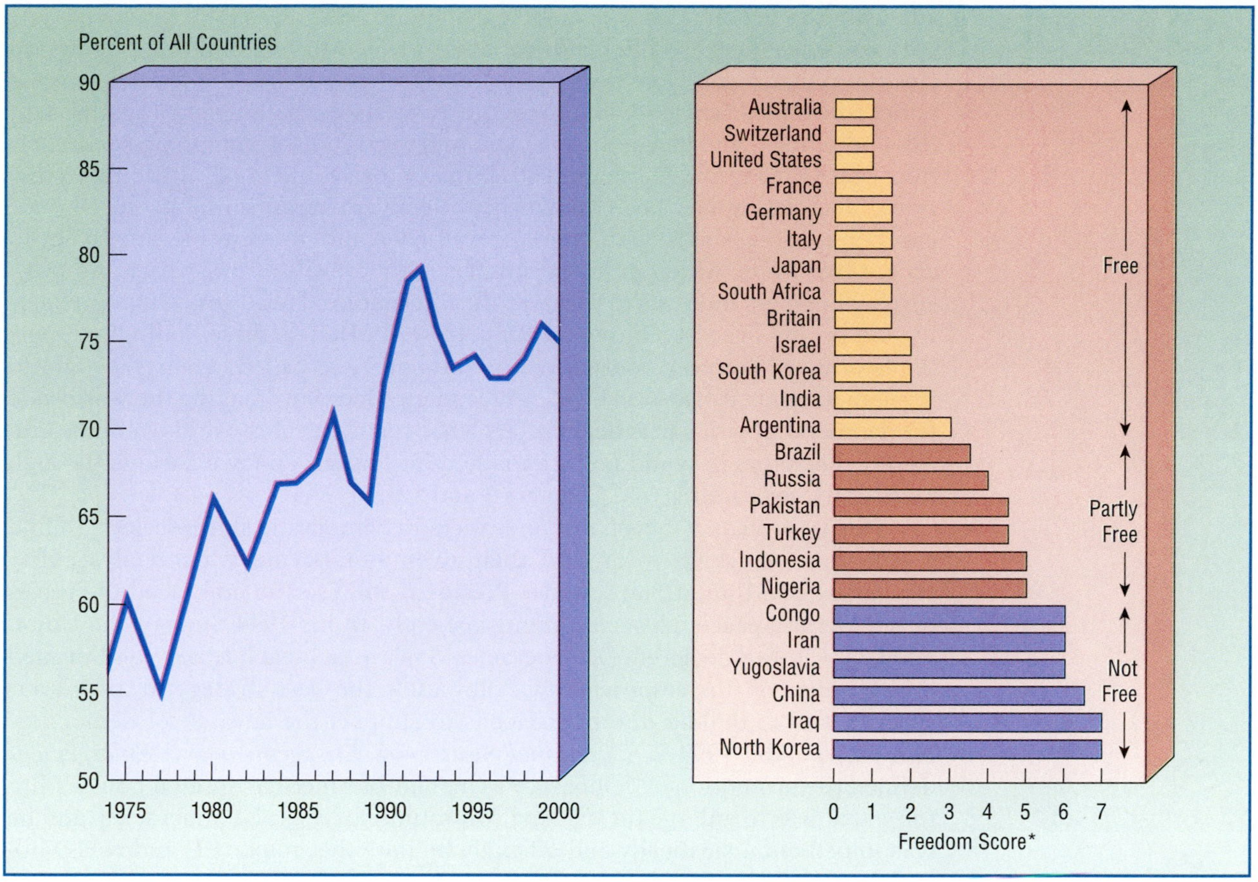

FIGURE 16.3
The Growth of Democratic Governance throughout the Globe since 1974

The number of free and partly free countries that are members of the community of democracies has increased as a percent of the world's state governments since 1974, in fits and starts. The human rights and civil liberties of populations living in relatively liberal states are protected (although some "illiberal" democratically ruled countries, such as Iran, Croatia, and Georgia, do not protect the civil rights of their minority populations). As the chart on the right shows, the "degree of freedom" of select countries in 1999 varied widely, with the "freedom score" of Australia seven times higher than that of the "not free" North Korea. Countries with free and fair elections benefit from the fact that when "people participate in making the decisions that affect them [democratization becomes] a key ingredient in the process of improving living standards—and thus in development" (World Bank 2000). Moreover, people in free societies with elections benefit from the tendency for their foreign relations with other democratically ruled countries to be peaceful.

*Combined average score for political rights and civil liberties, 1 = high degree of freedom, 7 = low degree of freedom.

SOURCE: Trends in the percentage of the globe's states that are democratic (on left), annual surveys of Freedom House as scaled by Harvey Starr; 1999 freedom scores for select states (on right), Freedom House as presented in *The Economist* (July 31, 1999), 13.

have never made war on one another [and] republics and only republics have tended to form durable, peaceful leagues" (Weart 1994 and 1998; see also Gowa 1999; Ray 1995; Russett 2001). Liberal reformers have ample reasons to advocate the promotion of democracy where it presently is not practiced as a path to peace, because the historical evidence is overwhelming that democracies not only do not wage wars against each other but also are less likely to be attacked by, or lose wars with, nondemocratic states; ballots deter against bullets and bombs, and give power in wars to free people fighting to preserve their freedoms (Kegley and Hermann 2001). In another vindication of Kant's predictions, democracy has been shown historically to be an antidote to war for another reason: states with free governments and free people are likely to accept free trade, which in turn generates higher levels of prosperity and pressure by business interests to preserve the international peace on which prosperity and profits depend (Oneal and Russett 1999). Hence, these findings support the liberal vision that Woodrow Wilson (and other so-called idealists) sought to implement after World War I, when Wilson pleaded that "making the world safe for democracy" was a practical peace plan, because a safer world would be created if the actors in world politics made their foreign policy decisions through democratic procedures (see Chapters 3 and 12).

This lesson has not been lost on leaders in democratic states seeking to find a principle on which to ground their twenty-first-century national security strategies. The United States under President Bill Clinton embraced the thesis of democratic-peace advocates enthusiastically. In his 1994 State of the Union address, Clinton declared, "Democracies don't attack each other," and argued that because of this empirical law, "ultimately the best strategy to insure our security and to build a durable peace is to support the advance of democracy elsewhere." The 1994 *U.S. National Strategy of Engagement and Enlargement* defined the promotion of democracy as a pillar of America's foreign policy. Clinton's goal was to enlarge the existing community of liberal democracies, and he was joined enthusiastically and officially by the other major EU and NATO liberal democracies whose members insist on states being democratically ruled as a condition for their inclusion as applicant-members or as beneficiaries of their political support.

■ **Group of Eight (G-8)** the major industrialized countries, including Russia, whose leaders participate in annual summit conferences to set economic, political, and military goals for the global future.

As the United States has pushed its democratization agenda to the forefront, many other democracies and international organizations have also embraced the aspiration. For example, the **Group of Eight (G-8)** has endorsed the promotion of democracy as a priority foreign policy goal. So, too, have the World Bank, the International Monetary Fund (IMF), and the Organization for Economic Cooperation and Development (OECD)—all of which have designated democratic reform as a condition for receipt of loans and development assistance. The OAS has similarly accepted the principle that it is permissible to export democracy. Its June 1991 Santiago Commitment to Democracy and Renewal of the Inter-American System established an OAS intervention policy to guarantee hemispheric democracy. Following suit, the UN has affirmed democratization as a human-rights entitlement in many of its recent resolutions. Thus, the United States and the democratic majority have the numbers to seek revision of international law. They are exercising their influence multilaterally by legitimizing military intervention to promote democratic reforms and protect the civil liberties and the human rights "entitlement," now embodied in international law, for people everywhere to democratically govern themselves (see Rosenberg 1999; von Glahn 1996). To promote peace and the growth of civil societies throughout the world, the liberal democratic community has taken a step toward accepting the use of intervention in nondemocratic sovereign states to force changes, allowing "democracy at the point of bayonets" to force reforms (Peceny 2000).

At the start of the twenty-first century, the critical question and heated issue concerns what democracies will do when a nondemocratic state fails to respect humanitarian law in its relations with its own citizens. Can the liberal democratic community build the necessary level of consensus to support the use of military means for the moral end of protecting oppressed peoples' human rights? The magnitude of the challenge is huge. "In the real world," U.S. President Bill Clinton told the UN General Assembly in September 1999, "priorities often collide, and tough choices must be made . . . I know that some are troubled that the United States and others cannot respond to every humanitarian catastrophe in the world. We cannot do everything everywhere." Indeed, providing humanitarian assistance and promoting civil liberties in many failed states and nondemocratic countries where repression and civil wars are occurring poses a huge problem. Kofi Annan observed that "There are a great number of peoples who need more than just words of sympathy." As much as a response is needed, there are limits to the willingness and capacity of the liberal democracies to police the problem through supranational IGOs. It is for this reason that many realists doubt if democracy and international institutions are truly antidotes to international and internal wars.

Some skeptics grounded in realism go even further. They question whether democracies will put their ideals for promoting liberties worldwide ahead of their narrow national interests by risking their soldiers' lives in humanitarian crusades in countries of low geopolitical importance. Worse still, some realists also question whether the interstate relations among democratic countries will remain peaceful. These skeptics look to the Boer War, the U.S. Civil War, the wars waged by the German Kaiser with the approval of an elected parliament against other democracies in World War I, and other factors such as warring democracies' alliances and high levels of competitive trade, and doubt if the relationship between democratization and peace is as strong as democratic-peace proponents maintain it is. Needless to say, confidence in the liberal path to peace through democratization will remain shaky in a precarious globalized world where the institutional foundations of lasting peace are themselves still unstable.

These doubts notwithstanding, past trends provide strong evidence to support the liberal tenet that democracy has the capacity to deter wars within and between members of the democratic community of states (Russett 2001). Simply put, "globalization needs a dose of democracy [because] a more democratic world, in which individuals and groups are less likely to perceive their rights as threatened, is a world more likely to be at peace" (Falk and Strauss 1999). Therefore, providing that democratic states continue to abide by their past record of dealing with conflicts by compromise through negotiation, mediation, arbitration, and adjudication, the existing liberal democracies' efforts to enlarge their community could potentially usher in a major transformation of twenty-first-century world politics. If so, and if "the worldwide democratic revolution" does not begin to "cool off around the globe" as some predict (Carothers 1997), liberalism will be vindicated; the future will witness less bloodshed, and the 1995 hopes Pope John Paul II expressed could make an ancient dream a reality: "No more war, war never again."

However, promise dictates neither performance nor destiny. As Prime Minister Ingvar Caarlsson of Sweden warned, "If we fail to nurture democracy—the most fundamental political project of this century—we will never be able to realize our goals and the responsibilities which the future will call for."

LIBERAL INSTITUTIONS AND WORLD ORDER: FROM SECURITY TO STABILITY?

Liberal and neoliberal theories that focus on international law, organization, integration, and democratization see armed conflict as deriving from prevailing and deeply rooted institutional deficiencies. Neoliberal reformers believe that the current anarchical system is the problem, not the solution, because weak institutions make security dear and global welfare subservient to national welfare. To change this, they advocate legal and institutional methods to pool sovereignty and reform the character of nondemocratic governments. Seeing the international system as underdeveloped and unstructured, advocates of these reforms believe that a rebuilt state system can best eliminate the roots of war. As one liberal scholar argues, global change requires innovation because "During the coming decades global challenges will continue and may increase. . . . There is more and more of an overlap between national interests and global responsibilities. The task of multilateral diplomacy is to cope with new issues, new demands and new situations [through] 'shared responsibilities' and 'strengthened partnership'" (Kinnas 1997).

To liberal advocates, the big problems on the global agenda are ones that simultaneously affect many states. They cannot be meaningfully managed unilaterally; they are transnational and cannot be met effectively with a national response. With respect to such global issues as free trade, environmental degradation, global warming, the control of AIDS, the global refugee crisis, failed states, and civil wars, a multilateral cooperative approach may be required under conditions of interdependent globalization. In this context, President Martii Athisaari of Finland in 1999 observed that "the world has turned from mere coexistence to cooperation [and it has] succeeded in reaching beyond the boundaries of state sovereignty." Whether multilateral IGOs such as the UN, the democratically driven EU, and the liberal community of states at large can orchestrate their collective opposition to interstate and civil war through multilateral action will determine if this liberal path to peace will ultimately succeed.

The contributions of the expanding number of international institutions created in the twentieth century to this grand purpose were, until recently, rather modest. Despite some promising developments, armed conflict has been frequent. This is not surprising in a system in which, during the mid-1990s, states allocated less than $2 for every man, woman, and child to the UN for humanitarian and security emergencies, while at the same time their combined annual defense expenditures exceeded $960 billion (Evans 1995, 8). However, the impact of multilateral management of strife-torn areas should not be minimized. As Inis L. Claude maintains,

> Particular *organizations* may be nothing more than playthings of power politics and handmaidens of national ambitions. But international *organization,* considered as an historical process, represents a secular trend toward the systematic development of an enterprising quest for political

> means of making the world safe for human habitation. It may fail, and peter out ignominiously. But if it maintains the momentum that it has built up in the twentieth century, it may yet effect a transformation of human relationships on this planet which will at some indeterminate point justify the assertion that the world has come to be governed—that mankind has become a community capable of sustaining order, promoting justice, and establishing the conditions of that good life which Aristotle took to be the supreme aim of politics. (Claude 1971, 447–448, emphasis added)

At the advent of the twenty-first century, liberal institutionalists have appropriately raised various concerns about the capacity of independent and competing sovereign states to engineer a hopeful future for humanity. On balance, sovereign states have not used their foreign policies to create a safe and secure global environment in which their youth can survive and propser. Instead, states have historically been instruments for making war with others, and recently national governments have proven inefficient at either preventing civil wars or commanding widespread loyalty and respect from their constituents. The global "crisis of confidence" in governments has resulted in the disintegration of failing states at the same time that these fragile states have become tied together in an interdependent globalized community. "Liberal internationalists see a need for international rules to solve states' problems, proclaim the end of the nation-state, [and see] transgovernmentalism rapidly becoming the most widespread and effective mode of international governance," said Anne-Marie Slaughter (1997) in defining the contemporary currents of public opinion. States are, to be sure, uniting by creating global institutions and a common culture to jointly protect themselves against the many shared problems they face. They appear to increasingly accept the once radical liberal view that, as Kofi Annan argued in 1999, "a new, broader definition of national interest is needed in the [twenty-first] century," which would unify states to work on common goals that transcend national interests. Borders and oceans cannot isolate or insulate states from these threats to security; they can only be controlled in the global commons by a collective effort. It is for this reason that many intergovernmental organizations (IGOs) originally came into being, and it is the persistence of collective threats produced by an increasingly globalized world that makes IGOs durable. As the globe shrinks and borders become even more porous, we can predict that liberal paths to peace and prosperity will continue to find favor, and policymakers will take seriously the call to help create what Swedish Foreign Minister Anna Lindh describes as "a global culture of conflict prevention." If pursued, will the liberal approaches to the control of armed conflict create a different pattern? The world awaits an answer.

KEY TERMS

neoliberal institutionalism
private international law
public international law
sovereignty
realism
sovereign equality
neutrality
nonintervention
diplomatic immunity
extraterritoriality
crimes against humanity
divine right of kings
statehood
diplomatic recognition
de facto recognition
de jure recognition
nonrecognition
mediation

good offices
conciliation
arbitration
adjudication
self-help
structural violence
positivist legal theory
security regimes
just war doctrine
morals
ethics
revolution in military affairs (RMA)
military necessity
noncombatant immunity
reprisals
retorsion
International Criminal Court (ICC)
permanent world criminal court
state-sponsored terrorism
war crimes
human rights
collective security
balance of power
peacekeeping
preventive diplomacy
peace making
peace operations
peace building
peace enforcement
selective engagement
regional collective defense
failed states
political integration
world federalism
absolute gain
relative gain
nationalism
nongovernmental organizations (NGOs)
functionalism
intergovernmental organizations (IGOs)
multinational corporations (MNCs)
ideology
intermestic
neofunctionalism
European Union (EU)
security community
spillover
spillback
spillaround
indigenous peoples
political disintegration
devolution
self-determination
democratic peace
behavioralism
Group of Eight (G-8)

SUGGESTED READING

Chalmers, Malcolm. *Sharing Security.* London: Macmillan/St. Martin's, 2000.

Doyle, Michael W. *Ways of War and Peace.* New York: Norton, 1997.

Held, David. *Democracy and the Global Order: From the Modern State to Cosmopolitan Governance.* New York: Polity Press, 1998.

Hsiung, James C. *Anarchy and Order: The Interplay of Politics and Law in International Relations.* Boulder, Colo.: Lynne Rienner, 1998.

Joyner, Christopher C. *International Law in the Twenty-First Century.* Boulder, Colo.: Rowman & Littlefield, 2000.

Lauren, Paul Gordon. *The Evolution of International Human Rights: Visions Seen.* Philadelphia: University of Pennsylvania Press, 1999.

Lockwood, Bert B., Jr., ed. *Human Rights Quarterly: A Comparative and International Journal of the Social Sciences, Humanities and Law.* Baltimore: Johns Hopkins University Press.

Lorenz, Joseph P. *Peace, Power, and the United Nations: A Security System for the Twenty-first Century.* Boulder, Colo.: Westview Press, 1999.

Mapel, David R., and Terry Nardin. *International Society: Diverse Ethical Perspectives.* Princeton, N.J.: Princeton University Press, 1998.

Ruggie, John Gerald. *Constructing the World Polity: Essays on International Institutionalization.* New York: Routledge,1998.

Russett, Bruce, and John Oneal. *Triangulating Peace: Democracy, Interdependence, and International Organization.* New York: Norton, 2000.

Shawcross, William. *Deliver Us from Evil: Peacekeepers, Warlords, and a World of Endless Conflict.* New York: Simon & Schuster, 2000.

Starr, Harvey. *Anarchy, Order, and Integration.* Ann Arbor: University of Michigan Press, 1997.

Wapner, Paul, and Lester Edwin J. Ruiz, eds. *Principled World Politics: The Challenge of Normative International Relations.* Boulder, Colo.: Rowman & Littlefield, 2000.

Woodhouse, Tom, Robert Bruce, and Malcolm Dando, eds. *Peacekeeping and Peacemaking.* London: Macmillan, 1998.

Ziring, Lawrence, Robert E. Riggs, and Jack C. Plano. *The United Nations: International Organization and World Politics,* 3rd ed. New York: Harcourt College, 2000.

WHERE ON THE WORLD WIDE WEB?

Carnegie Council on Ethics and International Affairs
http://www.cceia.org/

The best inventory of global issues, with Point of View commentary and links to other Web sites dealing with each issue.

Human Rights Watch
http://www.hrw.org/

Human Rights Watch (HRW) is an independent, nongovernmental organization dedicated to protecting the human rights of people around the world. To this end, the organization investigates and exposes human rights violations and holds abusers accountable. As Chapter 16 notes, the international community has impressively expanded the human rights protection granted under international law. HRW challenges governments to respect these laws. Its Web site houses stories on breaking news concerning human rights around the globe. A clickable map delivers HRW reports on specific country's human rights abuses. Which countries have the best and worst human rights records?

The International Court of Justice
http://www.icj-cij.org/

The International Court of Justice (ICJ) is the principal judicial organ of the United Nations. Examine the Court's statute to find out who can bring cases before the court. Then, read the biographies of the court's fifteen members. Finally, access the Decisions link to examine some of the ICJ's contentious cases. Which countries have brought the United States to court? What was the ICJ's ruling in these cases?

International Court of Justice Considers Genocide
http://oz.uc.edu/thro/genocide/index.html

Professor Howard Tolley of the University of Cincinnati has created an interactive Web site on which you can role-play the judge at the International Court of Justice when Bosnia brought charges against Yugoslavia in 1993. You can explore the facts, research the law, and consider opposing arguments, and then make your judgement. How does it compare to the court's actual decision?

International Criminal Tribunal for the Former Yugoslavia (ICTY)
http://www.un.org/icty/

Established by the United Nations Security Council in 1993, the ICTY is mandated to prosecute persons responsible for serious violations of international humanitarian law committed on the territory of the former Yugoslavia since 1991. Visit this Web site to see who was indicted for war crimes and what judgment was rendered. Do you believe that the international community's ability to punish individuals for war crimes will be a deterrent against futures acts of genocide and inhumanity?

Multilaterals Project
http://www.tufts.edu/fletcher/multilaterals.html

The Fletcher School of Law and Diplomacy makes available the texts of international multilateral conventions and other instruments. It has a searchable database as well as a list of conventions organized by subjects, such as the rules of warfare, the environment, cultural protection, or biodiversity. You can also view the Treaty of Westphalia and the League of Nations covenant. For thorough historical background on a subject, read the documents chronologically.

United Nations Peacekeeping Operations
http://www.un.org/Depts/dpko/

The United Nations has deployed numerous international military and civilian personnel to conflict areas to stop or contain hostilities and supervise the carrying out of peace agreements. View the World Map of All Missions on the homepage. Click on an ongoing mission and read about the profile, background, and facts and figures concerning the mission. Do the same thing for an older mission. Are there any similarities or differences?

Universal Declaration of Human Rights
http://www.un.org/Overview/rights.html

Table 16.2 chronicles the legal steps in the development of international human rights protections. Read the document that started it all—the Universal Declaration of Human Rights. Did you know that Eleanor Roosevelt, serving as a delegate to the United Nations, chaired the committee that produced this document?

ANK LTD.
TO VIET NAM
VISA
Welcome to the World of VISA

PART V

The Problematic Twenty-First Century

How are the trends that are emerging in world politics today likely to influence the global future? Will the twenty-first century find past approaches to world order useful, or will it reject past approaches as new questions that demand new answers arise?

Part V presents ten thought-provoking questions that ask how current trends in world politics are likely to impact the early part of the twenty-first century. These questions, originally introduced in Chapter 1, draw on ideas you have encountered as you have read this book. Thinking about possible answers will require you to analyze these ideas, looking ahead to the global future informed by your knowledge of the contemporary character of international relations and recent ideas about how world politics work.

CHAPTER 17

TEN QUESTIONS ABOUT TWENTY-FIRST-CENTURY GLOBAL PROSPECTS

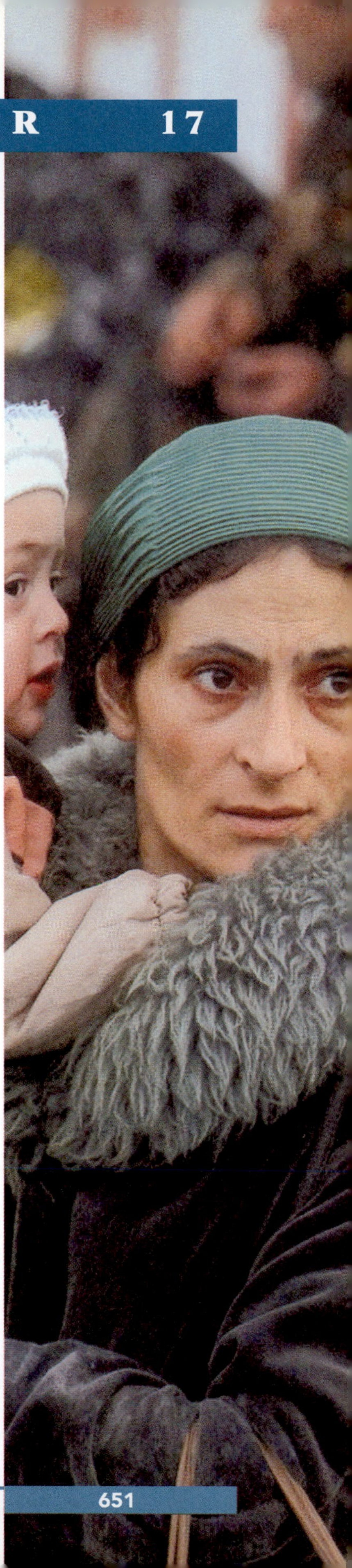

THEMES AND TOPICS

- What is the national interest?
- Of what value is military power?
- Is war between states obsolete?
- Will separatist conflict within states lead to hundreds of new states?
- Will the great powers intervene in the internal affairs of states for humanitarian purposes?
- What will be the impact of globalization?
- Is realism still realistic and is liberalism still too idealistic?
- Is the world preparing for the wrong war?
- Is this the "end of history"?
- Is there a reordered global agenda?

A Chechen refugee ponders her future.

Trend is not destiny.

—René Dubos, French author, 1975

On the cusp of epochal change, a new world seems to be emerging to dwarf even our most recent expectations, for better and for worse.

—Jim Hoagland, international journalist, 2000

The opposing trends toward integration and fragmentation point toward a new international global system—one whose character has yet to develop definition and coloration. Uncertainty and unpredictability thus define the mood at the start of the new millennium. But one thing is certain: The seismic shifts underway will challenge the wisdom of old beliefs and orthodox visions. Because turmoil and turbulence govern contemporary international affairs, they require that we ask unconventional questions about conventional ideas. They push us to try to think four-dimensionally in order to perceive how political, military, market, and environmental pressures—intensified through globalization—are increasingly being brought to bear on the countries of the world, the people who reside in them, and their interactions.

Chapter 1 suggested that the investigative challenge to interpreting the future of world affairs would require the consideration of five controversial questions:

1. Are states obsolete?
2. Is global interdependence a cure or a curse?
3. Is technological innovation a blessing or a burden?
4. Will geo-economics supersede geopolitics?
5. What constitutes human well-being on an ecologically fragile planet?

Answers to these questions are elusive. The conclusions boldly asserted by would-be prophets are not likely to prove definitive, because, as former United Nations (UN) Secretary-General Boutros Boutros-Ghali warned in 1996, "those caught up in revolutionary change rarely understand its ultimate significance." It is hard to recognize, and to describe, the bewildering array of problems that we carry into the new millennium. As President Bill Clinton lamented in his 1997 National Security Strategy of the United States,

> The dangers we face are unprecedented in their complexity. Ethnic conflict and outlaw states threaten regional stability; terrorism, drugs, organized crime and proliferation of weapons of mass destruction are global concerns that transcend national borders; and environmental damage and rapid population growth undermine economic prosperity and political stability in many countries.

Given this complex and dangerous environment, it is important to weigh plausible answers to these same five key questions as we attempt to prepare ourselves intellectually for understanding the problematic future of twenty-first-century world politics.

This final chapter addresses ten additional questions about the future, based on the preceding discussion of the major trends currently unfolding in world politics.

TOWARD THE FUTURE: CRITICAL QUESTIONS AT THE START OF THE NEW MILLENNIUM

Leaders and policy analysts worldwide are debating a number of controversial issues that require policy choices. How these and other questions are answered will significantly shape world politics in the twenty-first century.

1. What Is the "National Interest"?

What goals should states pursue? In earlier times, the answer was easy: The state should promote the internal welfare of its citizens, provide for defense against external aggression, and preserve the state's values and way of life.

Leaders pursue the same goals today, but their domestic and foreign policy options are increasingly limited. In an age of tradeoffs, many problems can be resolved only at the risk of worsening others. Under such conditions, the national quest for narrow self-advantage and global position often carries prohibitively high costs. The historic tendency toward chauvinism (my country, right or wrong) in defining national interests can be counterproductive domestically as well as internationally. No country can long afford to pursue its own welfare in ways that reduce the security and welfare of its competitors.

Those who questioned orthodox definitions of the national interest in the past seldom found support, but this is changing. As the eminent anthropologist Margaret Mead (1968) mused, "Substantially we all share the same atmosphere today, and we can only save ourselves by saving other people also. There is no longer a contradiction between patriotism and concern for the world." Former

U.S. Secretary of State Cyrus Vance voiced a similar idea when he observed that "more than ever cooperative endeavors among nations are a matter not only of idealism but of direct self-interest."

■ **realism**
the orthodox theory of world politics based on the assumption that because humans are born to seek self-advantage, international politics is doomed to be a struggle for power involving war (see p. 457).

E. H. Carr (1939), a British pioneer of **realism,** was convinced of the realism of idealism, maintaining that opposing the general interests of humankind does not serve a country's self-interest. Failing to recognize the plight of others can ultimately threaten one's own well-being—a view underscored by Martin Luther King, Jr., who urged that "injustice anywhere is a threat to justice everywhere." Indeed, it was largely enlightened awareness of the limitations of traditional notions of state sovereignty and the conventional ways in which states have defined their national interests that prompted UN Secretary-General Kofi Annan in September 1999 to warn: "The world has changed in profound ways since the end of the Cold War, but I fear our conceptions of national interest have failed to follow suit. A new, broader definition of national interst is needed . . . which would induce states to find greater unity in the pursuit of common goods and values." These proposals put human interests and global security ahead of national interests and national security. If such conceptions, largely rooted in the legacy of **liberalism,** gain a wider following in world public opinion in the twenty-first century, will the collective concerns of all humanity begin to better compete with states' continuing competitive preoccupation with their own narrow national interests?

■ **liberalism**
the optimistic view that because humans are capable of compassion, cooperation, and self-sacrifice for collective gain, it is possible for world politics to progress beyond narrow competition and war (see p. 28).

2. Of What Value Is Military Power?

In the past, military might enabled states to project power, exercise influence, and dominate others. Today nuclear and advanced (biological and chemical) weapons of mass destruction make the use of military might risky. Continuing arms proliferation raises new questions. Does the acquisition of more weapons increase **national security**—a psychological phenomenon? Or are preparations for war and defense responsible for the **security dilemma** that all countries face?

■ **national security**
a country's psychological freedom from fears that the state will be unable to resist threats to its survival and national values emanating from abroad or at home (see p. 456).

■ **security dilemma**
the propensity of armaments undertaken by one state for ostensibly defensive purposes to threaten other states, which arm in reaction, with the result that all arming states' national security declines as their arms increase (see p. 102).

Most leaders agree with the ancient Greek philosopher Aristotle, who argued that "a people without walls is a people without choice." Thus most accept the realist premise that preparing for war is necessary for peace. Yet the capacity to destroy does not always make for a convincing threat, especially against countries with the capacity to retaliate. Today, the threat of force often lacks credibility. Military power has become impotent by its very strength. And when military might no longer compels others' compliance, then weapons will have lost their primary role as a basis, or substitute, for diplomacy.

No level of military might can guarantee a state's invulnerability. And states' primary security problem today is the rise of internal, not external, aggression. Therefore, preparations for war can be assessed only in terms of other consequences. Thresholds may exist beyond which the addition of greater destructive power or the discovery of technologically revolutionary new kinds of lethal and nonlethal weapons is meaningless. Furthermore, excessive preparations for war may leave a country heavily fortified with little left to defend, as U.S. President Eisenhower warned in 1961.

Although immediate fears of another great-power conflict causing a world war have declined and further eroded justifications for acquiring military power, states' traditional quest for military advantage has not disappeared. Military

People Power? States continue to seek sovereignty and supremacy, but increasingly world politics is being transformed at the grassroots level by networks of nongovernmental organizations (NGOs) of people dissatisfied with states' definitions of national interests. Individuals have formed over 27,000 NGOs that advocate global changes and reforms. One such well-known NGO is Greenpeace, whose goal is to protect humanity from environmental degradation through countries' and companies' exploitation of the global commons for power and profit. Shown here are Greenpeace members in action. The Grand Peace Palace in Seoul, Korea—Asia's biggest performance hall and a symbol of world peace—hosted five thousand people representing more than eight hundred NGOs from over one hundred countries in October 1999 under the theme "The Role of NGOs in the Twenty-First Century: Inspire, Empower, Act!" NGOs have emerged as a major force to overcome global problems, such as war, famine, environmental pollution, human rights abuse, gender inequality, and income inequality, that many people feel are not being tackled effectively by states' governments; these organizations wish to see human interests reinterpreted as states' primary national interests.

spending by the United States, China, the European Union (EU), and other aspiring global powers is scheduled to climb. Another sign of the persistent belief that military power increases political influence and national security is found in the fact that the global trade in weapons is the world's largest industry. Nonetheless, the disarmament movement is progressing slowly, if erratically, and the pursuit of arms, arsenals, and armies has declined throughout much of the zone of peace in the Global North, where the expectation of foreign attack is nonexistent. Many governments have slashed military budgets in order to deal with the economic crises, which pose a greater threat to inflation, underemployment, and debt. Perhaps leaders in disarming states have begun to recognize that in the long run high military spending can reduce a state's industrial growth, weaken its global economic competitiveness, and ultimately undermine its ability to pursue and preserve dominance (Kennedy 1987). And when a government cannot satisfy citizens' cravings for a promising financial future and a standard of living comparable to that of people living abroad, protests against the state from discontented citizens can be expected, planting the seeds from which can potentially sprout **failed states,** civil war, and political disintegration.

■ **failed states** countries whose goverments have so mismanaged policy that they have lost the loyalty of their citizens who seek independence in order to create their own state (see p. 632).

However, as India's and Pakistan's quests for prestige through nuclear weapons suggests, many leaders will not take this lesson seriously. The one predicament that nearly every state finds unacceptable is being vulnerable to foreign aggression or subject to other states' dictates. Consequently, the pursuit of military power is likely to continue at the same time that concerns about the social and financial costs of preparations to use military force in war are likely to rise. Concurrently, in the Information Age states are increasingly likely to invest in nonmilitary methods of acquiring **soft power,** reasoning that "if a state can make its power legitimate in the eyes of others and establish international institutions that encourage others to define their interests in compatible ways, it may not need to expend as many costly traditional economic or military resources" (Keohane and Nye 2001). That outcome could diminish substantially states' traditional faith in the proposition that overwhelming military might is required to play the game of international **politics** because it gets others to accommodate themselves to the demands of a more militarily powerful state. If the power to destroy does not provide the power to control, then states' willingness to spend for destructive weapons will decline.

■ **soft power**
the ability to exercise influence in world politics due to intangible resources such as culture and ideas as opposed to methods that rely on military might (see p. 462).

■ **politics**
the pursuit and exercise of power to promote self-interests and goals (see p. 457).

3. Is War between States Obsolete?

Prevalent practices tend to wither away when they cease to serve their intended purpose, as the examples of slavery, dueling, and colonialism illustrate. Is war between states subject to these same forces? Since World War II, legal prohibitions against military aggression have expanded, and war has occurred almost exclusively in the Global South. The period since 1945 has been the longest span of great-power peace since the seventeenth century, raising expectations that the major powers have "retreated from doomsday" (Mueller 1989) and that large-scale wars between states will continue to decline and perhaps cease altogether. (This hope exists even as internal or civil wars are on the rise, and humanitarian concerns about genocide and war crimes increasingly require interventionary peacekeeping.) "For modern states the anticipated costs [of waging war], political and economic as well as human, generally exceed the benefits" (Mack 1996).

It is, of course, debatable whether the disincentives and dangers of using today's destructive weapons are truly making war between states obsolete. Instead, this kind of war may eventually disappear in another, far more frightening way—because resort to weapons of mass destruction will obliterate humankind. The puzzle, then, is when and by what means war will become obsolete. As Martin Luther King, Jr., put it, "The choice is either nonviolence or nonexistence."

4. Will Separatist Conflict within States Lead to Hundreds of New States?

Throughout the world's history, when distinct cultures have come into contact, either the collisions have sparked communication and a healthy respect for diversity or familiarity has bred contempt. When followers have embraced **ethnocentrism,** the view that their own group's values are inherently superior, animosity and disrespect for differences have been especially characteristic, and persecution and killing have often followed.

■ **ethnocentrism**
a propensity to see one's nationality or state as the center of the world and therefore special, with the result that the values and perspectives of other groups are misunderstood and ridiculed.

It appeared to many immediately after the Cold War's divisive ideological contest between capitalism and communism had disappeared that the globe was at last coming together, and that a new age of tolerance for differences was dawning. That hope was soon dispelled by the reappearance of another major divisive type of conflict, between not only what Samuel Huntington (1996, 1999) termed a **clash of civilizations** at the global level of analysis but also clashes *within* states between tribes, religions, and ethnic groups. In particular, an epidemic of often violent conflicts has erupted between nationalities whose identity is defined by a shared language, religion, or race that makes their members feel different from others. These perceived differences have bred hostilities, many long suppressed by strong state governments. In many countries where the dominant majority population has ruled without true representative democracy, minorities and indigenous peoples of the **Fourth World** have been persecuted through **state-sponsored terrorism** in campaigns that have resulted, at times, in **ethnic cleansing.** The former Yugoslavia, which fractured into a handful of separate states through a series of bloody civil wars, stands as the globe's foremost recent example of what can result when hypernationalists respect neither liberty nor life. But the civil wars that stemmed from the same roots in Burundi, Cambodia, East Timor, Rwanda, and Somalia are similar examples of the new face of violence within states in almost every corner of the globe. At the very moment in world history when the probability of war *between* states has greatly receded, the likelihood of wars *within* states has risen greatly. Such civil wars may break existing states into separate units, as the fragmentation of the former Yugoslavia and the separation of Eritrea from Ethiopia in 1993 illustrate.

"Peace is not only the absence of conflict," observed Juan Somavia, Chile's representative at the UN, in 1997. "It is the presence of human security—at the individual level, the family, the community. Peace is also positive things happening within a society. The two peaces are necessary. The problem today is that, yes, you have less major conflict, but you also have more human insecurity worldwide. The real security threat of the future is that people feel insecure in their own societies."

What does the future hold? That question cannot be answered with confidence. However, if the recent past is a guide, it appears likely that many existing states may splinter into newly independent states, in line with a trend that has been underway for the past two hundred years. "In the nineteenth century, new states were founded at an average rate of one every four years, accelerating to one every eighteen months in the first half of the [twentieth] century, and every five months in the second half" (Smith 1999). Between 1980 and 1998, thirty-two new states came into existence, with more than thirteen new states created on average each year in the last decade of the twentieth century to punctuate the growth of the rate of new state formation already well established (Enriquez 1999, 40).

The possible new explosion of new states is not widely seen as resulting from the kind of civil wars that end with the separation of an existing state into two or more independent states. It is now more commonly perceived as a product of the humanitarian disasters that result from failed or **failing states** where governments have lost the support of the population, can no longer maintain law and order, and have massacred rebelling peoples instead of protecting the human rights and lives of the inhabitants. Anarchy is a prelude to the eventual balkanization of states into smaller units composed of ethnic nationalities and

■ clash of civilizations
political scientist Samuel Huntington's controversial thesis that in the twenty-first century the globe's major civilizations will conflict with one another, leading to anarchy and warfare similar to that resulting from conflicts between states over the past five hundred years (see p. 136).

■ Fourth World
indigenous people or native ethnic and tribal groups who often live in poverty and deprivation within a state that occupies the land from which they originate (see p. 206).

■ state-sponsored terrorism
formal assistance, training, and arming of terrorists by a state in order to achieve foreign and domestic policy goals (see p. 613).

■ ethnic cleansing
the extermination of an ethnic minority group by a state, in violation of international law (see p. 211).

■ failing states
those governments that are in danger of losing the loyalty of their citizens, who are rebelling against corruption and administrative failure, and in the process tearing the country into separate political parts (see p. 441).

cultures seeking to secure an independent identity and territory for themselves to rule.

Nearly all the globe's 207 independent countries are made up of diverse nationalities and ethnic groups. In the past, countries like the United States and Canada have managed to forge a federal unity as they sought, and benefited from, a "melting pot" society that was enriched and strengthened by its differences. But today—for understandable reasons—many of the world's three thousand to five thousand indigenous peoples and ethnic minorities are seeking **self-determination.** They crave independence and sovereignty, just when the very concept of sovereignty in the borderless globalized world is under its strongest attack in four centuries and "the long-term trend is against sovereignty as it is generally understood" (Smith 1999). Separatist revolts and succession movements are rising fast throughout the globe, despite the fact that secessionist revolts are a threat to domestic stability and international security generally. If every major "political and ethnic and religious group" won independence, President Bill Clinton warned in October 1999, "we might have eight hundred countries in the world, [perhaps even] eight thousand. The great irony of the turning of the millennium is that we have more modern options for technology and economic advance than ever before, but our major threat is the most primitive human feeling—the fear of the other. We have to think of how we will live after the shooting stops, after the smoke clears, over the long run. National independence is often a questionable assertion in a global economy where cooperation pays greater benefits in every area than destructive competition."

■ **self-determination** the doctrine that asserts nationalities have the right to determine what political authority will represent and rule them (see p. 639).

The dilemma created by the striving for independence around the globe is that it pits important values against one another. Sovereign independence and human rights are treasured, but so are prosperity and peace. How will these values be reconciled, if at all? Would the breakup of states into smaller units be a blessing or a burden to the long-term collective interests of humanity?

5. Will the Great Powers Intervene in the Internal Affairs of States for Humanitarian Purposes?

Conflicts within countries are raging throughout the world, where, as noted, many failing states' threatened governments are resorting to mass violence and even genocide to restore stability. It is alarming enough that the human rights "entitlement" of all people to live in a democracy where they have a say in how they are governed that is outlined in international law has been frequently ignored or violated. Worse still, many civilians are the targets of overt oppression and violence by the governments presumably created to preserve law and order by peaceful means—in courts and through ballots. Of great concern, therefore, is whether the moral outrage of the globe's major powers will be sufficient for them to make concerted peacekeeping and peace-making interventions to end human rights abuses in those countries where acclaimed standards of conduct have been blatantly disregarded. Atrocities in many failed states are forcing a mass exodus of more than 20 million refugees each year, and another 80 million **displaced people** have left their homes to seek safety elsewhere within their countries. The global community is being put to a test of its true ideals and its capacity to defend them, at potentially high costs. Will a humanitarian concern for the victims targeted for extermination crystallize into a response? Or will the victims perish in a sea of indifference?

■ **displaced people** people involuntarily uprooted from their homes and forced either to flee outside their state or to seek sanctuary within their own countries (see p. 216).

Human rights law now provides unprecedented protection in principle for people everywhere to live in freedom without fear. The traditional legal rule of state sovereignty and its corollary—the **nonintervention** norm prohibiting external interference in the internal affairs of states—has been revised. In September 1999 UN Secretary-General Kofi Annan described well the redefinition when he noted that "States are now widely understood to be instruments at the service of their people, and not vice versa. At the same time . . . the fundamental freedom of each individual, enshrined in the charter of the UN and subsequent international treaties—[has] been enhanced by a renewed and spreading consciousness of individual [human] rights. When we read the charter today, we are more than ever conscious that its aim is to protect individual human beings, not to protect those who abuse them."

nonintervention
a fundamental international legal principle, now being challenged, that traditionally has defined interference by one state in the domestic affairs of another as illegal (see p. 531).

Principle is one thing; the reality of human suffering another. Will the great powers in the globalized community back their expressed convictions with deeds and action to free humanity from the oppression of mass murder? Can the great powers agree on a **doctrine** for **humanitarian intervention** that defines when it is legitimate to militarily respond to gross violations of "human rights, wherever they take place, and also on ways of deciding what action is necessary, and when, and by whom"? The challenge, Kofi Annan elaborated, is to transcend traditional notions of sovereignty. Those old ideas remain an "obstacle to effective action in humanitarian crises" that still encourages states "to stand idly by while the horror unfolds," instead of taking military action to enforce international human rights law. If the global community truly recognizes that all people have rights that transcend national borders, and defines those human rights as the core of the community's "common global interests," then it will have to answer and act on the essential unresolved questions: "What is the common interest? Who shall define it? Who shall defend it? Under whose authority? And by what means of intervention?" (Annan 1999). True global governance will begin to become a reality if a consensus can be reached on such monumental questions and the world's commitment to humanitarian action worldwide is then backed by collective action irrespective of region or state.

doctrine
a great power's statement of the principles its leaders will follow when making decisions about solutions to anticipated national security problems, such as the conditions under which it will use military power and armed force for political purposes abroad (see p. 522).

humanitarian intervention
the use of peacekeeping troops by foreign states or international organizations to protect endangered people from gross violations of their human rights and from mass murder and starvation.

6. What Will Be the Impact of Globalization?

In 1517, Martin Luther nailed his ninety-five theses to the door of a church in Wittenberg, Germany, and ignited the Protestant Reformation. To his surprise, his effort at religious reform undermined the Catholic church's authority over states. Ever since then, sovereign states have assumed primary responsibility for controlling affairs within their territorial borders and managing foreign relations with other, similarly empowered, secular state actors.

This system put sovereign states in charge of world affairs, without serious challenge. "People did what they were told to do because that is what one did. As a result, authority structures remained in place for decades, even centuries, as people tended to yield unquestionably to the dictates of governments" (Rosenau 1995).

That has changed. The power of "sovereign" states to control their internal affairs and external relations has eroded precipitously, instilling a widespread crisis of confidence in states' governing capabilities. As former Soviet President Mikhail Gorbachev observed in 1999, "Politics is being conducted in a terribly clumsy way everywhere." Why does it suddenly appear that the world and the

The Tumult of Separatism In the mid-1990s, Russia used force to prevent the breakaway province of Chechnya from secession. In the photo at left rebel leaders wave Chechnya's national colors from the roof of the destroyed presidential palace in the capital city of Grozny. Secession by force to gain independence is not recognized as a right in the UN Charter, and in 1999 and 2000 Russia acted again with military force to end Chechnya's separatist revolt, which Moscow feared would encourage the forty other active secessionist movements in various dissatisfied regions within Russia's sovereign borders. Shown at right, in February 2000 a Chechen woman glares at the ruins of a market in Grozny destroyed by the Russian military's razing of the city to end the Chechen rebellion. These kinds of revolts have a long history, as the U.S. Civil War illustrates. In the twenty-first century, a new surge appears likely which, if successful, could create a large number of new states.

■ **globalization**
the integration of states through increasing contact, communication, and trade to create a holistic, single global system in which the process of change increasingly binds people together in a common fate (see p. 41).

states within it are spinning out of control? The widely accepted code word is **globalization,** understood as a transforming force that is creating a sweeping governance crisis in a new age of increasing interdependent complexity. Globalization captures the idea that everyone and everything on the planet is now more closely connected than ever before, but on an institutional foundation that is shaky and unprepared for managing the massive adjustments brought on by accelerating worldwide changes. Most affected and at a loss are the so-called sovereign states, no longer able to exercise control over the economic, political, and environmental problems within their territories. States everywhere are experiencing a sense of lost sovereignty as they attempt to cope with the pressures originating outside their borders. Simply put, the communications and technology revolution has sped the flow of information, capital, people, and jobs across state boundaries, and the integration of the globe is forcing a redefinition—of historic proportions—of the role of states within this transformed, interconnected world.

With the demise of distance and the rise of states' vulnerability to external pressures, doubt has climbed about the capacity of governments to exercise control within their territories. The very concept of governmental authority is being challenged by public opinion, which no longer automatically accepts leaders' decisions as legitimate.

The shrinking of distances and knowledge and idea sharing characteristic of a borderless world and common culture have reduced old feelings of independence, identity, and autonomy and driven many states to surrender some of their sovereignty in order to benefit from collaborative participation in a competitive global marketplace. The message has been heard everywhere: borders and barriers cannot be revived in a nationalistic effort to close off a country in solitary isolation. "Join the world or become irrelevant" is the way Edward Balador, a former French prime minister, described "the end of **nationalism.**"

Many people feel that UN Secretary-General Boutros Boutros-Ghali was correct when in 1996 he wrote, "Globalization is the world's problem." To be sure, it is not just an opportunity, but a threat as well. When everyone depends on everyone else, they *must* work together. "People are recognizing that if there is a serious problem with the Brazilian economy," British Prime Minister Tony Blair counseled in 1999, "it develops into a serious problem for the British economy or the European economy or the American economy. It is similar with security problems." The challenge of globalization resides primarily in the fact that it reduces states' control over their national future and their capacity to govern, in conjunction with the pressing need to create stronger institutions of international governance to regulate the global system's integrated free market economy. The crisis of complexity makes it imperative that states work together and undertake bold departures from the **self-help** approaches of the past. The only practical prospect for universal peace [and prosperity] must be more civilization" through globalization, and so as to attain this goal "we should strive to create the largest social, economic, and political units possible, ideally one encompassing the whole world" (Keeley 1996). These observers see globalization optimistically as an unstoppable engine for unity and progress. They reason that people who trade have shared interests and fewer incentives to fight; by integrating countries' investments and consumers in the global economy, the capacity for troublemaking and warmaking among countries will be reduced. At the extreme is the celebratory view of Thomas Friedman (1999), who argues in his best-selling book *The Lexus and the Olive Tree: Understanding Globalization* that globalization is a **public good** to be promoted as a cause for human development because it will ultimately increase the wealth of everyone everywhere.

There are, in actuality, serious questions about whence the power to address future domestic and international problems will come in such a globalized world without organized global governance. These questions are prompted by the challenge of minority groups' quest for autonomy from within, and by the challenge of NGOs (such as Doctors without Borders and multinational corporations such as McDonald's) from outside. Many observers have blamed globalization for leaders' confusion about how to react, but the crisis of understanding may be deeper. "Globalization needs a human face," argue Klaus Schwab and Claude Smadja (1999) of the World Economic Forum. "We need to devise a way to address the social impact of globalization, which is neither the mechanical expansion of welfare programs nor the fatalistic acceptance that the divide will grow between the beneficiaries of globalization and those unable to muster the skills and meet the requirements of integration of the global system. . . . If we do not invent ways to make globalization more inclusive, we have to face the prospect of a resurgence of the acute social confrontations of the past, magnified at the global level."

To make globalization a green, clean, and compassionate process for engineering sustainable development for all humanity, a global civil society will require greater global governance to manage a world knit closer together. Globalization may have emasculated the sovereign power of states, but in various

nationalism
a mindset glorifying the nationalities of a people living in a state that assigns loyalty to the state's national interests as a supreme value (see p. 633).

self-help
the principle that because in international anarchy all global actors are independent, they must rely on themselves to provide for their security and well-being.

public goods
shared values from which everyone who has access to them benefits, such as safe drinking water, even if not everyone contributes to their preservation or creation.

A Worldwide Integrated Market Today, products made anywhere are available for sale everywhere. Internet access is common worldwide, even in countries such as China that fear the growth of electronic underground journals that circulate information critical of state policies. Here a billboard advertises for a computer company in Shenzen, China. The Information Age is rapidly making every place more like every place else, in part because "Computing power has doubled every eighteen months for the last thirty years. . . . Similarly, growth of the Internet and the World Wide Web has been exponential. Internet traffic doubles every 100 days" (Keohane and Nye 2001, 28).

respects this same force has strengthened many governments (Pfaff 2000). The question for the future is whether states can respond to the awesome challenge of adaptively steering global change in positive directions to enhance prosperity, human security, and peace. It is doubtful whether humanity can count on relatively powerless NGOs at the grassroots level seeking through global public policy networks to assume responsibility for engineering human progress. If states do not respond to the challenge, can the world's people expect a new global architecture with accepted supranational global governance and global norms to crystallize? This may be the most important issue facing twenty-first-century world politics.

7. Is Realism Still Realistic and Is Liberalism Still Too Idealistic?

Since the eve of World War II, leaders and scholars alike have organized their thoughts and images almost exclusively from the perspective of realism. Their reliance on realism to explain and predict international developments was understandable. Finding a fertile ground in which to flourish during the conflict-ridden fifty-year period between 1939 and 1989, realism accounted for the great powers' prevailing lust for power, the appetite for imperial expansion and struggle for hegemony, the all-consuming arms race, and the obsession with military security better than any other theoretical perspective.

Now, however, a window has opened to expose quite different dimensions of world politics that were previously neglected. The global agenda has shifted as new issues and problems have risen to prominence. "The problem . . . today is not new challengers for hegemony; it is the new challenge of transnational interdependence" (Nye 2001). Welfare, not warfare, is the primary global threat; global warming and trade balances now seem higher on the global agenda than does preventing the use of force by one state against another. As a consequence of these changing issues commanding the world's concern, the realist image of states as unitary rational actors has looked increasingly archaic. In the borderless global village, nongovernmental organizations (NGOs) composed of private citizen groups have flexed their muscles and raised their voices, and they are being heard and orchestrating changes in people's values. "More and more," observed Espen Barth Eide of the Norwegian Foreign Policy Institute in 1997, "the global agenda is being set by others . . . rather than [by] superpowers and governments."

To a number of theorists, the broadened and transformed global agenda goes beyond what realism can be expected to address accurately. To their minds, realist preoccupations threaten to mask the deeper political, economic, and social challenges in international affairs, and fail scientifically to "put existing findings and unresolved questions into a perspective that makes sense of both" (Vasquez 1993). Many critics are disturbed by realism's failure to anticipate the democratic revolutions that accompanied the Cold War's end, the voluntary retreat of the Soviet Union, and global change and cooperation generally. "The wisdom [that] calls itself 'realism,'" scolded Harvard University's Stanley Hoffmann (in Friedman 1993), "is utter nonsense today." Perhaps it was this sentiment that prompted Jeffrey Legro and Andrew Moravcsik (1999) to ask, "Is anybody still a realist?" If these critics of realism's receding accuracy and relevance are correct, then pressure will mount for a new theoretical approach that places less emphasis than realism, neorealism, and **neotraditional realism** on conflict in world politics and on military power and self-help to maintain international stability.

What a new theory will or should look like is not presently obvious, as challengers to realism differ in their prescriptions. Yet many agree with the general view that "it is time for a new, more rigorous idealist alternative to realism" (Kober 1990) and that "there are good reasons for examining aspects of the liberal international legacy once again" (Fukuyama 1992a) by giving Woodrow Wilson's liberal vision "the fair test it has never received" (Gaddis 1990). A number of scholars and policymakers have advocated a **neoliberal** approach for interpreting world politics and the transformed conditions of globalization. Such a new liberal approach emphasizes the transnational interdependence that drives cooperation in international affairs; it attaches importance to global governance, international law, and high ideals such as the promotion and protection of human rights and democracy as methods for reforming international anarchy and weapons proliferation and for creating a world order guided by a shared global consensus about international morality.

This liberal perspective places a greater value on principles than on power, on ideals rather than national self-interest. To the extent that global tensions recede and global harmony and cooperation prevail over warfare, neoliberalism is likely to grow increasingly popular as a way to describe and explain international relations. However, if the world experiences a new arms race and even another war between highly armed adversaries (e.g., India and Pakistan), then liberalism will once again be perceived as too idealistic and optimistic, as it was

■ **neotraditional realism**
a body of recent realist theorizing that departs from neorealism by stressing foreign policy more than international structure and that focuses on the internal influences on states' external behavior instead of the global determinants of states' foreign behavior (see p. 35).

■ **neoliberalism**
a perspective that accounts for the way international institutions promote global change, cooperation, peace, and prosperity through collective reform approaches (see p. 366).

when World War II began. In that case, realism and neorealism will regain popularity as theories of international security.

More probably, twenty-first-century world politics will continue to display combinations of both conflict and cooperation, unity and disunity, order and disorder. Should those dual properties simultaneously characterize the future of world politics, a synthesis of the rich insights of both realism and liberalism will be needed to capture the divergent trajectories. A reconstructed theory of world politics that fuses the most useful and reasonable assumptions of neorealist and neotraditional realist theories of international politics with those of neoliberalism may provide the intellectual framework needed to understand and guide policy making in twenty-first-century world politics.

8. Is the World Preparing for the Wrong War?

To preserve peace, one must prepare for war. That remains the classical realist formula for national security. But would states not be wiser to prepare to conquer the conditions that undermine prosperity, freedom, and welfare? "War for survival is the destiny of all species," observes philosopher Martin J. Siegel (1983). "In our case, we are courting suicide [by waging war against one another]. The world powers should declare war against their common enemy—the catastrophic and survival-of-the-fittest forces that destroyed most of the species of life that came before us."

Increasingly, fewer world leaders are succumbing to the single-mindedness of preparing to compete with other states. President François Mitterrand of France warned in 1983 that "together we must urgently find the solutions to the real problems at hand—especially unemployment and underdevelopment. This is the battlefield where the outlines of the year 2000 will be drawn." India's Prime Minister Indira Gandhi predicted that "either nuclear war will annihilate the human race and destroy the earth, thus disposing of any future, or men and women all over must raise their voices for peace and for an urgent attempt to combine the insights of different civilizations with contemporary knowledge. We can survive in peace and goodwill only by viewing the human race as one, and by looking at global problems in their totality." These prescriptions adhere to a fundamental premise, as expressed in 1995 by Martti Ahtisaari, president of Finland: "To deal with the great security challenges of our time, including population growth, the spread of weapons of mass destruction, crime, environmental degradation and ethnic conflicts, we must resolutely adopt new methods of managing change and building global security."

These rhetorical positions doubtless reflect the problems and self-interests the leaders faced at home and abroad. Nonetheless, they reveal a minority view. The war of people against people goes on. Human security remains precarious, as a large percentage of humanity faces famine, poverty, and a denial of their basic human rights; millions are threatened by genocide and terrorism sponsored by their own governments. Humankind may consequently self-destruct, not because it lacks opportunities, but because of its collective inability to see and to seize them. "Perhaps we will destroy ourselves. Perhaps the common enemy within us will be too strong for us to recognize and overcome," the eminent astronomer Carl Sagan (1988) lamented. "But," he continued, "I have hope. . . . Is it possible that we humans are at last coming to our senses and beginning to work together on behalf of the species and the planet?"

9. Is This the "End of History"?

To many observers, the history of world affairs is the struggle between tyranny and liberty. The contest has taken various forms since antiquity: between kings and mass publics; authoritarianism and republicanism; despotism and democracy; ideological principle and pragmatic politics. Labels are misleading and sometimes dangerous. However, they form the vocabulary of diplomacy and inform theoretical discourse about governance and statecraft. History, in this image, is a battle for the hearts and minds of civilizations. It is an ideological contest for the allegiance of humankind to a particular form of political, social, and economic organization.

Since the Bolshevik revolution in 1917 brought socialism to power in Russia and made Marxism a force in international affairs, the fight for allegiance in the twentieth century was dominated by the contests between communism, fascism, and democratic capitalism. With the defeat of fascism in World War II and the collapse of the international communist movement a generation later, it has become fashionable to argue that we have witnessed the end of a historic contest of epic proportions—and thus the triumph of liberalism and what Francis Fukuyama called the **end of history:**

end of history
the thesis that the philosophy of economic and political liberalism has triumphed throughout the world, ending the contest between market democracies and centrally planned governance (see p. 110).

> The twentieth century saw the developed world descend into a paroxysm of ideological violence, as liberalism contended first with the remnants of absolutism, then bolshevism and fascism, and finally an updated Marxism that threatened to lead to the ultimate apocalypse of nuclear war. But the [twentieth] century that began full of self-confidence in the ultimate triumph of Western liberal democracy seems at its close to be returning full circle to where it started: not to an "end of ideology" of a convergence between capitalism and socialism, as earlier predicted, but to the unabashed victory of economic and political liberalism. (Fukuyama 1989, 3; see also Fukuyama 1999b)

The abrupt repudiation of communism in Moscow and eastern Europe and China's embrace of a free-market economy have raised expectations that history has indeed "ended," in the sense that liberal democratic capitalism has triumphed throughout most of the world. Liberals, inspired by the belief that "liberal democracy and a market-oriented economic order are the only viable options for modern societies" (Fukuyama 1999b), are heartened by the doubling since the mid-1980s of the number of countries practicing multiparty elections and capitalism at home and in foreign trade. World order, they believe, can best be created by free governments practicing free trade. As Woodrow Wilson argued, making the world "safe for democracy" would make the world itself safe. From this liberal perspective, the diffusion of democratic capitalism bodes well for the future of world politics in the new millennium. This is why such a hard-core realist as former U.S. Secretary of State Henry Kissinger in 1997 concluded "it [is] essential to promote the democratic ideal by fostering close cooperation where it already exists [because] military conflict among these nations is nearly inconceivable."

A less reassuring possibility is that history has not "ended" and that the battle between totalitarian and democratic governance is not truly over. There remain many democracies ruled by one-party despots who, although elected, disregard constitutional limits on their power and deny their citizens basic civil, religious, and economic human rights. Fundamental civil liberties and freedoms continue to be ignored by many governments. This persistence of leaders not accountable to the electorate suggests that with the end of the ideological dimension to the Cold War we may be witnessing not history's end, but a watershed. Like previous turning points in history, tomorrow may signal history's resumption: the return to the ageless search for barriers against the resurgence of tyranny, nationalism, and war. Especially to followers of realpolitik, the most salient feature of world politics—the relentless competitive struggle for power under international anarchy—is permanent. There is no assurance that the global community has moved beyond tyranny or interstate competition and war. As former Soviet President Mikhail Gorbachev noted in 1992, "In the major centers of world politics, the choice, it would seem, has today been made in favor of peace, cooperation, interaction, and overall security." However, he warned, "A major international effort will be needed to render irreversible the shift in favor of a democratic world—and democratic for the whole of humanity, not just half of it."

10. Is There a Reordered Global Agenda?

The paradox of contemporary world politics is that a world liberated from the paralyzing grip of the Cold War must now face a series of challenges every bit as threatening and as potentially unmanageable. Globalization has simultaneously enlarged the responsibilities and expanded the issues to be confronted. As Bill Clinton observed, "Profound and powerful forces are shaking and remaking our world. And the urgent question of our time is whether we can make change our friend and not our enemy."

The changes in recent years have spawned transnational threats to world order, other than the resurgence of nationalism, ethnic conflict, failed states, and separatist revolts. These include acid rain, AIDS and other contagious diseases, drug trafficking, international organized crime, ozone depletion, climate change, obstacles to gender equality, energy and food insecurity, desertification and deforestation, financial crises and collapsing economies, and neomercantile trade protectionism.

The potential impact of these additional threats is formidable, as emerging trends suggest that nonmilitary dangers will multiply alongside the continuing threat of arms and armed conflicts in civil wars, as well as interstate wars in particular regions. As distance and borders cease to be barriers in the global village, low politics is becoming high politics; conversely, as weapons cut across state boundaries and reduce human security, whenever bombs and bullets are fired, killing people and degrading the environment, high politics has become low politics. Accordingly, the distinction between **high politics** (war and peace) and **low politics** (economic and other issues of human welfare) may disappear. How will humanity set priorities for action in a system crowded with so many interrelated issues and problems, all of which require attention if peace and prosperity with justice is to prevail?

■ **high politics**
geostrategic issues of national and international security that pertain to matters of war and peace (see p. 247).

■ **low politics**
the category of global issues related to the economic, social, demographic, and environmental aspects of relations between governments and people (see p. 247).

A NEW WORLD ORDER?

From our vantage point at the advent of the twenty-first century, the world appears to have undergone a fundamental transformation. Previously established patterns and relationships have been obliterated. Something revolutionary, not simply new, has unfolded.

Picturing Global Destiny Globalization "implies a holistic worldview and a rejection of the traditional realist paradigm. A globalist perspective embraces a much wider range of important international actors than realism does and addresses a much broader range of issues, as well as expanding the definition of existing concepts such as security" (Sheehan 1996). This view of a globe without borders is captured by this photo taken of the eastern Mediterranean from the Earth-orbiting space shuttle *Columbia*. It pictures an integrated world community, in which humanity shares a common destiny. It also captures the kinds of threats confronting humanity in a globalized world, where problems do not stop at borders. According to scientists studying this photo, the difference in visibility in this panorama suggests that a pollution event near the Black Sea contaminated the atmosphere.

Juxtaposed against the revolutionary is the persistent—the durability of accepted rituals, existing rules, established institutions, and entrenched customs that resist the pull of the momentous recent changes in world politics. Persistence and change coexist uneasily, and it is this mixture that makes the future so uncertain. The twin forces of integration and disintegration, continuity and change, create a mood of both confidence and disorientation. As Australia's Prime Minister John Howard put it in 1997, "In one sense, you are a remarkably lucky generation, but in another sense you have been born into a period of social and technological change . . . and economic evolution."

The outcomes of two races will determine the difference between the world that is and the world that will be. The first is the race between knowledge and oblivion. Ignorance stands in the way of global progress and justice. Advances in science and technology far outpace resolution of the social and political problems they generate. Building the knowledge to confront these problems may therefore present the ultimate challenge. "The splitting of the atom," Albert Einstein warned, "has changed everything save our modes of thinking, and thus we drift toward unparalleled catastrophe. Unless there is a fundamental change in [our] attitudes toward one another as well as [our] concept of the future, the world will face unprecedented disaster."

"Knowledge is our destiny," philosopher Jacob Bronowski declared. If the world is to forge a promising future, it must develop more sophisticated knowledge. Sophistication demands that we see the world as a whole, as well as in terms of its individual parts. We must overcome the temptation to picture others according to our images of ourselves and to project onto them our own aims and values. We must discard the belief in a simple formula for a better tomorrow and resist single-issue approaches to reform. Toleration of ambiguity, even the pursuit of it, is essential.

The future of world politics also rests on the outcome of a race between states' ability to cooperatively act in concert and their historic tendency to compete and fight. Paraphrasing a line from William Shakespeare's *Julius Caesar,* U.S. National Security Advisor Samuel Berger, noting in 1997 that it was time for the international community to get beyond settling conflicts by force, said, "I come not only to praise the post–Cold War era, but to bury it." Only concerted international cooperation can avert slipping back into regional conflicts guided by the belief that "might alone makes right." Because "policymakers have a deep-seated penchant for putting off hard choices as long as possible" (George 2000), the world's political will to implement the reforms necessary to meet global challenges is uncertain.

The future is cloudy, but it is ours to shape. The moving words of President John F. Kennedy thus describe a posture we might well assume: "However close we sometimes seem to that dark and final abyss, let no man of peace and freedom despair. For he does not stand alone. . . . Together we shall save our planet or together we shall perish in its flames. Save it we can, and save it we must, and then shall we earn the eternal thanks of mankind."

KEY TERMS

realism
liberalism
national security
security dilemma
failed states
soft power
politics
ethnocentrism
clash of civilizations
Fourth World
state-sponsored terrorism
ethnic cleansing
failing states
self-determination
displaced people
nonintervention
doctrine
humanitarian intervention
globalization
nationalism
self-help
public goods
neotraditional realism
neoliberalism
end of history
high politics
low politics

SUGGESTED READING

Blumfield, Yorick, ed. *Scanning the Future: Prospects for Tomorrow.* London: Thames & Hudson, 1999.

Dorn, Walter A., ed. *World Order for the New Millennium.* New York: St. Martin's, 1999.

Friedman, Thomas L. *The Lexus and the Olive Tree: Understanding Globalization.* New York: Farrar, Straus, Giroux, 1999.

Fukuyama, Francis. "Second Thoughts: The Last Man in a Bottle." *The National Interest,* 56 (Summer 1999): 16–33.

Gilpin, Robert. *The Challenge of Global Capitalism: The World Economy in the Twenty-First Century.* Princeton, N.J.: Princeton University Press, 2000.

Hopkins, Terence K., and Immanuel Wallerstein. *The Age of Transition: Trajectory of the World-System, 1945–2025.* London: Zed Books, 1996.

Hughes, Barry B. *International Futures: Choices in the Creation of a New World Order,* 3rd ed. Boulder, Colo.: Westview Press, 1999.

Keohane, Robert O., and Joseph S. Nye, Jr. "Globalization: What's New? What's Not? (And So What?)," *Foreign Policy* 118 (Spring 2000): 104–119.

Kennedy, Paul. *Preparing for the Twenty-First Century.* New York: Random House, 1993.

Krasner, Stephen D. *Sovereignty: Organized Hypocrisy.* Princeton, N.J.: Princeton University Press, 2000.

Legro, Jeffrey W., and Andrew Moravcsik. "Is Anybody Still a Realist?," *International Security* 24 (Fall 1999): 5–55.

Mazarr, Michael J. *Global Trends 2005.* New York: St. Martin's, 1999.

Ramonet, Ignacio. *Geopolitics of Chaos.* New York: Algrera, 2000.

Waltz, Kenneth N. "Globalization and Governance." *PS: Political Science and Politics* 32 (December 1999): 693–700.

Williams, Andrew. *Failed Imagination? New World Orders of the Twentieth Century.* Manchester, Eng.: Manchester University Press, 1998.

WHERE ON THE WORLD WIDE WEB?

International Futures Programme
http://www.oecd.org/sge/au/index.htm

The Organization for Economic Cooperation and Development (OECD) has designed a program to help decisionmakers in government and industry to deal with the formidable challenge of assessing the long-term trends that shape our global future. Scan the Web site and read about conferences and projects now under way. Do you think this is a good model for other organizations that strive to understand the changes occurring in the international system? What suggestions can you give?

World Citizen Web
http://www.worldcitizen.org/

As a student of international relations, you may ask yourself if there is a better way to organize international relations than the state system. The World Citizen Web site allows you to think about your world citizenship, asking how we, as sovereign world citizens, can collectively govern our world. The World Citizen Foundation believes that the Internet can help serve as a communication tool whereby the citizens of the world can vote on common global issues. Click on the spinning globe icon to enter the site. Click on the Tools Program to read about the World Syntegrity Project. Do you think this type of initiative is unrealistic or do you believe that one day soon we may be able to vote on world issues like we do national issues? Is it possible to form a world government?

World Future Society
http://www.wfs.org/

The last chapter of *World Politics* asks you to think about future global trends. To help with this task visit the World Future Society Web site. The World Future Society is a nonprofit educational and scientific organization whose main interest is how social and technological developments are shaping the future. Its Web site is a neutral clearinghouse for ideas about the future. Participate in the Big Ideas discussion forum. You can also read quotes offering wisdom on the new millennium. Feel creative? Submit your own quotes to be posted.

Glossary

absolute gains a condition in which all participants in exchanges become better off.
acid rain precipitation that has been made acidic through contact with sulfur dioxide and nitrogen oxides.
acquired immune deficiency syndrome (AIDS) an often fatal condition that can result from infection with the human immunodeficiency virus (HIV).
actor an individual, group, state, or organization that plays a major role in world politics.
adjudication a conflict resolution procedure in which a third party makes a binding decision through an institutional tribunal.
agenda setting the thesis that by their ability to identify and publicize issues, the mass media disseminate information and ideas which determine the problems that receive attention from governments and international organizations.
aid burden the ratio between aid and a donor's income as measured by gross national product.
alignments the acceptance by a neutral state threatened by foreign enemies of a special relationship short of formal alliance with a stronger power able to protect it from attack.
alliances coalitions that form when two or more states combine their military capabilities and promise to coordinate their policies to increase mutual security.
anarchy an absence of governmental authority, or an absence at the global level of a supranational authority to regulate relations between states.
antidumping duties duties imposed to offset the alleged selling of a product at below the cost to produce it.
antipersonnel landmines (APLs) explosives buried below the surface of the soil that detonate on contact with any person—soldier or citizen—stepping on them.
apartheid the former South African policy of racial separation.
appeasement a strategy of making concessions to an aggressor state without retaliation in the hope that, satisfied, it will not make additional claims on the territory of its neighbors.
arbitrage the selling of one currency (or product) and purchase of another to make a profit on the changing exchange rates; traders ("arbitragers") help to keep states' currencies in balance through their speculative efforts to buy large quantities of devalued currencies and sell them in countries where they are valued higher.
arbitration a conflict resolution procedure in which a third party makes a binding decision through an ad hoc forum.
armed conflict combat between the military forces of two or more states or groups.
arms control multilateral or bilateral agreements to contain arms races by setting limits on the number and types of weapons states are permitted.
arms control regimes rules, norms, and procedures accepted by the parties to treaties to prohibit the production, deployment, sale, or use of particular categories of weapons.
arms race the buildup of weapons and armed forces by two or more states that threaten each other, with the competition driven by the conviction that gaining a lead is necessary for security.
Asian Tigers the four Asian NIEs (Hong Kong, South Korea, Singapore, and Taiwan) that experienced far greater rates of economic growth during the 1980s than the more advanced industrial societies of the Global North; Hong Kong is now a part of China.
asylum the provision of sanctuary to safeguard refugees escaping from the threat of persecution in the country where they hold citizenship.
atrocities brutal and savage acts against targeted citizen groups or prisoners of war, defined as illegal under international law.
autocratic rule a system of authoritarian or totalitarian government where unlimited power is concentrated in a single ruler.
balance of payments a summary statement of a state's financial transactions with the rest of the world, including such items as foreign aid transfers and the income of citizens employed abroad who send their paychecks home.
balance of power the theory that peace and stability are most likely to be maintained when military power is distributed so that no single power or bloc can dominate the others.
balance of terror a concept used to describe situations of mutual nuclear deterrence.
balance of trade a state's net trade surplus or deficit, based on the difference in the value of its imports and exports.
balancer a role played by an influential global or regional great power that gives its support to the weaker side of a rivalry to ensure that the balance of power is preserved so that the stronger state does not achieve preponderance.
bandwagon the tendency for weak states to seek alliance with the strongest power, irrespective of that power's ideology or form of government, in order to increase security.
bargaining negotiation by states to try to settle their disputes without actually resorting to military force.
barter the exchange of one good for another rather than the use of currency to buy and sell items.

basic human needs adequate food intake (in terms of calories, proteins, and vitamins), safe drinking water, sufficient clothing and shelter, literacy, sanitation, health care, employment, and dignity.

beggar-thy-neighbor policies efforts to promote domestic welfare by promoting trade surpluses that can be realized only at the expense of other countries.

behavioralism an approach to the study of international relations that emphasizes the application of scientific methods.

behavioral scientists scholars who build theories of international relations through the application of the methods of modern social science.

bilateral relationships between two states.

bilateral agreements treaties negotiated between two states to ensure cooperation in some issue-area such as arms control.

biodiversity the variety of life on earth.

bipolar an international system with two dominant power centers.

bipolarity the division of the balance of power into two coalitions headed by rival military powers, each seeking to contain the other's expansion.

bipolarization the clustering of smaller states in alliances around two dominant power centers.

bipolycentrism the existence of military bipolarity between two rival hegemons, coupled with multiple political centers of independent foreign policy decisions.

bounded rationality the concept that decisionmakers' capacity to choose the best option is often constrained by many human and organizational obstacles.

boycotts concerted efforts, often organized internationally, to prevent relations such as trade with a state in order to express disapproval or to coerce acceptance of certain conditions.

brinkmanship the threat of escalation in a confrontation to compel submission, including the use of nuclear weapons.

bureaucracies the agencies, regulatory commissions, and departments that conduct the functions of a central government.

bureaucratic politics model an interpretation of policy making that stresses the bargaining and compromises among the contending governmental organizations that exert influence on the foreign policy choices of political leaders.

capital mobility hypothesis the proposition that MNCs' movement of investment capital has led to the globalization of finance.

carrying capacity the maximum biomass that can be supported by a given territory.

cartel an organization of the producers of a commodity that seeks to regulate the pricing and production of that commodity to increase revenue.

Carter Doctrine President Jimmy Carter's declaration of U.S. willingness to use military force to protect its interests in the Persian Gulf.

caucuses informal groups that individuals in government join to promote their common interests.

chain reaction arms race cycle arms races propelled when states increase their military capabilities to offset the expected growth of their adversaries' capabilities, which prompts other states to increase their capabilities in self-defense—an interaction that produces an upward spiral in weaponry but reduces every state's security.

chaos theory the application of mathematical methods to identify underlying and episodically recurring patterns in rapidly changing and seemingly unconnected relationships (as many global phenomena appear) in order to better interpret complex reality.

civil war war between factions within the same state.

clash of civilizations political scientist Samuel Huntington's controversial thesis that in the twenty-first century the globe's major civilizations will conflict with one another, leading to anarchy and warfare similar to that resulting from conflicts between states over the past five hundred years.

classical liberal economic theory a body of thought based on Adam Smith's ideas about the forces of supply and demand in the marketplace, emphasizing the benefits of minimal government regulation of the economy and trade.

Clinton Doctrine the Clinton administration's policy of active engagement in world affairs, pledging the United States to seek the enlargement of the peaceful liberal community of democratic states.

Club of Rome a private group that has popularized a neo-Malthusian interpretation of the limits to growth.

coercive diplomacy the use of threats or limited armed force to persuade an adversary to alter its foreign and/or domestic policies.

cognitive dissonance the general psychological tendency to deny discrepancies between one's preexisting beliefs (cognitions) and new information.

Cold War the forty-two-year rivalry between the United States and the Soviet Union, as well as their competing coalitions, which sought to contain each other's expansion through an arms race, and win worldwide predominance for capitalism (U.S.) or communism (USSR).

collective goods goods such as safe drinking water from which everyone benefits.

collective security a security regime created by the great powers that sets rules for keeping peace, guided by the principle that an act of aggression by any state will be met by a collective response from the rest.

colonialism the rule of a region by an external sovereign power.

commercial domino theory the notion that under conditions of globalization the depletion of one country's currency reserves panics investors worldwide and, like a contagious disease, spreads in a chain reaction to other countries which later witness the decline of their own currency reserves as the flight of capital also reduces the value of their currency, so that the world economy slumps through "financial contagion."

commercial liberalism an economic theory advocating free markets and the removal of barriers to the flow of trade and capital as a locomotive for prosperity.

commitment negotiator's promise during bargaining, designed to change the target's expectations about the negotiator's future behavior.

Common Foreign and Security Policy (CFSP) the agreement reached by the European Union defining the goals in foreign and defense policy the EU pledges to jointly pursue.

common market a form of economic integration in which restrictions on the free movement of commodities, capital, and labor among member states are abolished and a common external tariff is established.

common security a concept advocating replacing an anarchical system of states competing with one another for their own national security with collective security to promote the security of all states.

communism an ideology postulating that if society is organized so that every person produces according to his or her ability and consumes according to his or her needs, a community without class distinctions will emerge and sovereign states will no longer be needed.

communist theory of imperialism the Marxist-Leninist economic interpretation of imperial wars of conquest as driven by capitalism's need for foreign markets to generate capital.

comparative advantage a concept in liberal economics that a state will benefit if it specializes in those goods it produces comparatively cheaply and purchases through trade goods that it can only produce at a higher cost.

compellence the use of nuclear weapons as instruments of coercive diplomacy to make adversaries behave against their preferences.

complex interdependence a theory stressing the complex ways in which the growing ties among transnational actors make them vulnerable to each other's actions and sensitive to each other's needs.

concert a cooperative agreement among great powers to manage jointly the international system.

Concert of Europe a system of great-power conference diplomacy organized in Europe after the Napoleonic Wars.

conciliation a conflict resolution procedure in which a third party assists both negotiating sides in a dispute without proposing a solution.

conflict discord, often arising in international relations over perceived incompatibilities of interest.

consensus decision making in IGOs, voting by voice without a record of individual members' formal positions in order to reach agreement without generating criticism from opponents within the members' domestic systems.

constitutional democracy government processes that allow people or their elected representatives to exercise power and influence the state's policies.

constructivism a scholarly approach to inquiry emphasizing the importance of agents (people and groups) and the shared meanings they construct to define their identities, interests, and institutions—understandings that influence their international behavior.

containment a term coined by U.S. policymaker George F. Kennan for deterring the USSR's expansionist aims by counterpressures, which has since become a general term used by strategists to describe the methods used to prevent an expanding great power from flexing its military muscles.

Convention on Biodiversity a 1993 treaty obligating ratifying states to adhere to the agreement's rules for sharing the profits of biotechnological research discoveries and for protecting endangered species and habitats.

conventional deterrence dissuading an adversary from attacking by threatening retaliation with nonnuclear weapons.

Conventional Forces in Europe (CFE) Treaty a 1992 treaty that set ceilings on five categories of conventional arms.

conventional war armed conflicts waged with nonnuclear naval, air, and ground weapons.

cornucopians optimists who question limits-to-growth analyses and contend that markets effectively maintain a balance between population, resources, and the environment.

Council of Europe an organization founded in 1949, whose members now include forty states, for the purpose of promoting unity and preserving Europe's cultural heritage.

counterfactual reasoning thought experiments to consider the consequences that probably would have resulted had something not happened that actually did, such as speculating, "What if John F. Kennedy had not been assassinated?"

counterforce targeting strategy a doctrine based on targeting strategic nuclear weapons on particular military capabilities of an enemy's armed forces and arsenals.

countervailing duties tariffs imposed by a government to offset suspected subsidies provided by foreign governments to their producers.

countervalue targeting strategy a doctrine that targets weapons on the things an enemy most values, such as industrial and population centers.

countries in transition the remnant states of the former communist countries (Second World) in Central and Eastern Europe that are undertaking economic reforms to introduce capitalism.

covert operations secret activities undertaken by a state outside its borders through clandestine means to achieve specific political or military goals with respect to another state.

crimes against humanity a category of activities, made illegal at the Nuremberg war crime trials, condemning states that abuse the human rights of their citizens.

crisis a situation that threatens high-priority goals, restricts the time available for response, and surprises decisionmakers.

crisis decisions choices made in highly threatening and potentially grave situations, involving elements of surprise and restricted response time, by the highest level of authoritative decisionmakers.

Cuban missile crisis the showdown in October 1962 between the United States and the Soviet Union over the deployment of Soviet missiles in Cuba.

cultural conditioning the impact of national traditions and revered moral principles on international behavior, under the assumption that culture affects decision making about issues such as the acceptability of aggression.

cultural domains groups that share a common intellectual heritage and values and do not recognize national borders when they define their identities and loyalties.

current history approach a view of the purpose of inquiry which maintains that, to understand international relations, scholars should focus on the description of recent events, not theoretical explanations of their causes.

customs union a market in which sovereign states agree to remove taxes on goods exported across the borders of the union's members.

cyberspace metaphorical term used to describe the global electronic web of people, ideas, and interactions on the Internet, which is unencumbered by the borders of the geopolitical world.

cycles successions of periodically recurring events or phenomena.

debtor's cartel a proposal that Global South debtor states confront the creditor states with a coalition when pressing for a solution to the debt crisis.

decolonization the political process of freeing colonial peoples from their dependent status.

deconstruction postmodern theory that the complexity of the world system renders precise description impossible, and that the purpose of scholarship is to understand actors' hidden motives by deconstructing their textual statements.

de facto recognition a government's acknowledgment of the factual existence of another state or government short of full recognition of it as a sovereign member of the global community.

defense conversion the process of shifting resources from the production of military-related goods to civilian products.

deforestation the destruction of forests.

de jure recognition a government's formal, legal recognition of the sovereign existence of another government or state as a member of the community of states.

demilitarization the complete elimination of the military power or potential of a state.

democracy a government process of making foreign and domestic policy, which allows the mass public to exercise power and influence over the officials elected to formulate the state's policies.

democratic peace the liberal theory that, because democratic states do not fight each other, the diffusion of democratic governance throughout the world will reduce the probability of war.

demographic transition an explanation of population changes over time that highlights the causes of declines in birth and death rates so that a country's population achieves a stable level.

demography the study of population changes, their sources, and their impact.

dependency a condition of retarded economic growth believed to result from the Global South's subordination and structural exploitation by the Global North's advanced capitalistic market economies, making the Global South especially vulnerable to cycles of expansion and contraction.

dependency theory a perspective that perceives the international economic system as responsible for the less developed Global South countries' dependence on, and exploitation by, the wealthy Global North countries.

dependent development the industrialization of peripheral areas within the confines of the dominance-dependence relationship between Global North and Global South.

desertification the creation of deserts due to soil erosion, overfarming, and deforestation, which converts cropland to nonproductive, arid sand.

détente in general, a strategy of seeking to relax tensions between adversaries.

deterrence a preventive strategy designed to dissuade an adversary from doing what it would otherwise prefer to do.

developed countries a category used by the World Bank to designate those countries with a GNP per capita (in 1998) above $785 annually.

developing countries a category used by the World bank to designate those countries with a GNP per capita (in 1998) equal to or below $785 annually.

development the processes through which a country increases its capacity to meet its citizens' basic human needs and raise their standard of living.

devolution states' granting of political power to minority ethnopolitical national groups and indigenous people in particular national regions under the expectation that greater autonomy will curtail their quest for independence as a new state.

diaspora a dispersed emigrant community residing outside its homeland but preserving its identification with its country of origin.

digital world economy a system based largely on globalized electronic debt and credit systems.

diplomatic immunity the legal doctrine that gives ambassadors immunity from the domestic laws of the countries where their embassies are located.

diplomatic recognition the formal legal acceptance of a state's official status as a sovereign, independent country.

disarmament the reduction or elimination of weapons either by unilateral choice or through agreements between or among rival states.

displaced people people involuntarily uprooted from their homes but still living in their own countries.

diversionary theory of war the contention that leaders initiate conflict abroad as a way of increasing national cohesion at home by diverting national public opinion away from controversial domestic issues.

divine right of kings the realist doctrine that because kings are sovereign they have the right to rule their subjects authoritatively and are not accountable to the public because their rule is ordained by God.

doctrine the guidelines a state specifies to identify the conditions under which it will use military power and armed force for political purposes abroad.

domino theory a cold War metaphor which predicted that if one state fell to communism, its neighbors would also fall in a chain reaction, like a row of dominoes.

dualism the existence in many Global South less-developed countries of a rural, impoverished, and neglected sector of society alongside an urban, developing, or modernizing sector, with little interaction between the two.

dual-use production technologies technologies that have both commercial and military uses.

Earth Summit an international meeting held in 1992 in Rio de Janeiro, Brazil, aimed at creating a program of action to address a broad range of environmental and developmental issues.

ecological overshoot the exploitation of natural resources that exceeds the earth's carrying capacity.

ecological transition a process in situations of high population growth where human demands come to exceed sustainable yield.

economic sanctions government actions aimed at inflicting deprivation on a target state through the limitation or termination of economic relations.

ecopolitics how political actors influence perceptions of, and policy responses to, their environments.

electronic cash the instantaneous transfer of money for transnational purchases by computers and electronic telecommunications that, unregulated, can lead to global financial crises, corruption, and crime because these exchanges cannot be easily detected by traditional accounting methods.

elitism the argument that because a power elite really controls democratic governments for its own interests, ordinary citizens are given participation without power, involvement without influence.

embargo a government order prohibiting commerce with a target state.

emerging markets the Global South states whose domestic political economies have rapidly grown as a result of liberal economic reforms and foreign investment.

enclosure movement the claiming of common properties by states or private interests.

end of history the thesis that economic and political liberalism have triumphed as an accepted philosophy throughout the world, ending the seemingly timeless contest between market democracies and centrally planned governance.

enduring rivalries prolonged competition between great powers or other pairs of countries whose perpetual conflicting interests often lead to war.

engagement and enlargement strategy the Clinton administration's strategy that commits U.S. power to help manage conflicts throughout the world and to enlarge the community of liberal democracies.

Engels's law a principle espoused by Friedrich Engels that poorer families spend a greater percentage of their budget on food than do higher income families.

entente an agreement between states to work together in a close consultative relationship on security issues.

environmental security a concept recognizing that environmental threats to global life systems are as important as the threat of armed conflicts.

epistemic community a group of experts from around the world who, based on their knowledge, develop a shared understanding of a problem on the global agenda and a set of preferences for responding to it.

epistemology the philosophical examination of how knowledge is acquired and the analytic principles governing the study of phenomena.

ethics the criteria by which right and wrong behavior and motives are distinguished.

ethnic cleansing the extermination of an ethnic minority group by a state, in violation of international law since the mid-1990s, before which governments could treat the people within their territory as they wished.

ethnic group a group of people of the same nationality who share a common culture, set of ancestors, or language.

ethnic nationalism devotion to a cultural, ethnic, or linguistic community within an existing state.

ethnicity perceptions of likeness among members of a particular racial or linguistic grouping leading them to act prejudicially toward outsiders in other kinship or cultural groups.

ethnic warfare violence resulting from wars between two or more ethnic groups or from state-sponsored violence to terrorize or destroy an ethnic minority.

ethnocentrism a propensity to see one's nationality or state as the center of the world and therefore special, with the result that the values and perspectives of other groups are misunderstood and ridiculed.

ethnopolitical groups people whose identity is primarily defined by their sense of sharing a common ancestral nationality, language, cultural heritage, and kinship ties.

ethologists scholars who study animals in order to understand human behavior.

Euro-Atlantic Partnership Council (EAPC) a coordinating institution within NATO created in 1998 to manage the common political, military, financial, and security issues confronting Europe.

European Commission the executive organ administratively responsible for the European Union.

European Free Trade Association (EFTA) organization created in 1960 as a counterpoint to the European Economic Community.

European Political Cooperation (EPC) the ongoing effort of European Union members to devise a common position on foreign policy issues through regular meetings among EU foreign ministers.

European Union (EU) a regional organization created by the merger of the European Coal and Steel Community, the European Atomic Energy Community, and the European Economic Community; known as the European Community before November 1993.

exchange rate the rate at which one state's currency is exchanged for another state's currency in the global marketplace.

export-led industrialization a strategy that involves developing domestic export industries capable of competing in overseas markets.

export quotas a barrier to free trade imposed pursuant to negotiated agreements between producers and consumers.

extended deterrence strategies that seek to deter an adversary from attacking a state's allies.

externalities the side effects produced by economic activities, especially costs such as pollution.

extraterritoriality the legal doctrine that allows a state to maintain jurisdiction over its embassies in other states without interference from the host state.

extreme militant religious movements politically active organizations based on strong religious convictions, whose members are fanatically devoted to the global promotion of their religious beliefs.

failed states countries whose governments have so mismanaged policy that they have lost the loyalty of their citizens who, in rebellion, seek independence to create their own state.

failing states those governments that are in danger of losing legitimacy in the eyes of their citizens, who are revolting against corruption and administrative failure, and in the process tearing the country into separate political parts.

fascism a far-right ideology that promotes extreme nationalism and the establishment of an authoritarian society built around a single party with dictatorial leadership.

fast-track negotiating authority a concession by the U.S. Congress permitting the president to negotiate reciprocal tariff-reduction agreements with other countries, which, when granted, enables the United States to reach bilateral trade treaties more easily.

feminist theory a body of scholarship emerging from the social feminist movement to promote the political equality of women with men, critiquing sexual biases and challenging gender roles that encourage female subordination and warfare.

fertility rate the average number of children born to a woman (or group of women) during her lifetime.

firebreak the psychological barrier between conventional and nuclear war.

First World the relatively wealthy countries of the Global North that share a commitment to varying forms of democratic political institutions and developed market economies, including the United States, Japan, Canada, Australia, New Zealand, Israel, Malta, South Africa, and the countries of Western Europe.

fixed exchange rates a system under which states establish the parity of their currencies and commit to keeping fluctuations in their exchange rates within narrow limits.

floating exchange rates a system where market forces rather than government intervention determine the value of currencies.

food ladder a conceptualization based on the biological food chain, which observes that as personal income increases individuals move up the ladder, consuming grains indirectly as meat rather than directly.

food security access by all people at all times to enough food for an active, healthy life.

foreign aid economic assistance in the form of loans and grants provided by a donor to a recipient country for a variety of purposes.

foreign direct investment (FDI) an investment in a country involving a long-term relationship and control of an enterprise by non-residents and including equity capital, reinvestment of earnings, other long-term capital, and short-term capital as shown in the balance of payments.

foreign policy the decisions governing authorities make to realize international goals.

Fourth Way a strategy proposed for development in the Global South emphasizing government subsidies to help citizens contribute to growth within a free-trade market economy.

Fourth World a term used to recognize the native national groups residing in many so-called united states who, although often minorities, occupied the state's territory first and refuse to accept domination, seeking instead to create a new state for themselves by splitting existing states or to gain greater political freedom to govern themselves.

free riders those who enjoy the benefits of collective goods but pay little or nothing for their preservation and promotion.

Free Trade Area of the Americas (FTAA) a set of rules to promote free trade among thirty-four democracies in North and South America.

functionalism a bottom-up approach to fostering the political integration of states through transnational organizations that emphasizes pooling sovereignty.

gender empowerment the attempt to give women the same power as men within a society.

gender empowerment index the UN Development Program's attempt to measure the extent of gender equality across the globe's countries, based on estimates of women's relative economic income, high-paying positions, and access to professional and parliamentary positions.

gender inequalities differences between men and women in opportunity and reward that are determined by the values that guide states' foreign and domestic policies.

General Agreement on Tariffs and Trade (GATT) an international organization affiliated with the United Nations that promotes international trade and tariff reductions.

genetic engineering research geared to discover seeds for new types of plant and human life for sale and use as substitutes for those produced naturally.

genocide the deliberate extermination of an ethnic or minority group.

geo-economics the relationship between geography and the economic conditions and behavior of states that define their levels of production, trade, and consumption of goods and services.

geopolitics the relationship between geography and politics and their consequences for states' national interests and relative power.

global agenda the primary issues, problems, and controversies on which states and humanity concentrate their attention and to which they allocate resources.

global commons the entire environment considered to be the common heritage and property of the human race on the planet Earth, including the ocean floor under international waters, the Antarctic, and the celestial bodies in outer space.

Global Environment Facility (GEF) an instrument for resource transfers from Global North to Global South, as spelled out in the biodiversity convention.

globalization the integration of states, through increasing contact, communication, and trade, to create a holistic, single global system in which the process of change increasingly binds people together in a common fate.

globalization of finance the increasing transnationalization of financial markets.

global level of analysis an analytical approach to world politics that emphasizes the impact of worldwide conditions on the behavior of states, IGOs, NGOs, and other international actors.

global migration crisis the growing number of people moving from their home country to another country that has created a crisis because the sheer volume exceeds the ability of host countries to absorb the foreign migrants.

Global North a term used to refer to the world's wealthy, industrialized countries located primarily in the Northern Hemisphere.

Global South a term now often used instead of "Third World" to designate the less-developed countries located primarily in the Southern Hemisphere.

global system a system that international law still defines as composed primarily of states consisting of nationality groups who perceive themselves as unified by language, culture, or ethnic identity

global village popular image used to describe the growth of awareness that all people share a common fate, stemming from a cosmopolitan perspective that the world is an integrated and interdependent whole.

global warming the gradual rise in the average temperature throughout the globe, a suspected consequence of greenhouse gases trapping heat remitted from earth that would otherwise escape into outer space.

good offices the third-party offering of a location for discussions among disputants.

great powers the most powerful countries, militarily and economically, in the global system.

greenhouse effect the phenomenon producing planetary warming when gases released by burning fossil fuels act as a blanket in the atmosphere, thereby increasing temperatures.

green revolution the introduction of new high-yield grains to Global South countries.

gross national product (GNP) and gross domestic product (GDP) measures of the production of goods and services within a given time period, which differ only in whether nationality (GNP) or residency (GDP) is used to delimit the geographic scope of production. GNP measures production by a state's citizens or companies, regardless of where the production occurs. GDP measures production occurring within the territory of a state, regardless of the national identity of the producers.

Group of Seven (G-7)/Group of Eight (G-8) a group of the major most-advanced industrialized democracies, composed of the United States, Britain, France, Japan, Germany, Canada, and Italy, that meets in regular economic summit conferences; now known as the G-8 with the addition of Russia.

Group of 77 (G-77) a coalition of the world's poor countries formed during the 1964 United Nations Conference on Trade and Development (UNCTAD) in Geneva. Originally composed of seventy-seven states, the coalition now numbers over one hundred twenty developing countries and continues to press for concessions from the wealthy nations.

groupthink the propensity for members of a group to accept and agree with the group's prevailing attitudes, rather than speaking out for what they believe.

gunboat diplomacy a show of naval military force by a state to intimidate an enemy for the purpose of altering its behavior.

guns versus growth the trade-off that exists between military spending and economic development, and the controversy over the extent to which spending on weapons reduces the rate of growth of a state's economy.

hard power a state's ability to exercise influence in world politics because of its possession of tangible resources such as military and economic strength.

Heavily Indebted Poor Countries (HIPCs) the subset of countries identified by the World Bank's Debtor Reporting System whose ratio of government debt to gross national product is so substantial that they cannot meet their debt payment obligations without experiencing political instability and economic collapse.

hegemon a single dominant military and economic state that uses its unrivaled power to create and enforce rules aimed at preserving the existing world order with itself at the apex and its own superpower position in that order.

hegemonic stability theory the argument that a dominant state is necessary to enforce international cooperation, maintain international rules and regimes, and keep the peace.

hegemony the ability of one state to dominate the rules and arrangements governing international economics and politics.

high politics geostrategic issues of national and international security that pertain to matters of war and peace.

history-making individuals model an interpretation of foreign policy behavior that equates states' actions with the preferences and initiatives of the highest government officials.

horizontal nuclear proliferation an increase in the number of states that possess nuclear weapons.

human development the extent to which humans' ability to develop to their individual potential is protected, such that they are provided with sufficient schooling, income, and opportunity to live a full life.

human development index (HDI) an index that uses life expectancy, literacy, average number of years of schooling, and income to assess a country's performance in providing for its people's welfare and security.

human immunodeficiency virus (HIV) a virus that can progress to acquired immune deficiency syndrome (AIDS).

humanitarian intervention the use of peacekeeping troops by foreign states or international organizations to protect endangered people from gross violations of their human rights and from mass murder.

human rights the political rights and civil liberties recognized by the international community as inalienable and valid for individuals in all countries by virtue of their humanity.

human security a concept that refers to the degree to which the welfare of individuals is protected and advanced, in contrast to national security which puts the interests of states first.

idealists people inspired by the liberal theoretical tradition who believe that the pursuit of ideals like world peace can change the world by reducing the disorder often exhibited in world politics.

ideology a set of core philosophical principles that a group of leaders and citizens collectively hold about politics, the interests of political actors, and the ways people ought to ethically behave.

imperialism intentional imposition of one state's power over another, traditionally through territorial conquest but more recently through economic domination, denying the victim population's freedom to have a voice in the conquering regime's decisions.

imperial overstretch Paul Kennedy's thesis that hegemons decline becuase they make costly global commitments in excess of their ability to fulfill them.

import quotas nontariff barriers to free trade that involve limits on the quantity of particular products that can be imported.

import-substitution industrialization a strategy for economic growth that encourages domestic entrepreneurs to manufacture products traditionally imported from abroad.

indigenous peoples the native ethnic and cultural inhabitant populations within countries ruled by a government controlled by others, referred to as the "Fourth World."

individual level of analysis an analytical approach to the study of world politics that emphasizes the psychological and perceptual origins of the foreign policy behaviors of international actors, with special attention to leaders.

infant industry a newly established industry that is not yet strong enough to compete effectively in the global marketplace.

information warfare (IW)/infowar tactics attacks on an adversary's telecommunications and computer networks to penetrate and degradate an enemy whose defense capabilities depend heavily on these technological systems.

instrumental rationality a conceptualization of rationality that emphasizes the tendency of decisionmakers to compare options with one another and select the one which has the best chance of success.

integration the processes and activities by which the populations of two or more states or groups transfer their loyalties to a merged political and economic unit.

interdependence a situation arising when the behavior of international actors greatly affects others with whom they have contact, so that the parties to the exchange become mutually sensitive and vulnerable to the others' actions.

interethnic competition a struggle for supremacy within a geographic area between two or more ethnic groups.

intergovernmental organizations (IGOs) institutions created and joined by states' governments, which give them authority to make collective decisions to manage particular problem(s) on the global agenda.

Intermediate-range Nuclear Forces (INF) agreement the 1987 disarmament agreement between the United States and the Soviet Union to remove intermediate-range nuclear forces from Europe.

intermestic those issues confronting a state that are simultaneously international and domestic.

internally displaced people people who live in a refugee-like situation in their own countries.

International Criminal Court a court established by the United Nations for indicting and administering justice to people committing war crimes.

international liquidity reserve assets used to settle international accounts.

International Monetary Fund (IMF) a specialized agency of the United Nations that seeks to maintain monetary stability, assist member states in funding balance-of-payment deficits, and make long-term loans to its poorer members.

international monetary system the set of procedures used to calculate the value of foreign currencies and credits when capital is transferred across borders through trade, investments, and loans.

international organized crime (IOC) organized crime syndicates that use technology to cooperatively network with each other throughout the world.

international political economy the study of the intersection of politics and economics that illuminates the reasons why changes occur in the distribution of states' wealth and power.

international political system a pattern of interactions among political actors in international relations who have sufficient regular contact to make the behavior of each a central part of the calculations of the others.

international regime the set of rules, norms, and decision-making procedures that coordinates state behavior within a given issue area.

international terrorism the use of terrorism against targets in other countries.

interspecific aggression killing members of species other than one's own, such as lions attacking zebras for food.

intraspecific aggression killing members of one's own species, as humans sometimes do when they kill other human beings.

irredentism efforts by an ethnonational or religious group to regain control of territory by force so that existing state boundaries will no longer separate the group.

isolationism a policy of withdrawing from active participation with other actors in world affairs and instead concentrating state efforts on managing internal affairs.

just war the theory originating in the Middle Ages that identifies the conditions under which it is morally permissible, or "just," for a state to go to war and the methods by which a just war might be fought.

just war doctrine a set of ethical principles and legal rules that pertains to the moral considerations under which war may be undertaken and how it should be fought once it begins.

Kellogg-Briand Pact (Pact of Paris) a multilateral treaty negotiated in 1928 that outlawed war as a method for settling interstate conflicts.

laissez-faire economics from a French phrase (meaning literally "let do") that Adam Smith and other commercial liberals in the eighteenth century used to describe the advantages of the philosophical principle of free markets with little governmental regulation of the marketplace.

League of Nations mandate system the placement of colonies previously held by the Central Powers of World War I under the administration of certain Allied nations; implicit in the system was the idea that colonies were a trust rather than a territory to be exploited.

least developed of the less developed countries (LLDCs) the most impoverished members of the Third World in the Global South.

levels of analysis alternative perspectives on world politics that may focus on the personal characteristics of individual decisionmakers, the attributes of states, or the structure of the global system.

liberalism a paradigm predicated on the hope that the application of reason and universal ethics to international relations can lead to a more orderly, just, and cooperative world, and that international anarchy and war can be policed by institutional reforms that empower organizations and international laws for global governance.

liberal institutionalism the so-called neoliberal theory in international relations that advocates creating global institutions to promote peace and security among states.

Liberal International Economic Order (LIEO) the set of regimes, created after World War II, designed to promote monetary stability and reduce barriers to the free flow of trade and capital.

limited war the restrained use of armed force, short of full-scale warfare, to obtain limited objectives.

limits-to-growth proposition the theory that the earth's capacity to support life has natural limits and that if important resources such as fresh water are depleted, many will perish.

linkage strategy a set of assertions that claims leaders should take into account another country's overall behavior when deciding whether to reach agreement on any one specific issue.

Lomé Convention the series of agreements in 1975, inspired by the NIEO movement linking forty-six developing countries to Europe, that helps the African, Caribbean, and Pacific (ACP) countries stabilize their export earnings and provides them financial and technical assistance.

long-cycle theory an interpretation of world history that focuses on repeating patterns of interstate behavior, such as the outbreak of systemwide general wars at regular intervals, after long periods during which other patterns (global peace) were dominant.

long peaces long-lasting periods of great-power peace.

low-intensity conflict (LIC) fighting that falls below the threshold of full-scale military combat between modern armies.

low politics the category of global issues related to the economic, social, demographic, and environmental aspects of relations between governments and people.

machtpolitik the German realist philosophy in statecraft that sees the expansion of state power and territory by use of armed force as a legitimate goal.

macroeconomic the study of economic indicators such as GDP, the money supply, and the balance of trade that governments monitor to measure changes in the national economy.

Marxism-Leninism communist theory as derived from the writings of Karl Marx, V. I. Lenin, and their successors, which criticizes capitalism as a cause of class struggle, the exploitation of workers, colonialism, and war.

massive retaliation the strategic posture of the United States during the Eisenhower administration, which advocated the use of nuclear weapons to contain communism and Soviet expansionism.

mediation a conflict resolution procedure in which a third party offers a nonbinding solution to the disputants.

mercantilism a government trade strategy for accumulating state wealth and power by encouraging exports and discouraging imports.

migration movement by people from one place of abode to another.

militarized disputes confrontations short of war, characterized by the reciprocated threat, deployment, mobilization, or use of force.

military-industrial complex the term coined by U.S. President Eisenhower to describe the coalition among arms manufacturers, military bureaucracies, and top government officials that promotes unnecessary defense expenditures for their own profit and power.

military intervention overt or covert use of force by one or more countries that cross the borders of another country in order to affect the target country's government and policies.

military necessity the legal doctrine asserting that the violation of the rules of warfare may be excused during periods of extreme emergency.

military-technical revolution (MTR) the new generation of weapons systems created by the application of microprocessing and precision-guided technologies to fight wars with a minimum of civilian causalities.

mirror images the tendency of states and people in competitive interaction to perceive each other similarly—to see their enemy the same way the adversary perceives its enemy.

missile technology control regime (MTCR) an informal arrangement among the most advanced suppliers of missile-related equipment to control the export of ballistic and cruise missiles and associated technologies.

modernization a view of development popular in the Global North's liberal democracies which argues that wealth is created through efficient production, free enterprise, and free trade and that countries' relative ability to create wealth depends on technological innovation and education.

monetary policy the decisions made by states' central banks to regulate the economy and control inflation with policies such as changing the money supply and interest rates.

monetary system a stable and predictable method for calculating the value of sales and foreign investments.

money supply the total amount of currency in circulation in a state, calculated to include demand deposits, such as checking accounts, in commercial banks and time deposits, such as savings accounts and bonds, in savings banks.

morals principles or rules for behavior that differentiate right from wrong.

most-favored-nation (MFN) principle tariff preferences granted to one nation must be granted to all others exporting the same product.

muddling through the tendency for leaders to make foreign policy decisions that produce incremental policy changes through trial-and-error adjustments.

multilateral relationships among more than two states or other international actors for the purpose of collective action.

multilateral agreements treaties to manage common problems, such as arms control or global warming, negotiated among more than two global actors, such as states.

multinational corporations (MNCs) business enterprises headquartered in one state that invest and operate extensively in other states.

multiple advocacy the concept that better and more rational choices are made when decisions are reached in a group context, which allows advocates of differing alternatives to be heard so that the feasibility of rival options receives critical evaluation.

multiple independently targetable reentry vehicle (MIRV) a technological innovation permitting many warheads to be delivered from a single missile.

multipolar an international system with more than two dominant power centers.

multipolarity a global distribution of power in which three or more great powers or poles attain a disproportionate position of strength relative to all others, but with each power or pole approximately equal to the others.

mutual assured destruction (MAD) a system of mutual deterrence in which both sides possess the ability to survive a first strike and launch a devastating retaliatory attack.

nation a collection of people who, on the basis of ethnic, linguistic, or cultural affinity, perceive themselves to be members of the same group.

national character the collective characteristics ascribed to the dominant nationality group within a state.

national interest the goals that states pursue to maximize what is selfishly best for themselves.

nationalism a mindset glorifying a particular state and the nationality group living in it that sees the state's national interests as a supreme value.

national security a country's psychological freedom from fears that the state will be unable to resist threats to its survival and national values emanating from abroad or at home.

nature versus nurture the controversy over whether human behavior is caused by humans' biological traits or by the cultural conditions that influence human behavior.

negotiation the process and art of discussing and debating issues when a conflict arises, in order for the disputing parties to reach a mutually satisfactory compromise agreement to resolve the issue.

neocolonialism (neoimperialism) the economic rather than military domination of foreign countries.

neofunctionalism the revised functional theory which explains that the IGOs states create to manage common problems provide benefits that exert new pressures for further political integration, the creation of additional IGOs, and the globalization of international relations in an expanding network of interdependence that reduces states' incentives to wage war.

neoliberal institutionalism the recent liberal theoretical effort to explain how peace and prosperity instead of war might be created through law, global governance, and liberal democracies' cooperation to engineer international change.

neoliberalism a perspective that accounts for the way international institutions promote global change, cooperation, peace, and prosperity through collective reform approaches.

neoliberal theory a philosophy which maintains that peaceful change with prosperity can be encouraged through cooperation in institutions that knit the states and peoples of the world together into a true global community.

neo-Malthusians pessimists who warn of the global ecopolitical implications of uncontrolled growth.

neomercantilism a state trade policy that seeks to maintain a balance-of-trade surplus by reducing imports, stimulating domestic production, and promoting exports.

neonationalism the expression of communal or ethnic aspirations of a dissatisfied nationality group within a given state.

neorealism a theoretical, structural account of states' behavior that explains it as determined by differences in their relative power instead of by other factors, such as their values, types of government, or domestic circumstances.

neorealist theory the new realist theory that the behavior of competitive states is shaped by changes in the distribution of global power more than by changes in their domestic systems.

neotraditional realism a body of recent realist theorizing that departs from neorealism by emphasizing the motives behind states' foreign policy more than global structure and that focuses on the internal influences on states' external behavior instead of the global determinants of states' foreign behavior.

neutrality the legal doctrine that provides rights and duties for states who remain nonaligned with adversaries during wartime.

New International Economic Order (NIEO) a policy resolution backed by the Global South to replace the U.S.-sponsored Liberal International Economic Order (LIEO) with an international economic regime more favorable to the interests of developing countries.

newly industrialized economies (NIEs) the most prosperous members of the Global South, which have become important exporters of manufactured goods as well as important markets for the major industrialized countries that export capital goods.

New World Information and Communication Order (NWICO) a new regime demanded by the Third World for covering the flow of information between North and South due to dissatisfaction with the media coverage provided by news agencies from the developed countries.

Nixon Doctrine the position taken by President Richard Nixon that U.S. allies should bear a greater share of the burden for their own defense.

no first use the doctrine adhering to the principle that a nuclear-weapon state would not use its strategic weapons in the event of an attack on it with conventional weapons by another state.

Nonaligned Movement (NAM) a group of more than one hundred newly independent, mostly less-developed states that joined together as a group of neutrals to avoid entanglement with the superpowers' competing alliances and to advance the Global South's common interests in economic cooperation and growth.

nonaligned states countries that do not participate in military alliances with rival blocs because of a fear that formal alliance will lead to involvement in an unnecessary war.

nonalignment a foreign policy posture in which states do not participate in military alliances with competing great powers to avoid domination.

noncombatant immunity the legal principle that military force should not be used against innocent civilians.

nondiscrimination a principle for trade that proclaims that goods produced at home and abroad are to be treated the same for import and export agreements.

nongovernmental organizations (NGOs) transnational organizations of private citizens maintaining consultative status with the UN; they include professional associations, foundations, multinational corporations, or simply internationally active groups in different states joined together to work toward common interests.

nonintervention a fundamental international legal principle, now being challenged, that traditionally has defined as illegal interference by one state in the domestic affairs of another sovereign state.

nonlethal weapons the wide array of "soft-kill," low-intensity methods of incapacitating an enemy's people, vehicles, communications systems, or entire cities without killing either combatants or noncombatants.

nonproliferation a condition under which there are no arms races under way and, accordingly, weapons or technology do not spread to states that do not have them.

nonrecognition withholding official legal acceptance as a form of sanction against another established government recognized as an independent state by others.

nonstate actors all transnationally active groups other than states, such as organizations whose members are states (IGOs) and nongovernmental organizations (NGOs) whose members are individuals and private groups from more than one state.

nonstate nations national or ethnic groups struggling to obtain power and/or statehood.

nontariff barriers (NTBs) measures that discriminate against imports without direct tax levies and beyond the scope of international regulation.

North American Free Trade Agreement (NAFTA) an agreement that brings Mexico into the free-trade zone linking Canada and the United States.

North Atlantic Treaty Organization (NATO) a military alliance created in 1949 to deter a Soviet attack on Western Europe that now seeks to maintain peace and promote democracy.

Nth country problem the addition of new nuclear states.

nuclear deterrence dissuading an adversary from attacking by threatening retaliation with nuclear weapons.

nuclear freeze movement a popular revolt against the escalating strategic arms race in the 1980s that called for a suspension or freeze in building more nuclear warheads in the hopes that the threat of nuclear annihilation would be reduced.

Nuclear Nonproliferation Treaty (NPT) an international agreement that seeks to prevent horizontal proliferation by prohibiting nuclear weapons sales, acquisitions, or production.

nuclear utilization theory (NUTs) a body of strategic thought that claims deterrent threats would be more credible if nuclear weapons were made more usable.

nuclear winter the expected freeze that would occur in the Earth's climate from the fallout of smoke and dust in the event nuclear weapons are used, which would block out sunlight and destroy plant and animal life that survived the original blast.

official development assistance (ODA) grants or loans to countries from other countries, usually channeled through multilateral aid organizations, for the primary purpose of promoting economic development and welfare.

oil shocks the rapid increases in oil prices in the aftermath of Yom Kippur War, the revolution in Iran, and the invasion of Kuwait.

opportunity costs the concept in decision-making theories that when the opportunity arises to use resources, what is gained for one purpose is lost for other purposes, so that every choice entails the cost of some lost opportunity.

orderly market arrangements (OMAs) voluntary export restrictions that involve a government-to-government agreement and often specific rules of management.

Organization for Security and Cooperation in Europe (OSCE) a multilateral institution that led in the transformation of Europe from a system of counter-poised military alliances to one based on common principles for maintaining security in the post–Cold War world.

ozone layer the protective layer of the upper atmosphere over the earth's surface that shields the planet from the sun's harmful impact on living organisms on the planet.

pacifism a philosophy that rejects the right of people or states to kill, no matter what the provocation, and searches for nonviolent methods of resolving disputes, such as negotiation.

paradigm derived from the Greek *paradeigma,* meaning an example, a model, or an essential pattern; a paradigm structures thoughts about an area of inquiry.

Partnership for Peace (PfP) a plan proposed in 1993 by the United States that established limited military partnerships between NATO and the former Warsaw Pact countries.

pax atomica the notion that nuclear weapons have preserved peace.

peace building predominantly diplomatic and economic actions that strengthen and rebuild government infrastructure in order to avoid armed conflict.

peace dividend the global savings from arms expenditure reductions made possible by the end of highly hostile international rivalries such as the Cold War.

peace enforcement military actions undertaken to impose a peace settlement, truce, or agreement to surrender by a warring party, or to prevent the resumption of fighting by the participants in a past war.

peaceful coexistence in bitter interstate rivalries, the declaration that war will not be waged to settle the dispute, as illustrated by Soviet leader Nikita Khrushchev's 1956 doctrine that war between capitalist and communist states was not inevitable and that inter-bloc competition could be peaceful.

peacekeeping the efforts by third parties such as the UN to intervene in civil wars and/or interstate wars or to prevent hostilities between potential belligerents from escalating, so that by acting as a buffer a negotiated stttlement of the dispute can be reached.

peace making the process of diplomacy, mediation, negotiation, or other forms of peaceful ssettlement that arranges an end to a dispute, and resolves issues that led to conflict.

peace operations a general category encompassing both peacekeeping and peace enforcement operations undertaken to support diplomatic efforts to establish and maintain peace between disputants.

permanent world criminal court a standing international court to judge mass crimes such as genocide.

photovoltaic (PV) cells semiconductors that convert sunlight into electricity.

pluralism a model of the policy-making process that highlights the impact of competitive domestic groups in pressuring the government for policies responsive to their interests and needs.

polarity the degree to which power is concentrated among the major powers in the state system.

polarization the degree to which states cluster in alliances around the most powerful members of the state system.

policy agenda the changing list of problems or issues to which governments pay special attention at any given moment.

policy networks leaders and organized interests (such as lobbies) that form temporary alliances to influence a particular foreign policy decision.

political disintegration the fragmentation of a state into two or more separate sovereign states.

political economy a field of study that focuses on the intersection of politics and economics in international relations.

political efficacy a leader's belief in his or her power to control events politically.

political integration the process or the product of efforts to build new political communities and supranational institutions that transcend the state.

politics the exercise of influence.

polycentrism a concept used to describe the emergence of new centers of independent power within the polarized bloc structure of the Cold War.

pooled sovereignty the sharing of decision-making responsibility among several governments and between them and international institutions.

population momentum the concept that population growth will continue for several decades after replacement-level fertility is achieved.

positivist legal theory a theory that stresses states' customs as the most important source of law.

postbehavioral movement an approach to the study of international relations that calls for increased attention to the policy relevance of research conducted using the methods of behavioral science.

postmodern terrorism the prediction that in the twenty-first century technology has improved the prospects for terrorists to use new weapons to threaten their adversaries for political purposes.

power the factors that enable one actor to manipulate another actor's behavior against its preferences.

power potential the relative capabilities or resources that are presumed necessary for a state to achieve influence over others.

power transition a narrowing of the ratio of military capabilities between great power rivals that is thought to increase the probability of war between them.

power transition theory the theory that war is likely when a dominant great power is threatened by the rapid growth of a rival's capabilities, which reduces the difference in their relative power.

preemption a quick first-strike attack that seeks to defeat an adversary before it can organize a retaliatory response.

preventive diplomacy diplomatic actions taken in advance of a predictable crisis to prevent or limit violence.

price inelasticity of demand a condition where price increases have little impact on the amount of a commodity that is consumed.

private international law law pertaining to routinized transnational intercourse between or among NGOs or nongovernmental actors and sovereign states.

procedural rationality a method of decision making based on having perfect information and carefully weighing all possible courses of action.

product cycle theory a hypothesis that maintains that overseas expansion is a defensive maneuver designed to forestall foreign competitors and thereby reinforce the global competitiveness of domestically based industries.

proliferation the spread of weapon capabilities from a few to many states in a chain reaction, so that an increasing number of states gain the ability to launch an attack on other states with devastating (e.g., nuclear) weapons.

propaganda communications used to manipulate people's thoughts, emotions, or actions.

prospect theory the social psychological theory that international decision making is constrained by formed opinions and tendencies to overreact in crises, that decisions tend to be made based on the perceived prospects of choices to fulfill objectives, and that policymakers engage in risk-averse behavior in making choices about probable gains but are risk-acceptant when making choices about anticipated losses.

protectionism barriers to foreign trade, such as tariffs and quotas, that protect local industries from competition for the purchase of the products local manufacturers produce.

public goods shared values from which everyone who has access to them benefits, such as safe drinking water, even if not everyone contributes to their preservation or creation.

public international law law pertaining to government-to-government relations of sovereign states.

purchasing power parity (PPP) an index that calculates the true rate of exchange among currencies when parity—when what can be purchased is the same—is achieved; the index determines what can be bought with a unit of each currency.

rapprochement in diplomacy, a policy seeking to reestablish normal relations between enemies.

rational choice the theory that decisionmakers choose on the basis of what they perceive to be the best interests of themselves and their states, based on their expectations about the relative usefulness of alternative options for realizing goals. Sometimes called "expected utility theory," it was derived from realist theories.

Reagan Doctrine a pledge of U.S. support for anticommunist insurgents who sought to overthrow Soviet-supported governments.

realism a paradigm based on the premise that world politics is essentially and unchangeably a struggle among self-interested states for power and position under anarchy, with each competing state pursuing its own national interests.

realist theory the view that states are unitary global actors in relentless competition with each other for position and prosperity in the international hierarchy, dedicated to the promotion of their own interests at the expense of other states.

realpolitik the theoretical outlook prescribing that countries should prepare for war in order to preserve peace.

reciprocity a principle in international law and morality that actors should treat others as they wish to be treated, as seen in the realm of trade agreements that require countries to reduce their own tariffs in return for another's reductions.

refugees people who flee for safety to another country because of a well-founded fear of persecution.

regimes norms, rules, and procedures for interaction agreed to by a set of states.

regional collective defense organizations and military alliances within a specific region created to collectively preserve peace and security for their members.

regional currency union the pooling of sovereignty to create a common currency and single monetary system for members in a region, regulated by a regional central bank within the currency bloc to reduce the likelihood of large-scale liquidity crises.

relative burden of military spending the ratio of defense spending by a state relative to its gross national product.

relative deprivation the belief that one is unfairly deprived, in comparison to others, of the wealth and status that one deserves.

relative gains a measure of how much some participants in an exchange benefit in comparison with others.

religious movement a set of beliefs, practices, and ideas administered politically by a religious group to promote the worship of its conception of a transcendent diety or principles of conduct.

reparations compensation paid by a defeated state for damages or expenditures sustained by the victor during hostilities.

replacement-level fertility one couple replacing themselves with two children, so that a country's population will remain stable if this practice prevails.

reprisal hostile and illegal retaliatory acts against an enemy to punish previous actions that, according to international law, are prohibited.

retorsion hostile but legal retaliatory acts against an enemy for an act it has undertaken that, according to international law, is prohibited.

revolution in military affairs (RMA) the goal of seeking to increase military capabilities and effectiveness with new technology that does not rely on weapons of mass destruction.

revolution in military technology (RMT) the sophisticated new weapons technologies that make fighting without mass armies possible.

sanctions punitive actions by one state against another to retaliate for its previous objectionable behavior.

satisficing the tendency for decisionmakers to choose the first available alternative that meets minimally acceptable standards.

schematic reasoning the process of reasoning by which new information is interpreted according to a memory structure that contains a network of genetic scripts, metaphors, and stereotypical characters.

secession/separative revolts the attempt by a religious or ethnic minority to break away from an internationally recognized state.

second-strike capability a state's capacity to retaliate after absorbing a first-strike attack with weapons of mass destruction.

Second World a group of countries with centrally planned economies, consisting of the Soviet Union, its allies in Eastern Europe, and the People's Republic of China during the Cold War; with the termination of the Cold War, the "Second World" refers to the economies in transition that are adopting free-market capitalist economies.

security community a group of states whose high level of noninstitutionalized collaboration results in the settlement of disputes by compromise rather than by force.

security dilemma the propensity of armaments undertaken by one state for ostensibly defensive purposes to threaten other states, which arm in reaction, with the result that their national security declines as their arms increase.

security regime norms and rules for interaction agreed to by a set of states to increase their security.

selective engagement a great-power grand strategy using economic and military power to influence only important particular situations, countries, or global issues, by striking a balance between a highly interventionist "global policeman" and an uninvolved isolationism when crises erupt in a great power's sphere of influence.

self-determination the doctrine that asserts nationalities have the right to determine what political authority will represent and rule them.

self-fulfilling prophecy the tendency for one's expectations to evoke behavior that helps to make the expectations come true.

self-help the principle that because in international anarchy all global actors are independent, they must rely on themselves to provide for their security and well-being.

signaling in conflict situations, either explicit or implicit communication by states to reveal both their intentions and their capabilities.

semiperiphery to world system theorists, countries midway between the rich "core" or center and the poor "periphery" in the global hierarchy, at which foreign investments are targeted when labor wages and production costs become too high in the prosperous core regions.

size principle the propensity for competitors to form coalitions only large enough to ensure victory, even if by a narrow margin, with the result that over time opposed alliances tend to remain roughly equal to one another.

smart bombs precision-guided military technology that enables a bomb to search for its target and detonate at the precise time it can do the most damage.

social constructivism a liberal-realist theoretical approach advocated by Alexander Wendt that sees self-interested states as the key actors in world politics, whose actions are determined not by anarchy but by the ways states socially "construct" and then respond to the meanings they give to power politics so that as their definitions change, cooperative practices can evolve.

socialization the processes by which people learn the beliefs, values, and behaviors that are acceptable in a given society.

soft power the ability to exercise influence in world politics due to intangible resources such as culture and ideas, as opposed to methods that rely on military coercion.

sovereign equality the principle that states are legally entitled to equal rights under international law.

sovereignty/state sovereignty the legal doctrine that states have supreme authority to govern their internal affairs and manage their foreign relations with other states and IGOs.

sphere of influence a region of the globe dominated by a great power.

spillaround the stagnation or encapsulation of regional integration activities.

spillback the reversal of previous steps toward integration, reducing the number of sectors in which integrating states are engaged in cooperative exchanges.

spillover the propensity for successful integration across one area of cooperation between states to propel further integration in other areas.

spiral model a metaphor used to describe the tendency of efforts to enhance defense to result in escalating arms races.

stagflation a situation in which economic stagnation and high inflation occur at the same time and the usual tendency for an economic downturn to drive down prices does not occur.

standard operating procedures (SOPs) established methods to be followed for the performance of designated tasks.

state a legal entity with a permanent population, a well-defined territory, and a government capable of exercising sovereignty.

statehood as outlined by the Montevideo Convention of 1933, the legal criteria by which a country and its government become an independent sovereign state within the international community.

state level of analysis an analytical approach to the study of world politics that emphasizes how the internal attributes of states explain their foreign policy behaviors.

state sovereignty under international law, the status of states as equals in that within their territory they are subject to no higher external authority.

state-sponsored terrorism formal assistance, training, and arming of foreign terrorists by a state in order to achieve foreign policy goals.

state terrorism sovereign states' use of their armed forces and police to rule through fear and terror over targeted population groups within their borders.

Strategic Arms Limitations Talks (SALT) two sets of agreements reached during the 1970s between the United States and the Soviet Union that established limits on strategic nuclear delivery systems.

START (Strategic Arms Reduction) Treaty the U.S.-Russian series of negotiations that began in 1993 and, with the 1997 START-III agreement ratified in April 2000, pledged to cut the nuclear arsenals of both sides by 80 percent of their Cold War peaks, in order to lower the risk of nuclear war by making a successful preemptive strike impossible.

strategic concept NATO's 1999 set of plans identifying key strategic goals and the instruments that will be used to achieve them.

strategic corporate alliances cooperation between multinational corporations and foreign companies in the same industry, driven by the movement of MNC manufacturing overseas.

strategic defense initiative (SDI) a ballistic missile defense system using space-based laser technology.

strategic stockpile the inventory of nuclear warheads deployed for waging wars of mass destruction.

strategic trade policy an industrial policy that targets government subsidies toward particular national industries so as to gain a competitive advantage over foreign producers.

strategic weapons weapons of mass destruction (WMD) carried on either intercontinental ballistic missiles (ICBMs), submarine-launched ballistic missiles (SLBMs), or long-range bombers capable of annihilating an enemy state.

structuralism a neorealist theory that sees the changing distribution of power within the global system as the primary determinant of states' behavior and of whether coalitions will form and peace will prevail.

structural realism a theory associated with neorealism that emphasizes the influence of the structure of world power on the behavior of the states within it.

structural violence condition defined by Norwegian peace researcher Johan Galtung as the harm and injury caused by the global system's unregulated structure, which effectively allows strong states to victimize weak states that cannot protect themselves.

survival of the fittest a realist concept derived from Charles Darwin's theory of evolution that advises that ruthless competition is ethically acceptable to survive, even if the actions violate moral commands not to kill.

sustainable development economic growth that does not deplete the resources needed to maintain growth.

suzerainty the claim by a powerful state of the right to exercise influence over its neighbors.

system transformation a historic watershed in world history of profound changes occurring in the units that make up the international system, the predominant foreign policy goals that the units seek, or what the units can do to each other with their military and economic capabilities.

territorial imperative the term coined by anthropologist Robert Ardrey to popularize the proposition that people and nations will defend to the death their territory for the same reason animals do.

terrorism criminal acts and threats against a targeted actor for the purpose of arousing fear in order to get the target to accept the terrorists' demands.

theater missile defense (TMD) high-altitude defense systems to prevent strategic ballistic missiles from reaching their targets on land.

theory a set of hypotheses postulating the relationship between variables or conditions in order to describe, explain, or predict phenomena, and make prescriptions about how positive changes ought to be engineered to realize particular principles.

Third Way an approach to governance advocated primarily by European leaders such as British Prime Minister Tony Blair and France's socialist Prime Minister Lionel Jostin who, while recognizing few alternatives to liberal capitalism, seek to soften the cruel social impact of free-market individualism by progressively allowing government intervention to preserve social justice and the rights of individuals to freedom from fear of the deprivations caused by disruptions in the global economy.

Third World a term commonly used to refer to the world's poorer, economically less developed Global South countries.

total war wars, such as World Wars I and II, fought with all available weapons to threaten an enemy's survival, as opposed to limited wars waged with restricted capabilities for specific objectives.

trade integration the difference between growth rates in trade and gross domestic product.

tragedy of the commons a metaphor, widely used to explain the impact of human behavior on ecological systems, that explains how rational self-interested behavior by individuals may have a destructive collective impact.

transformation a change in the characteristic pattern of interaction among the most active participants in world politics of such magnitude that it appears that one "international system" has replaced another.

transgenetic crops new crops with improved characteristics created artificially through genetic engineering which combines genes from species that would not naturally interbreed.

transnational banks (TNBs) the globe's top banking firms, whose financial activities are concentrated in transactions that cross state borders.

Truman Doctrine the declaration by President Harry S Truman that the policy of the United States must be to support "free peoples who are resisting attempted subjugation by armed minorities or by outside pressures."

two-level games a concept referring to the growing need for national policymakers to make decisions that will meet both domestic and foreign goals.

Two Plus Four Treaty the 1990 agreement between four powers (the United States, the Soviet Union, Great Britain, and France) and the two Germanys (East and West) that ended the Four Powers' rights of occupation and enabled German reunification.

underemployment a condition critics trace to trade globalization in which a large portion of the labor force only works part time at low pay in occupations below their skill level.

unilateral a go-it-alone, self-reliant strategy for dealing with threats from another actor or global problem, as opposed to multilateral approaches, which involve working with allies or collective problem-solving institutions.

unipolarity a condition in which a global system has a single dominant power center, or pole.

unitary actor a transnational actor (usually a sovereign state) assumed to be internally united, so that changes in its internal circumstances do not influence its foreign policy as much as do the decisions that actor's leaders make to cope with changes in its global environment.

United Nations (UN) a global, multipurpose international, intergovernmental organization established in 1945, consisting of six major organs and numerous specialized agencies, conferences, and commissions.

United Nations Environment Program (UNEP) a UN agency created in 1972 to study environmental deterioration and propose regulations to protect the global environment.

Uruguay Round the multilateral trade negotiations of GATT that began in 1986 and concluded in 1994 with creation of the World Trade Organization.

verification processes through which signatories' adherence to arms control and disarmament agreements is confirmed.

vertical nuclear proliferation an increase in the capabilities of existing nuclear powers.

virtual corporations agreements between otherwise competitive multinational corporations, often temporary, to join forces and skills to coproduce and export particular products in the global marketplace.

virtual nuclear arsenals the next generation of near-nuclear military capabilities produced by the revolution in military technology that would put strategic nuclear weapons of mass destruction at the margins of national security strategies by removing dependence on them for deterrence.

virtuality imagery created by computer technology of objects and phenomena that produces a fictitious picture of actual things, people, and experiences.

voluntary export restrictions (VERs) a protectionist measure popular in the 1980s and early 1990s in which exporting countries agree to restrict shipments of a particular product to a country to deter it from imposing an even more onerous export quota.

war the use of states to resolve disputes by armed force—a condition under international law with rules for its initiation and conduct.

war crimes acts performed during war that the international community defines as illegal crimes against humanity, such as atrocities committed on an enemy's prisoners of war and civilians or the state's own minority population.

war weariness hypothesis the contention that a state at war will become exhausted and lose its enthusiasm for another war, but only for a time.

Western European Union (WEU) a European military pact composed of ten member and eighteen associate member countries.

World Bank also known as the International Bank of Reconstruction and Development (IBRD), the World Bank is the globe's major IGO for financing economic growth in the Global South.

world federalism an approach to integration based on the merger of previously sovereign states into a single federal union.

world-system theory a theory that claims there is an international division of labor in which core states specialize in the capital-intensive production of sophisticated manufactured goods and peripheral states concentrate on the labor-intensive production of raw materials and agricultural commodities.

World Trade Organization (WTO) a multilateral agency established as part of the trade reform pact signed by GATT negotiators in Morocco during 1994 that monitors the implementation of trade agreements, settles disputes among trade partners, and acts as the spearhead of the surge toward economic globalization.

xenophobia the suspicious dislike, disrespect, and disregard for members of a foreign nationality, ethnic, or linguistic group.

Yalta Conference the 1945 summit meeting among Franklin D. Roosevelt, Joseph Stalin, and Winston Churchill to resolve postwar territorial issues and voting procedures in the United Nations to collectively manage world order.

Yoshida Doctrine a security policy proposing that Japan should avoid international disputes, keep a low profile on divisive global issues, and concentrate on economic pursuits.

zeitgeist "the spirit of the times," or the dominant cultural norms assumed to influence the behavior of people living in particular periods.

zero-sum the perception in a rivalry that if one side gains, the other side loses.

References

Adelman, Kenneth L., and Norman R. Augustine. (1992) "Defense Conversion," *Foreign Affairs* 71 (Spring): 26–47.

Albright, David. (1993) "A Proliferation Primer," *Bulletin of the Atomic Scientists* 49 (June): 14–23.

Albright, Madeleine. (2000) "Time to Renew Faith in the Nonproliferation Treaty," *International Herald Tribune* (March 7): 8.

Allen, John L. (2000) *Student Atlas of World Politics,* 4th ed. New York: Dushkin/McGraw Hill.

———. (1998) *Student Atlas of World Politics,* 3rd ed. Guilford, Conn.: Dushkin/McGraw-Hill.

Allison, Graham, and Philip Zelikow. (1999) *Essence of Decision: Explaining the Cuban Missile Crisis,* 2nd ed. New York: Longman.

Allison, Graham T. (1971) *Essence of Decision: Explaining the Cuban Missile Crisis.* Boston: Little, Brown.

Al-Sammarrai, Bashir. (1995) "Economic Sanctions against Iraq," 133–139 in David Cortright and George A. Lopez (eds.), *Economic Sanctions.* Boulder, Colo.: Westview Press.

Altman, Roger C., and C. Bowman Cutter. (1999) "Global Economy Needs Better Shock Absorbers," *International Herald Tribune* (June 16): 7.

Ambrose, Stephen E. (1995) "The Bomb: It Was More Than Death," *New York Times* (August 5): A15.

Amoore, Louise, et al. (1997) "Overturning 'Globalisation,'" *New Political Economy* 2 (No. 1): 179–195.

Angell, Norman. (1910) *The Great Illusion: A Study of the Relationship of Military Power in Nations to Their Economic and Social Advantage.* London: Weidenfeld & Nicholson.

Annan, Kofi. (1999) "Two Concepts of Sovereignty," *Economist* (September 18): 49–50.

Appleby, R. Scott. (2000) *The Ambivalence of the Sacred: Religion, Violence, and Reconciliation.* Boulder, Colo.: Rowman & Littlefield.

Apter, David E., and Louis W. Goodman (eds.). (1976) *The Multinational Corporation and Social Change.* New York: Praeger.

Ardrey, Robert. (1966) *The Territorial Imperative: A Personal Inquiry into the Animal Origins of Property and Nations.* New York: Atheneum.

Arkin, William M. (1995) "The Pentagon's Blind Ambition," *New York Times* (May 10): A19.

Art, Robert J. (1999) "Geopolitics Updated: The Strategy of Selective Engagement," *International Security* 23 (Winter): 79–113.

Atwood, Brian. (1999) "Trade, Not Aid," *Christian Science Monitor* (July 6): 9.

Auguste, Byron G. (1999) "What's So New about Globalization?," 45–47 in Helen E. Purkitt (ed.), *World Politics 99/00,* 20th ed. Guilford, Conn.: Dushkin/McGraw-Hill.

Avery, Dennis. (1995) "Saving the Planet with Pesticides," 49–82 in Ronald Bailey (ed.), *The True State of the Planet.* New York: Free Press.

Ayoob, Mohammed. (1995) *The Third World Security Predicament.* Boulder, Colo.: Lynne Rienner.

Bagdikian, Ben H. (1992) *The Media Monopoly.* Boston: Beacon Press.

Baker, Raymond W., and Jennifer Nordin. (1999) "A 150-to-1 Ratio Is Far Too Lopsided for Comfort," *International Herald Tribune* (February 5): 6.

Balaam, David N., and Michael Veseth. (1996) *Introduction to International Political Economy.* Upper Saddle River, N.J.: Prentice Hall.

Baldwin, David A. (ed.). (1993) *Neorealism and Neoliberalism: The Contemporary Debate.* New York: Columbia University Press.

———. (1989) *Paradoxes of Power.* New York: Basil Blackwell.

Ball, Nicole. (1991) *Briefing Book on Conventional Arms Transfers.* Boston: Council for a Livable World Education Fund.

Barber, Benjamin R. (1998) "Fantasy of Fear: Huntington and the West versus the Rest," *Harvard International Review* 20 (Winter): 66–71.

———. (1995) *Jihad vs. McWorld.* New York: Random House.

Barbieri, Katherine, and Gerald Schneider. (1999) Globalization and Peace: Assessing New Directions in the Study of Trade and Conflict," *Journal of Peace Research* 36 (July): 387–404.

Barkun, Michael. (1968) *Law without Sanctions: Order in Primitive Societies and the World Community.* New Haven, Conn.: Yale University Press.

Barnet, Richard J. (1980) *The Lean Years.* New York: Simon & Schuster.

———. (1977) *The Giants: Russia and America.* New York: Simon & Schuster.

Barnet, Richard J., and John Cavanagh. (1994) *Global Dreams: Imperial Corporations and the New World Order.* New York: Simon & Schuster.

Barnet, Richard J., and Ronald E. Müller. (1974) *Global Reach: The Power of the Multinational Corporations.* New York: Simon & Schuster.

Baron, Samuel H., and Carl Pletsch (eds.). (1985) *Introspection in Biography: The Biographer's Quest for Self-Awareness.* Hillsdale, N.J.: Analytic Press.

Bayard, Thomas O., and Kimberly Ann Elliott. (1994) *Reciprocity and Retaliation in U.S. Trade Policy.* Washington, D.C.: Institute for International Economics.

Beckman, Peter R., and Francine D'Amico (eds.). (1994) *Women, Gender, and World Politics.* Westport, Conn.: Bergin & Garvey.

Beckman, Peter R., et al. (2000) *The Nuclear Predicament: Nuclear Weapons in the Twenty-First Century.* Upper Saddle River, N.J.: Prentice Hall.

Beer, Francis A. (1981) *Peace against War: The Ecology of International Violence.* San Francisco: Freeman.

Bell, Coral. (1995) "The Future of Power in World Affairs," *Quadrant* 39 (September): 49–56.

Belsie, Laurent. (1999) "Signs of the Food Fight to Come," *Christian Science Monitor* (March 10): 1, 4.

Benedick, Richard Elliot. (1991) "Protecting the Ozone Layer: New Directions in Diplomacy," 112–153 in Jessica Tuchman Mathews (ed.), *Preserving the Global Environment.* New York: Norton.

Bennett, A. Leroy. (1988) *International Organizations,* 4th ed. Englewood Cliffs, N.J.: Prentice Hall.

Bergesen, Albert, and Ronald Schoenberg. (1980) "Long Waves of Colonial Expansion and Contraction, 1415–1969," 231–277 in Albert Bergesen (ed.), *Studies of the Modern World-System.* New York: Academic Press.

Berghahn, Volker R. (1995) *Imperial Germany, 1871–1914.* Providence, R.I.: Berghahn Books.

Bergsten, C. Fred. (2000) "Free Trade Is a Real Boon for the Developing World," *International Herald Tribune* (February 9): 9.

———. (1997) "American Politics, Global Trade," *Economist* 344 (September 27): 23–26.

Bertelsen, Judy S. (ed.). (1977) *Nonstate Nations in International Politics.* New York: Praeger.

Bhagwati, Jagdish. (1999) *A Stream of Windows: Trade, Immigration, and Democracy.* Cambridge, Mass: MIT Press.

———. (1993) "The Case for Free Trade," *Scientific American* 269 (November): 41–49.

Bienefeld, Manfred. (1994) "The New World Order: Echoes of a New Imperialism," *Third World Quarterly* 15 (March): 31–48.

Birdsall, Nancy. (2001) "Life Is Unfair: Inequality in the World," 361–374 in Charles W. Kegley, Jr., and Eugene R. Wittkopf (eds.), *The Global Agenda,* 6th ed. Boston: McGraw-Hill.

Blainey, Geoffrey. (1988) *The Causes of War,* 3rd ed. New York: Free Press.

Blanton, Shannon Lindsey. (1999) "Examining the Impact of Arms Transfers on Human Development," *Journal of Third World Studies* 16 (Fall): 75–93.

Blanton, Shannon Lindsey, and Charles W. Kegley, Jr. (1997) "Reconciling U.S. Arms Sales with America's Interests and Ideals," *Futures Research Quarterly* 13 (Spring): 85–101.

Blechman, Barry M. (1995) "The Intervention Dilemma," *Washington Quarterly* 18 (Summer): 63–73.

Blechman, Barry M., and Stephen S. Kaplan, et al. (1978) *Force without War.* Washington, D.C.: Brookings Institution.

Block, Fred L. (1977) *The Origins of International Economic Disorder.* Berkeley: University of California Press.

Blumenthal, W. Michael. (1988) "The World Economy and Technological Change," *Foreign Affairs* 66 (No. 3): 529–550.

Blustein, Paul (1999a) "Currencies in Crisis," *Washington Post National Weekly Edition* (March 1): 6–7.

———. (1999b) "The Downside of an Upside: Last Year's Record Trade Deficit Signals Concern about the Impact of Faltering Economies," *Washington Post National Weekly Edition* (March 17): 19.

Bonnart, Frederick. (2000) "Europe Has Set Itself a Tough Military Challenge," *International Herald Tribune* (January 13): 8.

Boot, Max. (2000) "Paving the Road to Hell: The Failure of UN Peacekeeping," *Foreign Affairs* 79 (March/April): 143–148.

Borrus, Michael, Steve Weber, John Zysman, and Joseph Willihnganz. (1992) "Mercantilism and Global Security," *National Interest* 29 (Fall): 21–29.

Bostdorff, Denise M. (1993) *The Presidency and the Rhetoric of Foreign Crisis.* Columbia: University of South Carolina Press.

Boswell, Terry. (1989) "Colonial Empires and the Capitalist World-Economy: A Time Series Analysis of Colonization, 1640–1960," *American Sociological Review* 54 (April): 180–196.

Bozeman, Adda B. (1994) *Politics and Culture in International History.* New Brunswick, N.J.: Transaction.

Bracken, Paul. (1999) *Fire in the East: The Rise of Asian Military Power in the Second Nuclear Age.* New York: HarperCollins, 1999.

Brecher, Michael. (1993) *Crises in World Politics: Theory and Reality.* Oxford, Eng.: Pergamon.

Brecher, Michael, and Jonathan Wilkenfeld. (1997) *A Study of Crisis.* Ann Arbor: University of Michigan Press.

Brecke, Peter. (1999) "The Characteristics of Violent Conflict since 1400 A.D.," paper presented at the annual meeting of the International Studies Association, Washington, D.C., February 17–20,

Brierly, James L. (1944) *The Outlook for International Law.* Oxford, Eng.: Clarendon Press.

Broder, David. (1999) "Global Forces May Change Balance between States and Federal Government," (Columbia, S.C.) *The State* (August 11): A9.

Bronfenbrenner, Urie. (1971) "The Mirror Image in Soviet–American Relations," *Journal of Social Issues* 27 (No. 1): 46–51.

Brooks, Stephen G. (1997) "Dueling Realisms," *International Organization* 51 (Summer): 445–477.

Brown, Justin. (1999a) "Arms Sales: Exporting U.S. Military Edge?" *Christian Science Monitor* (December 2): 2.

———. (1999b) "Fight over Raptor Trims Military's Talons," *Christian Science Monitor* (October 18): 1, 3.

Brown, Lester R. (1999) "Feeding Nine Billion," 115–132 in Lester R. Brown, et al., *State of the World 1999.* New York: Norton.

———. (1995) *Who Will Feed China? Wake-Up Call for a Small Planet.* New York: Norton.

Brown, Lester R., et al. (2000) *State of the World 2000.* New York: Norton.

———. (1999) *State of the World 1999.* New York: Norton.

———. (1998) *State of the World 1998.* New York: Norton.

Brown, Lester R., and Brian Halweil. (1999) "How Can the World Create Enough Jobs for Everyone?" *International Herald Journal* (September 9): 9.

Brown, Lester R., and Christopher Flavin. (1999) "A New Economy for a New Century," 3–21 in Lester R. Brown, et al., *State of the World 1999.* New York: Norton.

Brown, Lester R., Gary Gardner, and Brian Halweil. (1999) *Beyond Malthus: Nineteen Dimensions of the Population Challenge.* New York: Norton.

Brzezinski, Zbigniew. (1998) "The Grand Chessboard," *Harvard International Review* 20 (Winter): 48–53.

Bueno de Mesquita, Bruce, (1975) "Measuring Systemic Polarity," *Journal of Conflict Resolution* 22 (June): 187–216.

Bueno de Mesquita, Bruce, and David Lalman. (1992) *War and Reason: Domestic and International Imperatives.* New Haven, Conn.: Yale University Press.

Bull, Hedley. (1977) *The Anarchical Society: A Study of Order in World Politics.* New York: Columbia University Press.

Bundy, McGeorge. (1990) "From Cold War to Trusting Peace," *Foreign Affairs* 69 (No. 1): 197–212.

Burkhart, Ross E., and Michael S. Lewis-Beck. (1994) "Comparative Democracy: The Economic Development Thesis," *American Political Science Review* 88 (December): 903–910.

Buzan, Barry, and Gerald Segal. (1998) *Anticipating the Future.* London: Simon & Schuster.

Cahn, Anne H. (1995) "Does the Defense Industry Really Need Welfare?" *Christian Science Monitor* (May 15): 19.

Caldwell, Dan. (1977) "Bureaucratic Foreign Policy Making," *American Behavioral Scientist* 21 (September–October): 87–110.

Calvocoressi, Peter, Guy Wint, and John Pritchard. (1989) *Total War: The Causes and Courses of the Second World War,* 2nd ed. New York: Pantheon.

Caporaso, James A., and David P. Levine. (1992). *Theories of Political Economy.* New York: Cambridge University Press.

Carment, David. (1993) "The International Dimensions of Ethnic Conflict," *Journal of Peace Research* 30 (May): 137–150.

Carothers, Thomas. (1997) "Democracy without Illusions," *Foreign Affairs* 76 (January/February): 85–99.

Carpenter, Ted Galen. (1991) "The New World Disorder," *Foreign Policy* 84 (Fall): 24–39.

Carr, Barry. "Globalization from Below: Labor Internationalism under NAFTA," *International Social Science Journal* 159 (March 1999): 49–59.

Carr, E. H. (1939) *The Twenty-Years' Crisis, 1919–1939*. London: Macmillan.

Carter, Ashton B. (1990–1991) "Chairman's Note," *International Security* 15 (Winter): 3–4.

Carter, Jimmy. (2000) "Lapsed Disarmament Brings on a Nuclear Crisis," *International Herald Tribune* (February 24): 6.

Cashman, Greg. (1993) *What Causes War? An Introduction to Theories of International Conflict*. New York: Lexington Books.

Caspary, William R. (1993) "New Psychoanalytic Perspectives on the Causes of War," *Political Psychology* 14 (September): 417–446.

Cerny, Philip G. (1994) "The Dynamics of Financial Globalization: Technology, Market Structure, and Policy Response," *Policy Sciences* 287 (No. 4): 319–342.

Chaliand, Gérald, and Jean-Pierre Rageau. (1993) *Strategic Atlas*, 3rd ed. New York: Harper Perennial.

Chan, Steve. (1997) "In Search of Democratic Peace: Problems and Promise," *Mershon International Studies Review* 41 (May): 59–91.

———. (1987) "Military Expenditures and Economic Performance," 29–37 in U.S. Arms Control and Disarmament Agency, *World Military Expenditures and Arms Transfers 1986*. Washington, D.C.: U.S. Government Printing Office.

———. (1984) "Mirror, Mirror on the Wall . . .: Are the Free Countries More Pacific?" *Journal of Conflict Resolution* 28 (December): 617–648.

Checkel, Jeffrey T. (1998) "The Constructivist Turn in International Relations Theory," *World Politics* 50 (January 1998): 324–348.

Chossudovsky, Michel. (1997) *The Globalisation of Poverty: Impacts of IMF and World Bank Reforms*. London: Zed Books.

Chubin, Shahram. (1998) "Southern Perspectives on World Order," 208–220 in Charles W. Kegley, Jr., and Eugene R. Wittkopf (eds.), *The Global Agenda*, 5th ed. New York: McGraw-Hill.

Cirincione, Joseph. (2000a) "The Asian Nuclear Reaction Chain," *Foreign Policy* 118 (Spring): 120–136.

———. (2000b) "The Assault on Arms Control," *Bulletin of the Atomic Scientists* 56 (January/February): 32–37.

Clad, James C. (1994) "Slowing the Wave," *Foreign Policy* 95 (Summer): 139–150.

Clancy, Tom, and Russell Seitz. (1991–1992) "Five Minutes Past Midnight—and Welcome to the New Age of Proliferation," *National Interest* 26 (Winter): 3–17.

Claude, Inis L., Jr. (1989) "The Balance of Power Revisited," *Review of International Studies* 15 (January): 77–85.

———. (1988) *States and the Global System: Politics, Law, and Organization*. New York: St. Martin's Press.

———. (1971) *Swords into Plowshares*, 4th ed. New York: Random House.

———. (1967) *The Changing United Nations*. New York: Random House.

———. (1962) *Power and International Relations*. New York: Random House.

Clausewitz, Karl von. (1976 [1832]) *On War*. Princeton, N.J.: Princeton University Press.

Clegg, Liz. (1999) "NGOs Take Aim" *Bulletin of the Atomic Scientists* 52 (January/February): 49–52.

Cobb, Roger, and Charles Elder. (1970) *International Community*. New York: Harcourt, Brace & World.

Cockburn, Andrew. (1995) "A U.S. Military Porkfest Fattens Contractors," *International Herald Tribune* (October 5): 9.

Cohen, Benjamin J. (2000) *The Geography of Money*. Ithaca, N.Y.: Cornell University Press.

———. (1996) "Phoenix Risen: The Resurrection of Global Finance," *World Politics* 48 (January): 268–296.

———. (1973) *The Question of Imperialism*. New York: Basic Books.

Cohen, Eliot A. (1998) "A Revolution in Warfare: The Changing Face of Force," 34–46 in Charles W. Kegley, Jr., and Eugene R. Wittkopf (eds.), *The Global Agenda*, 4th ed. New York: McGraw-Hill.

———. (1995) "The Future of Military Power: The Continuing Utility of Force," 35–43 in Charles W. Kegley, Jr., and Eugene R. Wittkopf (eds.), *The Global Agenda*, 4th ed. New York: McGraw-Hill.

Cohen, Joel E. (1998) "How Many People can the Earth Support?" *New York Review of Books* 45 (October 8): 29–31.

———. (1995) *How Many People Can the Earth Support?* New York: Norton.

Cohen, Roger. (2000) "A European Identity: Nation-State Losing Ground," *New York Times* (January 14): A3.

———. (1999) "Europe Seeks a New Parity: Dependence on U.S. Grows Uncomfortable," *New York Times* (June 15): A1, A14.

Commager, Henry Steele. (1983) "Misconceptions Governing American Foreign Policy," 510–517 in Charles W. Kegley, Jr., and Eugene R. Wittkopf (eds.), *Perspectives on American Foreign Policy*. New York: St. Martin's Press.

Commission on Transnational Corporations. (1991) "Recent Developments Related to Transnational Corporations and International Economic Relations," UN Doc. E/E.10/1991/2, United Nations Economic and Social Council.

Conger, Lucy. (1999) "A Fourth Way? The Latin American Alternative to Neoliberalism," 197–201 in Robert M. Jackson (ed.), *Global Issues 1999/00*. Guilford, Conn.: Dushkin/McGraw-Hill.

Connelly, Matthew, and Paul Kennedy. (1994) "Must It Be the Rest against the West?" *Atlantic Monthly* (December): 61–84.

Constable, Pamela. (1999). "India's Clock Just Keeps on Ticking," *Washington Post Weekly Edition* (August 30): 16.

Coplin, William D. (1971) *Introduction to International Politics*. Chicago: Markham.

———. (1966) *The Functions of International Law*. Chicago: Rand McNally.

———. (1965) "International Law and Assumptions about the State System," *World Politics* 17 (July): 615–634.

Cortwright, David, and George A. Lopez. (1995) "The Sanctions Era: An Alternative to Military Intervention," *Fletcher Forum of World Affairs* 19 (May): 65–85.

Coser, Lewis. (1956) *The Functions of Social Conflict*. London: Routledge & Kegan Paul.

Craig, Gordon A., and Alexander L. George. (1990) *Force and Statecraft*, 2nd ed. New York: Oxford University Press.

Crook, Clive. (1997) "The Future of the State," *Economist* 344 (September 20): 5–20.

Crossette, Barbara. (2000) "The UN's Unhappy Lot: Perilous Police Duties Multiplying," *New York Times* (February 23): A3.

———. (1999) "The Internet Changes Dictatorship's Rules," *New York Times* (August 1): Section 4, 1.

———. (1995) "The Second Sex in the Third World," *New York Times* (September 10): E1, E3.
Crump, Andy. (1998) *The A to Z of World Development.* Oxford, Eng.: New Internationalist Publications.
Curtis, Bronwyn. (1998) "What Asia Could Learn from Europe," *New York Times* (January 25): A12.
Dahrendorf, Ralf. (1999) "The Third Way and Liberty," *Foreign Affairs* 78 (September/October): 13–17.
D'Amato, Anthony. (1982) "What 'Counts' as Law?" 83–107 in Nicholas Greenwood Onuf (ed.), *Law-Making in the Global Community.* Durham, N.C.: Carolina Academic Press.
Daly, Herman E. (1993) "The Perils of Free Trade," *Scientific American* 269 (November): 50–57.
Daly, Herman E., and John B. Cobb, Jr. (1989) *For the Common Good.* Boston: Beacon Press.
Daniels, Ted (ed.). (1999) *A Doomsday Reader.* New York: New York University Press.
Davidson, Keay. (1991) "Slashing U.S. Nuclear Arsenal Now Thinkable," *Baton Rouge Sunday Advocate* (November 10): E1.
Davis, Bob. (1994) "Global Paradox: Growth of Trade Binds Nations but It Can Also Spur Separatism," *Wall Street Journal* (June 20): A1, A10.
Davis, Wade. (1999) "Vanishing Cultures," *National Geographic* (August): 62–89.
Deger, Saadet, and Ron Smith. (1983) "Military Expansion and Growth in Less Developed Countries," *Journal of Conflict Resolution* 27 (June): 335–353.
Dehio, Ludwig. (1962) *The Precarious Balance.* New York: Knopf.
Demko, George J., and William B. Wood. (1994) *Reordering the World: Geopolitical Perspectives on the Twenty-First Century.* Boulder, Colo.: Westview Press.
Dentzer, Susan. (1993) "Meet the New Economic Bogeymen," *U.S. News and World Report* (October 18): 67.
DeRivera, Joseph H. (1968) *The Psychological Dimension of Foreign Policy.* Columbus, Ohio: Merrill.
Desch, Michael C. (1998) "Culture Clash," *International Security 23* (Summer): 141–170.
de Tocqueville, Alexis. (1969 [1835]) *Democracy in America.* New York: Doubleday.
Deutsch, Karl W. (1974) *Politics and Government.* Boston: Houghton Mifflin.
———. (1953) "The Growth of Nations: Some Recurrent Patterns in Political and Social Integration," *World Politics* 5 (October): 168–195.
Deutsch, Karl W., et al. (2001) *Backgrounds to Community.* Columbia: University of South Carolina Press.
———. (1957) *Political Community and the North Atlantic Area.* Princeton, N.J.: Princeton University Press.
Deutsch, Karl W., and J. David Singer. (1964) "Multipolar Power Systems and International Stability," *World Politics* 16 (April): 390–406.
DeVecchi, Robert, and Arthur C. Helton. (1999) "The United Nations Requires an Upgrade," *International Herald Tribune* (September 20): 16.
Diehl, Paul F., and Gary Goertz. (2000). *War and Peace in International Rivalry.* Ann Arbor: University of Michigan Press.
Dillin, John. (2000) "Which Freedom First: Political or Economic?" *Christian Science Monitor* (February 7): 12–13.
Diouf, Jacques. (2000) "Global Trade Alone Will Not End World Hunger," *International Herald Tribune* (February 18): 8.
DiRenzo, Gordon J. (ed.). (1974) *Personality and Politics.* Garden City, N.Y.: Doubleday-Anchor.
Diwan, Isaac, and Ana Revenga. (1995) "Wages, Inequality, and International Integration," *Finance & Development* 32 (September): 7–9.
Dixon, William J. (1994) "Democracy and the Peaceful Settlement of International Conflict," *American Political Science Review* 88 (March): 14–32.
Doremus, Paul N., William W. Keller, Louis W. Pauly, and Simon Reich. (1998) *The Myth of the Global Corporation.* Princeton, N.J.: Princeton University Press.
Dorraj, Manochehr. (1995) "Introduction: The Changing Context of Third World Political Economy," 1–13 in Manochehr Dorraj (ed.), *The Changing Political Economy of the Third World.* Boulder, Colo.: Lynne Rienner.
Dos Santos, Theotonio. (1970) "The Structure of Dependence," *American Economic Review* 60 (May): 231–236.
Downs, George W. (ed.). (1994) *Collective Security beyond the Cold War.* Ann Arbor: University of Michigan Press.
Doyle, Michael W. (1997) *Ways of War and Peace.* New York: Norton.
———. (1995) "Liberalism and World Politics Revisited," 83–106 in Charles W. Kegley, Jr. (ed.), *Controversies in International Relations Theory: Realism and the Neoliberal Challenge.* New York: St. Martin's Press.
Doyle, Michael W., and G. John Ikenberry (eds.). (1997) *New Thinking in International Relations Theory.* Boulder, Colo.: Westview Press.
Drozdiak, William. (1999) "Germany Shifts Its Focus Eastward," *International Herald Tribune* (September 11–12): 1, 4.
Drucker, Peter F. (1997) "The Global Economy and the Nation-State," *Foreign Affairs* 76 (October): 159–171.
Dulles, John Foster. (1939) *War, Peace, and Change.* New York: Harper.
Dunn, Seth. (1999) "Cut Back on the Global Use of Coal," *International Herald Tribune* (August 30): 8.
Durbin, Andrea C. (1995) "Trade and the Environment," *Environment* 37 (September): 16–20, 37–41.
Durning, Alan Thein. (1993) "Supporting Indigenous Peoples," 80–100 in Lester R. Brown, et al., *State of the World 1993.* New York: Norton.
Dyson, Freeman. (1997) *Imagined Worlds.* Cambridge, Mass.: Harvard University Press.
Easton, David. (1969) "The New Revolution in Political Science," *American Political Science Review* 63 (December): 1051–1061.
Easton, Stewart C. (1964) *The Rise and Fall of Western Colonialism.* New York: Praeger.
Eberstadt, Nicholas. (1995) "Population, Food, and Income: Global Trends in the Twentieth Century," 7–47 in Ronald Bailey (ed.), *The True State of the Planet.* New York: Free Press.
The Economist. (1999a) *Pocket World in Figures, 2000.* London: Profile Books.
———. (1999b) *The World in 2000.* London: *Economist.*
Edwards, Stephen R. (1995) "Conserving Biodiversity: Resources for Our Future," 212–265 in Ronald Bailey (ed.), *The True State of the Planet.* New York: Free Press.
Eichengreen, Barry. (2000) "Hegemonic Stability Theories of the International Monetary System," 220–244 in Jeffry A. Frieden and David A. Lake (eds.), *International Political Economy.* Boston: Bedford/St. Martin's.
Eizenstat, Stuart. (1999) "Learning to Steer the Forces of Globalization," *International Herald Tribune* (January 22): 6.
Elliott, Kimberly Ann. (1998) "The Sanctions Glass: Half Full or Completely Empty?" *International Security* 23 (Summer): 50–65.
———. (1993) "Sanctions: A Look at the Record," *Bulletin of the Atomic Scientists* 49 (November): 32–35.
Elliott, Michael. (1998) "A Second Federal Democratic Superpower Soon," *International Herald Tribune* (November 24): 8.

Emerson, Sarah A. (1997) "Resource Plenty: Why Fears of an Oil Crisis Are Misinformed," *Harvard International Review* 19 (Summer): 12–15, 64.

Emmanuel, Arghiri. (1972) *Unequal Exchange: An Essay on the Imperialism of Trade.* New York: Monthly Review Press.

Enloe, Cynthia. (2000) *Maneuvers: The International Politics of Militarizing Women's Lives.* Berkeley: University of California Press.

———. (1993) *The Morning After: Sexual Politics at the End of the Cold War.* Berkeley: University of California Press.

Enriquez, Juan. (1999) "Too Many Flags?" *Foreign Policy* 116 (Fall): 30–50.

Etheredge, Lloyd S. (1999) "The Internet and World Politics," paper presented to the Columbia University Seminar on Human Rights, New York, May 10.

Etzioni, Amital. (1968) "Toward a Sociological Theory of Peace," 403–428 in Leon Bramson and George W. Goethals (eds.), *War.* New York: Basic Books.

Evans, Gareth. (1995) "A Struggling UN Must Now Appreciate the Art of the Possible," *International Herald Tribune* (October 7–8): 8.

Evans, Tony (ed.). (1997) *What a Way to Live!* Dallas, Tex.: Word Publishing.

Falk, Richard A. (2001) "The New Interventionism and the Third World," 189–198 in Charles W. Kegley, Jr., and Eugene R. Wittkopf (eds.), *The Global Agenda,* 6th ed. Boston: McGraw-Hill.

———. (1993) "Sovereignty," 851–854 in Joel Krieger (ed.), *The Oxford Companion to Politics of the World.* New York: Oxford University Press.

———. (1970) *The Status of Law in International Society.* Princeton, N.J.: Princeton University Press.

———. (1965) "World Law and Human Conflict," 227–249 in Elton B. McNeil (ed.), *The Nature of Human Conflict.* Englewood Cliffs, N.J.: Prentice Hall.

———. (1964) *The Role of Domestic Courts in the International Legal Order.* Syracuse, N.Y.: Syracuse University Press.

Falk, Richard, and Andrew Strauss. (1999) "Globalization Needs a Dose of Democracy," *International Herald Tribune* (October 5): 8.

Falkenheim, Peggy L. (1987) "Post-Afghanistan Sanctions," 105–130 in David Leyton-Brown (ed.), *The Utility of International Economic Sanctions.* New York: St. Martin's Press.

Fedarko, Kevin. (1995) "Louder Than Words," *Time* (September 11): 49–59.

Ferencz, Benjamin B., and Ken Keyes, Jr. (1991) *Planet-Hood.* Coos Bay, Ore.: Love Line Books.

Ferguson, Niall. (1999) *The Pity of War.* New York: Basic Books.

Festinger, Leon. (1957) *A Theory of Cognitive Dissonance.* Evanston, Ill.: Row, Peterson.

Fetter, Steve. (1991) "Ballistic Missiles and Weapons of Mass Destruction: What Is the Threat? What Should Be Done?" *International Security* 16 (Summer): 5–42.

Fieldhouse, D. K. (1973) *Economics and Empire, 1830–1914.* Ithaca, N.Y.: Cornell University Press.

Fitzgerald, Frances. (2000) *Way Out There in the Blue: Reagan, Star Wars, and the End of the Cold War.* New York: Simon & Schuster.

Flavin, Christopher, and Seth Dunn. (1999) "Reinventing the Energy System," 23–40 in Lester R. Brown, et al., *State of the World 1999.* New York: Norton.

Førland, Tor Egil. (1993) "The History of Economic Warfare: International Law, Effectiveness, Strategies," *Journal of Peace Research* 30 (May): 151–162.

Forsythe, David. (1997) "The International Court of Justice at Fifty," 385–405 in A. S. Miller et al. (eds.), *The International Court of Justice.* Amsterdam: Klumer Law International.

Francis, David R. (1999) "A Richer World—But Poorer Too," *Christian Science Monitor* (May 4): 1, 8.

———. (1997) "Welcome Mat Now Offered Foreign Firms," *Christian Science Monitor* (May 28): 1, 8–9.

Francis, Emerich K. (1976) *Interethnic Relations.* New York: Elsevier.

Frank, Andre Gunder. (1969) *Latin America: Underdevelopment or Revolution.* New York: Monthly Review Press.

Freeman, Orville L. (1990) "Meeting the Needs of the Coming Decade: Agriculture vs. the Environment," *Futurist* 24 (November–December): 15–20.

French, Hillary. (2000) *Vanishing Borders: Protecting the Planet in the Age of Globalization.* Washington, D.C.: Worldwatch Institute.

French, Hilary F. (1994) "Can the Environment Survive Industrial Demands?" *USA Today* 122 (January): 66–69.

Freud, Sigmund. (1968) "Why War," 71–80 in Leon Bramson and George W. Goethals (eds.), *War.* New York: Basic Books.

Fried, John H. E. (1971) "International Law—Neither Orphan nor Harlot, Neither Jailer nor Never-Never Land," 124–176 in Karl W. Deutsch and Stanley Hoffmann (eds.), *The Relevance of International Law.* Garden City, N.Y.: Doubleday-Anchor.

Friedheim, Robert L. (1965) "The 'Satisfied' and 'Dissatisfied' States Negotiate International Law," *World Politics* 18 (October): 20–41.

Friedman, Thomas L. (2000) "Corporations on Steroids," (Columbia, S.C.) *The State* (February 8): A9.

———. (1999a) "America's Technological Revolution," *International Herald Journal* (August 24): 11.

———. (1999b) *The Lexus and the Olive Tree: Understanding Globalization.* New York: Farrar, Straus, Giroux.

———. (1996) "Answers Needed to Globalization Dissent," *Houston Chronicle* (February 8): 30.

———. (1993) "Friends Like Russia Make Diplomacy a Mess," *New York Times* (March 28): E5.

Fukuyama, Francis. (1999a) *The Great Disruption: Human Nature and the Reconstitution of Social Order.* New York: Free Press.

———. (1999b) "Second Thoughts: The Last Man in a Bottle," *National Interest* 56 (Summer): 16–33.

———. (1992a) "The Beginning of Foreign Policy," *New Republic* (August 17 and 24): 24–32.

———. (1992b) *The End of History and the Last Man.* New York: Free Press.

———. (1989) "The End of History?" *National Interest* 16 (Summer): 3–16.

Fuller, Graham E. (1995) "The Next Ideology," *Foreign Policy* 98 (Spring): 145–158.

———. (1991–1992) "The Breaking of Nations—and the Threat to Ours," *National Interest* 26 (Winter): 14–21.

Gaddis, John Lewis. (1997) *We Now Know: Rethinking Cold War History.* New York: Oxford University Press.

———. (1991) "Great Illusions, the Long Peace, and the Future of the International System," 25–55 in Charles W. Kegley, Jr. (ed.), *The Long Postwar Peace.* New York: HarperCollins.

———. (1990) "Coping with Victory," *Atlantic Monthly* (May): 49–60.

———. (1983) "Containment: Its Past and Future," 16–31 in Charles W. Kegley, Jr., and Eugene R. Wittkopf (eds.), *Perspectives on American Foreign Policy.* New York: St. Martin's Press.

Galtung, Johan. (1969) "Violence, Peace, and Peace Research," *Journal of Peace Research* 6 (No. 3): 167–191.

Gardels, Nathan. (1991) "Two Concepts of Nationalism," *New York Review of Books* 38 (November 21): 19–23.

Garrett, Laurie. (1998) "Runaway Diseases," *Foreign Affairs* 77 (January/February): 139–142.

Garten, Jeffrey A. (1999). "Beware the Weak Links in Our Globalization Chain," *International Herald Tribune* (August 19): 8.

Garwin, Richard L. (2000) "The Wrong Plan," *Bulletin of the Atomic Scientists* 50 (March/April): 36–41.

Gedman, Jeffrey. (1999) "Continental Drift," *New Republic* (June 28): 23–24.

Gelb, Leslie H. (1993) "Tailoring a U.S. Role at the UN," *International Herald Tribune* (January 2–3): 4.

———. (1979) "The Future of Arms Control: A Glass Half Full," *Foreign Policy* 36 (Fall): 21–32.

Gelb, Leslie H., and Morton H. Halperin. (1973) "The Ten Commandments of the Foreign Affairs Bureaucracy," 250–259 in Steven L. Spiegel (ed.), *At Issue*. New York: St. Martin's Press.

Gelber, Harry. (1998) *Sovereignty through Interdependence*. Cambridge, Mass.: Kluwer Law International.

George, Alexander L. (2000) "Strategies for Preventive Diplomacy and Conflict Resolution," *PS: Political Science and Politics* 33 (March): 15–19.

———. (1992) *Forceful Persuasion: Coercive Diplomacy as an Alternative to War*. Washington, D.C.: United States Institute of Peace.

———. (1986) "U.S.–Soviet Global Rivalry: Norms of Competition," *Journal of Peace Research* 23 (September): 247–262.

———. (1972) "The Case for Multiple Advocacy in Making Foreign Policy," *American Political Science Review* 66 (September): 751–785.

German, F. Clifford. (1960) "A Tentative Evaluation of World Power," *Journal of Conflict Resolution* 4 (March): 138–144.

Gibney, Frank, Jr. (1999) "Birth of a Superpower," *Time* (June 7): 40–42.

Gill, Stephen. (1993a) "Group of 7," 369–370 in Joel Krieger (ed.), *The Oxford Companion to Politics of the World*. New York: Oxford University Press.

———. (1993b) "Hegemony," 384–386 in Joel Krieger (ed.), *The Oxford Companion to Politics of the World*. New York: Oxford University Press.

Gilpin, Robert. (2001) "Three Ideologies of Political Economy," 269–286 in Charles W. Kegley, Jr., and Eugene R. Wittkopf (eds.), *The Global Agenda*, 6th ed. Boston: McGraw-Hill.

———. (2000) *The Challenge of Global Capitalism: The World Economy in the Twenty-First Century*. Princeton, N.J.: Princeton University Press.

———. (1987) *The Political Economy of International Relations*. Princeton, N.J: Princeton University Press.

———. (1985) "The Politics of Transnational Economic Relations," 171–194 in Ray Maghroori and Bennett Ramberg (eds.), *Globalism versus Realism: International Relations' Third Debate*. Boulder, Colo.: Westview Press.

———. (1981) *War and Change in World Politics*. Cambridge, Eng.: Cambridge University Press.

———. (1975) *U.S. Power and the Multinational Corporation*. New York: Basic Books.

Glahn, Gerhard von. (1996) *Law among Nations*, 7th ed. Boston: Allyn & Bacon.

Gleditsch, Kristian S., and Michael D. Ward. (1999) "A Revised List of Independent States Since the Congress of Vienna," *International Interactions* 25 (No. 4): 393–413.

Gleditsch, Nils Petter. (1995) "35 Major Wars?" *Journal of Conflict Resolution* 39 (September): 584–587.

Gochman, Charles S., and Zeev Maoz. (1984) "Militarized Interstate Disputes, 1816–1976: Procedures, Patterns, and Insights," *Journal of Conflict Resolution* 28 (December): 585–616.

Goldgeier, James M., and Michael McFaul. (1992) "A Tale of Two Worlds: Core and Periphery in the Post–Cold War Era," *International Organization* 46 (Spring): 467–491.

Goldstein, Joshua S. ed. (1999) *Longman Atlas of War and Peace*. New York: Longman.

———. (1988) *Long Cycles: Prosperity and War in the Modern Age*. New Haven, Conn.: Yale University Press.

Goldstein, Morris. (1995) *The Exchange Rate System and the IMF: A Modest Agenda*. Washington, D.C.: Institute for International Economics.

Gordon, Michael R. (1999) "Russians Firmly Reject U.S. Plan to Reopen ABM Treaty," *New York Times* (October 21): A3.

Gottlieb, Gidon. (1982) "Global Bargaining: The Legal and Diplomatic Framework," 109–130 in Nicholas Greenwood Onuf (ed.), *Law-Making in the Global Community*. Durham, N.C.: Carolina Academic Press.

Gowa, Joanne. (1999) *Ballots and Bullets: The Elusive Democratic Peace*. Princeton, N.J.: Princeton University Press.

Graham, Bradley. (1995) "Revolutionary Warfare: New Technologies Are Transforming the U.S. Military," *Washington Post National Weekly Edition* (March 6–12): 6–7.

Graham, Edward M., and Paul R. Krugman. (1995) *Foreign Direct Investment in the United States*. Washington, D.C.: Institute for International Economics.

Grant, Rebecca, and Kathleen Newland (eds.). (1991) *Gender and International Relations*. Bloomington: Indiana University Press.

Green, Faktuurdatum. (1999) *The Contemporary Law of Armed Conflict*. Manchester, Eng.: Manchester University Press.

Greenberg, David. (2000) "The Empire Strikes Out: Why Star Wars Did Not End the Cold War," *Foreign Affairs* 79 (March/April): 136–142.

Greene, David. (1997) "Economic Scarcity: Forget Geology, Beware Monopoly," *Harvard International Review* 19 (Summer) 16–19, 65.

Greenfield, Meg. (1997) "Back to the Future," *Newsweek* (January 27): 96.

———. (1995) "When the Budget Is Colonized: Cutting a Program Is Like Bombing a Settlement," *Newsweek* (May 22): 78.

Greenstein, Fred I. (1987) *Personality and Politics*. Princeton, N.J.: Princeton University Press.

Grey, Edward. (1925) *Twenty-Five Years, 1892–1916*. New York: Frederick Stokes.

Grieco, Joseph M. (1995) "Anarchy and the Limits of Cooperation: A Realist Critique of the Newest Liberal Institutionalism," 151–171 in Charles W. Kegley, Jr. (ed.), *Controversies in International Relations Theory: Realism and the Neoliberal Challenge*. New York: St. Martin's Press.

Grimmett, Richard F. (1999) *Conventional Arms Transfers to Developing Nations, 1991–1998*. Washington, D.C.: Congressional Research Service.

Gulick, Edward Vose. (1955) *Europe's Classical Balance of Power*. Ithaca, N.Y.: Cornell University Press.

Gurney, Kevin Robert. (1996) "Saving the Ozone Layer Faster," *Technology Review* 99 (January): 58–59.

Gurr, Ted Robert. (2001) "Managing Conflict in Ethnically Divided Societies: A New Regime Emerges in the 1990s," 175–188 in Charles W. Kegley, Jr., and Eugene R. Wittkopf (eds.), *The Global Agenda*, 6th ed. Boston: McGraw-Hill.

———. (2000) *Peoples versus States: Minorities at Risk in the New Century*. Washington, D.C.: United States Institute of Peace Press.

———. (1998) "Communal Conflicts and Global Security," 197–207 in Charles W. Kegley, Jr., and Eugene R. Wittkopf (eds.), *The Global Agenda,* 5th ed. New York: McGraw-Hill.

———. (1994) "Peoples against States: Ethnopolitical Conflict and the Changing World System," *International Studies Quarterly* 38 (September): 347–377.

———. (1993) *Minorities at Risk: A Global View of Ethnopolitical Conflicts.* Washington, D.C.: United States Institute of Peace Press.

———. (1970) *Why Men Rebel.* Princeton, N.J.: Princeton University Press.

Haas, Ernst B. (1986) *Why We Still Need the United Nations: The Collective Management of International Conflict, 1945–1984.* Berkeley: Institute of International Studies, University of California.

Haas, Ernst B., and Allen S. Whiting. (1956) *Dynamics of International Relations.* New York: McGraw-Hill.

Haas, Peter M., Robert O. Keohane, and Marc A. Levy (eds.). (1993) *Institutions for the Earth: Sources of Effective International Environmental Protection.* Cambridge, Mass.: MIT Press.

Haass, Richard N. (1997) "Sanctioning Madness," *Foreign Affairs* 76 (December): 74–85.

Haffa, Robert P., Jr. (1992) "The Future of Conventional Deterrence," 5–30 in Gary L. Guertner, Robert Haffa, Jr., and George Quester (eds.), *Conventional Forces and the Future of Deterrence.* Carlisle Barracks, Pa.: U.S. Army War College.

Hagan, Joe D. (1993) *Political Opposition and Foreign Policy in Comparative Perspective.* Boulder, Colo.: Lynne Rienner.

Haggard, Stephan, and Beth A. Simmons. (1987) "Theories of International Regimes," *International Organization* 41 (Summer): 491–517.

Hajnal, Peter I. (2000) *The G7/G8 System: Evolution, Role, and Documentation.* Brookfield, Vt.: Ashgate.

Hall, John A. (1993) "Liberalism," 538–542 in Joel Krieger (ed.), *The Oxford Companion to Politics of the World.* Oxford, Eng.: Oxford University Press.

Hallenbeck, Ralph A., and David E. Shaver (eds.). (1991) *On Disarmament.* New York: Praeger.

Hammond, Grant T. (1996) "The Difficult Pursuit of Peace," *USA Today* 125 (November): 13.

Handbook of International Economic Statistics 1998 (1999) Langley, Va.: U.S. Central Intelligence Agency.

Hardin, Garrett. (1993) *Living within Limits.* New York: Oxford University Press.

———. (1968) "The Tragedy of the Commons," *Science* 162 (December): 1243–1248.

Harknett, Richard J. (1994) "The Logic of Conventional Deterrence and the End of the Cold War," *Security Studies* 4 (Autumn): 86–114.

Harries, Owen. (1995) "Realism in a New Era," *Quadrant* 39 (April): 11–18.

Heilbroner, Robert L. (1991) *An Inquiry into the Human Prospect.* New York: Norton.

Held, David, Anthony McGrew, with David Goldblatt, and Jonathan Perraton. (2001) "Managing the Challenge of Globalization and Institutionalizing Cooperation through Global Governance," 136–148 in Charles W. Kegley, Jr., and Eugene R. Wittkopf (eds.), *The Global Agenda,* 6th ed. Boston: McGraw-Hill.

———. (1999) *Global Transformations: Politics, Economics and Culture.* Stanford, Calif.: Stanford University Press.

Helman, Udi. (1995) "Sustainable Development: Strategies for Reconciling Environment and Economy in the Developing World," *Washington Quarterly* 18 (Autumn): 189–207.

Helms, Jesse. (1999) "An Epidemic of Sanctions? It's Sheer Nonsense," *International Herald Tribune* (December 16): 9.

Helprin, Mark. (1995) "What to Do about Terrorism, Really," *Wall Street Journal* (May 10): A14.

Henderson, Errol A., and Richard Tucker. (1999) "Clear and Present Strangers: The Clash of Civilizations and International Conflict," paper presented at the annual meeting of the American Political Science Association, Atlanta, September 2–5.

Heredia, Blanca. (1999) "Prosper or Perish? Development in the Age of Global Capital," 93–97 in Robert M. Jackson (ed.), *Global Issues 1999/00,* 15th ed., Guilford, Conn.: Dushkin/McGraw-Hill

———. (1997) "Prosper or Perish: Development in the Age of Global Capital," *Current History* 96 (November): 383–388.

Hermann, Charles F. (1988) "New Foreign Policy Problems and Old Bureaucratic Organizations," 248–265 in Charles W. Kegley, Jr., and Eugene R. Wittkopf (eds.), *The Domestic Sources of American Foreign Policy.* New York: St. Martin's Press.

———. (1972) "Some Issues in the Study of International Crisis," 3–17 in Charles F. Hermann (ed.), *International Crises.* New York: Free Press.

Hermann, Charles F., Charles W. Kegley, Jr., and James N. Rosenau (eds.). (1987) *New Directions in the Study of Foreign Policy.* Boston: Allen & Unwin.

Hermann, Margaret G. (1988) "The Role of Leaders and Leadership in the Making of American Foreign Policy," 266–284 in Charles W. Kegley, Jr., and Eugene R. Wittkopf (eds.), *The Domestic Sources of American Foreign Policy.* New York: St. Martin's Press.

———. (1976) "When Leader Personality Will Affect Foreign Policy: Some Propositions," 326–333 in James N. Rosenau (ed.), *In Search of Global Patterns.* New York: Free Press.

Herz, John H. (1951) *Political Realism and Political Idealism.* Chicago: University of Chicago Press.

Hiatt, Fred. (1997) "Globalization: Real Benefits, but Also Real Costs for Many," *International Herald Tribune* (June 12): 8.

Higgins, Benjamin, and Jean Downing Higgins. (1979) *Economic Development of a Small Planet.* New York: Norton.

Higgins, Rosalyn. (1994) *Problems and Process: International Law and How We Use It.* Oxford, Eng.: Oxford University Press.

Hilsman, Roger. (1967) *To Move a Nation.* New York: Doubleday.

Hirsh Michael, (1999) "At War with Ourselves," *Harper's* (July): 59–69.

Hoagland, Jim. (1999a) "At Present the Brutal Colonialists Aren't Westerns," *International Herald Tribune* (September 20): 12.

———. (1999b) "Is the Global Economy Widening the Income Gap?" *International Herald Tribune* (April 27): 6.

———. (1996) "Yes, Sanctions Can Be Effective, but You Have to Work at It," *International Herald Tribune* (February 8): 8.

———. (1993a) "A Breakthrough for Clinton Too," *Washington Post National Weekly Edition* (September 20–26): 29.

———. (1993b) "Economic Sanctions Sometimes Do More Harm Than Good," (Columbia, S.C.) *The State* (November 11): A12.

Hodges, Michael R., John H. Kirton, and Joseph P. Daniels. (2000) *The G-8's Role in the New Millennium.* Brookfield, Vt.: Ashgate.

Hoebel, E. Adamson. (1961) *The Law of Primitive Man.* Cambridge, Mass.: Harvard University Press.

Hoffmann, Stanley. (1998) *World Disorders: Troubled Peace in the Post–Cold War Era.* Lanham, Md.: Rowman & Littlefield.

———. (1992) "To the Editors," *New York Review of Books* (June 24): 59.

———. (1971) "International Law and the Control of Force," 34–66 in Karl W. Deutsch and Stanley Hoffmann (eds.), *The Relevance of International Law.* Garden City, N.Y.: Doubleday-Anchor.

———. (1961) "International Systems and International Law," 205–237 in Klaus Knorr and Sidney Verba (eds.), *The International System.* Princeton, N.J.: Princeton University Press.

Hollingsworth, J. Rogers, and Robert Boyer (eds.). (1997) *Contemporary Capitalism: The Embeddedness of Institutions.* New York: Cambridge University Press.

Holsti, Kalevi J. (2001) "Power, Capability, and Influence in International Politics," 13–25 in Charles W. Kegley, Jr., and Eugene R. Wittkopf (eds.), *The Global Agenda,* 6th ed. Boston: McGraw-Hill.

———. (1996) *The State, War, and the State of War.* New York: Cambridge University Press.

———. (1995) "War, Peace, and the State of the State," *International Political Science Review* 16 (October): 319–339.

———. (1992) *International Politics: A Framework for Analysis,* 6th ed. Englewood Cliffs, N.J.: Prentice Hall.

———. (1991) *Peace and War: Armed Conflicts and International Order, 1648–1989.* Cambridge, Eng.: Cambridge University Press.

———. (1988) *International Politics: A Framework for Analysis,* 5th ed. Englewood Cliffs, N.J.: Prentice Hall.

Holsti, Ole R. (2001) "Models of International Relations: Realist and Neoliberal Perspectives on Conflict and Cooperation," 121–135 in Charles W. Kegley, Jr., and Eugene R. Wittkopf (eds.), *The Global Agenda,* 6th ed. Boston: McGraw-Hill

———. (1989) "Crisis Decision Making," 8–84 in Philip E. Tetlock, et al. (eds.), *Behavior, Society, and Nuclear War.* New York: Oxford University Press.

Homer-Dixon, Thomas F. (1998) "Environmental Scarcities and Violent Conflict—Global Implications," 465–472 in Charles W. Kegley, Jr., and Eugene R. Wittkopf (eds.), *The Global Agenda,* 5th ed. New York: McGraw-Hill.

Hopf, Ted. (1998) "The Promise of Constructivism in International Relations Theory," *International Security 23* (Summer): 171–200.

Hopkins, Terence K., and Immanuel Wallerstein, eds. (1996) *The Age of Transitions: Trajectory of World Systems 1945–2025.* London: Zed Books.

Hottelet, Richard C. (1999) "Desertification: Forgotten Threat," *Christian Science Monitor* (December 15): 8.

House, Karen Elliot. (1989) "As Power Is Dispersed among Nations, Need for Leadership Grows," *Wall Street Journal* (February 21): A1, A10.

Howard, Michael E. (1983) *The Causes of War.* Cambridge, Mass.: Harvard University Press.

———. (1978) *War and the Liberal Conscience.* New York: Oxford University Press.

Howell, Llewellyn D. (2000) "Global Warming, Global Warning," *USA Today* 129 (March): 35.

———. (1998) "The Age of Sovereignty Has Come to an End," *USA Today* 127 (September): 23.

———. (1995) "Economic Sanctions as Weapons," *USA Today* 124 (July): 37.

Hufbauer, Gary Clyde. (1994) "The Futility of Sanctions," *Wall Street Journal* (June 1): A14.

Hufbauer, Gary Clyde, Jeffrey J. Schott, and Kimberly Ann Elliott. (1990) *Economic Sanctions Reconsidered: History and Current Policy,* 2nd ed. Washington, D.C.: Institute for International Economics.

Hughes, Barry B. (2000) *Continuity and Change in World Politics,* 4th ed. Upper Saddle River, N.J.: Prentice Hall.

———. (1999) *International Futures: Choices in the Face of Uncertainty,* 3rd ed. Boulder, Colo.: Westview Press.

Hughes, Emmet John. (1972) *The Living Presidency.* New York: Coward, McGann, & Geoghegan.

Huntington, Samuel P. (2001) "The Coming Clash of Civilizations or, The West against the Rest," 199–202 in Charles W. Kegley, Jr., and Eugene R. Wittkopf (eds.), *The Global Agenda,* 6th ed. Boston: McGraw-Hill.

———. (1999a) "Big Powers Have Little Sway When Rival Civilizations Clash," *International Herald Tribune* (December 17): 10.

———. (1999b) "The Many Faces of the Future," 15–18 in Robert M. Jackson (ed.), *Global Issues 1999/00,* 15th ed. Guilford, Conn.: Dushkin/McGraw Hill.

———. (1996) *The Clash of Civilizations and the Remaking of World Order.* New York: Simon & Schuster.

———. (1991a) "America's Changing Strategic Interests," *Survival* 33 (January/February): 3–17.

———. (1991b) *The Third Wave: Democratization in the Late Twentieth Century.* Norman: University of Oklahoma Press.

Hurwitz, Jon, and Mark Peffley. (1987) "How Are Foreign Policy Attitudes Structured? A Hierarchical Model," *American Political Science Review* 81 (December): 1099–1120.

Hutzler, Charles. (2000) "China Increases Military Spending," (Columbia, S.C.) *The State* (March 7): A4.

Hyndman, Jennifer. (2000) *Managing Displacement: Refugees and the Politics of Humanitarianism.* Minneapolis: University of Minnesota Press.

Ignatieff, Michael. (1999) "Human Rights: The Midlife Crises," *New York Review of Books* 46 (May 20): 58–72.

Ignatius, David. (1999) "A Dangerous Indifference to Global Warming," *International Herald Tribune* (June 2): 9.

———. "Webbing the World's Rich and Poor Together," *International Herald Tribune* (August 2): 8

Ikenberry, G. John. (1993) "Salvaging the G-7," *Foreign Affairs* 72 (Spring): 132–139.

Iklé, Fred Charles. (1991–1992) "Comrades in Arms," *National Interest* 26 (Winter): 22–32.

International Monetary Fund (IMF). (1999) *World Economic Outlook September 1999.* Washington, D.C.: International Monetary Fund.

———. (1997) *World Economic Outlook May 1997.* Washington, D.C.: International Monetary Fund.

Isaak, Robert A. (2000) *Managing World Economic Change: International Political Economy,* 3rd ed. Upper Saddle River, N.J.: Prentice Hall.

———. (1975) *Individuals and World Politics.* North Scituate, Mass.: Duxbury.

Isenberg, David. (2000) "Combat for Sale: The New Post–Cold War Mercenaries," *USA Today* 129 (March): 12, 16.

Jackson, John H. (1994) "Managing the Trading System: The World Trade Organization and the Post–Uruguay Round GATT Agenda," 131–151 in Peter B. Kenen (ed.), *Managing the World Economy: Fifty Years after Bretton Woods.* Washington, D.C.: Institute for International Economics.

Jacobson, Harold K. (1984) *Networks of Interdependence: International Organizations and the Global Political System.* New York: Knopf.

Jaggers, Keith, and Ted Robert Gurr. (1995) "Transitions to Democracy: Tracking Democracy's Third Wave," *Journal of Peace Research* 32 (November): 469–482.

Jain, Subhash, and Piotz, Chelminski. (1999) "Beyond Buzzwords—Defining 'Globalization,'" *International Herald Tribune* (April 25): 9.

Jakobson, Max. (1991) "Filling the World's Most Impossible Job," *World Monitor* 4 (August): 25–33.

James, Barry. (1995) "Religious Fanaticism Fuels Terrorism," *International Herald Tribune* (October 31): 6.

James, Patrick. (1993) "Neorealism as a Research Enterprise: Toward Elaborated Structural Realism," *International Political Science Review* 14 (No. 2): 123–148.

Janis, Irving. (1982) *Groupthink: Psychological Studies of Policy Decisions and Fiascoes,* 2nd ed. Boston: Houghton Mifflin.

Janning, Josef. (1999) "European Integration Needs to Expand Its Horizons," *International Herald Tribune* (July 24–25): 6.

Jenkins, Simon. (1995) "Dresden: Time to Say We're Sorry," *Wall Street Journal* (February 14): A22.

Jensen, Lloyd. (1982) *Explaining Foreign Policy.* Englewood Cliffs, N.J.: Prentice Hall.

Jervis, Robert. (1999) "Realism, Neoliberalism, and Cooperation: Understanding the Debate," *International Security* 24 (Summer): 42–63.

———. (1992) "A Usable Past for the Future," 257–268 in Michael J. Hogan (ed.), *The End of the Cold War.* New York: Cambridge University Press.

———. (1991–1992) "The Future of World Politics: Will It Resemble the Past?" *International Security* 16 (Winter): 39–73.

———. (1991) "Will the New World Be Better?" 7–19 in Robert Jervis and Seweryn Bialer (eds.), *Soviet-American Relations after the Cold War.* Durham, N.C.: Duke University Press.

———. (1982) "Security Regimes," *International Organization* 16 (Spring): 357–378.

———. (1976) Perception and Misperception in World Politics. Princeton, N.J.: Princeton University Press.

Joffe, Josef. (1990) "Entangled Forever," *National Interest* 21 (Fall): 35–40.

———. (1985) "The Foreign Policy of the Federal Republic of Germany," 72–113 in Roy C. Macridis (ed.), *Foreign Policy in World Politics,* 6th ed. Englewood Cliffs, N.J.: Prentice Hall.

Johansen, Robert C. (1995) "Swords into Plowshares: Can Fewer Arms Yield More Security?" 253–279 in Charles W. Kegley, Jr. (ed.), *Controversies in International Relations Theory: Realism and the Neoliberal Challenge.* New York: St. Martin's.

———. (1991) "Do Preparations for War Increase or Decrease International Security?" 224–244 in Charles W. Kegley, Jr. (ed.), *The Long Postwar Peace.* New York: HarperCollins.

Johnson, Kevin. (1999) "Law Enforcement Plays Catch-Up with Reorganized Crime," *USA Today* (September 2): 15A.

Jones, Dorothy V. (1991) *Code of Peace: Ethics and Security in the World of the Warlord States.* Chicago: University of Chicago Press.

Joyner, Christopher C. (2001) "The Reality and Relevance of International Law in the Twenty-First Century," 243–256 in Charles W. Kegley, Jr., and Eugene Wittkopf (eds.), *The Global Agenda,* 6th edition. Boston: McGraw Hill.

———. (2000) *International Law in the Twenty-First Century.* Boulder, Colo.: Rowman & Littlefield.

———. (1995) "Collective Sanctions as Peaceful Coercion," 241–270 in *The Australian Yearbook of International Law 1995.* Canberra: Australian National University.

Juergensmeyer, Mark. (1993) *The New Cold War? Religious Nationalism Confronts the Secular State.* Berkeley: University of California Press.

Kagan, Donald. (1995) *On the Origins of War and the Preservation of Peace.* New York: Doubleday.

Kaiser, David. (1990) *Politics and War: European Conflict from Philip II to Hitler.* Cambridge, Mass.: Harvard University Press.

Kane, Hal. (1995) *The Hour of Departure: Forces That Create Refugees and Migrants.* Washington, D.C.: Worldwatch Institute.

Kaplan, Morton A. (1957) *System and Process in International Politics.* New York: Wiley.

Kaplan, Morton A., and Nicholas DeB. Katzenbach. (1961) *The Political Foundations of International Law.* New York: Wiley.

Kaplan, Robert D. (1999) "China: A World Power Again," *Atlantic* 284 (August): 16–18.

Kaplan, Robert. (1994) "The Coming Anarchy," *Atlantic* 279 (February): 44–76.

Kaplan, Stephen S. (1981) *Diplomacy of Power.* Washington, D.C.: Brookings Institution.

Kapstein, Ethan Barnaby. (1991–1992) "We Are Us: The Myth of the Multinational," *National Interest* 26 (Winter): 55–62.

Kapstein, Ethan B., and Michael Mastanduno. (1999) *Unipolar Politics: Realism and State Strategies after the Cold War.* New York: Columbia University Press.

Keegan, John. (1999) *The First World War.* New York: Knopf.

Keeley, Lawrence. (1996) *War before Civilization.* New York: Oxford University Press.

Keeny, Spurgeon M., Jr. (1993) "Arms Control during the Transition to the Post-Soviet World," 175–197 in Joseph Kruzel (ed.), *American Defense Annual,* 8th ed. New York: Lexington Books.

Keeny, Spurgeon M., Jr., and Wolfgang K. H. Panofsky. (1981) "MAD vs. NUTS: Can Doctrine or Weaponry Remedy the Mutual Hostage Relationship of the Superpowers?" *Foreign Affairs* 60 (Winter): 287–304.

Kegley, Charles W., Jr. (ed.). (1995) *Controversies in International Relations Theory: Realism and the Neoliberal Challenge.* New York: St. Martin's Press.

———. (1993) "The Neoidealist Moment in International Studies? Realist Myths and the New International Realities," *International Studies Quarterly* 37 (June): 131–146.

Kegley, Charles W., Jr., and Margaret G. Hermann. (2001) "Democracy and Peace," forthcoming in Peter Schraeder, ed., *Exporting Democracy? Rhetoric versus Reality in the International Pursuit of Democratization.* Boulder, Colo.: Lynne Rienner.

———. (1997) "Putting Military Intervention into the Democratic Peace: A Research Note," *Comparative Political Studies* 30 (February): 78–107.

Kegley, Charles W., Jr., and Gregory A. Raymond. (1999) *How Nations Make Peace.* Boston: Bedford/St. Martin's.

———. (1994) *A Multipolar Peace? Great-Power Politics in the Twenty-First Century.* New York: St. Martin's Press.

———. (1990) *When Trust Breaks Down: Alliance Norms and World Politics.* Columbia: University of South Carolina Press.

Kegley, Charles W., Jr., Gregory A. Raymond, and Margaret G. Hermann. (1998) "The Rise and Fall of the Nonintervention Norm: Some Correlates and Potential Consequences," *Fletcher Forum of World Affairs* 22 (Winter/Spring): 81–101.

Kelman, Herbert C. (1965) *International Behavior: A Social-Psychological Analysis.* New York: Holt, Rinehart & Winston.

Kelsen, Hans. (1945) *General Theory of Law and State.* Cambridge, Mass.: Harvard University Press.

Kennan, George F. (1984a) *The Fateful Alliance: France, Russia, and the Coming of the First World War.* New York: Pantheon.

———. (1984b) "Soviet-American Relations: The Politics of Discord and Collaboration," 107–120 in Charles W. Kegley, Jr., and Eugene R. Wittkopf (eds.), *The Global Agenda.* New York: Random House.

———. (1982) *The Nuclear Delusion.* New York: Pantheon.

———. (1976) "The United States and the Soviet Union, 1917–1976," *Foreign Affairs* 54 (July): 670–690.

———. (1967) *Memoirs.* Boston: Little, Brown.
———. (1954) *Realities of American Foreign Policy.* Princeton, N.J.: Princeton University Press.
———. (1951) *American Diplomacy, 1900–1950.* New York: New American Library.
——— ["X"]. (1947) "The Sources of Soviet Conduct," *Foreign Affairs* 25 (July): 566–582.
Kennedy, Paul. (1999) "In the Shadow of the Great War," *New York Review of Books 45* (August 12): 36–39.
———. (1994) "Overpopulation Tilts the Planet," *New Perspectives Quarterly* 11 (Fall): 4–6.
———. (1993) *Preparing for the Twenty-First Century.* New York: Random House.
———. (1992) "A Declining Empire Goes to War," 344–346 in Charles W. Kegley Jr., and Eugene R. Wittkopf (eds.), *The Future of American Foreign Policy.* New York: St. Martin's Press.
———. (1987) *The Rise and Fall of the Great Powers.* New York: Random House.
Keohane, Robert O. (1989) "International Relations Theory: Contributions from a Feminist Standpoint," *Millennium* 18 (Summer): 245–253.
——— (ed.). (1986a) *Neorealism and Its Critics.* New York: Columbia University Press.
———. (1986b) "Realism, Neorealism and the Study of World Politics," 1–26 in Robert O. Keohane (ed.), *Neorealism and Its Critics.* New York: Columbia University Press.
———. (1984) *After Hegemony: Cooperation and Discord in the World Political Economy.* Princeton, N.J.: Princeton University Press.
———. (1983) "Theory of World Politics: Structural Realism and Beyond," 503–540 in Ada Finifter (ed.), *Political Science: The State of the Discipline.* Washington, D.C.: American Political Science Association.
Keohane, Robert O., and Stanley Hoffmann. (1991) "Institutional Change in Europe in the 1980s," 1–39 in Robert O. Keohane and Stanley Hoffmann (eds.), *The New European Community: Decisionmaking and Institutional Change.* Boulder, Colo.: Westview Press.
Keohane, Robert O., and Joseph S. Nye, Jr. (2001) "Power and Interdependence in the Information Age," 26–36 in Charles W. Kegley, Jr., and Eugene R. Wittkopf (eds.), *The Global Agenda,* 6th ed. Boston: McGraw-Hill
———. (2000) "Globalization: What's New? What's Not? (And So What?)," *Foreign Policy* 118 (Spring): 104–119.
———. (1989) *Power and Interdependence,* 2nd ed. Glenview, Ill.: Scott, Foresman/Little, Brown.
———. (1988) "Complex Interdependence, Transnational Relations, and Realism: Alternative Perspectives on World Politics," 257–271 in Charles W. Kegley, Jr., and Eugene R. Wittkopf (eds.), *The Global Agenda,* 2nd ed. New York: Random House.
———. (1977) *Power and Interdependence.* Boston: Little, Brown.
Khripunov, Igor. (1997) "Have Guns Will Travel," *Bulletin of the Atomic Scientists* 53 (May/June): 47–51.
Kidder, Rushworth, M. (1990) "Why Modern Terrorism?" 135–138 in Charles W. Kegley, Jr. (ed.), *International Terrorism: Characteristics, Causes, Controls.* New York: St. Martin's Press.
Kidron, Michael, and Ronald Segal. (1995) *The State of the World Atlas,* 5th ed. London: Penguin Reference.
Kim, Dae Jung, and James D. Wolfensohn. (1999) "Economic Growth Requires Good Governance," *International Herald Tribune* (February 26): 6.
Kim, Samuel S. (1991) "The United Nations, Lawmaking and World Order," 109–124 in Richard A. Falk, Samuel S. Kim, and Saul H. Mendlovitz (eds.), *The United Nations and a Just World Order.* Boulder, Colo.: Westview Press.
Kindleberger, Charles P. (1973) *The World in Depression, 1929–1939.* Berkeley: University of California Press.
Kinnas, J. N. (1997) "Global Challenges and Multilateral Diplomacy," 23–48 in Ludwik Dembinski (ed.), *International Geneva Yearbook.* Berne, Switzerland: Peter Lang.
Kissinger, Henry. (1999) *Years of Renewal.* New York: Simon & Schuster.
———. (1997) "A World We Have Not Known," *Newsweek* (January 27): 74–81.
———. (1994) *Diplomacy.* New York: Simon & Schuster.
———. (1992) "Balance of Power Sustained," 238–248 in Graham Allison, and Gregory F. Treverton (eds.), *Rethinking America's Security.* New York: Norton.
———. (1979) *White House Years.* Boston: Little, Brown.
———. (1969) "Domestic Structure and Foreign Policy," 261–275 in James N. Rosenau (ed.), *International Politics and Foreign Policy.* New York: Free Press.
Klare, Michael T. (1999) "The New Arms Race," 139–143 in Robert M. Jackson (ed.), *Global Issues 1999/00,* 15th ed., New Guilford, Conn.: Dushkin/McGraw-Hill.
———. (1994) "Adding Fuel to the Fires: The Conventional Arms Trade in the 1990s," 134–154 in Michael T. Klare, and Daniel C. Thomas (eds.), *World Security.* New York: St. Martin's Press.
———. (1990) "Wars in the 1990s: Growing Firepower in the Third World," *Bulletin of the Atomic Scientists* 46 (May): 9–13.
———. (1988) "Low-Intensity Conflict," *Christianity and Crisis* 48 (February 1): 11–14.
———. (1987) "The Arms Trade: Changing Patterns in the 1980s," *Third World Quarterly* 9 (October): 1257–1281.
———. (1985) "Leaping the Firebreak," 168–173 in Charles W. Kegley, Jr., and Eugene R. Wittkopf (eds.), *The Nuclear Reader: Strategy, Weapons, War.* New York: St. Martin's Press.
Klare, Michael T., and Daniel C. Thomas (eds.). (1991) *World Security: Trends and Challenges at Century's End.* New York: St. Martin's Press.
Kluckhohn, Clyde. (1944) "Anthropological Research and World Peace," 143–152 in L. Bryson, Laurence Finkelstein, and Robert MacIver (eds.), *Approaches to World Peace.* New York: Conference on Science, Philosophy, and Religion.
Knickerbocker, Brad. (1999) "Who Rules Next? Where America Stands among World Empires," *Christian Science Monitor* (December 29): 1, 4.
Knorr, Klaus. (1977) "International Economic Leverage and Its Uses," 99–126 in Klaus Knorr and Frank N. Trager (eds.), *Economic Issues and National Security.* Lawrence: Regents Press of Kansas.
Knorr, Klaus, and James N. Rosenau (eds.). (1969) *Contending Approaches to International Politics.* Princeton, N.J.: Princeton University Press.
Knorr, Klaus, and Sidney Verba (eds.). (1961) *The International System.* Princeton, N.J.: Princeton University Press.
Kober, Stanley. (1990) "Idealpolitik," *Foreign Policy* 79 (Summer): 3–24.
Kobrin, Stephen J. (1997) "Electronic Cash and the End of National Markets," *Foreign Policy* 107 (Summer): 65–77.
Kokoski, Richard. (1994) "Non-Lethal Weapons: A Case Study of New Technology Developments," 367–388 in the Stockholm International Peace Research Institute, *SIPRI Yearbook 1994.* New York: Oxford University Press.
Korany, Bahgat. (1986) *How Foreign Policy Decisions Are Made in the Third World.* Boulder, Colo.: Westview Press.

Korb, Lawrence J. (1995a) "The Indefensible Defense Budget," *Washington Post National Weekly Edition* (July 17–23): 19.

———. (1995b) "Our Overstuffed Armed Forces," *Foreign Affairs* 74 (November/December): 23–34.

Koretz, Gene. (1996) "Fewer Guns, More Butter," *Business Week* (July 1): 22.

Korten, David. (1995) *When Corporations Rule the World.* West Hartford, Conn.: Berrett-Koehler.

Krasner, Stephen D. (1993) "International Political Economy," 453–455 in Joel Krieger (ed.), *The Oxford Companion to Politics of the World.* New York: Oxford University Press.

Krauthammer, Charles. (1999) "The Limits of Humanitarianism," *Time* (September 27): 118.

———. (1991) "The Unipolar Moment," *Foreign Affairs* 70 (No. 1): 23–33.

Krepinevich, Andrew F., and Steven M. Kusiak. (1998) "Smarter Bombs, Fewer Nukes," *Bulletin of the Atomic Scientists* 54 (November/December): 26–32.

Kristof, Nicholas D. (1993) "The Rise of China," *Foreign Affairs* 72 (November/December): 59–74.

Krugman, Paul. (2000) "Some Don't Want to Be Saved from Globalization," *International Herald Tribune* (February 17): 7.

Kruzel, Joseph. (1993) "American Security Policy in a New World Order," 1–23 in Joseph Kruzel (ed.), *American Defense Annual,* 8th ed. New York: Lexington Books.

———. (1991) "Arms Control, Disarmament, and the Stability of the Postwar Era," 247–269 in Charles W. Kegley, Jr. (ed.), *The Long Postwar Peace.* New York: HarperCollins.

Kugler, Jacek. (1993) "War," 962–966 in Joel Krieger (ed.), *The Oxford Companion to Politics of the World.* New York: Oxford University Press.

Kunz, Josef L. (1960) "Sanctions in International Law," *American Journal of International Law* 54 (April): 324–347.

Landes, David S. (1998) *The Wealth and Poverty of Nations: Why Are Some So Rich and Some So Poor?* New York: Norton.

Laqueur, Walter. (2001) "Terror's New Face," 82–89 in Charles W. Kegley, Jr., and Eugene R. Wittkopf (eds.), *The Global Agenda,* 6th ed. Boston: McGraw-Hill

———. (1998) "Postmodern Terrorism," 89–98 in Charles W. Kegley, Jr., and Eugene R. Wittkopf (eds.), *The Global Agenda,* 5th ed. New York: McGraw-Hill.

———. (1986) "Reflections on Terrorism," *Foreign Affairs* 65 (Fall): 86–100.

Lauren, Paul Gordon. (1999) *The Evolution of Human Rights.* Philadelphia: University of Pennsylvania Press.

Lebow, Richard Ned. (1981) *Between Peace and War: The Nature of International Crisis.* Baltimore: Johns Hopkins University Press.

Lebow, Richard Ned, and Janice Gross Stein. (1994) *We All Lost the Cold War.* Princeton, N.J.: Princeton University Press.

Lee, Rensselaer W., III. (1995) "Global Reach: The Threat of International Drug Trafficking," *Current History* 94 (May): 207–211.

Legro, Jeffrey W., and Andrew Moravcsik. (1999) "Is Anybody Still a Realist?" *International Security* 24 (Fall): 5–55.

Leventhal, Paul L. (1992) "Plugging the Leaks in Nuclear Export Controls: Why Bother?" *Orbis* 36 (Spring): 167–180.

Levi, Isaac. (1990) *Hard Choices: Decision Making under Unresolved Conflict.* New York: Cambridge University Press.

Levine, Robert A. (1999) "The Global Market Holds Poor Nations at its Mercy," *International Herald Tribune* (October 17–18): 8.

Levingston, Steven. (1999) "Does Territoriality Drive Human Aggression?" *International Herald Tribune* (April 14): 9.

Levy, Jack S. (2001) "War and Its Causes," 47–56 in Charles W. Kegley, Jr., and Eugene Wittkopf (eds.), *The Global Agenda,* 6th edition. Boston: McGraw Hill.

———. (1998a) "The Causes of War and the Conditions of Peace," *American Review of Political Science* 1: 139–165.

———. (1998b) "Towards a New Millennium: Structural Perspectives on the Causes of War," 47–57 in Charles W. Kegley, Jr., and Eugene R. Wittkopf (eds.), *The Global Agenda,* 5th ed. New York: McGraw-Hill.

———. (1997) "Prospect Theory, Rational Choice, and International Relations," *International Studies Quarterly* 41 (March): 87–112.

———. (1992) "An Introduction to Prospect Theory," *Political Psychology* 13 (June): 171–186.

———. (1991) "Long Cycles, Hegemonic Transitions, and the Long Peace," 147–176 in Charles W. Kegley, Jr. (ed.), *The Long Postwar Peace.* New York: HarperCollins.

———. (1990–1991) "Preferences, Constraints, and Choices in July 1914," *International Security* 15 (Winter): 151–186.

———. (1989a) "The Causes of War: A Review of Theories and Evidence," 209–333 in Philip E. Tetlock, Jo L. Husbands, Robert Jervis, Paul C. Stern, and Charles Tilly (eds.), *Behavior, Society, and Nuclear War.* New York: Oxford University Press.

———. (1989b) "The Diversionary Theory of War: A Critique," 259–288 in Manus I. Midlarsky (ed.), *Handbook of War Studies.* Boston: Unwin Hyman.

Lewis, George, and Theodore Postol. (1997) "Portrait of a Bad Idea," *Bulletin of the Atomic Scientists* 53 (July/August): 18–24.

Lewis, Paul. (1999) "Corporate Conduct Code Is Proposed for Third World Nations," *New York Times* (April 29): A7.

Leyton-Brown, David. (1987) "Introduction," 1–4 in David Leyton-Brown (ed.), *The Utility of International Economic Sanctions.* New York: St. Martin's Press.

Libicki, Martin. (2000) "Rethinking War: The Mouse's New Roar?" *Foreign Policy* 117 (Winter): 30–42.

Lifton, Robert Jay, and Richard Falk. (1982) *Indefensible Weapons: The Political and Psychological Case against Nuclearism.* New York: Basic Books.

Lilly, James, and Carl Ford. (1999) "China's Military: A Second Opinion," *National Interest* 57 (Fall): 71–77.

Lind, Michael. (1993) "Of Arms and the Woman," *New Republic* (November 15): 36–38.

Lindblom, Charles E. (1979) "Still Muddling, Not Yet Through," *Public Administration Review* 39 (November/December): 517–526.

Lindsay, James M. (1986) "Trade Sanctions as Policy Instruments: A Re-examination," *International Studies Quarterly* 30 (June): 153–173.

Lipman, Masha. (2000) "In Russia's Future, Hard Work Instead of Tempests," *International Herald Tribune* (February 21): 8.

Liska, George. (1968) *Alliances and the Third World.* Baltimore: Johns Hopkins University Press.

———. (1962) *Nations in Alliance: The Limits of Interdependence.* Baltimore: Johns Hopkins University Press.

Lissitzyn, Oliver J. (1963) "International Law in a Divided World," *International Conciliation* 542 (March): 3–69.

Little, David. (1993) "The Recovery of Liberalism," *Ethics and International Affairs* 7: 171–201.

Lopez, George A., and David Cortright. (1995) "Economic Sanctions in Contemporary Global Relations," 3–16 in David Cortright and George A. Lopez (eds.), *Economic Sanctions.* Boulder, Colo.: Westview Press.

Lopez, George A., Jackie G. Smith, and Ron Pagnucco. (1995) "The Global Tide," *Bulletin of the Atomic Scientists* 51 (July/August): 33–39.

Lorenz, Konrad. (1963) *On Aggression.* New York: Harcourt, Brace & World.

Lundestad, Geir. (1994) *The Fall of the Great Powers.* Oslo: Scandinavian University Press.

Lumpe, Lora, (1999) "The Lender of the Pack," *Bulletin of the Atomic Scientists* 58 (January–February): 27–33.

Lutz, Wolfgang. (1994) "The Future of World Population," *Population Bulletin* 49 (June): 1–47.

Lynch, Colum. (2000) "Split U.S. Policy on Iraq: Bombing While Trading," *International Herald Tribune* (February 21): 1, 14.

Mack, Andrew. (1996) "Allow the Idea of Nuclear Disarmament a Hearing," *International Herald Tribune* (January 26): 8.

Mackinder, Sir Halford. (1919) *Democratic Ideals and Reality.* New York: Holt.

Mahan, Alfred Thayer. (1890) *The Influence of Sea Power in History.* Boston: Little, Brown.

Majeed, Akhtar. (1991) "Has the War System Really Become Obsolete?" *Bulletin of Peace Proposals* 22 (December): 419–425.

Mansfield, Edward D., and Jack Snyder. (1995) "Democratization and the Danger of War," *International Security* 20 (Summer): 5–38.

Marantz, Paul. (1987) "Economic Sanctions in the Polish Crisis," 131–146 in David Leyton-Brown (ed.), *The Utility of International Economic Sanctions.* New York: St. Martin's Press.

Markusen, Ann, Peter Hall, Scott Campbell, and Sabina Dietrick. (1991) *The Rise of the Gunbelt: The Military Remapping of America.* New York: Oxford University Press.

Marshall, Tyler. (1999) "Anti-NATO Axis Could Pose Threat, U.S. Analysts Say," *Los Angeles Times World Report* (October 11): 1, 4.

Mastanduno, Michael. (1991) "Do Relative Gains Matter? America's Response to Japanese Industrial Policy," *International Security* 16 (Summer): 73–113.

Masters, Roger D. (1969) "World Politics as a Primitive Political System," 104–118 in James N. Rosenau (ed.), *International Politics and Foreign Policy.* New York: Free Press.

Mathews, Jessica T. (1997) "Power Shift: The Rise of Global Civil Society," *Foreign Affairs* 76 (January/February): 50–66.

———. (1996) "Global Warming: No Longer in Doubt," *Washington Post National Weekly Edition* (January 1–7): 29.

McGowan, Patrick J. (1981) "Imperialism in World-System Perspective," *International Studies Quarterly* 25 (March): 43–68.

McGranahan, Donald. (1995) "Measurement of Development," *International Social Science Journal* 143 (March): 39–59.

McKibben, Bill. (1998) "The Fortune of Population," *Atlantic Monthly* (May): 55–78.

Mead, Margaret. (1968) "Warfare Is Only an Invention—Not a Biological Necessity," 270–274 in Leon Bramson and George W. Goethals (eds.), *War.* New York: Basic Books.

Mead, Walter Russell. (1995) "Forward to the Past," *New York Times Magazine* (June 4): 48–49.

Meadows, Donella H. (1993) "Seeing the Population Issue Whole," *The World & I* 8 (June): 396–409.

Meadows, Donella H., Dennis L. Meadows, Jørgen Randers, and William W. Behrens III. (1974) *The Limits to Growth.* New York: New American Library.

Mearsheimer, John J. (1990) "Back to the Future: Instability in Europe after the Cold War," *International Security* 15 (Summer): 5–56.

Medley, Richard. (1999) "Europe's Next Big Idea: Strategy and Economics Point to a European Military," *Foreign Affairs* 78 (September/October): 18–22.

Melanson, Richard A. (1983) *Writing History and Making Policy: The Cold War, Vietnam, and Revisionism.* Lanham, Md.: University Press of America.

Melko, Matthew. (1999). "Cycles of General War in World History," *International Interactions* 25 (No. 3): 287–299.

Metz, Steven, and James Kievit. (1995) *Strategy and the Revolution in Military Affairs.* Carlisle Barracks, Pa.: U.S. Army War College.

Midlarsky, Manus I. (1988) *The Onset of World War.* Boston: Unwin Hyman.

Miller, Judith. (1999) "Globalization Widens Rich-Poor Gap, UN Report ," *New York Times* (July 13): A8.

Miller, Marian A. L. (1995) *The Third World in Global Environmental Politics.* Boulder, Colo.: Lynne Rienner.

Mills, C. Wright. (1956) *The Power Elite.* New York: Oxford University Press.

Mitrany, David. (1966) *A Working Peace System.* Chicago: Quadrangle.

Mittelman, James H. (2000) *The Globalization Syndrome: Transformation and Resistance.* Princeton, N.J.: Princeton University Press.

Modelski, George (ed.). (1987a) *Exploring Long Cycles.* Boulder, Colo.: Lynne Rienner.

———. (1987b) "The Study of Long Cycles," 1–15 in George Modelski (ed.), *Exploring Long Cycles.* Boulder, Colo.: Lynne Rienner.

———. (1978) "The Long Cycle of Global Politics and the Nation-State," *Comparative Studies in Society and History* 20 (April): 214–235.

———. (1964) "The International Relations of Internal War," 14–44 in James N. Rosenau (ed.), *International Aspects of Civil Strife.* Princeton, N.J.: Princeton University Press.

Modelski, George, and William R. Thompson. (1999) "The Long and the Short of Global Politics in the Twenty-first Century: An Evolutionary Approach," *International Studies Review,* special issue, ed. by Davis B. Bobrow: 109–140.

———. (1996) *Leading Sectors and World Powers.* Columbia: University of South Carolina Press.

———. (1989) "Long Cycles and Global War," 23–54 in Manus I. Midlarsky (ed.), *Handbook of War Studies.* Boston: Unwin Hyman.

Moffett, George D. (1994) *Critical Masses: The Global Population Challenge.* New York: Viking.

Moisy, Claude. (1997) "Myths of the Global Information Village," *Foreign Policy* 107 (Summer): 78–87.

Møller, Bjørn. (1992) *Common Security and Nonoffensive Defense: A Neorealist Perspective.* Boulder, Colo.: Lynne Rienner.

Moon, Bruce E., and William J. Dixon. (1992) "Basic Needs and Growth—Welfare Trade-offs," *International Studies Quarterly* 36 (June): 191–212.

———. (1985) "Politics, the State, and Basic Human Needs: A Cross-National Study," *American Journal of Political Science* 29 (November): 661–694.

Moore, Mike. (1995) "Midnight Never Came," *Bulletin of the Atomic Scientists* 51 (November/December): 16–27.

Moran, Theodore H. (1999) *Foreign Direct Investment Development: the New Policy Agenda for Developing Countries.* Washington, D.C.: Institute for International Economics.

Moravcsik, Andrew. (1997) "Taking Preferences Seriously: A Liberal Theory of International Politics," *International Organization* 51 (Autumn): 513–553.

Morgan, T. Clifton, and Kenneth N. Bickers. (1992) "Domestic Discontent and the External Use of Force," *Journal of Conflict Resolution* 36 (March): 25–52.

Morgan, T. Clifton, and Sally Howard Campbell. (1991) "Domestic Structure, Decisional Constraints and War," *Journal of Conflict Resolution* 35 (June): 187–211.

Morgan, T. Clifton, and Valerie L. Schwebach. (1992) "Take Two Democracies and Call Me in the Morning: A Prescription for Peace?" *International Interactions* 17 (No. 4): 305–320.

Morgenthau, Hans J. (1985) *Politics among Nations,* 6th ed. Revised by Kenneth W. Thompson. New York: Knopf.

———. (1983) "Defining the National Interest—Again," 32–39 in Charles W. Kegley, Jr., and Eugene R. Wittkopf (eds.), *Perspectives on American Foreign Policy.* New York: St. Martin's Press.

———. (1959) "Alliances in Theory and Practice," 184–212 in Arnold Wolfers (ed.), *Alliance Policy in the Cold War.* Baltimore: Johns Hopkins University Press.

———. (1948) *Politics among Nations.* New York: Knopf.

Morris, Desmond. (1969) *The Human Zoo.* New York: Dell.

Mowlana, Hamid. (1995) "The Communications Paradox," *Bulletin of the Atomic Scientists* 51 (July): 40.

Mulhollin, Gary. (1994) "The Business of Defense Is Defending Business," *Washington Post National Weekly Edition* (February 14–20): 23.

Myers, Steven Lee. (1999) "Without Public Debate, Pounding of Iraq Goes On," (Columbia, S.C.) *The State* (August 20): A8.

Nardin, Terry. (1983) *Law, Morality, and the Relations of States.* Princeton, N.J.: Princeton University Press.

Nardin, Terry, and David R. Mapel (eds.). (1992) *Traditions of International Ethics.* New York: Cambridge University Press.

Nathan, James A. (1997) "Can Economic Sanctions Succeed as Foreign Policy?" *USA Today* 126 (September): 37.

Neild, Robert. (2000) "Expose the Unsavory Business behind Cruel Wars," *International Herald Tribune* (February 17): 6.

Nelson, Stephan D. (1974) "Nature/Nurture Revisited: A Review of the Biological Bases of Conflict," *Journal of Conflict Resolution* 18 (June): 285–335.

Neuman, Johanna. (1995–1996) "The Media's Impact on International Affairs, Then and Now," *National Interest* 16 (Winter): 109–123.

Newland, Kathleen. (1994) "Refugees: The Rising Flood," *World Watch* 7 (May/June): 10–20.

Nicholson, Michael. (1992) *Rationality and the Analysis of International Conflict.* Cambridge, Eng.: Cambridge University Press.

Niebuhr, Reinhold. (1947) *Moral Man and Immoral Society.* New York: Scribner's.

Nietschmann, Bernard. (1991) "Third World War: The Global Conflict over the Rights of Indigenous Nations," 172–176 in Robert M. Jackson (ed.), *Global Issues 91/92.* Guilford, Conn.: Dushkin.

Nikovich, Frank. (1999) *The Wilsonian Century.* Chicago: University of Chicago Press.

Nincic, Miroslav. (1982) *The Arms Race.* New York: Praeger.

Nnoli, Okwudiba. (1993) "Ethnicity," 280–284 in Joel Krieger (ed.), *The Oxford Companion to Politics of the World.* New York: Oxford University Press.

Nye, Joseph S., Jr. (2001) "The Changing Nature of World Power," 95–107 in Charles W. Kegley, Jr., and Eugene R. Wittkopf (eds.), *The Global Agenda,* 6th ed. Boston: McGraw-Hill.

———. (1990) *Bound to Lead: The Changing Nature of American Power.* New York: Basic Books.

———. (1987) "Nuclear Learning and U.S.-Soviet Security Regimes," *International Organization* 41 (Summer): 371–402.

Oberdorfer, Don. (1991) *The Turn: From the Cold War to a New Era.* New York: Poseidon.

O'Brien, Conor Cruise. (1993) "The Wrath of Ages," *Foreign Affairs* 72 (November–December): 142–149.

———. (1977) "Liberty and Terrorism," *International Security* 2 (Fall): 56–67.

O'Brien, Richard. (1992) *Global Financial Integration: The End of Geography.* New York: Council on Foreign Relations Press.

Odell, John S. (2000) *Negotiating the World Economy.* Ithaca, N.Y.: Cornell University Press.

Olson, Mancur. (1971) "Rapid Growth as a Destabilizing Force," 215–227 in James C. Davies (ed.), *When Men Revolt and Why.* New York: Free Press.

Oldstone, Michael B. A. (1998) *Viruses, Plagues, and History.* New York: Oxford University Press.

Oneal, John R., and Bruce Russett. (1999) "Assessing the Liberal Peace with Alternative Specifications: Trade Still Reduces Conflict," *Journal of Peace Research* 36 (July): 423–442.

Onuf, Nicholas. (2001) "Worlds of Our Making: The Strange Career of Constructivism in International Relations," forthcoming in Donald J. Puchala (ed.), *Visions of International Relations: Assessing an Academic Field.* Columbia: University of South Carolina Press.

———. (1989) *World of Our Making: Rules and Rule in Social Theory and International Relations.* Columbia: University of South Carolina Press.

———. (1982) "Global Law-Making and Legal Thought," 1–82 in Nicholas Greenwood Onuf (ed.), *Law-Making in the Global Community.* Durham, N.C.: Carolina Academic Press.

Opello, Walter C., Jr., and Stephen J. Rosow. (1999) *The Nation-State and Global Order: A Historical Introduction to Contemporary Politics.* Boulder, Colo.: Lynne Rienner.

Organski, A. F. K. (1968) *World Politics.* New York: Knopf.

Organski, A. F. K., and Jacek Kugler. (1980) *The War Ledger.* Chicago: University of Chicago Press.

Osgood, Robert E. (1968) *Alliances and American Foreign Policy.* Baltimore: Johns Hopkins University Press.

Ostrom, Charles W., and Brian L. Job. (1986) "The President and the Use of Force," *American Political Science Review* 80 (June): 554–566.

Owen, John M., IV. (1997) *Liberal Peace, Liberal War.* Ithaca, N.Y.: Cornell University Press.

Packenham, Robert. (1992) *The Dependency Movement: Scholarship and Politics in Dependency Studies.* Cambridge, Mass.: Harvard University Press.

Parry, Clive. (1968) "The Function of Law in the International Community," 1–54 in Max Sørensen (ed.), *Manual of Public International Law.* New York: St. Martin's Press.

Passel, Jeffrey S., and Michael Fix. (1994) "Myths about Immigrants," *Foreign Policy* 95 (Summer): 151–160.

Pastor, Robert A. (ed.) (1999) "The Great Powers in the Twentieth Century," 1–31 in *A Century's Journey: How the Great Powers Shape the World.* New York: Basic Books.

Payne, James E., and Anandi P. Sahu (eds.). (1993) *Defense Spending and Economic Growth.* Boulder, Colo.: Westview Press.

Pear, Robert. (1997) "AIDS' Numbers Make a Giant Leap," *International Herald Journal* (November 27): 1, 6.

Peceny, Mark. (2000) *Democracy at the Points of Bayonets.* College Station: Penn State Press.

Peirce, Neal R. (2000) "Keep an Eye on 'Citistates' Where Economic Action Is," *International Herald Tribune* (January 11): 8.

———. (1997) "Does the Nation-State Have a Future?" *International Herald Tribune* (April 4): 9.

Peterson, Erik. (1998) "Looming Collision of Capitalisms?" 296–307 in Charles W. Kegley, Jr., and Eugene R. Wittkopf (eds.), *The Global Agenda,* 5th ed. New York: McGraw-Hill.

Peterson, John L. (1999) "Getting Ready for the Twenty-First Century," *USA Today* 128 (May): 56–58.

Peterson, Niels Helveg. (1999) "Place Priority on Human Rights in Applying International Law," *International Herald Tribune* (July 27): 7.

Peterson, V. Spike, and Anne Sisson Runyan. (1993) *Global Gender Issues.* Boulder, Colo.: Westview Press.

Petit, Pascal, and Luc Soete. (1999) "Globalization in Search of a Future," *International Social Science Journal* 160 (June): 163–181.

Pfaff, William. (2000) "Look Again: The Nation-State Isn't Going Away," *International Herald Tribune* (January 11): 8.

———. (1999) "Getting the Facts on a Bumper Century for War Crimes," *International Herald Tribune* (September 4–5): 8.

———. (1996) "Seeking a Broader Vision of Economic Society," *International Herald Tribune* (February 3–4): 6.

Pfetsch, Frank L. (1999) "Globalization: A Threat and a Challenge for the State," paper presented at the European Standing Conference on International Studies, Vienna, September 11–13.

Philips, Rosemarie, and Stuart K. Tucker. (1991) *U.S. Foreign Policy and Developing Countries: Discourse and Data 1991.* Washington, D.C.: Overseas Development Council.

Pickering, Jeffrey. (1999) "The Structural Share of Force: Interstate Interaction in the Zones of Peace and Turmoil," *International Interactions* 25 (No. 4): 363–391.

Pierre, Andrew J. (1984) "The Politics of International Terrorism," 84–92 in Charles W. Kegley, Jr., and Eugene R. Wittkopf (eds.), *The Global Agenda.* New York: Random House.

Pincus, Walter. (1999) "Their Soldiers Aren't Ready to Fight," *Washington Post National Weekly Edition* (March 1): 18.

Pipes, Richard. (1977) "Why the Soviet Union Thinks It Could Fight and Win a Nuclear War," *Commentary* 26 (July): 21–34.

Pirages, Dennis. (1998) "An Ecological Approach to International Relations," 387–394 in Charles W. Kegley, Jr., and Eugene R. Wittkopf (eds.), *The Global Agenda,* 5th ed. New York: McGraw-Hill.

Pollack, Andrew. (1999) "Growing Pains: Why Hopes for a Global Biotech Treaty Withered," *International Herald Tribune* (February 25): 1, 4.

Pomfret, John. (1999) "China Maps Changes in Defense Strategy," *International Herald Tribune* (June 12–13): 1, 4.

Population Reference Bureau. (2000) *2000 World Population Data Sheet.* Washington, D.C.: Population Reference Bureau.

———. (1981) *World Population: Toward the Next Century.* Washington, D.C.: Population Reference Bureau.

Porter, Bruce D. (1994) *War and the Rise of the State.* New York: Free Press.

Porter, Gareth. (1995) "Environmental Security as a National Security Issue," *Current History* 94 (May): 218–222.

Porter, Gareth, and Janet Welsh Brown. (1996) *Global Environmental Politics,* 2nd ed. Boulder, Colo.: Westview Press.

Potter, William C. (1992) "The New Nuclear Suppliers," *Orbis* 46 (Spring): 199–210.

Pound, Edward T., and Jihan El-Tahri. (1994) "Sanctions: The Pluses and Minuses," *U.S. News & World Report* (October 31): 58–71.

Powell, Robert. *In the Shadow of Power: States and Strategies in International Politics.* Princeton, N.J.: Princeton University Press.

Powers, Thomas. (1994) "Downwinders: Some Casualties of the Nuclear Age," *Atlantic Monthly* (March): 119–124.

Puchala, Donald J. (2001) "Building Peace in Pieces: The Promise of European Unity," 160–174 in Charles W. Kegley, Jr., and Eugene R. Wittkopf (eds.), *The Global Agenda,* 6th ed. Boston: McGraw-Hill

———. (1994) "Some World Order Options for Our Time," *Peace Forum* 11 (November): 17–30.

Putnam, Robert D. (1988) "Diplomacy and Domestic Politics: The Logic of Two-Level Games," *International Organization* 42 (Summer): 427–460.

Quester, George. (1992) "Conventional Deterrence: The Past as Prologue," 31–51 in Gary L. Guertner, Robert Haffa, Jr., and George Quester, *Conventional Forces and the Future of Deterrence.* Carlisle Barracks, Pa.: U.S. Army War College.

Quinn, Dennis. (1997) "The Correlates of Change in International Financial Regulation," *American Political Science Review* 91 (September): 531–551.

Ralph, Jason G. (2001) *Beyond the Security Dilemma: Ending America's Cold War.* Brookfield, Vt.: Ashgate.

Rapkin, David, and William Thompson, with Jon A. Christopherson. (1989) "Bipolarity and Bipolarization in the Cold War Era," *Journal of Conflict Resolution* 23 (June): 261–295.

Ratner, Stephen A. (1997) *The New UN Peacekeeping: Building Peace in Lands of Conflict after the Cold War.* New York: St. Martin's Press.

Ray, James Lee. (1995) *Democracy and International Conflict: An Evaluation of the Democratic Peace Proposition.* Columbia: University of South Carolina Press.

Raymond, Gregory A. (1999) "Necessity in Foreign Policy," *Political Science Quarterly* 113 (Winter): 673–688.

———. (1994) "Democracies, Disputes, and Third-Party Intermediaries," *Journal of Conflict Resolution* 38 (March): 24–42.

Reardon, Betty. (1985) *Sexism and the War System.* New York: Teachers College Press.

Regan, Patrick M. (2000) *Civil Wars and Foreign Powers: Outside Intervention in Interstate Conflict.* Ann Arbor: University of Michigan Press.

———. (1994) *Organizing Societies for War: The Process and Consequences of Societal Militarization.* Westport, Conn.: Praeger.

Reich, Robert. (1990) "Who Is Us?" *Harvard Business Review* 68 (January–February): 53–64.

Reinicke, Wolfgang H. (1997) "Global Public Policy," *Foreign Affairs* 76 (November/December): 127–38.

Renner, Michael. (1999) "Arms Control Orphans," *Bulletin of the Atomic Scientists* 58 (January/February): 22–27.

Repetto, Robert, and Jonathan Lash. (1997) "Planetary Roulette: Gambling with the Climate," *Foreign Policy* 108 (Fall): 84–98.

Rice, Susan, and David Scheffer. (1999) "Sudan Must End Its Brutal War against Civilians," *International Herald Tribune* (September 1): 6.

Richardson, Lewis F. (1960a) *Arms and Insecurity.* Pittsburgh: Boxwood Press.

———. (1960b) *Statistics of Deadly Quarrels*. Chicago: Quadrangle.
Richardson, Michael. (1995) "Fears of a Militarily Resurgent Japan," *International Herald Tribune* (August 15): 1, 7.
Richardson, Neil R. (1995) "International Trade as a Force for Peace," 281–293 in Charles W. Kegley, Jr. (ed.), *Controversies in International Relations Theory*. New York: St. Martin's Press.
Riddell-Dixon, Elizabeth. (1995) "Social Movements and the United Nations," *International Social Science Journal* 144 (June): 289–303.
Ridley, Matt. (1998) *The Origins of Virtue: Human Instincts and the Evolution of Cooperation*. New York: Viking.
Rieff, David. (1999) "The Precarious Triumph of Human Rights," *New York Times Magazine* (August 8): 36–41.
Riggs, Robert E., and Jack C. Plano. (1994) *The United Nations: International Organization and World Politics*, 2nd ed. Belmont, Calif.: Wadsworth.
Riker, William H. (1962) *The Theory of Political Coalitions*. New Haven, Conn.: Yale University Press.
Roca, Sergio. (1987) "Economic Sanctions against Cuba," 87–104 in David Leyton-Brown (ed.), *The Utility of International Economic Sanctions*. New York: St. Martin's Press.
Rodrik, Dani. (1997a) *Has Globalization Gone Too Far?* Washington, D.C.: Institute for International Economics.
———. (1997b) "Sense and Nonsense in the Globalization Debate," *Foreign Policy* 107 (Summer): 19–37.
Rosa, Jean-Jacques. (2000) *Euro Error*. New York: Algrera.
Rosecrance, Richard. (1997) "Economics and National Security: The Evolutionary Process," 209–238 in Richard Shultz, Roy Godson, and George Quester (eds.), *Security Studies for the Twenty-First Century*. New York: Brassey's.
Rosenau, James N. (1998) "Disorder and Order in a Turbulent World: The Evolution of Globalized Space," 145–169 in Charles W. Kegley, Jr., and Eugene R. Wittkopf (eds.), *The Global Agenda*, 5th ed. New York: McGraw-Hill.
———. (1997) *Along the Domestic-Foreign Frontier: Exploring Governance in a Turbulent World*. Cambridge, Eng.: Cambridge University Press.
———. (1995) "Security in a Turbulent World," *Current History* 94 (May): 193–200.
———. (1990) *Turbulence in World Politics: A Theory of Change and Continuity*. Princeton, N.J.: Princeton University Press.
———. (1980) *The Scientific Study of Foreign Policy*. New York: Nichols.
Rosenberg, Shawn W. (1988) *Reason, Ideology and Politics*. Princeton, N.J.: Princeton University Press.
Rosenburg, Tina. (1999) "International Law Is Dissolving the World's Borders," *International Herald Tribune* (July 3–4): 6.
Rosenthal, Joel H. (1991) *Righteous Realists*. Baton Rouge: Louisiana State University Press.
Ross, Philip E. (1997) "The End of Infantry?" *Forbes* (July 7): 182–185.
Rosset, Peter. (1999) "Biotechnology Won't Feed the World," *International Herald Tribune* (September 2): 8.
Rostow, W. W. (1960) *The Stages of Economic Growth*. Cambridge, Eng.: Cambridge University Press.
Rothgeb, John M., Jr. (1993) *Defining Power: Influence and Force in the Contemporary International System*. New York: St. Martin's Press
Rowan, Carl. (1999) "U.S. Is on Right Side of History in Kosovo Campaign," (Columbia, S.C.) *The State* (March 30): A9.
Rubin, Nancy. (1999) "It's Official: All of the World Is Entitled to Democracy," *International Herald Tribune* (May 18): 8.
Ruggie, John Gerald. (1993) "Wandering in the Void: Charting the UN's New Strategic Role," *Foreign Affairs* 72 (November/December): 27–31.
———. (1983) "Continuity and Transformation in the World Polity: Toward a Neorealist Synthesis," *World Politics* 35 (January): 261–285.
Rummel, Rudolph J. (1994) *Death by Government*. New Brunswick, N.J.: Transaction Books.
———. (1983) "Libertarianism and International Violence," *Journal of Conflict Resolution* 27 (March): 27–71.
Runyan, Curtis. (1999) "NGOs Proliferate World Wide," 144–145 in Lester R. Brown, et al., *Vital Signs 1999*. New York: Norton.
Rupert, James. (1995) "The Cloud over Chernobyl," *Washington Post National Weekly Edition* (June 26–July 2): 6–7.
Rusi, Alpo. (1997) *Dangerous Peace*. Boulder, Colo.: Westview Press.
Russett, Bruce. (2001) "How Democracy, Interdependence, and International Organizations Create a System for Peace," 232–242 in Charles W. Kegley, Jr., and Eugene Wittkopf (eds.), *The Global Agenda*, 6th edition. Boston: McGraw Hill.
———. (1993) *Grasping the Democratic Peace: Principles for a Post–Cold War World*. Princeton, N.J.: Princeton University Press.
———. (1982) "Defense Expenditures and National Well-Being," *American Political Science Review* 76 (December): 767–777.
Russett, Bruce, and John Oneal. (2000) *Triangulating Peace: Democracy, Interdependence, and International Organization*. New York: Norton.
Russett, Bruce, and Harvey Starr. (1996) *World Politics: The Menu for Choice*, 5th ed. New York: Freeman.
Russett, Bruce, Harvey Starr, and David Kinsella. (2000) *World Politics: The Menu for Choice*, 6th ed. Boston: Bedford/St. Martin's.
Russett, Bruce, and James S. Sutterlin. (1991) "The UN in a New World Order," *Foreign Affairs* 70 (Spring): 69–83.
Sachs, Jeffrey. (1997) "The Limits of Convergence," *Economist* (June 14): 19–22.
Sadowaski. Yahya, (1998) "Ethnic Conflict" *Foreign Policy* 112 (Summer): 12–23.
Sagan, Carl. (1989) "Understanding Growth Rates: The Secret of the Persian Chessboard," *Parade* (February 14): 14.
———. (1988) "The Common Enemy," *Parade* (February 7): 4–7.
Sagan, Carl, and Richard Turco. (1993) "Nuclear Winter in the Post–Cold War Era," *Journal of Peace Research* 30 (November): 369–373.
Sandel, Michael J. (1996) "America's Search for a New Public Philosophy," *Atlantic Monthly* (March): 57–74.
Sandler, Todd, and Keith Hartley. (1995) *The Economics of Defense*. New York: Cambridge University Press.
Sanger, David E. (1998) "Contagion Effect: A Guide to Modern Domino Theory," *New York Times* (August 2): Section 4, 1, 5
Scarborough, Grace E. Iusi, and Bruce Bueno de Mesquita. (1988) "Threat and Alignment," *International Interactions* 14 (No. 1): 85–93.
Schelling, Thomas C. (1978) *Micromotives and Macrobehavior*. New York: Norton.
———. (1966) *Arms and Influence*. New Haven, Conn.: Yale University Press.
Schlagheck, Donna M. (1990) "Superpowers, Foreign Policy, and Terrorism," 170–197 in Charles W. Kegley, Jr. (ed.), *International Terrorism*. New York: St. Martin's Press.
Schlesinger, Arthur, Jr. (1997) "Has Democracy a Future?" *Foreign Affairs* 76 (September/October): 2–12.

———. (1986) *The Cycles of American History.* Boston: Houghton Mifflin.

———. (1983) "Pretension in the Presidential Pulpit," *Wall Street Journal* (March 17): 26.

Schmemann, Serge. (1999) "What Makes Nations Turn Corrupt?" *New York Times* (August 28): A15, A 17.

Schneider, Barry R., and Lawrence E. Grinter (eds.). (1995) *Battlefield of the Future: Twenty-First Century Warfare Issues.* Maxwell Air Force Base, Ala.: Air War College.

Schuler, Corinna. (1999) "Helping Children Warriors Regain Their Humanity," *Christian Science Monitor* (October 20): 1, 12–13.

Schwab, Klaus, and Claude Smadja. (1999) "Globalization Needs a Human Face," *International Herald Tribune* (January 28): 8.

———. (1996) "Start Taking the Backlash against Globalization Seriously," *International Herald Tribune* (February 1): 1, 8.

Schwartz, Regina M. (1997) *The Curse of Cain: The Violent Legacy of Monotheism.* Chicago, Ill.: University of Chicago Press.

Schwartz, Stephen I. (2000) "Outmaneuvered, Outgunned, and Out of Sight," *Bulletin of the Atomic Scientists* 56 (January/February): 24–31.

Schweller, Randall L. (1999) Review of *From Wealth to Power,* by Fareed Zakaria, *American Political Science Review* 93 (June 1999): 497–499.

———. (1992) "Domestic Structure and Preventive War," *World Politics* 44 (January): 235–269.

Seck, Manadon Manosour. (1999) "Shrinking Forests," *Christian Science Monitor* (May 3): 9.

Seib, Gerald F. (1999) "Another Great Threat Looms: China as New Demon," *Wall Street Journal* (May 26): A21.

Sellers, M. N. S. (1998) "Separatism and the Democratic Entitlement in International Law," in *The Challenge of Non-State Actors.* Washington, D.C.: American Society of International Law.

Sen, Amartya. (1994) "Population: Delusion and Reality," *New York Review of Books* 41 (September 22): 62–71.

Shannon, Thomas Richard. (1989) *An Introduction to the World-System Perspective.* Boulder, Colo.: Westview Press.

Shannon, Victoria. (1999) "What's Lurking behind Those Slow Downloads," *International Herald Tribune* (May 27): 6.

Shawcross, William. (2000) *Deliver Us from Evil: Peacekeepers, Warlords, and a World of Endless Conflict.* New York: Simon & Schuster.

Sheehan, Michael. (1996) "A Regional Perspective on the Globalization Process," *Korean Journal of Defense Analysis* 8 (Winter): 53–74.

Shultz, Richard, Roy Godson, and George Quester (eds.). (1997) *Security Studies for the Twenty-First Century.* New York: Brassey's.

Shultz, Richard H., Jr., and William J. Olson. (1994) *Ethnic and Religious Conflict: Emerging Threat to U.S. Security.* Washington, D.C.: National Strategy Information Center.

Siegel, Martin J. (1983) "Survival," *USA Today* 112 (August): 1–2.

Simmel, Georg. (1956) *Conflict.* Glencoe, Ill.: Free Press.

Simon, Herbert A. (1997) *Models of Bonded Rationality.* Cambridge, Mass.: MIT Press.

———. (1982) *Models of Bounded Rationality.* Cambridge, Mass.: MIT Press.

———. (1957) *Models of Man.* New York: Wiley.

Sinding, Steven W. (1999) "Now We Can Be Serious about Population Politics," *International Herald Tribune* (February 8): 8.

Singer, Hans W., and Javed A. Ansari. (1988) *Rich and Poor Countries,* 4th ed. London: Unwin Hyman.

Singer, J. David. (1991) "Peace in the Global System: Displacement, Interregnum, or Transformation?" 56–84 in Charles W. Kegley, Jr. (ed.), *The Long Postwar Peace.* New York: HarperCollins.

———. (1981) "Accounting for International War: The State of the Discipline," *Journal of Peace Research* 18 (No. 1): 1–18.

———. (ed.). (1968) *Quantitative International Politics.* New York: Free Press.

———. (1961) "The Level-of-Analysis Problem in International Relations," 77–92 in Klaus Knorr and Sidney Verba (eds.), *The International System.* Princeton, N.J.: Princeton University Press.

Singer, J. David, and Melvin Small. (1974) "Foreign Policy Indicators," *Policy Sciences* 5 (September): 271–296.

———. (1968) "Alliance Aggregation and the Onset of War, 1815–1945," 247–285 in J. David Singer (ed.), *Quantitative International Politics.* New York: Free Press.

Singer, Max (1999) "The Population Surprise," *Atlantic* (August): 22–25

Singer, Max, and Aaron Wildavsky. (1993) *The Real World Order: Zones of Peace/Zones of Turmoil.* Chatham, N.J.: Chatham House.

Sivard, Ruth Leger. (1996) *World Military and Social Expenditures 1996.* Washington, D.C.: World Priorities.

———. (1993) *World Military and Social Expenditures 1993.* Washington, D.C.: World Priorities.

———. (1991) *World Military and Social Expenditures 1991.* Washington, D.C.: World Priorities.

———. (1982) *World Military and Social Expenditures 1982.* Leesburg, Va.: World Priorities.

———. (1979) *World Military and Social Expenditures 1979.* Leesburg, Va.: World Priorities.

Siverson, Randolph M., and Julian Emmons. (1991) "Democratic Political Systems and Alliance Choices," *Journal of Conflict Resolution* 35 (June): 285–306.

Sivy, Michael. (1999) "The Buzz of Money in Motion," *Time* (July 26): 71.

Skjelsbaek, Kjell. (1991) "The UN Secretary-General and the Mediation of International Disputes," *Journal of Peace Research* 28 (February): 99–115.

Sklair, Leslie. (1991) *Sociology of the Global System.* Baltimore: Johns Hopkins University Press.

Slaughter, Anne-Marie. (1997) "The Real New World Order," *Foreign Affairs* 76 (September–October): 183–197.

Small, Melvin, and J. David Singer. (1982) *Resort to Arms: International and Civil Wars, 1816–1980.* Beverly Hills, Calif.: Sage.

———. (1976) "The War-Proneness of Democratic Regimes, 1816–1965," *Jerusalem Journal of International Relations* 1 (March): 50–69.

———. (1972) "Patterns in International Warfare, 1816–1965," 121–131 in James F. Short, Jr. and Marvin E. Wolfgang (eds.), *Collective Violence.* Chicago: Aldine-Atherton.

Smith, Dan. (1999) "The Norm of Sovereignty in the Age of Intervention," paper presented at the International Peace Conference, "Will World Peace Be Achievable in the Twenty-First Century," Kyung Hee University, Seoul, October 11–13.

———. (1997) *The State of War and Peace Atlas,* 3rd ed. New York: Penguin.

Smith, Ron P., and George Georgiou. (1983) "Assessing the Effect of Military Expenditures on OECD Economies: A Survey," *Arms Control* 4 (May): 3–15.

Smith, Steve. (1997) "Bridging the Gap: Social Constructivism," 183–187 in John Baylis and Steve Smith (eds.), *The Globalization of World Politics.* New York: Oxford University Press.

Smith, Steve, and Michael Clarke. (1985) *Foreign Policy Implementation.* London: Allen & Unwin.

Snidal, Duncan. (1993) "Relative Gains and the Pattern of International Cooperation," 181–207 in David A. Baldwin (ed.), *Neorealism and Neoliberalism: The Contemporary Debate.* New York: Columbia University Press.

Snider, Lewis W. (1991) "Guns, Debt, and Politics: New Variations on an Old Theme," *Armed Forces and Society* 17 (Winter): 167–190.

Snyder, Glenn H. (1991) "Alliance Threats: A Neorealist First Cut," 83–103 in Robert L. Rothstein (ed.), *The Evolution of Theory in International Relations.* Columbia: University of South Carolina Press.

———. (1984) "The Security Dilemma in Alliance Politics," *World Politics* 36 (July): 461–495.

Snyder, Glenn H., and Paul Diesing. (1977) *Conflict among Nations: Bargaining, Decision-Making, and System Structure in International Crisis.* Princeton, N.J.: Princeton University Press.

Snyder, Jack. (1993) "The New Nationalism: Realist Interpretations and Beyond," 179–200 in Richard Rosecrance, and Anthony A. Stein (eds.), *The Domestic Bases of Grand Strategy.* Ithaca, N.Y.: Cornell University Press.

Sobel, Andrew C. (1994) *Domestic Choices, International Markets: Dismantling National Barriers and Liberalizing Securities Markets.* Ann Arbor: University of Michigan Press.

Somit, Albert. (1990) "Humans, Chimps, and Bonobos: The Biological Bases of Aggression, War, and Peacemaking," *Journal of Conflict Resolution* 34 (September): 553–582.

Sommaruga, Cornelio. (1999) "Renew the Ambition to Impose Rules on Warfare," *International Herald Tribune* (August 12): 8.

Sørensen, Georg. (1995) "Four Futures," *Bulletin of the Atomic Scientists* 51 (July/August): 69–72.

Sorensen, Theodore C. (1963) *Decision Making in the White House.* New York: Columbia University Press.

Sorokin, Pitirim A. (1937) *Social and Cultural Dynamics.* New York: American Book.

Soroos, Marvin S. (2001) "The Tragedy of the Commons in Global Perspective," 485–499 in Charles W. Kegley, Jr., and Eugene R. Wittkopf (eds.), *The Global Agenda,* 6th ed. Boston: McGraw-Hill

Spector, Michael. (1998) "Low Birth Rates Cause Alarm," *New York Times International Edition* (July 11–12): 1, 10.

Spero, Joan E., and Jeffrey A. Hart. (1997) *The Politics of International Economic Relations,* 5th ed. New York: St. Martin's Press.

Speth, James Gustave. (1999a) "Debt Relief, Yes, but Development Aid as Well," *International Herald Tribune* (May 7): 6.

———. (1999b) "The Neglect of Growing Poverty Poses a Global Threat," *International Herald Tribune* (July 17–18): 6.

———. (1999c) "The Plight of the Poor," *Foreign Affairs* 78 (May–June): 13–17.

Spykman, Nicholas. (1944) *Geography of Peace.* New York: Harcourt Brace.

Stanley Foundation. (1999) *The United Nations and Civil Society.* Muscatine, Iowa: Stanley Foundation.

———. (1993) *The UN Role in Intervention.* Muscatine, Iowa: Stanley Foundation.

The State of Indigenous People. (2000) Olympia, Wash.: Center for World Indigenous Studies.

Starkey, Brigid, Mark Boyer, and Jonathan Wilkenfeld. (2000) *Negotiating a Complex World: An Introduction to International Negotiation.* Boulder, Colo.: Rowman & Littlefield.

Stein, Janice Gross. (1993) "Reassurance in International Conflict Management," 77–97 in Demetrios Caraly and Cerentha Harris (eds.), *New World Politics.* New York: Academy of Political Science.

Stein, Janice Gross, and Louis W. Pauly. (1993) *Choosing to Cooperate: How States Avoid Loss.* Baltimore: Johns Hopkins University Press.

Sterling, Claire. (1994) *Thieves' World: The Threat of the New Global Network of Organized Crime.* New York: Simon & Schuster.

Stevens, William K. (1997) "Five Years after Rio Summit, Old Ways Still Dominate," *International Herald Tribune* (June 18): 4.

Stevenson, Richard W. (1997) "The Cost of 'Fast-Track' Setback," *International Herald Tribune* (November 11): 3.

Stockholm International Peace Research Institute (SIPRI). (1999) *SIPRI Yearbook 1999.* New York: Oxford University Press.

Stokes, Bruce. (2000) "The Protectionist Myth," *Foreign Policy* 117 (Winter): 88–102.

Stopford, John (2000) "Multinational Corporations," *Foreign Policy* 117 (Winter): 12–20.

Strang, David. (1991) "Global Patterns of Decolonization, 1500–1987," *International Studies Quarterly* 35 (December): 429–545.

———. (1990) "From Dependence to Sovereignty: An Event History Analysis of Decolonization 1870–1987," *American Sociological Review* 55 (December): 846–860.

Strange, Susan. (1996) *The Retreat of the State.* Cambridge, Eng.: Cambridge University Press.

———. (1982) "Cave! Hic Dragones: A Critique of Regime Analysis," *International Organization* 36 (Spring): 479–96.

Strasser, Steven, and Mazumdar, Sudip. (1999) "A New Tiger," 119 in Robert Jackson, ed., *Global Issue 99/00,* 15th ed., Guilford, Conn.: Dushkin/McGraw-Hill.

Strom, Stephanie. (2000) "Group of G-8 Nations Seek Their Own Path to a Common Goal," *International Herald Tribune* (January 23): 4.

Sumner, William Graham. (1968) "War," 205–228 in Leon Bramson, and George W. Goethals (eds.), *War.* New York: Basic Books.

Talbott, Strobe. (1990) "Rethinking the Red Menace," *Time* (January 1): 66–72.

Tammen, Ronald J., et al. (2000) *Power Transitions: Strategies for the Twenty-First Century.* New York: Chatham House.

Taylor, Peter J. (ed.). (1990) *World Government.* New York: Oxford University Press.

Thakur, Ramesh. (1998) "Teaming Up to Make Human Rights a Universal Fact," *International Herald Tribune* (December 10): 10.

Thakur, Ramesh, and Steve Lee. (2000) "Defining New Goals for Diplomacy in the Twenty-First Century," *International Herald Tribune* (January 19): 8.

Thompson, Kenneth W. (1960) *Political Realism and the Crisis of World Politics.* Princeton, N.J.: Princeton University Press.

———. (1953) "Collective Security Reexamined," *American Political Science Review* 47 (September): 753–72.

Thompson, William R. (ed.). (1999a) *Great Power Rivalries.* Columbia: University of South Carolina.

———. (1999b) "Why Rivalries Matter and What Great Power Rivalries Can Tell Us about World Politics," 3–28 in William P. Thompson (ed.), *Great Power Rivalries.* Columbia: University of South Carolina Press.

———. (1988) *On Global War: Historical-Structural Approaches to World Politics.* Columbia: University of South Carolina Press.

Thurow, Lester C. (1999) *Building Wealth: The New Rules for Individuals, Companies, and Nations in a Knowledge-Based Economy.* New York: HarperCollins.

———. (1998) "The American Economy in the Next Century," *Harvard International Review* 20 (Winter): 54–59.

———. (1992) *Head to Head: Coming Economic Battles among Japan, Europe, and America.* New York: Morrow.

Tickner, J. Ann. (1999) "Searching for the Princess? Feminist Perspectives in International Relations," *Harvard International Review* 121 (Fall): 41–48.

———. (1997) "You Just Don't Understand: Troubled Engagements between Feminists and IR Theorists," *International Studies Quarterly* 41 (December): 611–632.

———. (1992) *Gender in International Relations: Feminist Perspectives on Achieving Global Security.* New York: Columbia University Press.

Tilford, Earl H., Jr. (1995) *The Revolution in Military Affairs: Prospects and Cautions.* Carlisle Barracks, Pa.: U.S. Army War College.

Tillema, Herbert K. (2001) *Overt Military Intervention in the Cold War Era.* Columbia: University of South Carolina Press.

———. (1994) "Cold War Alliance and Overt Military Intervention, 1945–1991," *International Interactions* 20 (No. 3): 249–278.

———. (1989) "Foreign Overt Military Intervention in the Nuclear Age," *Journal of Peace Research* 26 (May): 179–195.

Tillema, Herbert K., and John R. Van Wingen. (1982) "Law and Power in Military Intervention: Major States after World War II," *International Studies Quarterly* 26 (June): 220–250.

Timmerman, Kenneth. (1991) *The Death Lobby: How the West Armed Iraq.* Boston: Houghton Mifflin.

Todaro, Michael P. (2000) *Economic Development,* 7th ed. Reading, Mass: Addison-Wesley.

———. (1994) *Economic Development in the Third World,* 5th ed. New York: Longman.

Toffler, Alvin, and Heidi Toffler. (1993) *War and Anti-War: Survival at the Dawn of the Twenty-First Century.* New York: Little, Brown.

Toynbee, Arnold J. (1954) *A Study of History.* London: Oxford University Press.

Trachtenberg, Marc. (1990–1991) "The Meaning of Mobilization in 1914," *International Security* 15 (Winter): 120–150.

Triffin, Robert. (1978–1979) "The International Role and Fate of the Dollar," *Foreign Affairs* 57 (Winter): 269–286.

Tuchman, Barbara W. (1984). *The March of Folly.* New York: Ballentine.

———. (1962) *The Guns of August.* New York: Dell.

Tucker, Neely. (1999) "AIDS Slashes Life Expectancy Across Africa by 25 Years or More," (Columbia, S.C.) *The State* (March 19): A11.

Tucker, Robert C., and David C. Hendrickson. (1990) *Empire of Liberty.* New York: Oxford University Press.

Ullman, Richard. (1983) "Refining Security," *International Security* 8 (Summer): 129–153.

United Nations. (1999) *World Economic and Social Survey 1999.* New York: United Nations.

——— . (1998) *World Investment Report 1998.* New York: United Nations.

——— . (1995a) *World Economic and Social Survey 1995.* New York: United Nations.

———. (1995b) *World Population Prospects: The 1994 Revision.* New York: United Nations.

United Nations Development Program (UNDP). (2000) *Human Development Report 2000.* New York: Oxford University Press.

———. (1999) *Human Development Report 1999.* New York: Oxford University Press.

———. (1998) *Human Development Report 1998.* New York: Oxford University Press.

———. (1997) *Human Development Report 1997.* New York: Oxford University Press.

———. (1995) *Human Development Report 1995.* New York: Oxford University Press.

———. (1994) *Human Development Report 1994.* New York: Oxford University Press.

———. (1993) *Human Development Report 1993.* New York: Oxford University Press.

———. (1991) *Human Development Report 1991.* New York: Oxford University Press.

U.S. Arms Control and Disarmament Agency (ACDA). (1997) *World Military Expenditures and Arms Transfers 1995.* Washington, D.C.: U.S. Government Printing Office.

U.S. Commission on Integrated Long-Term Strategy. (1988) *Discriminate Deterrence.* Washington, D.C.: U.S. Government Printing Office.

U.S. Department of State. (2000) *Patterns of Global Terrorism: 1999.* Washington, D.C.: U.S. Department of State.

———. (1994) *Dispatch 5,* Supplement No. 8. (September): 9.

———. (1993) *State 2000: A New Model for Managing Foreign Affairs.* Washington, D.C.: Office of Management Task Force.

———. (1983) *Security and Arms Control: The Search for a More Stable Peace.* Washington, D.C.: U.S. Government Printing Office.

Urquhart, Brian. (1994) "Who Can Police the World?" *New York Review of Books* 41 (May 12): 29–33.

Van Evera, Stephen. (1999) *Causes of War: Power and the Roots of Conflict.* Ithaca, N.Y.: Cornell University Press.

———. (1990–1991) "Primed for Peace: Europe after the Cold War," *International Security* 15 (Winter): 7–57.

Vanhanen, Patu. (2000) "A New Dataset for the Measurement of Democracy 1810–1998," paper presented at the forty-first annual meeting of the International Studies Association, Los Angeles, March 14–18.

Vasquez, John A. (1998) *The Power of Power Politics: From Classical Realism to Neotraditionalism.* Cambridge, Eng.: Cambridge University Press.

———. (1997) "The Realist Paradigm and Degenerative versus Progressive Research Programs," *American Political Science Review* 91 (December): 899–912.

———. (1993) *The War Puzzle.* Cambridge, Eng.: Cambridge University Press.

———. (1991) "The Deterrence Myth: Nuclear Weapons and the Prevention of Nuclear War," 205–223 in Charles W. Kegley, Jr. (ed.), *The Long Postwar Peace.* New York: HarperCollins.

Väyrynen, Raimo. (1992) *Military Industrialization and Economic Development.* Aldershot, Eng.: Dartmouth.

Verba, Sidney. (1969) "Assumptions of Rationality and Non-Rationality in Models of the International System," 217–231 in James N. Rosenau (ed.), *International Politics and Foreign Policy.* New York: Free Press.

Vernon, Raymond. (1971) *Sovereignty at Bay.* New York: Basic Books.

Vital Signs 1999. (1999) Lester R. Brown, Michael Renner, and Brian Halweil (et al.), eds. New York: Norton.

Vital Signs 1997. (1997) Lester R. Brown, Michael Renner, and Christopher Flavin (et al.), eds. New York: Norton.

Walker, William O. (1991) "Decision-Making Theory and Narcotic Foreign Policy: Implications for Historical Analysis," *Diplomatic History* 15 (Winter): 31–45.

Wallace, Brian. (1978) "True Grit South of the Border," *Osceola* (January 13): 15–16.

Wallensteen, Peter, and Margareta Sollenberg. (1999) "Armed Conflict, 1989–98," *Journal of Peace Research* 36 (September): 593–606

———. (1998) "Armed Conflict and Regional Conflict Complexes, 1989–97," *Journal of Peace Research* 35 (September): 621–634.

Waller, Douglas. (1995) "Onward Cyber Soldiers," *Time* (August 21): 40–46.

Wallerstein, Immanuel. (1988) *The Modern World-System III: The Second Era of Great Expansion of the Capitalist World-System, 1730–1840.* San Diego: Academic Press.

———. (1980) *The Modern World-System II.* New York: Academic Press.

———. (1974a) *The Modern World-System: Capitalist Agriculture and the Origins of the European World-Economy in the Sixteenth Century.* New York: Academic Press.

———. (1974b) "The Rise and Future Demise of the World Capitalist System: Concepts for Comparative Analysis," *Comparative Studies in Society and History* 16 (September): 387–415.

Walter, Barbara F. (1997) "The Critical Barrier to Civil War Settlement," *International Organization* 51 (Summer): 335–364.

Walters, Robert S., and David H. Blake. (1992) *The Politics of Global Economic Relations,* 4th ed. Englewood Cliffs, N.J.: Prentice Hall.

Waltz, Kenneth N. (1999) "Globalization and Governance," *PS: Political Science and Politics* 32 (December) 693–700.

———. (1995) "Realist Thought and Neorealist Theory," 67–83 in Charles W. Kegley, Jr. (ed.), *Controversies in International Relations Theory: Realism and the Neoliberal Challenge.* New York: St. Martin's Press.

———. (1993) "The Emerging Structure of International Politics," *International Security* 18 (Fall): 44–79.

———. (1979) *Theory of International Politics.* Reading, Mass.: Addison-Wesley.

———. (1964) "The Stability of a Bipolar World," *Daedalus* 93 (Summer): 881–909.

———. (1954) *Man, the State, and War.* New York: Columbia University Press.

Ward, Michael D., David R. Davis, and Corey L. Lofdahl. (1995) "A Century of Tradeoffs: Defense and Growth in Japan and the United States," *International Studies Quarterly* 39 (March): 27–50.

Warrick, Joby. (1998) "Turning Cool toward the Kyoto Accords," *Washington Post National Weekly Edition* (February 23): 31.

———. (1997) "How Warm Will It Get?" *Washington Post National Weekly Edition* (December 1): 6–7.

Watson, Douglas. (1997) "Indigenous Peoples and the Global Economy," *Current History* 96 (November): 389–391.

Watts, Sheldon. (1998) *Epidemics and History: Disease, Power, and Imperialism.* New Haven, Conn.: Yale University Press.

Weart, Spencer R. (1998) *Never at War: Why Democracies Will Not Fight One Another,* New Haven, Conn.: Yale University Press.

———. (1994) "Peace among Democratic and Oligarchic Republics," *Journal of Peace Research* 31 (August): 299–316.

Weidenbaum, Murray. (1999) "Weighing U.S. Advantages in Global Marketplace," *International Herald Tribune* (March 18): 11.

Weinberg, Gerhard L. (1994) *A World at Arms: A Global History of World War II.* Cambridge, Eng.: Cambridge University Press.

Weiner, Myron. (1995) *The Global Migration Crisis: Challenges to States and Human Rights.* New York: HarperCollins.

Weiss, Stanley A. (1999) "Food Sanctions Are Bad Policy, So Just Lift Them," *International Herald Tribune* (March 18): 6.

Weldes, Jutta, Mark Laffe, Hugh Gusterson, and Raymond Duvall (eds.) (2000) *Cultures of Insecurity: States, Communities, and the Production of Danger.* Minneapolis: University of Minnesota Press.

Wendt, Alexander. (1992) "Anarchy Is What States Make of It: The Social Construction of Power Politics." *International Organization* 46 (Spring): 395–424.

Wendzel, Robert L. (1980) *International Relations: A Policymaker Focus.* New York: Wiley.

White, Donald W. (1998) "Mutable Destiny: The End of the American Century?" *Harvard International Review* 20 (Winter): 42–47.

White, Ralph K. (1990) "Why Aggressors Lose," *Political Psychology* 11 (June): 227–242.

Whiting, Allen S. (1985) "Foreign Policy of China," 246–290 in Roy C. Macridis (ed.), *Foreign Policy in World Politics,* 6th ed. Englewood Cliffs, N.J.: Prentice Hall.

Whitney, Craig R. (1999) "European Union Vows to Become Military Power," *New York Times* (June 4): A1, A16

Wilmer, Franke. (1993) *The Indigenous Voice in World Politics: Since Time Immemorial.* Newbury Park, Calif.: Sage.

Wilson, James Q. (1993) *The Moral Sense.* New York: Free Press.

Wohlforth, William C. (1999) "The Stability of a Unipolar World," *International Security* 24 (Summer): 5–41

Wolfers, Arnold. (1962) *Discord and Collaboration.* Baltimore: Johns Hopkins University Press.

Woodward, Bob. (1991) *The Commanders.* New York: Simon & Schuster.

Woodward, Bob, and Rick Atkinson. (1990) "Launching Operation Desert Shield," *Washington Post National Weekly Edition* (September 3–9): 8–9.

World Bank. (2000) *Entering the 21st Century: World Development Report 1999/2000.* New York: Oxford University Press.

———. (1999a) *Global Economic Prospects and the Developing Countries, 1998/99.* Washington, D.C.: World Bank.

———. (1999b) *World Development Report, 1998/99.* New York: Oxford University Press.

———. (1998) *World Bank Atlas.* Washington D.C.: World Bank.

———. (1997) *World Development Report 1997.* New York: Oxford University Press.

———. (1996) *World Debt Tables 1996,* vol. 1. Washington, D.C.: World Bank.

———. (1995a) *Global Economic Prospects and the Developing Countries 1995.* Washington, D.C.: World Bank.

———. (1995b) *World Development Report 1995.* New York: Oxford University Press.

———. (1992) *World Development Report 1992.* New York: Oxford University Press.

Wren, Christopher S. (1999) "UN Reporting Cuts in Global Drug Crops'" *New York Times* (July 11): 11.

Wright, Quincy. (1953) "The Outlawry of War and the Law of War," *American Journal of International Law* 47 (July): 365–376.

———. (1942) *A Study of War.* Chicago: University of Chicago Press.

Wright, Robert. (2000a) "Continental Drift," *New Republic* (January 17): 18–23.

———. (2000b) *Nonzero: The Logic of Human Destiny.* New York: Pantheon.

Yearbook of International Organizations, 1999/2000, vol. 3. Munich: K. G. Sauer.

Yoder, Edwin M., Jr. (1991) "Isolationists Would Put America on a Dangerous Course," (Columbia, S.C.) *The State* (December 14): A10.

Young, Oran R. (1995) "System and Society in World Affairs: Implications for International Organizations," *International Social Science Journal* 144 (June): 197–212.

Zacher, Mark W. (1987) "Trade Gaps, Analytical Gaps: Regime Analysis and International Commodity Regulation," *International Organization* 41 (Spring): 173–202.

Zacher, Mark W., and Richard A. Matthew. (1995) "Liberal International Theory: Common Threads, Divergent Strands," 107–149 in Charles W. Kegley, Jr. (ed.), *Controversies in International Relations Theory: Realism and the Neoliberal Challenge.* New York: St. Martin's Press.

Zagare, Frank C. (1990) "Rationality and Deterrence," *World Politics* 42 (January): 238–260.

Zakaria, Fareed. (1999) "The Empire Strikes Out: The Unholy Emergence of the Nation-State," *New York Times Magazine* (April 18): 99.

———. (1998a) *From Wealth to Power: The Unusual Origins of America's World Role.* Princeton, NJ: Princeton University Press.

———. (1998b) "The Future of Statecraft," 42 in *The World in 1999.* London: *Economist.*

———. (1992–1993) "Is Realism Finished?" *National Interest* 30 (Winter): 21–32

Zelikow, Philip. (1987) "The United States and the Use of Force: A Historical Summary," 31–81 in George K. Osburn, et al. (eds.), *Democracy, Strategy, and Vietnam.* Lexington, Mass.: Lexington Books.

Ziegler, David. (1995) Review of *World Politics and the Evolution of War,* by John Weltman, *American Political Science Review* 89 (September): 813–814.

Zimmerman, Tim. (1996) "CIA Study: Why Do Countries Fall Apart?" *U.S. News & World Report* (February 12): 46.

———. (1994) "Arms Merchant to the World," *U.S. News & World Report* (April 4): 37.

Zinnes, Dina A., and Jonathan Wilkenfeld. (1971) "An Analysis of Foreign Conflict Behavior of Nations," 167–213 in Wolfram F. Handieder (ed.), *Comparative Foreign Policy.* New York: McKay.

ACKNOWLEDGMENTS

Acknowledgments (continued from the copyright page)

Map 1.4: World Time View. Copyright © 1989 World View Time, Inc., P.O. Box 266, Brockville, Ontario, Canada K6V 5V5. Reprinted by permission.

Controversy: Can You Make a Difference in the World's Future? Tony Evans. Excerpt from *What a Way to Live* by Tony Evans, pp. 2–3. Copyright © 1997 by Word Publishers, Nashville, Tennessee. Reprinted with the permission of the publishers. All rights reserved.

Controversy: Are Democracies Deficient in Foreign Affairs? George F. Kennan. Brief excerpt from "Democracies in Foreign Affairs: A U.S. Policy-maker's Characterization," p. 59, in *American Diplomacy 1900–1950* by George F. Kennan. Copyright © 1951 by New American Library. Reprinted by permission of the author and The University of Chicago Press.

Map 3.2: The Flow of Freedom: Democratic Liberty at the Dawn of a New Century. From "Liberty's Ebb and Flow" in *The Christian Science Monitor* (May 9, 1997), pp. 18–19. Michael Kilborn/© *The Christian Science Monitor.* Data originally reported in Freedom House Survey, *Freedom in the World: The Annual Survey of Political Rights and Civil Liberties 1996–1997*. Reprinted by permission.

Map 4.1: Territorial Changes in Europe following World War I. From *Strategic Atlas, Comparative Geopolitics of the World's Powers,* revised edition by Gerard Chaliand and Jean-Pierre Rageau. Copyright © 1990 by Gerard Chaliand and Jean-Pierre Rageau. Reprinted by permission of HarperCollins Publishers, Inc.

Map 4.2: World War II Redraws the Map of Europe. Europe 1938 is based on map 5.3 (p. 118) in *A Multipolar Peace? Great-Power Politics in the Twenty-First Century* by Charles W. Kegley, Jr. and Gregory A. Raymond. Copyright © 1994 by St. Martin's Press, Inc. Reprinted by permission. Europe 1945 is from *Strategic Atlas, Comparative Geopolitics of the World's Powers,* third edition by Gerard Chaliand. Copyright © 1993 by Gerard Chaliand and Jean-Pierre Rageau. Reprinted by permission of HarperCollins Publishers, Inc.

Map 5.2: Wealth versus Population in the Global North and Global South. From *Entering the 21st Century: World Development Report.* Copyright © 2000 by The International Bank for Reconstruction and Development/The World Bank. Used by permission of Oxford University Press, Inc.

Map 5.4: The Global Income Gap: The Geographic Distribution of Gross National Product (GNP) per Capita. From *World Development Report 1998/1999* by the World Bank. Copyright © 1999 by the International Bank for Reconstruction and Development/The World Bank. Used by permission of Oxford University Press, Inc.

Table 5.1: Two Worlds of Development. From *World Development Report 1998/1999* by the World Bank. Copyright © 1999 by The International Bank for Reconstruction and Development/The World Bank. Used by permission of Oxford University Press, Inc.

Controversy: How Should National and Personal Wealth Be Measured? GNP per Capita versus "Purchasing Power Parity." From *The Economist* (May 8, 1999), p. 110. Copyright © 1999 The Economist Newspaper Group, Inc. Reprinted with permission. Further reproduction prohibited. <www.economist.com>. Citing data from the World Bank. From *World Development Report 1997*. Copyright © 1997 by The International Bank for Reconstruction and Development/The World Bank. Used by permission of Oxford University Press, Inc. Comparison of GNP per Capita and Purchasing Parity, Selected Countries. From *World Development Report 1998/1999*. Copyright © 1999 by The International Bank for Reconstruction and Development/The World Bank. Used by permission of Oxford University Press, Inc.

Table 5.2: Three Levels of Human Development: The 1999 Report on the Fastest and Slowest Progress in Selected Countries. Adapted from the United Nations Development Program, *Human Development Report 1999*. Copyright © 1999 by United Nations Development Program. Used by permission of Oxford University Press, Inc.

Figure 5.1: The Human Development Index. Adapted from the United Nations Development Program, *Human Development Report 1999*, and *The Economist* (July 17, 1999), p. 96. Copyright © 1999 by United Nations Development Program. Used by permission of the United Nations Bureau of External Relations. Copyright © 1999 by The International Bank for Reconstruction and Development/The World Bank. Used by permission of Oxford University Press. Copyright © 1999 The Economist Newspaper Group, Inc. Reprinted with permission. Further reproduction prohibited.

Figure 5.2: The Fluctuating Level of Bilateral and Multilateral Aid to Developing Countries since 1970. From *The Economist* (July 26, 1999), p. 24. Copyright © 1999 The Economist Newspaper Group, Inc. Reprinted with permission. Further reproduction prohibited.

Figure 6.1: The Number of States, IGOs, and NGOs since 1900. Figures for states are based on the Correlates of War (COW) project at the University of Michigan under the direction of J. David Singer. States, Polity III data (Jaggers and Gurr 1995); IGOs and NGOs, *Yearbook of International Organizations 1993/1994* (1993: p. 1699), and moving averages from selected prior volumes. Reprinted with permission of the Union of International Associations, Belgium.

Controversy: Who Should Be Allowed to Join the UN? The Case of Taiwan. From *The Economist* (December 10, 1994), p. 16. Copyright ©1994 The Economist Newspaper Group, Inc. Reprinted with permission. Further reproduction prohibited.

Figure 6.4: The European Union's Government Structure. From *The Economist* (October 23, 1999), p. 16. Copyright © 1999 The Economist Newspaper Group, Inc. Reprinted with permission. Further reproduction prohibited.

Maps 7.1 and 7.3: The Indigenous Cultures of the Fourth World, and Major Religions of the World. Adapted from *National Geographic,* August 1999 supplement: NG Maps/NGS Image Collection.

Figure 7.2: The World's Top Twenty Banks, 1999. From *The Economist* (July 10, 1999), p. 99. Copyright © 1999 The Economist Newspaper Group, Inc. Reprinted with permission. Further reproduction prohibited.

Table 7.4: Countries and Corporations: A Ranking by Size of Economy and Revenue. From *Fortune* (June 1999). Copyright © 1999 Time, Inc. Reprinted by permission.

Table 8.2 and Figure 8.1: Round and Round: A GATT-WTO Chronology. Adapted from *The Economist,* (May 16, 1998), p. 22. Copyright © 1998 The Economist Newspaper Group, Inc. Reprinted with permission. Further reproduction prohibited. Figure adapted from *The Economist* (August 28, 1998), p. 52. Copyright © 1998 The Economist Newspaper Group, Inc. Reprinted with permission. Further reproduction prohibited.

Map 8.2: Regional Free-Trade Blocs: Building Blocks or Road Blocks for Economic Growth? Adapted from *The Economist* (September 27, 1997), p. 23. Copyright © 1997 The Economist Newspaper Group, Inc. Reprinted with permission. Further reproduction prohibited.

Map 9.1: The Flow of Finance to Developing Countries. Adapted from *The Economist* (February 5, 2000), p. 102. Copyright © 2000 The Economist Newspaper Group, Inc. Reprinted with permission. Further reproduction prohibited.

Figure 9.2: The Growth of World Trade and Output since 1950. Adapted from *World Economic Survey* (1995), p. 35; and (1999 edition), p. 2. The United Nations is the author of the original material. Reprinted by permission of United Nations Publications.

Controversy: Is Globalization Producing Prosperity or Poverty? United Nations Development Program (1997), pp. 82-83. The United Nations is the author of the original material. Reprinted by permission of United Nations Publications.

Figure 9.4: The Changing Distribution of Foreign Direct Investment since 1970. Adapted from United Nations Development Program (1999), p. 26. The United Nations is the author of the original material. Reprinted by permission of United Nations Publications.

Map 10.1: Global Levels of HIV. From *International Herald Tribune* (November 27, 1997), p. 1. Copyright © 2000 by The New York Times Company. Reprinted by permission.

Figures 10.1, 10.2, 10.3, and 10.4: Adapted from *World Population Prospects*. The United Nations is the author of the original material. Reprinted by permission of United Nations Publications.

Table 10.1 and Figure 10.5: Rank by Size of the Twenty Largest Countries and Their Projected Population in 2050 and Total Grain per Person since 1950, with Projections to 2050. Adapted from figure on p. 34 and table on p. 21 in *Beyond Malthus: Nineteen Dimensions of the Population Chal-*

lenge by Lester R. Brown, Gary Gardner, and Brian Halweil. Copyright © 1999 Worldwatch Institute. Used by permission of W.W. Norton & Company, Inc. and Worldwatch Institute.

Controversy: Are National Security, Environmental Security, and Human Security Competing Goals? Gareth Porter. Excerpt from "Environmental Security as a National Security Issue" in *Current History* (May 1995), pp. 218–220. By permission of Current History, Inc.

Figure 11.1: Crude Oil Prices since 1861 and the Growth of Proven Oil Reserves. Adapted from *The Economist* (March 6, 1999), p. 23, and (July 3, 1999), p. 92. Copyright © 1999 The Economist Newspaper Group, Inc. Reprinted with permission. Further reproduction prohibited.

Figure 11.3: Rising Temperatures since 1860. Adapted from "Planetary Roulette: Gambling with the Climate" by Robert Repetto and Jonathan Lash in *Foreign Policy* 108 (Fall 1997), p. 93. Copyright © 1997 by The Carnegie Endowment for International Peace. Reprinted with permission from *Foreign Policy.*

Map 11.2: Biodiversity Bastions and Endangered Biodiversity Hot Spots. Adapted from *Time* (December 14, 1998), pp. 63–64, and *The Economist* (January 29, 2000), p. 126. Copyright © 1998 Time Inc. © 2000 The Economist Newspaper Group Inc. Reprinted with permission. Further reproduction prohibited.

Table 11.1: Post Rio Report Card on a Sustainable Global Commons. From *The Christian Science Monitor* (June 24, 1997), p. 11. Alexandra Marks/ © 1997 *The Christian Science Monitor*. Reprinted by permission.

Figure 12.3: The Long Cycle of Global Leadership and Global War, 1494–2000. Adapted from *Exploring Long Cycles* by George Modelski, ed., p. 6. Copyright © 1987 by Lynn Rienner Publishers, Inc. Reprinted by permission of the publisher.

Map 12.1: States Threatening to Collapse in Civil Wars, 1999. From *The Christian Science Monitor* (February 12, 1999), pp. 12–13. Dave Herring/© *The Christian Science Monitor*. Reprinted by permission.

Map 12.2: The Globalization of International Terrorism. From *Newsweek* (February 22, 1999), p. 64. Copyright © 1999 Newsweek, Inc. All Rights Reserved. Reprinted by permission.

Figures 13.1 and 13.2: Arms and Armies: The Twenty States with the Largest Military Budgets and Armed Forces, and World and U.S. Military Expenditures. Adapted from *Defense Monitor* 28 (No. 1, 1999), pp. 4–5. Reprinted by permission.

Figure 14.1: The Expansion and Reduction of Global Nuclear Arsenals since 1945. Adapted from data reported in "Global Nuclear Stockpiles, 1945–2000" by Robert S. Norris and William M. Arkin, *The Bulletin of the Atomic Scientists* (March/April 2000), p. 79. Copyright © 1999 by the Educational Foundation for Nuclear Science, 6042 South Kimbark, Chicago, Illinois 60637, USA. A one-year subscription is $28. Reprinted by permission of *The Bulletin of the Atomic Scientists*.

Controversy: Is the Balance of Power a Precarious and Failed Security System? Inis L. Claude, Jr. Excerpt from "The Balance of Power Revisited" published in *Review of International Studies* 15 (January 1989), pp. 77–85. Reprinted with the permission of Cambridge University Press.

Map 15.1: The Enlarged NATO and the New Geostrategic Balance of Power. Copyright © July 14, 1997, *U.S. News & World Report*. Visit us at our Web site at <www.usnews.com> for additional information.

Table 15.2: Major Multilateral Arms Control Treaties since 1945. Adapted from "Arms Control and Disarmament Agreements" by R. Ferm published in *Stockholm International Peace Research Institute Yearbook 1995: Armaments, Disarmament, and International Security* (Oxford University Press: Oxford 1995). Reprinted with the permission of SIPRI.

Figure 15.1: Countdown to Strategic Parity: The Negotiated End of the U.S.-Russian Arms Race. Based on data from Worldwatch data diskette, U.S. Arms Control Association Fact Files and *SIPRI Yearbooks*. Worldwatch data copyright © Worldwatch Institute. Reprinted with the permission of Worldwatch Institute and the Stockholm International Peach Research Institute.

Figure 16.1: The Legal Prohibition of Wars of Aggression since 1815. Adapted from Transnational Rules Indicators Project, as described in *When Trust Breaks Down: Alliance Norms and World Politics* by Charles W. Kegley, Jr., and Gregory A. Raymond. Copyright © 1990 by Charles W. Kegley, Jr., and Gregory A. Raymond. Reprinted with the permission of the University of South Carolina Press.

Figure 16.2: The Changing Status of the Nonintervention Rule in International Law since 1820. From Transnational Rules Indicators Project as measured in "The Rise and Fall of the Nonintervention Norm: Some Correlates and Potential Consequences" by Charles W. Kegley, Jr., Gregory A. Raymond, and Margaret G. Hermann from *The Fletcher Forum of International Affairs* (Winter 1998). Reprinted with the permission of The Fletcher Forum of World Affairs.

Map 16.1: UN Peace Missions since 1948. From the United Nations Department of Public Information. Copyright © 1998 by the United Nations. Reprinted with the permission of the UN Department of Public Information.

Map 16.2: A European Union on the Verge of Enlargement. Adapted from *The Economist* (July 31, 1999), p. 13. Copyright © 1999 The Economist Newspaper Group, Inc. Reprinted with permission. Further reproduction prohibited.

Photo Credits

Photos that appear on contents and part-opening pages are duplications of chapter photos.

Chapter 1: Pages 3 & 4: Christopher Morris/Black Star/Time Inc.; 7: Eric Bouvet/Liaison Agency; 14: Ron Haviv/Saba; 21: NASA.

Chapter 2: Pages 25 & 26: Ron Edmonds/AP/Wide World; 29: The Granger Collection, NY; Bettmann/CORBIS; 33: Scala/Art Resource, NY, Fuller: Thomas Hobbes, Bridgeman Art Library; 43: Erik Viktor/Science Source/Photo Researchers; 47: Arturo Mari/AP/Wide World.

Chapter 3: Pages 53 & 54: Michael Stephens/AP Photo/WPA POOL; 60: Jerome Delay/AP/Wide World; 68: Barbara Kinney/The White House/AP/ Wide World; 74: Reuters/Win McMamee/Archive Photos; 81: AP/Wide World.

Chapter 4: Pages 85 & 86: FDR Library; 90: Robert Harbison/The Christian Science Monitor; 98: Topham/Image Works; 109: Biber/Sipa; 114: Robyn Beck/AFP.

Chapter 5: Pages 123 & 124: Stephen Ferry/Liaison Agency; 130: Rene Burri/Magnum; 133: Bettmann/CORBIS, Bettmann/CORBIS; 144: Jean Pierre Laffont/Sygma; 147: Tim Holt/Photo Researchers; 155: D. Groshong/Sygma; 159: Les Stone/Sygma.

Chapter 6: Pages 171 & 172: Adam Nadel/AP/Wide World; 178: UN/DPI Photo; 189: Figaro Magazine/Liaison Agency.

Chapter 7: Pages 201 & 202: Mohammad Riaz/AP/Wide World; 205: Jeff Katz/Earthjustice; 208: Allan Tannenbaum/Sygma; 215: Seamus Conlan, F.S.P./Liaison Agency; 221: Peter Aventurier/Liaison Agency; 226: Esaias Baitel/Liaison Agency, Lemmer/Sipa, Ruth Fremson/AP/Wide World; 236: Robert Nickelsberg/Time Magazine.

Chapter 8: Pages 245 & 246 Ralph Radford/AP/Wide World; 256: Isabelle Rouvillois/AFP; Peter Dejong/AP/Wide World; 275: Frederick Brown/ AFP, Eric Feferberg/AFP; 277: Kurita/Murayama/Liaison Agency; 287: Jeffrey Aaronson/Network Aspen.

Chapter 9: Pages 291 & 292: Saleh Rifai/AP/Wide World; 295: Sally Wiener Grotta/The Stock Market; 313: Douglas Engle/AP/Wide World, Eraldo Peres/AP/Wide World; 319: Jeffrey Aaronson/Network Aspen; 321: Frank Fournier/Contact; 324: Ira Wyman/Sygma.

Chapter 10: Pages 329 & 330:Sherwin Castro/AP/Wide World; 345: Mariella Furrer/Saba; 350: Robert Harbison/The Christian Science Monitor; 357: Penny Tweedie/Panos Pictures.

Chapter 11: Pages 363 & 364: Douglas Engle/AP/Wide World; 365: NASA/AP File; 367: Graeme Ewens/Panos Pictures; 369: Ray Ellis/Photo Researchers, Steve Vidler/Leo de Wys; 371: Penny Tweedie/Panos Pictures; 384: Daniel Beltra/Greenpeace; 391: Wesley Bocxe/Photo Researchers; 393: Matthew Fearn/PA News.

Chapter 12: Pages 407 & 408: Charles Dharapak/AP/Wide World; 413: Mike Stewart/Sygma; 420: Noel Quidu/Liaison Agency; 430: U.S. ARMY/AP/ Wide World; 439: John Stanmeyer/Saba, John Stanmeyer/Saba; 441: A. Yagobzadeh/Sipa; 450: Reuters/Flash '90/Archive Photos.

Chapter 13: Pages 455 & 456: AP/Wide World; 467: Scott Peterson/Liaison Agency; 470: Steven R. Schaefer/AFP; 472: Alain McLaughlin/Impact Visuals; 474: AP/Wide World; 488: Reuters/Corinne Dufka/Archive Photos; 492: Lockheed Martin; 497: Chien-min Chung/AP/Wide World.

Chapter 14: Pages 507 & 508: Murad Sezer/AP/Wide World; 510: Dimas Ardian/AP/Wide World; 514: Copyright © NASM/Sygma; 517: Bernard Hermann/Liaison Agency; 530: AP/Wide World; 532: Santiago Lyon/AP/ Wide World; 538: AP/Wide World; 544: © Charles Crowell/Black Star.

Chapter 15: Pages 549 & 550: AP/Wide World; 554: The Granger Collection, NY; 565: Reuters/Archive Photos; 572: Reuters/Archive Photos; 577: UN/ DPI Photo by H. Ardvisson.

Chapter 16: Pages 595 & 596: Serge Ligtenberg/AP/Wide World; 607: Erich Lessing/Art Resource, NY; 613: Reuters/Ruben Sprich/Archive Photos, William Campbell/Time Magazine, Vienna Report/Sygma, Kathy Willens/AP/Wide World, P. F. Gero/Sygma, Matthieu Polak/Sygma, Sygma 614: AFP Photo; 628: Reuters/Peter Morgan/Archive Photos; 629: Maya Vidon/AFP; 632: Boris Grdanoski/AP/Wide World

Chapter 17 Pages 651 & 652: Mikhail Metzel/AP/Wide World; 655: Noresen/ Greenpeace; 660: Bettmann/CORBIS, AP Photo; 662: J. Van Hasselt/ Sygma; 667: NASA.

INDEX

Note: Glossary terms appear in **boldfaced** type. Page numbers followed by italicized letters *f, m,* and *t* indicate figures, maps, and tables, respectively.